710046279-6

LEEDS POLYTECHNIC BECKETT PARK LIBRARY

D1420567

71 0046279 UNIVERSITY TELEPEN
LEEDS BECKETT LIBRARY
DISCARDED

BIAS IN MENTAL TESTING

ARTHUR R. JENSEN

METHUEN

First published in Great Britain in 1980 by
Methuen & Co., Ltd.
11 New Fetter Lane, London EC4P 4EE

© 1980 by Arthur R. Jensen

All rights reserved. No part of this book may be reprinted
or reproduced or utilized in any form or by any electronic,
mechanical or other means, now known or hereafter invented,
including photocopying and recording, or in any information
storage or retrieval system, without permission in writing
from the publishers.

Printed in the United States of America

British Library Cataloguing in Publication Data

Jensen, Arthur Robert
Bias in mental testing.
1. Psychological tests
I. Title
152.8   BF176
ISBN 0-416-83230-X

710046279-6

LEEDS POLYTECHNIC

362193V

BP

23637

151·2   ← CLASSMARK

13·10·80   £15

COPYRIGHT ACKNOWLEDGMENTS

Permission to reprint the following materials, granted by publishers, authors, and other proprietors of copyrights, is gratefully acknowledged. Figure 1.1: Houghton Mifflin Company; copyright © 1937 by L. M. Terman and M.A. Merrill. Figure 1.2: Penguin Books Ltd, The Open Court Publishing Company; copyright © 1966 by H. J. Eysenck. Figure 4.3: D. Wechsler, Williams & Wilkins; copyright © 1944 by The Williams & Wilkins Co., Baltimore. Figure 4.4: Harcourt Brace Jovanovich, Inc. Figure 4.5: Houghton Mifflin Company; copyright © 1960 by Houghton Mifflin Company. Figures 4.6 and 4.7: Oxford University Press, Oxford. Figure 4.8: Cambridge University Press. Figure 4.9: Kathleen Durning. Figure 4.11: The British Psychological Society. Figure 4.14: W. Shockley. Figure 4.15: T. M. Sattler, W. B. Saunders Company. Figure 4.16: Prentice-Hall, Inc.; copyright © 1967. Figure 4.17: M. D. Dunnette and R. S. Elster, Educational and Psychological Measurements. Figure 4.21: W. A. Kennedy, The Society for Research in Child Development, Inc. Figures 4.22, 4.23, and 4.24: E. F. Wonderlic Associates, Inc. Figure 4.5: Robert R. Knapp. Page 155 (bottom) and page 156 (top, middle, bottom): Institute for Personality and Ability Testing, Inc.; copyright © 1950, 1961 by the Institute for Personality and Ability Testing, Inc. Page 157 (top): J. C. Raven Ltd. Page 157 (bottom): Robert R. Knapp. Page 158 (top): McGraw-Hill; copyright © 1967 by McGraw-Hill Book Company. Page 159 (middle and bottom): Educational Testing Service; copyright © 1962, 1976 by Educational Testing Service, Princeton, N.J. Page 161 (bottom): Philip E. Vernon. Page 163 (bottom): Alick Elithorn. Page 165 (bottom): Lauretta Bender, American Orthopsychiatric Association. Figure 6.3: Houghton Mifflin Company; copyright © 1977 by Houghton Mifflin Company. Figure 6.7: McGraw-Hill; copyright © 1956 by McGraw-Hill Book Company, Inc. Figure 6.11: Random House; copyright © 1954 by Random House, Inc. Figure 6.12: Methuen & Co. Ltd. Figures 7.3 and 7.4: Nancy Bayley, American Psychological Association; copyright © 1955 by the American Psychological Association. Figure 8.2: William D. Crano, American Psychological Association; copyright © 1972 by the American Psychological Association. Figure 8.3: Robert B. McCall, *Science;* copyright © 1977 by the American Association for the Advancement of Science. Figure 8.4: The Boxwood Press. Figure 9.3: American Institutes for Research in the Behavioral Sciences. Figure 9.5: American Educational Research Association; copyright © 1973 by the American Educational Research Association, Washington, D.C. Figure 11.4A: Lloyd Dunn. Figure 11.4B: J. C. Raven Ltd. Figure 11.6: L. E. Longstreth, American Psychological Association; copyright © 1978 by the American Psychological Association. Figure 14.1: Harcourt Brace Jovanovich; copyright © 1952, 1953 by Harcourt Brace Jovanovich, Inc. Figure 14.5: Elliot W. Eisner. Figure 14.14: Saul Sternberg, *Science;* copyright © 1966 by the American Association for the Advancement of Science. Figure 14.18: The University of Chicago Press; copyright © 1969 by The University of Chicago Press. Figure 14.19: William L. Mihal, American Psychological Association. Figure 15.1: Gerald S. Lesser; copyright © 1965 by the Society for Research in Child Development, Inc. Tables 6.9 and 6.13: *British Journal of Educational Psychology;* Scottish Academic Press (Journals) Limited. Table 6.12: The British Psychological Society. Table 7.2: Houghton Mifflin Company; copyright © 1960 by Houghton Mifflin Company. Table 7.6: Fels Research Institute. Table 7.8: University of California Press. Table 7.9: John Wiley & Sons, Inc. Table 7.10: Robert L. Thorndike, American Psychological Association; copyright © 1951 by the American Psychological Association. Table 7.11: National Society for the Study of Education. Table 7.12: Harper & Row; copyright © 1949 by Harper & Row, Publishers, Inc.; copyright © 1960 by Lee J. Cronbach. Table 8.3: The Psychological Corporation. Table 8.4: E. E. Ghiselli, American Psychological Association; copyright © 1953 by the American Psychological Association. Table 8.8: Harvard University Press; copyright © Harvard University Press. Table 10.1: Robert L. Thorndike. Tables 10.5 and 11.7: National Council on Measurement in Education, East Lansing, Michigan. Table 11.18: Houghton Mifflin Company: copyright © 1973 by Houghton Mifflin Company.

To the memory of the great pioneers:

Sir Francis Galton (1822–1911)

Alfred Binet (1857–1911)

Charles Spearman (1863–1945)

Contents

Preface

Many widely used standardized tests of mental ability consistently show sizable differences in the average scores obtained by various native-born racial and social subpopulations in the United States. Anyone who would claim that all such tests are therefore culturally biased will henceforth have this book to contend with.

My exhaustive review of the empirical research bearing on this issue leads me to the conclusion that the currently most widely used standardized tests of mental ability –IQ, scholastic aptitude, and achievement tests—are, by and large, *not* biased against any of the native-born English-speaking minority groups on which the amount of research evidence is sufficient for an objective determination of bias, if the tests were in fact biased. For most nonverbal standardized tests, this generalization is not limited to English-speaking minorities.

Research relevant to test bias is much more prevalent for black Americans than for any other group. The minority groups that have been the least researched with respect to test bias are Asian–Americans of Chinese and Japanese descent. Adequate evidence is lacking on these groups not because tests are less liable to culture bias for Asian–Americans than for any other minority group but probably because American-born Chinese and Japanese have generally fared quite well when tests are used in educational and occupational selection. It is when selection procedures yield markedly disproportionate rates of acceptance or rejection of minority and majority populations that tests are accused of bias and unfairness.

Claims of test bias and of the unfair use of tests cannot be ignored by psychologists. Such claims must be objectively investigated with all of the available techniques of psychometrics and statistical analysis. Where test bias is discovered, the test in question should either not be used on the group for which it is biased or should be used only in ways that permit the particular bias to be precisely and explicitly taken into account. Biased tests can often be revamped so as to greatly lessen, or even totally eliminate, their bias with respect to a particular subpopulation.

Before the use of tests is rejected outright, however, one must consider the alternatives to testing—whether decisions based on less objective means of evaluation (usually educational credentials, letters of recommendation, interviews, and biographical inventories) would guarantee less bias and greater fairness for minorities than would result from the use of tests.

These are exceedingly important questions for any society in which tests will almost

certainly be increasingly used—by schools and colleges, by the armed forces, and by the
job market. With enforced universal education now combined with the current trend
toward inflation of school grades, diplomas, and other formal credentials, selective colleges and employers will inevitably turn increasingly to the use of more precisely informative, objective, and valid methods for the selection of applicants and the assessment of
qualifications. Standardized tests have unquestionably proved their worth for these purposes. But what must also be determined is whether the tests serving any given purpose
are psychometrically *biased* with respect to the various subpopulations on which they are
used, and whether the selection procedure based on test scores is itself *fair* to all concerned. That is primarily what this book is about—the psychometric methods for objectively detecting *bias* in mental tests and for using tests *fairly* in any of the legitimate ways
that tests may be employed.

To treat these topics seriously and thoroughly requires that we delve far beyond the
level of popular discourse. The issues cannot really be understood in terms of the common
verbalisms regarding tests that are now so familiar to most laymen who read articles on
this topic in the popular press. Although I have intended this book to reach as wide an
audience with a serious interest in test bias as possible, it has obviously not been possible
to make this an "easy" book. The questions and answers in this field quickly, and
necessarily, force us into some highly technical aspects of psychometric theory and
methodology. However, I have designed the exposition so that even readers with no
psychometric or statistical background should not be at a loss at any point in the book,
provided that they are willing to read carefully, as one might study for a college-level
course, the early chapters (especially Chapters 4 through 8), which clearly define and
explicate nearly all the quantitative concepts that are frequently used throughout the rest of
the book—concepts such as the mean, standard deviation, standard score, standard error,
correlation, regression, reliability, validity, true score, factor, and so forth. For readers to
whom these concepts are already familiar, this book should present no special difficulties.
Many of the less crucial technical details, of interest more to students of psychometrics
than to the layman, are relegated to the notes at the end of each chapter. Also, technical
terms, which on their first appearance are marked by a star ($\star$), are defined in the
glossary.

Embedded more or less unobtrusively throughout the text is what amounts to practically a review of elementary statistics. I have found that many students in psychology and
education acquire a better appreciation of statistical concepts when they are presented, as
here, in the context of important substantive issues that are highly meaningful to them,
rather than as purely mathematical abstractions.

No less than the first eight chapters are, in a sense, introductory to the topic of test
bias per se, which is met head on for the first time in Chapter 9. But these introductory
chapters all deal with the most basic issues of psychometrics that are involved in criticisms
of mental tests and in arguments about test bias—the great variety of tests and test items,
the scaling of test scores and the form of the distribution of abilities in the population, the
quantification of subpopulation differences, the meaning of IQ and the psychological
nature of intelligence, and the reliability, stability, and validity of test scores. An understanding of these fundamental issues in testing is absolutely essential for a technical
understanding of the more specialized topic of test bias.

Professionals will quickly recognize that I have couched the discussion of bias mainly in terms of "classical test theory." This should not be misconstrued to imply that modern developments in so-called latent trait theories, which are applicable to many problems in psychometrics, are not potentially powerful methods for the study of test bias. However, we have scarcely begun to apply these relatively recent developments to empirical studies of test bias, and they are also much less familiar than classical test theory to the majority of psychologists and educators for whom the issue of test bias is of the most immediate concern.

Readers should note that I have intentionally omitted any discussion of theories and evidence as to the *causes* of the observed average differences in test scores between various racial and social groups, except insofar as these differences may be due to bias in the tests themselves or to the conditions under which tests are administered. It must be emphasized that test bias can be studied in its own right, quite independently of the broader question of the causes of individual and group differences in abilities, when such differences cannot be attributed to test bias. The question of test bias should not be confused with the question of the relative contributions of genetic and environmental factors to individual or group differences. In the terminology of genetics, test scores—*all* test scores—are measures of *phenotypes*, not of *genotypes*. The study of test bias, therefore, concerns only bias in the measurements of phenotypes. We need not be concerned with inferred genotypes in this inquiry. The answers to questions about test bias surely need not await a scientific consensus on the so-called nature–nurture question. A proper assessment of test bias, on the other hand, is an essential step toward a scientific understanding of the observed differences in test scores as well as the observed differences in all the important educational, occupational, and social correlates of test scores. Test scores themselves are merely correlates, predictors, and indicators of other socially important variables, which would not be altered in the least if tests did not exist. The problem of individual differences and group differences would not be made to disappear by abolishing tests. One cannot treat a fever by throwing away the thermometer.

My interest in test bias goes back to 1950, when I became personally acquainted with the late Kenneth Eells, one of the major pioneers in the study of cultural bias in tests. Eells had just completed his monumental work on social-class bias in group IQ tests when I did my own master's thesis under his tutelage. I frequently heard Eells talk about his fascinating research on test bias, and at that time I came to believe that nearly all standard IQ tests were grossly biased against virtually everyone but the white middle class. Eells's work involved only social-class differences within the white population, but everyone seemed to generalize what they perceived to be Eells's message to racial minorities as well. I can clearly remember how, at that time, audiences with a sympathy for the underdog received Eells's message with warm and heartfelt enthusiasm. I was among them. I say "message" because something rather different was communicated to Eells's audiences, perhaps at some unconscious emotional level, than what is actually conveyed by a close reading of the highly statistical and cautiously worded monograph describing his research (Eells et al., 1951). Eells's audiences relished seeing various well-known IQ tests and seemingly biased test items held up for criticism bolstered by tables and graphs. Our reactions were a mixture of scorn and hilarity, like seeing the villain in a play do a pratfall.

Tests indeed became popularly perceived as one of the villains in the 1950s. We have only recently begun to take a much more careful look at the more extravagant accusations made against tests during that socially conscious era, accusations that many well-intentioned persons thought would further the cause of social justice. The message essentially was that psychological tests are trivial, defective, and culture biased, and so we need not be concerned about the social group differences reflected by the tests: the differences were not "real" differences at all, but merely artifacts of the tests themselves. The tests' hidden purpose, whether intended or not, was to maintain the socioeconomic and political supremacy of the white middle and upper classes. Eells, always a careful scholar, must have been appalled by any such gross extrapolations from the important researches that he and Allison Davis had begun in the 1940s. To be sure, tests had been lambasted long before then (see the review by Cronbach, 1975), but most of the criticism came from outside the profession. Eells, as a psychologist trained in the psychometric tradition, was an "insider," and he made a far more valuable contribution to the analysis of test bias than had any of the critics on the "outside." Through my good fortune in becoming associated with Eells, I got in on the "ground floor" of the psychometric study of test bias.

I began to take a less one-sided view of Eells's interpretations of his findings when, in 1952, I wrote a student paper for Professor Irving Lorge extolling Eells's work. Lorge, who had been a protégé of E. L. Thorndike, was then one of the leaders in psychometrics, a president of the Psychometric Society, and editor of its journal, *Psychometrika*. And he was a most formidable professor. It turned out, to my dismay at the time, that Lorge himself had just written a paper (delivered at the annual convention of the American Psychological Association in 1952) that was highly critical of Eells's monograph. Lorge's only comment on my own paper was to give me a copy of his. Reading it made me feel a bit "softheaded" for my unquestioning and sentimental resonance to Eells's position. Lorge led me to see that one could take a more dispassionate, more incisively critical stance in psychological research than I had appreciated before my encounter with Lorge. He became one of my favorite professors, although I must admit I never felt at ease in his presence.

Since those days I have maintained a close watch on the controversy over bias in mental tests. But it was not until about 1970 that I began to take an active part in research on this topic. I was forced into it mainly out of my own concern with the possibility of culture bias in the tests I was using in my own research on the factors involved in the relatively poor scholastic performance of many minority children. One study led to another, and at the same time the technical literature on test bias was growing apace—it became a major task to keep on top of it. I was eager to get on with other research projects. But, by way of clearing the deck for new things, I felt the need first to digest as best as I could my expanding reprint files on test bias—four file drawers full—and to try to integrate it all with my own research and thinking in this sphere. This book is the result.

I have dedicated this book to the memory of Galton, Binet, and Spearman. Why just these three? I originally wanted to acknowledge the influence of all the great pioneers of mental testing. But where can one draw the line on such a list? Many other great names also came to mind—Edward L. Thorndike, Leon L. Thurstone, Lewis M. Terman, Sir Cyril Burt, and Sir Godfrey Thomson—to name several of the most prominent. Over the last couple of years I conducted an informal survey of colleagues and psychologists I met at conferences and conventions. I asked them, "Who in your estimateion are the greatest figures in the history of psychometrics?" Almost without exception the names of Galton,

Binet, and Spearman were given by everyone, and usually in the first three places. After those names there was considerable disagreement. If a fourth name were added to the list, I found there were arguments, but adding still another name would have led to even more dispute. After those indisputable first three, almost everyone I questioned seemed to have his own favorites or couldn't make up his mind as to who should be next on the list. So I stopped with three.

It is not hard to understand the unanimity of opinions on the first three. Almost every main theme in the history of mental measurement can be traced directly to Galton or to Binet or to Spearman.

Galton initiated the idea of measuring individual differences in mental abilities by purely objective methods. He devised some of the first techniques of mental measurement and tried them on thousands of subjects. He was the first to hypothesize the existence of a "general mental ability" in humans, and he was the first to apply statistical reasoning to the study of mental giftedness. Most important, he invented several of the most fundamental quantitative tools of psychometrics: the bivariate scatter diagram, regression, correlation, and standardized measurements.

Binet invented the first practically useful test of intelligence, which was the progenitor of all subsequent individual tests of intelligence and profoundly influenced the item contents of group tests as well. Binet also introduced the important concept of "mental age." (It was William Stern, however, who first divided the childs' mental age by his chronological age to yield the "intelligence quotient" or IQ.)

Spearman was the first to discover that all measurements of individual differences in complex mental performances are positively intercorrelated, which substantiated Galton's conjecture that there is a general factor of mental ability. Spearman gave the label g to this general factor, which is common to all complex mental tests, and he developed the method now known as factor analysis for determining the extent to which any given test measures g, or the general factor. Subsequent developments of factor analysis by Burt, Thurstone, and Thomson underlie our concepts of the psychological "structure" of abilities in terms of a limited number of factors or hypothetical sources of individual differences in abilities, which are measured in varying admixtures by the practically unlimited variety of ordinary mental tests.

There can be no question that the signal contributions of Galton, Binet, and Spearman have dominated the field of psychometrics from its beginnings in their pioneer efforts to the present day. All who work in the field of psychological measurement surely recognize the roots of their endeavors in the contributions of these three great pioneers.

Chapter 1

Mental Testing under Fire

Certainly no theory or practice in modern psychology has been more attacked than mental testing. The main targets have been "IQ tests" and similar measures of mental abilities and aptitudes. Most of the criticism in any scientific field or its applied aspects is professional and remains within the field. In the case of mental testing, however, the criticism has gone public (Cronbach, 1975). IQ tests are the only topic in psychology that in recent years has consistently been showered by brickbats from the popular media. Few of the theoretical and technical problems of real interest to testing experts ever get into the public debate. But most of the popular issues regarding testing, whatever their origin, have found their way into the literature of the behavioral sciences—in textbooks, in journals, and in official pronouncements by professional organizations.

Before passing any judgments on the criticisms of mental tests or examining the theory and evidence pertaining thereto, we had best begin by surveying the bare criticism itself. None of it should be ignored. Each criticism must finally be examined—semantically, logically, theoretically, or empirically. We first must order and classify the welter of published criticisms to discern all their essential points calling for detailed examination.

In a study of American attitudes toward intelligence tests, Brim (1965) found that antitesting sentiment, expressed both by lay and professional groups, involved one or more of the following issues:

1. Inaccessibility of test data
2. Invasion of privacy
3. Rigidity in use of test scores
4. Types of talent selected by tests
5. Fairness of tests to minority groups

But so compressed a summary falls far short of conveying the full sum and substance of the attack on tests.

In my own extensive reading on mental testing in the past several years, in professional and technical journals, college textbooks, and the popular press, I have made note of every critical statement about tests that I have come across. There are hundreds of criticisms in this collection. They constitute a large, representative sample of the variety of criticisms and antagonisms leveled at psychological testing in all its aspects. I have

1

classified all these into a number of main categories of criticism. Most merit separate consideration in the appropriate contexts of the later chapters of this book. In the present listing I have omitted only those criticisms that were couched strictly in technical terms or involve fine points in test theory that have never entered into the popular criticisms of tests. (Some of these technical points will necessarily enter into the discussion later on.)

Criticism of Tests

The full impact and character of the published criticisms cannot be savored by abstracting or summarizing them. Therefore, even at the risk of tedium, it seems worthwhile to present a number of typical examples of each category of criticism in their original wording. In this way few overtones of the critic's message are lost. Not that these overtones add to the clarity of the criticism; more often the contrary. But they reveal an important social-psychological aspect of the attack on mental testing, a phenomenon worthy of study in its own right.

By far most of the listed quotations used as examples of a particular type of criticism were gleaned from the professional literature, but a few are from the popular press. There are hardly any features that would intrinsically distinguish the two sources.

Cultural Bias

The most frequent of all criticisms is that tests are in various ways culturally biased so as to discriminate unfairly against racial and ethnic minorities or persons of low socioeconomic status. A thoughtful reading of some of the typical examples found in the following quotations reveals, in addition to the variety of explicit criticisms, many implicit and value-laden assumptions.

The majority of psychologists have concluded there is no such thing as a culture fair test.

A concept of intelligence testing is entirely a western notion, and so intelligence testing is culturally biased in itself.

Any attempt to measure intelligence must be culturally biased: what abilities one attempts to measure depend on what abilities are taken to be part of intelligence.

Intelligence tests are sadly misnamed because they were never intended to measure intelligence and might have been more aptly called CB (cultural background) tests.

IQ measures everyone by an Anglo yardstick. There is a conspiracy to make a narrow, biased collection of items the "real measure" of all persons.

IQ tests yield the best results when taken by those who come from the same cultural background as the devisers of the tests.

Tests are clearly discriminatory against those who have not been exposed to the culture, entrance to which is guarded by the tests.

Persons from backgrounds other than the culture in which the test was developed will always be penalized.

IQ tests are Anglocentric; they measure the extent to which an individual's background is similar to that of the modal cultural configuration of American society.

Racial, ethnic, and social class differences in mean IQ scores may not be due to genes or environment, but are probably inherent in the psycholinguistic, cultural, and temporal biases of the test.

Culturally unfair tests may be valid predictors of culturally unfair but nevertheless highly important criteria. Educational attainment, to the degree that it reflects social inequities rather than intrinsic merit, might be considered culturally unfair.

Aptitude tests reward white and middle class values and skills, especially ability to speak Standard English, and thus penalize minority children because of their backgrounds.

There are enormous social class differences in a child's access to the experiences necessary to acquire the valid intellectual skills.

How can a child who speaks Urdu or Lithuanian understand the questions much less the answers to an IQ test?

The middle-class environment is the birthright for IQ test-taking ability.

The IQ test is a seriously biased instrument that almost guarantees that middle-class white children will obtain higher scores than any other group of children. The more similar the experiences of two people, the more similar their scores should be.

IQ scores reported for blacks and low socioeconomic groups in the U.S. reflect characteristics of the test rather than of the test takers.

If children of Harvard University professors were raised in Africa they would test just like all other Africans. And if children of Africans were brought over here and raised they would have the same [IQ] distribution as American children.

Most of today's intelligence test items were written long ago during an age of even greater racial prejudice than now. These items correlate with race, since it was a prevailing belief then that race was a *criterion* of intelligence.

Tests have served as a very efficient device for screening out black, Spanish-speaking, and other minority applicants to colleges.

IQ tests are wholly inappropriate for making predictions about the academic potential of disadvantaged Negro children.

To correct the cultural bias of IQ tests, the thing to do is to add fifteen points to scores of black students. It will lift many of them from mentally retarded classes.

IQ tests do not and cannot measure the true potential of black children whose language and life styles are largely determined by the conditions of the ghetto.

The poor performance of Negro children on conventional tests is due to the biased content of the tests, that is, the test material is drawn from outside the black culture.

The words included in vocabulary tests are based on the frequency of their usage by whites. Blacks, who have differing vocabularies, may do poorly.

The whole IQ argument turns on the fact that black parents give their kids fewer jigsaw puzzles, Tinker Toys, and Erector Sets.

Criticism of Specific Test Items

Critics often try to ridicule tests by pointing to a specific test item as an example of culture bias or whatever point the critic wants to make. The implication to most readers is that the test as a whole measures no more than what the selected item seemingly measures. It is usually assumed that no other information than that of holding up the item itself is needed to evaluate the item or the test from which it was selected. Attention is directed entirely to the "face validity" of specific items. Yet no competent psychometrist would attempt to criticize or defend specific test items out of context. The importance of the "face validity" of an item depends, first, on the nature and purpose of the test in which it is included and, second, on certain "item statistics" that are essential to the psychometrist in evaluating any test item. Without such information, criticism of individual test items can carry no weight. Rarely does the test constructor attribute much importance to whether or not any given person knows the specific information content of any single item; rather, the chief concern is with the measurement of whatever is common to a number of quite diverse items. This is determined by summing the "rights" and "wrongs" over a large number of such items to obtain a total score. The specific features of single items thus average out, and the total score is a measure of whatever ability is common to the whole set of items. The more diverse the items, the more general is the ability measured by the total score. For this reason, criticism of item content, outside a context of essential psychometric information, is the weakest criticism of all.

The Comprehension test of the Wechsler Intelligence Scales is a favorite target for the critics of item content. For example, one critic points to the item "What would you do if you were lost in a forest?" and argues that "Urban black kids have not seen a forest. If you ask a black kid how to get from Lenox Avenue to Lexington Avenue, he can tell you." (Who cannot see the essential difference between these two questions?) Yet, interestingly, blacks have been found to perform better, relative to whites, on the Comprehension test than on any of the ten other subtests of the Wechsler (Shuey, 1966, p. 407). Another example is from the Wechsler Picture Completion test, in which the subject is asked to point to any missing essential feature in each of a set of pictures of familiar things. One item calls for noting a tooth missing from a comb. A critic claims:

> The ghetto child seldom sees a complete comb. A comb is useful even when teeth are missing, to be replaced when it is no longer of any use. The ghetto child may respond by saying "hair," or "brush" or "hand." The toothless comb is commonplace, not a rarity. Additionally, the physical aspects of Negro hair make it difficult to comb and the kinkiness often breaks off teeth more readily than does straight hair. Both economics and physiology influence this question.

It would be interesting to know how this item compares in difficulty with other seemingly less culture-biased items.[1]

---

[1] Notes are gathered at the end of each chapter.

Another favorite example is the "aesthetic comparison" test from the Year IV-6 level of the Stanford–Binet Intelligence Scale. The child is shown three pairs of pen sketches of faces and asked "Which one is prettier?" (See Figure 1.1) Two critics hold up this item as an example of cultural bias as follows:

> In all cases, the "correct" picture has the classic Anglo-Saxon features while the "incorrect" one has features common to other ethnic groups, e.g., a wide flat nose and thick lips in two cases, and a hooked nose in the last case.

Item statistics on the Stanford–Binet in the normative white and black samples, however, show that this particular item (out of the seven items at the Year IV-6 level) is the *easiest* item for blacks and only the third easiest for whites. That is the trouble with armchair criticisms directed at single items. Without knowing the item statistics, such criticism usually backfires. One critic used as an example of culture bias against blacks the test item shown in Figure 1.2, on the grounds that it would require blacks to deal with fourteen *white* faces.

Figure 1.1. The "aesthetic comparison" test of the Stanford-Binet scale (1937 and 1960) at Year IV-6. Of each pair of faces, the examiner asks "Which one is prettier?" A passing score is three out of three correct.

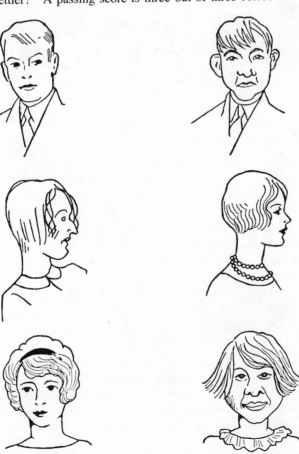

Figure 1.2.   Which one of the six faces in the bottom row should go into the space marked by the question mark in order logically to complete the pattern? (From Eysenck, 1971, p. 52)

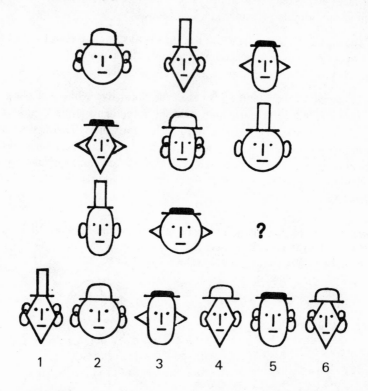

One critic of tests, Banesh Hoffman (1962), based an entire popular book on formal or rational criticisms of selected multiple-choice test items. His complaints are of a quite different character from those already displayed. He contends that IQ test questions are ambiguous in ways that will trap the creative and the overly thoughtful who recognize that more than one answer may be correct. He argues that multiple-choice tests deny creative persons an opportunity to demonstrate their creativity and that they favor the shrewd and facile candidate over the one who has something to say. Hoffman's argument rests on no empirical evidence but consists of armchair dissection of multiple-choice test items carefully selected to make his point. The items are most often of the type involving informational content, as are most commonly found in scholastic achievement tests. He has turned up some badly written items, to be sure, but no evidence is presented that they are typical. No consideration is given to the kinds of item statistics used by test constructors to evaluate the reliability and validity of test items. As Ebel (1973, p. 79) states, "These hyper-critics disdain the item and test statistics that challenge their beliefs. When they cannot find any published test item bad enough to clinch the point they are making, they invent one." Dunnette (1963) has written the most detailed and trenchant criticism of Hoffman's argument, pointing out that Hoffman attempts the impossible feat of using verbal analysis to overcome or reject empirical results.

Inability to Define or Measure Intelligence

This class of criticism argues that psychologists cannot define intelligence, or at least cannot agree on a definition, and therefore cannot possibly measure it.

It also includes variations on this theme, such as the idea that tests cannot get at the true essence of intelligence, or that definitions of intelligence are entirely arbitrary, or that tests are in some way inadequate to assess intelligence. Implicit in most of these criticisms is the assumption that there is some trait or essence in the individual that can be called his "real intelligence" (or even his "real worth" as a human being) and that for some reason this quality has eluded all attempts at objective measurement. Often the critic's expectations for a test are beyond anything ever dreamed of by the test constructor. Here are some examples.

If man has yet to define intelligence, how can he have the audacity to measure it?

We cannot possibly measure intelligence, since the measurement of effects is not necessarily the measurement of an entity.

In the final analysis the IQ does not measure anything real.

IQ tests do not identify or measure intelligence. Those who write IQ tests use their own perception of intelligent behavior to devise their measures.

What IQ measures is a value choice of the test makers; they measure culture-bound and value-laden abilities with no *a priori* justification.

No test can trick a person psychologically or otherwise into revealing how much brilliance or stupidity he possesses.

There is a clear and definite difference between intelligence, per se, and the concept of the intelligence quotient, or IQ.

IQ tests are not perfectly accurate nor are they a perfect indicator of potential.

The white middle-class Western community, like any moderately isolated social group, has created over the years a specialized vocabulary, reservoir of information, and style of problem-solving and communication which it summarizes under the concept "intelligence."

Intelligence is simply the ability to perform well at whatever one's social situations seem to require.

IQ tests do not measure perception, moral appreciation, and sensitivity to other people.

IQ tests do not indicate *why* a given student did poorly in a particular subject.

The IQ does not measure qualities such as creativity, imagination, insight, and original thinking.

These [IQ] tests do not measure the human quality of compassion, or sincerity, sensitivity, brotherhood, and any number of character traits which serve humanity.

We must demand a more accurate measuring device than the IQ test for these persons who will be specially rewarded and recognized. It must account for honesty, commitment to democratic values, and a well-integrated personality. These qualities are not measured by the IQ test.

The validity of IQ tests has not changed in 30 years.

A common form of criticism that we can place in this category consists of pointing out some very famous person or historic genius who is reputed to have done poorly in school. The implicit assumption is that the person would therefore also have obtained a low score on an IQ test. Yet low intelligence is obviously belied by the individual's outstanding achievements as an adult. This argument of course assumes a perfect correlation between scholastic performance or teacher's marks and IQ. But we know that the correlation between IQ and school marks is far less than perfect, and this fact alone guarantees that we should be able to find some very high-IQ persons who do poorly in school, whatever the reason. Also, as we shall see later on, intelligence is conceptually distinguishable from achievement. Hence it is a misfired criticism of IQ tests that what they measure is not completely redundant with assessments of achievement.

Tests Measure Too Narrow Abilities, or "Nothing But _____"

These criticisms generally equate IQ tests with scholastic skills or academic knowledge, or even something narrower, such as familiarity with "proper" English. The implication is that whatever it is that intelligence tests measure it is something much more limited and trivial than "intelligence." It is a debunking or "nothing but" style of criticism.

IQ tests are a sham and ought to be relegated to their proper status as parlor games where they were first inspired.

An IQ is nothing more than a score earned on a test.

IQ tests measure only the ability for doing well on IQ tests.

IQ tests perpetuate a narrow conception of ability.

IQ reflects rather than predicts a person's preparation for academic work.

We don't have intelligence tests. We have a measure for school achievement in a middle-class Anglo-Saxon–oriented school.

Children who have not had the opportunity to read widely or to acquire verbal facility must always be at a grave disadvantage on IQ tests.

IQ tests fail to measure "adaptive behavior," the capacity to survive in society, and place too high a premium on school intelligence.

A scholastic aptitude test is essentially a test of the student's command of standard English and grammar.

The games people are required to play on aptitude tests are similar to the games teachers require in the classroom.

While poor children score lower on IQ tests than the middle class and typically do not do well in school, these same children have normal intelligence outside of class and have no unusual problems succeeding in their adult occupational and family lives (except for discriminatory factors).

IQ tests treat intelligence (or more accurately, school intelligence) in aggregate terms, failing to recognize that a given student is likely to be competent at some things but not at others, and that combining those strengths and weaknesses into a single score necessarily misdescribes and oversimplifies the notion of intelligence.

If a candidate were chosen merely on the result of his IQ test score, only a small part of his total abilities would have been judged.

The IQ test does not measure all that we mean by mental ability.

To avoid the shortcomings of IQ tests, schools should rely more heavily on achievement tests.

Standardized achievement tests are often invalid because they do not measure what was taught in a particular school's curriculum.

Failure to Measure Innate Capacity

These criticisms exemplify the idea that individuals possess some innate ability, capacity, or potential that intelligence tests have been unable to measure. Because the critics making this claim do not acknowledge any valid measure of "innate intelligence," "capacity," or "intellectual potential," they never make clear just how they can determine the validity of their claim that IQ tests do not measure this innate capacity. Provided that the issue can be stated in such a way as to be theoretically meaningful and empirically testable, there happens to be a scientific methodology capable of answering the question of the extent to which any test measures innate (meaning genetically conditioned) factors. The methods of quantitative genetics were devised to deal scientifically with just this kind of question, but this is seldom mentioned by the critics who disparage tests on the grounds that they do not measure "innate intelligence."

Despite the name, intelligence tests do not measure "intelligence" or innate ability. No test does that.

IQ tests say nothing firm about capacity or about general learning ability.

These tests do not measure innate mental capacity in a cross-culturally valid and totally exhaustive way independent of socialization experience.

The great majority of psychologists and geneticists hold that there are no significant differences in intelligence between the races. If they are right, then IQ tests to identify mentally retarded school students should yield results closely corresponding to the racial make-up of the school population. But in San Francisco classes for EMR [educationally mentally retarded] children are 66% black though the student population in San Francisco is 28.5% black.

Unsuitable Norms

The standardization of a test is an elaborate procedure of sifting and selecting from a large pool of items according to a number of statistical and other criteria and finally trying out the finished test and standardizing the raw scores in a large representative sample of individuals from some specified reference population. The standardized scores are a mathematical transformation of the raw scores (number of items answered correctly) that permits a precise and meaningful interpretation, such as "Johnny's score on test X means that his performance on this test exceeded that of 86 percent of the children of his age in the normative or reference group."

One of the criticisms of tests is that the norms are inappropriate for some particular (usually low-scoring) group.

> The nature of psychological testing makes it logically necessary to use different norms for different ethnic groups, since identical cut-off points are inherently discriminatory.

> Blacks have been overlooked in devising questions for tests and were not included in the population used to standardize the figures used for the interpretation of test scores.

> Since Negro children are excluded from the norming sample, their score will make them look worse than they ought to.

> Aptitude tests, standardized (or "normed") for white middle class children, cannot determine the intelligence of minority children whose backgrounds differ notably from that of the "normed" population.

IQ Tests Measure Only Learned Skills

Underlying this line of criticism is the assumption that, if a test item depends on learned skills or knowledge, or if teaching, coaching, or practice on a class of test items will improve performance on similar items, any test composed of such items is invalidated as a test of intelligence or, at best, only measures something trivial or superficial. Also implicit in many of the criticisms in this category is the notion that the only true ability is the ability to learn and therefore that all that an IQ test can possibly measure is what the individual has already learned before taking the test.

> The IQ test is a measure of experience and learning rather than a measure of inborn capacity.

> IQ tests are basically tests of *learned* and *achieved* ability, not tests of mental capacity or potential.

> IQ tests measure essentially what children have learned.

> Standard IQ tests are based in large part on skills and information acquired in the school.

> Children must attend a school that adequately teaches the content of the IQ test in order to score well. Most ghetto schools fail at this task.

> Children can be taught to do intelligence tests just as they can be taught to do English and arithmetic, chess and crosswords.

IQ and aptitude tests can only test a student's present level of learning in certain skills and from that infer his capacity to learn further.

The IQ is just a number that reflects one form of general learning speed.

IQs Are Inconstant

A perennial argument concerns the "constancy" or lack of "constancy" of the IQ. But for a good many years now there has been no need for argument on this issue, as it is really an empirical question for which we have a great deal of highly reliable evidence. Yet we still read statements such as the following from recent articles:

> The IQ fluctuates from year to year. We have plenty of instances in which a child has gained or dropped as much as 50 points.

> IQ tests identify intelligence as static and not dynamic, and fail to account for the uneven growth patterns of children.

Test Scores Contaminated by Extraneous Factors

The claim is often made that external factors in the testing situation, such as the race of the tester as well as subjects' attitudinal and motivational disposition, contaminate test performance more for "minority" than for "majority" children.

> Disadvantaged children get low scores because of poor rapport with the examiner, especially when the examinee is black and the examiner is white.

> Minority children score higher on tests administered by someone of their own race, because of better communication and understanding.

> Black children often misunderstand the white middle class examiner's pronunciation.

> The traditional testing situation elicits deliberately defensive behavior from Negro examinees; the Negro child may not try to answer the questions.

> The impersonal environment in which aptitude tests are given depresses the scores of minority students who become anxious or apathetic in such situations.

> Ethnic minority group children and culturally disadvantaged children are handicapped in taking tests because of deficiencies in motivation, in test practice, and in reading.

> Specific cultural differences in *motivation,* unrelated to innate intelligence, can fully account for the lower IQ of blacks.

> These tests [Lorge-Thorndike IQ] penalize the slow, perfectionistic student who would score much higher if given more time.

Misuses, Abuses, and Undesirable Consequences of Testing

A large category of antitesting sentiment involves real or imagined misuses of tests and unjust or undesirable personal and social consequences of testing. Most of the criticism coming from professional testers falls into this category.

Tests are not given often enough, with the result that a few test scores have an enormous influence on a child's academic career.

Tests foster a rigid, inflexible, and permanent classification of individuals.

Standardized tests are the instruments by which we are routed into specific careers and pay levels.

Because teachers expect more of the high IQ scorers, those children do better than those who were assigned low IQ scores.

Tests contribute to their own predictive validity by functioning as self-fulfilling prophecies.

Often school officials and teachers view test scores punitively rather than remedially: They are used to label students as "smart" or "dumb" or to distinguish "college material" from future blue-collar workers.

School-age youths are increasingly subjected to internal and external testing programs from childhood onward. At age four the child is administered a pre-school test; at age five, a reading readiness test; and beginning with age six, annual batteries of language arts, math and IQ tests. The lives of serious-minded high school and college students become dominated by quizzes, course tests, qualifying exams, etc. Presently, 48% of the nation's youth enter college; but a mere 25% of those who start ever acquire the A.B. degree. A major obstacle affecting the life chances of today's youth is a test of some sort.

The minority, disadvantaged student may incur educational damage by being subjected to current standardized testing methods.

IQ tests are used to deny minority children educational opportunities by labeling them as uneducable, placing them in inappropriate ability groupings and special education classes.

Tests are inimical to the self-image and motivation of Black and Chicano children, shattering their self-confidence, lowering teacher and parental opinion, reinforcing negative expectations, and possibly contributing as much to the child's overall socio-educational deprivation as any other known factor.

By labeling a child who is performing adequately in his family environment, testing makes an otherwise invisible person visible and begins to create social problems where previously none had really existed.

There is too much secrecy surrounding test scores.

A test is a potential invasion of privacy because personal information is made available to others. Very important values in American society suggest that individuals have the right to decide to whom and under what conditions they will make available to others information about themselves.

Organized Opposition to Tests

Several national professional and political organizations are on record as opposing mental tests and have waged campaigns against them. The specific criticisms of tests encountered in the literature disseminated by these organizations are all much the same and include practically all the points found in the several categories of criticisms just reviewed, but the literature of the several organizations opposed to testing differs in tone, emphasis, and vehemence.

National Education Association

In February 1972, the National Education Association's Center for Human Relations held a three-day national conference in Washington, D.C., with the announced theme: "Tests and Use of Tests—Violations of Human and Civil Rights." The stated objectives of the program were

> To examine current attitudes about the educational value of standardized tests, especially as they affect the culturally different learner;
> To explore alternative measurement and evaluation processes that would be helpful tools in the educational process; and
> To create greater national awareness of an immediate need for concerted action to prohibit the use of IQ and other test scores as indicators of growth potential; especially for the culturally different learner.

All persons attending the conference were asked to fill out an "opinionnaire" indicating their degree of agreement with items such as

> IQ tests are not perfectly accurate nor are they a perfect indicator of potential.
> The IQ test is a measure of experience and learning rather than a measure of inborn ability.
> Most standardized tests are tests of developed abilities rather than measures of potential.
> Most colleges have developed procedures which minimize discrimination against minority group members on the basis of test scores.
> Given the possible negative effects of standardized tests, which of the following actions do you believe should be taken?
> (a) Eliminate the use of standardized tests entirely
> (b) Intensify efforts to develop culture free tests
> (c) Curtail the use of standardized tests except for research purposes
> (d) Conduct an intensive educational program to prevent misuses of tests

A press release put out by the National Education Association stated:

> The possibility that a third or more of American citizens are intellectually folded, mutilated or spindled before they have a chance to get through elementary school because of linguistically or culturally biased standardized tests, prompted the CHR to devote its annual conference to "Tests and Use of Tests—Violations of Human and Civil Rights."
>
> For the "average" middle class white American, the standardized gauntlet of tests through which he must pass in order to be classified "normal" may provide few, if any problems. The tests are written in his native language—English—the concepts directly relate to his everyday life, and the teacher who analyzes his responses comes from a similar and sympathetic cultural environment. But what if the rules of the game are changed, and you are the only player at the table who doesn't know the rules?

The press release contains a sample "IQ and Achievement Test" and invites the reader to try it. It consists of a set of five questions written in five foreign languages and a ghetto dialect, e.g.,

> Répondez au question suivante:
> Ist die Farbe des Wassers im Roten Meer rot?
> Décrivez ce qui se passe dans l'histoire suivante:
> "Quiet as its kept and man you'd better lay some chill, but this jive swab say the man eased into his crib last p.m., swung with his vee, his vines, and his sides. Even snatched some old roaches he savin' for hard times. The man took off with the brother right on his hine, hollerin' "Rip off, crab, 'fore I blow you away!"

The press release continues:

> If the average American's intelligence were to be graded according to the above test he or she would fail, be classified as mentally retarded, tracked in a slow learner grade, and rejected from higher education institutions or professions of any lucrative worth. Yet some 68 million Americans are daily subjected to tests that make about as much sense to them as the above Spanish–Hebrew–French–Greek–German–Ghettoese test would to the average English-speaking American.

The NEA press release stated further:

> America's tape measure of success depends on a child's ability to understand and communicate in "good" standard English, and to comprehend questions that relate to "good" standard middle-class, white concepts. For many of the 25 million Blacks, 12 million Spanish-speaking, nearly a million Indians, 18 million poor whites, 11 million first-generation foreign-born, and close to a million Orientals, a standard IQ or achievement test written in English and relating to middle-American concepts is about as understandable and relevant as purdah and sutee are to the average housewife in Dearborn, Michigan.

The two major results of the three-day NEA conferences were (1) a call for a moratorium on all standardized testing looking toward the possibility of eliminating testing completely and (2) a call for the abolition of the National Teacher's Examination. The main rationale given for both moves is the supposed bias of the tests against blacks and Chicanos.

Association of Black Psychologists

This professional organization, at its annual meeting in 1969, called for an immediate moratorium on the administration of ability tests to black children. The ABP charged (see Williams, 1971, p. 67) that ability tests

1. Label black children as uneducable,
2. Place black children in special classes,
3. Potentiate inferior education,
4. Assign black children to lower education tracks than whites,
5. Deny black children higher educational opportunities, and
6. Destroy positive intellectual growth and development of black children.

One of the leading spokesmen for the ABP, Dr. Robert L. Williams, has expressed attitudes about tests and testing such as the following:

> Black psychologists translated the whole abuse of testing issue into one of intellectual genocide of Black children. Tests do not permit the masses of Black children to develop their full potential. The tests are used to sort and consequently to misplace Black children in Special Education classes.   (1971, p. 67)

> [The testing industry] is a multimillion-dollar-a-year supermarket of oppression.   (1974, p. 34)

> IQ and achievement tests are nothing but updated versions of the old signs down South that read "For Whites Only."   (1974, p. 32)

> The testing arena is the place where blacks are literally thrown to the wolves.   (1974, p. 41)

Williams argues that "since [IQ] tests are biased in favor of middle-class Whites, all previous research comparing the intellectual abilities of Blacks and Whites should be rejected completely" (1971, p. 63). He claims "vast cultural differences in Black and White society" and emphasizes differences in language and dialect: "It is a common observation that Black and White children do not speak alike. The differences in linguistic systems favor White children since standard English is the *lingua franca* of the tests and the public schools" (1971, p. 66). The average lower scores of blacks on ability tests are explained by Williams as "manifestations of a viable and well-delineated culture of the Black American." His view is that "Blacks and Whites come from different cultural backgrounds which emphasize different learning experiences necessary for survival" (1971, p. 65). This "cultural difference model" is the chief rationale of the ABP's opposition to current standardized tests, which they largely blame for the disproportionate number of blacks in "special education" classes and classes for the mentally retarded.

The ABP has been the most vocal, and probably the most effective, in exerting various pressures on school boards to halt the testing of black children in the public schools. Some spokesmen for the ABP now call for more than merely a moratorium on testing. Williams advocates federal laws against the testing of blacks and urges black communities to "file class action law suits that demand an end to testing of black children for whatever reason" (1974, p. 41). Such actions were initiated by the ABP against the San Francisco, California, Board of Education in 1970 and eventuated in a court order banning testing of blacks and some other minorities in all state-supported California schools. This and other legal actions involving tests are discussed in the next chapter.

In 1968, largely in response to the ABP's manifesto demanding a moratorium on the use of psychological and educational tests with blacks, the American Psychological Association's Board of Scientific Affairs appointed an ad hoc committee of leading experts in the field of psychological testing to investigate and report to the APA on the validity of tests and testing practices in the schools. The committee's twenty-seven-page report was published in January 1975 in the APA's official journal, *American Psychologist* (Cleary et al., 1975). The Association of Black Psychologists replied to the report in the same issue, expressing strong disapproval and calling the APA report "blatantly racist" (Jackson, 1975). [A rebuttal to the ABP's charges was made by the APA committee chairman[2]

(Humphreys, 1975).] The ABP reply reiterated most of the same objections to tests already mentioned and asked, ''If a group of scholars charged with the responsibility of studying the problems inherent in testing after deliberation produces a document such as that of the [APA] Committee, to whom can we appeal for relief?'' (Jackson, 1975, p. 92). The ABP thus rejected the APA Committee's Report and reasserted its position in the strongest terms:

> Psychological testing historically has been a quasi-scientific tool in the perpetuation of racism on all levels of social or economic intercourse. Simultaneously, under the guise of scientific objectivity, it has provided a cesspool of intrinsically and inferentially fallacious data which inflates the egos of Whites by demeaning Black people and threatens to potentiate Black genocide.
>
> The general thesis [of the ABP] set forth in response to the [APA] Committee's position is that tests penalize minorities, supply inaccurate information to counselors and teachers, have a devastating effect on the self-image of minority students, and assist the white establishment in preventing Blacks and other minorities from gaining reasonable proportions in the professions, decision-making positions, corporate structures, and, in general, those areas which one attains through the educational enterprise. This, indeed, has been the history of psychological tests as such. Their misuses simply complement this abuse intrinsic to the tests.   (Jackson, 1975, pp. 88–92)

''Marxist'' Opposition to Tests

A number of rather small but vociferous groups in America and Great Britain that are self-identified as ''Marxist'' have waged propaganda campaigns against psychological tests. The best-known groups of this type in the United States are the Progressive Labor Party, an avowedly communist organization, and the Students for a Democratic Society (SDS), a small radical student organization once active on a number of university campuses in the United States.

The term ''Marxist'' is placed in quotes because there is nothing intrinsic in original Marxian theory that would oppose mental tests or any of the psychological and statistical principles on which they are based. Although there was a period when IQ tests were disdained in the Soviet Union, tests of scholastic achievement—essay and oral examinations—have long been used in the U.S.S.R. with an even greater emphasis on educational selection and grouping or tracking than is practiced in the United States. The selection and education of children with special academic talents, such as mathematical precocity, takes place much earlier in the Soviet child's educational career than is true of his or her American counterpart.

The official position of Soviet psychologists can be described as antihereditarian, but it has not precluded the study of individual differences in abilities or the practice of educational selection. In this process, however, more reliance has been placed on teachers' assessments than on standardized tests, at least in the early years of schooling. Some prominent Soviet psychologists, in presenting their views to audiences outside the U.S.S.R., have voiced the opinion that ability tests in capitalist countries are an instrument of political reactionary class aims, or, as one of them said, tests are ''used to prove that the level of ability is lower in children of workers and peasants than in children of the propertied classes, and that the abilities of children of subject people are lower than those of children of the so-called 'higher' peoples and 'higher' races. These tests serve as a foundation for the assertion that social inequality is based on and justified by such differences of aptitude'' (quoted by Goslin, 1966, p. 38).

In a similar vein, Marxists outside the U.S.S.R. have been most strongly opposed to ability tests, and some of their criticism has appeared in journals such as the *Marxist Quarterly, Communist Review,* and *Marxism Today.* The reader can find these neo-Marxian criticisms of tests and the psychological theories surrounding them expounded in *Intelligence, Psychology and Education: A Marxist Critique* by Brian Simon (1971), a British Marxist and educationist. Simon includes virtually nothing in his criticism of IQ tests that has not previously been listed, although they are often couched in the Marxist rhetoric of the class struggle.

[W]herever the [IQ] test is applied, it will discriminate between children on what can only be described as class lines. (Simon, 1971, p. 78)

Since, in a class society, *on average,* the higher the social status, the greater the likelihood that test questions of the kind described can be successfully answered; a test standardized this way is bound to set standards of ''intelligence'' which are largely class differences disguised. It is an inescapable fact that the middle-class child will always *tend* to do better than the working-class child, as a necessary result of the way in which the tests are constructed, validated and standardized. (Simon, 1971, p. 78)

[T]he ''intelligence'' measured by tests is a class-conditioned attribute. A class element enters into the practice of intelligence testing, at almost every stage; first, and most important, in the choice and character of the questions; second, in the method of putting the test questions together, and validating the test as a whole; finally, in the process of standardization. . . . It follows that an investigation of the class distribution of intelligence is bound to give precisely the result it does, and indeed these results are the best possible confirmation of our thesis. (Simon, 1971, pp. 78–79)

Intelligence tests can never be ''objective,'' can never reach the supposed elusive and independent inner essence of mind which psychologists attempt to measure. Instead they are bound sharply to discriminate against the working class. (Simon, 1971, p. 81).

A more recent Marxist book, by Lawler (1978), further exemplifies the strongly ideological and often sophistic flavor of Marxist disputation regarding mental testing and the study of individual and group differences.

Pamphlets circulated by the Progressive Labor Party and the Students for a Democratic Society go the limit in their interpretation of psychological tests as instruments of oppression promoted by the ''capitalist ruling class.'' One such pamphlet even suggested that the IQ be renamed the ''BQ'' or ''Bourgeois Quotient.'' The position of these groups is well summarized in the following quotations from their literature.

Intelligence testing is a political expression of those groups in society who most successfully establish behavior they value as the measure of intelligence.

The whole IQ test is constructed (contrived) to prove that the children of the upper class are the more intelligent section of the population.

IQ tests are used by the Establishment to promote its own goals and to hold down the downtrodden—those non-establishment races and cultures whose interests and talents are not fairly credited by intelligence tests.

The IQ test measures nothing inherently valuable and seems to test mainly things on which those with the right background and attitudes will score highly on. These attitudes are respect for authority, obedience, willingness to play the game and tendency toward isolation rather than social interaction.

[IQ test questions] seem to be measuring the extent to which children are willing to conform to the rules of society to do what they are told. Here intelligence seems to be equated with acceptance of the rules of the school and the society. Students are being tested to see if they are potentially dangerous, potentially rebellious and disrespectful toward authority.... What is measured is not intelligence, it is either a naive honesty, docility and respect for the system, or a clever, but mild dishonesty used to "make it" in the world of the school.

Explanations for Opposition to Tests

In reading many of the critics of mental testing one soon perceives a constellation of distinct themes and attitudes common to nearly all of them, with only superficial variations. Thus one can speak of an *antitest syndrome*. It has several clearly discernible features.

1. Most critics of tests are indiscriminate in their criticisms. They rarely point to specific tests or focus on specific shortcomings or abuses. Nearly all types of tests are referred to collectively as "IQ tests," and critics who state any one of the typical criticisms usually mention most of the others as well. All the criticisms seem to come from a common grab bag, are dispensed in a shotgun broadside, and convey attitudes and sentiments instead of information that would be needed to evaluate the arguments.

2. To most test critics there is a mystique about the word *intelligence* and a humanistic conviction that the most important human attributes cannot be measured or dealt with quantitatively or even understood in any scientifically meaningful sense. "Intelligence" is viewed as an attribute that eludes all scientists who have ever tried to study it or assess it objectively. There is an implicit reification and idealization of "intelligence" by the critic, who charges that tests do not or cannot measure "intrinsic merit," "true potential," "innate capacity," "real intelligence," "intelligence per se"—to use their own words. The problems of behavioral measurement are confused with the metaphysical and moral issue of the intrinsic worth of the individual. A sanctity and honorific valuation are often unconsciously attributed to "intelligence," as evinced, for instance, in one critic's objection that the general factor, or *g,* common to a large variety of cognitive tests is "anything *deserving* of the name 'general intelligence' " (italics added).

3. Critics give no empirical basis for their criticisms of tests, test items, or the uses of tests. They often attempt to refute empirical findings by logical or semantic analysis of test items rather than by pointing to any empirical counterevidence. Critics claim, for example, that a particular item in, say, the Comprehension subtest of the Wechsler, is biased against blacks; but it never seems to occur to them to cite any statistical evidence that the item singled out for this criticism is in fact relatively harder for blacks than other test items. Because of this nonempirical and nonresearch stance of the typical critic, the reader never sees, and indeed is never made aware of, the kinds of technical and statistical information that one would need to assess the merits of the critics' claims. The almost total lack of such essential information in most critical writings on tests leads one to suspect that the most valid and constructive criticism of tests are scarcely to be found in this literature.

   4. Critics fail to suggest alternatives to tests—or ways of improving mental measurement—or to come to grips with the problems of educational and personnel selection or the diagnosis of problems in school learning. In defense of tests, John Gardner (1961) argues:

> Anyone attacking the usefulness of tests must suggest workable alternatives. It has been proven over and over again that the alternative methods of evaluating ability are subject to gross errors and capable of producing grave injustices. Judgments, evaluations, predictions, and selections will be made, regardless. The only real question is whether we can make them more objective, more valid, and more fair in their use. To this end so far no one has proposed any method better than objective tests of abilities, aptitudes, skills, and achievements. Tests permit a more exact knowledge, examination, and quality control of the processes of assessment, prediction, and selection.

   Those who insist that IQ tests do not measure "intelligence" imply, whether they realize it or not, that they must know what intelligence is and how to measure it satisfactorily. But they never put forth the definition or the means of measurement that remains implicit in their arguments. Some anti-IQ critics, however, seem to favor tests of "creativity," often with the tacit supposition that persons who would score low on IQ tests are compensated with creativity and those with high IQs are apt to be lacking in creativity. (For a time in the 1960s there was a boom in "creativity" tests.) The apparent justice in this theory of the compensatory allocation of talents is unfortunately not supported by the evidence.

   5. Critics hardly ever mention the nonverbal and nonscholastic types of mental tests. They inculcate the notion that all intelligence tests simply tap word knowledge, bookish information, and use of "good English." This is exemplified by one critic who writes:

> [C]hildren who have not had the opportunity to read widely, or to acquire verbal facility, must always be at a grave disadvantage. Indeed, it is no exaggeration to say that the differences between social classes is most easily to be discerned in differences of expression, vocabulary, and sentence construction. The most common grammatical "errors," in the formal sense, are precisely those forms of speech which are generally current in local dialect. In short, it would be difficult to find a more effective method of differentiating children, according to social environment, than the standard verbal intelligence test.   (Simon, 1971, pp. 63–64)

6. Finally, criticisms are imbued with a sense of outrage at purported social injustices either caused or reinforced by tests. The sentiment is expressed also as antipathy for the measurement or the scientific study of human traits, for comparisons of persons or groups, or for judgments concerning the relative importance of various traits and abilities from the standpoint of society.

Sources of Antitest Sentiment

A number of psychologists have tried independently to find out who among the general public opposes tests. The question was studied systematically through public opinion surveys conducted by the Russell Sage Foundation in the early 1960s and summarized by Brim (1965).

A representative national sample of Americans over 18 were asked the following questions:

> Given tests as they are now, do you think it is fair (that is, just) to use intelligence tests to help make the following decisions?
> A. To decide who can go to certain colleges
> B. To put children into special classes in school
> C. To decide who should be hired for a job
> D. To decide who should be promoted

The percentages who opposed these listed uses of tests were (A) 41 percent, (B) 25 percent, (C) 37 percent, (D) 50 percent. In another survey of 10,000 high school students in a national sample of sixty secondary schools, the following percentages of opposition were found: (A) 54 percent, (B) 50 percent, (C) 53 percent, (D) 62 percent. The younger group, though probably having had more experience with tests, was the more opposed.

Antitesting sentiment expressed in the survey generally involved the issues of inaccessibility of test data (people generally wished that they had been better informed of their own test results or of their children's), invasion of privacy (who keeps the test results? who has access to one's scores?), rigidity in use of test scores (used too early, determines life chances, does not allow for future change), types of talent selected by tests (denies opportunity to person with different but valuable talents), and fairness of tests to minority groups (screens out from opportunities for advancement persons from culturally deprived backgrounds).

An interesting fact noted by Brim was that lower-social-class blacks have a more favorable attitude than whites or higher-social-class blacks toward the use of tests for job selection and promotion. Brim explains this finding:

> Those of culturally deprived backgrounds are frequently members of minority groups against which society discriminates. Minority groups, as such, should be favorably inclined toward the use of ability tests, since tests constitute a universal standard of competence and potential. When tests are substituted for discriminatory methods of educational placement and discriminatory methods of job selection and promotion, they increase the opportunities of minority group members because they measure ability rather than social status. Tests therefore should be viewed with favor by this segment of the culturally deprived. (Brim, 1965, p. 127)

Brim considers the personal and social characteritstics of antitest critics and suggests that their objections are often merely superficial expressions of more fundamental attitudes involving the individual's personality characteristics, his general system of values, his personal experience with intelligence tests ("antagonism is bred in the loss of self-esteem a person may have suffered as a result of poor performance"), and opposition due to any restriction on one's life opportunities that might have been associated with poor performance on tests.

As for the personality traits associated with antitest sentiments, Brim mentions hostility to any self-examination, introspection, or self-understanding.

As for the influence of one's values about how society is to be organized, Brim distinguishes three main philosophies: egalitarianism, inherited aristocracy, and open competition. Egalitarians generally scorn ability tests, as they are based on the assumption that there are important individual differences that can be measured; all persons are regarded by egalitarians as inherently equal, and the observed differences should be minimized by equalizing opportunities or by differential treatment. The aristocratic social order, based on family inheritance of wealth, privilege, and status, is challenged by a system of competition and selection based on tests that reflect genetically inherited abilities more than social status and thereby permit a greater educational and occupational mobility according to an individual's ability rather than to his social background. The open competition or meritocratic philosophy holds that society as a whole, as well as the individual, will benefit most by maximizing the discovery, development, and utilization of the society's most important natural resource—human talents; these can be most reliably discovered by tests. These views are here expressed in overly stark and simple terms only to emphasize their differences.

Brim's survey found that high school students are more "egalitarian" and adults more "aristocratic." More high school students than adults believe that there is no difference in intelligence among social groups and that everyone should go to college. Persons holding the egalitarian view most often said that intelligence tests are unfair.

Wounded self-esteem turned out to be relatively unimportant. Only about 60 percent of the high school respondents said that they had never received information about their own IQ scores, and, of those who did, 24 percent reported that the test information raised their estimate of their intelligence, 16 percent made no change, and 7 percent lowered their self-estimate. Brim suggests that the preponderance of raised estimates may be due to selective use of information to protect one's self-esteem. Those with lower scores than expected or hoped for forget them or explain them away. There is a trend for person's self-estimates of their intelligence to increase with age, and only a very small percentage see themselves as below average (e.g., only 8 percent of the high school pupils), although of course half the population scores below average. Another probable reason that people gradually raise their estimates of their intelligence is the fact, revealed in the survey, that the public thinks of intelligence more as knowledge and wisdom, which increase throughout life. Adults probably also have a narrower range of interpersonal contacts in which ability differences would be as salient as those to which they were exposed as high school students, and it becomes easier to avoid unfavorable self-comparisons. Studying hard in high school algebra and getting a grade of only D or F while some other pupils get A or B grades with little effort leaves a sharper impression on one's self-estimate than comparing oneself with Einstein. People understandably tend to move out of situations that too repeatedly highlight comparisons unfavorable to their self-esteem, and, when tests have contributed to such situations, though the scores may be forgotten, Brim speculates, "the residue of displeasure may well remain and be directed in general ways into resentment against tests.''

Tests and testing, of course, would not arouse strong reactions if people did not perceive tests or what they supposedly measure as being in some way important. As Goslin (1968, p. 851) has pointed out, "the high cultural value placed on intellectual abilities in our society also makes any instrument which purports to measure general intellectual abilities a source of fascination.... Intelligence and aptitude tests are implicitly assumed to measure a relatively deep and enduring quality. [They] therefore generate anxiety in people tested.'' It is noteworthy that, although a majority of the high schoolers in Brim's study were generally opposed to the use of tests, two-thirds of them said they believed that IQ test scores are accurate measures of intelligence, and only one-fifth thought them inaccurate. Their high valuation of intelligence is shown by the fact that, out of a long list of desirable attributes, the respondents rated intelligence as second only to good health in importance.

People's perception of the obvious and important *differences* between persons who stand at the opposite extremes of the intelligence distribution, from the mentally deficient to the gifted, lends credence to the significance of the trait, and any measure, such as the IQ test, that so clearly discriminates between the extremes most likely discriminates the intermediate gradations as well. This perception may offend one's sense of justice and stir one's sympathy for the underdog. Nearly everyone perceives the threshold property of intelligence, that there is some threshold of ability below which one's chances of success toward some desired goal are practically nil. On the above-average side of the intelligence distribution, such thresholds, though recognized to exist, seem tolerable. If one does not have what it takes to be an Einstein, perhaps one can be a successful high school or college physics teacher. But as the threshold moves further toward the bottom of the scale, the options appear less and less attractive, until finally a point is reached that is almost universally perceived as a grave misfortune in its implications. It is not surprising that the possession of good intelligence was rated second only to good health by the respondents in Brim's public opinion survey. But people have qualms about giving too explicit recognition to these perceived differences and their threshold implications, which tests and measurements make starkly explicit.

One critic of tests pointed out that "many of those who worry about the proper definition of IQ do so chiefly because they think it is becoming the central criterion for distributing the good things of life. People care about IQ because they regard it as the basis on which society's rewards and punishments are allocated; they believe that America is becoming a society in which status and power are now, and will increasingly be, a function of brains'' (Cohen, 1972, p. 54).

A large part of the public's receptivity to the critics of tests is probably based on misconceptions and a lack of understanding of the nature of tests and the traits and performances that they are intended to measure. People often equate intelligence with knowledge or experience, and so, of course, it is easy to believe that tests reflect only the rather superficial differences in what particular things people have learned, by choice or necessity. It is also easy, then, to believe that it should be a simple matter to raise one's IQ just by acquiring the "right'' kinds of knowledge.

The importance of motivation and industry are probably greatly overrated, as compared with capacity, by most persons. There is solace in the belief that success may depend more on one's self-willed efforts than on an inborn capacity over which one has little or no control. Thus, genius is defined as an unusual capacity for hard work or is claimed to be one-tenth inspiration and nine-tenths perspiration. Clark Hull (1928; reprinted in Wiseman, 1967, p. 90) explained this one-sided emphasis: "When a person is striving to achieve something, whatever special capacity he may have takes care of itself. The *capacity* requires no thought on the part of the striving individual. His attention is absorbed, instead, by the effort he is putting forth. When, therefore, a successful person is asked the secret of his success, he naturally finds little in his memory of the period preceding his success, except the effort." Sociologist Robert Gordon (1974) has noted: "Individuals awaken each morning with the same IQ, but often with widely different fluctuations in motivation toward school or work. Consequently, we experience considerable intra-individual variation in motivation, but no intra-individual variation in IQ, so that it appears to many of us that motivation far outweighs intellectual ability in human affairs." Gordon further notes that "the situational dimension is more hopeless still in these respects because it is totally unbounded. It is easier for one to imagine situations affecting IQ or achievement that would plausibly account for an observed difference without being aware that those situations never occur in the real world, or occur so very rarely as to make their explanatory power nil for a frequently observed phenomenon." Gordon mentions the well-known Coleman report as an example: "In sampling the existing universe of situations known as 'schools' it was found that within that range the quality of facilities and the money expended per pupil had little or no effect on student achievement. This outcome was the contrary even of Coleman's own intuitive predictions."

A not trivial objection to tests has been attributed to the "bluff factor," as explained by Goslin (1966, p. 124): "A test is a means whereby we are forced to lay bare our weakness as well as our strengths, with the choice of subject matter left to the tester. Imagine a poker game in which all the bluffs were called, and the winner determined purely on the basis of the cards held. A test is a means of calling our bluffs, either in the classroom or the outside world, and since we all bluff occasionally, tests can present a threat to our winning."

Thus anxiety about one's own status, or the importance of the traits measured by tests, or sympathy for the less fortunate, may prompt the acceptance of criticisms of tests without evidence, criticisms that may seem quite plausible in terms of one's own personal experiences. Yet there is now much objective evidence relevant to most of the criticisms and beliefs about mental tests listed in this chapter. We shall examine this evidence in later chapters.

SUMMARY

Mental testing has long been the subject of much public criticism and controversy, which have intensified in recent years. The chief criticisms directed against "IQ tests" are that they are culturally biased against minorities; that the test items appear schoolish, defective, or trivial; that psychologists cannot define intelligence and therefore cannot measure it; that the tests measure nothing but the ability to do well on similar tests; that the tests fail to measure innate capacity; that the norms are unsuitable for minorities; that the IQ is a measure only of specific knowledge and skills acquired in school or a cultured home; that the IQ is inconstant from early childhood to maturity; that test scores are lowered when the tester is of a different race; and that tests and test results have been misused.

The criticism of testing in the popular media, and much of it, even in textbooks, is largely emotional, ad hoc, often self-contradictory, and wholly lacking in consideration of the types of psychometric information needed for a proper evaluation either of the tests or of the broadsides directed against them. Although this type of popular fulmination against mental tests is undoubtedly of interest as a sociological phenomenon in its own right, it is of interest from a technical psychometric standpoint only as a possible source of researchable hypotheses. But, in this process of proper technical examination and analysis of the key issues in mental testing, the issues of most crucial importance from the standpoint of psychometrics necessarily become so transformed as to be scarcely appreciated by the popular critics of tests.

Psychological tests and the theories underlying them are surely not exempt from criticism. Yet, if tests as such are to be subjected to *real* critical scrutiny, it will have to come from psychometric and statistical analysis coupled with psychological theory. The verbal fulmination type of criticism carries no weight scientifically, although as propaganda its effects in the public sphere are undoubtedly considerable. Antitest propaganda has been energetically promoted by various political action organizations, most notably the National Education Association and the Association of Black Psychologists.

Certain ideological positions, particularly Marxism, are interpreted by some exponents as justifying opposition to mental tests. But much of the general public's uneasy feeling or even hostility toward tests probably comes about more from idiosyncratic personal factors involving threats to self-esteem, fear of self-examination, invasion of privacy, sympathy for the underdog, lack of knowledge about how tests work, and real or imagined abuses of test results, than from any consistent ideological position. Underlying all this, fundamentally, is the intuitive realization of most people that there are, in fact, individual differences in mental ability that have far-reaching and crucial implications educationally, occupationally, and socially. Any instrument purporting to "measure" such a highly valued human trait as intelligence is naturally viewed askance by the layman and, in the case of IQ, even by a good many professional psychologists.

NOTES

1. Analysis of item data from more than 1,000 WISC test protocols (60 percent white and 40 percent black) obtained in Georgia by R. T. Osborne shows that, for children from 5 to 11 years of age, when the 161 items of the WISC are ranked for difficulty (from the easiest item = 1 to the most difficult = 161) within each racial group, the rank order of difficulty for this item (i.e., WISC Picture Completion Item No. 1—a comb with some teeth missing) is 10 for whites and 8 for blacks. In other words, this item, relative to the other 160 items of the WISC, is in fact slightly *easier* for the blacks than for the whites.

2. Humphrey's rebuttal, which well summarizes the position of the APA committee's report, states:

The authors of the report also believe that test scores properly interpreted are useful. We do not and cannot support a moratorium on testing in the schools. Furthermore, many useful interpretations of test scores can be made without appreciable loss of accuracy in the absence of information about race, ethnic origin, or social class of the examinee. Whether demographic membership is needed is an empirical matter and not one decided on the basis of ideology.   (Humphreys, 1975, p. 95)

Chapter 2

Tests on Trial

In recent years, court actions and legislation have been directed at the uses of psychological tests in schools and industry. These actions have highlighted some of the main criticms involving the uses and abuses of tests. Often they have resulted in important legal decisions that drastically affect testing practices. Thus they command our attention.

Most of the legal actions directed against tests concern their uses for specific purposes and the alleged injustices, usually to minority groups, incurred by these uses. Aspects of the tests themselves are often a crucial part of the argument. Each of the cases I shall mention was chosen either because of its landmark significance for psychological testing or because it exemplifies a class of cases and issues that are important precedents for future actions.

Uses of Tests in Schools

The first court decision in which mental tests figured prominently is the now famous case of *HOBSON* v. *HANSEN*,[1] which resulted in abolishing the track system in the Washington, D.C., schools in 1967. The action was initiated by Julius W. Hobson, on behalf of his two children attending school in the District of Columbia, against Superintendent of Schools Carl F. Hansen and the Board of Education. The District of Columbia schools had three tracks in the elementary and junior high schools and four in the senior high. The tracking system or ability grouping in the predominantly black schools of Washington, D.C., instituted in 1956 after the official racial desegregation of the schools, resulted in a high degree of racial segregation within schools, with whites mostly in the higher tracks and blacks in the lower. The defendants claimed that ability grouping was intended to provide differential educational opportunities to children with widely ranging ability levels most suitable to their individual abilities and needs. It was argued that the resulting racial imbalances in the upper and lower tracks was an "innocent and unavoidable coincidence" of ability grouping and not evidence of racial discrimination per se. In his decision, Circuit Judge J. Skelly Wright stated that "there is no escaping the fact that the track system was specifically a response to problems created by the sudden commingling after racial desegregation of the schools in 1955 of numerous educationally retarded Negro students with the better educated white students." The plaintiffs contended that the tracking system was discriminatory along racial and socioeconomic lines rather than in terms of capacity to learn and that it resulted in unequal educational opportunity and subsequent life-long economic disadvantage. The decision of the court handed down by Judge Wright outlawed the tracking system of the District of Columbia as "irrational and thus unconstitutionally discriminatory." Judge Wright's decision stated:

> The track system simply must be abolished. In practice, if not in concept, it discriminates against the disadvantaged child, particularly the Negro. Designed in 1955 as a means of protecting the school system against the ill effects of integrating with white children the Negro victims of *de jure* separate but unequal education, it has survived to stigmatize the disadvantaged child of whatever race relegated to its lower tracks—from which tracks the possibility of switching upward, because of the absence of compensatory education, is remote. Even in concept the track system is undemocratic and discriminatory.

We shall not be concerned at this point with the pros and cons of ability grouping in general or of the District of Columbia's tracking system in particular, but with mental testing as it figured in the court's decision. It was the first legal decision in which explicit criticism of standardized ability tests played a central role. Judge Wright stated: "The court does accept the general proposition that tests are but one factor in programming students; but it also finds that testing looms as a most important consideration in making track assignments."

Ability grouping relied heavily on achievement and aptitude test scores, including IQs. The plaintiffs contended that (1) "tests were not given often enough, with the result that a few test scores have an enormous influence on a child's academic career," and (2) "the tests which were used, and which are of such critical importance to the child, are *wholly inappropriate for making predictions about the academic potential of disadvantaged Negro children, the tests being inherently inaccurate insofar as the majority of District schoolchildren are concerned*" (italics added). Both these conditions, it was claimed, "lead to artificial and erroneous separation of students according to status, and result in the undereducation of the poor and the Negro." The defendants disputed these points.

Judge Wright's decision is devoted to a discussion of tests and their application in terms of the key factors affecting his decision. He distinguished between achievement tests and scholastic aptitude tests. But, because the use of achievement tests was not seriously questioned by the plaintiffs, the discussion focused on aptitude or IQ tests.

> The skills measured by scholastic aptitude tests are verbal. More precisely, an aptitude test is essentially a test of the student's command of standard English and grammar. The emphasis on these skills is due to the nature of the academic curriculum, which is highly verbal; without such skills a student cannot be successful. Therefore, by measuring the student's present verbal ability the test makes it possible to estimate the student's likelihood of success in the future.
>
> Whether a test is verbal or nonverbal, the skills being measured are not innate or inherited traits. They are learned, acquired through experience. It used to be the prevailing theory that aptitude tests—or "intelligence" tests as they are often called, although the term is obviously misleading—do measure some stable, predetermined intellectual process that can be isolated and called intelligence. Today,

modern experts in educational testing and psychology have rejected this concept as false. Indeed, the best that can be said about intelligence insofar as testing is concerned is that it is whatever the test measures.

In plain words, this means that aptitude tests can only test a student's present level of learning in certain skills and from that infer his capability to learn further.

Of utmost importance is the fact that, to demonstrate the ability to learn, a student must have had the opportunity to learn those skills relied upon for prediction. In other words, an aptitude test is necessarily measuring a student's background, his environment.

Judge Wright goes on to describe the causes of low test scores besides innate limitations. He mentions lack of opportunity to acquire and develop the verbal and nonverbal skills needed to score well on tests and the pupil's emotional or psychological condition when he takes the test, such as a lack of motivation, anxiety, low self-esteem, or racial self-consciousness, which could lower test performance. Judge Wright states: "When standard aptitude tests are given to low income Negro children, or disadvantaged children . . . the tests are less precise and accurate—so much so that the test scores become practically meaningless." He mentions that the tests used in the District of Columbia were based on national norms and standardization and that the use of local norms would be an unsatisfactory solution because the "test questions are highly inappropriate to the background of the disadvantaged child."

"Consequently, the court finds that for a majority of District School children there is a substantial risk of being wrongly labeled as having abnormal intelligence, a label that cannot effectively be removed simply by interpreting aptitude test scores" [in light of the student's background].

Other objections to testing were that low test scores may cause teachers to underestimate pupils' capabilities; may increase the danger of the self-fulfilling prophecy, whereby a student may confirm his low aptitude test score by achieving at a correspondingly low level; may foster a competitive atmosphere in the pursuit of education, to the disadvantage of blacks; and may consign students to specially designated curricula, thereby making a student's status within the educational structure highly visible and reinforcing the undesirable psychological impact of being judged of low ability.

Several key points regarding the tests in this decision should be especially noted: (1) great emphasis is placed on the most superficial aspects of *verbal* tests of aptitude, such as "standard English and grammar"; (2) aptitude as measured by tests is repeatedly represented as consisting of *specific knowledge and skills* that can be taught and learned, and (3) the validity of the tests and their use is seen as hinging entirely on the question of the extent to which they measure *innate ability*. The last point seems crucial in the judge's decision:

> [R]egarding the accuracy of aptitude test measurements, the court makes the following findings. First, there is substantial evidence that the defendants presently lack the techniques and the facilities for ascertaining the innate learning abilities of a majority of District school children. Second, lacking these techniques and facilities, defendants cannot justify the placement and retention of these children in lower tracks on the supposition that they could do no better, given the opportunity to do so.

A legal scholar (Goodman, 1972, pp. 434–435) commenting on this aspect of Judge Wright's decision states:

> The difficulty in extending Judge Wright's approach lies in this initial premise. Few educators are so naïve as to suppose that an IQ or scholastic aptitude test reveals a child's inborn potential. Most realize that the attribute measured by such tests is the joint product of endowment and experience, that the verbal and conceptual skills demanded are acquired skills, and that children of minority and lower class background are at a disadvantage in obtaining them. But it by no means follows that such tests are an arbitrary or inappropriate basis upon which to classify students for purposes of educational grouping. Whatever may have been true in the District of Columbia, the declared purpose of homogeneous grouping in most school systems is not to pigeonhole the student on the basis of genetic potential, but to provide him an education better adapted to his present level of proficiency and better designed to meet his immediate learning problems than the standard fare he would receive in a heterogeneous classroom. So long as the aptitude or intelligence test accurately identifies those students who are not likely to do well in a heterogeneous classroom (and therefore stand to gain from a more specialized treatment), it accomplishes its purpose.

The Case of *DIANA et al.* v. *STATE BOARD OF EDUCATION*[2] in California in 1970 highlights the problems in testing immigrant or bilingual children and also sets the stage for further legal actions to restrict the use of tests in California schools. *Diana* was a class action suit on behalf of all bilingual Mexican–American children placed in classes for the educable mentally retarded (EMR) or who will be given an IQ test. Important in the background of this case was the fact that in California, at the time, about 3 percent of Mexican–American children were placed in EMR classes, as compared with only half that percentage of "Anglo" children. Assignment to EMR classes was based mainly on scores on individual IQ tests (Wechsler or Stanford–Binet), usually administered by testers who could not speak Spanish, which is either the only language or the predominant language used in the homes of many Mexican–American children. The principal plaintiffs were nine Mexican–American school children and their parents, who were primarily farm workers. The average IQ of the children when tested in English was 63.5, with a range from 30 to 72. (An IQ of 75 was the cutoff for placement in EMR classes.) When retested in Spanish, the children's IQs rose an average of 15 points, so that seven of the nine were above the EMR cutoff. One 8-year-old child, Diana, who had originally obtained a Stanford–Binet IQ of 30 when tested in English, scored 49 points higher on a Spanish version of the test. All these children's nonverbal performance IQs on the Wechsler Intelligence Scale for Children was above the EMR cutoff of IQ 75.

The plaintiffs in *Diana* contended, therefore, that the children were not retarded but were merely tested in the wrong language, because they spoke, predominantly, Spanish. They claimed that the children's IQs bore little relationship to their actual learning capacities and that placement in EMR classes denied their right to equal educational opportunity and was socially and academically damaging. The assessment procedures for placement in special classes, particularly the standard IQ tests, were declared inappropriate and unfairly discriminatory to Mexican–Americans. A study was cited claiming that retesting of Spanish-speaking children in EMR classes in their own language resulted in the reassignment to regular classes in nearly 90 percent of the cases.

The case of *Diana* was finally settled out of court, with the defendant (State Board of Education) agreeing to a number of stipulations:

1. All bilingual children must be tested in their primary language and in English.
2. Unfair verbal items such as vocabulary and general information may not be used, but pupils may be tested on the nonverbal or performance parts of standard tests.
3. Bilingual children presently enrolled in EMR classes must be retested in their primary language on nonverbal tests.
4. State psychologists are to develop an IQ test that reflects Mexican–American culture and obtain norms solely on a sample of Mexican–American children.
5. Any school district with a significant racial-ethnic disparity in regular and special classes must submit an explanation for the disparity.

The last point was undoubtedly the most important for future court cases involving testing in California. The notion that the percentages of every racial or ethnic group assigned to special classes should be the same as the percentages of these groups in the total school population of the district is based on the assumption that the same distribution of intelligence or scholastic aptitude is the same across all racial, ethnic, and socioeconomic groups and that such equal distributions pertain in every school district in the state. Some 300 school districts in the state, it turned out, had significant disparities between racial-ethnic groups in EMR classes. "Significant disparity" had been defined by the State Education Code as 15 percent or more. The State Board of Education was later cited for contempt of court for not equalizing these disparities except by definition (i.e., 15 percent). The plaintiff's lawyers would not accept 15 percent or even 2 percent as the criterion for disparity. Partly as a result of this action the number of children in EMR classes throughout California was decreased by 40 percent. The State Board of Education contended that of this 40 percent excluded from special classes at least half were not getting the necessary additional help to get along in regular classes.

An important aspect of the *Diana* case, as in most of the others, is the contention that placement of children in special classes on whatever basis of assessment is in effect a form of labeling, which carries a stigma. Legally, to claim "stigma," it must be demonstrated that children have been substantially harmed by the claimed "stigma" and that the harm is above and beyond that which naturally results from being a person who legitimately falls into the category represented by the classification. Thus this issue of stigma takes on legal importance when the methods of assessment used to determine educational classification are called into question. Contention that a standard test is invalid for a certain class of children is therefore a basis for claiming that such children, if educationally classified by such tests, have been deprived of their rights to a proper education. This has been legally interpreted as a violation of the "due process" and "equal protection" clauses of the Fourteenth Amendment to the Constitution of the United States.

STEWART et al. v. *PHILLIPS and MASSACHUSETTS BOARD OF EDUCATION*[3] was an action brought against the school system by parents in Boston. Like *Diana*, it involved the classification of children as mentally retarded and their placement in special

classes on the basis of IQ tests. (The state of Massachusetts uses a cutoff of IQ 79.)
Plaintiffs charged that an IQ of less than 80 is an inadequate basis for placement in special
education classes and that the tests are *unfair and biased against Negro children,* thereby
denying their right to equal protection of the laws in violation of the Fourteenth Amendment. They stipulated several conditions for placement in special classes, such as testing
by a qualified psychologist and the appointment of a commission to specify a battery of
tests from which the psychologist can select the most appropriate for a given case, with the
proviso that no child be placed in a special class solely on the basis of test scores.

In 1972 a bill (AB 438) was introduced in the California state legislature to abolish
statewide testing of IQ or scholastic aptitude and prohibit the use of any group tests of
aptitude in the schools. However, the bill permitted individual testing by a qualified
psychologist to determine a pupil's eligibility for special education classes. Although the
bill has been passed by the legislature on two occasions, it was vetoed both times by
California's governor. California has since elected a new governor, and, with impetus
from the black and Chicano communities, the antitesting bill has come before the legislature once again. A central argument in this bill is the self-fulfilling prophecy that test
scores may influence the teacher's expectancy for a child, which in the case of a low-
scoring child may hinder the future development of his intellectual potential.

LARRY P. et al. v. *WILSON RILES, Superintendent of Public Instruction for the
State of California,*[4] is probably the most crucial legal action to date with regard to school
testing. Its result so far has been to outlaw the administration of IQ tests to all black
children in California schools. The plaintiffs in this class action suit were the parents of
seven black children who had been placed in EMR classes largely on the basis of scoring
below IQ 75 on standard individual IQ tests. The children were retested by three members
of the Association of Black Psychologists that had previously presented a demand to the
San Francisco School Board for a moratorium on the IQ testing of black children. The
court's decision noted:

> They [the plaintiffs] claim that they are not mentally retarded and that they have
> been placed in EMR classes on the basis of tests which are biased against the culture
> and experience of black children as a class, in violation of their fourteenth amend-
> ment rights. In fact, plaintiffs have presented evidence, in the form of affidavits
> from certain black psychologists, that when they were given the same IQ tests but
> with special attempts by the psychologists to establish rapport with the test-takers,
> to overcome plaintffs' defeatism and easy distraction, to reword items in terms more
> consistent with plaintiffs' cultural background, and to give credit for non-standard
> answers which nevertheless showed an intelligent approach to problems in the
> context of that background, plaintiffs scored significantly above the cutting-off
> point of 75.[4]

One of the black psychologist's reports presented as an affidavit to the court indicated that some vocabulary and verbal comprehension items in the test (Wechsler Intelligence Scale for Children) were changed to be more suitable to the child's background
(e.g., changing "criminal" to "crook" and "cushion" to "pillow"). The child scored an
IQ of "91 to 94" as compared with the score of 70 obtained when the same test was
administered by one of the school system's psychologists. There was no attempt to show
that the vocabulary substitutions were in fact culturally more appropriate rather than being

merely easier words on which all children, not just blacks, would score higher. Another test report affidavit, that on Larry P., gave Verbal, Performance, and Full Scale IQs each of 100, in contrast to the IQs of 71, 85, and 75, respectively, previously obtained by the school psychologist. It is not clear if the test was administered in the standard way, but it is clear from the report that the conversion of the total verbal score to an IQ was done incorrectly,[5] spuriously adding 10 points to the Verbal IQ and 6 points to the Full Scale IQ. Under conditions of unspecified nonstandard administration and scoring of the tests and erroneous calculation of the IQ, almost any resulting IQ should not be surprising. The defendants did not challenge these results or raise the crucial question of whether the validity of the higher IQs obtained under these nonstandard testing conditions is enhanced or reduced.

The self-fulfilling prophecy, or teacher expectation notion, and the "Pygmalion in the Classroom" study by Rosenthal and Jacobson (1968), which purported to substantiate the expectancy hypothesis, were among the arguments put forth by the plaintiffs. These arguments were unchallenged by the defendants, although the well-known technical critiques that thoroughly discredited the study (Thorndike, 1968; Snow, 1969; Elashoff & Snow, 1971) had already been published, as had journal reports of nine independent attempts to replicate the results, all without success.

The claim was made by plaintiffs that IQ tests are culturally biased for blacks, without reference to any evidence other than restatements of this position by the plaintiffs' expert witnesses, one of whom, for example, stated:

IQ tests now being used by psychologists are, to a large extent, Anglocentric. They tend to measure the extent to which an individual's background is similar to that of the cultural configuration of Anglo, middle-class society and are not valid, as normed, for Mexican–American and Black populations.

The defendants acquiesced to the charge of test bias, offering the defense that "the tests, although racially biased, are rationally related to the purpose for which they are used because they are the best means of classification currently available."

The court accepted as *prima facie* evidence for test bias the plaintffs' statistics indicating that blacks comprise 9.1 percent of all school children in California but 27.5 percent of all school children in EMR classes, admission into which requires (among other things) a score below IQ 75 on an individually administered intelligence test. These undisputed statistics were claimed to support the charge of racially biased tests on the assumption that scholastic aptitude is equally distributed in all races, an assumption that went unchallenged. The presiding judge, Robert F. Peckham, therefore ruled that the burden of proof was on the defendants that the use of IQ tests was justified in placing black children in special classes. A key part of Judge Peckham's court order states:

The . . . assumption in the instant case would be that there exists a random distribution among all races of the qualifications necessary to participate in regular as opposed to EMR classes. Since it does not seem to be disputed that the qualification for placement in regular classes is the innate ability to learn at the pace at which those classes proceed . . . , such a random distribution can be expected if there is in turn a random distribution of these learning abilities among members of all races.

Defendants herein have not embraced any notion that inherited differences in intelligence exist among the races. They have suggested that since black people tend to be poor, and poor pregnant women tend to suffer from inadequate nutrition, it is possible that the brain development of many black children has been retarded by their mothers' poor diet during pregnancy. No affidavits have been presented to this Court substantiating this conclusion, however, or even explaining the alleged connection between the eating habits of pregnant mothers and the intelligence of their offspring. Since the Court cannot take judicial notice of such matters, there can be no basis for assuming otherwise than that the ability to learn is randomly spread about the population. And hence another reason exists for shifting the burden of proof to defendants . . . to justify the use of intelligence testing.

In conclusion the court ordered that "no black student may be placed in an EMR class on the basis of criteria which rely primarily on the results of IQ tests as they are currently administered, if the consequence of use of such criteria is racial imbalance in the composition of EMR classes." On October 16, 1979, Judge Peckham, then presiding over the U.S. District Court, ruled as unconstitutional the use of standardized IQ tests that result in placement of "grossly disproportionate" numbers of California black children in classes for the mentally retarded.

Prior to this ruling, school systems in a number of cities, including New York, Chicago, Los Angeles, and Houston, had already curtailed or eliminated the use of standardized tests of academic aptitude and achievement and were seeking other means of assessment to replace them (usually by "criterion-referenced" as opposed to "norm-referenced" tests; see index and glossary).

Another federal law with important implications for educational testing is the privacy provision of the Education Amendments of 1974, known as the "Family Educational Rights and Privacy Act" (PL93-380). This act opens all pupil records, including all test scores as well as evaluations by school personnel, to parents and to students over 18 years of age. It also permits the challenging of such records. Students' cumulative records, which often follow them through their entire school careers, have been charged with abuses such as information leaking, labeling, subjective comments, and discrimination, which gave impetus to this legislation. Educators opposed to the legislation hold that it will discourage teachers and counselors from making honest evaluations of pupils. A possible consequence could be that colleges and universities in screening applicants would be forced to rely even more on entrance examination test scores in place of the school's evaluations. The act also provides that educational researchers must make available for inspection by parents of children engaged in any research project any materials used in the research.

Testing for Personnel Selection and Promotion

Some 15 to 20 percent of the approximately 70,000 complaints filed annually with the Equal Employment Opportunity Commission involve alleged unfair discrimination by unfair testing (Ash & Kroeker, 1975, p. 486).

A pivotal court case in this field is *GRIGGS et al.* v. *DUKE POWER CO.*[6] Willie Griggs and twelve other black laborers at the Dan River Steam Station of the Duke Power Company in Draper, North Carolina brought a suit against Duke Power, charging discrimination against blacks. The power station had classified employees as laborers (sweeping and cleaning), coal handlers (shoveling coal), operators, maintenance workers, and laboratory workers. Hiring-in or promotion from one level to another was based on educational credentials and scores on certain tests. Fourteen of the ninety-five employees at the power station were black, and all but one of the fourteen were laborers. The next highest position of coal handler was open to any employee, provided he had a high school diploma and obtained "passing" scores on a general intelligence test (Wonderlic Personnel Test) and a mechanical aptitude test (Bennett Mechanical Comprehension Test). The case went all the way to the U.S. Supreme Court, whose decision focused on the general intelligence test that had rendered "ineligible a *markedly disproportionate* number of Negroes.'' Although the disproportionate number of whites and blacks qualifying for better jobs under the selection procedures was considered *prima facie* evidence of racial discrimination, the main thrust of the Supreme Court's decision in favor of Griggs et al. concerned the relevance and validity of the selection procedures. The court observed that "what is required by Congress [in Title VII of the Civil Rights Act of 1964, which prohibits racial discrimination by employers, agencies, and unions] is the removal of artificial, arbitrary, and unnecessary barriers to employment when the barriers operate invidiously to discriminate on the basis of racial or other impermissible classification."

The court ruled that when the plaintiff can show racially disproportionate consequences of the selection procedures "Congress has placed on the employer the burden of showing that *any given requirement must have a manifest relationship to the employment in question*" (italics added). The Duke Power Company argued that they believed that the diploma and test requirements "would improve the overall quality of the work force" and that they were not adopted to exclude blacks from the higher-paying jobs. The court rejected these arguments, however, stating that "good intent or absence of discriminatory intent does not redeem employment procedures or testing mechanisms that operate as 'built-in headwinds' for minority groups and are unrelated to measuring job capability."

Griggs v. *Duke Power* had a great impact on selection procedures, and many similar court cases followed. The requirement that the screening procedures should have a "manifest relationship to the employment in question" gives rise to a host of possible interpretations, debate, and technical psychometric questions concerning the meanings and criteria of test validity. Does "manifest relationship" mean simply that the test should have predictive validity, that is, that the test scores should be correlated with job performance? Or does "manifest relationship" also mean that the test items must resemble the tasks performed on the job? That is, must the selection test be a *work sample?* Is "general ability" over and above the *specific* skills involved in a particular job irrelevant to overall effectiveness on the job, or irrelevant to probability of promotion to "higher" jobs in those cases where a particular job in the employment hierarchy is merely viewed as a recruiting point and training ground for subsequent promotion to higher-level positions? Certain screening methods have been widely used that bear no manifest relationship to the job but nevertheless have substantial validity for predicting persistence and success in the job. The most striking example is the use of the "weighted biographical questionnaire." The job applicant fills out a form asking a number of quite routine-appearing questions concerning his age, place of birth, schooling, marital status, number and ages of children, place of residence, favorite sports and recreation, number and duration of jobs previously held, and the like. If there is some means for objectively rating success on the job, it is possible statistically to determine whether these biographical data are related to any criteria of job success and, if so, what are the optimal weights to be given each item of information to obtain a total "score" that will maximize prediction of success on the job. The predictive power is often quite good in an actuarial sense even though there is no · manifest relationship between the biographical data and the actual job requirements. For example, of what relevance is it to selling insurance whether a person prefers hunting to golf, or poker to chess? Yet expression of these preferences may add to the prediction of who will sell the most insurance policies. The only question then is not whether such biodata is a valid selection device but whether it is fair to individuals. According to the Supreme Court decision in *Griggs* v. *Duke Power,* an employer who screens applicants with tests or any other devices that depend upon abilities or personal characteristics not explicitly required of the particular job for which the applicant is being considered is breaking the law.

Prior to *Griggs,* courts ruled in a number of Title VII cases that tests were *prima facie* unfair if they resulted in disproportionate selection of whites and minorities. The *WESTERN ADDITION COMMUNITY ORGANIZATION* v. *ALIOTO*[7] (mayor of San Francisco), for example, challenged the use of a selection test by the San Francisco Fire Department. The plaintiffs charged that blacks were unfairly disadvantaged by the selection test, which was passed by 37 percent of white, 35 percent of Mexican–American, but only 12 percent of black applicants, or a 3-to-1 ratio disfavoring blacks. The Fire Department tried to improve the test by eliminating what seemed to be the most discriminatory items, but the court found for the plaintiffs, because under the new test 57 percent of whites and 20 percent of blacks attained passing scores, which was still close to the 3-to-1 ratio of the previously challenged test.

At present a lawsuit is pending in the U.S. District Court against the police department of Richmond, California, asking for federal orders to end alleged racial discrimination based on tests and to award $3 million damages to the plaintiffs, a group of black policemen. Written tests are used in hiring, job assignments, and promotions. Plaintiffs claim that the tests exclude three and one-half times as many minority as nonminority applicants and that the tests are not related to the *actual skills* needed by a policeman. Again, the ambiguity of the term *actual skills* raises difficult problems. Is general mental ability or "brightness" as measured by a standard IQ test relevant to performance as a policeman? Police duties presumably involve judgment in complex situations, interpreting clues and evidence, understanding legal implications, and writing clear, complete, and accurate reports—all "skills" that one might suspect are correlated to some degree with scores on standard intelligence tests. Does an intelligence test give a better prediction of how well a person can integrate a number of specific subskills effectively to perform a complex task than the prediction we could obtain from "work-sample" tests of the various subskills, each measured separately? If general intelligence is held to be an irrelevant requirement for a job, should it not be measured so as to statistically partial it out (i.e., remove its effects) from the scores derived from other assessments? These are the kinds of difficult questions to which the laws give rise. Such questions are especially highlighted when tests are used in screening individuals for occupations at the professional level, where written tests may be more directly and obviously related to the skills required by the profession, such as reading comprehension or mathematical skills or writing skills, as well as specific professional knowledge.

This issue was explicit in *DOUGLAS* v. *HAMPTON,*[8] a class action suit charging the U.S. Civil Service Commission with discrimination against blacks due to the "adverse impact'' of the selection tests, which screened out markedly disproportionate numbers of black applicants for civil service jobs. The Federal Service Entrance Examination, introduced in 1955, is a high-level test of verbal and quantitative reasoning not unlike the Scholastic Aptitude Test or the Graduate Record Exam. (In fact, applicants could offer scores on the GRE in lieu of the Federal Service Exam.) The Federal Service Entrance Exam was intended as a measure of general intellectual ability rather than as a test designed and validated to predict specific job performance, and it was used to select for entry into more than 200 widely varying professional, managerial, and technical positions in federal agencies. The chief defense of the Civil Service Commission was that the jobs for which the test was used required verbal and numerical abilities. The outcome of this case was that the commission abandoned the general verbal and numerical aptitude exam (FSEE) and proposed to use a new five-part Professional and Administrative Career Examination (PACE), which measures five types of abilities considered important at these occupational levels. The weighting of the five tests in the selection process would differ according to the specified demands of each job. Thus *Douglas* v. *Hampton* probably marks the demise of using unvalidated tests of general intellectual ability in personnel selection. Henceforth, selection tests would have to be tailored and validated in relation to the specific performance demands of a particular job.

Tests in Professional Selection

There have also been court cases involving the use of tests in professional selection or promotion, where racial discrimination has been blamed on the tests or examination procedures.

In *ARMSTEAD et al.* v. *STARKVILLE, Mississippi Municipal Separate School District*,[9] the court prohibited the school system from using the Graduate Record Examination (GRE) as a basis for hiring or retaining elementary and secondary teachers. The GRE is a high-level test of scholastic aptitude designed for the selection of college students applying for admission to graduate studies in universities and professional schools. An affidavit from an official of the Educational Testing Service (ETS), which publishes the GRE, declared that the GRE was inappropriate for screening applicants for teaching positions. The affidavit warned that the GRE might be less reliable for a group of teachers than for graduate students pursuing advanced studies at the doctoral level. The court-cited affidavit from the ETS official continued:

> In my judgment the use of the GRE . . . for selection and retention of teachers in Starkville School System . . . would be a blind use of these tests unless studies were first performed that would, as a minimum, establish the content validity★ and concurrent validity★ of these tests for the criteria of teacher effectiveness.

The affidavit also listed ways that aptitude and achievement tests in general discriminate against blacks:

1. The test may contain items that are specifically germane to the white, middle-class environment, thus placing Black students at a disadvantage.

★Starred terms are defined in the glossary at the back of the book.

2. Black students may be less familiar with test-taking strategies and will, because they are less skilled or "test wise," be less able to compete successfully.
3. The conditions under which students are required to take the tests are such that Black students may feel anxious, threatened and alienated, thereby impairing their ability to perform successfully on the test.
4. Tests measure abilities that are developed as a consequence of educational, social, and family experience over many years. One consequence of poverty, segregation, and inequality of educational opportunities to which Black students are more likely to have been subjected is reflected in lower scores on tests such as the GRE Aptitude and Advanced Test.

That the inappropriateness of the GRE for teacher certification was not really the central issue, however, was shown in *BAKER* v. *COLUMBUS MUNICIPAL SEPARATE SCHOOL DISTRICT*,[10] which charged "adverse impact" on blacks as a result of the school system's hiring or retaining teachers on the basis of the National Teachers Examination (NTE), a set of tests expressly devised for teacher selection. Plaintiff's charge of adverse impact was attested by the fact that only 11 percent of black as compared with 90 percent of white teacher applicants passed the test at the cutoff score used by the Columbus schools. The NTE consists of several parts designed to measure certain knowledge and abilities expected of every teacher (the "Common Examinations") and seventeen Teaching Area Examinations (of which the applicant has a choice) intended to assess preparation in specific teaching positions. The rather high intercorrelations among the parts of the Common Exam indicate that the total score is a measure largely of some general ability probably best labeled general academic aptitude and achievement when used in a college population. The test's publishers, the Educational Testing Service, never claimed that the NTE measured *all* the factors involved in effective teaching. The test is intended only to measure cognitive ability and knowledge thought relevant for teachers, and the test's most usual use is for setting minimal acceptable standards of knowledge for prospective teachers, with final selection based on a variety of other criteria involving interviews, personal recommendations, work experience, and the like. Because expert witnesses for both plaintiffs and defendants testified that the validity of the NTE as a predictor of a teacher's effectiveness in the classroom was undetermined, the court ordered the school system to cease using the test in hiring or rehiring teachers.

However, a validity study was later performed by the ETS that showed that the NTE met all the requirements under Title VII of the Civil Rights Act of 1964, and, in January 1978, the U.S. Supreme Court affirmed a federal district court decision approving the NTE for purposes of certification and promotion of teachers.

Although the relevance of a high level of academic aptitude for teaching effectiveness in elementary and secondary schools may reasonably seem questionable, attempts to abolish state bar examinations for lawyers seem to make a less convincing case. So far the courts of original jurisdiction have all turned back challenges to the state bar examinations, but appellate courts have not yet handed down their decisions.

In 1970 the National Bar Association, an organization of black lawyers, voted unanimously at its annual convention to take steps to abolish bar exams. Legal actions toward this end are now pending in nineteen states (Ash & Kroeker, 1975, p. 492). It was claimed that three out of four black law school graduates fail the bar exam, a mortality rate some two to three times that of their white counterparts. Thus bar exams were branded as "racist," and law school graduation is held to be a sufficient criterion of qualification to practice law. Bar exams are identified only by a code number and are scored "blind." Yet in Pennsylvania, in the period from 1955 to 1970, the initial pass rates of graduates of law schools on the approved list of the American Bar Association were 70 percent for whites and 30 percent for blacks, and the eventual pass rates (after successive tries) were 98 percent for whites and 60 percent for blacks (Bell, 1971). The Pennsylvania Board of Law Examiners, reviewing the entire bar examination process, declared: "Statistical evidence demonstrates that a grossly disproportionate percentage of blacks fail each examination, and there is lacking any available hypothesis other than race by which we can explain these proportions" (quoted in Bell, 1971, p. 1217). Even more disproportionate passing rates are reported in other states (Bell, 1971, p. 1217). A past president of the National Bar Association, E. F. Bell, has charged racial bias in the bar examination and grading procedures and points out that there are only four black bar examiners in the forty-six states that require bar exams (Bell, 1971, p. 1218). He asks:

> Why does a black law student who has successfully completed all his courses through high school, college and law school suddenly find that he is unable to pass that one final examination that permits him to engage in his chosen profession? I don't suggest there should be no black failures at the examination, but it is too much to expect that the failures will embrace such enormous proportions. The black law student has gone to the same school as his white counterpart and has taken the same courses. He has written the same examinations and passed them. He only fails the bar exam. This prompted a white judge from Pennsylvania to remark about blacks, "But they don't read quickly, they don't think quickly." Which prompts me to remark, "How do you think he arrived at the point to take a bar examination?"

The questions raised here obviously extend far beyond the issue of tests and testing per se. They go to the heart of the drive for equality, which is considered in relation to mental tests in the next chapter.

SUMMARY

A number of landmark court cases involving the use of tests in schools and in employment selection have resulted in legal decisions with far-reaching consequences for the practical application of tests. Many other cases involving tests are now pending in the courts. Key decisions already handed down are based largely on the premise, seldom challenged in any other court actions, that the distribution of ability is the same in all subgroups of the general population and that, therefore, any significant disproportions between racial groups in school "tracking" or placement in special classes, or in college admissions, or in employment selection or promotion based on test scores must be due to bias in the tests or testing procedures.

Specific court decisions have declared scholastic aptitude and IQ tests "inherently inaccurate" for black children, containing questions that are "highly inappropriate to the background of minority pupils"; and educational placement or ability tracking has been prohibited in schools, as these practices are based in large part on test scores that do not assess innate ability and therefore deny equal educational opportunity to children of poor backgrounds.

The "equal protection of the laws" clause of the Fourteenth Amendment of the United States Constitution is frequently invoked in decisions banning or restricting the use of tests. Courts have ruled that bilingual children must be tested in their native language or on nonverbal tests, and tests used in employment selection must be "manifestly related" to the capabilities required in performing the specific job for which the person is being hired. Also, the use of tests of general intellectual ability in personnel selection has been ruled against; if tests are to be used for hiring, courts have ruled that they should be tailor-made to predict success on the particular job, and evidence of such predictive validity for both minority and majority applicants must be secured. Cases involving tests of professional qualifications, such as the state bar examination, have not as yet resulted in any notable decisions.

NOTES

1. *Hobson* v. *Hansen*. U.S. District Court for the District of Columbia, 269 F. Supp. 401, 1967.

2. *Diana* v. *California State Board of Education*. U.S. District Court for the Northern District of California (consent decree), 1970.

3. *Stewart et al.* v. *Phillips and the Massachusetts Board of Education*. U.S. District Court for Massachusetts, Civil Action 70-1199F, 1970.

4. *Larry P.* v. *Wilson Riles*. U.S. District Court for the Northern District of California, No. C-71-2270RFP, 1972.

5. The Verbal IQ of the Wechsler Intelligence Scale for Children (WISC) is arrived at through a table that converts the total scaled scores on *five* of the verbal subtests to an IQ. When all *six* of the verbal subtests are given, the total of the scaled scores has to be prorated by five-sixths before conversion to an IQ. All six verbal subtests were used in testing Larry P., but the total score of 50 was not prorated, which would lower it to 42. On the other hand, only four of the six Performance (nonverbal) subtests were reported, and the total scaled score of 40 on these was properly prorated to raise it to 50.

6. *Griggs et al.* v. *Duke Power Company*. United States Supreme Court, No. 124–October Term, 1970 (March 8, 1971).

7. *Western Addition Community Organization* v. *Alioto*. U.S. District Court for the Northern District of California, 340 F. Supp. 1351, 1972.

8. *Douglas* v. *Hampton*. An appeal from the U.S. District Court for the District of Columbia, to the U.S. Circuit Court of Appeals of the District of Columbia, No. 72-1376, 1973.

9. *Armstead et al.* v. *Starkville Mississippi Municipal Separate School District*. U.S. District Court for the Northern District, Eastern Division, of Mississippi, Civil Action No. EC 70-51-5, 1972.

10. *Baker* v. *Columbus Municipal Separate School District*. U.S. District Court for the Northern District, Eastern Division, of Mississippi, 329 F. Supp. 706, 1971.

Chapter 3

The Drive for Equality

All tests discriminate. They would be utterly useless if they did not. As we have seen in the preceding chapters, most of the objections to tests involve the fact that tests often discriminate among certain *groups*. The legitimacy of tests discriminating among *individuals* is largely uncontested and generally taken for granted—unless the individuals are identified as members of different social, racial, or cultural groups that are known to show average differences in test scores. In the face of such discrimination—differences among group averages or among individuals from different groups—the test is said to be *biased,* and its use therefore is labeled *unfair.* No one advocates unfairness. Even though unfairness may be acknowledged to exist, or even to be inevitable, it is not viewed as a good thing by anyone, at least not openly. Fairness has all our moral sanctions, unfairness none. Most would agree that unfairness is to be condemned, fought against, minimized, or eradicated whenever and wherever possible.

A crucial question is whether tests increase or decrease the sum total of unfairness in society. The question cannot properly be answered by a simple statement. Although many persons may have already answered this question to their own satisfaction, a justified answer, or at least an explicitly considered one, is a big order indeed. The question is obviously not all of one piece. We must distinguish between tests and testing practices; between good tests and poor tests, good practices and bad practices; between current *de facto* uses (and abuses) and possible optimal uses; and between tests and testing as they are today and as they might be in the future.

But, before going any further, we must be more explicit about the meanings of some of the key terms that enter into such discussion. Some of the terms in the testing controversy have become emotionally loaded and now cannot be used without misunderstanding unless they are divested of their affective overtones. Also, the meaning of certain terms in the context of psychometrics does not coincide with their meaning in common parlance or with their dictionary definition. To get on with the job, we have to agree, for the time being at least, on the meaning of such terms as "discrimination," "bias," and "unfair."

"Discrimination"

"Discrimination," as used here, is a completely neutral term. Discrimination per se is neither good nor bad. It simply means a *reliable difference.* A reliable difference between individuals is an observed difference (in some behavior, attribute, characteristic, or some measurement or index thereof) that is not merely haphazard or due to chance or to errors of observation or measurement; it is relatively stable or repeatable from one observation to the next; and there is general agreement as to the difference by all observers. This says nothing whatever about the *cause(s)* of the difference, or whether it is important, or whether its implications or consequences are good or bad.

In psychometrics, discrimination occurs at several different levels. One can measure (1) differences between traits or abilities *within* a single person, such as noting that a particular baseball player is a good hitter but a slow runner, (2) differences *between individuals* on a particular ability, or (3) differences *between the averages of groups* of persons. If the groups are formed without reference to the test, or the test is constructed without reference to the groups, and there is a reliable difference between the averages of the groups, the discrimination is *incidental*.

Ability tests are explicitly designed to discriminate among individuals. I know of no ability tests that were ever designed for the purpose of discriminating *between* any social groups, although there have been attempts to design tests so as to minimize or eliminate differences between certain groups. (The most notable example is balancing the items in some tests so as to eliminate sex differences in the total score.) In contrast, some types of personality inventories are explicitly designed to discriminate between certain groups; the groups, in fact, are used as the main criterion in constructing the inventory—only those items that discriminate the most between the criterion groups are retained in the final version of the inventory. Such instruments are thus intentionally discriminatory for certain groups and are often used as a screening device to determine which individuals in an undifferentiated population are most like the members of the intentionally discriminated groups. A good example is the Minnesota Multiphasic Personality Inventory, or MMPI. It is a set of several inventories, comprising more than five hundred questions, that were selected so as to discriminate among several categories of psychiatric diagnosis, for example, hysteria, schizophrenia, paranoia, and depression.

Psychologists are generally agreed, with possible rare exceptions, that group discrimination by ability and aptitude tests is entirely *incidental* in the sense described here. No reputable standardized ability test was ever devised expressly for the purpose of discriminating racial, ethnic, or social-class groups. Yet, to hear some of the critics of tests, one might easily conclude that mental tests discriminate *primarily* in terms of racial and socioeconomic status. A member of the Fair Employment Practices Commission (FEPC) was quoted as saying that a certain standard IQ test that showed a group discrimination did so because it was a "culturally biased test." He said, "If you give the Otis test, the white applicant will beat the Negro applicant every time. Period. Anybody who wants to use the Otis can be damn sure what will happen." Such unsupported claims, often seen in the popular media, create an impression of gross, almost total, discrimination by tests along racial or social-class lines.

Yet the fact is that IQ tests, and probably most other kinds of tests as well, discriminate quite little among races or among socioeconomic groups, relative to other discriminations. To illustrate this point I have analyzed some data[1] on the Wechsler Intelligence Scale for Children (Revised) or *WISC-R* (Wechsler, 1974). By means of the statistical method known as the analysis of variance★ it is possible to apportion the total amount of all the discriminations (called the total variance★) made by test scores in a population into a number of "sources" of this discrimination or variation. The amount of variance in test scores attributable to each source can be expressed as a percentage of the total variance. WISC-R Full Scale IQs were obtained in a highly representative sample of 622 white and 622 black children, ages 5 to 12 years, from a random sample of 98 school districts in California. Determination was also made of each child's socioeconomic status (SES) on Duncan's SES index, a ten-point scale based on the parent's occupation. The percentages of the total variance attributable to each of several sources are shown in Table 3.1.[2]

We see that race and SES together contribute only 22 percent of the total IQ variance. (In this context "race" refers to the variance associated with classification as black or white, independent of any variance associated with SES as measured by the Duncan index. Thus the term "race" here is not exclusively a biological factor but some combination of *all* the factors associated with the racial classification except whatever socioeconomic factors are measured by the SES index.) More than three times as much of the variance as is due to race and SES combined is attributable to differences *between* families of the same race and SES level plus differences among children *within* the same family. In fact, the largest single source of the total variance is the within family differences, that is, differences among siblings.

The analysis shown in Table 3.1 is quite typical; it clearly belies many of the claims, such as those cited in Chapter 1, that IQ tests discriminate mostly along racial and social-class lines. Most of the heterogeneity in IQ in the population is found among siblings reared in the same family, whose race, socioeconomic status, and cultural backgrounds are as much alike as could be. And differences among families all of the same race and the same SES level (when SES is divided into ten levels) account for more of the IQ variance than do race and SES combined. Obviously the IQ test measures mainly *individual* differences, differences between persons that are very largely *not* attributable to differences in their racial and socioeconomic backgrounds.[3]

The reason that race and SES account for relatively little (i.e., 22 percent) of the total variance of IQ, of course, is that there is so much variability *within* racial and SES groups relative to the difference between the means. The analysis of variance highlights this important fact. Average differences among groups may seem overwhelming until they are viewed in the perspective of the total variation in the population. The average IQs of the separate racial groups across SES levels are shown graphically in Figure 3.1.

Table 3.1 Percentage of total variance[1] and average IQ difference[2] in WISC-R Full Scale IQs attributable to each of several sources.

Source of Variance	% of Variance[3]	Average IQ Difference[3]
Between *races* (independent of SES)	14 } 22%	12
Between *SES* groups (independent of race)	8	6
Between families (within race & SES groups)	29 } 73%	9
Within families	44	12
Measurement error	5	4
Total	100	17

[1]See note 2 at end of chapter.   [2]See note 4 at end of chapter.   [3]Rounded to nearest whole number.

Figure 3.1. Average Full Scale IQ on the Wechsler Intelligence Scale for Children (Revised), for random samples of white ($N = 622$) and black ($N = 622$) California school children in ten socioeconomic categories as measured on Duncan's index of SES.   (From Jensen & Figueroa, 1975)

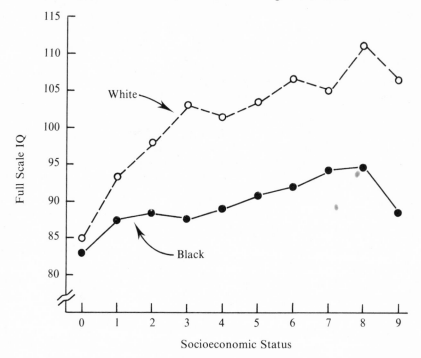

The overall IQ difference between whites and blacks is 15 points. Whites and blacks of the same SES differ by 12 points.[4] The average absolute difference among the means of SES groups of the same race is about 6 IQ points, or 9 IQ points among whites and 4 IQ points among blacks. But the average absolute difference among the means of families of the same race and SES is 9 IQ points, and the average difference among siblings in the same family is 12 IQ points (which is the same as the average IQ difference between races of the same SES).

The average difference between the IQs of the same person tested on two occasions about one month apart is 4 IQ points. The average absolute difference between random pairs of individuals picked from this sample regardless of race or SES is 17 IQ points. (These figures are shown in the last column of Table 3.1.)

Consequences of Discrimination

If discriminations, intentional and incidental, are a necessary and inevitable product of any good test, this is not the case for the *choice* of discrimination or its consequences. Whether one decides to discriminate at all, or which attributes one chooses to discriminate, and what decisions should follow from discrimination, are entirely matters of policy and judgment. They do not flow from the power of tests to discriminate.

Making discriminations by means of tests of one kind or another is often justified in theoretical or in practical terms. Tests and measurements serve a necessary function in theory-oriented scientific research on the nature of human differences in abilities and other traits. There is little disagreement on the importance of objective measurement for psychological research, although there may be considerable debate about which questions should or should not be researched. On the practical side, discrimination has four professed justifications: assessment, diagnosis, selection, and placement.

Assessment.   Assessment (or evaluation) per se is probably the least controversial of the practical uses of tests. Assessment is measurement of the results of a specific training or educational program, for the benefit of the teacher or educational administrator in evaluating the effect of the program or for the benefits of the assessee in evaluating his own progress. Scholastic achievement testing (where not used for selection or placement) is an example of assessment. The main justification for any test used in assessment is its *content validity*.★ A test has content validity to the degree to which its item content explicitly matches the knowledge or skills that the training was aimed to impart. Assessment testing may also consist of a pretest of the subject's knowledge or skill in the course content at the beginning of a course of training or study, as a baseline for evaluating progress and achievement due to the training itself rather than to prior attainment. Assessments may be used as ''informative feedback'' for the student or the teacher in evaluating progress in mastery of the course content, or in evaluating the effectiveness of different methods of instruction, or (less justifiably) for comparing teachers or schools. But, in every case, assessment is directed toward specific course content.

Diagnosis.   The observation of marked deviations from the class average or from some ''norm,'' revealed by assessment, may call for diagnosis involving the use of tests. Diagnosis is an attempt to understand the causes of deviations from the norm; it comes up especially when the individual's assessments indicate unusually poor progress. Diagnostic tests may have content validity relevant to the subject matter of the course, but they need not have content validity. Tests of other abilities or traits that are correlated with achievement may be useful for diagnosis. Special tests devised to measure fine-grained components of the course content, such as visual acuity, form perception, and eye movements, in the case of reading, may yield helpful information. So may tests of prerequisite knowledge or skills. Most often tests of general ability or IQ tests are used in diagnosis, with the rationale that such tests reflect the subject's achievements in a much broader sphere and thus may be indicative of his typical capacity for learning.

The justification of diagnosis, in psychology as in medicine, is to aid in prescription and remediation, if possible. It is at this point that other consequences of discrimination, such as placement, may enter the picture.

Placement.   Placement is of greater personal consequence than assessment and diagnosis per se. It means different treatments for different individuals. Good teaching always involves differential or individualized treatment to some extent, but it is informal, flexible, and geared to dealing with specific difficulties as they crop up from time to time. When differential treatment is relatively long term and is formalized or institutionalized, it is known as *placement*. Familiar examples are the school practices of ''tracking,'' ''streaming,'' or ''ability grouping,'' and placing pupils in ''special education'' classes for the ''educably mentally retarded,'' ''educationally handicapped,'' ''academically gifted'' or ''high potential,'' and the like. Ability and achievement tests usually play a large part in placement.

The only justification for placement is evidence that the alternative treatments are more beneficial to the individuals assigned to them than would be the case if everyone got the same treatment, with the slight variations in instruction that occur informally in the ordinary class. The supposed benefits of placement are often highly debatable. They are difficult to evaluate and are often undemonstrated. Placement is a complex matter, to say the least.

Even in the face of objective evidence, the evaluation of placement practices involves values and judgment in weighing real and supposed advantages against real and supposed disadvantages. It is no wonder that there is much disagreement about placement. Placement has significant consequences, for good or ill, for the individual. It becomes a socially sensitive and controversial issue when it affects various identifiable minorities disproportionally. Then there arise charges of stigma, unequal opportunity, and biased placement procedures, including biased tests.

Selection.   Equally contested from a societal standpoint is the use of tests for *selection* (or *screening*). Selection necessarily implies rejection. The pool of applicants is dichotomized: accepted/rejected.

There are two justifications for selection: (1) when the pool of applicants is larger than the number that can be accepted and (2) when the predictive validity of the selection procedure can be substantiated. A test or other selection procedure (the "predictor") is said to have *predictive validity*★ to the extent that it would discriminate between the performance (the "criterion") of selectees and rejectees if *all* of them had been accepted. A quantitative index of predictive validity, called a validity coefficient, is the correlation between individual differences on the predictor and criterion variables. Predictive validity is the essential justification for discriminatory selection. If the number of applicants does not exceed the number that can be accepted, and if there is no predictive validity in any selection procedure, there is of course no need for selection. If the number of applicants exceeds the number that can be accepted, but there is no selection procedure with predictive validity, there is no basis for discriminatory selection. Selection there must be, but only nondiscriminatory selection is justified. The only completely nondiscriminatory selection procedure is a random lottery. Randomness ensures that there is no correlation whatever between *any* attributes of the applicant and his chances of being accepted or rejected. When a degree of predictive validity for any selection procedure can be demonstrated, the possibility for discriminatory selection raises important questions: How high must the predictive validity be to justify selection? Are some predictors preferable to others, even though they may have the same validity? Is selection valid or warranted throughout the full range of the predictor variable, or is there some cutoff point on the predictor variable above which selection should be nondiscriminatory (i.e., random)?

It is convenient to speak of predictors as either *direct* or *indirect*. A *direct* predictor is information obtained from the person's own behavior, such as performance on a test. It is information generated by what the person *does* rather than information about who he is. Behavior samples of one kind or another, including test performances, may have predictive validity for selection. An *indirect* predictor is any information of an impersonal categorical nature. (It is impersonal in the sense that such information need not be obtained directly from the person, in contrast to such information as a score on a test or a rating in an interview, which can be obtained only from the person's own behavior.) Indirect predictors are items such as age, sex, race, place of birth, marital status, highest school grade completed, religious preference, number of children, father's occupation, home ownership, criminal record, political affiliation, and so on. Any such categories may have predictive validity for selection in a statistical sense. Used in an optimally weighted combination, they can have quite high validity as predictors of some criteria, even as high validity as a direct predictor. Does this justify the use of indirect predictors in selection—for jobs, training programs, and college entrance? An objection to indirect predictors is that they base selection on the average characteristics of persons in the categories of which the individual is a member and not on the characteristics of the individual himself. Hence atypical members of the category are discriminated "unfairly"—a term that I must clarify shortly. When impersonal categories are used as predictors, members of any category can claim unfair discrimination, regardless of the validity of the predictor. Title VII of the Civil Rights Act of 1964, in fact, prohibits discrimination in employment selection on the basis of race, color, or national origin, and subsequent legislation has moved against the use of sex and other indirect predictors for selection. It is now generally agreed that selection should be based exclusively on direct predictors, although, for certain specialized jobs and educational programs, there are still recognized exceptions involving age, sex, and amount of formal education.

But selection based on direct predictors raises thorny problems, too. First, of course, is the technical problem of establishing that the predictor is in fact substantially predictive. All selection procedures have a margin of error. The penalties of errors of prediction are borne by the rejectees as well as by the employer. Who pays the greater penalty? Obviously it is the rejectee, for to him rejection means total loss, unless he can be persuaded that rejection was in his own long-range interest. The employer can only gain by selection if the predictor is at all valid and is not more costly to use than are the consequences of not selecting at all. Errors in selection mainly affect the marginal rejectees. It has been argued that those who have been wrongly rejected would have been among the bottom in performance if selected, whereas those marginal cases who were wrongly selected would have been near the top of the class in which they are left if they had been rejected. Errors of selection are thus seemingly mitigated.

While it is easy to defend a selection threshold on the predictor below which utter failure on the criterion is practically certain, it may be more difficult to defend selection cutoffs at points above the threshold of competence. If the threshold for competence excludes, say, only the bottom 20 percent of job applicants on the distribution of the predictor variable, is the employer who can hire, say, only 30 percent of the applicants justified in using the predictor (e.g., a test score) to select the top 30 percent of applicants? Technically this should depend on the validity of the predictor above the threshold of competence; this can be determined by statistical analysis. But some would argue that, if the predictor puts an applicant above the threshold, any further selection should be nondiscriminatory, even if the predictor variable is significantly correlated with the criterion throughout its entire range. In terms of predictive validity, the idea that if a high score is good, a higher score must be even better is not always true. In practice, it is rare that a predictor can be shown to be valid throughout its entire range, and in some cases predictors have a marked curvilinear relationship to the criterion; that is, beyond some point on the predictor variable, higher scores predict *poorer* performance or other undesirable effects such as job dissatisfaction and greater turnover of employees.

Another problem in selection is that some selection tests are quite valid predictors of how fast new employees will learn to do a job but do not predict how effectively they will perform on the job *after* they have learned how to do it. Is such a selection test justified? It may be, if the time required for learning or the cost of training are considerable.

Selection procedures at times result in disproportional acceptance and rejection of members of some groups in the population. The courts have often referred to this as ''adverse impact'' of a selection procedure on some particular group, usually a racial minority. ''Adverse impact'' is often equated with biased selection, but this is wrong if the only evidence for ''adverse impact'' is a disproportional rejection of minority members. Selection having ''adverse impact'' may or may not be biased.

Bias.   There are a number of technical criteria of bias as well as statistical methods for detecting it. A proper discussion of all these calls for a separate chapter. (See Chapter 9.) But at this point we can hardly proceed without at least a capsule definition of bias.

Bias can enter into selection at any point in the process from the initial recruiting of applicants, to the testing of applicants, to the method for using test scores or other predictors in the final selection of applicants. Discrimination between groups in selection is not necessarily a sign of bias. To some it may come as a surprise to find that group discrimination is, in fact, neither necessary nor sufficient to establish bias. A highly biased test or selection procedure can result in perfectly proportional selection of applicants from different groups.

In the most general terms, bias exists when the method of selection discriminates individuals differently than does the criterion measure of performance. (This leaves out of the question for the moment the adequacy and possible bias in the criterion itself.) This may be stated in a number of ways. A predictor is biased if it either overestimates of underestimates an individual's criterion performance depending on his group membership. A predictor is biased if it correlates more with group membership than with the criterion it is intended to predict, for under this condition the selected or rejected applicants are being rewarded or penalized on the basis of their group membership rather than just on the basis of those individual traits that are in fact relevant to the criterion.

Bias can enter into the recruitment of the applicant pool, for example, when job openings are made known by word of mouth from the present employees or are advertised only in restricted neighborhoods that are vastly unrepresentative of the population in a larger area accessible to recruitment. Determining the extent of recruitment bias is more problematic in selection involving prior specialized training or educational requirements, as various racial or cultural groups may be very disproportionally represented among the eligible applicants for reasons unknown or beyond present control.

Bias enters into the testing aspect of selection when the test does not measure the same trait or ability when applied to different groups, or does not measure with the same reliability in different groups. The causes of any of these shortcomings may be attributable to the test itself or to factors operating in the testing situation, whieh may differentially affect the members of some groups, such as anxiety, fear of failure, or inhibition in the presence of an examiner of a different race or background.

Bias is essentially a form of error: it is error of measurement (unreliability) and error of prediction (invalidity) that are related to the individual's group membership. Measurement and prediction errors, of course, also exist independently of group membership and technically can be regarded as *individual* bias. An individual's test score is biased to the extent that it is unreliable or invalid. Because no tests are perfect, some degree of individual bias is inescapable. All we can hope is to minimize it as much as possible. Reliability★ and validity★ traditionally have been central considerations in setting standards of test usage. Psychometric science is preoccupied with estimating and reducing biases of every kind involved in testing.

Fairness and Unfairness.   These terms are often used more or less synonymously with "bias" (or the lack of it), but they carry additional moral overtones and thus imply subjective values and judgments beyond the objective and technical meanings of bias. Hence concepts of "fairness" or "unfairness" belong more to moral philosophy than to psychometrics. Even assuming that a test or selection procedure is totally without bias of any kind, the fact that it involves discrimination between persons may itself be questioned in terms of fairness. Is it fair that persons should be discriminated, even if the test accurately predicts the criterion? Is it fair that all persons not be given an equal chance to prove themselves on the criterion itself, rather than risk being screened out by an imperfect predictor test? Is it fair that members of different groups in the pool of applicants have different success rates in passing the selection tests, even when the test scores are equally predictive for all groups?

What are the alternatives? If there is competition for entry, as there must be for many positions in a complex society, discrimination is inevitable. The only question is *how* to discriminate. Would a random lottery be more fair than a validated selection procedure? A lottery gives everyone an equal chance for selection, but it protects no one from the risk of failure. Would failure to pass a selection test having high predictive validity be less costly to the individual than failure at the criterion performance? Is it more fair to predict and prevent highly probable failure? What about fairness to the employer who must risk his limited resources on the selectee's probability of success? Should the employer not be allowed to minimize his risk?

Such questions of fairness and unfairness ultimately lead to metaphysical debate and practically defy objective agreement. In the face of metaphysical disagreements we are thrown back on utilitarian considerations that at least are more amenable to objective analysis with the techniques of psychometrics and statistics.

Mental Tests and Social Justice

Time and again the case has been made that to abolish testing would only make selection more subjective, more biased, and more irrelevant to successful performance than if tests were used. Selection based on amount of formal education, personal recommendations, interview ratings, or teachers' grades all have been shown to be less reliable predictors than tests and to allow much more scope for the influence of background status, privilege, prejudice, politics, favoritism, and nepotism in determining who wins out in the competition for higher education and higher-status jobs. Generally, when ability tests have been substituted for other methods of selection, the result has been to favor socially underprivileged groups at the expense of the more privileged. This should not be surprising, since, as we have seen, individual differences in mental ability are widely distributed in every social class and therefore should contribute a large share of variance in educational and occupational achievement and income that is unrelated to social class of birth.

Compared with other methods of selection, tests are more impersonal, and yet more individual and objective, and hence tend to "read through" the veneer of social-class background that may carry undue weight in subjective ratings based on interviews and biographical data. As early as 1814, Thomas Jefferson showed his extraordinary social foresight by proposing that the Commonwealth of Virginia use tests to seek out the academically talented children of the poor so as to subsidize their education.

When early in this century intelligence tests began to be used in England to select students for secondary education, it came as a great surprise to many educators that more working-class children relative to middle-class children were selected than was the case when selection was based on teachers' grades and recommendations. The substitution of intelligence tests for traditional indices of scholastic attainment actually doubled the percentage of secondary school scholarship winners coming from working-class homes (those of skilled, semiskilled, and unskilled manual workers). When the use of intelligence tests for educational selection was abandoned because of political ideology in one county, in 1952, the percentage of children of manual workers admitted to academically oriented college preparatory schools fell from 14.9 percent to 11.5 percent, while the percentage of children of professional and managerial parents rose from 39.6 percent to 63.6 percent (Wiseman, 1964, pp. 155–156). Intelligence tests were opposed by upper- and middle-class parents whose children traditionally enjoyed the advantages of secondary education regardless of their ability.

Basing their conclusions on correlations between father's occupational status and the individual's school grades, test scores, occupational and educational aspirations in twelfth grade, educational attainment, and actual occupational status at age 25, Jencks et al. (1972, p. 194) state that "low-status boys will rise furthest if high-status occupations select on the basis of grades or test scores." Their analysis shows that test scores are considerably more advantageous to the upward mobility of low-status boys than are grades. Selection based on educational attainment (years of schooling) works to the relative disadvantage of the sons of manual workers. Jencks et al. point out that in their data the correlation between father's occupational status and son's status at age 25 is .331; it would only fall to .288 if the son's occupational status were determined solely by intelligence test scores. Jencks et al. conclude that "a system which allocates status on the basis of cognitive skills is likely to result in more social mobility than any of the obvious alternatives" (p. 195).

Other commentators have noted the actual and potential contributions of objective ability tests to educational and occupational mobility and hence to social justice:

> In view of the loose relationship between IQ and social class in the United States, it seems that one very constructive function of the ability measured by tests is that it serves as a kind of springboard, launching many men into achievements removing them considerable distances from the social class of their birth. IQ, in an achievement-oriented society, is the primary leaven preventing the classes from hardening into castes.   (Duncan, 1968, p. 11)

> Judging each person on the basis of his measured performance rather than on his family background, social status, or political connections has been a powerful agent of social change. Assuming unbiased, reliable measurement, what could be more just within the American concept of an egalitarian society than recognizing merit by objective tests of ability? Even today, college entrance examinations have made it possible for able but financially poor students to obtain scholarships in the best private colleges.   (Holtzman, 1971)

In the midst of today's charges that tests discriminate against certain social groups, it is worth reminding ourselves that impartial assessment has played a notable part in advancing children of the ethnic poor. In the United States the Jews, the Orientals, and the children of Germans and Scandinavians used the system of open, merit-based selection to attain social equality in the face of notorious preju-dice. (Cronbach, 1973)

Minority groups, as such, should be favorably inclined to the use of ability tests, since tests constitute a universal standard of competence and potential. When tests are substituted for [biased] methods of educational placement . . . job selection and promotion, they increase the opportunities of minority group members because they measure ability rather than social status. Tests therefore should be viewed with favor by this segment of the culturally deprived. (Brim, 1965, p. 127)

These writers seem to be thinking mostly of social class or white ethnic minority membership as the basis for prejudicial barriers to educational and occupational advance-ment that the use of ability tests has helped to overcome. Are these opinions at best naïve as applied to blacks, Puerto Ricans, and Mexican–Americans? Data are still insufficient for more than speculation regarding the latter two groups, but it is now quite evident that the use of ability tests has not had for blacks the beneficial results extolled in the preceding quotations. Opposition to the use of tests in placement, selection, and merit systems of employment and promotion was never generated among poor whites, ethnic minorities of European origin, or Orientals. These were the groups that seemed to benefit from selec-tion by merit. It is a fact that test-based placement and selection procedures discriminate strongly against blacks as a group, and most of the steam behind the current opposition to tests arises from this fact. Psychologists must face it: blacks as a group owe little to tests. Here then is understandably the prime focus for questions of bias and the unfair use of tests. Are the criticisms of tests by blacks and their white sympathizers ill-founded and misdirected, or are they just?

Jencks's analysis of the relation between occupational status and IQ scores led him to conclude:

If the occupational status of blacks has improved [since 1962], this has been because of direct efforts to eliminate discrimination and compensate for past discrimination. It has not been because blacks' test scores have risen or because they have appreci-ably more educational credentials than they did a decade ago." (Jencks, 1972, p. 191)

He later goes on to note that "a system which emphasizes cognitive skills would be far less satisfactory for blacks than for poor whites. For blacks, the ideal system is one which discounts test scores and emphasizes aspirations. Failing this, a system that emphasizes credentials is better for blacks than one that emphasizes test scores" (p. 195). Jencks's recent conclusions, arrived at from statistical analyses of relevant data, apparently were intuitively perceived years before by social reformers and political leaders of the black community. Thus began the relentless criticism of tests in employment selection and the increased emphasis on blacks' attaining the credentials conferred by educational institu-tions. The fact that tests are used most widely in school placement and selection for higher education has fueled the attacks on testing.

Equal Opportunity and Affirmative Action

Title VII of the Civil Rights Act of 1964, which forbids employment discrimination based on race, color, religion, national origin, or sex, had important beneficial effects for minorities with a long history of discrimination. Enforcement of the act under the provisions of the Equal Employment Opportunities Commission (EEOC) at least fostered what has been called "passive nondiscrimination." This, however, did not remove the disproportionate rates of unemployment of certain minorities or their marked underrepresentation in skilled and white-collar jobs. The perpetuation of these disproportions were attributed in large part to the effects of past inequalities in opportunity, as manifested in lack of knowledge of present job opportunities by many minority persons, or word-of-mouth recruitment of new employees and other informal networks of employment information, or job qualifications that are not directly related to actual job requirements.

To help overcome the lingering effects of past discrimination, a ruling known as Executive Order 11246 was made in July 1969 that requires employers receiving federal contracts to make self-analyses of their own employment practices and, if there is "underutilization" of minorities or women, to present and adopt "affirmative action plans" for remedying this imbalance. The regulations define "underutilization" as "having fewer minorities or women in a particular job classification than would reasonably be expected by their availability." The suggested remedies for underutilization of minorities and women involve affirmative actions in the areas of recruitment, training, promotion, counseling, and selection procedures.

Thus affirmative action clearly has important implications for selection or promotion based on tests when the percentages passing from different groups do not correspond to their representation in the pool of applicants. If minorities are underrepresented among the pool of applicants, special recruitment efforts may be deemed necessary. Although passive nondiscrimination requires the elimination of discrimination based on minority status, affirmative action requires more than mere neutrality with regard to race and sex. In fact, one official guideline goes so far as to state:

> Contractors may find that they will have to undertake a program to rebuild entirely the work habits of the people they hire. This may even require knocking on their door in the morning and providing transportation to the plant. The people we are talking about have been out of the mainstream of society for so long that they have not developed [the] values which the dominant white community takes for granted.

Affirmative action calls for "goals and time tables" by employers for hiring minorities. A "good faith" effort must be shown toward the attainment of these goals. The burden of proof of such effort is on the employer.

There has been a range of interpretations and implementation of affirmative action requirements, from passive nondiscrimination to hard quotas. In an article on affirmative action in *Fortune* magazine, Seligman (1973, p. 161) discerns four different postures on affirmative action: (1) *passive nondiscrimination,* which treats races and sexes alike in hiring, promotion, and pay; (2) *pure affirmative action,* which emphasizes recruitment efforts to expand the pool of applicants so as not to exclude members of formerly underrepresented groups, but hires the best qualified without regard to race or sex; (3) *affirmative action with preferential hiring* which not only recruits more widely but which systematically favors minority groups and women in hiring; qualifications may be relaxed to achieve more equal representation of all groups; (4) *hard quotas,* which specify specific numbers or proportions of minority persons that must be hired. There is little argument about points 1 and 2, and government officials deny the implications of affirmative action of point 4. Contention is mostly over point 3, that is, preferential hiring. Proponents claim that it is justified to right the wrongs of past racial discrimination; they view it merely as a temporary pump-priming measure needed at the beginning to attain the ultimate purpose of the affirmative action program, namely, proportional representation based on equal opportunity. They also argue in terms of the community's needs for services by racially diverse personnel, a factor that outweighs strictly educational or intellectual qualifications. Considering race among the selection criteria for public service positions in teaching, medical and legal services, social work, and law enforcement, it is argued, may better serve a racially diverse community. Critics, on the other hand, have characterized affirmative action as "reverse discrimination." One critic writes:

> Government officials continue to insist that "you never have to hire an unqualified person," and of course they avoid using terms like "reverse discrimination" and "quotas." But, given the many legal and economic weapons available to the government, the effect of affirmative action policies has been precisely to encourage employers and universities to practice discrimination against individuals who do not belong to those groups favored by affirmative action programs." (Ornstein, 1974, p. 481)

As examples, Ornstein claims that universities "frankly announce race and sex as qualifications for new students and faculty members" and notes that the chancellor of the City Colleges of Chicago "recently directed the presidents of the colleges to consider race the prime factor in hiring new faculty members; adding . . . that 'when 52 systemwide contracts expire in July for teachers, many qualified whites will not be rehired and blacks will be sought to fill their jobs'" (p. 481).

One of the most devastating critiques of the drive toward "preferential treatment" of blacks comes from a noted black economist, Thomas Sowell (1978), who claims that most blacks in the United States are opposed to preferential treatment for blacks in jobs or college admissions and notes that "the income of blacks relative to whites reached peak *before* affirmative-action hiring and has *declined* since" (p. 40).

The facts regarding the actual effects of affirmative action policies, and the validity of the assumptions on which these practices are based, are a subject for public evaluation. They are of concern here only insofar as they involve testing.

The implications of affirmative action for mental testing are clearly stated by the U.S. Commission on Civil Rights (1973, p. 18):

> Once a nondiscriminatory applicant pool has been established, the process of selection from that pool must itself be subjected to careful examination. All criteria used to select employees, whether or not they are discriminatory on their face, must be reviewed to determine if they have a disproportionately negative effect on minorities. If so, they must be further examined to determine whether they are relevant to the duties of the particular position in question.

Tests must be validated to insure that they are both job related and not culturally biased [italics added]. Other employment criteria must likewise be job related. This insures that they are not unnecessarily high and inadvertently discriminatory.

Such requirements raise innumerable questions and problems when applied to specific employment situations, and in many cases employers may be more inclined to practice reverse discrimination to comply rather than to embark on the possibly costlier prospect, at least in the short run, of carrying out the research to validate its procedures for testing and selecting personnel.

Colleges and universities are best equipped for research on test validation, as selection has long been based primarily on quantifiable data such as high school grades and college entrance examinations, and the validity criteria are readily available in the form of course grades and attainment of a college degree. Also it is relatively easy to make a case for the relevance of the usual selection criteria for success in college. Affirmative action policies in student admissions have been adopted by nearly all major universities and colleges.

Recruitment by individual colleges and Talent Search[5] centers scattered throughout the country have greatly increased the proportion of minority applicants, but there has also been a relaxation of the usual entrance requirements in many instances, particularly where selection by entrance examinations would have resulted in maintaining the *status quo* in minority admissions.

The claim of test bias with respect to minority students is harder to defend in college selection than in most employment situations, and this seems especially true when tests are used for determining admission to graduate programs and professional schools. Can it be convincingly argued that minority group college graduates seeking admission to professional schools suffer from cultural deprivation, or that graduate level aptitude tests are culturally biased for minority graduates? Whatever their family backgounds, they have gone through eight years of elementary school, four years of high school, and four years of college. Should not sixteen years of exposure to the majority culture be sufficient to make graduate aptitude tests appropriate for minority as well as majority students? Graduate aptitude tests, such as the Graduate Record Examination and the Medical and Law School Aptitude Tests, are after all intended to measure in large part the knowledge and intellectual skills acquired in school and college; and these are the factors that best predict success in specialized graduate programs. Is the question of cultural bias any longer relevant, then, in the case of a law school or medical school aptitude test, when the applicants to law school and medical school have all come through prelaw or premedical undergraduate curricula? At this point in the student's career, after some sixteen years of schooling, nationally standardized tests of academically relevant cognitive skills would seem to be a fair indicator of the student's manifest educational attainments and his probable capacity for further attainment in a similar academic program.

Yet such tests, when their use results in racially disproportionate admissions, are now frequently overridden by other considerations in line with affirmative action. The legality of such consideration, if applied differently to minority and majority applicants, has been contested in the courts. One action, the highly publicized *De Funis* case, was carried all the way to the U.S. Supreme Court, but without resulting in a decision by the court. The case is worth summarizing as an illustration of some of the practices and issues involved in affirmative action in graduate school admissions.

In 1971 Marco De Funis, a white, magna cum laude, Phi Beta Kappa graduate of the University of Washington, applied for admission to the university's law school. Applicants had to submit a personal statement, a list of their extracurricular college activities, at least two faculty recommendations, and a transcript of college grades. The application form requested information, which was optional, of "dominant ethnic origin." Applicants were also required to take the Law School Aptitude Test (LSAT), a nationally standardized test administered and scored by the Educational Testing Service of Princeton, N.J. No personal interview or report of economic status was required. In 1971, the law school could admit only 150 students out of the 1,601 applicants. Among the chief selection criteria was the Predicted First Year Average (PFYA), a validated formula worked out by the Educational Testing Service, which combines college grades and LSAT scores to predict academic performance in the first year of law school. White and minority applicants were ranked separately on the basis of their PFYA, so that whites were in competition with other whites and minority students with other minority students. Also, the selection committee had instructions when considering minority students to give more weight to such factors as potential community service, motivation, and maturity than to the PFYA, which was the primary selection criterion for whites. With each group judged separately and by a different weighting of the selection criteria, the best-qualified white and minority applicants were admitted.

Despite a nearly A grade-point average and a high LSAT score, De Funis was among the rejected applicants. When he discovered that a number of the admitted minority students had lower grade-point averages and LSAT scores than his own, he filed suit in the Superior Court of King County, Washington: *DE FUNIS* v. *ODEGAARD* (president of the University of Washington).[6] The suit charged the law school's rejection of De Funis was discriminatory, arbitrary, capricious, and unreasonable and in violation of the equal protection provision of the Fourteenth Amendment. The superior court judge ruled in favor of De Funis. In an oral decision, the judged stated:

> It seems to me that the law school here wished to achieve greater minority representation and in accomplishing this gave preference to the members of some races. ... Some minority students were admitted whose college grades and aptitude test scores were so low that had they been whites their applications would have been summarily denied. Excluding the Asians[7] only one minority student out of 31 admitted among the applicants had a predicted first-year average above the plaintiff's. Since no more than 150 applicants were to be admitted, the admission of less qualified resulted in a denial of places to those otherwise qualified. The plaintiff and others in this group, have not in my opinion been accorded the equal protection of the law guaranteed by the Fourteenth Amendment.[6]

De Funis was admitted to the University of Washington Law School. The university, however, appealed the case to the Washington State Supreme Court, which overturned the decision of the superior court. The Washington Supreme Court ruled 3 to 2 that it was within the law school's discretion to consider race as a factor in selecting the "best qualified'' for law school. The court upheld the constitutionality of affirmative action in student admissions, ruling that "the elimination of serious racial imbalances . . . constitutes a compelling state interest" and that underrepresentation of minorities in the legal profession is itself a subtle erosion of the equal protection guarantee of the Fourteenth Amendment.

Attorneys for De Funis then took the case to the U.S. Supreme Court, which, in April 1974, by a 5-to-4 vote, refused to review the case. The Supreme Court ruled the case was moot, since Mr. De Funis was in fact already enrolled as a student in the University of Washington Law School. The four Supreme Court justices who favored ruling on the De Funis case on the grounds that it affected many others offered their opinions. Justice William O. Douglas contended that the university was free to use any selection criteria it pleased but that it must apply them in a "racially neutral way." He said:

> A De Funis who is white is entitled to no advantage by reason of that fact; nor is he subject to any disability. . . . Whatever his race, he had a constitutional right to have his application considered on his individual merits in a racially neutral manner . . . .
> The Constitution commands the elimination of racial barriers, not their creation in order to satisfy our theory as to how society ought to be organized.

Finally, in the summer of 1978, the U.S. Supreme Court could not escape making a decision regarding whether a person's race is a proper consideration for college admission, in the now famous "Bakke decision." Allan Bakke was a white applicant to the University of California's Medical School (at Davis) who had been denied admission even though his college grades and score on the medical school admission test were higher than those of minority students who gained admission. The medical school's special admissions program, in line with its affirmative action policy, had set aside sixteen out of the one hundred openings for minority students. Bakke sued the university, and the California State Supreme Court rule in favor of Bakke, on the ground that his rejection had been racially discriminatory. The university appealed the case to the U.S. Supreme Court, which, in a 5-to-4 decision, ruled that Bakke's rejection by the medical school violated the "equal protection" of the Constitution because it was based on a racial quota, and so Bakke would have to be admitted to medical school. (He entered in the fall of 1978.) The Supreme Court, however, upheld the principle of affirmative action, saying that race might legitimately be an element in judging students for admission to universities, provided racial quotas are not involved. Thus the Supreme Court's decision is obviously ambiguous and will undoubtedly invite future legal actions not unlike the De Funis and Bakke cases. The arguments in such cases will extend far beyond questions of the objective validity of entrance tests and selection procedures. The debate involves fundamental philosophic positions and value judgments in the weighing of one social good against another, as the growing insistence on group rights runs head on into the traditional democratic belief in equality of individual opportunity. These questions of social policy cannot be answered by scientists. But in the controversy surrounding affirmative action there are implicit assumptions about the distribution of abilities and talents in the population, and these are susceptible to scientific analysis. In fact, the nature and consequences of racial and social-class discrimination cannot be properly understood without some knowledge of the statistical properties of ability distributions.

SUMMARY

Discrimination, that is, reliable measurements of differences between persons, or of differences *within* any one person, is fundamental in psychometrics. Discrimination per se is neutral and essential for the legitimate purposes of assessment, diagnosis, placement, and selection. Test discrimination between the statistical averages of different racial, cultural, or socioeconomic groups in the population is an incidental by-product of the test's discrimination among individuals *within* any group. No one constructs ability tests expressly to discriminate among social groups as such.

Discrimination, however, can be *biased,* although discrimination is not *necessarily* biased. Bias implies systematic (i.e., nonrandom) errors of measurement, or of predictions from measurements, in the test scores of individuals or groups. Thus, bias is essentially a *statistical* concept. Minimizing bias of all kinds in test scores has been a major aim of applied psychometrics.

The concept of "fairness" (or "unfairness") as applied to tests and the ways in which they are used is a *value* judgment based on broader social, moral, and philosophic considerations than just the statistical issue of bias.

In general, the use of objective tests in educational and employment selection has promoted social justice, and no other methods yet tried have proven to be as objectively impartial as the use of tests. For example, evidence indicates that, when tests are used in educational selection, the percentages of upper- and lower-socioeconomic-status pupils selected for "higher education" are more nearly equalized than by any other conventional methods of selection, such as school grades, teacher recommendations, and interview assessments. As assessments of ability, these conventional methods of selection and promotion do not "read through" the veneer of social-class and ethnic cultural differences nearly as well as do objective tests, which are less liable to personal bias or prejudice. Hence the use of tests has proven more advantageous to the upward mobility of low-status persons in our society than have such traditional criteria for advancement as amount of schooling, diplomas or other formal qualifications, school ties, and family connections.

These generalizations, however, may be seriously questioned in the case of black Americans, who, it can be legitimately claimed, have not benefited from tests to anywhere near the same extent as many other initially low-status minorities in American society. This fact, in part, has recently fostered the official policy of "affirmative action" or preferential recruitment and selection of blacks and certain other disadvantaged minorities in higher education and employment in higher-status jobs. The question of test bias and the fair use of tests, in the case of these minorities, has become a major concern to psychometric science.

NOTES

1. I am indebted for these data to Dr. Jane R. Mercer, who obtained the WISC-R IQs and SES ratings on representative samples of more than 1,200 white and black children in California schools.

2. The percentages of variance were estimated as follows. First, the following correlations were obtained:

$$\text{Race} \times \text{SES} = .4381$$
$$\text{Race} \times \text{IQ} = .4955$$
$$\text{SES} \times \text{IQ} = .4355$$

Then, partial correlations were obtained, partialing out SES from Race × IQ, and race from SES × IQ, yielding

$$(\text{Race} \times \text{IQ})/\text{SES} = .3765$$
$$(\text{SES} \times \text{IQ})/\text{Race} = .2797.$$

The proportion of IQ variance attributable to race and SES independently of one another is the square of the partial correlation, that is, .14 for race and .08 for SES.

The WISC-R Manual (Wechsler, 1974) gives .95 as the test–retest (one-month interval) reliability of Full Scale IQ in the age range of the present sample. This means there is 5 percent measurement error. Thus 14% + 8% + 5% = 27%, leaving 73 percent for variance between families (within racial and SES groups) and within families. By variance between families is meant the interfamily variability between the means of the siblings. Within families variance is variability among siblings within the same family. The between and within families variances were determined from the writer's study of sibling correlations in large samples of whites and blacks on a highly comparable IQ scale (Lorge-Thorndike IQ), which was .43 in both racial groups. This means that 43 percent of the variance within racial groups is attributable to differences between families, which includes SES differences. The remainder of the variance is due to variance *within* families and error variance. This means that if we exclude variance due to race (14 percent) we are left with 86 percent, and the sum of the SES variance plus variance between families (*within* SES groups) divided by 86 percent must be .43, that is, we solve $(8\% + x)/86\% = .43$, so $x = 29\%$, which is the percentage of variance between families within SES and racial groups. The remainder of 44 percent is the variance within families.

3. It is a quite separate question how much each of the variances in Table 3.1 is attributable to genetic and nongenetic or environmental factors. Most geneticists who have surveyed the evidence are agreed that some substantial part, probably as much as 80% or more of the IQ variance *within* families (i.e., between siblings) is genetic. Variance *among* families of the same race and SES level, the evidence indicates, is also at least 80 percent genetic. The genetic contributions to race and to SES variances are much more in doubt and at present highly controversial. A reasonable case can be made that some part of the SES variance is genetic; some would claim more than half, which would still only be about 6 percent of the total genetic variance within a racially homogeneous population. (But, as shown in Table 3.1, SES in any case does not account for much IQ variance, whether it is genetic or environmental or some combination of these factors. The idea of a genetic component in the racial (i.e., black–white) IQ differences is the most disputed and at present is generally regarded by geneticists as a scientifically legitimate but unproved hypothesis (Jensen, 1973b; Crow, 1975, Denniston, 1975; Loehlin, Lindzey, & Spuhler, 1975).

4. The average IQ difference among the races of the same SES and among SES groups of the same race were determined directly from the data. The average absolute differences in

IQ between families and within families and the average test–retest difference (measure-ment error) were determined indirectly by means of Gini's formula for the relationship between the variance and the average absolute difference among all possible random pairings of the values within the distribution of which the variance is known (Kendall, 1960, pp. 241–242). It assumes that the values are normally distributed; the distribution of IQs among and within families in the present sample very closely approximates the normal curve. Gini's formula is $|\bar{d}| = (4\sigma^2/\pi)^{\frac{1}{2}}$ where $|\bar{d}|$ is the average absolute difference among all randomly paired values, σ^2 is the variance, and π (pi) = 3.1416. In the present problem, σ^2 for each source of variance is of course the proportion of variance times the total variance of IQ in this sample (239.5).

5. Talent Search, which is funded by the U.S. Office of Education, has centers and programs in some seventy cities throughout the country; it finds and counsels black students and others from poor economic backgrounds who could profit from a college education. It has been well described in a feature article in *Science* by Bryce Nelson (1969).

6. *De Funis* v. *Odegaard*, No. 741727, Superior Court of King County, Washington, oral decision September 22, 1971, findings of fact and conclusions of law October 18, 1971.

7. Asian (i.e., Chinese and Japanese) students were not, in fact, included in the list of "favored minorities" by the University of Washington Law School, as Asians were not underrepresented when selected by the same criteria as whites. The "favored minorities" were blacks, Chicanos, American Indians, and Filipinos.

Chapter 4

The Distribution of Mental Ability

Reports of racial discrimination are usually presented to the public in terms of percentages. Group differences viewed in terms of percentages often appear startling and may give readers an impression of gross bias and unfairness in any testing, placement, or selection procedure that could result in such disparity between groups in the percentages who "pass" or "fail." For example:

[W]hile blacks constitue 28.5 percent of all students in the [San Francisco] district, 66 percent of all students in mentally retarded classes are black. (*San Francisco Chronicle*, June 24, 1972)

In classes for the gifted, only 5.5% are Black and 62.2% are white. (Report of the U.S. Commission on Human Rights)

There is no doubt that our classes for the intellectually gifted would have been totally segregated at that school if we had continued them. (Dr. R. T. Brande, School District Superintendent, quoted in *New York Times*, May 22, 1974)

The Oriental representation in EMR [educable mentally retarded] classes is disproportionately low for the overall Oriental school population, and the Spanish-surname representation is about equal to its percentage in the population. (Report of the U.S. Commission on Human Rights)

In the construction trades, new apprentices were 87 percent white and 13 percent black. [Blacks constitute 12 percent of the U.S. population.] For the Federal Civil Service, of those employees above the GS-5 level, 88.5 percent were white, 8.3 percent black, and women account for 30.1 of all civil servants. Finally, a 1969 survey of college teaching positions showed whites with 96.3 percent of all positions. Blacks had 2.2 percent, and women accounted for 19.1 percent. (U.S. Commission on Civil Rights, 1973)

Last year, the county's school system [Baltimore], the ninth largest in the Nation, reported 14,309 [disciplinary] suspensions. Forty-eight percent of the suspensions were of black students, although black students made up only 28 percent of the county's student body. On the elementary school level, where the student body is about 30 percent black, 67 percent of the suspensions involved black students (*Washington Post*, November 5, 1974)

All these disparities in percentages are, of course, evidence of discrimination in the neutral sense in which the term is used throughout this book. But such disparities cannot be taken as *prima facie* evidence of *biased* discrimination.

The percentage disparities seemingly show little consistency, which may suggest differences in bias from one situation to another. Black apprentices in the construction trades are 13 percent of the total—close to their percentage in the general population; blacks are only 8.3 percent of civil service workers, and 2.2 percent of college teachers. Do these marked differences indicate varying degrees of biased discrimination in the various occupations?

Percentages of the kind that we have just seen are the most commonly used index of group differences because they are easy to determine, they accord with the impressions one can gain directly from casual observation, and most persons easily understand what a percentage means. It turns out, however, that percentages are not the only way, or even the best way, for certain purposes, of describing these kinds of group differences. There is another, statistically more sophisticated, way of looking at these differences that makes them much less variable from one situation to another and makes them appear much less striking in magnitude. Most of the percentage differences, even those as great, for example, as the 96.3 percent white versus 2.2 percent black for college teachers, are seen to be consistent with actual group differences no greater than the differences typically found between members of the same family. Even average differences between groups that are in fact quite small, relative to differences between members of the same family, can, under certain conditions, result in extremely large differences in the percentages of each group that are selected; and this can be true even when selection is completely unbiased. This is an especially important fact wherever tests are used in selection. To understand it, however, one must first know something about the form and statistical properties of the distributions of abilities and traits in human populations.

Frequency Distributions of Test Scores

Raw Scores.   A test is composed of a number of items that the subject attempts to answer in the available testing time. The subject's answer to each item is classified on some quantitative scale, usually a two-category scale: Right–Wrong; or a three-category scale: Right–Wrong–Omitted (or Not Attempted). Each category is assigned a number, that is, Right = +1, Wrong = −1, Omitted = 0. These are called "item scores." The subject's total raw score on the test is then simply the sum of the item scores. The total possible range of raw scores will depend, of course, on the values assigned to the Right, Wrong, and Omitted categories, and on the number of items in the test. The simplest form of item scoring is Right = 1 and Wrong or Omitted = 0; the raw score then is simply the number Right, and the possible range of raw scores goes from zero to n, where n is the number of items in the test.

Score Distributions.   When a test is given to a number of persons, their raw scores can be tallied in the form of a frequency distribution. Say, a test made up of nine items is given to one hundred persons. The frequency distribution of raw scores might look like that in Table 4.1.

The number of persons obtaining each score is shown in the f (frequency) column. The cumulative frequency distribution (Cum. f) shows the number of persons who ob-

Table 4.1   Frequency distribution of a nine-item test.

Raw Score		f	Cum. f
High	9	2	100
	8	4	98
	7	9	94
	6	15	85
	5	20	70
	4	20	50
	3	15	30
	2	9	15
	1	4	6
Low	0	2	2

tained a given score or lower. If we divide f or Cum. f by $N,$ the total number of persons, and multiply by 100, the frequencies and cumulative frequencies are converted to percentages. (Since $N = 100$ in this example, the frequencies and percentages are the same.)

A frequency distribution can be shown graphically as a frequency polygon, as in Figure 4.1. This distribution approximates the so-called normal distribution as closely as is possible with 100 persons taking a nine-item test. (The "normal" curve will be explained shortly; the use of the term "normal" has a purely mathematical meaning here and does not have the popular connotation that contrasts normal to abnormal.)

Certain important features of a disbribution are quantified in terms of "descriptive

Figure 4.1.   A frequency polygon hypothetically based on 100 persons taking a nine-item test. With only 100 persons, this is as close as the frequency polygon can approximate the normal, or Gaussian, distribution, for a nine-item test.

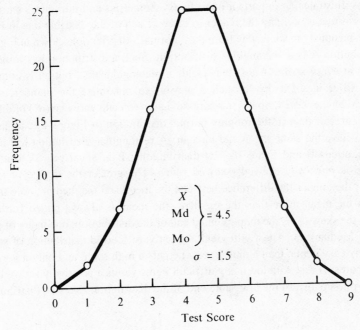

statistics.'' It is practically impossible to discuss score distributions without knowing the precise meaning of the most common descriptive statistics.

The *mean, median,* and *mode* are ways of describing the "central tendency" of the distribution, that is, the most typical or average score. The *mean* is simply the arithmetic average, that is, the sum of all the scores divided by the total number of scores. In statistics it is expressed as $\bar{X} = \Sigma\ X/N$, where X is a score, the symbol Σ means "the sum of,'' and N is the total number of scores. A bar over the X, called "X-bar'' ($\bar{X}$), signifies "the mean of all values of X in the distribution.'' The *median* is that score that divides the frequency distribution exactly in half; half the total number of obtained scores fall above the median and half below. (The Median is the same as the 50th percentile, since 50 percent are above and 50 percent are below the median.) The *mode* is the most frequently obtained score. (If two adjacent scores have the same highest frequency, the mode is the average of the two scores.) Some distributions have two modes and are called *bimodal*.

The *variance* $(\sigma^2)^\star$ and *standard deviation* $(\sigma)^\star$ are ways of describing the amount of dispersion, spread, or variability of the scores in the distribution. If everyone obtained the same score, there would be no variability, and σ^2 and σ would both equal zero. The *variance* is the average of the squared deviations of every score from the mean. (It is sometimes called the mean square deviation.) Algebraically it is expressed as $\sigma^2 = \Sigma(X - \bar{X})^2/N$. The *standard deviation*, σ, is simply the square root of the variance (σ and σ^2 are each useful in different kinds of statistical analysis: σ is the most commonly used to describe the dispersion of a distribution).

The frequency polygon can have almost any shape. For example, all the persons taking the test could have obtained a score of 9, or of 0, or any other score. A moment's reflection makes it obvious that the shape of the distribution will depend on the difficulty of the items for the persons taking the test. If all the items are very easy, for example, every person in the sample might get a score of 9.

Several characteristic types of distribution are shown in Figure 4.2. Each of these distributions illustrates an important point in psychometrics and introduces an often-used technical term that it will pay the reader to know. Each of the distributions in Figure 4.2 departs conspicuously in some way from the "normal" distribution shown in Figure 4.1.

Distribution A is a *rectangular* distribution. Such a distribution has roughly equal frequencies at every score. A test that yields a rectangular distribution is comprised of items that differ in difficulty in such a way as to maximize the number of persons discriminated by the scores. So the standard deviation (σ) and variance (σ^2) of distribution A are much greater than in the roughly normal distribution of Figure 4.1, although both distributions have the same mean and median. A rectangular distribution has no mode.

Distributions B and C are *skewed* distributions; B is *negatively* skewed (skewed left), and C is *positively* skewed (skewed right). The greater the degree of skew in a distribution, the greater the difference between the mean and the median; note that skewness moves the mean more than the median—the mean is always pulled further in the direction of the skew (i.e., the more pointed end of the distribution; one index of skewness is (Mean − Median)/σ). A test will yield a negatively skewed distribution of scores if it has too many easy items; then almost everyone gets a high score and only a very few get the lower scores. A test with too many difficult items yields a positively skewed distribution, with a pile-up toward the low-score end of the distribution. Skewed distributions can

Figure 4.2. Possible frequency distributions of a nine-item test taken by one hundred persons, with the form of the distribution determined by various item characteristics described in the text.

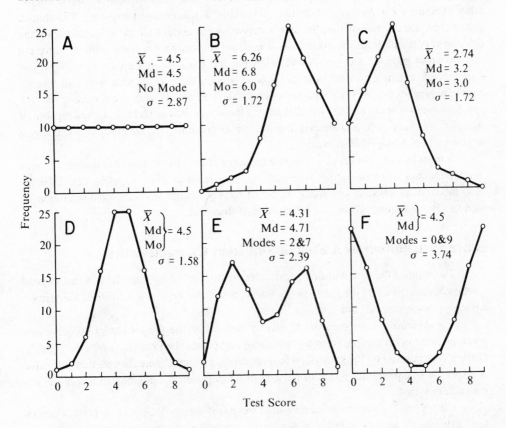

be made more symmetrical by including either more easy or more difficult items in the test. A test that has a symmetrical or normal distribution in one group, say, 10-year-olds, may yield skewed distributions in other groups, say, 6-year-olds or 14-year-olds.

Distribution D is a *leptokurtic* distribution. There are more scores at the extremes and more in the middle range. Consequently the standard deviation and variance can be greater than in the normal distribution. A test will yield a leptokurtic distribution if it contains too few very easy *and* too few very difficult items.

Distribution E is *bimodal*, with its major mode at score 2 and its minor mode at score 7. A bimodal distribution nearly always means that the sample of persons tested represents two different groups. If distributions were plotted separately for each of the groups, they would be unimodal. A bimodal distribution will result, for example, if the same test is given to groups of fourth-graders and sixth-graders and their scores are combined in a single distribution. When a statistician sees a bimodal distribution, his first impulse is to ask what are the two groups making up the distribution that, when separated, would produce two unimodal distributions.

Distribution F is said to be U-shaped. Such distributions are an extreme case of bimodality, with a marked piling up of the most extreme scores at both ends of the distribution. (If there is a piling up at only one extreme and the distribution trails off at the other extreme like a skewed distribution, it is called a J-shaped distribution.) A U-shaped distribution usually means that the test is very easy for about half the subjects taking the test and very difficult for the other half. We would suspect such a distribution to represent two different groups, and we should ask what the basis of this grouping is. One can imagine, for example, a math test that would be very easy for anyone who had taken a course in algebra but very difficult for anyone who had not. If such a test were given to a group of persons about equally divided among those who had or had not studied algebra, it would most likely yield a U-shaped distribution. If given to just one group or the other, it would yield a J-shaped distribution.

It must be fully obvious by now that the form of the distribution of test scores is very much a function of the difficulty levels of the items in the test. By juggling item difficulties, the psychometrician can make up a test having almost any kind of distribution he pleases. But not quite; there is a bit more to it than that.

Score Distribution as a Function of Item Characteristics

The form of the distribution of test scores is influenced by three factors that depend on the characteristics of the items in the test. These three item characteristics are termed *difficulty*, *homogeneity*, and *stability*.

The difficulty of an item is objectively defined as the proportion of subjects in a given population (or sample from a population) that passes the item (i.e., gets it ''right''). Difficulty is indexed by the symbol p (for proportion passing). Note than an item's p value is a specific to a particular group of persons or a sample of a population to whom the test was administered.

Homogeneity refers to the degree of correlation* among the items in a test. Correlation, symbolized as r, is an index of degree of association; it varies continuously from -1 (perfect negative association) to 0 (no association at all) to $+1$ (perfect positive association). The average correlation between all possible pairs of items in a test is a measure of homogeneity. Another measure of homogeneity is the average of the correlations between every item and the total scores on the test. (This, in fact, is equal to the square root of the average item intercorrelations.)

Stability here refers to the consistency of the subject's response to an item. If the subject's response to the item is highly variable, being easily affected by extraneous factors, such as the subject's momentary mood, the item is said to have low stability, and therefore variance among a subject's responses to the item is said to reflect largely measurement error. One way of determining measurement error (or, conversely, stability) is by giving the same test twice to the same subject. The correlation between the scores obtained on the two occasions is the stability (or test–retest reliability). (One can correlate the total scores on the test or scores on single items.) An item with low stability is often badly designed, ambiguous, or too dependent on how the subject just happens to look at it. Detecting and eliminating such defective items is a part of the process of test construction. Yet some margin of measurement error always remains; it can never be eliminated entirely. Test constructors can only try to minimize it.

Measurement error affects the form of the frequency distribution indirectly through its effect on the item intercorrelations or homogeneity of the test. Unreliable measurements cannot be highly correlated, and the measurement error in items weakens (or attenuates,★ to use the statistician's term) the correlations between items.[1] This actually simplifies our problem. Because item intercorrelations (homogeneity) are partly a function of item stability, we only have to deal directly with two parameters—item *difficulty* and item *homogeneity*—to explain the frequency distribution of total scores on a test.

The *mean,* $\bar{X}$ of the distribution is a function of the item difficulties. If p_i is the proportion of subjects passing a given item, the mean p value for the whole test is the sum of the p values of all items divided by the number of items, n, or $\bar{p} = \Sigma p/n$. The mean score on the test is $\bar{X} = \bar{p}n$, which is the same as the sum of the item p values. Obviously, adding more easy items to a test raises the mean and adding more difficult items lowers it.

The *variance* of the distribution is a function of the item difficulties and the item intercorrelations. This can be expressed as follows:

$$\sigma_X^2 = \Sigma\, pq + 2\Sigma r_{ij}\sigma_i\sigma_j, \tag{4.1}$$

where

$\sigma_X^2 = $ the variance of test scores
$p = $ the proportion passing an item,
$q = 1 - p,$ or the proportion not passing the item,
$r_{ij} = $ the correlation between any pair of items (designated i and j), and
σ_i and $\sigma_j = $ the standard deviations of items i and j. $\sigma_i = \sqrt{p_iq_i}$.

This equation can also be expressed in another way, as the variance of a single item σ_i^2 is simply p_iq_i and the covariance between two items C_{ij} is $r_{ij}\sigma_i\sigma_i$. Thus equation 4.1 can be rewritten to show that the variance of test scores is the sum of the item variances plus twice the sum of the item covariances:

$$\sigma_X^2 = \Sigma\sigma_i^2 + 2\,\Sigma C_{ij}. \tag{4.2}$$

To remove any mystery, let's see just where equation 4.2 (which is algebraically equivalent to equation 4.1) comes from. To illustrate, assume that we have a test of only two items, I and J. Assume also that answers to the items are scored Right or Wrong, that is, 1 or 0. Then a person's score, X, on the test will be the sum of his or her scores on the individual items, that is, $X = I + J$. Recall that the variance of the test scores, σ_X^2, is the mean of the squared deviations of all the X's from the mean of X. If, for simplicity, we represent raw scores as upper-case letters and deviations of scores from the mean of their distribution as lower-case letters, the variance of X is $\sigma_X^2 = \Sigma x^2/N$, where N is the number of subjects. Since $X = I + J$, $x = i + j$ and $\sigma_x^2 = \Sigma(i + j)^2/N$. If we square the expression $(i + j)$, we have

$$(i + j)^2 = i^2 + 2ij + j^2. \tag{4.3}$$

If we sum each of these terms over all persons and divide by the number of persons, N, we have

$$\frac{\Sigma(i + j)^2}{N} = \frac{\Sigma i^2}{N} + \frac{2\Sigma ij}{N} + \frac{\Sigma j^2}{N} = \frac{\Sigma x^2}{N} = \sigma_x^2. \tag{4.4}$$

Notice that $\Sigma i^2/N$ is the variance of item *I*, or σ_i^2, and that $\Sigma j^2/N$ is σ_j^2. The term $\Sigma ij/N$ is called the *covariance*, C_{ij}, of items *I* and *J*. (C_{ij} is the sum of the cross-products of individuals' deviation scores on items *I* and *J* divided by the number of individuals, *N*. The correlation r_{ij} is equal to $C_{ij}/\sigma_i\sigma_j$.)

So we see that the variance of test scores is made up of the variances of the single items and twice the covariances of all the possible pairs of items in the test. Readers who have not worked in psychometrics may wish to see a very simple example of all this worked out on some actual data.[3]

Let us note some of the important implications that equations 4.1 and 4.2 have for the distributions of test scores:

The variance will approach a maximum as (1) the difficulty level *p* of all items approaches .5 (since the item variance $pq = .25$ is at the maximum when $p = .5$) and (2) the inter-item correlations approach unity. The maximum possible variance $\sigma_{x\,\text{max}}^2$ is attained when $\bar{p} = .5$ and $r_{ij} = 1$ and is equal to

$$\sigma_{x_{\text{max}}}^2 = n\bar{p}^2 + n(n - 1)r_{ij}\bar{p}^2 = \bar{p}^2 n^2, \qquad (4.5)$$

where

> n = the number of items in the test (the expression $n(n - 1)$ is the number of all possible pairs—and hence the number of item intercorrelations—among *n* items),
>
> $\bar{p}$ = the mean of the items' *p* values, in this case .5, and
>
> $\bar{r}_{ij}$ = the mean of all the inter-item correlations, in this case 1.

Thus the maximum standard deviation that a test's raw scores can possibly have is $\sigma = \sqrt{.25n^2} = .5n$. The mean of such a test also equals .5n. But such a test would produce an extremely freakish distribution—a two-point distribution, with half of the subjects obtaining a perfect score and half of the subjects obtaining a score of zero. With perfect inter-item correlations, all items but one would be redundant. One need administer only a single item, which subjects would either pass or fail. This maximizes the variance, to be sure, but it is a poor test because it makes too few discriminations; it merely separates the sample of subjects into two broad categories—those who "pass" and those who "fail." Within each of these two broad categories, the test makes no discriminations.

For the test to make more discriminations, we would need to lower the item intercorrelations. (If the item intercorrelations were all perfect (i.e., $\bar{r} = 1.00$) and all we changed were the item difficulties, the test would make even fewer discriminations, since, with $\bar{p}$ less than or greater than .5, the distribution of scores would not be divided evenly between "pass" and "fail.") As the item intercorrelations progressively go down, the two-point distribution first changes to a U-shaped distribution (as with F in Figure 4.2), then to a bimodal distribution (E in Figure 4.2), then to a rectangular distribution (A in Figure 4.2), then to a normal distribution (Figure 4.1), then to a leptokurtic distribution (D in Figure 4.2), with σ finally reaching the minimum possible σ as r_{ij} becomes zero. The minimum possible σ is $\sqrt{\Sigma pq}$, which, by definition, is entirely error variance. At the same time, the variance of test scores will have diminished from the maximum (for the two-point distribution) to zero (for the one-point distribution). The desirable test must fall somewhere between these extremes. For reasons that I shall explain in the next section, the "normal" distribution is generally considered the most desirable. But actually the most ideal form of the distribution depends mainly on the use that one wishes to make of the test, and for some uses a normal distribution is of no particular advantage.

But let us turn back to equation 4.1 for a moment. Notice that it is made up of two components of variance, one, Σpq, due to *item difficulty levels*, and the other, $2\Sigma r_{ij}\sigma_i\sigma_j$, due to *item covariances*. An important point here is that the summation of the item variances is directly related to the number of items, n, whereas the number of covariances is much larger, namely, $n(n-1)$, so that adding more items to a test increases the covariance part of the total variance at a much greater rate than the part of the variance due to item difficulty per se. Thus item intercorrelations essentially are the most powerful determinant of the characteristics of the distribution of scores. Item difficulties alone affect skewness, whereas item intercorrelations affect the variance and the general shape of the distribution. An average item difficulty of greater than or less than $\bar{p} = .50$ results in positive or negative skewness. Moderately high inter-item correlations produce relatively flat ("platykurtic") or rectangular distributions; low inter-item correlations produce leptokurtic distributions; and moderate inter-item correlations produce a distribution resembling the normal curve.

The fact that the average inter-item correlation is positive means that most of the items must be measuring something in common for them to be positively correlated with one another. If the items were all measuring quite different abilities, the item intercorrelations would be zero, and the total variance would be Σpq. The total test scores would make no true discriminations at all. Without positive inter-item correlations, test scores would represent only error variance. What is called the internal consistency reliability r_{xx} of a test reflects the proportion of variance in test scores due to the covariance term (in equation 4.1); that is,

$$r_{xx} \approx \frac{2\Sigma r_{ij}\sigma_i\sigma_j}{\Sigma pq + 2\Sigma r_{ij}\sigma_i\sigma_j}. \qquad (4.6)$$

The maximum possible value of equation 4.6 for a test of n items is $(n-1)/n$; this is taken into account in a proper estimate of reliability.[4]

The reliability r_{xx} tells us the proportion of the variance in test scores that is attributable to whatever it is that the test is measuring, called *true score variance*. The remainder, $1 - r_{xx}$, is *error variance* made up of measurement error, item specificity (defined later), and a "difficulty factor" due to having a range of item p values, so that the term $2\Sigma r_{ij}\sigma_i\sigma_j$ in equation 4.6 is smaller relative to Σpq than would be the case if all p values were .50.

We have already seen that a hypothetical test composed entirely of items each having difficulty of $p = .50$ and perfect item intercorrelations, $r_{ij} = 1$, maximizes the variance but produces a two-point distribution, dichotomizing the group of subjects equally into two groups. Any single item of such a test could do the same thing. To make further discriminations we need items that will similarly dichotomize each of the two groups. Assuming perfect inter-item correlation and therefore equivalence of items, we could dichotomize the upper group with an item having $p = .25$ (in the combined groups), and we could dichotomize the lower group with an item having $p = .75$. So, with three items with difficulties of .75, .50, and .25, we have divided our sample evenly into fourths. Theoretically we could continue this process, dividing each of the groups further and further by finding items of intermediate difficulties, until we had made as many discriminations as we wished. If now we combined all these items ranging widely in difficulty into one test and gave the test to all the subjects, the resultant distribution of total test scores would tend to be rectangular. If we carried the dichotomization far enough, of course, no two persons would have the same score.

If it turns out that no person who passes any given item of difficulty p fails any item with a difficulty less than p, and no person who fails any item of difficulty p passes any item with a difficulty greater than p, the items form what is called a perfect Guttman scale.★ It is like a graded series of hurdles, each hurdle being equivalent to a test item. Any person who can jump over a 3-foot hurdle, for example, can jump all hurdles that are less than 3 feet; and anyone who fails to jump a 3-foot hurdle will fail all hurdles of more than 3 feet. In such an ideal scale we know that all the items must be measuring one and only one thing; thus such a scale is said to be *unidimensional*.

But here is an interesting point. Such a test as we have just made up by successively dichotomizing the distribution maximizes the number of *discriminations,* but it does not maximize the *variance* of the distribution of scores. One cannot possibly maximize both things at the same time. So we sacrifice some of the potential variance for the sake of greater discrimination. The reason that you cannot maximize both at the same time is that average item intercorrelation (and hence the average item covariance) decreases the more the items differ in difficulty.[5] This diminishes the covariance term in equation 4.1 and thereby reduces the total variance. Yet we have seen that the items must be spread over a wide range of difficulty level if they are to maximize discriminations.

In reality it turns out that perfect Guttman scales rarely if ever exist in mental tests composed of items, because no items measure perfectly—they all contain some error. That is, some of the variance pq on every item is error variance; this measurement error lowers the item intercorrelations, which in turn reduces the absolute variance of the test scores. But errors of measurement also have another important effect on the distribution. Because errors of measurement are by definition random and independent (i.e., totally uncorrelated with one another or with anything else), they are distributed according to the "laws of chance," which means that they are distributed "normally," that is, according to the normal curve. Hence, if we allow some measurement error to enter into the items of the imaginary "ideal" test we have constructed in the example preceding, the rectangular distribution of scores on the "ideal" test will be combined with the normal distribution of errors, making for a distribution that is something between the rectangular and the normal.

Also, in reality a single test item nearly always measures something that is not error but might as well be, as it does not correlate with any other item in the test. It is a unique source of variance entirely specific to a particular item. These uncorrelated components of variance in each item, called item *specificity,* have the same effect on the distribution of test scores, for all practical purposes, as errors of measurement.[6] (They are not *necessarily* normally distributed as are errors of measurement, but in actual fact they usually are.) Therefore when real items are selected according to their p values so as to maximally discriminate among individuals in any particular group of persons (say, all 10-year-olds), errors of measurement and item specificity tend to force the distribution of scores toward the form of the normal distribution. Because of error and item specificity, it is hard to avoid the test scores' falling into a distribution resembling the normal, so that even very casually constructed tests usually yield score distributions that look roughly normal. The most common departure from normality of casually made tests is skewness, which results when the item difficulties are not more or less evenly spread over the full range of difficulty and the average item difficulty $\bar{p}$ deviates from .50.

Although a rectangular distribution maximizes discriminations, there are a number of good reasons for preferring a test that yields a more or less normal distribution of scores.

The Normal Distribution

It is claimed that the psychometrist can make up a test that will yield any kind of score distribution he pleases. This is roughly true, but some types of distributions are much easier to obtain than others. However, the fact that the form of the distribution is merely a function of the item difficulties and item intercorrelations, as explicated previously, and the fact that these properties are rather easily manipulated by means of item selection, which is an important aspect of the whole process of test construction, surely means that there is nothing inevitable or sacred about any particular form of distribution with regard to mental test scores.

Why then have psychologists settled on the normal distribution in preference to other possible distributions in constructing mental tests? It is important to understand the main reasons for this preference, since many of the critics of mental tests have railed at what they view as the entirely arbitrary normal distribution of IQs or other mental test scores. It is even argued by some critics that mental test scores were made to yield a normal distribution of scores only to support the argument that a privileged elite—a small fraction of the population—have superior ability and therefore are justified in lording it over the vast majority of their fellows with mediocre ability and below, in other words, the large proportion of the population in the middle and lower part of the normal distribution (e.g., Simon, 1971, pp. 65-71).

Historically, the first workable mental tests were constructed without any thought of the normal distribution, and yet the distribution of scores was roughly normal. Alfred Binet, in making the first practical intelligence test, selected items only according to how well they discriminated between younger and older children, and between children of the same age who were judged bright or dull by their teachers, and by how well the items correlated with one another. He also tried to get a variety of items so that item-specific factors of ability or knowledge would not be duplicated (and so would not contribute to the inter-item correlations), and he tried to find items rather evenly graded in difficulty, so as to discriminate among children over a wide age range. Under these conditions it turned out, in fact, that the distribution of raw scores (number of items correct) within any one-year age interval was roughly normal.

The original Wechsler–Bellevue Intelligence Scale (Wechsler, 1944) was also constructed without reference to the normal curve. Wechsler sought items ranging widely in difficulty, spread more or less evenly from very simple to very difficult items, and having a considerable variety (which lowers the inter-item correlations, averaging only .10 in the Wechsler test). Items were not selected to produce a normal distribution. In fact, Wechsler states with reference to the usefulness of a scale:

> In general it is desirable that the range [of scores] be as wide as possible, that the measures be continuous, and that there be no piling up of scores at any point. Some

authors also believe that the resulting frequency curve ought to be Gaussian [i.e., normal] or as nearly Gaussian as possible. The last requirement seems to be a result of the wide-spread but mistaken belief that mental measures distribute themselves according to the normal curve of error.   (Wechsler, 1944, p. 126)

Yet the distribution of IQs on Wechsler's test turned out to be a slightly negatively skewed normal curve, that is, with an excess of very low scores, as shown in Figure 4.3. Because the *p* values or difficulty levels of the hardest items in the Wechsler are as low as .01, adding still more difficult items would not appreciably alter the skewness of the curve; only about the upper 1 percent of the distribution would be further spread out by having more difficult items. There will be more to say about this skewness later on.

Another test, the Pintner Ability Test, dating from 1923, which was not constructed with reference to the normal curve showed the following distribution of IQs among a national sample of fourth-graders (Figure 4.4). The obtained distribution is shown in the form of a bar graph (or histogram); a normal curve is superimposed for comparison. There is still a slight negative skewness, but the excess of very low IQs seen in Figure 4.3 is lacking, as most children with extremely low IQs are not found in the public schools, in which this sample of 7,273 children was tested.

The well-known Stanford–Binet Intelligence Test, like the original Binet test, was not constructed with the normal distribution as a criterion for item selection, but the IQs in the 1937 standardization sample are close to normally distributed, again with a slight excess at the lower end of the distribution, as shown in Figure 4.5.

The simple fact is that a test unavoidably yields a near normal distribution when it is made up of (1) a large number of items, (2) a wide range of item difficulties, (3) no marked gaps in item difficulties, (4) a variety of content or forms, and (5) items that have a significant correlation with the sum of all other item scores, so as to ensure that each

Figure 4.3.   Distribution of Full Scale IQs on the Wechsler–Bellevue Intelligence Scale for 1,508 persons of ages 10 to 60 years.   (From Wechsler, 1944, p. 127)

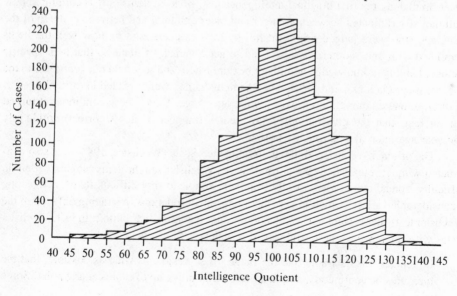

Figure 4.4.   Distribution of IQs on the Pintner Ability Test in a national sample of 7,273 fourth-grade children. A smooth normal curve is superimposed on the actual distribution, which is shown in the form of a histogram or bar graph.   (From Lindvall, 1967, p. 89)

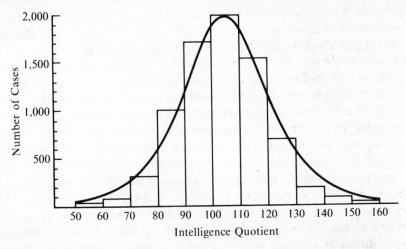

item in the test measures whatever the test as a whole measures. (Items that are uncorrelated or negatively correlated with the total score can only add error to the total scores.) These are all desirable features of a test. Critics never seem to attack these commonsense features of tests that inevitably lead to a close approximation to the normal distribution. One would have to violate all these commonsense *desiderata* to produce a test that would yield a distribution of scores that departs at all radically from the normal.

But there are more fundamental and theoretical reasons to justify the normal distribution of mental test scores. After all, we could simply ignore the "accident" of roughly normal distributions that result when tests are constructed without specific reference to the

Figure 4.5.   Distribution of 1937 Stanford-Binet IQs of 2,904 persons of ages 2–18 years.   (From Terman & Merrill, 1960, p. 18)

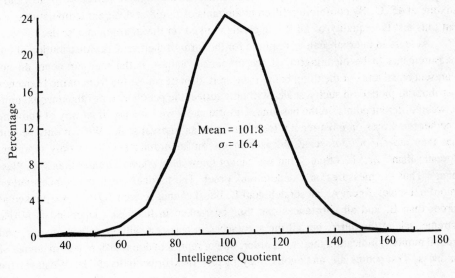

form of the distribution, and work at it to make the score distributions take on some other shape. Why argue for a normal distribution?

To proceed any further with the argument, it must be made clear why there should be any argument at all. Scientists have never argued about the distribution of height, or brain weight, or life span, or pulse rate, or the air capacity of the lungs. So why should there be any dispute about the distribution of mental measurements?

The Scale Problem.   Each of the physical measurements just mentioned constitutes an *absolute* scale; that is, the measuring instrument in each case has a true zero point and the units of measurement are equal intervals throughout the entire scale. The measurements therefore have two important properties: (1) they are additive and (2) they can yield meaningful ratios. (Thus an absolute scale is also called a *ratio* scale.) Unless the units of measurement are equal intervals at every part of the scale, they cannot be additive. If our yardstick did not have equal intervals, 4 inches plus 5 inches would not necessarily total the same actual length as 3 inches plus 6 inches, and the distance between the 2-inch and 12-inch marks would not necessarily be the same as the distance between the 20-inch and 30-inch marks. Also, if there were no true zero point on the scale, our measurements could not form meaningful ratios; the ratio of 2 inches to 1 inch would not be the same as the ratio of 8 inches to 4 inches. Without a true zero point on our scale for measuring weight, we could not be sure that a 200-pound man is twice as heavy as a 100-pound man. All we would know is that the 200-pound man is 100 pounds heavier than the 100-pound man; but we could not say he is twice as heavy.

An *interval* scale has equal units but no *true* zero point; the zero point on such a scale is arbitrary. The ordinary thermometer is a good example of a measuring device that is only an interval scale; the zero point of the centigrade thermometer is arbitrarily set at the freezing point of water and 100° C is arbitrarily set at the boiling point of water (at sea level); the distance between those points is divided into equal units. (It was not until long after the invention of the centigrade thermometer that it was known that the absolute zero of temperature is at $-273°$ C.) So we cannot say that 60° C is twice as hot as 30° C. But, since we have an interval scale, we can say 45° C is halfway between 30° C and 60° C, and we can demonstrate this by mixing equal quantities of liquid at 30° C and 60° C to yield a mixture at 45° C. By combining different amounts of liquid at different temperatures, we can thus test the equality of all the intervals marked on the thermometer scale.

At least an interval scale is required for the form of the frequency distribution of our measurements to be meaningful. If the numerical values of the measurements do not represent equal units of the thing being measured, then of course the form of the frequency distribution, plotted on such a scale, will only reflect the peculiarities of the unequal units between different points on the baseline. Unfortunately we have no direct way of knowing whether the scores on most mental tests constitute an interval scale. We can only be sure that they are an *ordinal* scale. Measurements on an ordinal scale can only represent "greater than" or "less than"; but we cannot know *how much* "greater than" or "less than." Thus the measures only denote rank order. The hardness of gems is measured on an ordinal scale; if gem A can scratch gem B, but B cannot scratch A, then A is ranked as harder than B, and all substances can thus be ranked in hardness. Diamond is at one extreme, talc at the other, but all the substances in between, although they are assigned ordinal numbers indicating their rank order, do not represent equal differences in degree of hardness. Test scores are analogous; they merely rank order individuals. Whatever the numbers assigned to the scores, they can only be compared with one another in terms of "greater than" or "less than." Individuals' test scores could be changed to any other numbers that one pleased as long as their rank order remained the same. Obviously then, the shape of the frequency distribution of scores that are only an ordinal scale is quite meaningless, or at best trivial.

How can we get a mental test that will yield scores on an interval scale, so that the shape of the frequency distribution of scores is meaningful? We have no independent yardstick of ability as we have when we measure height. (It is easy to test whether the marks on your yardstick for measuring height are equal intervals; for example, if we cut the yardstick at the 18-inch mark, will the two pieces when laid side by side have the same length?) The mental test itself is our yardstick, but the scale properties of the scores are what we do not know. So how can we ever make sure that the test scores represent an interval scale?

We simply *assume* what the distribution of scores should look like if we had an ideal test that measured the trait or ability in question on a perfect interval scale. Then, if we can construct an actual test that in fact yields a score distribution like the one we have assumed, we can be absolutely certain that the scores are on an equal-interval scale— provided, of course, that we are correct in our initial assumption about the true shape of the distribution. For most mental abilities, and particularly general intelligence, psychologists have *assumed* that the true distribution is the normal distribution. *Ipso facto,* any test of intelligence that yields a normal distribution of scores must be an interval scale. The logic boils down to the one crucial question: What is the justification for the assumption of normality?

Physical Measurements.   Many physical traits measured on an absolute scale show approximately normal distributions, and usually the larger the sample of measurements, the closer is the distribution to the normal. For example, Figure 4.6 shows the distribution of height in 91,163 young men called up for military service in England in 1939; a normal curve (dashed line) is superimposed. It can be seen that the actual distribution of height is extremely close to normal, except for a slight excess at the lower end of the distribution, similar to that in Figure 4.3. Brain weight is another example, as shown in Figure 4.7.

The distribution of birth weight, shown in Figure 4.8, is nearly normal, but again with a slight skewness at the lower end of the scale.

Because many human physical traits are closely in accord with the normal curve, it is assumed by analogy that mental ability is also.

Most physical *abilities,* too, show a normal distribution when they can be measured on an absolute scale, such as strength of hand grip (measured as pounds of pressure), simple reaction time, running speed (in feet per second), jumping distance, tapping rate (number of taps with pencil per minute), the number of X's (of a standard size) that a person can make with a pencil in one minute. Because there is no clear point that separates physical from mental abilities, we may presume that mental abilities are also normally distributed.

A few mental abilities can be measured on an absolute scale; for example, the number of digits that a person can repeat in the correct order when he sees or hears a series of n digits and n is varied over a reasonable range. Durning (1968) gave such a test to 5,539 U.S. Navy recruits. Digit series of from four to ten digits were read aloud at the rate

Figure 4.6. Distribution of stature in young Englishmen called up for military service in 1939. The position of the mean ($\bar{x}$) is indicated by a solid vertical line and of the standard deviation (σ) as vertical broken lines. A normal, or Gaussian, curve with the same mean and standard deviation is superimposed on the actual data. (From Harrison et al., 1964, p. 201)

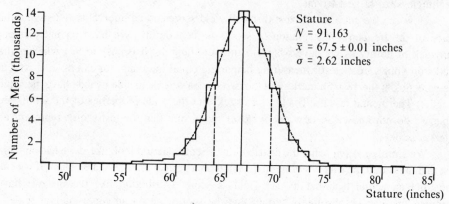

Stature
N = 91,163
$\bar{x}$ = 67.5 ± 0.01 inches
σ = 2.62 inches

of 1 second per digit and subjects scored one point for every digit recalled in the correct order, with a possible range of scores from 0 to 49. The test is repeated three times, so that the possible range of total scores goes from 0 to 147. The distribution of scores on this 147-point interval scale is almost perfectly normal (see Figure 4.9), except for a slight truncation at each end: at the upper end undoubtedly due to the fact that the test was not

Figure 4.7. Distribution of brain weights (obtained directly by use of the balance) of European males aged 21 years and over. (From Baker, 1974, p. 430)

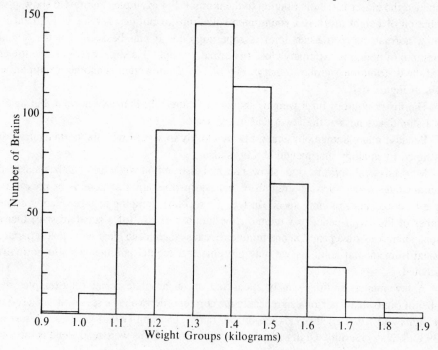

Figure 4.8.   Distribution of birth weights of 13,730 human infants in England.   (Based on data from Karn & Penrose, 1952)

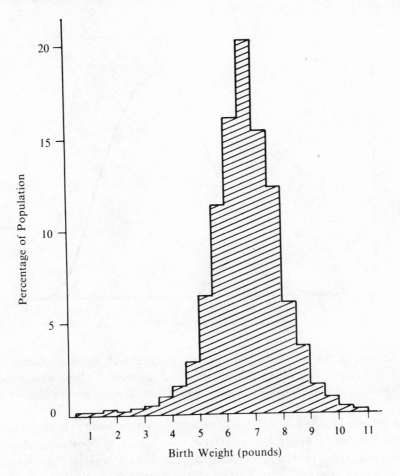

quite hard enough, and at the lower end because Navy recruits are selected on mental tests with cutoff scores that exclude the lower 10 percent of the population. Digit memory tests consisting of one to fifteen digits would certainly come very close to yielding a normal distribution of scores in the general population.

As we move on to even more intellectually loaded performances that can be measured on an absolute or interval scale, we find that the distribution of measurements still approximates the normal curve. For example, vocabulary is highly correlated with other measures of intelligence. The size of a person's vocabulary constitutes an absolute scale, with the word as the unit. Some vocabulary tests are made up by selecting words at random from a dictionary, and scores on such vocabulary tests should be distributed approximately the same as the distribution of total vocabulary. It is consistently found that vocabulary so measured is approximately normally distributed within any given age group. Figure 4.10 shows the distribution of vocabulary scores in a group of 360 11-year-old boys.

Thus it seems a reasonable presumption from the distribution of relatively simple

Figure 4.9.   Smoothed frequency distribution of total scores on a digit-span memory test given to 5,539 U.S. Navy recruits. The total possible range of scores is 0 to 147.   (From Durning, 1968)

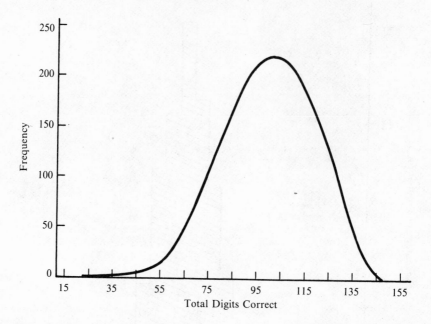

mental performances, for which the interval scale properties of the measurements are self-evident, that mental ability in general is normally distributed. But there are also more important lines of reasoning than this argument, which is based only on generalization and analogy.

Psychophysical Scaling of Test Items.   Burt (1957) constructed an intelligence test by means of a technique in psychophysics known as scaling by "just noticeable differences" or *jnd*'s. It is a method for obtaining an equal-interval scale of a psychological variable, in this case, item difficulty. A large number of intelligence test items, like those found in IQ tests such as the Stanford–Binet, were presented in all possible pairs to twenty teachers, who were asked to judge whether the two items of a pair were approximately the same or different in difficulty and to indicate which item they thought was the more difficult. A pair of items having a "just noticeable difference" in difficulty would be judged as being the same in difficulty by 50 percent of the judges and as being different by 50 percent of the judges. By obtaining such 50:50 judgments on a large enough number of items, it was possible to rank order test items differing by one *jnd* in judged difficulty. This set of items, therefore, was selected entirely without reference to actual difficulty level in terms of item *p* values. The items thus scaled in terms of *jnd*'s constitute a psychophysical scale of equal-appearing intervals based on judgments of item difficulty. When this set of scaled items was administered as a test to a large random sample of London school children, the resulting distribution of scores was approximately normal, except for a slight excess of very low scores. The distribution, furthermore, was almost identical to the distribution of Stanford–Binet IQs in the same population (shown in Figure 4.11), although the Stanford–Binet test items had not been scaled by this method.

Sibling Differences. It has been argued that, if intelligence is normally distributed in the population and if intelligence test scores are normally distributed, it must mean that the scores are an equal-interval scale. Now, if we really have an equal-interval scale, we should expect that, if we pick a person with a score near the high end of the scale of measurements, that individual should differ from his or her own siblings by the same amount as does a person with a score equally far toward the low end of the scale. There is no theoretical reason to believe that sibling differences should be greater or smaller above the mean than below the mean. If the test scores were not an interval scale throughout the full range, and the differences between high scores were not really the same as nominally equal differences between low scores, we should expect sibling differences to vary systematically at different points on the scale. But this is not the case. Sibling differences, on average, are the same for high as for low IQs, until we come to the very low IQs below about 50, where the normal curve no longer holds.

Furthermore, we have a theory of intelligence—the polygenic theory—that is entirely independent of any test of intelligence. (The same essential polygenic theory applies also to all continuous characteristics in all plants and animals.) The theory, which will be explained later, predicts the magnitude of the difference between siblings, provided the measurements are an interval scale. It predicts that, on the average, the score of a person's sibling will fall halfway between the score of the person and the mean score in the population from which the person is selected. This phenomenon is known as *regression to the mean*. It results because each full sibling inherits a random half of the parental genes (i.e., half of each parent's genes combine in the fertilized ovum from which the new individual develops); siblings therefore, on the average, have half of their segregating genes (i.e., genes that make for variance in the trait) in common, causing them to be correlated .50. A sibling correlation of .50 implies that for persons who deviate from their

Figure 4.10. Distribution of scores on a vocabulary test given to 360 11-year-old boys. (From Garrett, 1951, p. 268)

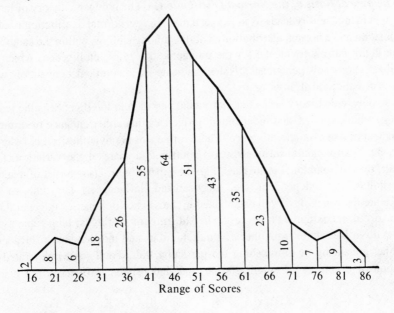

Figure 4.11.   Distribution of Stanford-Binet IQs in 2,835 children between ages 6 and 11 years randomly drawn from London schools. The dashed curve shows a normal curve fitted to the mean and standard deviation of the actual data.   (From Burt, 1957, p. 171)

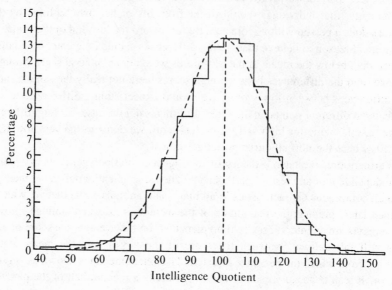

population mean by X units, their siblings, on the average, will deviate $.50X$ units from the mean. This prediction is derived from purely theoretical considerations that are entirely independent of any intelligence tests. Yet the prediction of the sibling differences could be borne out accurately only if the measurements were on an interval scale. The prediction has in fact been borne out in many studies using standardized intelligence tests constructed entirely without reference to polygenic theory.

Theoretical Basis of the Normal Distribution.   The polygenic theory of individual variation in mental ability leads us to expect a more or less normal distribution of ability in the population and a normal distribution of ability among siblings within the same family.[7] Without going into the evidence for the polygenic theory of intelligence, which is now generally accepted by geneticists, I shall indicate its theoretical connection with the normal distribution of ability.

The polygenic theory holds that individual variation in intelligence is the result of a number of small, similar, and independent influences that either enhance or diminish the development of a person's intelligence. These influences are hypothesized to be primarily genetic, but environmental influences also contribute a share of the variation. (For the most part, the environmental influences, like the genetic ones, also consist of a number of small, similar, and independent, i.e., uncorrelated, influences.) The units of genetic influence are the genes. It is well established in the science of genetics in general that the genes involved in continuous traits (e.g., height, fingerprint ridges, lung capacity, blood pressure) do in fact act as a number of small, similar, and independent influences, each gene either enhancing or diminishing the particular trait. Total scores generated by the summation of a number of small, similar, and independent influences are distributed according to the binomial distribution, $(A + B)^n$, which approaches the normal distribution as n increases. Imagine flipping a single coin many times, assuming that heads (H) and tails (T) have perfectly equal probabilities ($\frac{1}{2}$); this is represented as $(\frac{1}{2}H + \frac{1}{2}T)^1$ and it yields a two-point distribution approximating 50% H and 50% T, coming closer to these figures the larger the number of tosses. If we toss *two* coins simultaneously, we would have $(\frac{1}{2}H + \frac{1}{2}T)^2$, which yields a three-point distribution: 25% HH, 50% HT (or TH), and 25% TT. Tossing four coins produces a five-point distribution, as shown in Figure 4.12.

It can be seen that even with only five independent events the frequency distribution begins to resemble the normal curve. Figure 4.13 shows the distributions that would result from a large number of tosses of 2, 4, 6, 12, and 16 coins, respectively; in each case the normal curve is superimposed to show the increasing approximation of the binomial distribution to the normal curve.

The polygenic theory is analogous to the coin-tossing example. Each of a number of genes (i.e., coins) either enhances (i.e., heads) or does not enhance (i.e., tails) the trait. In the process of gametogenesis (formation of germ cells), each parent contributes a random assortment of one-half of his or her genes to each sperm or ovum. Random assortment means that each parental gene has a 50:50 chance of being passed on to any one offspring (like each tossed coin having a 50:50 chance of coming up heads). If in the whole population the total number of enhancing genes is equal to the number of nonenhancing genes (as the number of heads equals the number of tails in our batch of coins), the distribution of scores (i.e., the sum of the enhancing genes, as if heads scored 1 and tails scored 0) will be normal. If the relative frequencies of enhancing and nonenhancing genes are unequal, the distribution will be skewed, but the skewness will be less, the larger the

Figure 4.12.   The theoretical frequency distribution that would result from tossing four coins simultaneously an indefinitely large number of times. The relative frequencies (percentages) are given by the expansion of the binomial $(\frac{1}{2}H + \frac{1}{2}T)^4$.

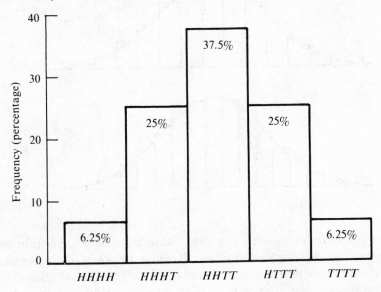

Figure 4.13. Frequency distributions of relative numbers of heads and tails on each toss that would result from tossing $n = 2, 4, 6, 12$, or 16 coins simultaneously an indefinitely large number of times, with a normal curve superimposed on the obtained distribution. Note that, as n increases, the obtained distribution more closely approximates the normal curve.

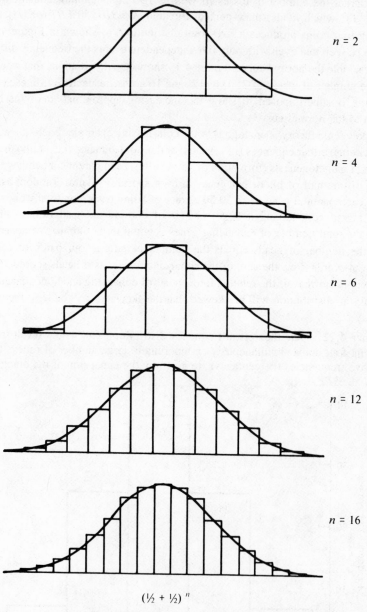

$$(\tfrac{1}{2} + \tfrac{1}{2})^n$$

number of genes involved. Even a very great difference in the proportions of enhancing and nonenhancing genes, such as .90 versus .10, will result in only a slight departure from the normal curve when there is a large number of genes. The IQ distribution of Terman's gifted subjects (more than 1,500 persons selected for having Stanford–Binet IQs of 140 and above, with an average IQ of 152) is extremely skewed, and also, but to a lesser degree, is the distribution of their spouses, with an average IQ of 125. Yet the IQ distribution of the children born to the Terman gifted subjects does not depart significantly from the normal curve (although the mean IQ is 132.7), as can be seen in Figure 4.14.

The so-called microenvironmental factors that contribute to the nongenetic part of the intelligence differences between children reared together in the same family act in much the same way, that is, by the laws of chance, and therefore are also normally distributed.[8] The deviations of intelligence due to environmental variation *among* families could not depart very much from normality, either, since combining a markedly nonnormal distribution with the normal distributions produced by both genetic and *within*-family environmental effects would not yield the normal distribution of IQs that, in fact, is generally found when large random samples of the population are tested.

Departures from the Normal Curve.   It was noted in Figures 4.3, 4.6, and 4.11 that the distributions depart somewhat from the normal curve mainly because of an excess of frequencies at the lower end of the scale. This departure from normality is seen in the frequency distribution of height as well as of intelligence. The excess at the lower end is not a sampling error. It is a genuine departure from normality and shows up in every study of the distribution of IQ (and height) based on large, representative samples of the population, both in Europe and America. This anomaly in the distribution is caused by

Figure 4.14.   Distribution of Stanford-Binet IQs of the 1,525 offspring of Terman's gifted subjects. A normal curve is fitted to the actual data indicated by crosses. Terman and Oden's (1959, Table 61) data were plotted in this figure by W. Shockley, who notes that "the offspring have an accurately normal distribution in the same IQ range in which the parents do not fit the tail of a normal distribution" (personal communication). This point is interesting in that this result is predictable from a polygenic model with a large (i.e., > 20) number of loci and a considerable amount of heterozygosity in the parents. Under these conditions, theoretically, the offspring should show a nearly normal distribution despite marked skewness of the distribution of parental values, and this in fact is what is found in these data.

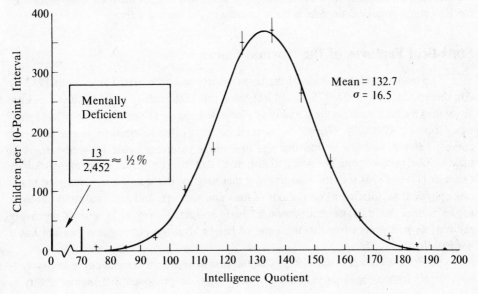

rare, major adverse influences that override the polygenic and environmental factors involved in the normal variation in intelligence (or height). These unusual adverse influences consist of serious diseases, injuries (often prenatal), single mutant genes having major effects, and chromosomal anomalies such as Down's syndrome ("mongolism"). Genetic mutations are much more likely to diminish ability than to enhance it, just as damage or defective parts in an automobile engine are more apt to impair than to improve its performance. Thus, we see, for instance, midgets and dwarfs, whose stature may be due to any one of various genetic anomalies that overrides the whole polygenic system accounting for normal variation in height. Analogously, in the case of intelligence, we see various clinical types of mental deficiency, such as the genetic defects of microcephaly, Tay–Sachs syndrome, phenylketonuria (PKU), and Down's syndrome (mongolism), as well as brain damage due to diseases, such as German measles (in the pregnant mother) and encephalitis, or to birth trauma, such as asphixia. Some 20 to 25 percent of all the mentally retarded (IQs below 70) are of this abnormal type, mostly concentrated in the range of IQs below 50. The remainder of IQs below 70, some 75 to 80 percent, are the result of variation in the normal polygenic and multifactorial environmental influences on mental development.[9] The vast majority of IQs between 50 and 70 thus are to be regarded as biologically normal in the same way that most persons of short stature (except midgets and dwarfs) are regarded as biologically normal.

Within the IQ range from about 60 to 150, the IQ distribution does not depart significantly from the normal curve. But there is an excess of high IQs beyond about 150. Like the excess of very low IQs, it is a genuine phenomenon, though less pronounced. It is generally not statistically detectable in samples numbering fewer than two or three thousand. The causes of this excess of IQs above 150 are not certain, but two factors most likely account for it: (1) a high degree of assortative mating (like marrying like) among highly intelligent parents and (2) covariance of favorable environmental and genetic influences. It can be shown theoretically that either of these factors, or both combined, would have the effect of elongating the upper tail of an otherwise normal distribution. But the most important point for all practical purposes is that at least the middle 98 percent of the IQs in the population conform quite closely to the normal curve.

Statistical Features of the Normal Curve

The mathematical equation of the normal curve was formulated as early as 1733 by Abraham de Moivre (1667–1754), and its central role in the theory of probability was later developed by such mathematical giants as Pierre de Laplace (1749–1827) and Carl Friedrich Gauss (1777–1855). (Hence the normal curve is often referred to as the Gaussian curve.) Later it was discovered that the magnitude of errors made by astronomers in making observations are normally distributed, and the Belgian astronomer Adolphe Quetelet (1796–1874) was the first to show that heights, chest measurements, and many other physical measurements on persons of the same age, sex, and ancestral stock conform to the normal curve. (The distribution of body weight, however, is always positively skewed, as it is proportional to the cube of height. But the cube root of weight has a normal distribution.)

Sir Francis Galton (1822–1911) was the first to apply the normal curve in psychology. In his famous book *Hereditary Genius* (1869) he proposed that mental ability is normally distributed, arguing from analogy to normally distributed physical characters such as head circumference, brain weight, and number of brain cells, as well as from the roughly normal distribution of examination marks of competitors for public appointments and college admission.

Fitting a normal curve to any distribution depends on only two parameters of the distribution, the mean, $\bar{X}$, and standard deviation, σ.[10] The goodness of fit of the normal curve to the observed distribution can be tested statistically to determine if the discrepancies between the two are within the limits of sampling error.[11] The method of fitting the normal curve, of course, ensures that it will have the same mean and standard deviation as the obtained scores. But the obtained distribution may differ from normality in *skewness* and *kurtosis* (i.e., degree of peakedness of the distribution). Calculation of certain simple statistics (called "moments") on the obtained scores provides indices of the degree of departure from normality.[12]

Areas under the Normal Curve. The most important feature of the normal curve from a practical standpoint is that we can know precisely the *area* of the curve marked off by any two scores, or the sizes of the areas that lie on either side of any given score. If the total area under the curve is called 100 percent, any subdivision of the curve will represent the percentage of scores falling within that subdivision. In other words, the area under the curve represents relative frequency (expressed as a percentage). If we have a normal distribution of our measurements, we can answer such questions as what percentage of the population will fall above or below score x_1? or what percentage will fall between scores x_1 and x_2? Figure 4.15 shows the areas (as percentages) under the normal curve when it is

Figure 4.15. Areas (in percentages) under the normal curve and the baseline of the curve scaled to various types of standard scores. (From Sattler, 1974, p. 124)

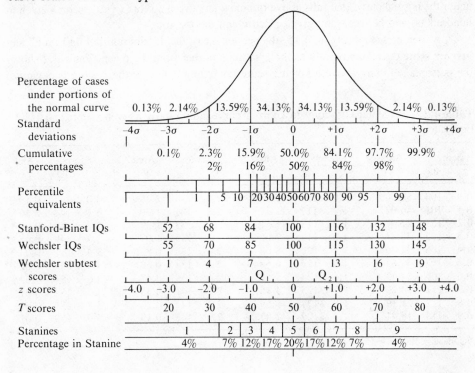

divided into standard deviation units. Also shown are where different types of scaled scores fall on the baseline.

The baseline scale in σ units can be further subdivided into tenths or hundredths. Scores on such a scale, expressed in terms of σ deviations from the mean, are called z scores. Any obtained score X on a test with a standard deviation σ may be converted to a z score:

$$z = (X - \bar{X})/\sigma. \tag{4.7}$$

(Thus a distribution of z scores always has a mean of 0 and a standard deviation of 1.) This is a useful method for putting the raw scores of different tests all on the same scale. All scores then can be expressed in terms of z scores, indicating how many σ units they deviate from the mean. Also, z scores are the first step in transforming raw scores to a scale with *any* desired mean and σ. Because Stanford–Binet IQs have a mean of 100 and a standard deviation (σ) of 16, for example, we can transform the raw scores on any test to the same scale as Stanford–Binet IQs by first converting the raw scores to z scores (by equation 4.7) and then by transforming the z scores; thus

$$IQ = 16\, z + 100.$$

In this way, height or any other measurements can be put on the same scale as IQ or vice versa. In general, a transformed score X on any desired scale having a mean of $\bar{X}$ and standard deviation of σ can be obtained via a z score by the equation

$$X = \sigma z + \bar{X}. \tag{4.8}$$

Almost every book on statistics contains a table giving the percentage of the area under the normal curve that falls above or below any given z score (with z scores given in hundredths) and between any given z score and the mean.

As can be seen in Figure 4.15, the percentage of the distribution falling beyond any given z score decreases rapidly as the z score is farther from the mean. Table 4.2 shows the percentage falling above a given z score (or falling below, if the z score is negative)

Table 4.2. Percentage of scores in a normal curve falling above a given z score and its IQ Equivalent.[1]

| Score | | Area | Score | | Area | Score | | Area | Score | | Area |
z	IQ	%	z	IQ	%	z	IQ	%	z	IQ	%
0.0	100	50.00%	1.0	115	15.87%	2.0	130	2.28%	3.0	145	0.13%
0.1	101	46.02	1.1	117	13.57	2.1	131	1.79	3.1	147	0.10
0.2	103	42.07	1.2	118	11.51	2.2	133	1.39	3.2	148	0.07
0.3	105	38.21	1.3	119	9.68	2.3	135	1.07	3.3	149	0.05
0.4	106	34.46	1.4	120	8.08	2.4	136	0.82	3.4	151	0.03
0.5	107	30.85	1.5	123	6.68	2.5	137	0.62	3.5	153	0.02
0.6	109	27.43	1.6	124	5.48	2.6	139	0.47	3.6	154	0.02
0.7	111	24.20	1.7	125	4.46	2.7	141	0.35	3.7	155	0.01
0.8	112	21.19	1.8	127	3.59	2.8	142	0.26	3.8	157	0.01
0.9	113	18.41	1.9	129	2.87	2.9	143	0.19	3.9	159	0.01

[1]IQ mean $= 100$, $\sigma = 15$.

along with the IQ equivalents of the z scores (assuming an IQ scale with mean = 100, σ = 15).

From such a table, one can read off the probability of obtaining a score as high or higher than any given z score. It is also possible, using this table, to "normalize" any unimodal distribution (except a J-curve) of obtained raw scores. One simply determines the percentage of the distribution that falls above (or below) each raw score, and from this percentage one reads off the corresponding z score in a table of the normal curve (such as Table 4.2). Whatever the shape of the raw score distribution, the transformed z scores will have a normal distribution. The normalization procedure is considered justifiable if the sample is large and representative, and if it is believed that the trait being measured should be normally distributed in the population. Under this condition the normalization procedure puts the trait measurements on an interval scale of z scores, rather than merely on an ordinal scale represented by the original raw scores.

Lack of Competing Evidence for Other Forms of the Distribution of Intelligence. Finally, psychologists accept the idea that intelligence is normally distributed because no compelling alternative theory or evidence for any other kind of distribution has ever been proposed. Critics of intelligence tests often attack the contention that mental ability is distributed in the population according to the normal curve. But I have never found an instance of critics' having proposed any other form of distribution. Criticism of the theory that intelligence is normally distributed, if it is to be scientifically productive, must posit an alternative hypothesis and demonstrate its cogency in terms of evidence and theoretical analysis. Because this has never been done, the normal distribution of intelligence is probably the most unrivaled theory in all of psychology.

Overlap and Group Differences. From the table of the normal curve we can tell what percentage of any group, assuming that its scores are normally distributed, falls beyond a particular score, such as the "cutting score" used in a selection procedure. And we can also compare different groups in terms of the percentages of each that fall above (or below) any given score. The procedure can also be worked in reverse; that is, if we know the percentage of each group that falls above a given score, we can determine the mean difference between the groups on an interval scale. In actual practice, these determinations are never exact, of course, because obtained distributions and percentages are subject to sampling error; and all the populations being compared may not conform perfectly to the normal distribution. Yet most predictions made on the assumption of normality, where abilities are concerned, prove to be fairly accurate.

Group differences in general can be expressed quantitatively in any one of five ways that are independent of the original scale of measurement, so that group differences on various measures are directly comparable.

1. The *sigma* (σ) *difference* (or z score difference) is the simplest and most frequently used index of group differences. It is simply the difference between the group means divided by the average of the standard deviations of the two groups:

$$\sigma \text{ Diff.} = (\bar{X}_1 - \bar{X}_2)/[(\sigma_1 + \sigma_2)/2]. \qquad \textbf{(4.9)}$$

(A better method is to use the square root of the average of the two variances in the denominator of equation 4.9, i.e., $(X_1 - \bar{X}_2)/\sqrt{(\sigma_1^2 + \sigma_2^2)/2}$.) A variation of this is to express the mean difference in the units of either σ_1 or σ_2, e.g., $(X_1 - \bar{X}_2)/\sigma_1$. One should always be explicit as to which formula is used, because they may give somewhat different results.

2. *Percentage of variance* tells us what percentage of the total variance in the scores of all persons in the combined groups is attributable to the average difference between the groups. It can be derived either directly from a one-way analysis of variance (*between* groups and *within* groups) or simply by squaring the point-biserial correlation between the dichotomized variable (groups) and the continuous variable (scores).

3. *Point-biseral correlation* goes from 0 to ± 1 and is interpreted like any other correlation coefficient. It is really a Pearson product-moment correlation between a dichotomized variable, such as group membership, and a continuous variable, such as test scores. Members of the two groups (e.g., males and females) are quantized as 0 and 1, respectively, and these dichotomized scores are correlated with the test scores in the same fashion as computing the Pearson r. The resulting correlation is called the point-biserial correlation, r_{pbs}. It can be obtained more easily from the following formula:[13]

$$r_{pbs} = \frac{(\bar{X}_1 - \bar{X}_2)\sqrt{N_1 N_2}}{\sigma_t(N_1 + N_2)}, \tag{4.10}$$

where

$\bar{X}_1$ and $\bar{X}_2$ = the means of groups 1 and 2,
N_1 and N_2 = the numbers in each group, and
σ_t = the standard deviation of the combined groups.[14]

The square of the point-biserial correlation, r_{pbs}^2, is the proportion of the total variance of all the scores that is attributable to the mean difference between the two groups. (r_{pbs}^2 is termed eta squared, η^2, in the context of the analysis of variance.)

4. *Median overlap* is the percentage of scores in the group with the lower mean that exceeds the median score of the group with the higher mean. Because 50 percent of a group exceeds its own median, an overlap of 50 percent indicates that the medians of the two groups do not differ (although the groups still may differ in means and standard deviations if the distributions are not normal). Figure 4.16 shows a median overlap of 25 percent.

An advantage of median overlap as a measure of group difference is that it makes no assumptions whatever about the form of the distribution or the scale of measurement. If both distributions are normal, however, there will of course be a systematic relationship between the σ difference and the median overlap. The σ difference, which is the same as

Figure 4.16. Two overlapping normal distributions illustrating the concept of *median overlap*; the shaded area shows the 25 percent of the lower-scoring group that exceeds the median score of the higher-scoring group. (From Garrett, 1951, p. 280)

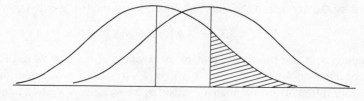

Figure 4.17. Overlap (shaded area) between two groups expressed as the percentage of persons in one group whose scores are matched by persons in the second group. (From Elster & Dunnette, 1971, p. 686)

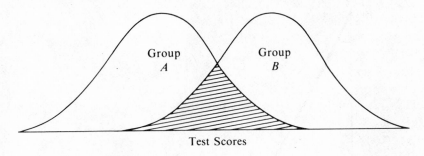

the z difference, can be looked up in the table of the normal curve to find the corresponding percentage overlap (see Table 4.2). If the mean of Group *A* is, say, one standard deviation below the mean of Group *B*, the median overlap is approximately 16 percent.

The limitation of median overlap as a measure of group differences is that it becomes quite unreliable when the overlap is small, say, less than 5 percent, and the sample sizes are not very large. Also, median overlap cannot measure a larger group difference than is indicated by a median overlap of zero.

5. *Total percentage overlap* meets this problem and is therefore preferable to median overlap as an index of group difference. The total percentage overlap is the percentage of persons in one of the groups whose scores may be matched by persons in the second group (Tilton, 1937). Total overlap of 20 percent is shown in Figure 4.17. This scale goes from 0 to 100 percent overlap, and, assuming normality of the distributions in the population, this measure of overlap has been shown to be fairly insensitive to sampling error for sample sizes greater than one hundred (Elster & Dunnette, 1971). Skewness of the population distributions results in an overestimate of the percentage overlap when overlap is determined on the assumption of normality. Figure 4.18 shows the percentage of overlap for group mean differences, expressed as σ differences (equation 4.11) of from zero to five standard deivations. (The percentages are tabled precisely in 1 percent steps from 1 percent to 100 percent by Elster & Dunnette, 1971, p. 687.)

Applications of the Normal Curve

Consider two populations of equal size whose IQ distributions are as shown in Figure 4.19. The means of the two distributions are 92 and 100, respectively. In each distribution $\sigma = 15$. Thus, the average difference of 8 IQ points can be expressed in terms of the five scale-free measures described in the preceding section:

1. σ Diff. = 0.53.
2. Percentage of variance = 6.65%.
3. r_{pbs} = .258.
4. Median overlap = 29.81%.
5. Total overlap = 79%.

Figure 4.18. The percentage of totally overlapping scores in the distributions of two groups (with equal standard deviations) as a function of the mean difference between the groups in standard deviation (σ) units.

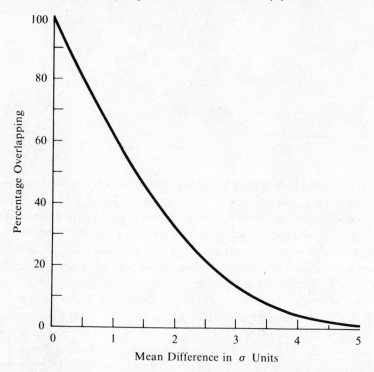

Say that admission to a highly selective school is based on IQ, with a cutting score at $X' =$ IQ 120. What percentage of each group falls above the cutting score X'? For the higher group (with a mean IQ of 100), an IQ of 120 is equivalent to a z score of $(120 - 100)/15 = 1.33$ (see equation 4.7). The area of the normal curve falling above $1.33z$ is 9.18 percent. So we would expect about 9 percent of the higher group to qualify for admission. For the lower group (with a mean IQ of 92), an IQ of 120 is equivalent to a z score of $(120 - 92)/15 = 1.87$. The area of the normal curve falling above $1.87z$ is 3.07 percent. So only about 3 percent of the lower group would qualify for admission. Note that, even with an average difference of only 8 IQ points, that is, about half a standard deviation, a cutting score as high as IQ 120 results in three times as many who qualify for admission from the higher group as from the lower group. If the cutting score X' were moved up to IQ 135 (the usual criterion for admission to classes for the "academically gifted" or "high potential"), the percentages qualifying for admission from the two groups would be 1 percent and 0.21 percent, or a ratio of about 5 to 1. It can be seen that the higher the cutting score, the greater will be the disparity between the groups in terms of the ratio of admissions.

At the lower end of the scale, say there is a cutoff $X =$ IQ 70 for admission to a special class (IQ below 70 or 75 is the usual criterion for "educable mentally retarded," or EMR, classes). The z scores corresponding to IQ 70 for the higher and lower groups are -2.0 and -1.47, respectively; and the percentage of each group falling below these points would be 2.3 percent and 7.1 percent, or a ratio of about 1 to 3. Thus three times as many of the lower as of the higher group would be eligible for the special class.

The process can be worked in reverse; if we know the percentages of each of the groups falling above (or below) a given cutting score (which need not be known), we can determine the difference between the group means. Say that 15 percent of Group A and 3 percent of Group B fall above a given score. How large a difference on an equal-interval scale of the trait in question does this percentage difference represent? Assuming a normal distribution of the trait and the same standard deviation in each group, we find, in the table of the normal curve (Table 4.2), the z scores corresponding to 15 percent and 3 percent, which are $1.03z$ and $1.88z$, respectively. The difference between the z scores is the difference between the means of the groups, that is, $1.88z - 1.03z = 0.81z$, which on an IQ scale with $\sigma = 15$ is equal to a difference of 12 IQ points.

When percentage differences are thus transformed to z differences, the data often appear much more orderly. Percentage differences fluctuate greatly depending on the location of the cutting score. When the varying percentage differences are transformed to the equal-interval z scale, it is usually found that the group difference in z units is reasonably constant. What usually differs is the location of the cutting score.

Turning back to the examples of percentage differences given at the beginning of this chapter, we can now convert them to z differences. Then they do not seem nearly so capricious and arbitrary as the percentage figures might have led us to believe.

In Example 1 (p. 61), we can predict what percentage of students in mentally retarded classes in the San Francisco schools would be black given (1) the percentage of blacks in the entire school district is 28.5 percent, (2) the IQ cutoff for eligibility for EMR classes is IQ 75, and (3) the assumption that the average IQ of blacks in the San Francisco schools is 85 as compared with the white 100, which are the best estimates of the average Wechsler Full Scale IQs of blacks and whites in California. Under these conditions, and assuming an IQ below 75 as the only criterion for placement in EMR classes, we should expect such classes to have 68 percent blacks and 32 percent whites. The actual percentage of blacks reported as evidence of biased discrimination in Example 1 is 66 percent— very close to the expected percentage. There is no evidence, therefore that whites and

Figure 4.19. Two hypothetical normal distributions of IQs with means at 92 and 100. The selection cutoffs at X and X' are used in the text to illustrate the statistical effects of a mean difference of 8 IQ points on the proportions of each distribution that fall above and below the two cutting scores at IQ 70 and IQ 120.

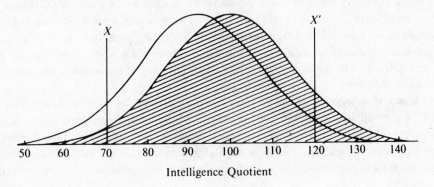

Intelligence Quotient

blacks were treated differently with regard to placement in EMR classes. To support a claim of racial bias in the placement procedure, it would have to be shown that the test itself is biased in its discrimination between whites and blacks.

In Example 2 (p. 61), which also refers to the San Francisco schools, if (1) blacks constitute 28.5 percent of all pupils, (2) the white and black IQ means are 100 and 85, respectively, and (3) the cutoff for placement in gifted classes is an IQ of 135, then we should expect the gifted classes to have 2 percent blacks and 98 percent whites. The fact that there are 5.5 percent blacks could mean either that a lower selection cutoff than IQ 135 was used or that different selection criteria were used for blacks and whites. If whites, in fact, constitute only 62.2 percent of the gifted classes, the remaining 32.3 percent must be mostly Orientals, who are a smaller percentage of the school population than blacks. But we cannot predict their percentage for lack of information on their exact percentage in the population and their mean IQ. All we can conclude here is that the actual percentage of blacks in the gifted classes is more than twice the expected percentage if an IQ over 135 were the only criterion for placement.

In Example 5 (p. 61), there is apparently no evidence of discrimination in the construction trades, as the percentage of black apprentices (13 percent) is about the same as the percentage of blacks in the general population (12 percent) and is close to the percentage one should expect to find if selection were completely random, that is, no discriminative selection at all. For Civil Service employees at the GS-5 level, with 88.1 percent white and 8.3 percent black, we cannot make a prediction because we do not know the z score equivalent of the cutoff for level GS-5. If we assume that the Civil Service exam resulting in this differential selection behaves like an IQ test and use the best estimate of the general population white–black IQ differences of one standard deviation (15 IQ points), then the lowest cutoff that would yield the actual percentages of blacks and whites reported above (assuming 12 percent of blacks in the general population) is a z score of approximately $-.32\sigma$ below the black mean, which would be equivalent to an IQ of 80. In other words, if the Civil Service selection were based on measured intelligence and the selection process excluded all persons below cutoff IQ 80, we would expect the percentages of acceptable whites and blacks to be 88.1 percent and 8.3 percent, respectively.

In Example 5 the percentages of 96.3 percent versus 2.2 percent for whites and blacks in college teaching positions would result if the cutting score were at IQ 112, again assuming 12 percent blacks in the general population and white and black IQ means of 100 and 85. If the cutting score for college teaching were at IQ 120, the expected percentages of white and black college teachers would be 99 percent and 1 percent. Of course we cannot necessarily assume the same cutting score for blacks and whites if there is biased discrimination. The reported figures are what would be found only under the stated assumptions. Without the assumptions (or actual data in place of the assumptions), percentage differences between groups by themselves can provide no evidence whatsoever of biased discrimination.

Mean of a Segment of the Normal Curve.   At times it is useful to estimate the mean of a group selected from some segment of a normally distributed population. If exactly the same selection cutoff is maintained for all persons regardless of the population from which they are selected, and if the population means differ, the means of the selected members of these populations will also differ, but only by a small amount. Thus selection tends strongly to equalize the selected groups, even though they may be selected from populations that differ considerably, and this trend toward equalization of the selected groups increases as the cutting score becomes more extreme.

$$\text{The mean } \bar{z}_1 = \frac{y_1}{\text{Area beyond } z_1} \ , \tag{4.11}$$

where y_1 is the value of the ordinate of the normal curve at z_1.[15] The mean of a segment lying between z_1 and z_2 is

$$\bar{z}_{1-2} = \frac{y_1 - y_2}{\text{Area between } z_1 \text{ and } z_2} \ .$$

Say we select persons from two populations whose means on an IQ test differ by one standard deviation, as do the black and white populations, with means of 85 and 100. The mean IQs of the selected subjects for various cutting scores then would be as shown in Table 4.3.

Table 4.3 highlights two important points. First, the more extreme the selection cutoff, the more it equalizes the means of the selected groups from different populations. Conversely, the closer the selection cutting score is to the general mean of the combined populations, the greater is the risk of group discrimination by any subsequent selection or competition attrition within the initially selected groups. Second, with more extreme selection cutoffs, selectees from different populations, once selected, have equal chances of success (to the extent that the selection criterion is a valid predictor); selectees can know that they are on a par in terms of the selection criterion regardless of their group membership, for the group difference among selectees is indeed negligible. (These conclusions, however, depend on the *reliability* of the test scores; see the discussion in the following two sections.) These advantages of a common cutting score for selection should be weighed against arguments for using different cutting scores or selection criteria for different groups in the population.

Table 4.3. Mean IQs of whites and blacks above or below various cutting scores on the IQ scale.

Cutting Score IQ		Mean IQ of Selected Group		
		Whites	Blacks	Diff.
Below	60	55.4	53.8	1.6
	70	64.5	62.1	2.4
	80	73.1	69.7	3.4
	90	81.0	76.0	5.0
Above	90	106.4	100.3	6.1
	100	112.0	107.9	4.1
	110	119.0	116.2	2.8
	120	126.9	125.0	1.9
	130[a]	135.5	135.4	0.1

[a]Higher cutting scores yield effectively no difference in the selected group means.

Measurement Error and Selection Cutoff.   A technical question arises involving the fact that measurement error is greater for more extreme scores. This shows up on retest or on an equivalent form of the test as "regression to the mean," which simply means that, on average, retest scores will fall closer to the mean by an amount that is predictable from the test's standard error of measurement, SE_m, or its reliability, r_{XX}. Because all obtained scores contain some error, scores that are more extreme deviations from the mean are more likely to contain larger error deviations than less extreme scores. Therefore, a more extreme selection cutoff for any group is bound to result in more error than a less extreme selection cutoff, as the regression is toward the mean of the population from which one is selected. One could ignore this problem and thereby give selectees drawn from the population whose mean is farthest from the selection cutoff the "benefit" of the measurement error. Or one could correct for group differences in measurement error by using *estimated true scores* instead of obtained scores. Because estimated true scores are always closer to the population mean than are obtained scores, persons who obtain high scores are apt to complain that they have been cheated out of a few score points by conversion to estimated true scores.

True score is a theoretical abstraction in psychometrics. It is the hypothetical score that would have been obtained, had there been absolutely no measurement error. It is a *hypothetical* score because, of course, in reality there is no perfect measurement. But, by making the reasonable assumption, which is universal in scientific measurement, that errors of measurement are random, uncorrelated, and normally distributed, we can make a statistical best estimate of an individual's hypothetical true score from his obtained score on a test, provided that we know the mean and the reliability of test scores in the population from which the individual was selected. The estimated or regressed true score, $\hat{X}$, as it is called, is given by the following formula:

$$\hat{X} = r_{xx}(X - \bar{X}) + \bar{X}, \qquad (4.12)$$

where

$\hat{X}$ = the estimated true score,
X = the individual's obtained score,
$\bar{X}$ = the mean of the population, and
r_{xx} = the reliability coefficient of the test.

For example, if a person from a population with a mean IQ of 100 obtains an IQ of 129, his estimated true score would be 126.1, if the test's reliability is .90. If another person from a population with a mean IQ of 85 obtains an IQ of 131, his true score would be 126.4. It can be seen that it makes but little difference when the test reliability is fairly high. (Tests with reliability of less than .90 probably should not be used, except in combination with other measures, for making decisions that affect individuals.) But what if the selection cutting score were an obtained IQ of 130? If the individual's score were close to the selection cutoff, a small difference could affect a sizable number of individuals whose scores were very close to the cutting score. How this should be handled in practice is usually not a strictly psychometric problem but a policy decision based on numerous considerations. For individuals with scores close to the cutoff, obtained scores are *biased* (because of measurement error) in favor of individuals from whichever population has its mean farther away from the cutoff score. This constitutes a form of biased discrimination, which, from a strictly psychometric standpoint, it is desirable to minimize. The best available method for doing so is to use estimated true scores.

Theoretically, there are essentially only three types of selection procedures: (1) selection based on unbiased discrimination, (2) selection based on biased discrimination, and (3) selection without discrimination, that is, purely random selection. Which of these is to be preferred in any actual situation is a matter of policy or of practical limitations. But psychometric techniques can be used to detect selection biases and to estimate their magnitudes. Psychometric techniques can also be used to minimize biases. It is best from our standpoint to keep the policy matters and the psychometric matters as clearly distinct as possible.

Separate Norms for Different Populations

Critics of mental testing often argue that IQs or other derived test scores should be based on separate racial and ethnic norms. In other words, an individual's score essentially would represent his deviation from the mean of his own racial or ethnic group. Hence, with separate norms, the same raw score on a test, reflecting a certain absolute level of performance, would result in different standardized scores for different groups. It is hard to see any practical utility in this proposal. It would greatly complicate the interpretation of test scores, since, if one were to use the scores for prediction of some criterion such as grades or job performance, or as an indication of relative standing in the knowledge or skills measured by the test, one would have to know the subject's group membership and make the necessary statistical adjustments for the scores to have the same meaning and predictive validity across groups. Also, an individual could raise his or her standardized score merely by claiming membership in a group with lower norms. There is also the problem of how many different sets of norms there should be; every ethnic group and religious group in every geographical region of the country could insist on its own norms.

Common sense as well as psychometric and statistical considerations dictate that test scores should have the same scale for everyone at a given age. That is, all scores should be scaled on homogeneous age groups within a single normative population. How well the normative sample was chosen is a separate consideration and depends in part on the nature and purpose of the test and the populations in which it is to be used. The psychometrist aims to maximize the theoretical meaningfulness and practical usefulness of tests and the scores derived from them. Scores scaled to separate norms for different groups would solve no real problems and would create a practical nuisance, much like having to contend with different currencies and exchange rates in going from one country to another. If tests are biased for some groups in the population, the bias should be recognized rather than obscured by having separate norms for that group.

Distribution of Achievement

As we have seen, there are a number of reasons for believing that mental ability is normally distributed in the population. But this generalization most likely does not extend to manifestations of ability in individual achievements, output, acquired knowledge, developed skills, occupational success, earnings, and the like. There is good reason to believe that achievement, in contrast to more elemental traits and abilities, is not normally distributed in the general population but that it has a markedly skewed distribution, like that in Figure 4.20.

When frequency distributions are plotted for accomplishments that can be counted, and thus are measurable on an absolute scale, the distributions are found to be markedly skewed. Examples are number of patents held by inventors, number of publications of research scientists and university professors, amount of music written by composers, and yearly earnings.

The skewness of the distribution of accomplishments also accords with subjective impressions of the absolute differences between persons lying at various percentile points on the scale of accomplishments in any field. The difference in chess skill between world champions and the average chess player certainly seems greater than the difference between the average player and the chess duffer. An Olympics champion is much farther above the average person in his particular athletic skill than the average person is above those who are just barely capable of displaying the particular skill at all.

A similar skewness is found for scholastic achievement and measures of general knowledge. Most scholastic achievement tests, however, are constructed in such a way as not to reveal the skewed distribution of achievement. In the first place, the usual achievement tests given in any grade in school have too little "top," that is, too few hard items, thereby cutting off the long upper tail of the skewed curve. The reason for this is that the usual achievement tests are intended to measure the achievement of a particular grade and do not include information and skills that are a part of the curriculum of higher grades. The eighth-grader who has mastered calculus could never show it on the usual math achievement tests given to eighth-graders. In the second place, most scholastic achievement tests today are in a sense double-duty tests; they are designed to measure not only what the child has learned in a given grade in school, but to test his intelligence as well.

Figure 4.20.   Theoretical distribution of achievement as measured on a scale of equal intervals. Notice that, even with this marked positive skewness of the distribution, the median and mean are quite close together but that the mean is pulled in the direction of the skew.

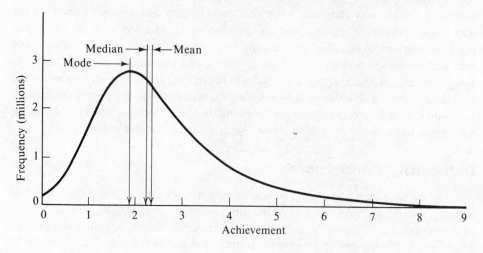

Knowledge acquisition is substantially correlated with intelligence, but not to the extremely high degree suggested by the correlation between the usual group verbal IQ test and the usual achievement test. A large number of the items in achievement tests requires the subject to use his or her acquired knowledge to solve novel problems, to reason, compare, generalize, and figure out answers to questions that may be unlike anything he or she has been taught in school, except that the information required to solve the problems has been taught. The ability to use information in reasoning and problem solving is more a matter of intelligence than of how much information the child has acquired in class, and so a larger proportion of the variance in achievement will represent intelligence variance than variance in how much children have actually learned from their lessons. Thus, when achievement tests are made to resemble intelligence tests in this way, and also are made to restrict the range of informational content sampled by the test, it should not be surprising that the distribution of achievement scores on such tests is much like the distribution of intelligence test scores. Because their informational content is so restricted, the usual grade-level achievement tests can be made difficult enough to spread students out into a normal distribution only by increasing the level of reasoning and problem-solving ability required by some of the items, making them very much like intelligence test items.

But achievement tests can be constructed to measure knowledge of things taught in school, rather than reasoning ability; the items sample knowledge at all levels over a wide range of fields, so that the test has virtually no ceiling and few if any subjects at any age could obtain a perfect score. An example of such a test is the General Culture Test (Learned & Wood, 1938), which was originally devised to assess all-around scholastic achievement in the high schools and colleges of Pennsylvania. The test contains some 1,200 questions involving information on all the fine arts, all periods of history, social studies, natural sciences, and world literature. The test has plenty of bottom and plenty of top for high school and college students. The total range of scores in a group of 1,503 high school seniors was from 25 to 615. The highest score found in a sample of 5,747 college sophomores was 755; the highest among 3,720 college seniors was 805, which is only about two-thirds of the maximum possible score. The distribution of scores in a large sample of high school seniors was quite skewed (10 percent less skew than in Figure 4.20).[16]

If achievement depends on other normally distributed factors in addition to ability, such as motivation, interest, energy, and persistence, and if all these factors act *multiplicatively*, then theoretically we should expect achievement to show a positively skewed distribution. The greater the number of factors (each normally distributed), the more skewed is the distribution of their products. The products of normally distributed variables are distributed in a skewed way such that the distribution of products can be normalized by a logarithmic transformation. A logarithmic transformation of achievement scores in effect makes the component elements of achievement additive rather than multiplicative. Theoretically a multiplicative effect of ability and motivation (or other traits involved in achievement) makes sense. Imagine the limiting case of zero ability; then regardless of the amount of motivation, achievement would equal zero. Also, with zero motivation, regardless of the amount of ability, achievement would equal zero. Great achievers in any field are always high in a number of relevant traits, the multiplicative interaction of which places their accomplishments far beyond those of the average person—much farther than their standing on any single trait or a mere additive combination of several traits. A superior talent alone does not produce the achievements of a Michelangelo, a Beethoven, or an Einstein. The same can be said of Olympics-level athletic performance, which depends on years of concentrated effort and training as well as certain inborn physical advantages. Thus it is probably more correct to say that a person's achievements are a *product,* rather than a *summation,* of his or her abilities, disposition, and training.

Form of the IQ Distribution in the Black and White Populations in the United States

Because much of the controversy over mental testing involves the claim that the tests are biased against blacks and certain other minority groups, it seems appropriate at this point to examine the form of the distribution of test scores in the black population. There have not been large-scale normative studies of racial or ethnic groups other than blacks and whites in the United States that provide information about the *form* of the distribution of scores, although for some other minority groups there is substantial information about means and standard deviations.

Standardized intelligence tests of practically every description show an average white–black difference of very close to one standard deviation, with over 90 percent of the published studies reporting differences between $\frac{2}{3}\sigma$ and $1\frac{1}{3}\sigma$, which on the IQ scale (with $\sigma = 15$) is between 10 and 20 IQ points, with a mean of 15 IQ points difference. There are regional variations in both black and white mean IQ and Armed Forces Qualification Test Scores, and the regional variations are similar for blacks and whites, with the result that the approximately one standard deviation mean difference is fairly constant from one region to another. In the United States, for whites as well as for blacks, there is a general increasing gradient of mean test performance that fans outward from the deep South to the North and West. A good part of this gradient is associated with population densities in rural and urban areas, and agricultural versus industrial employment opportunities. Urban versus rural differences in test performance are a universal finding wherever tests have been used throughout the world.[17]

Two large sets of published data on black test performance provide the best available evidence on the distribution of scores in specified representative black populations.

Figure 4.21 shows the distribution of Stanford–Binet IQs in a representative sample of 1,800 black children in the first to sixth grades in schools in five southeastern states (Kennedy, Van de Riet, & White, 1963). The mean IQ of blacks in this region is about five points below best estimates of the black national average, and also the standard deviation is probably slightly less. But it is the only published data that show the form of the IQ distribution in a large random sample of blacks. The distribution can be compared with that of the white standardization data based on a fairly representative sample of the U.S. white school-age population. The white normative distribution is as near to normal as can be. An index of skew shows it to be zero. The black distribution is positively skewed, with an index of skew[16] equal to .10. It is also more leptukurtic than the white distribution. The shortness of the lower tail as compared with the upper tail cannot be attributed in this case to a "floor effect," that is, too few easy items, because no subject in the entire sample came near obtaining the lowest possible score. In this population, at

Figure 4.21.   Stanford-Binet IQ distribution of black children in five Southeastern states and the white children in the 1960 normative sample.   (From Kennedy, Van de Riet, & White, 1963)

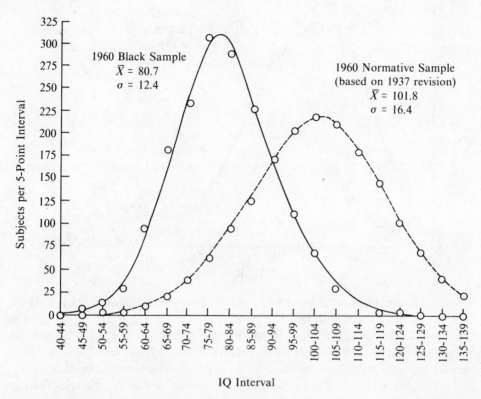

least, the positive skew is most likely a real phenomenon. It is possible to make both distributions almost perfectly normal and equalize their variances by a particular logarithmic transformation of the IQ scale,[18] but this would hardly seem justifiable unless it could be shown that such a transformation had other theoretically desirable conse- quences, such as making for a closer fit of the data to kinship regressions and correlations predicted from genetic principles. There are a number of possible and plausible causes of the skew of the black IQ distribution. It could mean that (1) the distribution of genotypes for IQ is skewed (as would result if the proportion of genes enhancing IQ was markedly less than 50 percent of the black gene pool), or (2) the environmental factors influencing the development of intelligence have a highly skewed distribution in this black population, or (3) the Stanford–Binet is more an achievement test and less an intelligence test for blacks than for whites, or (4) it is a scale artifact due to unequal intervals on the IQ scale. (Item 4 seems the least likely. See Chapter 9, pp. 428–429.)

Figure 4.22 shows the raw score distributions on the Wonderlic Personnel Test of 38,452 black and 142,545 white job applicants of both sexes for 80 occupations in 1,071 business, industrial, and government organizations in every part of the United States (Wonderlic, 1972). The Wonderlic Personnel Test is a fifty-item measure of general intelligence; because the item content is highly iverse, the total score reflects a quite general cognitive ability in persons with at least a high school education. (Means for high

Figure 4.22.   Distribution of raw scores on the Wonderlic Personnel Test of black and white job applicants in eighty occupations nationwide.   (Data from Wonderlic, 1972)

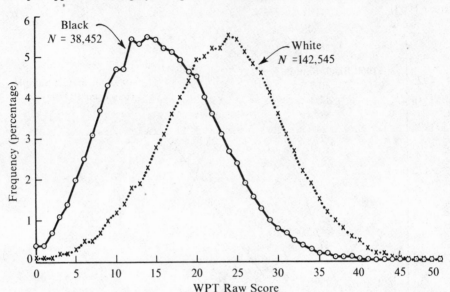

school graduates: black = 15.79, white = 22.29; for college graduates: black = 23.26, white = 29.96.) The overall white–black mean difference of 1.03σ and the normality of the white distribution suggest that the samples are probably quite representative of the noninstitutionalized adult white and black populations. An index of skew[16] is very close to zero for the white and .12 for the black curve. In this case the skew of the black curve is undoubtedly due to there not being quite enough "bottom" in this test, that is, not enough very easy items so as to permit the lowest tail of the curve to go all the way down to zero. (In a practical sense there would be no point in adding easier items, as this test is never used for making discriminations at that low level of ability in adults. A raw score of zero on the Wonderlic would correspond to an IQ of about 55.) With the addition of several easier items, both curves would be as near perfectly normal as could be statistically expected for samples of this size. It suggests that the distribution of general cognitive skills differs very little in the white and black populations of adults seeking employment, except for the location of the mean.[19]

Self-selection and the Normal Curve

Applicants for any particular college, training program, or job are, of course, not a random sample of the total population. They are self-selected even before they enter the selection process that follows application for the job. Some knowledge of the educational prerequisites for a particular job on the part of potential applicants, as well as the nature of the job itself, restricts the range of applicants with respect to mental ability. Different jobs, for example, attract applicants from different segments of the normal distribution of ability, so that the applicant pools for various jobs are centered about different means. Of course there is also a great spread of talent in any applicant pool; if there were not, there would be little need for further selection—anyone who applied would be well suited for the ability demands of the job. The correlation between persons' aspirations for particular jobs and their aptitudes for these jobs is very far from perfect.

An interesting and important fact is that *job applicants are self-selected, not in terms of an absolute standard of aptitude requirements, but from the same relative position in their own racial, ethnic, or cultural group's distribution of aptitude.*

This phenomenon can be seen quite clearly in data on the Wonderlic Personnel Test (WPT), described in the preceding section. Because scores on the WPT are very close to normally distributed in both the white and black populations of job applicants, it is reasonable to infer an interval scale throughout the total range of scores, permitting meaningful comparisons of the means of white and black applicants for various jobs. If job applicants were self-selected in terms of an absolute standard, there should be very little average difference between the aptitudes of white and black applicants. But in fact the average difference between self-selected white and black job applicants for any given job is only about 10 percent to 20 percent smaller than the total population difference of approximately one standard deviation. Because of the more restricted range of applicants' abilities for any given job, the white–black difference within the applicant groups is often greater, in relation to the standard deviation in the particular applicant group, than the one standard deviation difference found in the general population. Wonderlic (1972) presents mean scores of white and black applicants in eighty job categories from unskilled and semiskilled (e.g., custodian, laborer, maid, picker) to highly skilled technical and managerial jobs (e.g., accountant, administrator, general manager, laboratory technician), with median WPT scores ranging from 9 to 30—a range of nearly three standard deviations. The average difference between the white and black median scores of the eighty job categories is 6.1 (the difference between the means is 5.9), as compared with the population difference of 7 to 8 points. The distribution of median white–black differences for the eighty job categories is shown in Figure 4.23. It can be seen that the differences cluster around the average population difference. The correlation (Pearson *r*) between the white and black means in the eighty job categories is .87, which means that white and black job applicants are highly similar in self-selection for these eighty types of jobs. The self-selection of whites and blacks is in terms of *similar percentile positions in their own population distributions.*

Job qualifications are perceived largely in terms of educational level, and so we should expect white and black applicants for a given job to be more similar in educational background than in the kind of general mental ability measured by the WPT. This is in fact true. Because WPT scores show a regular increase with years of schooling and because there is a fairly consistent white–black difference in the mean WPT score at all educational levels, we should expect the observed high correlation between the racial groups' mean WPT scores across jobs as well as the mean within-jobs racial difference of 5.9 score points. This is very close to the mean difference of 5.8 points between whites and blacks of the same educational level. Figure 4.24 shows the mean WPT scores of blacks and whites by years of education.

Why the Standard Deviation of IQ Is 15 or 16

IQs are never raw scores on any test. They are derived scores, and there are two methods of derivation, each yielding roughly comparable results.

Figure 4.23. The distribution of white–black mean raw score differences on the Wonderlic Personnel Test of self-selected applicants in eighty job categories.

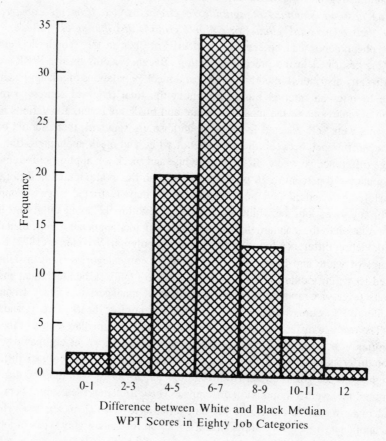

Difference between White and Black Median
WPT Scores in Eighty Job Categories

The original Binet intelligence test was scaled according to mental age.[20] This was an obvious choice due to the fact that between the ages from about 4 years to 16 years, raw scores on tests composed of items more or less evenly graded over a wide range of difficulty show a fairly linear increase with age. The mental-age equivalent of a given raw score on such a test is determined from the mean raw score obtained by all children of any given chronological age. Thus, if the average raw score of 10-year-old children is 60, a raw score of 60 is equivalent to a mental age (MA) of 10 years. By "norming" the test on large representative samples of children at every age in one-month intervals (as in the Stanford–Binet scale) and plotting raw scores against age in months, one can directly read off the MA equivalents of the raw scores, as shown in Figure 4.25.[21]

For example, a raw score of 60 on this test would be equivalent to a mental age of 10 years. The actual mean score at each age is plotted (circles) and a smoothed curve (heavy line) is fitted to the data points, on the reasonable assumption that the slight deviations of the data points from the smoothed curve represent sampling error and the smoothed curve better represents the population values. The fine lines bound plus or minus one standard deviation (in raw score units) from the mean at each age. (In a normal distribution, 68 percent of the scores fall within plus or minus one standard deviation of the mean.) Notice that the standard deviation of raw scores increases steadily with age. Consequently, the standard deviation of mental age also increases with age. A 4-year-old whose raw score is one standard deviation above the mean of 4-year-olds will have a MA of 4.6 years, or about 4 years and 7 months, whereas a 12-year-old whose raw score is one standard deviation above the mean of 12-year-olds will have a MA of 13.8 years, or about 13 years and 10 months. At each age, the raw scores, and consequently their MA equivalents, have an approximately normal distribution.

Figure 4.24. Wonderlic Personnel Test raw score means of blacks (*N* = 38,293) and whites (*N* = 140,684) by years of education. (Data from Wonderlic, 1972)

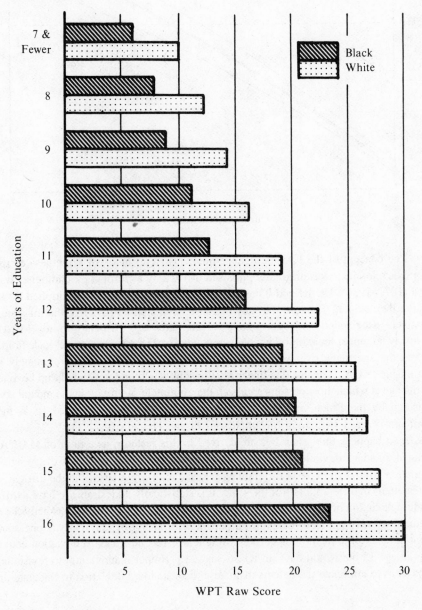

Figure 4.25. Raw scores on a test are converted to a mental-age (MA) scale via the smoothed curve of the raw score means based on normative groups at each chronological age. For example, on this hypothetical test, a raw score of 60 is the mean attained by 10-year-olds and corresponds to a MA of 10 years. The diverging thin lines are one standard deviation above and below the smoothed curve through the means (circles).

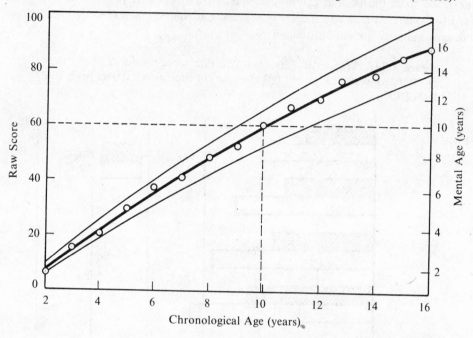

The concept of the IQ (intelligence quotient) as an index of brightness or *rate* of mental development was originally proposed in 1912 by a German psychologist, William Stern (1871–1938). He defined IQ as mental age/chronological age, multiplied by 100 to remove the decimal. Because the growth curve of mental ability, like that of stature, is negatively accelerated and begins to level out after age 16, the formula MA/CA is obviously no longer meaningful beyond about age 16. The ratio has useful scale properties only in the age range over which raw scores on the test have an approximately linear relationship to CA. Because this linear relationship was found not to hold up beyond age 16, the age at which most persons approach the asymptote of growth in the mental abilities measured by the Binet scales, it became conventional to use a CA of 16 as the denominator of the IQ equation for all persons of age 16 and over.

It so happens that when IQs are derived in this fashion, as a ratio of MA/CA, the obtained standard deviation of the IQ is about 15 or 16 IQ points at every age. The fluctuation around 15 or 16 at different ages was due to irregularities in the difficulties of the test items in different parts of the scale. It is statistically undesirable to have a different standard deviation of IQ at various ages, since then the IQ does not have exactly the same meaning at every age. For example, a person with an IQ of, say, 116 is one standard deviation above the mean at age 10 and might still be one standard deviation above the mean at age 15 but would have an IQ of, say, 113. Rather than attempt to revise the test items so as to eliminate the defects that cause the ststandard deviation to fluctuate unsystematically from one age to another, test constructors used a simpler device. They applied a statistical transformation of the raw scores, converting them directly to IQs, without first determining the MA equivalents of the raw scores. For each age group (in one-month intervals) they determined the mean and the standard deviation of raw scores. Each raw score X was converted to a z score, thus

$$z = (X - \bar{X})/\sigma.$$

The IQ equivalent of a given z score thus is

$$IQ = 15z + 100,$$

which yields a distribution of IQs at each age with a mean of 100 and a σ of 15.

The MA can then be determined, if one wishes to obtain it, from the equation MA = (CA $\times$ IQ)/100. All the Wechsler tests have always derived IQs in this fashion (with σ = 15). The Stanford–Binet tests since the 1960 revision have also used the z scores transformed to IQs, but with σ = 16. The standard deviation was kept at 16 because the normative sample of the 1937 revision, based on IQ = 100 MA/CA, had a standard deviation of 16. Practically all other modern IQ scales are based on the z score transformation, with mean = 100 and σ = 15 or 16.

There is some value in retaining this scale for IQ, as its standard deviation is close to that obtained from the MA/CA ratio, and from it we can make a fair estimate of the MA level at which a child is functioning by knowing his IQ. We can say, for example, that a 12-year-old with an IQ of 80 is performing like an average child of 9 years 7 months in the kinds of cognitive skills measured by the test.

Caution is needed, however. Not all tests yield a standard deviation of 15 or 16 for IQs when derived from the MA/CA formula. "Culture fair" tests composed of nonverbal, nonscholastic, noninformational types of reasoning problems, based on figural materials, have a larger standard deviation of ratio IQs. Cattell's Culture Fair Test of g, for example, has a standard deviation of 24 IQ points. Tests that are culturally and educationally loaded tend to have a more restricted variation of raw scores (and hence MAs) in any given age group. This will be reflected in the steepness of the gradient of percentage passing as a function of age for single items, as shown in Figure 4.26. Items (like item B in Figure 4.26) that depend more exclusively on reasoning ability, in contrast to items (like item A in Figure 4.26) that call for specific information or school-type skills as are found in many verbal IQ tests, generally show a less steep age gradient; and a test made up of a large number of such (B-type) items will have a greater spread of mental ages at any given chronological age, because the item variances and interitem covariances are larger for B-type than for A-type items.

Interpretation of IQ

We have seen that a general intelligence test that yields IQs with a standard deviation of 15 or 16 can be roughly interpreted in terms of mental age—that is, MA = (IQ $\times$ CA)/100—between the ages of about 4 to 16. A child's MA, regardless of his CA (chronological age), tells us that his general knowledge and general cognitive ability for reasoning, problem solving, and comprehension are much like that of the average or typical child of the same CA. To characterize the intellectual ability of a 10-year-old child

Figure 4.26. "Item characteristic curves," showing percentage of the population passing two test items, A and B, at every age from 5 to 12 years. Item A is more typical of items in culture-loaded tests, that is, items that call for specific knowledge acquired prior to taking the test. Item B is more typical of items in culture-reduced tests, that is, items based more on reasoning, grasping relationships, and problem solving than on informational content per se.

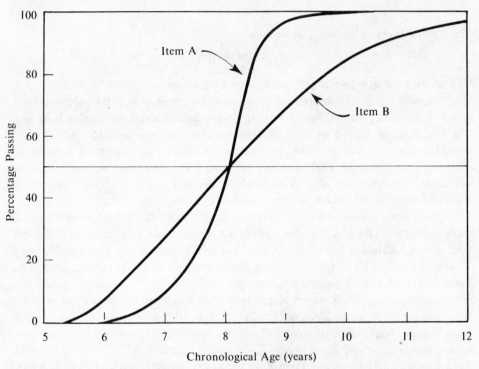

with an IQ of 70, for example, one thinks in terms of the cognitive capabilities of the typical 7-year-old.

If it is difficult by casual observation to "see" much intellectual difference between the typical 10-year-old and the typical 11-year-old, it is equally difficult to "see" a difference between two 10-year-olds, one with a MA of 10 and one with a MA of 11, that is, having IQs 100 and 110, respectively. IQ differences smaller than about 10 points are not generally socially perceptible. They are confounded with too many other personality variables, special abilities, developed skills, and the like to be accurately judged by observing a person's behavior in the usual activities of daily life. As IQ differences increase beyond about 10 points, they become noticeable, first only in intellectually demanding activities and finally in almost every form of behavior. The behavioral differences between persons at the ninety-ninth percentile of IQ (i.e., an IQ of 135) and at the first percentile (IQ of 65) are as completely obvious in any situation making any intellectual demands as a corresponding difference in height (6 feet 3 inches versus 5 feet 3 inches) would be on the basketball court.

The best way to appreciate the meaning of different levels of IQ is to work closely with children varying over a wide range of IQs and to note their learning capabilities, how fast they "catch on" to new instructions, the kinds of problems they can solve, the kinds of errors they make, and the kind and amount of instruction they need to understand a given concept. At any given age, the above-average IQ child (110 or above) will appear quite different from the below-average (below 90) child in cognitively demanding situations. In many other situations that involve mainly physical or social skills, IQ seems not to be a salient characteristic until it falls below some quite low point, such as IQ of 60 or 70, and even then it is not crucial in some cases. Not all activities, by any means, put a premium on the kind of mental ability measured by IQ tests. But some activities put a very high premium on IQ. A low IQ is disabling in mathematics, for example, and in English composition and reading comprehension.

The importance of IQ, therefore, depends to a great extent on the type of activity in which the individual is involved. Misjudgments of an individual's general intelligence are usually a result of basing judgment on an atypical aspect of the person's behavior. Almost everyone may do or say something that is particularly clever or bright or sagacious now and then, or may behave quite stupidly on occasion. If we give too much weight to these atypical occurrences in our subjective judgment of a person's mental capacity, we are apt to take exception to his or her tested IQ. Parents seem especially prone to judge their own children by their atypical performances. Each person's abilities vary about his own mean, and we usually notice the deviations more than the mean. Prejudices and the like may cause us consistently to give greater weight to the positive deviations than to the negative for some persons and vice versa for others. School teachers, who observe large numbers of children of similar age over a wide range of ability, are usually better judges of intelligence than parents are. I once had occasion to interview independently the mothers and the classroom teachers of a number of children to whom I had given individual IQ tests. I found that the teachers had a much better estimate than the mothers of a given child's rank in the total distribution of IQs. In giving their reasons for their estimate of a particular child's IQ, the teachers usually noted the child's typical behavior in cognitively demanding situations, whereas mothers more often pointed out exceptional instances of clever behavior. On this basis, low-IQ children especially are often rated average or above by their parents. Very-high-IQ children, on the other hand, are often *underrated* by their parents, who are usually surprised to learn that their child is quite exceptional. Parental judgments of children's intelligence tend to cluster more closely around the mean (or slightly above) than do the children's IQs. Personality factors affect subjective judgments, too, for both parents and teachers. The socially outgoing, extraverted child tends to be overrated as compared with the more shy, quiet, or introverted child.

In lieu of much direct experience with persons of different IQs, one can gain some idea of what MAs and IQs mean by observing the typical performance of persons on test items for which there are good normative data. The best items are usually retained in tests when they are "normed." Unfortunately one cannot publish these copyrighted items without violating the norms of standardized tests. But a few items have been published as examples. It is interesting to see what the average adult can do. For example, 55 percent of a national sample of adults[22] were able to fill in a correct word for this completion item:

A five-pound rock is dropped from a cliff 500 feet high. The longer the rock falls, the greater is its _____.

Fifty percent of adults can solve the following problem:

> A motor boat can travel five miles an hour on a still lake. If this boat travels downstream on a river that is flowing five miles per hour, how long will it take the boat to reach a bridge that is ten miles downstream?

Responses to the following item are quite revealing of the cognitive ability of a national sample of 9-year-olds:

> A pint of water at 50° Fahrenheit is mixed with a pint of water at 70° Fahrenheit. The temperature of the water just after mixing will be about:

Answers	% of 9-year-olds
20° F	4%
50° F	2
60° F	7
70° F	5
120° F	69
I don't know	12
No response	0

The majority of 9-year-olds can obviously add 50 + 70, but they apparently do not have the concept of "average" and do not appreciate the physical absurdity of the answer 120° F. The knowledge of simple arithmetic required by this item is possessed by the vast majority of 9-year-olds, but the level of reasoning required is clearly beyond the typical 9-year-old.

Psychologists have generally followed a convention in labeling levels of intelligence by dividing the normal curve into a number of segments of equal IQ intervals. The unit of division is the probable error (P.E.), which is about two-thirds of a standard deviation ($.6745\sigma$, to be exact). The normal curve is divided into seven probable error segments and each of these is given the conventional labels shown in Table 4.4. Also shown are the corresponding IQs on the Wechsler Adult Intelligence Scale and the theoretical percentage of the population falling within each interval.

These classifications have little, if any, real utility. They are by no means clear-cut or rigid categories, and there is considerable overlap between behavioral capabilities and social adjustment of persons with IQs in these ranges. This is to be expected, because IQ

Table 4.4.   Conventional intelligence classification.

Classification	Interval in P.E. Units	IQ Interval[1]	% Included
Retarded	−3 P.E. and below	69 and below	2.2%
Borderline	−2 to −3 P.E.	70–79	6.7
Dull-normal	−1 to −2 P.E.	80–89	16.1
Average	−1 to +1 P.E.	90–109	50.0
Bright-normal	+1 to +2 P.E.	110–119	16.1
Superior	+2 to +3 P.E.	120–129	6.7
Very superior	+3 P.E. and above	130 and above	2.2

[1]IQ based on Wechsler Adult Intelligence Scale, with $\bar{X} = 100$, $\sigma = 15$.

has a low correlcation with many of the usual criteria of adjustment and success. One can justifiably describe the mental capabilities of each classification only in terms of the average or modal characteristics of all persons falling within the classification, at the same time realizing that there are many exceptions and variations. Such characterizations lose accuracy and meaningfulness for the individual directly to the extent that they go beyond intellectual skills, particularly those involving reasoning and problem solving based on language, numbers, or symbols. The classifications are generally quite congruent with indices of performance in traditional academic curricula, especially the more complex, symbolic, and conceptual subjects, such as composition, mathematics, and science.

The "retarded" category is traditionally described as IQ below 70, but this is rather arbitrary. Psychologists, educators, and social workers, however, show little disagreement that the vast majority of persons with IQs below 70 have unusual difficulties in school and generally have difficulties of an intellectual nature as adults. There are few jobs in a modern industrial society for which persons below IQ 70 are capable without making allowances for their intellectual disability or restructuring the usual requirements of the job so as to bring it within the capabilities of the retarded person. Persons below IQ 70 have difficulty in managing their financial affairs and other ordinary demands involving arithmetic and reading comprehension. Many school systems set the retarded classification at IQ 75 or even 80, because such children so often require special instruction to learn the basic school subjects. Even then these children find it very difficult to keep pace with their classmates, because, with a mental age a year or more below the average of their classmates, they lack the conceptual readiness for the scholastic subjects that are taught in a given grade. The armed forces exclude most persons who score below an equivalent of about IQ 75 or 80 on the Armed Forces Qualification Test. There are too few useful occupations that these low-IQ recruits can be successfully trained to perform, with limited time for training.

The American Association of Mental Deficiency has recommended that the borderline of mental retardation be set at between IQ 70 to 85, defining as "subnormal" IQ deviations of more than one standard deviation below the general mean of the population. But this is a matter of statistical definition and does not agree with the general practice of basing classification as retarded not only on IQ but on various criteria of the individual's social adjustment and adaptive behavior. The majority of adults with IQs between 70 and 85 are not retarded by ordinary criteria of social adjustment. In one large study, for example, it was found that 84 percent of such persons had completed at least eight years of school, 83 percent had held a job, 65 percent had a semiskilled or higher occupation, 80 percent were financially independent or a housewife, and almost 100 percent were able to do their own shopping and travel alone (Mercer, 1972a).

The AAMD further subdivides the retarded classification as follows:

IQ 85–70	Borderline retardation
IQ 69–55	Mild retardation
IQ 54–40	Moderate retardation
IQ 39–25	Severe retardation
IQ 24 and below	Profound retardation

The vast majority, some 70 percent to 80 percent, of persons below IQ 70 are biologically normal; no brain damage, disease, or genetic defect is detectable. They are a part of normal variation in the combination of polygenic and environmental factors that contribute to variance in IQ. The remaining 20 percent to 30 percent show "clinical" signs, either due to brain damage from injury or disease, or they show the medically recognizable signs of one or another of the more than eighty specifically identifiable syndromes associated with a single defective gene or chromosomal anomaly. The bulk of such individuals are found in the IQ range below 50 and nearly all persons with IQs below 35 or 40 are the "clinical" type.

All levels of retardation, except perhaps some of those at the "profound" level, are amenable to various forms of therapy, conditioning, or training that can make their social behavior and their lives more satisfactory, both to themselves and to those who must take care of them, although such training has no appreciable effect on the IQ. The mildly or educably retarded can benefit from schooling when it is properly geared to their level of readiness and conceptual capabilities.

Moving up the IQ scale to the 80 to 90 range, which is traditionally but unfortunately labeled "dull normal," the typical picture is that of quite normal children or adults whose only consistently distinguishing feature is greater than average difficulty in the more academic school subjects. Such children are generally slower to "catch on" to whatever is being taught if it involves symbolic, abstract, or conceptual subject matter. In the early grades in school they most often have problems in reading and arithmetic and are sometimes labeled "slow learners." But it is really not that they learn slowly as that they lag behind in developmental readiness to grasp the concepts that are within easy reach of the majority of their age mates. Such children will eventually grasp these basic subjects fairly easily, but about a year or two later than their age mates. They are better thought of as "slow developers" than as "slow learners." The child with an IQ of 80 to 90, it seems, has to be *explicitly taught* more of what he must learn, in or out of school, than the brigher child, who picks up much more knowledge and skills on his own, without need of direct intervention by parents or teachers. The lower-IQ child does not as readily absorb as much from his own experiences as the brighter child. Most low-IQ children do *not* eventually catch up with their age mates. Because of the fairly high degree of constancy of the IQ (see Chapter 7, p. 277), low-IQ children differ increasingly from their average age mates in mental age as they advance in school.[23] Children in the IQ range of 80 to 90 are usually not noticed to be intellectually different in any way until they enter school. Their scholastic problems become more evident with each higher grade, since they are further behind their classmates in mental age.

Because of this increasing lag in the academic subjects, most of these children, when they reach junior or senior high school, elect the less academic courses. The elective system allows them to choose courses in which they are more apt to succeed and from which they are more apt to profit in the world of work when they leave school. By high school age many such children, because of their earlier scholastic difficulties, have already acquired a definite dislike for the academic subjects and tend to drop out of high school if it has little else to offer besides the traditional curriculum. Algebra and geometry, foreign languages, English literature, and physics and chemistry are not these pupils' forte; unless strenuously pressured by parents, they usually avoid these traditionally college preparatory courses. They prefer the more practical and vocational courses, which are less symbolic and abstract. Not surprisingly, as adults they have few if any intellectual interests to speak of; they are generally poorly informed on world affairs, science, the arts, or other types of information gained through reading. They are usually employed in jobs that depend little on scholastic skills or in which advancement depends on individual study or training courses involving "book learning," "examinations," or other school-like requirements.

The 50 percent of the population classed as "average" and falling between IQs 90 and 110 hardly needs description. They differ from those below and above on the IQ scale only in degree. The schools, the world of work, and the entertainment industry are largely geared to this average majority of the population. Persons with IQs closer to 110, because of their usually more favorable experiences in elementary and high school are more likely to seek advanced training or even college than those with IQs closer to 90. The myriad of occupations below the highly technical and professional levels are mostly occupied by persons in this IQ range. There is virtually no limitation on such persons in fields that are not dependent on university- or graduate-level education or in occupations that require special talents, such as athletics, art, acting, and musical performance. At least an average IQ is usually needed to compete successfully in such fields, but, beyond that, a high level in special talents and personal qualities are the crucial factors in success.

IQs between 110 and 130 are typically found in children who do well in school subjects, who catch on easily to what is being taught at their grade level, and who take a liking to the academic curriculum. They are typically good readers from an early age; they enjoy reading, and they do more of it than most children without encouragement from others. There are great individual differences in interests and special abilities in this group, and these differences are reflected in the variability of these children's performances in various scholastic subjects. But usually children with IQs above 115 or so can perform outstandingly in any school subject to which they may apply themselves, barring special disabilities such as aphasia and dyslexia. These above-average children show a wider range of interests than the average, they tend to be self-learners, and their hobbies are usually more complex, advanced, well planned, and long term than one sees in their more average age mates. Colleges and universities obtain their students almost entirely from the range above IQ 110. Entering freshmen in most selective colleges average in the 115 to 120 range, and graduates from these colleges average about 120 to 125. The vast majority of persons in skilled, managerial, and professional occupations are from this group. Manual or "blue-collar" workers in this IQ range generally become the master carpenters, skilled mechanics, technicians, foremen, and contractors with earnings on a par with or exceeding those of many white-collar and professional workers.

Persons with IQs above 130 usually find school easy, or even perhaps boring for lack of intellectual challenge. Some are not very enthusiastic students until they reach college. With average interest, motivation, and application, they tend to be in the upper half of their college class in grade-point average. With better than average effort and persistence, they can succeed in virtually any occupation except those requiring special talents, among which I would include mathematics; at an advanced level mathematics seems to require not only a high level of general intelligence but also something more in the nature of a special talent. (As in high-level talent for musical composition and in playing chess, there is also a marked sex difference in high-level mathematical ability. Also, it is interesting that authentic child prodigies are found only in chess, music, and mathematics.) Beyond IQ 130, factors other than general intelligence largely account for what these persons make of their careers. Personality factors, interests, drive, stability, perseverance, general health, cultural background, educational opportunities, and special talents become the main determining factors once a high level of general intelligence is present. Outstanding achievement, as Galton noted, depends on at least three things: exceptional general mental ability, exceptional drive, and exceptional perseverance. These qualities are almost invariably illustrated, for example, in the biographies of persons whose achievements are judged sufficiently outstanding to be included in the *Encyclopaedia Britannica*.

Even persons above IQ 140 as a group are extremely varied in interests, accomplishments, and conventional criteria of "success," as shown by Lewis M. Terman's (1877–1956) famous study of "gifted" children, described in Terman's four volumes of *Genetic Studies of Genius* (1925–1929). In 1921, from some 160,000 school children in California, Terman selected 1,528 with Stanford–Binet IQs above 140. The children were described in terms of medical examinations, physical measurements, scholastic achievement, character tests, interests, books read, and games known. These children on the whole were superior physically, averaging more than an inch taller than their age mates in elementary school. They also have above-average birth weight. In the 1920s, before the era of social promotions in school, seven out of eight of the gifted group were in grades ahead of their age group and none was below grade level. They had wider interests and read more than their age mates. They were also superior in leadership and in social responsibility. Terman and his co-workers made follow-up studies of these children all the way into their adulthood and middle age (Terman & Oden, 1959).

Their adult achievements were far beyond expectancy for the general population. A much higher pecentage completed college, entered the professions, worked up to high managerial positions at a comparatively early age, published books and articles, and achieved distinctions meriting biographical citations in *American Men of Science* and *Who's Who*. Their incomes were well above the average, and their divorce rate was below the national average. Their spouses averaged about 125 IQ and their children's IQs were, interestingly enough, normally distributed about a mean IQ of 133, with a standard deviation of 16, ranging all the way from IQs below 70 to above 200. (The Terman gifted subjects themselves had an average Stanford–Binet IQ of 152 when tested as children.) When the more than 1,500 gifted subjects were classified as adults into three groups from least to most successful in terms of conventional criteria of success, such as outstanding achievements and public or professional recognition, it was found that the most and the least successful groups (the top and bottom 20 percent) differed on average by only 6 IQ points. This highlights the fact that beyond an IQ of 140, personal factors other than intelligence are the main determinants of "success."

Children selected from the range of IQs above 150 show quite remarkable capabilities. A recent study (Stanley, Keating, & Fox, 1974) of exceptionally gifted children found that many of them by the sixth to eighth grade were fully capable of more than holding their own in math and science courses at Johns Hopkins University, a highly selective institution. Most of these students, while still in junior high school, scored far above the average of college freshmen on the Scholastic Aptitude Test (SAT). One 12-year-old, for example, scored 800 (the highest possible score) on the SAT math test—three standard deviations above the average college freshman score! Five of these youngsters between 13 and 14 years of age were experimentally enrolled in a college algebra class at Johns Hopkins University. It was found that these students participated more in the discussions than the average university student taking the course, and they all earned A grades.

Estimates of the IQs of famous geniuses in history, based on biographical information of their capabilities at definitely known ages as children, show many of them to have been mentally very precocious, much like the children described in the preceding paragraph (Cox, 1926). The average estimated IQ of three hundred historical persons (from a list of the one thousand most eminent men of history) on whom sufficient childhood evidence was available for a reliable estimate was IQ 155. Many were as high as 175 and several as high as 200. Very few were below IQ 120, and in most of these cases there was too little evidence of the early years, so that the evidence available resulted in an estimate of the *minimum* IQ consistent with what these persons were known to have done at a particular age in childhood. Thus the majority of these eminent men would most likely have been recognized as intellectually gifted in childhood had they been given IQ tests.

By way of summary, it may be useful to look at Table 4.5 compiled by Cronbach (1960, p. 174) from estimates in the research literature of the typical IQ levels or requirements for the various listed criteria. At best, it gives only an approximate and limited indication of what persons at the various IQ levels are most typically capable of achieving, and it would be easy to find many exceptions. At every IQ level above 40 or 50, a rather wide range of practical accomplishments and capabilities is found, first, because a certain level of ability is usually only a necessary but not sufficient condition for any particular achievement and, second, because many socially useful and valued activities do not depend to any large extent on the kind of mental ability measured by IQ tests. This is not a fault of the tests, but rather a virtue. A single score or measurement is necessarily unidimensional if it is to have any real meaning. A single number like an IQ cannot reflect two or more uncorrelated attributes, and there are many uncorrelated factors that determine human behavior. But a mental test score can reflect one part, often an important and stable part, of the many diverse factors that contribute to variability in performance in particular situations and to lifetime accomplishments in general.

Although IQs are an interval scale, the practical, social, economic, and career implications of different IQs most certainly do not represent equal intervals. Again, this is

Table 4.5.   Typical IQ levels for various criteria.

IQ	Criteria
130	Mean of persons receiving Ph.D.
120	Mean of college graduates.
115	Mean of freshmen in typical four-year college. Mean of children from white-collar and skilled-labor homes.
110	Mean of high school graduates. Has 50:50 chance of graduating from college.
105	About 50:50 chance of passing in academic high school curriculum.
100	Average for total population.
90	Mean of children from low-income city homes or rural homes. Adult can perform jobs requiring some judgment (operate sewing machine, assemble parts).
75	About 50:50 chance of reaching high school. Adult can keep small store, perform in orchestra.
60	Adult can repair furniture, harvest vegetables, assist electrician.
50	Adult can do simple carpentry, domestic work.
40	Adult can mow lawns, do simple laundry.

not a fault of the IQ scale, but is the result of personal and societal values and demands. The implications and consequences of, say, a 30-point IQ difference is more significant between IQs of 70 and 100 than between IQs of 130 and 160. The importance of a given difference depends not only on its magnitude, but on whether or not it crosses over any of the social, educational, and occupational *thresholds* of IQ. To be sure, these thresholds are statistical and represent only differing probabilities for individuals' falling on either side of the threshold. But the differential probabilities are not negligible. Such probabilistic thresholds of this type occur in different regions of the IQ scale, not by arbitrary convention or definition, but because of the structure of the educational and occupational systems of modern industrial societies and their correlated demands on the kind of cognitive ability measured by IQ tests.

The four socially and personally most important threshold regions on the IQ scale are those that differentiate with high probability between persons who, because of their level of general mental ability, can or cannot attend a regular school (about IQ 50), can or cannot master the traditional subject matter of elementary school (about IQ 75), can or cannot succeed in the academic or college preparatory curriculum through high school (about IQ 105), and can or cannot graduate from an accredited four-year college with grades that would qualify for admission to a professional or graduate school (about IQ 115). Beyond this, the IQ level becomes relatively unimportant in terms of ordinary occupational aspirations and criteria of success. That is not to say that there are not real differences between the intellectual capabilities represented by IQs of 115 and 150 or even between IQs of 150 and 180. But IQ differences in this upper part of the scale have far less personal implications than the thresholds just described and are generally of lesser importance for success in the popular sense than are certain traits of personality and character.

The *social* implications of exceptionally high ability and its interaction with the other factors that make for unusual achievements are considerably greater than the personal implications. The quality of a society's culture is highly determined by the very small fraction of its population that is most exceptionally endowed. The growth of civilization, the development of written language and of mathematics, the great religious and philosophic insights, scientific discoveries, practical inventions, industrial developments, advancements in legal and political systems, and the world's masterpieces of literature, architecture, music and painting, it seems safe to say, are attributable to a rare small proportion of the human population throughout history who undoubtedly possessed, in addition to other important qualities of talent, energy, and imagination, a high level of the essential mental ability measured by tests of intelligence.

SUMMARY

Differences between various subpopulations in selection ratios for educational and occupational selection cannot be properly understood without reference to the total distributions of ability in the subpopulations. Seemingly very large subpopulation differences when expressed in terms of selection ratios (i.e., the percentage of a group falling above or below some selection cutting score) are shown to correspond to smaller and much less erratic differences between the total distributions of abilities in the subpopulations.

The form of the frequency distribution of test scores depends on certain statistical characteristics of the test items, namely, the item difficulties (i.e., the percentage of the population passing each item) and the item intercorrelations. Manipulation of these two item characteristics can produce marked variations in the form of the frequency distribution of test scores. Tests of mental ability are devised to yield a normal distribution of scores in the population, as a number of cogent arguments can be brought to bear in support of the hypothesis that *general mental ability* is distributed in the population approximately in the form of the normal curve, with certain systematic departures from normality occurring both above and below about two standard deviations from the mean. No contrary hypothesis regarding the distribution of ability has ever gained theoretical or empirical support. The distribution of *achievement,* on the other hand, is not normal but is markedly skewed to the right, if measured on an absolute scale. This finding is consistent with the hypothesis that achievement is a multiplicative (or some other nonadditive) function of a number of simpler, normally distributed factors, including general mental ability.

The traditional mean and standard deviation of IQ as 100 and 15, respectively, were originally derived from the relationship of mental age to chronological age. The MA/CA ratio, however, has certain psychometric disadvantages, and today IQs are generally expressed as standardized scores (with mean = 100, σ = 15) at every age level.

The cumulation of many years of experience with the IQ and its many educational, occupational, and social correlates permits rough general descriptions of the kinds of probabilistic performance expectancies associated with the various broad divisions of the IQ distribution above and below the general population mean. There are several critical probabilistic thresholds within the total range of IQ, each having important educational and occupational consequences for individuals. It is largely the layman's perception of this critical threshold property of intelligence, and the fact of its objective measurement by the IQ, that lends the IQ its importance in the public eye and makes it such a sensitive and controversial topic.

It is an interesting and important fact that white and black applicants for a wide variety of jobs (and probably also applicants to institutions of higher learning) with differing ability demands are self-selected from the same *relative* positions in their *own* population's distribution of aptitude and not in terms of one and the same scale of aptitude for the whole population.

Test scores scaled differently for various subpopulations in terms of separate standardization norms based on the different subpopulations have no legitimate practical utility. Separate norms for different subpopulations merely obscure actual test biases.

NOTES

1. The highest possible correlation between two variables, x and y, is the square root of the product of their reliabilities, that is, $\sqrt{r_{xx} \times r_{yy}}$, where r_{xx} and r_{yy} are the reliabilities of x and y, respectively. In the case of dichotomously scored items (such as Right = 1, Wrong = 0), the size of the highest possible correlation between two items is also a function of the item difficulties (p values). The more that two items differ in difficulty, the lower is their highest possible correlation, even when there is no measurement error.

2. In algebra, squaring a binomial such as $(a + b)$ is accomplished by multiplication, as follows:

$$
\begin{array}{r}
(a + b) \\
\times\ (a \times b) \\
\hline
ab + b^2 \\
a^2 +\ ab \\
\hline
a^2 + 2ab + b^2
\end{array}
$$

3. Consider the data in Table 4N.1, which shows the results of ten subjects who have taken a test made up of two items, *I* and *J,* with the answer to each item scored as Right $(= 1)$ or Wrong $(= 0)$. The variance of σ_i^2 of a single item is pq, where $p =$ the proportion passing and $q = 1 - p$. The variance of total scores σ_x^2 is $\Sigma x^2/N$, where x is the deviation of each person's total score from the mean. The covariance C_{ij} between items is the cross-products of the item deviation scores for each person, summed over all persons, and divided by N (the total number of persons). In the example in Table 4N.1, these values are

$$
\text{Item variances } \sigma_i^2 \begin{cases} \sigma_i^2 = .25. \\ \sigma_j^2 = .24. \end{cases}
$$

$$
\text{Item covariance } C_{ij} \quad = .10.
$$

$$
\text{Total variance } \sigma_x^2 \quad = .69.
$$

Table 4N.1

	Raw Scores[1]			Deviation Scores[2]		
	Item Score		Test Score	Item Score		Test Score
Subjects	*I*	*J*	*X*	*i*	*j*	*x*
a	1	1	2	+0.5	+0.4	+0.9
b	1	1	2	+0.5	+0.4	+0.9
c	1	1	2	+0.5	+0.4	+0.9
d	1	1	2	+0.5	+0.4	+0.9
e	1	0	1	+0.5	−0.6	−0.1
f	0	1	1	−0.5	+0.4	−0.1
g	0	1	1	−0.5	+0.4	−0.1
h	0	0	0	−0.5	−0.6	−1.1
i	0	0	0	−0.5	−0.6	−1.1
j	0	0	0	−0.5	−0.6	−1.1
Total	5	6	11	0	0	0
Mean[3]	.5	.6	1.1	0	0	0
σ^2	.25	.24	.69	.25	.24	.69

[1]Right = 1, Wrong = 0.
[2]The deviation score (denoted by lower-case letters) is the raw score minus the mean, for example, $x = X - \overline{X}$.
[3]Note that the item mean is the same as the item's p value (proportion passing). The mean of the distribution of test scores is the sum of the item means (or p values).

In equation 4.2 we see that $\sigma_x^2 = \Sigma\sigma_i^2 + 2\ \Sigma C_{ij}$. Substituting the values from our example into this equation, we see that

$$.69 = (.25 + .24) + 2(.10).$$

The correlation r_{ij} between items i and j is their covariance divided by the product of their standard deviation, that is $r_{ij} = C_{ij}/\sigma_i\sigma_j$. In the example preceding, the correlation r_{ij} between items i and j is $.10/(.5 \times .4899) = .4082$.

In practice, however, this is not the usual way of determining item intercorrelations. The most common method is by the phi coefficient, which is a product-moment correlation for dichotomized data. The relationship between a pair of items scored pass or fail is represented in a 2×2 contingency table, where A, B, C, and D are the frequencies in each of the four cells:

		Item J		
		Wrong	*Right*	
	Right	A	B	(A + B)
Item I				
	Wrong	C	D	(C + D)
		(A + C)	(B + D)	

The letters in the cells represent the number of subjects in each cell. The phi coefficient, ϕ_{ij}, which is exactly the same as the correlation coefficient r_{ij}, is

$$\phi_{ij} = \frac{BC - AD}{\sqrt{(A + B)\ (C + D)\ (A + C)\ (B + D)}} . \qquad \textbf{(4N.1)}$$

In terms of our example in Table 4N.1, this is

		Item J		
		Wrong	*Right*	
	Right	A 1	B 4	5 (A + B)
Item I				
	Wrong	C 3	D 2	5 (C + D)
		4 (A + C)	6 (B + D)	

$$\phi_{ij} = \frac{(4 \times 3) - (1 \times 2)}{\sqrt{5 \times 5 \times 4 \times 6}} = \frac{10}{24.4949} = .4082.$$

4. Equation 4.6 is related to the well-known Kuder–Richardson formula (K-R 20) for estimating the internal consistency reliability, r_{xx}, of a test:

$$r_{xx} = \left(\frac{\sigma_x^2 - \Sigma pq}{\sigma_x^2}\right) \left(\frac{n}{n - 1}\right), \qquad \textbf{(4N.2)}$$

where

$$\sigma_x^2 = \text{the total variance of test scores,}$$
$$\Sigma pq = \text{the sum of the item variances, and}$$
$$n = \text{the number of items in the test.}$$

The expression involving n is a correction factor needed to permit the maximum possible r_{xx} to equal 1. A test length limits the proportion of total variance that is attributable to the item covariances; the maximum possible value of this proportion is $(n - 1)/n$.

5. The size of the correlation between items depends in part on the difference in their difficulties. Only items of the same difficulty can have $r_{ij} = 1$. The maximum possible correlation is increasingly less than unity the greater the difference in item difficulties. Take two items i and j, with p values of .8 and .6, respectively. The following contingency table shows the proportion of subjects needed in each cell to produce the highest possible correlation, which is $r_{ij} = .6124$.

		Item *J*		
		Wrong	*Right*	
Item *I*	*Right*	.2	.6	.8 p_i
	Wrong	.2	0	.2 q_i
		.4	.6	
		q_i	p_i	

The highest possible correlation between two items with $p_i = .9$ and $p_j = .1$ is only $r_{ij} = .11$. The average item intercorrelation $\bar{r}_{ij}$ of a nine-item perfect Guttman scale is only .486; $\bar{r}_{ij}$ decreases as the number of items increases in a Guttman scale. The nine-item Guttman scale would yield the rectangular distribution of scores shown in part A of Figure 4.2. The variance components are

$$\sigma_x^2 = \Sigma pq + 2\Sigma r_{ij}\sigma_i\sigma_j,$$
$$8.25 = 1.65 + 6.60,$$

and the internal consistency reliability r_{xx} (by the Kuder–Richardson formula, see equation 4N.2) is .90. The highest possible correlation that a test score can have with another variable is the square root of its reliability. This perfect Guttman scale (of only nine items) thus cannot be correlated more than $\sqrt{.90} = .95$ with whatever it is that it measures, that is, the scores are a less than perfect measure of the hypothetical trait in question, yet it is the best measure possible with a test of only nine items. A perfect Guttman scale of ninety items, on the other hand, would be correlated .9945 with whatever trait it measures.

6. The average item intercorrelations $\bar{r}_{ij}$ of actual tests are quite low, generally falling between .10 and .20. Examples are Raven's Colored Progressive Matrices Test, $\bar{r}_{ij} = .20$; the Peabody Picture Vocabulary Test, $\bar{r}_{ij} = .14$; the Wechsler Adult Intelligence Scale, $\bar{r}_{ij} = .10$. Because these tests all have fairly large numbers of items (Raven = 36, PPVT = 150, WAIS = 153), their internal consistency reliabilities (see note 4) are quite high (Raven = .90, PPVT = .96, WAIS = .97).

7. Because the number of siblings within any one family is too small ever to demonstrate a normal distribution on any trait, the method of showing the normality of the distribution

of test scores within families has to be indirect. Differences between family means cannot enter into the distribution. Therefore we plot the distribution of absolute differences between all pairs of siblings within each family. When this has been done in large samples, it turns out that the distribution of absolute differences among sibling pairs does not differ appreciably from the form of the χ (chi) distribution, which is the theoretical distribution of absolute differences between all possible pairs of values in the normal distribution. Thus we can infer that the siblings' scores are normally distributed within families. The variance of this normal distribution is of course less (by approximately one-half) than the variance in the total population, which is comprised of the variance *within* families plus the variance *between* families.

8. The study of identical twins provides good evidence that the environmental influences on IQ are normally distributed. Because identical twins have exactly the same complement of genes, any difference between them must be attributable to environmental factors and errors of measurement. The distribution of absolute differences in IQ between identical twins reared apart does not differ significantly from the chi distribution, which means that the environmental components in the twins' IQs are normally distributed (see note 7; Jensen, 1970a).

9. Burt (1957) tried to determine whether this excess in the lower range of the IQ distribution is due to brain damage or other environmental factors as compared with purely genetic factors. He began with an unselected group of several thousand London children. Any child with signs of brain damage (other than low IQ) or from an extremely unfavorable environment was excluded. The resulting distribution of Stanford–Binet IQs of the remaining 4,523 children is shown in Figure 4N.1. This IQ distribution comes quite close to the normal curve (dashed line), but a statistical test for the goodness of fit shows that it departs significantly from normality. A discrepancy of this magnitude could occur by random sampling fluctuation less than once in a million samples if the distribution in the population were strictly normal, so it seems safe to say that this departure from normality is a genuine fact of nature. Again, the discrepancy consists of an excess of very low IQs. Thus, the true distribution of intelligence is represented not by the normal curve but by a particular kind of skewed curve that statisticians refer to as a Type IV curve (the continuous line shown in part B of Figure 4.2), so named by the English statistician Karl Pearson. The fact that there remains an excess of IQs below 60 despite the attempt to screen out cases of brain damage and severe environmental handicap strongly suggests that at least some part of this "bulge" at the lower end of the distribution has a genetic basis. It should be noted that the obtained distribution of IQs fits the normal curve almost perfectly in the IQ range from about 60 to 150.

10. The formula for the normal curve is

$$y = \frac{N}{\sigma\sqrt{2\pi}}\, e^{-(X-M)^2/2\sigma^2},$$

where

$y = $ the frequency of score X,
$M = $ the mean of the distribution,
$\sigma = $ the standard deviation of the distribution,
$N = $ the total number of scores or measurements,
$\pi = $ the mathematical constant 3.1416, and
$e = $ the base of natural logarithms, with a fixed value of 2.718.

Figure 4N.1.   Distribution of Stanford–Binet IQs of a sample of 4,523 London children from which all cases of diagnosed brain damage and extreme environmental deprivation have been excluded. A normal curve (dashed line) and Pearson's Type IV curve (continuous line) are superimposed on the actual data (stepwise curve). Note that the Type IV curve shows a closer fit to the data than does the normal curve.   (From Burt, 1963, p. 180)

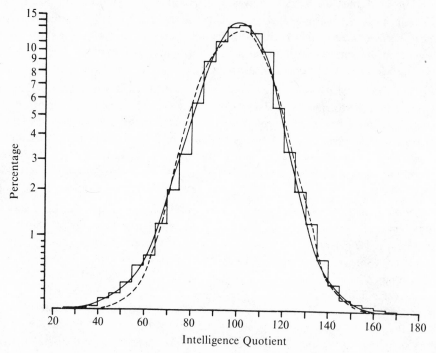

11. The usual statistical method for testing the goodness of fit of a theoretical curve to the obtained measurements is the χ^2 (chi squared) test, which is explicated in most statistics textbooks. It tells us the chance probability of finding discrepancies as large as were actually found between the theoretical (e.g., normal) distribution and the obtained distribution. If the chance probability is very small, say, 5 percent or 1 percent or less, we may feel safe in concluding that the discrepancy between the theoretical and obtained distributions is real and not merely the result of chance fluctuations due to imperfect sampling of the population. Figure 4N.2 shows a normal curve fitted to a distribution of 486 actual test scores. A χ^2 test shows that the discrepancies of the obtained values (the data in each column) differ from the normal curve by an amount that would occur by chance fluctuations in 15 percent or more of all similar samples from the population. A probability of 15 percent is much too large for us to be quite confident that the obtained sample distribution came from other than a normal distribution of scores in the population, and so we accept the hypothesis that the population distribution is normal.

12. The moments (m) about the mean of a distribution consist of the raw score deviations from the mean raised to the powers of 1, 2, 3, 4, and so on. Statisticians rarely use moments beyond the fourth.

The first moment is $\qquad\qquad m_1 = \Sigma(X-\bar{X})^1/N = 0.$
The second moment is the *variance*: $m_2 = \Sigma(X-X)^2/N = \sigma^2.$

The third moment is $m_3 = \Sigma(X-\bar{X})^3/N$.

The fourth moment is $m_4 = \Sigma(X-\bar{X})^4/N$.

An index of *skewness*, α, is $\alpha = m_3/\sigma^3$. For the normal curve $\alpha = 0$. Positive values of α indicate positive skewness and negative values indicate negative skewness.

An index of *kurtosis* (peakedness) is $\beta = m_4/\sigma^4$. For the normal curve, it is $\beta = 3$. Values of β greater than 3 indicate leptokurtosis (greater peakedness or piling up of scores in the middle of the distribution). Values of β less than 3 indicate platykurtosis (flattening of the distribution).

13. When the two groups are of the same size and have the same standard deviation, the formula for the point-biserial correlation depends only on the mean difference $\bar{d}$; the relationship between $\bar{d}$ and r_{pbs} is shown in Figure 4N.3.

14. The standard deviation σ_t of combined groups 1 and 2 may be obtained by the following formula, in which the subscript t refers to the total (i.e., combined) groups:

$$\sigma_t = \sqrt{\frac{N_1\,(\bar{X}_1^2 + \sigma_1^2) + N\,(\bar{X}_2^2 + \sigma_2^2)}{N_1 + N_2} - \bar{X}_t^2}\ . \qquad \textbf{(4N.3)}$$

15. The ordinate y of the normal curve for any value of z is the height of the curve at z, with y expressed on a scale that goes from 0 to .3898, which is the range of values of y between plus or minus infinity and the mean of z; that is, $y = .3898$ is the highest point of the curve. In mathematical terms,

$$y = \frac{1}{\sqrt{2\pi}}\, e^{-z^2/2}\ ,$$

where π is 3.1416 and e is the base of natural logarithms, 2.718. Values of y as a function of z are usually given in tables of the normal curve.

Figure 4N.2. A normal curve mathematically fitted to an actual distribution of 486 IQ scores. In this sample the obtained distribution does not depart significantly from the normal curve. (From Lewis, 1960, p. 229)

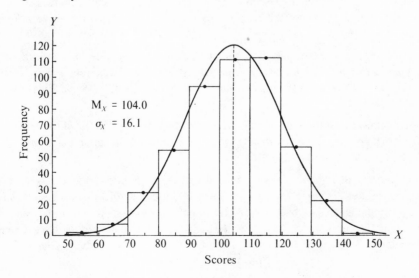

Figure 4N.3.   The relationship between the point-biserial correlation (r_{pbs}) and the mean difference ($\bar{d}$) between groups in σ units on the continuous variable, assuming equal σ's and equal N's in the two groups.

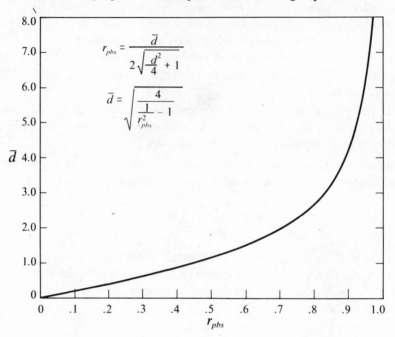

16. An index of skewness that can be applied to these data as presented is

$$\text{Skew} = \frac{(X_{90} - X_{50}) - (X_{50} - X_{10})}{(X_{90} - X_{10})} \, ,$$

(4N.4)

where X is the raw score at the percentile represented by the subscript. This index is an absolute scale of skewness ranging from 0 to ± 1. This index of skewness applied to a raw score distribution of 1,503 high school seniors taking the General Culture Test yields Skew = .21. For comparison, the normal curve has Skew = 0 and the curve in Figure 4.20 has Skew = .31.

17. Reviews of the extensive evidence for the approximately one standard deviation white–black difference in IQs and other mental test scores are to be found in Dreger and Miller (1960, 1968); Jensen (1973b); Loehlin, Lindzey, and Spuhler (1975); Shuey (1966); and Tyler (1965).

18. The logarithmic transformation of the IQ is $100[1 + \ln (IQ/100)]$, which leaves the transformed IQ of 100 still equal to 100. (ln = the natural or Napierian logarithm, which is 2.3026 times log n to the base 10.)

19. It also suggests that the more skewed distribution of Stanford–Binet IQs of black school-age children shown in Figure 4.21 is a result of the fact that these school children, though a random sample of blacks in the five southeastern states in which they attended school, are not a representative sample of the entire black population of the United States. The Wonderlic sample is probably more representative, but this is only speculative, since unfortunately the Wonderlic data, although obtained from every part of the United States, are not a random sample of the U.S. population but, rather, a self-selected sample of applicants for jobs in organizations that use the Wonderlic Personnel Test. Such persons may be less representative of the black than of the white population.

20. A good historical account of the development of the Binet scale and its descendants is provided by Tuddenham (1962, pp. 481–494).

21. Notice that this method of deriving mental age (MA) from the regression of raw score means on chronological age (CA) is equivalent to defining MA in terms of the average raw score obtained by a normative sample of a given CA. But MA could also be determined from the regression of mean CA on raw scores, which would define MA in terms of the average age of all persons attaining a given raw score. Because raw scores and CA are far from being perfectly correlated, the two regression lines (i.e., raw score on age and age on raw score) do not coincide. Therefore the MA would be different depending on which method is used. (Conventionally, the first method is most commonly used.) In a beautifully lucid and now famous article, L. L. Thurstone (1926) severely criticized the mental-age concept because of this ambiguous aspect of its definition; he urged that "we should discard the awkward mental age concept," and suggested replacing it with percentile scores or standardized scores (z scores) based on the mean and standard deviation of raw scores of the normative population within each CA interval. This, in fact, is what has been done in all modern intelligence tests, including the Stanford–Binet since 1960.

22. These examples are from the National Assessment Tests (Womer, 1970).

23. The best prediction that one can make of a person's future IQ on the basis of his or her present IQ is given by the formula

$$\hat{IQ} = r_{PF} (IQ - \overline{IQ}) + \overline{IQ},$$

where

$\hat{IQ}$ = the predicted future IQ,
r_{PF} = the known correlation between IQ at present (P) and future (F) ages, and
$\overline{IQ}$ = the mean IQ in the population of which the person is a member.

The standard error of estimate (i.e., of $\hat{IQ}$) is

$$SE_{\hat{IQ}} = \sigma \sqrt{1 - r_{PF}^2} ,$$

where σ is the standard deviation of the IQ in the population. Values of r_{PF} are discussed in Chapter 7, pp. 277–284.

Chapter 5

Varieties of Mental Test Items

Critics of mental testing rely heavily on popular misconceptions concerning the nature of the items or questions that make up intelligence tests. The public generally think of "IQ tests" as lists of questions calling for specific knowledge or information, especially of the kinds most apt to be acquired in school, in highbrow books, or in a cultured home. It is easy to pick out for display single items from the more than one hundred published intelligence tests that will reinforce this impression. To gain a more accurate idea of what makes up an intelligence test, we need to look at a representative sample of the varieties of items that are actually used in the many tests of general ability. In fact, in the measurement of *general* ability, it might be said that *variety* is the name of the game, and necessarily so.

Here we shall consider only the varieties of items that make up tests of general mental ability or intelligence, as these are the tests that are the most disputed and most misunderstood. The contents of many other types of tests, such as achievement tests in specific scholastic subjects and work-sample aptitude tests for specific vocational skills, can be more easily imagined than the contents of intelligence tests. Intelligence tests constitute only about 10 percent of all published psychological tests currently in print. Table 5.1 shows the main types of published standardized psychological tests.

Here we shall focus on types of *items* rather than on whole tests, because nearly all intelligence tests consist of some selection of these various types of items. Examination of item types is the most direct way of gaining some insight into the mental processes called for in tests of intelligence. Descriptions and critical reviews of each of the many published tests can be found in the seven *Mental Measurement Yearbooks* edited by Oscar K. Buros (1938, 1941, 1949, 1953, 1959, 1965, 1972). Several well-known textbooks on psychological testing also present detailed descriptions of some of the more widely used tests (Anastasi, 1976; Cronbach, 1970; Vernon, 1960).

Overview

A few general principles about intelligence test items should be kept in mind while examining any specific item.

Lack of Resemblance to "Real Life." At the outset, one should realize that test items, and even whole tests, are in an important sense much more simple and clear-cut

Table 5.1. Psychological tests by major classifications. (From Buros, 1972, p. xxxi)

Classification	Number	% of Total
Vocations	181	15.6%
Personality	147	12.7
Miscellaneous	129	11.1
INTELLIGENCE	121	10.5
Reading	102	8.8
Mathematics	96	8.3
Science	80	6.9
Foreign languages	75	6.5
English	55	4.8
Social studies	53	4.6
Speech & hearing	38	3.3
Achievement batteries	36	3.1
Sensory-motor	20	1.7
Fine arts	14	1.2
Multi-aptitude	10	0.9
Total	1,157	100.0%

than most "real-life" situations that one thinks of as showing intelligence. This is an intentional and practical necessity in a standardized test. An essential part of the meaning of "standardized" is that the stimulus or situation eliciting the behavior that is to be observed, rated, or graded should be relatively unambiguous and objective, in the sense that it is perceived consistently as the same task by all persons and by the same person at different times. It should present no choice and no difficulty in terms of the subject's knowing what he or she is *supposed* to do. (Whether the subject *can* do it or not is another matter; that is what the test item is intended to determine.) To achieve this simplicity and clarity of purpose usually results in what may appear to be a kind of artificiality or impracticality of the test items, a lack of resemblance to the kinds of problems on which most of us actually have to use our "brains" in our everyday lives. But this may not be a serious matter if it can be successfully argued that the complex situations of real life that call for intelligence or demonstrate intelligent behavior can be analyzed into essentially the same basic components of ability or mental processes that are called on in a simpler, more pure form in the items of intelligence tests. The fact that intelligence test scores can predict practical, real-life criteria and accord with commonsense judgments of intelligence, brightness, cleverness, and the like is good evidence that the "unrealistic" test items must share something in common with the complex real-life situations in which a person's intelligence is judged in commonsense terms.

By analogy, consider a test of running ability. All contestants start in a certain position with their toe on a line. They are required to run 100 yards down a straight and narrow path marked off by white lines, and they are not to begin until they hear a gunshot. Each contestant's score is the number of seconds that it takes him or her to run to the finish line. What could be a more artificial situation? We are never called on to do this in real life. When we have to run to catch our bus, for example, we may not be on a smooth dirt track but on a slippery wet street; we may be carrying a briefcase, an umbrella, or packages; we may have to dodge other pedestrians; and so on. The real situation always seems to involve many other factors and conditions than the test situation. Yet our simple running test may be a better predictor of how fast persons can run overall in a great variety of real-life situations than we could predict from any single one of those more complex situations, any one of which would require that we take into consideration all the other factors in addition to running ability that entered into the situation. If running ability per se, as we intended to measure it in one test, is an *unimportant* factor in real-life situations that involve running, it should not correlate with speed in these real-life situations. We might find, for example, that we could make better predictions if our test combined the running speeds measured under a number of different conditions—running on a slippery versus a dry surface, a clear runway versus dodging obstacles, running along straight versus zigzag lines, and so on. All these conditions could not effectively be combined in a single 100-yard running trial, equivalent to a single test item, but several trials could be given, each incorporating a different feature. The subject's total score summed for all the conditions would be a measure of his general running ability. The test as a whole still will not closely resemble all the running situations that one encounters in life, but it will contain the essential components of most such situations. Much the same sort of thing is also true of intelligence tests. To understand this properly involves discussing definitions and theories of intelligence, but such discussion is best postponed until we have taken a look at the kinds of items that actually make up intelligence tests.

Indifference of the Indicator.   It is important to understand the principle enunciated by the English psychologist Charles E. Spearman (1923), known as "the indifference of the indicator" (or "the indifference of the fundaments"). It means that in an intelligence test the specific content of the items is unessential, so long as it is apprehended or perceived in the same way by all persons taking the test. Any given item cannot, of course, be without content, but the content is a mere vehicle for the essential elements of intelligence test items. The essential elements involve the expression of relationships. According to this view, there is no limit to the number or specific kinds of items that can measure intelligence. The number and variety of items that can be invented for intelligence tests is limited only by the imagination of the test constructor. But, if the items are to measure intelligence, they must all possess certain abstract properties, described by Spearman as presenting the possibility for *eduction of relations and correlates*. This has much the same meaning as inductive ("relations") and deductive ("correlates") reasoning. *Eduction of relations* means inferring the general rule from specific instances (i.e., induction). *Eduction of correlates* means making up or recognizing a specific instance when given one other specific instance and the general rule (i.e., deduction). Later on we shall see how Spearman's principle of "eduction of relations and correlates" applies to a great variety of specific items.

Spearman's principle of "indifference of the indicator" had its origin as a corollary of his two-factor theory of intelligence, which held that every cognitive test or test item measured a general factor g that is common to all items and a specific factor s that is unique to the particular item and not shared by any other items. When a large number of item scores is summed, the uncorrelated specific factors cancel out, so that the total score reflects individual differences only in the factor common to all of the items, called the g factor. But it was later discovered that, in addition to the two factors g and s, there are also "group factors" that are common to groups of items, such as verbal, numerical, and spatial. Items thus can measure certain group factors as well as the general factor common to all items, and this fact, later acknowledged by Spearman, necessitates some qualification of his principle of "indifference of the indicator." When we admit the existence of group factors, as the evidence now compels us to do, we must logically recognize that items may be composed in such a way as to measure g plus one or more group factors.

Only by including a great variety of items that measure many different group factors as well as g can we determine (by means of factor analysis) the degree to which the total scores on the test reflect individual differences in g and how much of the variance is attributable to various group factors. All present-day intelligence tests predominantly measure g, but they differ somewhat from one another in the extent to which the scores also represent an amalgam of g plus certain group factors. After g, a verbal factor is most prominent in most intelligence tests, especially in group intelligence tests intended to measure scholastic aptitude.

If intelligence could be measured only by certain standard or conventional test items, however, the principle of "indifference of the indicator" would be wholly invalid, and it would be impossible to go on making up "new" and "different" intelligence tests that all measure pretty much the same thing. But it is a fact of the utmost importance that the very same intelligence can be measured by tests that differ markedly in form and content, just so long as they at some point require the process of relation eduction. Test constructors and publishers would be in serious trouble if this were not the case, as tests and test items are copyrighted. If one wants to publish a new or better test, one cannot borrow the test items from all the other tests but must make up one's own items from scratch. In practice, however, no modern test constructor ignores what has been learned from analyses of past and present tests or from the important principles discovered by Spearman. As a consequence, new tests of intelligence do not look very new, although they may differ in every detail of form and content or other superficial properties. One still can easily see Spearman's principle of "eduction of relations and correlates" in most of the items. No attempt to ignore this principle in intelligence test construction and yet produce either a practical or a theoretically defensible test of intelligence has had much success.

Low Item × Total Score Correlation.   One must realize that no single test item is a very good measure of intelligence (or whatever it is that the total score on the test measures). This fact is in large part the basis for the plausibility of those criticisms of IQ tests that consist of singling out specific items as examples of the supposed triviality of what is measured by the test. For the most part, this is a psychometrically unwarranted basis for criticism, as any *single* item in a good intelligence test measures intelligence much *less* than it measures a number of other factors. This is true even of the items in the best intelligence tests available. *There simply are no "pure" measures of intelligence at the level of single items.*

Items are very "impure" measures indeed. The average correlation of Stanford–Binet test "items" with total score is about .60, which means that only about 36 percent of the variance in the typical "item" reflects the intelligence measured by the Stanford–Binet total score or IQ. The remaining 64 percent of the "item's" variance reflects something other than intelligence, assuming that the total score or IQ is a good index of intelligence. I have used the word "item" in quotes, because many of the Stanford–Binet "items" on which this correlation was based are not really single items, but are small subtests, or groups of items, or two or three trials on a single type of item. When we look at the correlation of really single items with total score on most intelligence tests, we seldom find correlations higher than about .40, and the average correlation is closer to .30. To get a direct impression of what a correlation of .40 consists of, imagine that we have a single hypothetical item that is a perfect measure of intelligence and that divides the population exactly in half. (In other words, the hypothetical and actual items both have a difficulty, *p,* of .50.) A correlation of .40 between the hypothetical perfect item and the actual item, both given to the same group of one hundred persons, would look like this:

		Perfect Item		
		Fail	*Pass*	
	Pass	15	35	50
Actual Item				
	Fail	35	15	50
		50	50	100

Notice that the actual item correctly classifies 70 percent of the persons and misses on 30 percent. But even a correlation of zero would result in 50 percent "hits" and 50 percent "misses," just by the laws of chance. So the result on the actual item predicts the result on the perfect item only 20 percentage points better than chance. Remember, this is about the best we can expect to find for single items in our current tests of intelligence. If the average correlation of items with the total test score is between .3 and .4, as is the case for most tests of intelligence, and if the total score on such tests is not a *perfect* measure of intelligence, as we know is the case, then a prediction of 20 percentage points better than chance is probably close to the upper limit of the power (or validity) of our best test items, taken singly, for reflecting intelligence. It is little wonder that inspection of single items leaves one with the feeling, "Could passing or failing this trivial-looking item really measure anything important?"

Single items gain their importance only by the summation of a large number of them. Each and every item must correlate with intelligence to at least a small degree, so that this small factor in each item is, so to speak, distilled out by summation, and whatever else it is that each item measures must be sufficiently varied from item to item so that it will tend to average out, that is, algebraically sum to zero. The total score then should be a measure of intelligence more than of anything else. The oft-asked question "But does it *really* measure intelligence?" is postponed to the next chapter.

Eduction of Relations and Correlates.   The common factor in the test items that summate in the total score was described by Spearman as eduction—"the eduction of relations and correlates." In viewing typical items from a variety of tests, one is usually able to discern the eductive element in the item. It most often assumes one of two forms—relations or correlates—which Spearman (1923) illustrated in the following way.

In the first diagram, *A* and *B* are what Spearman called *fundaments,* which are given, and *R* is a relationship between them, to be educed by the subject (hence the broken line). Fundaments are the mental elements between which a relation mediates. A fundament calls for *apprehension* rather than eduction. *Apprehension,* in Spearman's terminology, is the principle that any lived experience tends to evoke immediately a knowing of its character and experience. It is direct perception without inference, or recognition based on familiarity. Apprehension is thus more primal than eduction. A simple example of diagram 1: *A* and *B* are the words "good" and "bad"; the relationship is "opposite." In the second diagram the subject is given a fundament *A* and a relation *R* and must educe a correlate *C*. For example, "good"—"opposite" = "bad." Many test items will be seen to take one of these forms, which most seem to characterize items that have the largest correlations with the total score. (However, there are some noteworthy exceptions, to be mentioned shortly.) The content or vehicle for the eduction of relations and correlates is quite unimportant, with the proviso that the given fundaments are clearly perceived and known to the subject by apprehension, as Spearman used this term. The subject must first know the elements of the test item and understand the requirements of the task for it to reflect the subject's power of eduction. It is largely because these prerequisites for testing intelligence are so difficult to fulfill in the case of very young children that "infant intelligence tests" are made up of quite different kinds of items than those in tests that are appropriate for older children and adults. Also, infant tests clearly do not measure the same ability that we identify as intelligence in older children. This is not because intelligence itself is mainly learned or acquired through experience, but because the vehicles for testing it—a wide variety of fundaments—depend on learning and experience for their acquisition. The infant intelligence tests are better called tests of perceptual-motor development. They assess apprehension of fundaments much more than eduction of relations and correlates. But, beyond early childhood, standard intelligence tests attempt to assess mainly the subject's ability to *think,* as reflected in the mental manipulation of words, numbers, symbols, concepts, and ideas.

Classification of Tests and Items

Intelligence tests and items can be classified in several ways: individual and group; verbal, nonverbal, and performance; culture loaded and culture reduced; altitude and breadth; speed and power. The reader should gain some familiarity with each of these terms.

Individual and Group Tests. Individual tests, like the Stanford–Binet and Wechsler, are administered individually by a trained tester. Individual administration is required for many of the items in such tests because they involve equipment that has to be manipulated and presented in standard ways by the tester, and in some cases the subject's performance on a given task has to be timed with a stopwatch. Also, individual tests contain items in which the subject's performance usually has to be observed directly to be recorded and scored by the tester. The subject does not write his or her answers, and many of the responses are nonverbal performances, such as putting colored blocks together in a certain pattern, working a kind of jigsaw puzzle, or arranging pictures in a logical sequence.

The chief advantage of an individual test is that the tester is usually able to tell whether a subject has understood the directions, and, if the child has not, to repeat them. Also, the tester observes whether or not the subject is conscientiously attending to the assigned tasks and is putting forth effort to comply with the tester's requests. A clinical psychologist's test report usually comments on these points. The clinician also takes note of external distractions should they occur, as well as the emotional state of the subject and the possibility of internal distractions such as anxiety, too great wariness, or response inhibition. Through the personal experience of testing a great many persons under standard conditions, the good clinician develops a "feel" for whether he or she is obtaining a "good" test in any particular case, and, if the tester feels some doubt about the results or the conditions under which the test results were obtained, the tester will state this in his or her report and recommend retesting the subject on another occasion. Usually more than one test will be given to see if they all yield similar results.

At times a clinician will see a child on several occasions in a play therapy room before testing the child, to ensure that the child will feel familiar and at ease with the tester when it comes to the test situation. A clinician tries, within the constraints of the standardized administration procedures, to elicit the best performance of which the subject is capable. Individual administration also permits observation of the nonscorable or qualitative aspects of the subject's performance. Was the subject cooperative? Did the child try? Does the child give up easily on the harder items? Does the child's attention wander? Does the child make unusual or bizarre responses? Is the child slow and deliberate, or overly quick and impulsive? Is the child verbose or taciturn? And how might any of these attitudes affect the score? The clinician is also called on to *interpret* the subject's test score against the background of the testing conditions, the subject's attitudes and personality, emotional state, and cultural and educational background. I recall giving the Wechsler Adult Intelligence Scale to a particularly hostile young man on whom a clinical assessment, including intelligence testing, was ordered by the juvenile court. On the verbal subtests—Information, Similarities, Comprehension, and so on—he formally scored below 80 IQ. Yet on nearly every item he said something to reveal that he actually knew the correct answer. His responses usually took the form of criticizing the items. To the hardest Information question, "What is the Apocrypha?" he answered, "How would I know? Why don't you ask a priest that one? I personally think the *whole* Bible is bunk." I estimated his Verbal IQ at 140 plus, despite his apparent unwillingness to give strictly scorable answers to all but the simplest verbal items. For some reason he showed no such antipathy for the nonverbal or performance subtests and obtained a Performance IQ of 136.

Individual testing is indicated whenever the test score (and its interpretation) enter into a decision of any personal importance concerning an individual. Selection testing for higher education, the armed forces, and personnel selection seems to be a warranted exception to this rule, for in these cases the subject is an applicant trying to qualify for admission and is presumably self-motivated to do his best. Even in these situations where group tests are used there should always exist the opportunity to be retested on an equivalent form of the test.

Group tests, administered to a number of subjects at once, invariably require the subjects to write answers or make marks on specially prepared answer sheets. The test instructions are usually printed on the first page of the test for all subjects to read, and usually the tester also reads the instructions aloud and asks the subjects if there are any questions about the instructions before they begin. Group tests may or may not be timed. Timed tests are more usual, however, because they are administratively convenient and also because timing makes for more standardized testing conditions. Except for the fact that group tests obviously do not permit the clinical observations that are possible in individual testing, the scores derived from the two types of tests are highly comparable in the vast majority of subjects. Group testing, however, has a greater risk of error for the atypical subject.

Most, but not all, group tests are verbal and involve reading or writing. It should always be determined independently if the test and instructions are appropriate for the literacy level of all the individuals taking the test.

Verbal, Nonverbal, and Performance Tests.   Verbal items involve language, spoken or written. They are therefore generally unsuitable for persons who are not familiar with the language. Individually administered verbal tests depend on the subject's understanding the spoken language of the tester, but they seldom require the subject to read anything. The subject must also be able to respond in spoken language.

Verbal items in group tests are of two types: one requires only the ability to understand spoken language, the other requires reading. In the first case the tester asks questions to which the subject responds by making appropriate marks on the test sheet, as in response to the tester's question: "Which of the pictures in this row is of a dog? Draw a circle around the dog." Such verbal group tests are commonly used in testing children in the primary grades, where reading skills are not yet sufficiently developed to serve as a medium for test items.

Verbal items that depend on reading are usually constructed in such a way that the cognitive demands of the item are considerably greater than the reading demands per se. For example, a 10-year-old verbal intelligence test item will have a reading difficulty at the 7- or 8-year level, so as to minimize variance due to reading ability per se and maximize the variance on eduction or reasoning. Given the ability to read, therefore, tests of verbal intelligence are not primarily measures of reading ability. Because reading is merely a vehicle for the items, it is kept as simple as possible. For this reason we usually find a higher correlation between verbal and nonverbal IQ tests than between the verbal IQ and scores on a reading test. In a large sample of school children who had taken the Lorge–Thorndike Intelligence Test, for example, we found that the correlation of a reading test (Paragraph Meaning subtest of the Stanford Achievement Test) with verbal IQ is .52; but the reading scores correlate almost as highly (.47) with the nonverbal IQ, which requires no reading at all. The correlation between the verbal and nonverbal IQs is .70 in this sample. Obviously the verbal IQ reflects reading ability per se to only a relatively small degree. (The partial correlation between reading and verbal IQ, holding nonverbal IQ constant, is .29.)

Nonverbal tests require no reading but are based on figural materials, pictures of objects, geometric patterns, symbols, and the like. The directions are usually verbal, but a good nonverbal test begins with items of any particular type that are so simple that virtually all subjects can catch on to the requirements of the task without verbal instructions, or with pantomimed instructions by the tester. Such tests are suitable for nonliterate subjects or those who know only a foreign language. Nonverbal items are answered by making marks of some kind on the test or on a specially prepared answer sheet.

Performance tests are nonverbal and require the subject to perform some action or manipulation, although the items are not intended to measure manipulative skill or manual dexterity per se. Perceptual-motor skills contribute very little to the variance of performance tests of intelligence, which consist of items such as form boards, paper folding, block designs, jigsaw puzzles, mazes, stringing beads to match a pattern, and copying simple geometric figures. The scoring criteria on performance tests are often complex: they take account of the correctness of the performance (e.g., how well does the subject's block design match the model he was supposed to copy?); the time taken to complete it (or whether the criterion performance was reached within a given time limit); or the resemblance between the subject's product (e.g., the subject's attempt to copy a geometric figure) and standard specimens that have been scaled or rated.

Culture Loaded versus Culture Reduced. This distinction must be viewed as a continuum rather than a dichotomy. Items that make use of scholastic types of knowledge or skills (e.g., reading, arithmetic) or items in which the fundaments consist of artifacts peculiar to a particular period, locality, or culture are considered to be "culture loaded." (Culture *loaded* should not be confused with culture *biased;* this is an important distinction to be elaborated in Chapter 9. Culture-loaded items may or may not be culture biased.) Culture-reduced items are nonverbal and performance items that do not involve content that is peculiar to a particular period, locality, or culture, or skills that are specifically taught in school. Items involving pictures of cultural artifacts such as vehicles, furniture, musical instruments, or household appliances, for example, are culture loaded as compared with culture-reduced items involving lines, circles, triangles, and rectangles.

Breadth and Altitude. This distinction was first suggested by the famous American psychologist Edward Lee Thorndike (1874–1949) in his pioneering book *The Measurement of Intelligence* (1927). "Breadth" of intellect is reflected in the amount of relatively simple information that a person has acquired about a wide variety of things. The more information the individual possesses about the world, the greater is said to be that person's intellectual "breadth." "Altitude," on the other hand, has to do with mental power—how difficult or complex a problem the person can solve in any given sphere. Conceptually, breadth and altitude are quite different. Think of passing the introductory course in every department of a university as compared with going all the way through a course of study, from introductory course to Ph.D., in one field, especially if the subject matter is very hierarchical, as in mathematics or the physical sciences. Or consider the difference between knowing how to play moderately well each of twenty different games—checkers, chess, backgammon, and bridge, for example—and being a world-champion chess player. Or knowing how to play a dozen different musical instruments as compared with playing one instrument like a Heifetz or Rubinstein.

According to Thorndike, tests could be designed to reflect either altitude or breadth. Altitude items generally call for eduction, reasoning, problem solving, and they minimize the importance of specific factual knowledge in arriving at the correct answer. Breadth items involve a wide variety of information, no item of which is conceptually complex, difficult, or esoteric. For example, a vocabulary test of the words: *clef, countersink, deciduous, half-nelson, halogen, light-year, parboil, starboard.* Each of these is "easy" for anyone with even a casual and superficial knowledge of music, carpentry, botany, wrestling, chemistry, astronomy, cooking, and sailing. One can imagine a 100-item test of this type, based on simple knowledge in a great many different spheres. It would constitute a test of *breadth* of intellect.

The distinction between breadth and altitude is seldom seen in the recent literature on intelligence, most likely because, even though altitude and breadth are a formally or conceptually valid distinction, they apparently do not represent essentially different mental abilities. Correlational analyses (e.g., *factor analysis,* ★ to be explained in Chapter 6) do not distinguish separate abilities involved in measures of breadth and altitude. The measures are so highly correlated as to seem to be measuring essentially the same general ability. E. L. Thorndike (1927, pp. 388–397) reported correlations between various measures of altitude and breadth in the range from .8 to .9; corrected for attenuation (i.e., unreliability of measurement), the correlations are close to unity. An adequate theory of intelligence should be able to account for the high correlation between altitude and breadth. More intelligent persons not only can reason through more complex and difficult problems, they also acquire more bits of simple information from their life experiences.

Speed and Power.   In taking most *individually* administered tests, the subject does not have to attempt every item in the whole test. The items are arranged in order of difficulty, from easy to hard, and the tester usually begins testing the subject at a point in the sequence where it seems likely that the subject will be able to get, say, at least five (or some other specified number) consecutive correct answers. If the subject fails one of the first five items given to him or her, the tester moves down the scale of difficulty until the subject has obtained five consecutive correct answers. Then the subject moves up the scale of difficulty until he or she has, say, five consecutive failures (or fails, say, six out of the last eight items presented). Because the items are steeply graded in level of difficulty, there is a high probability that the subject would have passed all the items that rank easier than the first five consecutive items he or she got right, and so the subject is given full credit for all the easier items without having to take them. Likewise, there is a high probability that none of the more difficult items would be passed beyond the five consecutively failed items, and so it is assumed that the subject would have failed all the rest. This procedure makes testing more efficient, it saves the subject from the boredom of too many easy items and the discouragement of too many failed items, and it ensures that most of the testing time will be spent on those items of the test that are the most discriminating at the particular subject's level of ability.

In group testing, this desirable procedure obviously cannot be applied. All subjects must start at the very beginning of the test. How far a subject can go will depend on the number and difficulty of the items and the time allowed. If there are a great many very easy items and the time allowed is too short to permit even the fastest subjects to attempt every item, the test stands at the one extreme of the speed test–power test continuum. If enough time is allowed for even the slowest subject to attempt every item, but the items are steeply graded in difficulty so that they will discriminate among subjects even with unlimited time, the test stands at the other extreme of the speed–power continuum.

Most group tests in current use stand somewhere between these two extremes. They are timed, but they allow enough time for the majority of subjects to reach their own ceiling of difficulty. That is, the items are graded steeply enough in difficulty so that beyond some point for a given individual there is very low probability that the subject will get the item right even if there was no time limit at all—that person simply does not know the answer or cannot solve the problem and begins to guess at the answers. Enough time is allowed for the majority of subjects to reach this difficulty ceiling, which of course differs from one subject to another. Subjects spend little time on the easy items and increasingly more time as the items increase in difficulty, until a sheer guessing level is reached, beyond which time is practically irrelevant.

The effect of the time limit on test scores should be known for every timed test. However, this information is commonly lacking in test manuals. Investigations have shown that, when the items are evenly graded in difficulty and have plenty of "top" (i.e., very difficult items), and the test is not too long for the time available (i.e., the fast students can finish although they reach their difficulty ceiling before the end of the test), giving subjects additional time beyond the prescribed time limit adds very little to the score and has little effect on the rank order of subjects' scores. Studies of the Otis IQ test illustrate this nicely (Cronbach, 1960, p. 222). The Otis Verbal IQ test has a time limit of 30 minutes. When subjects are allowed an extra 15 minutes (i.e., 50 percent more time), they increase their total score an average of 1.5 percent. The Otis Non-Verbal IQ test allows 20 minutes; when subjects are given an extra 30 minutes (i.e., 150 percent more time), they increase their scores an average of 1.7 percent. The Henmon–Nelson IQ test has a time limit of 30 minutes; giving subjects an extra 20 minutes (i.e., 67 percent more time) increases their scores an average of 6.3 percent.

If the increase in score leaves unaltered the subject's rank order, the speed factor is of little importance. That is, the time or speed factor does not contaminate the scores with some ability or trait extraneous to what the test attempts to measure, in this case, intelligence. Usually the correlation between strictly timed and leniently timed administration is as high as the reliability of the test. When the correlation between the two timed conditions falls significantly below the reliability, the recommended time limit should be viewed with suspicion. It means that the speed factor is given too much weight in the test scores, when what we really want to measure is mental power rather than some kind of "personal tempo" factor. The personal tempo factor actually has little if any correlation with intelligence. E. L. Thorndike (1927, pp. 400–401) tried to determine the correlation between speed and altitude. To measure speed he used a large number of quite easy items and recorded the time that subjects required to complete a given number of such easy items without error. To measure altitude he gave subjects a succession of items steeply graded in difficulty; the altitude score was the difficulty level beyond which the subject failed 50 percent or more of the items. The correlations between the measure of speed (the reciprocal of time) and of altitude averaged about .40 in several groups (about .46 when corrected for attenuation).

This correlation suggests that the time that subjects require for the easy items that they all can do is not measuring the same thing as the number of steeply graded items that persons can get right without time limit. In other words, it indicates the presence of a speed factor that is independent of a power or altitude factor as a source of variance in test scores. The correlation of about .40 does not necessarily mean that the speed factor is correlated at all with the altitude factor, because the items used to measure speed still had some low level of difficulty so that these items were not a pure measure of the speed factor. We know that the average time required per item is correlated with the item's difficulty.

One can measure a speed factor in almost pure form only by divesting the timed task as completely as possible of any cognitive difficulty whatsoever. The Making X's Test is such a device. Subjects are asked to make X's in rows of "boxes," 300 "boxes" in all, with a time limit of 3 minutes. The subject's score is the number of X's he makes in this time. There are highly reliable individual differences. It was found in large samples of children 9 to 12 years of age that scores on this speed test had low but significant correlations (averaging about .20) with a general intelligence factor determined from timed tests (Jensen, 1971a). The factor common to both the speed test (Making X's) and the timed intelligence tests may be motivation, as it is generally believed that motivation affects speed but not power. Speeded tests composed of many easy items have been shown to reflect motivation much more than untimed or liberally timed "power" tests. As Guilford (1954, p. 369) notes in reviewing this evidence, "Thus, speed conditions where items are not very easy open the door to many uncontrolled determiners of individual differences in scores."

In what is probably the best experimental study of the matter, the correlation between subjects' speed scores and power scores, when difficulty level and response accuracy were controlled, is close to zero for all kinds of test items (Tate, 1948). Thus it appears that a personal speed factor exists that is independent of mental power but that can contribute to variance on mental tests that are timed inappropriately. An important part of the validity evidence for all time tests should be some indication of the extent to which a speed factor enters into the score variance.

The items in some tests, like Raven's Progressive Matrices, are arranged in cycles of graded difficulty, each group beginning with easy items and gradually advancing to more difficult. The full range of difficulty is repeated in each of the several cycles comprising the test. Such a test must be administered with a liberal time limit so that all subjects may attempt every item. If a more severe time limit must be imposed, it should apply to each of the separate cycles of the test, so that every subject gets a chance at the easy items at the beginning of each section and does not waste too much time on the items that lie beyond the subject's difficulty ceiling.

How Tests Are Constructed

A standardized mental test is a product of creative invention, critical judgment, and statistical winnowing. The process begins, of course, with some definitions or notions of the trait that one wants to measure and some idea of the kinds of behavior that would constitute observable and quantifiable instances of the trait in question. This aspect is largely a matter of experience, psychological insight, and the test constructor's particular theory, whether explicit or implicit, of the essential nature of the trait that the constructor wishes to measure. A test gains acceptance to a large extent in terms of consensus among psychometricians that the specific bits of behavior elicited by the test are adequately representative of the trait the test claims to measure.

Such is the general background for item invention. One keeps in mind, too, characteristics of the population for which the test is to be appropriate—age, educational level, language, and cultural background—and whether it is to be an individual test or a group test, for this will determine the types of items that can be included.

After a large pool of items is constructed—perhaps anywhere from fifty to several hundreds—they are submitted one by one to careful scrutiny and critical judgment, either by the "item writer" (as he or she is usually labeled) or by a panel of several judges. This step in test construction, if properly done, is laborious and painstaking. Each item is critically examined for what might be termed formal defects, as in the case of verbal items: Is the question as clearly and simply stated as possible? Does the punctuation add to clarity? Are the distractors (i.e., error choices in multiple-choice items) stylistically similar so as not to give hints as to which is the correct answer? Is the level of reading difficulty appropriate for the majority of the intended population? Are words with peculiar regional or local meanings avoided? In the case of nonverbal and performance items: Are the pictures or figures clear and aesthetically spaced? Do the tasks make too much demand on sensory or motor abilities when these are not the main factor the test purports to measure? Are two or more items so similar as to be redundant? And so on. The directions to the subject for taking the tests are also scrutinized for possible ambiguities, difficulty level, and so on. In the process of item editing, some items are retained, some are discarded, and others are revamped in hopes of improving them.

The next step is item tryout. The whole pool of items is given as a test to a large number of subjects who are typical of the population for which the test is intended. These data then are used for an elaborate set of statistical procedures known as *item analysis.* We cannot go into all the technical aspects of item analysis at this point. But the main points of information it yields are (1) *item difficulty,* that is, percentage passing each item, which may be determined separately for each age group and each sex; (2) *item discrimination,* that is, the correlation of each item with the total score on the test, which indicates to what extent a particular item measures whatever is measured by the test as a whole; (3) *error or distractor analysis,* that is, in multiple-choice items with several response alternatives we wish to know if each of the distractors (wrong alternatives) has a fair proportion of the error responses. Distractors that are very seldom selected as compared with others are nonfunctional, and their presence may spuriously affect the difficulty of the item or weaken its correlation with the total score. Items with a seldom-used distractor are discarded or rewritten.

This item analysis information is the basis for selecting the items that will go into the test for standardization. Those items are selected that show the best correlation with total score and also result in a suitable and evenly graded range of item difficulties. (In some tests, items are discarded if they discriminate between the sexes, or the items are selected so as to balance out the sex discriminations, thereby making the overall average item difficulty the same in both groups.) The total number of items included in the final version of the test will depend on practical considerations, such as testing time available in a given setting, or a tolerable time limit for a particular age group, and on the reliability of the test. The reliability of a test increases with the number of items, but the increase in reliability as a function of test length follows a curve of diminishing returns.

The final step is the standardization or norming of the test by giving it to a large representative or random sample of a clearly specified population as a basis for computing the mental age, percentile, standard score, or IQ equivalents of the obtained raw scores.

These are the bare essentials of test construction. Depending on the nature and purpose of the test, there may be additional procedures, such as selecting items in terms of their correlations with other standardized tests claiming to measure the same trait or in terms of their correlation with outside criteria, such as school grades, ratings of job performance, or ability to succeed in some course of training. These so-called validation procedures are usually undertaken over a long period of time after the initial standardization of the test. It is largely for this reason that older tests on which much validation data have accumulated are so hard to replace by newer tests, however excellent. Test users rely considerably on the cumulative evidence of a test's validity or on some kind of experience with the meaning of its scores. Therefore test users are often reluctant to exchange old and tried tests for newer models whose properties are not yet so fully known. For a new test to compete successfully in the market with already established tests demands a tremendous expenditure in test development and research, which can be afforded by only the largest test-publishing firms such as the Psychological Corporation and the Educational Testing Service. To produce a new general intelligence test that would be a really significant improvement over existing instruments would be a multimillion-dollar project requiring a large staff of test construction experts working for several years. Today we possess the necessary psychometric technology for producing considerably better tests than are now in popular use. The principal hindrances are copyright laws, vested interests of test publishers in the established tests in which they have already made enormous investments, and the market economy for tests. Significant improvement of tests is not an attractive commercial venture initially and would probably have to depend on large-scale and long-term subsidies from government agencies and private foundations.

Development of Tests of General Ability

The Mental Tests of Galton and Cattell

The first systematic attempts actually to *measure* intelligence are generally credited to the British scientist Sir Francis Galton (1822–1911) and the American psychologist James McKeen Cattell (1860–1944). Cattell, after receiving his doctorate in experimental psychology in Wilhelm Wundt's (1832–1920) laboratory in Leipzig, Germany, spent several postdoctoral years working with Galton. Cattell later headed Columbia University's Psychology Department and became a founder of the American Psychological Association.

The Galton–Cattell approach to the measurement of mental ability proved disappointing at the time, even in the eyes of its originators. The fault was not with Galton's notions about general mental ability, but with an historically unfortunate choice of measuring instruments, dictated largely by the prevailing ideas at that time about how psychology could become a science. The experimental physical sciences, especially chemistry, were held up as a model for the development of psychological science, with the emphasis on analytical laboratory measurement of human faculties, as if to try to analyze complex mental experience into its most elemental constituents, much as the chemist analyzes substances to determine their basic elements.

Wundt in Germany and Galton in England established laboratories for the measurement of human traits and faculties. Galton hypothesized the existence of a hereditary general mental ability that entered into every intellectual endeavor. But his theory about how this general ability could be objectively measured proved unfruitful in its own day, when the statistical methodology that might have found order in the data was not yet developed. He believed that one should try to measure separately all the simplest, most elemental constituents of mental functioning, which presumably constituted the building blocks of general mental ability. Galton invented many ingenious laboratory devices and techniques for measuring separately these various elemental aspects of mental ability. His student James McKeen Cattell added many other tests to the battery.

It was Cattell who originally coined the term "mental test." Because commonsense notions of intelligence, along with a few quite casual experiments, suggested to Galton that the most intelligent persons showed "fine discrimination," "discernment," "subtlety," and "quickness of mind," he thought that, by measuring sensory discriminations and speed of motor reactions to visual and auditory stimuli, one could get at the essence of general mental ability. Below are listed some of the many tests invented by Galton and his student Cattell:

Size discrimination	Reaction time to light
Weight discrimination	Reaction time to sound
Pitch discrimination	Speed of perception
Color discrimination	Speed of movement
Discrimination of rhythm	Resistance to fatigue
Discrimination of time intervals	Strength of handgrip
Speed of color naming	Speed of word associations
Visual acuity	Visual imagery
Hearing acuity	Auditory and visual memory span
Skin sensitivity	Logical memory
(two-point discrimination)	
Sensitivity to pain	Retrospective memory

Thousands of persons were given various of these tests in Galton's Anthropometric Laboratory in the Natural Science Museum of South Kensington, London, and in Cattell's Psychological Laboratory at Columbia University in New York before the turn of the century. Other investigators, too, were busy collecting data with these and similar tests.

The main upshot of these studies was that the tests appeared generally unpromising as measures of intelligence. The tests failed to correlate very significantly among themselves, suggesting that they each measured rather different abilities and not a single mental ability and that they failed to correlate consistently or substantially with various commonsense criteria of intelligence. A historically fateful study by Clark Wissler (1870-1949), one of Cattell's own Ph.D. students in psychology at Columbia University, effectively signaled the demise of the Cattell battery of tests as a measure of intelligence (Wissler, 1901). In its time Wissler's study was methdologically the most carefully executed and statistically sophisticated investigation of Cattell's battery. The study's conclusions were so strong as to encourage psychologists to look in quite other directions than the psychological laboratory of that day for methods for measuring intelligence. In retrospect it seems likely that more advanced statistical analyses of Wissler's data might have resulted in somewhat different conclusions. (See Chapter 14, p. 686.) In 1900 statistical thinking was not up to the task of reaching the correct conclusions from Wissler's data.

Wissler administered Cattell's battery of "mental tests" to some seventy undergraduate students in Columbia University, one of the nation's academically most selective colleges. The students who remained each successive year, from the entering freshman class to the end of the senior year, were retested each year. Correlations were computed among various pairs of tests, but only a fraction of all the possible intercorrelations were determined. The idea of analyzing a total intercorrelation matrix had not yet occurred in psychology. Hand calculation of Pearson correlations was just too laborious, and Wissler had to choose from among all the variables the ones to be correlated. There were more than 600 possible correlations that could be computed among Wissler's tests, but he actually computed only 42 correlations, based on pairs of tests selected for psychological importance and likelihood of yielding the largest correlations. Some of the tests were also correlated with academic class standing, based on course grades in mathematics, Latin, rhetoric, French, German, and Greek. The intercorrelations among the mental tests were very low, though nearly all were positive, ranging from −.08 to +.39, with a mean of only .12, which is not significantly greater than a chance correlation for the size of sample used by Wissler. The separate correlations of the various tests with class standing ranged from −.09 to +.23, with a mean of +.09. The correlations between class standing in various subjects ranged from +.30 to +.75, with a mean of +.56. Wissler concluded that (1) the tests did not correlate better than chance among themselves, and therefore were not measuring a general mental ability, and (2) they did not correlate better than chance with class standing, and therefore did not measure a commonsense criterion of intelligence.

At least two major shortcomings in Wissler's analysis would now stand out as conspicuous to any present-day graduate student in psychology.

In the first place, Wissler took no account of the great restriction of "range of talent" in his highly selected sample of intellectually able Columbia College students, all of whom were probably in the top 5 or 10 percent of the total population in general intelligence. Restriction of range of scores on one or both of the variables entering into a correlation makes the correlation lower than it would be with an unrestricted range of scores. For example, the correlation between height and weight in the general population is about .55. When the correlation is computed among the top-league basketball players, the correlation shrinks to about .12.

In the second place, Wissler took no account of the errors of measurement in his tests. The degree to which scores or measurements can correlate with one another is limited by the reliability of the measurements. A test's reliability, r_{xx}, is the proportion of true variance as opposed to error variance in the scores. The highest possible correlation between two tests is the square root of the product of their reliabilities, that is, $\sqrt{r_{xx}} \times \sqrt{r_{yy}}$. If Wissler had taken into account these two factors—the weakening of correlations by restriction of range and by imperfect reliability—he might well have drawn quite different conclusions and set the course of the history of mental measurement in a different direction.

Just three years after the publication of Wissler's monograph, Charles Spearman (1904), in what is now regarded as one of the three or four most important papers in the history of mental measurement, pointed out these statistical deficiencies in Wissler's analysis and showed that, when they were corrected, the Galton and Cattell type of laboratory measurements of discrimination are (1) positively intercorrelated, thereby revealing a common or general factor, and (2) significantly correlated with school marks among groups of children who were not selected for ability—just the opposite of Wissler's conclusions. Spearman's statistical methodology was a most important advance. Although the data on which Spearman based his conclusions were far from definitive, they were sufficient to suggest that the Galton–Cattell ideas about mental measurement were not as wholly unpromising as Wissler's analysis concluded.

Yet the Galton–Cattell laboratory tests were unattractive in a practical sense. They required quite special and complicated laboratory equipment, and time-consuming re-peated measurements were needed to obtain satisfactory reliability. Also, the tests of reaction time and of various modalities of sensory discrimination measured very much less of the general ability common to all the tests than of the specific factor peculiar to each single test. Thus, despite Spearman's important theoretical and methodological attempt to rescue the Galton–Cattell approach to mental measurement, Spearman's work was little appreciated at the time, and so the laboratory study of individual differences in mental abilities was virtually abandoned. Less than a year after the appearance of Spearman's contribution in 1904, mental measurement was set in a different direction by an histori-cally momentous development in France.

Binet's Test

Alfred Binet (1857–1911), a French psychologist, and Théophile Simon (1873–1961), a psychiatrist, were commissioned in 1904 by the Ministry of Education in France to devise a practical means for distinguishing between mentally retarded and normal school children, so that retarded children could be quickly identified and provided special education. Binet, who had begun as an experimental psychologist, had already given up laboratory research on elemental sensory functions in the Wundtian tradition and had turned his attention to the "higher mental processes." He assumed that intelligence was not much involved in the elemental sensory–motor tasks of the psychological laboratory, but in tasks calling for more complex mental processes, especially *judgment,* which Binet viewed as the *sine qua non* of intelligence. He emphasized the distinction between elemental sensory capacities and judgment. In the same way, he distinguished between judgment and simple memory. Yet he retained Galton's tests of weight discrimination and short-term memory span in his battery of tests, because they showed good age discrimina-tions and correlated well with an independent diagnosis of mental retardation. Binet's idea of intelligence is summed up in his words:

> It seems to us that in intelligence there is a fundamental faculty, the alteration or lack of which is of the utmost importance for practical life. This faculty is judgment, otherwise called good sense, practical sense, initiative, the faculty of adapting one's self to circumstances. To judge well, to comprehend well, to reason well, these are the essential activities of intelligence. A person may be a moron or an imbecile if he is lacking in judgment; but with good judgment he can never be either. Indeed the rest of the intellectual faculties seem of little importance in comparison with judg-ment.   (Binet & Simon, 1905)

The Binet-Simon tests were innovative because of their simplicity and the ease and quickness with which they could be individually administered. This was an explicit aim in their construction, an essential feature if the tests were to be practical and widely used in the schools of France. Data gained in the first few years after publication of the Binet test led to published revisions in 1908 and again in 1911, the year of Binet's untimely death at the age of 54. The final form in which Binet left the tests, arranged in age groups, consisted of the following:

Age 3
1. Points to nose, eyes, and mouth.
2. Repeats two digits.

3. Enumerates common objects in a picture.
4. Gives family name.
5. Repeats a sentence of six syllables.

Age 4

1. Gives own sex.
2. Names key, knife, and penny.
3. Repeats three digits.
4. Compares two lines.
5. Strings seven beads.

Age 5

1. Compares two weights.
2. Copies a square.
3. Repeats a sentence of ten syllables.
4. Counts four pennies.
5. Unites the halves of a divided rectangle.

Age 6

1. Distinguishes between morning and afternoon.
2. Defines familiar words in terms of use.
3. Copies a diamond.
4. Counts 13 pennies.
5. Distinguishes pictures of ugly and pretty faces.

Age 7

1. Shows right hand and left ear.
2. Describes a picture.
3. Executes three commands given simultaneously.
4. Counts the value of six sous, three of which are double.
5. Names four cardinal colors.

Age 8

1. Compares two objects from memory.
2. Counts backward from 20 to zero.
3. Notes omissions from pictures of familiar objects.
4. Gives day and date.
5. Repeats five digits.

Age 9

1. Gives change from 20 sous.
2. Defines familiar words in terms superior to use.
3. Recognizes nine common coins.
4. Names the months of the year in order.
5. Comprehends and answers "easy questions."

Age 10

1. Arranges five blocks in order of weight.
2. Copies two drawings from memory.
3. Criticizes absurd statements.

4. Comprehends or answers "difficult questions."
5. Uses three given words in not more than two sentences.

Age 12
1. Resists suggestion as to length of lines.
2. Composes one sentence containing three given words.
3. Names 60 words in three minutes.
4. Defines three abstract words.
5. Discovers the sense of a disarranged sentence.

Age 15
1. Repeats seven digits.
2. Finds three rhymes for a given word in one minute.
3. Repeats a sentence of 26 syllables.
4. Interprets pictures.
5. Interprets given facts.

Adult
1. Solves the paper-cutting test.
2. Rearranges a triangle in imagination.
3. States differences between pairs of abstract terms.
4. Gives three differences between a president and a king.
5. Gives the main thought of a selection that he has heard read.

The Binet test was quickly taken up in England and the United States. Lewis M. Terman (1877–1956), a psychologist at Stanford University, made the most important adaptation and standardization of the test for use in America in 1916, known as the "Stanford Revision of the Binet Scale" and later simply as the Stanford–Binet. Terman added thirty-six more items (bringing the total to ninety), improved the calibration of the scale, and made use of the IQ score obtained from the quotient of *mental age / chronological age*. Further revisions or restandardizations of the Stanford–Binet were published in 1937 and 1960; the 1960 version was last renormed in 1972.

The Stanford–Binet has been translated and adapted in many countries throughout the world. For more than half a century it has been the most widely used individual test of intelligence. It has often served as a standard for the construction and calibration of other tests.

The Wechsler Scales

The only individual intelligence tests that have rivaled the Stanford–Binet in popularity and in recent years have become the preferred tests of clinical and school psychologists are the battery authored by David Wechsler (born 1896), formerly chief psychologist at Bellevue Psychiatric Hospital in New York City. His first test became known as the Wechsler–Bellevue (1938). It was the first successful individual test of adult intelligence. Although the Stanford–Binet ranged from age 2 to adult level, the adult part of the scale consisted of only twenty of the ninety items making up the entire test. Clinicians felt that they needed a more extensive and varied set of tests for assessing the intelligence level of adults. The Wechsler–Bellevue test filled this need. It was extensively revised and restandardized on a national sample in 1955 and became the Wechsler Adult Intelligence Scale

(WAIS). In 1949 Wechsler published the Wechsler Intelligence Scale for Children (WISC), which was revised and renormed in 1974 as the WISC (R). In 1963 there appeared the Wechsler Preschool and Primary Scale of Intelligence (WPPSI). The WPSSI is normed for ages 4 years to 6½ years, the WISC (R) for ages 6 years to 16 years 11 months, and the WAIS for ages 16 to 75 years and over. The background and history of the development of the Wechsler tests, along with a comprehensive review of the published research on the tests, are provided by Matarazzo (1972).

All the Wechsler tests follow the same plan, consisting of several verbal tests and several performance tests. Scores on the verbal tests are combined in a statistically appropriate manner to yield a Verbal IQ; similarly the Performance IQ. All the tests together yield the Full Scale IQ. The same types of verbal and performance tests are found in the WPSSI and WISC and WAIS, but the items are at different difficulty levels. Items in each subtest are presented in order from easy to difficult. The examples given here are not actually from the WAIS test, which for obvious reasons cannot be published, but are made up to resemble as much as possible the typical items in each subtest of the WAIS.

Verbal Subtests

1. *Information* (29 questions)

   What does the Fourth of July celebrate?

   At what temperature does water freeze?

   How far is it from San Francisco to New York?

   Who wrote *The Republic?*

2. *Comprehension* (14 questions)

   Why are traffic lights needed?

   Why is gold worth more than copper?

   What is the meaning of the saying "A bird in the hand is worth two in the bush"?

3. *Arithmetic* (14 questions)

   If a man buys sixty cents worth of groceries and gives the clerk a dollar, how much change should he get back?

   How many inches are there in three and one-half feet?

   If six men can finish a job in three days, how many men would be needed to finish it one day?

4. *Similarities* (13 questions)

   In what way are DOG   and CAT   alike?

   "   "   "   "   NOSE   " CHIN   " ?

   "   "   "   "   SPERM   " OVUM   " ?

   "   "   "   "   FEAR   " HATE   " ?

   "   "   "   "   SYMPHONY " JAZZ   " ?

5. *Digit Span*

   Digits forward: The subject is asked to repeat a series of digits, going from three to nine digits, after hearing them spoken by the tester at the rate of one digit per second.

   Digits backward: The subject repeats three to nine digits backward, that is, in reverse of the order of presentation.

6. *Vocabulary* (40 words)

The subject is asked to explain the meaning of words, going from very easy familiar words like *summer* and *strange* to more rare and difficult words like *adumbrate* and *cacophony*.

Performance Subtests

1. *Digit Symbol*

The subject has to translate the numerals from 1 to 9 into code symbols (e.g., ⊔, ⊥, ∧, etc.), where the digits are listed in several rows in a random order. The score is the number completed correctly in 90 seconds.

2. *Picture Completion* (21 items)

Twenty-one pictures, each of a familiar object or scene; the subject must tell what essential feature is missing or what is wrong in each picture, e.g., a clock without "hands," a violin being played without strings, a flag blowing one way in the wind while smoke from a nearby chimney is blowing in the opposite direction.

3. *Block Design* (10 designs)

The subject is shown a series of cards with designs in red and white and is asked to duplicate the designs with a set of 1-inch wooden cubes painted red and white. The designs go from very simple (requiring four blocks) to quite complex (sixteen blocks). Time as well as accuracy enters into the scoring.

4. *Picture Arrangement* (8 items)

The subject is presented with several series of cartoon pictures in a haphazard order and is asked to arrange them in a row so as to make a logical sequence or story. For example, pictures A, B, and C show (A) a man jacking up an automobile, (B) the car starting up, (C) a car standing with a flat tire; the correct response is to arrange the pictures in the order CAB. The subject's score is based on time and accuracy.

5. *Object Assembly* (4 items)

These are four jigsaw puzzles, each of an extremely familiar object and each involving only a few pieces. The pieces are presented haphazardly; in this form it is not always immediately obvious what object is represented, though it is always instantly recognizable when assembled.

The various subtests of the Wechsler differ in reliability and in contribution to the total score. The pair of tests that together best predict the Full Scale IQ are Vocabulary and Block Design, with a correlation approaching .90. The weakest subtests are Digit Span, Digit Symbol, and Object Assembly.

Verbal Item Types and Examples Used in Group Tests of Intelligence

Vocabulary.   Word knowledge figures prominently in standard tests. The scores on the vocabulary subtest are usually the most highly correlated with total IQ of any of the other subtests. This fact would seem to contradict Spearman's important generalization that intelligence is revealed most strongly by tasks calling for the eduction of relations and correlates. Does not the vocabulary test merely show what the subject has learned prior to taking the test? How does this involve reasoning or eduction?

In fact, vocabulary tests are among the best measures of intelligence, because the acquisition of word meanings is highly dependent on the *eduction* of meaning from the contexts in which the words are encountered. Vocabulary for the most part is not acquired by rote memorization or through formal instruction. The meaning of a word most usually is acquired by encountering the word in some context that permits at least some partial inference as to its meaning. By hearing or reading the word in a number of different contexts, one acquires, through the mental processes of generalization and discrimination and eduction, the essence of the word's meaning, and one is then able to recall the word precisely when it is appropriate in a new context. Thus the acquisition of vocabulary is not as much a matter of learning and memory as it is of generalization, discrimination, eduction, and inference. Children of high intelligence acquire vocabulary at a faster rate than children of low intelligence, and as adults they have a much larger than average vocabulary, not primarily because they have spent more time in study or have been more exposed to words, but because they are capable of educing more meaning from single encounters with words and are capable of discriminating subtle differences in meaning between similar words. Words also fill conceptual needs, and for a new word to be easily learned the need must precede one's encounter with the word. It is remarkable how quickly one forgets the definition of a word he does not need. I do not mean "need" in a practical sense, as something one must use, say, in one's occupation; I mean a conceptual need, as when one discovers a word for something he has experienced but at the time did not know there was a word for it. Then when the appropriate word is encountered, it "sticks" and becomes a part of one's vocabulary. Without the cognitive "need," the word may be just as likely to be encountered, but the word and its context do not elicit the mental processes that will make it "stick."

During childhood and throughout life nearly everyone is bombarded by more different words than ever become a part of the person's vocabulary. Yet some persons acquire much larger vocabularies than others. This is true even among siblings in the same family, who share very similar experiences and are exposed to the same parental vocabulary.

Vocabulary tests are made up of words that range widely in difficulty (percentage passing); this is achieved by selecting words that differ in frequency of usage in the language, from relatively common to relatively rare words. (The frequency of occurrence of each of 30,000 different words per 1 million words of printed material—books, magazines, and newspapers—has been tabulated by Thorndike and Lorge, 1944.) Technical, scientific, and specialized words associated with particular occupations or localities are avoided. Also, words with an extremely wide scatter of "passes" are usually eliminated, because high scatter is one indication of unequal exposure to a word among persons in the population because of marked cultural, educational, occupational, or regional differences in the probability of encountering a particular word. Scatter shows up in item analysis as a lower than average correlation between a given word and the total score on the vocabulary test as a whole. To understand the meaning of scatter, imagine that we had a perfect count of the total number of words in the vocabulary of every person in the population. We could also determine what percentage of all persons know the meaning of each word known by anyone in the population. The best vocabulary test limited to, say, one hundred items would be that selection of words the knowledge of which would best predict the total vocabulary of each person. A word with wide scatter would be one that is almost as likely to be known by persons with a small total vocabulary as by persons with a large total vocabulary, even though the word may be known by less than 50 percent of the total population. Such a wide-scatter word, with about equal probability of being known by persons of every vocabulary size, would be a poor predictor of total vocabulary. It is such words that test constructors, by statistical analyses, try to detect and eliminate.

It is instructive to study the errors made on the words that are failed in a vocabulary test. When there are multiple-choice alternatives for the definition of each word, from which the subject must discriminate the correct answer among the several distractors, we see that failed items do not show a random choice among the distractors. The systematic and realiable differences in choice of distractors indicate that most subjects have been exposed to the word in some context, but have inferred the wrong meaning. Also, the fact that changing the distractors in a vocabulary item can markedly change the percentage passing further indicates that the vocabulary test does not discriminate simply between those persons who have and those who have not been exposed to the words in context. For example, the vocabulary test item ERUDITE has a higher percentage of errors if the word *polite* is included among the distractors; the same is true for MERCENARY when the words *stingy* and *charity* are among the distractors; and STOICAL – *sad,* DROLL – *eerie,* FECUND – *odor,* FATUOUS – *large.*

Another interesting point about vocabulary tests is that persons *recognize* many more of the words than they actually know the meaning of. In individual testing they often express dismay at not being able to say what a word means, when they know they have previously heard it or read it any number of times. The crucial variable in vocabulary size is not exposure per se, but conceptual need and inference of meaning from context, which are forms of eduction. Hence, vocabulary is a good index of intelligence.

Picture vocabulary tests are often used with children and nonreaders. The most popular is the Peabody Picture Vocabulary Test. It consists of 150 large cards, each containing four pictures. With the presentation of each card, the tester says one word (a common noun, adjective, or verb) that is best represented by one of the four pictures, and the subject merely has to point to the appropriate picture. Several other standard picture vocabulary tests are highly similar. All are said to measure *recognition* vocabulary, as contrasted to *expressive* vocabulary, which requires the subject to state definitions in his or her own words. The distinction between *recognition* and *expressive* vocabulary is more formal than psychological, as the correlation between the two is close to perfect when corrected for errors of measurement.

General Information.   The range of a person's knowledge is generally a good indication of that individual's intelligence, and tests of general information in fact correlate highly with other noninformational measures of intelligence. For example, the Information subtest of the Wechsler Adult Intelligence Scale is correlated .75 with the five nonverbal Performance tests among 18- to 19-year-olds.

Yet information items are the most problematic of all types of test items. The main problems are the choice of items and the psychological rationale for including them. It is practically impossible to decide what would constitute a *random* sample of knowledge; no "population" of "general information" has been defined. The items must simply emerge arbitrarily from the heads of test constructors. No one item measures *general* information. Each item involves only a specific fact, and one can only hope that some hypothetical general pool of information is tapped by the one or two dozen information items that are included in some intelligence tests.

Information tests are treated as *power* tests; time is not an important factor in administration. Like any power test, the items are steeply graded in difficulty. The twenty-nine Information items in the WAIS run from 100 percent passing to 1 percent passing. Yet how can one claim the items to be *general* information if many of them are passed by far fewer than 50 percent of the population? Those items with a low percentage passing must be quite specialized or esoteric. Inspection of the harder items, in fact, reveals them to involve quite "bookish" and specialized knowledge. The correlation of Information with the total IQ score is likely to be *via* amount of education, which is correlated with intelligence but is not the cause of it. A college student is more likely to know who wrote *The Republic* than is a high school dropout. It is mainly because college students, on average, are more intelligent than high school dropouts that this information item gains its correlation with intelligence. The Information subtest of the WAIS, in fact, correlates more highly with amount of education than any other subtest (Matarazzo, 1972, p. 373).

Information items should rightly be treated as measures of *breadth*, in Thorndike's terms, rather than of *altitude*. This means that informational items should be selected so as to all have about the same low level of difficulty, say, 70 percent to 90 percent passing. Then they could truly be said to sample general or common knowledge and at the same time yield a wide spread of total scores in the population. This could only come about if one selected such an extreme diversity of such items as to result in very low inter-item correlations. Thus the individual items would share very little common variance. The great disadvantage of such a test is that it would be very low in what is called internal consistency, and this means that, if the total score on such a test is to measure individual differences reliably, one would need to have an impracticably large number of items. There would be little point to it, as there are much more efficient and theoretically defensible ways of measuring intelligence than by means of information items. Information items are much more suited to scholastic and vocational achievement tests, where a more limited and clearly defined domain of knowledge can be adequately sampled and the items' face validity and relevance to the purpose of the test are unquestionable.

Verbal Oddity Problems.   This type of verbal item clearly involves eduction of a classification. The subject is instructed to underline the one word in each set that does not belong with the others.

1. *door   kitchen   painted   garage   porch*
2. *sculptor   painter   singer   author   composer*
3. *car   train   bus   plane   tram   road*
4. *hear   taste   see   food   smell*

Verbal Similarities.   In these the subject underlines the two words in each set that mean most nearly the same.

1. *person   man   lad   youth*
2. *stupid   idle   activity   inactive*
3. *soft   fragile   severed   brittle*

Similar–Opposite Words. The subject indicates with letter S or O which pairs of words are more similar or more opposite in meaning.

1. *serene – tranquil*
2. *logical – preposterous*
3. *conquer – vanquish*
4. *accelerate – retard*

Sentence Completion. The subject inserts the missing word in each blank.

1. The _____ way to _____ is by airplane.
2. Two pounds of silver are _____ more than two pounds of iron.
3. A body of _____ entirely surrounded by _____ is called an _____.

Scrambled Sentences. The words are scrambled in each of the following statements. The subject has to figure out the correct word order and indicate whether the statement is true (T) or false (F).

1. Envy traits malice are bad and.
2. Sand and made is salt of bread.
3. Has triangle every three sides.
4. A is water gas.

Verbal Analogies. The subject underlines the one word that best completes the analogy.

1. *Cat* is to *kitten* as *dog* is to
    beast   bark   puppy   chase.
2. *Prisoner* is to *jail* as *water* is to
    prison   drink   tap   bucket.
3. *Artist* is to *beauty* as *farmer* is to
    picture   plough   usefulness   musician.
4. *Cliff* is to *steep* as *plain* is to
    rugged   mountain   even   level.

Another form of verbal analogy is the completion item. The subject is instructed to fill in the blank.

1. *Tall* is to *height* as *heavy* is to _____.
2. *Before* is to *behind* as *future* is to _____.

Still another form of analogy requires the subject to underline the two words in each set of four words that have the same relationship as the pair of words in capitals.

1. SECOND – TIME   ::   *ounce   return   minute   weight*
2. PREDICTION – FUTURE   ::   *past   absence   memory   present*
3. COMPOSER – OPERA   ::   *music   author   read   novel*
4. SQUARE – CUBE   ::   *curve   circle   round   sphere*

Proverbs. The interpretation of proverbs is generally a good measure of intelligence because it calls for abstraction and generalization of meaning. (The following examples are from Thorndike, 1927, p. 167.) In each set of sentences the subject selects the two that mean most nearly the same as the first sentence.

1. Today is worth two tomorrows.
   _____ Time is an herb that cures all diseases.
   _____ A bird in the hand is worth two in the bush.
   _____ To speed today is to be set back tomorrow.
   _____ There is no time like the present.
2. Faint heart never won fair lady.
   _____ Nothing ventured, nothing gained.
   _____ Marry in haste, repent at leisure.
   _____ Fools rush in where angels fear to tread.
   _____ Fortune favors the brave.
3. Fight fire with fire.
   _____ Set a thief to catch a thief.
   _____ Knavery is the best defense against a knave.
   _____ Sow the wind, reap the whirlwind.
   _____ Fire that's closest kept burns fiercest.

Logical Reasoning.   The subject is given a set of relationships from which to deduce the answer to the question.

1. Bill is taller than John. Ralph is shorter than Bill. Who is the tallest?
2. Five girls are sitting side by side on a bench. Jane is in the middle and Betty sits next to her on the right. Alice is beside Betty, and Dale is beside Ellen, who sits next to Jane. Who are sitting on the ends?
3. In a race the dog runs faster than the horse, which is slower than the cow, and the pig runs faster than the dog. Which one finishes last?

Verbal Classification.   The subject underlines the one word in small print that goes best with the preceding set of words in large letters.

ARM   HAND   FOOT   NECK   ::   *body   man   knee   tall*
ANGRY   ANXIOUS   HAPPY   SAD   ::   *fearful   funny   laugh   tragic*
SUE   BETTY   MARY   JANE   ::   *girl   name   Carol   Smith*

Syllogisms.   These are another form of logical reasoning. They have gone out of favor in tests of intelligence because knowledge of a simple method of solution by the use of Venn diagrams makes the solution of any syllogism a simple matter. Too much of the variance on this type of item is attributable to whether or not persons know how to solve the problems by means of Venn diagrams, rather than to a general intelligence factor.

1. All liquid is fluid.
   All milk is liquid.
   Therefore, all milk is fluid.   True or false?
2. All girls are scholars.
   Some boys are scholars.
   Therefore, some boys are girls.   True or false?
3. All champions are strong.
   All athletes are strong.
   Therefore, all champions are athletes.   True or false?

4. All musicians can hear.
   No deaf person can hear.
   Therefore, no musicians are deaf.   True or false?

Synonyms.   The subject has to fill in the blank with a single word that when substituted for the word in brackets will not essentially change the meaning of the sentence.

1. He placed the table near the [middle] of the room. _____
2. The house is very [big]. _____
3. The twins were of the same [stature]. _____
4. The image was [enlarged] by the microscope. _____

Inferential Conclusions.   These items do not depend on strict logical deduction but on reasonable inference and judgment based on the information given. These items are similar in form to items in tests of reading comprehension, except that in intelligence tests the level of vocabulary and reading difficulty are kept simple so that the items measure reasoning ability more than vocabulary or reading level per se.

1. In a particular meadow there are a great many rabbits that eat the grass. There are also many hawks that eat the rabbits. Last year a disease broke out among the rabbits and most of them died. Which one of the following things then most probably occurred?
   (a) The grass died and the hawk population decreased.
   (b) The grass died and the hawk population increased.
   (c) The grass grew taller and the hawk population decreased.
   (d) The grass grew taller and the hawk population increased.
   (e) Neither the grass nor the hawks were affected by the death of the rabbits.

(In a random sample of the U.S. adult population, 52 percent chose the keyed correct answer, *c;* see Womer, 1970.)

Syntactic Inference.   This is a test of one's ability to infer the syntactic form of a word from its context in a sentence. It is a good measure of general intelligence at high school age and above. The subject is instructed to mark the "word" that *best* fills the blank in the second of two sentences.

1. A gelish lob relled perfully.
   I grolled the _____ meglessly.
   (a) *gelish*   (b) *lob*   (c) *relled*   (d) *perfully*
2. Four gobable trains krinned and zagged terfily.
   I yammed porishly whenever they trinned so _____.
   (a) *gobable*   (b) *trins*   (c) *zagged*   (d) *terfily*
3. The dandable rals niddered zorfully, but I didn't bek.
   Those rals have _____ gofishly, too.
   (a) *dandable*   (b) *rals*   (c) *niddered*   (d) *zorfully*

Pedigrees.   This type of item consists of a family pedigree diagram followed by a list of questions based on it. The pedigree diagrams differ in size and complexity, from very simple family relationships (as shown in the following example) to very complex relationships involving some ten to fifteen "persons." Pedigree items are inappropriate for persons who do not know the meanings of such terms as *sister, brother, daughter, aunt, uncle, cousin, brother-in-law, grandson*, and so on.

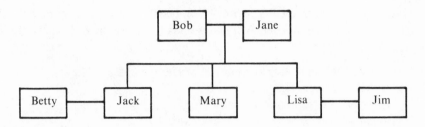

This chart shows that Bob and Jane were married and had three children: Jack, Mary, and Lisa. Jack married a woman named Betty, and Lisa married a man named Jim. The subject is instructed to answer the following questions by looking at the chart and circling the right answer.

1. Bob is Jane's   father   husband   brother   son   uncle.
2. Mary's brother is   Jack   Bob   Jim   Betty   Lisa.
3. How many children has Jane?   1   2   3   4   5
4. Lisa's sister-in-law is   Jane   Betty   Mary   Jack   Jim.
5. Betty's mother-in-law is   Jane   Mary   Lisa   Jack.

Numerical Reasoning Items.   There is a clear distinction between arithmetic computation (or mechanical arithmetic) and arithmetic problem solving. Computation is a quite poor measure of intelligence; numerical problem solving is one of the best measures, assuming that the subject is able to read the problems and perform the computations called for. When arithmetic operations are incorporated in intelligence test items, the reading level and the arithmetic computations called for are kept at a much lower level of difficulty than the reasoning called for to solve the problem. Here is a typical example:

1. John is twice as old as his sister Mary, who is now 5 years of age. How old will John be when Mary is 30 years of age?

Over 20 percent of the adult population fail this item, but nearly all who fail show that they can do the arithmetic calculations by giving the answer "sixty" and by answering correctly the simpler item: "Mrs. Jones bought a loaf of bread for 30¢ and a bar of candy for 5¢. How much did she spend all together?"

Number Series.   These are the most commonly used numerical reasoning items found in intelligence tests; they assume only a knowledge of the cardinal numerals and the simple arithmetic operations taught in elementary school.

1. At the end of each line, the subject is to write the number that most logically continues the series.
   (a) 3, 5, 7, 9, ____
   (b) 35, 28, 21, 14, ____
   (c) 1, 2, 4, 8, ____
   (d) 3, 6, 5, 10, 9, ____

Another form of number series:

2. The subject is to fill in the blank with the number that will make the third pair of numbers related in the same way as the first two pairs.
    (a) (1, 3)   (4, 6)   (7, _____)
    (b) (1, 1)   (2, 4)   (3, _____)
    (c) (2, 8)   (4, 64)   (3, _____)

Number matrices involve much the same principle:

3. The subject is to fill in the blank cell.

7	5	2
6	4	

45	15	5
90	30	

Number series and matrices items can be made to range in difficulty from close to 100 percent passing to less than 1 percent passing, even among college students. A popular criticism of such problems is that there are theoretically many correct answers besides the one that is keyed as correct to any given problem. This is an utterly trivial criticism, however, because the other correct solutions are usually possible only for a mathematician; they involve a level of mathematical sophistication far beyond that required for the most obvious solution. Even an expert mathematician who *could* figure out other possible solutions would not do so in a test situation, because it would take so much more time, and anyone capable of figuring out one of the more complex solutions would certainly have no difficulty arriving at the simplest solution, which in every item is the keyed answer.

Number series have their parallel in *letter series,* which are also used in some tests. The subject is instructed to fill in the blank with the letter or letters that most logically continue the series.

1. d, ee, fff, _____
2. a, z, b, y, c, _____

Nonverbal Item Types and Examples Used in Group Tests of Intelligence

Pictorial Tests

Nonverbal items are intended to obviate the need for reading or the overt use of language. Hence nonverbal items are particularly useful for testing young children, illiterates, persons with language problems, and the deaf. Nonverbal items may range from highly culture-loaded pictorial items to very culture-reduced geometric forms. One class of nonverbal items is pictorial, using pictures of familiar things. Most pictorial items involve the subject's ability to induce a generalization or classification from a series of five or six pictures and then decide which one of several multiple-choice alternatives belongs to the same classification.

Pictorial Oddities.   The oddity problem, described under verbal tests, can also be presented in pictorial form. The subject is asked to select the one picture in each set that does not belong with the others.

Faulty Pictures.   Familiar objects are pictured with essential faults, incongruities, or missing parts, which the subject is asked to detect.

Figure Analogies.   In a set of drawings, such as those shown below, the first two drawings go together in a certain way. The subject is to find the drawing at the right that goes with the third drawing in the same way that the second goes with the first.

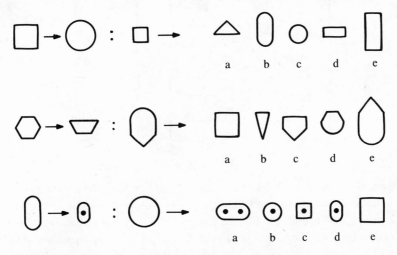

Spatial Analogies.   These differ slightly from figure analogies in that spatial analogies call for the mental ability to rotate figures in space to determine which pair of figures is congruent.

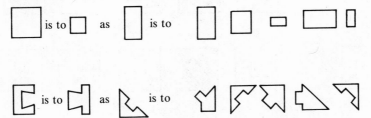

Figure Series.   The subject is asked which figure at the right logically continues the series of the three figures at the left. The sample items shown here are from R. B. Cattell's Culture Fair Test of *g*.

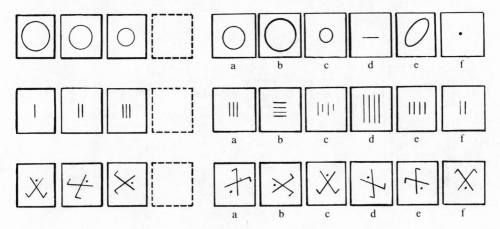

Figure Classification.   The subject is asked which two figures in each series go together. The sample items shown here are from R. B. Cattell's Culture Fair Test of *g*.

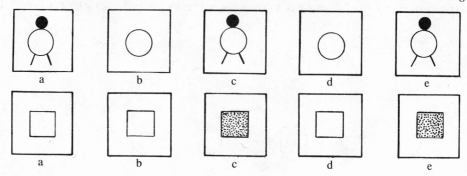

Figure Generalization.   Here the subject must figure out the general rule for where the dot is to be placed. In the first example shown below, for instance, the rule is that the dot is inside the rectangle but outside the circle. In only one alternative of each series can the rule be applied. The subject is to infer the rule and pick the figure at right to which it applies. The sample items shown here are from Cattell's Culture Fair Test of *g*.

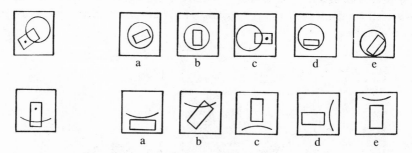

Figure Matrices.   These take several forms and are among the best tests of eduction. The sample items shown here are from Cattell's Culture Fair Test of *g*. The subject is to determine which of the five alternatives at the right most logically completes the matrix pattern on the left.

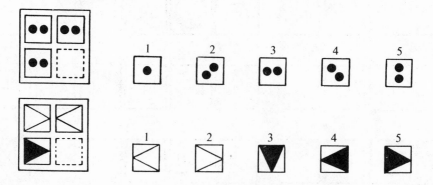

The best-known form of matrices test is Raven's Progressive Matrices, which was devised in England by J. C. Raven, a psychologist, and L. S. Penrose, a geneticist, with the aim of measuring as completely as possible in a single test the eduction processes that Spearman regarded as the essence of intelligence. The Raven Matrices Tests are discussed in more detail in Chapter 14 (pp. 645–648). The two shown below are typical. The subject must indicate which of the several alternatives below each matrix most logically fills the blank space to complete the matrix pattern.

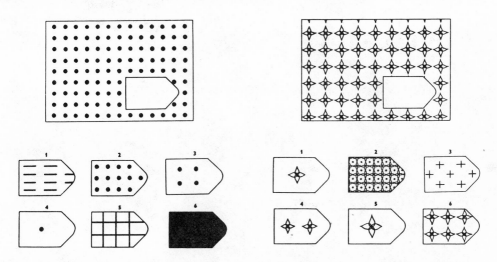

Imbedded Figures. In these items, also called Gottschaldt figures after the German psychologist who invented them, the subject must be able to analyze complex figures into their simpler components to find which of the several figures in the bottom row contains the figural component in the top row.

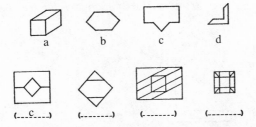

Gestalt Completion. Familiar words and objects are shown in various degrees of "mutilation" and the subject must infer what the word or object is. Performance is scored according to the average time taken per item or the number of items completed within a given time limit. The difficulty of any particular item is a function of its familiarity and the extent of the "mutilation"; these can be varied independently in making up items. However, so far as I know, no one has thought of giving a posttest of all the failed items in unmutilated form to establish a baseline for the subject's recognition of the items under optimal conditions for recognition. Gestalt completion items, which are known to be a good measure of the general intelligence factor (as well as of a small group factor labeled speed of closure), merit further experimental investigation in their own right. The following are examples of easy and difficult items used on the test.

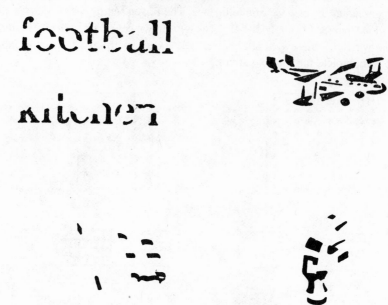

Reversed Figures.   These require that the subject mentally manipulate geometric figures so as to tell how a particular figure looks when its spatial position is changed. In the items shown here, for example, which of the four figures on the right is the same as the figure on the left flipped over and around? This type of item measures a special ability—spatial visualization—as well as general intelligence. The next chapter explains how it is possible to analyze the various abilities that enter into performance on any particular kind of test.

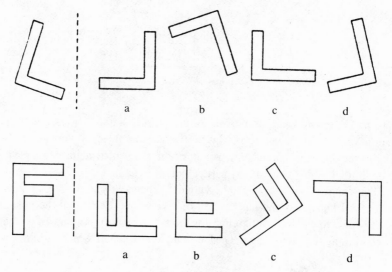

Block Counting.   This is another type of test that involves spatial visualization ability as well as general intelligence. From a drawing of a pile of blocks, such as that shown below, the subject is required to count the total number of blocks in the pile, including those he cannot see. This calls for an important aspect of general intelligence: the ability to imagine what is not directly perceived by the senses.

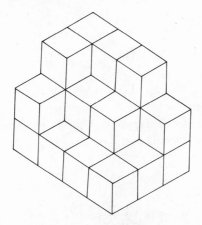

Cube Comparisons.   This type of item, originated by the eminent American psychometrician Louis Leon Thurstone (1887–1955), also calls for mental manipulation and spatial visualization. The subject must figure out whether the blocks in each pair can be the same or must be different.

Surface Development.   This test was also originated by Thurstone. The subject must imagine how a piece of paper can be folded to form some kind of object. For orientation, one surface of the object is always indicated by an X, which also appears on the unfolded piece of paper. The subject is to indicate which edges of the object (indicated by letters) correspond to the edges of the unfolded piece of paper (indicated by numbers).

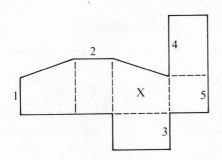   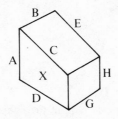

1:	H
2:	
3:	
4:	C
5:	

Spatial Visualization.   The subject is asked to visualize the three-dimensional object that will result from folding a two-dimensional pattern. In the item shown here, the subject is to determine which of the five boxes at the right can be made from the pattern shown at the left.

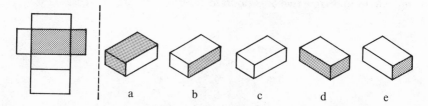

a   b   c   d   e

Object–Aperture Test.   The subject is presented with drawings of a three-dimensional object and a series of five two-dimensional apertures. If mentally turned to the correct position, the object could pass through only one of the apertures. The subject is to indicate which one it is.

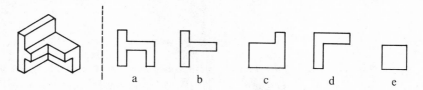

a   b   c   d   e

Perspective Reasoning.   This test consists of a variety of items that involve changes in perspective. In the first item shown here, the subject is to indicate how the three-dimensional model on the left would appear if viewed from directly above. In the second item, depicting a solid object that is to be cut in half, the subject is to determine which of the three alternatives given will be the shape of the cut face.

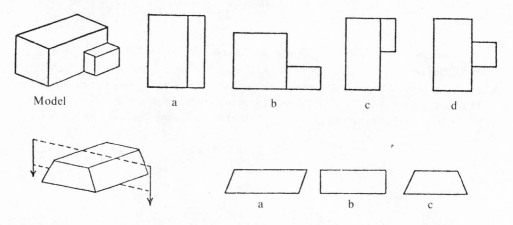

Model   a   b   c   d

a   b   c

Performance Tests

Performance tests require the subject to draw or construct something rather than merely select the correct answer. For this reason they must be individually administered. The scoring of the tests that involve drawing requires a trained and experienced scorer. A number of performance tests have already been described in the preceding discussion of the Wechsler tests. There are a great number of other types of performance items that have been used in tests of general intelligence. Only a few of the better-known examples are presented in the following paragraphs.

Bead Patterns.   This test is appropriate for children in the preschool years and in its simplest form is included at the 3-year-old level in the Stanford–Binet. The child is given a box full of large wooden beads of various shapes and colors that can be strung on a shoestring with a knot at one end. The tester, in full view of the child, strings a particular sequence of several beads, places it in front of the child, and asks him or her to make one just like it. The number of beads and complexity of the sequence can be varied so as to make for a considerable range of difficulty for preschool children.

Form Board.   There are a number of form boards in use. They range widely in difficulty. One of the easiest and the best known in testing children is the Seguin Form Board, shown below. The subject's performance is timed as he or she inserts the wooden objects (which are actually stacked in three piles) into the loose-fitting holes of the form board. The board is large, and very little if any variance in motor skills per se is involved in the scores on this test. The subject's score is usually the average time required over three trials.

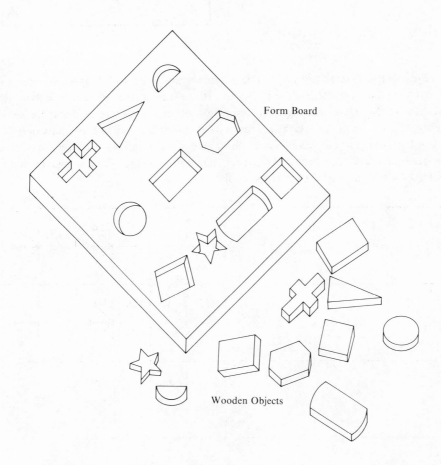

Form Board

Wooden Objects

Paper Folding.   In this test the tester, in view of the subject, slowly folds a sheet of paper (about 8 inches square) and, with a paper punch, punches a hole in the folded sheet of paper. The folded sheet is placed on the table before the subject. The subject is then given a pencil and another sheet of paper of the same size and is asked to draw all of the folds and holes just as they will appear when the paper is unfolded. (A multiple-choice form of this test has also been devised for group testing.)

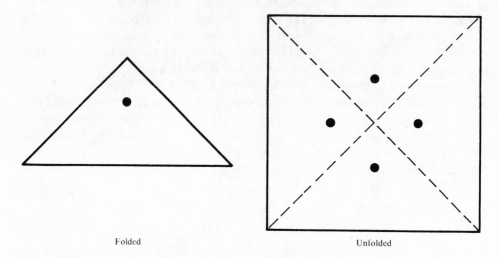

Folded   Unfolded

Figural Reasoning Matrices.   These items resemble Raven's Progressive Matrices test, but there are no multiple-choice answers. It is a performance test because the testee must draw in the figure that logically completes the matrix pattern in the space in the lower right novenant of the matrix. All the correct figures are easy to draw, although they can involve quite difficult problems in the eduction of relations and correlates. Performance is scored for conceptual correctness, not draftsmanship. The test is much more a measure of *g* than of spatial or perceptual abilities.

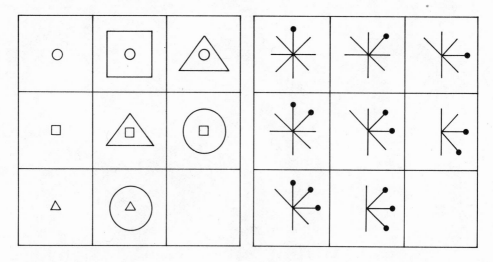

Maze Tests.   The subject has to draw an unbroken pencil line from the starting point, S, to the exit out of the maze; the line must not touch or cross the sides of the alleys or enter blind alleys. Violations of these rules subtract from the total score. An elaborate graded series of mazes, extensively used in cross-cultural research on mental ability, was devised by Stanley D. Porteus, who has written a comprehensive review of research on the maze tests (Porteus, 1965). The Porteus maze shown here is graded at the adult level.

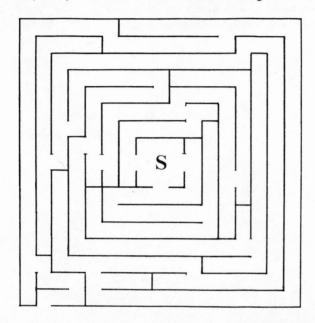

Another type of maze is the lines-and-dots maze, devised by Elithorn. The subject begins with his or her pencil on the dot nearest the bottom. The task is to draw a line that goes from the bottom to the top such that a line goes through a specified number of the large dots (in this case, ten). The subject must stay on the lines and may move in any direction except down. Scoring is based on accuracy and speed.

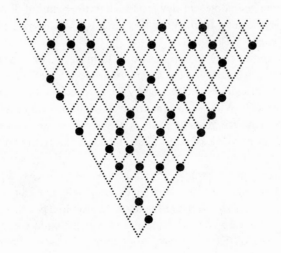

Leiter International Performance Scale.   This test can be given entirely without the use of language by either the tester or the subject. Wooden frames with a number of "slots" are placed before the subject. Below each slot is a figure, and the series of figures has some systematic or logical property. The subject is given a set of wooden insets bearing other figures that can be arranged in a way analogous to those on the frame, as shown below. The problems begin at such an easy level that virtually everyone gets the idea of what is required without any verbal instructions. The "items" are graded in difficulty so that the test is suitable from age 2 years to adult.

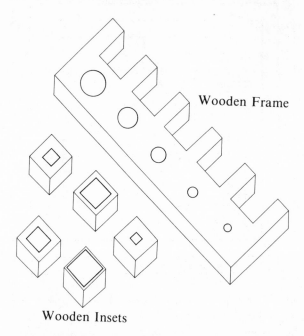

Wooden Frame

Wooden Insets

Figure Copying.   The ability to copy simple geometric forms is one of the oldest tests of children's intelligence. Binet incorporated several figures for copying in his early tests, and these are retained in present-day tests such as the Stanford–Binet, the Wechsler Preschool and Primary Scale of Intelligence (WPPSI), the McCarthy Scales of Children's Abilities, and the Bender–Gestalt test.

The child is asked to copy each figure so as to make it as much like the model as possible. On the facing page are the ten forms used in the Gesell Figure Copying Test, presented in order of difficulty as determined by the percentage of children who can copy each figure at a given age. With a constant criterion of 50 percent passing, these figures span an age range from about 3 years to 12 years. Copying tests are not useful with normal children beyond 10 to 12 years of age, where the quality of performance closely approaches the adult asymptote.

The copying test is given without time limit, and the subject is urged to attempt to copy every figure. A pencil with an eraser is an essential feature of the testing procedure, so that the subject can erase and improve his drawing at will. The most fascinating thing about this test is the great ease and correctness with which a child will copy some of the first figures and the great difficulty, in fact virtual impossibility, in copying later figures.

For example, a child will be able to copy perfectly every figure up to and including the triangle; he will have difficulty with the criss-cross rectangle, and will find the diamond and all the succeeding figures just impossible, no matter how hard he tries or how much he erases and redraws. His failing attempts lack certain essential features. The difficulty is a conceptual one; it is not a perceptual or motor problem. More is said about this test in Chapter 14 (pp. 662–665).

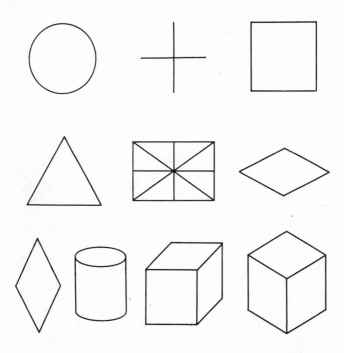

Another well-known figure-copying test is the Bender–Gestalt, consisting of eight figures, mostly of greater complexity than the Gesell figures. For normal children, it is essentially a measure of general intelligence, just like the Gesell figures. But the Bender–Gestalt is more often used in the clinical assessment of adults suspected of brain damage. The normal adult has no difficulty in copying all the figures. Many persons with brain damage, however, find the test inordinately difficult and often are unable to copy a number of the figures anywhere near correctly. Below are the figures used in the Bender–Gestalt test.

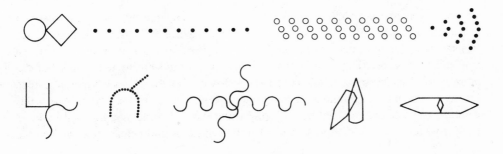

Draw-a-Man Test. The subject is given a blank sheet of paper and a pencil and is simply asked to "draw a man." Various features of children's drawings reveal the child's mental maturity. The drawings of preschoolers differ conspicuously from those of sixth-graders, and there are of course continuous gradations in between these age groups, so that the tests can be scored on a scale of mental age in terms of definite criteria and by comparison with models typical of the drawings of children at each age. Scoring standards and norms were originally provided by Florence L. Goodenough (1926) and have been revised by Dale B. Harris (1963). The test, now called the Goodenough–Harris Drawing Test, is discussed further in Chapter 14 (pp. 660–662). Below are specimen drawings that have been scored according to the Goodenough–Harris criteria.

Man: Raw Score 7	Woman: Raw Score 31	Man: Raw Score 66
CA 5-8 IQ 73	CA 8-8 IQ 103	CA 12-11 IQ 134

SUMMARY

The identification and measurement of general mental ability depends on a great variety of test items. The items that can measure general intelligence are virtually unlimited. All items that involve some degree of conscious mental effort, mental complexity, and mental manipulation are positively correlated with one another in unrestricted samples of the population. This means that all mental test items having the characteristics just cited measure something in common, although any single test item usually measures this common factor to only a slight degree; it measures more of something that is peculiar to itself. By composing tests of a large number of such items, individual differences in the factor common to all of the items emerge clearly above the background "noise" that is specific to each item. Thus, even though each single item measures the common factor to a much smaller degree than it measures something else, the sum total of a large number of items yields a highly reliable measure of the general factor that is common to all items. The total variance (individual differences) in test scores is comprised mostly of the sum of the covariance (correlations) among all of the items.

In view of these factors, items cannot be properly evaluated or criticized (except for strictly formal defects) as to their psychometric effectiveness outside the context of the test as a whole. An item's psychometric effectiveness is determined by a procedure known as *item analysis,* which looks at the difficulty levels of the items and their intercorrelations with other items or with the total score on the test, within a given population.

Charles E. Spearman subsumed these empirical observations in his principle of "the indifference of the indicator," which means that the common factor of general mental ability, which Spearman labeled g, can be measured in a great variety of ways. This fact has given rise to a multitude of intelligence tests comprised of items that are superficially quite different in appearance but that all measure essentially the same thing: g or the general intelligence factor. The taxonomy of mental tests and test items includes such classifications of tests as group or individually administered tests, verbal, nonverbal, performance, speed versus power, breadth versus altitude, and culture-loaded versus culture-reduced. Examples of each type of test are displayed in this chapter, which also reviews briefly the history of the discovery and development of tests of general ability by such pioneers of psychometrics as Galton, McKeen Cattel, Binet, Spearman, E. L. Thorndike, Terman, and Wechsler.

Chapter 6

Do IQ Tests Really Measure Intelligence?

It is difficult to imagine that the concept of intelligence, by one name or another, has not been around at least since *Homo sapiens* appeared on the earth. Individual differences in ability that do not stem directly from differences in sensory and motor functions have been noticed by virtually all humans in all times and places. The words for "intelligence" vary according to time and place, of course, but the concept itself is ancient. The earliest-known literature makes use of some concept of intelligence and recognizes individual differences in intelligence. The concept of intelligence is found in the three-thousand-year-old Upanishads, sacred writings of Hinduism, and in the writings of the ancient Greek philosophers Plato (427–347 B.C.) and Aristotle (384–322 B.C.). The great orator and educator of ancient Rome, Quintillian (A.D. 35–95), gave the following advice to teachers, which looks much like something one might read about individual differences in a modern textbook of educational psychology:

> It is generally, and not without reason, regarded as an excellent quality in a master to observe accurately differences of ability in those whom he has undertaken to instruct, and to ascertain in what direction the nature of each particularly inclines him; for there is in talent an incredible variety, and the forms of mind are not less varied than those of bodies.   (As quoted in Stoddard, 1943, p. 79)

Thomas Aquinas (1225–1274) defined intelligence as the "power to combine and separate," that is, the ability to see the similarity among dissimilar things and the dissimilarities among similar things, which is a fair characterization of a good many of the items found in present-day intelligence tests.

Today, if the word "intelligence" were to be included in the Vocabulary test of the Wechsler Adult Intelligence Scale, it would undoubtedly rank as one of the easier items in the order of difficulty.[1] Most adults could correctly define "intelligence" in the lexical sense. It is defined in *Webster's New Collegiate Dictionary* (1974) as follows: "the ability to learn or understand or to deal with new or trying situations: REASON." In popular parlance the term and its antonym "unintelligent" are most often used in their adjective form. The many more or less synonymous adjectives that come to mind for most people in connection with the words "intelligent" and "unintelligent" are found listed in *Roget's Thesaurus:*

> **Adj.** *intelligent,* quick of apprehension, keen, acute, alive, brainy, awake, bright, quick, sharp; quick-, keen-, clear-, sharp-, -eyed, -sighted, -witted; wide

awake; canny, shrewd, astute; clear-headed; far-sighted; discerning, perspicacious, penetrating, piercing, nimble-witted; sharp as a needle; alive to; clever; arch.

wise, sage, sapient, sagacious, reasonable, rational . . .

Adj. *unintelligent,* -intellectual, -reasoning; brainless; having no head; not bright; inapprehensible.

addle-, blunder-, muddle-, pig-, -headed.

weak-, feeble-minded; shallow-, rattle-, lack-, -brained; half-, nit-, short-, dull-, blunt-, -witted; shallow-, addle-, -pated; dim-, short-, -sighted; thick-skulled; weak in the upper storey.

shallow, weak, wanting, soft; dull; stupid . . .

The strictly verbal definitions of ''intelligence'' by leading psychologists are little if any improvement on the general dictionary definitions or those given by the layman. Here are some examples:

The power of combination.   (Herman Ebbinghaus, 1897)

The power to think abstractly.   (Lewis M. Terman, 1921)

The power of good responses from the point of view of truth.   (Edward Lee Thorndike, 1921)

That which can be judged by the incompleteness of the alternatives in the trial and error life of the individual.   (Leon Lee Thurstone, 1921)

Comprehension, invention, direction, and censorship; intelligence lies in these four words.   (Alfred Binet, 1910)

Intelligence is: (1) tendency to take and maintain a definite direction, (2) capacity to make adaptations for the purpose of attaining a desired end, and (3) power of autocriticism.   (Lewis M. Terman, 1916)

Measureable intelligence is simply what the tests of intelligence test, until further scientific observation allows us to extend the definition.   (Edwin G. Boring, 1923)

Intelligence is the ability to undertake activities that are characterized by (1) difficulty, (2) complexity, (3) abstractness, (4) economy, (5) adaptiveness to a goal, (6) social value, and (7) the emergence of originals, and to maintain such activities under conditions that demand a concentration of energy and a resistance to emotional forces.   (George D. Stoddard, 1943)

Intelligence is defined as the entire repertoire of acquired skills, knowledge, learning sets, and generalization tendencies considered intellectual in nature that are available at any one period of time.   (Lloyd G. Humphreys, 1971)

According to Humphreys, the category of knowledge and skills considered ''intellectual in nature'' is a matter of consensus among psychologists at any given time.

Other definitions emphasize the *capacity to acquire* knowledge and skills. Others stress assimilation, analysis and synthesis, and communication. David Wechsler (1975) probably best represents the viewpoint of most clinical psychologists in interpreting intelligence as an aspect of the total personality—an effect of multiple causes rather than as a cause iteslf. Intelligence is seen by Wechsler as involving personality and values as well as cognition. Because intelligence is viewed as a complex of many abilities and traits, Wechsler believes it cannot be measured separately and independently. Wechsler states:

> What we measure with [intelligence] tests is not what tests measure—not information, not spatial perception, not reasoning ability. These are only a means to an end. What intelligence tests measure, what we hope they measure, is something much more important: the capacity of an individual to understand the world about him and his resourcefulness to cope with its challenges.   (Wechsler, 1975, p. 139)

Acting "intelligently," either in taking a test or in any other situation, involves a certain self-discipline to think before acting, to be self-critical, to "keep one's eye on the ball," to persist in the face of difficulty, and so on. These may be regarded as personality traits more than as cognitive abilities. Thus response to an intelligence test task has been characterized by Cronbach (1976) as "an orchestration of knowledge and judgment and temperament" (p. 209).

Some critics of IQ tests have seized on such notions and, by extrapolation, argue that IQ tests measure just about everything *except* intelligence: personality traits, cultural background, opportunity, quality of schooling, values, interests, attentiveness, distractability, and so on.

Purely verbal or lexical definitions are obviously unsatisfactory for scientific purposes. They lack precision and they vary from one authority to another; they only roughly outline a broad domain of mental or behavioral phenomena rather than a criterion for objective measurement. The semantic, logical, and scientific problems of defining a term like "intelligence" have been brilliantly analyzed by T. R. Miles, who concluded: "The important point is not whether what we measure can appropriately be labelled 'intelligence,' but whether we have discovered something worth measuring. And this is not a matter that can be settled by an appeal to what is or is not the correct use of the word 'intelligent'" (Miles, 1957, p. 157).

No attempts to define intelligence that I have ever come across have included purely sensory or motor abilities or physical strength or endurance in the concept of intelligence, and nowhere is a behavioral disability resulting from a sensory or a motor handicap thought of as a lack of intelligence. The deaf-mute is not thought of as "unintelligent," neither is the blind nor the physically disabled. The idea of intelligence is clearly independent of sensory–motor functions.

Many formal definitions, and popular conceptions as well, suggest some kind of distinction between *intelligence* and *performance*. It is recognized that a highly intelligent person might also be very lazy and therefore never accomplish much. So there is an implied distinction between intelligence and achievement, yet it is a quite blurred distinction in popular discourse. The possession of knowledge is a form of achievement. Yet the amount of knowledge that a person seems to display, as well as the type of knowledge, are often interpreted as signs of the person's intelligence level. On the other hand, it is seldom the case that a lack of formal education per se is equated with a lack of intelligence; opportunity and interest are taken into account. The popular conception of intelligence is that it is more a property of the individual himself than of his or her circumstances.

Because people assign such a variety of meanings to "intelligence," often vague or inconsistent meanings, people's ranking of their own acquaintances in terms of "intelligence" are not likely to be a highly consistent or valid criterion. If intelligence test scores do not correlate perfectly with subjective judgments of persons' intelligence, it does not necessarily mean that the test scores are in error. Perhaps our subjective judgments are more in error. But how can we know this? Of course, if there were no correspondence at all between our subjective impressions of various persons' intelligence and their test scores, there would be good reason to doubt that the test measured intelligence at all. In fact, most persons probably do not think of others as ranked along a single dimension of general intelligence, but in terms of rather specific capabilities and talents. Persons tend more to be known and valued for what they can actually do rather than in terms of a general overall level of ability or potential.

The properties measured by our instruments usually begin as subjective judgments. Temperature is a good example. People were aware of variations in temperature long before there were any objective measurements of temperature. Judgments of temperature are imperfectly correlated among different persons, or even the same person at different times, depending on the humidity, the person's activity level and age, surrounding air currents, and so on. The idea that anything as subtle and complex as all the manifestations of changes in temperature could be measured and quantified on a single numerical scale was scoffed at as impossible, even by the leading philosophers of the sixteenth century.

The first thermometer invented by Galileo in 1592 did not go far in dispelling the notion that temperature was inherently unmeasurable, because the earliest thermometers, for about their first hundred years, were so imperfect as to make it possible for those who wished to do so to argue that no one could ever succeed in measuring temperature. Temperature was then confounded with all the subtleties of subjective judgment, which easily seem incompatible with a single numerical scale of measurement. How could the height of a column of mercury in a glass tube possibly reflect the rich varieties of temperature—damp cold, dank cold, frosty cold, crisp cold, humid heat, searing heat, scalding heat, dry heat, feverish heat, prickly heat, and so on?

The early thermometers were inconsistent, both with themselves and with each other. Because they consisted of open-ended glass tubes, they were sensitive to changes in barometric pressure as well as to temperature. And there were problems of calibration, such as where to locate the zero point and how to divide the column of mercury into units. It was believed, incorrectly, that all caves had the same temperature, so thermometers were calibrated in caves. The freezing and boiling points of water were also used in calibration, but, as these vary with impurities in the water and the barometric pressure, the calibration of different thermometers at different times and places resulted in thermometers that failed to correlate perfectly with one another in any given instance. They lacked reliability, as we now would say.

All the while, no one knew what temperature is in a theoretical or scientific sense. There was no theory of thermodynamics that could explain temperature phenomena and provide a complete scientific rationale for the construction and calibration of thermometers. Yet quite adequate and accurate thermometers, hardly differing from those we use today, were eventually developed by the middle of the eighteenth century. Thus the objective measurement of temperature considerably preceded the development of an adequate theory of temperature and heat, and necessarily so, as the science of thermodynamics could not possibly have developed without first having been able to quantify or measure the temperatures of liquids, gasses, and other substances independently of their other properties. Measurement and theory develop hand in hand; it is a continuing process of improvements in the one making possible advances in the other.

The measurement and theoretical understanding of intelligence are quite analogous to the case of temperature, except that in psychology we have not yet arrived at a unified theory of intelligence at all comparable with the thermodynamic theory of physics in completeness and unanimous assent. But today we are far from being totally in the dark concerning the nature of what intelligence tests measure.

For one thing, they do in fact correlate, though far from perfectly, with subjective judgments of intelligence. But we should not expect more than positive but imperfect correlation, for much the same sort of reason that subjective judgments of temperature cannot correlate perfectly with thermometer readings. There are too many confounding factors in subjective judgments.

Just how do people go about making judgments of intelligence when asked to do so? On what observations do they base their judgments? Children are generally judged as more intelligent when they display knowledge, vocabulary, language usage, and a level of comprehension that are advanced for their age. The 5-year-old who talks and acts in many ways like a typical 7-year-old is regarded as a bright youngster. The child who easily learns certain cognitive skills that are either very difficult or practically impossible for most children his own age is universally seen as possessing superior intelligence. Another factor that enters into judgments of children's intelligence is the child's interests and spontaneous play activities. Children who read a good deal, collect things, build things, write stories, ask questions, acquire a detailed knowledge about certain things on their own—animals, airplanes, automobiles, music, science, or whatever—are usually regarded as bright. The child who quickly catches on to games requiring some thought—checkers, chess, card games, Monopoly, and the like—and can more or less consistently beat his age mates or even older siblings who have had at least equal experience in the game is also viewed as bright.

IQ tests are in large part an attempt to observe, under standardized conditions, many of these commonsense and practically universal indicators of "brightness" or intelligence. It turns out, in fact, that the IQ scores are very substantially correlated with parents' and teachers' and peers' judgments of children's brightness, relative to their age mates'. Parents can rank order their own children with fair accuracy, and school teachers do even better when asked to rank the children in their own classes, provided that the teacher has had time to become acquainted with all the pupils. The correlations between the teachers' ranking of pupils for "brightness" and their tested IQs are typically between .60 and .80.

We may ask why the correlations are not higher than this. What are the factors that make for discrepancies between teachers' judgments of intelligence and tested IQs? Most important probably is the fact that teachers tend to judge in terms of *mental age* rather than IQ, so that older children in the class are rated too high and the youngest in the class are underrated. In a study we did on this point, it turned out that, although teachers' ratings correlated close to .60 with Lorge–Thorndike IQs, they correlated closer to .80 with mental age on the test. Teachers also overrate girls and underrate boys, whereas the tested IQs show no appreciable difference between the sexes. In teachers' ratings docile behavior and nice manners are somewhat confounded with judgments of intelligence.

Other confounding factors are social extraversion and eagerness. Pupils who speak up more, who most eagerly raise their hands to be called on to recite, who volunteer for activities, and the like are understandably the most often overrated by teachers. This is not to say that these traits may not be considerable assets, but they are more a matter of personality than of intelligence and are not reflected in IQ scores.

In conducting one study in which I wished to obtain rather extreme groups of children with high and low IQs where IQ tests had not previously been used, each teacher in the elementary school was requested to submit the names of the two brightest and two dullest children in her class, according to her own judgment. I then personally tested all the nominated children on the Wechsler Intelligence Scale for Children. There was a very clear separation of the IQs of the two groups for the most part, but there were also some interesting anomalies that highlighted the causes of the imperfect correlation between teachers' judgments and measured IQ.

What struck me most, however, is that, while administering the WISC to the few children whose actual IQs were most discrepant from the teachers' judgments, I myself was surprised at the results when I scored the tests. A few children seemed quite bright who in fact were not at all exceptional in IQ, and a few fairly high-IQ children gave the appearance of being rather dull. For example, a painfully shy 9-year-old fourth-grade girl who had been nominated the dullest in her class (which was a quite random group) turned out to have a WISC Full Scale IQ of 116. It surprised me because the girl was so taciturn and each response was so hesitant and minimal that one got the superficial impression of failing performance at every step of the way. Yet it objectively scored up as IQ 116. On the other hand, a 9-year-old boy whose teacher nominated him to the "brightest" group (accompanied by the teacher's notation, "the brightest kid in the whole school, not just in my class") tested out as quite average. Again, I was rather surprised in scoring his test, because his behavior during the whole session gave the impression of "brightness." Even with only a quite average IQ, which I think was probably quite accurate in this case, I believe that this boy will probably go far in the world, though his greatest assets are clearly not in the cognitive sphere. He was a handsome boy with a very "bright" appearance, an extraverted, self-confident and eager personality; he was talkative and gave quick and often clever-sounding answers to the questions; he attacked the nonverbal performance items with obvious relish. Yet it all added up to a Full Scale IQ of only 105, with no discrepancy between the Verbal and Performance IQs! But these cases were the instructive exceptions. In the vast majority of cases the teachers had correctly selected children with extreme deviations from the average IQ.

It is probably more difficult directly to judge the intelligence of adults, and we are inclined to rely more on indirect clues such as the person's level of educational attainment or occupation (or of the spouse's). Breadth and detail of knowledge displayed in conversation as well as articulateness of expression also undoubtedly influence judgments. Difficulty in judging, especially in casual situations, stems from the fact that adults have become much more specialized than children in their knowledge and skills. The knowledge and skills that people possess in connection with their different occupations cannot easily be equated, nor can knowledge associated with different interests. The sportsman, the baseball fan, the opera buff, the political enthusiast—all seemingly know a lot about different things. To rank them in intelligence, one would need to estimate how much they know about many different things in general, as well as the level of complexity and cognitive skills that are typically demanded by their occupations. Yet there is such great latitude in these kinds of criteria that one could venture judgments only within a very broad range. I do not know of any study of overall subjective judgments of adult intelligence, but there is much evidence (reviewed in Chapter 8) that indirect clues such as education and occupation are substantially correlated with mental test scores. And, because spouses' IQs are known to be correlated as much as siblings' (about 0.50), one can guess a person's intelligence better than chance just from an estimate of the intellectual level of the person's spouse. If you know one and not the other, the statistically best guess is that the unknown is halfway between the known and the average of the general population. But the margin of probable error in such a statistical estimate is, of course, great for any single instance.

Animal Intelligence

If the concept of intelligence were really just a human fiction invented by the "establishment" to justify social inequalities and perpetuate various forms of social injustice, as some critics of IQ tests have claimed, then it should seem surprising indeed if a similar concept of intelligence arose independently in the field of zoology, from the comparative study of animal behavior. In trying to gain some understanding of the nature of intelligence, it should prove instructive to note the features that characterize differences in the cognitive capabilities of various phyla and species of animals. Why is there almost universal assent that some animals are more intelligent than others? By what criteria do we judge the dog to be more intelligent than the chicken, the monkey more intelligent than the dog, the chimpanzee more intelligent than the monkey, and the human more intelligent than the chimp? Zoologists, ethologists, and comparative psychologists have amassed a great deal of substantial information in answer to this question.[2] Some of the findings that are the most pertinent to our discussion are worth reviewing briefly.

The main indices of intelligence in animals are the speed of learning and the complexity of what can be learned, the integration of sensory information to achieve a goal, flexibility of behavior in the face of obstacles, insightful rather than trial-and-error problem-solving behavior, transfer of learning from one problem situation to somewhat different situations, and capacity to acquire abstract or relational concepts. There is a definite relationship between high and low ratings of animals' performances along these dimensions (all of which involve a common factor of differences in complexity) and the animals' phylogenetic status. Numerous ingenious behavioral tests have been devised to investigate this relationship, tests that permit comparisons of behavioral capacities of quite differing animals despite their often vast differences in sensory and motor capacities. It is possible to give such diverse species as fish, birds, rats, cats, and monkeys essentially equivalent forms of the same test problems. In terms of measured learning and problem-solving capacities, the single-cell protozoans (e.g., the ameba) rank at the bottom of the scale, followed in order by the invertebrates, the lower vertebrates, the lower mammals, the primates, and man. The vertebrates have been studied most intensively and show fishes at the bottom of the capacity scale, followed by amphibians, reptiles, and birds. Then comes the mammals, with rodents at the bottom followed by the ungulates (cow, horse, pig, and elephant, in ascending order), then the carnivores (cats and dogs), and finally the primates, in order: new world monkeys, old world monkeys, the apes (gibbon, orangutan, gorilla, chimpanzee), and, at the pinnacle, humans. Because of individual differences within species, there is considerable overlap between adjacent species and even adjacent phyla in the phylogenetic hierarchy.

Behavioral differences among species, like physical differences, are a product of evolution. Natural selection, by acting directly on the behavior involved in the animal's coping with the environment, indirectly shapes the physical structures underlying adaptive behavior, of which the nervous system is the most important. There is much evidence for evolutionary continuity in the behavior of organisms, just as there is in their morphology. The phylogenetic differences in the complexity of behavioral capacities are clearly related to brain size in relation to body size, and to the proportion of the brain not involved in vegetative or autonomic and sensory-motor functions. Development of the cerebral cortex, the association areas, and the frontal lobes phylogenetically parallels behavioral complexity (Jerison, 1973). Also we know that the higher the animal ranks in the phyletic scale, the more seriously do lesions in the cortex of the brain affect its objectively measured behavioral capacity. Thus, differences in behavioral complexity of mammalian species are definitely linked to evolutionary status and the size and structure of the brain. Cranial capacity, which is closely correlated with brain size, is known to have increased markedly over the five million years of human evolution, almost tripling in size from the earliest fossils of Australopithecus up to present-day man.

It is most instructive to note the essential features of the various behavioral tests that most clearly reveal the increasing complexity of adaptive capacities of animals, going from lower to higher classes. Virtually all animals, certainly all those above the level of worms, are capable of the simplest forms of learning—habituation and the formation of stimulus–response association or conditioned responses. But these simplest forms of learning show up only relatively small differences among the phyla. At the level of conditioning the octopus acquires simple stimulus–response connections almost as quickly as the dog, which does not differ appreciably from monkeys and humans. Speed of simple learning, in short, does not much distinguish phylogenetic levels. Nor is speed of simple stimulus–response learning or conditioning correlated with intelligence assessments among humans, except at the lowest extreme of pathological mental defect.

Behaviorally, the phylogenetic hierarchy shows an increasing complexity of adaptive capabilities and an increasing degree of intersensory integration and greater breadth of transfer and generalization of learning as we move from lower to higher phyla. The degree of complexity and abstractness of what can be learned, given any amount of time and training, shows quite distinct differences going from lower to higher phyla. Each phyletic level in general possesses all the learning capacities (although not necessarily the same sensory and motor capacities) of the levels below itself, in addition to new emergent abilities, which can be broadly conceived of as an increase in the complexity of information processing. This increase of complexity of information processing is the common dimension along which all animal tests of intelligence can be ordered.

Trial-and-error learning is just one step above simple conditioning, and it shows greater phyletic differences than stimulus–response conditioning—differences in speed of learning rather than distinct discontinuities in capability from one phylum to another. In the purest forms of trial-and-error learning, which do not allow any possibility for solving the problem or for "catching on," so to speak, humans do not perform conspicuously better than lower animals. In the absence of visual cues, rats can learn by trial-and-error to run through a complicated maze, finally avoiding all the blind alleys, in about as many trials as it takes for college students.

The kinds of test situations that show the most marked differences among species are those that pose a problem, or series of problems, for the animal and allow the possibility of more than just trial-and-error learning, that is, the possibility of "catching on" by discriminating and integrating a number of features of the problem situation— "sizing it up," so to speak. This is very much the essence of what is involved in many human intelligence test items.

Habit reversal is a common experimental method in comparative psychology. It begins with simple trial-and-error learning. The animal must learn by trial-and-error to discriminate between two stimuli (say, a white triangle and a black triangle); response to one stimulus is consistently followed by no reward or by punishment (e.g., electric shock), whereas response to the other is rewarded, usually with food. Learning is complete when the animal consistently chooses the positive (i.e., rewarded) stimulus in a succession of, say, ten trials, in which the positive and negative stimuli are randomly presented on the right or left side on each trial. Depending on the type of animal (below man), learning such a discrimination may take anywhere from a dozen (or fewer) trials up to several hundred. Once the animal has learned the discrimination, the two stimuli are *reversed,* that is, response to the previously rewarded stimulus is now unrewarded and the previously unrewarded stimulus is now rewarded. The animal then is required to learn the new discrimination to the same criterion of mastery as the first one, for example, ten successive responses to the rewarded stimulus. The two stimuli are reversed again, and the animal has to learn to reverse its discriminative response. And so on.

Various versions of this reversal discrimination problem, which are made appropriate for different species' sensory and response capacities, and with appropriate forms of reward for different species, have been tried on animals at different levels of the phyletic scale—that is, earthworms, crabs, fishes, turtles, pigeons, rats, and monkeys (Bitterman, 1965, 1975). The principal finding is that these various animals do not differ so much in the number of trials that it takes them to learn the first discrimination, but in how quickly they can learn each of the successive reversals. Fish (and animals below them in the phyletic scale) show no sign of "catching on" or "learning to learn." For the fish, each reversal of the positive and negative stimuli is like an entirely new problem and takes just as long to learn as the first problem. The turtle, which is phylogenetically higher than the fish, shows a slight improvement from one reversal to the next. The pigeon does considerably better, whereas the rat improves markedly in its speed of learning, from one reversal to the next. Monkeys learn still more quickly and, after a comparatively few reversals, will take only one trial to learn each successive discrimination. Immediately after the very first instance that the reward does not follow the positive stimulus, the monkey consistently selects the other stimulus until the first time it is not followed by the reward, and then the monkey immediately reverses its choice. He can be said to have "caught on" completely. Psychologists refer to this kind of learning as "learning to learn" or the formation of a "learning set." The speed of acquiring learning sets is one of the most sensitive and clear-cut indices of species differences.

It is most interesting that, when portions of the rat's cerebral cortex are removed, thereby reducing the most prominent evolutionary feature of the mammalian brain, the learning capacity of the decorticated rat in the discrimination reversal experiment is like that of the turtle, an animal with little cerebral cortex, and it would probably be like that of the fish if all the rat's cortex could be removed. The fish has no capacity at all for acquiring learning sets.

The same learning-set discrimination reversal problems have been given to monkeys and human children of varying ages (see Hunt, 1961, pp. 80–83). In one study, children 2 to 5 years old, on the average, acquired the discrimination reversal learning set in about half the number of trials as rhesus monkeys. The rhesus monkey, in turn, develops discrimination learning sets much more quickly than the phylogenetically more primitive marmoset and squirrel monkey (Harlow, 1959, p. 506). The chimpanzee stands between the rhesus monkey and nursery school children in rate of learning-set formation. Harry F. Harlow, the leading researcher on learning-set acquisition in primates, makes the following observation: "All existent discrimination LS [learning set] data on all measured species are in keeping with the anatomical data bearing on cortical complexity, and it is obvious that LS techniques are powerful measures for the intellectual ordering of primate and possibly even nonprimate forms" (Harlow, 1959, p. 507).

The same type of learning-set formation in children is definitely related to IQ as measured by standard tests (Hunt, 1961, p. 83). Mentally retarded children with IQs ranging from 50 to 75 require many more trials to attain a criterion of perfection in learning sets than do average children with IQs in the 90 to 109 range, and one study found that most of the severely retarded, with IQs ranging between 14 and 48, do not acquire learning sets of this type at all.

A more complex type of learning set is the so-called *oddity problem*. The animal is presented with three (or more) stimulus objects—two are alike and one is different, for example, two circles and a square. Response (e.g., picking it up) to the odd one is always rewarded. As soon as the animal learns the first oddity problem up to some criterion of mastery, it is given a completely new set of three stimulus objects, with one different from the other two, say, two triangles and a star. Improvement in performance, that is, fewer trials needed to master each successive new oddity problem, indicates that the animal is catching on to an abstract concept—the concept of oddity. It is interesting that the capacity to acquire this concept is absent in animals below a certain level of cortical development. No animals below primates are known to have mastered the oddity problem no matter how much training they are given. In fact, the oddity problem is beyond the capacity of the young human child.

One can differentiate between different species of primates by varying the complexity of the oddity problem, as in the so-called combined oddity–nonoddity problem. In this problem the animal must learn to respond to the odd item if the background on which all the stimulus objects are presented is colored, say, *green* and respond to one of the nonodd stimuli if the background is *red*. This problem can be mastered only by the higher primates—monkeys and apes as adults and normal human children of school age. If we add one more dimension of complexity—a triple-ambiguity problem in which selection of the odd or nonodd item depends simultaneously on two different attributes of the background, such as color and shape, then it is beyond the capabilities of all lower primates, given any amount of training, except a few of the brightest chimpanzees. It is beyond most humans below a certain age and cannot be mastered even by some human adults.

Notice that the *complexity* of the oddity problem (the number of features that must be taken into consideration simultaneously) as well as its *abstract* nature (the actual stimuli in no two problems are alike) are the crucial features in the test's discrimination between species at the primate level. Sensory capacities and memory per se are quite unimportant variables in this hierarchical differentiation.

In tests of sensory acuity, in visual and auditory discrimination per se, many animal species outperform humans. In certain tests of simple memory, humans do little better than chimpanzees. In one memory study (cited by Harlow & Harlow, 1962, p. 34), human adults, children, and chimpanzees were compared on a rather difficult memory task involving the location of rewards (e.g., candy or fruit) that the experimenter had placed under different objects in the room while the animal or human subject watched. At some time later the subject had to retrieve the hidden rewards, and the memory score depended on how few objects not containing the rewards the subject had to pick up before locating each reward. The chimpanzees scored better than any of the human children, who were 8 years old, and they did almost as well as the human adults. The Harlows point out: "Since one would expect that the translation of object and position cues into language—an automatic response of older children and adults in a learning situation—would be of some help, one is led to doubt that humans are superior to chimpanzees in basic memory capacity." This being the case, it would seem surprising if tests of sheer memory would be very good as a measure of individual differences in human intelligence. As we shall see later, simple learning and memory tests, even though they may be highly reliable measures, are not highly correlated with general intelligence.

Another type of test that discriminates between lower and higher primates, as well as between younger and older human children is *cross-modal transfer*. The animal learns to discriminate the positive (rewarded) stimulus object from other nonrewarded objects in one sensory modality, say, visual, and then can immediately transfer this learning to another situation in which the same set of stimuli is presented in another sensory modality, say, tactile. To learn to discriminate an object shaped as a triangle from objects shaped as a circle and a square entirely by sight, and then to be able immediately to make the same discrimination in the dark simply by handling the objects, is an example of cross-modal transfer. The immediate transfer from visual recognition to tactile recognition implies that the animal has acquired some abstract mental representation or concept of the distinguishing features of the rewarded object. Monkeys and most preschool children cannot do it, whereas some chimpanzees and most school-age children are capable of cross-modal transfer in the visual and tactile modalities.

A somewhat similar but simpler form of transfer is *relational learning,* or transposition generalization. The animal learns to discriminate between, say, a dime and a nickel, with the larger of the two (i.e., the nickel) always rewarded. Then it is presented with a quarter and a half-dollar piece. Choosing the quarter would be an example of primary stimulus generalization, because the quarter is closer in size to the previously rewarded nickel. Choosing the half-dollar would be an example of transpositional generalization— the nickel was the larger of two things in the first problem, and now in the second problem the half-dollar is the larger of two things. The response in this case is not to a specific object or other objects that most closely resemble it, but to a *relationship*. The capacity for transpositional generalization increases going from lower to higher phylogenetic levels and increases in children from infancy to about school age. Cats and monkeys are capable of auditory transposition, that is, discriminating a particular short melody when it is played in different keys and in different octaves. Lower animals are apparently incapable of this kind of relational learning. Their learning is much more attached to specific stimuli, except for the little flexibility allowed by primary stimulus generalization.

Detour problems also illustrate the capacity to "size up" the elements of a problem situation. Detour problems show marked differences between species much lower than primates in the phylogenetic scale. A hungry animal, *A,* is placed in a large screened enclosure with one side open, and food, *F,* is placed outside, like this:

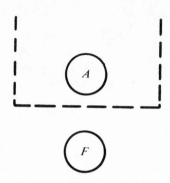

A hungry chicken, seeing a heap of grain through the wire mesh, will run back and forth inside the fence for a long time, seemingly unable to turn its back on the food; only in its increasing excitement in rushing about does it get out of the enclosure merely by chance. A hungry dog or cat placed in the same situation, with meat on the other side, behaves very differently: a dog or cat looks back and forth once or twice, may even run from one side to the other, but then the situation is quickly sized up and the animal runs directly around the barrier to the food. A rat engages in much more trial and error than a cat or dog, but a rat is far superior to a chicken in solving this problem.

Now, what if we close all *four* sides of the cage and attach a single *conspicuous* piece of string to the food, with a knob on the other end inside the cage, in such a way that the animal can easily pull the food into the cage. Here the dog and cat are helpless. They never see the possibility on their own; their eyes do not follow the string to the piece of food—they do not "see" the connection. Monkeys, however, have no problem; they "get the idea" almost immediately, and the only way that one can make a discriminating intelligence test out of it for monkeys is by complicating the problem by using two or more strings laid down in ways that make the problem quite tricky. Figure 6.1 shows various positions of the strings in one experiment and the percentage passing (i.e., pulling the correct string on the first trial) among a group of rhesus monkeys. (The 50 percent passing the most difficult two-string problem is no better than chance.)

In more complex string-pulling tasks, which use pulleys or other means whereby pulling the string makes the desired object move away from the cage before it moves back toward the cage, the lower primates cannot do the problem at all, but chimpanzees can solve the problem. For them, solution is possible even when it does not involve bringing the object closer all the time. This reflects the chimp's ability to "see," that is, understand, the more complex relationships involved in the pulley problems.

This superiority of chimps over monkeys is illustrated also in their use of tools. If a stick with a small rake on the end of it is left outside the cage within reach of the animal,

Figure 6.1. String-and-food problems of various levels of complexity given to animals. Food is represented by circles. The wire mesh that separates the animal from the food is represented by dashed lines.

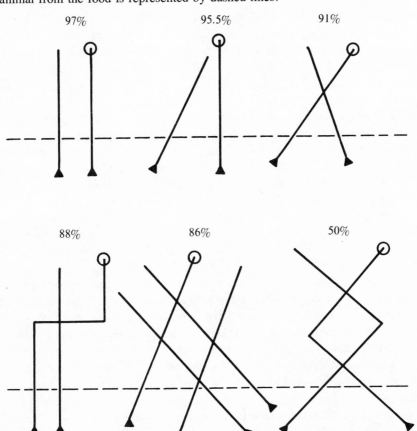

both rhesus monkeys and chimps will use it to rake in a piece of food that is out of reach. But this occurs only if the rake and the food are simultaneously within the field of vision. The chimp, however, can mentally bridge a larger gap between the stick and the food and will use a stick from inside its cage. If there are two shorter sticks in the cage, neither of which is long enough to reach the food but which can be joined by inserting the end of one into the other to make a stick twice as long, some chimps can figure this out and use the joined sticks to reach the food. But they can do this only when both of the unjoined sticks are simultaneously in the field of vision. Their intelligence is essentially object bound. All the elements needed for the solution of the problem must be physically present to the animal's senses for the solution to occur. In humans, however, the greater capacity for abstraction permits the purely mental visualization or imagination of the complete solution before any overt action is taken, even when the action is taken at a much later time or in a different location. Only chimps with a good deal of experience at using sticks to get food will go in search of sticks when food is out of reach. Monkeys apparently never do this, and it is not universal in chimps, who have little organized memory to call on, as compared with simple recognition memory. Wolfgang Köhler (1887–1967), the great pioneer of research on primate behavior, remarked that "the time in which the chimpanzee lives is limited in past and future" (quoted in Viaud, 1960, p. 35, from Köhler's *The Mentality of Apes*, 1917).

Notice that the problems that Köhler and others found to distinguish most among primates are those that permit the animal to "catch on" to a set of relationships rather than problems that can be solved only gradually by trial and error. It is also this type of problem, requiring insight or the grasping of the essential elements and relationships in a posed problem, that most characterizes the test items that best represent the general intelligence factor of standard intelligence tests for humans.

In fact, many of the experimental procedures used to study the mentality of monkeys and apes have been directly applied to human children. There is considerable overlap between apes and children in problem-solving capabilities. In the problem of assembling sticks to reach a reward, for example, the performance of the brightest chimps is equaled only by normal children of 9 or 10 years of age. Younger children and retarded children do not solve the problem without instruction. Normal children and institutionalized children with varying degrees of mental retardation, as independently diagnosed, have been given the battery of tests that Köhler used with chimpanzees and that other investigators have used with monkeys. Exactly the same *rank order of difficulty* of these problems emerged for human children as for chimpanzees and other apes, suggesting that these tests reflect some similar mental functions or behavioral capacities across species of primates, including man (Viaud, 1961, pp. 44–45). This general factor seems to be related to the *complexity* of the problems and the degree to which they permit solution by seeing relationships in contrast to merely hitting on the solution by more or less random trial-and-error behavior. This complexity factor common to such experimental problems rank orders children in the same way that standard IQ tests do. Thus the kind of ability to deal with complexity that is measured by such tests is not just peculiar to individual differences among human children within a particular culture but, rather, is continuous with broader biological factors of neural organization reflected as well in individual differences within other primate species and even in the evolutionary differences in behavioral capacities between various species. In this sense, intelligence is as much a biological reality, fashioned by evolution, as the morphological features of the organism.

Armchair Analysis versus Empirical Investigation

Subjective judgments and semantic or logical analysis by themselves are entirely inadequate for an understanding of human intelligence in a scientifically meaningful sense. At most they can only roughly outline the territory in need of empirical investigation. In the early history of psychology, philosophic armchair analysis based on each psychologist's introspection into his own mental processes and the contents of his conscious experience gave rise to "faculty psychology," which thought the mind to be composed of many distinct faculties. Individual differences in mental abilities were viewed as differences in the degree of development of the various faculties. It was believed that the main function of education was to train and develop the mental faculties. Intelligence was defined in terms of these faculties, and psychologists differed from one to another in the faculties or combinations of faculties that they included in their conceptions of mental ability. Here, listed alphabetically, are some of the mental faculties mentioned most often in the early psychological literature: abstraction, aesthetic, attention, autocriticism, comprehension, dexterity, discrimination, foresight, imagination, insight, inventiveness, judgment, kinaesthetic, language, memory, motor control, prudence, reason, recollection, sensory acuity.

As Spearman (1904) first pointed out, faculty psychology's armchair analysis of mental abilities does not tell us what kinds of tests can best measure intelligence, and in fact it assumes a large number of distinct abilities each of which would have to be measured separately. But do all the verbal labels for various faculties really represent different mental processes and abilities? Is "foresight" different from "prudence"? "Memory" from "recollection"? "Imagination" from "inventiveness"? "Reason" from "insight" or "judgment"? As long as psychologists debated these questions at the level of purely verbal and logical analysis, there was no way to resolve their arguments.

Spearman pointed out that, if one could make up tests that measure each of these faculties of the mind, and if they were truly independent faculties, then they should be uncorrelated, and it would make no sense to add up the scores on the various tests to obtain a single overall score by means of which persons could be ranked along a single dimension of general mental ability. The faculty theory thus seemed theoretically incompatible with Galton's notion of a general all-around ability as accounting for the largest part of the differences among persons' intellectual achievements.

But, in fact, when tests were devised to measure various faculties, it was commonly found that they were not completely independent. Although these intercorrelations, which were nearly all positive, were far from perfect and varied widely, they were substantial enough for Spearman to insist that any satisfactory theory of intelligence would have to account for the positive correlations among nearly all objective measures of human abilities. Spearman's chief importance in the history of psychology stems from his pioneering the development of the objective quantitative method, known as factor analysis, for investigating the organization or structure of mental abilities. Factor analysis helped to break through the semantic deadlock of introspective faculty psychology.

I do not wish to leave the impression that logical analysis is inappropriate to all of the issues in this field. Far from it. Such analysis is an essential formality for keeping clear just what it is that we are talking about at any given time. Semantic explicitness in this sense is an essential aspect of objectivity and is one of the scientific virtues. A good example of such a useful logical formulation is D. O. Hebb's (1949) distinction between *Intelligence A* and *Intelligence B* and Philip E. Vernon's (1969) further distinction of *Intelligence C*. It will pay to keep these distinctions in mind throughout this book. If at this stage one does not wish to concede even the usefulness of the term "intelligence," one can just as well use a more neutral term such as *ability* and simply refer to abilities *A, B,* and *C.* At this point, it is the distinction among *A, B,* and *C,* more than the nature of the trait itself, that is the important thing to understand.

Intelligence A refers to the individual's genotype, that is, the complement of genes, or the genetic blueprint, so to speak, that conditions the individual's intellectual development. The genotype is itself a theoretical construct. No one can look at a genotype for intelligence under a microscope or isolate it in a test tube. Yet we know that there is a genetic basis for the development of intelligence and that genetic factors are involved in individual differences in intelligence. The methods of quantitative genetics permit us to make certain inferences about the probable extent to which individual differences in any measured trait are due to genetic variation, and, in some cases, we can even make inferences about the nature of the genetic influence, such as the number of genes involved, the proportions of dominant and recessive genes, and the sex linkage of genes affecting the trait. We cannot go into all of this here. It is a highly technical subject that would require a whole book to do it justice.

The important point for our present purpose is to understand that *Intelligence A* is a theoretical construct and cannot be observed or measured directly. In other words, no test scores are measures of *Intelligence A.* But this does not mean that *Intelligence A,* or the individual's genotypic value (i.e., genetic deviation from the population mean) cannot be statistically estimated, within the limits of a certain probable error, on the basis of test scores, at least in principle. I add "in principle," because the theoretical chain of reasoning going from an individual's actual test score or other measurement to an estimate of the individual's genotypic value on the trait in question is a theoretically long and complicated one, and the crucial links or parameters in it are no stronger than the quality and generalizability of the empirical data that went into estimating them. In any case, estimating genotypic values is an exercise in quantitative genetics. It has had no place in the practice of mental testing.

Intelligence A is important in the theory of intelligence, however, because the pattern of correlations among IQs of persons of various degrees of genetic relatedness, whether reared together or reared apart, must be adequately accounted for by any complete theory of intelligence. Genetical models that are based on general principles of genetics and are applicable to metric traits in all plants and animals fit the various kinship correlations for IQ remarkably well (Jensen, 1973a; Jinks & Fulker, 1970). On the other hand, no theoretical model that ignores genetics has ever been formulated that can explain the distinctive pattern of kinship correlations found for intelligence test scores, a pattern that is typical of many hereditary physical traits as well. So there seems to be no escaping the fact that an adequate theory of intelligence will have to be closely linked to genetical theory.

Intelligence B is the individual's phenotypic intelligence. It is the final product, at any given time in the individual's life span, of the genotype and all the environmental factors that have interacted with the genotype from the moment of conception. The phenotype is not a constant value like the genotype, but is altered by constitutional and experiential factors. While it is usually said that the phenotype is what can be actually observed or measured, and this is what Hebb had in mind as *Intelligence B,* it is really better to think of *Intelligence B* as one step removed from what we can observe or measure at any given moment or by any single test. *Intelligence B* is best regarded as an average of many measurements over a limited period of time, so as to average out momentary and idiosyncratic features of specific tests and situations. *Intelligence B* is the individual's *general* intelligence, not his performance in any specific situation or his score on any particular test. The idea of general intelligence is itself an abstraction, a theoretical construct, that cannot be properly understood without some basic conception of factor analysis, from which the notion of general intelligence gains its scientific meaning.

Intelligence C is the sample of "intelligent" behavior that we can actually observe and measure at a given point in time. *Intelligence C* is a *sample* of *Intelligence B,* or an imprecise estimate thereof. Scores on any particular intelligence test do not correlate perfectly with scores on the same test taken at another time, and scores on different intelligence tests are highly but not perfectly correlated. Each of these separate measurements is an instance of *Intelligence C*. They all vary somewhat, but also they are all measures of something in common, as shown by their substantial intercorrelations. The "something in common" is mainly *Intelligence B*. Whenever we talk about a score on any particular intelligence test, we are talking about *Intelligence C*. Some test scores are better estimates of *Intelligence B* than others. We can determine this by means of factor analysis, a mathematical technique for analyzing the matrix of intercorrelations among a number of tests. The meanings of *Intelligences A, B,* and *C* are summarized in Figure 6.2. Each can be thought of in terms of the sources of variance that enter into it. *Intelligence C* includes sources of variance (i.e., causes of individual differences) that are not included in *Intelligence B*, which in turn includes sources of variance that are not included in *Intelligence A*. To understand this in any further depth requires that we introduce some of the basic concepts of the factor analysis of human abilities.

Factor Analysis

I had originally thought of including a "technical appendix" on factor analysis at the end of the book. Then I realized that many readers who know little or nothing about factor analysis would be too apt to skip it and muster through the rest of this book with at most only the vaguest notion of what factor analysis is all about. That would be most unfortunate. The basic vocabulary, concepts, and typical results of factor analysis are so absolutely central to any theoretical understanding of intelligence and to the scientific definition of the concept itself that the reader who does not possess some idea of how factor analysis works will simply run the risk of reading the whole remainder of this book with misapprehension every time certain key terms are used, including the key concept of "intelligence." There is a point in any scientific understanding of a subject beyond which popular verbalism simply cannot proceed. A somewhat more technical and quantitative form of expression becomes essential if one is to get even a glimmer of understanding of what the scientists who work in the field are really talking about. I will try to keep the exposition of factor analysis as basic, simple, and nontechnical as possible, consistent with conveying those ideas most essential for understanding the main themes of this book. There are a number of excellent textbooks[3] on factor analysis for readers who wish to pursue the subject at a more detailed and technical level, but all texts on the subject presuppose a background of statistics equivalent to a two-year college course. The follow-

Figure 6.2.   The relationships of *Intelligences A, B,* and *C.*

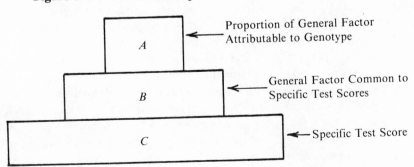

ing presentation of factor analysis presupposes no more than the ability to read. It is conceded that, as compared with a regular course on factor analysis, this brief explanation is almost like describing Beethoven's Fifth Symphony in terms of its first four notes.

Factor analysis is a method for expressing the variation in a number of different measurements (or *variables*) in terms of a (usually) smaller number of theoretical dimensions called *factors*. Essentially, the method of factor analysis converts a matrix of intercorrelations among a number of different variables (called a *correlation matrix*) into a *factor matrix* that shows the correlations of each of the variables with a smaller number of factors or hypothetical sources of the variance in the original measurements. To proceed beyond this very brief and rather abstruse description of factor analysis, we have to be clear about the terms "variable," "variance," and "correlation."

Variable.   A variable is any measurement that varies from person to person in the population or from time to time in the same person—such as height, weight, blood pressure, age, income, family size, and scores on a particular test.

Variance.   This is a precise quantitative expression of the amount of variation in a given variable in a particular population or a sample from that population. The variance, symbolized as σ^2, is also referred to as the "mean squared deviation," since it is the mean of the squared deviations of every score from the mean of all the scores,[4] that is,

$$\sigma^2 = \Sigma(X - \bar{X})^2/N, \qquad\qquad (6.1)$$

where

Σ = "the sum of,"
X = a score,
$\bar{X}$ = the mean of all scores, and
N = the total number of scores.

(The well-known *standard deviation,* σ, is simply the square root of the variance.) It is obvious from equation 6.1 that the variance could never be less than zero. When there is absolutely no variability among the scores, the variance is zero.

The variance is a more general and useful index of variability than the standard deviation, the reason being that variances are additive and standard deviations are not. For example, consider the distribution of adult height in the population. The variance of height measurements in the population can be thought of as a linear or additive composite of variation due to sex (because, on average, males are taller than females) and to individual variation within each sex, plus variation due to errors of measurement or unreliability. (If we measure everyone twice, there will not be perfect agreement in the measurements, due to unreliability of measurement.) The total population variance in height can be expressed as the sum of the separate variances due to each of these three sources, that is, sex difference plus individual differences within sexes plus measurement error. The variance of the means of the two sexes, plus the average of the variances for men and for women separately, plus variance due to measurement error (i.e., the variance of the differences between the first and second measurements) all add up to the total variance for all the measurements. Thus, we are able to partition the variance into a number of smaller component variances that make up the total variance. It is called a linear or additive model, because it expresses the total variance as a linear equation, that is, one in which the several components of variance simply add up to the total variance.

At times it is convenient to "standardize" the scores on a number of different variables so that they all can be expressed in the same units and all of them will have the same mean and the same variance. These are called standard scores or z scores. They express the original measurements or scores in terms of their deviation from the mean in units of the standard deviation. Understanding z scores will facilitate the following discussion of correlation. An obtained measurement or raw score X is transformed to a z score as follows:

$$z = (X - \bar{X})/\sigma, \qquad\qquad (6.2)$$

where $\bar{X}$ is the mean of all the raw scores and σ is the standard deviation of the distribution of raw scores. A distribution of z scores, therefore, will always have a mean of 0, a standard deviation of 1, and a variance of 1.

Correlation. "Correlation" was originally spelled "co-relation." It is a quantitative index of the degree of relationship between two variables. The idea of a quantitative index of co-relation originated with Sir Francis Galton, who was interested in expressing precisely the degree of resemblance between parents and their children (and other kin) in various measurable physical traits. Galton invented the coefficient of correlation, which was further developed by the English statistician Karl Pearson (1857–1936), who has been called "the founder of the science of statistics." The most useful and the most commonly used measure of correlation is called the *Pearson product–moment coefficient of correlation*, or just "Pearson correlation," or "Pearson r" for short. In statistics it is always symbolized by a lower-case r. Just what does it tell us? There are several possible ways of explaining r; each one gives a helpful insight into the meaning of correlation.

To take a simple example, what is the correlation between height and weight? We can measure the height and weight of each of fifty 12-year-old boys and plot the measures as a bivariate distribution, as shown in Figure 6.3. Each of the fifty boys' height and weight is represented by a single point located in this two-dimensional space. (Such a graph is called a "scatter diagram" or "scattergram.") When a smooth line is drawn so as to just encompass all of the points, we see that it forms an ellipse. Casual inspection of Figure 6.3 reveals that the taller boys tend to weigh more than the shorter boys, so there is visibly some relationship between height and weight. But it is also clear that it is not a perfect relationship, for, if it were, all the points would be located exactly on the straight line running through the long axis of the ellipse. The fact that the data points show some scatter about this straight line means that the correlation is less than perfect. The more scatter, the lower the correlation. If there were no correlation at all, the data points would be scattered about so that a smooth line encompassing them would be a circle instead of an ellipse. As the correlation gradually increases, the circular shape of the scattergram becomes more and more elliptical until finally, when there is a perfect correlation and there is no scatter at all, the ellipse becomes a straight line.

The correlation is said to be *positive* when high values on one variable go with high values on the other, as in Figure 6.3. When high values on one variable go with low values on the other, the ellipse would tilt in the opposite direction, and the correlation would be *negative*. An obvious example of a negative correlation would be the correlation between the *average rate of speed* in miles per hour of automobiles traveling from San Francisco to Los Angeles and the number of *hours of travel time*.

We can express the degree of relationship between height and weight shown in

Figure 6.3.   A scatter diagram of the heights and weights of fifty 12-year-old boys. The coefficient of correlation between these measurements of height and weight is .75.   (From Blommers & Lindquist, 1960, p. 365)

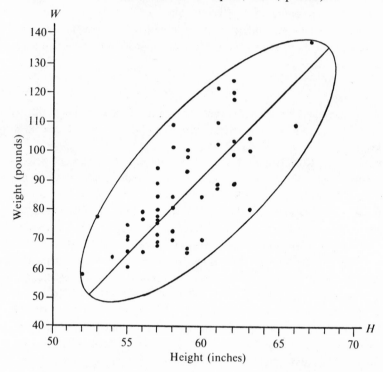

Figure 6.3 very precisely by means of Pearson's *r*. Textbooks on statistics show various ways of computing *r*, using a calculator, but the simplest method to explain (although not the easiest to compute on a calculator) is to convert all the height and weight measurements to *z* scores, as described in equation 6.2. Then we multiply each boy's *z* score on height by his *z* score on weight, sum all of these products, and divide by the number of boys. The result is Pearson's *r*, expressed symbolically[5] as

$$r = \Sigma xy/N, \tag{6.3}$$

where

$$r = \text{Pearson's coefficient of correlation,}$$
$$x \text{ and } y = \text{the two variables expressed as } z \text{ scores, and}$$
$$N = \text{the number of persons (or pairs of measurements).}$$

For the data in Figure 6.3, the *r* is +0.75.

Pearson *r* is a continuous metric on a scale ranging from -1 to 0 to $+1$, that is, from a perfect negative correlation to zero correlation to a perfect positive correlation.

Knowing the *r* between any two variables permits one to predict the most likely value of an individual's score on one variable from a knowledge of his score on the other variable and to know the margin of probable error in making such a prediction. If we know an individual's z score on variable X, the individual's predicted z score on variable Y will be

$$\hat{y} = r_{xy}x, \tag{6.4a}$$

where

$\hat{y} =$ the predicted z score on Y,
$x =$ the known z score on X, and
$r_{xy} =$ the correlation between X and Y: $r_{xy} = r_{XY}$.

The z scores can easily be transformed back into the original measurements; for example,

$$X = x\sigma_X + \bar{X},$$
$$\hat{Y} = r_{xy}(\sigma_Y/\sigma_X)(X - \bar{X}) + \bar{Y}. \tag{6.4b}$$

Equation 6.4b, which predicts $\hat{Y}$ from X, is known as the *regression equation*. Notice that, when the correlation is less than perfect (i.e., $r < 1$), the predicted score $\hat{Y}$ is closer to the mean than the predictor score X. The predicted score $\hat{Y}$ shows regression toward the mean of Y. In the example in Figure 6.3, we would find that the tallest boys are not so far above the mean in weight as they are above the mean in height and that the shortest boys are not so far below the mean in weight as they are in height. Notice that regression works in both directions, that is, $\hat{x} = r_{xy}\hat{y}$ and $\hat{y} = r_{xy}x$.

Error of Estimate and Interpretations of the Correlation Coefficient

Just how *accurate* is such a prediction based on a correlation? It will be completely accurate only if the correlation is perfect; then, given X, we can predict Y with complete certainty. When the correlation is less than perfect but is greater than zero, we can predict only with some *error of estimate*, as it is called—the greater the correlation, the smaller is the error of estimate. The quantitative index of this error is the *standard error of estimate*, which is simply the standard deviation of all the actual values of Y for any given predicted value, $\hat{Y}$. In other words, the obtained values of Y will be scattered around the predicted value $\hat{Y}$ and the standard deviation of this scatter is the *standard error of estimate*, or SE_E. Two-thirds of the obtained values of Y will fall within the range of one SE_E of the predicted value. In predicting Y from X, the SE_E of $\hat{Y}$ is

$$SE_E = \sigma_Y \sqrt{(1 - r_{xy}^2)\left(\frac{N-1}{N-2}\right)}, \tag{6.5}$$

where

$\sigma_Y =$ the standard deviation of Y,
$r_{xy}^2 =$ the square of the correlation coefficient, and
$N =$ the number of persons in the sample on which r_{xy} is based.

Obviously, when the correlation is perfect ($+1$ or -1), $SE_E = 0$; and when the correlation is zero, $SE_{Ey} = \sigma_Y$, (i.e., the standard deviation of Y). If we have no knowledge of the individual's score on X, or of the correlation between X and Y, the best prediction we can make of the individual's score on Y is the mean, $\bar{Y}$, and our error of estimate will be σ_Y. If we know r_{xy} we can predict $\hat{Y}$ with an error of estimate $= SE_{Ey}$, and, if $r > 0$, SE_{Ey} will be less than σ_Y. And so we can think of r in terms of the proportion of reduction in our error of estimate; that is,

$$r_{xy} = (\sigma_Y - SE_{Ey})/\sigma_y. \tag{6.6}$$

Thus we can say that $r \times 100$ is the percentage of improvement in prediction over the prediction when $r = 0$. Statisticians prefer to square both sides of equation 6.6, so that r^2 expresses the proportion of *variance* in Y that is predicted by or associated with X, and $1 - r^2$ is the proportion of residual variance in Y not accounted for by X. You will recall that variances are additive, and that is why equation 6.6 has to be squared—to express all the elements as variances—if we want to talk about the proportion of *variance* in one variable accounted for by the other.

Another interpretation of correlation is in terms of the *slope* of the regression line. Consider Figure 6.4. This scatter diagram shows the relationship between variables X and Y, both transformed to z scores z_x and z_y. The two heavy lines are the regression lines. Both regression lines pass through the mean on each variable; in this case the mean is 0, as the variables are expressed as z scores. The regression line labeled $\hat{y}$ on x is the one and

Figure 6.4. Regression lines (of the regression of variable x on y and of y on x) in a correlation scatter diagram. X is the best predicted value of x for any given value of y, and $\hat{y}$ is the best predicted value of y for any given value of x.

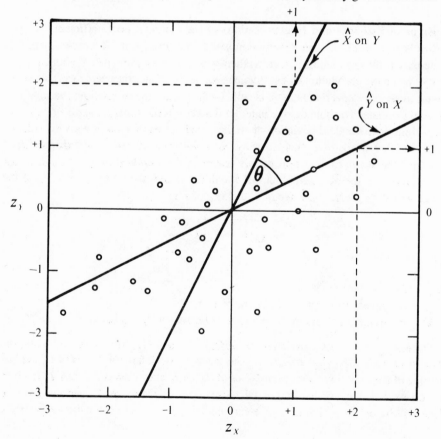

Figure 6.5.   Correlation between variables X and Y depicted as the number of elements (N_c) common to both X and Y. The variance of each variable is represented by the total area of each square. (See text for full explanation.)

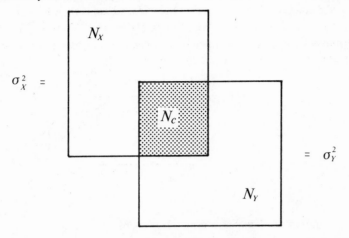

only straight line that predicts the value of y for any given value of x with the minimum error of estimate. It is the best-fitting straight line to all the actual values of y for any particular value of x. It is referred to as the linear regression of y on x, and all the predicted values of y, , that is, $\hat{y}$, for every value of x falls on this line. Likewise, the line $\hat{x}$ on y is the one line that best predicts the value of x for any given value of y. For example, for individuals with $z_x = +2$, the best prediction of their $\hat{z}_y$ is seen to be $+1$; just follow the broken line from $+2$ on the z_x scale up to the regression line of y on x and then over to the y axis. It works the same way in predicting $\hat{z}_x$ from $z_y = +2$; follow the broken line from the z_y axis over to the regression line of $\hat{x}$ on y and up to the x axis.

The positions of the two regression lines can be determined with exactitude by the method of least squares, a mathematical procedure that we need not go into here. It is explicated in most textbooks on statistics.

But notice that we can obtain the ratio of any predicted value of $\hat{y}$ for any given value of x, that is, $\hat{y}/x$. This ratio is equal to the correlation r_{xy}. When both variables are expressed as z scores, $\hat{y}/x = \hat{x}/y = r$, and r can be defined as the *slope* of the regression line; that is, for every unit that we deviate from the mean of variable x, we deviate ry units on variable y; and for every unit that we deviate from the mean of variable y, we deviate rx units on variable x. In Figure 6.4 it can be seen that $r = 0.50$.

The *sine* of the angle θ subtended by the two regression lines is related to the correlation coefficient; $r = 1 - \text{sine } \theta$. In Figure 6.4, the angle θ is $30°$, the sine of $30°$ is 0.50, and $r = 1 - 0.50 = 0.50$. When the correlation is perfect, the two regression lines come together, so that θ is $0°$, the sine of $0°$ is 0, and $r = 1$. When there is no correlation at all, the two regression lines are at right angles to one another, so that $\theta = 90°$, the sine of $90°$ is 1, and $r = 0$.

Especially in understanding factor analysis, it is most helpful to think of correlation in terms of the proportion of *variance* shared in common by two variables. Think of the variance as an *area* containing a number of elements. To make it visually clear, we can show the area as a square containing N elements, as shown in Figure 6.5. The variance,

σ_x^2, of variable x contains $N_x + N_c$ elements, the variance, σ_y^2, of y contains $N_y + N_c$ elements. (Because we are dealing with z scores, both x and y have the same unit variance, i.e., $\sigma_x^2 = \sigma_y^2 = 1$.) Now, the correlation between variables x and y can be represented by the amount of *overlap* of the two areas, which is the variance or number of elements, N_c, they have in common. We can express the correlation r_{xy} in terms of the following formulas, which are algebraically equivalent to the previously given formulas for r_{xy} (equations 6.3 and 6N.1|[in the notes]):[6]

$$r_{xy} = \frac{N_c}{\sqrt{N_x + N_c} \times \sqrt{N_y + N_c}} , \qquad (6.7)$$

or

$$r_{xy} = \frac{2N_c}{(N_x + N_c) + (N_y + N_c)} , \qquad (6.8)$$

where

N_c = the number of elements common to variables x and y,
N_x = the number of elements unique to x, and
N_y = the number of elements unique to y.

As can be seen in Figure 6.5, one-fourth, or .25, of the area (variance) of each square (variable) is shared in common by the other. Because σ_x^2 and $\sigma_y^2 = 1$, and $N_c = .25$, we can write, according to equation 6.7,

$$r_{xy} = \frac{.25}{\sqrt{.75 + .25} \times \sqrt{.75 + .25}} = .25.$$

Thus, the correlation can be thought of as the proportion of variance shared in common. The proportion that is *unique* to each variable, therefore, is $1 - r$.

We can use the same method to determine the correlation between one area and just that part of the area that is shared in common, as depicted in Figure 6.6. Again, using equation 6.7,

$$r_{xc} = \frac{.25}{\sqrt{.75 + .25} \times \sqrt{0 + .25}} = .50.$$

Thus, the *correlation* between variable x and just what it shares in common with variable y is .50. (We also see that $\sqrt{r_{xy}}$ is equal to the correlation between x and the elements common to x and y.) The part of the total variance in x that is shared with y accounts for (or "predicts") .25 of the total *variance* in x. Notice that the variance in variable x accounted for by what it has in common with variable y is the square of the correlation between variable x and the element common to both x and y. The common elements or area of overlap is called a *factor*. *Factor analysis*, then, is a method for determining the factors that exist among a number of variables. But, before we pursue this point further, a few words are in order about the psychological, as contrasted to just the statistical, nature of correlation.

Figure 6.6.   Illustration of the correlation between variable X and the proportion of elements that it shares in common (shaded area) with another variable. As in Figure 6.5, the variances are represented by areas, that is, N_c is one-fourth or 25 percent of the total N.

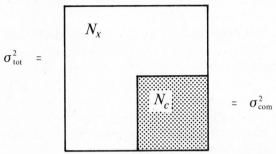

Causes of Correlation

Textbooks constantly remind us that correlation does not necessarily imply causation. Two variables with no direct causal connection between them may be highly correlated as a result of their both being correlated (causally or not) with a third variable. Even if $r_{xy} = 0$, we cannot be sure there is no *causal* connection between x and y. A causal correlation between x and y could be statistically *suppressed* or obscured because of a negative correlation of x with a third variable that is positively correlated with y. A variable that, through negative correlation with x (or y) and a positive correlation with y (or x), reduces the correlation r_{xy} is called a *suppressor*★ variable.

To establish causality, other information than correlation is needed. Temporal order of the correlated variables increases the likelihood of causality, that is, if variable x precedes variable y in time, it is more likely that x causes y. But even correlation plus temporal order of the variables is insufficient as a proof of causality. To prove causality we must resort to a true *experiment,* which means that the experimenter (rather than natural circumstances) must randomly vary x and observe the correlated effect on y. If random experimental manipulation (i.e., experimenter-controlled variation) of variable x is followed by correlated changes in y, we can say that variation in x is a *cause* of variation in y. This is why experimental methods are so much more powerful than correlation alone. Unfortunately, much of the raw material found in nature that we wish to subject to scientific study cannot be experimentally manipulated—to do so may be practically unfeasible or it may be morally objectionable. It is largely for these reasons that experimental plant and animal genetics have been able to make much greater scientific strides than human genetics.

Although it is a commonplace truism that "correlation does not prove causation," one seldom sees any discussion of the *causes* of correlation between psychological variables. I shall here briefly summarize the five main causes of correlation between measurable psychological variables, using as examples the correlations between scores on any two tests, call them x and y, in the abilities domain.

1. Common Sensory–Motor Skill.   Variables x and y may be correlated because they involve the same sensory-motor capacities. This is a practically negligible cause of correlation among most tests of mental ability. That is, very little, if any, of the test variance in the normative population is attributable to individual differences in visual or auditory acuity or to motor coordination, physical strength, or agility. Persons with severe sensory or motor handicaps must, of course, be tested for mental ability on specially made or carefully selected tests on which performance does not depend on the particular sensory or motor function that is disabled.

2. Part–Whole Relationship.   Variables x and y may be correlated because the skills involved in x are a subset of the skills required in y. For example, x is a test of shifting automobile gears smoothly and y is a driving test; or x is a test of reading comprehension and y is a verbal test of arithmetic problem solving. Transfer of skill from one situation to another, due to common elements, also comes under this heading. Playing the clarinet and playing the saxophone are more highly correlated because of common elements of skill than the correlation between playing the clarinet and playing the violin, which involves fewer elements in common.

3. Functional Relationship.   Variables x and y may be functionally related in the sense that one skill is a prerequisite for the other. For example, a performance on a digit-span test of short-term memory may correlate with performance on an auditory test of arithmetic problem solving, because the subject must be able to retain the essential elements of a problem in his memory long enough to solve it. Memory may not be intrinsic to arithmetic ability per se (i.e., it is not a part–whole relationship), as might be shown by a much lower correlation between auditory digit-span and arithmetic problems presented visually so that the person does not have to be able to remember all the elements of the problem while solving it.

4. Environmental Correlation.   There may be no part–whole or functional relationship whatever between x and y, and yet there may be a substantial correlation between them because the causes of x and y are correlated in the environment, whether x and y be specific skills or items of knowledge. For example, there is no functional or part–whole connection between knowledge of hockey and knowledge of boxing, yet it is more likely that persons who know something about hockey will also know something more about boxing than they will about say, the opera. And it is more likely that the person who knows something about symphonies will also know something about operas. In all such cases, correlated knowledge is a result of correlated environmental experiences. The same thing applies to skills; we would expect to find a positive correlation between facility in using a hammer and in using a saw, because hammers and saws are more correlated in the environment than are, say, hammers and violins. Different environments and different walks of life can make for quite different correlations among various items of knowledge and specific skills. On the other hand, a common language, highly similar public schools, movies, radio, television or other mass media, and mass production of practically all consumer goods and necessities all create a great deal of common experience for the vast bulk of the population.

5. Genetic Correlation.   Variables x and y may be correlated because of common or correlated genetic determinants. There are three kinds of genetic correlation that are empirically distinguishable by the methods of quantitative genetics: correlated genes, pleiotropy, and genetic linkage.

Correlated genes, through selection and assortative mating—segregating genes that are involved in two (or more) different traits, may become correlated in the offspring of mated pairs of individuals both of whom carry the genes of one or the other of the traits.

For example, there may be no correlation at all between height and number of fingerprint ridges. Each is determined by different genes. But, if, say, tall men mated only with women having a large number of fingerprint ridges, and short men only with women having few ridges, in the next generation there would be a positive genetic correlation between height and fingerprint ridges. Tall men and women would tend to have many ridges and short persons would have few. Breeding could just as well have created a negative correlation or could wipe out a genetic correlation that already exists in the population. A genetic correlation may also coincide with a functional correlation, but it need not. Selective breeding in experimental animal genetics can breed in or breed out correlations among certain traits. In the course of evolution, natural selection has undoubtedly bred in genetic correlations among certain characteristics. Populations with different past selection pressures and different factors affecting assortative mating, and consequently different evolutionary histories, might be expected to show somewhat different intercorrelations among various characteristics, behavioral as well as physical.

Pleiotropy is the phenomenon of a single gene having two or more distinctive phenotypic effects. For example, there is a single recessive gene that causes one form of severe mental retardation (phenylketonuria); this gene also causes light pigmentation of hair and skin, so that the afflicted children are usually more fair complexioned than the other members of the family. Thus, there is a pleiotropic correlation between IQ and complexion within these families.

Genetic linkage causes correlation between traits because the genes for the two traits are located on the same chromosome. (Humans have twenty-three pairs of chromosomes, each one carrying thousands of genes.) The closer together that the genes are located on the same chromosome, the more likely are the chances of their being linked and being passed on together from generation to generation. Simple genetic correlation due to selection can be distinguished from correlation due to linkage by the fact that two traits that are correlated in the population but are not correlated *within* families are not due to linkage. Linkage shows up as a correlation between traits *within* families. (In this respect it is like pleiotropy.)

There are methods in quantitative genetics by which we can analyze the correlation between two traits into two components—genetic correlation and nongenetic or environmental correlation (e.g., Falconer, 1960, Ch. 19). To the best of my knowledge, these methods have not been applied to human behavioral data. They have been used almost exclusively in agricultural and animal genetics. Their use with humans in natural environments would involve inordinate methodological difficulties because of the correlation between genotypes and environments.

The various causes of correlation listed in the preceding paragraphs are not in the least mutually exclusive; any one or any combination of them may be involved in any measured correlation between two mental test variables. Usually all we can say is that the correlated variables have some component in common, and we do not know what the nature of the common component is, although we may try to set up testable hypotheses as to its nature.

Influences on Obtained Correlations

It is also important to understand that obtained correlations in any particular situation are not Platonic essences. They are affected by a number of things. Suppose that we are considering the correlation between two variables, x and y. We give tests X and Y to a group of persons and compute r_{xy}. Now we have to think of several things that determine this particular value of r_{xy}:

1. First, there is the correlation between X and Y in the whole population from which our group is just a sample. The correlation in the population is designated by the Greek letter rho, ρ_{xy}. Obviously the larger our sample, the closer r_{xy} is likely to come to ρ_{xy}. Any discrepancy between r_{xy} and ρ_{xy} is called sampling error and is measured by the *standard error of the correlation, SE*$_r$ (not to be confused with the standard error of estimate). $SE_r = (1 - r^2)/\sqrt{N - 1}$, where N is the number of persons (or pairs of correlated measurements) in the sample. (When ρ is zero, $SE_r = 1/\sqrt{N - 1}$.) The sample size does *not* affect the *magnitude* of the correlation, but only its *accuracy,* and SE_r is a measure of the degree of accuracy with which the correlation coefficient r obtained from a sample estimates the correlation ρ in the population. So we should always think of any obtained correlation as $r \pm SE_r$; that is, r is a region, a probabilistic estimate that tells us that r is most likely in the region of $+1SE_r$ to $-1SE_r$ from the population correlation ρ. The expression $r = .55 \pm .03$, for example, means that .55 most likely (i.e., more than two chances out of three) falls within the range of plus or minus .03 of ρ; or, to put it another way, that ρ most probably lies somewhere between .52 and .58. The larger the sample, the smaller is SE_r and the more accurate is r as an estimate of ρ. We are usually more interested in r as an estimate of ρ than in the sample r for its own sake.

2. The so-called *range of talent* in one or both variables also affects the correlation. This is an important factor to consider in making inferences from the sample r to the population ρ, because generally the range of talent in the samples used in most research studies is considerably more restricted than the range of talent in the general population. *Restriction of range* in either variable (or both) lowers the correlation. For example, the correlation between height and weight in the general population is between 0.6 and 0.7. But, if we determine the correlation between height and weight among a team of professional basketball players, the correlation will drop to between 0.1 and 0.2. The full variation in height and weight found in the general population is not found in the basketball team, all of whom are tall and lean. Figure 6.7 illustrates the effect of restriction of range on the correlation scatter diagram. The moral is that in viewing any correlation, and particularly discrepancies between correlations of the same two variables obtained in different samples, we should consider the range (or variance) of the variables in the particular group in which the correlation was obtained. For example, correlations among ability tests are usually much lower in a college sample than in a high school sample, because the college population has a much more restricted range of intellectual ability—practically the entire lower half of the general population is excluded. Thus the more selective the college, the less will students' scores on the entrance exam (or other tests of mental ability) correlate with the students' grade-point averages.

3. The reliability of the tests or measurements affects the correlation. The upper theoretical limit of the correlation between any two measures, say, X and Y, is the square root of the product of their reliabilities, i.e., the maximum possible $r_{xy} = \sqrt{r_{xx}r_{yy}}$, where r_{xx} and r_{yy} are the reliability coefficients of X and Y, respectively. The test's reliability can be thought of as the test's correlation with itself.[7] If we wish to know what our obtained correlation r_{xy} would be if our measures were perfectly reliable, we can make a *correction for attenuation*. The corrected correlation, $r_c = r_{xy}/\sqrt{r_{xx}r_{yy}}$.

Figure 6.7. The effect of extreme restriction of range on the correlation. The coefficient of correlation represented by the scatter diagram over the complete range is above .90; the correlation in the restricted range is near zero. (From Guilford, 1956, p. 457)

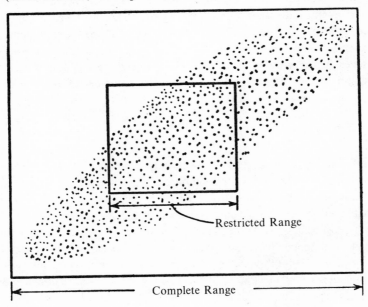

Restricted Range

Complete Range

The Correlation Matrix

When we are dealing with more than two variables, the number of correlations among the variables is $n(n - 1)/2$, where n is the number of variables. A correlation matrix is the most convenient way of displaying the intercorrelations among n variables. If there are six variables (labeled a, b, c, d, e, f) the number of correlations will be $6(6 - 1)/2 = 15$, and the correlations can be displayed in a matrix, as follows:

Variable	a	b	c	d	e	f
a	$(r_{aa} = 1)$	r_{ab}	r_{ac}	r_{ad}	r_{ae}	r_{af}
b	r_{ab}	$(r_{bb} = 1)$	r_{bc}	r_{bd}	r_{be}	r_{bf}
c	r_{ac}	r_{bc}	$(r_{cc} = 1)$	r_{cd}	r_{ce}	r_{cf}
d	r_{ad}	r_{bd}	r_{cd}	$(r_{dd} = 1)$	r_{de}	r_{df}
e	r_{ae}	r_{be}	r_{ce}	r_{de}	$(r_{ee} = 1)$	r_{ef}
f	r_{af}	r_{bf}	r_{cf}	r_{df}	r_{ef}	$(r_{ff} = 1)$

Notice that the matrix is symmetrical, with every correlation appearing above and below the *principal diagonal*, which contains the self-correlations, that is, those in parentheses. (The correlations between empirically measured variables are sometimes referred to as *zero-order correlations*. First-order correlations are correlations with one (other) variable partialed out; second-order correlations are correlations with two (other) variables partialed out, and so on.) No importance attaches to the arrangement of the variables in the matrix—it is a completely arbitrary matter, and we may rearrange the order of the variables in any way that we please. Doing so may help to highlight some interesting feature of the intercorrelations. For example, there might be a descending order of magnitude of the correlations, that is, $r_{ab} > r_{ac} > r_{ad}$, and so on, and $r_{bc} > r_{bd}$, and so on. Then the largest correlations will be nearest the principal diagonal. Such an arrangement of the correlations is called a *hierarchical matrix*. Not all correlation matrices can be so arranged. If the correlations can be arranged so as to reveal this hierarchical feature of the matrix, more or less, it is evidence of a large general factor common to all the variables. Or perhaps the correlations can be arranged in such a way as to reveal several rather distinct clusters of high correlations standing out against a background of quite low correlations. This suggests that there are a number of different factors in the matrix, the so-called *group factors*.

The General Factor

The theoretically simplest factor analysis possible involves only two variables, A and B, measured in a sample from the population. The correlation r_{AB} is the proportion of their total variance that variables A and B have in common; $\sqrt{r_{AB}}$ is the correlation of each variable with the element common to both variables; and r_{AB}^2 is the proportion of variance in one variable that is predictable from a knowledge of the other variable. The common element shared by the two variables we shall call g for "general," as it is common or *general* to both variables. Notice that we have not measured g directly; we have measurements only on variables A and B. Therefore, g is not a directly observable or directly measurable variable, but a hypothetical *factor*. At this point we are not saying anything at all about the nature of this factor; all we are saying is that it is general (i.e., common) to A and B. The proportion of the total variance in each variable that is not general to both is called their *uniqueness* and is $1 - r_{AB}$. The test's *uniqueness* has two components: random *error* of measurement, e, and *specificity*, s, which is a reliable (nonerror) component entirely specific to the particular test and not shared by the other test(s). Again, representing the total variance on each test as an area, the correlation r_{AB} can be depicted as the overlapping area in common (the error component is omitted for the sake of simplicity):

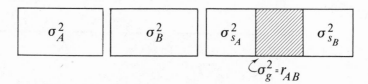

The area of overlap is the correlation and the general factor variance of these two tests; the nonoverlapping parts are the variances specific to tests A and B.

There is still another way we can look at the correlation r_{AB}: in terms of *principal axes* (also called *principal components*). Consider the correlation scatter diagram between variables A and B, as shown in Figure 6.8. The degree of relationship between A and B is shown by the scatter of the data points, each one representing an individual's pair of measurements on variables A and B. Now let us find the one straight line that lies closer to all the data points than any other straight line. This line is called a "least-squares best-fitting line," because the sum of the squared deviations (i.e., where the deviations are the shortest distances) of each of the data points from this one and only straight line is a minimum. This particular best-fitting line is called the first principal component of our

Figure 6.8. A scatter diagram for the correlation of variables A and B, and the principal components I and II of the bivariate distribution.

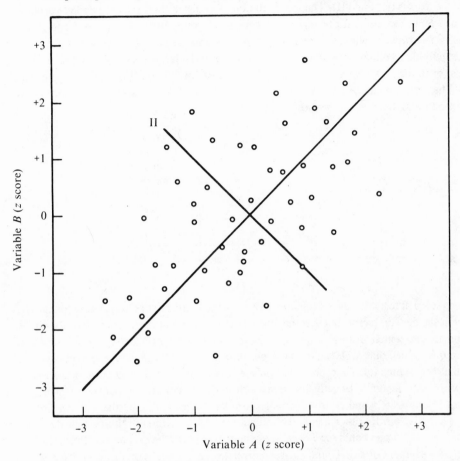

correlation r_{AB}; it is designated by the roman numeral I. It is the *general factor* in this correlation matrix.

The first principal component has this important feature: it "accounts for" more of the variance common to both of the variables A and B than any other possible component (i.e., straight line). We can give each individual a "score" based, not on the two tests A and B, but on the shortest projection of the paired AB data points on the line I in Figure 6.8. Such a derived score is called a *factor score*. It measures, in a single score, what is common to tests A and B.

The second principal component, labeled II in Figure 6.8, is defined as the one straight line at right angles to the first principal component, I, about which the squared deviations of the data points are a minimum. It, too, is a best-fitting straight line, and it accounts for the part of the total variance that is not accounted for by the first principal component. Being at right angles, the two components are said to be *orthogonal*. This also means that the two principal components are not correlated. That is, just as we can give individuals factor scores on principal component I, we can do the same on principal component II, and we will find that the correlation between these two sets of factor scores is zero.

Thus, what we have done in this simplest possible example of a principal components analysis is to exchange one set of reference axes (viz., *A* and *B*) for another set of reference axes (viz., I and II). The same amount of variance (in this case the total variance in *A* and *B*) is accounted for by either set of axes. The only difference is that *A* and *B* are *correlated variables,* whereas I and II are *uncorrelated factors.* In other words, we can locate individuals either in the *test space* in terms of the reference axes *A* and *B* (i.e., test scores) or in the *factor space* in terms of the reference axes I and II (i.e., factor scores).

The factor analysis of our two tests has consisted of transforming a correlation matrix into a factor matrix, as shown below:

Correlation Matrix

Test	*A*	*B*
A	r_{AA}	r_{AB}
B	r_{AB}	r_{BB}

Factor Matrix

Test	|	Factor I	Factor II	h^2
A	|	r_{AI}	r_{AII}	h_A^2
B	|	r_{BI}	r_{BII}	h_B^2
% Var.	|	I%	II%	

First notice that tests *A* and *B* each correlate $+.90$ with the first principal component (I), which is the general factor, but that they have symmetrically opposite correlations with the second factor, which in this simple case is the *uniqueness* of each test. Look again at Figure 6.8; notice that *high* scores on *A* are projected onto the *higher* segment of axis I and that low scores on *A* are projected on the *low* segment of I. Thus test *A* correlates *positively* with factor I. Exactly the same is true of the correlation between test *B* and factor I. Both tests *A* and *B* are positively correlated with I, that is, the *general factor.* With factor II, on the other hand, the situation is quite different. Notice that the *high* scores on test *A* project onto the *lower* segment of axis II and *low* scores on *A* project onto the *higher* segment of axis II; thus test *A* correlates *negatively* with factor II. Test *B,* on the other hand, correlates *positively* with factor II, that is, *low* scores on *B* project onto the *lower* segment of II and *high* scores on *B* project onto the *higher* segment of II. Factor II is therefore called a *bipolar* factor, as it correlates positively with one test and negatively with the other. Persons with high scores on test *A* will have low factor scores on factor II whereas persons with high scores on test *B* will have high factor scores on factor II. Factors I and II have zero correlation with each other.

The correlation between a test and a factor (e.g., r_{AI}) is called the test's *factor loading* or *factor saturation.* The proportion of the test's variance accounted for by a given factor is the square of the factor loading.

The percentage of variance (% Var.) accounted for by each factor is shown in the bottom row of the factor matrix. It is the mean of the squared loadings $\times$ 100.

The column headed h^2 is known as the test's *communality*, the proportion of the test variance accounted for by the common factors. The test's communality, h^2, is the sum of all the squared factor loadings on the common factors of that test. In the present example, $h^2 = .81$ for each test. The test's communality, h^2, is the unit total variance of the test scores minus the proportion of variance that is *specific* to the particular test and the proportion of error variance (*unreliability*) in the test scores.

In the preceding example only one common factor, namely, I, is needed to account for the intercorrelation between the tests. The rule is that the intercorrelation between any two tests is equal to the sum of the products of their loadings on the common factors, which of course excludes the *uniqueness* of each test, as it cannot enter into the correlation between the tests. In our simple example, $r_{AB} = r_{AI} \times r_{BI}$.

What have we gained by transforming our correlation matrix to a factor matrix? At the outset, notice that we can quite well describe a person's performance levels on two tests in terms of that person's standing on only one factor. Because each test correlates .90 with factor I, a factor score based on factor I gives a good indication of a person's standing on both tests. More important, the factor I score indicates the person's standing on just the ability that the two tests measure in common. If the ability that is general to both tests is of greater interest to us than are whatever abilities are specific to each test, factor analysis shows us how much of the test variance is attributable to the general factor and permits us to assign scores to persons showing their relative standing on the general factor.

Our preceding example of factor analysis, however, is much too simple to illustrate the advantages of factor analysis realistically. The importance of factor analysis depends on correlations among many more than just two variables. But, to make the point most simply, let us look at a hypothetical situation of three intercorrelated variables, that is, r_{AB}, r_{AC}, and r_{BC}. In terms of overlapping common elements, the three variables may be pictured as follows:

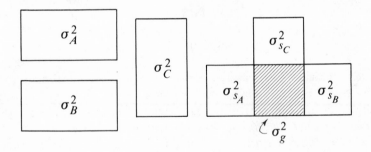

Here we see only one general factor common to all three tests; the remaining variance is entirely unique to each test. In other words, all the correlations are explainable in terms of the fact they all measure a single general factor, g. The correlations are less than perfect because each test also measures some specific factor, s.

But there are other possibilities for the intercorrelations among our three variables, like the following:

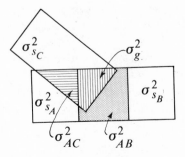

Here we see that variables *A, B,* and *C* all share *g* in common (σ_g^2) and that each has *specific* variance ($\sigma_{s_A}^2$, $\sigma_{s_B}^2$, and $\sigma_{s_C}^2$). But there are also two other factors here: one that is common to only variables *A* and *C* (σ_{AC}^2) and one that is common to only variables *A* and *B* (σ_{AB}^2). These are technically called *group factors.* They are factors that are common to some of the variables in the correlation matrix but are not common to all of the variables. (In actual practice psychologists usually do not accept as true group factors any that do not substantially involve at least three or more different tests.) Group factors are what remain after taking out the general factor and after excluding specific factors and error variance. Thus, the total variance in scores on a test (σ_X^2) may be thought of as the sum of a number of smaller variances due to the general factor (σ_g^2), one or more group factors ($\sigma_{F_1}^2$, $\sigma_{F_2}^2$, $\sigma_{F_3}^2$, etc.), a specific factor (σ_s^2), and error of measurement (σ_e^2); thus,

$$\sigma_X^2 = \underbrace{\sigma_g^2 + \sigma_{F_1}^2 + \sigma_{F_2}^2 + \cdots + \underbrace{\sigma_s^2 - \sigma_e^2}_{}.}_{}$$

$$\text{communality } (h^2) \qquad\qquad \text{uniqueness}$$

(6.9)

The *communality, h^2,* expresses the proportion of variance in the test scores attributable to common factors (including *g*). The test's *uniqueness* is that part of its variance which is not shared by any other tests in the correlation matrix; it is true variance *specific* to the particular test plus random *error* variance.

If the variance in test scores can be partitioned in this fashion, we can also think of a single test score *X* as comprised of the corresponding components:

$$X = g + \underbrace{F_1 + F_2 + \cdots + \underbrace{s_X + e}_{}.}_{}$$

$$\text{group factors} \qquad\qquad \text{uniqueness}$$

By means of factor analysis we can give persons separate factor scores on *g, F_1, F_2,* and so on. If the factors are uncorrelated, these separate scores will be uncorrelated.

Where do group factors come into the picture in Figure 6.8? As we have seen, to obtain a group factor in addition to the *g* factor we need at least three variables. To picture three variables in Figure 6.8 one has to imagine, instead of a two-dimensional square bounded by variables *A* and *B,* a three-dimensional egg-shaped swarm hanging in midair within the cube. The first principal component, I, would again be the one straight line about which all the squared deviations are a minimum; it thus best describes and accounts for most of the variance simultaneously now in all three of the variables. The first principal component is the general factor. The second principal component, always at right angles to the first, will account for the maximum amount of the variance left unaccounted for by principal component I. It is a group factor. The third principal component, at right angles to I and II, will account for the remainder of the variance; it is a specific factor. (Measurement error cannot be extracted as a separate "factor," but it can be determined independently.) Each successive component always accounts for less of the total variance than the preceding one.

Now we can go on adding more tests, but we can no longer picture their intercorrelations graphically, as we did for two tests in Figure 6.8. If the scatter diagram of the correlation between two tests requires a two-dimensional space, and the intercorrelations among three tests require a three-dimensional space, then the scatter diagram of the intercorrelations among four tests requires a four-dimensional space; five tests require a five-dimensional space, and *n* tests require an *n*-dimensional space. (Spaces beyond three dimensions are called *hyperspace.*)

An *n*-dimensional space is impossible to visualize, but this is no handicap to the purely mathematical procedure for determining the principal components of a correlation matrix of *n* tests (Hotelling, 1933). When we do a principal components analysis of a large correlation matrix, we can easily see the efficiency of this kind of analysis. Because each successive principal component extracts a smaller proportion of the total variance from the correlation matrix than was extracted by each preceding component, the percentage of variance accounted for by the latter principal components becomes so small as to be practically negligible. When the percentage of variance accounted for by a principal component (and *ipso facto* by all the subsequent components) is no greater than the percentage of error variance, it only makes sense to stop extracting any more principal components. Theoretically there are as many principal components as there are tests, but in practice the number of significant principal components that can be extracted from the intercorrelation matrix of a large number of tests is far fewer than the number of tests. This is because so many of the tests overlap each other in what they measure that, say, twenty tests might in fact really be measuring no more than four or five factors, each of which is common to three or more of the tests. Any other factors (i.e., principal components) that emerge after these first few large ones have been extracted are so small as to be swamped by the error variance, or they are too small in terms of the percentage of variance they account for to be of any practical value. No one is very interested in a factor that accounts for less than 2 or 3 percent of the variance in any test.

As has already been pointed out, the matrix of intercorrelations can be recreated from the factor matrix when the factors are orthogonal (i.e., uncorrelated). Then the correlation between any pair of tests is the sum of the products of their loadings on each of the factors. The number of factors that need to be extracted from a correlation matrix to "explain" all the correlations, therefore, is determined by the number of factors needed to recreate the matrix accurately within the margin of sampling error. If we can subtract each of our recreated correlations from each of the original correlations and the remainders (called the *residual matrix*) are not significantly larger than zero, then we know we have extracted enough factors to account for the significant variance in our correlation matrix. A simpler conventional rule among factor analysts is to go on extracting principal components until the *eigenvalue* of the principal component falls below 1. The eigenvalue is the sum of the squared loadings on the principal component in question. (I am here using the terms "principal component" and "factor" interchangeably, although there is a technical distinction that it would not be necessary or helpful to go into in this brief account.)[8]

An Artificial Example of Factor Analysis

For illustrative purposes let us perform a factor analysis on six hypothetical tests labeled *A, B, C, D, E,* and *F,* given to a sample of one hundred persons. The correlation matrix is shown in Table 6.1.

First, we must determine whether the correlation matrix is even worth factor analyzing. If in the sample all of the correlations could have resulted by mere chance, that is, they are just happenstance correlations among the variables in the particular sample, but

Table 6.1.   Correlation matrix for six hypothetical tests, with estimated communalities in the main diagonal (in brackets).

Test	A	B	C	D	E	F	Total
A	[.56]	.56	.48	.40	.32	.24	2.56
B	.56	[.56]	.42	.35	.28	.21	2.38
C	.48	.42	[.48]	.30	.24	.18	2.10
D	.40	.35	.30	[.40]	.20	.15	1.80
E	.32	.28	.24	.20	[.32]	.12	1.48
F	.24	.21	.18	.15	.12	[.24]	1.14
Total	2.56	2.38	2.10	1.80	1.48	1.14	11.46
Factor loadings (1)	.76	.70	.62	.53	.44	.34	3.39

are really not correlated variables in the population, then the obtained correlations represent nothing more than *sampling error*. There is, of course, no point in analyzing random error. A glance at Table 6.1 makes it obvious that the correlations are not random. All the correlations are positive and many are substantial. In case we are in doubt, however, there is a method for determining whether the correlation matrix as a whole is statistically significant.[9]

The first step in a factor analysis is called *estimating the communalities.* (The closer our initial estimates are to the true values, the less will be our computational work.) We do not know the communalities at the outset. The best estimate of a test's communality is the squared multiple correlation (R^2) between the given test and every other test in the matrix. But getting (R^2) itself involves considerable computational labor, and so an easy but very rough estimate of a test's communality is simply the largest correlation it has with any other test in the matrix. We enter these estimates in brackets in the principal diagonal, as shown in Table 6.1. Then, we total the rows and columns, and obtain the square root of the grand total, that is, $\sqrt{11.46} = 3.39$. Dividing each of the column totals by 3.39 gives us factor loadings (1), that is, our first crude estimates of the tests' loadings on the general factor. Because we only roughly estimated the communalities by the simple rule of inserting the highest r in each row, we can be sure that our factor loadings are not accurate this first time around; but they are a rough approximation.

After extracting the general factor, we are ready to extract the second factor. To do this we must first subtract out of our matrix that part of each correlation that is due to the

Table 6.2.   Estimated correlations between tests due to the general factor.

Test	A	B	C	D	E	F
A		.53	.47	.40	.33	.26
B	.53		.43	.37	.31	.24
C	.47	.43		.33	.27	.21
D	.40	.37	.33		.23	.18
E	.33	.31	.27	.23		.15
F	.26	.24	.21	.18	.15	

general factor. So we determine the correlations between the tests attributable to the general factor from the principle that the correlation between two tests is the sum of the products of their factor loadings. Thus, the correlation between tests *A* and *B* due to the general factor will be .76 × .70, and so on. All these correlations due to the general factor are shown in Table 6.2.

Now, after we subtract the matrix in Table 6.2 from the matrix in Table 6.1, we have a *residual matrix,* shown in Table 6.3. The first thing we notice about this residual matrix is that the correlations are extremely small. Can we possibly extract any more factors from it? A statistical test for the significance of the matrix[9] shows that it is completely nonsignificant; the small correlations are merely sampling error residue. Therefore, no more factors can be extracted. However, if we had found a statistically significant residual matrix, we would extract the next factor. Then we would compute the correlations due to the second factor by multiplying the factor loadings, and by subtraction obtain another residual matrix. If it is significant, we will repeat the process. Finally, the residual matrix will diminish to the point of nonsignificance, and that ends our analysis—but not quite.

When we have extracted all the significant factors, we then use them to make better estimates of the communalities. (Recall that the test's communality, h^2, is the sum of its squared factor loadings.) We then insert these better estimates of the communalities into the main diagonal of the original matrix and repeat the whole process all over again. We get a new, more accurate set of estimates of the communalities and insert these into the original matrix, and we go through the whole process again. By such successive *iterations,* our estimates gradually converge toward the true communalities. When further iterations result in no further significant change in the estimated communalities, the factor problem is solved and we can determine the true values of the factor loadings. It is laborious, to be sure. Fortunately we now have high-speed computers that can go through many iterations in a matter of seconds.

The example given here is very simple, because only one factor, the general factor or *g*, exists in the matrix. Successive iterations finally converge on the following values of the factor loadings in Table 6.4.

Incredibly neat—but of course this simple didactic example was specially contrived to turn out this way. Notice that the original correlations can be exactly reproduced by multiplying the factor loadings of the various pairs of tests. This proves that all the correlations in the matrix can be explained in terms of only one factor that all the tests share in common, plus a factor specific to each test. Every test measures *g* + *s* (a specific

Table 6.3. Residual matrix (from original correlations in Table 6.1).

Test	A	B	C	D	E	F
A		.03	.01	.00	−.01	−.02
B	.03		−.01	−.02	−.03	−.03
C	.01	−.01		−.03	−.03	−.03
D	.00	−.02	−.03		−.03	−.03
E	−.01	−.03	−.03	−.03		−.03
F	−.02	−.03	−.03	−.03	−.03	

Table 6.4.   Factor loadings on g.

Test	First Estimate	Final Value	h^2
A	.76	.80	.64
B	.70	.70	.49
C	.62	.60	.36
D	.53	.50	.25
E	.44	.40	.16
F	.34	.30	.09
% Var.	34	33	

factor) and nothing else. Test A has a lot of the g factor and not much of its s; test F has relatively little g and a lot of its s.

A Realistic Example of Factor Analysis

Some further points about factor analysis can be illustrated by means of a more realistic analysis, using measurements of certain physical abilities that involve skills and muscle groups that are more easily observed and understood than the entirely covert processes involved in mental tests.

Table 6.5 shows correlations among ten physical and athletic tests. The labels of the tests are all quite self-explanatory, except possibly for variables 7 and 8. In no. 7 the person is required to trace a drawing of a five-pointed star while observing his own performance in a mirror. In no. 8 the person must try to keep a stylus on a small metal disc, called the "target," about the size of a nickel, while it rotates on a larger hard rubber disc like a phonograph turntable at about one revolution per second. Electrical contact of the stylus with the small metal disc operates a timing device that records the number of seconds per minute that the stylus is in contact with the target.

Inspection of the correlation matrix in Table 6.5 shows that it is not random—there are too many high correlations, all positive, and the large correlations can be seen to be grouped or clustered in different parts of the matrix. The fact that all the r's are positive indicates that there is a substantial general factor in this matrix, and the clustering of high correlations suggests that there are probably also one or more group factors in addition to the general factor.

Table 6.5.   Correlation matrix for physical ability measures.

Variable	1	2	3	4	5	6	7	8	9	10
1. Softball throw		.76	.78	.32	.32	.29	.30	.44	.12	.16
2. Hand grip	.76		.93	.47	.47	.00	.00	.00	.14	.19
3. Chinning	.78	.93		.39	.39	.00	.00	.00	.15	.20
4. 50-yard dash	.32	.47	.39		.84	.00	.32	.32	.28	.22
5. 100-yard dash	.32	.47	.39	.84		.13	.28	.48	.65	.62
6. One-leg balance	.29	.00	.00	.00	.13		.00	.38	.27	.28
7. Mirror star tracing	.30	.00	.00	.32	.28	.00		.68	.09	.05
8. Pursuit rotor tracking	.44	.00	.00	.32	.48	.38	.68		.48	.47
9. 1-mile run	.12	.14	.15	.28	.65	.27	.09	.48		.93
10. 5-mile run/walk	.16	.19	.20	.22	.62	.28	.05	.47	.93	

Table 6.6 shows the first four principal components extracted from the correlation matrix in Table 6.5. Only four components were extracted. Together they account for 89.1 percent of the total variance in the ten variables. The remaining six components, if extracted, would account for only 10.9 percent of the total variance, averaging about 1.8 percent of the variance for each component. Thus none of the six remaining components is retained, as each one accounts for so little as not to be needed to recreate the original correlation matrix, which can be recreated, within the margin of sampling error, using only the first four components. Thus, in a sense, we have reduced ten intercorrelated variables to only four independent factors. The communality, h^2, indicates the proportion of variance in each variable that is accounted for by the four components. All the communalities are quite large, the smallest being .73.

After this purely objective mathematical process of extracting the factors, we are left with the more subjective and judgmental task of interpreting or naming the factors, if possible. We would like to be able to understand the nature of the factors underlying the pattern of correlations. We do this by examining the magnitudes of the factor loadings on the various tests. The largest factor loadings are clues to the nature of the factor.

The first principal component, I, is the general factor, and the main question is, how large is this general factor, that is, how much of the variance does it account for? In this case it accounts for 41.1 percent of the total variance or 46 percent of the total communality. Thus it is a quite large general factor, almost twice as large as the next largest factor, which accounts for only 21.6 percent of the variance. Only two of the tests have relatively small loadings on the general factor—no. 6 (one-leg balance) and no. 7 (mirror star tracing). The best single test of the g factor in this battery is the 100-yard dash, with a g loading of .86. The remaining tests are all pretty much alike in their g loadings.

The second principal component, II, we see, has some large negative as well as large positive loadings; it is therefore called a bipolar factor. What this means is that, when persons are equated on g, those who score high on the tests at one end of the bipolar factor will score low on the tests at the other end. The bipolar factor thus can be inter-

Table 6.6. Unrotated factor matrix (principal components) for physical ability measures.

Variable	Unrotated Factors[1]				
	I	II	III	IV	h^2
1. Softball throw	.70	−.45	.27	.42	.95
2. Hand grip	.67	−.70	−.13	.04	.96
3. Chinning	.65	−.70	−.13	.11	.94
4. 50-yard dash	.70	−.11	.14	−.52	.79
5. 100-yard dash	.86	.14	−.11	−.38	.92
6. One-leg balance	.30	.31	−.03	.73	.73
7. Mirror star tracing	.38	.26	.80	−.14	.88
8. Pursuit rotor tracking	.63	.52	.47	.17	.92
9. 1-mile run	.66	.53	−.45	−.02	.92
10. 5-mile run/walk	.67	.48	−.48	.05	.91
% Var.	41.1	21.6	14.4	12.0	89.1

[1]I = General factor. II = Bipolar hand-and-arm strength versus long-distance running and tracking. III = Hand-eye coordination. IV = Body balance.

preted as two factors that are negatively correlated with each other. The high negative loadings on II are handgrip ($-.70$) and chinning ($-.70$), followed by a softball throw (-45). This pole of factor II obviously involves hand-and-arm strength—it might be labeled "upper-limb strength." The positive pole is less distinct, with largest loadings on pursuit rotor, 1-mile run, and 5-mile run/walk. This is hard to decipher or to label, as these three tests appear so dissimilar. It is hard to imagine why they go together and we can only speculate at this point. The best speculation is that all involve resistance to fatigue of the leg muscles. The short-distance running tests have negligible loadings on this factor. Pursuit rotor tracking is performed standing up, and persons commonly report feeling some fatigue of their leg muscles after working 10 minutes or so at the pursuit rotor. We could experimentally test this hypothesis by giving the pursuit rotor to persons sitting down. Under this condition pursuit rotor performance should have a negligible loading on factor II, if our hypothesis is correct that the positive pole of factor II represents resistance to leg fatigue. This is how factor analysis can suggest experimentally testable hypotheses about the nature of abilities.

Factor III has its largest positive loadings on mirror star tracing ($+.80$) and pursuit tracking ($+.47$). It might be labeled "hand–eye coordination," as that is what these two tests seem to have in common. The long-distance running tests are negatively loaded on this factor, and the other tests have practically negligible loadings.

Factor IV has its largest loading on one-leg balance ($+.73$) and is also positively loaded on softball throw ($+.42$), which suggests that it is a body balance factor. It is not a very important factor for most of the tests (accounting for only 12 percent of the total variance).

In any one such analysis our labeling of the factors must always be regarded as speculative and tentative. By repeating such analyses on various groups of subjects, and by including other tests that we hypothesize might be good measures of one factor or another, we can gradually clarify and confirm the nature of the basic factors underlying a large variety of athletic skills. In this particular analysis, we might tentatively summarize the factors as follows:

> Factor I   General athletic ability.
> Factor II   Bipolar: Hand-and-arm strength versus resistance
>   to fatigue of leg muscles.
> Factor III   Hand–eye coordination or fine-motor dexterity.
> Factor IV   Body balance.

In labeling the first factor "general athletic ability," we run the risk of over-generalization if our battery of tests contains only a limited sample of athletic skills. For example, there are no *jumping* tests; no *aiming* tests, such as throwing a ball at a target or "making baskets" as in basketball; no *dodging* obstacles while running, as would be involved in football; and so on. Thus, the general factor derived just from this battery of only ten tests is probably an overly narrow general factor as compared, say, with the general factor extracted from a correlation matrix of twenty different athletic skills. The more different tests we can put into our original correlation matrix, the more sure we can be of the generality of the "general factor" or first principal component. We would most likely find that certain of our tests always have high *g* loadings regardless of the other tests in the battery, so long as there were a reasonable number and diversity of tests. These tests of more or less consistently high *g* loadings would therefore be regarded as good indices of *g*. The best measure of *g,* of course, would be factor scores based on the *g* loadings of a large and diverse battery of tests. Essentially, these factor scores are a weighted average of the standardized scores on each of the tests, the weights being proportional to each test's loading on the general factor. (Factor scores on the other factors are obtained by a different algorithm.) Thus, in terms of our example in Table 6.6, a person who is exactly one standard deviation above the mean on each of the ten tests would have a factor score on the general factor of 0.62 (i.e., the average of the products of the factor loading on each test times the person's test score in standard deviation units). The unweighted average of the test scores provides only a rough approximation to the general factor, "contaminated" by other factors to the extent that the various tests are not loaded on the general factor.

Because our four factors account for most of the variance in all ten tests, we could more efficiently describe the abilities of each person in terms of four factor scores instead of ten test scores. Even if we added ten more tests, we may still have only five or six (or even four) factor scores. It becomes more and more difficult to add further tests that involve any significant proportion of variance not already accounted for by the several factors involved in all the other tests. Thus factor scores can be a much more efficient means of describing abilities than test scores.

Rotation of Factors.   The reader will have noticed that Table 6.6 is labeled "unrotated" factor matrix. This means that the principal components are given just as they emerge from the mathematical analysis, each accounting for the largest possible linear component of variance that is independent of the variance accounted for by all of the preceding components.

Looking back to Figure 6.8 we see two principal components, I and II. We can *rotate* these axes on their point of intersection, while keeping everything else in place. When rotated into any other position than that shown in Figure 6.8, they are no longer principal components, but *rotated factors*. The first factor after rotation is no longer a general factor in the sense that it accounts for the maximum amount of variance in all of the tests. Some part, perhaps a large part, of the variance on the first principal component is projected onto the other axes as a result of rotation, depending on the degree of rotation. The total variance remains, of course, unchanged, as all the data points remain fixed in space. Rotation merely changes the reference axes.

Rotation of axes becomes too complex to visualize when there are more than three factors. One would have to imagine four or more straight lines, each one at right angles to each of the others, being rotated around a single point in *n*-dimensional space!

Why do we bother to rotate the axes? Rotation is often done because it usually clarifies and simplifies the identification, interpretation, and naming of group factors. Other positions of the reference axes may give a more meaningful, practical or intuitive picture. Rotation will not create any new factors that are not already latent in the principal components, but it may permit them to stand out more clearly. It does so, however, at the expense of the general factor (first principal component), the variance of which gets distributed over the rotated factors. Rotation is quite analogous to taking a picture of the same object from a different angle. For example, we may go up in a helicopter and take an aerial photograph of the Grand Canyon, and we can also take a shot from the floor of the canyon, looking through it lengthwise, or from any other angle. There is no one "really correct'' view of the Grand Canyon. Each shot better highlights some aspects more than others, and we gain a better impression of the Grand Canyon from several viewpoints than from just any single one. Yet certain views will give a more informative overall picture than others, depending on the particular viewer's interest. But no matter what the angle from which you photograph the Grand Canyon, you cannot make it look like the rolling hills of Devonshire, or Victoria Falls, or the Himalayas. Changing the angle of viewing does not create something that is not already there; it may merely expose it more clearly, although at the expense of perhaps obscuring some other feature.

In the early days of the development of factor analysis, theorists had heated arguments over whether factors should be rotated, and, if so, just *how* they should be rotated. Nowadays, there is little if any real argument over this issue. Deciding whether unrotated factors or various rotations are more or less meaningful than others must be based on criteria outside factor analysis itself. The main justification for rotation is to obtain as clear-cut a picture as possible of the latent factors in the matrix. To achieve this, one should look at both the unrotated and rotated factors.

But into what position should the factors be rotated? Again, there is no sacrosanct rule. The main idea is to rotate the axes into whatever position gives the clearest picture of the factorial structure of all the tests. But obviously we need some notion of what we mean by the "clearest picture."

Thurstone (1947) proposed a criterion for factor rotation that he named *simple structure*. He believed that *simple structure* reveals the psychologically most meaningful picture of the factorial structure of any set of psychological tests. Thurstone's idea of simple structure has become the most common basis for rotation, the aim being to approximate as closely as possible, for any given matrix, the criterion of simple structure. Simple structure is approximated to the extent that the factors can be simultaneously rotated so as to (1) have as many zero (or nearly zero) loadings on each factor as possible and (2) concentrate as much of the total variance in each test on as few factors as possible. Table 6.7 shows an idealized factor matrix with perfect simple structure. You can see that the interpretation of the factors in terms of the tests they load on is greatly simplified, as is the interpretation of the tests in terms of the factors they measure. Each test represents a

Table 6.7.   Idealized factors rotated to perfect simple structure.

Test	Rotated Factors			
	I	II	III	IV
A	+1	0	0	0
B	+1	0	0	0
C	+1	0	0	0
D	0	+1	0	0
E	0	+1	0	0
F	0	+1	0	0
G	0	0	+1	0
H	0	0	+1	0
I	0	0	0	+1
J	0	0	0	+1

single factor. Such tests would be called factor-pure tests because they measure only one factor, uncontaminated by any others. It was Thurstone's dream to devise such factor-pure tests to measure the seven "Primary Mental Abilities" represented by the seven factors that he succeeded in extracting reliably from multitudes of highly diverse cognitive tests.

The *general* factor worked against this dream. It pervaded all the tests and thereby made it impossible to do more than approach simple structure; the tests always had substantial loadings on more than one factor, because the rotation spreads the general factor over the several rotated factors, so that simple structure, while it can be more or less approximated, cannot be fully achieved as long as there is a substantial general factor.

To get around this problem, Thurstone adopted the method of *oblique* factor rotation. When all the rotated axes are kept at right angles to one another, regardless of the final position to which they are all simultaneously rotated, the rotation is termed *orthogonal*. When simple structure cannot be closely approximated by means of orthogonal rotation (which will always be the case when there is a large general factor), one can come closer to simple structure by letting the factor axes assume oblique angles in relation to one another, rather than maintain all the axes at right angles. The axes and angles, then, are allowed to move around in any way that will most closely approximate simple structure. But recall the fact that, when the angles between axes are different from 90°, that is, when they are oblique angles, the factors are no longer uncorrelated. Oblique rotation makes simple structure possible by making for correlations between the factors themselves. In other words, one gets rid of the general factor in each of the rotated primary factors by converting this general factor variance into covariance (i.e., correlation) among the factors themselves.

Thus the correlations among oblique factors can themselves be subjected to factor analysis, yielding *second-order factors,* which are of course fewer in number than the primary factors. Usually with cognitive tests only one significant second-order factor emerges—the general factor. If there are two or more second-order factors, they too can be obliquely rotated and their intercorrelations factor analyzed to yield third-order factors. At some point in this process there will be just one significant factor—the general factor—at the top of the *hierarchical* factor structure, as pictured in Figure 6.9. The general factor will show up as the first unrotated factor, or as the highest factor in a hierarchical analysis of rotated oblique factors, as shown in Figure 6.9. One can arrive at essentially the same *g* factor from either direction. It is seldom a question of whether there is or is not a *g* factor, but of how large it is in terms of the proportion of the total variance it accounts for.

Now let us see what orthogonal rotation to approximate simple structure does to our matrix of physical variables. Table 6.8 shows the rotated factors for the physical ability measures. An objective mathematical criterion of simple structure was used, called *varimax,* because it rotates the factors until the variance of the squared loadings on each factor is maximized (Kaiser, 1958). Obviously the variance of the squared loadings on any given factor will be maximized when the factor loadings approach either 1 or 0. The method (now usually done by computer) rotates all the factors until a position is found that simultaneously maximizes all the variances of the squared loadings on each factor, that is, produces as many very large and very small loadings as the data will allow.

We could obtain an even closer and more clean-cut approximation to simple structure had we allowed oblique factors in our rotation. But obliqueness also introduces

Figure 6.9. Diagram showing the hierarchical relationship among factors that may emerge from a factor analysis of a number of diverse tests each composed of highly similar (homogenous) items.

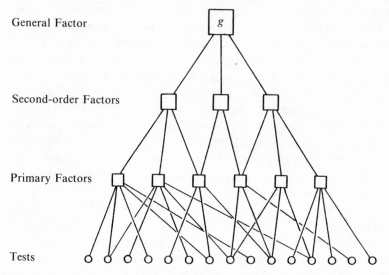

General Factor

Second-order Factors

Primary Factors

Tests

greater sampling error, and we therefore have less confidence in the stability of our results than if we maintained orthogonality.

The rotated factors in Table 6.8 are quite clear. The general factor has been submerged in the rotated factors. Notice that the communalities, h^2, remain unchanged and that the four factors account for 89.1 percent of the variance but that each factor now accounts for a more equal share of the total variance than was the case with the unrotated factors. The general factor, which had carried so much of the variance (41.1 percent), is now spread out and submerged within the four "simple structure" factors. The rotated factors, just like the unrotated principal components, will reproduce, to the same degree of approximation, all the correlations in the original matrix, by applying the same rule that the correlation between any two variables is the sum of the products of their loadings on each of the factors.

Factor I, with very large loadings on the first three tests, is clearly a "hand-and-arm strength" factor. (It is the same factor that we identified as one pole of the bipolar factor II in the unrotated factor matrix; see Table 6.6.)

Factor II, with its largest loadings on variables 9 and 10, and also a moderately large loading on variable 5, is a running or leg strength factor, and suggests resistance to fatigue of leg muscles, as it is most heavily loaded on the most arduous and fatiguing running tasks. In fact, it could even be a general resistance to fatigue or a general endurance factor. (It is essentially the same factor as one pole of bipolar factor II in the unrotated matrix.)

Factor III, with its only large loadings on mirror star tracing and pursuit rotor tracking, is clearly a hand–eye coordination or fine muscle dexterity factor. (It is the same as factor III in the unrotated matrix.)

Factor IV has its only large loading on one-leg balance and is thus a body balance factor, the same as factor IV in the unrotated matrix.

The approximation to simple structure achieved by the varimax rotation in Table 6.8

has made the factors stand out more clearly than in the unrotated factor matrix. But it is important that we look at the unrotated factors to see how important the general factor is, because this point is obscured by rotating the factors. When only one factor matrix is presented, it is probably most useful, for theoretical interpretation, to present the general factor (or first principal component) followed by the rotated factors, as in Table 6.8.

Factor Analysis of Mental Tests

Since factor analysis was first invented by Spearman, countless hundreds if not thousands, of factor analyses have been performed on innumerable and varied cognitive tests. Perusal of many of these analyses in the technical literature gives a fairly consistent picture, varying in predictable ways in terms of the number and variety of mental tests that have been entered into any given analysis.

It is a well-worn cliché that nothing comes out of a factor analysis that the investigator did not put into it in the first place. This is true in the sense that factors that are not latent in the original correlation matrix cannot possibly come out of any factor analysis of the matrix. It is false, however, in this sense: one begins with correlations among variables and obtains factors that were not known to begin with, though their existence might have been hypothesized beforehand. The method of factor analysis precludes detecting factors that may exist in only one of the tests in the matrix, as this would then be a specific factor in that particular matrix, rather than a common factor. Two or more tests containing the same factor are needed if the method of factor analysis is to reveal the factor, and the proportion of variance attributable to the factor must of course be large enough to be statistically detectable.

Tests that were not devised with factor analysis in mind are often factorially complex; that is, they have significant loadings on two or more factors. It is possible to devise tests that are quite homogeneous in terms of the similarity of the mental processes involved in every item, and such tests are more likely to be factorially simple. But this is not

Table 6.8. Physical ability measures: General factor (g) and varimax rotated factors to approximate simple structure.

Variable	g	Rotated Factors[1]				h^2
		I	II	III	IV	
1. Softball throw	.70	.86	.00	.34	.32	.95
2. Hand grip	.67	.96	.14	−.05	−.11	.96
3. Chinning	.65	.96	.11	−.07	−.04	.94
4. 50-yard dash	.70	.43	.42	.43	−.50	.79
5. 100-yard dash	.86	.37	.76	.35	−.29	.92
6. One-leg balance	.30	.08	.23	.13	.80	.73
7. Mirror star tracing	.38	.01	−.02	.93	−.06	.88
8. Pursuit rotor tracking	.63	.03	.39	.81	.33	.92
9. 1-mile run	.66	.02	.94	.07	.16	.92
10. 5-mile run/walk	.67	.07	.93	.02	.21	.91
% Var.	41.1	29.1	27.4	19.8	12.8	89.1

[1] I = Hand-and-arm strength. II = Running factor. III = Hand–eye coordination. IV = Body balance.

necessarily the case, and one can find this out only by doing a factor analysis. One can often be surprised at the outcome. An apparently very homogeneous test, for example, is the Pitch Discrimination Test of Seashore's battery of musical aptitude tests. The Pitch Discrimination Test consists of ten subtests that assess one's ability to discriminate various tones differing in pitch by 30, 23, 17, 12, 8, 5, 3, 2, 1, or 0.5 cycles per second. A factor analysis of these ten subtests shows that pitch discrimination ability is not a unitary factor (Guilford, 1941). Three factors are involved in these ten subtests of pitch discrimination, and there is not even a general factor common to all ten of the tests. It is a clear demonstration that armchair inspection of tests, along with introspection and speculation as to their psychological nature, is actually quite a poor guide as to the psychological analysis of tests or test items. Subjectively one would have imagined that pitch discrimination is a highly unitary ability.

Originally Spearman hypothesized a two-factor theory of intelligence that held that every cognitive test measured only a general factor, *g,* common to all other cognitive tests, and a specific factor, *s,* unique to the particular test. His original theory is pictured in Figure 6.10. Some tests had more *g* and less *s* than others, and tests with no *g* at all were regarded as outside the cognitive domain—they may be tests of purely sensory or motor abilities or of personality traits, but could not be called cognitive or intellectual.

Spearman's two-factor model soon proved much too simple. Thurstone and other pioneers in the development of factor analysis, such as Sir Cyril Burt (1883–1971) and Sir Godfrey Thomson (1881–1955) and finally even Spearman himself, found that there were also other factors besides *g* common to groups of tests and hence called *group factors.* By factor analyzing large batteries of as many as sixty or more tests at one time, Thurstone,

Figure 6.10. Illustration of Spearman's two-factor theory of abilities, in which every test measures a general factor *g* common to all mental tests and a specific factor *s* that is unique to each test.

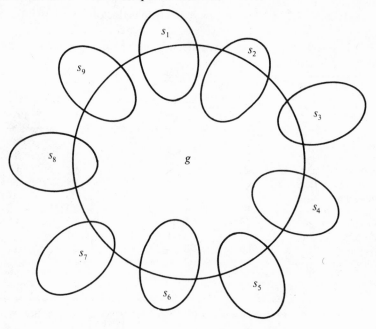

Figure 6.11.   Thurstone's Primary Mental Abilities, showing their intercorrelations and the correlation of each PMA test with the general factor g.   (From Bischof, 1954, p. 14)

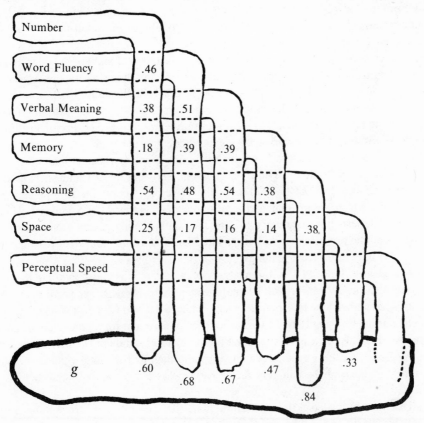

using oblique rotation to approximate simple structure, found seven stable group factors that, in one large study, were intercorrelated as shown in Figure 6.11.

Thurstone (1938) called these factors *primary mental abilities*, and he and Thelma Gwinn Thurstone, his wife and research collaborator, developed special tests to measure each of the primary abilities in as "factor-pure" a form as possible. This set of tests is known as the Primary Mental Abilities, or PMA, test. But it turns out that each of the various PMA subtests measures g as much as, or even more than, it measures the particular primary ability. It is apparently impossible to devise any kind of test involving complex cognitive functions that does not have a considerable loading on g. But it is possible to construct tests that load on g and only one group factor, as do Thurstone's PMA tests.

Factor analysis of the PMA tests (or of the intercorrelations among the primary factors) reveals two major or second-order group factors, which Vernon (1950) has labeled *v:ed,* representing verbal–educational aptitudes, and *k:m,* representing spatial, mechanical, and "practical" aptitudes. Numerical, verbal, and logical reasoning tests are loaded on the *v:ed* factor; tests involving spatial visualization and understanding of physical and mechanical principles are loaded on the *k:m* factor.

The most reasonable overall picture that emerges from all the factor analytical studies of mental abilities has been pictured by Vernon (1950) as a branching hierarchy, going from the most general factor, *g,* to the major group factors, *v:ed* and *k:m,* then to the minor group factors or primary abilities, and finally to the small factors specific to each test, as shown in Figure 6.12.

Table 6.9 shows a factor analysis by Eysenck (1939) of sixty of the cognitive tests used by Thurstone. The tests are extremely varied, involving abstraction (tests 4–8), verbal knowledge and skills (9–16, 52–60), spatial visualization (17–25), number or mechanical arithmetic (30–35), numerical reasoning (36–39), verbal reasoning (40–42), nonverbal and spatial reasoning (43–45), and rote learning (46–51). Factor loadings too small to be of statistical significance are omitted, and the tests are grouped together according to the "group factors" on which they are most significantly loaded. The most important feature of Table 6.9 is the first column, showing the *g* loadings. Note that in this battery of sixty quite diversified tests, the *g* factor accounts for 30.8 percent of the total variance, which is more than all the group factors combined (23.5 percent), and more than half of the tests have a larger *g* loading than their loading on any group factor. (The average correlation of all the tests with *g* is .555. Three of the nonverbal reasoning tests (41, 43, 44) have significant loadings only on *g*.)

Let us now look at a factor analysis of a test that is most familiar to clinical psychologists, the Wechsler Adult Intelligence Scale (WAIS), consisting of eleven subtests—six verbal and five performance. Table 6.10 shows a factor analysis of the normative group for ages 18 to 19 years. Four factors account for 65.5 percent of the total variance in these eleven tests. Extraction of more factors would not be interpretable in this battery. Notice that the *g* factor accounts for more than half the total variance and about four times as much of the common factor variance as the remaining three factors combined.

The most *g*-loaded tests are Information, Similarities, and Vocabulary. But the relative sizes of the factor loadings are not meaningful in any general psychological sense unless they have been corrected for attenuation. Because the various subtests differ in reliability, the relative sizes of the loadings reflect, in part, the reliabilities of the tests. The maximum theoretical correlation that any test can have with any factor is the square root of the test's reliability. Thus we can correct the factor loadings for attenuation by

Figure 6.12. Vernon's hierarchical model of the organization of ability factors. *g* = general factor, *v:ed* = verbal–educational aptitude, *k:m* = spatial–mechanical aptitude.

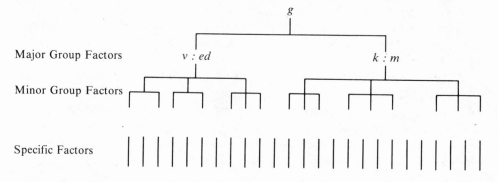

Table 6.9. Factor loadings (group factor analysis) of sixty of Thurstone's cognitive tests. (From Eysenck, 1939)

Test	Factor[1]								
	G	V	L	A	S	C	M	R	Z
4	.554	.483	——	——	——	——	——	——	——
5	.662	.525	——	——	——	——	——	——	——
9	.293	.531	——	——	——	——	——	——	——
10	.649	.511	——	——	——	——	——	——	——
11	.669	.492	——	——	——	——	——	——	——
16	.611	.437	——	——	——	——	——	——	——
52	.533	.496	——	——	——	——	——	——	——
56	.497	.404	——	——	——	——	——	——	——
58	.398	.832	——	——	——	——	——	——	——
59	.237	.265	——	——	——	——	——	——	——
60	.741	.465	——	——	——	——	——	——	——
12	.605	——	.351	——	——	——	——	——	——
13	.537	——	.548	——	——	——	——	——	——
15	.437	——	.628	——	——	——	——	——	——
57	.688	——	.351	——	——	——	——	——	——
30	.678	——	——	.448	——	——	——	——	——
31	.032	——	——	.649	——	——	——	——	——
32	.395	——	——	.575	——	——	——	——	——
33	.349	——	——	.743	——	——	——	——	——
34	.461	——	——	.641	——	——	——	——	——
35	.565	——	——	.444	——	——	——	——	——
37	.627	——	——	.313	——	——	——	——	——
38	.483	——	——	.465	——	——	——	——	——
39	.683	——	——	.446	——	——	——	——	——
8	.444	——	——	——	.424	——	——	——	——
17	.389	——	——	——	.589	——	——	——	——
18	.495	——	——	——	.606	——	——	——	——
19	.520	——	——	——	.512	——	——	——	——
20	.340	——	——	——	.750	——	——	——	——
21	.670	——	——	——	.489	——	——	——	——
22	.504	——	——	——	.622	——	——	——	——
23	.510	——	——	——	.497	——	——	——	——
24	.565	——	——	——	.453	——	——	——	——
27	.367	——	——	——	.555	——	——	——	——
28	.575	——	——	——	.382	——	——	——	——
29	.561	——	——	——	.336	——	——	——	——
36	.304	——	——	——	.214	——	——	——	——
45	.696	——	——	——	.325	——	——	——	——
53	.299	——	——	——	.525	——	——	——	——
6	.814	——	——	——	——	.436	——	——	——
7	.684	——	——	——	——	.364	——	——	——
14	.657	——	——	——	——	.427	——	——	——
26	.418	——	——	——	——	.549	——	——	——
51	.309	——	——	——	——	.445	——	——	——
46	.361	——	——	——	——	——	.499	——	——
47	.527	——	——	——	——	——	.569	——	——
48	.420	——	——	——	——	——	.457	——	——
49	.472	——	——	——	——	——	.404	——	——
50	.370	——	——	——	——	——	.495	——	——

(*continued on next page*)

Table 6.9 (*continued*)

Test	G	V	L	A	S	C	M	R	Z
					Factor[1]				
40	.688	——	——	——	——	——	——	[.575]	——
42	.653	——	——	——	——	——	——	[.575]	——
54	.409	——	——	——	——	——	——	——	[.520]
55	.707	——	——	——	——	——	——	——	[.520]
25	.584	——	——	——	——	——	——	——	——
41	.824	——	——	——	——	——	——	——	——
43	.868	——	——	——	——	——	——	——	——
44	.772	——	——	——	——	——	——	——	——
% Var.	30.80	5.00	1.65	4.58	6.61	1.74	1.79	[1.16]	[.097]

[1]G = General factor of mental ability. V = Verbal–Literary factor. L = Verbal-Linguistic factor. A = Arithmetical factor. S = Visuo-Spatial factor. C = Classification factor. M = Memory factor. R = Relational factor. Z = Audio-Rhythmic factor.

dividing each factor loading by the square root of the test's reliability. Table 6.10 also shows the factor loadings after correction for attenuation, using the split-half reliabilities (r_{xx}) for the same age group. (Split-half reliabilities are not appropriate for the Digit Span and Digit Symbol tests.) Only factor loadings larger than .20 are corrected. The tests hardly differ enough in g loadings after correction for attenuation to warrant comparisons on this basis. The diversity of the subtests and their almost uniformly high g loadings

Table 6.10. Factor analysis of WAIS (ages 18–19), showing factor loadings before and after correction for attenuation.

Subtest	Factor Loadings[1]					Corrected Factor Loadings[2]				
	I g	II v	III p	IV m	h^2	I g	II v	III p	IV m	r_{xx}
Information	.83	.38	.12	.04	.83	.87	.40			.91
Comprehension	.69	.38	.11	.09	.64	.78	.43			.79
Arithmetic	.68	.10	.13	.34	.60	.77			.38	.79
Similarities	.81	.27	−.09	.05	.74	.87	.29			.87
Digit Span	.63	−.12	−.12	.29	.51	—[a]	—	—	—	—
Vocabulary	.86	.28	−.12	.09	.84	.89	.29			.94
Digit Symbol (Coding)	.66	.09	.19	.08	.49	—[a]	—	—	—	—
Picture Completion	.76	.08	.12	−.01	.60	.84				.82
Block Designs	.71	−.03	.46	.13	.73	.77		.50		.86
Picture Arrangement	.66	.16	.32	−.11	.58	.81		.39		.66
Object Assembly	.65	−.09	.46	.05	.64	.81		.57		.65
% Var.	52.7	4.5	6.0	2.3	65.5					

[1]g = General factor of intelligence. v = Verbal factor. p = Performance factor. m = Short-term Memory factor. h^2 = Communality. r_{xx} = Split-half reliability of test.
[2]Only loadings larger than .20 are corrected for attenuation.
[a]No split-half reliability on this test.

suggest that the Full Scale IQ on the WAIS is a very good estimate of the general factor of mental ability. The Full Scale IQ correlates about .90 with the g factor, which means that about 80 percent of the variance in Wechsler IQs is g, about 15 percent is attributable to group factors (verbal and performance) as well as to specific factors in each test, and about 5 percent is measurement error.

Factor analysis of the Wechsler Intelligence Scale for Children (WISC), which has the same subtests, though at a lower level of difficulty, yields very similar results. The g factor is highly stable across age groups, and verbal and performance factors emerge at every age level, but factors beyond these first three are quite small, unstable, and often psychologically uninterpretable. Factor analytic studies of the Wechsler tests have been reviewed by Matarazzo (1972, Ch. 11).

The items of the 1937 Stanford–Binet have also been factor analyzed by a number of investigators, reviewed by Sattler (1974, pp. 129–131). Most of the Stanford–Binet items load heavily on the g factor, which accounts for some 80 percent of the variance. The g factor is highly stable over successive age levels. Besides g there are a few small group factors (e.g., verbal, spatial, memory) that are not very stable across age levels and do not always show up.

Table 6.11 shows the factor loadings of thirteen quite diverse tests given to 1,000 British army recruits (Vernon, 1947). Again we see a large g factor accounting for more than half the total variance and more than three times as much as the other four factors combined. The Dominoes test is the only one that measures no other factor but g, among the factors found in this battery. The Dominoes is a nonverbal test of inductive reasoning. The only test that does not have its largest loading on g is a mechanical assembly test. All

Table 6.11. Factor analysis of group tests in a representative British army population of 1,000 recruits.   (After Vernon, 1947)

Test	Factor Loadings[1]					
	I g	II $k{:}m$	III ed	IV v	V n	h^2
Matrices	.79	.17				.65
Dominoes (Nonverbal)	.87					.75
Nonverbal Group Test	.78	.13				.62
Squares	.59	.44				.54
Assembly	.24	.89				.85
Bennett Mechanical Aptitude	.66	.31				.54
Verbal	.79		.29	.45		.90
Dictation	.62		.54	.48		.90
Spelling	.68		.41	.43		.82
Following Instructions	.87		.23	.09		.82
Arithmetic, I	.72		.49		.39	.91
Arithmetic, II	.80		.38		.16	.81
Arithmetic, III	.77		.36		.32	.82
% Var.	52.5	8.7		6.9		76.5

[1] g = General factor. $k{:}m$ = Spatial-perceptual-motor factor. ed = Educational aptitude factor. v = Verbal factor. n = Numerical factor.

the other tests measure g more than anything else, and, if a total score were obtained for the entire battery, it would be a good measure of individual differences in g.

The more highly diverse a battery of tests, the less the percentage of total variance accounted for by g, because the diverse battery will involve more group and specific factors. This can be seen in the factor analysis of a very diverse battery of sixteen tests given to 4,925 U.S. Navy recruits, shown in Table 6.12. In this analysis a general factor was extracted, and then all five of the significant principal components were rotated to simple structure to highlight the group factors. (After rotation g is submerged in the group factors.) Despite the great diversity of these tests, g still accounts for 31.3 percent of the total variance and 50 percent of the common factor variance. The General Classification Test, devised as a verbal test of general intelligence, has the largest g loading. Other tests with high g loadings involve some form of verbal or quantitative reasoning, while those with the smallest g loadings involve mainly visual–motor skills or simple recognition memory of previously learned material.

Table 6.13 shows a factor analysis of an even more diverse collection of tests, several of which scarcely belong in the cognitive domain. Such tests, when factor analyzed along with more cognitive tests requiring knowledge, reasoning, and problem solving, have comparatively small loadings on the g factor. The tests in Table 6.13 were obtained on 166 boys between 10 and 11 years of age, in 4 London schools representing the average elementary school population (Maxwell, 1972). The twenty various tests were selected to represent four levels of complexity of mental organization: *relational* (tests 1–7), *associative* (8–11), *perceptual* (12–16), and *sensory-motor* (17–20). In this analysis, the g factor (first principal component) was extracted, and the remaining four

Table 6.12. Factor analysis of battery of diverse tests given to 4,925 U.S. Navy Recruits.

Test	g	Rotated Factors[1]				h^2
		I	II	III	IV	
Armed Forces Qualification Test						
Verbal	.65	.65	.08	.25	−.14	.51
Mathematics	.71	.81	.01	−.04	.13	.67
Mechanical Knowledge	.27	.01	.85	−.06	.01	.73
Spatial Visualization	.59	.50	.34	.00	.23	.42
Manual Speed Test	.06	−.15	.08	.10	.72	.56
Hand Steadiness Test	.35	.09	.00	.50	.59	.61
Digit Span Memory	.46	.42	−.21	.48	.01	.45
General Classification Test (Verbal)	.84	.80	.12	.32	.00	.76
Arithmetic Reasoning	.76	.85	−.01	.02	.14	.74
Mechanical Comprehension	.46	.15	.89	.09	.08	.83
Clerical Speed & Accuracy	.31	.26	−.08	−.04	.75	.64
Sonar Pitch Memory Test	.36	.03	.20	.78	−.01	.65
Radio Code Aptitude Test	.51	.30	−.05	.63	.26	.56
Electronics Technician Selection Test	.79	.76	.20	.16	.07	.65
Shop Procedures (Tools & Uses)	.50	.26	.79	.08	−.10	.71
Achievement Test in Basic Training	.68	.64	.25	.17	−.07	.51
% Var.	31.3	25.8	15.5	10.9	10.3	62.5

[1]Group factors: I = $v{:}ed;$ II = mechanical; III = auditory memory; IV = visual–motor speed and dexterity.

Table 6.13.   Factor analysis of twenty tests given to London school boys, ages 10 to 11 years.   (From Maxwell, 1972)

Test	*g* I	Rotated Factors				h^2
		II	III	IV	V	
1. Mental age	.84	.37	.11	.03	−.03	.86
2. Synonyms & opposites	1.00	0	0	0	0	1.00
3. Number series	.79	.35	.11	.07	.06	.77
4. Nonverbal analogies	.79	.41	.11	.05	.03	.80
5. Completion	.84	.31	.05	−.01	−.02	.81
6. Syllogisms	.79	.37	.03	.11	.00	.77
7. Verbal analogies	.79	.44	.04	−.05	.02	.83
8. Association	.62	.08	.39	.09	.05	.56
9. Memory for shapes	.51	.16	.60	.10	.08	.66
10. Imagery	.55	.11	.56	.12	.06	.65
11. Memory for numbers	.46	.26	.47	.13	.14	.52
12. Perception of parts	.35	.07	.12	.36	.23	.32
13. Sorting shapes	.31	.16	.18	.55	.00	.45
14. Perception of patterns	.24	.23	.19	.45	.11	.36
15. Counting	.37	−.04	.11	.39	.15	.32
16. Checking	.38	−.04	−.01	.43	.15	.35
17. Writing speed	.25	−.00	.06	.16	.43	.27
18. Reaction time	.22	.07	.03	.15	.45	.28
19. Weight discrimination	.23	−.02	.07	.11	.45	.28
20. Touch discrimination	.24	−.01	.06	.02	.51	.32
% Var.	34.3	5.3	6.0	5.5	5.0	56.1

significant factors were rotated to simple structure. It is instructive to view the loadings on *g* in terms of the four levels of mental organization listed. Notice that the size of the *g* loadings systematically decreases going from the *relational* to the *sensory-motor* level. The average *g* loadings for the different levels are *relational* (.84), *associative* (.54), *perceptual* (.33), *sensory-motor* (.23). Also, the fact that the communalities (h^2) decrease going from relational to sensory-motor tests indicates that the less complex tests have much more specific variance than the more complex tests, which have more common factor variance. Inspection of the size of the loadings of factors II to V on the various tests would lead to their being labeled as *relational, associative, perceptual,* and *sensory-motor* factors, respectively.

Hakstian and Cattell (1974) administered 57 ability tests to 343 adults averaging 23.7 years of age. The tests were extremely diverse and probably constitute one of the most complete samplings of the domain of cognitive tests to be found in the entire literature. Each of the fifty-seven tests was homogeneous in content so as to be highly representative of a particular primary mental ability. It would be hard to imagine a much greater variety of mental tests than the fifty-seven tests included in this battery. Hakstian and Cattell factor analyzed the battery, which yielded nineteen significant interpretable primary factors that were rotated to oblique simple structures, that is, the primary factors were intercorrelated. Each of the nineteen primary factors is represented by three similar tests.

I have factor analyzed the matrix of intercorrelations among the nineteen primary

Table 6.14. Second-order factor analysis of nineteen oblique primary factors derived from a factor analysis of fifty-seven diverse cognitive tests.[1]   (From Hakstian & Cattell, 1974)

Primary Factors[2]	Rotated Second-Order Factors[3]					h^2
	g	I	II	III	IV	
Verbal	.68	.16	.41	.53	.40	.64
Numerical	.67	.43	.13	.52	.26	.54
Spatial	.56	.70	.14	.05	.26	.59
Perceptual Speed & Accuracy	.47	.62	.04	.12	.02	.40
Speed of Closure	.77	.46	.32	.53	.08	.60
Inductive Reasoning	.72	.66	.30	.25	.09	.60
Associative Memory	.56	.38	.28	.37	−.25	.42
Mechanical Knowledge	.26	.19	.12	.00	.65	.47
Flexibility of Closure	.61	.56	.39	.09	.11	.49
Memory Span	.43	.37	.02	.30	.16	.26
Spelling	.56	.09	.13	.78	−.10	.65
Aesthetic Judgment	.60	.35	.41	.28	.10	.38
Meaningful Memory	.57	.35	.36	.34	−.19	.40
Originality I	.70	.31	.50	.42	.01	.52
Ideational Fluency	.58	.05	.50	.46	.10	.47
Word Fluency	.63	.17	.29	.65	−.02	.54
Originality II	.51	.04	.56	.26	.22	.44
Aiming	.42	.36	.25	.17	−.22	.27
Representational Drawing	.57	.41	.57	.05	−.02	.50
% Var.	36.7	34.1	6.5	4.6	3.1	48.3

[1]Given to 343 adults, mean age = 23.7, SD = 8.7.
[2]Each primary factor is represented by three tests.
[3]Orthogonal (varimax) rotation to approximate simple structure.

factors. The results are shown in Table 6.14. (The factors resulting from a factor analysis of oblique primary factors are called *second-order factors*.) Again we see very substantial *g* loadings on most of the primaries; *g* accounts for 36.7 percent of the total variance and 86 percent of the common factor variance. The highest *g* loadings are found on *speed of closure* (.77) and *inductive reasoning* (.72). *Speed of closure* involves the ability to complete a gestalt when parts of the stimulus are missing. Time needed for recognition of multilated words is a measure of this ability. It involves a kind of perceptual inference, of mentally filling in the gaps or "seeing" the relationships among the parts to form a recognizable or familiar whole. *Inductive reasoning* involves reasoning from the specific to the general.

The primary factor with the smallest *g* loading is *mechanical knowledge*, which, as represented by the tests in this battery, involves knowledge of physical principles, tools, electrical and automotive facts. It has a larger experiential component than most of the other factors.

The rotated second-order factors are not especially clear but could be labeled as follows: (I) *k:m,* or "fluid intelligence"; (II) artistic ability; (III) *v:ed,* or "crystalized intelligence," (IV) mechanical knowledge. The terms "fluid" and "crystalized" are explained later in this chapter. They are only roughly similar to the *k:m* and *v:ed* factors described earlier.

The Nature of *g*

We have now seen what *g* is in purely mathematical terms. And we have seen that a large general factor can usually be extracted from the matrix of correlations among a number of mental tests of various sorts. Standard intelligence tests, when included in such a matrix, show especially large *g* saturations. The *g* factor is whatever it is that a variety of tests measure in common. It is an average or linear composite of a person's performance on a number of different items or tests. But it is not a simple arithmetic average, as is the total score on most tests. It is a weighted average in which each unit (item or subtest) in the composite is weighted in such a way as to maximize the variance (i.e., a measure of the amount of individual differences in the population) of the composite scores. No other set of weights of the subscores of a test will yield total scores with as great a variance as that of the *g*-weighted total.[10]

The *g*-weighted composite score is a linear dimension on which individuals can be ordered. If a test comprises a large number of *g*-loaded units, the simple unweighted sum of the scored units (assuming, of course, that they are standardized scores) will be highly correlated with the *g*-weighted sum of the scored units. This is the same as saying that total scores on a test of many *g*-loaded items will order individuals in about the same way as the individuals would be ordered in terms of their *g* factor scores. The reason, of course, is that, when subscores are totaled, the correlated or common elements (*g*) consistently cumulate, whereas the uncorrelated elements (group factors, specific factors, and measurement error) tend to average out.

Take, as an example, physical stature, which everyone agrees is a true linear scale on which individuals can be ordered. Imagine that we cannot measure an individual's height directly but can measure only the lengths of (1) lower leg, (2) upper leg, (3) torso, (4) neck, and (5) head. Imagine also that we have no absolute units of measurement, so that the individual's measurement on each of these five items is expressed merely as a standard score. Now for each individual we can obtain the simple sum of the standard scores on each of the five variables, and we can rank order individuals in terms of this sum. Call this the rank of unweighted sums. We can also obtain the intercorrelations among the five variables and extract the first principal component, or *g*, and then weight each of the five standard scores by its *g* loading and obtain the *g*-weighted sum for each individual. We can rank order individuals in terms of this sum; call it the rank of *g*-weighted sums. But now suppose finally that we can measure every individual's height on a true scale and rank all individuals on this scale. What we would most likely find is that the *g*-weighted sum has a higher rank order correlation with the true scale measurements of height than does the unweighted sum.[11] The five subscores are all measuring something in common and whatever this is adds up to the individual's relative standing in total height when each subscore is weighted in the sum proportionately to how much it measures of whatever all of the subtests have in common.

Much as we can order persons in overall physical stature by measuring and summing a number of different but intercorrelated parts of the body, so we can order persons in overall mental "stature" by summing scores on a number of different but intercorrelated mental test items.

We identify intelligence with g. To the extent that a test orders individuals on g, it can be said to be a test of intelligence. Not all so-called intelligence tests meet this criterion equally well, and even the best tests can only approximate it, as g is a hypothetical construct and is not itself directly measureable. Yet IQ tests such as the Stanford–Binet and the Wechsler Scales would probably correlate between .8 and .9 with a hypothetical true scale of g in the normative population.

The Problem of Domain and the Uniqueness of *g*

Because the g factor (i.e., first principal component) is a function of the composition of the correlation matrix from which it is derived, we are faced with the question of the uniqueness of g. How can we identify intelligence with g if there are many different g's depending on which particular matrix of intercorrelations we choose to factor analyze? What claim can be made for g if it is not unique or invariant? For example, we would not expect the g factor extracted from the intercorrelations among a large number of body measurements to be the same as the g factor extracted from a number of mental tests. In fact, the two g's might even be correlated zero. If this is true of the correlation between the g of body measurements and the g of mental tests, then, at least in principle, it could be true for two different sets of mental tests. If test set A yields g_A and test set B yields g_B, and if there is little or no correlation between g_A and g_B, how is one to decide which g should be called "intelligence"? If one could show that there are many different g's depending on the particular selection of tests that one happens to factor analyze, it would seem reasonable to argue that there is no such thing as a general ability called intelligence, and it necessarily follows that it would be impossible to rank order individuals in terms of intelligence. One could only describe individuals' abilities in highly specific terms of how well or poorly any given individual performs each particular task.

A few psychologists argue that there really is no g factor of mental ability. The eminent psychologist J. P. Guilford is probably the leading exponent of this view. The cornerstone of this argument is the existence of zero correlations among mental tests. A tabulation of more than 7,000 correlations among various mental tests used in 13 studies in Guilford's laboratory revealed that some 17–24 percent of the correlations could be considered not to differ significantly from zero (Guilford, 1964). (Most of the samples on which the correlations were based exceeded 200 in number.)

Does the finding of zero correlations among some tests rule out the existence of g? It would do so only if our theory of g required that every conceivable kind of mental test have a sufficiently substantial loading on g to produce consistently significant correlations with other tests in any reasonably sized sample of the population. (Recall that the correlation between any two tests due to g is the product of each of the tests' correlations with g, i.e., $r_{xy} = r_{xg} \times r_{yg}$.) On the other hand, g may be a valid theoretical concept even if it does not extend throughout the entire domain of human abilities. Even Spearman acknowledged that various kinds of tests had different g loadings and that these loadings could presumably range between 0 and 1. Our task then would be to discover the essential characteristics of tests standing at various points on the scale of g loadings.

Guilford's research program, over the years, has concentrated on devising a large number of very narrow or specialized tests that intercorrelate as little as possible. Guilford's Structure of Intellect model posits 120 ability factors (Guilford, 1959; 1967), and his aim has been to devise tests to measure each of these abilities in such a way that each test will be significantly loaded on only one primary factor when the factor axes are rotated orthogonally. As Guilford points out, "there is a frank effort to achieve minimal correlation between every pair of tests of two different factors" (Guilford, 1964, p. 462). This means that Guilford's tests are specially devised and selected to minimize their g loading. Moreover, most of the tests used in this tabulation were tests of divergent-production abilities (sometimes called "creativity tests"), which, Guilford claims, "usually correlate low, even zero, with tests of the traditional types of IQ tests, such as Reading Comprehension" (1964, p. 403). Most divergent-production tests do not have keyed "right" answers; the person's responses to the items are generally scored for quantity and novelty or originality in answering questions such as "How many different uses of a brick can you think of?" Other investigations have found even that many of these tests are substantially g loaded, as shown by their sizable correlations with standard IQ tests (see studies reviewed by Yamamoto, 1964, and a critique of Guilford's claims by McNemar, 1964, p. 878).

Then, too, Guilford's samples were not representative of the range of ability in the general population but undoubtedly had a restricted range on g, a fact that would necessarily lower the intercorrelations among tests due to g. Guilford (1964, p. 403) states, "Most of the analyses were based upon subjects who were males with generally higher-than-average IQ levels, near the age of 20, in military training that ordinarily led to officer commissions." These subjects for the most part were college-level youths, with few if any having IQs below 100, and we know that variance on the g factor must always be shrunken when the range of intellectual talent is restricted. So Guilford's evidence for the unimportance of g is not at all compelling. Other objections to g are overcome as soon as we acknowledge, as all factor analysts now do, that g is not the only factor involved in the correlations among tests. There are a number of smaller group factors (or "primary mental abilities") as well.

Guilford's Structure of Intellect model of 120 abilities rises from a threefold classification of mental tests in terms of four types of *contents* (figural, symbolic, semantic, behavioral) × five hypothetical types of mental *operations* called for (cognition, memory, divergent production, convergent production, evaluation) × six types of *products* resulting from the mental operations (units, classes, relations, systems, transformations, implications), or $4 \times 5 \times 6 = 120$ abilities. The model is better thought of as one possible classification scheme for tests. It may have some possible value in suggesting types of tests that have not yet been devised. (In fact tests have not yet been devised for some of the cells in the model.) It has not been satisfactorily demonstrated that each of the 120 cells represents a different ability, except in the trivial sense, that any tests that correlate with all the other tests less than perfectly, after correction for attenuation, represent separate ability factors. The method of factor analysis allows almost infinite subdivision of abilities if one wishes to identify factors that reliably account for almost vanishingly small percentages of variance among all ability tests.

In a factor analysis of a large number of diverse mental tests including a number of different memory tests, for example, one might find a memory factor that accounts for, say, 10 percent of the total variance. One can then do a separate factor analysis on just the memory tests and find two or three factors among them, such as meaningful memory, paired-associate rote memory, and span memory (as in the digit-span test). One can then make up a variety of tests within any one of these categories, say, span memory. We can test memory span for digits, for letters, for words, and for pictures. Using several tests of each of these types, we can do still another factor analysis and perhaps find memory factors for digits, letters, and so on. Then within any one type of test, say, digits, we can elaborate other variations, such as requiring subjects to recall digit series in a forward or in a reverse order, or to recall the series immediately after presentation or after a 10-second delay, or to recall them after visual or after auditory presentation, and we could factor analyze the correlations among these various forms of digit-span test and find still more factors. But the factors yielded at each stage of this increasing fractionation of tests are narrower and narrower, involving diminishing fractions of the total variance in human abilities. They become trivial in any practical sense involving the predictive use of tests and are reflected in no observable real-life behavioral differences among persons. As Eysenck (1967, p. 82) has remarked,

> There is a possibility of infinite sub-division inherent in the statistical method employed [by Guilford], and evidence is lacking that further and further sub-factors add anything either to the experimental analysis of intellectual functioning or the practical aim of forecasting success and failure in intellectual pursuits.

In principle, the *g* factor cannot be regarded as unique, because it is determined by the nature of the variables that have gone into the analysis. But this is not as great a problem as it may seem, once we agree that we are interested only in the *g* of a limited domain. Correlation and factor analysis help to define the domain. But rational judgment too must enter into the process. This element of judgment, however, does not determine which variables belong to a certain domain or their loadings on the *g* factor in that domain. These aspects can be objectively determined by mathematical analysis. Our judgment in this whole process is involved only in selecting the domain of interest.

To illustrate this point, let us suppose that we obtain an extremely large number of assessments of human characteristics, including any variables that anyone can think of and that can be objectively assessed. Our list would include many body measurements (the garment industry, for example, takes into account individual differences in some fifty different body measurements in designing various wearing apparel); various measures of physical abilities (strength and endurance of different body parts, "wind" or vital capacity, walking and running speeds, jumping of various types, etc.); measures of eye, hair, and skin pigmentation; fingerprint measurements; physiological measures (temperature, blood pressure, pulse rate under rest and after exercise, basic metabolic rate, to name a few); individual histories including birthweight, maternal age, and ancestry; sensory acuity in every sensory modality; personality traits or dispositions; attitudes, likes and dislikes, food preferences, interests; and tests of every conceivable kind of ability or skill that persons might display—intellectual, artistic, musical, mechanical, social, and so on. We could include all existing psychological and educational tests of every variety. In short, we would include every conceivable assessment of any human characteristics, physical or behavioral, that anyone can think of. There could be literally thousands of different measurements. Above all, we would not want there to be any *selection* of variables; none should be excluded.

Now, if we obtained all these measurements on a large representative sample of the population (say, 10,000 persons) and intercorrelated all the measurements, what would we find? First, we would notice that the correlation matrix contains values over the whole possible range from -1 to $+1$, with many low and near zero correlations. Second, we could rearrange the order of the variables in the matrix in such a way that the most highly intercorrelated variables are grouped together in the list. So rearranged, the matrix would show numerous clusters of substantial (positive or negative) correlations, with each cluster separated from the others by small and zero correlations. These clusters of large correlations standing out against the background of more or less negligible correlations represent the subdomains existing within the total domain of human characteristics.

If now we do a principal components analysis of the entire correlation matrix, we will find a large number of significant components, but none that could be regarded as a general factor for the whole set of variables. In such an extremely diverse collection of variables, the first principal component would probably not account for a much larger proportion of the total variance than would many other of the components, and not all the variables, by any means, would have significant or positive loadings on the first principal component. It would therefore have no claim to being a general factor.

But now we can rotate the principal components to approximate simple structure. The rotated factors then will clearly reveal the various subdomains that we discerned in the clusters of large correlations. If, from among all of the rotated factors (and there would undoubtedly be very many factors in such a large and diverse collection of variables), we removed all the variables with significant loadings on any one factor and did a principal components analysis of just this set of variables, we would find a large first principal component on which all the variables in the set would have substantial positive loadings. The first principal component of this set or subdomain would therefore qualify as a general factor. Thus there would conceivably exist many general factors—one for each subdomain of the total domain of human characteristics. Separate factor analyses within each subdomain would reveal other smaller group factors in addition to the general factor.

How we *label* the various subdomains revealed by this analysis, and which one we may choose to focus on for further scientific study, are entirely matters of the investigator's judgment and purpose. Some psychologists have mistakenly believed that, because the labeling of a domain is an arbitrary matter (as is the labeling of anything else), the domain itself is an arbitrary figment of personal or ideological preference. The subdomains of course exist, regardless of the various labels that we may give to them. If a variable is significantly correlated with the first principal component of a domain (in which the first principal component is a general factor), then the variable can be included in that domain. If it does not correlate, it either belongs to some other domain or is so highly specific or unreliable as to be incapable of correlating with any other variable. (Whether it is an unimportant variable for this reason is a separate consideration.)

No one has ever assembled or factor analyzed such a comprehensive matrix of intercorrelated measures of all human characteristics as described in the preceding discussion. But, from existing factor analyses on a more modest scale, we can make some good guesses about what some of the more prominent subdomains would be.

Body measurements would be one domain. Factor analyses of body measurements reveal a large general factor corresponding to overall body size and two large group factors, which might be labeled ''longitude'' and ''latitude.'' Height and weight both have their largest loadings on the general factor of size, but height loads highly only on the "longitude" factor and weight loads highly only on the "latitude" factor. Then there are a number of smaller factors involving legs, arms, torso, and so on. For example, imagine two persons who are the same on the general size factor and on logitude and latitude (i.e., they are the same height and weight), but they differ in leg length and torso length—one has long legs and a short torso and the other is the reverse. These variations would produce leg and torso factors. Still smaller factors might involve differences between lower- and upper-leg lengths, and so on.

In the behavioral realm, two or three, or possibly more, domains would appear, each with a general factor and a number of group factors. Personality measures and ability measures would fall into distinct domains, and each of these would undoubtedly have subdomains. At least two large domains of abilities would be distinguishable: one involving physical measurements of strength, dexterity, speed of movement, motor coordination, and the like and the other involving what we would term mental abilities. The latter, of course, covers a broad territory. But, if ability measures within this territory are obtained in a representative sample of the population so that the appearance of zero or negative correlations among ability measures cannot be attributed to the artifact of restriction of range, virtually all measures of what we would call mental ability would have positive loadings on the general factor of this domain, within the limits of test reliability and sampling error.

The term "ability" itself here needs clarification. How is a measure of ability distinguishable from a measure of personality or attitude or preference? The term "ability" is never used to refer to involuntary behavior. Thus variations in blood pressure are not differences in ability, unless it is shown that the individual has voluntary control over his blood pressure. Then we could say he has the ability to raise or lower his blood pressure, meaning that he can do it when he consciously wishes to do so or is told to do so. In the realm of voluntary behavior, essentially, an ability measurement (whether physical or mental) involves an objective (i.e., universally agreed on) criterion of better or porrer, higher or lower, performance. The performance measure may be dichotomous (e.g., right or wrong, pass or fail, can or cannot, $+$ or $-$) or continuous (e.g., distance jumped, speed of running, reaction time, etc.). But everyone would agree that jumping 6 feet is a "better" score than jumping 4 feet; solving a puzzle in 2 minutes is "better" than solving it in 5 minutes; knowing the conventional meaning of a particular word is "better" than not knowing it; giving the correct answer to an arithmetic problem is "better" than giving an incorrect answer. These examples are all distinguishable from performances that are not gradeable in terms of better or porrer or that are elicited from the person with the understanding that there is no criterion of goodness of performance. Personality and interest inventories are of this nature. In these inventories we are interested in knowing the subject's typical behavior, attitude, or preference. Notice that such devices could be made into ability measures of a kind, if we instructed the person to try to meet a particular criterion, such as answering all questions the way he thinks that the average person, in some defined population, would answer them. The degree of congruence between the person's answers and the typical answers in the population (i.e., the objective criterion in this case) would then constitute a measure of the person's *ability* to judge what the typical response to each item would be in the defined population.

Because all measurements that fall within the mental abilities domain are positively intercorrelated, they all share some general factor. But they do not share it equally. The very fact that various mental tests have different loadings on g provides leverage for discovering the psychological nature of g.

What Characterizes the More Highly g-Loaded Tests?

Spearman originally tried to fathom the psychological nature of g by factor analyzing more than one hundred tests, each fairly unitary or homogeneous in content, and then comparing their g loadings (Spearman & Jones, 1950, Ch. 8). His analysis was based on the classical method of agreement and difference. He inquired as to which ways are all possible paired comparisons of the various tests (1) *similar,* and in which ways are they (2) *different,* when (a) both tests have *large g* loadings, (b) both tests have *small g* loadings, and (c) one test has a *large g* loading and the other a *small g* loading. By trying to answer these questions for each pair of tests, Spearman reached the conclusion that "*g is essentially characterized by the combination of noegenesis with abstractness*" (Spearman & Jones, 1950, p. 72).

By "noegenesis" Spearman means the "eduction of relations and correlates," that is, perceiving relationships, inducing the general from the particular, and deducing the particular from the general. Noegenesis is inductive or inventive as contrasted with reproductive or rule-applying behavior. "Abstractness" refers to ideas, relationships, and concepts in contrast to properties that can be directly perceived by the senses. Spearman found that the most highly g-loaded tests were those involving both noegenesis and abstraction. Substantial g loading depends on the combination of these two characteristics.

The most g-loaded test in the whole battery was Raven's Progressive Matrices, which depends almost entirely on perceiving key features and relationships and discovering the abstract rules that govern the differences among the elements in the matrix. The second highest in g loading was a test of verbal generalizations (e.g., in what ways are pairs of abstract words, such as "triumph" and "victory," the same and different?).

Other very highly g-loaded tests are

Verbal analogies: such as "*Cut* is to *sharp* as *burn* is to   *fire   flame   hot   hurt.*"
Series completion: such as "1, 2, 4, 7, 11, ____, ____ "
   and "a, z, b, y, c, x, d, ____."
Arithmetic problem reasoning: such as "John is 6 years old or just half as old as his sister. What will be John's age when his sister is 40?"
Paragraph comprehension: making conclusions and inferences based on the content but not explicit in the paragraph.
Figure analogies and *Figure classifications*: correlating common characteristics.

Spearman noted that tests of arithmetic separate on g depending on whether they consist of *problem* arithmetic, in which the arithmetic operations are not explicit and are up to the subject to choose, or *mechanical* arithmetic in which all the operations called for are entirely explicit (e.g., addition, subtraction, multiplication, etc.). Problem arithmetic has very high g loadings (.7 to .8), whereas the g loadings on mechanical arithmetic are generally moderate (.4. to .6).

Tests with quite moderate g *loadings (.4 to .5) are*

> Several tests of spatial visualization ability involving direct perception
>   and manipulation, such as form boards and puzzles
> Sentence completion
> Figure recognition
> Handwriting speed
> Counting speed
> Paired-associate learning
> Pitch, delayed discrimination

Tests with very low g *loadings (below .30) include*

> Simple addition (speed)
> Counting groups of dots
> Crossing out designated letters or numbers
> Recognition memory (words and numbers)
> Rote memory tasks
> Tapping speed
> Dotting speed

We can add other instructive examples to Spearman's list. Tests of "closure" are especially interesting in this context because they are perceptual and seemingly nonabstract and yet are quite highly g loaded. These tests consist of black silhouettes (on a white background) depicting highly familiar objects, but the silhouettes have been mutilated or broken up. In their unmutilated form they are instantly recognized by virtually everyone. In their mutilated form it takes a matter of seconds, sometimes even minutes, of intensive examination before the object becomes apparent. Sooner or later the viewer suddenly experiences "closure" of the broken parts and thereupon has not the slightest doubt as to what is pictured. It becomes obvious all at once. The average speed of attaining closure on a number of such items is a good measure of g. Note that the essential mental requirement of this task is that of synthesis or integration of what at first appear to be meaningless parts into a meaningful whole. It is making order out of chaos. Subjective reports by persons taking the test suggest that it also involves processes of classification (category inclusion and exclusion) and invention and rejection of successive inferences as to what the mutilated picture might be, mental processes often occuring rapidly and at times on a nonverbal level.

It is also instructive to note the kind of changes in a given task that will increase its g loading. Take simple reaction time to a visual stimulus, such as a light bulb going "on." The subject simply takes his finger off a telegraph key as quickly as possible when he sees the light go on. This performance, measured as the time (in milliseconds) it takes the person to remove his finger from the telegraph key, has a g loading close to zero. But if we have two light bulbs, and either one or the other goes on at random, and the subject is required to touch the one that goes on as quickly as possible, his reaction time to get off the telegraph key will be slower and will have some slight but significant loading on g. If we have as many as eight lights going on in a random order, the subject's reaction time will be three times as long as the difference in his reaction times to one light and two lights. And the *difference* between the reaction times to one light and to eight lights has a *g* loading of about .30 to .40. In short, simple reaction time has practically no *g* loading (at least in normal adults), whereas choice reaction time has a slight, but significant, *g* loading. The increase in task complexity and associated increase in the subject's mental processing time are related to the *g* loading of the performance measure (Eysenck, 1967; Jensen, 1979; Jensen & Munro, 1979).

A similar case in point is the difference between forward and backward digit span. Forward digit span is the number of digits the subject can repeat in the order of presentation after hearing them once at the rate of one digit per second. Backward digit span is the number that can be recalled in reverse of the order of presentation. Backward digit span has a significantly higher *g* loading than forward digit span. The backward span is clearly the more complex task. It is the increased complexity and greater demands on mental manipulation that are the crucial factors, rather than an increase in task difficulty per se. The *g* loading of the digit-span task does not vary as a function of the number of digits in the series but as a function of forward versus backward order of recall (Jensen & Figueroa, 1975).

Thus, task complexity and the amount of conscious mental manipulation required seem to be the most basic determinants of the *g* loading of a task. If we distill this summary generalization still further, the amount of conscious mental manipulation set off by the input would seem to be the crucial element. The degree of complexity of the task is merely the occasion for mental manipulation. Task complexity may be correlated with difficulty, but complexity is not the same thing as difficulty, and the two need not be positively correlated. We have found, for example, that serial and paired-associate learning tasks can be made much more difficult for everyone simply by increasing the speed of presentation of the items during the learning trials, so that subjects may take twice as many trials to learn the list, on the average. Yet speeding up the presentation beyond a certain point *decreases* the correlation between learning performance and IQ. In other words, the more difficult task in this case is less *g* loaded than the easier task. The most reasonable explanation is that the more highly speeded presentation of the items to be learned allows subjects less time to think, that is, to engage in the mental manipulations that can give the kind of meaning and organization to the material that promotes recall. The recruitment of *g* for any given task takes some time, which when not available forces the subject to fall back on simpler mental processes. Thus tasks that by their nature can be mastered only by these simpler processes, such as by trial and error and by rote learning, show less correlation with *g* than do tasks that permit or require more elaborate mental manipulations.

Conscious mental manipulation is specified, because many components of a complex performance can take place without conscious effort or awareness of the mental processes as a result of practice and overlearning. It is a common finding that individual differences during the acquisition phase of learning many complex skills are more highly correlated with *g* than are individual differences in the final performance levels attained after training. The reader may recall his or her own experience in learning to drive an automobile. The initial stages involve considerable conscious mental effort and demand all of one's attention. The beginning driver finds it practically impossible to shift gears and carry on a conversation at the same time. Individual differences in learning to drive are probably moderately correlated with *g*. But the *g* loading decreases as the skill becomes highly practiced and the various components become fully integrated and more automatic.

Thus some degree of novelty is a common feature of g-loaded tests, because novelty elicits conscious mental activity; the subject cannot fall back on already well learned or practiced skills. Carl Bereiter once gave an informal definition of intelligence as ''What you do when you don't know what to do.'' Various evidence in the literature on learning and intelligence suggest that when persons are given intensive instruction and prolonged practice in any particular type of highly g-loaded test items and are then tested on similar type items (but not the ones used for training), these items show diminished g loadings when factor analyzed among a number of other types of g-loaded tests on which the persons were not specially trained.

Age and g.   In Chapter 5 it was noted that one of the criteria used by Binet for selecting items for his intelligence test was that the item should discriminate well between children of different ages. Items that correlated highly with age were thought to be good measures of general intelligence. Factor analysis, however, reveals that there is neither a high nor a necessary correlation between a test's (or item's) correlation with age and its loading on g within a homogeneous age group.

A clear illustration of this is a study by Garrett et al. (1935). These investigators factor analyzed a battery of ten quite diverse tests in large groups of children of ages 9, 12, and 15 years. Some of the tests were typical of highly g-loaded tests, such as vocabulary and problem arithmetic, whereas others were typical of lowly g-loaded tests, such as motor speed, digit span, and rote memory. When the factor analyses were performed separately in each of the three homogeneous age groups, the g factor accounted for about 25 percent of the total variance and 58 percent of the common factor variance. (Four factors including g were extracted in each age group.) But, when factor analysis was done in all three age groups combined, the g factor accounted for 48 percent of the total variance and 85 percent of the common factor variance. The increased variance on g in the combined group is, of course, attributable to age differences in performance on all the tests.

Thus it would appear on first impression that the age differences are mainly g. But in fact this is not the case. If age variance on the various tests were mainly g, we should expect the tests with the highest g loadings in the homogeneous age groups to increase the most in g loadings when the tests are factor analyzed in the heterogeneous age group. And tests with the lowest g loadings in the homogeneous age groups should show the least increase in g loading in the heterogeneous age group.

In fact, just the opposite is found. Tests with low g loadings in the homogeneous age groups increase their g loadings more in the heterogeneous age group. In the heterogeneous group, *developmental* differences become a large part of the g factor, and not all of this developmental variance is the same as the g factor found in homogeneous age groups. The rank order of magnitudes of the g loadings on the ten tests are not the same for homogeneous and heterogeneous groups. (The rank order correlation is about .50.) One can readily see why this is the case by considering a variable such as strength of hand grip, which shows a marked correlation with age, but an almost zero g loading when factor analyzed among a battery of mental tests within a homogeneous age group. But in a heterogeneous age group, hand-grip strength (and all other variables which show age differences) will show substantial loadings on the general factor.

Thus it is essential in factor analyzing mental tests to remove the effects of age. This is best done by using homogeneous age groups with no more than a one-year interval and partialing age (in months) out of the intercorrelations among the tests. Nearly all the correlation between test scores and age is linear within a one-year interval or less, and so partial correlation removes virtually all of the effects of age. Because the regression of test scores on age over intervals greater than one year is often nonlinear, partial correlations cannot remove all of the effects of age. Factor analyses of mental abilities based on heterogeneous age groups, even when age is partialled out, are therefore usually suspect, unless nonlinear components of age (e.g., age^2, age^3, age^4, etc.) are also partialled out of the intercorrelations among the various tests.[12]

Uniqueness of g. Is the g of one battery of mental tests the same g as that obtained in a different battery of mental tests? If g is something different from one set of tests to another, it is not unique and therefore will not be a very important theoretical construct. Spearman believed that g is unique, and he offered a formal proof that the g of one set of tests is the same as the g of another set, provided that the correlation matrices of each set are hierarchical (i.e., that each test involves only g plus a specific factor) and that two (or more) tests are common to both sets (Spearman & Jones, 1950, pp. 17–19). But these are very limiting and unrealistic assumptions. Spearman's proof of the uniqueness of g does not hold when there are group factors in addition to g and s. Then no purely mathematical proof of the uniqueness of g is possible, and the answer to the question devolves on empirical evidence.

It seems a safe generalization that the g of a *large* and *diverse* set of mental tests is the same as the g of a different large and diverse set of mental tests. By ''large,'' I mean ten or more tests; by ''diverse,'' I mean tests sampled from a wide domain of informational content, types of problems, and task demands, involving verbal, figural, and numerical materials. If all the tests are verbal, for example, the resultant g factor will really be $g +$ v, because there will be no chance for separation of the general and verbal factors.

Take the Wechsler Adult Intelligence Scale as an example. The six verbal subtests (information, vocabulary, comprehension, arithmetic, similarities, digit span) are all very different in content and task demands from the five performance subtests (digit symbol, picture completion, block design, picture arrangement, object assembly). Yet it can be determined that in the normative adult population the correlation is at least .80 between the general factor of the six verbal subtests and the general factor of the five performance subtests (Matarazzo, 1974, p. 243). The Verbal IQ and the Performance IQ each correlates at least .90 with the same g. This is almost as high a correlation as the reliability of the tests will permit. In other words, we have here two phenotypically very different sets of tests, yet each set has essentially the same g factor as the other.

Let us push the issue to an even greater extreme. Garrett et al. (1935) factor analyzed a battery of six varied memory tests (meaningful prose, paired-associates, free recall of words, digit span, memory for forms, memory for objects) and extracted the general factor. This battery of tests then was factor analyzed along with four other diverse tests not especially involving memory (motor speed, vocabulary, arithmetic, form board). The g loadings of the memory tests in the two analyses correlated .80. The overall correlation between g factor scores based on just the memory tests and g factor scores based on just the nonmemory tests is .87. This is evidence that the g of the six memory tests is the same g as the g of the nonmemory tests. To be sure, the memory tests are not highly loaded on g (average g loading $= .42$) as compared with vocabulary and arithmetic (average g loading $= .65$), but what little g the memory tests have is much the same g as is found in the nonmemory tests.

Thus it is reasonable to conclude that g is the same common factor in different sets of mental tests, provided that each set is reasonably large and quite heterogeneous in content.

Fluid and Crystalized g

If we factor analyze a large number of highly diverse mental tests and rotate the factor axes so as to allow them to be oblique (i.e., correlated) to approximate the criterion of simple structure as closely as possible and then factor analyze the correlations among the primary factors so as to obtain second-order factors, which we also rotate to simple structure, we will usually come out either with one factor or with two large factors, that is, either g or g_f and g_c. Even when g_f and g_c are found in place of a unitary g, they are usually highly correlated. Raymond B. Cattell (b. 1905) first discovered these two correlated aspects of g, which sometimes emerge as second-order factors, and named them *fluid* and *crystalized* general intelligence (Cattell, 1963; 1971b, Ch. 5). Cattell's theory of fluid and crystalized intelligence is especially important in any discussion of cultural or educational bias in mental testing.

The essential distinction between fluid and crystalized general intelligence, or g_f and g_c for short, can be gleaned in part from noting the kinds of tests that load most heavily on one or the other factor. Tests loaded mostly on g_f are those that have little informational content but demand the ability to see relationships, often complex relationships, between relatively simple elements: number series and letter series, figure classification, figure analogies, spatial visualization, closure tests, embedded figures tests, block designs, and matrices. Tests loaded mostly on g_c are those that have informational content and draw on the subject's already acquired knowledge and skills: general information, vocabulary, arithmetic, mechanical information and tool identification, verbal syllogisms and other formal logical reasoning problems, and abstruse verbal analogies.

Notice that the g_c–g_f distinction is not the same as the verbal–nonverbal distinction. For example, verbal analogies based on highly familiar words, but demanding a high level of relation eduction are loaded on g_f, whereas analogies based on abstruse or specialized words and terms rarely encountered outside the context of formal education are loaded on g_c. Compare the following:

Typical g_f item:
  Grass is to *cattle* as *bread* is to   *man   butter   water   bones.*
Typical g_c item:
  Pupil is to *teacher* as *Aristotle* is to   *Socrates   Plato   philosopher   Homer.*

The demands on relation eduction are greater in the first than in the second analogy item, which requires almost no reasoning at all but depends entirely on the subject's having acquired (probably in college) the rather specialized bit of knowledge that Aristotle was a pupil of Plato.

Because persons who are high in g_f generally also tend to acquire information more rapidly, thoroughly, and broadly, there is usually a high correlation between g_f and g_c, often so high a correlation that these two aspects of g are not clearly distinguishable by means of factor analysis. Fluid and crystalized general factors are harder to distinguish in children and young adults who have had very similar cultural and educational opportunities than in populations that are very heterogeneous in cultural and educational background. Individuals *invest* their g_f, so to speak, in somewhat different subject matters, in terms of their opportunities, interests, values, motivations, and external pressures from family and peers. Thus individuals with the same g_f may show quite different patterns of performance on various tests loaded mainly on g_c. Because of different backgrounds or interests, they will have invested g_f in different ways. However, common schooling and other aspects of a common culture, such as a common language, the popular media, and the like, make for considerable homogeneity of experience, especially in school-age persons, so that measures of g_f and g_c will be quite highly correlated. Thus some types of tests, such as problem arithmetic, load substantially on both g_f and g_c factors. Arithmetic skills have to be learned, but nearly everyone has the opportunity for such learning in school, and those with more g_f learn these skills faster and better and can make better use of them in novel problems.

Even though g_f and g_c are not always clearly distinguishable in factor analyses, the distinction gains conceptual validity from other lines of evidence, which are more impressive than the evidence from factor analysis. Scores on tests with high g_f or high g_c loadings show different age trends (Cattell, 1971b, Ch. 7; Horn, 1967; Horn & Cattell, 1967). For one thing, g_f shows a growth curve much more like that of various physical growth curves than does g_c. The growth of g_f is steady but relatively rapid and reaches a maximum in the late teens or early twenties, after which it shows a gradual decline; the decline becomes more accelerated after 55 or 60 years of age. Such a curve of growth and decline closely parallels measures of physical strength, air capacity of the lungs (called "vital capacity"), and brain weight. (Average brain weight decreases some 3 to 4 percent from the late teens to the middle fifties.) Scores on tests highly loaded on g_c, on the other hand, show a more gradual increase from infancy to maturity, and, although the rate of increase is negatively accelerated in the teens, decline does not set in until relatively late in life, usually not until about 60 to 70 years of age.

Although performance on Raven's Matrices peaks at around 20 years of age, for example, vocabulary scores go on increasing very gradually up to 60 or 70 years of age. So does the amount of general information. In persons over 60 years of age, scores on g_c tests such as information and vocabulary are a better indication of the person's past level of g_f than of his present functioning level of g_f. High vocabulary and general information scores would be very unlikely in a person who had never been high in g_f. But, in old age, scores on tests of crystalized intelligence can be somewhat likened to hollow shells that no longer contain the g_f that was invested in the past and has since diminished, leaving only an indicator of the fluid ability that once existed. Clinicians working with the aged are familiar with the person who has a large vocabulary, a large fund of information, highly developed and still useful technical skills, yet who finds it extremely difficult to learn something quite new and is at an almost total loss when confronted with a very novel problem in which his crystalized knowledge or skills are of little use. The extent to which performances on different tests do or do not hold up in old age coincides closely with the tests' relative loadings on g_c and g_f (Horn, 1973).

Another difference between g_c- and g_f-loaded tests noted by Cattell (1971b, pp.

138–148) is that g_f tests have a standard deviation almost 50 percent greater than that of g_c tests, when scores are expressed as a ratio of mental age to chronological age. That is, at any given age level, there are greater individual differences in g_f than in g_c. The 10-year-old who is one standard deviation above the population mean on a highly g_c-loaded test has a performance equivalent to that of the average child of 11 years and 6 months of age. The same 10-year-old, if he is also one standard deviation above the mean on a highly g_f loaded test, would be exhibiting a level of performance equal to that of the average child at about 12 years and 3 months.

The Organic Substrata of g

Wechsler (1958, p. 121) has stated that g " is independent of the modality or contextual structure from which it is elicited; g cannot be exclusively identified with any single intellectual ability and for this reason cannot be described in concrete operational terms." He goes on to note that g "is not a factor at all in the sense that verbal comprehension, memory, etc., are factors of the mind. . . . One should note . . . that un-like all other factors [g] cannot be associated with any unique or single ability; g is involved in many different types of ability; it is in essence not an ability at all, but a property of the mind" (p. 124).

Other psychologists have likened g to the concept of the *efficiency* of a machine. A machine's efficiency cannot be found in any of the components of the machine or in an average measure of all the separate components. Efficiency is a function of how well all of the parts work together to accomplish a particular purpose. Thus, if g is a kind of mental efficiency, it is unlikely to be identified with the quality of any single neural structure or biochemical element of the brain, but would reflect the integrated action of the many elements called into play by any complex situation.

It makes little sense to say that g is more an aspect of the tests than of persons. The magnitude of the g loadings of various homogeneous tests is not related to their type of content or other identifiable common elements. The loadings of tests on verbal, nu-merical, and spatial factors, for example, are clearly related to common elements in such items. But there are no surface-level common elements among test items that have high g loadings. Such g-loaded items, as we have noted, seem to have in common a degree of complexity of some sort and require conscious mental manipulation, but these characteris-tics can apply to any kind of item content and are not elements of the items as such. What elements do verbal analogies, block designs, and number series have in common? The "common elements" are something in the brain, not in the test items as such.

Spearman regarded g as a kind of general mental energy available to the brain, the physiological basis of which is as yet unknown, and in which persons differ innately. He wrote: "The brain may be regarded (pending further information) as able to switch the bulk of its energy from any one to any other group of neurons; . . . accordingly, the amount and the direction of the disposable energy regulate respectively the intensity and the quality of the ensuing mental process" (Spearman, 1923, p. 346).

This theory of g as a kind of general neural energy that can be applied to any of the brain's functions, however, does not easily explain why some mental tests are so much more g loaded than others. If a homogeneous neural energy were involved in every mental act, then every mental test should be an equally good measure of g, allowing for dif-ferences in reliability of measurement. Any sample, no matter how small, of a homogeneous or unitary "substance" should be as representative as any other, and the size of the sample should affect only its reliability or error of measurement. Thus, if *g* were a unitary energy homogeneously available throughout the brain, all tests equated for reliability should show the same *g* loading. But this theoretical result does not seem to accord with Spearman's own statistical formulation of the total test variance as comprised of a *general factor* plus *specific factor* plus *error variance*. If the specific factor *s* involves nonerror variance, as it most certainly does, we are left with the question of its nature and why it enters into some tests more than others. Spearman's (1923, pp. 5–7) answer was that different parts of the cerebral cortex have localized or specific energies. Various tests involve different groups of neurons and thus tap not only the general energy common to the entire cerebrum but also the specific energies involved in the particular tasks. He likened the specific areas of the cortex to different engines (with individual differences in efficiency), and the general neural energy of the whole cerebrum was likened to the fuel (with individual differences in its quality or potential energy). "In this manner, successful action would always depend partly on the potential energy developed in the whole cortex and partly on the efficiency of the specific group of neurons involved" (Spearman, 1923, p. 6).

Edward L. Thorndike (1927, pp. 415–422) saw no need to posit the existence of a general energy, but instead viewed *g* as the total number of available neural connections. According to Thorndike, the more intelligent person has more neural connections or "bonds," as he called them. A person's educability depends on the potential connections available for learning; the efficiency of problem solving is a function of the number and speed of the neural connections that are brought to bear. Tests are loaded on *g* in direct proportion to the number of connections they involve. The solution of complex problems would depend on the utilization of many neural connections, and individual differences in *g* reflect differences in the quantity of available connections. Thorndike wrote:

> This greater fund of ideas and connections is partly due to larger life and more varied and stimulating life, but it may be and certainly is partly due to original nature. It has some anatomical or physiological cause or parallel. Our hypothesis regards this anatomical cause or correspondent of the original possibility of having more such connections (call it C) as the cause of the original differences in intelligence among men. (1927, p. 420)

In summary, Thorndike states, "The gist of our doctrine is that, by original nature, the intellect capable of the higher reasoning and adaptability differs from the intellect of an imbecile only in the capacity for having more connections of the sort described" (p. 422).

Sir Godfrey H. Thomson (1881–1955), in his now famous work *The Factorial Analysis of Human Abilities* (1951), elaborated on Thorndike's theory and showed mathematically that the results of factor analysis, with its hierarchical structure involving a general factor and a number of group factors, could be neatly explained in terms of a "sampling" model in which the elements sampled are small, numerous, diverse, and need not be specified as to their physiological nature, knowledge of which would depend on appropriate investigations of the brain itself.

The action of the brain can be thought of as involving a large number of elements of various types: the number and amount of branching of brain cells, synaptic conductivity, threshold of activation of neural elements, production of neurochemical transmitters such as acetylcholine and cholinesterase, the blood supply to the brain and the richness of the capillary network in different parts of the brain, and so on. If various kinds of behavioral tasks involve different samples of these many elements, the degree to which performance is correlated across tasks will depend on the number of elements that they have in common. The more elements that are sampled by a given task, the more highly will it be correlated with other tasks. Thus tasks are *g* loaded in proportion to the number of such elements that they involve. This is illustrated in Figure 6.13. The many small circles represent various neural elements, connections, and the like. The three large areas represent different test items. Each item samples a number of elements, and some of the elements are sampled in common by two or three of the test items, causing them to be correlated. The elements in areas *A, B,* and *C* are specific to each item. Areas *AC, AB,* and *BC* correspond to group factors, that is, elements sampled in common by some but not all of the items. Very simple items that sample very few elements are less apt to sample elements in common with other items. More complex items will sample more elements in common. Increasing the number of items, provided that they are sufficiently complex and diverse, increases the number of elements sampled. A score on a test made up of complex items, each of which samples a relatively large number of elements, will represent an average of more elements than a score on a test made up of simple items, each of which samples relatively few elements. The more diverse and complex tests have more common elements and hence a greater *g* loading than simple and homogeneous tests. See, for example, the factor analysis of the diverse battery of tests shown in Table 6.13.

This model is consistent with a common empirical observation in psychometrics, which was first clearly enunciated by Clark L. Hull (1884–1952). In examining the intercorrelations among an extremely great variety of tests, including sensory-motor skills, coordination, reaction time, rhythm, balancing, memory, tapping, card sorting, and verbal and nonverbal intelligence tests of various types, Hull reached the conclusion

Figure 6.13. Illustration of Thomson's sampling theory of abilities, in which the small circles represent elements or bonds and the large circles represent tests that sample different sets of elements (labeled *A, B,* and *C*). Correlation between tests is due to the number of elements sampled in common, represented by the areas of overlap.

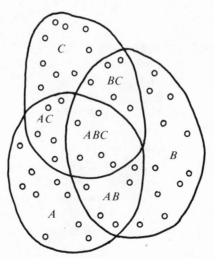

that "the highly complex intellectual activities correlate highly with each other, the less complex correlate with each other to an intermediate degree, and the relatively simple motor activities correlate with each other only slightly" (Hull, 1928, Ch. 6). Hull explained this "law," as he called it, in terms of the same kind of sampling model later propounded by Thomson.

As an example, Hull assumed that the total number of neural elements was 1,300. He then showed the size of correlation that would result between pairs of tests that randomly sample different numbers of elements or "determiners." A complex activity involving a random sampling of, say, 800 of the total 1,300 elements would correlate, on the average, +.61 with other tests of the same degree of complexity. Tasks involving a random sample of 400 elements would correlate +.31, and tasks involving only 50 elements would correlate +.04. (In general, if test 1 samples the proportion P_1 of the total elements and test 2 samples P_2, the correlation between tests 1 and 2 will be $\sqrt{P_1 P_2}$.) The correlations of +.61, +.31, and +.04 are typical of the intercorrelations that Hull found among intellectual, complex motor, and simple motor tasks, respectively.

According to the sampling model, the elements that are sampled by tests are not themselves abilities in the behavioral sense. Abilities, as we observe and describe them behaviorally, are a resultant of the simultaneous actions of some aggregate of substrata elements that await description ultimately in neurophysiological and biochemical terms.

Intelligence and Achievement

The claim is often made that intelligence tests are really just achievement tests. After all, the Wechsler tests, for example, ask the subject for items of information and for the solutions to problems in arithmetic, and these are obviously achievements—the information and the skills involved have had to be learned. Can we, then, properly make any meaningful distinction between intelligence (or aptitude) and achievement? (This question has been considered in great depth by seventeen prominent scholars who met for a three-day conference on the topic, the proceedings of which were published; see Green, 1974, and, for a penetrating discussion, Humphreys, 1978.)

All performance is a form of achievement, and of course there is no psychological test that is performance free. In every case, the subject must say something, write something, or do something to score on the test. In this trivial sense, all tests are achievement tests. No clear-cut *operational* distinction can be made between aptitude *tests* and achievement *tests,* because some form of achievement must always be the vehicle for measurement. Attempts to distinguish between *aptitude* (or intelligence) and *achievement* at the operational level of tests have pointed to the following features:

1. Intelligence test items sample much broader and more heterogeneous forms of achievement based on a wider variety of experiences than do achievement tests, which sample specific types of knowledge and skills associated with formal schooling or special instruction.

2. Intelligence tests sample cumulated knowledge and skills from all times in the individual's past experience, whereas achievement tests usually sample knowledge or skills acquired in the recent past, usually in connection with a course of instruction and study.

3. Intelligence (*g*) can be measured by an almost infinite variety of test items so long as they involve some complexity, whereas achievement of any particular kind can only be measured by a narrow and clearly definable class of items. "General achievement" is probably indistinguishable operationally (though not conceptually) from "general intelligence." That is, composite tests of either kind would probably measure the same general factor in a culturally homogeneous population.

4. Intelligence and aptitude tests predict future intellectual achievements, even though the contents of the achievements have nothing in common with (i.e., are not sampled by) the aptitude test.

5. Most intelligence measures are more stable across time and are less susceptible to the influence of instruction or training than is the case of most achievement measures.

6. The total score on an intelligence test represents a second-order factor (e.g., g or g_c or g_f) that is not itself describable in terms of test content or specific items of knowledge or skill, whereas achievement test scores (unless combined from a great variety of achievement tests) represent primary factors that are describable in terms of specific content and the specific behavioral aspects of successful performance.

None of these criteria is without important exceptions, and all represent only points along a continuum rather than discrete differences between intelligence tests and achievement tests.

As we shall see in Chapter 8, there is generally a high correlation between IQ and scholastic achievement. For individuals who have had an equality of experiential opportunities equivalent to the equality of backgrounds found for, say, siblings reared in the same family, there is such a high correlation between intelligence test scores and scholastic achievement test scores as to make the two kinds of scores operationally indistinguishable. It is only when there have been considerable differences among individuals in experiential opportunities or motivations for certain classes of achievement that we find a low correlation between certain intelligence and achievement measures. This is especially true of achievements that are not deemed essential by the schools or for which there are not strong social sanctions against poor performance. Achievement in reading or arithmetic, for example, is more highly correlated with IQ (or g) than is achievement in, say, music. A large part of the reason for this is that virtually all children are under pressure from school and home to acquire the 3 R's, whereas musical instruction is much less uniformly insisted on and is begun at various ages over a wide range for different children, and failure is not generally considered a serious handicap. If musical achievements were treated with the same uniformity and persistence of instruction throughout the school years that we see in the case of reading or arithmetic, we can be fairly sure that IQ tests would show a much higher correlation (though not a perfect correlation, because of special talents) with musical accomplishment than is now the case.

The validity and importance of the aptitude–achievement distinction are conceptual and theoretical. Differences in aptitude are inferred when individuals with roughly equal or equivalent experience, opportunity, and motivation to acquire some particular knowledge or skills, show marked differences in their rates of acquisition and level of performance after a given amount of exposure. A concept of aptitude is needed to account for the acquisition of a broad class of knowledge and skills in which the main sources of individual differences are not linked essentially to any particular sensory or motor capabilities.

Such a concept of aptitude is also needed to account for the fairly high consistency shown by the intercorrelations of individual differences on a variety of tasks. Rates of knowledge and skill acquisition are not highly particularistic but, rather, show considerable consistency from early childhood to maturity and beyond, though in some spheres of achievement there are outstanding variations depending on special aptitudes such as in music, art, and athletics, which generally involve particular sensory and motor functions.

Achievement is also conceptually (and, at times, empirically) distinguishable from aptitude in the sense that individual differences in achievement also involve other traits besides aptitude, as well as opportunity. A familiar formulation is

$$Aptitude \times Motivation \times Opportunity = Achievement.$$

Measures of certain personality factors predict a significant proportion of the variance in scholastic achievement independently of intelligence (Cattell, 1971b, pp. 376–398). Tests of crystalized intelligence g_c, which most closely reflect past achievements, are usually better predictors of future achievement than are tests loaded mainly on fluid ability g_f, as g_c-loaded tests reflect not only the past effects of g_f but some of the personality, motivational, and past opportunity factors involved in achievement. For short-term prediction, the individual's recent past achievement is, generally, the best predictor of his or her achievement in the near future.

In a series of large statistical analyses, too complex to be explicated here in detail, William D. Crano has attempted to determine the direction of causality between intelligence and achievement (Crano, et al., 1972; Crano, 1974). The investigation used a technique known as cross-lagged correlation analysis. In brief, intelligence tests and a variety of scholastic achievement tests were given to large samples of school children in Grade 4 and two years later in Grade 6. The key question is, Do the Grade 4 achievement tests predict Grade 6 IQ more or less than Grade 4 IQ tests predict Grade 6 achievement? If the correlation from Grade 4 to 6 is higher in the direction $IQ_4 \rightarrow Achievement_6$ than in the direction $Achievement_4 \rightarrow IQ_6$, it can be reasonably argued that individual differences in IQ have a causal effect on individual differences in achievement. This, in fact, is what was found for the total sample of 5,495 pupils. However, when the total sample was broken down into two groups consisting of pupils in suburban schools and pupils in inner-city schools (in other words, middle- and lower-socioeconomic-status groups), the cross-lagged correlations showed different results for the two groups. The suburban group clearly showed the causal sequence $IQ_4 \rightarrow Achievement_6$ at a high level of statistical significance, whereas the results of the inner-city group were less clear, but suggested, if anything, the opposite causal sequence, that is, $Achievement_4 \rightarrow IQ_6$, at least for verbal IQ. (The $Ach_4 \rightarrow Nonverbal IQ_6$ was significant only for arithmetic achievement.) Also a high-IQ sample (one standard deviation above the mean) showed a much more prominent $IQ_4 \rightarrow Ach_6$ cause–effect correlation than did a low-IQ sample (one standard deviation below the mean). The predominant direction of causality is from the more abstract and g-loaded tests to the more specific and concrete skills. For example, in the total sample and in both social-class groups, Verbal IQ in Grade 4 predicts spelling in Grade 6 significantly higher than spelling in Grade 4 predicts Verbal IQ in Grade 6.

Factor analysis has shown that the Verbal IQ of the Lorge–Thorndike Intelligence Test used in Crano's study measures mainly crystalized intelligence g_c, whereas the Nonverbal IQ is mainly fluid ability g_f (Jensen, 1973d). Consistent with Cattell's theory of g_f and g_c, Crano et al. (1972) found that Grade 4 Nonverbal IQ (g_f) predicts Grade 6 Verbal IQ (g_c) more highly than Grade 4 Verbal IQ predicts Grade 6 Nonverbal IQ, and this is true in both social-class groups. Thus, g_f can be said to cause g_c more than the reverse. Crano et al. (1972, p. 272) conclude as follows:

> The findings indicate that an abstract-to-concrete causal sequence of cognitive acquisition predominates among suburban school children. The positive and often statistically significant cross-lagged correlation values... also indicate that the concrete skills act as causal determinants of abstract skills; their causal effectiveness, however, is not as great as that of the more abstract abilities. Taken together, these results suggest that the more complex abstract abilities depend upon the acquisition of a *number* of diverse, concrete skills, but these concrete acquisitions, taken independently, do not operate causally to form more abstract, complex abilities. Apparently, the *integration* of a number of such skills is a necessary precondition to the generation of higher order abstract rules or schema. Such schema, in turn, operate as causal determinants in the acquisition of later concrete skills.   (italics added)

It would be hard to find a better statement of the relationships among g_f (as basic integrative ability), g_c (as higher order schema), and the acquisition of specific scholastic knowledge and skills.

"Capacity" and "Potential"

Warren's *Dictionary of Psychology* (1934) defines "capacity" as "the full potentiality of an individual for any function, as limited by his native constitution and as measured, theoretically, by the extent to which that function would develop under optimal conditions." "Potential" is defined as "pertaining to characteristics which are not present or manifest in an organism at the given moment, but may develop or appear later."

The terms "capacity" and "potential" have gone out of favor in modern psychometrics, and for good reason. The concepts that these terms may originally have intended to convey have since been reformulated in a scientifically more satisfactory fashion.

We no longer speak of any kind of test score as a measure of a person's capacity or potential. Tests obviously measure what the individual can do at the time of taking the test and not what he was born with or what he *could* do under some other conditions or at some future time. The notions of capacity and potential suggest some clear-cut and inexorable upper limit of development. But this is a metaphysical rather than a strictly scientific notion.

Scientifically, all we can do in any test situation is measure an individual's performance then and there on the particular test at that particular time with that particular examiner. Performance is a function of numerous variables, including the demands of the task, situational factors affecting the person's effort, willingness, and persistence, the person's understanding of the task, the past acquired knowledge and developed skills that he or she brings to the task, as well as internal organismic factors. From this performance measure—the test score—we can make *conditional probability* statements based on research with the particular test. If the test has no research behind it and is not highly similar to other tests about which a great deal is known, then no inferences about the meaning of the score are possible. Conditional probability is the likelihood (expressed as a proportion of all possible outcomes) of an event (i.e., a value, performance, test score, etc.), given certain specified conditions.

Conditional probability statements based on empirical research simply do not include or require the notions of capacity or potential.

Evidence on the *reliability* or *stability* of the test permits a probabilistic estimate of the individual's score if he or she is tested again at some specified future time, assuming, of course, that the individual can be regarded as a member of the population in which the reliability evidence was obtained.

Evidence on the *validity* of the test permits probabilistic statements about the subject's performance on other tests, on other criteria such as scholastic achievement, success in special training programs, efficiency in a particular job, and so on. (The topics of reliability, stability, and validity of mental tests are discussed more fully in the next two chapters.)

Evidence on the *heritability* of the test scores in the population permits conditional probabilistic statements about the individual's genotypic value on the characteristic or trait measured by the test. Theoretically the individual's genotypic value can be defined as the average value (i.e., measurement or score) of all persons in the population who have the same genotype (as the given individual's) for the trait in question. Notice how the concept of genotypic value differs from the notion of capacity. Capacity is defined as what the individual's value on the trait would be if the trait had developed to its "full value" under "ideal" conditions. "Full value" and "ideal" conditions are mystical ideas that have no operational meaning. In principle, we have no way of knowing *a priori* what level an individual's performance might attain under unspecified environmental conditions or even under some novel specified conditions that have never existed before.

Genotypic value, on the other hand, is the level of performance attained by all identical genotypes (for the given trait) averaged over the total range and frequency of environmental conditions that actually exist in the population here and now and contribute to individual differences in performance on the test in question. Environmental factors that do not influence performance make no contribution to variance (i.e., individual differences) and therefore are of no explanatory interest. The range of variation in performance of identical genotypes in the existing population of environments is termed the *reaction range*. It indicates the range of performance values that can be expected for a given genotype under the range of environmental conditions that actually exists in the population. Notice that the concept includes no notion of ideal or unknown or unspecified environmental conditions of development. In short, the phenotypic expression of a given genotype has a range of values depending on other conditions.

There are no operational means, in principle, for estimating capacity or potential. But genotypic value can, in principle, be estimated in operational, empirical terms. An individual's estimated genotypic value $\hat{G}_i$ on any measurable phenotypic characteristic P_i (e.g., height in inches, weight in pounds, test performance in IQ units, etc.) is

$$\hat{G}_i = h^2 (P_i - \bar{P}_p) + \bar{P}_p, \qquad (6.10)$$

where h^2 is the broad heritability of the trait and $\bar{P}_p$ is the mean of the population. The formula assumes that the individual for whom $\hat{G}_i$ is estimated is a member of the population in which h^2 and $\bar{P}_p$ are determined and that h^2 and $\bar{P}_p$ are determined in the same population. (They need not be determined in the same sample from the population.)

Heritability, signified by h^2, is the proportion of phenotypic variance attributable to genetic factors. It can also be thought of as the squared correlation between genotype and phenotype. The coefficient of nongenetic determination e^2 is $1 - h^2$. The nongenetic variance is comprised of all environmental influences (pre- and postnatal) and errors of measurement. Estimation of h^2 for the measurements of any given trait is a highly technical and complex affair involving the principles and methods of quantitative gene- tics. The reader is referred elsewhere for an explication of the theory and methodology of heritability estimation (Burt, 1971; Jensen, 1973b, pp. 366–375; 1975a; 1976; Li, 1975; McClearn & DeFries, 1973).

Estimates of h^2 (i.e., "broad heritability," which includes all of the genetic var- iance) for various standardized tests of intelligence vary from about .50 to .90 in different samples and populations, with a central tendency close to .75. But it should be noted that there are a number of theoretical assumptions involved in estimating h^2 by any of the several most common methods, and in practice it is rarely the case that the data meet all the assumptions underlying any one method. Thus, although there is general agreement among most behavioral geneticists that the hertability of intelligence is substantial, there is much less agreement that any given empirical determination of h^2 is an entirely satisfac- tory estimate. In any particular study, one can always find methodological reasons for some doubt. The convergence of evidence from many studies using different methods, however, leaves little if any doubt concerning the relatively high heritability of IQ. From the existing studies, it would be difficult indeed to make a case for the hypothesis that the heritability of IQ is less than .50.

The standard error $SE_{\hat{G}}$ of the estimated genotypic value for an individual as estimated from equation 6.10 is

$$SE_{\hat{G}} = \sigma_P h \sqrt{1 - h^2}, \tag{6.11}$$

where σ_P is the standard deviation of the measurement in the population. Assuming that the individual is a member of the population for which h^2 is estimated, and assuming no error in the estimates of h^2 and σ_P, we can determine the standard error of the estimated genotypic values for any given estimate of h^2 based on a σ_P of 15, which is the population standard deviation of IQ. The standard errors are shown in Table 6.15 for values of h^2 be- tween .50 and .90, along with the corresponding confidence intervals, that is, the probabil- ity that the true genotypic value lies within $\pm x$ IQ points of the estimated value. For exam- ple, if we assume $h^2 = .50$, we can be confident of being right 75 percent of the time in concluding that an individual's estimated genotypic value differs by no more than ± 8.6 IQ points from the true genotypic value. The confidence interval for the genotypic dif- ference between two randomly selected persons is the *standard error of the difference*, that is, $\sqrt{2} SE_{\hat{G}}$. If $h^2 = .50$, two persons would have to differ in estimated genotypic values by more than $\sqrt{2} \times 14.7 = 20.8$ IQ points for confidence at the 95 percent level that the estimated difference represents a true difference.

The lower-limit estimate of h^2 is set at .50, as there is no body of evidence that can reject the hypothesis that the broad heritability of IQ is greater than .50, whereas the evidence is overwhelming for rejecting the hypothesis that h^2 is less than .50. In fact, as noted earlier, h^2 is more probably near .75. As can be seen from Table 6.15, even assuming a heritability of as low as .50, it is highly improbable (i.e., less than 1 chance in 100) that two individuals from the same population whose estimated genotypic values differ by 30 IQ points or more actually have equal genotypes for IQ. But note that to have this degree of confidence (i.e., 99 percent), and assuming $h^2 = .50$, the two individuals might have to differ in IQ by about 55 points. Even if h^2 is assumed to be .75, two individuals might have to differ by at least 36 IQ points to warrant 99 percent confidence

Table 6.15. Standard error and confidence intervals of the estimated genotypic value on an IQ scale (with $\sigma = 15$) for various estimates of heritability (h^2).

h^2	$SE_{\hat{G}}$	Confidence Interval (Probability)					
		.75	.80	.85	.90	.95	.99
.90	4.50	±5.2	±5.8	± 6.5	± 7.4	± 8.8	±11.6
.85	5.36	±6.2	±6.9	± 7.7	± 8.8	±10.5	±13.8
.80	6.00	±6.9	±7.7	± 8.6	± 9.9	±11.8	±15.5
.75	6.50	±7.5	±8.3	± 9.3	±10.7	±12.7	±16.7
.70	6.87	±7.9	±8.8	± 9.9	±11.3	±13.5	±17.7
.65	7.15	±8.2	±9.2	±10.3	±11.8	±14.0	±18.4
.60	7.35	±8.5	±9.4	±10.6	±12.1	±14.4	±18.9
.55	7.46	±8.6	±9.6	±10.7	±12.3	±14.6	±19.2
.50	7.50	±8.6	±9.6	±10.8	±12.3	±14.7	±19.3

that they differ in genotypes for IQ. In making such estimates, it is assumed that we possess no knowledge of the individual other than his test score and the fact that he is a member of our reference population. If more is known about the individual's background and personal history, these factors might be taken into account in estimating the individual's genotypic value and its standard error. Brain damage, for example, would increase the standard error of estimate, whereas a comprehensive knowledge of the individual's environment throughout the course of development would give us greater confidence in our estimate.

The preceding examples clearly illustrate the wide margin of uncertainty involved in drawing genetical conclusions from any individual's test score. But tests are rarely, if ever, used to estimate an individual's genotype, although they may do so about as accurately as they predict school grades or job performance. Testers, however, are more interested in using tests to predict behavior in specified situations than to estimate a hypothetical construct such as the individual's genotype, which is of practical interest only insofar as it may predict other criteria. Because these criteria can be predicted just as well from the test scores themselves and because we have no estimate of the individual's genotype that is independent of the test score, there is really no point in estimating genotypic values. The nearest we can come to giving any scientific meaning to the disfavored notions of "capacity" and "potential" is the concept of genotypic value. But, as has been shown in the foregoing discussion, this concept has quite different meanings and implications than "capacity" and "potential," and, furthermore, it can only be estimated from test scores probabilistically, with a rather wide margin of error for any individual.

Intelligence as Learned Strategies

A popular view held by many psychologists in recent years is that what we call intelligence and measure by means of IQ tests consists only of various acquired "strategies" for efficient learning, thinking, and problem solving. Implicit in this view is the notion that there are no individual differences in the brain itself but only differences in how persons *use* their brains. The low-IQ person has simply not *learned* the efficient strategies that have been learned by the person with a high IQ. Teach the low-IQ person the same strategies that give the high-IQ person an advantage in intellectual performance, and the difference between them will be reduced or eliminated.

It is true that many of the tasks that are used in IQ tests and are good measures of g can be subjected to a ''task analysis,'' which consists of inferring the kinds of psychological processes that enter into efficient and successful performance. These processes are thought of as specific bits of teachable behavior that the subject can engage in when confronted with a certain class of intellectual problems. For example, we can analyze our own thought processes as we solve problems in arithmetic, isolate the discrete behavioral acts, and express these in terms that can be generalized to the class of all similar problems, such as ''first get an overview of the problem, then determine the relevant information and discard the irrelevant, then break the problem down into the particular arithmetic operations it calls for, determine the order in which these operations should be performed,'' and so on. Each step is a teachable skill or stratagem for solving problems. Many problem tasks typical of those found in IQ tests lend themselves to this kind of task analysis.

The trouble is that the effect of training on such strategies is very narrow in its degree of transfer to other classes of problems. Moreover, there are still marked individual differences in the benefits derived from strategy training. The brighter subjects learn the strategies more readily, generalize them to a wider class of problems, and are more flexible in choosing and adapting different strategies according to the particular requirements of any given problem. A child thoroughly trained in strategies for arithmetic problem solving (a highly g-loaded type of test) does not thereby become more proficient in dissimilar but highly g-loaded tasks, such as figure copying, block designs, and matrices.

Performance on any g-loaded task may be introspectively analyzed into a sequence of specific verbal, subvocal, or other behavioral acts, but these behaviors themselves do not constitute g. The g factor of ability is a planning and integrative function that calls forth and governs verbal and behavioral acts appropriate to all kinds of problems. When different specific strategies are learned for different types of problems, then superstrategies are needed to govern the choice of the appropriate strategy for any given problem and to coordinate a number of simpler strategies for the solution of more complex problems. Then, too, strategies are needed for inventing new strategies when novel problems are confronted that do not lend themselves to the already available strategies. The ability to acquire and use such strategies and superstrategies is itself highly g loaded.

The field of mathematics is an elaborate example of formalized problem-solving strategies. But, as we well know, individual differences in learning mathematics are highly correlated with other (nonmathematical) measures of g. The acquisition, by direct teaching and through incidental learning, of cognitive strategies and their efficient utilization are themselves highly dependent on g. To mistake the cognitive strategies themselves for g is to confuse cause and effect. This is not to say, however, that the teaching or the learning of efficient strategies for certain classes of problem solving is not valuable in its own right. In fact, it is largely what formal education is all about.

The popular confusion of g with strategies per se is a legacy of the radical behaviorism of John B. Watson (1878–1958), who, in the early 1900s, taught that all complex human behavior is built up of a myriad of specific conditioned responses and that individual differences in all forms of complex behavior (including intelligence) are merely the result of different experiences and histories of conditioning. In Watson's view, thinking is no more than subvocal speech—a muscle activity. This peripheralist notion, which denies the importance (or even the existence) of central cerebral mechanisms, except insofar as they are the site of conditioning, still influences much of psychological thinking. Some psychologists, following Watson, view individual differences in intelligence simply as differences in what has been learned. This belief that the brain is a *tabula rasa* switchboard, or learning machine, however, is contradicted by the convergence of many lines of evidence from research on brain physiology, the genetics of mental abilities, factor analysis of innumerable highly diverse tasks revealing substantial g loadings, the narrow transfer of training of cognitive processes, the relatively low correlations between learning rates and the g of intelligence tests, and the biological correlates of g, such as brain size and changes with age.

Cultural Relativism and the Ubiquity of g

Another popular view is that intelligence is culturally determined, with the implication that what constitutes intelligence in one time or place could be something quite different from what constitutes intelligence in some other time or place. Jerome Kagan (1971b, p. 658) has expressed this idea as follows:

> Although it is reasonable to believe that intelligence is the ability to acquire the abstract mental skills promoted by a culture, it should also be clear that the specific skills promoted in Western society are culturally determined. At another place and time a different set of skills might be primary and the child who was intelligent in terms of the first set might be very unintelligent in terms of the second.

The reader will recognize that this cultural relativism view of the nature of intelligence is closely allied to the notion of intelligence as a set of specific acquired skills or strategies, as described in the preceding section. But as was pointed out, this confuses intelligence, or g, with the vehicle for measuring it. The vehicles for measuring g are undoubtedly cultural, in the sense that the subject must have had some experience with the basic contents of the test—Spearman's *fundaments*—for the test to be usable at all. To give an exclusively English-speaking person a verbal analogies test in Mandarin or Tamil would be ridiculous. But the person's score on a well-standardized vocabulary test in English would probably afford the best prediction we could make of his vocabulary in Tamil if he had had comparable exposure to that language. It seems safe to assume that, had Shakespeare grown up in a Hindu family in Madras, he would have had a large vocabulary in Tamil and would have performed quite well on a verbal analogies test in that language. But would anyone argue that the g loading of vocabulary and analogies tests in Tamil is a different g from that of vocabulary and analogies tests in English—or French, or German, or whatever? Thus, we should not equate g with the means used for measuring it.

Furthermore, we should not equate g necessarily with the abilities that are most valued or most salient in a given culture. Intelligence is not defined in terms of the trait (or constellation of traits) that is of the greatest importance or is valued the most in a particular culture. Visual acuity, running speed, and motor coordination may be of supreme importance for survival in a tribe of hunters, and individual differences in the kinds of abilities most representative of *g* might go largely unnoticed. But we would not say, therefore, that a test of *intelligence* in this hunting tribe would consist of measures of visual acuity, running speed, and coordination. It would consist of whatever means are appropriate in terms of the tribe's cultural experiences for eliciting the eduction of relations and correlates and other complex problem-solving skills and the extraction of a general factor from such items. This is the central problem of cross-cultural testing, which is treated further in Chapter 14, pp. 636–643. The problem is essentially no different from that of devising cross-species tests of mental ability. We have already noted that the same or highly similar tests with high *g* loadings have been used successfully with monkeys, apes, and humans.

The trait of intelligence representing essentially a single *g* factor in all humans (and probably even all primates) is probably recognized in all human groups, even though the trait may not be especially valued in some groups. Even in a group as culturally different as the Kalahari Bushmen of Africa, scores on *g*-loaded cognitive performance tests show considerable correspondence to the Bushmen's own notions of cleverness. A psychologist who tested large numbers of Bushmen on a variety of Western *g*-loaded tests of the performance type, noted that the tests had face validity for the Bushmen themselves, who

> accepted as a matter of fact that the "clever ones" would do well on them. The kind of individual the Bushmen recommended to us, e.g., as a guide when we needed one or as one whose opinion in important matters must be obtained, tended to have above average scores on our tests. The Bushmen's concept of "practical intelligence" does not appear to differ essentially from ours. (Reuning, 1972, p. 179)

Yet there are considerable technical problems involved in measuring a *g* factor in widely differing cultures and testing the hypothesis that it is essentially one and the same *g* that is being measured across cultures. Of these problems, more will be said in Chapter 14.

As for the ubiquity of *g* across the time span of human history, it seems most unlikely that a different *kind* of intelligence from that defined by our present conception of *g* was involved in the architectural and engineering feats of the ancient Egyptians and the Mayans or in the profound literary, philosophic, and mathematical achievements and the intricate artistic productions of ancient India and China. It would be hard to believe that the then-recognized geniuses of the great ancient civilizations were not well above the average in the kinds of behaviors that best characterize the *g* of present-day intelligence tests.

The ubiquity of the concept of intelligence is clearly seen in discussions of the most culturally different beings one could well imagine—extraterrestrial life in the universe. Scientists find little difficulty at least in wondering if there is intelligent life on other planets. What are the criteria by which this question would be answered if extraterrestrial forms of life were indeed discovered? Can one easily imagine "intelligent" beings for whom there is no *g*, or whose *g* is qualitatively rather than quantitatively different from *g* as we know it?

SUMMARY

"Intelligence," at the lexical level, has multiple definitions with largely similar connotations corresponding to the layman's conception of intelligence as mental power, quickness, brightness, cleverness, judgment, the ability to learn, to "catch on," to "get the idea," to solve problems, and the like.

From a scientific perspective, intelligence is not an entity, but a theoretical construct. Scientists do not begin their investigations by first trying to define theoretical constructs, which must develop from the investigation itself, abetted by the scientist's creative imagination.

Scientifically, little or nothing follows from definitions as such. A definition is neither correct nor incorrect. But a definition can aim for clarity and can be agreed on to get on with the job of scientific investigation. At the beginning, all that needs to be agreed on is the identification of some clearly delineated natural phenomenon that the scientist thinks is worth investigating.

One of the most striking and most firmly established phenomena in all of psychology is the fact of ubiquitous positive correlations among virtually all tests of mental ability, no matter how diverse the mental skills or contents they call on, when they are obtained in an unselected or representative sample of the population. This is simply a raw fact of nature.

Charles Spearman was apparently the first psychologist to be amazed by the consistently positive correlations among all kinds of mental tests. He hypothesized that there is some "general factor" of ability, to which he gave the neutral label g, that is measured in common by all of the intercorrelated mental tests. The g factor may also be termed a theoretical construct, which is intended to explain an observable phenomenon, namely, the positive intercorrelation among all mental tests, regardless of their apparently great variety.

Spearman developed the mathematical method known as factor analysis to prove the existence of g and to make possible the identification and quantification of g in various tests. By means of factor analysis it is possible to determine the proportion of the total variance in scores on any given test that is measured in common by all of the other diverse tests included in the factor analysis. The square root of this proportion of common variance is known as the test's g loading. It can be interpreted as the correlation between the particular test and the hypothetical general factor that is common to all of the tests included in the analysis.

A working definition of intelligence, then, is that it is the g factor of an indefinitely large and varied battery of mental tests. By "mental" we simply mean that very little or none of the variance in test scores in the general population is attributable to individual differences in sensory or motor capacities. No single test can be a perfect measure of g, so defined, although some tests are quite highly correlated with g. The g factor is remarkably robust across different batteries of tests, provided that the tests in each battery are diverse. In large and diverse batteries of tests, g is also quite robust across different populations and across different appropriate methods of factor analysis.[13] At the strictly empirical or observational level, g is best thought of only as a mathematical transformation of the correlations among the tests that permits us to summarize the raw fact of the test intercorrelations in terms of each test's correlation with g, that is, its g loading. This, however, is not a trivial piece of information. It tells us how much any particular test is correlated with other tests in general and, more precisely, how much it is correlated with whatever it is that all of the other tests measure in common. For this reason, g is a more interesting object of our scientific curiosity than any particular test.

Factor analysis by itself does not and cannot explain the basis for the existence of *g*, that is, the essential nature of *g* itself. Spearman himself stated that factor analysis cannot reveal the essential nature of *g*, but only reveals where to look for it. As Spearman (1927, p. 76) put it, factor analysis is a way of "defining *g* by site rather than by nature," and "This way of indicating what *g* means is just as definite as when one indicates a card by staking on the back of it without looking at its face."

By examining the surface characteristics of a great variety of tests in connection with their *g* loadings, we may arrive at some descriptive generalizations about the common surface features that characterize tests that have relatively high *g* loadings as compared with tests that have relatively low *g* loadings. Today we have much more test material to examine for this purpose than was available to Spearman more than half a century ago. This permits broader generalizations about *g* than Spearman could safely draw. Spearman characterized the most *g*-loaded tests essentially as those requiring the subject to grasp relationships—"the eduction of relations and correlates." That is all perfectly correct. But now we can go further. The *g* factor is manifested in tests to the degree that they involve *mental manipulation* of the input elements ("fundaments" in Spearman's terminology), *choice, decision, invention* in contrast to reproduction, *reproduction* in contrast to selection, *meaningful memory* in contrast to rote memory, *long-term memory* in contrast to short-term memory, and *distinguishing relevant information* from irrelevant information in solving complex problems. Although neither the forward nor backward digit-span tests of the Wechsler Intelligence Scale, for example, has much *g* loading, the slightly greater *mental manipulation* required by backward than by forward recall of the digits more than doubles the *g* variance in backward as compared with forward digit span (Jensen & Figueroa, 1975). We have seen many examples in which a slight increase in task complexity is accompanied by an increase in the *g* loading of the task. This is true even for the most mundane and seemingly nonintellectual tasks. Virtually any task involving mental activity that is complex enough to be recognized at the commonsense level as involving some kind of conscious mental effort is substantially *g* loaded. It is the task's *complexity* rather than its *content* that is most related to *g*. In fact, the magnitudes of *g* loadings seem to show no systematic relationship to the types of tests or test items in terms of sensory modality, substantive or cultural content, or the form of effector activity involved in the required response. This fact is the basis for Spearman's principle of "the indifference of the indicator" when it comes to measuring *g*.

We are forced to infer that *g* is of considerable importance in "real life" by the fact that *g* constitutes the largest component of total variance in all standard tests of intelligence or IQ, and the very same *g* is by far the largest component of variance in scholastic achievement. IQ jointly with scholastic performance predicts more of the variance among persons in adult occupational status and income than any other known combination of variables, including race and social class of origin.

No really clear distinction can be made operationally at the level of tests between *intelligence* and intellectual *achievement*, although intelligence and achievement can be clearly distinguished at the conceptual or theoretical level. The concepts of "capacity" and "potential" as applied to mental ability are found to be conceptually defective and have been superseded by more satisfactory formulations based on concepts from quantitative genetics.

The essential features of mental tests designed for humans that most manifest *g* are found also in various tests of animal intelligence, suggesting that *g* is a concept with relevance not only to individual differences in humans but also to understanding species differences in individually adaptive behavioral capacity. Consideration of the common features of experimental tests developed by comparative psychologists that most clearly distinguish, say, chickens from dogs, dogs from monkeys, and monkeys from chimpanzees suggests they are roughly scalable along a g dimension. Various animal tests of problem solving that discriminate among species and show individual differences among chimpanzees also show the same rank order of difficulty among human children, and children's performance on these animal tests is correlated with their intelligence levels.

The idea that g can be viewed as an interspecies concept with a broad biological and evolutionary basis culminating in the primates, particularly Homo sapiens, stands in striking contrast to the limited popular view of the intelligence measured by IQ tests as a purely human artifact of modern Western industrial civilization. The substantial heritability of all highly g-loaded tests is, of course, proof of a biological basis for individual differences in g, whatever g is. There is our really interesting question: What is g? Can g itself be analyzed?

Attempts to explain the *nature* of g, almost without exception, take an analytic stance and make reference to some hypothetical process underlying test performance in which there are individual differences. Accordingly, tests are correlated with one another to the extent that they involve the same hypothetical processes. The various conjectures concerning the nature of these common processes by the classic theorists of intelligence are remarkably alike, differing more in terminology than in substance. Spearman (1927, Ch. 9) conceived of the basis of g as some kind of electrochemical energy available to the brain for problem solving, with some types of tests requiring more mental energy than others and some persons possessing more of this energy than others. E. L. Thorndike (1927) thought of intellectual capacity as involving the number of modifiable neural connections available in the brain, with persons differing in the total number of potential connections and tests differing in the number of connections they call upon. Godfrey Thomson (1948) had a very similar explanation of g in terms of the differential sampling of neural "elements" by various tests, with more of the elements sampled by the more complex tests, hence more overlap of the samples and consequently higher correlations among the more complex tests. Cyril Burt's theory is best summarized in his own words: "It is the general character of the individual's brain tissue—viz., the general degree of systematic complexity in the neural architecture—that seems to represent the general factor..." (1961, pp. 57–58). Burt noted that the cerebral cortex in mental defectives often shows less density and less branching of neurones than in normal persons. But none of these theoretical conjectures says essentially anything more than the others. All theoretical speculations, so far, have been quite lacking in the kind of heuristic power needed to get on with the empirical job of hypothesis testing, which is the *sine qua non* of theory building. At present, it seems safe to say, we do not have a true theory of g or intelligence, although we do know a good deal about the kinds of tests that are the most g loaded and the fact that the complexity of mental operations called for by a test is related to g.

NOTES

1. It can be estimated that the word "intelligence" would rank somewhere between WAIS vocabulary items 7 and 14, out of the forty items arranged in order of difficulty, going from item 1 (100 percent passing) to item 40 (5 percent passing). By plotting the percentage passing the forty WAIS vocabulary items as a function of the Thorndike–Lorge (1944) word count (i.e., the frequency of occurrence of a given word per million words in a varied sample of American books, magazines, and newspapers), we can estimate the difficulty level (for the WAIS standardization sample) of the word "intelligence" to be between 90 percent and 95 percent passing.

2. For an introduction to the comparative psychology of animal intelligence, the reader is referred to Bitterman (1975), Nissen (1951), Stenhouse (1973), Viaud (1960), Warden (1951), and Warden et al. (1934).

3. Probably the clearest textbook on factor analysis ever written is Thomson (1951), but the most popular text in college courses today, because it is the most comprehensive and up to date, is Harman (1967). Cattell (1952) provides a good theoretical introduction for psychology students, although the older computational methods have become obsolete with the availability of high-speed computers. Cattell (1978), an excellent new book on factor analysis, is especially suitable for students of psychology who know only the basics of statistics. Lawley and Maxwell (1963) is a more statistically advanced and specialized text. Exceptionally well written classic works in the field, besides Thomson (1951), are Burt (1940) and Thurstone (1947). Maxwell (1968) and Humphreys (1968) provide brief accounts of the mathematical theory and psychological applications of factor analysis.

4. When the variance in a population is estimated from a random sample of the population, the formula is

$$s^2 = \Sigma(X - \bar{X})^2/(N - 1), \qquad \text{(6N.1)}$$

where s^2 is the sample estimate of the population variance σ^2, and the other symbols are the same as in equation 6.1.

5. Pearson's r obtained from *raw* scores is

$$r = \Sigma\,[(X - \bar{X})(Y - \bar{Y})]\,/\,N\sigma_x\sigma_y\,, \qquad \text{(6N.2)}$$

where

$$X \text{ and } Y = \text{raw scores,}$$
$$\bar{X} \text{ and } \bar{Y} = \text{the mean of the } X \text{ and } Y \text{ variables,}$$
$$N = \text{the number of } XY \text{ pairs, and}$$
$$\sigma_X \text{ and } \sigma_Y = \text{the standard deviations of } X \text{ and } Y.$$

The *covariance* of X and Y is equation 6N.2 with $\sigma_x\sigma_y$ omitted in the denominator. The covariance can also be expressed as Cov $XY = r_{xy}\,\sigma_x\,\sigma_y$.

Another kind of correlation coefficient, known as the intraclass correlation, r_i, is

$$r_i = \frac{2\mathrm{Cov}_{xy}}{(\sigma_x^2 + \sigma_y^2)}. \qquad \text{(6N.3)}$$

The intraclass correlation is equal to the Pearson r only when $\bar{x} = \bar{y}$ and $\sigma_x^2 = \sigma_y^2$.

6. Recall that when two variables X and Y, are expressed in the form of standard scores (z scores), x and y, the correlation between the variables is simply $\Sigma xy/N$. Remember that in terms of standard scores $\sigma_x = \sigma_y = 1$.

We can conceive of each x score as composed of two components, one that is *unique* to x, to which we shall give the label x', and one that is *common* to both x and y, to which we shall give the label c. So $x = x' + c$. Likewise, each y score is composed of a unique component y' and the c component that y shares in common with x. So $y = y' + c$. Saying that x' and y' are each unique means that they have nothing at all in common with each other or with c; in other words, by definition there is zero correlation between x' and y', between x' and c, and between y' and c.; that is, $r_{x'y'} = 0$, $r_{x'c} = 0$, and $r_{y'c} = 0$.

If $r_{xy} = \Sigma xy/N$, then also

$$r_{xy} = \frac{\Sigma\,[(x' + c)(y' + c)]}{N}\,. \tag{6N.4}$$

Multiplying the two expressions in the numerator, summing, and dividing by N, gives

$$r_{xy} = \frac{\Sigma\,(x'y' + x'c + y'c + c^2)}{N}\,. \tag{6N.5}$$

Since by definition all the correlations among x', y', and c are zero, the sums of the cross-products $\Sigma x'y'$, $\Sigma x'c$, and $\Sigma y'c$ will all be zero, and so these terms drop out of the above equation, which becomes simply

$$r_{xy} = \Sigma c^2\,/\,N, \tag{6N.6}$$

which is the *variance* of the component common to x and y, that is, σ_c^2. (Remember that c is expressed as a z score and that the variance of a set of z scores is $\sigma_z^2 = \Sigma z^2/N$.) So $\sigma_c^2 = \Sigma c^2/N = r_{xy}$.

Therefore, the correlation r_{xy} may be regarded as the proportion of the combined variance in x and y that they share in common. The combined variance of x and y is $\frac{1}{2}\,(\sigma_x^2 + \sigma_y^2)$. So the proportion p_c of common variance is

$$p_c = \frac{\sigma_c^2}{\frac{1}{2}\,(\sigma_x^2 + \sigma_y^2)}\,, \tag{6N.7}$$

and, because x and y are z scores, $\sigma_x^2 = \sigma_y^2 = 1$, so $p_c = \sigma_c^2 = r_{xy}$.

There is a very common but mistaken notion that one must square the correlation r_{xy} to express the proportion of variance that variables X and Y share in common. The analysis here clearly reveals that this notion is incorrect. The correlation itself is the proportion of common variance, that is, the proportion of variance that X has in common with variance in Y, and the proportion of variance in Y that is common to X. It is only in the case where we have a correlation between a variable X and a common component C, that is, r_{xc}, that we must square the correlation to determine the proportion of variance in X that is accounted for by variance in C, that is, $r_{xc}^2 = \sigma_c^2 \sigma_x^2$. We can see why. Again, in the form of standard (z) scores, $x = x' + c$; that is, each x score is composed of a unique and a common element. Although x (as a z score) has $\sigma = 1$, we do not know the standard deviation of the common component c, but we do know that $\sigma_c < \sigma_x$. We must include σ_x and σ_c in the denominator of the formula for correlation. (This was not necessary in the formula for the correlation between x and y, since, as z scores, $\sigma_x = \sigma_y = 1$, and $\sigma_x \sigma_y = 1$, so that $r_{xy} = \Sigma xy/N\sigma_x\sigma_y = \Sigma xy/N$.) Thus the correlation between x and c can be expressed as

or

$$r_{xc} = \frac{\Sigma (x' + c)c}{N\sigma_x\sigma_c} \tag{6N.8}$$

$$r_{xc} = \frac{\Sigma x'c + \Sigma c^2}{N\sigma_x\sigma_c} . \tag{6N.9}$$

Since by definition x' and c are uncorrelated, the term $\Sigma x'c$ is zero and therefore drops out, leaving

$$r_{xc} = \Sigma c^2/N\sigma_x\sigma_c , \tag{6N.10}$$

which, after dividing the numerator by the denominator, becomes

$$r_{xc} = \frac{\sigma_c^2}{\sigma_x\sigma_c} = \frac{\sigma_c}{\sigma_x} . \tag{6N.11}$$

Therefore, to show the proportion p_c of the total *variance* in x accounted for by variance in the common component, we have to square both sides of the equation; thus

$$p_c = \sigma_c^2 / \sigma_x^2 = r_{xc}^2 . \tag{6N.12}$$

The idea of squaring r_{xy} itself only has to do with the proportional reduction in the variance of one variable as *predicted* from the other variable. We can predict y for any value of x (in z scores) from the regression equation $y = r_{xy}x$. The *standard error of estimate*, SE_E, is the standard deviation of the discrepancies between the predicted and the obtained values of y; that is,

$$SE_E = \sqrt{\frac{\Sigma (\hat{y} - y)^2}{N}} . \tag{6N.13}$$

The total variance of the obtained values of y is $\sigma_y^2 = 1$ (in z score form). The total variance of y, that is, σ_y^2, may be thought of as composed of two parts—the part that is not predictable from x, which is SE_E^2, and the part that is predictable from x, which is $\sigma_y^2 - SE_E^2$. Thus, the proportion of the total variance in y that is predictable from x is

$$p = \frac{\sigma_y^2 - SE_E^2}{\sigma_y^2} = 1 - \frac{SE_E^2}{\sigma_y^2}, \tag{6N.14}$$

which in z score form (since $\sigma_y^2 = 1$) is the same as $1 - SE_E^2$.

Now, the correlation between obtained y and predicted $\hat{y}$ is exactly analogous to the preceding example of the correlation between x and c, that is, between a variable and a component that is common to the variable. The variable y can be thought of as composed of a component unique to y, namely, y', and a component predicted by (and therefore common to) x, namely, $\hat{y}$. So the correlation is

$$r_{y\hat{y}} = \frac{\Sigma\,(y' + \hat{y})\hat{y}}{N\sigma_y\sigma_y} \qquad (6\text{N}.15)$$

or

$$r_{y\hat{y}} = \frac{\Sigma\,\hat{y}y' + \Sigma\,\hat{y}^2}{N\sigma_y\sigma_{\hat{y}}}\,, \qquad (6\text{N}.16)$$

and, since by definition $r_{\hat{y}y'}$ is zero, the sum of the cross-products $\Sigma\hat{y}y'$ drops out; dividing, we have

$$r_{y\hat{y}} = \frac{\sigma_{\hat{y}}^2}{\sigma_y\sigma_{\hat{y}}} = \frac{\sigma_{\hat{y}}}{\sigma_y}\,. \qquad (6\text{N}.17)$$

So, to get the proportion p of the total *variance* in y that is accounted for by variance in $\hat{y}$ (which is predicted by x), we must square both sides of the equation:

$$p = \frac{\sigma_{\hat{y}}^2}{\sigma_y^2} = r_{y\hat{y}}^2\,. \qquad (6\text{N}.18)$$

The correlation $r_{y\hat{y}}$ is equal to r_{xy}, so r_{xy}^2 is also the proportion of variance in y predicted by its association with x (and vice versa). Note that, since $\hat{y} = rx$, we can express the correlation $r_{y\hat{y}}$ as

$$r_{y\hat{y}} = \frac{\Sigma\,y(rx)}{N\sigma_y(r\sigma_x)}\,, \qquad (6\text{N}.19)$$

and, since in standard score form $\sigma_y = \sigma_x = 1$, by dividing the numerator by the denominator, we have

$$r_{y\hat{y}} = \frac{\Sigma\,yx}{N} = r_{xy}. \qquad (6\text{N}.20)$$

Thus, when we wish to express the proportion of the total variance in one variable that is predictable from another variable, we use r^2. When we speak of the proportion of the total variance that the two variables have in common, we use r. The correlation of a variable with just the component that it shares in common with another variable is the square root of the correlation between the two variables, that is, $r_{xc} = r_{yc} = \sqrt{r_{xy}}$. And the proportion of the total variance in one of the variables that is also common to the other variable is $r_{xy} = r_{xc}^2 = r_{yc}^2$. Note the following relationships (in standard score form):

$$r_{xy} = r_{y\hat{y}} = r_{x\hat{x}} = \sigma_{\hat{y}} = \sigma_{\hat{x}} = \sigma_c^2$$

where

$$r = \text{the Pearson correlation,}$$
$$x \text{ and } y = \text{variables (in standard scores),}$$
$$\hat{y} = \text{the predicted } \hat{y} \text{ from } x, \text{ that is } \hat{y} = r_{xy}x,$$
$$\hat{x} = \text{the predicted } \hat{x} \text{ from } y, \text{ that is, } \hat{x} = r_{xy}y,$$
$$\sigma = \text{the standard deviation,}$$
$$\sigma^2 = \text{the variance, and}$$
$$c = \text{the component common to } x \text{ and } y.$$

Also,

$$r_{xc} = r_{yc} = \sigma_c = \sqrt{\sigma_{\hat{x}}} = \sqrt{\sigma_{\hat{y}}}$$

$$\sigma_{\hat{x}} = \sigma_{\hat{y}} = \sqrt{\sigma_{\hat{x}}\sigma_{\hat{y}}} = \sigma_c^2.$$

Understanding these relationships and their derivations should give the student a rather complete understanding of the statistical properties of correlation.

7. If a test score X is thought of as consisting of a true component t and an error component e due to random errors of measurement, the correlation of the test scores obtained on the same persons on two occasions will be (in z score form)

$$r_{XX'} = \frac{\Sigma\,(t + e)(t + e')}{N}. \tag{6N.21}$$

Since errors are random, they are uncorrelated with each other and are uncorrelated with t. Therefore the product of $(t + e)(t + e') = t^2$, and

$$r_{XX'} = \Sigma t^2 / N = \sigma_t^2, \tag{6N.22}$$

which is the variance of the true-score components.

8. Principal components analysis begins with unities (i.e., the tests' self-correlations) in the principal diagonal of the correlational matrix, and each extracted component is a proportion of the total test variance. Common factor analysis, strictly speaking, begins with estimates of the communalities in the principal diagonal, and each extracted factor is some proportion of the common factor variance (represented by the test's communality, h^2). Principal components analysis is sometimes used to determine the communalities, which are then used for the factor analysis. In brief, principal components analysis involves the total variance, whereas common factor analysis involves only the common factor variance (i.e., total variance minus test-specific and error variance).

9. A statistical test for the significance of a correlation matrix is

$$\chi^2 = (N-1)\Sigma r_{ij}^2, \tag{6N.23}$$

where

χ^2 = chi squared,
N = the sample size, and
Σr_{ij}^2 = the sum of the squared correlations (in just half of the matrix as divided by the principal diagonal).

Chi squared has $n(n - 1)/2$ degrees of freedom, where n is the number of variables.
    Table 6.1 has $6(6 - 1)/2 = 15$ *df.* With 15 *df,* chi squared must be equal to at least 25.0 to be statistically significant at the 5 percent level of confidence. The chi squared for Table 6.2 is 154.9, which is significant well beyond the 0.1 percent level. The residual matrix in Table 6.3 has a chi squared of 0.91, which is nonsignificant.

10. Factor scores are conventionally standardized so that scores on each factor are made to have the same mean and variance. If the factor scores are not standardized with respect to variance, however, the factor variances are directly proportional to their eigenvalues, and the first principal component or g factor always has the largest variance.

11. It is usually empirically true, but not necessarily mathematically true, that the first principal component factor scores will have a higher correlation with any outside variable than will total scores based on any other weighted composite of the subscores, including the unweighted composite (i.e., equal weights for the subscores).

12. An easy method for partialing linear and nonlinear components of age out of the correlation matrix of a battery of tests is to include age (in months) and various higher powers of age (e.g., age^2, age^3, age^4, etc.) among the intercorrelated variables in the matrix. (Usually nothing further is gained by including powers beyond age^5.) A varimax rotation of the principal components, then, puts all the powers of age onto a single factor, along with any linear and nonlinear correlations that age may have with the other variables in the matrix. This age "factor" then can be removed prior to obtaining other rotational solutions or to reconstituting the matrix of intercorrelations among all the test variables (now with the several powers of age partialed out) and extraction of the first principal component or g factor.

A slightly more exact method, which usually will yield negligibly different results from the varimax rotation method just described, is to rotate the principal components (including age, age^2, etc.) so as to maximize the sum of the squared loadings of just the several age variables (i.e., powers of age) on the age factor. (Varimax rotation, on the other hand, maximizes the variance of the squared loadings over all the variables on every factor.)

13. I must here vent my opinion on a rather technical matter, namely, the kind of factor analysis and the type of rotation of factors that should be used in the abilities domain. We can forget Spearman's (1927, Appendix) original method, which is entirely inadequate when more than one common factor is involved in the intercorrelations among tests. With the availability of high-speed electronic computers, we can also forget all the older desk-calculator methods, such as Thurstone's (1947) centroid method, Holzinger's (1935) bifactor method, and Burt's (1941) methods of simple and weighted summation, which are merely simplified approximations to more laborious but more exact solutions that can now be done by computers. Also, completely objective analytic rotation of factors by computer has virtually done away with the practice of subjective rotation using graph paper and eyeball. So what we are left with are choices between principal components (putting unities in the principal diagonal of the correlation matrix) or principal factors (also called common factor analysis, putting communalities in the principal diagonal), with or without rotation of the axes, and in which rotation can be either orthogonal (uncorrelated) or oblique (correlated). These options make altogether six kinds of analyses from which to choose. I propose two more: extract the first principal component (or principal factor) and then orthogonally rotate the remaining components (factors) having eigenvalues greater than 1, to approximate simple structure. (To be exact, one should rotate the remaining components [with eigenvalues greater than 1] plus one additional component, i.e., the component with the next largest eigenvalue.)

Out of all eight of these distinct possible methods, I think only two constitute a flagrant conceptual and scientific blunder when applied in the abilities domain. I refer to orthogonal rotation of principal components or factors without first extracting the general factor (i.e., the first principal component or first principal factor). From a strictly mathematical standpoint, it makes absolutely no difference whether you do or do not rotate the factors, or how you rotate them. The extracted factors, in any case, will all equally well regenerate the original correlations to the same approximation by a simple algorithm, if that is all you want from the factor analysis. Scientifically, however, we want considerably more than that. Orthogonal rotation of an ability matrix is scientifically an egregious error for two reasons. (1) Most important, it artificially hides or submerges the large general factor—it is "rotated away," so to speak—and the orthogonally rotated analysis therefore misrepresents or obscures the raw fact of nature that anyone can see immediately in the test correlation matrix: the predominantly positive intercorrelations. (2) The main purpose of rotation is to attain some kind of clarity or simplicity in the pattern of factor loadings, such as Thurstone's criterion of *simple structure,* to make the factors easier to interpret psychologically. But orthogonal rotation in the abilities domain cannot begin to approximate *simple structure*—the large general factor prevents it. Consequently, orthogonal rotation forces a conceptually messy and distorted picture. Thurstone himself clearly perceived this fact and advocated oblique rotation of factors in order to achieve *simple structure*. The correlations among oblique factors are indicative of a general factor, which can be recovered by factor analyzing the correlations among the oblique primary factors. Thus one can find g in either of two ways: it can be obtained by a so-called hierarchical analysis, that is, it is the first principal component extracted from the intercorrelations among the obliquely rotated primary factors. Essentially the same g emerges in either case, although the loadings on the various tests may differ somewhat in the two methods due to sampling error. The first principal component extracted from the zero-order correlations seems safest, because the general factor obtained through a hierarchical analysis (extracted from the intercorrelations among obliquely rotated factors) is at the mercy of sampling error at two stages of the analysis instead of only one—errors in the zero-order correlations and in the correlations among the oblique primary factors. Sampling errors thus tend to be compounded by the hierarchical extractions of g, making the g rather unstable. In large samples, however, I have generally found the difference in g attained by the two methods to be practically negligible if there is a good sampling of tests. The same thing is true (but only with regard to the g factor) whether one uses principal components or common factor analysis. Usually the differences among the g loadings of the same tests are practically negligible. However, if we wish to obtain factor scores on a number of factors, principal components analysis is preferable.

Chapter 7

Reliability and Stability of Mental Measurements

Unreliability and instability of test scores are the most fundamental forms of test bias. Most people usually think of bias only as unfair discrimination that favors or disfavors members of particular groups. But unreliability and instability of measurement are sources of individual bias that involve *all* persons on whom tests are used, regardless of their group membership. Also, when tests are used for selection, unreliability and instability contribute to group biases in selection and rejection, even when the tests are completely fair and unbiased in all other respects.

If our tests scores are unreliable or unstable, members of one group in the population may be selected (or rejected) more frequently than would be the case if the scores were perfectly reliable and stable. Thus, erroneous rejection and selection and inaccurate prediction, which inevitably result from unreliability and instability of test scores, are clearly forms of test bias affecting both individuals and various groups in the population. Such bias can only be minimized but can never be eliminated completely, as no actual measurements, either mental or physical, have perfect reliability. However, present-day standardized aptitude and achievement tests usually have very high reliability, even comparable with the reliability of physical measurements.

Fundamental Variables in Measurement Theory

To understand the above generalizations, a few fundamental concepts of classical psychometric theory need to be explicated. The essential variables are

1. The individual's obtained (i.e., observable) test score, X,
2. The individual's hypothetical true score, T, and
3. The individual's obtained score on some criterion, C.

Reliability. The population correlation between X and T, r_{XT}, is the *index of reliability* of the test. The square of this value, r_{XT}^2, is the *reliability* of the test. The *index of reliability* tells us how accurately the test measures whatever it is that it measures, with accuracy expressed as the correlation between the *observed* scores and the hypothetical *true* scores. The reliability, r_{XT}^2, tells us the proportion of the total variance in obtained scores (σ_X^2) that is attributable to variance in the true scores (σ_T^2). Thus, the reliability

259

coefficient is σ_T^2/σ_X^2. Consequently, the proportion of the total variance due to error (i.e., unreliability) is $1 - (\sigma_T^2/\sigma_X^2)$. The reliability can also be thought of as the theoretical self-correlation of a test's obtained scores, symbolized as r_{xx}, which is the most common expression for reliability. Figure 7.1 illustrates the concept of reliability in a two-item test.

Relevance.   The population correlation between T and C, r_{TC}, is called the test's *relevance*. It tells us how closely related the true scores are to the criterion of interest, in other words, how *relevant* the test is to the criterion C.

Validity.   The correlation between X and C is the test's *validity coefficient.* The validity tells us how closely the actual test scores are related to the criterion scores, that is, scores on the variable that the test is intended to predict, such as scholastic achievement or job performance.

The validity of a test is equal to the product of its index of reliability and its relevance, that is, $r_{XC} = r_{XT} \times r_{TC}$. Note that high validity requires both high reliability and high relevance; each one is necessary and neither one alone is sufficient. It also follows from this formulation that a test's validity can never be higher than its index of reliability or than its relevance.

Distinction between Reliability and Stability

Reliability.   Reliability is the proportion of true-score variance in scores on a particular test at the time it was taken. It indicates how well the test scores measure whatever it is that the test as a whole is measuring at the time it was given in the particular population of persons who took the test.

The concept of a "true score," as compared with an actual (or obtained) score, may sound rather mystical at this point, but in fact it is a quite straightforward and objective mathematical construct. To put it into words, think of an individual's obtained score X_i on

Figure 7.1.   Illustration of test reliability in terms of overlap. Items A and B share variance in common (σ_T^2); this represents the true-score variance of this hypothetical two-item test. Also, some of the variance in items A and B is unique to each item (i.e., unshared); this is considered to be error variance (σ_e^2).

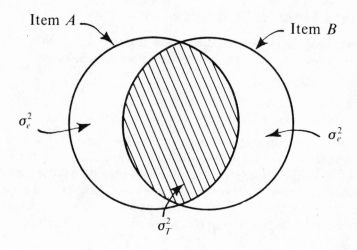

a test as a deviation from the mean, $\bar{X}$, of all the obtained scores in the population of which he or she is a member. Thus the individual's observed deviation is $D_i = X_i - \bar{X}$. The individual's *true-score deviation* is defined as that part of D_i that is due to the intercorrelations among all of the single test items that have entered into the total score on the test. Without a preponderance of positive correlations among the test items, everyone's true score would be zero (or indeterminate); the obtained scores would not represent any unitary trait, disposition, or ability. From a psychometric standpoint the obtained scores would consist only of error. So we say that an obtained score deviation from the mean is comprised of a true-score deviation and an error deviation. *Each item in a test contributes to the true score only to the extent that the item is correlated with other items in the test.*

Test scores are said to be reliable to the extent that their true-score components are large and that their error components are small. Reliability is often redundantly called *internal consistency reliability*. By "internal consistency" of a test is meant the degree to which the items are correlated with one another, that is, the extent to which they measure something in common. In fact, the reliability (r_{xx}) of a test may be described in terms of the mean of all of the item intercorrelations ($\bar{r}_{ij}$) and the number of items in the test (n); thus,

$$r_{xx} = \frac{1}{1/n\ (1/\bar{r}_{ij} - 1) + 1}\ . \tag{7.1}$$

Reliability is seldom if ever computed from this formula, because there are other formulas that, although algebraically equivalent, involve simpler computations.

Stability.   Conceptually, the *stability* of a test is something altogether different from its reliability, as was just defined. The property of stability should not be confused conceptually with reliability as technically defined, and so usage of the outmoded term *test–retest reliability* instead of *stability* should be avoided.

Stability refers to the consistency of test scores over time. It is indexed by the correlation between scores obtained on the same test given to the same group of persons on two occasions separated in time. The amount of time separation can be anything from minutes up to many years. Specification of the time interval between the two testings is an essential feature of reporting the stability coefficient, that is, the correlation between test and retest scores.

Often a different (but statistically parallel) form of the test is used on the retest, in which case the test–retest correlation reflects both reliability and stability, mixed in unknown degrees, and can never be higher (and is virtually always lower) than either the reliability or the stability.

A test may be highly reliable, but have very low stability, and vice versa. For example, a highly sensitive measure of a person's mood at a given point in time could be very reliable, accurately reflecting his mood at the time, but it could be very unstable, as person's particular moods usually last only a short time and may change quite markedly from one day to the next. On the other hand, a person's reasponses to a list of questions in a biographical questionnaire may have almost no reliability (i.e., there is little correlation among the items), but persons answer all of the questions exactly the same at one time as at another. Such a questionnaire would have near zero reliability and perfect stability.

A test's reliability and stability are both important to know, and the evaluation of each depends on what one intends to measure with the test and the use one wishes to make of the measurement. If the aim is to measure an enduring trait or disposition of individuals, then both high reliability and high stability are important, and, if one wishes to predict the future status of an individual, then high stability is essential.

Although reliability and stability are theoretically and conceptually distinct, it turns out empirically that the two are quite closely related. This is not a logically necessary relationship that follows automatically from the mathematical definitions of reliability and stability. It is merely an empirical generalization: the most reliable tests also tend to be the most stable. There are of course many exceptions, since there is no mathematically necessary relationship between reliability and stability.

A Hypothetical "Perfect" Test

We may gain a deeper insight into the meaning of reliability by considering an idealized "perfect" test. "Perfect" is in quotes because even conceptually there is not just one set of criteria for a perfect test. A test that is ideal for one purpose may be unsuitable for another. Any given test—even an idealized "perfect" test—represents a compromise between a number of desirable but inherently contradictory criteria.

Consider the following list of desirable features of an ability test.

1. The test measures a broad or general trait.
2. The test scores have the maximum possible variance in the population.
3. The test makes the maximum possible discriminations among persons.
4. The scores are an equal-interval scale, so that the frequency distribution of scores reflects the true form of the population distribution of the measured trait.
5. The test has perfect reliability.
6. The test has maximal internal consistency, that is, all the correlations between items are unity.
7. The test is short, consisting of just a few items, so that little testing time is required.
8. When the test items are arranged in the order of percentage of the population passing each item, from the easiest to the most difficult, every person obtains his total raw score on the test by passing all the easier items up to a given item and failing all the more difficult items. In this case no two persons could obtain the same total score by passing and failing different items. Thus, given any person's total score, one would know automatically which items had been passed and failed. (Such a test is called a perfect Guttman scale.)

Each of these eight characteristics would be a highly desirable feature of a test. Unfortunately, however, many of them are mutually contradictory. So we have to make trade-offs among the various desirable features in terms of our aims in constructing a particular test. For example, in the list of criteria just given, the psychometrically incompatible or mutually contradictory features are

No. 1 is incompatible with 6, 7, and probably 8.
No. 2 is incompatible with 3.
No. 3 is incompatible with 4, 5, 6, and 7.

No. 4 is incompatible with 5, 6, and probably 7.

No. 5 and No. 6 are incompatible with 8.

In all these cases, if we wish to maximize one feature, we must sacrifice another, or find some compromise or balance among the various features that will yield the most desirable test for our purposes. In the case of physical measurements, such as height and weight, for example, we give much more weight to some of the criteria listed at the sacrifice of others. Consider measurements of weight, assuming perfect accuracy of our scales. If we regard each ounce of weight as analogous to a single test item that can be "passed" or "failed," weight measurements maximize criteria no. 4 (equal intervals) and no. 8 (Guttman scale), but in doing so must sacrifice maximizing criteria nos. 1, 2, 3, 5, 6, and 7.

Let us make up a fictitious test that will maximize a number of the listed criteria, so we can observe how the features of such a test influence its reliability and how changes in those features of the test will alter the reliability.

The Persons × Items Matrix.   The clearest means of observing the results of a test is in terms of the persons × items matrix, which shows what every person in the tested sample did on every item of the test. For the sake of simplicity we shall imagine a short test (ten items) administered to a small sample (eleven persons). In this example, we assume that all the persons attempted every item in the test and that no items were gotten right by guessing or by "luck." The criteria we wish to maximize are

No. 3 (the maximum possible discriminations among persons). To discriminate among N persons (i.e., for the test to yield N different scores), we need at least $N - 1$ items.

No. 7 (a short test). The shortest test that will maximize the number of discriminations among eleven persons will be $N - 1 = 10$ items.

No. 8 (a perfect Guttman scale, i.e., the order of difficulty of the items is the same for all persons).

By maximizing these three features, we cannot maximize any of the others. We simply have to take the statistically inevitable consequences of having chosen these particular three criteria. (We can, of course, compromise and relax these criteria to some extent if we wish to enhance the test on some of the other criteria. This is the necessary trade-off among various criteria of a test.)

Table 7.1 shows the persons × items matrix of our fictitious test that maximizes criteria nos. 3, 7, and 8. For clarity the persons are arranged in order from the highest to the lowest total score. Performance on each item is scored Right (=1) or Wrong (=0). (We assume in this idealized case that all items are attempted by all persons and that none of their correct answers is achieved by guessing. We shall see later the consequences of not attempting all the items and of guessing at the answers.)

Notice the following points in Table 7.1:

1. Every person has obtained a different total score (criterion no. 3).
2. The test is short, achieving the maximal discrimination among eleven persons with the fewest possible items, namely, ten (criterion no. 7).
3. Every person passes all the items up to his first failure and from there on fails all the items (criterion no. 8).

Table 7.1. Persons × items matrix of a hypothetical "perfect" test of 10 items taken by 11 persons.

Persons	Test Items										Total Raw Score[1]
	1	2	3	4	5	6	7	8	9	10	
A	1	1	1	1	1	1	1	1	1	1	10
B	1	1	1	1	1	1	1	1	1	0	9
C	1	1	1	1	1	1	1	1	0	0	8
D	1	1	1	1	1	1	1	0	0	0	7
E	1	1	1	1	1	1	0	0	0	0	6
F	1	1	1	1	1	0	0	0	0	0	5
G	1	1	1	1	0	0	0	0	0	0	4
H	1	1	1	0	0	0	0	0	0	0	3
I	1	1	0	0	0	0	0	0	0	0	2
J	1	0	0	0	0	0	0	0	0	0	1
K	0	0	0	0	0	0	0	0	0	0	0
Total (+)	10	9	8	7	6	5	4	3	2	1	
% Passing	91	82	73	64	55	45	36	27	18	9	

[1]Mean of total raw scores = 5.0. Standard deviation of total raw scores = $\sqrt{10}$ = 3.1623. Reliability of total raw scores = 10/11 = .9091. Mean inter-item correlation = 1/2 = .50.

There are a number of ways of computing the reliability of a test, given the persons × items matrix. We need not go into these technical matters here.[1] (Stanley, 1971c, presents the clearest, most comprehensive coverage of this topic at an advanced level.) The reliability of the total scores on our hypothetical test is .9091. The only way that we could obtain a higher reliability would be by relaxing one or more of the criteria we have aimed to maximize. To increase the reliability to unity, we would have to sacrifice the number of possible discriminations. If half the persons received scores of 10 and the other half scores of 0, we would maximize the variance and increase the reliability to 1. But we would have only two classes of persons and could discriminate only between those who pass and those who fail. This would be all right if we wished to select exactly half the persons and reject the other half. But what if we wanted a finer discrimination and the option of selecting and rejecting different proportions of the samples at different times? Then persons would have to be spread out over more scores. For the increased discriminability, we would sacrifice some degree of reliability. But, as can be seen in this example, even by maximizing the discriminability of the test, we have not sacrificed the reliability by very much: it is .9091 and that is a quite high reliability.

Another way that we could increase the reliability is by increasing the number of items in the test. If we add more items of the same kind as those already in the test, the reliability will rise by a predictable amount.[2] For example, if we add ten more items with the same difficulties and item intercorrelations as the original ten items, the reliability of our new twenty-item test will be .9524. As long as we retain the feature of a perfect Guttman scale (criterion no. 8), the reliability will always be equal to $n/(n + 1)$, where n is the number of items. With 100 items, the reliability will be equal to $100/101 = .99$. Thus we can sacrifice a shorter test for higher reliability. There is a trade-off between test length and reliability.

What happens if we retain criterion no. 3 (maximum discriminability) but relax criterion no. 8 (Guttman scale)? (That is, the total scores will still be 10, 9, 8, . . . , 1, 0, but the sequence of "rights" and "wrongs" (1's and 0's) will not be perfectly regular as in Table 7.1.) The reliability then will be lower. It could be as low as .7346 if the item difficulties (i.e., percentage passing) were as alike as possible (i.e., half the items would have five persons, or 45 percent, passing and half would have six persons, or 55 percent, passing). But then we could boost the reliability of .7346 back up to .9091 by increasing the length of the test to thirty-six items.[3]

What if we sacrifice maximum discriminability, as would happen if unequal numbers of persons obtained each of the possible scores on the test? For example, the distribution might be more like the normal bell-shaped distribution, with many persons close to the average and fewer at the extremes. Then the reliability would be lower. But we could raise it again by increasing the length of the test, while retaining the normal distribution.

Note also that, if the test is too difficult (i.e., too many items that are failed by nearly everyone), the reliability will be less than $n/(n + 1)$. Items that do not discriminate among persons are nonfunctional: they add nothing to the discriminability of total scores, or to the variance of scores, or to the reliability or validity of the test. But such nonfunctional items do not detract from the test's reliability except insofar as too many difficult items encourage guessing at the answers and a certain proportion of items are gotten "right" by chance, which lowers the reliability.

On the other hand, if the range of difficulty of the items is too narrow, the test will not reflect the true range of differences in the group being tested. The remedy is to add more difficult or more easy items of the same type. This then simultaneously increases the test's discriminability and its reliability.

The hypothetical test exemplified in Table 7.1 is incompatible with criterion no. 1, that is, measuring a broad or general ability. By having a perfect Guttman scale, we have guaranteed the highest possible average item intercorrelation (given the constraint of maximum discriminability of total scores). But why is having the highest possible item intercorrelations incompatible with measuring a broad factor of ability? The reason is that, if all the item intercorrelations are very high, it means that they are all measuring a great deal in common and are therefore probably very much alike on the *content* (e.g., verbal, pictorial, numerical, figural), *form* (e.g., matrices, classification, analogies, opposites), and *process* (e.g., discrimination, generalization, induction, deduction, visualization, memory) involved. If we are interested in measuring an ability that is common to a wider variety of contents, forms, and processes, we will have to diversify these features of our test items and thereby sacrifice high inter-item correlations. But the total score on our more diverse test will represent a broader factor of ability, one that is common to a considerable variety of test items. The broader the factor we wish to measure, the more heterogeneous must the items be, and consequently the lower the inter-item correlations. To compensate for this, the test must contain more items to have high reliability. To maintain a given reliability, there is a necessary trade-off between inter-item correlation and test length.

So the only way that we can be sure initially that we are measuring an ability factor that has considerable generality is to include a wide variety of items in the test, as did Binet and Wechsler in making their respective tests. By means of factor analysis, we may later find that some types of items measure the general factor common to all of the items better than do other types of items, and yet do not measure any other factors to an appreciable degree. These kinds of items then may be used to form a shorter and more homogeneous test that measures the same general factor as the much longer and more heterogeneous test. Raven's Progressive Matrices is a good example of a quite homogeneous test that nevertheless measures much the same general factor (and little else) found in much more heterogeneous intelligence tests. (The Progressive Matrices Test is discussed in more detail in Chapter 14.)

Conditions That Influence Test Reliability

Scoring.   The scoring of many of the items in individually administered intelligence tests, such as the Stanford–Binet and the Wechsler scales, requires a subjective judgment on the part of the tester as to whether the examinee passed or failed the item. For example, in the vocabulary test the tester has to decide whether the definitions given by the examinee are to be scored right or wrong. (In the Wechsler tests the answer to each vocabulary item is scored 2, 1, or 0, depending on the quality of the examinee's response.) To the extent that testers do not agree on the scoring of a given response, the reliability of the total score is lowered. To keep the scoring reliability (i.e., agreement among testers) as high as possible, the scoring instructions are made quite explicit in the test manual, with many examples of passing and failing responses to each item. Moreover, the standard for passing any given item is made very lenient, so that a failing response is quite easily agreed on. Doubtful and ambiguous "correct" responses are generally scored as correct, so there will be high agreement among different scorers as to which answers are *clearly* wrong. (The Stanford–Binet scoring criteria are more lenient in this respect than the Wechsler's.)

Besides having explicit scoring criteria, individually administered tests should be given and scored only by trained persons. An essential part of such training consists of supervision and criticism of the trainee's performance in ways that make the procedures of testing and scoring more uniform and standardized and hence more reliable. With such training the agreement among scorers can be made very high, with interscorer correlations in the high .90s. Less than perfect agreement among scorers will be reflected in the test's reliability coefficient. If the test's reliability is adequately high for one's purpose, it follows that the reliability of the scoring itself is satisfactory, as the scoring reliability cannot be less than the test's internal consistency reliability.

It is commonly believed that, by uniformly relaxing the administration procedures or scoring criteria for all testees, the less able will enjoy an advantage. That is, everyone's score would rise, but the low scorers would rise relatively more under more lenient conditions. When this has been tried, the brighter testees benefit most in absolute score, but the rank order of subjects is hardly changed. Little and Bailey (1972), for example, gave the WAIS Comprehension and Similarities subtests to college students under conditions that would maximize their performance, by urging the students to give all the correct answers they could think of to each question, without time limit. Scores were obtained by giving credit for *all* correct answers on each item, as contrasted with the standard WAIS scoring procedure of giving a maximum of two points to each item. The result of the more "generous" procedure was to spread the higher- and lower-scoring students farther apart, while the "generous" and standard scores correlated very highly ($r = .93$ for Comprehension, .84 for Similarities). This shows that even when the conditions of administration and scoring are altered quite drastically, provided that it is done uniformly for all testees, the rank order of persons' scores is little changed. There is little statistical interaction of testees and scoring procedures. Thus the scoring criteria themselves, if uniformly applied, are not a potent influence on test reliability.

The same thing is usually true of allowing unlimited time on normally timed tests. The untimed condition will result in higher scores, but the correlation between the timed and untimed scores will be very high. Persons' scores on a *power test* maintain much the same rank order for various time limits, provided that the time limit is the same for everyone. A power test is one in which the items are arranged in order of increasing difficulty, and the time limit is such that most testees run out of ability, so to speak, before they run out of time, so that increasing the time limit has little effect on the score. Most tests of intelligence and achievement are power tests. In contrast, *speed tests* are comprised of many easy items all of which nearly everyone would answer correctly if there were no time limit. Tests of clerical and motor skills are commonly of this type.

Most group-administered tests have completely objective scoring, so there is no question of scoring reliability, barring clerical inaccuracies due to carelessness or to defects in the equipment in the case of machine-scored tests. Such clerical errors are generally rare, and precautions can be taken to reduce their occurrence, such as by having every test scored independently by two persons (or machines) and checking disagreements.

Standardized tests administered and scored by classroom teachers who are untrained and unsupervised in their testing procedures can yield highly unreliable and invalid scores. It is not the rule, fortunately. But we have found numerous deplorable instances in our retesting of teacher-tested classes, on the same tests, by trained testers, under very careful standardized conditions. Some of the teacher-administered test results were found highly discrepant, usually due to incomplete or improper test instructions, lax observance of time limits on timed tests, and a poor testing atmosphere resulting from a disorderly class. Tests administered under such conditions are useless, at best. (This problem is discussed more fully in Chapter 15, pp. 717-718.)

Guessing.   Most objective tests are of the multiple-choice type, in which the testee must select the one correct answer from among a number of incorrect alternatives called *distractors*. The testee who does not know the correct answer to a given item may leave it unanswered or may make a guess, with some chance of picking the correct answer. When there are many difficult items, there is apt to be more guessing. A corollary of this is that persons with lower scores are more likely to guess on more items, as there are fewer items to which they know the answers.

Guessing lowers the reliability of test scores, because items that are gotten right merely by chance cannot represent true scores. "Luck" in test taking is simply a part of the error variance or unreliability of the test. The larger the number of multiple-choice alternatives, the smaller the chances of guessing the correct answers, and, consequently, the less damage to the reliability of the test. True–false items are in this respect the worst, as there is a 50 percent chance of being right by guessing. Recall tests are the best, as no alternatives are given and the testee must produce his own answer. (This is the case in most individual tests of intelligence.) A study by Ruch (cited by Symonds, 1928) illustrates the effect of the number of multiple-choice response alternatives on the reliability of equivalent tests of one hundred items:

Type of Answer	Reliability Coefficient
Recall	.950
7-alternative multiple choice	.907
5-alternative multiple choice	.882
3-alternative multiple choice	.890
2-alternative multiple choice	.843
True–false	.837

Test constructors have devised complex ways of scoring tests, taking account of right, wrong, and unanswered items and the number of multiple choice alternatives, so as to minimize the effects of guessing on the total scores and on their reliability.[4] Most modern standardized tests take account of these factors in their scoring procedures, and their reliabilities can be high despite persons' tendency to guess when they are unsure of the right answer.

Range of Ability in the Sample.   Reliability is not a characteristic of just the test, but is a joint function of the test *and* the group of persons to which it is given. A test with high reliability in one group may have much lower reliability in a different group.

The principal condition that causes variations in a test's reliability from one group to another is the range of test-relevant ability in the group. A test administered to a group that is very homogeneous in the ability measured by the test will have lower reliability in that group than the same test administered to a more heterogeneous group.

Any decrease in the range of obtained scores or any piling up of scores in one part of the scale automatically lowers reliability. Piling up of scores occurs when a test is too difficult or too easy for a given group, or when persons at the upper and lower extremes of ability have been excluded. (The most dependable index of the score dispersion in a group is the standard deviation, because it takes *all* the scores into account, not just the most extreme values, which define the range.)

Tests have their maximum reliability when the average item difficulty is 50 percent passing. In this case, the frequency distribution of the total scores will be symmetrical about the group mean.

Another way of saying all this is that to have maximum reliability a test must tap the full range of ability in the group. Otherwise the test is said to have a *ceiling effect*★ or a *floor effect*★ that results in inadequate discriminatory power at the high or low ends of the scale.

Consequently, a test standardized in one population cannot be assumed to have the same reliability in a different population. The test's reliability has to be demonstrated anew. If the score distribution is more restricted or is markedly more asymmetrical in the second than in the first population, it is generally safe to infer that the test will also have lower reliability in the second population.

Miscellaneous Sources of Unreliability. Of the numerous other factors that can reduce a test's reliability, the most often recognized are

1. Interdependence of items lowers reliability; that is, the answer to one item is suggested in another, or knowing the answer to one item presupposes knowing the answer to another item. The effect on reliability is like that of reducing the number of items in the test.
2. Dissimilarity in the experiential backgrounds of persons taking the test can lower reliability. Conversely, tests that sample the more common elements of experience are more reliable. Thus tests of knowledge and skills acquired in school are likely to be more reliable than tests of knowledge and skills acquired in the home, other parameters of the tests being equal.
3. For reasons related to factor 2, scholastic achievement tests administered late in the school year tend to have higher reliability than those given at the beginning of the year.
4. "Tricky" questions or "catch" questions lower the reliability of a test.
5. Wording of test items—words that are overemphasized and may mislead, emotionally toned words that distract from the main content, overly long wording of the question, strange and unusual words, poor sentence structure and unusual word order—all these features lower the reliability.
6. Inadequate or faulty directions or failure to provide suitable illustrations of the task requirements can lower reliability. Giving several easy practice items at the beginning of the test can increase reliability.
7. Accidental factors such as breaking a pencil or interruptions and distractions lower reliability, especially in timed tests.
8. Subject variables such as lack of effort, carelessness, anxiety, excitement, illness, fatigue, and the like may adversely influence reliability.

It is because of an amalgam of all these factors in varying degrees that mental tests fall short of perfect reliability. The remarkable thing is that the reliabilities of most mental tests are as high as they are in fact.

Empirical Reliabilities of Standard Tests

Individually Administered IQ Tests.   The Stanford–Binet and the Wechsler tests are the most widely used individual tests of intelligence. Their reliabilities merit detailed examination.

The reliability of the Stanford–Binet is based on the correlation between the alternate forms (L and M) of the test. Alternate-forms reliability is usually slightly lower than reliability derived from split-half correlations or other methods of measuring a test's internal consistency. The alternate-forms reliability of the Stanford–Binet computed within twenty-one different age groups ranged from .85 to .95, with a median of .91. The median for ages 2 to 6 was .88, and for ages above 6 it was .93 (Terman & Merrill, 1937, p. 47). These are considered very high reliabilities. The IQs are less reliable at lower ages and are more reliable at the lower IQ levels than at the higher.

Table 7.2 shows the extremes of the reliabilities in three age groups at the upper and lower extremes of the IQ distribution. The reliabilities of intermediate IQs fall between these extremes. It is in the lower range of IQ that high reliability is most important, because usually more personally crucial decisions involve very low levels of IQ rather than average or superior levels.

The three Wechsler tests span a total age range from 4 years to 74 years (Preschool and Primary, 4–6½; Children, 5–16; Adult, 16–74). The reliabilities of the various Wechsler subscales and of the Verbal, Performance, and Full Scale IQs are shown for selected age groups in Table 7.3. Notice that the subtests have considerably lower reliabilities than the composite IQ scores. This is because many of the subtests are quite short. The Full Scale IQ, however, has exceptionally high reliability.

Reliabilities reported for well-known individual tests for infants and preschoolers are Bayley Scales of Infant Development, .81–.91; McCarthy Scales of Children's Abilities, .93 (average of ten half-year age groups); Cooperative Preschool Inventory, .86–.92; Pictorial Test of Intelligence (ages 3–8), .87–.93. Reliabilities are lowest for the youngest age groups in each of these sets.

Group Administered Tests.   Table 7.4 shows the reliabilities of 33 standard group tests of intelligence or general mental ability as reported in the publishers' test manuals.

Table 7.2.   Reliability (alternate form) of Stanford–Binet intelligence test.   (From Terman & Merrill, 1960, p. 10)

	IQ Range	
Age (years)	60–69	140–149
2½–5½	.91	.83
6–13	.97	.91
14–18	.98	.95

Table 7.3. Reliability coefficients of Wechsler intelligence test scales.

Subtest	WPPSI[1]	WISC[2]	WAIS[3]
Information	.81	.80	.91
Comprehension	.81	.73	.77
Vocabulary	.84	.91	.95
Similarities	.83	.81	.85
Arithmetic	.82	.84	.81
Sentences	.85		
Digit Span	—	.59	.66
Picture Completion	.83	.66	.85
Picture Arrangement	—	.71	.60
Block Design	.82	.87	.83
Object Assembly	—	.63	.68
Animal House	.77[a]	—	—
Mazes	.87	.81	—
Geometric Design	.82	—	
Verbal IQ	.94	.96[b]	.96
Performance IQ	.93	.89[c]	.93
Full Scale IQ	.96	.95[b,c]	.97

[1] Preschool and Primary Scale of Intelligence. Average reliability of six age groups at half-year intervals from 4 years to $6\frac{1}{2}$ years.
[2] Intelligence Scale for Children, age $10\frac{1}{2}$.
[3] Adult Intelligence Scale, ages 25–34.
[a] Test–retest reliability.   [b] Without digit span.   [c] Without mazes.

Where a range of values is given for a test, it indicates the range of reliabilities in different age groups or for various subscores.

The average reliability over all these tests is close to .90. Most test experts are critical of using tests with reliabilities of less than .90 as a basis for individual decisions, unless the test scores are statistically combined in optimal ways with other quantitative information of high reliability as the basis for decision. Reliabilities of .90 and above are generally considered satisfactory and compare favorably with individually administered tests.

Standard scholastic achievement tests have reliabilities at least comparable to those for ability tests, and a few are extremely high, even reaching .99. The reliabilities reported in the manuals of some of the most popular scholastic achievement tests are given in Table 7.5.

Consequences of Inadequate Reliability

The consequences of unreliability follow directly from the mathematical relationship between the reliability coefficient and the *standard error of measurement*. Probably the easiest way to understand the meaning of the standard error of a given person's obtained score, X, on a test is to begin by pretending that we know the person's *true score*, T. Since, by definition, errors of measurement E are random (and therefore uncorrelated with true scores) and normally distributed, and since any given $X = T + E$, we can say that obtained scores are randomly distributed about the person's true score. The

Table 7.4. Reliability coefficients[1] of group mental ability tests based on normative samples.

Test Title	Reliability
ACT (College Aptitude Test) Composite Score	.86
Academic Alertness Test	.92
Analysis of Learning Potential	.92–.97
Analysis of Relationships (Various groups)	.70–.90
Boehm Test of Basic Concepts (Young Children)	.60–.90
California Analogies and Reasoning Test	.88–.94
California Test of Mental Maturity (Age 8+) Total Score	.93–.96
Cognitive Abilities Tests	.90
College Board Scholastic Aptitude Test	.90+
Cooperative Academic Ability Test (Total Score)	.89–.94
Cooperative School and College Ability Tests (Total Score)	.94
D-48 Test (Nonverbal Reasoning)	.89
Doppelt Mathematical Reasoning Test	.78–.85
Figure Reasoning Test (Nonverbal Intelligence)	.96
Goodenough–Harris Drawing Test (Scorer Reliability = .90)	.70s–.80s
Graduate Record Examination	.90–.92
Henmon–Nelson Tests of Mental Ability	.94–.95
Illinois Index of Scholastic Aptitude	.85–.90
IPAT Culture Fair Intelligence Test	over .80
Junior Scholastic Aptitude Tests	.91–.95
Kuhlman-Anderson Intelligence Tests	.85–.95
Lorge–Thorndike Intelligence Tests. Verbal, Nonverbal	.90–.93
Miller Analogies Test	.91
Otis Group Intelligence Scale[2]	.97
Otis–Lennon Mental Ability Test[2]	
Grade 4 and below	.83–.89
Beyond Grade 5	above .90
Preliminary Scholastic Aptitude Test	.86–.91
Quick Word Test	.90
RBH Test of Nonverbal Reasoning (Long form)	.86
SRA Pictorial Reasoning Test	.60–.75
Safran Culture Reduced Intelligence Test	.76
Test of Adult College Aptitude	.95–.96
Tests of General Ability: Inter-American Series[2]	.72–.90
Wonderlic Personnel Test[2]	.95

[1]Reliabilities measured by internal consistency, e.g., split-half and Kuder–Richardson formulas, except where indicated by footnote.
[2]Reliability coefficient is the correlation between alternate forms.

standard deviation of the theoretical (normal) distribution of obtained scores about the person's true score is called the *standard error of measurement.* Since the distribution of all possible obtained scores is assumed to be normal, we can say that the probability is 68 percent (i.e., the chances are roughly two out of three) that the person's obtained score falls within the range of scores extending one standard error ($\pm 1SE_X$) above and below his true score. Conversely, knowing the person's obtained score, we can say that the probability is 68 percent that his true score falls within the range of $\pm 1SE_X$ of his obtained score, that is, T is embraced in the score interval defined by $X \pm 1SE_X$.

If we want to be more confident than 68 percent regarding the interval embracing the person's true score, we merely extend the limits of the confidence interval. For example, the probability is 95 percent that the person's true score falls within the score interval of $X \pm 2SE_X$. And the probability is 99.7 percent that the person's true score falls within the score interval of $X \pm 3SE_X$. An interval of $\pm 4SE_X$ has a probability of 99.99 percent of containing the true score. One chooses the confidence interval depending on how certain one wishes to be.[5] For example, one would normally be willing to bet much more that an individual's true score falls in the interval $X \pm 2SE_X$ than in the narrower interval $X \pm 1SE_X$.

The standard error of measurement, *SE*, is related to the reliability, r_{xx}, by the following formula:

$$SE_X = \sigma_X \sqrt{1 - r_{xx}}, \qquad (7.2)$$

where σ_X is the standard deviation of scores in the normative population. Notice that if reliability were perfect (i.e., $r_{xx} = 1$), then SE_X would be zero. If there were zero reliability, the SE_X would be equal to the standard deviation in the population, in which case the probability that a person's true score falls within the interval $X \pm 1SE_X$ is the same as the probability of *any* score drawn at random from the whole population falling within that interval. In other words, with zero reliability, an individual's obtained score tells us absolutely nothing about the probable location of his true score on the scale of measurement that we cannot determine from just the population statistics, without knowing anything about the given individual.

Obtained scores should be reported and thought of in the form $X \pm 1SE$, because what we are really interested in knowing is the interval within which the person's true score most likely falls. As long as reliability is less than perfect, we can legitimately think of scores only in terms of an interval or range that most probably embraces the true score. As an example, say that a person obtains an IQ score of 120 on a test with a reliability of .97 and a standard deviation of 15 (as would be the case for the Wechsler Adult

Table 7.5.   Reliability coefficients of standard achievement tests.

Test Title	Reliability
American College Testing Program Examination–Composite	.95
ACTP Various Subtests	.85–.90
Bristol Achievement Tests	.92–.96
California Achievement Tests	.90–.95
Iowa Tests of Basic Skills (Composite)	.98–.99
Metropolitan Achievement Tests, Various Subtests	.70s–.80s
National Merit Scholarship Qualifying Test (Composite)	.97
Pupil Record of Educational Progress—Total Score	.93–.95
SRA Reading and Arithmetic Indexes	.87–.95
Secondary School Admissions Test	.89–.92
STS Educational Development Series (Composite)	.97–.98
Stanford Achievement Test (High School Level)	above .90
Sequential Tests of Educational Progress (STEP) Various Subtests	.80s–.90s
Survey of College Achievement	.57–.77
Tests of Academic Progress	.80s–.90s
Wide Range Achievement Test	.90–.98

Intelligence Scale). The standard error then would be $15 \times \sqrt{1 - .97} = 2.6$, and the person's IQ would be thought of as 120 ± 2.6, which means that the probability is 68 percent that his true IQ is within the interval from 117.4 to 122.6, or 97 percent that it is within the interval $(X \pm 2SE_X)$ from 114.8 to 125.2, or 99.7 percent that it is within the interval $(X \pm 3SE_X)$ from 112.2 to 127.8. The probability that the person's true score is more than 10 IQ points above or below his or her obtained score is practically nil (or to be more exact, about one chance in ten thousand).

Do not confuse this degree of precision with the *temporal stability* of the person's score. The reliability coefficient only tells us how accurately a test measures whatever it is that it measures at a given point in time. The person may have been coming down with the flu while taking the test, in which case the obtained test score reflects the person's true score while suffering from the flu, plus some error component. The person's hypothetical true score is his or her true score on that occasion and not necessarily an enduring characteristic. The test's *stability coefficient*, rather than its reliability coefficient, is the relevant statistic when we are estimating the standard error so as to take account of persons' temporal fluctuations in performance.

Reliability of Score Differences.   When test scores are used as the basis for selection, the test's power to discriminate accurately between persons whose scores lie near the selection/rejection threshold is an important consideration. Say that the selection cutting score is set at 100. Jones, with a score of 99, is rejected, and Smith, with a score of 101, is accepted. Is there a true score difference between them, or is the difference merely a result of the test's unreliability?

We can determine the probability that the obtained score difference between Jones and Smith represents a true score difference if we know the test's standard error of measurement, SE_X. We simply divide the obtained score difference $(X_1 - X_2)$ by the standard error of the difference SE_D, which is $\sqrt{2}SE_X$.

$$z = (X_1 - X_2)/\sqrt{2}SE_X. \qquad (7.3)[6]$$

The z is a unitized deviate of the normal curve. In a table of areas under the normal curve, we can look up the unitized area (i.e., proportion) of the curve falling below any given value of $+z$; this is the probability that the observed score difference $X_1 - X_2 > 0$ represents a true score difference in the direction $T_1 - T_2 > 0$.

In our example of Jones and Smith, say that the test they took has a SE_X of 5. Then $z = (101 - 99)/\sqrt{2} \times 5 = 0.28$. The corresponding probability level of $+z$ of 0.28 is 61 percent. This is a very poor probability, being only slightly better than pure chance, which is 50 percent. Thus we are not very confident that Smith's true score is higher than Jones's. Selecting Smith and rejecting Jones on the basis of this score difference is unfair. It gives Smith the benefit of the test's lack of perfect reliability, and it penalizes Jones for the same reason.

If we want to be at least 99 percent confident in our decision, we would find the z value in the table of the normal curve corresponding to 99 percent, which is 2.33, and work backward from equation 7.3 to determine the size of obtained score difference we would need to be 99 percent confident that the true scores differ. Thus, since at the 99 percent confidence level $z = 2.33$, we solve the following equation for D when $D = X_1 - X_2$:

General form: $D/\sqrt{2} SE_X = z$
Substituting actual values: $D/\sqrt{2} \times 5 = 2.33$
Rearranged: $D = \sqrt{2} \times 5 \times 2.33 = 16.5.$

In other words, Smith would have to score 16.5 points higher than Jones for us to be 99 percent confident that Smith's true score is higher than Jones's true score.

So, if we wish to set our cutting score at some point X_c and give all examinees the benefit of the doubt, with the confidence that we will err only 1 percent of the time by rejecting those who should have been accepted, we would accept all applicants with scores above a point that is actually 2.33 SE_X below the cutting score. Of course, the price for giving the benefit of the doubt (i.e., the test's unreliability) to the examinees is that we must also accept those examinees whose true scores are below the cutting score and therefore should have been rejected. Obviously the location of the cutting score is an economic decision in the broad sense, rather than a purely statistical decision. The statistics only spell out the consequences of any given economic decision, which will be based on a number of considerations, such as the supply or availability of qualified candidates, minimizing the costs of errors in selection, and maximizing opportunity to all possibly qualified applicants. In making such decisions, high reliability (and hence a small standard error) makes for fewer decision errors and greater fairness for all concerned in any selection procedure. At the present stage of test development, the reliabilities of most standardized tests are sufficiently high to allow little grounds for criticism on this score, and the test's predictive *validity* becomes the chief concern.

A test's reliability derives its chief importance through its effect on the test's validity, which cannot be greater than the square root of the test's reliability.

Regression and Estimated True Scores.   When any actual measurements have less than perfect reliability, the corresponding true scores *on the average* lie somewhat closer to the mean of the group than the obtained measurements. This is a statistical certainty and it applies to all forms of measurement, not just psychological measurement. The reason for this becomes clear if we think of scores as deviations from the group mean. Each deviation, then, consists of a true deviation plus or minus an error deviation.

The larger score deviations (positive or negative) from the mean are, on the average, larger in part due to larger error (i.e., chance) deviations. Thus the hypothetical true deviations are closer to the general mean. If the test were given again, the errors of measurement, being random, would not likely be attached to the same true scores on retest; others would be "lucky" or "unlucky" due to the errors of measurement, so that the persons with the more extreme scores on the first test will, on the average, have somewhat less extreme scores on the retest. This effect is known as *regression toward the mean* due to unreliability of measurement.

The average amount of score regression theoretically is the discrepancy between the person's obtained score and his true score. The person's true score is a purely hypothetical construct and cannot be known, but we can statistically infer its most likely value, which is called an *estimated true score* (or a "regressed" or "predicted" true score), symbolized as $\hat{T}$. If we know a person's obtained score X, the reliability of the test r_{xx}, and the mean $\bar{X}$ of the group of which the person is a member, we can compute the person's estimated true score $\hat{T}$ from the following formula:

$$\hat{T} = r_{xx} (X - \bar{X}) + \bar{X}. \qquad (7.4)$$

Estimated true scores have the advantage of being more accurate than obtained scores. That is, the standard error of estimated true scores is smaller, and so the confidence interval embracing the true score is narrower than for obtained scores.[7] But, if the reliability is very high, the discrepancy between X and $\hat{T}$ will be quite small, so it is usually not considered worthwhile to compute estimated true scores. In any case, if all persons are regarded as members of the same group, the $\hat{T}$ scores will preserve exactly the same ranking of persons as the X scores. If all we are interested in is a person's rank, there is no point in computing that person's estimated true score. Estimated true scores are more important when measurements are on an *absolute* scale (e.g., height, weight, blood pressure, pulse rate, reaction time) and the selection cutoff is a point on such a scale.

Regression toward Which Mean?   Estimated true scores are a more important consideration when the persons taking a test belong to different groups that are defined independently of their scores on the test, for example, groups defined in terms of sex, race, social class, geographic region, school district, neighborhood, and the like. Persons' scores regress toward the mean of their own group. Consequently, we can compute even more accurate estimated true scores by using, not the general mean in equation 7.4, but the mean of the particular subgroup of which the person is a member. If the subgroup means differ appreciably, the estimated true scores may have a different ranking than the obtained scores.

The net effect of using such estimated true scores, besides increasing the accuracy of measurement, is to reduce the higher scores of persons belonging to low-scoring subgroups and boost the lower scores of persons belonging to high-scoring subgroups. Such an outcome may seem unfair from the standpoint of members of the lower-scoring subgroups, but it is merely the statistically inevitable effect of increasing the accuracy of measurement. When higher scores are preferred in the selection procedure, the "luck" factor resulting from unreliability statistically favors persons belonging to lower-scoring groups. The "luck" factor is minimized by using estimated true scores instead of obtained scores.

Say, for example, that we are selecting high school seniors for entrance to a college that wishes to maintain a high academic standard and yet not have to fail many students. This can be achieved by admitting only those students above a certain level of scholastic aptitude, which can be measured with a college aptitude test. The purpose of testing applicants will be to predict as accurately as possible who will and will not be most apt to succeed in this college. A cutoff score will be placed at a point that past experience has shown will keep the failure rate in this college below, say, 10 percent (or whatever percentage the college wishes to tolerate without lowering its academic standards). Now, say that we have applicants from two high schools, HS A in which the mean aptitude score of applicants is 120, and HS B with a mean applicant aptitude score of 90.[8] The fact is that we can more accurately predict who will and will not succeed in the college if we select on the basis of estimated true scores, using the mean of each applicant group in equation 7.4, instead of the students' obtained scores. Also, if the reliability of the test differs in the two groups, we will increase our accuracy by using the different reliabilities for each group in computing the estimated true scores. (Usually, however, the reliability varies much less from one group to another than does the mean.)

Say that we have two applicants, Anderson from HS A and Bronson from HS B, both with the same aptitude score of 110. Then, if the test's reliability is .90 for the applicants from each school, these students' estimated true scores will be

$$\text{Anderson's } \hat{T} = .90 \ (110 - 120) + 120 = 111.$$
$$\text{Bronson's } \hat{T} = .90 \ (110 - 90) + 90 = 108.$$

If the selection cutting score happens to be 110, Anderson is accepted and Bronson is rejected. (It is assumed that the test has the same validity for applicants from both high schools.) If there are many applicants from both schools whose scores are near the cutoff, the use of estimated true scores could make an appreciable difference in the test's validity for selecting so as to minimize academic failures. If test reliability is quite high (i.e., above .90), however, the slight gains in accuracy and predictive validity from using estimated true scores may hardly repay the extra computational effort.

Temporal Stability

Just as the reliability coefficient indicates how accurately a test score measures whatever trait it measures at a given point in time, the *stability coefficient* indicates how consistent or stable the test scores are from one occasion to another. This is an important consideration when the test is intended to measure a trait, ability, or aptitude, because we think of these as being relatively stable and enduring characteristics of persons that should not change like the weather. When we obtain a person's test score today, we would like to have some assurance that the person's score is likely to be very similar if tested again tomorrow, or next week, or even after a year or more. The test's stability coefficient tells us the degree to which this is the case.

The stability coefficient is simply the correlation between scores on the same test (or parallel forms of the test) obtained at two points in time.

At the outset, let us be clear about what the stability coefficient does and does not represent. It does not necessarily represent the degree of *constancy* of the measurements themselves. It does represent the degree of *constancy in the person's relative standing* among others on the same test. If everyone's actual scores changed over time at the same rate, or by the same amount, the test would be said to have perfect stability, and the stability coefficient r_{12} (i.e., the correlation between the test scores obtained at time 1 and at time 2) would be equal to 1. Everyone's height, for example, increases from infancy to maturity, but children maintain pretty much the same rank order in height among their age peers from year to year, and so we would say that height measurements have rather high stability throughout the course of growth. For very short intervals the stability of height is nearly perfect.

Stability of Mental Test Scores

How stable are scores on intelligence tests? The psychological literature contains a tremendous amount of evidence on this point. One of the best reviews and discussions is to be found in *Stability and Change in Human Characteristics* by Benjamin Bloom (1964). From all this evidence we can make some summarizing generalizations.

1. The stability coefficient is a function of the characteristic being measured. It differs for different physical and mental measurements.

2. The stability coefficient is generally less than the square root of the product of the reliabilities of the tests on the two occasions on which they were administered, that is, $r_{12} \leqq \sqrt{r_{11} \times r_{22}}$.

3. The stability coefficient is a function of the amount of time separation between measurements.

4. The stability coefficient is a function of chronological age, CA, at the time of measurement.

The relationship among these factors can be shown in a simple formula that gives a reasonably good fit to the actual stabilities of intelligence test scores reported in the literature:

$$r_{12} = \sqrt{r_{11} \times r_{22}} \times \sqrt{\frac{CA_1}{CA_2}}, \tag{7.5}$$

where r_{11} and r_{22} are the reliabilities of the test on occasions 1 and 2, respectively, and CA_1 and CA_2 are the person's chronological age on occasions 1 and 2. The formula gives a good approximation to the empirical findings only up to age 10 years for CA_2. After age 10, intelligence test scores become so stable that the best prediction of r_{12} for any subsequent time interval up to maturity (age 18+) is that r_{12} will fall between $r_{11} \times r_{22}$ and $\sqrt{r_{11} \times r_{22}}$.

It should be obvious from this formulation that the closer that CA_1 and CA_2 are together, the closer does the stability coefficient r_{12} approach the reliability of the test (r_{11} or r_{22}). For very short intervals, the stability is only slightly lower than the reliability. For example, the manual of the *McCarthy Scales of Children's Abilities* shows the following reliability (r_{xx}) and stability (r_{12}) coefficients for the total scores when the time between test and retest is three to five weeks (McCarthy, 1970, pp. 31–34):

Age Groups (years)	r_{xx}	r_{12}
3–3½	.95	.91
5–5½	.94	.89
7–8½	.93	.90

Another implication of equation 7.5 is that scores obtained at early ages correlate relatively poorly with scores obtained at much later ages. This can be seen in the matrix of intercorrelations of Stanford–Binet IQs from a group of eighty children tested at regular intervals from age 2½ to 17 years by the Fels Research Institute, shown in Table 7.6.

The correlations in Table 7.6 are quite typical of those found in other studies. The matrix of age-to-age correlations of mental test scores always approximates what is called a *simplex,* its main feature being that the correlations show a regular decrease as the temporal distance between tests increases.

The last column in Table 7.6 shows the first principal component (P.C. I) of the correlation matrix. The values in this column represent the correlation of the test scores at each age with the first principal component or general factor that is common to the scores across all age levels. This general factor accounts for 77 percent of the total variance in IQs between the ages 2½ and 17 years.

Table 7.6.   Intercorrelations (decimals omitted) of Stanford–Binet IQs at various ages in a group of eighty children.[1]

Age (years)	2½	3	3½	4	4½	5	5½	6	7	8	9	10	11	12	14	15	P.C. I[2]
2½																	.77
3	93																.81
3½	85	82															.83
4	86	86	86														.88
4½	76	78	83	88													.91
5	80	78	83	88	90												.90
5½	68	71	75	80	85	86											.89
6	68	70	77	83	83	87	88										.91
7	66	70	73	78	82	84	84	90									.92
8	59	65	69	74	82	80	78	83	87								.93
9	58	66	66	75	81	79	81	83	88	91							.93
10	59	67	66	72	78	74	77	80	87	91	92						.93
11	57	65	63	71	78	74	78	80	83	90	71	94					.92
12	55	62	62	68	75	70	74	77	77	89	89	92	93				.90
14	49	57	59	65	73	65	68	72	75	83	84	86	86	90			.86
15	48	55	58	62	70	63	65	73	77	84	84	86	86	90	88		.86
17	36	43	47	49	56	49	54	62	62	65	67	69	67	74	71	89	.71

[1]Correlations courtesy of Dr. Robert McCall and the Fels Research Institute.
[2]P.C. I is the first principal component derived from this correlation matrix (see text).

Group tests show the same pattern of age-to-age correlations and are remarkably stable when used during the school years, as shown in Table 7.7, which is based on the Otis group tests of IQ given to the same children every year from Grade 1 to Grade 6. Notice that the scores obtained in any given grade correlate between .90 and .94 with the general factor (P.C. I) common to all the scores. The general factor in Table 7.7 accounts for 86 percent of the total variance in all test scores between Grade 1 and Grade 6. This represents a quite substantial degree of stability.

How does the stability of mental test scores compare with the stability of other growth measurements such as height and weight? Height is considerably more stable than

Table 7.7.   Intercorrelations (decimals omitted) of Otis IQs at six grade levels in a group of 343 children.   (Data from Hirsch, 1930)

Grade in School	1	2	3	4	5	P.C. I[1]
1						94
2	86					90
3	86	86				94
4	82	74	85			92
5	85	79	84	87		94
6	79	76	77	81	89	91

[1]First principal component of correlation matrix.

Table 7.8. Interage correlations (decimals omitted) of height (above diagonal) and weight (below diagonal) for 66 males. (From Tuddenham & Snyder, 1954)

Age (years)	2	4	6	8	10	12	14	16	18	Height P.C. I
2		83	77	75	72	67	61	62	60	79
4	82		93	91	88	82	73	74	75	91
6	77	87		97	95	88	77	79	81	95
8	62	72	92		98	92	82	83	85	97
10	53	60	85	96		96	86	88	88	98
12	42	50	74	89	94		94	89	83	96
14	34	40	64	81	85	95		92	79	90
16	39	43	62	76	80	89	93		93	92
18	32	39	53	67	70	80	82	93		90
Weight P.C. I	65	72	89	96	95	94	89	89	81	

mental age, especially during the years before puberty. Age-to-age correlations for height are approximated by the formula $r_{12} = \sqrt[4]{CA_1/CA_2}$, that is, the fourth root of the ratio of the ages at the time of the first and second measurements. The age-to-age correlations of weight are similar to those for IQ, although the reliability of weight is so high as to be practically equal to 1, so that for weight, $r_{12} = \sqrt{CA_1/CA_2}$ is a good approximation to the interage correlations. The interage correlations for height and weight measurements are shown in Table 7.8, which may be compared with Tables 7.6 and 7.7 for intelligence measurements.

Table 7.9 shows the stability coefficients for a variety of standard intelligence tests given to unselected groups of school children at various age intervals.

Robert L. Thorndike (1933) examined stability coefficients of the 1916 Stanford–Binet in 36 studies totaling 3,840 children. He fitted an equation to the data that best

Table 7.9. Stability coefficients of standard intelligence tests over various age intervals in years. (From Bloom, 1964, pp. 66–67)

Test	N	Age 1	Age 2	r_{12}
Stanford–Binet (1937)	52	2, 3	12, 13	.58
Stanford–Binet (1916)	100	$4\frac{1}{2}$	$13\frac{1}{2}$	.59
Stanford–Binet (1916)	74	8	12	.68
Stanford–Binet (1916)	139	$4\frac{1}{2}$	$7\frac{1}{2}$	.72
Otis	160	7, 8	12, 13	.80
Henmon–Nelson	54	10	14	.83
Calif. Test of Mental Maturity	169	$13\frac{1}{2}$	17	.68
ACE Psych. Exam. (HS)	2,169	14	17	.80
Kuhlman–Anderson	59	6	9	.65
Henmon–Nelson	113	15	17	.70
Thorndike CAVD	59	8	10	.76
Dearborn	575	6	7	.72
SAT Verbal Test	2,000	16	17	.94

Table 7.10. Average stability coefficients of Stanford–Binet (1916) as a function of test–retest interval. (From R. L. Thorndike, 1933, p. 547)

Test–Retest Interval (months)	r_{12}
0	.889
10	.868
20	.843
30	.814
40	.781
50	.743
60	.698

predicted the stability coefficient for any given number of months of separation up to sixty months. The results are summarized in Table 7.10.

The obvious practical conclusion from all these data is that the more recent the test, the better it assesses the person's current status; and less stock should be placed in scores, the further removed they are in time. This is especially true of tests in the age range below 4 years. Test scores below that age, although reliable and stable over short periods of time, have little long-term predictive value for the individual child. In fact, below age 5 one can better predict what a child's IQ will be at age 15 from a knowledge of the average IQ of the parents than from any test score obtained on the child.[9] Below age 4 or 5 years, scores should be treated only as indicators of the present level of performance, not as dependable and enduring measures of intellectual status throughout the entire course of development. It should be noted, however, that the same kind of limitation holds for height and weight and other developmental characteristics. The imperfect stability of mental test scores over long intervals during the most rapid periods of the child's growth is not so much a criticism of the tests as a fact of nature that is paralleled by many physical traits as well. As the child approaches maturity, the measurements increase in stability and power for predicting future status on comparable measuring instruments. The systematic pattern of age-to-age correlations of test scores clearly reveals the extent to which long-term stability increases with age, and it needs to be taken into account in the interpretation of any given test scores.

Interpretation of a Stability Coefficient

Like the reliability coefficient, the stability coefficient may be interpreted in terms of a confidence interval, namely, the interval within which a retest score, at some future time, is most likely to fall. To determine the obtained score interval in which the person's hypothetical true score is most like to be located, we use the standard error of measurement (equation 7.2). But to determine the interval in which the person's obtained retest score will most likely fall, when tested at some future time, we use the standard error of an individual's predicted retest score $\hat{X}_2$, the formula for which is given (in an algebraically equivalent form) by Dixon and Massey (1951, p. 159):

$$SE_{\hat{X}_2} = \sqrt{\sigma_{X_2}^2 \left(1 - r_{12}^2\right)\left(\frac{N-1}{N-2}\right)\left(1 + \frac{1}{N} + \frac{(X_1 - \overline{X}_1)^2}{(N-1)\sigma_{X_1}^2}\right)}, \qquad \textbf{(7.6)}$$

where

σ_{X_1} = the standard deviation of scores on the first test,

σ_{X_2} = the standard deviation of retest scores,

r_{12} = the stability coefficient (i.e., the test–retest correlation for a given age and interval),

X_1 = the person's score on the first test,

$\overline{X}_1$ = the mean of all the scores on the first test in the sample on which the r_{12} is based, and

N = the size of that sample.

The interpretation of $SE_{\hat{x}_2}$ or SE_{est} in terms of confidence intervals is the same as for the standard error of measurement SE_X. Say that we obtain a child's IQ at age 6 and wish to estimate the interval in which his or her IQ is likely to fall at, say, age 15. The Stanford–Binet stability coefficient for the interval between ages 5 and 15 is about .70. Say that the child's IQ is 130 at age 5. The best prediction we can make of IQ at age 15 is given by the following regression equation:

$$\text{Predicted IQ} = r_{12}(\text{IQ}_o - \text{IQ}_m) + \text{IQ}_m,$$

where

r_{12} = the stability coefficient,

IQ_o = the obtained IQ, and

IQ_m = the mean IQ in the population of which the person is a member.

So this child's predicted IQ is

$$\hat{\text{IQ}} = .70\,(130 - 100) + 100 = 121.$$

The standard error of estimate of $\hat{\text{IQ}}$ is

$$SE_{est} = 16\,\sqrt{1 - (.70)^2} = 11.4.$$

If the sample size is large (say, $N > 200$), equation 7.6 can be greatly simplified with little loss in accuracy, to the much more familiar formula for the *standard error of estimate:*

$$SE_{est} = \sigma_{X_2}\,\sqrt{1 - r_{12}{}^2} \qquad\qquad \textbf{(7.7)}$$

When $N < 200$, the standard error of estimate should be computed from equation 7.6. Thus there is approximately 68 percent probability that this 5-year-old child's Stanford–Binet IQ at age 15 will fall within the interval 121 ± 11.4, or roughly 110 to 132. The 95 percent confidence interval is 121 ± 22.3, or roughly 99 to 143. The 99 percent confidence interval is 121 ± 29.4, or roughly 92 to 150. This means there is only one chance in a hundred that a child whose IQ is 130 at age 5 will obtain an IQ below 92 or above 150 at age 15. This wide confidence interval clearly underlines the very inexact predictive value of the IQ over long intervals going from early childhood to adolescence. Even if we were using Stanford–Binet IQ at age 5 to predict IQ at age 6, the SE_{est} of the predicted IQ would be about 7.9, giving a 99 percent confidence interval of ± 20 IQ points.

From the SE_{est} we can also estimate the average absolute change (up or down) in scores that will be found among a group of children when they are retested at some later time. The average absolute change in scores is simply $2SE_{est}/\sqrt{\pi}$ or $1.13\ SE_{est}$. Thus a test with a one-year interval stability coefficient of .90 and a standard deviation of 15 will show an average change in retest scores a year later of

$$\text{Average absolute change} = 1.13 \times 15 \times \sqrt{1 - (.90)^2} = 7.4 \text{ score points.}$$

Small changes are common, large changes rare. Figure 7.2 shows the distribution of Stanford–Binet (1916) IQ changes on retest after an interval of 15 months among children between ages 7 and 14 years.

Table 7.11 shows the frequencies of various amounts of IQ change for test–retest intervals greater than two and one-half years among children in three elementary schools in New York. Retest scores in this sample show an average gain of 2.8 IQ points and an average absolute change (i.e., either up or down) of 10.5 IQ points. Some 68 percent of the children's retest scores fall within ±12 of their original scores, but there are also some enormous decreases and increases in retest scores. How can they be accounted for?

One of the most popular topics for argument in psychology years ago involved the questions of the "constancy of the IQ" and "fixed intelligence." A casual inspection of the age-to-age correlations of mental measurements reveals much less than perfect "constancy" or "fixity" of the IQ over the course of development from infancy to maturity. So there is really nothing to argue about on this point. The empirical data tell the whole story, which is that test scores maintain considerable stability of rank order for the majority of persons but show quite marked fluctuations for a few. The larger the fluctuations, the more rare they are in the population. All this is summarized in the fact that the distribution of IQ changes is approximately normal.

Figure 7.2. Frequency distribution of the changes in Stanford-Binet (1916) IQs of school children (ages 7 to 14 years) with a test–retest interval of 15 months. (From Cronbach, 1960, p. 177, based on study by A. W. Brown, 1930)

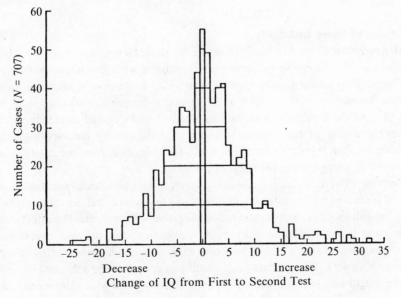

Table 7.11. Percentage of elementary school children showing a given change in Stanford–Binet IQ on retest after a minimum of $2\frac{1}{2}$ years.   (From R. L. Thorndike et al., 1940)

Amount of Change in IQ Points	Frequency	%
48 to 52	2	0.17%
43 to 47	3	0.25
38 to 42	7	0.60
33 to 37	11	0.94
28 to 32	15	1.29
23 to 27	45	3.86
18 to 22	60	5.14
13 to 17	105	9.00
8 to 12	154	13.20
3 to 7	179	15.34
−2 to 2	176	15.08
−7 to −3	166	14.22
−12 to −8	123	10.54
−17 to −13	80	6.75
−22 to −18	21	1.80
−27 to −23	8	0.68
−32 to −28	4	0.34
−37 to −33	6	0.51
−42 to −38	1	0.09
−47 to −43	1	0.09

Number	1,167
Mean IQ gain	+2.8
Standard deviation	12.9
Mean absolute IQ difference	10.5

Causes of Score Instability

Measurement Error Per Se.   These are the same factors that lower the reliability, mentioned earlier, and can show up as score instability with test–retest intervals of less than a week. They involve scoring errors, variability in the testing situation itself, and short-term fluctuations in the testee's attentiveness, willingness, emotional state, health, and the like. All these influences on stability are quite minor contributors to the long-term test–retest instability of test scores, however, as indicated by the very high stability coefficients for short test–retest intervals, which scarcely differ from the reliability coefficients based on a single administration of the test.

Practice Effects.   Gaining familiarity with taking tests results in higher scores, usually of some 3 to 6 IQ points—more if the same test is repeated, less if a parallel form is used, and still less if the subsequent test is altogether different. Practice effects are most pronounced in younger children and persons who have had no previous experience with tests. In a minority of such cases retest scores show dramatic improvements equivalent to 10 or more IQ points. The reliability and stability of scores can be substantially improved by giving one or two practice tests prior to the actual test on which the scores are to be used. The effects of practice in test taking rapidly diminish with successive tests and are typically of negligible consequence for most school children beyond the third grade unless they have had no previous exposure to standardized tests.

Because nearly all persons show similar effects of practice on tests, practice has little effect on the ranking of subjects' scores except for those persons whose experience with tests is much less or much greater than for the majority of the persons who were tested.

Environmental Changes. Large shifts in IQ are traceable in some cases to rather drastic changes in the child's environment, such as moving from an orphanage to a good adoptive home, or losing the parents, or marked changes in family circumstances that may affect interests and opportunities for intellectual development.

Emotional Problems. We refer here not to the person's momentary emotional state at the time of testing, but to the more serious emotional problems that some children experience during one or more periods in the course of their development. These periods of emotional stress, in some instances even amounting to a "nervous breakdown" and recovery therefrom, often result in quite extreme slumps and gains in relative standing on test scores. Fluctuations of as much as 20 to 40 IQ points are not uncommon in severely emotionally disturbed persons. Often atypical inconsistencies in the person's test performance reveal emotional disturbance, such as missing very easy questions but getting some very difficult items correct, or great discrepancies between certain subtest scores. A good psychological clinician is keenly alert to factors in the person's present emotional behavior and in his current life situation that could adversely affect test performance, and he will interpret the person's score accordingly.

Remediation of Physical Deficiencies. Poor eyesight, hearing loss, and endocrine gland dysfunctioning, after being corrected or compensated for, will often improve test performance, in some cases dramatically. All these conditions, especially the possibility of thyroid deficiency, should be medically checked in any child who repeatedly scores very low on a competently administered mental test.

Remediation of Scholastic Deficiencies. Most group tests for children beyond the second grade require some reading skill. Children with a specific disability in reading are therefore handicapped in such tests and will show marked gains in test scores when the specific disability is overcome, either spontaneously or through special treatment. Children with specific disabilities that respond to remedial treatment are often first discovered by means of mental tests, and as a consequence of the ensuing treatment their test scores may go up considerably.

Aside from stable gains arising from remediation of specific physical or scholastic deficiencies, "late bloomers" are quite rare as far as IQ is concerned. Mental growth begins to slow up in the teens, and, if it has only reached a low level by then, it does not usually gain much in relative status in subsequent years. Most anecdotal accounts of late bloomers, when examined, turn out to be explained in terms of confusing ability with achievement. There are notable late bloomers in scholastic and intellectual *achievements* (e.g., Charles Darwin and Winston Churchill), but authentic comparable shifts in general intelligence per se are practically impossible to find in the absence of amelioration of a pathological condition or extreme environmental deprivation.

Individual Differences in Rate of Maturation. Even when all of the other causes of score instability are accounted for, some fluctuation in scores still remains, however, becoming less and less as children approach maturity. These fluctuations are due to intrinsic individual differences in rate of development. They are apparent in physical as well as in mental growth. Growth of any kind does not proceed at a constant rate for all individuals; there are spurts and lags at different periods in each person's development. These, of course, contribute to lower stability coefficients of scores over longer intervals. Figure 7.3 shows individual mental growth curves from 1 month to 25 years for five boys. One clearly sees both stability and instability of the mental growth rates in these graphs.

Spurts and lags in the rate of mental development are conditioned in part by genetic factors, as indicated by the fact that the pattern of spurts and lags in mental development scores, at least in the first two years, coincides more closely for identical than for fraternal twins (Wilson, 1972). On the other hand, the constant aspect of mental growth rates appears to be much more genetically determined than the pattern of lags and spurts, which evidently reflects changing environmental influences to a considerable extent (McCall, 1970).

Changes in Factor Composition.   The very same test items cannot be used over very long test–retest intervals during childhood. Items that discriminate at ages 2 to 4 are

Figure 7.3.   Individual growth curves of intelligence, from age 1 month to 25 years, measured on an absolute scale, for five boys.   (From Bayley, 1955)

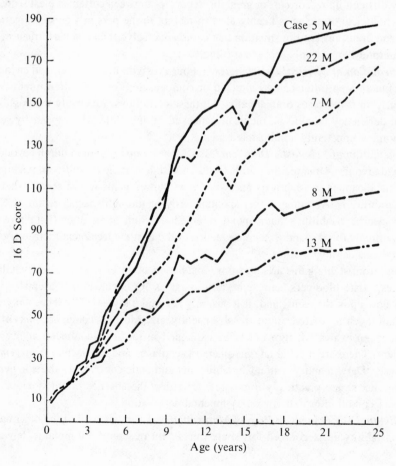

Table 7.12.   Stability coefficients of the subtests of the general aptitude test battery of the U.S. Employment Service.   (From Cronbach, 1960, p. 275)

	Correlation with Twelfth-Grade Scores of Tests Given in Grade			
	8 $N = 53$	9 $N = 61$	10 $N = 61$	11 $N = 53$
G—General	.75	.82	.80	.84
V—Verbal	.70	.76	.73	.82
N—Numerical	.76	.77	.81	.85
S—Spatial	.76	.86	.86	.88
P—Form Perception	.61	.65	.71	.75
Q—Clerical Perception	.77	.80	.86	.89
A—Aiming	.55	.58	.69	.64
T—Motor Speed	.59	.61	.78	.75
F—Finger Dexterity	.59	.66	.68	.72
M—Manual Dexterity	.65	.65	.71	.73

much too easy and therefore nondiscriminatory at ages 6 to 8. Consequently, the item composition of tests must necessarily change from year to year over the interval from infancy to adolescence if the tests are to be psychometrically suitable at every age. Changing the items in tests to make them appropriate, reliable, and discriminating for each age may introduce changes in the factor composition of the test, so that the test does not actually measure exactly the same admixture of abilities at every age level. To the extent that the factor composition of the test changes at different age levels, the age-to-age correlations are reduced. Infant tests consisting of items that are appropriate below 2 years of age, for example, measure almost entirely perceptual–motor abilities, attention, alertness, muscular coordination, and the like. There are a few simple verbal commands and some assessment of the quality of the infant's vocalization, but there are no items that call for abstraction, generalization, reasoning, or problem solving. Such items can be successfully introduced only after about age 2 or 3, and then only in a rudimentary form. Hence, tests before about age 4 or 5 are not as highly *g* loaded as later tests and are therefore rather poor predictors of scores on the much more *g*-loaded tests given to school-age children and adults. Below 2 years, scores on infant tests of development correlate negligibly with school-age IQs, and below 1 year of age the scores have zero correlation with IQ at maturity, provided that one excludes infants who are obviously brain damaged or have other gross pathological conditions.

Beyond age 2, however, most of the variance in Stanford–Binet IQs is attributable to the same general factor at every age level, steadily rising from about 60 percent *g* variance at age 2 to about 90 percent by age 10. The same thing is very likely true also of the Wechsler scales, in which the same types of subtests (though of course different items) are used throughout the age range from 5 years to adult.

Different abilities show varying degrees of stability from age to age. More complex and "higher," or *g*-loaded, functions, such as reading, arithmetic, spelling, sentence completion, composition, and the like have been found to be more stable than simpler abilities such as number checking, handwriting, auditory memory span, and the like (Keys, 1928, p. 6). The various subtests of the General Aptitude Test Battery (developed by the U.S. Employment Service) display the typical differences in stability of various abilities, as shown in Table 7.12.

After *g,* verbal facility and knowledge appear to be the most stable, especially after maturity. The more fluid abilities such as abstract reasoning, problem solving, and memory are somewhat less stable after maturity, showing greater individual differences in rates of decline, especially in adults past middle age. In adults, crystalized abilities, as measured for example by tests of general information and vocabulary, go on gradually increasing up to middle age and often beyond, whereas the fluid abilities (e.g., matrices, block design, figure analogies, and memory span) show a gradual decline with advancing age. Overall ability level on omnibus tests of general intelligence shows little change throughout adulthood until advanced old age, as the gradual decline in fluid abilities is compensated for by the gradual increase in crystalized abilities.

Scale Artifacts.   Studies of IQ stability based on age-to-age *differences* in IQ often show more instability of scores than would be inferred from age-to-age *correlations*. The explanation is that interage score *differences* are much more sensitive to imperfect scaling than are interage score *correlations*. If the units of the IQ scale are not equal from one age to another, a person will show IQ differences when there is really no change at all in his mental status relative to his age peers. The 1916 and 1937 editions of the Stanford–Binet had this scale defect as a result of calculating IQs as the ratio of mental age to chronological age (i.e., IQ = 100 MA/CA). Because this ratio had slightly different standard deviations at different ages, a constant IQ from one age to another could not represent a constant relative status. Conversely, if the person's relative status remained stable from one year to the next, the IQ would have to change. Such a change is pure artifact due to inequalities in the IQ scale from year to year. This was the main reason for abandoning the ratio IQ and using instead a deviation IQ, which is a standardized score that represents the person's deviation from his or her age-group mean in standard deviation units. Deviation IQs, which were adopted in the 1960 revision of the Stanford–Binet (as well as in all of the Wechsler tests and virtually all modern group tests of intelligence), maintain the same relative status from one age to another. The end result of changing from ratio IQs to deviation IQs is to reduce the age-to-age difference in IQ, although the age-to-age correlations remain the same. For example, an analysis of Stanford–Binet IQ changes in forty-two children between 6 and 12 years of age showed an average absolute change of 12.9 points for ratio IQs but only 9.8 points for deviation IQs (Pinneau, 1961).

An implication of using deviation IQs, which is too often forgotten, is that they cannot be used to compute mental age from the formula MA = CA × IQ/100. (The 1960 Stanford–Binet Manual, Part III, presents a table of the correct conversions from MA to IQ and vice versa.)

The Quantitative Nature of Mental Growth

We cannot directly plot mental test scores as a function of age to produce a meaningful mental growth curve in the same sense that we can show growth curves for measurements of physical traits such as height and weight. Raw scores and mental-age scores are not absolute scales with a true absolute zero and the assurance of equal intervals throughout. Without such an absolute scale, the exact *shape* of the growth curve is an artifact of the peculiarities of the particular scale of measurement. One other essential requirement is that the measurements represent one and the same factor or dimension at every age covered by the growth curve. These are very difficult requirements to meet in the case of mental test data.

Attempts to solve these problems so far have not been completely convincing in the degree to which each of these criteria is rigorously satisfied.

The usual method of establishing factorial uniformity over a wide age range, when the test items themselves necessarily differ from one age level to the next, is to factor analyze the same and the different test items in adjacent overlapping age groups. For example, the 5- and 6-year test items would be given to age groups of 5-, 6-, and 7-year-olds, and the 6- and 7-year items would be given to groups of 6-, 7-, and 8-year-olds, and so on, and it is shown that the general factor extracted at one age from the set of items is the same general factor extracted at an adjacent age from another set of items.

The usual method of putting all age groups on a common scale is to use one age group (say, age 10) as a reference group and assign standardized scores to all the other age groups on the basis of the mean and standard deviation of raw scores in the reference group. Again, the method depends on using overlapping adjacent age groups and making the assumption that the raw score intervals represent the same differences in mental ability at each age level.

The method of finding the absolute zero of the scale is based on the assumption (for which there is some empirical evidence) that the absolute variance in the population is directly proportional to the mean level of ability at any given age. Because the variance of scores increases systematically with age, we can extrapolate the relationship between variance and mean downward along the age scale until we reach the point at which the variance is zero. (The variance can never be less than zero.) This point on the age scale, then, is assumed to be the true absolute zero of the scale on which the trait is measured. It may fall at some point on the age scale well below the age at which the tests can be given (Thurstone, 1928).

When a method intended to meet these criteria, known as Thurstone's (1925) *absolute scaling* method, has been applied to mental test scores, the true zero point of mental ability lies on the age scale slightly before birth, and the resulting sigmoid form of the mental growth curve is very similar to the growth curve for weight. The average mental growth curve (and its standard deviation) based on absolute scaling of test scores from several IQ tests is shown in Figure 7.4.

The Simplex Property of Mental Growth. As noted in Tables 7.6 and 7.7, the pattern of age-to-age correlations of mental test scores (as well as of height and weight shown in Table 7.8) form what is known as a simplex, with the correlations decreasing regularly with the increase in age difference between tests. (Scholastic achievement scores display the same phenomenon.) The importance of noting that the age-to-age correlation matrix is a simplex is that we know the essential underlying mathematical properties of the simplex and can explicitly describe these in terms of a quite simple model, which can serve to generate hypotheses about the nature of mental growth.

The simplex model of growth involves variance in only a single factor that remains constant (or maintains a constant rank order in each individual across time) plus other sources of variance that are uncorrelated with the constant factor, or with each other, or from one age to another, and thus, in effect, are random variation.

Assume that the individual's constant factor C represents an innate latent ability to consolidate one's experience into cognitive structures that make for the kind of manifest performance called intelligence as measured by IQ tests. Persons differ in C. Also assume that persons encounter various experiences E at random across time. That is, the various

Figure 7.4. Mean growth curve of intelligence and its standard deviation represented on an absolute scale. (From Bayley, 1955)

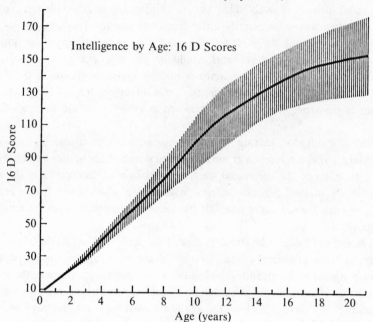

experiences are not correlated with C or with each other from one time to another, and every person has equal chances of having the same or equivalent experiences at one time or another in the course of development. Mental growth, then, would consist of the cumulation of cognitively consolidated experiences, each increment of which can be expressed as $C \times E_t$, where C is the individual's constant consolidation factor and E_t is the experience at a given time t. The person's intellectual status S_t at a given time is the sum of all $C \times E$ increments up to that time. Certain parameters must be entered into the equations to reproduce the following main features of empirical data: (1) sigmoid growth curve, (2) normal distribution of scores at any given age, and (3) simplex pattern of age-to-age correlations.[10]

This simplex model probably is the simplest model that will simulate the actual age-to-age correlations of intelligence test scores, as well as reproduce such well-established empirical findings as (1) the increasing variability among persons as age increases, (2) the greater variability and less age-to-age stability of scores among persons in the upper half of the ability distribution than among those in the lower half, (3) the very low correlations between gains in one year and gains in another, and (4) assuming that the C factor represents mainly genotypic potential, the model predicts the gradually increasing correlations between parents' and children's IQs as the children grow from infancy to maturity. (This parent–child correlation appears even in the case of adopted children who have never known their biological parents; in contrast, the correlation between adoptive children and their adoptive parents decreases with age (Munsinger, 1975, p. 649).)

In the model, E may be thought of as learning experiences of all kinds and C as a capacity for consolidating what is learned into the kinds of cognitive structures that permit for later retrieval, generalization, and transfer of past learning to new experiences. Unless learning experiences are consolidated in such a fashion, they contribute little to that aspect of the individual's cumulative mental growth that shows up as the g factor in factor analyses of a wide variety of cognitive skills. The best estimate of the general capacity corresponding to C in this model would be factor scores derived from the general factor g (or the first principal component) in a large and diverse battery of mental tests. The model is entirely consistent with the following summarization of research findings on mental development put forth by a group of British psychologists in a government report on secondary education:

> Intellectual development during childhood appears to progress as if it were governed by a single central factor, usually known as "general intelligence," which may broadly be described as innate all-round intellectual ability. It appears to enter into everything which the child attempts to think, to say, or do, and seems on the whole to be the most important factor in determining his work in the classroom. (Spens report, 1958, quoted in Simon, 1971, p. 50)

SUMMARY

Test *reliability* is an index of the degree of internal consistency with which a test comprised of a number of items (or other units) measures whatever trait, knowledge, skill, or characteristic that it measures. A test's reliability is a monotonically* increasing function jointly of the inter-item correlations and the number of items in the test. The coefficient of reliability can be estimated by several methods: split-halves, equivalent forms, the Kuder–Richardson formulas, and analysis of variance. Some methods are preferable to others, according to the purposes and computational resources of the investigator.

Reliability is affected by a host of conditions, including method of scoring the test, amount of guessing and the probability of guessing the correct answers, the number of items in the test and the number of items actually attempted by subjects, the range of ability in the sample, the average item difficulty, and ceiling and floor effects.

Unreliability (the complement of reliability) constitutes a form of individual bias in test scores, bias being defined as a systematic error of measurement. In this case, the error of measurement may be conceived of as the discrepancy between the subject's obtained score and the subject's hypothetical *true score*. (True scores can only be estimated statistically; they can never be known exactly.) When reliability is less than perfect, the obtained scores of high-scoring subjects (i.e., those above the population mean) are systematically biased by *over*estimating the subjects' true scores. The obtained scores of low-scoring subjects are systematically biased by *under*estimating their true scores. The use of estimated true scores corrects for these biases, although the amount of correction is quite small for the majority of subjects when the test's reliability is high (e.g., over .90), as is usually the case for standardized tests. The use of estimated true scores, however, may significantly reduce group biases when test scores are used for selection of persons from a pool comprised of groups from two or more populations having considerably different means on the test.

The *standard error of measurement* is an index of the degree of accuracy of test scores expressed in the units of the scale of test scores. It is the average standard deviation of the distribution of obtained scores for every true score; it is estimated from the reliability and standard deviation of obtained scores.

The reliabilities of current standardized tests of mental abilities and of scholastic achievement are generally quite high, averaging over .90. For most tests, unreliability is not an important source of bias, and what little bias there is may be corrected or reduced by the use of estimated true scores.

Stability is conceptually altogether different from reliability. Stability refers to the consistency of test scores (or exactly, standardized scores indicating relative standing in the total distribution of scores) across time. The stability coefficient is the correlation between scores on the same test administered on two occasions, which may be separated by an interval of time for which one wishes to determine the test's temporal stability.

The stability of tests of mental ability is jointly a monotonically *decreasing* function of the length of the time interval between the first and second administrations of the test and an *increasing* function of the child's age at the first administration. A number of other factors—physical, maturational, psychological, and situational—affect the temporal stability of test scores. Practice and coaching on similar tests may also influence stability.

In some tests scale artifacts spuriously attenuate the stability of scores, as when the standard deviation of the IQ fluctuated markedly at different age levels in the older (1916 and 1937) standardizations of the Stanford–Binet.

The stability of mental test scores during the period from infancy to maturity is roughly comparable to the stability of height and weight measurements, although mental measurements more closely resemble weight measurements in this respect. Mental test scores become increasingly stable over any given time interval as the chronological age of the subjects increases, from infancy to adulthood.

The *standard error of estimate* is a crucial consideration in using any test scores to predict future status on a test of the same ability. The large size of the standard error of estimate for making predictions of future status over intervals of more than a year may come as a shock to many, especially in predicting the future mental status of children under 5 or 6 years of age. It should caution against using mental tests for long-range predictions, and it underlines the importance of frequent and up-to-date assessments of children whose tested level of ability is of concern.

NOTES

1. All methods of determining the reliability of tests are related to the complete analysis of variance of the persons × items matrix. The popular split-half method consists of dividing the test into two halves (e.g., odd- versus even-numbered items), giving every person a score based on each half, obtaining the correlation between the two half-scores, and then boosting the correlation to give the reliability of a test twice as long, using the Spearman–Brown formula (see note 2). But split-half reliability is only a crude estimate, as there are many possible ways of splitting a test in half. Any one split-half reliability coefficient is merely a selection of only one reliability from all possible reliabilities for all of the many split-halves that could be made up from the test. What we would really like to

Table 7N.1

Source of Variance	Sum of Squares	df	Mean Square	F ratio
Between items	7.50	9	.83	8.30
Between persons	11.00	10	1.10	11.00
Interaction: items × persons	9.00	90	0.10	
Total	27.50	109		

know is the average reliability determined from all possible split-halves. A test of n items has $n!/2[n/2)!]^2$ possible split-halves, where $n!$ is n factorial, that is, $n \times (n-1) \times (n-2) \times \cdots \times [n-(n-1)]$. A mere 10-item test would have 126 possible split-halves. It would be practically prohibitive to calculate the reliabilities of all possible split halves of a test of, say, 50 or 100 items.

Fortunately, the analysis of variance of the persons × items matrix quite simply yields the reliability that would be obtained from the average of all possible split-half reliabilities. It is beyond the scope of this book to explicate the analysis of variance, but, for readers who are already familiar with this statistical method, it is most instructive to note how the reliability is obtained from the two-way analysis of variance of the persons × items matrix.

As an example, we can perform an analysis of variance on the matrix in Table 7.1, with the results shown in Table 7N.1. If the between persons F ratio (i.e., between persons *mean square*/interaction *mean square*) is not large enough to be statistically significant, the test's reliability cannot be assumed to be greater than zero, and the computation of the reliability coefficient is not warranted. In the present example $F = 11$; with 10 and 90 degrees of freedom it is significant at well beyond the .001 level, so we are justified in calculating the reliability, which is simply $r_{tt} = (F-1)/F$, or $10/11 = .9091$. The average inter-item correlation is also derivable from the between persons F ratio:

$$\bar{r}_{ij} = (F-1)/(F+n-1),$$

where n is the number of items in the test. In the present example, $\bar{r}_{ij} = 10/20 = .50$.

It can be seen from the analysis of variance that the condition that favors high reliability is a large mean square for persons and a small mean square for the items × persons interaction.

2. The Spearman–Brown formula gives the reliability r_{nn} of a test with n times as many items as a given test with a reliability of r_{tt}, assuming that the test length is changed by adding (or eliminating) items that are statistically equivalent to those already in the test. (Equivalent means having the same difficulty levels and inter-item correlations.)

$$r_{nn} = \frac{nr_{tt}}{1 + (n-1)r_{tt}} \qquad (7N.1)$$

3. From the Spearman–Brown formula (note 2) one can derive the amount by which a test must be lengthened (or shortened) to achieve a given reliability. If r_{tt} is the reliability of

the test and r_{nn} is the desired reliability, the original test must be made n times as long to change the reliability from r_{tt} to r_{nn}, where

$$n = \frac{r_{nn}\,(1 - r_{tt})}{r_{tt}\,(1 - r_{nn})}.$$ (7N.2)

4. Because this book is not a treatise on test construction, a proper discussion of scoring formulas is beyond its scope. A good introduction to the subject is Chapter 18 ("Methods of Scoring Tests") in the textbook by Gulliksen (1950).

5. Students of statistics will recognize these probabilities as areas under the normal curve, which are given in tables of the normal curve (found in most statistics textbooks) in terms of the proportion of the total area of the curve between the mean and any given z score, where the z score corresponds to the unitized standard error of measurement. Because we wish to know the area between the interval $-SE_x$ and $+SE_X$, we must double the tabled area between the mean and z. In choosing any desired confidence level, one can determine the corresponding $\pm SE_X$ interval from the table of areas under the normal curve.

6. The generalized formula for the standard error of a score difference $X_1 - X_2$ is $SE_D = \sqrt{SE_1^2 + SE_2^2}$. When $SE_1 = SE_2 = SE_X$, the formula simplifies to $SE_D = \sqrt{2}\,SE_X$.

7. The standard error of measurement of estimated true scores is $SE_t = r_{xx}SE_x$, where r_{xx} is the reliability of the obtained scores and SE_x is the standard error of measurement of the obtained scores. (For the derivation, see Stanley, 1971c, pp. 380–381.) In this sense, the estimated true scores are more accurate than obtained scores, but their reliabilities are exactly the same, as estimated true scores are a linear transformation of obtained scores and a correlation coefficient is not changed by a linear transformation of either one or both of the variables.

8. Note that the relevant mean in this case is the mean of the college applicants from each high school, not the mean of all students in the school, as the college applicants are not a random sample, but a self-selected sample of all the students.

9. Because the empirical regression of child's IQ (after age 10) on the midparent (i.e., average of both parents) IQ is found to be close to two-thirds, the regression equation for predicting the child's IQ from the midparent IQ is

$$\hat{IQ}_c = 2/3\,(IQ_{\bar{p}} - IQ_m) + IQ_m,$$

where

$\hat{IQ}_c$ = child's predicted IQ,
$IQ_{\bar{p}}$ = midparent IQ, and
IQ_m = mean IQ of the population of which the parents are members.

The standard error of estimate of the predicted $\hat{IQ}_c$ is $\sigma_{\hat{IQ}_c}\sqrt{2/3}$, which, for tests with a standard deviation of 15, is 12.25. Hence this is not a very precise prediction. The 95 percent confidence interval is $\hat{IQ}_c \pm 24.01$.

10. A growth model that reproduces quite well several features of empirical data on the growth of general mental ability as measured by IQ tests is the following. (The mental status score at each point in time is on an absolute scale and can be transformed to mental-age units, IQs, weight, or any other scale of measurement. The units of measurement of the present absolute scale are purely arbitrary.)

S is a person's score or status at a given point in time (measured on an absolute scale) indicated by the subscript.

C is an experiential or learning consolidation factor, constant for each person, sampled from a normal distribution of values ranging from 0.1 to 0.9. C is likened to the person's genotypic value on the trait in question.

E is the quantity and quality of environmental experience or input relevant to the development of the trait in question. It is a random variable at each point in time, randomly sampled from a normal distribution of values ranging from 1 to 9. The subscripts of E correspond to the time period in which E occurs (i.e., is randomly sampled from the total range of values of E). The coefficients of E $(1, 2, 3, \dots)$ in each equation increase with the person's age; that is, they represent a developmental or maturational factor for increasing awareness or utilization of environmental inputs.

A single growth curve is simulated by the following model:

$$S_0 = \log_2 (5E_0)$$
$$S_1 = \log_2 (C1E_0 + 5E_1)$$
$$S_2 = \log_2 (C1E_0 + C2E_1 + 5E_2)$$
$$S_3 = \log_2 (C1E_0 + C2E_1 + C3E_2 + 5E_3)$$
$$\vdots$$
$$S_{18} = \log_2 (C1E_0 + \dots + C17E_{17} + 5E_{18}).$$

The coefficients of E do not increase beyond point 17; at this point in time the growth of maturational factors is assumed to be complete. Using logarithms to the base 2, which converts the values in parentheses to *bits* (i.e., binary digits) in terms of information processing theory, gives the growth curve the sigmoid shape and negative acceleration typical of actual physical growth curves (and mental growth curves when represented on an absolute scale). The model thus implies that the growth of the number of elements (an interaction of C and E or genotype and environment) is related to growth in mental ability, as manifested in performance on tests, as a function of $\log_2$, the measure of information processing capacity.

Chapter 8

Validity and Correlates of Mental Tests

Validity is the most central concept in the whole testing enterprise. It is the main goal toward which reliability and stability are aimed. However elegantly a test may be constructed in terms of all the other essentials of psychometrics, without validity it comes to naught. *A test's validity is the extent to which scientifically valuable or practically useful inferences can be drawn from the scores.*

From this most general definition of validity, it is obvious that validity is a complex concept requiring further analysis and explication. There are four main types of validity, and the demonstration of a test's validity may be based on any one or any combination of these, easily remembered as the four *C*'s: *content* validity, *criterion* validity, *concurrent* validity, and *construct* validity.

Content Validity

This type of validity is most relevant to achievement tests, job-knowledge tests, and work-sample tests. A test has content validity to the extent that the items in the test are judged to constitute a representative sample of some clearly specified universe of knowledge or skills. This judgment is usually based on a consensus of experts in the field of knowledge or skill that the test items are intended to sample. For example, if it is a test of general musical knowledge (not musical talent), the items, in the judgment of musicians, would have to represent a sufficiently broad and varied selection of factual information about music: notation, musical vocabulary, orchestral instruments, music history and theory, composers, and so on. Any musician examining the test should be able to agree that it is a test of musical knowledge. The test then would be said to show good content or face validity. Tests of knowledge about specific jobs are evaluated in terms of content validity. So are work-sample tests, which are performance tests consisting of a representative sample of the kinds of skills that analysis of a particular job reveals a person must actually possess to perform adequately on the job, for such occupations as typist, computer programmer, welder, electrician, and machinist, among others.

Specific aptitude tests (clerical, mechanical, musical, etc.), often aim for content validity, but it is not a crucial feature in such tests, which must depend mainly on other types of validation. The kinds of items that measure an aptitude need not closely resemble the final kind of performance for which the aptitude is a prerequisite. It may be possible to measure a person's musical aptitude before he has learned to play an instrument or before he has had any kind of training in music. The musical aptitude test, tapping such elemental capacities as discrimination and short-term memory of pitch, loudness, duration, timbre, and rhythmic patterns, would obviously have some degree of content validity, but its validation would have to rest chiefly on criterion validity, that is, the correlation of the aptitude test scores with assessments of later success in musical training. The aptitude test itself may predict but does not sample the criterion performance, knowledge, or skills acquired through training.

Criterion Validity

This is the ability of test scores to predict performance in some endeavor that is external to the test itself, called the *criterion*. A test's validity coefficient is simply the correlation between the test scores and measurements of the criterion performance. For example, a college aptitude test would be said to have good criterion validity (also called *predictive validity*) to the extent that the test scores are correlated with grades in college (the criterion).

The criterion performance may be measured by other tests (e.g., scholastic achievement tests and job-knowledge tests), by grades in courses, by supervisor's ratings of performance on the job, or by direct indices of work proficiency and productivity, such as the number of articles assembled per hour, number of sales per month, number of pages typed per hour, and the like.

Criterion validity is probably the most important, defensible, and convincing type of validation in the practical use of psychological tests. In many cases it is regarded as crucial. Increasingly in recent years the use of tests in educational and employment selection can be justified only in terms of the test's criterion validity. It is a reasonable and scientifically and economically defensible requirement benefiting both the student and the school, the job applicant and the employer.

Criterion validity does not rest on the content or statistical analysis of the test per se, or on expert opinion or testimony, but depends entirely on empirical demonstration. This consists of establishing the correlation between the test scores and some clearly specified and quantified criterion. The criterion itself, of course, must be open to critical scrutiny.

Analysis of the criterion, in fact, is often the first step in the procedure of establishing a test's criterion validity. The criterion performance itself is systematically examined and analyzed to determine the kinds of abilities, knowledge, and skills that it involves, as a means to formulating hypotheses as to the kinds of test items that would most likely predict the criterion. A test is constructed accordingly and is then tried out. In a test to predict performance in a clerical job, for example, it would seem reasonable to include items that measure perceptual speed and accuracy, knowledge of alphabetizing, tabulation, and the like.

Once a test is thus selected or designed for predicting a particular criterion, one of four procedures is used for determining the test's validity coefficient (i.e., correlation with the criterion):

Method 1. The most completely satisfactory method is to test all the job applicants but not use the test scores in any hiring decisions. The scores are then later correlated with measurements or ratings of success in training or job performance. It is important that the scores be kept secret so as not to risk contaminating the criterion measures used in determining the test's validity for the particular criterion.

This method has many statistical advantages over all the others, because it enables one to estimate accurately the degree of improvement in selection decisions that can result from using the test as compared with whatever other basis for selection was being used. If the test shows a significant validity coefficient (i.e., correlation between test scores and the criterion measure), one can determine the most suitable cutoff score for selecting applicants in such a way as to maximize success in the criterion performance, which may be successfully completing a course of training, proficiency on the job, job satisfaction, or probability of qualifying for promotion to a higher level job that requires the experience of the hiring-in job.

The only disadvantages of this method are that (1) it takes more time than other methods, because of the necessary interval between initial testing and the later assessment of performance, and (2) no direct benefit in employee selection can be gained from the test results in the first validation group of applicants, as their scores are not used in hiring, and, if there is some prior evidence of the test's validity for similar criteria, this information can have no effect on the initial hiring decisions.

Method 2. The second method gets around these disadvantages of the first method. Employees already on the job are tested and their scores are correlated with assessments of their job performance. This correlation is best described as a *restricted* validity coefficient. It is valuable information, but it usually underestimates the true validity of the test because of the restriction of range of test scores and of the criterion measure. Present employees to some extent have already been selected for success on the job. The least successful have quit or been fired. If there is a correlation between test scores and job performance, we may presume that the on-the-job selection process by and large would have eliminated persons with lower test scores. When the range of predictor scores and criterion measures is thus restricted, the correlation between them is necessarily shrunken and may greatly underestimate the validity that the test would have if it were used in the initial selection of job applicants. The effect of restriction of range is seen most strikingly in highly selective colleges. If all applicants with a high school diploma were indiscriminantly admitted to the college, the college aptitude test scores would correlate very highly with grades and persistence to graduation, assuming that the college maintains its academic standards. But, when admissions are limited only to students who earned excellent grades in high school and obtained high scores on the college aptitude test, the scores will show relatively little correlation with success in college.

In general, a test that has been used as the basis for selection cannot then be adequately validated on the selected group. This is especially true when there is a non-linear relationship between test scores and the criterion, as when the test score acts as a threshold variable, discriminating well between those who fail and those who succeed, but not discriminating well between varying degrees of success. This is often the case when success on the job depends on a number of traits, each of which is necessary but not sufficient and only one of which is measured by the predictor test. For example, a person with poor pitch discrimination will not succeed as a violinist, whatever other assets he may possess, and so unsuccessful violin students could be confidently predicted by a test of pitch discrimination alone. But prediction of degree of success at the violin would be only very weak for pupils with good pitch discrimination, because talent for the violin involves many other aptitudes and personal qualities as well.

Method 3.   The third method is usually used only in choosing or designing a suitable test to predict a particular criterion, but it may be the sole method of test validation when selection of applicants is clearly essential but validity studies of the first two types are not feasible. Selecting the first astronauts is a good example of the necessity of careful selection of personnel in the absence of any validation of the selection tests in terms of later actual performance.

The best method in such a case is systematic analysis of the job or criterion performance into its various component knowledge and skills and selection (or construction) of validated tests of these components of the criterion performance. For example, in the judgment of psychologists trained in "task analysis," the job may require perceptual speed, motor coordination, and the capacity quickly to grasp and interpret numerical information presented simultaneously on an instrument control panel. The selection battery then will include tests of these abilities and any others that the job analysis suggests are important in successful performance, including perhaps certain physical attributes and personality traits.

What cannot be determined in this type of analysis are the ideal weights that should be assigned to each of the component measures to achieve maximal validity in predicting final performance. (Determining the ideal weights to give every subtest in the total predictor score is completely possible by method 1 and, to a limited extent, by method 2.)

Also, it should be emphasized that selecting predictor tests on the basis of job analysis is really a psychologically sophisticated art involving experience and good judgment concerning the higher-order cognitive abilities required by the person to integrate the more obvious subskills revealed by job analysis. The capacity to integrate a number of subskills effectively may be a more important source of individual differences in the criterion performance than are individual differences in the separate subskills per se. This kind of general integrative capacity is usually best measured by tests that are highly loaded in what we have termed g, such as most tests of general intelligence.

Method 4.   Another method, which is better viewed merely as an aid to finding potentially useful selection tests rather than as a means of validating them, is to look for tests that show differences, on the average, between successful employees in different kinds of jobs (or students in different kinds of colleges). If the average test scores differ significantly for persons who are successful in different jobs, it is evident that the test measures factors relevant to job selection, success, and possibly satisfaction and persistence in the job. If test scores do not show significant differences, on the average, between persons in quite different jobs, it is less likely that they will have substantial validity for predicting success in any specific job.

Multiple Prediction

Very often in practice a validity coefficient is based on a *multiple correlation* (symbolized as R) rather than on a simple correlation (r) between a single test and the criterion. A multiple correlation is the correlation between (1) a best-weighted composite score from a number of different tests (called the predictor variables) and (2) the criterion. If the two or more different predictor variables in the composite are well chosen, the multiple correlation, *R,* of the composite score with the criterion may be appreciably larger than the simple correlation, *r,* of any one of the predictor tests with the criterion.

The predictor tests that work best in combination are those that are not highly correlated with one another but are each separately correlated significantly with the criterion. Even if each test separately has only a quite moderate or even low correlation with the criterion, the tests in combination may correlate very substantially with the criterion, provided that the tests are not highly correlated among themselves. For a multiple correlation to be worthwhile, one needs a number of predictor tests that do not overlap too much in the abilities that they measure. Thus each test measures some aspect of ability relevant to the criterion that is not measured by any of the other tests in the combination of predictors.

The scores on each of the several predictor tests are combined into a composite score in such a way as to maximize the multiple correlation between the composite score and the criterion. The statistical device for achieving this is called a multiple regression equation. The method, which is mathematically quite complex, is explicated in most statistical textbooks. The main aim of the method is to determine precisely the optimum values (called *regression coefficients*) by which to weight each of the predictor scores so as to make the composite score (i.e., the sum of the separate weighted predictor scores) have the highest correlation with the criterion.

The multiple correlation is rarely increased significantly by adding in more tests beyond the first few, because there is diminishing likelihood that any new test added to the composite will measure any appreciable part of the criterion-relevant abilities that are not already included in the first few tests. The statistical technique of multiple regression, in fact, permits the investigator optimally to select from a very large number of tests the few tests that are capable of maximizing the prediction of the criterion. It has been amply demonstrated that even the most expert human judgment and intuition cannot compete with the precision of the multiple regression equation as a means for choosing and weighting the final combination of tests (or other variables) that can best predict any given criterion (Meehl, 1954).

A multiple *R* validity coefficient is interpreted in exactly the same way as a simple *r* validity coefficient.

Concurrent Validity

This label has been used in the testing literature to refer to two quite distinct types of validity. It is always confusing in science when different concepts are given the same label. The remedy is simply to redefine or delimit old definitions and consistently stick to the new definition.

"Concurrent validity" traditionally has referred to (1) the correlation between a test and a criterion when both measurements are obtained at nearly the same point in time (as when a scholastic aptitude test and scholastic achievement test are administered on the same day or within a few days) and (2) the correlation between a new, unvalidated test and another test of already established validity.

The first case is really a form of criterion validity, that is, a correlation between a test and a criterion. A test's criterion validity can be studied as a function of the temporal interval between giving persons the test and measuring their criterion performance. The temporal interval between test and criterion should be an essential part of reporting the criterion validity of any test. The interval over which a test will predict a criterion, and with how much precision, is a wholly empirical matter. One could label criterion validity *predictive* criterion validity when there is a reasonably long interval between the test and the criterion, but this would be merely an arbitrary rather than a conceptual distinction, as the interval between test and criterion is a continuous variable.

Therefore, the term concurrent validity should be used only to refer to the second case, that is, the correlation of a previously unvalidated test with an already validated test.

There are dangers in this type of validation. The risk is perhaps least when the unvalidated test is merely a parallel form or shortened version of the validated test, as when only a few of the eleven subscales of the Wechsler Intelligence Scale are used to determine the Full Scale IQ.

Concurrent validation may be resorted to, with greater risk, by finding a shorter, more efficient test, or one that is easier to administer, that can be shown to correlate highly with a much longer or more cumbersome test of established validity for the criterion of interest. Thus group-administered tests are sometimes validated against tests that require individual administration.

Concurrent validity rests on the soundness of the inference that, since the first test correlates highly with the second test and the second test correlates with the criterion, the first test is also correlated with the criterion. It is essentially this question: If we know to what extent A is correlated with B, and we know to what extent B is correlated with C, how precisely can we infer to what extent A is correlated with C? The degree of risk in this inference can be best understood in terms of the *range* within which the actual criterion validity coefficient would fall when a new test is validated in terms of its correlation with a validated test. Call the scores on the unvalidated test U, scores on the validated test V, and measures on the criterion C. Then r_{VC}, the correlation between V and C, is the *criterion validity* of test V; and r_{UV}, the correlation between U and V, is the *concurrent validity* of test U. The crucial question, then, is what precisely can we infer concerning r_{UC}, that is, the probable criterion validity of test U?

If we know r_{VC} and r_{UV}, the upper and lower limits of the possible range of values of r_{UC} are given by the following formulas:

$$\text{Upper limit of } r_{UC} = r_{VC}r_{UV} + \sqrt{r_{VC}^2 r_{UV}^2 - r_{VC}^2 - r_{UV}^2 + 1}$$

$$\text{Lower limit of } r_{UC} = r_{VC}r_{UV} - \sqrt{r_{VC}^2 r_{UV}^2 - r_{VC}^2 - r_{UV}^2 + 1}$$

It may come as a sad surprise to many to see how very wide is the range of possible values of r_{UC} for any given combination of values of r_{VC} and r_{UV}. The ranges of r_{UC} are shown in Table 8.1, from which it is clear that concurrent validity inspires confidence only when the two tests are very highly correlated and the one test has a quite high criterion validity. Because it is rare to find criterion validities much higher than about .50, one can easily see the risk in depending on coefficients of concurrent validity. The risk is greatly lessened, however, when the two tests are parallel forms or one is a shortened form of the other, because both tests will then have approximately the same factor composition, which means that all the abilities measured by the first test that are correlated with the criterion

Table 8.1. Upper and lower limits of the possible range of criterion validity coefficients (r_{UC}) for test U, when the criterion validity of test V is r_{VC} and the concurrent validity of test U is r_{UV}.

r_{UV} (or r_{VC})	r_{VC} (or r_{UV})								
	.10	.20	.30	.40	.50	.60	.70	.80	.90
.95	.41	.49	.58	.67	.75	.82	.89	.95	.99
	−.21	−.11	−.01	.09	.20	.32	.44	.57	.72
.90	.52	.61	.69	.76	.83	.89	.94	.98	1.00
	−.34	−.25	−.15	−.04	.07	.19	.32	.46	.62
.85	.61	.69	.76	.82	.88	.93	.97	1.00	.99
	−.44	−.35	−.25	−.14	−.03	.09	.22	.36	.53
.80	.68	.75	.81	.87	.92	.96	.99	1.00	.98
	−.52	−.43	−.33	−.23	−.12	.00	.13	.28	.46
.75	.73	.80	.85	.91	.95	.98	1.00	1.00	.96
	−.58	−.50	−.41	−.31	−.20	−.08	.05	.20	.39
.70	.78	.84	.89	.93	.97	.99	1.00	1.00	.94
	−.64	−.56	−.47	−.37	−.27	−.15	−.02	.28	.32
.65	.82	.87	.92	.96	.98	1.00	1.00	.97	.92
	−.69	−.61	−.53	−.44	−.33	−.22	−.09	.06	.25
.60	.85	.90	.94	.97	.99	1.00	.99	.96	.89
	−.73	−.66	−.58	−.49	−.39	−.28	−.15	.00	.19

also exist in the second test. The two tests should thus have fairly comparable correlations with the criterion, which is a necessary inference to justify concurrent validity.

Construct Validity

Although criterion validity is the most important kind of validity in the practical use of tests, *construct validity* is the most important from a scientific standpoint. The idea of construct validity is more difficult to explain. It concerns our attempt scientifically to understand, in psychological terms, what the test measures. For criterion validity we need not have this understanding. If the test predicts the criterion, that is all we need to know for it to be potentially useful in educational and vocational counseling and personnel selection. We can use the test's criterion validity to advantage without ever needing to understand what it involves in psychological terms.

Construct validity becomes a consideration as soon as we have some theory (or "construct") as to the psychological nature of the trait that we wish to measure. A theoretical formulation in psychology, as in any other science, is a formal set of propositions about the nature of something, from which we can logically deduce certain consequences or hypotheses, given certain conditions. A hypothesis, usually in the form of a prediction of what will happen under certain specified conditions, can be put to an empirical test to determine its truth or falsity. The theory from which the hypotheses are derived is progressively modified by the results of these empirical tests of the hypotheses. The greater the range and variety of the hypotheses that are borne out by methodologically sound investigations, the more credence we have in the theory. This of course assumes that the tested hypotheses are really proper deductions from the theory itself.

A theory about a psychological trait calls for a great deal of this kind of hypothesis-testing research. First, it is necessary to determine whether such a trait can even be claimed to exist, because it is possible to posit a trait (i.e., a more or less consistent and enduring constellation of behavioral tendencies) and not be able to adduce any objective evidence of its existence. The next step is to discover the psychological nature of the trait.

A test devised to measure the trait is said to show construct validity if the test predicts the behavior in specific situations that would be deduced from our theory of the trait. For example, if our theory of intelligence involves the idea of an ability to deal effectively with complexity in any form, we might then hypothesize that an intelligence test should be a better predictor of performance on complex jobs than on simpler jobs. We could then ask a group of judges to rank a number of jobs in terms of their complexity. Finally, we would correlate our intelligence tests with employees' performance ratings in these various jobs. If the correlation increases as a function of the job's rank order in judged complexity, we would say that the intelligence test scores behave as our theory of intelligence should predict. Such a finding would be evidence for the test's construct validity as a measure of intelligence.

The task of construct validation is never really completed. A test's construct validity is further enhanced by every such theoretical prediction that is borne out in fact.

Factor analysis is another means of demonstrating a test's construct validity. If the factors that emerge in a factor analysis of a large battery of measurements are unambiguous and well established, and a new test has a high loading on one of the factors, the test is said to show *factorial validity*. This is a form of construct validity, because factors may be viewed as theoretical constructs used to explain the sources of individual differences in a variety of psychological measurements.

Construct validity is most important for tests that claim to measure some broad psychological trait and for which the demonstration of validity in terms of the test's correlation with any *single* criterion would be either inadequate or impossible.

The term ''face validity'' is frequently heard in discussions of tests, but it is actually a misnomer, since it has only a subjective and incidental relationship to the other forms of validity, that is, the four *C*'s. It refers to the degree to which the test items give the *appearance,* in the eyes of the person taking the test or of the person interpreting the test scores, of being a reasonable and appropriate indicator of what the test is supposed to measure.

Such appearance may or may not be related to the actual validity of the test, which is a matter for empirical determination. However, face validity could influence a person's attitude toward the test and affect his effort and test performance. Especially in the domains of ability and achievement, it is advantageous for the test items to have the appearance of being reasonable and appropriate questions for what the test purports to assess. Tests or test items that fail to meet this condition are said to have poor face validity. Such items make easy targets for popular ridicule. No test, of course, can stand on mere face validity alone; but it is possible that an objectively valid test may be scorned if it is deficient in face validity. Test makers now are paying more attention to this public relations aspect of people's attitudes toward tests, which depend to a considerable extent on the test's face validity.

The Interpretation of a Validity Coefficient

There are three main ways of interpreting a validity coefficient. Each gives a view from a different perspective. The perspective of choice depends on one's purpose in using the validity coefficient. The three types of interpretations of validity are (1) improvement over chance prediction of a point estimate, (2) prediction of odds for success, and (3) prediction of the efficiency of performance.

Improvement over Chance Prediction. This interpretation of validity is based on the standard error of estimate, which we have encountered before (p. 281), as $SE_{est} = \sigma_c \sqrt{(1 - r_{xc}^2)[(N - 1)/(N - 2)]}$, where σ_c is the standard deviation of all the criterion measures, r_{xc} is the validity coefficient, that is, the correlation between test scores (x) and the criterion (c), and N is the sample size. (The expression $(N - 1)/(N - 2)$ may be omitted from the formula when $N > 200$.) SE_{est} is the standard deviation of the actual criterion measures around the *predicted* values of the criterion (i.e., the regression line). One can see from the formula that, if the validity is zero, SE_{est} is equal to σ_c and therefore that using the test does not make for better than chance prediction. The percentage of improvement in accuracy of prediction by using the test scores, over mere chance prediction, therefore, is equal to $100[1 - (SE_{est}/\sigma_c)]$. We can rewrite this formula solely in terms of the validity coefficient: $100 (1 - \sqrt{1 - r_{xc}^2})$. This value is known as the *index of forecasting efficiency.*

It is important to note that the *index of forecasting efficiency* (IFE) tells us the percentage of improvement over chance in the accuracy of prediction when we are predicting *a specific point on the scale of criterion measurement*. To predict the *precise* value of an individual's criterion performance requires very high validity if the prediction is to be a marked improvement over chance. (The best *chance* prediction is the same value for every person and is the mean of the distribution of all criterion measurements.) To predict 50 percent better than chance (i.e., an IFE of 50 percent), we would need a validity coefficient of .866. In practice, however, most validity coefficients do not exceed .50 or .60, and usually are even lower. Yet a validity coefficient of .60 corresponds to an IFE of only 20 percent.

In terms of the index of forecasting efficiency, then, a realistic validity coefficient does not look very impressive, and validities below about .50 would hardly seem worth considering. But recall that the IFE concerns the accuracy of predicting a *specific point* on the criterion scale. This is an extremely stringent demand on any prediction test, and one that, in practice, is almost never required. For example, we are much more often concerned with predicting who will succeed or fail on a particular criterion, but we are not so concerned with predicting the specific rank order in performance on the criterion among those who fail or among those who succeed. If we can predict that Bill and Sue will both easily succeed on the job, we may not care, as far as our selection procedure is concerned, whether Bill or Sue performs better.

Therefore, when we are not primarily concerned with the accuracy of prediction at every single point throughout the entire range of measurement of the criterion, the index of forecasting efficiency is a much too stringent interpretation of the validity coefficient; it grossly underestimates the benefit gained from using the test in selection. For this reason the index of forecasting efficiency is very seldom considered in the practical use of tests in educational and personnel selection. It does not tell the test user what he or she usually most wants to know. For this we turn to the following more practical interpretations of validity.

Prediction of Odds for Success.　In the practical use of tests for selection we are usually concerned with the test's accuracy of predicting success or failure on the criterion. The dividing line between success and failure is defined in terms of some level of performance on the criterion, such as ability to obtain passing marks in a course of training or to perform on a job in a way deemed satisfactory by the employer. The test user tries to determine the best *cutoff score* on the predictor test (or combination of tests) to maximize the selection of applicants who will prove successful, given the constraints of (1) the number of persons who can be selected and (2) the total number of applicants. The ratio of condition 1 to condition 2 is termed the *selection ratio*. It is expressed as a proportion and is a crucial factor in the interpretation of a test's validity coefficient. The one other crucial parameter in the interpretation of validity is the *failure rate* on the criterion performance among selectees who were selected entirely without reference to their scores on the test in question. If there are no failures on the criterion, there is of course no need for the selection test in the first place. The test could not improve on whatever selective factors were already in effect. It should be remembered that applicants for any particular college or occupation are usually an already highly self-selected group with respect to the relevant requirements. The crucial question is how much the use of a test will improve selection (in terms of decreasing the failure rate) over and above whatever other selective factors are already operating.

The optimal cutoff score on a selection test with *perfect* validity would divide the pool of applicants into two groups: (1) those who score above the cutoff and *succeed* on the criterion (called *positives*) and (2) those who score below the cutoff and *fail* on the criterion (called *hits*). But when the test's validity is less than perfect, there will be created two other groups of applicants: (3) those who score above the cutoff but fail on the criterion (called *misses*) and (4) those who score below the cutoff but succeed on the criterion (called *false positives*). A test is regarded as valid to the extent that it minimizes the proportions of misses and false positives (and, conversely, maximizes the proportion of selectees who succeed on the criterion) for any given selection ratio (i.e., the proportion of the applicant pool that can be selected).

Taylor and Russell (1939) have devised a set of tables that take all these parameters into account to show the proportion of successes that should result from the use of a selection test with a given validity. One of the Taylor–Russell tables is presented in Table 8.2. The figures in the body of the table are the proportion of successes that would be expected for a given test validity and a given selection ratio, when the proportion of successes without selection on the basis of test scores is .60. The selection ratio determines the location of the cutoff score: the smaller the proportion of applicants that one needs, the higher can be the cutoff score on the selection test, and the greater is the payoff (in terms of the proportion of successful selectees) for any given validity coefficient.

A greater appreciation of the practical meaning of a given validity coefficient may be had by converting the proportions of success in the Taylor–Russell tables into the predicted odds for success when the test is or is not used. If the success rate without test

Table 8.2. Proportion of successes expected through the use of a test of given validity, when the proportion of successes is .60 without use of the test. (From Taylor & Russell, 1939, p. 576)

Validity	Selection Ratio										
	.05	.10	.20	.30	.40	.50	.60	.70	.80	.90	.95
.00	.60	.60	.60	.60	.60	.60	.60	.60	.60	.60	.60
.05	.64	.63	.63	.62	.62	.62	.61	.61	.61	.60	.60
.10	.68	.67	.65	.64	.64	.63	.63	.62	.61	.61	.60
.15	.71	.70	.68	.67	.66	.65	.64	.63	.62	.61	.61
.20	.75	.73	.71	.69	.67	.66	.65	.64	.63	.62	.61
.25	.78	.76	.73	.71	.69	.68	.66	.65	.63	.62	.61
.30	.82	.79	.76	.73	.71	.69	.68	.66	.64	.62	.61
.35	.85	.82	.78	.75	.73	.71	.69	.67	.65	.63	.62
.40	.88	.85	.81	.78	.75	.73	.70	.68	.66	.63	.62
.45	.90	.87	.83	.80	.77	.74	.72	.69	.66	.64	.62
.50	.93	.90	.86	.82	.79	.76	.73	.70	.67	.64	.62
.55	.95	.92	.88	.84	.81	.78	.75	.71	.68	.64	.62
.60	.96	.94	.90	.87	.83	.80	.76	.73	.69	.65	.63
.65	.98	.96	.92	.89	.85	.82	.78	.74	.70	.65	.63
.70	.99	.97	.94	.91	.87	.84	.80	.75	.71	.66	.63
.75	.99	.99	.96	.93	.90	.86	.81	.77	.71	.66	.63
.80	1.00	.99	.98	.95	.92	.88	.83	.78	.72	.66	.63
.85	1.00	1.00	.99	.97	.95	.91	.86	.80	.73	.66	.63
.90	1.00	1.00	1.00	.99	.97	.94	.88	.82	.74	.67	.63
.95	1.00	1.00	1.00	1.00	.99	.97	.92	.84	.75	.67	.63
1.00	1.00	1.00	1.00	1.00	1.00	1.00	1.00	.86	.75	.67	.63

selection is .60, then the predicted odds in favor of any person's succeeding is in the ratio of .60 to .40, or 1.5 to 1, regardless of the selection ratio. But say that we use a test with a validity of .40 and the selection ratio is .30. Then the predicted odds in favor of any selectee succeeding will be in the ratio of .78 to .22, or 3.5 to 1. In other words, the use of a test with a validity of .40 in this situation would increase the odds in favor of success by 3.5 to 1.5, or 2.33 times greater than the odds in favor of success if we had not used the test. The higher the validity and the lower the selection ratio, the more one can increase the odds in favor of success by using the test in selection. With a validity of .60 (which is about the top validity for college entrance exams) and a selection ratio of .10, the odds in favor of succeeding are almost 16 to 1, which is more than ten times better odds than if no selection test had been used. It can be seen that *test validity gains greater potency as the selection ratio becomes more stringent.*

Another set of tables has been devised to show the probability of success for persons selected from different deciles in the distribution of scores on the selection test (Wesman, 1953). (Deciles divide the total frequency distribution equally into tenths, going from the lowest 10 percent of the scores, decile 1, to the highest 10 percent, decile 10.) Table 8.3 shows that percentage of successes for persons selected from different deciles when the failure rates are 20 percent, 30 percent, or 50 percent and the test validity (*r*) ranges from .30 to .60.

From Table 8.3 we can determine the predicted odds in favor of success for persons scoring in any given decile on the selection test. When the overall failure rate is 20 percent

Table 8.3. Percentage of successful persons in each decile on test score. (From Wesman, 1953)

Standing on the Test		When the Total Percentage of Failures is 20%, and				When the Total Percentage of Failures is 30%, and				When the Total Percentage of Failures is 50%, and			
Percentile	Decile	r = .30	r = .40	r = .50	r = .60	r = .30	r = .40	r = .50	r = .60	r = .30	r = .40	r = .50	r = .60
90–99	10	92%	95%	97%	99%	86%	91%	94%	97%	71%	78%	84%	90%
80–89	9	89	91	94	97	81	85	89	92	63	68	73	78
70–79	8	86	89	91	94	78	81	84	88	59	62	65	69
60–69	7	84	86	88	91	75	77	80	83	55	57	59	61
50–59	6	82	84	85	87	72	74	75	77	52	52	53	54
40–49	5	80	81	82	83	70	70	70	71	48	48	47	46
30–39	4	78	77	77	78	67	66	65	64	45	43	41	39
20–29	3	75	73	72	71	63	61	59	56	42	38	35	31
10–19	2	71	68	64	61	59	55	50	45	37	33	28	22
1–9	1	63	56	49	40	50	43	35	27	29	23	16	10

and the test validity is .60, for example, the odds in favor of success for persons in the 10th decile are 99 to 1, as compared with the odds of 0.67 to 1 for persons in the 1st decile. The 10th decile's chances of success are 148 times greater than the 1st decile's chances. If no test were used, the odds for all persons would be 4 to 1 that they would succeed. Notice how markedly the odds are increased by selecting persons in the higher deciles. Even when the test validity is as low as .30, the odds favoring success for selectees in the tenth decile are 11.5 to 1, which is almost three times better odds than if no selection test were used. If one views test validity as would a gambler trying to find the best odds to maximize the payoff on his or her bets, even a test with a quite low validity would yield odds favoring the gambler that are impressively better than the base rate of success if no selection test were used. Gamblers would all be billionnaires if they could predict half as well as do tests with validities even much lower than .30. It is also worth noting that the typical validity coefficients of psychological tests compare quite favorably with the reliability of medical diagnoses, which is near .40 (Cronbach, 1960, p. 349).

Validity as a Proportional Increase in Criterion Performance. Another interpretation of validity is in terms of the average level of productivity, proficiency, or other index of performance that would result from using a selection test of a given validity, as compared with not using the test. Brogden (1946) has proved the following relationship:

$$r_{xc} = \frac{S - U}{P - U},$$

where

r_{xc} = the test's validity (i.e., the correlation r between the test scores x and the criterion measures c),

S = the mean level of performance of the persons who were selected on the basis of test scores,

U = the mean level of performance of persons who were selected at random (i.e., without the aid of the test), and

P = the mean level of performance of *perfectly* selected persons, as would be the case if $r_{xc} = 1$.

For example, say that we were selecting salesmen and that the performance criterion is the salesman's average number of sales per month over a period of one year. And say that we need to hire 50 salesmen from a pool of 200 job applicants. We could then do the following experiment. First, give the test to all the applicants. Then, draw 50 applicants at random; they are group U, that is, unselected by the test. Then, from the remaining 150 applicants we would select the 50 with the highest scores on the test; they are group S. Then we employ all 200 applicants and determine the average monthly sales of group U and of group S, which are, say, 40 and 30 sales per month, respectively. Finally, we determine the average monthly sales of the 50 salesmen who actually turned out to have the highest sales records; they are group P, that is, the 50 best applicants who hypothetically would have been chosen if we had used a *perfect* selection test. Say that their average sales are 60 per month. The validity of our selection test, then, can be expressed as the proportional improvement in employee performance over the base level resulting from using the test, as compared with a hypothetical test of perfect predictive validity. Thus, in the example,

$$\text{Validity} = \frac{S - U}{P - U} = \frac{40 - 30}{60 - 30} = \frac{1}{3},$$

which is to say that employee selection by means of this particular test increases the average level of performance $33\frac{1}{3}$ percent over what it would be without the use of the test. This is numerically the very same validity coefficient that is usually defined as the correlation between test scores and criterion measures. The $33\frac{1}{3}$ percent improvement in employee performance or productivity, which in this example could be achieved by hiring the 50 applicants who scored highest on a test having a validity of only .33, would not be regarded as a trivial gain by most employers.

Brown and Ghiselli (1953) have expressed criterion performance as a standard score scale with a mean of zero and standard deviation of one when there has been no selection of applicants. The effects of selection (for any given selection ratio) by means of a test (with any given validity coefficient) can then be expressed in terms of the mean increase in criterion performance (in standard score units) over what it would be if the test were not used. These values computed by Brown and Ghiselli are presented in Table 8.4. For example, if one hired the highest-scoring 50 percent of applicants on the selection test (i.e., a selection ratio of .50), and, if the test's validity coefficient is .25, then the average level of job performance of these selected employees would be 0.2 standard deviations higher than the average performance level of an unselected group. But notice that, even if we had *perfect* validity in selection and a selection ratio of .50, the average performance of the selected employees would be 0.8 standard deviations higher than that of an un-selected group. Thus, selection by means of our test (with a validity of only .25) results in an average employee performance gain over unselected employees that is 25 percent as good as the maximal selection procedure could possibly yield. Again, as with Brogden's formula, the *test's validity* ($\times$ 100) *may be interpreted as the average percentage gain in criterion performance resulting from use of the test in selection.*

Factors Influencing Validity

One may wonder why there is a "prediction ceiling" such that validity coefficients seldom exceed .50 or .60 and in most cases are considerably lower. Several main factors have been found to influence the validity coefficient.

Criterion Reliability. Very often the criterion is not measured with sufficient precision or consistency to permit any other variable to correlate with it highly. The highest possible validity coefficient cannot exceed the square root of the reliability of the criterion measurements. The criterion, when consisting of grades or ratings, often has considerably lower reliability than the predictor test itself. Considering the reliabilities of both the test and the criterion, the highest possible validity coefficient is the square root of the product of the two reliabilities, that is, $\sqrt{r_{tt} \times r_{cc}}$.

Restriction of Range. The possible size of the correlation between any two variables is affected by the range or spread of scores on each variable. For example, we would expect to find a much lower correlation between height and weight among the

Table 8.4. Mean standard criterion score of selected persons in relation to test validity and selection ratio.
(From Brown & Ghiselli, 1953, p. 342)

Selection Ratio	Validity Coefficient																				
	.00	.05	.10	.15	.20	.25	.30	.35	.40	.45	.50	.55	.60	.65	.70	.75	.80	.85	.90	.95	1.00
.05	.00	.10	.21	.31	.42	.52	.62	.73	.83	.94	1.04	1.14	1.25	1.35	1.46	1.56	1.66	1.77	1.87	1.98	2.08
.10	.00	.09	.18	.26	.35	.44	.53	.62	.70	.78	.88	.97	1.05	1.14	1.23	1.32	1.41	1.49	1.58	1.67	1.76
.15	.00	.08	.15	.23	.31	.39	.46	.54	.62	.70	.77	.85	.93	1.01	1.08	1.16	1.24	1.32	1.39	1.47	1.55
.20	.00	.07	.14	.21	.28	.35	.42	.49	.56	.63	.70	.77	.84	.91	.98	1.05	1.12	1.19	1.26	1.33	1.40
.25	.00	.06	.13	.19	.25	.32	.38	.44	.51	.57	.63	.70	.76	.82	.89	.95	1.01	1.08	1.14	1.20	1.27
.30	.00	.06	.12	.17	.23	.29	.35	.40	.46	.52	.58	.64	.69	.75	.81	.87	.92	.98	1.04	1.10	1.16
.35	.00	.05	.11	.16	.21	.26	.32	.37	.42	.48	.53	.58	.63	.69	.74	.79	.84	.90	.95	1.00	1.06
.40	.00	.05	.10	.15	.19	.24	.29	.34	.39	.44	.48	.53	.58	.63	.68	.73	.77	.82	.87	.92	.97
.45	.00	.04	.09	.13	.18	.22	.26	.31	.35	.40	.44	.48	.53	.57	.62	.66	.70	.75	.79	.84	.88
.50	.00	.04	.08	.12	.16	.20	.24	.28	.32	.36	.40	.44	.48	.52	.56	.60	.64	.68	.72	.76	.80
.55	.00	.04	.07	.11	.14	.18	.22	.25	.29	.32	.36	.40	.43	.47	.50	.54	.58	.61	.65	.68	.72
.60	.00	.03	.06	.10	.13	.16	.19	.23	.26	.29	.32	.35	.39	.42	.45	.48	.52	.55	.58	.61	.64
.65	.00	.03	.06	.09	.11	.14	.17	.20	.23	.26	.28	.31	.34	.37	.40	.43	.46	.48	.51	.54	.57
.70	.00	.02	.05	.07	.10	.12	.15	.17	.20	.22	.25	.27	.30	.32	.35	.37	.40	.42	.45	.47	.50
.75	.00	.02	.04	.06	.08	.11	.13	.15	.17	.19	.21	.23	.25	.27	.30	.32	.33	.36	.38	.40	.42
.80	.00	.02	.03	.05	.07	.09	.11	.12	.14	.16	.18	.19	.21	.22	.25	.26	.28	.30	.32	.33	.35
.85	.00	.01	.03	.04	.05	.07	.08	.10	.11	.12	.14	.15	.16	.18	.19	.20	.22	.23	.25	.26	.27
.90	.00	.01	.02	.03	.04	.05	.06	.07	.08	.09	.10	.11	.12	.13	.14	.15	.16	.17	.18	.19	.20
.95	.00	.01	.01	.02	.02	.03	.03	.04	.04	.05	.05	.06	.07	.07	.08	.08	.09	.09	.10	.10	.11

players on a professional basketball team than in the general population, in which there is much greater variability in height and weight. If applicants are already highly self-selected on job-relevant characteristics, then a predictor test cannot show as high a validity coefficient as it would in an unselected group. Validity coefficients may even be reduced to zero if the test scores themselves are the basis for stringent selection and then are correlated with the criterion grades or performance ratings. If the test has high predictive validity and succeeds in eliminating applicants who would not excel on the criterion, then we should expect to find a low correlation between test scores and criterion performance in a highly selected group. The correlation between test scores and criterion in such a case is not a proper estimate of the test's validity. Yet many reported validity coefficients are determined on test-selected groups and consequently underestimate the test's potential validity.

Criterion Contamination.   In determining validity, it is essential that the criterion ratings be made "blind," that is, without the rater's having any knowledge whatsoever of the ratee's score on the selection test. Such contamination usually inflates the validity coefficient.

Variable Criteria.   The criterion itself may not actually be the same for all selectees, which may drastically lower the validity coefficient. Examples of this are grades in school or college. Grading standards differ from one teacher to another, from one course to another, and from one department to another. A grade of A in one course may be equivalent to a C in another, in terms of the level of aptitude and effort required. Also, weaker students tend to seek out the easy courses and the teachers reputed to have the most lenient grading standards. These factors all work against high correlations between scholastic aptitude test scores and grades.

A similar effect occurs in ratings of job performance when the rated employees have somewhat different duties that may make for different rating standards.

Training versus Final Level of Performance.   It is a consistent finding that validity coefficients are higher for predicting success in training than for predicting the final level of performance reached after training and experience on the job. In a thorough survey of the reported validities of many tests in numerous and varied training and employment settings, Ghiselli (1966, p. 125) concluded: "Taking all jobs as a whole . . . it can be said that by and large the maximal power of tests to predict success in training is of the order of .50, and to predict success on the job itself is of the order of .35. . . ." The range of the average validity coefficients was .27 to .59 for training criteria and .16 to .46 for job proficiency criteria. Abilities that are important in the early stages of learning a new set of skills, and that may be measured well by aptitude tests, are sometimes of much less importance in the performance of the skills once they are learned and have become well practiced. The training phase may involve skills, such as reading ability, that are not even a part of the final job. In some cases, quite different tests may be needed to predict speed of progress in training and final level of job performance, because these two aspects can involve different abilities and personality characteristics.

Usually, new learning makes greater demands on *g* than does the final practiced performance, and most aptitude tests have a fairly substantial *g* loading. As a simple example, think of when you first learned to drive an automobile. It took all your concentration and considerable mental effort to recall and coordinate in sequence all the correct actions that were explained by the instructor. The ease and quickness with which the learner "catches on" could be predicted to some extent by a *g*-loaded paper-and-pencil test. But with prolonged practice the task of driving becomes less and less mentally demanding. One's final level of driving performance will be more related to personality factors and very specific aptitudes (such as developing a "feel" for the performance capabilities of the vehicle itself) than to the g of mental ability per se. And so it is with training on many jobs. If the training itself is not too extensive or costly to the employer, and if trainability is not highly correlated with the final level of proficiency, one may question the use of selection tests that predict only success in training.

In predicting success in training, the validity of the predictor test will depend also on the form of instruction. Success in training that emphasizes abstract and conceptual understanding of what is being taught will be more predictable from g-loaded tests than will training that emphasizes practice on specific component skills and imitative learning in an apprenticeship fashion. In one training program, for example, changes in the methods of instruction reduced the validity of a mathematical aptitude test in predicting success in training from better than .50 to approximately zero, although under the modified instruction, those who were low in mathematical aptitude took 50 percent longer to complete the training. Most of these low-math-aptitude trainees would have failed the course altogether under the old method of instruction (Ford & Meyer, 1966).

Correlates of IQ and g-Loaded Tests

It would be practically impossible to review all the published evidence on the validity of all types of mental tests, even in a volume twice the length of this book. Validity coefficients are highly specific to the particular test, the particular criterion with which the test is correlated, and the particular population involved. Generally the best sources of information on the validity of any published test are the publisher's test manual and the *Mental Measurements Yearbook* edited by Oscar K. Buros. The *MMY* contains detailed, critical reviews, often by two or more expert reviewers, of all published psychological tests. Reviewers usually pay particular attention to the nature, extent, and statistical quality of the evidence for the test's validity. Readers seeking descriptive and evaluative information on any specific test are urged to consult the *Mental Measurements Yearbook,* of which seven large volumes have appeared, along with a new volume devoted exclusively to critical reviews of all published intelligence tests.

Rather than try to summarize the evidence for the validity of numerous specialized tests, I will confine the following review to typical examples of the wide variety of well-established correlates of intelligence tests or highly g-loaded tests. All intelligence or IQ tests are highly g loaded, but not all highly g-loaded tests are labeled as intelligence tests. In recent years test publishers have often substituted new labels for intelligence tests, such as tests of "cognitive ability," "general aptitude," and "learning potential." Most all such tests are found to be highly g loaded when factor analyzed along with other tests and are virtually indistinguishable from traditional intelligence tests in item content, statistical properties, and correlations with external criteria.

IQ has more behavioral correlates than any other psychological measurement. The external correlates of IQ are an empirical fact that must be recognized regardless of one's theoretical position regarding the existence or nature of intelligence, the causes of individual differences in IQ, or the causes of the correlations between IQ and other behavioral criteria. We may gain further insights into the nature and importance of IQ by surveying

Table 8.5. Correlations between various standard intelligence tests reported in the literature. (Data from Buros, 1972, Vol. I; Matarazzo, 1972, pp. 245–246; Sattler, 1974, pp. 125, 155, 236–246, Appendix B)

Tests	Correlations[1]
Wechsler–Bellevue I ×	
Stanford–Binet (1937)	.62, .86, .89
Raven Progressive Matrices	.55
Army Alpha	.74
Army General Classification Test	.83
Kent EGY	.65, .69
Shipley–Hartford	.72, .76
Thorndike CAVD	.69
Otis	.73
Wechsler Adult Intelligence Scale ×	
Stanford–Binet	.40–.83 (.77)
Raven Progressive Matrices	.53, .72, .83
SRA Nonverbal	.81
Army General Classification Test	.74
Army Beta (Revised)	.37, .82, .83
Ammons Picture Vocabulary	.76–.84 (.83)
Peabody Picture Vocabulary	.86
Kent EGY	.70, .77
Shipley–Hartford	.73–.86 (.77)
Otis	.78
Thurstone Test of Mental Alertness	.62
Wechsler Intelligence Scale for Children ×	
Stanford–Binet (47 studies)	.43–.94 (.80)
Columbia Mental Maturity Scale	.50–.76 (.64)
Draw-a-Man	.04–.59 (.36)
Raven Progressive Matrices	.27–.91 (.15)
Quick Test	.35–.84 (.41)
Peabody Picture Vocabulary Test	.30–.84 (.63)
Pictorial Test of Intelligence	.65, .71, .75
Slosson Intelligence Test	.50–.84 (.67)
Hiskey–Nebraska Test of Learning Aptitude	.82
Stanford–Binet ×	
Peabody Picture Vocabulary (37 studies)	.22–.92 (.66)
Pictorial Test of Intelligence	.38–.78 (.69)
Columbia Mental Maturity Scale	.39–.87 (.71)
Slosson Intelligence Test	.60–.94 (.90)
Cooperative Preschool Inventory	.39–.65
Hiskey–Nebraska Test of Learning Aptitude	.78–.86
Kahn Intelligence Test	.62, .75, .83
California Test of Mental Maturity	.66–.74
Peabody Picture Vocabulary Test ×	
Pictorial Test of Intelligence	.77
Columbia Mental Maturity Scale	.53
A Variety of (24) Other Ability Tests (not including WISC and S–B)	.06–.90 (.53)
Pictorial Test of Intelligence ×	
Columbia Mental Maturity Scale	.53
Leiter International Performance ×	
S–B and WISC (8 studies)	.56–.92 (.83)

Table 8.5   (*continued*)

Tests	Correlations[1]
Lorge–Thorndike × Analysis of Learning Potential	.83
Academic Alertness × Wonderlic Army Beta AGCT	.69–.88

[1]Where more than three correlations are reported, only the range and median (in parentheses) are indicated. In some cases in the literature, the range of correlations is reported but not the median.

the variety and characteristics of the many variables that show a correlation with IQ. Measurements of human individual differences that show few or negligible correlations with other aspects of life are usually of little or no interest. There are marked and highly reliable individual differences, for example, in fingerprints and form of the outer ear, but, because these features show correlations with hardly anything else, they are of no interest to anyone, except as a reliable means of identification. The great and persistent interest in IQ, on the other hand, is a direct result of the readily perceived and undeniable fact that IQ is correlated with so many other variables that are deemed important in life by almost everyone.

   Concurrent Validity of IQ Tests.   How well do scores on different IQ tests agree with one another? Do different IQ tests measure one and the same intelligence? There are hundreds of studies of correlations between various IQ tests. Table 8.5 shows a compilation of reported correlations between some of the most well-known standardized tests of intelligence.

   It can be seen that the correlations range widely, with an overall mean of +.67. Many studies have been summarized in terms of the total range of correlations (i.e., the lowest and highest *r*'s that are found in any of the studies) and the median value of the entire set of correlations (indicated in parentheses in Table 8.5). The mean of the median values is +.77. The mean of all the lower values of the range of correlations is +.50, and the mean of all the higher values of the range is +.82. Thus the correlations among various IQ tests can be said to be most typically in the range from about +.67 to +.77. The lower limit of the range of correlations between certain tests is often the result of studies based on small samples or on atypical groups, such as retardates, psychiatric patients, college students, or other groups with a restricted range of scores. Correlations are generally higher in studies based on representative samples of the general population. Also, some of the tests showing the lowest correlations with other tests (e.g., ''Draw-a-Man'' and the ''Quick Test'') may be questioned as measures of intelligence even on the basis of other psychometric criteria than their poor correlations with a quite good test of intelligence such as the WISC.

   Correlations between IQ tests in the range from .67 to .77 are just about what one should expect if the *g* loadings of most IQ tests range from .80 to .90 and the tests have little variance other than *g* in common. The reader may recall from Chapter 6 that the correlation between any two tests can be expressed as the sum of the products of the tests' loadings on each of the common factors. By far the largest common factor in IQ tests is *g*.

Tests with g loadings in the .80 to .90 range, therefore, would show intercorrelations ranging from .64 to .81. Other common factors, such as verbal ability, would tend to raise the correlations only slightly. The fact that the median correlation between the Wechsler Intelligence Scale for Children and the Stanford–Binet in forty-seven studies is .80 suggests that these two tests have g loadings of close to .90 (i.e., $\sqrt{.80}$), which is only slightly less than the reliabilities of these tests (i.e., about .95).

It should be remembered that the correlation between tests indicates mainly the degree to which persons maintain the same relative standing on the various tests. A high correlation does not guarantee that the IQ scores themselves will be alike on every test. It is often noticed that even though individuals remain in very much the same rank order on two different IQ tests, meaning there is a high correlation between the tests, the actual IQ scores may be quite discrepant on the two tests. The discrepancies in the two IQs may show up consistently throughout the whole range, or they may differ in direction and magnitude in the lower, middle, and upper ranges of the IQ scale. Hence the various IQ scales themselves, although they may be highly correlated, are not exactly equivalent in an absolute sense. In this respect mental testing is currently in the situation similar to the measurement of distance and weight before the adoption of uniform international standards of measurement. Unfortunately, at present we have no standard IQ test corresponding to the platinum meter bar that is kept in the International Bureau of Standards in Paris.

The most common causes of the IQ scale discrepancies among various intelligence tests are the following:

1. The tests were standardized on somewhat different populations, with different absolute means or different standard deviations, or both.
2. The IQ scales were arbitrarily assigned different standard deviations. For example, the standard deviation of IQ on the Wechsler scales is 15 and on the Stanford–Binet it is 16.
3. The IQ is a standardized score on one test and on another is derived from the MA/CA ratio (which results in a variable standard deviation at different ages).
4. The IQ scores of one or both tests are not on an equal-interval scale throughout the whole range.
5. The factorial composition of the two tests is not quite the same, at all levels of difficulty. Scores in the high, medium, or low range may be more g loaded on the one test than on the other, even though both tests overall are equally g loaded.

Scholastic Achievement

In the seventy years since the publication of the Binet–Simon intelligence scale there have been thousands of studies of the correlation between intelligence test scores and scholastic performance. So generally consistent and statistically incontestable are these massive results that even the harshest critics of mental testing wholly concede the substantial relationship between IQ and scholastic achievement. They even exaggerate the relationship and claim that IQ differences reflect *nothing but* differences in educational advantages, in school, and in the home. In general, no other single fact that we can determine about a child after the age of 5 better predicts his or her future educational progress and attainments than the IQ. Children with higher IQs generally acquire more scholastic knowledge more quickly and easily, get better marks, like school better, and stay in school longer.

A detailed review of all the evidence cannot be attempted here. Readers who wish to pursue the evidence further are referred to reviews by Cattell and Butcher (1968, Ch. 3), Lavin (1965, Ch. 4), Matarazzo (1972, Ch. 12), and Tyler (1965, Ch. 5). The evidence, however, is fairly easy to summarize, because there is now so much of it that a number of firm generalizations quite clearly emerge.

Intelligence and achievement are correlated but are not synonymous. Because they are not the same thing, it should not be surprising that the correlation between them is considerably less than perfect, even when the correlation is corrected for measurement error. Even if measurements of intelligence and of scholastic achievement were found to be perfectly correlated, however, it would not necessarily mean that intelligence, as a theoretical construct, is the same thing as achievement. Correlation does not prove synonymity. Diameters and circumferences of circles are perfectly correlated, but no one would claim that they are the same thing. Many actual tests of intelligence and scholastic achievement, however, are not completely distinct; they often have many elements in common. Tests of abilities, aptitudes, and achievement can be thought of as lying on a *continuum* (in that order) that consists of the amount of specific learning and information involved in the test items. Tests of "scholastic aptitude" contain more items involving the kinds of knowledge and skills specifically taught in school than do most tests of general intelligence. Aptitude test items sample rather broadly from the domain of past achievements that are quite closely related to the future achievements that the aptitude test is specifically intended to predict. Past progress in a specific field is the best predictor of future progress in the same field. Hence the shift from the use of IQ tests to the use of scholastic aptitude tests at higher and more specialized levels of education. Increasing the proportion of test items that tap specific past academic achievements increases the test's predictive validity, the more as students advance in school and increase their scholastic skills and knowledge, as these in turn are good predictors of students' future acquisitions in the academic sphere.

It is an important fact, however, that IQ *pre*dicts about as well as it *post*dicts scholastic achievement. That is, the IQ can predict individual differences in a particular area of cognitive or scholastic achievement before the individuals have any achievement at all in that area, and even when there are no items in the IQ test that show any resemblance to the predicted achievement in specific skills or informational content. In fact, in the elementary school grades, at least, present IQ predicts future scholastic achievement slightly but significantly better than present scholastic achievement predicts future IQ (Crano, Kenny, & Campbell, 1972). But the cause-and-effect relationship between performance on intelligence tests, and even more so on scholastic aptitude tests, on the one hand, and scholastic achievement, on the other, is best thought of as working to some extent in both directions. Scholastic achievement involves more different identifiable causal factors and correlates than IQ, which is simply the single most important factor. Achievement may be thought of as the product of intelligence × motivation, emotional stability, persistence, work habits, interests and values, and certain personality traits.

Educational Level and Predictive Validity of IQ. The most frequently mentioned value of the typical correlation between IQ and scholastic achievement is .50. This is a good estimate of the overall average of all estimates of the predictive validity of IQ for scholastic achievement. To gain some sense of the degree of relationship represented by a correlation coefficient of .50, it is instructive to examine a correlation scatter diagram, as shown in Figure 8.1. The "bivariate normal" scatter plot is here divided into four sections by the regression of achievement scores on IQ (middle line) and the deviations of one standard deviation above and below the regression line, as indicated by the upper and lower broken lines. Traditionally, persons whose achievement score is more than one standard deviation above the regression line (i.e., their predicted achievement on the basis of IQ) have been referred to as "overachievers" (dots in Figure 8.1), and persons whose achievement is more than one standard deviation below their predicted scores have been called "underachievers." Actually these designations are quite arbitrary and really mean little more than the fact that IQ and achievement are far from perfectly correlated even if one corrects for measurement error. Because intelligence is not the only determinant of achievement, it is inevitable that there should be less than a perfect correlation, and hence the existence of "underachievers" and "overachievers." R. L. Thorndike (1963a) has expanded on this point.

Figure 8.1. A bivariate normal scatter diagram showing a correlation of .50, typical of correlations between scholastic achievement and IQ. "Underachievers" (circles) and "overachievers" (dots) are those persons whose achievement scores deviate more than one standard deviation from the regression line.

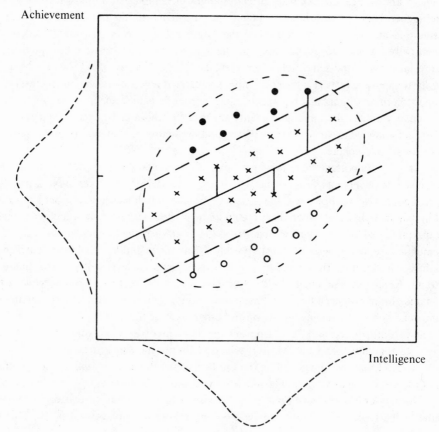

Every bit as important as the overall correlation of .50, from a psychological standpoint, is the great variation above and below this average value from one study to another. Much of this variation in the size of the correlation between IQ and scholastic achievement is quite systematic and is worth noting.

The first fact that stands out when reviewing all the evidence is that the higher that one moves up the educational ladder—from elementary school to high school, to college, and finally to graduate school—the lower in general is the correlation between IQ (or scores on scholastic aptitude tests) and indices of achievement. The typical range of most of the validities of a single IQ score for predicting academic achievement are the following for the various levels of schooling:

Elementary school	.60–.70
High school	.50–.60
College	.40–.50
Graduate school	.30–.40

The lower correlations at higher educational levels have a number of causes, which are discussed later in this chapter. But it should be emphasized that none of the causes implies in the least that intelligence becomes any less important at more advanced levels of education.

IQ Not a Threshold Variable for Scholastic Achievement.   Note that the regression line of achievement on intelligence in Figure 8.1 is linear throughout the entire range of IQ scale. This is typical of the findings of the many studies that have investigated the form of the regression of achievement on IQ. The findings are unequivocal. There is no point on the IQ scale below which or above which IQ is not positively related to achievement. This means that IQ does not act as a threshold variable with respect to scholastic achievement, as has been suggested by some of the critics of IQ tests, for example, McClelland (1958, p. 13), who wrote: "Let us admit that morons cannot do good school work. But what evidence is there that intelligence is not a threshold type of variable; that once a person has a certain minimal level of intelligence, his performance beyond that point is uncorrelated with ability?" There is plenty of evidence that this is not the case. The evidence is overwhelming that scholastic achievement increases linearly as a function of IQ throughout the entire range of the IQ scale so long as scholastic achievement itself is measured on a continuous scale unrestricted by the artifacts of ceiling or floor effects due to the achievement tests not including simple enough or advanced enough items. Even items such as "can button shirt," "can tie own shoe laces," "can eat with a fork," and "can say own name" are achievements that are positively correlated with IQ at the lower end of the intelligence scale. At the other end of the scale, for IQs of 140 and above, there are still achievement differences related to IQ, as can be seen by contrasting the typical school-age intellectual achievements of Terman's (1925) gifted group with IQs above 140 (the top 1 percent) with Hollingworth's (1942) even more highly gifted group with IQs above 180. Some of the differences in the intellectual achievements even among children in the IQ range from 140 to 200 are quite astounding. Over fifty years ago, Hollingworth and Cobb (1928) strikingly demonstrated marked differences in a host of scholastic achievements between a group of superior children clustering around 146 IQ and a very superior group clustering around IQ 165. The achievement differences between these groups are about as great as between groups of children of IQ 100 and IQ 120. It is also noteworthy that the superior (IQ 146) and very superior (IQ 165) groups do not differ in the least in ratings of the quality of their home backgrounds.

Grades versus Objective Test Scores.   Part of the variation in validity coefficients from one study to another is due to *heterogeneity of the criteria,* as it is called by psychometricians. This means that different studies have used different criteria for measuring scholastic achievement. The most conspicuous source of differences in validity coefficients involves using teachers' *grades* versus *scores* on objective achievement tests as the criterion of achievement to be predicted by IQ or scholastic aptitude scores. Grades assigned by teachers typically have correlations with IQ some .10 to .20 lower than the correlation between IQ and achievement test scores.

Not all this difference is due merely to the lower reliability of grades than of test scores. There are also systematic biases in teacher-assigned grades. For example, teachers give higher marks to girls than to boys who are their equals on IQ and achievement as measured by objective tests. In elementary school, the more outgoing, socially extraverted children receive higher marks than more introverted children with the same IQ and achievement scores. Teachers' grades tend to confound achievement with deportment. Many teachers use good grades to reward effort as well as achievement. Grades are also influenced by the general level of aptitude of the particular class; a grade of A in a class of low average ability may be equivalent to the grade of C in a high-ability class, in terms of actual achievement. All these conditions work to lower the correlation between IQ and school grades as compared with achievement test scores.

Sex.   In elementary school girls score slightly higher on achievement tests than do boys of the same IQ, although the sex difference is not nearly as pronounced as in the case of school grades. Girls excel particularly in subject matter involving language. With increasing grade level boys outperform girls in arithmetic and subjects involving numerical reasoning. The sex difference in overall scholastic achievement as measured by tests decreases at the higher grade levels and is practically negligible in high school, although girls still receive considerably higher grades from their teachers than do boys. Because of these sex differences, the correlation between IQ and achievement (whether assessed by grades or test scores) is generally about .10 higher when computed separately for boys and girls than when computed for the combined sexes.

Differences in School Subjects.   IQ does not correlate equally with all school subjects. There are systematic differences in the average correlations between IQ and various subjects. Performance in the more highly academic and abstract subjects, such as English, mathematics, and science, is more highly predictable from IQ than is performance in subjects that depend more on special abilities, such as music and art, or acquisition of specific skills requiring narrower perceptual-motor abilities and improvement of skills through prolonged practice, such as typing and shorthand and the manual arts. Even within a specialized field such as music, IQ is probably differentially predictive for certain aspects of the field. Learning to play a musical instrument is probably less predictable from IQ than is learning harmony and counterpoint. Achievement in foreign languages shows low or intermediate correlations with IQ as compared with other academic subjects.

These differences in correlations are not the result of various subjects' having more or less content in common with IQ tests, but arise from the fact that some subjects are more *g* loaded than others; that is, they involve more of the ability for abstraction and the "eduction of relations and correlates," to use Spearman's characterization of *g*. A content analysis of achievement tests in, say, algebra and shorthand shows no more resemblance of one or the other test to such highly *g*-loaded components of general intelligence tests as vocabulary, block designs, figure analogies, and embedded designs. Yet these tests predict performance in algebra much more highly than in shorthand. The same is true of achievement in English composition as compared with spelling or arithmetic concepts and reasoning problems as compared with arithmetic computation or so-called mechanical arithmetic.

IQ predicts achievement better in subjects that are hierarchically ordered in complexity and in the sequence of cognitive skills and knowledge that are prerequisite to more advanced achievement, as in mathematics, the physical sciences, and engineering, than in less hierarchical subjects such as history and the social sciences. The biological sciences are intermediate in this respect.

In general, the correlation between IQ and achievement is *lower* for subject matter in which there is a high correlation between achievement or the amount learned and the amount of time spent in study. But, when study time is held constant, the IQ–achievement correlation is increased. The IQ–achievement correlation is highest for subject matter that involves difficulty due to the increasing complexity of the material. It has also been found that in any subject area the correlation between IQ and achievement can be increased by eliminating the easier items in the achievement test. An easy item that, say, 80 percent of the students pass and 20 percent fail has the same statistical capacity to correlate with IQ as a more difficult item that is passed by only 20 percent and failed by 80 percent. Yet the easier item in fact correlates less with IQ. High-IQ pupils tend to miss those achievement test items that involve material that they did not study or that was presented by the teacher on the day that the student was absent. In addition to these kinds of failures, low-IQ pupils tend more to miss those achievement items that are abstract or conceptually complex, for example, *thought* problems in arithmetic, the proper *application* of the relevant formulas in physics and chemistry, the logical *inferences* and interpretation of meaning involved in the reading comprehension of literature, history, and the social sciences. In short, IQ predicts scholastic achievement because, and to the extent that, achievement is dependent on those kinds of cognitive processes that characterize *g*. *The correlation does not come about because IQ tests only measure knowledge that has been taught in school.*

Other Factors That Lower the Predictive Validity of IQ.   While there can be no doubt that IQ measures aptitude for academic education, it is also important to note that IQ accounts for only about half, or less, of the variance in measured achievement at any given point in the course of schooling. Why is the correlation between IQ and achievement not higher?

For one thing, the achievement tests themselves differ in *content validity* from one class to another and from one school to another. That is, the item composition of any given standardized achievement test is a less than perfect sample of the subject matter that has actually been presented in a particular class in the months preceding the administration of the achievement test. Scores on an achievement test that is tailored specifically to what was actually taught in a given class, assuming that the test has all the other desirable psychometric features of the best standardized tests, would yield a higher correlation with IQ than do the usual standardized tests. A corollary of this is that, when teachers are familiar with the content and nature of the standardized achievement tests to be used in their class at the end of the school year and "teach to the test," it most likely has the effect of increasing the correlation between IQ and achievement test scores. *IQ correlates best with achievement scores when there has been uniformity of exposure of pupils to all of the subject matter sampled by the achievement test.*

Another factor that lowers the IQ–achievement correlation is the greater restriction of range on many achievement tests as compared with IQ tests, on which there is virtually no restriction of range in the general school population. Achievement tests are usually designed to assess achievements for the subject matter content of a particular grade level in school. Such tests fall far short of sampling the full range of scholastic knowledge that exists in the total pupil population at any one grade level. The achievement tests thus have "ceiling" and "floor" effects that restrict the possible size of the obtained correlation with IQ. Laymen scarcely appreciate the actual spread of scholastic achievement that exists within any one grade level in the typical large city school system. The total range of scholastic knowledge and skills increases with every grade, and by high school the students falling below the 10th percentile may average six or seven grade levels below the students who score above the 90th percentile in achievement. The top high school students possess greater scholastic knowledge than the majority of college graduates, whereas the poorest high school students are academically on a par with the average second or third grader. But the high school junior who knows calculus and Boolean algebra cannot show this on the standard achievement tests typically used in high school. Nor are the academic limitations of the poorest students revealed by such tests, because rarely are high school students given tests that are appropriate for second and third-graders—the level of test that would have to be used fully to reveal the actual range of academic achievement among high school students.

Motivational factors undoubtedly play a part in achievement, and the imperfect correlation between motivation and IQ can therefore lower the predictive validity of IQ. But the contribution of motivational differences is probably overrated, for the following reason: there is a positive correlation between academic aptitude (i.e., IQ) and academic motivation, and the correlation increases throughout the course of schooling. The positive correlations among ability, achievement, and motivation work to enhance the correlation between IQ and achievement. Nothing reinforces the behavioral manifestations of motivation as much as success itself. Abler students are rewarded by greater success, which in turn reinforces the kinds of behavior—attention, interest, persistence, and good study habits—that lead to further academic success. The repeated failures of less able students generally have just the opposite effect. A pupil's self-perceived failure, even when it is not explicitly pointed out by the teacher, is a kind of punishing or at least unrewarding kind of experience from which the student is anxious to escape. Thus the academically less successful students tend to withdraw from academic pursuits and seek out other areas for enhancing their self-esteem. The greatest efforts are made by the most successful. The teacher and pupil alike are usually not very highly motivated to move the pupil's performance from the 1st percentile to the 10th percentile. At the other extreme, one often sees phenomenal efforts on the part of some students, such as scholarship winners, who are already at the 99th percentile and wish to climb to the 99.9th percentile, or from the 99.9th to the 99.99th percentile. The most striking examples of this kind of motivation and effort to exceed excellence are seen in great musical virtuosos, world chess champions, and Olympic athletes.

There are temporal fluctuations in people's performance both in achievement and in

IQ tests due to irregularities and the ups and downs that everyone experiences, some much more than others. Persons differ from day to day and even over somewhat longer periods in their lives in how effectively they use the abilities they possess and how they deploy their investments of attention, interest, and energy. At the extreme, for example, we know that psychiatric patients or persons suffering from severe emotional disorders often show great fluctuations in performance on IQ tests amounting to twenty or thirty points or more, along with a temporary impairment of the ability to accomplish anything that demands sustained mental effort. At a lesser extreme, everyone is familiar with "off days" or being in the doldrums for even a week or more.

Because of such fluctuations in the conditions affecting performance, more accurate assessments of ability and achievement and a consequently higher predictive validity of IQ can be secured with repeated measurements spread over a period of time, as was first demonstrated by Noel Keys (1928). By averaging various IQ and achievement test results over several years, the correlations between and among the tests approach the magnitude of the general factor common to all of the IQ and achievement tests—correlations between .80 and .90. Hence, with temporal fluctuations averaged out over the years, the correlation between IQ and scholastic achievement approximates the g saturation of IQ tests. Over the entire course of schooling from kindergarten to college, IQ and objective measures of academic achievement probably have as much as 90 percent or more of their variance in common.

This is illustrated by test data from 274 pupils in an integrated suburban school district on whom were obtained IQs, achievement scores, and teachers' marks in every grade from third through high school (Vane, 1966). The average correlation between IQ and scholastic achievement in any single grade was .67, with a range of correlations from .56 to .71 across grades. From the data given in Vane's Table 1, we can extract a general factor (i.e., first principal component) from the matrix of intercorrelations among achievement measures at every grade level; this large general achievement factor accounts for no less than 82 percent of the total variance in achievement at all grade levels. The IQ, measured at any single grade level, correlates on the average .79 with the general achievement factor, which is close to the correlation between the IQ obtained at any single administration and the g factor loading of any single group IQ test.

Prediction of Achievement by Multifactor Tests of Ability. Numerous studies have shown that by far the largest share of the validity of mental ability tests for predicting scholastic achievement is attributable to the g factor. Mental ability factors other than g, as measured by multifactor tests such as Thurstone's Primary Mental Abilities, the Differential Aptitude Tests, and the General Aptitude Test Battery of the U.S. Employment Service, add surprisingly little to the prediction of overall scholastic achievement or even of achievement in specific academic subjects. Rarely is the multiple correlation between a number of differential aptitude tests and achievement measures more than .10 greater than the simple correlation between IQ and achievement.[1] Verbal ability contributes more to the prediction of scholastic achievement independently of g than does any other ability factor.

Although multifactor ability tests predict only slightly better than a single IQ score, the prediction of achievement is considerably enhanced by the use of composite achievement scores, mainly because a number of different achievement tests provide a broader sampling of students' achievements than any single achievement test. Composite scores on multiachievement batteries have been found to correlate close to .80 with single IQ scores at the elementary school level where there is no restriction of range and all children are exposed to the same curriculum.

Achievement in Elementary School.   Results quite typical of those found in most studies of the predictive validity of IQ are seen in a large-scale study by Crano, Kenny, and Campbell (1972). It has the added advantage of showing both the concurrent and predictive validities of IQ. Achievement was measured by a composite score on the Iowa Tests of Basic Skills, which measure achievement and skills in reading, language (spelling, punctuation, usage, etc.), arithmetic, reading of maps, graphs, and tables, and knowledge and use of reference materials. IQ was measured by the Lorge–Thorndike Intelligence Test. The tests were taken by a representative sample of 5,495 children in the Milwaukee Public Schools in Grade 4 and parallel forms of the tests were obtained again in Grade 6. Figure 8.2 shows all of the correlations among the four sets of measurements. Notice that the predictive validity of IQ over an interval of two years (IQ_4–Ach_6) is nearly as high as the concurrent validity (IQ_4–Ach_4 and IQ_6–Ach_6). As is typically found, past achievement predicts future achievement slightly better than IQ.

One might wonder to what extent the common factor of reading ability per se involved in group tests of IQ and achievement plays a part in such intercorrelations. It is not as great as one might imagine. Although the verbal items of group IQ tests usually involve reading, the reading level is deliberately made simpler than the conceptual demands of the items, so that individual differences in the IQ scores are more the result of general cognitive ability than of reading ability per se. The reading requirements of an IQ test for sixth-graders, for example, will typically involve a level of reading ability within the capability of the majority of fourth-graders. The Lorge–Thorndike IQ test has both Verbal and Nonverbal parts; the Verbal requires reading, the Nonverbal does not. In a large study (Jensen, 1974b) of children in Grades 4 to 6, a correlation of .70 was found between the Verbal and Nonverbal IQs. The correlation between Verbal IQ and the reading comprehension subtest of the Stanford Achievement Test was .52. The correlation between Nonverbal IQ (which involves no reading) and reading comprehension scores

Figure 8.2.   Correlations among IQ and achievement test scores on 5,495 children in Grades 4 and 6.   (From Crano, Kenny & Campbell, 1972)

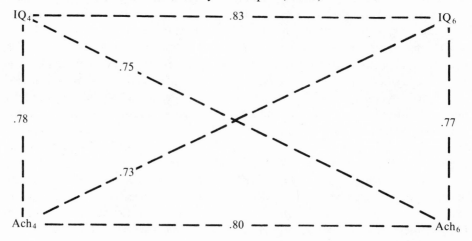

was .47. The correlation between Verbal IQ and reading comprehension after Nonverbal IQ is partialled out is only .29. The Verbal IQ test obviously measures considerably more than just reading proficiency.

IQ and Learning to Read. Pupils' major task in the primary grades (i.e., Grades 1 to 3) is learning to read. There are two main aspects of reading skill: *decoding* and *comprehension.* Decoding is the *translation* of the printed symbols into spoken language, and *comprehension,* of course, is *understanding* what is read. The learning of decoding (also called *oral reading*) is somewhat less predictable from IQ than is reading comprehension, which, once decoding skill has been achieved, quite closely parallels mental age. When elementary school children (all of the same age) are matched on decoding skill, their rank on a test of reading comprehension is practically the same as on IQ. In fact, reading comprehension per se is almost indistinguishable from oral comprehension once decoding is acquired. Most students with poor *reading* comprehension perform no better on tests of purely *oral* comprehension. But the reverse does not hold: there are some children (and adults) whose oral comprehension is average or superior, yet who have inordinate difficulty in the acquisition of decoding. When such disability is severe and unamenable to the ordinary methods of reading instruction, it is referred to as *developmental dyslexia.* Dyslexia seems to be a specific cognitive disability that does not involve *g* to any appreciable extent. Some dyslexics obtain high scores on both the verbal and nonverbal parts of individual IQ tests that require no reading, and they can be successful in college courses, especially in mathematics, physical sciences, and engineering, provided that someone reads their textbooks to them. There is no deficiency in comprehension per se. The vast majority of poor readers, however, are poor readers not because they lack decoding skill, but because they are deficient in comprehension, which, as measured by standard tests of reading comprehension is largely a matter of *g* (E. L. Thorndike, 1917; R. L. Thorndike, 1973–74.)

Here are some typical results. The Wechsler Preschool and Primary Scale of Intelligence (WPPSI), which does not involve reading, was given to children in kindergarten prior to any instruction in reading and was correlated with tests of reading achievement in first grade after one year's instruction in reading (Krebs, 1969). Achievement was measured by the Gilmore Oral Reading Test (a test of decoding) and the reading subtests of the Stanford Achievement Test (SAT), which involves word meaning and paragraph comprehension as well as decoding. The one-year predictive validities of the WPPSI IQ scales are as follows:

WPPSI	Gilmore Oral Reading	SAT Reading Comprehension
Verbal Scale IQ	.57	.61
Performance Scale IQ	.58	.63
Full Scale IQ	.62	.68

When the sample was divided into lower- and upper-socioeconomic-status groups, it was found that the predictive validity of IQ was higher in the lower-SES group than in the higher-SES group (e.g., SAT reading scores correlated .66 versus .40 with Full Scale IQ).

Group tests of *reading readiness* look a good deal like group IQ tests in item content. They are intended to predict reading achievement in the primary grades and can be taken by children prior to having received any instruction in reading. Lohnes and Gray (1972) factor analyzed seven reading readiness tests and an IQ test given to 3,956 pupils in 299 classrooms in the first weeks of the first grade, before they could read. The IQ test correlated .84 with the general factor (i.e., first principal component) common to the reading readiness tests, a higher correlation than that of any of the readiness tests themselves, which showed correlations with the general factor ranging from .44 to .81, with a median of .60. Two years later, when the same pupils were in the second grade, they were given ten reading and language achievement tests and one arithmetic computation test. These were factor analyzed, yielding correlations with the general factor of the achievement battery ranging from .64 (arithmetic computation) to .87 (reading vocabulary), with a median correlation of .80. The general factor of the reading readiness battery (including IQ) correlated .81 with the general factor of the achievement battery. Lohnes and Gray conclude:

> There is no question that reading skills of pupils were observed by the criterion measurement instruments [i.e., the achievement tests given in second grade]. What these analyses reveal is that the most important single source of criterion variance, or to put it differently, the best single explanatory principle for observed variance in reading skill, was variance in general intelligence.   (p. 475)

IQ, Learning Ability, and Retention.   The relation between intelligence and learning ability has long been a puzzle to psychologists. It is still not well understood, but a number of consistent findings permit a few tentative generalizations.

Part of the problem has been that "learning ability" has been much less precisely defined, delimited, and measured than intelligence. The psychometric features of most measures of "learning ability" are not directly comparable with tests of intelligence, and it is doubtful that much further progress in understanding the relation between learning and intelligence will be possible until psychologists treat the measurement of individual differences in learning with at least the same degree of psychometric sophistication that has been applied to intelligence and other abilities.

One still occasionally sees intelligence defined as learning ability, but for many years now, since the pioneer studies of Woodrow (1938, 1939, 1940, 1946), most psychologists have dropped the term "learning ability" from their definitions of intelligence. To many school teachers and laymen this deletion seems to fly in the face of common sense. Is not the "bright," or high-IQ, pupil a "fast learner" and the "dull," or low-IQ, pupil a "slow learner?" Simple observation would surely seem to confirm this notion.

The ability to learn is obviously a mental ability, but it is not necessarily the same mental ability as intelligence. Scientifically the question is no longer one of whether learning ability and intelligence are or are not the same thing, but is one of determining the conditions that govern the magnitude of the correlation between measures of learning and measures of intelligence.

The Woodrow studies showed two main findings. (1) Measures of performance on a large variety of rather simple learning tasks showed only meager intercorrelations among the learning tasks, and between learning tasks and IQ. Factor analysis did not reveal a general factor of learning ability. (2) Rate of improvement with practice, or gains in proficiency as measured by the difference between initial and final performance levels, showed little or no correlation among various learning tasks or with IQ. Even short-term pretest–posttest gains, reflecting improvement with practice, in certain school subjects showed little or no correlation with IQ. Speed of learning of simple skills and associative rote learning, and rate of improvement with practice, seem to be something rather different from the *g* of intelligence tests. Performance on simple learning tasks and the effects of practice as reflected in gain scores (or final performance scores statistically controlled for initial level of performance) are not highly *g* loaded.

Many other studies since have essentially confirmed Woodrow's findings. (Good reviews are presented by Zeaman and House, 1967, and by Estes, 1970.) The rate of acquisition of conditioned responses, the learning of motor skills (e.g., pursuit rotor learning), simple discrimination learning, and simple associative or rote learning of verbal material (e.g., paired associates and serial learning) are not much correlated with IQ. And there is apparently no large general factor of ability, as is found with various intelligence tests, that is common to all these relatively simple forms of learning.

The same can be said of the *retention* of simple learning. When the degree of initial learning is held constant, persons of differing IQ do not differ in the retention of what was learned over a given interval of time after the last learning trial or practice session.

But these findings and conclusions, based largely on simple forms of learning traditionally used in the psychological laboratory, are only half the story. Some learning and memory tasks do in fact show substantial correlations with IQ. This is not an all-or-none distinction between types of learning, but a continuum, which in general can be viewed as going from the simple to the complex. What this means needs to be spelled out more specifically. Individual differences in learning proficiency show increasingly higher correlations with IQ directly in relation to the following characteristics of the learning task.

1. Learning is more highly correlated with IQ when it is *intentional* and the task calls forth conscious mental effort and is paced in such a way as to permit the subject to "think." It is possible to learn passively without "thinking," by mere repetition of simple material; such learning is only slightly correlated with IQ. In fact, *negative* correlations between learning speed and IQ have been found in some simple tasks that could only be learned by simple repetition or rote learning but were disguised to appear more complex so as to evoke "thinking" (Osler & Trautman, 1961). Persons with higher IQs engaged in more complex mental processes (reasoning, hypothesis testing, etc.), which in this specially contrived task only interfered with rote learning. Persons of lower IQ were not hindered by this interference of more complex mental processes and readily learned the material by simple rote association.

2. Learning is more highly correlated with IQ when the material to be learned is *hierarchical,* in the sense that the learning of later elements depends on mastery of earlier elements. A task of many elements, in which the order of learning the elements has no effect on learning rate or level of final performance, is less correlated with IQ than is a task in which there is some more or less optimal order in which the elements are learned and the acquisition of earlier elements in the sequence facilitates the acquisition of later elements.

3. Learning is more highly correlated with IQ when the material to be learned is *meaningful,* in the sense that it is in some way related to other knowledge or experience already possessed by the learner. Rote learning of the serial order of a list of meaningless three-letter nonsense syllables or colored forms, for example, shows little correlation with IQ. In contrast, learning the essential content of a meaningful prose passage is more highly correlated with IQ.

4. Learning is more highly correlated with IQ when the nature of the learning task permits *transfer* from somewhat different but related past learning. Outside the intentionally artificial learning tasks of the experimental psychology laboratory, little that we are called on to learn beyond infancy is *entirely* new and unrelated to anything we had previously learned. Making more and better use of elements of past learning in learning something "new"—in short, the transfer of learning—is positively correlated with IQ.

5. Learning is more highly correlated with IQ when it is *insightful,* that is, when the learning task involves "catching on" or "getting the idea." Learning to name the capital cities of the fifty states, for example, does not permit this aspect of learning to come into play and would therefore be less correlated with IQ than, say, learning to prove the Pythagorean theorem.

6. Learning is more highly correlated with IQ when the material to be learned is of *moderate difficulty* and *complexity.* If a learning task is too complex, everyone, regardless of his IQ, flounders and falls back on simpler processes such as trial and error and rote association. Complexity, in contrast to sheer difficulty due to the amount of material to be learned, refers to the number of elements that must be integrated simultaneously for the learning to progress.

7. Learning is more highly correlated with IQ when the *amount of time* for learning is fixed for all students. This condition becomes increasingly important to the extent that the other conditions listed are enactive.

8. Learning is more highly correlated with IQ when the learning material is more *age related.* Some things can be learned almost as easily by a 9-year-old child as by an 18-year-old. Such learning shows relatively little correlation with IQ. Other forms of learning, on the other hand, are facilitated by maturation and show a substantial correlation with age. The concept of *learning readiness* is based on this fact. IQ and tests of "readiness," which predict rate of progress in certain kinds of learning, particularly reading and mathematics, are highly correlated with IQ.

9. Learning is more highly correlated with IQ at an *early stage* of learning something "new" than is performance or gains later in the course of practice. That is, IQ is related more to rate of acquisition of new skills or knowledge rather than to rate of improvement or degree of proficiency at later stages of learning, assuming that new material and concepts have not been introduced at the intermediate stages. Practice makes a task less cognitively demanding and decreases its correlation with IQ. With practice the learner's performance becomes more or less automatic and hence less demanding of conscious effort and attention. For example, learning to read music is an intellectually demanding task for the beginner. But for an experienced musician it is an almost automatic process that makes little conscious demand on the higher mental processes. Individual differences in proficiency at this stage are scarely related to IQ. Much the same thing is true of other skills such as typing, stenography, and Morse code sending and receiving.

It can be seen that all the conditions listed that influence the correlation between learning and IQ are highly characteristic of much of school learning. Hence the impression of teachers that IQ is an index of learning aptitude is quite justifiable. Under the listed conditions of learning, the low-IQ child is indeed a "slow-learner" as compared with children of high IQ.

Very similar conditions pertain to the relation between memory or retention and IQ. When persons are equated in degree of original learning of simple material, their retention measured at a later time is only slightly if at all correlated with IQ. The retention of more complex learning, however, involves meaningfulness and the way in which the learner has transformed or encoded the material. This is related to the degree of the learner's understanding, the extent to which the learned material is linked into the learner's preexisting associative and conceptual network, and the learner's capacity for conceptual reconstruction of the whole material from a few recollected principles. The more that these aspects of memory can play a part in the material to be learned and later recalled, the more that retention measures are correlated with IQ.

These generalizations concerning the relationship between learning and IQ may have important implications for the conduct of instruction. For example, it has been suggested that schooling might be made more worthwhile for many youngsters in the lower half of the IQ distribution by designing instruction in such a way as to put less of a premium on IQ in scholastic learning (e.g., Bereiter, 1976; Cronbach, 1975). Samuels and Dahl (1973) have stated this hope as follows: "If we wish to reduce the correlation between IQ and achievement, the job facing the educator entails simplifying the task, ensuring that prerequisite skills are mastered, developing motivational procedures to keep the student on the task, and allocating a sufficient amount of time to the student so that he can master the task."

IQ and College Grades.   The predictive validity of IQ for success in college has to be dealt with separately, as it involves problems peculiar to this level. For one thing, omnibus achievement tests are seldom given to college students. Students' academic achievements are assessed only in those courses that they have taken in college, and this criterion measure is usually just the final grade received in the course. College grades constitute a five-point scale (A, B, C, D, and F), usually with a highly skewed distribution (i.e., many more A's and B's than D's and F's). Hence this is a quite crude scale and far from statistically optimal as a criterion measurement against which to determine the validity of any predictor variables. Most studies of predictive validity use grades averaged over all of the courses the student has taken in college, the grade-point average or GPA, obtained by assigning numerical values to the letter grades.

According to Lavin's (1965, p. 51) review of the literature, the validity of college entrance exams, such as the Scholastic Aptitude Test (SAT), for predicting college grade-point averages ranges from about .30 to .70, with an average correlation of about .50. Other reviews of this voluminous literature cited by Lavin give highly similar values as typical. When multiple predictors based on tests of specific aptitudes relevant to different courses of study are used to predict GPA, the multiple correlation coefficients reported may be as high as .60 to .70. But it now appears that this increase in validity is not so much the result of using multiple predictors (i.e., differential aptitude tests) as it is a result of using more homogeneous criteria, namely, predicting GPA *within* groups majoring in the same subjects. If grades are not strictly comparable across different fields of study, this fact can only weaken the correlation between any predictor variable and grades when students from all fields are pooled together.

College aptitude tests such as the SAT are not, strictly speaking, general intelligence tests, although they would no doubt show a quite high correlation with IQ. The aptitude tests are a kind of hybrid, combining items typical of those found in IQ tests and items typical of those found in high school achievement tests. Including the assessment of high school achievement significantly enhances the predictive validity of the college aptitude test. This should not be surprising, because academic knowledge and skills gained in high school are a prerequisite for many college courses. High school grades or the student's rank in his or her graduating class generally predict college GPA at least as well as scores on college aptitude tests.

There are few studies of the correlation between standard intelligence tests (in contrast to scholastic aptitude tests) and college grades. The Full Scale IQ of the Wechsler Adult Intelligence Scale correlated .44 with college freshman GPA in a college where the mean IQ of freshmen is 115. (The correlation of WAIS IQ with rank in high school graduating class, with a mean IQ of 107, was .62; see Matarazzo, 1972, p. 284.)

The most extensive evidence that I have been able to find of the correlation between general intelligence and college grades is based on the general intelligence test of the General Aptitude Test Battery (GATB) developed by the U.S. Employment Service (Manpower Administration, U.S. Department of Labor, 1970). The general intelligence test of the GATB is a good measure of g and correlates .89 with the WAIS Full Scale IQ. Table 8.6 shows the frequency distribution of correlations between GATB intelligence test scores and college grades (usually GPA) in 48 different samples (totaling 5,561 students) from diverse colleges and for various majors within the colleges. The median correlation is .40.

A number of conditions contribute to the considerable variation in correlations between IQ and college grades.

Sex differences in the predictability of college grades are a quite consistent finding, with higher predictive validities for females than for males. This is also true at the high school level. The causes of this sex difference are obscure. (See Chapter 13, pp. 628–630, for a discussion of this.)

Table 8.6. Correlations between scores on the general intelligence test of the GATB and college grades in 48 college samples. (From *Manual of the GATB*, Sec. III, pp. 205–219, Manpower Administration, U.S. Department of Labor, Washington, D.C., 1970)

Correlation	Frequency	Percentage
.60–.64	1	2%
.55–.59	1	2
.50–.54	8	17
.45–.49	4	8
.40–.44	10	21
.35–.39	5	10
.30–.34	8	17
.25–.29	3	6
.20–.24	5	10
.15–.19	1	2
.10–.14	2	4

Selection of students in terms of high school grades and scholastic aptitude scores lowers predictive validity by restriction of range on both predictor and criterion variables.

Field of study is also related to the predictive validity of IQ. Grades in mathematics and the sciences generally show the highest predictive validities, followed by the social sciences and humanities, and finally by the arts. These differences are attributable mainly to three factors: (1) the hierarchical nature of the subject matter in math and science and the fact that IQ at all ages is quite highly related to capacity for mastering material that is hierarchically ordered in terms of increasing complexity in which the simpler elements are prerequisite for the more complex; (2) the greater objectivity and reliability of the criteria for assessing achievement in math and science than in the humanities and the arts; and (3) the important role of special talents in the arts.

Self-dependence of college students is greater than of pupils in elementary and high school and works to lower the validity of IQ and scholastic aptitude tests in predicting college grades. There is much less parent and teacher supervision of the student's study habits in college. Class attendance is seldom mandatory, and the time spent in classes is only a small fraction of the total study time needed to obtain passing grades, time that the student must allocate wisely on his own. Individual differences in self-discipline, study habits, and the like lessen the correlation between ability and achievement.

Variable grading standards is the most important cause of attenuation in predicting college grade-point average from intelligence and aptitude tests. The GPA is a composite scale of *nonequivalent* components, that is, grades in different courses. Hence the GPAs of students who have taken different courses are not equivalent in their regressions on ability. This has been conclusively shown in research by Roy Goldman and his associates (Goldman, Schmidt, Hewitt, & Fisher, 1974; Goldman & Slaughter, 1976; Goldman & Hewitt, 1976). Their studies justify the conclusion that GPA is a very poor criterion against which to judge the validity of tests for predicting *actual* achievement in college. GPA per se is a poor index of actual achievement.

Goldman et al. have shown that grading standards differ from one field to another and from one course to another within fields. What is more important is that the stringency of grading standards is positively related to the average level of student ability within a field or within a course in a given field. High-ability students can perform well in any field, but low-ability students can pass only in certain fields and courses with lax grading standards. This is evident in the preponderant direction of changes in college major, which is from ''harder'' to ''easier'' fields in terms of the level of ability required to obtain passing grades. Low-ability students tend to gravitate toward fields and courses with lax grading standards. This condition obviously plays havoc with the predictive validity of aptitude tests for predicting composite GPA. Taking into account differences in reliability of grades and restriction of range in different courses, the validities of the SAT are considerably higher for grades within separate fields than for overall GPA and are still higher for grades in separate classes.

In other words, the aptitude tests predict actual achievement in college better than they have been given credit for when judged in terms of their correlation with GPA. Goldman and Slaughter (1976) conclude:

As long as there are radical differences in grading standards, and students are able to choose most of their classes, then *no predictor* will have more than moderate validity for predicting GPA. There are several remedies for this situation, but none of them seem politically palatable. One solution would be to create a conversion system for equating grades in one class with grades in another. Although this presents some technical difficulties, they are not insurmountable. Nevertheless, we imagine that there will be a great deal of resistance to such a suggestion, although it has been implicitly adopted for many purposes: medical schools, for example, tend to weight grades from different classes with greater or lesser values depending on the perceived difficulties of the classes. Another possible solution would be to use the GPA in a particular field as the success criterion. This too would present problems. In sum, we believe that the validity problem in GPA prediction is a result of the shortcomings of the GPA criterion rather than the tests that are used as predictors. Recognition of this phenomenon would eliminate much pointless argument about the merits of standardized tests for college student selection.   (p. 14)

Goldman and Hewitt (1976) also discovered the interesting fact that the SAT–Verbal score is more predictive of grades (even in the sciences) than the SAT–Math score. On the other hand, SAT–Math is more predictive of the student's major field and career choice. College courses can be arranged along a quantitative–nonquantitative continuum, and the mean scores of students in the courses so ordered show a steeper gradient in SAT–Math scores than in SAT–Verbal, although the two abilities are correlated. The continuum is as follows: physical sciences (including mathematics), biological sciences, social sciences, humanities, fine arts. Which of these areas a student is most apt to major in is determined largely by his mathematical aptitude; but the grades that he receives within his chosen field are determined more by verbal ability. Nonscience students are below science students in mathematical ability; but, contrary to popular belief, nonscience students are not higher than science students in verbal ability.

The ratio of males to females in different college majors seems to be largely "explainable" in terms of the sex difference in mathematical aptitude. The correlations between sex and major field (which range from .15 to .28 in four colleges) are greatly reduced (to values from .07 to .17) when males and females are statistically equated on the verbal and the math SAT scores.

Prediction of Grades in Graduate School.   The same conditions that work against predictive validity in undergraduate college operate even more strongly in graduate and professional schools. In most graduate and professional schools, such as law and medicine, the ratio of applicants to selectees varies from about 10 to 1 to 100 to 1. This high degree of selection implies a severe restriction of range on the predictor variables. Last year at the University of California in Berkeley, for example, none of the finally selected students admitted to the graduate program in the Mathematics Department scored below the 98th percentile on the Graduate Record Examination, a high-level scholastic aptitude test standardized on college seniors and graduates. Moreover, at the graduate level, course grades usually constitute only a three-point scale (grades of A, B, C), with the vast majority of grades consisting of A's and B's. Such conditions militate severely against high correlations between the predictor and criterion variables. Hence grades in graduate school typically correlate with aptitude scores in the range from .30 to .40. The median correlation between first-year average grades in twenty-eight law schools and scores on the Law School Aptitude Test (essentially a high-level verbal intelligence test) was .30, ranging from .01 to .40 (Pitcher & Schrader, 1969). (Correlation of under-graduate grades with law school grades was only .27.)

A much more potent factor than stringent selection (and the consequent restriction of range) operates to lower the predictive validity of aptitude tests in graduate school. The method of selecting students, by most graduate schools, statistically guarantees a low correlation between the predictor and the criterion. Students are selected on the basis of undergraduate grades and aptitude scores such that among the accepted students there is a substantial *negative* correlation between undergraduate grades and aptitude scores. Be-cause both undergraduate grades and aptitude scores are each positively correlated with grades in graduate school, when the two variables are negatively correlated with each other in the selected sample, it makes it mathematically impossible for either predictor variable (i.e., undergraduate grades and aptitude scores) to be highly correlated with the criterion (i.e., grades in graduate school). This observation has been clearly explicated by Dawes (1975). The most prestigious and highly selective graduate schools admit almost exclusively students who have *high* GPA and *high* aptitude scores. There is poor predic-tive validity in this select group mainly due to restriction of range. Students who do not make it on both points gain admittance to other graduate schools if they have *high* GPA and *low* aptitude (i.e., high or low relative to the median of all other applicants) or *low* GPA and *high* aptitude. (Few graduate schools would normally select low-GPA–low-aptitude students.) This results in a negative correlation between GPA and aptitude, making it impossible for either predictor variable to correlate highly with the criterion, as explained. There is simply no way in which the single correlations between predictors and criterion can be high. Because of these peculiar conditions in the selection of graduate students, the correlations between aptitude scores and grades are not a fair assessment of the actual validity of aptitude tests for predicting the achievement of graduate students.

IQ and Amount of Formal Education. Number of years of schooling is a com-mon criterion of educational achievement, mainly because it is so easy to ascertain. For the past decade or more, however, it has been a relatively poor index of actual educational achievement, so great are the average differences between various colleges as well as the range of individual differences in achievement within any given college population. One large study using a very broad general scholastic achievement test (the General Culture Test) found that about 10 percent of high school seniors exceeded the median achievement level of college seniors (Tyler, 1965, pp. 104–105). If diplomas were awarded to the upper fifth of the entire college student body on the basis of tested knowledge rather than on hours and credits, the composition of the "graduating" class would consist of 28 percent seniors, 21 percent juniors, 19 percent sophomores, and 15 percent freshmen; and 10 percent of high school seniors could be awarded the diploma before ever having entered college.

The differences between colleges are enormous. When the Selective Service Col-lege Qualification Test was given to more than 74,000 men in colleges throughout the United States in 1952, in some colleges as many as 65 percent failed the test as compared with 2 percent in some other colleges (Tyler, 1965, p. 106). There are even colleges that graduate some students who fail the Armed Forces Qualification Test, the failing score on which is equivalent to an IQ of less than 80. There are also large differences in the percentage passing the Selective Service College Qualification Test in different college majors, from 69 percent passing in physical science and mathematics to 30 percent passing in education, with an average of 54 percent over nine majors (Tyler, 1965, p. 106).

Considering the wide margin of discrepancy between objectively tested attainments and years of education, diplomas, and credentials, it seems an obvious conclusion that most employers and our social institutions in general have put far too much stock in sheer amount of schooling and formal credentials and not enough in objectively assessed actual achievement.

Despite these conditions that attenuate amount of education as an index of real educational achievement, there is still a quite substantial correlation between IQ and amount of schooling. The IQ is clearly not a *result* of the amount of schooling, as childhood IQ predicts the final level of education attained by adulthood. For example, in a group of 437 adults there was found a correlation of .58 between their IQs measured in the sixth grade (at age 12) and the amount of education they had attained by the age of 45 (Bajema, 1968).

IQ is positively correlated with school persistence even if we do not consider schooling beyond high school graduation. Dillon (1949) followed the high school careers of 2,600 pupils who took an IQ test in the seventh grade. The percentage of pupils within each of five IQ intervals who persisted to high school graduation was as follows:

IQs less than 85	4%
IQs 85–94	54%
IQs 95–104	63%
IQs 105–114	76%
IQs 115 and above	86%

Longitudinal data from the Fels Research Institute (McCall, 1977) shows the correlations between IQ measured at various intervals between 3 and 18 years of age and adult educational and occupational attainment in samples of 94 males and 96 females all of at least 26 years of age. The group was considerably above average, with a mean IQ of 117, standard deviation of 15.9. Among the women 3 percent did not graduate from high school, 31 percent graduated but did not go beyond high school, and 34 percent graduated from college. The comparable figures for men were 1 percent, 22 percent, and 56 percent, respectively. Figure 8.3 shows the correlations of IQ × adult educational and occupational attainments for males and females. Notice that by 7 years of age, the IQ predicts adult educational and occupational levels with a validity coefficient of .40 to .50. IQ at age 40 (data from a study by Honzik, 1972), as shown in Figure 8.3, is considerably more predictable from childhood IQ than are educational and occupational attainments. Also it is interesting that females' adult attainments are more predictable from IQ at an early age than is the case for males. The cause of this sex difference is open to speculation.

IQ Not a Stand-in for Socioeconomic Status.   The claim has been made that IQ as a predictor of amount of education attained by adulthood is merely a "stand-in" for socioeconomic status. SES is indexed mainly by the father's occupational status and the educational level of both parents. If a child's SES determines his educational achievement or number of years spent in school, we should not expect to find a significant correlation between IQ and years of schooling among brothers reared together in the same family. Yet among brothers there is a correlation of about .30 to .35 between IQ and years of schooling as adults when IQ is measured in elementary school. (This correlation can be inferred

Figure 8.3. Correlation between IQ at ages from 3 to 16 years and IQ at age 40, adult occupational status, and final educational level attained by adulthood, shown separately for males and females. (From McCall, 1977)

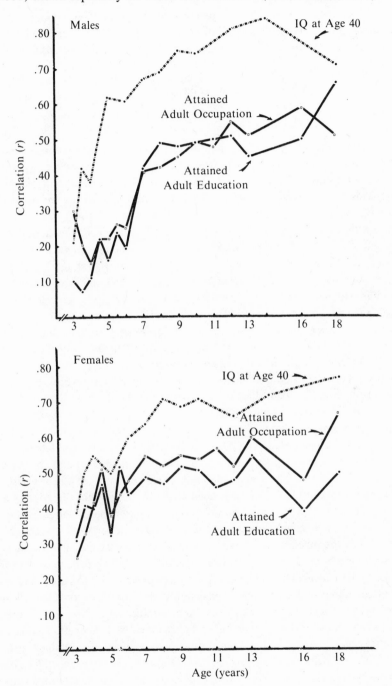

from data presented by Jencks, 1972, p. 144.) Within-family differences in educational attainments for same-sex siblings cannot be attributed to differences in SES, "cultural differences," or "family background."

A study in Britain (Kemp, 1955) determined the correlations among IQ, tested scholastic achievement, and SES, with all of the intercorrelated variables consisting of the mean values obtained on these characteristics in fifty schools. The intercorrelations were as follows:

> IQ and scholastic achievement   = .73
> IQ and SES   = .52
> SES and scholastic achievement = .56

When IQ is partialled out (i.e., held constant statistically) of the correlation between SES and scholastic achievement, the partial correlation drops to .30. However, when SES is partialled out of the correlation between IQ and achievement, the partial correlation drops only to .62. This means that IQ independently of SES determines achievement much more than does SES independently of IQ.

Because father's education and occupation are the main variables in almost every composite index of SES or "family background," it is instructive to look at the degree of causal connection between these variables and a child's early IQ (at age 11), the child's level of education (i.e., highest grade completed) attained by adulthood, and the child's IQ as an adult. The intercorrelations among all these variables were subjected to a "path coefficients analysis" by the biometrician C. C. Li (1975, pp. 324–325).

Path analysis is a method for inferring causal relationships from the intercorrelations among the variables when there is prior knowledge of a temporal sequence among the variables. For example, a person's IQ can hardly be conceived of as a causal factor in determining his or her father's educational or occupational level. The reverse, however, is a reasonable hypothesis. The path diagram as worked out by Li (from data presented by Jencks, 1972, p. 339) is shown in Figure 8.4.

In path diagrams the observed correlations are conventionally indicated by curved lines (e.g., the observed correlation of .51 between father's education and father's occupation). The temporal sequence goes from left to right, and the direct paths, indicating the unique causal influence of one variable on another independently of other variables, are represented by straight lines with single-headed arrows to indicate the direction of causality. (Arrows that appear to lead from nowhere (i.e., from unlabeled variables) represent the square roots of the residual variance that is attributable to variables that are unknown or unmeasured in the given model.) We see in Figure 8.4 that the direct influences of father's education and occupation contribute only $.14^2 + .20^2 = 6$ percent of the variance in the child's final educational attainment (i.e., years of schooling) as an adult, whereas the direct effect of the child's IQ at age 11 in determining final educational level is $.44^2$, or 19 percent of the variance. In brief, childhood IQ determines about three times more of the variance in adult educational level than father's educational and occupational levels combined. Notice also that the father's education and occupation combined determine only $.20^2 + .20^2 = 8$ percent of the variance in childhood IQ. Li concludes: "The implication seems to be that it is the children with higher IQ who go to school rather than that schooling improves children's IQ. The indirect effect from early IQ to adult IQ via education is $(0.44)(0.25) = 0.11$" (p. 327).

Figure 8.4. Path diagram showing analysis of the network of some of the causal influences on IQ from early childhood (early child IQ) to adult (adult child IQ). (From Li, 1975, p. 325)

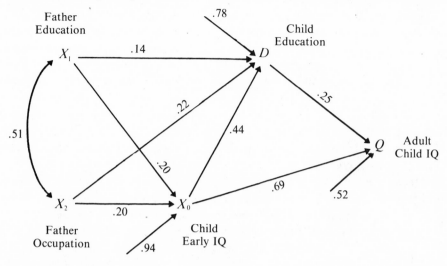

IQ and Evaluations by Parents, Teachers, and Peers

As was pointed out in Chapter 6, teachers' ratings of pupils' intelligence correlate between .60 and .80 with IQ scores. Teachers' ratings of ability generally show a sex bias slightly favoring girls, probably because deportment and scholastic achievement enter into teachers' judgments of intellectual ability. Yet teachers' and pupils' ratings of mental ability show a remarkably high agreement as evinced by the correlations between teacher ratings of pupils' intelligence and pupils' ratings of one another on intelligence—a raw correlation of .85 (or .95 when corrected for unreliability of the ratings) for girls and of .76 or .90 corrected) for boys (Thorndike, Lay, & Dean, 1909). The correlations of the ratings with school marks was .60 for teachers' ratings and .40 for pupils' ratings, which are values similar to the correlations of IQ scores with school marks.

IQ and other measurements of general intelligence also show significant correlations with interpersonal ratings and behaviors even when the raters have not been instructed to rate on intellectual ability per se. A study of 7,417 children of ages 6 to 11, sampled so as to be representative of the school population of the United States, showed significant relationships between children's intellectual ability and various behavioral indices of social acceptance by their classmates and peers (Roberts & Baird, 1972). In competitive game activities, for example, the first few children chosen for a team were much more often (54 percent versus 8 percent) selected from among the higher-IQ children (upper quartile) in the class than from among the lower-IQ children (lower quartile). The frequency with which children were chosen as leaders by their peers was also related to ability level. A number of other studies have shown essentially the same thing: the more intelligent school children are usually better accepted socially by their classmates than are the less intellectually favored children and the retarded (Baldwin, 1958; Barbe, 1954; Epperson, 1963; Gallagher, 1958).

Parental attitudes along a continuum of acceptance–rejection of their children are significantly correlated with the children's IQs, especially in the case of mothers and daughters, showing an average correlation of .42 (or .55 corrected for unreliability) between daughters' IQs and accepting attitudes by their mothers (Hurley, 1965). The correlations were significantly lower for boys. The direction of the causality of the correlation between parental attitudes and child's IQ is unknown, but the lack of sex differences between all four possible sex combinations of parent–child IQ correlations (which average close to .50) would suggest that the child's IQ causes the parental attitudes rather than the reverse.

Adults' ratings of one another also reflect IQ to some extent even when the basis of rating is not intelligence per se but a quality only indirectly correlated with intelligence. Izard (1959) found low but significant correlations between group intelligence test scores (as well as certain personality traits) and peer nominations for leadership ability among military personnel. Among student nurses, peer predictions of success in nurses' training were significantly related to measures of verbal and numerical ability (Poland, 1961).

In a study by Schmidt (unpublished manuscript), trainees for foremen in a large manufacturing concern were asked to rate each of their peers' probable degree of future success on the job as foremen. Among white ratees, the peer ratings (made by whites and blacks) correlated .385 with the unweighted composite score on a battery of eight diverse mental tests. (Such a composite score should be a good measure of g). Future success ratings of blacks by black raters correlated .421 with the composite mental test score, but the ratings of blacks by whites was not significantly correlated with test score ($r = .088$). Trainees also rated one another for "drive and assertiveness." These ratings, too, correlated significantly ($r = .409$) with composite test score in the white sample, but again ratings of blacks by whites were not significantly correlated with test scores, although blacks' ratings of whites showed a significant correlation (.367) with test score. It is not known why the ratings of blacks by white raters are so much less correlated with the ability measures than the ratings of blacks by blacks or the ratings of whites by whites *or* blacks. One may wonder if a similar pattern of correlations would have resulted if the raters were asked to estimate the general intelligence level of their co-workers.

"Assortative mating" is the term used by geneticists to refer to the degree of positive correlation between mates on any given observable or measurable characteristic. It is a fact of considerable interest that among married couples the degree of assortative mating for IQ is higher than for any other trait, physical or mental. Studies of assortative mating for IQ show correlations between spouses ranging between $+.40$ to $+.60$, with a mean of $+.50$ (Jencks, 1972, p. 272). (This is about the same as the correlation between brothers and sisters.) A correlation of .50 is equivalent to an average absolute difference between spouses (or siblings) of 12 IQ points. Assuming that the IQ tests have a reliability of .95, the correlation between spouses after correction for attenuation becomes $+.53$. (The marital correlation for physical stature is about $+.30$.) It is hard to imagine how such a correlation could come about if IQ were not a socially important variable and if a host of personal cues and other social determinants in mate selection were not correlated with IQ, since prospective marriage partners ordinarily do not give one another IQ tests or have access to one another's IQ scores in old school files. The correlation of about .50 between spouses' IQs implies a correlation of at least .70 between measured IQ and one's ability to estimate the intelligence of oneself and of others who are known quite well in a variety of contexts. Apparently a person is perceived as less attractive as a possible marriage partner when his or her intelligence as perceived by the partner (a perception that may be based on a host of observable correlates of intelligence) departs more than a certain amount from the partner's self-perception of his or her own intelligence level. Too great a discrepancy between these perceptions of the partner's intelligence and the person's own intelligence decreases the probability of the persons' marrying one another. If we assume that the validity of the perceptions of intelligence is .71, as measured against the criterion of measured IQ, and that mates' self-perceptions of their intelligence are perfectly correlated, then we should expect their IQs to be correlated .71 × 1.0 × .71 = .50, as shown in Figure 8.5.

But mates' self-perceptions of their own intelligence are most likely not perfectly correlated, because there is a mutual "trade-off" between perceived intelligence and other assets that determine overall attractiveness. Hence it could be argued that there is an even higher correlation than .71 between perceived intelligence and measured IQ to account for the correlation of .50 between mates' measured IQs. Another possibility is that one does not marry another person unless the other person's overall assets, as perceived by oneself, are *at least* equivalent to one's own overall self-perceived assets. This requirement on the part of both mates would ensure a near perfect correlation between their overall self-perceived assets. The correlation, then, between these self-perceived total assets and measured IQ would have to be at least .71 to account for the observed correlation of .50 between spouses' measured IQs.

Occupational Level, Performance, and Income

Not the judgment of the "average" person, but the *averaged judgments* of many persons can show an extraordinary consistency across quite diverse groups of persons, and from one generation to the next, as well as remarkably high correlations with certain independent objective criteria. Such is the case with people's average subjective judgments of occupational "level" and their high correlation with the average tested IQs of persons in various occupations. This striking finding has been demonstrated to about the same high degree in numerous studies and has been contradicted by none. (For more

Figure 8.5. Path diagram of marital correlation.

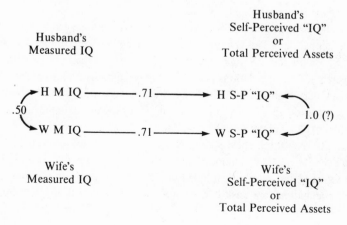

extensive reviews of this evidence the reader is referred to Matarazzo, 1972, Chs. 7 and 12; and Tyler, 1965, Ch. 13.)

People's average ranking of occupations is much the same regardless of the basis on which they were told to rank them. The well-known Barr scale of occupations was constructed by asking 30 "psychological judges" to rate 120 specific occupations, each definitely and concretely described, on a scale going from 0 to 100 according to the level of general intelligence required for ordinary success in the occupation. These judgments were made in 1920. Forty-four years later, in 1964, the National Opinion Research Center (NORC), in a large public opinion poll, asked many people to rate a large number of specific occupations in terms of their subjective opinion of the *prestige* of each occupation relative to all of the others. The correlation between the 1920 Barr ratings based on the average subjectively estimated *intelligence requirements* of the various occupations and the 1964 NORC ratings based on the average subjective opined *prestige* of the occupations is .91. The 1960 *U.S. Census of Population: Classified Index of Occupations and Industries* assigns each of several hundred occupations a composite index score based on the average income and educational level prevailing in the occupation. This index correlates .81 with the Barr subjective intelligence ratings and .90 with the NORC prestige ratings.

Rankings of the prestige of 25 occupations made by 450 high school and college students in 1946 showed the remarkable correlation of .97 with the rankings of the same occupations made by students in 1925 (Tyler, 1965, p. 342). Then, in 1949, the average ranking of these occupations by 500 teachers college students correlated .98 with the 1946 rankings by a different group of high school and college students. Very similar prestige rankings are also found in Britain and show a high degree of consistency across such groups as adolescents and adults, men and women, old and young, and upper and lower social classes. Obviously people are in considerable agreement in their subjective perceptions of numerous occupations, perceptions based on some kind of amalagam of the prestige image and supposed intellectual requirements of occupations, and these are highly related to such objective indices as the typical educational level and average income of the occupation. The subjective desirability of various occupations is also a part of the picture, as indicated by the relative frequencies of various occupational choices made by high school students. These frequencies show scant correspondence to the actual frequencies in various occupations; high-status occupations are greatly overselected and low-status occupations are seldom selected.

How well do such ratings of occupations correlate with the actual IQs of the persons in the rated occupations? The answer depends on whether we correlate the occupational prestige ratings with the *average* IQs in the various occupations or with the IQs of individual persons. The correlations between *average* prestige ratings and *average* IQs in occupations are very high—.90 to .95—when the averages are based on a large number of raters and a wide range of rated occupations. This means that the average of many people's subjective perceptions conforms closely to an objective criterion, namely, tested IQ. Occupations with the highest status ratings are the learned professions—physician, scientist, lawyer, accountant, engineer, and other occupations that involve high educational requirements and highly developed skills, usually of an intellectual nature. The lowest-rated occupations are unskilled manual labor that almost any able-bodied person could do with very little or no prior training or experience and that involves minimal responsibility for decisions or supervision.

The correlation between rated occupational status and *individual* IQs ranges from about .50 to .70 in various studies. The results of such studies are much the same in Britain, the Netherlands, and the Soviet Union as in the United States, where the results are about the same for whites and blacks. The size of the correlation, which varies among different samples, seems to depend mostly on the *age* of the persons whose IQs are correlated with occupational status. IQ and occupational status are correlated .50 to .60 for young men ages 18 to 26 and about .70 for men over 40. A few years can make a big difference in these correlations. The younger men, of course, have not all yet attained their top career potential, and some of the highest-prestige occupations are not even represented in younger age groups. Judges, professors, business executives, college presidents, and the like are missing occupational categories in the studies based on young men, such as those drafted into the armed forces (e.g., the classic study of Harrell & Harrell, 1945).

Evidence contradicts the notion that IQ differences between occupations are the result rather than a cause of the occupational difference. Professional occupations do not score higher than unskilled laborers on IQ tests because the professionals have had more education or have learned more of the test's content in the pursuit of their occupations. A classic study (Ball, 1938) showed that childhood IQs of 219 men correlated substantially with adult occupational status as measured on the Barr scale some 14 to 19 years later—a correlation of .47 for a younger sample of men and of .71 for a sample of older men just five years further into their careers. Thorndike and Hagen (1959) analyzed data on the tested abilities of 10,000 World War II airforce cadets, *all of them high school graduates with IQs above 105,* who were tested at age 21, and their postwar occupations (classified into 124 occupational categories) at 33 years of age. Recall that this was an above-average group in IQ (and education) to begin with, constituting the upper 35 percent of the general population. Yet their scores on a test of general intelligence at age 21 show a marked relationship to their occupational classifications 12 years later. For example, men in the following high-status occupations (listed alphabetically) averaged .53 standard deviations *above* the mean of the whole group of 10,000 in "general intelligence" score: accountants, architects, college professors, engineers, lawyers, physicians, scientists, treasurers and comptrollers, and writers. The following occupations of lower-status occupations (not the lowest, as these were not represented in this above-average sample) averaged .54 standard deviations *below* the overall mean: bus and truck drivers, guards, miners, production assemblers, tractor and crane operators, railroad trainmen, and welders. (Day laborers and unskilled manual occupations are not represented in this group.) In an informal study, mean prestige ratings made by a group of college students of 42 of the 124 occupations in the Thorndike and Hagen list correlated .74 with the occupations' average intelligence scores (R. J. Herrnstein, personal communication, 1971).

To gain an accurate impression of the full range of mean intelligence differences between occupational levels, we must look at a representative sample of the working population that has not been previously selected on intelligence or education. The U.S. Department of Labor has obtained such information (see Manpower Administration, 1970). A representative sample of 39,600 of the employed U.S. labor force in the age range from 18 to 54 years was given the U.S. Employment Services General Aptitude Test Battery. The sample contains 444 of the specific occupations listed in the U.S. Department of Labor's *Dictionary of Occupational Titles* (1965). (Certain occupations were not included in the sample: all farmers and farm workers and foremen, proprietors, managers and officials, and service workers.) The overall mean GATB General Intelligence score is 100, with a standard deviation of 20. The means of the 444 specific occupations range from 55 (tomato peeler) to 143 (mathematician). Thus the total range of occupational means embraces 4.45 standard deviations on the scale of the distribution of intelligence test scores in the general working population of men and women in the United States, with the exception of the excluded occupations noted. Figure 8.6 shows the frequency distribution of the means of the GATB intelligence test scores of the 444 occupations. Superimposed on it is the normal distribution. Even though the *Dictionary of Occupational Titles* was not made up with reference either to intelligence or to the normal distribution nor was the sampling of these 444 occupations or the 39,600 men and women in them, it is interesting to see that the distribution of occupational means is roughly symmetrical but departs significantly from the normal curve. The distribution of occupational means is quite *leptokurtic;* that is, there is a piling up of scores in the middle of the distribution with too few scores at the extremes for a truly normal curve. The lack of perfect symmetry of the distribution, with too small frequencies in the range from 60 to 80, may well be due in part to the exclusion from the sample of all farm workers and the unemployed. We know from other studies that intelligence test scores from the lower half of the normal distribution are overrepresented among farm workers and the unemployed. The smaller frequencies in the

Figure 8.6.   Frequency distribution (shaded histogram) of *mean* intelligence test scores of 444 occupational categories. A normal curve (smooth line) shows the theoretical distribution of *individual* scores in the population.

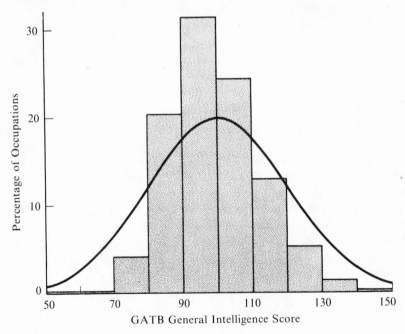

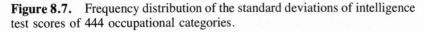

Figure 8.7. Frequency distribution of the standard deviations of intelligence test scores of 444 occupational categories.

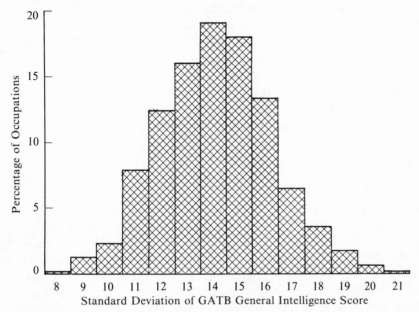

lower tail of the distribution are also due to the fact that the distribution of scores within the lowest occupational categories is quite positively skewed, which pulls up the mean of the occupational group. (Median scores would be expected to show a more normal distribution than mean scores.) Hence it appears that the frequency distribution of the average intellectual requirements of existing occupations corresponds somewhat to the distribution of general intelligence in the working adult population with the marked exception that the percentage of jobs of average ability (i.e., within plus or minus one standard deviation of the mean) is greater than the percentage of persons of average ability. This is because so many of these middle-level jobs contain persons scoring over quite a wide range, so that the *average* score within each job category is pulled toward the middle of the distribution.

Thus at least as important a fact as the differences *between* the means of occupations is the wide distribution of individual scores *within* occupations. Figure 8.7 shows the frequency distribution of the standard deviations of GATB intelligence scores in 444 occupations. They range from a standard deviation of 8 to a standard deviation of 21, with a mean standard deviation of 14.6. These standard deviations may be compared with the standard deviation of 20 for the distribution of individual scores in the total population. The full *range* of scores in different occupations is of course much greater. Analysis of variance shows that of the total population variance in test scores, 47 percent of it is variation *between* the means of occupations and 53 percent is individual variation *within* occupations. (From these figures, it follows statistically that the correlation between individual intelligence scores and occupational classifications is $\sqrt{.47} = .69$). The distribution of individual scores *within* occupations is roughly normal for most occupations but tends to become skewed to the right in the occupations lowest on the intelligence scale; in these groups there is a greater piling up of low scores with a long narrow tail of the distribution extending up to quite high scores.

It is a consistent finding in all the studies of occupations and IQ that the standard deviation of scores within occupations steadily *decreases* as one moves from the lowest to the highest occupational levels on the intelligence scale. In other words, a diminishing percentage of the population is intellectually capable of satisfactory performance in occupations the higher the occupations stand on the scale of occupational status. Almost anyone can succeed as a tomato peeler, for example, and so persons of almost every intelligence level except the severely retarded may be found in such a job. But relatively few can succeed as a mathematician; no persons in the lower half of the intelligence distribution are to be found in this occupation in which nearly all who succeed are in the upper quarter of the population distribution of IQ. Thus the lower score of the total range of scores in each occupation is much more closely related to occupational status than is the upper score of the range.

For example, in a study using the Army General Classification Test (with an overall mean of 100 and a standard deviation of 20), the range of scores for engineers is 100 to 151 (with a mean of 127) whereas the range for farmers is 24 to 147 (with a mean of 93) (Harrell & Harrell, 1945). From the "lowest" to the "highest" occupations, the top of the score range varies only 12 points (from 145 to 157), whereas the bottom score of the range varies 86 points (from 16 to 102). This threshold quality of general intelligence with respect to occupational status was first stated clearly by Harrell and Harrell (1945, p. 239):

> Evidently a certain minimum of intelligence is required for any one of many occupations and a man must have that much intelligence in order to function in that occupation, but a man may have high intelligence and be found in a lowly occupation because he lacks other qualifications than intelligence.

A certain threshold level of intelligence is a necessary but not sufficient condition for success in most occupations. Therefore a low IQ is much more predictive of occupational level than is a high IQ. A person with a high IQ may be anything from an unskilled laborer to a Nobel Prize-winning scientist. But low-IQ persons are not found at all in the sciences or in any of the learned professions. The range of WAIS IQs of 80 medical students in one year's class of the University of Oregon Medical School goes from 111 to 149 (with a median of 125.5). But the lowest IQ of 111 still exceeds the IQs of 77 percent of the general population (Matarazzo, 1972, p. 177). WAIS IQs of 148 members of the Cambridge University faculty ranged from 110 to 141 (with a mean of 126.5) (Matarazzo, 1972, p. 180). A group of 243 policemen and firemen had a range of WAIS IQs from 96 to 130, with a median of 113. In this group there was one exceptional outlier with an IQ of 86 (Matarazzo, 1972, p. 175). Almost no professional, technical, or highly skilled job has a median IQ below 100. Typical jobs with median IQs falling slightly below this point are crane operator, cook, weaver, truck driver, laborer, barber, lumberjack, farmhand, and miner (Harrell & Harrell, 1945).

Terman's famous follow-up study of some 1,500 school children with IQs of 140 and above (with an average IQ of 152) showed that this group by middle age attained a far higher level of occupational status than would have been expected for a random sample of persons of comparable childhood backgrounds or even of college graduates (Terman & Oden, 1959). Among the men in Terman's study, the ten most frequent occupations were lawyers, engineers, college professors, major business managers, financial executives, scientists, physicians, educational administrators, top business executives, and accountants—in that order. Over 85 percent of the men in the Terman group were employed in these high-level occupations. Only about 3 percent were farmers or semiskilled laborers, and virtually none were unskilled laborers.

The Terman sample also had earnings well above the income level of the general population and higher than persons of the same education and occupation. In fact, in this very superior group, amount of formal education seemed to make relatively little difference in income. For example, even those in the Terman sample who had not gone beyond high school had earnings comparable with those who had graduated from college with a bachelor's degree; and of the six men with the highest incomes in the entire sample, only one was a college graduate.

In the general population, however, there is a closer link between education and income than was found for the Terman gifted group. It has been argued by a number of sociologists and economists that the correlation between IQ and income (as well as between IQ and occupational status) is largely *indirect;* it is *mediated* via the correlation of IQ with amount of education and of education with occupation and income (e.g., Bajema, 1968; Bowles & Gintis, 1973; Eckland, 1965; Jencks, 1972). This conclusion is based on the observation that the *partial correlation* between amount of education (i.e., highest grade completed) and occupational status (statistically holding IQ constant) is much higher than the partial correlation between IQ and occupational status (statistically holding education constant). Table 8.7 shows the simple correlations and partial correlations found in two typical studies. What these partial correlations mean is that occupational status is related to IQ for all persons having the same educational level.

But the interpretation of such partial correlations is very tricky. They are easily misleading. The high partial correlation of education and occupation, for example, would seem to imply that almost anyone, given the necessary amount of education, could attain the corresponding occupational status more or less regardless of his or her IQ, as the partial correlation of IQ and occupation is quite low. But this would be a false inference, because not everyone can attain the educational thresholds required by the higher occupa-

Table 8.7. Simple and partial correlations between IQ, amount of education, and occupational status in two samples. (Above diagonal, data from Bajema, 1968; below diagonal, data from Waller, 1971)

	Simple Correlation		Partial Correlation	
	Education	*Occupation*	*Education*	*Occupation*
IQ[1]	.58 / .52	.46 / .50	.42 / .27	.15 / .21
Education		.63 / .72		.50 / .63

[1]IQ in the Bajema study is Terman Group Test given in the sixth grade. IQ in the Waller study is Otis and Kuhlman group tests given in school at a mean age of 13.38 years.

tions. Holding IQ constant statistically, as a partial correlation, only means that, among those whose IQs are above the threshold required for any given occupation, educational attainment then becomes the chief determinant of occupational level. The low partial correlation between IQ and occupation does not contradict the importance of the threshold property of IQ in relation to occupational status. If the true relationship between IQ and occupation were as low as the partial correlations would seem to suggest, we should find every level of IQ in every type of occupation. But of course this is far from true, even in occupations to which entry involves little or no formal education. Moreover, not all high-IQ persons choose to enter the professions or other high-status occupations, but those who do so work to attain the required educational levels; and hence educational level is more highly correlated with occupational level than is IQ per se.

The causal relationships between IQ, education, and occupational status are too complex to be explained satisfactorily in terms of partial correlations, as the forms of the correlation scatter diagram between these variables do not all involve to the same degree the property of being "necessary and sufficient" types of correlations.[2] (A statistician would note that the bivariate distributions are not *homoscedastic,*★ which makes partial correlations hazardous.) Because of the practically inextricable causal connections among IQ, education, and occupations, probably the least contentious kind of correlation that one can report is the multiple correlation R between the *combined* effects of IQ and education, on the one hand, and occupational level, on the other. The R based on the data in Table 8.7 is .64 for the Bajema study and .73 for the Waller study.[3]

Some economic and social theorists (e.g., Bowles & Gintis, 1973) would like to have us believe that occupational level is not causally related to IQ but is almost wholly a result of privilege associated with the individual's social-class background, especially the educational and occupational level of the parents, as well as sheer "luck" (which only means as yet unexplained sources of variance). This claim is only partly true. It is partly true because of the correlation between education and occupation and the fact that education has some relationship to social class independently of IQ. Youths from low-socioeconomic backgrounds are less likely to finish high school or graduate from college than are youths of higher SES but of the same IQs. This is more true at mediocre levels of IQ; SES makes a considerably greater educational difference for the mediocre than for those at the upper end of the IQ scale.

The fact that privilege associated with family background is not the whole story in occupational level is shown by the great variability in occupation and income among members of the same family. Inequality in occupational status between brothers is about 82 percent of status inequality in the general population; the correlation between brothers' occupational statuses is only about .30 (Jencks, 1972, pp. 198, 343). Moreover, a substantial part of the status inequality within families is related to IQ differences within families. This is clearly seen in a study by Waller (1971), which found that the discrepancy between father's and son's adult occupational status correlated + .368 with the difference in their IQs. The IQs were obtained from high school records for both fathers and sons. Sons with IQs higher than their fathers' IQs tended to attain higher occupational levels than their fathers, and sons with lower IQs than their fathers' generally fell below their fathers' occupational levels. Waller concludes that intelligence produces variation in persons' occupational attainments that is unrelated to the status of their family origin.

Income, like occupational level, is causally related to IQ in a complex fashion. The simple correlation between IQ and earnings is about .30 for white males and only about .10 for black males, and the simple correlations between education and earnings are about the same (Brown & Reynolds, 1975). Jencks (1972, p. 240) estimates the correlation between intelligence (AFQT scores) and income, after correction for unreliability of measurement, to be .349. A correlation this size, though seemingly small, still has considerable consequences in terms of dollars and cents. As Jencks (1972, p. 220) notes, men who scored above the 80th percentile on the Armed Forces Qualification Test (AFQT) after the Korean War had personal incomes 34 percent above the national average, whereas men who scored below the 20th percentile had incomes about 34 percent below the average; this amounts to the first group's earning about twice as much as the second group. Jencks's analyses of the best available income and IQ data led to the conclusion that ''about half the observed relationship between test scores and income persists after we control family background and [educational] credentials'' (p. 221).

Citing other evidence on the relation of earnings to IQ and education, Leona Tyler (1974, p. 47) draws the following conclusion:

> These figures show that the more college education a high school graduate obtained, the higher his income turned out to be; but they also show that with any amount of education beyond high school, persons who as children scored in the top ten percent [i.e., IQ 119 and above] on an intelligence test had a distinct advantage over the rest. What the figures suggest is that measured intelligence is related not solely to school success and survival but also to the kinds of real life success reflected in income differences. If this is true, some advantage of high scores may remain even if schools and colleges cease to carry out the screening that has been a major source of the relationship between educational aptitude and occupational success.

Tested Ability and Performance within Occupations.   The IQ and other ability test scores are considerably better at predicting persons' occupational statuses than at predicting how well they will perform in the particular occupational niche they enter. Some one-fourth to one-half of the total IQ variance of the employed population is already absorbed in the allocation of persons to different occupations, so that there is less IQ variation left over that can enter into the correlation between IQ and criteria of success *within* occupations.

Restriction of range, however, is not the major factor responsible for the often low correlations between test scores and job performance. For one thing, in the vast majority of jobs, once the necessary skills have been acquired, successful performance does not depend primarily on the ability we have identified as *g*. Other traits of personality, developed specialized skills, experience, and ability to get along with people become paramount in job success as it is usually judged. It has been said that in the majority of jobs, as far as employers are concerned, the most important ability is not intellectual ability but *dependability*.

Another factor that lowers predictive validity is the lack of standardization of the criterion. The criterion of successful job performance is usually a judgment of the worker's immediate supervisor. Supervisor ratings have notoriously poor reliability compared with objective measures of performance. The assessment of job success is often based on more objective indices such as actual production records, sales records, and tested job-related knowledge and skills. In many test validation studies based on various criteria of job performance, inconsistent criteria are used for different employees on the same job. For example, Mr. X, a stockman, receives a low rating because, although seemingly conscientious, he is judged to be slow and inaccurate in his work; Mr. Y in the same job, although he is fast and accurate, receives the same rating as Mr. X because Mr. Y is often late to work, overextends coffee breaks and lunch hour, and is often seen socializing rather than working on the job. Both men are given low job ratings by their supervisor for such different reasons that it would seem miraculous if their IQs were at all correlated with their ratings.

Yet despite these kinds of limiting conditions, there are still sufficiently substantial predictive validities of ability tests for many jobs to be of considerable value in personnel selection.

A review of the entire literature on the validity of tests for predicting job performance found that intelligence tests correlate on the average in the range of .20 to .25 with ratings of actual proficiency on the job (Ghiselli, 1955). An equally important finding of Ghiselli's review is that the average validity of intelligence scores for predicting proficiency differs systematically for various types of jobs. For example, here are the ranges for the majority of validity coefficients for the following groups of occupations:

.00 to .19   Sales, service occupations, machinery workers,
               packers and wrappers, repairmen
.20 to .34   Supervisors, clerks, assemblers
.35 to .47   Electrical workers, managerial and professional

These results suggest the hypothesis that the predictive validity of tests is related in part to the *g* demands of the job.

Another important conclusion from the Ghiselli monograph is that test validities for training criteria (e.g., course grades, instructor ratings, time required to meet training criteria) are considerably higher than for actual job proficiency criteria after training. Training criteria correlate close to .50 with IQ and other ability tests. Often the abilities that best predict success in training for a particular job are not the same abilities that best predict success on the job after training. The most *g*-loaded tests have their highest validity for predicting success in *training*. After training is completed, special abilities—numerical, spatial, perceptual, motor—gain in importance, relative to *g*, for predicting actual job performance.

Ghiselli's 1955 review includes a great variety of tests with different psychometric properties, a fact that could itself contribute to the great variability he observed in the validity coefficients for many jobs. The extensive validation studies carried out by the U.S. Employment Service using a single standardized test battery—the General Aptitude Test Battery, or GATB—overcomes this objection. Yet the results are still very similar to those by Ghiselli.

The GATB was devised according to factor analytic principles and yields scores on the following factors:

G – General Intelligence
V – Verbal Aptitude
N – Numerical Aptitude
S – Spatial Aptitude

P – Form Perception
Q – Clerical Perception
A – Aiming
T – Motor Speed } *K* – Motor Coordination
F – Finger Dexterity
M – Manual Dexterity

A total of 537 predictive and concurrent validity coefficients, based almost entirely on supervisory ratings, were obtained on large samples of workers in 446 different occupational categories listed in the *Dictionary of Occupational Titles.* Validity coefficients were determined on the basis of the optimally weighted composite of the various GATB scores for predicting performance ratings in each occupation, as well as for each of the ten separate factors. Figure 8.8 shows the frequency distributions of validity coefficients for the multifactor battery and for *G,* the general intelligence score, which is factorially about the same as scores on most standard IQ tests. It can be seen that multiple predictors yield somewhat higher validities than *G* alone. The median validity for multiple predictors is +.36; for *G* it is +.27.

Notice also that the distribution of validities for *G* has a wider spread than the distribution of multifactorial validities. In the latter case, of course, a different best-weighted combination of tests is used to maximize the validity for each occupation. Against this multifactor standard, *G* alone stands up remarkably well.

As noted in the Ghiselli review, there are occupational differences in validity coefficients, and these are much more highly related to *G* validities than to multifactor validities. In general, occupations with the greatest cognitive demands, the "knowledge

Figure 8.8. Frequency distribution of 537 validity coefficients of the General Aptitude Test Battery for 446 different occupations. *G score* is general intelligence; multifactor validity is based on a weighted composite of GATB subtests.

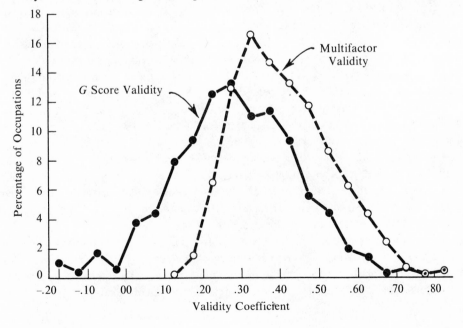

jobs'' and those requiring higher education or technical training show the highest G validities. Jobs showing negligible (or even negative) G validities are on the whole the least skilled and least complex jobs that involve rather simple, repetitive, or routine work, such as onion corer ($-.15$), metal chair assembler ($-.19$), and letter-opener operator ($-.08$).

It is also interesting to note that although the G validities are higher for training criteria than for job proficiency criteria, the multifactor validities show no difference in this respect. It is also interesting that *predictive* validites average slightly higher (by .04) than *concurrent* validities, probably because the latter are based on tests given to persons who have already survived in the given job for some time and they are therefore a more highly selected sample in terms of job performance and suitability for the job.

The fact that general intelligence correlates significantly with performance ratings in so very many ordinary jobs that have little or no formal educational requirements calls for closer psychological scrutiny into the specific aspects of these jobs that account for the correlation between job proficiency ratings and general intelligence.

The Human Resources Research Organization, better known as ''HumRRO,'' has done intensive research on just this question (Vineberg & Taylor, 1972). The test of general intelligence they used was the Armed Forces Qualification Test. The subjects of the study were 1,544 inducted and enlisted men in the army distributed about equally in four specific job categories: armor crewman, repairman, supply specialist, and cook. At the time of the study all the men were working daily in their jobs. Job experience ranged from one month to over twenty years. Job proficiency was measured by objective job-sample tests. These tests were made up by having persons in the jobs make up inventories of the specific activities involved in the performance of the job. Because the job of cook will be more familiar than the other jobs to most readers, it provides the best example. The inventory of duties contains twenty-nine items, for example, prepares cook's worksheet and other forms, takes inventory of food products and kitchen equipment, stores and inspects food, prepares beverage, cooks meat, fish, poultry, prepares desserts, cleans or disassembles equipment, cooks soups, and so on. Under each of these categories are a number of even more specific jobs, such as ''makes scrambled eggs,'' ''makes jellyroll,'' ''makes cocoa.'' These many specific jobs constitute the ''items'' of the job-sample test. (The tests contain 359 items for armor crewmen, 176 for repairmen, 156 for supply specialist, and 158 for cooks.) The person's score is simply the percentage of the total items that the person could perform unassisted. (Prompts were allowed on some of the more complex items, which were given part-scores that added to the total score only when prompts for the various subtasks were not needed.)

First, it was shown that there is a significant correlation between AFQT and scores on the job-sample tests. The partial correlations, which remove from the AFQT × job-sample correlation the effects of years of education, number of months on the job, and age, are the most relevant here. The partial correlations for the four jobs are armor crewman, .36; repairman, .32; supply specialist, .38; cook .35.

It is interesting to compare these partial correlations with the corresponding partial correlations between AFQT scores and supervisor ratings of job performance; armor crewman, .26; repairman, .15; supply specialist, .11; cook, .15. The AFQT correlates significantly higher with the objective job-sample tests than with supervisor ratings. (The simple correlations between job-sample scores and supervisory ratings for the four jobs are .27, .20, .28, and .28.)

A paper-and-pencil job-knowledge test was also given. Its validity is attested to by its partial correlations (controlling for AFQT, education, and age) with *months on the job,* ranging from .48 to .66, with an average of .56 in the four jobs. The partial correlations (controlling education, age, and months on job) between job knowledge and AFQT scores were armor crewman, .54; repairman, .42; supply specialist, .37; cook, .47. Thus AFQT correlates somewhat higher with job-knowledge than with job-sample scores.

Finally, the most important from a theoretical standpoint are the analyses that highlight the aspect of job performance, as assessed by the job-sample tests, that is most responsible for its correlation with general intelligence as measured by the AFQT. Subjects were classified into four mental groups in terms of AFQT score, as follows:

Mental Group	AFQT Percentile	WAIS IQ Equivalent
I	93–100	122 and above
II	65–92	105–121
III	31–64	93–104
IV	10–30	81–92

The AFQT percentiles are based on all U.S. males, ages 18 to 26, who have come up for the armed forces draft. The Wechsler Adult Intelligence Scale (Full Scale) IQs corresponding to the same percentiles in the general population are listed as a frame of reference. The mean job-sample scores of the AFQT groupings show clear separation out to at least five years of experience on the job, after which there is some, but not complete, convergence of mean scores.

Correlations between AFQT and job-sample scores are mainly a function of the empirically determined difficulty level of the subtests. The easiest job-sample problems (in terms of percentage of subjects passing the item) discriminated the least between the AFQT Mental Groups. The more difficult and complex items discriminated more highly between the groups. For example, comparing the percentage of cooks in category IV with the percentage in categories I to III who can scramble eggs, an easy task, we see a nonsignificant difference of 77.5 percent versus 79.0 percent. For the somewhat more complex task of making a jellyroll, there is a significant difference of 59.9 percent versus 70.3 percent. In fact, the only single subtest in all of the 849 subtests for the four jobs that showed no significant difference between the AFQT categories was making scrambled eggs—the easiest of all the test items for cooks! A graph of the percentage passing the repairman's job-sample subtests as a function of AFQT Mental Category, task difficulty, and months on the job clearly illustrates the greater separation of the AFQT groups on the difficult than on the easy job performance items, a difference that persists to some degree throughout all months on the job, as shown in Figure 8.9. Similar trends were found in the other three job categories.

The trends of the means, which are theoretically important for understanding the nature of general ability, should not detract from the considerable amount of overlap of the AFQT mental groups in their performance on the various jobs. Substantial percentages of

Figure 8.9.   Mean scores on job-sample tests for repairman as a function of task difficulty (easy, medium, or difficult), intelligence level (AFQT categories), and number of
months on the job.   (From Vineberg & Taylor, 1972, p. 56)

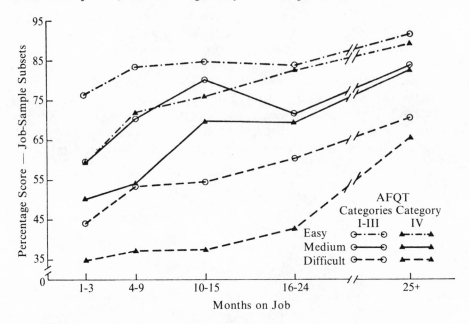

every mental group performed above and below the median on the job-sample tests. With
increasing months of job experience, an increasing percentage in the AFQT Group IV
were able to perform at acceptable levels on these particular army jobs.

Another army study carried out by HumRRO psychologists (Fox & Taylor, 1967)
demonstrated most clearly the interaction between general intelligence level and task
complexity, even when the tasks are extremely simple and variation in degree of task
complexity is minimal. Two artificial "jobs" were devised, both at a simple stimulus–
response level of performance, but one task involved only simple reaction time, the other
complex reaction time. The authors described these two tasks as follows:

> [S]equential monitoring tasks which fall at the simplest level of complexity. In fact,
> they are so simple that no learning is required for performance. These tasks have
> elements in common with many military jobs. . . . Task 1 (T_1) is a Simple Sequen-
> tial Monitoring Task. The trainee was told that his "control" panel was part of a
> communications system that became overloaded when a red light came on. His task
> was simply to "reset" the control panel by pressing the lever when a red light
> appeared. The control panel apparatus was programmed so that white lights flashed
> intermittently across the panel accompanied by loud clicking noises. After an inter-
> val which varied from 15 to 205 seconds, the white lights went out and one of the
> four red lights came on. The trainee was required to "reset" the panel a total of
> twenty times over a forty-minute period. The second task (T_2) is a Choice Sequen-
> tial Monitoring Task and uses the same apparatus as the previous task except for
> additional response levers. The trainee was to respond to one of the four red lights,

labeled A, B, C or D, by pressing the corresponding lever. All procedures and programming were identical for both tasks.

The subject's performance was measured in terms of reaction time, that is, the time interval between the appearance of the red light and the subject's pressing the lever.

The tasks were given to two groups of army recruits from mental categories I and IV on the AFQT, labeled "Hi" and "Lo" AFQT, respectively. The results are shown in Figure 8.10. Notice that for both AFQT groups choice monitoring resulted in greater response times than simple monitoring and that the separation between the Hi and Lo AFQT groups was greater for the slightly more complex task, even at this relatively simple level. This result shows that subjects who are selected on general intelligence differ even on performance of very simple tasks. The general ability factor thus extends over an enormous range of complexity and types of performance.

IQ and Creativity

In recent years, the popular psychological and educational literature has promulgated the notion of "creativity" as a psychological trait quite distinct from, or even opposed to, general intelligence. The belief is probably born of the hope that, if a person is deficient in intelligence, there is a chance that he may possess an abundance of something at least equally valuable—*creativity*. However, there is no sound scientific basis for this hope.

The term "creativity" is in quotes because it means so many different things to different investigators and has no standard operational definition. The use of the term in the psychological literature often refers to types of behavior that scarcely correspond to

Figure 8.10.   Reaction times on simple and choice monitoring tasks by high and low scorers on the Armed Forces Qualification Test.   (From Fox & Taylor, 1967)

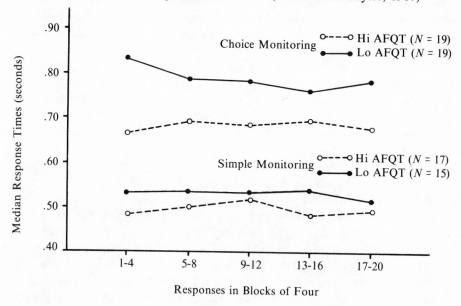

what the layman means by creativity. The laymen's concept of creativity generally involves the characteristics both of *originality* and *quality* of performance. To devise objective measures of "creativity" that have as little correlation with IQ as possible, psychologists have had to leave out of consideration altogether the concept of quality of performance.

There exists at present no validated test of "creativity" in the sense of being able to predict who will be socially judged as creative in the arts or sciences. The existing tests of "creativity" are more accurately referred to as tests of *divergent thinking*. The usual IQ tests involve mainly *convergent thinking*. That is, the mental manipulations called forth by a given test item lead to a single correct solution. Items in a test of divergent thinking, in contast, are intended to lead to a large number and diversity of possible answers, none of which is either correct or incorrect. The person's responses are scored for *fluency* (i.e., number of responses to a question), *flexibility* (i.e., diversity of responses), and *originality* (i.e., uncommonness of the responses). A typical example of a divergent thinking test item is the "unusual uses" type of item, such as the question "How many uses can you think of for a brick?" Answers such as the following would score low on flexibility and originality: "To build a house," "To build a fireplace," "To build a wall," "To pave a walk." Higher-scoring answers would be "As a doorstop," "A pillow for an ascetic monk," "An abrasive to strike matches on," "As a bedwarmer or footwarmer after heating it in a stove."

Critical reviews of attempts to measure creativity have concluded that various creativity tests show hardly any higher correlations with one another than with standard tests of intelligence (Thorndike, 1963b; Vernon, 1964). The *g* factor is common to both kinds of tests, and there seems to be no independent substantial general factor that can be called creativity. Besides *g*, creativity tests involve long-recognized smaller group factors usually labeled as verbal and ideational fluency. Differences between persons scoring high and persons scoring low on "creativity" tests, when they are matched on IQ, invariably consist of descriptions of *personality* differences rather than of characteristics that would be thought of as any kind of *ability* differences. Thus "creativity," at least as presently measured, apparently is not another type of ability that contends with *g* for importance, as some writers might lead us to believe (Getzels & Jackson, 1962; Wallach & Kogan, 1965). While "creativity" tests may be related to certain personality characteristics, they have not been shown to be related to real-life originality or productivity in science, invention, or the arts, which are what most people regard as the criteria of creativity.

For a time it was believed that the research of Wallach and Kogan (1965) contradicted the conclusion of earlier reviews to the effect that "creativity" and intelligence are not different co-equal abilities or even factorially distinguishable traits. Wallach and Kogan had claimed that the failure of earlier researches to separate creativity and intelligence was a result of the fact that the creativity tests were usually given in the same manner as the usual psychometric tests, with time limits, as measures of some kind of ability, in an atmosphere conducive to competitiveness and self-critical standards. These conditions, it was maintained, were antithetical to the expression of creativity. So Wallach and Kogan gave their tests of creativity (better labeled as *fluency*) without time limits, in a very free, nonjudgmental, play-like, game-like atmosphere. Under these conditions, they found negligible correlations between several verbal intelligence tests and their "creativity" tests. The "creativity" scores, however, account for only a small percentage (2 percent to 9 percent) of the variance in any of the dependent variables measured in this study. High scorers in general tended to be less inhibited or less constricted in producing responses; they responded more energetically and fluently in the game-like setting in which the "creativity" tests were given.

In a penetrating and trenchant methodological critique and reanalysis of the Wallach–Kogan data, Cronbach (1968) concluded:

> My final impression is that the F [i.e., fluency or "creativity"] variable has disappointingly limited psychological significance. It can scarcely be considered a measure of ability or creativity; there is no evidence that high F children produce responses of superior quality in any situation. It is correlated with other measures of social responsiveness, but not strongly.   (p. 509)

In one of the earliest works on the psychology of creativity, Spearman (1930) argued that socially recognized creativity exemplified the very process that most characterizes g—"the eduction of relations and correlates." Creativity could be characterized as "the eduction of *new* relations and correlates." This is the essence of invention and innovation—in science, in the arts, in politics. According to Spearman, a high level of g is a necessary but not sufficient condition for creativity in the nontrivial sense. Creative persons may possess certain traits of personality and character not found as often in noncreative persons, but none is poorly endowed on g.[4]

Most present-day researchers on creativity, such as MacKinnon, Barron, and Torrance, acknowledge the *threshold relationship* of intelligence to creativity. Beyond a certain threshold level of intelligence, which is probably about one standard deviation above the mean IQ of the general population, there is little relationship between IQ and rated creativity; below the threshold there is simply no creativity to speak of in any culturally significant sense. Below the threshold, tests of "creativity" are factorially hard to distinguish from tests of general intelligence.

If there were actually no relationship of any kind between creativity and intelligence, as some popular writers would have us believe, we should expect to find the same proportion of mentally retarded persons (with IQs below 70) among the acknowledged creative geniuses of history as is found in the general population. Biographical research on the childhoods of famous creative persons in history, however, has revealed that in 300 cases on whom sufficient data were available, all of them without exception showed childhood accomplishments that would characterize them as of above-average intelligence, and the majority of them were judged to be in the "gifted" range above IQ 140 (Cox, 1926).

Donald W. MacKinnon has actually obtained the Wechsler (WAIS) Full Scale IQs of 185 noted architects, mathematicians, scientists, and engineers who were selected from a national sample on the basis of ratings by other professionals in these fields as being among the most creative contributors to these socially significant fields (MacKinnon & Hall, 1972). In this highly select group, the judged ranking in creativity correlated only +.11 with WAIS IQ. But the more important fact, which is often neglected in popular accounts, shows the threshold relationship of IQ to creativity: the total IQ variance in this group of creative persons is *less than one-fourth* of the IQ variance in the general population. The entire creative sample ranges between the 70th and 99.9th percentiles of the population norms in IQ (i.e., IQs from 107 to 151), with the group's *mean* at the 98th percentile (IQ 131). To the extent that these groups are typical of persons whom society regards as creative, it can be said that some 75 to 80 percent of the general population would be excluded from the creative category on the basis of IQ alone. Despite claims that IQ has little or nothing to do with creativity, no one has ever published the crucial evidence that would necessarily follow from this position: a distribution of IQs among persons of generally acknowledged creativity that differs nonsignificantly from the distribution of IQs in the population. It would be absolutely astounding if such evidence could ever be found.

Nonintellectual Correlates of IQ

Intelligence tests have never been specifically devised to measure anything other than general intellectual ability and scholastic aptitude, and so it is especially interesting to note that, despite this fact, IQ has a number of nonintellectual and nonacademic behavioral correlates. The *causal* connection between IQ and nonintellectual behavior, such as personality adjustment, social responsibility, delinquency, and crime, is complicated. The links in the chain of causality are not at all clearly worked out in most studies. Social-class and cultural differences are undoubtedly involved to some degree in such correlations, but they are not the whole story. Frustration due to repeated failures in a society that makes many intellectual demands, particularly during the school years, can lead, for those who are less able to compete intellectually, to aggression, or withdrawal, or other forms of socially maladaptive behavior.

In a highly organized social system of a technological bent that tends to sort out people according to their abilities, and rewards them more or less accordingly, it seems not surprising to find that those traits of personality and temperament that complement and reinforce the development of intellectual skills requiring persistent application, practice, freedom from emotional distraction, and resistance to mental fatigue and boredom in the absence of physical activity, should become genetically assorted and segregated, and thereby be genetically correlated with the socially valued mental abilities that require the most education for their full development and utilization in the world of work.

Thus ability and personality traits tend to work together in determining a person's overall capability in the society. For example, Cattell (1950) has found that certain personality traits are correlated to the extent of about 0.3 to 0.5 with the general mental ability factor. He concludes: "There is a moderate tendency . . . for the person gifted with higher general ability, to acquire a more integrated character, somewhat more emotional stability, and a more conscientious outlook. He tends to become 'morally intelligent' as well as 'abstractly intelligent' " (pp. 98–99). The connection between intelligence and moral behavior has been further investigated in recent years by Harvard psychologist Laurence Kohlberg (1969), who concludes that a person's complexity and maturity of moral judgments depend in large part on his level of general cognitive ability. Because the correlation, though substantial, is not perfect, we can all, of course, point out notable exceptions.

Adjustment and Adaptive Behavior. "Adjustment" is a broad term in psychology and mental hygiene, referring to a complex of behaviors involving such features as emotional stability, freedom from neurotic symptoms, responsibility, getting along with people, social participation, realistic self-confidence, absence of socially disruptive and self-defeating behavior, healthy attitudes about sex and bodily functions, marital success, possessing more than superficial or fleeting interests and values (whatever they may be), and displaying a capacity for self-discipline and planful and sustained goal-directed effort. What psychoanalysts term "ego strength" is an amalgam of these indices of "adjustment." Adjustment is usually assessed by means of interviews, detailed ratings by parents, teachers, or peers, and self-report adjustment inventories or questionnaires.

A number of studies (see reviews by Anderson, 1960; Kohlberg, LaCrosse, & Ricks, 1970; White et al., 1973, pp. 207–209) have found substantial correlations between IQ and various assessments of adjustment. The validity of IQ for predicting adjustment generally ranges from 0.4 to 0.6, even when several years intervene between the IQ and adjustment assessments. IQs measured in Grades 6 to 9, for example, show correlations of about 0.50 with various assessments of adjustment in early adulthood. A review of longitudinal studies relating IQ to later indices of adjustment reached the following conclusion: "[A] crude quantitative estimate of the predictive power of IQ is the statement that 20% to 30% of the reliable variation in gross ratings or estimates of adjustment in a representative sample of adults can be predicted from elementary school IQ scores" (Kohlberg et al., 1970). It was also noted that high IQ predicts very good adjustment somewhat better than low IQ predicts very poor adjustment.

Curiously, two of the most extreme forms of maladjustment—psychosis and suicide—seem to be unrelated to IQ. Terman's "gifted" group of 1,500 persons with IQs above 140, for example, showed at age 40 better than average adjustment on all criteria considered except the incidence of psychosis and suicide, which were about the same as in the general population (Terman & Oden, 1959).

The extent to which there is a direct *causal* connection between IQ level and adjustment is still obscure. All we can say for certain on the basis of the present evidence is that IQ *predicts* adjustment to some extent as a result of both IQ and adjustment being correlated elements in a complex causal network involving other factors such as social class, cultural values, styles of child rearing, physical health and appearance, and probably some degree of criterion contamination (i.e., indicants of intelligence, per se, influencing ratings of adjustment).

Adaptive behavior is somewhat akin to adjustment, but it also involves to a greater extent the implication of personal and social *competence*. In the words of Matarazzo (1972, pp. 147–148):

> *Adaptive behavior* refers primarily to the effectiveness with which the individual copes with, and adjusts to, the natural and social demands of his environment. It has two principal facets: (a) the degree to which the individual is able to function and maintain himself independently, and (b) the degree to which he meets satisfactorily the culturally imposed demands of personal and social responsibility. It is a composite of many aspects of behavior . . . [subsumed] under the designation intellectual, affective, motivational, social, motor, and other noncognitive elements [that] all contribute to and are a part of total adaptation to the environment.

The concept of adaptive behavior, also referred to as social maturity, has evolved largely in connection with the diagnosis of mental retardation. It is now generally agreed that the diagnosis of mental retardation must be based on a broader set of criteria than just performance on an IQ test. The list of additional criteria are termed indices of adaptive behavior, and a number of adaptive behavior rating scales including these criteria have been devised to improve the reliability and objective validity of assessments of these forms of adaptive behavior.

The American Association on Mental Deficiency has expended considerable research effort in the development of adaptive behavior rating scales (Nihira, Foster, Shellhaas, & Leland, 1969). These scales consist of more than a hundred specific descriptive behavioral items involving three broad factors: personal independence, social maladaptation, and personal maladaptation. Because the scales are intended primarily for use with the mentally retarded, the items are much more discriminating in the lower half of the IQ distribution than in the upper half. Adaptive behavior scales necessarily have too low a ceiling for the above-average segment of the population. Many items, for example, involve quite simple everyday skills such as handling money, personal care and hygiene, telling time, domestic skills, ability to go shopping alone, and the like. (In normal children items of this kind are correlated .60 to .70 with Stanford–Binet mental age and some 117 such items have been age graded to form the well-known Vineland Social Maturity Scale; see Doll, 1953, 1965.)

Adaptive behavior, as rated on such scales, is substantially, but far from perfectly, correlated with IQ among retardates. Correlations in a number of institutional samples range from .58 to .95 (Leland, Shellhaas, Nihira, & Foster, 1967, p. 368). (See also Chapter 14, pp. 681–685.)

School Deportment.   A study of 7,119 school children aged 6 to 11, by Roberts and Baird (1972), shows a relationship between a pupil's intelligence (as rated by their teachers) and the frequency with which the teacher reports the pupil's behavior in school results in disciplinary action on the teacher's part. At all ages, for both boys and girls, there is a negative relationship, corresponding to an overall correlation of about $-.30$, between rated intelligence and frequency of disciplinary action. Although disciplinary action was less frequent for girls than for boys, it had about the same correlation with intelligence as was found for boys. A possibly serious shortcoming of this study, of course, is that, because both the assessments of intelligence and of frequency of disciplining were based on teacher judgments, there could be an undetermined degree of criterion contamination[*] or "halo effect"[*] involved in the correlation between these two variables. However, other evidence on the negative correlation between measured IQ and delinquent behavior suggests that the correlation between teacher ratings of intelligence and deportment is not mainly due to a halo effect.

Activity Level in Early Childhood.   Harvard psychologist Jerome Kagan was the first to report the observation of a *negative* correlation between degree of motoric hyperactivity (hyperkinesis) in young children (ages 3 to 6 years) and their intellectual level at maturity (Kagan, 1971; Kagan, Moss, & Sigel, 1963). It is as if the inability to inhibit gross motor activity in early childhood interferes with development of the capacity for sustained involvement in cognitive tasks. Hyperactivity, impulsivity, and short attention span all work together to hinder the child's acquiring as much information as he should from interaction with the physical and social environment.

Another possible explanation of the negative correlation between degree of early hyperactivity and later cognitive ability is that both variables are related to some third variable that mediates the correlation. This hypothesis is suggested by some excellent recent research by Halverson and Waldrop (1976), who found that early childhood activity level is "highly related to an index of minor physical anomalies" (p. 107). The correlation between physical anomalies, including motor coordination problems, and activity rating in children at $2\frac{1}{2}$ years of age is .51; in the same children at $7\frac{1}{2}$ years of age the correlation is .44. All the sixty-two unselected nonclinical children in this longitudinal study were white middle class, from intact families, who were attending a nursery school. Activity level during free play was rated through systematic observations by trained observers and was also measured objectively by means of a mechanical activity recorder fastened to the child's clothing during free play periods. (When included in a factor analysis of the observers' ratings of activity level, according to various criteria, the activity recorder has a factor loading of .83 on the general factor of activity level.)

Measurements taken from the activity recorder and behavior ratings during free play at age $2\frac{1}{2}$ years show a highly significant correlation of $-.47$ with the Full Scale WISC IQ obtained at age $7\frac{1}{2}$ years. (Verbal and Performance IQs correlate with activity level $-.38$ and $-.40$, respectively.) These are remarkably high correlations, considering that the correlations of IQ with itself between the ages of $2\frac{1}{2}$ and $7\frac{1}{2}$ is only about .50. In other words, at age $2\frac{1}{2}$, objectively measured motoric activity level during free play predicts IQ at age $7\frac{1}{2}$ almost as well as an IQ test itself given at age $2\frac{1}{2}$. The correlation between activity level and later IQ is negative, which means that the young children who show the most fast-moving, vigorous, impulsive behavior during play turn out, on average, to have the lower IQs later on.

There was found to be considerable stability of individual differences of activity level over the five-year period between ages $2\frac{1}{2}$ and $7\frac{1}{2}$. Activity ratings at age $7\frac{1}{2}$ still correlate significantly ($r = -.31$) with IQ at age $7\frac{1}{2}$. The highly g-loaded Embedded Figures Test (given at age $7\frac{1}{2}$) also shows a significant negative correlation ($-.34$) with activity level at age $2\frac{1}{2}$.

Delinquency and Criminal Behavior. A number of studies show that IQ is associated with delinquency and criminality within the white population (Burt, 1925; Caplan, 1965; Glueck & Glueck, 1950; Gordon, 1975; Merrill, 1947; Siebert, 1962). Delinquents with court records average some 10 to 12 IQ points below the mean IQ of nondelinquents. Delinquents come preponderantly from the lower half of the IQ distribution and as a group average only about 3 IQ points higher than the mean IQ of 89 that would be obtained by excluding all IQs above the mean of the general population. Recent research by sociologist Robert A. Gordon (1975b, 1976) presents strong evidence that delinquency is related to IQ to much the same degree in the black as in the white population and that racial, ethnic, social-class, and regional differences in the prevalence of delinquency are highly predictable from the mean IQs of the persons comprising each of these groups. *Across various racial and social-class groups, the prevalence of delinquency is approximately the same at any given IQ level.* In other words, if one controls for IQ, the marked racial and social-class differences in delinquency rates disappear. Minority racial and ethnic groups with mean IQs at or above the general population mean, such as Orientals and Jews, show correspondingly lower rates of delinquency to the same extent that minorities with mean IQs below the population average show correspondingly higher rates. (It should be noted that even quite small but statistically significant correlations between two variables based on individual measurements can result in extremely high correlations between group means on the two variables.) From such findings, Gordon (1975b, 1976) argues that general cognitive ability, as indexed by IQ, must be regarded as a central variable in the development of a scientific theory of delinquency and criminality. This viewpoint has recently been strongly reinforced by an excellent review of the research on intelligence and delinquency by Hirschi and Hindelang (1977), who show that IQ has an effect on delinquency independent of class and race.

Juvenile delinquency and adult criminality show a negative curvilinear relationship to IQ, with delinquency and crime rates diminishing markedly below IQ 50 and above IQ 100. (Just the simple within-race linear correlation (point-biserial r) between court-recorded delinquency and IQ is between $-.4$ and $-.5$.) The highest rates of delinquency and crime fall in the IQ range from 70 to 90. Apparently the majority of persons below IQ 50 are either under close enough supervision by parents and relatives to be kept out of serious trouble or are too incompetent or socially isolated to become involved in the kinds of serious delinquent activities that would come to legal attention. To steal an automobile, for example, one has to be at least smart enough to be able to break in, start the car without a key, and know how to drive—all skills that it would be rare to find in a person below IQ 50.

IQ does not predict delinquency rates across the sexes. Males and females do not differ in IQ, but males show much higher rates of delinquency and adult crime than females. Within each sex, separately, however, there is about the same degree of relationship between IQ and delinquency.

Is the association between IQ and delinquency explainable by the fact that both are correlated (in opposite directions) with social class, low income, and poverty? Apparently not, as research on full siblings reared together in the same families shows almost the same degree of association between IQ and delinquency as is found in the general population (Healy & Bronner, 1936; Shulman, 1929, 1951). Delinquents show lower IQs, on the average, than their nondelinquent siblings of the same sex. Hirschi and Hindelang (1977) have hypothesized that the child's school experience mediates the correlation between IQ and delinquent behavior. A similar theory, with some supporting evidence that delinquency is often a reaction to a learning disability in school, has been advanced by Berman (1978).

Obviously many factors in addition to IQ must be involved in delinquency and antisocial behavior, as the majority of persons at every level of IQ and in every race and social class are nondelinquent. A low IQ is neither a necessary nor a sufficient condition for delinquent behavior. But there is a heightened probability of delinquency in the low-IQ child, even as compared with his or her own siblings of higher IQ. The correlation is most likely mediated by the frustrations arising from possessing less than average general ability, with its consequences of more frequent failures in competition with age peers and in winning recognition and approval from significant persons in the environment. The school, as presently constituted, is generally a potent source of such frustration for children in the lower quarter of the IQ distribution, that is, IQs below 90.

Miscellaneous Behavioral Correlates of IQ.   Intelligence test scores have been shown to have significant low to moderate positive correlations with a variety of other variables, such as *honesty* (Mussen, Harris, Rutherford, & Keasey, 1970); nonacademic attainment in *extra-curricular activities* (Kogan & Pankove, 1974); children's *appreciation of humor* as judged from response to cartoons of varying subtlety and sophistication (Zigler, Levine, & Gould, 1966); ability to solve *anagrams* (Gavurin, 1967); untrained *musical aptitude* (Wing, 1941); speed of learning a number of relatively complex (but not simple) *motor skills* (Noble, 1974); susceptibility to certain *optical illusions* and various *perceptual phenomena* (studies reviewed by Honigfeld, 1962); and amount of specific *information retained* from viewing a television feature program, especially the incidental, unemphasized bits of information (Nias & Kay, 1954).

Physical Correlates of IQ

A number of anthropometric and physiological measurements show reliable small to moderate correlations with measured intelligence.

Brain Size.   A most thorough and methodologically sophisticated recent review of all the evidence relevant to human brain size and intelligence concludes that the best estimate of the within-sex correlation between brain size and IQ is about 0.30, taking proper account of physical stature, birthweight, and other correlated variables (VanValen, 1974). Such a correlation is considered quite important from a biological and evolutionary standpoint, considering that much of the brain is devoted to noncognitive functions. The author argues that there has been a direct causal effect, through natural selection in the course of human evolution, between intelligence and brain size. The evolutionary selective advantage of greater brain size was the greater capacity for more complex intellectual functioning. "Natural selection on intelligence at a current estimated intensity suffices to explain the rapid rate of increase of brain size in human evolution" (VanValen, 1974, p. 417).

Brain size is correlated with head size, and thus it is noteworthy that the Harvard anthropologist Ernest Hooton (1939) found that the head circumferences of Boston whites in various occupational levels are in about the same rank order as is usually found when occupations are ranked according to their average IQs, as shown in Table 8.8. A chi squared test shows that the means of the eight occupational categories differ significantly ($\chi^2 = 84.4$, $df = 7$, $p < .001$).

Brain Waves.   IQ is correlated with various indices involving the speed and amplitude of electrical potentials in the brain, evoked by visual and auditory stimuli, and measured by the electroencephalogram (Callaway, 1975). This topic is considered in greater detail in Chapter 14, pp. 707–710.

Stature.   In American and European Caucasian populations there is a significant low within-sex correlation (ranging in various studies from about .1 to .3, with an average

Table 8.8.   Head circumferences (in millimeters) of Boston whites in various occupational categories.   (From Hooton, 1939)

Occupational Category	N	Mean	SE_M
Professionals	25	569.9	1.9
Semiprofessionals	61	566.5	1.5
Clerical	107	566.2	1.1
Trades	194	565.7	0.8
Public service	25	564.1	2.5
Skilled trades	351	562.9	0.6
Personal services	262	562.7	0.7
Laborers	647	560.7	0.3

of about .25) between IQ and physical stature (Stoddard, 1943, p. 200; Paterson, 1930). This correlation almost certainly involves no causal or functional relationship between stature and intelligence but is a result of the common assortment of the genetic factors for both height and intelligence. These are both perceived in our society as desirable characteristics, and there is a fairly high degree of assortative mating for both characteristics. This results in a between-families genetic correlation between the traits. There appears to be no within-families correlation, as indicated by the fact that, on the average, there are no differences in height or other physical characteristics between gifted children (average IQ 141) and their nongifted siblings (average IQ 109), yet gifted children, on the average, are taller for their age and have generally better physiques than the average child (Laycock & Caylor, 1965). This finding is precisely what we should expect if the correlation between stature and intelligence is a between-families correlation, due to common genetic assortment of the two traits, rather than a correlation due to pleiotropy, genetic linkage, or functional relationship. (See Chapter 6, pp. 193–195.)

Basal Metabolic Rate and Obesity.   The evidence is somewhat equivocal on BMR, showing correlations with IQ running from close to zero to as high as .80 in various studies. It appears that there may be significant correlations in childhood, during the most rapid growth period, and that the significant correlations diminish and finally disappear from adolescence to adulthood (Stoddard, 1943, pp. 206–407; Tyler, 1965, p. 429).

The diagnosis of obesity (defined as 20 percent or more overweight for age, height, and build) has been found to have a quite marked inverse relationship to IQ in women (Kreze, Zelina, Juhas, & Garbara, 1974). The percentages of women in the lower and upper quartiles of IQ who were classified as obese are 41.4 percent and 10.7 percent, respectively. (The corresponding percentages for men are 17.0 percent and 9.3 percent.) The negative relationship between IQ and obesity is more likely mediated in large part by the variable of social class, which was uncontrolled in this study, but which is known from other studies to be correlated (in opposite directions) with IQ and obesity.

Myopia.   Near-sightedness or myopia is believed to be attributable to genetic factors, most probably recessive inheritance with full penetrance. Myopia is quite markedly associated with higher IQ. Myopes average about 8 IQ points higher than nonmyopes. Because no purely environmental explanation for this striking relationship (a point-biserial correlation of about .25 between IQ and the diagnosis of myopia) has been found to withstand critical scrutiny in light of evidence, it is suggested that there is a pleiotropic effect of the myopia gene on intelligence. The evidence has been reviewed by Karlsson (1978, Chs. 9 and 10), who concludes that "the myopia gene has an important stimulant effect on brain activity. It thus becomes the first identified specific gene which appears to contribute significantly to intelligence" (p. 78).

SUMMARY

Test validity is the extent to which scientifically or practically useful inferences can be drawn from test scores to behaviors outside performance on the test itself. The four main types of validity, known as the *four C*'s, are content validity, criterion validity, concurrent validity, and construct validity. Each is appropriate for a particular purpose. The methods for determining a test's validity, of course, depend on the type of validity.

For the practical use of tests in educational and employment selection, criterion (or predictive) validity is the most important; it is indexed by the correlation coefficient between test scores and some measure of the criterion performance.

The validity coefficient is open to several different statistically correct interpretations, depending on the purpose for which the test is used. The practical efficiency or utility of a test used for selection depends on more than just its validity coefficient; the test's utility depends also on the selection ratio, that is, the proportion on the total number of applicants who can be selected and the success–failure ratio of randomly selected applicants. Under certain realistic conditions, even tests with only moderate criterion validity can have great utility.

Because much of the debate concerning bias in mental tests involves the concept of *differential validity* of a test for minority and majority groups, it is essential fully to understand the meanings of validity in its technical sense.

Validity coefficients, and particularly their practical interpretations, have some degree of situational specificity, involving not only the test itself but also the reliability and validity of the criterion and the nature of the population and the circumstances in which the test is used. However, the situational specificity of test validity has been exaggerated and overemphasized in the past. It is now realized that much of the apparent specificity of test validity, as indicated by fluctuations of the raw validity coefficient from one study to another, is due to statistical artifacts; and, when these are taken into account, test validity is quite generalizable across situations (Schmidt & Hunter, 1977).

A review of the correlates of highly *g*-loaded tests, such as standard IQ tests, reveals that *g* has many correlates with variables outside the realm of the tests themselves, probably more correlates with more far-reaching personal and social significance than any other psychological construct. IQ alone predicts scholastic performance better than any other single variable or combination of variables that psychologists can measure. This is especially true of performance in the more academic school subjects, such as reading comprehension, mathematics, and written composition. The high predictive validity of *g*-loaded tests in this sphere is not at all due to common learned content between the tests and the school subjects, but to essential mental processes common to both spheres. Test performance and scholastic performance both involve essentially the same *g* factor of mental ability of acquired scholastic knowledge and skills. Thus there is a clear conceptual distinction between mental ability and scholastic attainments, even though these variables are highly correlated with one another. The validity coefficients of IQ tests for predicting school grades or achievement as measured by tests decrease from elementary school to high school and from high school to college, for reasons extraneous to the tests themselves. It is important to understand the several conditions that spuriously lower the obtained validity coefficients of IQ tests at each successively higher stage of the educational ladder.

IQ is correlated only slightly with simple rote learning and memory abilities but shows higher correlations with forms of learning that permit transfer from previous learning, insight, seeing relationships, spontaneous organization of complex material, and the like.

IQ also has important nonscholastic correlates: occupational level attained in adulthood and income level (within occupations). IQ has a threshold property for success in many occupations. There is some point on the IQ scale below which the probability of success in a particular occupation is practically nil. For persons above the threshold of IQ needed for a given occupation, other personal factors besides IQ become relatively more important determiners of success. Amount of education, which is highly related to IQ, mediates much of the correlation between IQ and occupational status, but this cannot be validly interpreted to imply that amount of education per se is the *cause* of occupational status. Educational attainment, however, is causally dependent on IQ.

IQ is also correlated with a host of other traits and behaviors in which often the causal connections are still quite obscure: leadership qualities, socially recognized creativity, personality adjustment, social competence, and adaptive behavior. IQ is negatively correlated with proneness to delinquency. IQ also has a number of physical correlates, including brain size, amplitudes and latency of evoked brain electrical potentials, stature, metabolic rate in childhood, obesity, and myopia. It is clear that IQ tests and other highly *g*-loaded tests measure something considerably more profound and far-reaching than merely knowledge and skills acquired in school or in a cultured home.

NOTES

1. In comparing a multiple correlation R with a simple correlation r, it is proper to correct the multiple R for "shrinkage." Multiple R capitalizes on mere chance association, the more the greater the number of predictor variables k and the smaller the number of subjects N. When the number of variables is as large as the number of subjects, the multiple correlation can be perfect ($R = 1$), even when the true correlation between the predictors and the criterion is zero. The correction for shrinkage is

$$R_c = \sqrt{1 - (1 - R_o^2)\frac{N - 1}{N - k - 1}},$$

where

R_c = the shrunken (or corrected) multiple correlation coefficient,
R_o = the observed multiple correlation,
N = the sample size, and
k = the number of predictor variables used in the multiple correlation.

2. The correlation scatter diagram can take many forms other than the most common form, an ellipse. Three of the forms are shown in Figure 8N.1. (All represent positive correlations.) In each case the form of the correlation between variables X and Y can be described in terms of "necessary/sufficient." In form A (the usual ellipsoid scatter diagram), X is *necessary and sufficient* for Y. In form B, X is *necessary but not sufficient* for Y. In form C, X is *sufficient but not necessary* for Y. (In the case of zero correlation, i.e., a circular scatter diagram, it would be said that X is *neither necessary nor sufficient* for Y.) Notice that in form A all values of X are equally predictive of Y (a condition known in statistics as homoscedasticity), whereas in form B low values of X are more highly predictive of Y than are high values of X, and in form C high values of X are more predictive of Y than are low values of X. (Forms B and C are called heteroscedastic.)

The scatter diagram of forms B and C have been called "twisted pear" correlations, because the shape of the scatter diagram resembles a silhouetted twisted pear. For

Figure 8N.1. Types of scatter diagrams. Form *A* is bivariate normal. Forms *B* and *C* are "twisted pear" correlations and are heteroscedastic. (See text.)

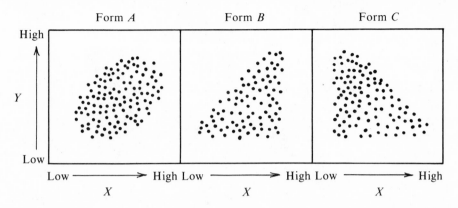

further discussion of the interpretation of "twisted pear" correlations in psychological research, the reader is referred to Fisher (1959) and Storms (1960).

3. Given the Pearson correlations r_{ab}, r_{ac}, and r_{bc} among three variables *a, b, c,* the *partial correlations* (i.e., the correlation between each pair of variables, holding the third variable constant or "partialing out" its effect) are as follows:

$$r_{ab \cdot c} = \frac{r_{ab} - r_{ac} r_{bc}}{\sqrt{(1 - r_{ac}^2)(1 - r_{bc}^2)}},$$

$$r_{ac \cdot b} = \frac{r_{ac} - r_{ab} r_{bc}}{\sqrt{(1 - r_{ab}^2)(1 - r_{bc}^2)}},$$

$$r_{bc \cdot a} = \frac{r_{bc} - r_{ab} r_{ac}}{\sqrt{(1 - r_{ab}^2)(1 - r_{ac}^2)}}.$$

The *multiple correlation R* between the combination of any two variables and the third variable (called the dependent variable or the criterion) is of the following form:

$$R_{c \cdot ab} = \frac{r_{ac}^2 + r_{bc}^2 - 2 r_{ab} r_{ac} r_{bc}}{1 - r_{ab}^2},$$

where $R_{c \cdot ab}$ is the multiple correlation between the independent variables *a* and *b* and the dependent variable *c*. $R_{c \cdot ab}^2$ is the proportion of the total variance in the dependent variable *c* accounted for jointly by the independent variables *a* and *b*.

4. One of the soundest, objective research-based discussions of the personality characteristics associated with creativity is in *The Prediction of Achievement and Creativity* (1968) by Cattell and Butcher, particularly Chapters 14 and 15.

Chapter 9

Definitions and Criteria of Test Bias

The question of "cultural bias" in mental tests arose shortly after the first practical test of intelligence came into use in 1905. Binet and Simon acknowledged the problem when their new test, which they had first developed and standardized on children of the Parisian working class, was applied to groups of children of higher social status, whose test scores were invariably higher, on the average, than the scores of the working-class children. This was found in France, in Belgium, in Germany, and in the United States.

Did the social-class differences in test scores represent real differences in intelligence between the social classes, or were they an artifact of the test—a result of an inadvertently biased selection of test items more specifically attuned to the cultural experiences of the upper than of the lower classes?

Binet never formally researched that question. But he fully recognized that language, cultural background, and a common background of experience were necessary *vehicles* for the measurement of intelligence. Unless the vehicles are carefully sampled by the test, the measurement of intelligence could be biased or contaminated for certain individuals or for groups with very atypical educational and cultural experiences. It is clear from Binet's writings that he gave great importance to the distinction between general intelligence, on the one hand, and specific information acquired in school or a cultured home, on the other. He intended his test to measure mainly the former (Binet & Simon, 1916). Binet made this point most explicitly when explaining the rationale of his second revision of the Binet–Simon scales in 1911. He had thoughtfully scrutinized all the test items for possible educational–cultural bias, and he eliminated a number of the items that seemed overly dependent on specific information of the kind most apt to be acquired in school or an educated home. Some of the specific items that Binet thought it well to eliminate from his original test included those that involved knowing one's age, counting one's fingers, distinguishing the words "evening" and "morning," naming four coins, copying a model of penmanship, writing a sentence from dictation, naming the days of the week, and reading a short passage and recalling six facts from it. Elimination of these and similar items, however, did not appreciably reduce the average social-class differences in overall test scores. Social-class differences showed up more or less on all the test items, not just on those most obviously cultural or scholastic. In fact, Binet found that the items that were based more on scholastic knowledge and home training did not at all consistently show the largest social-class differences; such items were hardly different, on the average, from any of the other types of items in their tendency to discriminate between social classes. Therefore, Binet wisely did not interpret the fact of social-class differences in test scores as *prima facie* evidence that the tests themselves were biased against children of the working class. But Binet did not investigate the matter further. He died in 1911, the same year that he published the revisions of his scale that were intended to minimize social-class bias.

Since then, many other psychological investigators, too numerous to mention, have reported social-class differences in intelligence test scores and have speculated as to the causes. (For a brief review of early studies, especially those attributing social-class differences to culture-biased tests, see Eells et al., 1951, Ch. 2.) Psychologists soon discovered the need for tests of mental ability that were appropriate for illiterates, the poorly educated, and the non-English speaking. Performance tests such as the Knox (1914) battery and the Pintner–Paterson Scale of Performance Tests (1927) were developed for this purpose. These tests consisted of form boards, object assembly, picture completion, and the like and were the forerunners of the Performance Scale subtests of the present-day Wechsler intelligence tests. In World War I, the U.S. Army psychologists devised the well-known Army Alpha group test of general intelligence for selection of draftees and assignment of recruits, and along with it they developed the first important nonlanguage paper-and-pencil group test, the Army Beta, for assessing the mental ability of illiterate, unschooled, or non-English speaking draftees. Whereas the Army Alpha included such verbal and scholastic items as synonyms and antonyms, disarranged sentences, verbal analogies, and arithmetic problems, the Army Beta minimized verbal and scholastic knowledge by using items involving mazes, cube counting, continuing series of X's and O's in a particular pattern, noting missing parts of pictures of familiar objects, geometrical constructions, and the like. Yet some of the nonverbal items of the Beta were still of a specifically culture-linked nature, such as detecting the missing parts in pictures of a pistol (trigger), light bulb (filament), tennis court (net), and violin (strings). One can easily believe that a good many American men at the time of World War I had never been exposed to some of these things.

The term "culture free" with reference to tests first appeared in the psychological literature in 1940, when Raymond B. Cattell (b. 1905) proposed a "culture free" intelligence test (Cattell, 1940). The meaning of the term "culture free" in the abstract sense intended by Cattell was widely misunderstood, and it became a popular cliché among psychologists, sociologists, and anthropologists to declaim that a "culture free" test is an impossibility, a contradiction in terms, an illusory goal, an elixer, a deception. Cattell later substituted the term "culture fair," which gained greater acceptance, as did the term "culture reduced."

Systematic large-scale investigation of the extent of culture bias in the existing standardized tests when they are used with certain cultural subgroups within the United States was not initiated until 1945, in the investigations of sociologist Allison Davis and psychologist Kenneth Eells of the University of Chicago. The classic study by Eells (1951), which is described in detail in Chapter 11 (pp. 520–524) made explicit the concept of cultural bias in testing and illustrated a methodology for investigating it. Cultural bias in test items was viewed as one of several factors hypothesized to account for differences in mean IQ between various cultural groups. The other hypothesized factors were genetic ability, developmental factors, test motivation, and test work habits or test skills. Eells pointed out that the last two factors, as well as cultural bias, differ from the first two in one important respect:

> Both genetic and developmental factors are presumed to determine the actual intelligence of the child as it might be evidenced in thinking clearly and in solving appropriate problems in real-life situations. . . . [C]ultural bias in test items, test motivation, and test work habits or test skills, on the other hand, are oriented toward the test situation as such and are assumed to affect the pupil's ability to score well on the test but not to affect materially his ability to think clearly and to solve appropriate problems in real life situations.   (Eells et al., 1951, p. 58)

Eells defined cultural bias as follows:

> By *cultural bias in test items* is meant differences in the extent to which the child being tested has had the opportunity to know and become familiar with the specific subject matter or specific process required by the test item. If a test item requires, for example, familiarity with symphony instruments, those children who have opportunity to attend symphony concerts frequently will presumably be able to answer the question more readily than can those children who have never seen a symphony orchestra. To the extent that intelligence-test items are drawn from cultural materials of this sort, with which high [socioeconomic] status pupils have more opportunity for familiarity, status differences in I.Q.'s will be expected.   (p. 58)

Following Eells's pioneering study, the literature on test bias and culture fair testing becomes increasingly confused, partly due to inconsistencies in terminology and a lack of conceptual clarity in the meanings of "bias" and "unfairness" as these and other terms were used by various authors. "Culture bias" was a common cliché in popular and superficial explanations of social-class and racial group differences in IQ test scores. But few writers bothered to examine the concept critically or to provide truly objective criteria for the recognition of test bias. Those who proclaimed most vociferously that mental tests are biased against racial minorities and the poor have actually contributed the least to a working scientific definition of culture bias or to establishing objective criteria for assessing the extent of bias in any specific test. Critics of tests did not seem to think it necessary to do empirical studies to determine whether the criticized tests do in fact show evidence of bias in terms of objectively defined criteria.

The lack of conceptual clarity and objective criteria hindered the scientific investigation of test bias. The demand for such investigation took on greater urgency in the 1960s with the increasing national concern over the generally lower scholastic performance of the "culturally disadvantaged" and certain racial minorities. Much of the blame for their educational plight was heaped onto the tests of IQ, scholastic aptitude, and achievement that so clearly revealed the disparities among ethnic groups, particularly blacks and whites. The tests were condemned as culturally biased against blacks. Such was the prevailing popular opinion throughout the 1960s.

Surprisingly, it was not until the 1970s that the concepts of test bias and fairness came under thorough critical scrutiny in terms of definitions, objective criteria, and empirical analysis undertaken by a number of specialists in the field of psychometrics itself. Until then, the literature on test bias was much more in the province of sociologists, cultural anthropologists, educators, and the critics of mental testing who stood outside the field. Only recently has the topic of test bias become of major theoretical and empirical interest to psychologists who specialize in psychometrics.

Inadequate Concepts of Test Bias

There are three inadequate or improper concepts of test bias frequently seen in the literature. They should be laid to rest before explicating a scientifically defensible definition of test bias. We can label these three inadequate concepts as (1) the *egalitarian fallacy,* (2) the *culture-bound fallacy,* and (3) the *standardization fallacy.*

Egalitarian Fallacy. This concept of test bias is based on the gratuitous assumption that all human populations are essentially identical or equal in whatever trait or ability the test purports to measure. Therefore, any difference between populations in the distribution of test scores (such as a difference in means, or standard deviations, or any other parameters of the distribution) is taken as evidence that the test is biased. The search for a less biased test, then, is guided by the criterion of minimizing or eliminating the statistical differences between groups. The perfectly nonbiased test, according to this definition, would reveal reliable individual differences but not reliable (i.e., statistically significant) group differences, with the exception, of course, of groups that were comprised of persons previously selected on the basis of their scores on the test in question (or on a closely related test).

Probably no psychologist today would hold to this extreme concept of bias with respect to all tests or for all traits, or even for all abilities. There are just too many examples for which it can be easily and obviously proven false, as in the case of population differences in certain physical traits and sensory capacities. Also, with respect to scholastic performance there is now general agreement that group differences in *achievement test* scores are not wholly due to test bias. The achievement differences between groups are more often attributed primarily to inequalities in schooling and home background. The egalitarian definition of bias is most commonly applied to tests of intelligence. IQ is the main target. The assumption of equal or equivalent intelligence across all human populations lies at the heart of most of the criticism of IQ tests.

This assumption, whatever its ideological basis, is scientifically unwarranted. The egalitarian assumption obviously begs the question in such a way as to completely remove itself from the possibility of scientific investigation. By definition, measured group differences are indicative of bias in the measuring instruments rather than of true group differences in the trait being measured; and therefore it is forever impossible either to prove or disprove the hypothesis that groups actually differ in the trait. Science, of course, does not operate in this way. The *a priori* agreed-on assumptions in science are of a purely definitional and formal logical nature. They do not involve substantive questions of fact. Therefore, the egalitarian definition of test bias is scientifically useless, and from this standpoint it must be rejected outright.

The egalitarian definition of bias is sometimes stated in a statistical form in terms of the point-biserial correlation coefficient, that is, the correlation between a continuous variable (e.g., test scores) and a dichotomous variable (e.g., male/female), in which the dichotomous variable is membership in one or the other of two groups, scored as 0 and 1 (or any arbitrary pair of numerals). According to the egalitarian concept, a test is biased if the absolute value of the point-biserial correlation $|r_{xg}|$ between test scores x and group membership g is greater than zero, that is, $|r_{xg}| > 0$. An unbiased test is defined as one for which $r_{xg} = 0$.

Culture-bound Fallacy. This fallacy is based on the content validity (or face validity) of test items. A subjective judgment is made as to the degree to which particular test items are "culture bound." If a test contains items that someone (usually a critic of tests) has judged to be "culture bound," the test is declared to be culturally biased and hence unfair to some particular cultural group. The subjective criteria for judging one test item as more or less culture bound than another item are seldom clearly specified. Usually items that involve scholastic or "bookish" vocabulary or knowledge or knowledge of the fine arts or items that reflect what are imagined to be the moral, ethical, or aesthetic values of the white middle class are judged to be culture bound and hence unfair to nonwhites and persons of low socioeconomic status. The following items are examples of the kinds of items most typically judged to be culture bound.

1. *Sonata* is a term used in   drawing   drama   music   poetry   phonetics.
2. *Author* is to *novel* as *composer* is to   *book   work   symphony   statue   piano.*
3. Who wrote *Hamlet?*
4. Why does the state require people to get a marriage license?
5. What should you do if a child much smaller than yourself tries to pick a fight with you?

The presumption is that certain groups in the population have experienced different cultural backgrounds that do not include these kinds of knowledge. This position was first stated clearly by Kenneth Eells (1951, p. 4):

> [I]f (*a*) the children from different social-status levels have different kinds of experiences and have experiences with different kinds of material, and if (*b*) the intelligence tests contain a disproportionate amount of material drawn from the cultural experiences with which pupils from the higher social-status levels are more familiar, one would expect (*c*) that children from the higher social-status levels would show higher IQs than those from the lower levels. This argument tends to conclude that the observed differences in pupil IQ's are artifacts dependent upon the specific content of the test items and do not reflect accurately any important underlying ability in the pupils.

The fallacy is not in the possibility that some test items may discriminate between different cultural groups because of the groups' differences in experience but that such items can be identified or graded as to their degree of culture-boundness merely by casual inspection and subjective judgment. As the evidence reviewed in Chapter 11 will show, many items subjectively judged by test critics to be "culturally unfair" for some particular group actually show the group to be less disadvantaged on those items than on other items that were not judged to be so culture bound. It is easy to demonstrate with evidence that culture *bias* in test items cannot be accurately judged in terms of the item's content or face validity. Thus claims of test bias cannot be supported by subjective judgments regarding the item content. A test comprised of culture-bound items, so judged, need not therefore be a biased test. The determination of bias must be based on objective psychometric and statistical criteria.

It is a significant fact that those who have most strongly claimed the existence of cultural bias in intelligence and aptitude tests have done so entirely on the basis of subjective judgments regarding the culture-boundness of specific items in the tests.

Standardization Fallacy.   This claims that, because a test was standardized on a given population, it is *ipso facto* biased or unfair when used in any other population. It is a popular criticism of tests that were originally standardized on the white population but came to be used with blacks as well, such as the Stanford–Binet and the earlier editions of the Wechsler tests. The fact that a test was standardized in one population, however, does not support the claim that the test is biased for members of another population. Such a claim must depend on other forms of evidence.

When a test is used with members of a different population from that in which the test was standardized, however, we need to determine if the test is appropriate for the second population. Reliability and validity for any population group other than the standardization population cannot be taken for granted, but must be investigated in their own right.

There are two main aspects of test standardization: (1) *item selection* and (2) *scaling* of the scores. The first is an important consideration for culture bias; the second is trivial, because a change of scale does not alter the rank ordering of individuals and has no effect whatsoever on the amount of overlap (either median overlap or total overlap) among different groups.

The item selection aspect of standardization is based essentially on some form of item correlation, for example, the average correlation of each item with all other items in the test, or of each item with the total score, or of each item with some external criterion measurement that the test is intended to predict, or usually some combination of these. Items are also selected with respect to difficulty level so that an even gradation of item difficulties, from very easy to very difficult, exists in the standardization population, and with as few nondiscriminating items as possible (i.e., items that are so easy everyone gets them right or so difficult that everyone misses them). It is in the aspects of item intercorrelations and the distribution of item difficulties that a test could be biased for members of any population that were not included in the standardization sample. The psychometric properties of a test are a direct result of the item selection procedures. If the criteria for item selection resulted in a different set of items when standardized on one population group than on another, the test could be said to be biased with respect to any uses involving the comparison of members of these two groups. As we shall see, one method for assessing test bias is to investigate whether certain psychometric characteristics of a test, which are determined by item selection during the original standardization process, differ significantly in samples from populations that were not included in the standardization population.

Merely rescaling or renorming a given test on a sample from a different population than the one on which the test was originally standardized accomplishes nothing of fundamental significance. It merely assigns different numerical values to the mean and standard deviation of the standardized scores of a particular group. It does not change the relative positions of persons within the groups or the relative difference between the groups. It merely puts these differences on a different numerical scale without essentially changing them, like shifting from a Fahrenheit to a Celsius thermometer.

How should a minority group be taken account of in the original standardization process? Is it enough merely to include a number of minority persons in the standardization sample corresponding to their percentage in the general population and then simply proceed with the standardization procedures on the composite sample, without further separate analyses of the subgroups? Although this is a common procedure with tests that claim to have included blacks or other minorities in their standardization, it by no means assures that the test will be unbiased for the minority group, especially if it constitutes only a small percentage of the total standardization sample. The statistical criteria for item selection may actually differ in the subgroups for many items, but this would remain unknown unless the item selection procedures were carried out separately in each of the subgroups. For example, the internal consistency reliablities could differ markedly across the subgroups, but one could not tell this from the reliability of the composite sample, which might well misrepresent the separate reliabilities within each subgroup.

Proper standardization for different subgroups should consist of comparable item selection procedures performed separately within each subgroup. The subgroups should be approximately equal in size, or at least each one should be large enough to permit comparable statistical inferences regarding the psychometric properties of the test. Only in the final norming (i.e., the computation of normalized standardized scores) for the composite sample should the subgroups be combined in proportion to their numbers in the general population.

Standardization within subgroups aims not at equalizing the means of the subgroups but at achieving highly similar reliability, factorial composition, predictive and construct validity, and range of item difficulties while at the same time minimizing item × subgroup interactions (i.e., the items should have the same rank order of difficulties across subgroups).

Some Essential Terminology

One cannot read very far in the literature on culture bias without encountering a plethora of inconsistent terminology. Undefined terms with subjective or vaguely implied meanings are common. Even when writers have given explicit and precise definitions of terms in their own particular usage of them, there is a lack of uniformity of meanings from one writer to the next. In the following discussion, to hold to the same terminology used by each writer in discussing his or her particular contribution to the understanding of test bias would only compound confusion.

Therefore, before proceeding further with the discussion of test bias, I will set forth a number of fundamental definitions and use them consistently throughout. I shall not attempt to observe the many differences in terminology used by different writers in this field in paraphrasing their contributions, but will translate their varying terms into a common set of clearly defined terms.

Culture Free, Culture Fair, Etc. "Culture reduced," "culture loaded," and "culture bound" are other variations in this set of terms. As generally used in describing tests, these various terms have no exact or clearly distinguishable meanings.

"Culture free" may be criticized on the ground that any kind of test of mental ability depends on some experiential background acquired in some culture, that is, in interpersonal interactions with other members of one's family or social group. A mental test that could measure a person's ability unaffected by all his past experience would be about as impossible as having a pair of scales that could measure a person's present weight unaffected by his health history and dietary habits.

"Culture fair" as applied to tests per se can be criticized on the ground that the notion of "fairness" is best thought of not as an attribute of tests themselves but of the particular use of tests—in educational and personnel selection, clinical decisions, and the like.

"Culture reduced" seems the preferable term for what many writers mean by "culture free" and "culture fair."

"Culture bound" and "culture loaded," of course, are generally used as the opposites of "culture free," "culture fair," and "culture reduced."

To be given any scientifically useful meaning, these terms, as applied to tests rather than to the ways in which the tests are used, are best thought of as describing variation along a *hypothetical continuum*. The end points of such a continuum need not be attainable in reality for the continuum itself to be a meaningful one. *Elasticity* is such a useful continuum in physics, although in reality there are no materials that are either perfectly elastic or perfectly inelastic. Actual materials, however, can be ordered between these hypothetical extremes on the continuum of elasticity. "Culture free" and "culture bound" may be regarded as the hypothetical end-points of the continuum of culture loading along which actual tests may be ordered. Going in one direction, tests may be described as more and more "culture reduced" and, going in the other direction, as more and more "culture loaded." No actual tests stand at the hypothetical or idealized end-points of the continuum.

How can this "culture-free–culture-bound" continuum be characterized? A test item's location on the continuum, relative to all other items, reflects the degree of its generality across subpopulations, both with respect to the content of the item and the formal demands of the item (i.e., understanding the test instructions or what one is expected to do with the item). By "generality" is meant the number of different subpopulations (however defined) in which the item can be deemed appropriate in terms of the subpopulation's background and experience. This is admittedly a highly subjective judgment, and that is why this particular hypothetical continuum is of quite limited usefulness and not of crucial importance in the objective study of mental tests.

Among various judges, however, there is a high degree of subjective agreement as to the relative positions of many test items on the continuum. By using the average rankings of the culture loading of items by a number of judges from different subpopulations and backgrounds, it is possible to select test items from the large pool of ranked items that stand at clearly separated points on the culture-loaded continuum. Tests that are termed "culture free," "culture fair," or "culture reduced" usually consist of items that have been judged to be less culture loaded than the items typically found in other tests in which item selection was not based primarily on this kind of judgment.

Culture-reduced items, so judged, are usually those that are nonlanguage and nonscholastic and do not call for any specific prior information for a plus-scored response, assuming, of course, that the test instructions are themselves clearly understood by all persons taking the test. Pictorial items in culture-reduced tests usually avoid pictures of artifacts that are peculiar to any particular culture, geographical location, or historical period. An item picturing a musical instrument, or the Eiffel Tower, or a helicopter, for example, would be ranked fairly high in culture loading as contrasted with, say, an item involving the comparison of squares, triangles, and circles.

Subjective judgments, even when they represent a high degree of concordance among many judges, do not prove the objective correctness of an item's relative position on the culture-loading continuum. A high degree of subjective plausibility does not constitute scientifically objective evidence. A faith in plausibility at times leads to a disconcerting surprise in the face of objective evidence.

I have not found in the literature any defensible proposal for a purely objective set of criteria for determining the *culture-loadedness* of individual test items, and perhaps none is possible. This is not the same as saying that there are not objective measures for determining test *bias,* a topic to be taken up shortly. As we shall see, one can determine with objective statistical precision how and to what degree a test is *biased* with respect to members of particular subpopulations. But no such objective determination can be made of the degree of *culture-loadedness* of a test. That attribute remains a subjective and, hence, fallible judgment. Because there is no *a priori* basis for assuming that all subpopulations are equal in the ability that a particular test is intended to measure, items cannot be ordered on the culture-loading continuum simply according to how much they discriminate among various subpopulations.

Discrimination. This term has three common interpretations in the literature. It is used to mean (1) to "treat unfairly because of one's group membership," or (2) to "treat differently," or (3) to show a reliable (i.e., statistically significant) difference between individuals or groups on some measurement, index, or descriptive statistic. Note that the third meaning of discrimination, unlike the first two, is purely statistical and wholly neutral in terms of "fair" and "unfair" or in terms of the *causes* of statistically significant differences. (We know the causes of statistically *nonsignificant* differences—they are due to random error, either measurement error* or sampling error.*)

Throughout this book, the term "discrimination" (and the verb "to discriminate") is used strictly in the third sense, and absolutely no other overtones should be read into it. It is the only way to avoid future confusion.

Bias. This term is used henceforth also in a strictly statistical sense. As such, the term "bias" is to be kept distinct from the concept of fairness–unfairness.

In mathematical statistics, "bias" refers to a *systematic* under- or overestimation of a population parameter by a statistic based on samples drawn from the population. In psychometrics, "bias" refers to systematic errors in the *predictive validity* or the *construct validity* of test scores of individuals that are associated with the individual's group membership. "Bias" is a general term and is not limited to "culture bias." It can involve any type of group membership—race, social class, nationality, sex, religion, age. The assessment of bias is a purely objective, empirical, statistical and quantitative matter entirely independent of subjective value judgments and ethical issues concerning fairness or unfairness of tests and the uses to which they are put. *Psychometric bias is a set of statistical attributes conjointly of a given test and two or more specified subpopulations.* As we shall see in terms of certain criteria of fairness, unbiased tests can be used unfairly and biased tests can be used fairly. Therefore, the concepts of bias and unfairness should be kept distinct. The main purpose of this chapter is to explicate the statistical meaning of test bias and to examine various criteria of the fair use of tests.

Fair and Unfair.   These terms refer to the ways in which test scores (whether of biased or unbiased tests) are *used* in any *selection* situation. The concepts of fairness, social justice, and "equal protection of the laws" are moral, legal, and philosophic ideas and therefore must be evaluated in these terms. Consequently, persons holding divergent philosophies about these matters will understandably differ in their interpretations of "fairness" and "unfairness" in selection procedures based on tests. They will legitimately disagree about the criteria for deciding the fairness of a selection procedure involving members of different racial, social, or cultural groups. This itself is not a statistical decision. Hence a number of different, and often mutually contradictory, criteria for fairness have been proposed, and no amount of statistical or psychometric reasoning per se can possibly settle any arguments as to which is best. That must remain a policy decision based on philosophic, legal, or practical considerations, rather than a statistical decision.

Once such a policy decision as to the meaning of "fairness" has been made, however, the matter from that point on becomes purely statistical. Then clear-cut, entirely objective, statistical criteria can be established for the fairness, as defined, of the selection procedure. Most of the recent literature in this field has been devoted to formulating statistical criteria for differing definitions of "fairness." Although the authors of many of these discussions often use the terms "biased" and "unfair" indiscriminately, it is usually clear from their context what they mean in terms of the distinction proposed here, which will be maintained consistently to avoid confusion.

Major and Minor Groups.   Because the following discussion of bias and fairness is theoretical and general, we need abstract terms to represent without any loss of generality the specific subpopulations that would actually be involved in any empirical study. Thus the terms "major group" and "minor group" will be used to refer to any two subpopulations that one might wish to consider.

The major group can usually be thought of as (1) the larger of the two groups in the total population, (2) the group on which the test was primarily standardized, or (3) the group with the higher mean score on the test, assuming that the major and minor groups differ in means. (In some cases, of course, the minor group may actually have a higher mean score than the major group, but for simplicity of discussion only the reverse case will be used in all the examples, without any loss in generality.)

For simplicity of statistical notation, in subscripts and the like, the *major* and *minor* groups are always labeled A and B, respectively.

Test and Criterion.   In psychometrics *test scores* (or any other predictor variables) are labeled X. The measurements of the *criterion* variable are labeled Y. In the bivariate scatter diagram of the correlation between test scores and criterion, X is always plotted on the *abscissa* (i.e., horizontal axis) and Y on the *ordinate* (i.e., vertical axis).

Overview of Bias and Unfairness

Because the issues in this chapter are the most complex in the entire book, it will aid the reader first to have a brief overview of what lies ahead.

The criteria of test bias fall under two main headings: (1) *predictive validity* criteria and (2) *construct validity* criteria.

Predictive validity criteria are a much narrower topic, but predictive validity is most germane for the practical use of tests. *Construct validity* criteria are a much broader and more open-ended area of scientific and theoretical importance for the understanding of the nature of group differences; it also has important implications for predictive validity.

Construct validity criteria of bias can be considered under two main categories: *external* and *internal*. *External* refers to the correlations of test scores with other variables independent of the test itself. (Thus a test's predictive validity also may enhance its construct validity.) *Internal* refers to various quantifiable features of the test data themselves, such as reliability, item discriminability indices, item intercorrelations, and other item statistics, as well as to the factorial structure of the test.

Situational bias refers to influences in the test situation, but independent of the test itself, that may bias test scores. Examples are the race, age, and sex of the tester, the emotional atmosphere created in the testing situation, cooperativeness and motivation of the person taking the test, time pressure, time of day, and the tone and content of the test instructions. These factors, whether or not they are specifically identified, are usually reflected in the predictive and construct validity criteria of bias. Situational bias, however, is treated separately in Chapter 12.

Because the question of fairness involves the use of tests in selection, this topic logically follows the topic of criteria of bias in predictive validity. The more complex topic of construct validity criteria of bias will come last.

Predictive Validity Models of Test Bias

These statistical models of test bias are all based on the linear regression of the criterion variable Y on test scores X in the major and minor groups. The expression "the regression of Y on X" is merely the statistician's way of saying "Y as a (linear) *function of X.*" From the standpoint of prediction, the regression line indicates the most likely value of Y for a particular value of X. The predicted value of Y for any given value of X is $\hat{Y}$ (called "y-hat"). Regression is shown graphically in Figure 9.1. Several points should be noted.

The formula for the regression line $\hat{Y}$ is

$$\hat{Y} = \frac{\Delta Y}{\Delta X} X + k. \qquad (9.1)$$

The *slope* of the regression line is indicated by the expression $\Delta Y / \Delta X$ ("delta Y over delta X"); it is the rate of change in Y with respect to X. In statistics it is called the *regression coefficient* and is symbolized b_{YX}. (In mathematics it is known as the *constant of proportionality*.) The *regression coefficient* is related to the *coefficient of correlation* between X and Y as follows:

$$b_{YX} = r_{XY} \frac{\sigma_Y}{\sigma_X} , \qquad (9.2)$$

where σ_Y and σ_X are the standard deviations of variables Y and X. (Notice that when variables X and Y are expressed in standard form, so that $\sigma_X = \sigma_Y = 1$, the regression coefficient is equal to the correlation coefficient (i.e., $b_{YX} = r_{XY}$; also $r_{XY} = \sqrt{b_{YX} \cdot b_{XY}}$) and $k = 0$.)

Figure 9.1. Graphical representation of the regression of variable Y on variable X, showing slope b of regression line $\hat{Y}$, the Y intercept k, and the standard error of estimate $SE_{\hat{Y}}$. Unfortunately, there is no satisfactory way to represent $SE_{\hat{Y}}$ graphically; this figure is intended only to convey the idea that $SE_{\hat{Y}}$ is the standard deviation of the dispersion of all of the obtained scores Y about all of the predicted scores $\hat{Y}$ (i.e., the regression line). $SE_{\hat{Y}}$ is not the same as the standard deviation of obtained scores about any *particular* predicted score, which is the standard error of a single predicted score (see equation 9.6). The exact meaning of $SE_{\hat{Y}}$ is most accurately conveyed only by its mathematical expression $SE_{\hat{Y}} = \sqrt{\Sigma(Y - \hat{Y})^2/(N - 2)}$, which is algebraically equivalent to equation 9.5.

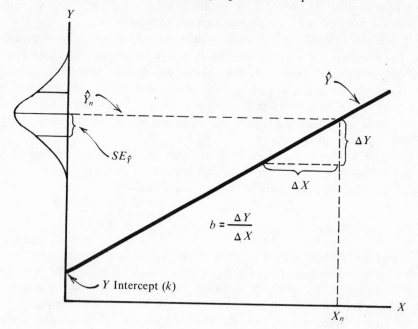

The *Y intercept* (symbolized by the letter k) is the point on the Y axis that is cut by the regression line. Because

$$k = \bar{Y} - b_{YX}\bar{X},\qquad(9.3)$$

where $\bar{Y}$ and $\bar{X}$ are the means of X and Y, we can rewrite regression equation 9.1 in its more familiar form:

$$\hat{Y} = b_{YX}(X - \bar{X}) + \bar{Y}.\qquad(9.4)$$

Thus, with equation 9.4, for any given person's test score X, we can make a "best" prediction $\hat{Y}$ of that person's score on Y. By "best" it is meant that the discrepancies between the predicted $\hat{Y}$ and the obtained Y's are minimized. They are said to meet the least-squares criterion of best fit, such that the sum of $(\hat{Y} - Y)^2$ over all persons is a minimum; that is, no other predicted values would show as small discrepancies from the actually observed values of Y.

The *standard error of estimate,* symbolized $SE_{\hat{Y}}$, is an index of the amount of error in prediction, that is, the scatter of observed scores around the predicted score. This is shown in Figure 9.1 as a normal distribution of the obtained Y scores around the predicted

$\hat{Y}_n$ for the given value of X_n. The standard deviation of that distribution is called the *standard error of estimate, $SE_{\hat{Y}}$*, and its numerical value is obtained from the following formula:

$$SE_{\hat{Y}} = \sigma_Y \sqrt{(1 - r^2_{XY})[(N - 1)/(N - 2)]}, \qquad (9.5)$$

where σ_Y is the standard deviation of all the Y scores. $SE_{\hat{Y}}$ tells us in general how confident we can be about our predictions. Notice that the larger the correlation r_{XY} (i.e., the test's validity coefficient), the smaller is $SE_{\hat{Y}}$. Thus, higher validity means lesser errors in prediction.

The standard error of estimate $SE_{\hat{Y}}$, it should be recalled, is simply the standard deviation of all of the residual errors of prediction $\hat{Y} - Y$. It is not, as is so often mistakenly supposed, the standard error of prediction of a single individual's Y_i value from a single observation of his X_i value. The standard error of a single predicted value, here symbolized as $SE_{\hat{Y}_i}$, is larger than the standard error of estimate and is defined by the following formula (Dixon & Massey, 1951, p. 129):

$$SE_{\hat{Y}_i} = SE_{\hat{Y}} \sqrt{1 + \frac{1}{N} + \frac{(X_i - \overline{X})^2}{(N - 1)\sigma^2_X}}, \qquad (9.6)$$

where

N = the sample size from which the regression equation (and $SE_{\hat{Y}}$) is derived,
$\overline{X}$ = the mean of the sample on variable X,
σ^2_X = the sample variance on X, and
X_i = the individual's score on X from which is derived his predicted score $\hat{Y}_i$.

Notice, however, that, as N increases, $SE_{\hat{Y}_i}$ approaches $SE_{\hat{Y}}$ asymptotically, so that, when N is quite large (e.g., $N > 200$), one can use the more common simplified formula for the standard error of estimate for individual predicted scores as well, with little loss of accuracy:

$$\text{Simplified } SE_{\hat{Y}_i} = \sigma_Y \sqrt{1 - r^2_{XY}}. \qquad (9.7)$$

An Essential Definition of Predictive Test Bias. Now we are in a position to give a basic statistical definition of predictive bias.

A test with perfect reliability is a biased predictor if there is a statistically signifi- cant difference between the major and minor groups in the slopes b_{YX}, or in the intercepts k, or in the standard error of estimates $SE_{\hat{Y}}$ of the regression lines of the two groups. Conversely, an unbiased test with perfect reliability is one for which the major and minor groups do not differ significantly in b_{YX}, k, or $SE_{\hat{Y}}$.

In other words, for a perfectly reliable and unbiased test, the major and minor groups share one and the same regression line, and any given test score X predicts the same criterion score $\hat{Y}$ for a member of either group, with the same probability of error $SE_{\hat{Y}}$. There is no systematic under- or overprediction of criterion performance for persons of either group; and persons whose test scores are at any given selection cutoff score have equal probabilities of success on the criterion regardless of their group membership. Knowledge of a person's group membership, therefore, can neither enhance nor diminish the test score's accuracy of prediction of the particular criterion in question. (The test could, of course, be a biased predictor of some different criterion.) Notice that this definition says nothing at all about the groups' having the same mean score on the tests. But it implies that, if the groups differ on the test, they must differ on the criterion as well, by an amount equal to $b_{YX}\bar{d}$, where $\bar{d}$ is the group mean difference in test scores.

Such is the core definition of an unbiased test in terms of its predictive validity. But it is such a stringent definition, given that no actual tests are perfectly reliable, that it must be viewed as a theoretical model that can only be roughly approximated in practice. Yet theoretically, by itself, this definition says all that need be or can be said. Nothing can be added to it that would make a test a less biased predictor, and any departure from any one of the three conditions of the definition, statistically speaking, introduces a form of bias. This definition, therefore, is all-inclusive. All other statistical definitions of predictive bias that are to be found in the literature (excepting those that are fallacious, as noted on pp. 370–373) are implicit in this core definition. However, not all the other definitions include all the conditions of the core definition, and so they are regarded as "relaxed" definitions, as they do not insist on one or another of the essential conditions of the core definition. We will critically review these other definitions shortly. They properly belong under the heading of statistical criteria for the *fair use* of tests, as "relaxed" definitions of test bias really amount only to a subjective, nonstatistical judgment as to which particular aspects of bias can be ignored while still claiming that the predictive use of the test is fair. In terms of prediction, no definition of test bias other than the one given here can be viewed as wholly adequate or acceptable. *Selection bias* is quite another matter and comes under the heading of *fair use* of tests. But first we must understand the core definition in greater detail.

Two points in the definition should be especially noted. First, notice that the emphasis is on the *predictive* bias of a test and not on some intrinsic property of the test itself. The definition is of a *biased predictor,* not of a biased test per se. We are concerned here with a test's usefulness as a predictor of a particular criterion and with whether the test has the same predictive efficiency in different subpopulations. Thus it is a wholly pragmatic definition of bias. Predictive bias means *systematic error* (as contrasted to random errors of measurement) in the prediction of the criterion variable for persons of different subpopulations as a result of basing prediction on a common regression equation for *all* persons regardless of their subpopulation memberships, or basing prediction for persons of one subpopulation on the regression equation derived on a different subpopulation. Notice that one and the same test that is a biased predictor for different subpopulations, if predictions for all persons are based on any single regression equation, can be an unbiased predictor when predictions are based on different regression equations, each one derived on a particular subpopulation and applied only to members of the particular subpopulation. It is important to understand that the question of the presence or absence of predictive bias per se is crucial with respect to the practical use of tests and to their fair use in selection, but it is actually quite uninformative with respect to the construct validity of the ·test in question.

A test could have the same high degree of construct validity in both the major and minor groups and yet be a biased predictor of some particular criterion for the major and minor groups, even when the predictor variable has the same reliability in both groups. A good intuitive example is the prediction of an infant's height as an adult, using as the predictor variable the midparent height (i.e., the average of the heights of the infant's mother and father). Midparent height is a biased predictor of the infant's adult height if the prediction is based on a common regression line for males and females but is an unbiased predictor if different regression lines are used for males and females. Yet no one would argue that measurements of height per se are biased measurements for males or females, or for parents or offspring. But the midparent height is in fact a biased predictor of the offspring's height unless we take sex of offspring into account in making the prediction. Thus it is evident that the regression model alone can neither prove nor disprove that a test is biased in terms of its construct validity. The regression model can tell us only whether the test is or is not an unbiased predictor of a particular criterion.

Second, note that the definition refers to a "test with perfect reliability." This would appear to be an impractical and unrealistic condition to include in the definition of bias, as all real tests or measurements of any kind have less than perfect reliability. Then why include this condition in our definition? It is included to get around a seeming paradox, to wit: If the major and minor groups (with differing means on X and on Y) have one and the same regression line for a test (i.e., predictor variable) that has imperfect reliability (regardless of whether the reliabilities of the major and minor groups are or are not equal), the test would indeed serve as an unbiased predictor of the criterion. But it would seem paradoxical to call such a test unbiased (even though it is, in fact, an unbiased *predictor*) if by simply *improving* the test's reliability (say, by increasing its length, changing the time limit, or eliminating poor items), thereby increasing the accuracy of the test scores, we cause the test to become a biased predictor. How can a test become more biased by being made a more accurate measuring instrument? This is the seeming paradox. It is easily resolved, of course, if we realize the conceptually important distinction between (1) the validity of the test score X as a measure of some ability, trait, or characteristic of the individual (i.e., the test's construct validity) and (2) the validity of the test score X as a predictor of a particular criterion variable Y. It seems preferable, logically, to think of an unbiased test (in either sense, 1 or 2) as a hypothetical ideal that is approached by *improving* a test's accuracy (i.e., reliability), rather than by means of lowering its reliability or causing it to have different reliabilities in different groups.

One implication of our definition of bias is that all real tests, because they have less than perfect reliability, are thereby doomed to condemnation as biased, *even* when, under certain conditions, they can serve as unbiased predictors, as we soon shall see. But the fact is that sheer unreliability (i.e., random errors of measurement) can cause an otherwise unbiased test to be biased when the common regression line is used for two groups with different means. In such a case, the bias due solely to unreliability will always "favor" (i.e., overpredict the actual criterion value) members of the group with the lower mean. This source of predictive bias can be overcome either by using estimated true scores for all persons and deriving the common regression equation from the estimated true scores or by using different regression equations derived separately on each group for predicting the criterion performance for persons of the corresponding groups.

In light of the preceding, it should be noted that our first definition of predictive test bias can be given a theoretically equivalent but more realistic definition in terms of estimated true scores, as follows:

A test is a biased predictor if there is a statistically significant difference between the major and minor groups in the slopes b_{YX}, or in the intercepts k, or in the standard error of estimates $SE_{\hat{y}}$ of the regression lines of the two groups, when *these regression parameters are derived from the estimated true scores of persons within each group.*

Previous literature on predictive bias has virtually ignored the issue of test reliability, probably because when test reliability is high (say, $r_{XX} > .90$) as it often is, the fact that it is short of perfection (i.e., $r_{XX} = 1$) actually contributes relatively little to predictive bias. (The amount of predictive bias contributed by imperfect reliability can be precisely calculated, as shown in the section entitled "Effects of Reliability on Test Bias.")

Finally, it should be noted that the definition of bias pragmatically refers to a *statistically significant difference* between the major and minor groups' regression parameters, as these parameters, like any other statistics, are subject to sampling error. However, because the sample regression parameters k, b, and $SE_{\hat{y}}$ are unbiased estimates of the population parameters (that is, the sampling error does not have a *systematic* effect on any of the regression parameters), sampling error has no systematic effect on predictive test bias from one sample to another.

Reliability of Group Differences.   The definition of test bias states that the major and minor groups must show a statistically significant difference in slopes or intercepts or standard error of estimates, after each of these has been corrected for attenuation or when they are based on estimated true scores, for bias to be claimed. Each of these parameters, of course, can be tested for significance, using the appropriate formulas.[1] But, if the sample sizes are quite large, even quite small group differences in b_{YX}, k, and $SE_{\hat{y}}$ can be statistically significant. Even so, the test must be regarded as biased according to our definition, although for all practical purposes the amount of the bias may be trivial.

If the test is known to be significantly biased, then two main questions must be considered. How much test bias is to be tolerated in practice in the given circumstances? And what other measures (outside the test itself) can be taken to mitigate or counteract the test's bias when the scores are used in selection?

The amount of test bias regarded as tolerable is a judgment that should be based on the probable bias or error that would result from some alternative selection procedure. Even a significantly biased test might result in more fair selection than some alternative means of selection for which no assessment of bias has been made, say, interviews, biographical data, previous school or employment record, and the like. As we soon shall see, there are ways of meliorating a biased test in the selection procedure itself. Although an unbiased test is certainly to be desired, any test with validity, unbiased or not, can always improve selection. The problem is in using the test in a way that is the most "fair" to everyone.

Equal Validity Coefficients Not Essential.   The definition of an unbiased test just given does not require equal test validities in the two groups, and it does not require that both groups have the same σ_X and σ_Y. This, of course, is because both b_{YX} and $SE_{\hat{y}}$ are complex functions of r_{XY}, σ_X and σ_Y, for which many different sets of values can result in a single value for b_{YX} or $SE_{\hat{y}}$. If the groups do not differ significantly in σ_X or σ_Y, however, then they cannot differ significantly in their validity coefficients for the test to be considered unbiased. When the two groups differ nonsignificantly in σ_X and σ_Y, as is often the case in reality, an unbiased test can be defined as one in which the major and minor groups have nonsignificantly different validity coefficients and nonsignificantly different Y intercepts of the regression lines. This definition, of course, is algebraically equivalent to our original definition of an unbiased test.

It should be noted that, when two such groups are pooled into one large group, the regression line remains unchanged (i.e., b_{YX} and k are the same in the pooled as in the separate groups), but r_{XY} will be increased in the pooled data if the true correlation is greater than zero and the group means differ on X; also σ_X and σ_Y are increased for the pooled groups.[2] Because the regression line remains unchanged, the predicted $\hat{Y}$ from any given value of X for an individual is the same for the pooled groups as for the groups separately, and $SE_{\hat{Y}}$ is also the same, regardless of the individual's group membership.

The Criterion Problem. The definition of test bias given depends on the assumption that the criterion itself is unbiased. We know that this is not always the case, especially when criterion measurements are based on ratings rather than on more objective observations. A biased criterion is one that consistently overrates (or underrates) the criterial performance of the members of a particular subpopulation. A good example is sex bias in school grades: teachers generally give slightly higher grades to girls than to boys, even when the sexes are perfectly matched on objective measures of scholastic achievement.

When the criterion itself is questionable, we must look at the various construct validity criteria of test bias. If these show no significant amount of test bias, it is likely (although not formally proved) that the criterion, not the test, is biased. In a validity study, poor criterion measurement can make a good test look bad. We have to make sure, before revising or throwing out the suspect test, that the criterion measure itself is not at fault. A well-constructed test is often likely to be a technically sounder, more sophisticated measuring instrument than the means of measuring the criterion performance. The reliability of the criterion measurements is not nearly so important a consideration from our standpoint as is the absence of any group bias in the criterion measurements.

The Effects of Reliability on Test Bias. In reality no test has perfect reliability, so we must now consider in detail the effects of unreliability on our basic model of test bias. We are here using the term reliability in the broad sense, to include internal consistency, parallel forms, and test–retest (i.e., stability) types of reliability.

Because test bias has been defined primarily in terms of three features of regression—slope, intercept, and standard error of estimate—we need to look at the effect of unreliability on each of these parameters. It turns out that each parameter is sensitive to test reliability, and consequently what may be mistaken as cultural bias in the test may actually be due only to unreliability. Reliability can be raised, such as by lengthening the test and other purely psychometric means, without essentially altering the test's content, factorial structure, or essential validity (i.e., the test's validity coefficient after correction for attenuation). Therefore, before concluding that a test is intrinsically biased, it should be determined how much of the apparent bias is attributable to the unreliability of the test.

To the critics of tests who complain that because of tests' imperfect reliabilities they work to the disadvantage of groups that, on the average, score below the mean of the general population, it may come as a surprise to find that just the opposite is true. Unreliability, as we shall see, actually gives a disadvantage to *high-scoring* persons (regardless of their group membership). Hence any group with fewer high-scoring persons is thereby *favored,* as a group, by a test's unreliability. One can easily see why this is so. Take height as an example. Imagine two persons, A and B. Say that A's true height is greater than B's true height. Then, if we obtain measurements of their heights that have perfect reliability, A will have a 100 percent probability of measuring taller than B. But, if our measurements have less than perfect reliability, then there is some probability that A will measure shorter than B. If the measurements have no reliability at all, then, of course, A has a 50 percent chance of measuring shorter than B. As the reliability of measurement increases, the probability of A's measuring taller than B also increases. The same applies to groups. For example, the amount of the average difference in height between men and women would be reduced, in relation to the standard deviation of height within sexes, if height were measured with less reliability. Similarly, an IQ test with low reliability will show more overlap between the score distributions of blacks and whites, for example, than will the same test with improved reliability. In more general terms, *whatever statistical discriminability a test has, it is only accentuated by improving its reliability.*

Now, looking back at Figure 9.1, imagine that the regression line depicted represents that of an *unbiased* test with *perfect reliability;* by definition the slope, intercept, and standard error of estimate are one and the same (within the limits of sampling error) for both the major and minor groups. What will happen if now we make the test *unreliable,* that is, its reliability r_{XX} is now something less than 1? Also, assume that r_{XX} is the same for the major and minor groups.

The observed slope b_{YX} then becomes $r_{XX}b_{YX}$. Thus we can say that *unreliability reduces the slope* by an amount equal to $\Delta b = (1 - r_{XX})b_{YX}$. With zero reliability the regression line would be perfectly horizontal. Note that there is no major/minor *differential* effect of test unreliability on the slope b_{YX} unless the reliability differs in the two groups.

Also, *unreliability produces a group difference in the Y intercepts.* If the intercepts are the same for the major and minor groups when the test has perfect reliability, then, with an unreliable test, the difference between the intercepts of the two groups will be increased by an amount equal to $\Delta(k_A - k_B) = b_{YX}(1 - r_{XX})(\bar{X}_A - \bar{X}_B)$, where $\bar{X}_A$ and $\bar{X}_B$ are the means of the major and minor groups, respectively. When $\bar{X}_A$ is greater than $\bar{X}_B$, the intercept of the major group will be *above* that of the minor group. This means that we would make systematic errors of prediction, which constitutes *biased* prediction, purely due to the unreliability of the test, if we used the common regression line or used the regression line of one group for predicting the criterion performance of a person from the other group. Using the major group's regression line to predict for the minor group, for example, with an unreliable test we would predict members of the minor group to do better on the criterion than they actually do; hence the test is said to *over*predict the criterion. Conversely, if we used the minor group's regression line the test would *under*predict the criterion for members of the major group. However, each group's own regression line yields an unbiased prediction of the criterion for members of the respective group. That is, there is neither systematic over- nor underprediction of the criterion values; the effect of lower reliability is simply to increase the standard error of estimate, $SE_{\hat{y}}$.

It is interesting that, by far, most of the instances of test bias found empirically for whites and blacks are of the kind just described, where the intercept of the black group is below that of the white group and the slopes are the same—a form of bias that favors the black group in any selection procedure based on the white regression line (or the common regression line) and a common selection cutoff score. Hunter and Schmidt (1976, p. 1056) have suggested, for example, that test unreliability alone would account for perhaps half the overprediction of black grade-point averages reported in the literature.

For both the major and minor groups, *test unreliability increases the standard error of estimate* $SE_{\hat{y}}$ by an amount equal to $\Delta SE_{\hat{y}} = \sigma_Y(\sqrt{1 - r_{XY}^2 r_{XX}} - \sqrt{1 - r_{XY}^2})$. Thus unreliability makes prediction less accurate.

Test unreliability also *reduces the validity coefficient* r_{XY} by an amount equal to $\Delta r_{XY} = (1 - \sqrt{r_{XX}})r_{XY}$, for both groups.

The amount of overlap of the distributions of *predicted* criterion scores of the major and minor groups is *increased* by test unreliability. Also, *test unreliability decreases the standard deviation of the predicted criterion measure* $\sigma_{\hat{y}} = \sigma_Y \sqrt{r_{XX}}$ by an amount equal to $\Delta \sigma_{\hat{y}} = (1 - \sqrt{r_{XX}})\sigma_{\hat{y}}$.

The effects of test unreliability are summarized graphically in Figure 9.2.

Since in practice we are always dealing with less than perfect reliability, we can determine how much of the test bias, as indicated by group differences in k and $SE_{\hat{y}}$ is attributable to the test's unreliability by using the formulas for Δk and $\Delta SE_{\hat{y}}$ given above. To conclude that there is significant predictive bias other than that due to unreliability, one should first correct the group differences in the regression parameters for attenuation (i.e., unreliability) before subjecting them to the appropriate statistical tests of significance. (These tests are given in note 1 at the end of this chapter.) The simplest method for

Figure 9.2. Illustration of the effects of test unreliability on the regression of Y and X in groups A and B, with test means of $\bar{X}_A$ and $\bar{X}_B$. Solid line represents a hypothetical unbiased test with perfect reliability; broken lines represent the effect on regression of adding error variance (i.e., lowering the reliability from 1 to .40) to the same test. (See caption to Figure 9.1 regarding $SE_{\hat{y}}$.)

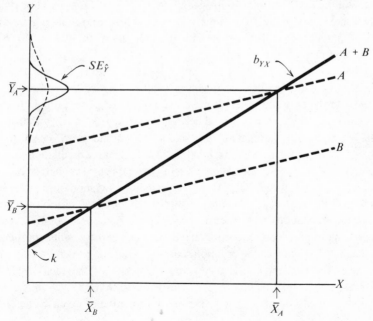

correcting the group differences for attenuation is to subtract Δk from the observed difference in intercepts of the two groups, subtract Δb from the observed difference in slopes, and subtract $\Delta SE_{\hat{y}}$ from the difference between the observed values of $SE_{\hat{y}}$ in the two groups. Of course, when the regression parameters have been corrected for attenuation, one must then use not the test scores themselves but the estimated true scores as the predictor variable in the regression equation. The regression equation can be corrected for attenuation of X as follows:

Uncorrected: $\quad \hat{Y} = (\overline{Y} - b_{YX} \overline{X}) + b_{YX} X.$

Corrected: $\quad \hat{Y}_c = \left(\overline{Y} - \left(\dfrac{b_{YX}}{r_{XX}}\right) \overline{X}\right) + b_{YX}(X - \overline{X}) + \overline{X}.$

It should be noted that $\hat{Y} = \hat{Y}_c$ for all persons from the same subpopulation with means $\overline{X}$ and $\overline{Y}$.

Although the use of estimated true scores (see Chapter 7, pp. 275–276) cannot improve predictive validity *within* any subgroup, the bias due to test unreliability when predictions are made from a single regression equation for two or more subgroups can be obviated by using estimated true scores. Each person's score is regressed toward the mean of his own group to an extent determined by the test's reliability for that group. Although this method would surely reduce bias in prediction, it could be objected to as being "unfair" according to some definitions of fairness (which are discussed in the latter part of this chapter), as the method requires identification of a person's group membership to reduce prediction bias due to unreliability by using estimated true scores.

What are the corresponding *effects of unreliability in the criterion?* They are quite a bit simpler. Most important, the slope and intercept of the regression line are completely independent of the reliability of the criterion r_{YY}. If the slope of the true regression line is b_{YX}, the slope of the observed score regression line is simply $r_{XX} b_{YX}$, and obviously r_{YY} does not enter into it at all. Similarly, if the Y intercept of the true-score regression line is $k = \overline{Y} - b_{YX} \overline{X}$, the intercept of the observed regression line is simply $k = \overline{Y} - b_{YX} \overline{X} r_{XX}$, and r_{YY} does not enter into it.

The reliability of the criterion r_{YY} does, however, affect the standard error of estimate, as it affects the validity coefficient r_{XY} and σ_Y, which both enter into $SE_{\hat{y}}$. If we assume that test scores and criterion measures both have perfect reliability, then the true-score standard error of estimate would be $SE_{\hat{y}} = \sigma_Y \sqrt{1 - r_{XY}^2}$, and the standard error of estimate based on the unreliable observed scores would be $SE_{\hat{y}'} = (\sigma_Y / \sqrt{r_{YY}}) \sqrt{1 - r_{XY}^2 r_{XX} r_{YY}}$. Thus it can be seen that unreliability of either the predictor or the criterion measures will increase $SE_{\hat{y}}$. Notice that unreliability increases the standard deviation; thus, if the standard deviation of true scores is σ_T, the standard deviation of the unreliable observed scores will be $\sigma_T / \sqrt{r_{XX}}$, where r_{XX} is the reliability of the observed scores. Correction of $SE_{\hat{y}}$ for attenuation of the criterion, or of the test score, or of both is accomplished by applying the appropriate corrections for attenuation both to the validity coefficient, r_{XY}, and to the standard deviation of the criterion scores σ_Y. For the reader who does not have a clear grasp of the concept of estimated true score and of the relationships among obtained scores, true scores, estimated true scores, reliability, and validity, correlation, and regression, a brief summary of this essential information is given at the end of this chapter (pp. 462–463).

Trouble-shooting Test Bias. Test bias has been defined as significant subgroup differences in one or more of three features of the regression system: slopes, intercepts, and errors of estimates, that is, b_{YX}, k, and $SE_{\hat{y}}$, respectively.

If a test of statistical significance reveals a significant difference between the major and minor groups on any one or a combination of these aspects of the regression of the criterion on test scores, then what? Obviously the test in question has thereby failed to qualify as an unbiased predictor. But this does not necessarily imply that the test is useless or should be immediately discarded. The source of bias might be easily remediable. And, if not, even an irremediably biased test, if properly used, might be more fair for selection purposes than no test at all.

As Hunter and Schmidt (1976, p. 1065) have noted, "Elimination of valid psychological tests will usually mean their replacement with devices or methods with less validity (e.g., the interview), thus increasing further the 'unfairness' to individuals and/or groups." Therefore, when a test is found to be biased in terms of our definition, further analysis is called for. We can go about this most systematically in the fashion of trouble-shooting defects in mechanical and electronic equipment. There is a routine of examina-tion that exposes first the most accessible and easily remediable causes of the trouble.

We have already noted that the slope, intercept, and error of estimate are complex functions of several other more elemental statistics that can vary between subgroups. These are the validity coefficient, r_{XY}; the standard deviations of the predictor (test) and the criterion, σ_X and σ_Y; and the reliability coefficients of the predictor and criterion, r_{XX} and r_{YY}. Thus there are five elements on any of which a significance test might reveal that the two subgroups are either the *same* or *different*. So, with five such binary decisions, there are $2^5 = 32$ possible ways that a test could fail to meet our definition of an unbiased predictor. Some are much more serious than others.

1. *Unequal Slopes*. Because $b_{YX} = r_{XY}(\sigma_Y/\sigma_X)$, one must look at each of these elements to locate the source of the inequality. First, correct b_{YX} for attenuation (unrelia-bility) of the test scores: $_cb_{YX} = b_{YX}/r_{XX}$, where $_cb_{YX}$ is the slope corrected for attenua-tion and r_{XX} is the test's reliability *within each subgroup*. (As noted earlier, the reliability of the criterion r_{YY} does not affect the slope.)

If the subgroups do not differ in $_cb_{YX}$, then we can assume that the group difference in b_{YX} is due to differential unreliability of the test scores in the two groups. In this case, the remedy for unequal slopes is a simple one statistically, although it may not be acceptable in terms of certain definitions of fairness, as it requires identification of every person's group membership. The purely statistical remedy, however, is to correct the test scores themselves for unreliability by converting them to *estimated true scores*. A per-son's estimated true score is $\hat{T}_X = r_{XX}(X_o - \bar{X}_g) + \bar{X}_g$, where X_o is the person's observed score and $\bar{X}_g$ is the mean test score of the subgroup of which the person is a member. This procedure eliminates the bias in the slopes and the intercept (but not in the error of estimate, as the reliability of estimated true scores is the same as the reliability of obtained scores) due to unreliability in the test scores. Remember that such bias can exist even when the test's reliability is exactly the same in both subgroups.

If the subgroup reliabilities r_{XX} differ significantly, however, every effort should be made to reduce or eliminate the difference before resorting to the use of estimated true scores. Often it will be found that the subgroup reliabilities differ because of floor or ceiling effects that cause a piling up of scores at the bottom or the top of the frequency distribution.* There are great advantages to improving the test reliability and equalizing it as nearly as possible in all subgroups, as compared with using estimated true scores. When the reliabilities are high and not significantly different in the subgroups, however, the use of estimated true scores will practically eliminate slope and intercept bias due to unreliability in the test scores.

If, however, there are significant subrgoup differences in $_cb_{YX}$, we know that the differences are not the result of test unreliability but must be due to something else. The next step then is to test the significance of the difference between the subgroups' validity coefficients corrected for attenuation: $_cr_{XY} = r_{XY} / \sqrt{r_{XX}r_{YY}}$. If the subgroups differ significantly in $_cr_{XY}$, there is, unfortunately, no easy solution. Although the test is biased, unbiased selection might still be possible, as we shall see later in this chapter; but it is not possible on the basis of the test scores alone. If one's aim is to have an unbiased test, rather than just an unbiased selection strategy, the only remedy for unequal validities is a fundamental redesigning of the test in the hope that it will be possible to create at least as valid a test but with *equal validities* in both subgroups. If this is deemed unfeasible, whatever the reason, then of course one is left with the choice either of discarding the test or of using it, along with certain other information, in a way that could be considered unbiased.

If $_cb_{YX}$ differs in the subgroups and $_cr_{XY}$ does not differ, then the difference must be due to subgroup inequalities in σ_X and σ_Y. This can be checked by first correcting σ_X and σ_Y for attenuation ($_c\sigma_X = \sqrt{r_{XX}}\sigma_X$ and $_c\sigma_Y = \sqrt{r_{YY}}\sigma_Y$) and then testing the significance of the subgroup difference in either $_c\sigma_X$ or $_c\sigma_Y$ by means of the variance ratio $F = {_c\sigma_L^2}/{_c\sigma_S^2}$, with $N_L - 1$ and $N_S - 1$ degrees of freedom, where $_c\sigma_L^2$ is the larger corrected variance (for either subgroup) and $_c\sigma_S^2$ is the smaller corrected variance and N_L and N_S are the corresponding sample sizes. A significant F then means the test is biased with respect to regression slopes because of subgroup inequalities in either σ_X or σ_Y, or both.

Is there a remedy for unequal σ's? The simplest remedy, but one that might not always work, is a *nonlinear transformation of the scale* of scores (i.e., test scores or criterion scores, as the case may be). The very same transformation must be applied to all scores regardless of subgroup membership. (Converting original scores to standard scores is not a suitable transformation procedure in this case, as it involves a different transformation equation for each subgroup.) A linear transformation (such as standard scores) would be of no avail, of course, as it only alters the means and standard deviations of the subgroups in equal proportions. Nonlinear transformations are generally exponential or logarithmic, for example, $X' = X^a$ (or $X' = X^{-a}$), or $X' = \log X$, where X is the original score, X' is the transformed score, and a is an exponent. Complex combinations and variations of these types of transformation provide many possible ways to transform the original scale of scores so that the transformed scores will have some desired property such as equal σ's in various subgroups of the population. If subgroup σ's are proportional to their means, for example, such that $\sigma/\overline{X} = C$ (a constant) across subgroups, some type of exponential transformation (e.g., $X' = \sqrt{X}$) may remove the proportionality, so that on the transformed scale X' will still show mean differences between subgroups but no differences in σ's.

We cannot here go further into the technical aspects of transformations of scale; for a good introduction the reader is referred to Mueller (1949). But, before leaving the topic of transformations, it should be noted that the scientifically unsophisticated often hold the mistaken notion that a transformation of the scale perpetrates a kind of legerdemain that is not quite cricket. This is nonsense. The transformation merely makes the scale more useful for a given purpose. There is no metaphysical "ultimate reality" underlying the original scores that the transformed scores obscure or distort. If the transformed scores have more desirable properties for our purpose than the original scores, then we are fully justified in using the transformed scores. In the present context, test bias may be reduced or even eliminated if it is due solely to unequal σ's in the subgroups (for either X or Y or both) and a transformation of the scale can be found that equalizes the σ's across subgroups. It is important to note that, if a scale transformation of test scores can eliminate bias by equalizing subgroup σ_X's, the test can be regarded as an unbiased test, as the bias is not inherent in the test itself but is merely an artifact of the particular scale on which the test scores are expressed. There is no rule in science that any one scale is better than any other in an absolute sense. One uses whichever scale will yield some theoretical or practical advantage—in this case, the least biased test scores.

If a suitable transformation cannot be found to equalize the subgroup σ's, the only remedy, if one wishes to have an unbiased test, is to alter the test itself in some way that could equalize the subgroup σ_X's, such as by adding more difficult or more easy items or by item selection aimed at increasing or reducing item intercorrelations, and the like. It may be much more difficult to alter subgroup σ_Y's on the criterion measures, if there is no suitable transformation.

2. *Unequal Intercepts.* Because the Y intercept $k = \bar{Y} - b_{YX}\bar{X}$, the correction of the intercept for attenuation is $_ck = \bar{Y} - _cb_{YX}\bar{X}$. If the subgroups do not differ significantly in $_ck$, the same remedies for low or unequal subgroup reliabilities described in the previous section apply here as well. But, if the subgroups differ significantly in $_ck$, the trouble is inherent in $_cb_{YX}$ and calls for the same analytic procedures and remedies, if any are possible, as were indicated for subgroup differences in $_cb_{YX}$. Whatever methods will correct attenuation bias in slopes will also necessarily correct attenuation bias in intercepts.

3. *Unequal Errors of Estimate.* The standard error of estimate $SE_{\hat{Y}}$ when corrected for attenuation is $_cSE_{\hat{Y}} = \sqrt{r_{YY}}\,\sigma_Y\sqrt{[1 - (r_{XY}^2/r_{XX}r_{YY})][(N - 1)/(N - 2)]}$. If the subgroups do not differ significantly in $_cSE_{\hat{Y}}$, the indicated remedies for low or unequal reliabilities are applied. But, if the subgroups differ significantly in $_cSE_{\hat{Y}}$, the cause may be inequality of σ_Y (in which case a transformation of the criterion scale might help) or inequality in $_cr_{XY}$ (in which case a redesigning of the test itself is the only remedy for making the test unbiased).

In all three features of the regression system reviewed here, it can be seen that the most intractable source of bias is subgroup inequality in $_cr_{XY}$, that is, the validity coefficients corrected for attenuation (technically known as the *relevance* of the test). That is the main reason that test experts give prime attention to subgroup differences in validity as a crucial criterion of test bias. Bias due to low test reliability (if r_{XX} is the same in all subgroups) can be corrected by using estimated true scores, or by raising the reliability of the test by lengthening it, or by doing both these things. Bias due to subgroup inequalities in σ_X or σ_Y can often be corrected simply by a transformation of the scale. But bias due to subgroup inequality in $_c r_{XY}$ has no remedy short of altering the inherent structure of the test. Because a test's validity is the result of factors common to both the test and the criterion, subgroup differences in validity indicate subgroup differences either in the factorial structure of the test, or of the criterion, or of both. Factor analysis of the test items (or subsets of items) within each subgroup will tell us whether the test scores have a different factor composition in the various subgroups. If so, then fundamental alterations of the test become necessary to make it unbiased. If there are no significant subgroup differences in the test's factor structure, then we must look to the criterion measurement for the source of the bias. A biased criterion variable does not readily yield to analysis if it is based on the global subjective judgments of teachers or work supervisors, and it may be necessary to substitute more objective and analytical measures of performance. We either do that, or we ignore predictive validity as a criterion of test bias and fall back on the test's construct validity in the various subgroups, one aspect of which is the test's factorial composition, as the basis for judging whether the test is biased for the particular subgroups in question.

The Bartlett–O'Leary Models of Test Bias. Bartlett and O'Leary (1969) have described eleven different "models" of the various forms of predictive validity that theoretically could occur for any two subgroups on a particular test. These "models" can be represented in the form of correlation scatter diagrams, in which an ellipse represents a significant correlation between the predictor and criterion variables and a circle represents zero correlation. The location of their centers indicates the absence or presence of subgroup mean differences in the predictor X or criterion Y. The eleven "models" are shown in Figure 9.3.

Model 1 is the only one that represents an unbiased test. The remaining models have been used to classify test validation studies based on two or more subgroups in terms of the types of bias that they reveal. In a large number of validation studies of a variety of

Figure 9.3. Correlation scatter diagram representations of the Bartlett–O'Leary models of the relationships between predictor (X) and criterion (Y) variables in the major and minor groups. (After Farr et al., 1971, pp. 4–5)

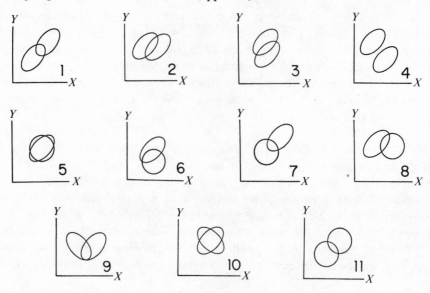

Table 9.1. Checklist of hypotheses about types of group differences (indicated "yes" or "no") in a test validation study involving two groups, A and B, and the corresponding Bartlett–O'Leary models

Hypothesis	Bartlett–O'Leary Models										
	1	2	3	4	5	6	7	8	9	10	11
$\bar{X}_A = \bar{X}_B$	No	No	Yes	No	Yes	Yes	No	No	Yes	No	No
$\bar{Y}_A = \bar{Y}_B$	No	Yes	No	No	Yes	No	Yes	No	Yes	Yes	No
$\sigma_{X_A} = \sigma_{X_B}$	Yes	Yes	Yes	Yes	?	?	?	?	Yes	Yes	Yes
$\sigma_{Y_A} = \sigma_{Y_B}$	Yes	Yes	Yes	Yes	?	?	?	?	Yes	Yes	Yes
$r_{XX_A} = r_{XX_B}$	Yes	?	?	?	?	?	?	?	?	?	?
$r_{YY_A} = r_{YY_B}$	Yes	?	?	?	?	?	?	?	?	?	?
$r_{XY_A} > 0$	Yes	Yes	Yes	Yes	Yes	Yes	Yes	No	Yes	Yes	No
$r_{XY_B} > 0$	Yes	Yes	Yes	Yes	No	No	No	Yes	Yes	Yes	No
$r_{XY_A} = r_{XY_B}$	Yes	Yes	Yes	Yes	No	No	No	No	No	No	Yes
$b_{YX_A} = b_{YX_B}$	Yes	Yes	Yes	Yes	No	No	No	No	No	No	Yes
$k_A = k_B$	Yes	No	No	No	No	No	No	No	No	No	No
$SE_{\hat{Y}_A} = SE_{\hat{Y}_B}$	Yes	Yes	Yes	Yes	No	No	No	No	Yes	Yes	Yes

tests and criteria for white and black groups, it was found that out of 765 of the validity studies 357, or only 47 percent, could be roughly classified into one or another of the Bartlett–O'Leary models. Obviously these eleven models describe only a very limited subset of all the possibilities that actually occur empirically. They take into account only a few of the basic elements that can make for test bias and consider only a few of the many possible combinations of these.

Table 9.1 gives a checklist of the ways in which two groups, subscripted A and B, may or may not differ significantly in a test validation study. Each item in the list may be regarded as the statement of a hypothesis that can be subjected to a statistical test and answered "yes" or "no" at a given level of significance. The combinations of "yes" and "no" that describe the eleven Bartlett–O'Leary models are shown on the right. Only the first is one possible model of an unbiased test. The question marks indicate relevant variables that are ambiguous or unspecified in the Bartlett–O'Leary models. It is apparent that these models do not go very far in describing all the possible varieties of validation outcomes or test biases involving two groups. But Table 9.1 illustrates an important point: there is no single statistic that is adequate to define an unbiased test; a combination of all three (viz., b_{YX}, k, and $SE_{\hat{Y}}$) is crucial, and a significant subgroup difference on any one of these is sufficient to define a test as biased. Notice that no other statistical features of the validation process listed in Table 9.1 have this critical defining power. Even the validity coefficient itself can be the same in both subgroups and still the test can be biased.

Philosophies of Fair Selection

Before going into the specifics of how a test is used in accord with different selection strategies based on different, often incompatible, concepts of fairness, we shall have to examine three basic conceptions or philosophies of fairness. They define three broad, mutually exclusive categories into one or another of which every strategy for fair selection thus far proposed in the literature can be classified. Hunter and Schmidt (1976) have labeled these conceptions *unqualified individualism, qualified individualism,* and *quotas.* Each of these philosophies of selection has different implications for selection based either on an *unbiased* test or on a *biased* test. The intersection of the three philosophies with the unbiased versus biased tests theoretically forms $3 \times 2 = 6$ categories of selection strategies, as shown in Table 9.2. However, only five categories need to be considered, since for an unbiased test, categories 1a and 1b lead to exactly the same selection strategy. The five selection strategies will each be taken up in the order 1 to 5 as shown in Table 9.2. But first we must understand the three basic philosophies of fair selection.

Unqualified Individualism. This philosophy maintains that a fair selection strategy is one that selects from the available pool of applicants those individuals with the highest predicted criterion performance, using whatever predictor variable (or optimally weighted combination of variables) yields the highest predictive validity. There are no holds barred on the nature of the predictor variables, which in addition to test scores may include quantitized★ demographic and biological information such as sex, race, socioeconomic status, religion, years of schooling, parental education, location of residence—in general, any variable that is at all correlated with the criterion is regarded as a legitimate predictor. Whether it is used or not depends solely on the statistical consideration of whether it adds a statistically significant increment to the overall predictive validity and the practical value of such an increment as weighed against the cost and feasibility of obtaining the particular information on which it is based.

Moreover, according to unqualified individualism, the same test or other predictor variables need not be used for all applicants. Different predictors may be used according to applicants' group membership. If any one test has higher validity for members of one subgroup and a different test has higher validity for members of another subgroup, then each subgroup is given the test with the higher validity for that subgroup. Or all applicants are tested on *both* tests, and the separate scores, along with a quantitized score indicating subgroup membership, are optimally combined in a multiple prediction equation.

Applicants are selected in rank order from the top down in terms of predicted

Table 9.2. Five categories of fair selection strategies.

Selection Philosophy	Test	
	Unbiased	Biased
Unqualified individualism	1a ⎫	3
Qualified individualism	1b ⎭ 1	(4)[a]
Quotas	2	5

[a]Category 4, as explained later in this chapter, is illusory and actually falls into category 5.

criterion performance until all the available positions are filled or until the predicted performance falls below some cutoff point below which performance is regarded as unacceptable.

Advocates of this position regard it as fair for the following reasons.

1. This philosophy of selection guarantees the highest average level of criterion performance of the selected applicants. Short of clairvoyance, any other possible selection strategy (given the same available information) will necessarily yield an overall lower criterial performance by the selectees. Maximizing criterial performance is of course especially desirable from the employer's standpoint, and for certain jobs (e.g., surgeon, airlines pilot) it would be considered crucial by the public as well.

2. No one is selected (or rejected) because of his or her race or sex or other subgroup membership. Selection is solely on the basis of the best available prediction of performance. If group membership is a valid predictor, there is no concern with why it predicts, that is, with the complex chain of causality between group membership and criterial performance. The aim is to maximize accuracy of prediction and not to try to determine what each individual's criterial performance might be if he or she had had a different past history, with different cultural and environmental advantages or disadvantages, or a different set of genes. Thus, if a person from a particular subgroup is rejected by our selection strategy, it is not because the person is a member of that subgroup, but because of the best prediction that can be made of that person's performance. Our prediction will be wrong less often by this strategy than by any other possible strategy.

3. This type of selection strategy minimizes (but does not necessarily eliminate) average subgroup differences in criterial performance among those who are selected. The advantage of this may be considerable in terms of the morale of employees, cutting down job turnovers or rate of firing, and especially in terms of equalizing the chances of the subgroups for further promotions within the organization. For example, Hunter and Schmidt (1976) describe the case of a company that "deliberately reduced its entrance standards so as to hire more blacks. However, these people could not then pass the internal promotion tests and hence accumulated in the lowest level jobs in the organization. The government then took them to court for discriminatory promotion policies!" (p. 1069).

4. This type of selection strategy is deemed fair also to those who are rejected, as it predicts more accurately than any other strategy which persons will not succeed on the criterion (assuming that the criterial standard of success or failure remains the same for all selectees regardless of their group membership). Those who would not succeed are thus best identified by this strategy and are spared the unpleasantness of failure, or of a dead-end job without a reasonable probability of future promotion, or of wasting time and money in a college, a job-training program, or a job that only leads to failure or intolerable frustration from inability to meet the normal expectations for performance.

5. Selection errors do occur, of course. There will always be some selectees whose criterial performance will not be so good as that of some of the rejectees had they been given the same opportunity. But such errors of prediction are inevitable in any selection situation for which the predictive validity is less than perfect, as is always the case in reality. The best we can possibly do with the available information on the applicants is to try to *minimize* errors of prediction, and that is exactly what this type of strategy statistically guarantees.

What are the main objections to this philosophy? They are spelled out by the other philosophies, but the one that may be the most troublesome, even to the most committed advocates of unqualified individualism, should be emphasized at this point. If for one subgroup no valid predictor is available, or if the predictor has appreciably lower validity than that for other subgroups, then the most capable members of that subgroup will have less chance of being selected than will equally capable members of other subgroups. In this sense, the selection strategy may be regarded as unfair to members of the subgroup in which the predictor has relatively low validity. Imagine the extreme case where the predictor has zero validity for one subgroup. Then, the regression line for that group will be perfectly horizontal, with its intercept at the subgroup's mean on the criterion (Y axis), and the best prediction of the criterion performance for every member of the subgroup will be the subgroup's mean. If that mean is *below* the criterion success–failure cutoff point, then no one from that subgroup will be selected. If the subgroup mean is *above* the cutoff point, then all members of the subgroup are equally eligible for selection, with no selection advantage given to the really more capable members. In the first case the selecting institution also loses, because the invalid predictor cannot identify the most potentially successful applicants of that particular subgroup, which may contain some highly valuable persons in terms of their criterial performance. And, in the second case, the selecting institution also loses, because a great many of the nonvalidly selected persons will prove to be incompetent.

The first case may be less serious to the selecting institution if the supply of qualified talent in any one subgroup with high test validity is greater than the number of persons that can be selected. That state of affairs may cause the selecting institution to have little incentive to try to improve the validity of its predictor variables for the subgroups in which the test has low validity. Improvements in validity can often involve costly and time-consuming research, with no guarantee as to the outcome. Therefore, the advocate of unqualified individualism, to be fair, must be able to satisfy him- or herself that an adequate effort has been made to find or devise the most valid predictors for every subgroup and to ensure that there is as little discrepancy between subgroup validites as possible. If this should turn out not to be possible, the condition should be acknowledged as something to worry about in terms of a fair selection policy. Other solutions may be in order, based on some alternative conception of fairness. An uncompromising advocate of unqualified individualism, however, will still argue that in this admittedly imperfect world, where selection is required (because there are more applicants than available positions), no other alternative is preferable to selection from the top down, based on the best possible prediction of each individual's criterial performance, thus minimizing errors of prediction. Almost everyone might agree with this philosophy in selection for those rare jobs where competence or incompetence can mean a matter of life or death. For the ordinary run-of-the-mill situations where selection is required, however, many persons might prefer to adopt a different concept of fairness.

Qualified Individualism.   This philosophy, like unqualified individualism, advocates maximizing predictive validity for all individuals. But as a matter of principle it imposes one fundamental constraint: *identification of an individual's group membership should not enter into the selection procedure.* If an unbiased test is available, the selection strategy advocated by qualified and unqualified individualism is the same, because any given score on an unbiased test yields the same prediction for individuals regardless of their group membership. But, if the test is biased, the qualified individualist is in a quandary. He or she cannot use *different* tests for different groups, as an individual's group identity is prohibited. The qualified individualist obviously cannot use group membership itself as a predictor or moderator* variable in a multiple regression equation, even if doing so would markedly increase the validity of prediction.

If a test predicts differentially for members of two or more groups (i.e., is biased), one can equalize prediction, according to this philosophy, only by adding other variables to the prediction equation that do not involve identification of a person's group membership. This may lead one to seek easily measured variables that are correlated both with group membership and with the criterion. Information about place of residence, birthplace, amount of education, and other biographical data may serve this purpose. Is using such information to boost predictive validity any more fair than using group membership itself as a predictor, for example, race, sex, or religion? Certain other variables can act as *indirect indicators of race or other group membership. An indirect indicator* has been defined as any variable that correlates more highly with group membership than with the criterion. But this definition has little to recommend it, theoretically or practically, as we shall see.

The most scrupulous adherents to qualified individualism would frown on the use of such indirect indicators of group membership on the grounds that they have only incidental or extrinsic validity rather than *intrinsic validity* as predictors of the criterion. They would argue that one is obliged to discover variables with *intrinsic validity* for predicting criterion performance. If the variable of *race,* for example, predicts some proportion of the variance in criterion performance that is not predicted by the test, it is presumed that this is because the test does not measure all the intrinsic factors involved in the criterion performance, and therefore what one needs to do is find other tests that measure these factors. The variable of *race* then does not have to serve as a "stand-in" for psychological factors that can be (and *should* be) measured as *individual* differences.

The most that the terms "extrinsic" and "intrinsic" can be made to mean in this context is as follows.

An *extrinsic* predictor is one for which the *cause* of its correlation with the criterion is unknown or at best obscure. The chain of causality between predictor and criterion is not readily apparent and may even be unanalyzable by any present methodology. *Race,* as a predictive variable, is a good example of an extrinsic predictor. Race undeniably has substantial predictive validity for certain scholastic and job performance criteria. But the basic *causes* of this predictive validity are still a matter of scientific controversy and cannot be answered without recourse to other lines of investigation outside the domain of test validation.

An *intrinsic* predictor is one that seems to show some fairly obvious functional relationship to the criterion performance. If we are to select applicants for the job of postal clerk, for example, a card-sorting test, among others, might be regarded as an intrinsic predictor if scores on such a test were shown to be correlated with proficiency on the job. It would seem easy to explain the correlation in terms of common behavioral elements between predictor and criterion. But notice that this perception of causality underlying the correlation is a *subjective* judgment, however plausible it may seem to everyone concerned. Theoretically, it leaves room for argument. The unqualified individualist would argue that *any* predictor is intrinsic if it involves a significant correlation, whether or not we are able directly to perceive the essential cause of the correlation; and plausibility is beside the point.

The only objective and operational distinction that one can make between extrinsic and intrinsic predictors, if one wishes to enforce the distinction, is this: a predictor is *intrinsic* if it shows predictive validity for persons *within* a particular group. A predictor is *extrinsic* if it has nonsignificant validity *within* a group and has validity only when groups are pooled. Group membership per se as a predictor is extrinsic by this definition; since there is no predictor variance *within* groups, there can be no within-groups correlation between predictor and criterion.

How large the within-group validity coefficient should be for the predictor to be judged as intrinsic remains an arbitrary decision. Statistical significance can only set the *lower* limit, since even a very small and practically useless correlation can be statistically significant if the sample size is very large. A decision rule proposed by Darlington (1971) is that a predictor variable is acceptable if the partial correlation $r_{XG \cdot Y} = 0$, where X is the predictor, G is group membership (quantitized as 0 or 1), and Y is the criterion. That is, the correlation between the predictor and group membership, with the criterion partialled out (statistically held constant), is zero. This is another way of saying that persons of the major and minor groups who are matched on the criterion variable Y should not differ on the predictor variable X. But this rule runs into serious difficulty, for it contradicts our core definition of an unbiased test except in the unrealistic limiting case where the test has *perfect* validity, that is, $r_{XY} = 1$. The reason, of course, is that, if $r_{XY} < 1$, the regression of X on Y is not the same line as the regression of Y on X. Members of the major and minor groups who by selection are matched on X will *ipso facto,* on the average, also be matched on Y, *if the test is unbiased;* but members of the major and minor groups who by selection are matched on Y will then *not* be matched on X. In other words, only a *biased* test (or other biased predictor) can possibly satisfy the condition $r_{XG \cdot Y} = 0$. In short, if we define an unbiased test score as one that predicts the same average level of criterion performance for individuals regardless of their group membership, then it cannot also be true (except when the test has perfect validity) that members of the major and minor groups who are matched on the criterion will, on the average, have the same test scores. Darlington's condition that $r_{XG \cdot Y} = 0$, therefore, can be regarded as acceptable only under a *quota* philosophy of fair selection. It will be considered later in that context.

The main advantages of qualified individualism, according to its proponents, are that it selects the best qualified applicants and is eminently fair because it does not make any use of the group identity of the individual applicants. It is willing, if necessary, to sacrifice some degree of predictive validity in exchange for preserving the racial (or other group) anonymity of the applicants in those cases where the predictive validity could have been improved by using group membership as a predictor or moderator variable, or where the use of different tests for different groups would have improved validity or equalized validites across the groups. Above all, no person could ever justifiably complain that this selection procedure treated him or her differently than anybody else because of his or her group identity.

Also, this philosophy forces the designers of selection procedures to seek more and better intrinsic predictors of the criterion.

The objections to this philosophy are, first, that it handicaps the attainment of maximal validity, given all the available information; second, that it makes an unnecessary metaphysical distinction between extrinsic and intrinsic predictors based on notions of the ultimate causes of correlations that have no necessary role in the objective procedures for establishing the predictive validity of variables; and, third, at worst it can lead to including among the predictor variables subtly disguised indirect indicators of group membership, even including culturally biased items in the test itself as a substitute for group membership, when group membership predicts the criterion independently of other unbiased predictors. The unqualified individualist would argue that it is preferable to maximize predictive validity using any variables available, while openly acknowledging agnosticism as to the causality of the intercorrelations involved in the most effective prediction equation.

Quotas.   According to this philosophy, fair selection does not consist in treating everyone alike regardless of their group membership, or in trying to maximize predictive validity and minimize errors of selection. A fair selection strategy involves some degree of trade-off of these admitted advantages for certain other desired advantages that may be deemed as having greater social importance. It may be regarded as important, for example, to select a greater proportion of minority group applicants than would be selected under the philosophies of unqualified or qualified individualism, to compensate for past exclusion of minority applicants and redress their grievances over former injustices and unequal opportunity. It may be regarded as socially and economically important that a minority group be adequately represented in a school or an occupation, even if bringing this about means lowering the selection cutoff for minority applicants and incurring a higher failure rate among the selectees or readjusting the failure rate by tolerating a somewhat lower level of performance.

A quota strategy of selection may be explicit or it may be implicit and "hidden" in the statistical procedures for selection, but a quota system can be claimed in fact whenever selection standards are applied to members of the major and minor groups such that one sacrifices maximizing criterial performance and minimizing errors of prediction. An argument may be made that the longer-range and broader social benefits of quota selection more than outweigh the lowering of criterial performance.

The main problem of quota selection is in gaining a consensus as to which groups are to be favored or disfavored by the quota. For a quota, of course, cuts two ways. It admits less qualified applicants (in terms of the best prediction of their future performance) of one subgroup in preference to better qualified applicants of another subgroup. Applicants in the favored group who are selected are apt to approve of quota selection for the advantage it gives them, whereas those in the unfavored group, who had equally high test scores but were rejected, are apt to complain. The argument is unresolvable in any psychometric or statistical terms and must be decided on other grounds. However, if a quota philosophy is decided on, there are precise mathematical strategies for determining the optimal cutting scores for different groups and calculating the most probable consequences of a given strategy. Once a quota is decided on, then purely technical considerations are involved in the method of selecting applicants from each subgroup. Usually a selection strategy is preferred that will maximize criterial performance or minimize prediction errors *within* each subgroup.

Other objections to the quota philosophy are all corollaries of the central fact that is made statistically inevitable by *any* kind of quota strategy: the average level of performance of the selected applicants is lowered overall, and the average difference between the selected majority and minority applicants is increased. Hunter and Schmidt (1976) point out some of the specific consequences of this statistical inevitability:

> In college selection, for example, the poor risk blacks who are admitted by a quota are more likely to fail than the higher scoring whites who were rejected because of the quota. Thus, in situations where low criterion performance carries a considerable penalty being selected on the basis of quotas is a mixed blessing.
>
> If lowered performance is met by increased rates of expulsion or firing, then the institution is relatively unaffected but (1) the quotas are undone and (2) there is considerable anguish for those selected who didn't make it. On the other hand, if the institution tries to adjust to the candidates selected by quotas, there may be great cost and inefficiency. Finally, there is the one other problem which academic institutions must face. Quotas will inevitably lower the average performance of graduating seniors, and hence lower the prestige of the school. Similar considerations apply in the case of the employment setting. In both cases, the effects of these changes on the broader society must also be considered. These effects are difficult to assess, but they may be quite significant.   (p. 1069)

Another objection, overlooked by Hunter and Schmidt, comes from those minority applicants who are selected under a quota system but who also would have been selected under unqualified individualism and must therefore pay the price, in lowered prestige and self-esteem, of the overall lower average performance of minority selectees, which is due mostly to the lower peformance of those minority selectees who were accepted in preference to better qualified but rejected majority applicants.

Selection Models with an Unbiased Predictor

A number of different models for selection that are considered fair in terms of one or another of the three philosophies of fairness that were just described have been proposed in the literature. These models are most easily explicated first for the case of an *unbiased* predictor as it would be used in terms of each philosophy.

Unqualified and Qualified Individualism

For an unbiased predictor, these two philosophies make no distinction between the selection models that are deemed fair. Because an unbiased test by definition does not predict differentially in terms of some specified group membership, one and the same regression equation is applicable to all applicants. No account needs to be taken of each applicant's group identity in the selection process, which, for any given test validity, ensures a maximum criterial performance of the selectees and a minimum of predictive errors, provided that applicants are selected solely on the basis of their test scores in rank order from the top down. (This, of course, assumes *linear* regression of the criterion measures on the test scores, a point that is established in the process of test validation. Nonlinear regression is rarely a serious problem and can usually be rectified by a suitable transformation of the test scores.)

Curiously enough, this selection model is the only one of many in the previous literature that has not been given a name. It is here labeled the ***Equal Risk Regression Model,*** as selection is based on one and the same regression line for all applicants, and all selectees or rejectees with the same score, regardless of group membership, involve the same risk or prediction error. When the test is unbiased, this selection model results in exactly the same selection decisions and *more* than satisfies the Regression Model of fairness proposed by Cleary (1968) and the Equal Risk Model proposed by Einhorn and Bass (1971), both of which logically are best described under the heading "Selection with Biased Tests."

Selection from the top down can stop at one of two points: (1) at a predetermined cutoff score below which the predicted criterial performance is deemed unacceptable or (2) if the number of applicants scoring *above* the cutoff score exceeds the number who can be selected, one selects the first N highest-scoring applicants.

Given an unbiased test, this model for selection is deemed as fair according to the proponents both of unqualified and qualified individualism. From the standpoint of both, it is the ideal model, because it selects solely on the basis of the best possible prediction of each individual's performance without need of any reference whatsoever to the individual's group membership. It is fair to individuals, and it maximizes the benefits of selection for the institution doing the selecting.

Quota Selection

In general, a quota is implied in any selection model that has the effect of selecting any applicant who is less qualified than is some rejected applicant, when "qualified" means the best available prediction of the applicant's criterial performance. A quota model does not necessarily imply that subgroup membership is explicitly taken into consideration. It is true of all quota systems, by definition, that they do not aim to maximize the level of criterion performance by selection. But the loss of this advantage is traded for other purported advantages that are deemed socially more important, at least temporarily.

A number of selection models having the essential feature of a quota model have been proposed in the literature; but, interestingly, very few are explicitly characterized as quota models, which they all in fact are. Each of these models is described here in terms of its application to selection with an *unbiased* test, assuming that the advocates of quotas would subscribe to the use of selection tests at all.

The ***Proportional Representation Model*** is the most straightforward of all quota models. It is the model of choice for those who believe that the proportions of selectees from various subgroups should represent their proportions in the total population or of the applicant population. For example, one often sees arguments that the percentage of black applicants admitted to a college should be the same as the percentage of blacks in the U.S. population (or in the population served by the particular college), or that the percentage of blacks admitted to special classes for the educationally retarded or for the gifted should be no greater or no less than the percentage of blacks in the school population. (Or the number of children selected for the special classes should constitute the same percentage of each racial group.)

The method of selection in such a case is to allot some specified quota to be selected from each subgroup and, then, within each subgroup, select in rank order from the top down on the basis of test scores until the quota is filled.

How well different subgroups will fare under this method of selection will depend, of course, on the proportional quota allotted to each subgroup and the mean of each subgroup's distribution of scores on the predictor variable. How the quota for each subgroup is determined is of crucial importance, but it is a policy decision and not a statistical matter. For any given quota, however, the statistical consequences can be calculated, such as the overall mean of selectees on the criterion and the most probable criterion means of each subgroup of selectees, the amount of overlap of subgroups in criterial performance, and their probable failure rates, assuming that after selection uniform standards of performance are applied to all selectees. All these consequences and their broader social effects must, of course, be carefully weighed in any rational application of quota selection.

Each of the quota models discussed here can be neatly summarized in terms of Figure 9.4, which shows the bivariate frequency distribution (i.e., scatter diagram) between test (X) and criterion (Y) cut into four regions, A, B, C, and D, by the accept-reject cutting score X^* on the test and the corresponding success–failure point Y^* on the criterion. The location of the point Y^* (and, consequently, of the cutting score X^*) is set by the selecting institution, and the four regions of the bivariate distribution formed by their intersection have *areas* corresponding to the *proportions* of the sample of applicants. (The regression line of Y on X, which is not shown in Figure 9.4, of course, goes through the point of intersection of X^* and Y^*.) The efficiency of the selection strategy for any group can be expressed in terms of the ratio $[(A + C) - (B + D)]/(A + C)$, where the four regions represent proportions totaling unity.

The Proportional Representation Model, then, can be described as a form of selection that sets the test's cutoff score X^* (and hence the corresponding Y^*) differentially for the major and minor groups so as to make the accept/reject ratio $(A + D)/(B + C)$ exactly the same for both groups.

The *Constant Ratio Model,* proposed by Robert L. Thorndike (1971a), holds that in a fair selection procedure "the qualifying scores on a test should be set at levels that will

Figure 9.4. Bivariate frequency distribution (ellipse) with test cutting score set at X^*, showing the four types of outcomes in a selection procedure.

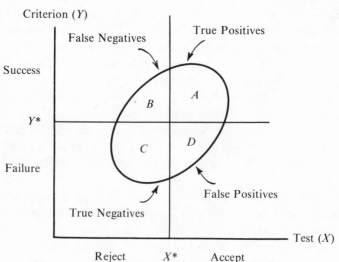

Figure 9.5. Illustration of the selection problem that inspired Thorndike's Constant Ratio Model. (From Linn, 1973, p. 147)

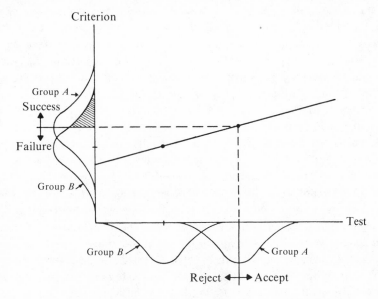

qualify applicants in the two groups in proportion to the fraction of the two groups reaching a specified level of criterion performance'' (Thorndike, 1971a, p. 63).

Thorndike was led to this definition of fairness by considering the selection situation depicted in Figure 9.5. Notice that groups A and B differ much more on the test than on the criterion and that the common cutting score on the test would reject virtually all applicants from group B, even though some proportion of group B applicants, if selected, would succeed on the criterion (i.e., the shaded area in Figure 9.5). What Thorndike proposes is that the cut score should be set differentially for the two groups so that the ratio of *accept* to *success* is constant for both groups. In terms of Figure 9.4, the ratio $(A + D)/(A + B)$ should be the same for the major and minor groups. For example, if 50 percent of group A and 20 percent of group B succeed on the criterion, then the test's cut scores should be set so as to select the top 50 percent of group A applicants and the top 20 percent of group B applicants.

Notice that Thorndike's proposal seems to become more cogent when the test's validity is low, because with low predictive validity the cutoff score has to be placed very high and many persons are rejected who, if accepted, would have succeeded, and this effect is exaggerated in the lower-scoring group (e.g., group B in Figure 9.5).

But it should also be noted that for any test with less than perfect validity, the N applicants accepted by this procedure are not all the very same persons as the N persons who would have succeeded had everyone been given the chance. With imperfect validity, the test is fallible, and so a predictable percentage of the N top-scoring persons accepted from either group will fail on the criterion. This percentage will inevitably be greater for group B. Also, for those who succeed, the mean level of criterial performance for group B will fall further below the level of group A than would be the case if a common cutting score were used for both groups.

Thorndike's Constant Ratio Model qualifies as a quota system, because it sets different cutoff scores for applicants from different groups and sacrifices maximizing the criterial performance of the selectees for the sake of the fairness implied by this model. Notice that, like all quota systems, it focuses the concept of fairness on *groups* rather than on *individuals.* An individualist selection system that accepts, say, only 10 percent of the minor group when, say, 20 percent of the minor group could succeed on the criterion is deemed as unfair to the *group* per se, despite the fact that all members of both groups have been selected without regard to their group membership.

The fairness of the Constant Ratio Model runs into a disturbing logical contradiction if we simply apply it to the converse categories of *reject* and *failure*. Petersen and Novick (1976) have labeled this the ***Converse Constant Ratio Model.*** (In terms of Figure 9.4, the ratio $(B + C)/(C + D)$ must be constant across groups.) If the *accept/success* ratio is made constant for both groups, the converse *reject/failure* ratio, given the same test cut scores, will not necessarily be constant. (It will be constant only in the rare case where the ratio *accept/success = reject/failure = 1*, or in the case where the major and minor groups are equal on the criterion.) In other words, according to the Constant Ratio Model of fair selection, if one wishes to be *fair* to the minor group in terms of the proportion who are *accepted,* then, by applying the very same logic one must simultaneously be *unfair* to the minor group in terms of the proportion who are *rejected.* Thus the model is *internally inconsistent.* If the Constant Ratio Model is considered fair, then the Converse Constant Ratio Model, by the very same logic, must be considered unfair, and vice versa.

The ***Conditional Probability Model*** was proposed by Cole (1973), as follows: "[F]or both minority and majority groups whose members can achieve a satisfactory criterion score $[Y > Y^*]$ there should be the same probability of selection regardless of group membership" (p. 240). Referring to Figure 9.4, the cutoff scores are set differentially for the major and minor groups so as to yield the same ratio $A/(A + B)$ for both groups.

The Conditional Probability Model results in a slightly different cutoff score for the minor group than the Constant Ratio Model. Given the same cutoff score in the major group for both models, the Conditional Probability Model requires an even lower cutoff score for the minor group than does the Constant Ratio Model, with the consequence that in the Conditional Probability Model the minor group will have a somewhat lower average level of criterial performance, as compared with the major group, than would result from the Constant Model, which, in turn, results in a greater average criterion difference between major and minor groups than would result from the Equal Risk Regression Model.

Cole (1973, p. 253) urges the general adoption of the Conditional Probability Model for educational and employment selection, with the following rationale;

> In the regression model and equal risk model, the concern is solely with the importance of the criterion at the expense of ideas of fairness to the applicant. Both models provide high expected success rates among the selectees and are therefore advantageous to the selecting institution, and they also minimize the ill effects of selection followed by failure. However, the potentially successful applicant's concern is often primarily that there be a fair chance of selection regardless of the group membership rather than a guarantee of success. In cases in which the regression line

for the group is such that, even though many of that group could succeed, they will have less chance of selection than members of other groups, no selecting institution's concern with selection of applicants with higher predicted criterion scores will receive much sympathy from those applicants. And when poor prediction in one group is the only cause of chances of selection being lowered, the applicant will rightly blame the institution for its failure to find a good predictor—a situation for which the applicant should not be penalized.

In a trenchant critique of various selection models, Hunter and Schmidt (1976, p. 1064) have this to say about Cole's arguments for the Conditional Probability Model:

Although Cole's argument sounds reasonable and has a great deal of intuitive appeal, it is flawed by a hidden assumption. Her definition assumes that differences between groups in probability of acceptance given later success if selected are due to discrimination based on group membership. Suppose that the two regression lines of criterion performance as a function of the test are equal [i.e., the test is unbiased]. If a black who would have been successful is rejected while a white who fails is accepted, this need not imply discrimination. The black is not rejected because he is black, but because he made a low score on the ability test. That is, the black was rejected because his ability at the time of the predictor test was indistinguishable from that of a group of other people (of both races) who, on the average, would have low scores on the criterion.

Whereas the Conditional Probability Model advocates selecting equal proportions of potentially successful applicants from each subgroup, the other side of the same coin, called the *Converse Conditional Probability Model* by Petersen and Novick (1976), argues from the same logic that the potential failures on the criterion should be rejected in equal proportions in each subgroup. (In terms of Figure 9.4, the ratio $C/(C + D)$ should be the same for the major and minor groups.) But achieving this "fairness" to the potential failures is incompatible with being "fair" to the potentially successful. It is then a subjective decision as to whether "fairness" should focus on decreasing minority applicants' risk of failure or on increasing their chance of acceptance and success. One cannot have both selection strategies simultaneously. Thus, like the Constant Ratio Model, the Conditional Probability Model is shown by its converse to be logically inconsistent. If (in Figure 9.4) the ratio $A/(A + B)$ is constant across groups, then, with the same test cutoff scores, the converse ratio $C/(C + D)$ cannot also be constant across groups (except in the unlikely case where the major and minor groups do not differ on either the criterion or the test).

The *Equal Probability Model,* which was first described by Linn (1973, p. 153) and later named by Petersen and Novick (1976, p. 13), is based on the argument that all applicants who are selected should have the same chance of being successful regardless of their group membership. Therefore, the test cutoff scores for the major and minor groups are set so that the proportion of selectees who will succeed on the criterion will be constant across groups. In terms of Figure 9.4, the ratio $A/(A + D)$ is the same for the major and minor groups.

The Equal Probability Model, however, runs into trouble, because it cannot be applied when the major and minor groups differ too widely on the test and there is a high cutoff on the criterion. Then there will be no possible test cutoff point that will equalize the $A/(A + D)$ ratio in the major and minor groups, unless one selects applicants *below* a given cutoff from the major group and *above* a given cutoff from the minor group. In short, under some conditions one can achieve equal probabilities of success, given selection, only by selecting the top scores from one group and the bottom scores from another group. (This situation is shown in Figure 9.6, panel 5.) Taken literally, the rather bizarre result is that the Equal Probability Model would demand in some circumstances that the best qualified applicants of the major group (assuming that it is the higher-scoring group) would be rejected in favor of the lowest-scoring members of the major group to equate their probability of success, once selected, with the highest-scoring applicants selected from the minor group. Many would call it a travesty of fair selection.

Also, the Equal Probability Model is inconsistent with the **Converse Equal Probability Model,** which holds that applicants who are rejected by the test cutoff should have equal probabilities of *failure* on the criterion regardless of their group membership. In terms of Figure 9.4, the major and minor groups should have the same ratio of $C/(B + C)$. But, if that ratio is made the same in both groups, the Equal Probability Model's ratio of $A/(A + D)$ will not result in the same test cutoff score in both groups, except in the unusual case where the groups do not differ on the test *and* do not differ on the criterion. Thus the model is internally inconsistent and results in different selection strategies depending on whether one is more concerned with fairness to *selectees* or with fairness to *rejectees*. By its own definition of fairness, if the Equal Probability Model is fair to minority selectees, it cannot at the same time be fair to minority rejectees.

Figure 9.6 graphically compares the foregoing quota models with each other and with the Equal Risk Regression Model for the case of an *unbiased* test. To make clear the differences between the models, the means of the major and minor groups A and B are set quite far apart and the minimum acceptable cutoff point on the criterion Y^* is set quite high. The test cutoff score X^* is set uniformly for group A so that 50 percent of applicants are selected and 50 percent of the selectees will succeed on the criterion. (The correlation r_{XY} between test and criterion is 0.43 in this example.) Under these rather extreme conditions, the Equal Risk Regression Model does not select any applicant from group B. (The shaded areas in Figure 9.6 represent the proportions of applicants from each group selected by the various models.) The Equal Probability Model (Figure 9.6, panel 5) in this case results in selection of group A applicants scoring at or *below* X^* while selecting applicants from group B scoring at or *above* X^*. Notice that the Equal Probability Model cannot possibly be satisfied in the present case if group A's test cutoff score is at the same point X_A^* as in all the other models.

There are analytical methods for determining precisely the minor group's test cutoff score X_B^* so as to satisfy any one of the quota models. (Some of these methods have been explicated by Cole (1973).) These analytic methods for locating X_B^* are not given here, as all of the quota models, as indicated, are logically deficient in one or more respects, and none is recommended for actual use. The only quota model that can be recommended is the Expected Utility Model, to be explicated later in this section.

The **Probability Weighted Model,** first proposed by Carl Bereiter (1975), is unique in that it is the only selection model that gives every applicant some chance of being selected regardless of his test score. But the *chances* of being selected are not the same for everyone; they are determined by each person's probability of success if selected, as predicted from the person's test score. The procedure is illustrated in Figure 9.7.

Figure 9.6. Graphic representation of various selection models (with an unbiased test), given the same criterion success–failure cutoff Y^* and test accept–reject cut score X^* for the major group (A) in all models (except model 5, see text for explanation). Panels 1 to 5 represent (1) Equal Risk Regression Model, (2) Proportional Representation Model, (3) Constant Ratio Model, (4) Conditional Probability Model, and (5) Equal Probability Model.

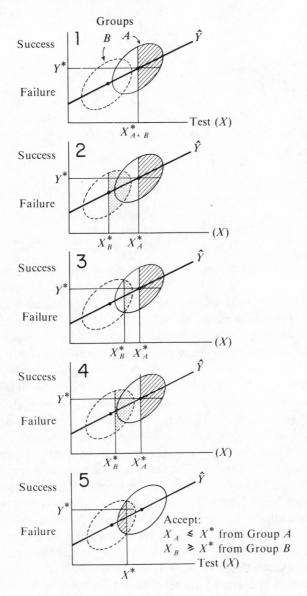

A *success–failure* cutoff point Y^* on the criterion scale below which performance is regarded as unacceptable is determined by the selecting institution. The location of Y^* depends on the minimal level of performance that the institution is willing to tolerate, for example, the minimum grade-point average required to remain in college. The corresponding test score that best predicts Y^* is X^*, as determined from the regression line $\hat{Y}$.

Figure 9.7. Illustration of Bereiter's Probability Weighted Model. X_A and X_B represent the test scores of two individuals, *A* and *B*, with predicted criterion measures $\hat{Y}_A$ and $\hat{Y}_B$.

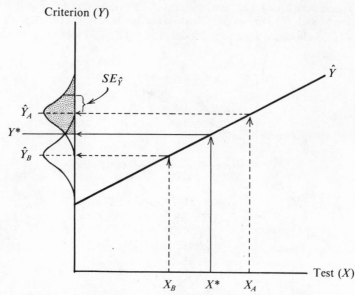

In the usual selection procedure, no applicants with test scores below X^* would be considered for selection. In the Probability Weighted Model, however, *all* applicants, whatever their test scores, have a chance of selection, their chances being the *probability* that their level of criterial performance will exceed the cutoff value Y^*. Figure 9.7 shows the situation for two persons, *A* and *B*, with test scores X_A and X_B and predicted criterion values $\hat{Y}_A$ and $\hat{Y}_B$. The errors of prediction (or errors of estimate) are normally distributed about the predicted values. The key question is "What proportion of the area under the curve of the errors of prediction for each person exceeds the cutoff value Y^*?" This can be determined precisely, given the person's predicted value $\hat{Y}$, the cutoff value Y^*, and the standard error of estimate $SE_{\hat{Y}}$. We simply obtain $Z = (Y^* - \hat{Y})/SE_{\hat{Y}}$, and from the tables of the normal curve we find the proportion of the area under the curve that falls above Z. In Figure 9.7, for example, 93 percent of the area under the curve of person *A* falls above the cutoff Y^*, and only 7 percent of the area under the curve of person *B* falls above the cutoff. Hence person *A*'s name is placed in the lottery 93 times and person *B*'s name is placed in the lottery only 7 times. The same procedure is followed for every applicant, and then the names are drawn strictly at random until the required number of applicants have been selected. In this way, every applicant has a chance of being selected, but the chances are related to the predicted probability of success on the criterion. By the standard selection procedure, on the other hand, person *B*'s chance of being selected would be absolutely zero, as his predicted $\hat{Y}_B$ is below the cutoff. But with the Probability Weighted Model even the person with the very lowest test score (X) has *some* chance of being selected, albeit a very small chance if the cutoff is set very high.

As it stands, this model is especially disadvantageous to the relatively few persons obtaining the highest scores on the test, as they are only a small proportion of the entire pool of applicants and are outproportioned by applicants with more mediocre test scores.

Although no *single* mediocre individual has a better chance of being selected than does any *single* high scorer, in the aggregate the mediocre scorers, because there are so many more of them in a roughly normal distribution of test scores, have a greater chance of selection than the few highest scorers. This disadvantage can be meliorated as follows: the probability p that an individual's criterial performance will exceed the cutoff value Y^* is weighted (i.e., multiplied) by the reciprocal of the ordinate y of the normal curve at z, where z is the individual's standardized test score. Thus an individual is represented in the random lottery with a relative frequency of p/y. With this method, if the score distribution is roughly normal, the chances of extreme scorers (whether high *or* low) being selected in accord with their probability of exceeding the criterial cutoff value will not be overwhelmed by the aggregate chances of the much larger number of persons near the middle of the distribution of test scores.

This Probability Weighted Model is disadvantageous to the selecting institution, as compared with the Equal Risk Regression Model with a point cutoff, if the same cutoff value is adopted in both models. The mean performance level in that case will be lower (and the failure rate slightly higher) for selectees by the Probability Weighted Model than for selectees by the standard cutoff model, because the Probability Weighted Model accepts some small percentage of persons with less than, say a 50 percent chance of success, whereas the least promising selectees by the standard cutoff model have *at least* a 50 percent chance of success. The Probability Weighted Model can compensate for this disadvantage, however, simply by setting a higher cutoff on the criterion, such that the average level of performance and the failure rate of those who are selected will be equal to that of selectees chosen by the Equal Risk Regression Model (with a lower cutoff Y^*).

An advocate of the Probability Weighted Model would argue that it is more fair for individuals, as well as for subgroups with differing means, than the point cutoff models, given an unbiased test, because it recognizes the probabilistic nature of prediction. Anyone with a nonzero probability of success (as must always be the case for any test with less than perfect validity) has a nonzero chance of being selected. Unlike the cutoff models, it does not dichotomize the probability of selection as 0 or 1, but treats selection more realistically as a *continuous* variable, namely, the person's probability of success, which ranges continuously between 0 and 1 and is monotonically related to scores on the selection test.

Because the Probability Weighted Model, when used with an unbiased test, takes no account of subgroup membership, it might seem to give the appearance of being compatible with the philosophy of individualism rather than being a quota system. But this is wholly illusory. Although the Probability Weighted Model is a more disguised form of quota system than any other quota model, it is nevertheless in effect a quota model. Interestingly, it achieves the same purpose as the Constant Ratio Model, but with somewhat less efficiency. That is, it selects from each subgroup a proportion of the subgroup that equals the proportion that would exceed the criterion cutoff. But the persons selected are not necessarily the same as those selected by the Constant Ratio Model, which selects persons from within subgroups (i.e., from the top down) so as to *maximize* the criterion performance of the selectees within each subgroup. The random selection aspect of the Probability Weighted Model, on the other hand, *prevents* it from maximizing criterion performance within subgroups. A possibly undesirable consequence of this, which must be taken into account, is that selectees from various subgroups that differ on the test will differ more in criterion performance than would be the case with the Constant Ratio Model.

In general, the introduction of any *randomness* into the selection procedure has the same effect as lowering the reliability of the test (or other predictors). That is, its effect is to select less qualified persons in place of the better qualified in terms of the best prediction of their criterion performance. Therefore, the Probability Weighted Model turns out to be a statistically rather disguised form of quota that inevitably favors lower-scoring individuals and consequently also lower-scoring subgroups.

The ***Culture-modified Criterion Model*** was proposed by Darlington (1971), with the aim of making explicit the exact amount of trade-off between selection quotas and the level of criterion performance of the major and minor groups that the selecting institution wishes to sanction. Darlington proposed that an adjustment be made in the criterion scores that will reflect the amount of criterion performance that one wishes to trade for group membership or cultural differences. In other words, the criterion to be predicted by the test is not *just* the criterion performance per se but some weighted composite of criterion performance *and* group membership. Hence, instead of predicting criterion Y from test score X, as in the usual regression model, we use the test score X to predict $Y - kG$, where k is the "trade-off" value and G is group membership, which is quantitized (e.g., 0 or 1 for male/female or white/black, or is some continuous value between 0 and 1 for, say, socioeconomic status).

The value of k is based on a subjective judgment or a consensus of concerned persons. In deciding on the value of k in terms of the criterion scale Y, one asks "How many units of Y are of equivalent value to a unit of G?" Or, put another way, "How much decrement in Y are we willing to tolerate to accept a less-qualified applicant from group B in preference to a better-qualified applicant from group A?" In other words, we explicitly make group membership a part of the qualification for selection, and we can be precise as to how much a person's group membership contributes to his or her qualification.

For example, if the selecting institution wishes to increase the percentage of selectees among applicants from group B as compared with group A, it decides how many units k of criterion performance Y should be equivalent to the value of selecting applicants from group B in preference to applicants from group A. Then, if groups B and A are quantitized as $G_B = 1$ and $G_A = 0$, respectively, a test would be devised such that the scores on it will predict the criterion values $Y - kG_B$ and $Y - kG_A$ for applicants of groups B and A, respectively. Such a test would have to be *biased* by our definition, since the regression lines would have equal slopes but their intercepts would differ by the amount k.

It can be seen that with an unbiased test this procedure simply amounts to equalizing the predicted criterion values for the two groups by subtracting some value k from the predicted criterion performance of group A. The score on an unbiased test that will best predict the criterion value $Y - kG_B$ (which is equal to Y) for group B is simply X_B, that is, the unadjusted score on an unbiased test. But the test score on an unbiased test that will best predict the criterion value $Y - kG_A$ for group A is $X_A - (k\sigma_X/r_{XY}\sigma_Y)$. In other words, for an unbiased test the scores of the two groups are differentially adjusted by subtracting the value in parentheses from the test scores of every applicant from group A; and then, using these adjusted scores, we select from the top down in the combined pool of applicants from the two groups. If there is to be a cutoff score on the test, it is determined in the same way. Group B's test cutoff will be lower than group A's by an amount equal to $k\sigma_X/r_{XY}\sigma_Y$. Any desired quota can be achieved by manipulating the value of k.

The value of k is determined by the selecting institution's considerations involving the supply and qualifications of its pool of applicants, its view of its social responsibility, its policy regarding quotas, and many other factors. The only advantage of this rather complicated quota strategy is that it explicitly forces examination of the trade-off between the quota and the criterion performance. It can generate statements such as "The selecting institution holds that a member of group $B,$ if selected, is worth k more units on the scale of criterion performance than a member of group A whose actual criterial performance is equivalent." The trade-off then is made entirely explicit so that it can be openly debated by all concerned.

If one chooses to adopt a quota system, what is really desired is a strategy that simultaneously takes into account all four of the possible outcomes of any selection strategy, as shown in the four cells of Table 9.4, and assigns explicit relative values to each of these outcomes. Then, given a minimum level of satisfactory performance on the criterion (designated by the criterion cutoff Y^*) and a selection ratio (i.e., the proportion of all applicants who can be selected), it is possible to determine precisely the cutoff score X^* on the test (or other predictors) for any two (or more) subpopulations that will maximize the overall desirability or *utility* of the selection outcomes in terms of the relative values assigned to the cells of the fourfold table. This strategy is referred to as the **Expected Utility Model.** By "utility" is meant the relative desirability (a subjective judgment) of various outcomes of the decision process. The aim is to make selection decisions in such a way as to *maximize* the overall *utility* of the selection process.

The statistical logic and methodology for maximizing the utility of selection decisions have been presented by John von Neumann and Oskar Morgenstern in their *Theory of Games and Economic Behavior* (1944) and by Abraham Wald in *Statistical Decision Functions* (1950). The applicability of this statistical decision model to quota selection has been advocated and explicated by Gross and Su (1975), Petersen (1975), and Petersen and Novick (1976). In recommending this selection strategy in preference to all others, Petersen and Novick (1976, p. 25) state:

> Most statisticians interested in decision problems accept the correctness of the von Neumann and Morgenstern–Wald Model and the incorrectness of any statistical decision procedure that does not conform to that model. It seems clear that the Constant Ratio Model, the Conditional Probability Model and the Equal Probability Model [and their converses] do not conform to that model, though the ideas that are at their bases may well be reformulated in a coherent manner.

The Equal Risk Regression Model does conform to the von Neumann–Morgenstern–Wald formulation; it is merely a special case of the Expected Utility Model in which group membership per se does not have differential utility.

Let us see how the Expected Utility Model would be applied to the selection of majority and minority applicants, using an *unbiased* test. The basic conceptual units of this model, applied to each person, are the *conditional probability* of an outcome (success or failure) on the criterion, given a particular test score, and the *utility* (i.e., desirability) of that outcome. The selection decision for any applicant is based on the sum of the *products* of the conditional probabilities of each outcome and their utilities. This sum of products is the *expected utility* of the individual decision. When these values are summed over all applicants, we have the overall *expected utility of the selection process*. The model ensures that this overall value will be maximized and, therefore, that it is the optimum selection strategy.

Assigning utilities is a wholly subjective matter. But at least the Expected Utility Model forces an explicit evaluation of the utilities assigned to every possible outcome of the selection process for every single person involved.

The Expected Utility Model, like all selection strategies, must begin with two constraints: (1) the minimum level of criterion performance (success–failure threshold) Y^* that can be tolerated by the selecting institution and (2) the selection ratio, that is, the proportion of all applicants who can be selected, assuming some limited number of openings. Within these given constraints, then, we select each applicant by setting the test cutoff score X^* so as to maximize the overall expected utility in accord with the relative values that we have subjectively assigned to all of the possible outcomes of our selection procedure, which are shown in Figure 9.8. (Only two subpopulations are considered here, although the model is generalizable to any number of subpopulations.)

We see in Figure 9.8 that there are eight possible outcomes $(O_1, O_2, \ldots, O_8)$ of the selection process: outcomes O_1 to O_4 for major group applicants and the corresponding outcomes O_5 to O_8 for minor group applicants. The various possible outcomes can be described as follows:

O_1 and O_5: Applicant is accepted and is successful. (true positive)
O_3 and O_7: Applicant is rejected and would have failed if accepted. (true negative)
O_2 and O_6: Applicant is rejected and would have succeeded if selected. (false negative)
O_4 and O_8: Applicant is accepted and fails. (false positive)

The next step is to assign a *utility* value U to each of these eight outcomes. Obviously, correct selection decisions (true positives and true negatives) have greater

Figure 9.8. Hypothetical utilities assigned to the various outcomes of a selection procedure in the major and minor groups.

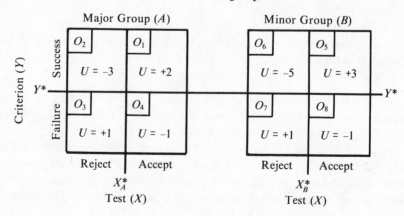

utility for all concerned than incorrect decisions (false positives and false negatives), and so we generally assign *higher* utility values to the outcomes O_1 and O_3 (and O_5 and O_7) than to O_2 and O_4 (and O_6 and O_8). The false positive and false negative outcomes, O_2 and O_4 (and O_6 and O_8), can be viewed as disutilities; these are generally assigned *negative* values. (Thus the saddle point between *utility* and *disutility* is conveniently set at zero.)

Figure 9.8 shows some hypothetical utilities assigned to the various outcomes. In this hypothetical case, for example, greater utility is placed on true positives than on true negatives, that is, $U(O_1) > U(O_3)$ and $U(O_5) > U(O_7)$. The least desired outcome in this example is false negatives, since $U(O_2) = -3$ and $U(O_6) = -5$. Also, notice that, in this example, *different* utilities are assigned to the major and minor groups. False negatives are here considered more undesirable (and are therefore more to be avoided) for minority than for majority applicants, that is, $U(O_6) = -5$ and $U(O_2) = -3$. Also, true positives are seen as more desirable for minority than for majority applicants, that is, $U(O_5) = +3$ and $U(O_1) = +2$. On the other hand, in this example, group membership does not distinguish between the utilities assigned to true and false negatives.

Finally, it should be made clear that any other utility values that one chooses can be assigned to each of the outcomes. Probably not everyone will agree with any given set of values. The assigned utilities are open to discussion and debate by all concerned, and the numerical values assigned to the utilities will depend on various considerations involving the immediate and long-range economic, social, and ethical values of all the parties affected by the particular selection process. When the *same* utility values are assigned to the major and minor groups, as would be dictated by the philosophy of individualism (both unqualified and qualified), the Expected Utility Model results in the very same selection decisions as the Equal Risk Regression Model for any given selection ratio and values of Y^* and X^*. Thus, when group membership per se has no utility as far as the selection process is concerned, one and the same cutoff score X^* is applied to all applicants regardless of their group membership. In a quota system, on the other hand, it is decided that different utilities should be assigned to different groups, and this then means that *different* test cutoff scores must be applied to applicants from different groups. The next problem then is to set the test cutoff scores X_A^* and X_B^* for the major and minor groups so as to *maximize* the expected utility of the whole selection process in accord with our assigned utilities.

Recall that the expected utility $E(U)$ is the product of the utilities for each outcome and the probability P of each outcome summed over all applicants. P is simply the probability that an applicant with a given test score X will fall into each of the eight possible outcomes shown in Figure 9.8. Our problem finally is to determine the test cutoff scores X_A^* and X_B^* that will maximize the sum of $P \times U = E(U)$ over all applicants. The mathematical solution[3] to this problem involves solving two simultaneous equations containing two unknowns, X_A^* and X_B^*, in addition to the following known quantities: the overall selection ratio, the proportions of majority and minority applicants, and the validity coefficient r_{XY} of the test for each group. (For an unbiased test, r_{XY} is the same in each group.) The method of solution and its mathematical rationale have been given detailed explanation and further references by Gross and Su (1975). These authors are also able to infer the exact utilities that are implicit in several of the various quota models previously described. They correctly point out that the assignment of utilities is always made, explicitly or implicitly, knowingly or unknowingly, in every selection model. By using the Expected Utility Model, the assigned utilities can be openly identified and studied.

Selection Models with a Biased Test

Even when a selection test is biased according to our definition of test bias, it is possible to use the test in ways that meet certain concepts of fair selection. Some selection models may be described as *relaxed,* in that they impose somewhat less stringent criteria of fairness. This means that one or another of the essential criteria of an unbiased test is relinquished. First, we shall consider the two selection models of this type that are compatible with the philosophy of unqualified individualism, the Regression Model and the Equal Risk Model. For an *unbiased* test they are, in effect, indistinguishable and are the same as the Equal Risk Regression Model described earlier.

Regression Model.   Originally put forth by Cleary (1968), this model relaxes the requirement of equal (i.e., nonsignificantly different) standard errors of estimate $SE_{\hat{Y}}$ of the predicted criterion $\hat{Y}$ in the major and minor groups. The test, however, must still have the same regression slope and intercept in both groups. The same test cutoff is used for the selection of applicants from both groups, and group membership is not taken into account in the selection process. Applicants are selected on the basis of their predicted performance on the criterion, and, for any given test score, this prediction is the same regardless of group membership. What *can* vary with group membership, however, is the *risk of failure* (or, conversely, the *probability of success*) if selected. If the predicted values of $\hat{Y}$ have different standard errors of estimate $SE_{\hat{Y}}$ in the major and minor groups, it means that, even though the best prediction of criterion performance may be the same for a majority and minority applicant, the prediction for one of them involves a greater risk of error than for the other. However, in this case where $\hat{Y}$ is the same for both applicants, the Regression Model shows no preference for one or the other. The outcome of this selection model will be that there will be more erroneous predictions (false positives), that is, more failures among the selectees, of whichever group has the larger standard error of estimate.

It could be argued that this model is *unfair* to members of whichever group has the smaller $SE_{\hat{Y}}$, because the prediction of criterion performance for these applicants involves smaller risk of error. In other words, for any given predicted value $\hat{Y}$, they are a safer bet.

The size of $SE_{\hat{Y}}$ is a function of the group's standard deviation σ_Y on the criterion and the correlation r_{XY} between test and criterion, that is, $SE_{\hat{Y}} = \sigma_Y \sqrt{1 - r_{XY}^2}$. Since the Regression Model requires equality of regression slopes b_{YX} in the two (or more) subpopulations, and since $b_{YX} = r_{XY}(\sigma_Y/\sigma_X)$, it can be seen that, for a constant σ_X, whichever group has the smaller r_{XY} must also have the larger σ_Y, and assuming σ_X is the same in both groups, when the test is biased with respect to $SE_{\hat{Y}}$, the Regression Model tends to *favor* the group with the *lower* test validity r_{XY}, since the selection of applicants from the group with lower test validity (and consequently larger $SE_{\hat{Y}}$) entails greater risk of error, that is, an increased risk for selectees from one group that would not be taken with an *unbiased* test. From the standpoint of the selecting institution, the Regression Model is satisfactory if there is no utility to minimizing the risk of errors in selection, but that would be a most unusual situation and practically intolerable in cases where criterion performance above some minimal level is crucial.

Equal Risk Model. This selection model, proposed by Einhorn and Bass (1971), puts the emphasis on the applicant's risk of failure if selected and selects applicants in terms of the same degree of risk regardless of their group membership. The model can be applied to unbiased tests (in which case it is identical to the Equal Risk Regression Model) or to biased tests for which there are significant group differences in the regression slope, the intercept, or the standard error of estimate. In fact, even different predictor tests may be used for the major and minor groups if that will improve the validity of the predictors.

Applicants are selected in order in terms of their risk of falling below the minimum acceptable performance on the criterion Y^*, which is set by the selecting institution. The more desirable applicants are those who have the smallest risk, and so are selected first. Also, a *maximum* degree of risk of selection errors that the selecting institution is willing to take is set by the institution and is constant for all groups. All applicants with a risk greater than the set maximum are rejected.

One first decides the maximum probability P of a selection error (i.e., a false positive) that one is prepared to tolerate. Regarding P as a percentile of the normal curve, one then determines its corresponding z_P value from a table of the normal curve, where z is the unit normal deviate, with mean $= 0$, $\sigma = 1$. If, for example, we will tolerate *at most* a 25 percent probability of a selection error (i.e., the applicant if selected has one chance in four of failing on the criterion), then the corresponding value of $z_{.25}$, from the table of the normal curve, is $-.6745$. Then for each applicant, we make a prediction $\hat{Y}$ of the criterion performance, based on the applicant's test score and the regression equation for that applicant's group. We can determine the applicant's risk of failure, if selected, from the following formula:

$$z = (Y^* - \hat{Y})/SE_{\hat{Y}}, \tag{9.8}$$

where

$z =$ the deviate of the normal curve,
$Y^* =$ the criterion success–failure threshold,
$\hat{Y} =$ the applicant's predicted level of criterion performance, and
$SE_{\hat{Y}} =$ the standard error of estimate of $\hat{Y}$ in the applicant's group.

The percentile corresponding to z in the table of the normal curve is the applicant's probability of failure, if selected. If that probability is greater than the tolerated degree of risk, the applicant is rejected. Thus, in our 25 percent risk example, we would reject all applicants for whom the value of z (obtained from equation 9.8) is greater than $z_{.25} = -.6745$. And we would select the remaining applicants in order, with preference for the z values that fall farthest below $-.6745$, since they imply the least risk of failure.

Note that the Equal Risk Model makes the best prediction of performance for every person, given all the available information, including group membership. But beyond that point every applicant is selected or rejected solely on the basis of his or her risk of failure if selected. This does not imply, of course, that the *average risk* overall will be the same for each group. Nor is any quota implied.

The *fairness* of the Equal Risk Model becomes open to argument especially when the following situation arises, as it must in some cases when the test is biased. An applicant from group A has a higher test score X_A and therefore a higher predicted criterion score $\hat{Y}_A$ than that of an applicant from group B, that is, $\hat{Y}_A > \hat{Y}_B$; but the standard error of estimate is smaller in group B than in group A, so that the group B applicant has a smaller risk of failure. Because the Equal Risk Model dictates that we should prefer the applicant with the smaller risk of failure, we select the applicant from group B. This situation is illustrated in Figure 9.9, in which the shaded area under the normal curve falling below the criterion cutoff Y^* indicates the degree of risk (i.e., probability P) of failure for applicants A and B. The standard error of estimate $SE_{\hat{Y}}$ in group A is 2.2 times larger than in group B. The group A applicant can complain that he or she should be preferred because of his or her higher predicted performance (albeit with a greater risk that the prediction is wrong). Why should the applicant be penalized for being a member of a group that has a larger $SE_{\hat{Y}}$ than some other group? The size of $SE_{\hat{Y}}$, after all, is in part a function of a psychometric property of the test (viz., its validity), and the applicant is in no way responsible for that.

There are two answers to this complaint. The first answer holds for all tests and selection strategies: none is perfect and each depends on the statistical properties of the test, the criterion, and the subpopulations involved. Every selection strategy short of perfection will result in some proportion of false positives and false negatives, and the most that any strategy can claim is that it has made the *best* decision possible with the available information. The Equal Risk Model is no different from any other in this respect. But what about this model's seeming ambiguity with respect to choosing between the probability of failure and the level of predicted performance?

Einhorn and Bass (1971) correctly point out that this is really a question of *utilities,* and it can only be answered in terms of considerations outside the model itself. For

Figure 9.9.   Illustration of the Equal Risk Model when persons A and B are from groups having different standard errors of estimate $SE_{\hat{Y}}$, resulting in different probabilities (5.2% versus 9.7%) of each person's falling below the success–failure cutoff Y^*.

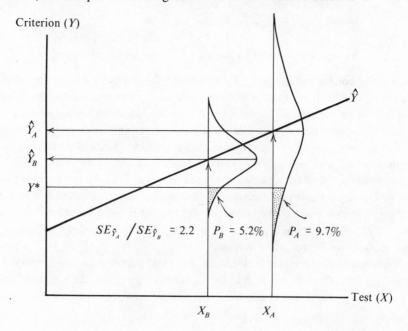

example, the selecting institution might believe that individual differences in criterion performance above a certain threshold Y^* are of no consequence; that is, performance differences above the threshold Y^* have no utility. Instead, all the utility is assigned to the importance of a person's performance level being *above Y^** (no matter how far above). In that case, risk of failure (i.e., being *below Y^**), rather than the predicted performance level $\hat{Y}$, is the appropriate basis for decision.

On the other hand, the selecting institution might believe that differences in the level of performance above Y^* are also of some importance. It may wish to promote personnel to higher positions on the basis of performance in entry level jobs and therefore wishes to have as many high-level performers as possible to choose from, even at the risk of a higher failure rate among the selectees in their entry level jobs. In that case, some *utility* value is assigned to predicted performance level. Hence, there will be two items of information entering into the select–reject decision for every applicant: (1) the applicant's risk of failure P (determined from equation 9.8) and (2) the applicant's predicted performance on the criterion $\hat{Y}$ (determined from the regression equation for the applicant's group). The values of $1/P$ and $\hat{Y}$ are put on a common scale, each is multiplied by its relative utility (as decided on by all parties concerned), and the two products are summed. This weighted sum is an overall index of the applicant's desirability, in terms of his or her predicted performance and risk of failure and the utilities explicitly assigned to each. Applicants then are selected from the top down on the basis of their standing on this index. Thus modified, the Equal Risk Model becomes a sort of hybrid—a utility weighted hybrid—between the pure Equal Risk Model and the Regression Model and is preferable to either one when the test is *biased*. As noted earlier, when the test is *unbiased,* these two selection models are both equivalent to the Equal Risk Regression Model, in which there is never any discrepancy between predicted performance $\hat{Y}$ and the risk of failure P. $\hat{Y}$ and P are perfectly correlated when the test is unbiased.

Multiple Regression Model. When first advocated by Quinn McNemar (1975), this model gave rise to a little flurry of argument (Angoff, 1976; Bass, 1976), which McNemar (1976) effectively quelled in terms of sheer psychometric and statistical logic. True, this model would not be acceptable from the viewpoint of qualified individualism or of quotas. But from the standpoint of unqualified individualism, it is the most appealing and statistically the most sophisticated selection model available when the test is *biased*. If the model is used with an *unbiased* test, the selection decisions will not differ significantly from those of the Equal Risk Regression Model. Both models have the same purpose: to select applicants according to the best possible prediction of their criterion performance and to maximize the average level of performance of the selectees, without regard to group membership. (In these two models, as in all nonquota models, group membership per se has zero utility.)

The main appeal of the Multiple Regression Model is that it provides an *unbiased* selection strategy even though the selection test itself is biased. Whether the Multiple Regression Model is regarded as *fair* or not depends, of course, on one's philosophy. It is fair from the standpoint of unqualified individualism. But aside from philosophies, in the strictly statistical sense, it is an *unbiased* selection strategy, with the one qualified exception that under certain conditions it is not an equal risk strategy, as will be explained later.

Consider the case in which the test bias consists only of there being different intercepts for the major and minor groups, as shown in Figure 9.10. If the minor group's

Figure 9.10. A biased test in which the major and minor groups, *A* and *B,* have regression lines differing only in intercepts. The slopes of the regressions are the same.

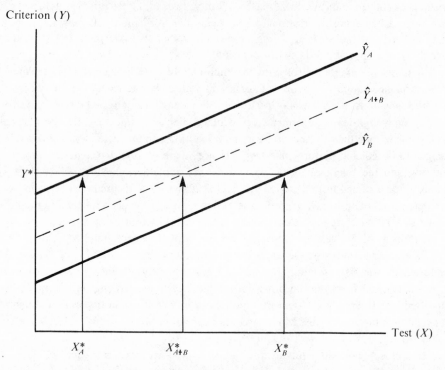

intercept is below the major group's, as shown here, then the use of a common regression line for both groups will result in *over*prediction of the criterion performance of the minor group selectees and *under*prediction of the performance of the major group selectees. We can improve our predictions and eliminate the intercept bias from our selection procedure by using different regression lines (and, consequently, different test cutoff scores) for the major and minor groups. We would select from the top down according to the applicant's predicted criterion performance $\hat{Y}$, with the prediction being based on the regression equation for the applicant's own group.

The very same thing is accomplished by the Multiple Regression Model; it is done by using group membership (quantitized as 2 and 1 for the higher- and lower-scoring groups, respectively), along with test scores, in a multiple regression equation to predict criterion performance. Applicants then are selected from the top down on the basis of their $\hat{Y}$ scores, that is, the best prediction of performance. The essential information needed for the multiple regression equation is the following set of correlations: r_{XY} (in the combined groups), r_{XG} and r_{YG} (where X is the test, Y is the criterion, and G is group membership). Because G is a dichotomous variable, scored 1 or 2, whereas X and Y are continuous variables, the correlations r_{XG} and r_{YG} are technically known as *point-biserial* correlations, the computation of which is explicated in most statistics textbooks. In the case of an *unbiased* test, of course, the multiple correlation $R_{Y \cdot GX}$ will not differ significantly from the simple correlation r_{XY}, as group membership adds nothing to the prediction of the criterion over and above what is measured by the test. If the test fails to measure some source of variance in the criterion that is related to group membership (whatever is the cause of this relationship), it is by definition a *biased* test, and this bias can be remedied (and prediction improved) by including group membership as a variable in the multiple regression equation for predicting the criterion.

In brief, the Multiple Regression Model, instead of selecting on the basis of test scores alone, selects on the basis of a *predictive index* that is a best-weighted linear composite of test score *and* group membership. ("Best-weighted" means that errors of prediction are *minimized*. "Linear," from "linear equation," means *additive*.)

Consider now the case of a test that is biased both with respect to the *intercepts* and the *slopes* of the regression lines of the major and minor groups, as depicted in Figure 9.11. This could result, for example, when the test has different validities in the two groups. Two possible criterion cutoff values, Y_1^* and Y_2^*, are shown here. Notice that when the criterion cutoff is low (Y_1^*), the test cutoff scores for groups A and B are such that $X_{A_1}^* > X_{B_1}^*$, but, for a high criterion cutoff (Y_2^*), the test cutoffs for the groups are reversed, that is, $X_{B_2}^* > X_{A_2}^*$. In such a case, there is said to be an *interaction* between *test scores X* and *group membership G* in relationship to the criterion *Y*. Such an interaction is symbolized as $G \times X$. When there is a $G \times X$ interaction, a higher test score consistently predicts a higher *criterion* value *only if we know to which group the test score belongs.* Hence it is said that the correlation r_{XY} between test and criterion is *moderated* by the variable of group membership. In this case, group membership is called a *moderator*

Figure 9.11. A biased test for which the regression lines of the major and minor groups, *A* and *B*, differ both in intercepts and in slopes.

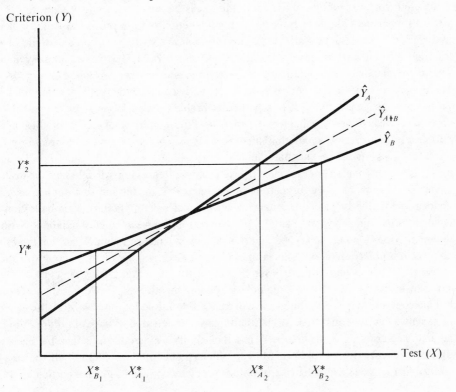

variable. In general terms, a moderator variable is any characteristic in which persons vary that makes their performance on a given criterion consistently more (or less) predictable from their score on a particular test. Test X, for example, may correlate highly with performance Y for men, but may have a significantly lower correlation for women. Sex, in this case, is called a moderator variable.

In the example in Figure 9.11, which depicts a $G \times X$ interaction, the moderator variable is groups (A and B). This *slope* bias is handled in the Multiple Regression Model by including the $G \times X$ interaction term as a predictor variable in the multiple regression equation, along with X and G. The variable $G \times X$ is just what it appears to be: the simple product of the person's test score X and his quantitized (1 or 2) binary group membership G. Adding the interaction term to the multiple regression equation (now containing $X + G + (G \times X)$, with each term multiplied by its appropriate regression weight b) both increases the predictive validity and eliminates the selection bias due to the groups' having unequal slopes and intercepts. Each applicant is selected on the basis of the best possible prediction of his or her performance, given the available information, and errors of prediction are reduced to a minimum. It is regarded as a statistically unbiased selection procedure, since there is no systematic under- or overestimation of either group's mean performance on the criterion.

There is still the possible complaint that applicants with a higher predictive index from the group with the lower predictive validity are penalized to some extent by the fact of lower validity; that is, they may be rejected even though their predictive indices and criterion performance are as high or higher than some members of the higher validity group who are selected. Lower validity (either of a single test or of a multiple composite) of the predictor disfavors the more able individuals on the criterion, as it identifies them with less precision. The only remedy for this condition is to improve the validity of the predictors by finding other variables or inventing new tests that will predict some of the criterion variance that is not predicted by the set of variables that are already in the multiple prediction equation. Other tests and their interactions with groups can be added to the multiple regression equation so as to more nearly equalize the predictive validities for the two groups separately. But this particular problem is, in fact, largely hypothetical, since, as we shall see in Chapter 10, there is little empirical evidence of differential validities in the practical prediction situations for which tests are most commonly used.

Test bias involving unequal standard errors of estimate in the major and minor groups is not automatically eliminated by the Multiple Regression Model. This means that it does not always have the properties of an equal risk model and that applicants with identical predictive index values may not have equal risks of failure. This condition of unequal $SE_{\hat{y}}$ would arise, for example, if the two groups have unequal standard deviations on the criterion. It could be argued that this is a given "fact of nature" and that therefore the selection procedure should not artificially make corrections for it. A more practical answer, however, is that, if there is some *utility* involved in minimizing the risk of failure and in ensuring that all selectees, regardless of group membership, have less than a certain designated uniform risk of failure, one can treat the Multiple Regression Model in exactly the same way as the Equal Risk Model. Utilities are assigned to the risk of failure P and to the predicted criterion performance $\hat{Y}$, and their utility weighted sum is then the basis for selection. The Multiple Regression Model, with its higher predictive validity in the case of a biased test, ensures a smaller risk of failure for every applicant, given a particular value of Y^*, than could be achieved with any other method. The standard error of estimate of the multiple predictive index is $SE_{\hat{y}} = \sigma_Y \sqrt{1 - R^2}$, where R is the multiple correlation.

Thus, one can hardly lose by using the Multiple Regression Model. The predictive index that it yields can easily be used in any of the quota models. When two or more tests are entered into the multiple regression equation, the predictive index would increase the precision of the Expected Utility Model. Recall that the correlation between the multiple predictive index and the criterion is the multiple correlation R, and R must always be equal to or greater than the simple correlation r_{XY}. A biased test, of course, is not inherently a problem to any quota system, since here the concept of fairness is focused on the *quotas* rather than on *unbiased selection* that minimizes errors of prediction and maximizes the criterial performance of those who are selected.

The qualified individualists are bound to be the most troubled by a biased test, because fewer options are allowed to them for making the best of the situation. Qualified individualists cannot enter the variable of group membership into the Multiple Regression Model to eliminate intercept and slope biases. The Multiple Regression Model is still usable, of course, but one must enter other variables instead of group membership (or indirect indicators of group membership) that are correlated with the criterion. The only variables that, when added to the multiple regression equation, will reduce or eliminate intercept and slope biases are variables that are significantly correlated with both group membership and with the criterion. Logically it can be argued that *any* variable that is correlated both with group membership and with the criterion is to that extent an indirect indicator of group membership, and therefore the position of the qualified individualist is essentially untenable. Carried to its logical extreme, it would require that no test (or other variable) could be used that in any way discriminates between groups. But, if the groups differ on the criterion, a predictor that did not discriminate between the groups would necessarily have lower predictive validity than a variable that correlated with both the criterion *and* group membership. Consider a hypothetical example. Say that our criterion performance involves both "brains" and "brawn" but that we use only an IQ test in our selection procedure. Men and women will not differ on the average on the selection test (IQ), but they will differ on the criterion. By using a common regression line (as qualified individualism would dictate), we would underpredict the performance of men and over-predict the performance of women. The qualified individualist would have to be satisfied with this situation. Sex cannot be added as a predictor variable along with IQ in a multiple regression equation, and, if a test of physical strength is added instead, the qualified individualist could be accused of using an indirect indicator of sex, as measures of physical strength would surely discriminate between the sexes.

On the other hand, there would be nothing to stop the unqualified individualist from boosting the predictive validity by adding both the variables of sex and physical strength to the multiple regression equation, along with IQ, thereby increasing the predictive validity, diminishing errors of prediction, and eliminating bias (i.e., the systematic under- and overprediction for males and females) in the selection procedure. If either sex or strength does not make a significant independent contribution to the criterion variance, it is simply dropped from the prediction equation. Except when an unbiased test is available, the *qualified individualist* with a biased test finds himself in the very peculiar position of being forced to advocate a *less valid* and *more biased* selection strategy than the strategy that would be used by the *unqualified individualist*. If lower validity and group bias are regarded as unfair to individuals, as both types of individualists would agree, then it must be concluded that the *qualified individualist* is willing to sacrifice fairness to individuals for the appearance of fairness to groups and that is essentially a *quota* philosophy, albeit unwitting. Hence the qualified individualist, faced with a biased test, must advocate a selection strategy that absolutely contradicts his own philosophy!

The upshot, of course, is that there are really only two selection philosophies—*unqualified individualism* and *quotas*—and we are only fooling ourselves in thinking there is any third alternative. With an *unbiased* test the selection strategy of *qualified individualism* is identical to that of *unqualified individualism,* that is, the Equal Risk Regression Model; and with a *biased* test, *qualified individualism* sanctions an inefficient and biased selection procedure having the statistical properties of a *quota* system, with the added disadvantage that its utilities are inexplicit and inadvertent.

Internal and Construct Validity Criteria of Bias

So far in this chapter we have dealt only with criteria of bias that are based on the test's external validity, that is, some criterion independent of the test itself that presumably the test is intended to predict for some practical purpose. But there is another large group of criteria for detecting test bias that does not depend on external criteria or direct evidence of the test's predictive validity. These criteria of test bias that do not depend on the test's predictive validity per se are referred to as *internal* criteria and *construct* criteria of bias.

The validity of many tests does not or cannot depend on predictive validity. Often there is no single clear-cut external criterion for what the test is intended to measure. This is certainly true of intelligence tests, as intelligence itself is a hypothetical construct that the test attempts to measure. It has no single objectively measurable external referent. This is not to say that an intelligence test cannot also have practical predictive validity, as we surely know it has in predicting, say, scholastic achievement; but an intelligence test *qua* a test of *intelligence* depends on *construct validity,* which is a complex, open-ended affair. The question here is, how do we identify cultural bias in tests that depend on construct validity?

The same question may be asked of tests that depend on *content validity.* Most achievement tests, many Civil Service tests, and the state bar exams are all examples of tests that are justified by their content validity rather than by predictive validity. A test's content validity is determined by a consensus of experts in the particular content field covered by the test. But, once the test's content validity is determined, how are we to determine that the test items involving this content are free of cultural biases for the various populations that may be required to take the test? Such signs of cultural bias must be sought in the internal characteristics of the test itself.

Internal criteria of bias are important even for tests that are mainly dependent on predictive validity, since internal signs of bias make it increasingly likely that the test will show predictive bias as well. Thus internal criteria of bias are useful in test construction, as potentially biased items in the predictive sense can be weeded out during initial item selection, even prior to any attempts to examine the test's predictive validity in various populations.

When the criterion for establishing a test's predictive validity is itself accused of being culturally biased, then the failure to demonstrate significant differential predictive validity in two or more cultural groups that differ both on the test and the criterion is not deemed as evidence that the test does not reflect cultural bias. The test may merely contain the same cultural bias that exists in the criterion, so that the biased test therefore "predicts" the similarly biased criterion. One can get around this objection in two main ways: (1) by examining the test's correlations with other external criteria besides the criterion suspected of cultural bias and (2) from certain internal analyses of the test itself that are capable of revealing cultural bias if indeed it exists to a statistically significant degree.

The remainder of this chapter describes the various methods of analysis, not involving predictive validity, for detecting cultural bias in tests.

The Cultural Difference Hypothesis

All the types of analyses described in this section are aimed essentially at testing the *cultural difference hypothesis,* which, in its simplest terms, holds that certain racial-cultural groups are so different (for whatever reason) that the same common psychological dimensions or traits either cannot be identified in the two or more diverse cultural groups or, if they do possess the same traits, they cannot be measured by the same instruments in the diverse groups. This is essentially the claim made by those who argue that such and such a test is inappropriate for this or that minority group. Lloyd G. Humphreys (1973) has caricatured this cultural difference hypothesis in its most extreme form as follows: "Minorities probably do not belong to the same biological species as the majority; but if they do, the environmental differences have been so profound and have produced such huge cultural differences that the same principles of human behavior do not apply to both groups" (p. 2). Humphreys notes that this point of view is apparently explicitly advocated by at least one psychologist, Robert L. Williams, whom Humphreys quotes as follows: "[Y]ou never compare black and white people. We are Afro-Americans, and whites are either Euro-American or Euro-Asians" (p. 2).

Humphreys totally rejects this point of view on theoretical and empirical grounds, and offers the following counterhypothesis:

> [T]here is every reason to accept a single biological species for blacks and whites and a high degree of cultural similarity as well. *While there are obvious environmental differences, these differences are not so profound as to require different psychological principles in the explanation of black and white behavior.* The two groups use a highly similar (if not identical) language, attend similar schools, are exposed to similar curricula, listen to the same radio programs, look at the same television programs, live in the same cities, and buy the same commodities, etc. Cultural differences are a question of degree, not of kind.   (pp. 2–3)

What is needed, then, are forms of analysis of test results based on samples of majority and minority populations that can detect the degree to which the two groups differ in ways that would be consistent with the cultural difference hypothesis, aside from differences in overall mean level of performance. Group differences in mean level of performance, as argued at the beginning of this chapter, cannot be presumed to be zero *a priori*. But, if the results of other internal analyses of the test data are in accord with expectations from the cultural difference hypothesis, it makes it reasonable to conclude that all or part of the group mean difference in level of performance on the test could be an artifact of culturally biasing factors in the test.

Correlation between Test and Construct

Construct validity may be defined theoretically as the correlation between test scores X and the construct C the test is intended to measure, that is, r_{XC}. In reality, of course, the problem is that we have no direct measure of C. And so the process of construct validation is roundabout, consisting mainly of showing in more and more different ways that the test scores behave as should be expected if, in fact, the test measures the construct in question. Thus construct validity rests on a growing network of theoretically expected and empirically substantiated correlations and outcomes of specially designed experiments to test the construct validity of the measuring instrument.

Rarely would it be claimed that any single test is a perfect measure of a complex theoretical construct such as intelligence. A test score is viewed as merely an imperfect index of the construct itself, which is to say that, for any given test that attempts to measure the construct, the correlation r_{XC} is less than 1, even after correction for attenuation (unreliability). If, for example, we define the construct of intelligence as the g factor common to an indefinitely large and diverse battery of mental tests, the construct validity (or, more narrowly, the factorial validity) of a given IQ test is estimated by its g loading when it is factor analyzed among a large battery of other tests. The variance contributed by any given test's group factors, specificity, and unreliability, of course, all tend to lower the test's correlation with g.

Because no single test is a perfect measure of the construct that it aims to measure, what is the consequence of this one fact alone for group mean differences on such an imperfect test?

Considerable conceptual confusion on this theoretically important point has been introduced into the literature on test bias by Block and Dworkin (1974, pp. 388–394). These writers state:

> Given linearity [of the regression of IQ scores on the hypothetical construct of intelligence] and the obvious fact that IQ tests are less than perfect as measures of intelligence, a rather surprising conclusion follows: if IQ tests are color-blind on an *individual* basis, they are likely to be biased against racial *groups,* such as blacks, which score below the population mean.   (p. 388)

There follow three pages of statistically fallacious reasoning by Block and Dworkin to "prove" that, even if the test is unbiased for individuals, the observed black–white mean IQ difference of 15 points (85 versus 100) is *greater* than the true intelligence difference, since IQ is only an imperfect measure of intelligence. They say, "Thus, on the average, people with below-average IQs have their intelligence underestimated by IQ tests. . . . It follows that the black intelligence expected on the basis of IQ is higher than 85" (p. 389).

In fact, Block and Dworkin's argument is entirely wrong, and just the opposite conclusion is correct. The fallacy in their reasoning is due to their failure to recognize that (1) a group mean (and consequently a group mean difference) is a statistically unbiased estimate of the population value, (2) the reliability or validity of the measurements do not in themselves systematically affect the sample mean, and (3) removal of the error variance and the variance that is nonrelevant to the construct (assuming that the groups do not differ on the nonrelevant factors, which is presumably what Block and Dworkin mean by the test's being "color-blind on an *individual* basis") would actually create a *larger* difference between the black and white group means when measured in standard deviation units or in terms of the percentage of overlap of the two distributions.

To put it in more general terms, assume that on a particular test two populations A and B differ in observed means, $\bar{X}_A - \bar{X}_B$; and assume that the test's construct validity is r_{XC} in both groups and that the test is color-blind on an individual basis; that is, it measures no factors on which the groups differ other than the construct purportedly measured by the test. Then the group mean difference on the construct itself, expressed in standard deviation (σ) units will be $\bar{D}_{A-B} = (\bar{X}_A - \bar{X}_B)/\sigma r_{XC}$. Thus, when the test is an imperfect measure of the construct, that is $r_{XC} < 1$, the mean score difference between two groups *underestimates* the group mean difference in the construct itself, by an amount proportional to r_{XC}. If we wish to retain the same measuring scale and the same σ for the construct as for the obtained scores, the group mean difference on the construct will be simply $\bar{D}_{A-B} = (\bar{X}_A - \bar{X}_B)/r_{XC}$. Thus, for example, Block and Dworkin (p. 389) assume the construct validity of IQ to be 0.50, in which case the observed white–black mean IQ difference of 15 points would represent a true intelligence difference, measured on the same scale, of $\bar{D} = (100 - 85)/0.50 = 30$ points. (Probably for the purposes of their argument, Block and Dworkin assumed an excessivly low value of .50 for the construct validity of IQ. Values in the range from .70 to .90 are probably closer to the truth, which would make the true mean intelligence difference between blacks and whites equivalent to only some 17 to 21 points on an IQ scale, or about 1.1σ to 1.4σ.)

Because a test underestimates group mean differences in a latent trait to the extent that the test's construct validity falls short of perfection, it would not be surprising, consequently, to find that improvement of a test's construct validity can actually augment group mean differences, if the groups in fact differ in the latent trait that the test attempts to measure and do not differ in other factors that the test might measure. A test fails to be color blind and may be regarded as biased to the extent that it measures group differences that are irrelevant to (i.e., uncorrelated with) the test's construct validity.

What we need to be sure of, of course, is that the test measures the same construct equally well in the various populations in which it is intended for use and does not also measure some other characteristic on which the groups differ but which is uncorrelated with the construct purportedly measured by the test. The probability that these conditions are true is increased by showing that the groups do not differ in certain other properties of the test besides its construct validity. Every validity coefficient the test demonstrates in terms of various external criteria, when the validity coefficient is the same in the major and minor groups, is an additional point of evidence increasing the probability that the test is an unbiased measure of the same construct in both groups.

Positive, Negative, and Reverse Bias. It can be seen from the preceding discussion that, with respect to a test's construct validity, we must make a theoretical distinction between three possible types of test bias—*positive, negative,* and *reverse* bias.

If the true difference between the means of the major and minor groups in the construct is $\bar{D}_{\bar{t}} = \bar{t}_A - \bar{t}_B$, then a test is positively biased if the mean score difference between the groups, $\bar{X}_{\bar{X}} = \bar{X}_A - \bar{X}_B$, is greater than $\bar{D}_t$.

A test is negatively biased if $\bar{D}_{\bar{X}}$ is less than $\bar{D}_{\bar{t}}$.

A test is reverse biased if $\bar{D}_{\bar{t}}$ and $\bar{D}_{\bar{X}}$ have opposite signs, that is, if $\bar{t}_A$ is greater than $\bar{t}_B$ and $\bar{X}_A$ is less than $\bar{X}_B$, or $\bar{t}_A$ is less than $\bar{t}_B$ and $\bar{X}_A$ is greater than $\bar{X}_B$.

Most discussions of test bias refer to *positive* bias, and, when the nature of the bias is not specified, it is generally safe to assume that positive bias is being referred to. "Culture biased" almost always means positive bias. One condition is necessary for positive bias: the test must measure, in addition to the construct it purports to measure, some other characteristic or factor that is completely uncorrelated with the construct and on which the major group, on the average, exceeds the minor group. A typical example is the case in which the major and minor groups differ in their native language. A person's native language is presumably not correlated with the construct of intelligence. If the test involves the native language of the major group exclusively and the minor group has a different language, the test will most likely be positively biased in favor of the major group. In other words, the test is measuring something (in this case a specific language) in addition to the construct that it purports to measure, which condition favors the major group.

Two conditions may separately or conjointly result in *negative* bias: The first condition is test unreliability (i.e., random errors of measurement) or any factors measured by the test that are not correlated with the construct but do not discriminate between the major and minor groups. (This is the case of the "color-blind" test described by Block and Dworkin, discussed in the preceding pages.) Any source of individual differences (variance) in the test scores that is irrelevant to the construct and is not systematically related to group characteristics decreases the group mean difference as measured in standard deviation units or the percentage of overlap between the groups' test score distributions.

The second condition is some factor measured by the test that is not correlated with the construct and on which the minor group exceeds the major group. In other words, the test measures the construct plus some other irrelevant factor that discriminates the groups *oppositely* from the construct, but not to such an extent as to completely counteract the group difference on the construct or reverse the direction of the group mean difference.

Reverse bias results when the test measures some other factor besides the construct that discriminates between the groups in the opposite direction to the construct to such a degree that the groups' mean difference in test scores is the reverse of the groups' mean difference on the construct nominally measured by the test. An example would be a group of mentally retarded English children obtaining a higher mean score than a group of normal native-speaking Chinese children on a verbal IQ test in English.

Theoretically Predicted Correlates of Test Scores

A test's construct validity depends in large part on the test's correlations with other external measures that in some way exemplify the construct or would be related in some predictable way to the extent that the test is in fact a measure of the construct. If these predictable relationships, then, are not significantly different in any two racial, cultural, or socioeconomic groups, they constitute further evidence that the test measures the same construct in both groups. Each such theoretically expected relationship that is borne out equally in both groups increases our confidence that the test is not a biased measure of the construct in the groups in question.

Age Correlations. The construct of general intelligence implies a systematic growth in mental ability from infancy to maturity. Consequently, the raw scores on a test of general intelligence should show a positive correlation with chronological age. And, if the test measures the same construct in both the major and minor groups, they should both show a positive correlation between raw score and age, but not necessarily the same correlation, except under rather special conditions, as noted in the paragraphs following.

Because mental growth is approximately linear between about 5 and 15 years of age, most of the relationship between raw scores and age will be accounted for by linear regression, that is, Pearson r. To determine if there is any significant nonlinear trend in the raw scores $\times$ age relationship, one can use multiple correlation, with powers of age (i.e., age^1, age^2, age^3, age^4, etc.) as the independent (i.e., predictor) variables and raw score as the dependent (i.e., predicted) variable. If the shrunken squared multiple correlation R^2 (i.e., the proportion of variance in the dependent variable accounted for by the independent variables) is not significantly larger than the squared simple correlation r^2, one may conclude that linear regression accounts for all the reliable variation in raw scores as a function of age.

If the age $\times$ test score correlation is similar across both groups, this is a point in favor of the test's being unbiased, but this fact by itself does not prove the absence of bias, as a test with a systematic bias against one group could still yield scores that are related to age in that group. But it would be a rather improbable coincidence if there were a test bias that nevertheless resulted in similar age correlations in both groups. On the other hand, a zero age correlation in one group, or a marked discrepancy in the correlations across groups, warrants a much stronger conclusion, namely, that the test does not behave the same in both groups, and that is evidence of some kind of bias. Many statistical tests of bias have this one-way characteristic: the lack of a group difference does not establish the absence of bias but only increases the probability of its absence, whereas a marked and significant group difference may definitely indicate bias.

It should be noted that, if two groups have different mental growth rates, the *slope* of the regression of raw scores on age will differ in the two groups, even when the score $\times$ age correlation is the same in both groups. When there are group differences in mental growth rate, and the standard deviation as well as the mean of the measurements increases systematically with age, the group with the lower rate should have a smaller standard deviation at any given chronological age; the standard deviation of the lower group should be approximately the same as the standard deviation of the higher group at the earlier age at which its mean score is equal to the lower group's mean at the given age. The slightly lower standard deviation of blacks' IQs, as compared with whites', which is generally found, can be attributed to their different growth rates in mental age (or raw test scores). Because IQ = 100 MA/CA, if MA has a smaller standard deviation for blacks than for whites at any given CA, the IQ also will have a smaller standard deviation in the black group. When the black mean $\overline{X}_B$ and standard deviation σ_B are based on the white-normed IQ scale, then we should expect $\overline{X}_B / \overline{X}_W = \sigma_B / \sigma_W =$ a constant.

We can test this on the largest set of black normative data collected on the Stanford–Binet Intelligence Test, by Kennedy, Van de Riet, and White (1963), with the following statistics:

	Mean	σ
White IQ	101.8	16.4
Black IQ	80.7	12.4

Thus, $80.7/101.8 = .79$, and $12.4/16.4 = .76$, and $.79 - .76 = .03$, which is a nonsignificant difference between the two ratios.

The difference in white and black IQ standard deviations, therefore, is entirely consistent with the differences in mental growth rates as indicated by the different slopes of the regression of raw scores (or their white normative mental-age equivalent) on chronological age.

It follows, then, that if the overall mean test score of the minor group B is *below* that of the major group A, at every age, the slope b_{sa} of the regression of test score on age is *lower* in the minor than in the major group. For example, the regression slope of Stanford–Binet mental age on chronological age is lower for blacks than for whites, in about the ratio of $b_B/b_W = 0.85$, on the average. The regression slopes of intelligence test raw scores on age in the two races could be expected to show about the same proportionality. This being the case, we should expect the Pearson *correlations* of test scores with age to be the same in both groups *only* if the standard deviation of test scores is smaller in the minor than in the major group, in the same proportion as for the regression slopes. That is, σ_B/σ_A should be approximately equal to b_B/b_A. Without this condition, the expectation that the test score $\times$ age correlation should be the *same* in both groups does not hold. This can be seen from consideration of the relationship between correlation and regression,

$$r_{sa} = b_{sa}\,\frac{\sigma_a}{\sigma_s}\,,$$

where s stands for *score* and a for *age,* and b_{sa} is the slope of the regression of scores on age. With proper sampling for this type of age $\times$ score analysis (i.e., a constant proportionality of the sample sizes of the major and minor groups in every age interval), σ_a should be the same in the major and minor groups. Therefore, if b_{sa} is smaller in the minor than in the major group, σ_s will also have to be proportionally smaller, if r_{sa} is to be equal in both groups. If, for whatever reason, σ_s is equal in both groups or larger in the minor group, we should expect the score $\times$ age correlation r_{sa} to be *lower* in the minor group. Notice that this is a case where the group with the larger variance (but smaller b_{sa}) shows the *smaller* r_{sa}. (This is the exception to our general statistical reflex of explaining a small r as being due to restricted variance.)

Because of the noted limitations (i.e., the constant proportionality of b_{sa}/σ_s in the major and minor groups) on the interpretation of a difference between the correlation of test scores with age in the major and minor groups, this cannot be regarded as a statistically rigorous criterion of test bias. In such a case, a simple graph showing test scores (on the ordinate) plotted as a function of age (on the abscissa) for each group in question should provide adequate evidence of whether the test scores increase with age in a strictly monotonic fashion in all groups. Any appreciable deviations from strict monotonicity in any one of the groups under comparison should arouse suspicion of test bias.

Another use of age for investigating test bias depends on longitudinal data, in which the same group of children is repeatedly given the same test at different ages. The age $\times$ age correlations (i.e., the correlation between scores at one age and scores at another age) of the test scores (either raw scores or any derived standardized scores) should be the same, within the limits of sampling error, in the major and minor groups if the test is unbiased, making allowance for the effects of differing standard deviations on the size of the correlation coefficient.[4]

Kinship Correlations and Differences

No standard tests of intelligence (or of other abilities) have been devised with the intention of finding certain regularities in the correlations between the test scores of persons having different degrees of genetic relationship to one another. For a number of highly heritable physical characteristics that are continuously (and usually normally) distributed in the population, such as height, weight, head size, and number of fingerprint ridges, such kinship correlations show a quite distinctive pattern. Therefore, if our construct of intelligence includes the idea that intelligence has a biological basis, being a product of organic evolution like many physical features of the species conditioned by genetic factors, then the finding of a pattern of kinship correlations for intelligence test scores similar to that of indisputably physical and highly heritable traits, such as height and weight, may be viewed as an important line of evidence for the construct validity of intelligence tests.

Innumerable studies over the past seventy years have found that intelligence test scores do, in fact, show a pattern of kinship correlations very similar to that found for heritable physical traits. The correlation or degree of resemblance between relatives decreases in a regular stepwise fashion the more distantly they are related. The order of the correlations is predictable from basic principles of genetics. Identical (or monozygotic) twins, who inherit exactly identical sets of genes, whether reared together or apart, are the most alike in IQ of any kinships, just as they are physically the most alike. Fraternal (dizygotic) twins, who have only about half of their segregating genes in common, like ordinary siblings, are considerably less alike in IQ than identical twins and show about the same degree of resemblance as ordinary siblings. Parents and their children also have about half of their genes in common (since each parent contributes randomly half of each child's genes), and the correlation between parents' and their children's IQs is just about the same as the correlation between siblings. Genetically unrelated children who are reared together from early infancy in adoptive families show much less correlation in IQ than do ordinary siblings. Also their IQs show very little correlation with the IQs of their adoptive parents but significantly greater correlation with the intelligence levels of their biological parents whom they have never known (Munsinger, 1975).

From such kinship data, experts in quantitative genetics can derive estimates of the so-called *heritability* of trait measurements such as height or IQ. Heritability is defined as the proportion of the total variance in the measurements that is attributable to genetic factors. Most published estimates of IQ heritability fall in the range from .6 to .9, with a median of about .7. Heritability estimation is a highly technical matter involving many possible theoretical and empirical difficulties and pitfalls for the technically unsophisticated in quantitative genetics. Because even an elementary explication of heritability analysis is beyond the scope of this book, the interested reader must be referred elsewhere for an introduction to the subject. (See Burt, 1971, 1972; Falconer, 1960; Jensen, 1973b, Appendix A; Jinks & Fulker, 1970; Loehlin, Lindzey, & Spuhler, 1975; McClearn & De Fries, 1974.)

Now what has all this to do with test bias? Just this: the construct validity of a test in any two population groups is reinforced if the test scores show the same kinship correlations (or absolute differences) in both groups. If a given mental test does not measure the same construct in two populations, it is possible, but quite improbable, that the test will show the same kinship correlation or the same pattern of various kinship correlations in both populations. If the IQ correlations of identical twins or fraternal twins or ordinary siblings, or any other kinships, are nonsignificantly different in the major and minor populations, for example, the fact that the test scores thus behave in the same way with respect to the particular kinship correlations in both populations would constitute presumptive evidence that the test measures the same construct in both populations. This conclusion becomes especially compelling, of course, when such a finding is viewed in conjunction with other forms of evidence that the test scores behave in the same way across the two populations.

Two kinds of kinship comparisons are useful in this respect: (1) the similarity between two groups in the correlations of different kinships (twins, siblings, parent–child, etc.) for a single test and (2) the similarity between two groups in the correlations of a variety of different mental tests for a single kinship. Various tests that reflect genetic and environmental factors to different degrees will usually show different correlations for any given kinship, and, if such correlations are ordered the same in two populations, it is further evidence that the tests measure the same factors in both populations.

Checking for Interval Scale in Kinship Differences. It follows necessarily that kinship correlations are systematically related to the average absolute difference between relatives of a given kinship—the higher the correlation, the smaller the difference.[5] Kinship absolute differences in standardized test scores can also be used to check the interval scale property of the scores across two populations that may differ in means and standard deviations. We might wish to know, for example, whether the test is measuring the IQs of, say, blacks and whites on the same interval scale and that the score intervals are equal in every part of the full range of scores in both groups. We can use sibling absolute differences for this analysis, although any other kinship would do. But siblings are easier to find in large numbers than any other type of kinship.

Because there is no theoretical reason why siblings in one part of the score range should differ any more or less than siblings who score in another part of the range, we may assume that any systematic relationship between the mean score of sibling pairs, $\overline{X}_S = \frac{1}{2}(X_1 + X_2)$ and the absolute difference between the siblings' scores, $D_S = |X_1 - X_2|$, must indicate a departure from an equal-interval scale of test scores. The hypothesis of an interval scale can be rigorously tested by determining if there is a significant correlation between the sibling means and differences. This should be done in each population sample separately and then in the two samples combined. Because there could be some nonlinear form of relationship between sibling means and differences, one must check for possible nonlinear trends between the means and differences. This is best done by a multiple regression technique in which we determine the multiple correlation R between a set of independent variables and a dependent variable. In this case, the set of independent variables consists of the first five powers of the sibling mean and the dependent variable is the sibling absolute difference. If the multiple correlation R (after correction for shrinkage; see Chapter 8, note 1) is significantly greater than zero, we may reject the hypothesis that the test scores lie on an interval scale. If, however, R is nonsignificant, we perform a further statistical test, this time using the first five powers of the sibling absolute difference as the independent variables and the sibling means as the dependent variable. If the resulting shrunken R is also nonsignificant, we may presume that the test scores are an interval scale. (In any kind of measurement scale, of course, there are always random errors of measurement, and mental test scales are no exception.) The multiple regression paradigm just described can be summarized as follows:

	Independent Variables	Dependent Variable
First stage	$\overline{X}_S^1, \overline{X}_S^2, \overline{X}_S^3, \overline{X}_S^4, \overline{X}_S^5 \longrightarrow$	D_S
Second stage	$D_S^1, D_S^2, D_S^3, D_S^4, D_S^5 \longrightarrow$	X_S

If the shrunken R is nonsignificant at both stages within each population sample, one then performs the same two analyses for the combined samples. If the shrunken R at both stages is still nonsignificant, one may conclude that the test measures both populations on the same interval scale. Because the absence of a correlation between sibling (or other kinship) means and absolute differences is not something that test constructors have purposely tried to build into any test's psychometric characteristics, it constitutes an independent check on the test's scale properties. Of course, the form of the frequency distribution of test scores is meaningful only if the scores are on an interval scale, which is indicated by a zero correlation between kinship means and differences. The fact that IQs derived from most standard intelligence tests are distributed approximately normally in the population, at least within the IQ range from about 60 to 140, in conjunction with the fact that there is no significant correlation between sibling IQ means and differences, thus indicating an interval scale of IQ, can be interpreted as evidence that the construct of intelligence itself, and not just the IQ, is normally distributed in the population.

These analyses were performed on large samples from two quite different populations with respect to their IQ distributions: black and white school children in the same school district in rural Georgia (Jensen, 1977b). The California Test of Mental Maturity, a standard group test, was used. The IQ distributions of these two groups are so widely separated, with a black mean IQ of 71 and a white mean of 102, that there is naturally some question as to whether the IQs lie on one and the same interval scale for both groups. Each of the analyses described revealed negligible and nonsignificant values of R for whites and blacks, separately and combined, for verbal, nonverbal, and total IQ. Thus it was concluded that the IQs are measured on the same interval scale throughout the full range of scores for whites and blacks. This would seem an exceedingly unlikely finding if the test did not measure the same construct in both racial groups.

Internal Detection of Test Bias

Most tests are composed of a number of items that singly and in relationship to one another have a variety of statistical properties that can be compared across different populations. If certain of these statistical properties of the test differ significantly in any two populations, it is *prima facie* evidence that the test internally behaves differently in the two populations and one may suspect that the test is biased with respect to these particular populations.

Of course, not all the statistical features of a test are suitable for the detection of bias. As was emphasized in the first part of this chapter, the test score means or medians of various populations may reflect true differences in the construct that the test is intended to measure, and therefore group mean differences per se cannot be interpreted as evidence of bias. The same thing can be said about group differences in the standard deviation of test scores. However, there are other important statistical properties of tests that are indifferent to the population mean (or other measures of central tendency) but that are crucial to its adequacy as a measuring instrument and to its construct validity. It is in the comparison of these particular properties of a test across different racial, socioeconomic, and cultural groups that bias may be detected.

Temporal Stability. If a test is unbiased, test–retest correlation, of course with the same interval between testings for the major and minor groups, should yield the same correlation for both groups. Significantly different test–retest correlations (taking proper account of possibly unequal variances in the two groups) are indicative of a biased test. Failure to understand instructions, guessing, carelessness, marking answers haphazardly, and the like, all tend to lower the test–retest correlation. If two groups differ in test–retest correlation, it is clear that the test scores are not equally accurate or stable measures for both groups.

Internal Consistency Reliability. This depends on the intercorrelations among the test items. Item intercorrelations are diminished by failure to understand the items, guessing, carelessness, or any general test-taking attitudes that are unrelated to the specific cognitive demands of each item. If the reliability coefficients are very high ($r_{xx} > .95$) in the major and minor groups, there is little need to be further concerned about group differences in reliability. A very high reliability coefficient in both groups tells us that in both groups the test is measuring whatever it measures with reasonable accuracy. In such a case, the reliability coefficients are not indicative of bias, but neither can they prove its nonexistence, as the test could possibly measure different things in the two groups with comparably high reliabilities.

A test's internal consistency reliability proves to be a sensitive indicator of test bias if the major and minor groups show significantly different reliability coefficients, especially if in one of the groups the reliability coefficient is below an acceptable standard, say, $r_{xx} < .90$.[6] But a significant difference between groups in internal consistency reliability coefficients is not by itself sufficient to establish bias. If a significant group difference in reliabilities is found, it then has to be determined whether the groups' reliability coefficients differ because of group differences in item difficulty, or because of group differences in item intercorrelations, or both.

The reader will recall that the total variance in test scores is composed of two components: (1) the sum of the item variances, Σpq (where p and q are the proportions passing and failing the item, and $p + q = 1$), and (2) twice the sum of all the item covariances, $2\Sigma r_{ij} \sqrt{p_i q_i p_j q_j}$, where r_{ij} is the correlation between a pair of items. Thus, the total variance $\sigma_X^2 = \Sigma pq + 2\Sigma r_{ij} \sqrt{p_i q_i p_j q_j}$. The internal consistency reliability, then, is, $r_{xx} = 2\Sigma r_{ij} \sqrt{p_i q_i p_j q_j}/\sigma_X^2$. Obviously the reliability coefficients of two groups on the same test may differ because of group differences in Σpq, owing to group differences in item difficulty levels, or because of group differences in the sum of the item intercorrelations Σr_{ij}, or both these components of variance. A group difference in reliability coefficients resulting only from group differences in item difficulties cannot be considered an aspect of test bias, as the items may truly be more difficult for one group than for the other. A group difference in the item intercorrelations, however, is a more serious matter and may indicate bias.

If the groups differ in the sum of the item intercorrelations Σr_{ij}, one further analysis is required to establish bias, because the size of the correlation between any two items is itself affected by the item difficulties. (Recall that restriction of variance in one or both variables restricts the size of the correlation between them and that the variance of a single test item is pq, where p is the proportion of the sample passing the item and $q = 1 - p$. Items, therefore, obviously will differ in variance depending on their difficulty in the sample of subjects.) We would like to know if the major and minor groups would differ in the inter-item correlations even if the groups did not evince differences in item difficulties. That is, we wish to determine the *intrinsic* correlation between any two items, i and j, free from the influence of item difficulty per se on the obtained correlation between the items.

The obtained correlation between any two items i and j can be represented in the form of a 2×2 contingency table:

		Item j		
		Fail	Pass	
Item i	Pass	a	b	p_i
	Fail	c	d	q_i
		q_j	p_j	$p + q = 1$

The proportions of the total sample that fall into each of the four cells are indicated by a, b, c, and d. The correlation based on such a 2×2 contingency table is called a *phi coefficient*, ϕ. It is algebraically equivalent to the Pearson r. Using this information, the phi coefficient (and Pearson r) is

$$\phi = (cb - ad)/\sqrt{p_i q_i p_j q_j}. \tag{9.8}$$

(Notice that all the entries in this formula can be *either* proportions *or* frequencies.) However, the upper limit of phi is determined by the item difficulties, that is, p_i and p_j. Only if the two items have the same difficulty, that is $p_i = p_j$, can phi be equal to 1 if there is intrinsically a perfect correlation between i and j. Therefore, if the items differ in difficulty, then to determine the intrinsic correlation between i and j free of the influence of differences in item difficulty, we must divide the obtained phi by the maximum value of phi that could possibly be obtained with the given marginal frequencies p_i and p_j. This maximum possible value of phi is called phi max, or ϕ_{max}; it is most easily obtained by the following formula:

$$\phi_{max} = \sqrt{\frac{B\,(T - A)}{A\,(T - B)}}, \tag{9.9}$$

where A is the *largest* of any of the four marginal frequencies (or proportions), B is the *second largest* of any of the marginal frequencies (or proportions), and T is the total frequency (or the sum of the proportions $= 1$) in the 2×2 contingency table. (When two frequencies, or proportions, are equal, use either one.)

When each of the inter-item phi coefficients has been divided by its respective ϕ_{max}, we may sum them all and compare $\Sigma(\phi/\phi_{max})$ in the two population samples, which should not differ significantly if the test is unbiased.[7] In other words, if the populations differ significantly in their reliability coefficients on the test but do not differ significantly in $\Sigma(\phi/\phi_{max})$, we know the reliability difference is due only to group differences in item difficulties, which by itself does not indicate bias. Low reliability due to a markedly skewed distribution of item difficulties, however, is an undesirable feature in its own right and may warrant the rejection of a test on that basis alone.

A marked group difference in the average item intercorrelation indicates that the items do not measure the same abilities in both groups, which means that the test is biased. The overall sum of item intercorrelations, of course, may average out and obscure particular deviant items. Specific item correlation analyses for the detection of such biased items in a test in which most of the items are not biased are described in a later section.

Groups × Items Interaction.   The statistical concept of interaction, derived from the analysis of variance, provides the basis for several of the most important objective techniques available for detecting test bias. The interaction between population groups and test items, referred to as the groups by items (or groups × items) interaction, is the central focus of this type of analysis.

Probably the easiest way to grasp the concept of a groups × items interaction is to examine the complete data matrix of a hypothetic test for which the groups × items interaction is zero, despite the fact the groups differ in their overall means. Such a test can be regarded as unbiased in the statistical sense of a failure to reject the null hypothesis. More accurately, we would say that a potential indicator of bias, namely, a groups × items interaction significantly greater than zero, has failed to materialize, and therefore we cannot reject the null hypothesis, which states that there is no groups × items interaction. With failure to reject the null hypothesis, all we can conclude is that there is no evidence of bias, which, of course, does not prove that bias does not exist. But in statistics it is axiomatic that the null hypothesis can never be proved. If, however, a significant groups × items interaction were found, we could then reject the null hypothesis and conclude that the test items are subject to some kind of bias, possibly cultural, with respect to the two groups under consideration. We might then proceed to try and determine precisely the nature of the item biases. But that is quite another problem, to be dealt with later.

The complete data matrix (more specifically termed "items × subjects matrix") of a hypothetic perfectly unbiased test is shown in Table 9.3. For the sake of simplicity, this "test" has only ten items, and we have administered it to only twenty "subjects" in each group. Groups A and B are assumed to be random samples drawn from populations A and B. (In practice, A and B may be different ethnic groups, social classes, nationalities, religions, sexes, etc.) Also, to simplify inspection of the matrix, the subjects in each group are arranged in the order going from the highest to the lowest test scores (see column headed Score), and we have arranged the test items in the order of their p values (proportion passing), from the easiest to the hardest (see rows labeled p_A and p_B). Two conspicuous features of Table 9.3 should be noted.

1. In both groups the test items are a perfect *Guttman scale*. This means that, if we know any subject's total score on the test, we also know exactly which items he or she passed or failed; and, of course, we also know that any two subjects with the same score have passed or failed exactly the same items. This is true irrespective of which group a

Table 9.3. Items × subjects matrix[1] of a hypothetical "perfectly unbiased test" for groups A and B.

Group A

Subject No.	1	2	3	4	5	6	7	8	9	10	Score X
					Test Items						
1	1	1	1	1	1	1	1	1	1	1	10
2	1	1	1	1	1	1	1	1	1	1	10
3	1	1	1	1	1	1	1	1	1	0	9
4	1	1	1	1	1	1	1	1	1	0	9
5	1	1	1	1	1	1	1	1	0	0	8
6	1	1	1	1	1	1	1	1	0	0	8
7	1	1	1	1	1	1	1	0	0	0	7
8	1	1	1	1	1	1	1	0	0	0	7
9	1	1	1	1	1	1	0	0	0	0	6
10	1	1	1	1	1	1	0	0	0	0	6
11	1	1	1	1	1	0	0	0	0	0	5
12	1	1	1	1	1	0	0	0	0	0	5
13	1	1	1	1	0	0	0	0	0	0	4
14	1	1	1	1	0	0	0	0	0	0	4
15	1	1	1	0	0	0	0	0	0	0	3
16	1	1	1	0	0	0	0	0	0	0	3
17	1	1	0	0	0	0	0	0	0	0	2
18	1	1	0	0	0	0	0	0	0	0	2
19	1	0	0	0	0	0	0	0	0	0	1
20	1	0	0	0	0	0	0	0	0	0	1
p_A	1.0	.9	.8	.7	.6	.5	.4	.3	.2	.1	$\bar{X}_A = 5.5$ $\sigma_A = 2.872$

Group B

Subject No.	1	2	3	4	5	6	7	8	9	10	Score X
					Test Items						
21	1	1	1	1	1	1	1	1	1	0	9
22	1	1	1	1	1	1	1	1	1	0	9
23	1	1	1	1	1	1	1	1	0	0	8
24	1	1	1	1	1	1	1	1	0	0	8
25	1	1	1	1	1	1	1	0	0	0	7
26	1	1	1	1	1	1	1	0	0	0	7
27	1	1	1	1	1	1	0	0	0	0	6
28	1	1	1	1	1	1	0	0	0	0	6
29	1	1	1	1	1	0	0	0	0	0	5
30	1	1	1	1	1	0	0	0	0	0	5
31	1	1	1	1	0	0	0	0	0	0	4
32	1	1	1	1	0	0	0	0	0	0	4
33	1	1	1	0	0	0	0	0	0	0	3
34	1	1	1	0	0	0	0	0	0	0	3
35	1	1	0	0	0	0	0	0	0	0	2
36	1	1	0	0	0	0	0	0	0	0	2
37	1	0	0	0	0	0	0	0	0	0	1
38	1	0	0	0	0	0	0	0	0	0	1
39	0	0	0	0	0	0	0	0	0	0	0
40	0	0	0	0	0	0	0	0	0	0	0
p_B	.9	.8	.7	.6	.5	.4	.3	.2	.1	.0	$\bar{X}_B = 4.5$ $\sigma_B = 2.872$

[1] Each item for a given subject is marked as passed (= 1) or failed (= 0).

433

subject belongs to, as the items are the same Guttman scale in both groups. When the items are a Guttman scale, we know they are all measuring only one and the same trait or factor. They are said to be unidimensional, and *ipso facto* the test as a whole must also be unidimensional, measuring only one and the same trait in all subjects in both groups. The more closely items approximate a Guttman scale in both the major and minor groups, the less is the likelihood that the test is biased in respect to these groups.

But a test can be unbiased even without resembling a Guttman scale, as long as there is no significant groups × items interaction, which brings us to the second, crucial point.

2. In Table 9.3 notice that, although each item's p value is lower in group B than in group A, the two sets of p values, p_A and p_B, are perfectly correlated between the two groups. If in group A we subtract the mean p value ($\bar{p}_A = .55$) from every item's p value, the two resulting sets of remainders will be identical for the two groups. This shows, in other words, that the groups differ only in their overall mean level of performance, and not in respect to any particular items. A less than perfect correlation between the two sets of p values would indicate a groups × items interaction. That is, the items would have different relative difficulties (p values) within each population group. The items then would not maintain either the same rank order of p values or the same relative differences among the p values within each group. And, of course, subtracting each group's mean p value from every item's p would not render identical sets of remainders in the two groups. If what is an easy item in group A is a hard item in group B, or vice versa, we may suspect the item is biased. It does not behave the same, relative to the other items, within both groups; and its deviance, therefore, is less apt to reflect equally in both groups whatever general ability is reflected in the test's overall mean in each group.

It is instructive to represent interactions graphically, as in Figure 9.12. Note that, when there is no groups × items interaction, the plots of the items' p values in the two

Figure 9.12. Graphic representation of items × groups interaction for a hypothetical five-item test. The ordinate is an index of item difficulty.

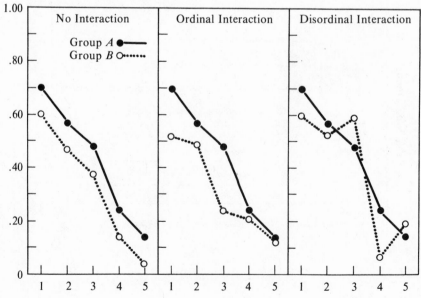

Table 9.4. Summary of the analysis of variance of the data in Table 9.3.

Source of Variance	Sum of Squares	Degrees of Freedom	Mean Square	F Ratio	η^2 ($\times$ 100)[1]
Between groups	1	1	1.00	1.15[a]	1
Between items	33	9	3.667	38.00[b]	33
Between subjects (within groups)	33	38	.868	9.00[c]	33
Groups $\times$ items	0	9	0	0	0
Subjects $\times$ items (within groups)	33	342	.096		33
Total	100	399			100

[1]Eta squared is the sum of squares for each source divided by the total sum of squares. Multiplied by 100, it is the percentage of the total variation in the data accounted for by each source. (It is a mere coincidence in this case that the sum of squares totals 100 and is therefore the same as eta squared $\times$ 100.)
[a]The F ratio is the groups mean square (MS)/subjects MS.   [b]F is items MS/subjects $\times$ items MS.
[c]F is subjects MS/subjects $\times$ items MS.

groups are perfectly parallel. There are two types of interaction—*ordinal* and *disordinal*—as shown in Figure 9.12. The two essential features of an *ordinal* interaction are (1) the items' p values are *not parallel* in the two groups but (2) the p values are in the *same rank order* in both groups. The essential feature of a *disordinal* interaction is that the p values have a *different rank order* in the two groups. (Whether the two lines cross over one another or do not is wholly irrelevant to the essential distinction between ordinal and disordinal interactions.)

Spearman's rank order correlation (ρ, or rho), if computed on the two sets of item p values, will be 1 when there is no interaction and also when there is ordinal interaction. The Pearson r computed on the same data will be 1 when there is no interaction and will be something less than 1 when there is either an ordinal or a disordinal interaction. (This is true except in the rare case where the ordinal interaction is due only to a difference in the variances of the two sets of p values, in which case the Pearson r between the two sets of p values will equal 1.) Thus, the difference between rho and r computed on the same sets of p values provides an indication of the relative amounts of the total interaction that are attributable to ordinal and disordinal effects. Disordinal effects, as indicated by a significant difference between rho and r, are generally a more compelling sign of biased items. In an unbiased test the rank order of item difficulties should not differ significantly between the major and minor groups.

It should be kept in mind that a significant and large groups $\times$ items interaction can exist even though the groups do not differ at all in their overall mean test score. This means that, according to the criterion of a groups $\times$ items interaction, a test may be markedly biased without there being an iota of difference between the group means. Some tests, for example, contain sex-biased items but maintain an equality of the two sexes in overall mean score by balancing the number of sex-biased items that favor or disfavor each sex.

A complete analysis of variance (abbreviated ANOVA) of the item score matrix yields much of the statistical information one needs to detect item biases in a test. This can be illustrated by presenting the ANOVA of the hypothetic data matrix in Table 9.3. The results of the ANOVA are given in Table 9.4. This kind of table will look familiar to readers who are versed in the analysis of variance. (The computations involved in the ANOVA cannot be explicated here; they can be found in most modern statistics textbooks and are a standard part of advanced courses in statistical methods.) The first four columns of figures in Table 9.4 are the usual ANOVA, which tabulates the sample values of the mean square (*MS*) by dividing the sum of squares (*SS*) by its degrees of freedom (*df*). The variance ratio *F* is the ratio of two mean squares and tests the statistical significance of a given source of variance. An *F* value less than 1 is always interpreted as nonsignificant in this context. An *F* greater than 1 is significant or not depending on the *df* associated with the numerator and denominator that entered into the *F* ratio. In our example, the between-groups $F = 1.15$, with 1 and 38 *df,* is nonsignificant; that is, we cannot reject the null hypothesis, namely, that the populations of which the groups *A* and *B* are random samples do not differ in means on this particular test. The differences between item means (i.e., item *p* values) with $F = 38$ (1 and 342 *df*) are highly significant, as are the differences between the individual subjects within each group.

The groups × items interaction *MS* is zero, which means the items maintain exactly the same relative difficulties within each group. If the groups × items interaction term were greater than zero, it would be tested for significance by the *F* ratio = the groups × items *MS*/subject × items *MS*, with 9 and 342 *df*.

The last column in Table 9.4 gives eta squared. Eta squared merely indicates the proportion of the total variation in all the data contributed by each source. It is an important calculation for our purposes, because we wish to know not only the statistical significance of any given source of variance, but also its size relative to other sources of variance. A source of variance that may be significant in the statistical sense may also be so small a percentage of the variance as to be utterly trivial for any practical considerations.

Reliabilities and Correlations from the ANOVA.   The complete ANOVA of the item score matrix, as in Table 9.4, yields, with a little extra computation, certain coefficients of reliability and correlation of importance in assessing test bias. All but one of the formulas make use of the mean squares (*MS*). The commonly used Kuder–Richardson formula[8] for the internal consistency reliability gives exactly the same population estimate of the reliability that is obtained directly from the ANOVA.

Internal consistency reliability:

$$r_{xx} = 1 - \frac{\text{Subjects} \times \text{Items } MS}{\text{Between Subjects } MS} . \tag{9.10}$$

Example:

$$r_{xx} = 1 - \frac{.096}{.868} = .89.$$

Increasing the length of the test by adding more of the same type of items will increase r_{xx} to $r'_{xx} = (1 + n/N)/(r_{xx}^{-1} + n/N)$, where *N* is the number of items in the original test and *n* is the number of new items added to it; this formula is just another form of the well-known Spearman–Brown formula.

Intraclass correlation of the item p values between groups:

$$r_{p_A p_B} = \frac{\text{Items } MS - \text{Groups} \times \text{Items } MS}{\text{Items } MS + \text{Groups} \times \text{Items } MS} . \tag{9.11}$$

Example:

$$r_{p_A p_B} = \frac{3.667 - 0}{3.667 + 0} = 1.$$

This correlation between the sets of p values in the two groups is an *intraclass* correlation, r_i. (The Pearson r is an *interclass* correlation.) Both r_i and Pearson r are estimates of the same population value of the correlation ρ (although, of course, the *sample* values of Pearson r and r_i may differ) only if it can be assumed that the means and variances of the two correlated variables do not differ in the population. (Thus any sample differences in means and variances are due only to sampling error and are therefore nonsignificant.) The Pearson r and the intraclass r_i are identical, when computed on the same set of data, only when the correlated variables have the same mean and the same variance; otherwise, r_i is smaller than Pearson r. (In the present example, based on the mean squares derived from a complete ANOVA, the group mean difference in p values is removed from the mean squares used in the formula for the intraclass correlation $r_{p_A p_B}$, so that this correlation would differ from the Pearson r only if the A and B sets of p values had different variances.) The standard error of the sample intraclass r is smaller (by a factor of $\sqrt{N-1}/\sqrt{2(N-1)}$, where N is the number of paired values) than that of Pearson r, which is thus a slightly less accurate estimate of ρ (the correlation in the population) than is r_i. (See Fisher, 1970, p. 222.)

However, the intraclass correlation between the p values, as derived from the ANOVA by the formula, is theoretically less defensible than using Pearson r as an indicator of the groups' similarity in p values (or, more exactly, the deviations of p values from their respective group means). The reason, of course, is that, in testing for culture bias, we are not justified in assuming that the population means or variances of the major and minor groups' sets of p values are the same, which is the assumption underlying the use of the intraclass correlation. Therefore, the Pearson r is required in this case. Unfortunately, it cannot be derived from the ANOVA table but must be calculated directly from the paired p values. In practice we have generally found only small and usually negligible differences between r_i, as derived from the ANOVA, and the Pearson r. Both the intraclass r and the Pearson r between groups' item p values are usually increased by increasing the number of subjects (provided that all of the subjects within a given group are a random sample from the same population), only because increasing the number of subjects improves the reliability of the p values.

Average reliability of p values within groups:

$$\bar{r}_{pp} = \frac{\text{Items } MS - \text{Subjects} \times \text{Items } MS}{\text{Items } MS + \text{Subjects} \times \text{Items } MS} . \tag{9.12}$$

Example:

$$\frac{3.667 - .096}{3.667 + .096} = .949.$$

The average *reliability* of the p values within each of the two groups separately establishes the highest correlation that could possibly be obtained *between* the groups' p values, and therefore the average reliability $\bar{r}_{pp}$ can be used to correct for attenuation the Pearson correlation $r_{p_A p_B}$ between the groups' p values. In general terms, the highest possible correlation between any two variables X and Y is the geometric mean of their respective reliabilities, that is, $(r_{XX}r_{YY})^{\frac{1}{2}}$.

The reliability of the item p values is increased by increasing the number of subjects, provided that they are all randomly drawn from the same population. (That is, all subjects in sample A are drawn from the population A and all subjects in sample B are from population B.)

The index of group similarity in p values, corrected for attenuation (unreliability) of the p values, then, is Pearson $r_{p_A p_B}/\bar{r}_{pp}$. For an unbiased test, this index should be close to unity.

A z test of the significance of the difference $\bar{r}_{pp} - r_{p_A p_B}$ is a statistical indicator of bias, since, for an unbiased test, the Pearson r between the groups' p values should be an estimate of the average reliability of the p values, and $\bar{r}_{pp}$ and $r_{p_A p_B}$ should not differ, except by sampling error. The proper test of the significance of the difference is obtained by transforming each r to the corresponding Fisher's Z (see note 9), and then obtaining the difference d_z between the transformed Z's corresponding to $\bar{r}_{pp} - r_{p_A p_B}$. The standard error of the difference[10] is

$$SE_{d_z} = \sqrt{\frac{1}{N - 3/2} + \frac{1}{N - 3}} , \qquad (9.13)$$

where N is the number of items in the test, and $d_z/SE_{d_z} = z$ is a standard deviate of the normal curve, the tabled values of which may be referred to for the corresponding probability value (i.e., the proportion of the area under the normal curve that falls above z). Customarily, if this probability value is not less than .05, the null hypothesis is not rejected, and thus we would conclude that there is no reliable evidence for test bias in terms of this particular criterion. (The same conclusion, of course, should follow from the nonsignificant groups $\times$ items interaction.)

One other correlation of possible interest that can be derived from the ANOVA table is the point-biserial correlation[11] r_{pbi}, which is a product–moment correlation, equivalent to the Pearson r, expressing the degree of relationship between a dichotomized variable (in this case *groups*) and a continuous variable (e.g., test scores). It is a way of expressing a group mean difference on a continuous variable on the same scale as the correlation coefficient. The more disparate the group means are, in relation to the total amount of variation among subjects within groups, the larger is r_{pbi}. The value r_{pbi}^2 is the proportion of the total variance among subjects (in the combined groups) that is attributable to the dichotomous variable on which the subjects are classified into two groups.

The point-biserial correlation can be most easily calculated from the ANOVA sum of squares (SS) for between groups and between subjects (within groups):

$$r_{pbi} = \sqrt{\frac{\text{Groups' } SS}{\text{Groups' } SS + \text{Subjects' } SS \text{ (within groups)}}} . \qquad (9.14)$$

Example: $r_{pbi} = \sqrt{1/(1 + 33)} = .1715.$

When the N's of the two samples, A and B, are not equal, the r_{pbi} must be multiplied by $2\sqrt{N_A N_B}/(N_A + N_B)$.

The sample *variance s_X^2 of the test scores* of subjects of both groups combined can be obtained from the sum of squares for groups and subjects (within groups):

$$s_X^2 = \left(\frac{n}{N}\right) \text{(Groups' } SS + \text{Subjects' } SS \text{ [within groups]),} \qquad \textbf{(9.15)}$$

where n is the number of items in the test and N is the number of subjects in the combined groups. (Using $N - 1$ instead of N yields the estimate of the population value σ_X^2.)

Example:

$$s_X^2 = \left(\frac{10}{40}\right)(1 + 33) = 8.5.$$

Transformation of the Scale of Item Difficulty. As a scale of item difficulty, p values have the one advantage of representing directly the proportion of all subjects passing any given item. But the one great disadvantage of p values is that they do not represent item difficulty on an interval scale. Thus, the difference between the item difficulties of two items with p values of .90 and .80 cannot be interpreted as the same degree of difference in difficulty as the difference between two items with p values of .60 and .50. In short, equal intervals on the scale of p values do not represent equal intervals on a true scale of item difficulty. This is certainly true unless one can defend the very unlikely assumption that the common ability measured by the items comprising the test has a rectangular distribution, that is, a distribution with uniform frequencies at every level of ability in the population.

We should like to transform the observed item p values to an interval scale of difficulty. We can do this easily if we make the much more defensible assumption that the ability measured by the items is normally distributed (see Chapter 4). Then the p value of any given item is seen as the proportion of the total area under the normal curve that passed the item, and $q = 1 - p$ is seen as the proportion of the area under the normal curve that failed the item. The vertical line that cuts the total area under the normal curve into areas p and q intersects the baseline of the curve, which is the z scale of deviations of the normal distribution with a mean of 0 and a standard deviation of 1. The z scale of the normal curve thus represents an interval scale of item difficulty. The difficulty of any given item on the z scale is simply the value of z on the baseline of the normal curve that is intersected by the vertical line that divides the curve into areas p and q, where p is always the upper (i.e., right) tail of the curve. An item of average difficulty would be a p value of .50, thus cutting the normal curve exactly in half, with a corresponding z scale value of 0. Easier items would have z values less than 0 and more difficult items would have z values greater than 0. (Notice that large z values indicate greater difficulty, just the reverse of the p values, which are inversely related to difficulty; simply remember that p values greater than .50, i.e., the easier items, must always have *negative z* values.) The value of z corresponding to any given p can be found in the table of the normal curve.

Another commonly used interval scale of item difficulty is the delta scale, which is simply a linear transformation of the z scale described earlier, that is, $\Delta = 4z + 13$. Thus the Δ values are an interval scale with a mean of 13 and a σ of 4. This scale has two advantages: it completely obviates negative values, and it ranges from 0 (for p values

Table 9.5. Transformation of item p values to normal standard (z) and delta (Δ) scales.

	Scales of Item Difficulty		
	p	z	Δ
Difficult	.10	+1.2816	18.126
	.20	+.8416	16.366
	.30	+.5244	15.098
	.40	+.2533	14.013
	.50	.0000	13.000
	.60	−.2533	11.987
	.70	−.5244	10.902
	.80	−.8416	9.634
Easy	.90	−1.2816	7.874

greater than .999) to 26 (for p values less than .001). The values of z and Δ corresponding to various values of p are shown in Table 9.5.

The z and Δ scales of item difficulty also have two other advantages over the p scale. Since z and Δ are interval scales, they allow linear transformations, which is an advantage if we wish to represent the item difficulties for two different populations on a scale with the same mean and standard deviation for both populations. Also, the standard error of z and Δ is constant at all levels of item difficulty, whereas the standard error of p values varies directly as a function of $\sqrt{pq}$. The standard error of z is always $SE_z = 1/\sqrt{N-1}$, and the standard error of Δ is always $SE_\Delta = 4/\sqrt{N-1}$. A constant standard error at all levels of item difficulty greatly simplifies certain statistical operations that can be used to detect item biases.

One statistical test of bias in single items uses Δ values. This test assumes that a group difference in the means or standard deviations of the item difficulties (Δ values) is no indication of bias but that a singificant group difference in the relative difficulties of the items is an indicator of bias. Therefore, we begin by transforming the item Δ values of the minor group (B) so as to have the same mean $\overline{\Delta}$ and standard deviation σ_Δ as the major group.

The linear transformation of the minor group's delta value for item i is

$$\Delta'_B = (\sigma_{\Delta_A}/\sigma_{\Delta_B})(\Delta_{B_i} - \overline{\Delta}_B) + \overline{\Delta}_A,$$

where

σ_{Δ_A} and σ_{Δ_B} = the standard deviations of the item Δ values in groups A and B,

Δ_{B_i} = the Δ value of item i in group B, and

$\overline{\Delta}_A$ and $\overline{\Delta}_B$ = the mean $\overline{\Delta}$ in groups A and B.

This transformation removes any group differences in the mean or standard deviation of the Δ values and any group differences in Δ values that then remain represent group differences in the items' *relative* difficulties, which is a criterion of item bias.

Next, for each item we obtain

$$\chi^2 = [(\Delta_A - \Delta'_B)^2 - \sigma^2_{\Delta_A}(1 - \bar{r}_{ii})]/SE^2_{\Delta_{\text{diff}}},$$

(9.16)

where

$$\chi^2 = \text{chi squared with one degree of freedom,}$$
$$\Delta_A, \Delta'_B, \text{ and } \sigma_{\Delta_A} = \text{as already defined,}$$
$$\bar{r}_{ii} = \text{the average reliability}[12] \text{ of the item difficulties, and}$$
$$SE_{\Delta_{\text{diff}}} = \text{the standard error of the difference}[13] \text{ between the } \Delta \text{ values.}$$

The second term involving the reliability of the item difficulties estimates the average size of the item Δ differences (squared) if each group were compared with itself, as by obtaining differences between the Δ values in random halves of one group.

Chi squared with one degree of freedom must equal or exceed 3.84 to be significant at the .05 level of confidence, which is the conventional level of rejection of the null hypothesis. Items showing χ^2 values greater than 3.84 can be suspected of bias. By chance alone, of course, we should expect 5 percent of the test items to have χ^2 values greater than 3.84. A statistical test of item biases in the test as a whole is simply the sum of all of the χ^2 values for the single items, which is χ^2 with $n - 2$ degrees of freedom, where n is the number of items. (Note: 2 df are lost in equating the means and σ's of the Δ values in the two groups.) If this overall χ^2 is not significant, it means that there are no more χ^2 values greater than 3.84 for the single items than would be expected by chance, and hence the test as a whole cannot be regarded as significantly biased.

A first step toward improving a significantly biased test is to eliminate all items with χ^2 values greater than 3.84. The sum of the χ^2 values (with $df = n - 2$) of the remaining items then should not be significant.

The direction of the significant item biases may favor either the major or minor group or may cancel each other altogether, but, whichever of these possibilities is the case, such items are nevertheless biased. A test does not become less biased by merely balancing significantly biased items. A test in which large item biases balance each other so as not to favor either group in the total score is no more desirable or defensible than a test in which the item biases preponderantly favor one group. There is only one satisfactory solution for significantly biased items: elimination.

Rank Order of Item Difficulties and Delta Decrements. The groups $\times$ items interaction is composed of ordinal and disordinal components and their interaction. The *disordinal* component is the result of items having a different *rank order* of difficulties (i.e., p or Δ values) in the major and minor groups. The *ordinal* component is a result of relative differences in item difficulties that nevertheless have the same rank order of difficulty in both groups. The interaction of the ordinal and disordinal components reflects differences in the relative difficulties of items owing to their having different rank orders of difficulty in the two groups.

If the groups $\times$ items interaction in the ANOVA of the items $\times$ subjects $\times$ groups matrix is significant, we may wish to analyze the interaction further to determine whether it is due mostly to ordinal or disordinal group differences in item difficulties. Or, even if the groups $\times$ items interaction is not significant, we may wish further to demonstrate the degree of similarity between the groups by showing the degree of their similarity on the ordinal and disordinal effects separately.

This analysis can be achieved by the following method:

1. All the test items are simply *ranked* for difficulty within groups A and B, and Spearman's rank order correlation, rho or ρ_{AB}, is computed between the two sets of ranks. (It makes no difference whether we rank the item p values or Δ values, as they have exactly the same rank order.) The coefficient ρ is a correlation coefficient, interpreted like the Pearson r. In this case ρ indicates the degree of similarity between the groups in the order of item difficulties. The value of $1 - \rho^2$ estimates the proportion of the groups $\times$ items interaction variance attributable to the purely disordinal aspect of the groups $\times$ items interaction.

2. Within the major group, the n items of the test are ranked in the order of their Δ values, going from the largest to the smallest. The items are arranged in exactly the same order in the minor group (regardless of the items' actual order of difficulty in the minor group).

3. Then the Δ decrements are obtained within each group. A Δ decrement is the difference in Δ values between adjacent items when the items are ranked as just described.[14] For example, if there are four items, numbered 1 to 4, which in the major group have a rank order of Δ values of 1, 2, 3, 4, respectively, then the Δ decrements will be $\Delta_1 - \Delta_2$, $\Delta_2 - \Delta_3$, and $\Delta_3 - \Delta_4$. In the major group all the Δ decrements are necessarily zero or greater than zero. It can be seen that all the inter-item variance (in the major group) due to the rank order of item difficulties is completely eliminated by this procedure, leaving only the variance due to the unequal difficulty decrements between items.

4. Finally, we compute the Pearson r between the Δ decrements of the major and minor groups. The r indicates the degree of group resemblance in relative item difficulties when the rank order of item difficulties is eliminated, and r^2 is the proportion of variance in the minor group's Δ decrements that is predictable from the items' Δ decrements in the major group. The value $\rho^2(1 - r^2)$ is the proportion of the groups $\times$ items interaction variance that is due to group differences in the relative difficulties of items over and above that which is attributable to the items' differences in rank order; in other words, it is the purely ordinal component of the groups $\times$ items interaction. The *residual* proportion of the groups $\times$ items interaction variance, that is, the part attributable jointly to the interaction of group differences in the ordinal *and* disordinal aspects of item difficulties, is $\rho^2 r^2$. The following table summarizes the analysis of the groups $\times$ items interaction variance, where ρ is the rank order correlation between the groups' item difficulties and r is the Pearson correlation between the groups' Δ decrements:

Source of Interaction Variance	*Proportion of Variance*
Disordinal, i.e., group differences in rank order of item difficulties	$1 - \rho^2$
Ordinal, i.e., group differences in Δ decrements	$\rho^2(1 - r^2)$
Residual, i.e., interaction of disordinal $\times$ ordinal	$\rho^2 r^2$

The Item Characteristic Curve. The ICC is commonly used to reveal generally defective items in a test, but it is also one of the most direct and sensitive methods for detecting biased items. The ICC is a graph of the percentage passing an item as a function of total raw score on the test.[15]

If the test scores measure a single ability throughout their full range, and if every item in the test measures this same ability, then we should expect that the probability of passing any single item in the test will be a simple increasing monotonic function of ability, as indicated by the total raw score on the test. Ideally, the function approximates the ogive* of the normal curve. Persons with more of the ability (i.e., a higher score) measured by the test should, on the average, have a higher probability of passing any given item in the test than persons with less ability (i.e., a lower score). The graph of this relationship of the percentage of all persons at each raw score who pass a given item is the item characteristic curve (ICC). The ICCs of three items are shown in Figure 9.13.

Item 1 is an example of a defective item, as revealed by the anomalous ICC. An item with such an ICC should be eliminated from the test, as the percentage passing the item is not a monotonically increasing function of the raw score. Persons of high ability on the test as a whole do less well on item 1 than do persons of intermediate ability. In many cases, the nature of the item's defect can be inferred from a critical examination of the item. For example, the following item from a college test of general cultural knowledge produced an ICC like that of item 1 in Figure 9.13.

A musical work entitled "The Emperor" was composed by
(*a*) Haydn,   (*b*) Mozart,   (*c*) Beethoven,   (*d*) Schubert,   (*e*) Wagner.

Beethoven is keyed as the correct answer. Many persons only slightly acquainted with classical music have heard of Beethoven's "Emperor Concerto." But more knowledgeable music lovers will also think of Haydn's "Emperor Quartet," which is generally less known than the Beethoven concerto (and probably unknown to the item writer). Thus the responses of the most knowledgeable persons are divided between the multiple-choice alternatives *a* and *c*, which causes the more informed persons to do less well on this item than persons with only moderate musical knowledge.

Figure 9.13.   Item characteristic curves of three test items. Item 1 is a clearly defective item.

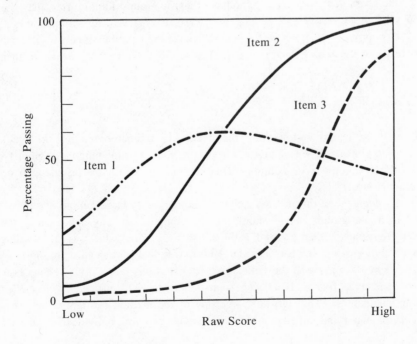

Items 2 and 3 both show highly acceptable ICCs. Item 3 is obviously much more difficult than item 2.

Notice that the ICC does not depend on the form of the distribution of raw scores. Therefore, if the test measures the same ability in two or more different groups, we should expect the groups to have the same ICC for any given item in the test, regardless of any difference between the groups in the distribution of total scores on the test.

Hence, a reasonable statistical criterion for detecting a biased item is to test the null hypothesis of no difference between the ICCs of the major and minor groups. In test construction, the items that show a significant group difference in ICCs should be eliminated and new ICCs plotted for all the remaining items, based on the total raw scores after the biased items have been eliminated. The procedure can be reiterated until all the biased items have been eliminated. The essential rationale of this ICC criterion of item bias is that any persons showing the same ability as measured by the whole test should have the same probability of passing any given item that measures that ability, regardless of the person's race, social class, sex, or any other background characteristics. In other words, the same proportions of persons from each group should pass any given item of the test, provided that the persons all earned the same total score on the test. In comparing the ICCs of groups that differ in overall mean score on the test, it is more accurate to plot the proportion of each group passing the item as a function of *estimated true scores* within each group (rather than raw scores on the test), to minimize group differences in the ICCs due solely to errors of measurement.

Chi squared provides an appropriate statistical test of the null hypothesis in this case. For a given item, one determines the obtained frequencies O and the expected frequencies E of *passes* (+) and *failures* ($-$) in the major (A) and minor (B) groups for each total score. The obtained frequencies O_A^+ and O_B^+ and O_A^- and O_B^- are simply the numbers of persons with a given total score in the major or minor groups who passed or failed the given item. Under the hypothesis that the groups do not differ, the expected frequency for group A is $E_A = N_A(O_A + O_B)/(N_A + N_B)$, and for group B it is $E_B = N_B(O_A + O_B)/(N_A + N_B)$, where N_A and N_B are the total number of persons in groups A and B, respectively, who earned the same total score on the test. Chi squared, then, is

$$\chi^2 = \sum \left[\frac{(O_A^+ - E_A^+)^2}{E_A^+} + \frac{(O_B^+ - E_B^+)^2}{E_B^+} + \frac{(O_A^- - E_A^-)^2}{E_A^-} + \frac{(O_B^- - E_B^-)^2}{E_B^-} \right]. \qquad (9.17)$$

($\sum$ indicates that the expression within the brackets is summed over all of the total score cohorts.) The χ^2 has $s(g - 1)$ degrees of freedom, where g is the number of groups and s is the number of total score cohorts. (This method can of course be adapted for any number of groups.)

A disadvantage of this method is that it requires a very large sample size in both the major and minor groups, as χ^2 should not be computed in any cohort in which the expected frequency, either E_A or E_B, is less than 10. The usual way of handling the computation of χ^2 when any E is less than 10 is to combine enough adjacent score cohorts to yield E's of 10 or more. If the samples are not especially large, it may be necessary to combine as many as five or six adjacent score cohorts to yield sufficiently large E's from which to calculate χ^2. The statistical precision of the method is slightly weakened, of course, if the major and minor groups' scores are not proportionally distributed the same within each combined score interval, and usually they will not be distributed the same if there is a marked difference between the overall groups' means. The overall lower group will tend to have the lower mean score within any score interval. This can be corrected by eliminating persons from the larger group to make the proportional distributions of scores within the interval nearly the same for both groups. When this is done, even quite coarse grouping, creating as few as five or six score intervals in all, can result in a satisfactory chi squared test of item bias.

Usually not all significantly biased items are biased in the same direction. Some item biases favor the major group and some favor the minor group in the total score. One can estimate the net amount of directional bias by determining the difference between the group means when the significantly biased items are included in the total score on the test and when they are excluded. A *t* test for correlated means can then be applied to determine whether this mean difference is statistically significant (see Guilford, 1956, p. 186). The outcome of such an analysis would indicate whether the various item biases in the test significantly favor the major or the minor group in the overall score. However, the test may be biased *whether or not* it systematically favors one group, if there is a larger number of significantly biased items than could be expected by chance alone. A test composed of a large proportion of significantly biased items, some that favor the major and some the minor group, but in which the item biases are balanced out so as not to favor either group in the overall test score, cannot be claimed to measure one and the same ability on the same scale in both groups.

Item Correlation Methods. In test construction, one of the principal criteria for item selection is the item's correlation with total score on the test. Items that do not correlate significantly with the total score cannot contribute to the true variance in test scores but only to the error variance; they are therefore discarded in the process of test construction. Items, of course, differ in their degree of correlation with the ability measured by the test, as indexed by the total score, so that there is always a range of item × total score correlations, all of which are distributed significantly above zero in a well-constructed test.

In an unbiased test ideally the item × score correlation for any given item should be the same in the major and minor groups. Unfortunately, this hypothesis is difficult to test rigorously, for three reasons: (1) the item × score correlation has a rather large sampling error, (2) the item × score correlations are usually fairly homogeneous, and (3) the item × score correlation is affected by the difficulty of the item, so that if the difficulty of the item is markedly different in the major and minor groups, the item × score correlations in the two groups will not be directly comparable. (The biserial correlation[16] r_b seems preferable to the point-biserial correlation r_{pbi} because it is somewhat less affected by item difficulty.) Despite these limitations, certain indications of bias may be gleaned by comparing the item × score biserial correlations in the major and minor groups. The frequency distributions of all the r_b values for the *n* items in the test should be approximately the same for both groups. The number of nonsignificant correlations should be very few and not differ significantly in the two groups. When nonsignificant correlations are found, one should look for ceiling or floor effects, that is, extremely easy or extremely difficult items, that result in low correlations because of the restriction of variance on the item. We should also expect to find a significant positive correlation between the item × score biserial correlations of the major and minor groups, although this correlation could be greatly attenuated by the homogeneity of r_b, sampling error, and perturbations due to group differences in item difficulty. No one has yet devised a satisfactory statistical test of the overall significance of the differences between the major and minor group's item × score biserial correlations. However, the most probably biased items may be identified as those for which the item × score biserial correlation differs between groups by more than twice the standard error of the difference between the r_b values.

The item × test biserial r_b makes possible the testing of a hypothesis of considerable interest. If the test measures the same ability in the major and minor groups, and if the groups differ on this ability measured by the score on the whole test, then we should expect that the items that best measure ability *within* each group (i.e., those items with the largest item × score r_b) should also discriminate most *between* the groups. This hypothesis can be tested by first obtaining the item × score r_b for every item, within each group, then obtraining the item × groups correlation (phi/phi max),[17] and finally obtaining the correlation (r) between r_b and phi/phi max over all of the items, for each group. If this correlation is positive and significant, the hypothesis is borne out; namely, those items that correlate most highly with the ability measured by the test *within* each group also discriminate most highly *between* the groups. By splitting the major group (and the minor group) into random halves and performing this analysis in the two halves, one can determine if the correlation between the item × score correlation and item × groups correlation is significantly larger for the split-halves of the *same* group or for the split-halves *across* the major and minor groups. A same-group split-halves correlation significantly larger than the across-groups split-halves correlation would indicate bias.

Factor Analysis Criteria of Bias.   In the first part of this chapter it was noted that a test can be regarded as unbiased if it predicts the performance of different persons on an external criterion with equal accuracy regardless of their group memberships. One condition that we should expect if this is true is that the correlation between test scores and criterion measures should be the same in the major and minor groups.

The test and the criterion are correlated because they share certain factors in common. If, for example, the test score X measures a single factor F in common with the criterion measures C, then the correlation r_{XC} between test scores and criterion measures can be expressed as the product of their correlations with the common factor, that is, $r_{XC} = r_{XF} \times r_{CF}$. Therefore, if the test score measures different factors in the major and minor groups, that is, if r_{XF} is different in the two groups, then it is highly improbable that r_{XC} will be the same in both groups. (It could conceivably be the same, however, if the test measured two different factors, F_1 and F_2 in the major and minor groups, respectively, and yet each factor had exactly the same correlation with the criterion, that is, $r_{F_1C} = r_{F_2C}$.) If it can be shown that r_{XF} is significantly different in the major and minor groups, it is so highly likely that the test will predict a criterion differentially for persons depending on their group membership as to constitute strong evidence of bias. As Humphreys and Taber first pointed out,

> Regression differences can confidently be expected across groups . . . if the initial factor analyses of scores in the two groups indicate factorial dissimilarity. Comparability of factors and factor loadings in the groups is not a necessary condition for near identity of slopes of regression lines in the mathematical sense, but the probability that factor loadings of a given criterion would exactly compensate for dif-

ferences in predictor loadings is very small. If the predictors are to be used for several criteria, the probability that factor loadings for every criterion will compensate for differences in predictors becomes vanishingly small. . . . If factor loadings are comparable, it is reasonable to expect parallel or very nearly parallel regression lines for advantaged and disadvantaged groups.   (Humphreys & Taber, 1973, pp. 107–108)

Thus, factor analysis of a test or a battery of tests or other predictors in adequate samples of the major and minor groups can be used to detect predictive bias indirectly, without need for the more time-consuming and expensive direct determination of the test's predictive validity in terms of an external criterion.

The concept of construct validity also implies that the test score variance has the same factorial composition in the major and minor groups.

Therefore, if we can reject the null hypothesis that there is no difference between groups in the factorial composition of their test scores, we can claim that the test is biased. For this statistical purpose, a principal components analysis seems preferable to any rotated factor solution, because the process of factor rotation itself can magnify the effects of sampling errors in the basic correlations. (However, rotated factors may be more amenable to psychological interpretation). Furthermore, if we are concerned about bias in the total score on the test (or test battery), our attention should be primarily focused on the first principal component, as it accounts for the largest proportion of the variance in total scores. The variance of total scores on a good test is concentrated mostly in the first principal component, and, therefore, we should be most concerned that the first principal component is the same, within the margin of sampling error, in the major and minor groups if the test scores are to be interpreted as unbiased measures.

Principal components analysis can be applied to the matrix of correlations among the single items comprising the test or to the correlations among subtests (homogeneous groups of items) that make up the total test. If items are used, the item intercorrelations should be obtained by phi/phi max, so that group differences in item difficulty will not enter into the matrix of intercorrelations and produce a ''difficulty factor'' on which the major and minor groups may differ. As emphasized previously, a group difference in difficulty cannot itself be a criterion of test bias, because it completely begs the question of whether the groups differ because of test bias or because of some other factors.

Since either items or subtests may be subjected to principal components analysis, for simplicity we shall henceforth refer to either item scores or subtest scores as *units* of the test. A principal components analysis of the units is performed in the major and minor groups separately. Two questions, then, must be answered: (1) ''Do the same factors emerge in the major and minor groups?'' and (2) ''Do the units have the same factor loadings in the two groups?'' Both conditions are important, because, even if the test measures the same factors in both groups but the units have different loadings on the factors in the two groups, the factors will be weighted differently in the total score depending on the person's group membership. The total score, therefore, would not be an equivalent measure for persons from different groups, even when such persons have numerically equal scores. An objective criterion, such as varimax, for orthogonal rotation of the principal components to approximate simple structure facilities identification of the factors measured by the test. The same criterion for the number of principal components to be rotated, such as retaining only those components with eigenvalues greater than 1, should apply to both the major and minor groups. Simple inspection of the rotated factors usually reveals whether the same factors have emerged in both groups, although sophisticated statistical tests of factorial invariance across groups have been devised (e.g., McGaw & Jöreskog, 1971).

If one of the two groups yields one or more different or additional factors than are found in the other group, it is instructive to examine the units that contribute the most variance to these factors, that is, the units with the largest factor loadings. They are very likely biased units; discarding them should produce greater factorial similarity of the groups.

Factor analysts have devised rather complex methods for comparing factors across different populations (see Cattell, 1978, pp. 251–270; Kaiser, Hunka, & Bianchini, 1971), but a rough and ready index of factorial similarity that is probably satisfactory for our purpose is simply the Pearsonian correlation between the factor loadings of the major and minor groups for any given factor. This does not provide a statistical test of significance, but only an index of factorial similarity between groups. If the total score of the test is the point of contention with respect to bias, then the correlation between the two groups' loadings of the test's units on the first principal component is of primary interest, since the first principal component is the largest source of variance in the total scores. If we can reject the null hypothesis that the groups do not differ on the first principal component, we need go no further and can conclude that the test's total scores are biased. Elimination of the offending units (i.e., those units whose factor loadings show the greatest discrepancies between groups) may be found to improve the test upon reanalysis, using the same method.

We shall consider two statistical tests of the null hypothesis of no group difference in the loadings of the test's units on the first principal component.

1. This method should be used only if the major and minor samples have equal N's and if N is at least 200 in each sample. It is a test of the hypothesis that the *pattern* of loadings of the test's units on the first principal component (or any other component or factor to which the method is applied) is not significantly different in the major and minor groups.

Randomly split both the major and minor groups into split-halves; do a principal components analysis on each of the four split halves; obtain correlations among the loadings of the first principal components of all six of the possible combinations of the split-halves. That is, if the two halves of the major group are A and a and the two halves of the minor group are B and b, then we obtain the correlations r_{Aa} and r_{Bb} (i.e., the within-group split-half correlation) and r_{AB}, r_{Ab}, r_{aB}, r_{ab} (i.e., the between-group split-half correlations). Average the two within-group correlations via Fisher's z transformation, to obtain $\bar{z}_W$; and average the four between-group correlations to obtain $\bar{z}_B$. If the test's first principal component is the same factor in the major and minor groups, the pattern of loadings on the first principal component should be as alike *between* the major and minor groups as *within* the groups. The null hypothesis, then, is the expectation that $\bar{z}_W = \bar{z}_B$ or $\bar{z}_W - \bar{z}_B = 0$. A chi squared test of the null hypothesis is

$$\chi^2 = (n - 3)(\bar{z}_W - \bar{z}_B)^2/2. \tag{9.18}$$

with 1 *df*, where *n* is the number of units of the test that went into the principal components analysis.

2. This is a test of the overall difference between the loadings of the first principal components (or other factors) of the major and minor groups; it simultaneously tests for differences in *pattern* of loadings and *size* of loadings and, therefore, is a more complete and stringent test than the previously described method. Also, it does not require that the major and minor samples be of equal size.

First, each of the loadings of the first principal component (or other factor) is transformed to Fisher's *z*. For each unit, then, the transformed loadings in the major and minor groups are z_A and z_B, respectively. A chi squared test of the null hypothesis that the loadings of the first principal component do not differ between the groups is

$$\chi^2 = \frac{\sum\limits_{1}^{n} (z_A - z_B)^2}{\dfrac{n}{N_A - 3} + \dfrac{n}{N_B - 3}} \, , \tag{9.19}$$

with 1 *df*, where *n* is the number of units of the test and N_A and N_B are the number of subjects in the major and minor groups, respectively.

3. Finally, because principal components and factor analysis are based on the matrix of intercorrelations among all of the variables (in this case the units of the test), one can test the null hypothesis that the correlation matrices of the major and minor groups do not differ in the population and that all the observed differences between the correlation matrices of the two samples are attributable to sampling error. Two correlation matrices that do not differ significantly can be presumed to have the same factorial structure.

Unfortunately, there is no computationally simple but exact statistical test of the significance of the difference between correlation matrices obtrained in samples from two populations. The fact that the correlations are correlated among themselves within each sample shrinks the standard error of the difference between correlations. Because the root mean squared differences between correlations are more or less correspondingly shrunken, however, a simple but only approximate chi squared test of the difference between the correlation matrices in two samples is possible, as follows. The $k(k - 1)/2$ correlations, where *k* is the number of variables, in each matrix are transformed to Fisher's *z*'s. The squared differences between the analogous transformed correlations z_{ij} of the major (*A*) and minor (*B*) groups are averaged and divided by the standard error of the difference. This can be written as

$$\chi^2 = \frac{\Sigma(z_{ij_A} - z_{ij_B})^2}{\dfrac{n}{N_A - 3} + \dfrac{n}{N_B - 3}} \, , \tag{9.20}$$

with 1 *df*, where *n* is the number of correlations (i.e., $n = k(k - 1)/2$, where *k* is the number of variables in the correlation matrix) and N_A and N_B are the numbers of subjects in the major and minor groups. Because this test is only approximate, it probably should not be interpreted when the χ^2 falls between 1.64 and 6.64, that is, unless *p* is greater than .20

(nonsignificant) or less than .01 (significant). If p falls between .01 and .20, the results of this approximate test are in doubt, and one must resort to some more exact but much more complex and laborious statistical test of the equality of two correlation matrices (see Timm, 1975, pp. 547–549).

When the major and minor samples are large, each with $N > 200$, one can obtain a simple index of the degree of similarity between the correlation matrices of the two groups. *Similarity* between two correlation matrices refers here not to the overall magnitude of the correlations in the matrix but to the *pattern* of the correlation coefficients. The factorial structure of a correlation matrix is related to the pattern of correlations rather than to their absolute magnitude.

Each group is randomly split in half, and the $k(k - 1)/2$ intercorrelations among the k variables are obtained within each random half-sample. (The four half-samples are labeled A and a for the major groups and B and b for the minor groups.) Then Pearson r is obtained between the six pairs of correlation matrices (i.e., the $k(k - 1)/2$ paired sets of analogous correlations from two matrices), $A \times a$, $B \times b$, $A \times B$, $A \times b$, $a \times B$, and $a \times b$.

The key question, then, is whether the *within*-group correlations ($A \times a$ and $B \times b$) are significantly larger than the *between*-group correlations ($A \times B$, $A \times b$, $a \times B$, and $a \times b$). The correlations are transformed to Fisher's z's, and the mean of the two within-group transformed correlations, $\bar{z}_W$ is compared with the mean of the four between-group transformed correlations, $\bar{z}_B$. If $\bar{z}_W$ is less than $\bar{z}_B$, there is no basis for claiming that the correlation matrices of major and minor groups have different patterns and hence different factorial structures. If $\bar{z}_W$ is greater than $\bar{z}_B$, the difference can be tested for significance by means of chi squared:

$$\chi^2 = \tfrac{1}{4} (\bar{z}_W - \bar{z}_B)^2 (k^2 - k - 6), \qquad \textbf{(9.21)}$$

with 1 df, where k is the number of variables entering into the original correlation matrix. The corresponding p value of the χ^2 is just half the tabled p value in this case, as it is a one-tailed test of the hypothesis that $\bar{z}_W$ is greater than $\bar{z}_B$. (The hypothesis that $\bar{z}_W$ is greater than *or* less than $\bar{z}_B$ would call for a two-tailed test.)

Matched Groups and Pseudogroups. All the foregoing methods of internal analysis for detecting culture bias in tests depend on two basic assumptions. The first basic assumption underlying the foregoing methods of internal analysis is that cultural differences between groups will interact with item content or item types and that group differences in cultural background should not produce equal effects on all of the items in a heterogeneous test. Rejection of this assumption can be cogent only if evidence can be adduced for the presence of some cultural factor that is hypothesized to have a uniformly enhancing or depressing effect across all the items in the test. Such a hypothesis must, of course, be formulated so as to be empirically testable if it is to be of any scientific value.

The second basic assumption underlying the foregoing methods of internal analysis is that cultural groups × items interaction is not perfectly correlated with ability levels × items interaction *within* the cultural groups. If the test score distributions of the major and minor groups differ in mean or variance and there is a significant groups × items interaction (or other internal indicator of bias), it must be determined whether the interaction is attributable solely to differences in ability level rather than to some other aspect of the group difference. It is quite ossible that ability level interacts with item difficulty, in which case a significant groups × items interaction might reflect only the fact of the groups' mean difference in the ability measured by the test rather than a difference involving cultural bias. In other words, we need to distinguish between a *culture* × *item* interaction and an *ability* × *item* interaction. This distinction can be made by means of matched-groups and pseudogroups designs.

In the *matched-groups design* we test the hypothesis that the major and minor groups, when matched on total test score distributions, do not differ on any of the internal indices of cultural bias, such as groups × items interaction, rank order of item difficulties, correlation of delta decrements, and factorial structure. The hypothesis states, in other words, that there are no features of the test that discriminate between individuals from the major and minor groups who obtain the same total score on the test.

If any of the previously described methods of detecting bias should produce significant results on random samples of the major and minor groups, the method should be reapplied to the major and minor groups after they have been matched on ability, to see if the significant effect was the result of an ability difference between the groups rather than a cultural difference. The best method for obtaining matched groups is to pair up individuals from the major and minor groups with identical total test scores, obtaining as many identically matched pairs of major–minor persons as possible from the available test data. A *cultural* difference, if it exists, should be detectable by the internal analyses even when the major and minor groups are matched on overall test score. If the result of the analysis is nonsignificant after matching, it can be concluded that the significance of the result from the unmatched groups was due to the groups' difference in ability level rather than to cultural bias.

The *pseudogroups design* permits a further test of this hypothesis. In the pseudogroups design a subgroup of persons from the major group is formed that conforms to the distribution of total test scores in the minor group, or vice versa. Thus, we create a pseudo minor group or a pseudo major group for comparison with the real major group or the real minor group, respectively. Then, for example, if the pseudogroups × items interaction is of about the same magnitude as the real groups × items interaction, it is reasonable to conclude that the interaction is due to an ability difference rather than to a culture difference, as the real group and pseudogroup in this analysis are both made up of persons from the same cultural group.

If it is argued that the different ability levels of racial groups are related to *social-class* cultural differences rather than to racial differences, then one must divide the major and minor groups into subgroups on the basis of social class and test for social class × item interactions, within racial groups. It must also be determined if the social class × items interaction is not attributable to an ability levels × items interaction, by using the matched-group design (i.e., matching social-class groups on overall score and testing the matched groups × items interaction).

The most powerful pseudogroups design for detecting ability × item interaction free of culture × item interaction can be achieved by making up two pseudogroups out of pairs of siblings who differ as much in total test score as do the major and minor groups. Siblings reared together show ability differences, but such differences cannot be due to differences in cultural background. If two groups of siblings, with one member of each sibling pair assigned to each group, are selected so as to reproduce the means and variances of the major and minor groups, and if these two sibling groups then simulate the actual major versus minor groups × items interaction (or other internal indices of bias), it can be presumed that the interaction, and so on, is an ability × items interaction rather than a sign of cultural bias. The only possible alternative conclusion would be that the cultural differences between groups simulate ability differences within either cultural group. This would not seem to be a very compelling conclusion in the absence of independently supporting evidence.

In testing children, *age differences* in total test score within a given group may be used like pseudogroups formed on the basis of total score. If the internal analyses show major versus minor groups × items interaction, and so on, these may be due to group differences in developmental rates rather than to cultural differences. To test this hypothesis, we repeat the internal analyses, contrasting the major and minor groups each at *different ages,* to see what happens to the groups × items interaction. The groups × items interaction could disappear when the major group is compared with a minor group one or two years older (or younger). Conversely, one may be able to simulate the major versus minor groups × items interaction by contrasting different age groups *within* either the major or minor group. The finding that the groups × items interaction can be made to appear or disappear by the manipulation of age of the contrasted samples, *between* the major and minor groups and *within* either group, is consistent with the hypothesis that the groups × items interaction is attributable to the major and minor groups' differential developmental status rather than to cultural bias. The only possible counterhypothesis would be that cultural differences between groups simulate developmental differences within groups in respect to interactions with items, factorial structure of the item intercorrelations, and so on. As an ad hoc hypothesis, this carries no conviction. Independently supporting evidence would be required to lend scientific credibility to this counterhypothesis.

Distractor Analysis

Many objective-type tests are composed of items with multiple-choice response alternatives, usually five or six, one of which is keyed as the correct answer. The incorrect alternatives are termed *distractors*. Although test constructors usually try to make all the distractors more or less equally attractive to all persons who do not select the correct answer, the attempt is seldom entirely successful. More often we find that the several distractors for any given item differ quite markedly in attractiveness, as shown by the percentages of the group that select each distractor. Although it presumably requires more knowledge or ability to select the correct answer than an incorrect answer, there is little doubt that partial knowledge or ability often make for differential elimination among the several distractors. Also, it is well known that the persons who miss a given item do not pick a distractor at random. Guessing is rarely a random action; it is usually based on partial information, misinformation, a misunderstanding of the question, or a conscious error in reasoning. The person's choices of distractors usually have as much test–retest stability as his or her choices of correct responses.

If a test is unbiased with respect to two groups, we should expect the distractors to have the same relative degree of attraction within each group, in which case the distractors for any given item would have the same relative frequencies of "takers" in both groups.

Thus, for every item, we can test the null hypothesis that the major and minor groups do not differ in the relative frequencies of choices of distractors. Items for which the null hypothesis can be rejected at some predetermined level of significance p are thereby identified as probably biased. Because the number of items showing a significant group difference at the given p level expected by sheer chance is pn, where n is the number of items, we can firmly establish that the significant items are biased only by replication of the analysis with new samples of the major and minor populations. However, if the number of significant items is appreciably greatly than pn, the test as a whole may be suspected of bias.

The simplest statistical test of the null hypothesis in this case is chi squared. The correct response, of course, is omitted from the error analysis, and the frequencies of the major and minor groups are compared across distractors. For example,

Test Item No. 10	*Distractors*			
	1	*2*	*3*	*4*
Group *A*	60	25	41	16
Group *B*	76	32	58	35

$$\chi^2 = 2.66, \quad df = 3, \quad .30 < p < .50.$$

If our level of significance for rejecting the null hypothesis is any value of p less than .30, we could not reject the null hypothesis. In other words, groups A and B do not differ significantly in their choice of distractors on test item no. 10.

If a significant chi squared is found, then, to conclude that there is bias, one must rule out that it is not an overall ability level $\times$ distractor interaction responsible for the significant chi squared. This calls for applications of the same type of matched-groups or pseudogroups treatment described in the preceding section. In analyzing possible bias in children's tests, age manipulation of the contrasted samples, as indicated in the previous section, is also highly advisable, as the relative attractiveness among some distractors has been found to be age related in connection with developmental trends in cognitive ability.

SUMMARY

This chapter presents definitions of test bias and the rationale for various criteria and methods for the statistical detection of test bias. (The empirical results of applying these criteria and methods to test data on various racial and cultural groups in the United States are presented in Chapters 10 and 11.)

The presence of a difference in central tendency between the distributions of test scores obtained by two populations is not in itself evidence that the test is biased with respect to one or both populations. Also, the fact that a test has been standardized in a particular population does not imply *ipso facto* that the test is biased when used in a different population. A clear conceptual distinction is made between the *culture loading* of a test and *test bias*. Culture loading per se is not evidence of bias. Culture loading is a subjective judgment of the temporal and cultural specificity or generality of test items. Bias is a purely statistical concept that is applicable to a test when it is used in two or more distinguishable populations.

Bias is also clearly distinguished from the concept of "unfairness." The concept of "unfairness" versus the "fair" use of tests is a judgment based on a philosophic position regarding the way that test scores should be used, particularly in educational and employment selection. Once a policy on the fair use of tests in selection has been decided on philosophic grounds, objective statistical criteria can be applied to determine if the test and selection procedures in fact meet the specified conditions for fairness.

The main philosophic positions underlying differences in policy regarding the fair use of tests in the selection of majority and minority applicants are unqualified individualism, qualified individualism, and quotas. *Unqualified individualism* aims to maximize predictive validity for individuals by using any predictor variables available. *Qualified individualism* has the same aim, with the restriction that the individual's group membership (e.g., race, sex, social class) per se cannot be used as a predictor variable. *Quotas* permit the use of different selection criteria for different groups to achieve more equal representation of the different groups among those who are selected. Different "statistical models" of selection are consistent with one or another of these philosophic positions regarding fair selection.

Examination of various selection models proposed in the literature reveals that (1) some models are internally inconsistent in terms of their own implicit or explicit philosophic position, (2) some models that superficially appear to be nonquota models are in fact disguised methods of quota selection, (3) some selection models can result in "fair selection" using *either* unbiased *or* biased tests, whereas other selection models can achieve "fair selection" only with the use of unbiased tests, and (4) only one selection model (Expected Utility Model) is capable of being entirely internally consistent and generalizable to any selection strategy, with the great advantage that every element of the particular philosophic position governing the selection process is wholly explicit. Every other selection model, in fact, is merely a special case of the Expected Utility Model, which is the only model that is entirely defensible from a statistical and logical standpoint, regardless of one's philosophy of fair selection. The Expected Utility Model is applicable to every selection philosophy and forces the implications of one's philosophy of fair selection to be absolutely explicit in the selection procedure.

Psychometric bias per se can be defined and identified in terms of two main classes of statistical criteria: (1) external or predictive validity criteria and (2) internal or construct validity criteria.

In terms of predictive validity, a test is defined as biased with respect to two (or more) groups when either the regression of the criterion variable on estimated true scores or the standard error of estimates, or both, are different (i.e., a statistically significant difference) for the two groups. This means that for an unbiased test any given estimated true score based on the test yields the same prediction of criterion performance, with the same degree of accuracy, regardless of the group membership (e.g., race, class, sex) of the person obtaining that score. If we cannot reject the null hypothesis (i.e., no difference in the regressions or standard errors of estimate for the two groups), the test is presumed to be *unbiased,* although of course this can never be absolutely proved, for the simple reason that in statistics one can never prove the null hypothesis.

It may come as a surprise to many that even a biased test, as here defined, can nevertheless be used to achieve fair selection, provided that the selection philosophy permits the use of the persons' group membership as well as test scores as predictor variables.

Internal and construct validity criteria of psychometric bias, although wholly objective and statistical, are much more complex than criteria involving merely predictive validity. Statistical and psychometric methods of "internal" and construct analysis of tests are explicated that permit the testing of various hypotheses of differences that would seem highly probable if the test were in fact culturally biased with respect to any two or more groups of interest. If, however, the test behaves in essentially the same way for different groups with respect to a number of features of test performance, the test is presumed to be unbiased for those groups. The more features of the test on which the groups do not differ, the stronger is the presumption that the test is unbiased. The features on which tests are hypothesized to differ in various populations if the tests are in fact culturally biased include internal consistency reliability, temporal stability, correlation of raw scores with chronological age, kinship correlations and absolute differences between persons of a given degree of kinship (e.g., siblings), the statistical interaction of test items by group membership, the rank order of item difficulties, item intercorrelations, the factor structure of tests (or items) and the magnitudes of factor loadings, the item characteristic curve, and the frequencies of choice of the various error distractors in multiple-choice test items. Methods are also described for determining whether group differences in any of these features are merely a result of a difference in overall level of ability, as compared with a true cultural difference. The two cannot be distinguished, of course, if one proposes the purely ad hoc and quite implausible hypothesis that the cultural differences *between* two population groups perfectly simulate all the "internal" psychometric effects associated with ability level differences *within* each population group.

Significant internal evidences of bias, as described here, often do not consistently favor (or disfavor) one or the other of two subpopulations, as the various item biases tend to cancel one another in the total score. However, a test in which the item biases with respect to different subpopulations are "balanced out" is still regarded as a biased test from a psychometric standpoint. Objectively identified test biases of any kind, regardless of whether they "favor" or "disfavor" any particular subpopulation in which the test is used, are psychometrically undesirable, and every effort should be made to minimize or eliminate bias. Methods for "trouble-shooting" test bias are proposed, in addition to methods for achieving the fair use even of biased tests, which is possible *if* the tests have adequate predictive validity *within* each subpopulation.

NOTES

1. The *standard error of the regression slope* b_{YX} is

$$SE_{b_{YX}} = \frac{\sigma_Y}{\sigma_X} \sqrt{\frac{1 - r_{XY}^2}{N - 1}} = \frac{SE_Y}{\sigma_X \sqrt{N - 1}} , \qquad (9N.1)$$

where N is the number of persons in the sample.

The standard error of the difference between the regression slopes in two independent samples, A and B, is

$$SE_{b_{\text{diff}}} = \sqrt{SE_{b_{YX_A}}^2 + SE_{b_{YX_B}}^2}.$$ (9N.2)

The appropriate test of significance is the t test:

$$t = (b_{YX_A} - b_{YX_B})/SE_{b_{\text{diff}}}, \quad \text{with } df = N_A + N_B - 4.$$ (9N.3)

The *standard error of the Y intercept k* is

$$SE_{k_Y} = SE_{b_{YX}} \sqrt{\Sigma X^2/N}.$$ (9N.4)

Equation 9N.4 is used for testing the significance of the difference between the obtained sample intercept and some theoretical value or a population value, but it is seldom used in computing the standard error of the difference between the intercepts of two samples. It is not a sufficiently stringent test, because the standard error increases with distance from the mean and therefore is quite large for values as far out on the score distribution as the intercept usually is.

The significance of the difference between two sample intercepts is properly tested by the analysis of covariance, with the predictor variable X as the control variable and the criterion variable Y as the adjusted variable. If the covariate-adjusted means of Y in the major and minor groups differ from one another significantly as determined by the F statistic of the analysis of covariance, one can conclude that the intercepts also differ significantly. The validity of this test of the intercepts depends on failure to reject a prior test of the hypothesis of equality of the slopes of the two regression lines. If the two regression lines deviate significantly from parallel (i.e., they have different slopes), the analysis of covariance is an inappropriate test of the significance of the difference between the intercepts. The theory and computational procedures of this covariance test are described by Marascuilo (1971, Ch. 18).

The analysis of covariance, of course, requires that we possess all the scores. But what if we wish to test the equality of intercepts and do not have at our personal disposal all of the original measurements? There is a satisfactory solution to this problem that will lead to the same conclusion as the analysis of covariance method, and it is applicable if we cannot reject the null hypothesis that the regression lines of the two groups are parallel. This method takes a different approach based on the fact that, if the regression lines are parallel and if their intercepts do not differ, then the predicted mean of the minor group, when it is estimated from its own regression equation, symbolized as $\hat{Y}_{B \cdot \bar{X}_B}$ (which is the same as $\bar{Y}_B$), will be equal to the predicted mean of the minor group, when it is estimated from the regression equation of the major group, the estimate symbolized as $\hat{Y}_{B \cdot X_A}$. (Notice that $\bar{X}_B = X_A$ is a fixed value of X.) Therefore, we test the null hypothesis that $\hat{Y}_{B \cdot \bar{X}_B} - \hat{Y}_{B \cdot X_A} = 0$. The value of $\hat{Y}_{B \cdot \bar{X}_B}$ is exactly the same as the observed mean $\bar{Y}_B$. The value of $\hat{Y}_{B \cdot X_A}$ is

$$\hat{Y}_{B \cdot X_A} = \bar{Y}_A + b_{yx_A} (\bar{X}_B - \bar{X}_A),$$ (9N.5)

where the subscripts A and B indicate on which group the various parameters are based.

The standard error of $\hat{Y}_{B \cdot \bar{X}_B}$, which is the same as the standard error of $\hat{Y}_B$, is

$$SE_{\hat{Y}_{B \cdot \bar{X}_B}} = SE_{\hat{Y}_B} \sqrt{1/N_B},$$ (9N.6)

where $SE_{\hat{Y}_B}$ is the standard error of estimate for group B (i.e., the minor group) and N_B is the sample size of group B.

The standard error of $\hat{Y}_{B \cdot X_A}$ for a given fixed value of X is

$$SE_{\hat{Y}_{B \cdot X_A}} = SE_{\hat{Y}_A} \sqrt{\frac{1}{N_A} + \frac{(\bar{X}_B - \bar{X}_A)^2}{(N_A - 1)\sigma_{X_A}^2}} . \tag{9N.7}$$

The standard error of the difference between $\hat{Y}_{B \cdot \bar{X}_B}$ and $\hat{Y}_{B \cdot X_A}$ is

$$\sqrt{SE_{\hat{Y}_{B \cdot \bar{X}_B}}^2 + SE_{\hat{Y}_{B \cdot X_A}}^2} ,$$

and t is the difference divided by the standard error of the difference, with $df = N_A + N_B - 4$. If t is significant, we can reject the hypothesis of equality of intercepts, but, of course, only if we have failed to reject the prior hypothesis of equality of slopes.

The standard error of the standard error of estimate is not used for determining the confidence limits for $SE_{\hat{Y}}$, because the sample values of this parameter are not symmetrically distributed about the population value (the sampling distribution is skewed: the smaller the sample size the greater the skewness). Therefore, the confidence interval for the standard error of estimate is determined from considering that $SE_{\hat{Y}}^2 (N - 2)/\sigma_{\hat{Y}}^2$ (where $\sigma_{\hat{Y}}^2$) is the population value of $SE_{\hat{Y}}^2$) is distributed as χ^2 with $df = N - 2$. From this fact, it follows that the appropriate test for the significance of the difference between the standard errors of estimate of two independent samples is the F test:

$$F = SE_{\hat{Y}_L}^2/SE_{\hat{Y}_S}^2, \quad \text{with } df = N_L - 2 \text{ and } N_S - 2,$$

where $SE_{\hat{Y}_L}$ is the larger of the two standard errors of estimate and N_L is its corresponding sample size.

A commonly used chi squared test of the significance of the differences between regressions has been proposed by Gulliksen and Wilks (1950). This method consists of testing sequentially three hypotheses concerning whether the populations from which two samples were drawn are equal in (1) standard errors of estimate, (2) slopes, and (3) intercepts. The three hypotheses are tested sequentially in that order, so that, when the null hypothesis is rejected for any one, the subsequent hypotheses are not tested, and it is concluded that the regressions are not homogeneous for the groups in question.

2. The standard deviation of the pooled scores of groups A and B is

$$\sigma_T = \sqrt{\frac{N_A \sigma_A^2 + N_B \sigma_B^2 + N_A (\bar{X}_A - \bar{X}_T)^2 + N_B (\bar{X}_B - \bar{X}_T)^2}{N_A + N_B}} , \tag{9N.8}$$

where

σ_T = the standard deviation of the total pooled scores,
N = the number of scores in each group, A or B,
σ_A and σ_B = the standard deviations of groups A and B, separately,
$\bar{X}_A$ and $\bar{X}_B$ = the means of the separate groups, and
$\bar{X}_T$ = the mean of the total pooled scores: $\bar{X}_T = (N_A \bar{X}_A + N_B \bar{X}_B)/(N_A + N_B)$.

3. For notational simplicity, we express the test X and criterion Y variables in standardized score form, z, separately for each group A and B, (i.e., standardized variables have a mean of 0 and standard deviation of 1 within each group). Thus the success/failure

threshold on the criterion in standardized form for group A is $z_{Y_A^*} = (Y^* - \bar{Y}_A)/\sigma_{Y_A}$, where Y_A and σ_{Y_A} are the mean and standard deviation of the criterion variable for group A. The test cutoff score in standardized form for group A is $z_{X_A^*} = (X_A^* - \bar{X}_A)/\sigma_{X_A}$. The corresponding $z_{Y_B^*}$ and $z_{X_B^*}$ for group B are obtained by substituting B in the subscripts of these formulas.

Let P_A stand for the probability under the normal curve that a standardized score z exceeds a value of $(z_{Y_A^*} - r_{XY}z_{X_A^*})/\sqrt{1 - r_{XY_A}^2}$, where r_{XY_A} is the correlation between test and criterion in group A; and substituting B in the above subscripts let P_B be the corresponding probability for applicants of group B.

Then, for any given selection ratio (SR = number of applicants who can be selected divided by total number of applicants), it can be proved mathematically that the test cutoff scores of $z_{X_A^*}$ and $z_{X_B^*}$ that will maximize the overall expected utility $E(U)$ of selection must satisfy the following equation (with reference to notation in Figure 9.8):

$$[P_A][U(O_2) - U(O_1) + U(O_4) - U(O_3)] - [U(O_4) - U(O_3)]$$
$$= [P_B][U(O_6) - U(O_5) + U(O_8) - U(O_7)] - [U(O_8) - U(O_7)]. \quad \textbf{(9N.9)}$$

For example, in terms of the utilities assigned to the various outcomes in Figure 9.8, equation 9N.9 becomes

$$P_A(-7) + 2 = P_B(-10) + 2 \quad \text{or} \quad P_B/P_A = 7/10. \quad \textbf{(9N.10)}$$

Equation 9N.9 can also be expressed as

$$\frac{P_B[z \geq -r_{XY_A}z_{x_B^*}]\sqrt{1 - r_{XY_B}^2}}{P_A[z \geq -r_{XY_A}z_{x_A^*}]\sqrt{1 - r_{XY_A}^2}} = \frac{7}{10}. \quad \textbf{(9N.11)}$$

The selection ratio SR can be expressed as

$$SR = q_A P_A(z \geq z_{X_A^*}) + q_B P_B(z \geq z_{X_B^*}), \quad \textbf{(9N.12)}$$

where q_A and q_B are the proportions of applicants from groups A and B, respectively, and P is the probability (for group A or B, according to the subscript) of a standard score z equaling or exceeding the test cutoff score z_{X^*} for the particular group. Because the value of P_B/P_A can be calculated from equation 9N.9 and because the values of q_A and q_B and r_{XY} and SR are all known, equations 9N.11 and 9N.12 can be solved for the only two values that are unknown, namely $z_{X_A^*}$ and $z_{X_B^*}$. (The solution of such simultaneous equations is of course most easily obtained by means of a computer routine devised for this purpose.) If, for example, we assume that $q_A = q_B = .50$, and $r_{XY_A} = .60$, $r_{XY_B} = .40$, $SR = .20$, and $z_{Y^*} = 0$, then, solving simultaneously equations 9N.11 and 9N.12, we obtain the test cutoff scores $z_{X_A^*} = 1.33$ (for group A) and $z_{X_B^*} = .51$ (for group B). These cutoff scores would result in the selection of 9 percent of group A (majority applicants) and 31 percent of group B (minority applicants) in this particular example. Obviously, in this example, minority group membership has a high utility. If, on the other hand, the minor group B were assigned the same utilities as are assigned to the major Group A (in Figure 9.8), so that minority group membership per se has no utility whatsoever, the test cutoff scores would be $A_{X_A^*} = .64$ and $z_{X_B^*} = 1.09$. (These are the same cutoff scores that would result from the Equal Risk Model, described in the next section, if the test had the given validities in the two groups.) These cutoffs would result in the selection of 26 percent of the majority applicants and 14 percent of the minority applicants, which is a quite different situation from that in which minority group membership is assigned greater utility than majority group membership.

4. The correction of the correlation r_{XY} between variables X and Y for restriction of variance on variable X is given by McNemar (1949, p. 126) as

$$r_c = \frac{r_u(S_X/s_X)}{\sqrt{1 - r_u^2 + r_u^2(S_X/s_X)^2}}, \tag{9N.13}$$

where

$\quad r_c$ = the corrected correlation,
$\quad r_u$ = the uncorrected correlation,
$\quad S_X$ = the standard deviation of the unrestricted distribution of variable X, and
$\quad s_X$ = the standard deviation of the restricted distribution of variable X.

To correct r_{XY} for restriction of variance on both X and Y, use this formula to correct first for restriction of variance in variable X and then enter the corrected value r_c (in place of r_u) and S_Y and s_y in the formula to correct for restriction of variance in variable Y. This procedure, of course, yields the same final result regardless of the order in which the two operations are performed with respect to correcting for restriction of variance in X and Y. However, McNemar (1949, p. 127) warns against double correction of the r.

5. Assuming a normal distribution of scores, the average absolute difference $|\bar{d}|$ between relatives of a given kinship is estimated by the formula $|\bar{d}| = (2\sigma\sqrt{1 - r})/\sqrt{\pi}$, where σ is the standard deviation of the scores, r is the correlation between relatives, and π is 3.1416.

6. Internal consistency reliability may be estimated by a number of different methods that are algebraically more or less equivalent. The least favored method for making group comparisons is the split-half reliability coefficient, since different ways of assigning the test items to each half can often yield quite different correlations between the two halves. What we would like to know is the average correlation between all possible split-halves. This can be most easily obtained from the analysis of variance of the subjects $\times$ items matrix or from the Kuder–Richardson formula (K-R 20). These and other methods for computing internal consistency reliability are clearly explicated in Guilford's *Psychometric Methods* (1954, pp. 373–398). The significance of the difference between the reliability coefficients is determined by the same method used in testing the difference between two correlation coefficients, using Fisher's z transformation of r (see Guilford, 1956, pp. 182–183, 194).

7. To test the significance of the difference between groups A and B in the values of $\Sigma(\phi/\phi_{\max})$, one treats $\phi/\phi_{\max}$ for each pair of items as an observation and performs a correlated t test of the mean difference in $\phi/\phi_{\max}$ between the two groups, A and B. The $k(k - 1)/2 = n$ pairs of correlated items (where k is the number of items in the test) each yields a $\phi/\phi_{\max}$. The correlation r_{AB} between the corresponding sets of $\phi/\phi_{\max}$ in the two groups is determined, along with the standard deviation σ of $\phi/\phi_{\max}$ in each group. The standard error of the group mean difference in $\phi/\phi_{\max}$ then is

$$SE_{\text{diff}} = \sqrt{\frac{\sigma_A^2 + \sigma_B^2 - 2r_{AB}\sigma_A\sigma_B}{n - 1}}. \tag{9N.14}$$

The t test, of course, is

$$t = \frac{\Sigma \; (\phi/\phi_{\max})_A \; - \; \Sigma \; (\phi/\phi_{\max})_B}{n(SE_{\text{diff}})} \; . \tag{9N.15}$$

This is a test of the hypothesis that the n values of $\phi/\phi_{\max}$ for each group, A and B, are random samples of all of the $2n$ values of $\phi/\phi_{\max}$.

A much simpler nonparametric test of the same hypothesis that does not assume an approximately normal distribution of the values of $\phi/\phi_{\max}$, as does the t test, is the median test based on the chi squared statistic. One simply obtains each of the n differences of the corresponding pairs of $\phi/\phi_{\max}$ in each group, that is, $\phi/\phi_{\max_A} - \phi/\phi_{\max_B}$ for each of the n correlated pairs of items. If the values of $\phi/\phi_{\max}$ for groups A and B are random samples of all the $2n$ values, there should be as many $\phi/\phi_{\max_A} - \phi/\phi_{\max_B}$ differences greater than zero as less than zero. The chi squared test, with 1 df, therefore is

$$\chi^2 = 4(N - n/2)^2/n, \tag{9N.16}$$

where N is the number of differences between the corresponding pairs of $\phi/\phi_{\max_A} - \phi/\phi_{\max_B}$ that are *greater* than zero and n is the total number of differences.

8. There are various Kuder–Richardson (1937) formulas for estimating the population value of a test's internal consistency reliability from the item statistics, but only one of their formulas (K-R 20) is exact and statistically defensible,

$$r_{xx} = \left(\frac{n}{n-1} \right) \left(1 - \frac{\Sigma \; pq}{\sigma_t^2} \right), \tag{9N.17}$$

where

$$\begin{aligned} n &= \text{the number of items in the test,} \\ \Sigma pq &= \text{the sum of the item variances, and} \\ \sigma_t^2 &= \text{the total variance of subjects' scores on the tests.} \end{aligned}$$

9. Fisher's z transformation of r is $z = \frac{1}{2}\log_e (1 + r) - \log_e(1 - r)$, where $\log_e$ is the natural or Napierian logarithm and r is the correlation coefficient.

10. The reason for the different denominators in this formula is that this is the standard error of the difference between an intraclass correlation ($\bar{r}_{pp}$) and a Pearson (interclass) correlation ($r_{p_A p_B}$). The z transformation of the intraclass correlation has a standard error that is only $\sqrt{(N-3)/(N-3/2)}$ times as large as the standard error of the z transformation of Pearson r, where N is the sample size, which in this example is the number of items in the test.

11. The usual formula for computing the point-biserial correlation is

$$r_{pbi} = \frac{(\bar{X}_A - \bar{X}_B)\sqrt{N_A N_B}}{N\sigma_t}, \tag{9N.18}$$

where

$$\begin{aligned} \bar{X}_A \text{ and } \bar{X}_B &= \text{the means of groups } A \text{ and } B, \\ N_A \text{ and } N_B &= \text{the number of subjects in each group,} \\ N &= N_A + N_B, \text{ and} \\ \sigma_t &= \text{the standard deviation in the combined groups.} \end{aligned}$$

Notice that, when $N_A = N_B$, the formula simplifies to

$$r_{pbi} = \frac{\overline{X}_A - \overline{X}_B}{2\sigma_t} \ . \qquad\qquad \text{(9N.19)}$$

12. The average reliability $\bar{r}_{ii}$ of the item difficulties can be obtained from the ANOVA of the items $\times$ subjects matrix for each group separately, (i.e., $r_{ii} = 1 - $ (items $\times$ subjects MS/items MS)), and then averaged by obtaining the geometric mean (i.e., the square root of the product) of the two reliabilities. One may obtain $\bar{r}_{ii}$ also by randomly splitting each sample in half, obtaining the correlation r_{hh} between the item Δ values of the two halves, then boosting the split-half correlation by the Spearman–Brown formula to obtain the reliability of the Δ's in the whole sample, that is, $r_{ii} = 2r_{hh}/(1 + r_{hh})$, and finally obtaining the geometric mean of r_{ii} for the two groups. The split-half method is less precise than the ANOVA method, especially if the size of either sample is less than 200. For very large samples, the two methods generally yield practically the same estimate of the reliability of the item difficulties.

13. The standard error of the difference between the Δ values of a given test item in groups A and B, with sample sizes of N_A and N_B, is

$$SE_{\Delta\text{diff}} = \sqrt{[4/(N_A - 1)]^2 + [(4/(N_B - 1)]^2}. \qquad \text{(9N.20)}$$

14. Delta decrements should be used rather than p value decrements, as Δ values come closer to representing item difficulties on an interval scale than do p values, as explained earlier in chapter 9. It is a necessary rule that the items must be ranked in the order of the Δ values in the major group for obtaining the Δ decrements. This minimizes the correlation between the Δ decrements of the major and minor groups. Otherwise, various correlations could be obtained depending on the arbitrary order of the items in the test. For example, if the two groups have a similar rank order of item difficulties, it would be possible to produce a spuriously high correlation between the groups' Δ decrements by ordering the items so as to alternate easy and difficult items. The Δ decrements would then have alternatingly positive and negative values in both the major and minor groups, consequently producing a high correlation between the groups. The correlation would represent a complete confounding of ordinal and disordinal effects and hence would defeat the purpose of the analysis here proposed.

15. It is beyond the scope of this book to go into the modern developments in *latent trait theory* that have sprung basically from statistical consideration of the item characteristic curve. Latent trait models are prominent in recent developments in item analysis and test construction. An introduction to this topic is provided by Baker (1977). More detailed discussions are to be found in a series of articles on latent trait models in the *Journal of Educational Measurement* 14 (Summer 1977).

16. The biserial correlation between an item and total test score is

$$r_b = (\overline{X}_p - \overline{X}_t)/\sigma_t \times p/y, \qquad\qquad \text{(9N.21)}$$

where

$\overline{X}_p$ = the mean test score of all persons who pass the item,
$\overline{X}_t$ = the mean test score of the total sample,
σ_t = the standard deviation of test scores in the total sample,

p = the proportion of the sample passing the item, and

y = the ordinate of the unit normal curve at the point of division of the curve into p and $1 - p$ proportions.

The standard error of r_b is $SE_{r_b} = 1/\sqrt{N}[(\sqrt{pq}/y) - r_b^2]$.

17. The phi coefficient divided by phi max (see pp. 431–432) is one suitable method for correlating dichotomized items (i.e., pass versus fail) with dichotomous groups (e.g., major versus minor group). Another measure of association, simpler but quite satisfactory for the present purpose, is Yule's Q. Computed from the frequencies in a 2×2 contingency table, $Q = (ad - bc)/(ad + bc)$, where a, b, c, d, are the frequencies in the upper left, upper right, lower left, and lower right cells of the 2×2 table, respectively. Q is monotonically related to the phi coefficient and, like phi/phi max, ranges from -1 to $+1$, regardless of the marginal frequencies.

SUMMARY OF PSYCHOMETRIC VARIABLES

X is the *observed score* for an individual.

Y is the *criterion measurement* for an individual.

$\bar{X}$ and $\bar{Y}$ are the means of the frequency distributions of variables X and Y.

r_{XX} is the *reliability* (self-correlation) of X scores.

T_X is the hypothetical *true score* corresponding to an observed score X. T_X can never be measured directly; it can only be estimated.

$\hat{T}_X$ is an *estimated* (or *regressed*) *true score;* that is, it is an estimate of T_X:

$$\hat{T}_X = r_{XX} (X - \bar{X}) + \bar{X}.$$

r_{XT_X} is the *index of reliability:*

$$r_{XT_X} = r_{T_X T_X} = \sigma_{T_X}/\sigma_X = \sqrt{r_{XX}}.$$

(σ is the standard deviation.)

$\sigma_T = \sigma_{\hat{T}} = \sqrt{r_{XX}} \cdot \sigma_X$ = the *standard deviation of true scores.*

r_{XY} is the *validity* of the X variable as a predictor of the Y variable:

$$r_{XY} = r_{T_X Y} \cdot r_{T_X X}.$$

$r_{T_X Y}$ is the *relevance* (or intrinsic validity) of X scores for predicting the Y variable:

$$r_{T_X Y} = r_{XY}/\sqrt{r_{XX}}.$$

b_{YX} is the *slope* of the regression of variable Y on variable X:

$$b_{YX} = r_{XY}(\sigma_Y)/(\sigma_X).$$

b_{YT_X} is the slope of the regression of criterion scores Y on test true scores T_X:

$$b_{YT_X} = b_{Y\hat{T}_X} = r_{T_X Y} (\sigma_Y/\sigma_{T_X}) = b_{YX}/r_{XX}.$$

$\hat{Y}$ is the "best" (i.e., most likely in the least-squares sense) prediction of an individual's Y value, given the person's X scores, from the regression equation:

$$\hat{Y} = (\overline{Y} - b_{YX}\overline{X}) + b_{YX}X.$$

The expression in parentheses is termed the Y *intercept*.

Another algebraically equivalent form of the regression equation is

$$\hat{Y} = b_{YX}(X - \overline{X}) + \overline{Y}.$$

The regression equation corrected for attenuation is

$$\hat{Y} = (b_{YX}/r_{XX})(\hat{T}_X - \overline{X}) + \overline{Y}.$$

The correction for attenuation has no effect on the predicted value $\hat{Y}$ for any given group or for groups with the same values of r_{XX}, $\overline{X}$, and $\overline{Y}$. The corrected regression equation, however, yields more accurate predictions of Y when the same regression equation is used for two or more groups that differ in $\overline{X}$ or r_{XX}, or both. Then, of course, the value of r_{XX} based on each particular group must be used in the correction for attenuation, and the estimated true scores of each individual $\hat{T}_X$ must be derived from the parameters r_{XX} and $\overline{X}$ of the group of which the individual is a member.

Chapter 10

Bias in Predictive Validity:
Empirical Evidence

General Caveats in Evaluating Evidence of Bias

The present evidence on the predictive bias of mental tests certainly does not allow broad generalizations encompassing every variety of test in every minority subpopulation for every predictive purpose. But the evidence now at hand does discredit certain broad generalizations about test bias that were proclaimed in the recent past. For example,

M. D. Jenkins, a psychologist and past president of predominantly black Morgan State College in Baltimore, stated in 1964 that "it is well known that standardized examinations have low validity for individuals and groups of restricted experiential background" (quoted by Stanley, 1971a, p. 640).

The *Guidelines for Testing Minority Group Children* (Fishman et al., 1964), published by the Society for the Psychological Study of Social Issues, stated that the "predictive validity [of standardized tests] for minority groups may be quite different from that for the standardization and validation groups..." (p. 130).

Clark and Plotkin (1963), in their study of alumni of the National Scholarship Service and Fund for Negro Students, concluded that "scholastic aptitude test scores are not clearly associated with college grades. It is suggested that college admissions officers weigh test scores less, since they do not predict the college success of Negro students in the same way they do for whites."

The California Association of Black Psychologists, who have demanded a moratorium on the IQ testing of minority children, asserted that "the overwhelming body of scientific evidence—clearly, indicates that those individual and group tests of intelligence and scholastic ability currently in use by the State Board of Education are questionable and invalid as measures of the intellectual and scholastic ability of Black children" (quoted by Thorndike, 1971b).

Although these generalizations must now be regarded as seriously misleading in view of the overwhelming preponderance of evidence on the validity of general intelligence and aptitude tests for predicting the scholastic performance of native-born Americans, either white or black, we should be circumspect in generalizing about the counterconclusions that are indicated by the bulk of the data.

465

Students of test bias are in general agreement that the results of any one study, however well designed, based on a single test and a single criterion and comparing only one minority group with the majority, can only answer a quite limited question: namely, does this particular test give a biased prediction of the criterion for this particular minority group in this particular institution? Few experts would be confident in generalizing the results of the one study, whatever the level of statistical significance, beyond the particular test involved (or, at most, to highly similar tests) or beyond the minority group in question, with due caution concerning the age range, the locality, the educational level, and the conditions of recruitment or self-selection of the study samples. Finally, the results of one study cannot be generalized safely beyond the nature and quality of the predicted criterion measures to include all other possible indices of achievement or success.

Every properly designed study of test bias allows the possibility of rejecting the null hypothesis (i.e., "no bias") and, if it is rejected, there should be an assessment of the amount of the bias and an evaluation of its practical consequences in the light of alternative selection procedures. As the number of studies increases, especially as they involve variations in the tests, subject populations, and the criteria, and, as they consistently either fail to reject the null hypothesis or to find amounts of bias large enough to have any practical implications, the more we should be surprised by any new study that seems to show the contrary. The investigator then is prompted to examine the anomalous study to find out in what crucial conditions it differs from the other studies yielding contrary results. Scientific investigation is the analysis of variables, not just a box score tallying how many studies are pro or con some conclusion. Bray and Moses (1972), reviewing studies of test bias in personnel selection in the *Annual Review of Psychology,* make the following observation:

> Do aptitude test scores, obtained under proper conditions of administration, show significantly different validities for minority and majority group members in predicting a pertinent measure of job proficiency? This question is still open since there are few such studies. It does appear, however, that the closer the study design comes to the ideal, the less likelihood there is of finding differential validity.   (p. 554)

Several of the most telling points for the evaluation of study designs for assessing bias in predictive validity are the following.

Differential Selection of Major and Minor Groups.   If more rigorous selection for abilities relevant to the criterion has been applied to one of the groups than to the other, creating group differences in the variances of the test scores or criterion measures, it can result in significantly different validity coefficients for the two groups. One should be most alert for this effect especially in studies involving affirmative action programs in which a greater latitude in selection criteria is allowed for minority than for majority applicants. Under differential conditions of selection, validity coefficients may differ more *or less* than they would under more uniform conditions of selection. This holds true whether the differential selection is based on the test in question or on some other predictive variables such as past grades in school.

Group differences in predictor or criterion variances will inevitably affect validity coefficients, but not necessarily regressions, unless the restriction of variance is due to floor or ceiling effects on the predictor or criterion measures. For this reason, regression information is much more valuable than correlations (i.e., validity coefficients) alone for assessing test bias, as explained in the paragraphs that follow.

Floor and Ceiling Effects.   When a test is too easy for one group, so that its distribution of scores piles up at the high end of the scale (ceiling effect), or is too difficult, so that the scores pile up at the low end (floor effect), the regression of the criterion measures on the test scores is distorted. (This is a form of bias due to the inappropriate difficulty level of the test for one of the groups.) Studies of test bias should first rule out ceiling and floor effects and ensure that the scale of test scores is capable of measuring the full range of ability in both the major and minor groups. Only then can a group difference in the regressions of criterion measures on test scores serve as a proper indicator of test bias.

Combining Heterogeneous Samples.   To increase the total sample size (of either the major or minor group), investigators occasionally perform a validity study on the combined data from a number of different sources. The danger in this practice is that the several samples entering into the total combined sample may not all represent samples from the same population. That is, the differences between the several samples in the distributions of test scores or criterion measures are attributable to more than just sampling error. When there are systematic differences between the samples, the results of a validity study based on a composite of the samples not only has no practical generality but can, in fact, seriously misrepresent the actual validity that the test might have for any one of the samples in the composite. A flagrant example is the correlation of college aptitude test scores with grade-point averages (GPA) in samples of students from several colleges with widely differing academic standards. A grade of A in one college may be equivalent to a C in another in terms of actual academic achievement. Although the test scores may have substantial predictive validity *within* each of the several colleges, the validity could be near zero for the *combined* samples from these colleges. (The various ways in which heterogeneous composite samples can distort correlations and regressions are discussed more fully by Guilford, 1956, pp. 322–324.) Some reasonable approximation to a common scale for the measurement of the criterion across samples is a necessary condition for combining the samples, and, when this is not assured, the results of the validity study should be viewed skeptically. In addition, the samples entering into a composite should not differ significantly from one another in the distributions of either the test scores or criterion measures. This can be adequately determined from the F test for the significance of differences among means and Bartlett's test for homogeneity of variances (see Guilford, 1956, pp. 242–244). If the results of these two tests permit rejection of the hypothesis that the combined groups are random samples of the same population, the only correct procedure for a validity study is to determine the correlations (or the regression parameters) between test scores and criterion within the separate groups. They should not be averaged if they differ significantly (Fisher, 1970, p. 206).

Noncomparable Criterion Measures.   One must ensure reasonable comparability of the criterion measures in the major and minor groups. For example, the validity of an IQ test for predicting grade-point average is much lower in vocational and practical arts courses than in academic and college prep courses. If a larger proportion of the majority than of minority students are enrolled in academic curricula, the validity coefficient can be expected to be lower for the minority, not necessarily because the IQ test is biased, but because the GPA is not a comparable criterion for both groups. In a study of predictive bias, the major and minor groups should be matched on the courses on which the GPA is based. Similarly, studies of the validity of IQ or other aptitude tests for predicting scholastic achievement as objectively measured by achievement tests in the various school subjects are based on the assumption, which must be assured in fact, that the major and minor groups have been exposed to a common curriculum with respect to the subject matter content of the achievement tests.

A study of the Verbal Reasoning subtest of the Differential Aptitude Tests for predicting the four-year GPA of students in a single New York high school found that for students in the academic college preparatory curriculum the correlation of Verbal Reasoning with GPA was .64 for boys and .62 for girls. But for boys in the practical arts curriculum the r was only $-.07$. For boys in the "general" curriculum the r was .39, and for girls in the commercial curriculum the r was .41 (Bennett, Seashore, & Wesman, 1966).

The obvious point is that, in comparing validity coefficients or regressions of the major and minor groups, it should not be assumed that criteria such as GPA or supervisor's ratings of job performance are comparable criteria across different curricula or different jobs. In short, predictive bias can be determined only if the test is used to predict a common criterion in the major and minor groups.

Prediction versus Postdiction.   Reports of a test's criterion validity occasionally fail to be clear as to whether the test was actually used *pre*dictively, that is, obtained at some time *before* the criterion was assessed, or obtained concurrently with the criterion measure (such as an achievement test), or used *post*dictively, that is, obtained at some time *after* the criterion was measured. Although a proper report should certainly provide this information, the empirical fact is that the distinction among predictive, concurrent, and postdictive validity makes much less difference than is commonly supposed.

There have been two mutually contradictory popular beliefs on this matter, neither of which can be supported by the present evidence. One is that predictive validity should be higher than concurrent or postdictive validity, because the predictive measure (e.g., an IQ test) acts as a self-fulfilling prophecy, causing the criterion (e.g., scholastic achievement) to conform to the prediction. The other belief is that the IQ or aptitude test really only measures what has already been learned and therefore that it should *post*dict past achievement or correlate concurrently better than it predicts future achievement. But in fact there is remarkably little difference among the predictive, concurrent, and postdictive validity coefficients reported in the literature.

One of the largest relevant studies, based on over 5,000 elementary school pupils in Milwaukee, found a correlation (predictive validity) of .75 between fourth-grade IQ and sixth-grade scholastic achievement test scores, a r (concurrent validity) of .77 between sixth-grade IQ and sixth-grade achievement, and a r (postdictive validity) of .73 between sixth-grade IQ and fourth-grade achievement (Crano, Kenny, & Campbell, 1972). The differences among these coefficients, although statistically significant and of some theoretical interest (see Chapter 8, p. 324), are negligible for all practical purposes. Although generally the criterion validity of a test, within limits, can be determined with approximate equivalence by predictive, concurrent, or postdictive designs, studies of test bias cannot be rigorously interpreted if the validity coefficients are not based on the same design in the major and minor groups.

Generalizability of Tests. It is problematic to what degree we can generalize the results of a study of bias based on one test to other similar tests. We have to know what we mean by "similar." Similar in item content, or similar in factorial structure?

Intuitive inspection of item content is an undependable basis for generalization. Similarity of tests in their factorial structure, in both the major and minor groups, particularly in their loadings on the general factor or first principal component, which accounts for most of the variance in total scores, is the more objective basis for generalizing the findings from one test to another similar test. (More is said on this in Chapter 11.)

Many IQ tests and scholastic aptitude tests are highly similar in factorial composition, and test manuals often show the particular test's correlations with other comparable tests. The correlations between different tests often meet the criteria for "equivalent forms" of the same test; that is, they are as high as the average correlation (boosted by the Spearman–Brown formula for a test of full length) between all possible split-halves of the same test.

Even tests with quite different titles, such as the Scholastic Aptitude Test (SAT), the Medical College Admission Test, the Law School Aptitude Test, and the Graduate Record Examination (GRE), are almost as highly correlated with one another as are equivalent forms of the same test. Benno Fricke (1975), the director of the Evaluation and Examination Office of the University of Michigan, gives a good summary of the situation:

> In my opinion the GRE aptitude test has no special psychometric advantage over many other ability tests that could be used for assessing the academic strength of prospective graduate students. The GRE is just another test—it measures essentially the same thing that is measured by practically all of the other academic selection and intelligence tests (i.e., conceptual ability). More specifically, judging from the available evidence it would seem that the quality of students admitted to a graduate program would be about the same if the test used for selecting them were the GRE, the Miller Analogies Test, the CEEB–SAT, the ACT, the Law School Admission Test, the Medical College Admission Test, or some other admission test. Similarly, all of these tests would be more or less equally satisfactory for selecting among applicants to a law school, a medical school, or some other professional program. Scores from each of these tests correlate very highly with scores from the others. Also, students who score high on any one of them differ substantially in conceptual ability from those who score low. The content flavoring of the various aptitude tests has very little to do with how well students perform ... the multiplicity of tests measuring the same thing is at least partly due to various professional and other groups wanting "their own test." (p. 71)

As a striking illustration of the similarity between two of the tests mentioned, Fricke (1975, pp. 71–72) points out that the correlation is .80 between the SAT scores used for college admission and the GRE scores used for admission to graduate school for more than 1,400 students tested on the SAT and GRE *four years apart*. This correlation is not significantly lower than the test–retest reliability of either test.

A safe rule for generalizing the results of a bias study from one test to another is to do so only if the correlation between the two tests is not significantly lower than the equivalent forms, boosted split-half, or internal consistency reliability of each of the tests in both the major and minor groups.

Comparison of Validity Coefficients in Major and Minor Groups. If a test's validity coefficient is the same (i.e., not significantly different) in the major and minor groups, it does not necessarily guarantee that the test is not biased for one group, as the regressions could differ between the groups. But equal validities does mean that the test can be used fairly in both groups, either by using separate regression lines for predicting the criterion in each of the groups or by including group membership as a dichotomous variable in a multiple regression equation. Validity coefficients, therefore, are useful, though limited, for assessing test bias.

The only proper test for possible bias in terms of differential validity is the z test of the significance of the difference between the validity coefficients in the major and minor groups. Some investigators, however, have based a verdict of test bias on the incorrect procedure of testing the validity coefficients, separately within each group, for differing significantly from zero and if the validity differs significantly from zero in one group but not in the other, the test is considered biased. The fault in this method is that the key question as concerns bias is whether the validities are significantly *different* in the two groups, and this question is not answered by a test of the hypothesis that the validity in one or the other group is not significantly different from zero. Because the significance of r depends on the sample size, and because the minor group sample is often much smaller than the major sample, some investigators (e.g., Kirkpatrick et al., 1968, p. 132) using the improper method have concluded there was bias when the r was not significantly greater than zero in the minor group, even though the r was exactly the same in the major and minor groups!

Validity and bias are separate questions. The question of validity can apply to a single group. The question of bias, on the other hand, always implies a comparison of two or more groups. A test that is either valid or invalid in one or more groups may be either biased or not biased with respect to any two of the groups.

Correlations or Regressions? Older studies and test manuals usually report only validity coefficients, that is, the correlation between test scores and criterion measures. But only limited conclusions regarding bias can be drawn from correlations alone. Information on the regression parameters—intercept, slope, and standard error of estimate—are all essential for a definitive statistical test of the null hypothesis regarding bias, as explained in Chapter 9 (see esp. Figure 9.1). (If validity coefficients as well as the means and standard deviations on the test and criterion are given, the value of all of the regression parameters can easily be derived from this information.[1])

If the regressions of the major and minor groups do not differ significantly, the test is unbiased and may be used in the combined groups without predictive bias for members of either group.

If the regression lines are parallel (i.e., nonsignificant difference in slope) but differ significantly in intercept, the test will be biased for the combined groups, *underpredicting* the criterion performance of the higher-scoring group and *overpredicting* the performance of the lower-scoring group. The test can be used, however, with equal validity *within* each group and therefore can be used fairly in selection. The test with equal regression slopes but different intercepts in the major and minor groups can be used fairly for prediction in the combined groups if the prediction is based on a *multiple* regression equation that includes two predictor variables—test score *and* group membership quantitized as 2 and 1 for the higher- and lower-scoring groups, respectively.

When the slopes are unequal (i.e., nonparallel) the test predicts with unequal accuracy in the two groups. This poses a much more serious problem for the fair use of the test than the case of unequal intercepts, as pointed out in Chapter 9 (pp. 387–389). The "trouble-shooting" procedures outlined in Chapter 9 will indicate how remediable is the bias due to unequal slopes. If this form of bias is irremediable by any combination of these trouble-shooting measures, the biased test, if used at all, is best used for selection under the rubric of the Multiple Regression Model, as described in Chapter 9. Whether or not this is deemed a fair use of a biased test depends, of course, on other than purely statistical considerations. But our aim in this chapter is not to determine whether tests are used fairly in any given setting but, rather, whether they are biased according to the purely objective statistical definitions set forth in Chapter 9 (pp. 379–382). An important part of this consideration is the practical assessment of the *amount* of predictive bias involved when the null hypothesis can be statistically rejected.

Rejection and Nonrejection of the Null Hypothesis.   The proper strategy is, first, to determine if the null hypothesis of no bias can be rejected at a given level of confidence, and, second, to assess the practical consequences if the null hypothesis is rejected.

If the null hypothesis is not rejected (i.e., if there are nonsignificant differences between the major and minor groups in the slopes, intercepts, and standard error of estimates of the regression of criterion measures on test scores), one cannot conclude that the test is biased. But this may be a strong or a weak conclusion depending on the sample sizes involved and hence of the power of the study for rejecting the null hypothesis.

There is fortunately a simple and clear-cut procedure in this case for determining whether the study is in fact capable of rejecting the null hypothesis if it is false. The method consists simply of reversing the predictor (e.g., test scores) and criterion variables and testing the significance of the difference between the major and minor groups in the regression parameters for the regression of test scores on the criterion measures. If the correlation between test scores and criterion is less than perfect in both the major and minor groups, which is always the case in reality, and the groups differ in means, then, if the regression of the criterion on test scores is the same in the two groups (i.e., no bias), the regression of test scores on the criterion *cannot* be the same for both groups. If the intercepts are the same for both groups in predicting from test to criterion, they will necessarily differ between groups when predicting in the other direction. If a study cannot reject the null hypothesis of no difference for the regressions in either direction, the verdict is clear: the study is not statistically strong enough adequately to test the null hypothesis. (It is rare in applied statistics that we have such a clear-cut objective criterion for determining whether a study is or is not adequate to test the null hypothesis.) Thus a statistical test of the null hypothesis with respect to bias, strictly speaking, can clearly have one of three decision outcomes: *accept, reject,* or *moot.* Unfortunately, no studies, to the best of my knowledge, have explicitly recognized the third category of decision.

Statistical rejection of the null hypothesis, provided that there is a true nonzero difference, however small, between the groups in the population, can always be accomplished simply by increasing the sample size sufficiently. The question, then, is whether the difference is so small as to be trivial in terms of any practical use of the test. If the difference is so small as to be trivial, the test can be treated as unbiased for all practical purposes, even though the hypothesis of no bias has been statistically rejected. The answer to that question will depend on the available alternatives to use of the test. How valid and unbiased are other available predictors? Is the error of prediction introduced by treating the test as if it were unbiased (i.e., by using a common regression line for the major and minor groups) greater than the sampling error incurred by using a separate regression equation for the minor group if the regression parameters are based on a much smaller sample than are the parameters for the major group? Finally, in which group is the criterion performance underpredicted, and by how much? In most cases, these group errors of prediction due to a biased test can be minimized or eliminated altogether when using the test for selection by entering the test scores along with group membership in a multiple regression equation. (See the discussion of the Multiple Regression Model in Chapter 9.)

Test Bias in Predicting Scholastic Performance

Elementary School. The published evidence here is surprisingly meager, proba-bly for two main reasons: (1) because tests are not generally used for selection in the elementary grades (1 to 8), there has been little concern with their predictive validity, as compared with, say, college and vocational aptitude tests; and (2) teachers' marks in elementary school are not a very solid criterion for studies of predictive validity.

Nevertheless, the few available studies suggest that standard IQ tests have quite comparable validities for blacks as for whites in elementary school. Sattler (1974, pp. 43–44) has reviewed some of this evidence. A study of 1,800 black elementary school children, ages 5 to 16, in the southeastern United States showed a correlation of .69 between Stanford–Binet MA and California Achievement Test Scores and .64 to .70 with grades in academic subjects, but only .32 with overall teacher ratings. In other studies the Stanford–Binet correlated .67 with the Metropolitan Achievement Test in a disadvantaged sample, ages 8 and 11, of whom 80 percent were black. Stanford–Binet also correlated .57 with the reading achievement of second- and third-grade black boys. There are significant correlations ranging from .38 to .61 between the WISC and the Wide Range Achievement Test in samples of 6-year-old white and black children. None of these findings is very informative, but they do indicate that significant validities of about the same magnitude as are generally found in the white school population are also found in the black.

Thorndike (1971b) provides comparative data on the validity of the Lorge–Thorndike Verbal and Nonverbal IQ for white and black pupils in one Maryland county. (See Table 10.1.) Thorndike remarks:

> Correlations do average somewhat lower for black students, reflecting in part smaller variability in this black group of students, but the correlations clearly follow much the same pattern and are of the same order of magnitude. The abilities needed . . . to master academic materials know no color line. Reading, science, mathematics make the same demands on blacks as on white students. The same abilities are needed to cope with them in either case.   (1971, p. 1)

A study by Crano, Kenny, and Campbell (1972) gives predictive validities of the Lorge–Thorndike total IQ for large samples of inner-city ($N = 1,499$) and suburban ($N = 3,992$) school children. The correlation of IQ obtained in Grade 4 with a composite score on scholastic achievement tests (Iowa Test of Basic Skills) obtained in Grade 6 was .73 for

Table 10.1.   Correlations of Lorge–Thorndike Verbal and Nonverbal IQs with school criteria for white and black pupils.   (From Thorndike, 1971b)

	Correlations			
	Verbal IQ		Nonverbal IQ	
Criterion	White	Black	White	Black
Reader completed at end of year	.69	.53	.50	.56
Eighth-grade achievement test composite	.83	.72	.69	.53
Composite of teachers' grades	.41	.26	.41	.25

the suburban sample and .61 for the inner-city sample. The significant difference found between these correlations cannot be interpreted from the evidence given, and we cannot determine whether the different correlations result in significantly different regressions in the two groups. For making these evaluations we would need to know the groups' means, standard deviations, and reliabilities of both the IQs and achievement scores. Unfortunately this information is not provided by Crano et al.

The appropriate regression statistics, however, were obtained in a recent study of the validities of verbal and nonverbal IQ tests for predicting scholastic performance as indexed by grade point average (GPA) in large samples of elementary school children in England (Messé, Crano, Messé, & Rice, 1979). The data were analyzed separately in high, middle, and low SES samples. The predictive validity coefficients average about 0.60 and do not differ as a function of SES. The regressions of grade point average on IQ, determined separately in the low, middle, and high SES samples, do not differ significantly in standard error of estimate or in slope, but they do show a slight but significant intercept bias. IQ significantly *over*estimates GPA in the low SES sample and significantly *under*estimates GPA in the middle SES sample. That is, the predictive bias of the IQ "favors" the lower SES children.

Jensen (1974d) examined the validity of a number of ability, socioeconomic, and personality variables (eleven in all), in addition to sex, age, and ethnic group membership for predicting scholastic achievement (Stanford Achievement Test) in various school subjects (eight in all) in Grades 1 to 8 in California schools comprised of whites ($N = 2,237$), blacks ($N = 1,694$), and Mexican–Americans ($N = 2,025$). The predictor measures were obtained at the beginning of the school year and the achievement tests at the end.

The predictive validity (multiple R) of this battery in the combined groups ranged from .60 to .80 for various school subjects, in different grades, with an overall average validity of $R = .70$. The Lorge–Thorndike IQ contributed by far the most of this multiple correlation. The validities steadily and markedly increase going from the first to the eighth grades.

But the more important point of this study is that overall the addition of ethnic membership to the thirteen other predictors in the multiple regression equation does not add a significant increment to the R, despite the large sample sizes. If the battery of predictor variables was biased with respect to any of these ethnic groups, we should expect the addition of ethnicity as a predictor variable to significantly enhance the R. But in fact the independent contribution of ethnicity was generally negligible. For example, the average point-biserial correlation between ethnicity and achievement was .522 for white–black and .314 for white–Mexican. When the thirteen predictor variables were partialled out of these correlations, they dropped to nonsignificant values of .055 (p = .379) and −.083 (p = .237), respectively. In other words, the contribution of pupils' ethnic group membership to the prediction of scholastic performance, independently of psychometric, personality, and status variables, was practically nil. Thus, with a good choice of predictor variables, such as were used in this study, it is possible to predict scholastic achievment in the elementary grades with considerable validity (about .70) for white, black, and Mexican–American children without having to take their ethnicity into account.

High School.   Here, too, the evidence is surprisingly scant. Test manuals commonly give the validity of IQ and other scholastic aptitude tests for predicting high school grades and achievement test scores, but they say nothing about differential validity in major and minor groups. Such information should be included in test manuals, preferably in the form of complete regression information on the different population groups most likely to be subjected to the test, particularly whites, blacks, males, females, urban, rural, and suburban. But, because the generalizability of the regression parameters may be problematic when samples of certain subpopulations are not large or representative, test publishers could argue that each school district should conduct its own studies of differential validity so that they will be more precisely applicable to the particular subpopulations represented in the district.

The study with the most extreme finding of differential validity of aptitude tests for predicting high school grade-point average (GPA) compared 104 male and 129 female eleventh-grade blacks from two Detroit high schools with 254 male and 261 female eleventh-grade whites from nine high schools in eight Michigan cities (Green & Farquhar, 1965). The School and College Ability Test (SCAT) Verbal scores were used on the two Detroit samples, and the Differential Aptitude Test (DAT) Verbal Reasoning scores were used in the nine other Michigan samples. They were correlated with GPA based on ninth- and tenth-grade academic subjects, as follows:

	Correlation with GPA			
	Males		*Females*	
Test	*White*	*Black*	*White*	*Black*
SCAT-V	—	−.01	—	.25
DAT-VR	.62	—	.21	—

The difference in validities between the black and white males is significant ($p < .001$) as is the difference between black males and females ($p < .05$).

The nonsignificant validity for black males and the quite low validities for females of both races in this study are markedly out of line with the findings of other studies. This may be attributable to the heterogeneity of the samples from eleven different schools across which the GPAs could well be noncomparable and therefore unsuitable as criterion measures. Also, as Stanley and Porter (1967, p. 202) have noted in commenting on this study, if many of the black males were enrolled in the practical arts curriculum, their GPAs may have been based on too few miscellaneous academic courses per pupil to be reliable. Moreover, as noted by Stanley and Porter (p. 201), we are not told which level(s) of the SCAT was used or the standard deviations of the scores, and, therefore, cannot judge whether the test was of an appropriate level of difficulty for these subjects. And nothing is said about the time span between predictors and criterion. Thus, we can put little stock in the results and conclusions of this poorly designed and inadequately reported study.

A study by Boney (1966) showed quite different results. DAT–Verbal Reasoning scores in the twelfth grade correlated with high school GPA .65 for 109 black males and .65 for 118 black females. The DAT–Numerical Ability scores correlated .67 and .62, respectively. The DAT-VR and DAT-NA scores together gave a multiple correlation with GPA of .72 and .71 for males and females; and the Cooperative School Ability Test scores correlated .66 and .70 with GPAs. These validities are quite comparable to those found with white high school students.

I have found only one high school study that provides the complete regression information required for a proper statistical test of bias. Farr et al. (1971) studied the validity of the California Test of Mental Maturity (CTMM), a widely used IQ test, in ninth- and twelfth-grade racially integrated classes in North Carolina public schools. Unfortunately, the samples are not very large: ninth grade, 166 whites and 55 blacks; twelfth grade, 245 whites and 58 blacks. The criteria were teachers' grades in English, math, science, social studies, and total GPA. Also, teacher ratings were obtained on leadership (class participation, initiative, dominance, acceptance by others, etc.) and creativity (generalization of new ideas, seeks new solutions, independence, originality, interest in outside activities, etc.). Twelfth-graders were also assigned a "rank in class" for academic performance (position divided by class size).

Whites and blacks in the ninth grade differed an average of 12.2 IQ points (or .84σ in terms of the within-groups standard deviation); the average racial difference in the twelfth-grade sample was 17.4 IQ points (or 1.37σ). Whites and blacks differed less in overall GPA: .58σ in the ninth grade and .69σ in the twelfth grade. This is a general finding in many other studies: blacks and whites differ somewhat less in school grades than in IQ or in objective test measures of scholastic achievement. Table 10.2 shows the correlations between CTMM IQ and teachers' grades and ratings. The black and white regressions also were compared on each of these variables. The type of bias, in terms of the Bartlett-O'Leary models (see Chapter 9, pp. 390-391) is indicated in the column headed "Model." Model 1 represents "no bias," that is, nonsignificantly different slopes and intercepts in the two groups. Model 2 represents intercept bias, with the whites having the higher intercept, thus resulting in underprediction of the criterion for whites and overprediction for blacks when the common regression (based on the combined groups) is used for prediction. In Grade 9 only science grades show this type of bias. The CTMM predicts all the other measures without slope or intercept bias. In Grade 12, the Bartlett-O'Leary model 8 is represented in both English and science grades and in leadership ratings. In model 8 the predictor is valid for whites but not for blacks, and there are significant mean differences on both the predictor and the criterion. In Grade 12, the predictive validity of the CTMM for math grades was nonsignificant in both groups. But in both grades the CTMM IQ predicted the overall GPA without bias as well as rank in

Table 10.2.   Correlations[1] of CTMM IQ with school grades and teacher ratings.   (From Farr et al., 1971)

	Grade 9				Grade 12			
Criterion[2]	White	Black	Total	Model[3]	White	Black	Total	Model[3]
English	.38	.65[a]	.48	1[b]	.50	(.15)[a]	.50	8
Math	.52	.54	.55	1	(.26)	(.38)	(.28)	—
Science	.52	.47	.53	2	.39	(.27)	.42	8
Social studies	.34	.56	.42	1[b]	.51	.47	.51	1[b]
Overall GPA	.52	.62	.58	1	.50	.34	.51	1
Rank in class					−.53	−.55	−.54	1
Leadership[4]	.54	.52	.58	1	.29	(.29)	.33	8
Creativity[4]	.62	.53	.64	1	.36	.44	.42	1[b]

[1] All correlations are significant at the .01 level except those in parentheses, for which $p > .05$.
[2] Sample sizes vary slightly for different criteria. Average N: ninth grade, 156 whites and 45 blacks; twelfth grade, 189 whites and 31 blacks.
[3] The regressions correspond to the designated Bartlett-O'Leary models shown in Figure 9.3. Model 1 represents no bias in slope or intercept. Model 2 represents intercept bias. Model 8 represents slope and intercept bias.
[4] Based on teacher ratings.
[a] Indicates that the correlation for blacks is significantly different from that for whites.
[b] The standard error of estimate of the criterion variable is significantly ($p < .05$) larger in the white than in the black group.

class for twelfth-graders. In the four (out of fifteen) comparisons that showed significant bias, in every case it would "favor" the black groups, that is, the use of the white regression line or the common regression line for all students would result in *over*prediction of the blacks' criterion performance. We shall see in the next section that this is a common finding also in the prediction of college GPA. In those cases where predictive bias is found, the use of the majority regression line or the common regression line almost invariably favors blacks relative to whites.

Although the study tested for bias in slopes and intercepts, it did not compare the standard error of estimates in the white and black groups. So I have done this, using the data provided by the authors. Significantly different standard error of estimates indicate that the predictions for the two groups are of unequal reliability; that is, they do not involve equal risk of errors in prediction. There are four instances in which the standard error of estimates differs significantly at the .05 level (as indicated by a superscript *b* in the "Model" column of Table 10.2); in each instance, the standard error of estimate is larger for the white group—that is, errors of prediction are greater for whites than for blacks. But the only two criteria, out of a total of eight, for which there is any significant predictive bias of any kind at both grade levels is for grades in English and in social studies.

A related study by Fox (1972) involved more than 11,000 ninth- and twelfth-grade students of both races in thirty-nine high schools from nine districts in North Carolina, representing a stratified random sample of North Carolina high school students. It shows the correlation of CTMM IQ with items of a biographical inventory that discriminate significantly between the races. A random half of the total sample ($N = 5,524$) was given an inventory of three-hundred questions (with from three to five multiple-choice answers) concerning a great variety of biographical information. The items that discriminated beyond the .01 level of confidence between the races were then cross-validated in the other random half of the sample ($N = 5,524$), and only the items that discriminated significantly in the second sample were retained. It is noteworthy that a total of only forty-nine of the three-hundred biographical items significantly differentiated race (white versus black) for males (twenty-seven items), females (thirty-six items), or both sexes (twenty-three items). One might expect the items of a biographical inventory to be much more "culture loaded" than the items of an IQ test, and yet only about 8 to 16 percent of the three hundred biographical items discriminated significantly between the races. Yet, even though intelligence test items are not selected in terms of racial criteria, virtually all the items of standard group IQ tests discriminate significantly between whites and blacks in samples of comparable size to those used in the present study. Apparently, in a broad catalog of life experiences, whites and blacks do not differ as much as many would imagine. Of course, none of the biographical items pertain to race per se, but they do pertain to socioeconomic factors, family size, parental education and occupation, interests, values, likes and dislikes, and a great variety of social and cultural experiences.

The finally selected items were keyed so that higher scores were indicative of white biographical experiences. Scores on the Biographical Race Key in the total sample have a point-biserial correlation with actual racial classification (black = 1, white = 2) of .56. (This corresponds to a mean white–black difference on the Biographical Race Key of approximately 1.35σ.) The correlations (curved lines) and partial correlations (straight lines) shown in Figure 10.1 are of particular interest. The point-biserial correlation of .45 between race and IQ corresponds to a mean difference of approximately 1σ or 15 IQ points. Notice that, when the racially differentiating biographical factors are partialed out of this correlation, it drops from .45 to .27, indicating that IQ measures some substantial

Figure 10.1. Correlations (curved lines) and partial correlations (straight lines), with other variable partialed out, between race, IQ, and biographical inventory keyed to discriminate between races (i.e., white and black).

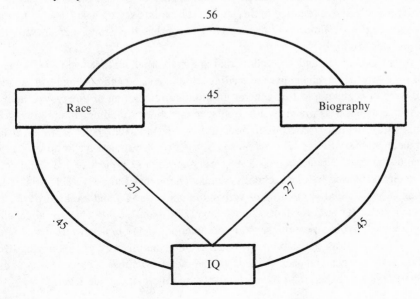

difference between the races that is wholly independent of those life experience differences between the races assessed by the biographical inventory. However, one cannot prove from such correlational data that any part of the race correlation with IQ is *caused* by the biographical differences. We can say only that the CTMM IQ reflects something more than just these biographical differences.

Note, too, that biography is correlated .27 with IQ after race is partialed out, which means that there is a correlation between IQ and the biographical factors *within* each racial group. Finally, much of the biographical variance is associated with race independently of IQ, as indicated by the partial correlation of .45. Those who argue that all the racial IQ variance merely reflects differences in life experience, values, and attitudes, such as are tapped by the biographical inventory, should be able to devise a biographical inventory on which the correlation of race and IQ (with biography partialed out) is nonsignificantly different from zero. The obtained correlation of .45 between race and IQ thus would have to be accounted for through the indirect effects of race on biography and of biography on IQ, which requires that the product of the partial correlations race × biography (partialing out IQ) and biography × IQ (partialing out race) must equal .45. This would obviously call for a biographical inventory having a very much higher partial correlation either with race or with IQ (or both) than does the present inventory. If such an inventory could be devised, it would be instructive to examine its item content. Would it reflect the kinds of cultural learning experiences that some critics claim make IQ tests racially biased?

Comparisons of Predictive Test Bias in Various Ethnic Groups.   Although the well-known Coleman report, *Equality of Educational Opportunity* (Coleman et al., 1966), made no attempt to examine test bias, it provides massive data (in the Supplemental Appendix, Sec. 9.10) from which we can make such an examination. This nationwide survey of scholastic aptitudes and achievements involved the testing of more than 645,000 children in 4,000 public schools, which constitutes the largest school testing program ever undertaken using a common battery of aptitude and achievement tests. Children were tested only in grades 1, 3, 6, 9, and 12, and larger numbers of various minorities were included than their proportions in the population, to ensure adequate-sized samples for the many statistical analyses required in this study. The sample sizes are so large, in fact, that the sampling error of almost any descriptive statistic based on the Coleman samples is practically negligible.

In Grades 3, 6, 9, and 12, both verbal and nonverbal aptitude tests were given, as well as scholastic achievement tests in reading comprehension and mathematics. Grades 9 and 12 were also given a test of general information, consisting of ninety-five items on such diverse subjects as practical arts (tools, automobiles, building, food, sewing, decorating, etc.); natural science; literature, music, and art; and social science (history, government, public affairs). The scholastic achievement tests are made up of standard tests produced by the Educational Testing Service and are typical of the standardized achievement tests used by most school systems. The verbal and nonverbal aptitude tests are taken from standard group tests of verbal and nonverbal IQ and are highly typical of most such group IQ tests used in schools, involving items such as picture vocabulary, picture association, classification, sentence completion, and figural and verbal analogies.

Table 10.3 shows the amount by which each of the minority groups deviates from the white majority mean on each of the tests; the mean difference is expressed in units of the white standard deviation on the particular test at the given grade level.

Table 10.3. Difference between white majority mean and minority group mean expressed in standard deviation units.[1] (Calculated from data in Coleman et al., 1966, Supplemental Appendix, Sec. 9.10)

Test	Grade	Black	Mexican	Indian	Oriental
Verbal IQ	3	0.66	0.64	0.67	0.41
	6	1.10	1.12	0.93	0.42
	9	1.16	0.89	0.79	0.28
	12	1.24	0.91	0.93	0.28
Nonverbal IQ	3	0.75	0.50	0.38	0.16
	6	1.12	1.12	0.83	0.30
	9	1.01	0.82	0.54	−.01
	12	1.31	0.82	0.57	−0.04
Reading Comprehension	3	0.86	0.70	0.61	0.28
	6	0.87	0.94	0.81	0.34
	9	0.95	0.77	0.68	0.19
	12	1.05	0.85	0.84	0.35
Math Achievement	3	0.85	0.66	0.60	0.28
	6	1.07	1.00	0.93	0.38
	9	0.98	0.80	0.72	0.04
	12	1.13	0.72	0.70	0.07
General Information	9	1.18	0.95	0.83	0.26
	12	1.27	0.98	0.82	0.36
Average		1.03	0.84	0.73	0.25

[1]Raw score means and standard deviations were used: (white mean − minority mean)/white standard deviation.

We can determine the degree of predictive bias in these typical verbal and nonverbal "IQ" tests for various minority groups by seeing how accurately scores on these ability tests can estimate (or "predict") the mean performance of various minority groups on the achievement tests, basing the estimate on the regression equation derived from the white majority.[2] The estimated means for the minority groups can then be compared with their actually obtained means on the achievement tests. The amount of the discrepancy (D) between the estimated mean ($\hat{\bar{Y}}$) and the obtained mean ($\bar{Y}$), expressed as a proportion of the total standard deviation (σ) of the achievement scores for the particular group in question, that is $D = (\hat{\bar{Y}} - \bar{Y})/\sigma$, is an index of the amount of predictive bias of the IQ test. A positive value of D indicates *over*prediction of the criterion; that is, in using the prediction equation derived from the white majority to predict the mean achievement test score of the minority group, the aptitude test (verbal or nonverbal IQ) predicts a higher mean on the criterion measure (achievement test) than was actually obtained.

The results of this analysis are shown in Table 10.4 for blacks, Mexican–Americans, American Indians, and Orientals (Chinese- and Japanese-Americans). To gain some idea of how much of the predictive discrepancy (D) might be attributed solely to test unreliability, another value, labeled Dc, has been calculated to show the estimated value of D if the tests had perfect reliability. This is achieved simply by correcting the regression equation for attenuation,[3] assuming that the actual reliability of all of the tests

Table 10.4.   Deviation (D) in standard deviation units of predicted mean from obtained mean on criterion test in minority groups.   (Calculated from data in Coleman et al., 1966, Supplemental Appendix, Sec. 9.10)

Predictor/Criterion	Grade	Black		Mexican		Indian		Oriental	
		D [1]	Dc [2]	D	Dc	D	Dc	D	Dc
Verbal IQ									
Reading Comprehension	3	.648	.579	.481	.415	.347	.280	.108	.072
	6	.060	−.173	.120	−.098	.121	−.055	.019	−.046
	9	.110	−.098	.113	−.032	.104	−.034	−.011	−.055
	12	.091	−.126	.138	−.011	.119	−.036	.126	.080
Math Achievement	3	.607	.536	.418	.348	.331	.260	.090	.055
	6	.397	.190	.274	.087	.322	.168	.093	.032
	9	.227	.058	.198	.077	.203	.083	−.121	−.158
	12	.408	.257	.195	.085	.168	.057	−.075	−.108
General Information	9	.271	.007	.229	.049	.189	.034	.026	−.026
	12	.336	.095	.270	.114	.102	−.052	.140	.092
Nonverbal IQ									
Reading Comprehension	3	.637	.565	.558	.510	.490	.455	.204	.191
	6	.380	.222	.428	.282	.423	.317	.166	.135
	9	.436	.304	.318	.221	.401	.331	.186	.187
	12	.390	.243	.406	.320	.520	.459	.303	.299
Math Achievement	3	.581	.504	.491	.438	.472	.433	.184	.171
	6	.594	.433	.460	.316	.528	.423	.213	.180
	9	.399	.261	.301	.203	.404	.331	.041	.042
	12	.428	.282	.276	.186	.373	.310	.049	.044
General Information	9	.762	.613	.539	.432	.555	.487	.254	.255
	12	.654	.487	.542	.451	.493	.431	.322	.317
Average		.421	.262	.338	.220	.333	.239	.116	.088

[1]Positive values of D indicate overprediction of criterion score. Calculation of D is based on the white majority regression equation.

[2]Dc is the deviation calculated from the white majority regression after correction for attenuation, assuming a reliability of .90 for all tests.

is .90, which is a typical reliability coefficient for most standard group tests of IQ and scholastic achievement. Because the Coleman report provides no information on the reliability of these tests in the various groups, the calculation of Dc based on the reasonable assumption of a test reliability of .90 in all samples is done merely to illustrate in a general way the approximate effect of correcting the regression equation for attenuation (i.e. test unreliability). The effect, in general, is to decrease the amount of overprediction by about .07σ.

As can be seen in Table 10.4, the minority group means on the criterion tests are generally overpredicted by the IQ tests, using the regression equation based on the white majority pupils. Blacks evince the largest degree of overprediction, Orientals the least, with Mexican–Americans and Indians intermediate. Except for Orientals, the amount of predictive bias (i.e., overestimation of minority achievement test means) is considerable, amounting to as much as half a standard deviation or more in some instances. In other words, the verbal and nonverbal IQ tests tend to overestimate the mean level of reading comprehension and mathematics achievement and general information of the minority pupils. That is, white pupils with the very same IQ scores as the mean IQ of a minority group actually obtain higher achievement scores. This finding is just the opposite of the popular notion that the usual IQ tests are biased so as to underestimate the actual scholastic performance of minority pupils.

Notice also that the verbal IQ shows less predictive bias than the nonverbal IQ, and this is true even for the minority groups in which bilingualism is most common. This finding, too, goes counter to popular expectations. The reason for it is that verbal IQ has considerably higher validity than nonverbal IQ for predicting scholastic achievement and general information within every ethnic group. In a factor analysis, scholastic achievement scores are highly loaded not only on *g* but also on a verbal ability factor measured in the language of instruction in the school.

It should be remarked that the predictive bias might be lessened considerably if the verbal and nonverbal IQ tests were combined in a multiple regression equation instead of being used separately in simple regression equations as was done in Table 10.4. Our purpose here, however, was not to determine the maximum predictive validity that could possibly be obtained from these particular tests, but to determine the *direction* of the predictive bias of typical verbal and nonverbal aptitude tests in the various minority groups. In this respect, the Coleman data are quite consistent with the general findings of most of the other studies reviewed in this chapter, namely, that standard aptitude tests, when found to be significantly biased, are most often biased in the direction of *over*predicting the minority group's actual achievement.[4]

The validity of the Wechsler Intelligence Scale for Children (Revised) (WISC-R) for predicting scholastic achievement in reading and math (as measured by the Metropolitan Achievement Tests) was investigated by Reschly and Sabers (1979) in a stratified random sample of children from four ethnic groups in the schools of an Arizona county with a large urban population. Pupils were selected in equal numbers from Grades 1, 3, 5, 7, and 9. The four ethnic groups were whites (called Anglos), blacks, Mexican–Americans, and Indians (Native American Papago). The predictor variable was the WISC-R Full Scale IQ; the two criteria were the reading and math scores of the MAT.

The regressions of the criterion scores on the predictor scores were compared simultaneously across the four ethnic groups at each grade level by means of the Gulliksen–Wilks procedure, which tests sequentially for significant differences in standard error of estimate, slope, and intercept. The hypothesis of the same regression equation for all groups was rejected at the .05 level at every grade, for the prediction of both reading and math. Most of the significant differences were differences in intercepts. Thus by this stringent statistical criterion the WISC-R is an ethnically biased predictor of reading and math achievement.

So we must go on to examine the direction and magnitude of the predictive error when the common (i.e., based on the combined groups) regression equation is used for each ethnic group, to gain some idea of the practical consequences of the predictive bias for each group. This is given in Table 10.5, in which I have averaged the authors' results over grades, since there appears to be no systematic effect of grade level for those

Table 10.5. Predictive validity of WISC-R IQ for Metropolitan Achievement Tests of Reading and Math and the deviation of predicted (*P*) from actual (*A*) achievement scores expressed in standard deviation units,[1] with prediction based on the regression equation for the combined groups.   (From Reschly & Sabers, 1979)

Subgroup	*N*	Validity Coefficient		Deviation[2]	
		Reading	Math	Reading	Math
Anglo	250	.59	.55	−.16	−.14
Black	222	.64	.52	+.00	+.05
Mexican–American	215	.55	.52	−.04	−.14
Indians (Papagos)	223	.45	.41	+.33[a]	+.38[a]

[1]$(P - A)/SD$, where *SD* is the obtained subgroup standard deviation.
[2]Positive deviation indicates *over*prediction of actual scores.
[a]$p < .01$.

statistics. First, note the validity coefficients (i.e., the Pearson correlation between the Full Scale IQs and the MAT scores); only the Papago Indians show appreciably lower values than the other three groups, which differ only slightly. The deviations of the predicted achievement scores from the actual achievement scores are expressed in units of each subgroup's own standard deviation. It can be seen that these discrepancies between predicted and obtained scores are quite small and statistically nonsignificant for all groups except the Indians, whose actual achievement is significantly *over*predicted by the WISC-R IQ. At the other extreme, the Anglo group's actual achievement is slightly, but not significantly, *under*predicted by the common regression equation. For practical purposes, this small amount of bias, except for the Indians, would hardly justify the use of separate regression equations for each group. The WISC-R Full Scale IQ appears to have very much the same meaning for white, black, and Mexican–American pupils in relation to their achievement in reading and math.

Prediction of College Grades and Academic Achievement

There are many more methodoligically sound studies of white–black bias in scholastic aptitude tests for predicting academic performance in college than for any other type of predictive validity of psychological tests. This should not seem surprising, since in no other realm are tests so widely or so crucially used for selection as in college admissions. The contention of bias in these selection procedures, and particularly in the tests on which they are based, has gained prominence in the crusade for equality of educational opportunity of the past decade, as the tests screen out a larger proportion of black than of white applicants.

My aim here is not to examine the validity per se of college aptitude tests, but to determine to what extent they are differentially valid for majority and minority groups or yield biased predictions of the future academic performance of minority students. The number of applicants to most colleges far exceeds the number of possible admissions, and admissions officers try to select those applicants who are most likely to succeed academically in their college careers and are most likely to persist to graduation. This obviously calls for an assessment of the applicant's aptitude for the kinds of verbal and quantitative comprehension and abstract conceptual reasoning abilities that are essential to most college-level courses and are presumed to have been developed throughout the student's prior educational experiences. Stanley (1971a, 1971b) gives a thoughtful overview and discussion of the problems of college admission for disadvantaged students, along with a review of much of the evidence for the predictive validity of tests and other selection criteria. (For a critique of one point in Stanley's review see Clark and Plotkin, 1971, and the rebuttal by Cleary and Stanley, 1972.)

One test for college selection strikingly dominates the field, and also the empirical research literature on test bias: the College Entrance Examination Board's Scholastic Aptitude Test, better known as the College Boards, or the SAT. The CEEB administers the SAT throughout the nation's high schools to all students who wish to take it. The CEEB sends the results to the student and to the colleges to which the student seeks admission. Most selective colleges in the United States today require SAT scores from all applicants. Colleges, however, differ markedly in how they use the SAT scores in their selection procedures, in the minimum score allowed for admission, and in the relative weights given to test scores among other selection criteria. In the United States, the variance among college *means* on the SAT is almost as great as the variance among individuals. The saying that one can find a college suitable for every level of ability is only a slight exaggeration.

The SAT is a timed paper-and-pencil, group-administered, objective test comprised of 150 five-option multiple-choice items. It has two main parts, Verbal and Mathematical, labeled SAT-V and SAT-M. The SAT-V items involve reading comprehension, antonyms, verbal analogies, and sentence completion. The SAT-M consists of numerical and quantitative reasoning items but not formal mathematical knowledge per se. The SAT total score would undoubtedly be a very high g-loaded variable in a factor analysis that included a variety of other mental ability tests. The SAT-V scores generally have a higher correlation with college grades than SAT-M scores. Each scale is standardized to a mean of 500 and a standard deviation of 100 nationwide. Scores range from 200 to 800. (Chance scores are about 220 for SAT-V and 270 for SAT-M). Only 45 percent of all high school seniors are estimated to obtain SAT-V scores of 400 or more and only 20 percent score above 500; the corresponding estimates for blacks are 15 percent and 1 or 2 percent, respectively (Stanley, 1971a, p. 643). Many of the more selective colleges use a cutoff of 600 or higher for admission. Brown University, for example, defines SAT-V scores below 620 as "academic risks" for that university; only about 4 percent of all high school seniors would exceed a score of 620. The mean SAT-V of Cornell University freshmen over the years from 1965 to 1969 ranged from 660 to 703 (Stanley, 1971a, p. 643). Such mean scores are typical of most of the "big name" colleges and universities in the country.

The many studies of "bias" in the SAT can be classified into two main categories: studies of differential validity and studies of regression. The former can tell us whether or not the SAT is equally useful for predicting the academic performance of blacks as of whites; but only the latter can determine the presence of predictive bias when the test scores are used without regard to individuals' racial or ethnic classification.

Studies of Differential Validity.   The SAT does not seem an ideal test for many black college applicants. It is too difficult for many, which causes a piling up of scores at the low end of the scale. Such a pile-up of scores due to a "floor effect" limits the test's discriminability; it reduces the variance of scores, which adversely affects the validity. Despite these adverse conditions in most black samples involved in studies of the differential validity of the SAT, the validity coefficients obtained are generally quite substantial and even on a par with those typically obtained for whites.

These points are well illustrated in a methodologically careful study by Stanley and Porter (1967). Students in three all-black coeducational four-year state colleges in Georgia were compared with students in fifteen predominantly white state colleges in Georgia. The data consist of students' SAT scores and their freshman grades in all these institutions over the six-year period 1959–1965. The black mean SAT-V was 266 as compared with about 400 for whites; and the authors claim the test is too difficult for approximately one-third of the black students. Indeed, the modal score in the blacks' distribution is 200, which is the lowest obtainable score on the SAT-V, with the chance guessing level being a score of about 220. Despite this considerable restriction of range, the average multiple correlation between SAT-V + SAT-M and freshman grades were nonsignificantly different for white and black males and black females, averaging about .50 over the six tests. The validity of SAT-V + SAT-M for white females was significantly higher, averaging about .65. When the high school GPA was combined with SAT scores in the best-weighted linear composite, the multiple correlations with college freshman grades were as follows:

	White	Black
Males	.60	.60
Females	.72	.63

College grades are significantly ($p < .01$) more predictable for white females than for any of the three other groups, which do not differ significantly. These results, viewed in terms of the variances of SAT scores in each of the groups, suggest that the validity of the SAT would be even higher for blacks than for whites if the range of the test were extended downward by adding a number of easier items. The standard deviations of SAT scores in these groups were as follows:

	SAT-V		SAT-M	
	White	*Black*	*White*	*Black*
Males	82	52	80	51
Females	85	45	77	42

All the white–black contrasts are highly significant.

Stanley and Porter conclude:

> [I]n view of the detailed analysis of the Georgia data and several related studies, it seems likely that SAT-type test scores are about as correlationally valid for Negroes competing with Negroes and taught chiefly by Negroes as they are for non-Negroes competing chiefly with non-Negroes and taught chiefly by non-Negroes. (1971, p. 216)

McKelpin (1965) found that for somewhat higher-scoring black students in a southern predominantly black state college, the median predictive validities for the SAT were .64 for men and .66 for women. Roberts (1964; cited in Stanley & Porter, 1967, p. 216) found median predictive validities in fifteen private predominantly black colleges of .64 for men and .67 for women. Munday (1965) reported that the American Council on Education Test (ACE), which is another college entrance examination similar to the SAT, operated with "typical predictive efficiency" at five predominantly black colleges.

Hills (1964) investigated the validity of SAT-V and SAT-M for predicting freshman GPA in three predominantly black four-year colleges as compared with the predominantly white Georgia Institute of Technology. He summarizes the results as follows:

> [T]he mean [SAT]-V for males at these [three predominantly black colleges] was approximately 270, with an average standard deviation of approximately 45. The mean and standard deviation of SAT-M were approximately 305 and 48. At the other extreme, the means and standard deviations for [Georgia Tech] males were approximately 500 and 87 for SAT-V and 580 and 77 for SAT-M. Yet the average [multiple-correlation coefficient R] for males at the [three black colleges] is .57, while at [Georgia Tech] the average R for the five years is .581.   (p. 158)

Baggio and Stanley (1964, cited in Stanley & Porter, 1967) later showed that, when the black validity coefficients in Hill's (1964) study were corrected for restriction of range, they were significantly higher for blacks than for whites.

Hills and Stanley (1970) tried giving an easier test than the SAT to entering students in three black four-year colleges in the South to see if the greater range afforded by an easier test would increase the correlation between test scores and freshman GPA. They used Level 4 of the School and College Ability Test (SCAT). Level 4 of the SCAT is designed for elementary school Grades 6 to 8. Whereas the SAT scores were markedly skewed in these black colleges, the SCAT scores had a nearly normal distribution, with means on the Verbal and Quantitative scales at the 60th and 35th percentiles, respectively, for eighth-grade national norms. The average validities of the SAT-V + SAT-M and SCAT-V + SCAT-Q were .41 and .55, respectively. Yet there was considerable variation in validities among the three colleges and between the sexes, which reinforces the test experts' prevailing admonition to admissions officers that each college conduct its own test validation studies for the particular subpopulations it serves.

When high school GPAs were included along with the test scores in the multiple R, the average SAT + HSGPA and SCAT + HSGPA validities were .60 and .65, respectively. In these samples, high school GPA correlates about .50 with college freshman GPA and, when combined with the test scores, clearly adds a significant increment to the overall predictive validity.

A general finding of several other studies has been that high school GPA predicts college GPA better than SAT or ACE scores in whites but that the reverse is true for blacks (Munday, 1965; Farr et al., 1971; McKelpin, 1965; Thomas & Stanley, 1969; Cleary, 1968; Funches, 1967; Perlberg, 1967; Peterson, 1968).

Studies Comparing Regressions.   These studies provide the complete and necessary statistical information for determining the significance and magnitude of test scores' predictive bias. Fortunately, in recent years there have appeared a number of methodologically exemplary studies of this type, as well as excellent reviews of the main findings (Stanley, 1971a, 1971b; Linn, 1973; Cleary, Humphreys, Kendrick, & Wesman, 1975).

The first important study of this type, by T. Anne Cleary (1968), compared the slopes and intercepts of the regression of GPA (at the end of the freshman year) on SAT-V and SAT-M for white and black students in three racially integrated state-supported colleges, two in the East and one in the Southwest. Nearly all the black students ($N = 273$) enrolled in these colleges were included in the study, but only a random sample of the white students ($N = 2,808$) and a smaller sample of white students ($N = 318$) who were matched with the blacks on sex, class, and curriculum. (Cleary, 1968, p. 119, found that curriculum differences contribute to the variation in validity coefficients.)

First, the SAT-V and SAT-M validity coefficients for blacks and whites were highly comparable, averaging .47 for blacks, .47 for the matched whites, and .43 for the random whites.

Second, the results of the regression tests showed that the hypothesis of equality of slopes for blacks and whites could not be rejected in any of the six black–white comparisons (i.e., three colleges × matched and random comparisons). The hypothesis of equality of intercepts was not rejected for the two eastern colleges but was rejected for the southwestern college. Thus there was no significant sign of predictive bias in two of the three colleges. There was no slope bias in any of the comparisons, and the intercept bias that appeared in the one college of course does not preclude using the SAT; it merely indicates that separate regression equations should be used for each group or that group membership be entered into the prediction equation. In the one college showing intercept bias, the black students' GPA was *over*predicted by the SAT when the white or the common regression line was used. When high school grades or rank in high school class were used in addition to the SAT as predictors, the degree of positive bias favoring black students increased. Prediction from the SAT alone overestimated the black GPA by a practically trivial amount, about one-tenth of a standard deviation. Thus the SAT, if used for selection without regard to race in this college, would be only slightly biased in favor of black applicants.

This finding, which came as a surprise to most people, has proved to be typical in the light of many subsequent studies. The popular belief was that the actual college grades of black students would be *higher* than the tests predicted. But, in fact, just the opposite is true. When significant regression differences are found, it is usually *intercept* bias, and in virtually every case it consists of *over*prediction of the black GPA when the white or the common regression equation is used (Centra, Linn, & Parry, 1970; Davis & Kerner-Hoeg, 1971; Davis & Temp, 1971; Kallingal, 1971; Pfeifer & Sedlacek, 1971; Temp, 1971; Wilson, 1970). Linn (1973, p. 143), in reviewing the homogeneity of regressions of GPA on SAT scores for blacks and whites in studies of 22 racially integrated colleges, noted that the actual GPA of blacks was *over*predicted in 18 of the 22 comparisons when prediction was based on the regression equation for white students, and in no college was black GPA significantly *under*predicted.

I have been able to find only one study (Bowers, 1970) in the whole literature with results that appear to be contrary to the general finding that where regression bias exists it overpredicts black performance. But Bowers's contrary finding seems to be the result of an artifact. Black GPA was significantly *under*predicted (about $.25\sigma$) by the SCAT-V and SCAT-Q. However, the black students were those in a Special Educational Opportunities Program, offering tutorial and remedial services as well as special courses in several departments and special teaching sections in many courses. It turns out that the number of special courses taken by these black students was negatively correlated with their SCAT scores and positively correlated with their earned GPAs. In other words, the less able students were enrolled in the special courses, which gave higher grades, thereby lowering the correlation between SCAT scores and GPAs. This particular study therefore cannot in the least countervail the findings of the studies reported for twenty-two other colleges.

The American Psychological Association, in response to the Association of Black Psychologists' demand for a moratorium on psychological testing at the APA's national convention in 1968, commissioned a panel of experts in psychometrics to investigate the ABP's charges of test bias. The panel's report was published in the APA's official organ, *American Psychologist* (Cleary et al., 1975; for dissenting opinions see Bernal, 1975; Jackson, 1975; and the rebuttal to these by Humphreys, 1975). The panel's conclusion regarding the findings of the studies reviewed above was succinct:

> In summary, when the criterion to be predicted is GPA in a regular college program, almost all of the research demonstrates that standardized tests are useful, both within and between groups. The predictions within black and white colleges are comparable, and within integrated colleges the usual regression equations lead to comparable predictions for black and white students.   (p. 31)

This conclusion is largely correct for the practical use of tests in predicting college performance. But it should be noted that, in the majority of the colleges studied, the hypothesis of homogeneity (i.e., equality) of regressions can be statistically rejected, with respect to standard error of estimates, slopes, or intercepts. Linn (1973) points out that, in fourteen of the twenty-two colleges included in his review of virtually all the large-scale regression studies, the null hypothesis of equality of regressions for blacks and whites can be rejected at the .05 level of significance for at least one or another feature of the regression, the most frequent being differences in intercepts, as already noted. Much of this bias could probably be greatly reduced or even eliminated altogether by using esti-mated true scores (see Chapter 9, pp. 387–389) instead of the actual test scores.

But how much does this bias (i.e., overprediction of black GPA) actually amount to in terms of the difference between the predicted GPA and the actual GPA? Linn (1973, p. 144) presents an elaborate table that answers this question; it can easily be summaried. For all twenty-two colleges Linn computed the discrepancy between the actual college GPA of blacks and the predicted GPA when the white regression equation was used. The dif-ference between the actual and the predicted GPAs is a practical measure of the amount of bias. This discrepancy was determined at three levels of ability—for black students 1σ below the black mean on the SAT, for those scoring at the mean, and for those scoring 1σ above the mean. For each of these levels, the black GPA was *over*predicted by .08, .20, and .31 points, respectively. In relation to the overall standard deviation of the black GPA ($\sigma = .69$), these *over*predictions measured in sigma units are .11σ, .29σ, and .45σ, respectively. Thus, the *over*prediction of GPA is greatest for the highest-scoring black students.

A prediction and regression study by Farr et al. (1971) is of particular interest, because, in addition to using the SAT and high school GPA as predictors of college GPA for blacks and whites, it also examined the predictive validities of scores on eighteen personality scales of the California Psychological Inventory (CPI), eleven scales of the Holland Vocational Preference Inventory (HVPI), and seventeen items of an opinion questionnaire about college called the University Student Census (USC). The subjects were all the black students ($N = 126$) entering a large state university in 1968 and a random sample of white students ($N = 178$) from that institution. The validities of the test scores were as follows:

	SAT-V	SAT-M	HSGPA
White	.46	.31	.64
Black	.50	.41	.44
Total	.54	.43	.60

There was equality of the regressions for the SAT scales but not for high school GPA, which had significantly different regression slopes for the two groups. (The various inventories, by and large, showed unimpressive validities.)

Perhaps the most interesting feature of the Farr et al. data is the fact that, while the black and white means differ by $.88\sigma$ on SAT-V and 1.02σ on SAT-M, there are so few significant differences on the eighteen CPI scales (six significant at $p < .05$, the largest mean difference being 0.38σ), or on the eleven HVPI scales (one significant, with a mean difference of 0.51σ), or on the seventeen items of the USC (seven significant, the largest mean difference being 1.35σ on the opinion item "The University should actively recruit black students"—answered "yes" by more blacks than whites). One might well expect cultural differences to show up on personality, interest, and opinion inventories even more than on tests of verbal and quantitative reasoning. Yet very few of the personality, interest, and opinion inventories show either significant or substantial white–black differences, whereas all cognitive ability tests consistently show white–black differences of about one standard deviation in representative samples. This finding may lead one to suspect that the differences on cognitive tests probably reflect something other than just cultural differences.

Only one white and black college prediction study has used a more exact and objective criterion than GPA. Centra, Linn, and Parry (1970) looked at the ability of the SAT-V and SAT-M to predict scores on achievement tests in the areas of the students' college major—the Area Tests of the Graduate Record Examination. These tests assess broad knowledge in the liberal arts. Students from seven predominantly black and seven predominantly white four-year liberal arts colleges, majoring in natural sciences (N), humanities (H), and social sciences (SS) were given the GRE tests in N, H, and SS, respectively. The seven white colleges were selected from among ninety white colleges so as to be as nearly equal as possible to the seven black colleges in preentry SAT scores; even so, the white mean was about one-half a standard deviation above the black mean.

The predictive validities (i.e., multiple R with SAT-V + SAT-M as predictors of total GRE achievement) for students in all majors were .78 for blacks ($N = 327$) and .74 for whites ($N = 406$). There was equality of white and black regressions for predicting achievement in the natural sciences and the social sciences and on total GRE scores, but there was a significant ($p < .05$) inequality in the regressions (due to significantly different error of estimates) for predicting achievement in the humanities. Overall, the predicted mean for blacks was slightly but not significantly higher than for whites, that is, the typical *over*prediction of the lower-scoring group.

Prediction of GPA of Other Ethnic Minorities. There have been peculiarly few studies of test bias in predicting college grades for other ethnic minorities. I have found only three such studies. They all involve Mexican–American (Chicano) students in selective colleges. The first is a very small-scale study with questionable results; the others are large-sample regression analyses of test bias.

The first study (Spuck & Stout, 1969, cited in Cleary et al., 1975, p. 31) was based on a sample of thirty-two low-socioeconomic-status Mexican–American freshmen admitted to the Claremont Colleges under a "program of Special Directed Studies." The predictor tests given prior to admission were the California Test of Mental Maturity (Verbal and Nonverbal IQ), the SCAT-V and SCAT-Q, and Cattell's Culture Fair Tests. All the correlations between these tests and GPA were nonsignificant and four of the six correlations were negative!

The second study (Goldman & Richards, 1974) examined the validity of SAT-V and SAT-M for predicting GPA of Chicanos in a medium-sized four-year liberal arts college (the University of California at Riverside). It was found that the SAT had slightly lower validity for Chicanos than for majority students; the regressions of GPA on test scores were unequal; the regression equation for the Chicano sample placed zero weight on SAT-M; and the use of the majority-derived regression equation slightly *over*predicted Chicano GPAs.

The third study (Goldman & Hewitt, 1975) carries the most weight, being based on all of the undergraduate Chicano students (total $N = 656$) in four campuses of the University of California. The Anglo-American comparison sample had a total N of 17,188. All campuses have the same admission standards, based on SAT scores and high school GPA in academic subjects. The Chicanos' mean SAT scores were about 1.0σ to 1.5σ below the Anglo-Americans', and the Chicano GPAs averaged about $.5\sigma$ to $.8\sigma$ below the average Anglo–American GPA. The main results were as follows: (1) the average validity (multiple R with SAT-V + SAT-M predicting GPA) was significantly lower for Chicanos ($R = .25$) than for Anglos ($R = .38$); (2) when high school GPA was added to the multiple prediction equation the average R's were .36 for Chicanos and .45 for Anglos; (3) the regressions were significantly nonparallel but by a practically trivial amount, such that the use of different regression equations for Chicanos and Anglos would account for only an additional 0.4 percent of the variance in GPA predicted by a common regression equation; (4) the predictors (SAT-V, SAT-M, and HSGPA) do not systematically *under*predict or *over*predict mean GPA of Chicano students when prediction is based on the Anglo-derived regression equation. In conclusion, for practical purposes the SAT was not a biased predictor for Chicano students, although its predictive validity was not impressive and the SAT adds little predictive precision over what is achieved by high school GPA alone. Goldman and Hewitt did not report the standard error of estimates of the predicted GPAs, which I have calculated from their data as .53 for Chicanos and .50 for Anglos, a statistically significant ($p < .01$) but practically negligible difference. The variance in college GPAs accounted for by SAT scores is unimpressive in both samples. Note that the total standard deviations of GPA are .55 for Chicanos and .54 for Anglos, which are not much different from the standard error of estimates.

Prediction of GPA for Different Socioeconomic Levels. The two available studies of prediction of college GPA for students from different socioeconomic backgrounds give no indication of test bias disfavoring lower-status students. More than one thousand students at Tulane University were divided into three levels of socioeconomic status (SES) on the basis of father's occupation, and the regression of GPAs on test scores was compared across the three SES groups. There were no differences in regression lines for women students, but the test scores overpredicted the GPA of men students in the lowest-SES category (Wing & Kitsanes, 1960). In a study by Hewer (1965) the regressions of GPA on test scores were compared across large groups of students classified into nine SES levels according to father's occupation. Although, with the large samples involved, there were significant but slight differences among the regressions, there was no consistent tendency for the common regression equation to either *over-* or *under*predict for either high- or low-SES groups.

Predictive Bias in the Armed Forces

In recent years, personnel psychologists in the U.S. armed forces have conducted investigations of predictive bias in the tests most commonly used for the selection and assignment of recruits to various specialized training programs. Almost invariably the studies have investigated test bias only with respect to black–white comparisons. The performance criteria have usually been final marks or rank in the training course or supervisor's ratings on the job. Nearly all the studies have been described in mimeographed technical reports and very few have been published. I shall concentrate on those that provide the most complete information regarding validities and regressions of the criterion measures on test scores and involve tests of rather general ability as contrasted to the many narrowly specific aptitude tests used in some branches of the armed forces.

When the number of persons who must be selected and assigned to various training programs and jobs is enormous, as it is in the case of the armed forces, even slight improvements in the predictive validity of aptitude test batteries have great financial importance. In recent years, the total annual savings in training costs to the armed forces as a result of test selection and classification of enlisted personnel has been estimated at $442 million. Biased predictions for some large subgroups within the armed forces, therefore, can be extremely costly. Tests are intended primarily to predict success in various kinds of training, that is, the probability of completing the training program and attaining the requisite level of useful skill in the job for which the training is designed. Because the aptitude demands vary widely among different training courses and jobs, and aptitudes vary widely among individuals, training costs can be greatly reduced by the efficient matching of individuals' aptitudes to specific training demands.

The relevance of scores on general ability tests to armed forces training is clearly manifested in studies comparing performance in training of personnel with low, medium, and high scores. For example, in one study (Fox, Taylor, & Caylor, 1969), such groups of recruits were all trained on tasks of visual monitoring, rifle assembly, missile preparation, phonetic alphabet learning, map plotting, and combat plotting. To acquire these skills the low-aptitude group needed two to four times more training time, two to five times more training trials, and two to six times more prompting than the middle- and high-aptitude groups.

Armed Forces Qualification Test.   The Armed Forces Qualification Test (AFQT) is a 100-item multiple-choice group test of general ability used for selection into the military and for the classification of those accepted (scores above the 9th percentile) into four "Mental Categories," as follows:

Category	Percentile Score	Raw Score
I	93–100	89–100
II	65–92	74–88
III	31–64	53–73
IV	10–30	25–52
V (Rejectees)	9 and below	1–24

A study comparing the performance of 26,915 men in category IV accepted into the air force with that of men in the top three categories, concluded that the category IV men were less likely to complete basic training, had more unsuitable discharges, and were less likely to attain the required levels of skill (Grunzke, Guinn, & Stauffer, 1970). The correlation of AFQT scores with job-training grades is about .5, but generally drops to about .2 to .3 for ratings of performance on the job. Also, it has been found that men scoring low on the AFQT have a greater tendency to become disciplinary cases.

Because the distributions of whites and blacks in the various Mental Categories on the basis of AFQT scores differ considerably, it is a matter of major concern to the military whether the AFQT scores result in biased predictions of training and job performance when the same prediction equation is used in both racial groups. The percentages of each racial group's falling into each of the AFQT categories in 1968 (the last year on which complete nationwide statistics were published by the Office of the Surgeon General, in 1969) are as follows:

Category	White	Black
I	6.9%	0.3%
II	34.2%	4.8%
III	36.3%	22.2%
IV	17.1%	43.1%
V	5.5%	29.6%

Is the AFQT biased? The largest study of bias in the AFQT that I have found was conducted in the U.S. Navy (Thomas, 1972). It involved a total of 104,683 white and 2,067 black recruits enrolled in twenty-two different "Class A" schools for training in a variety of specialized navy occupations such as electronics repairman, signalman, quartermaster, ordinance man, and communications yeoman. The criterion measures were the grades given on graduation from the school (final school grade). The grades were standardized within schools to a mean of 50 and standard deviation of 10, so that the AFQT (as well as other tests) could be used to predict the final grades in all of the schools combined.

General Classification Test.   The General Classification Test (GCT) was also used in this study; it is a test of general mental ability much like the AFQT, but probably even somewhat more highly *g* loaded. The validity coefficient on the AFQT was .34 for whites and .26 for blacks, and on the GCT was .39 for whites and .25 for blacks. These white–black validities differ significantly at the .01 level. Notice that these validities are lower than is generally found for the prediction of college grades. This is consistent with the findings of many other studies showing that the predictive power of tests of general ability is related to the degree of abstractness and the conceptual level of the criterion performance. Many of the navy's training courses evidently are not as abstract or conceptual as most college courses, but involve acquisition of more purely factual information and technical skills rather than the more general principles and concepts typical of much of the academic curriculum in college. However, using a combination of other more specialized aptitude tests in the prediction equation very significantly increases the precision of predicting grades in the navy schools, with multiple correlations as high as .50 to .60.

The differences between the regressions of final school grades on AFQT and GCT in the white and black groups were found to be significant for both tests. The standard error of estimates do not differ significantly, but the slopes and intercepts do differ, as shown in Figures 10.2 and 10.3. These figures are worth examining because they are so typical of so many of the findings of studies of test bias in the armed forces. There is a consistent difference in the findings for prediction of college GPA and of final grades in armed forces courses or job performance ratings. Slope bias is rare in college studies (where the bias, if any, is in the intercepts), whereas slope bias is the most common type of bias found in regression analyses of armed forces data.

Level I and Level II Types of Tests.   How can we account for this difference? The best hypothesis, I would suggest, is that the difference in the two types of regression bias found in college and in the armed forces is the result of a difference in the factorial composition of the criterion measures. In extensive studies, we have found that the regression of relatively simple learning and memory measures on highly g-loaded measures (such as IQ, SAT, AFQT, and GCT) differ in whites and blacks in exactly the same way that the regressions of armed forces training final grades on AFQT or GCT scores differ in whites and blacks. Figure 10.4, for example, shows the regression of scores on a

Figure 10.2.   Regression lines of final school grades on Armed Forces Qualification Test score for whites and blacks in training schools of the U.S. armed forces.   (From Thomas, 1972)

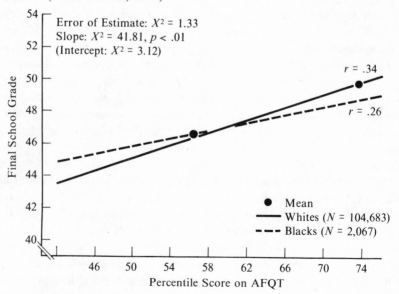

Figure 10.3.   Regression lines of final school grades on the General Classification Test for whites and blacks in training schools of the U.S. armed
forces.   (From Thomas, 1972)

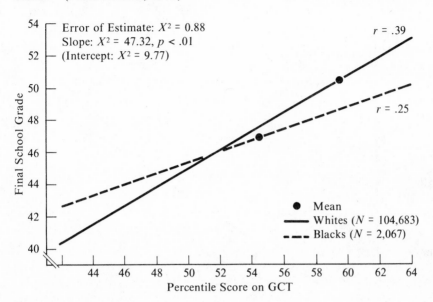

simple memory for numbers test on Lorge–Thorndike nonverbal intelligence test raw
scores in large samples of white and black school children (Jensen, 1974b). Notice how
similar these regressions are to those in Figures 10.2 and 10.3. There generally seems to
be less difference between whites and blacks on performance involving rote learning and
memory (which I have labeled level I ability), than on tasks involving abstract conceptual
ability (level II ability); also, level I and level II abilities are slightly less correlated in
blacks than in whites (Jensen, 1974b). I conjecture that the content of most armed forces
training courses involves relatively more level I ability than the content of academic
courses in college, and this results in the differing slopes of the white and black regression
lines. College GPA, in contrast to final grades in armed forces training schools, is
probably almost as highly loaded on level II ability (after correction for attenuation) as are
the predictor tests.

How serious is the degree of bias in the AFQT and GCT as shown in Figures 10.2
and 10.3? The Gulliksen–Wilks (1950) chi squared test of the significance of the difference between the white and black regressions shows that, even with these very large
samples, the standard error of estimates do not differ significantly, which means that
errors of prediction are essentially no different for the two groups when prediction is based
on each group's regression line. The slopes, however, differ very significantly. (A test of
the intercept difference is uncalled for when the slopes differ significantly.) If the white
regression equation were used for predicting the final school grades of blacks, it would
*under*predict for low-scoring blacks and *over*predict for high-scoring blacks on both the
AFQT and GCT. At the points of over- or underprediction of the final school grade the
average error of prediction amounts to slightly less than one-fourth of the white standard
deviation for the GCT and one-sixth of a standard deviation for the AFQT. The final

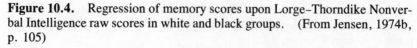

Figure 10.4.   Regression of memory scores upon Lorge–Thorndike Nonverbal Intelligence raw scores in white and black groups.   (From Jensen, 1974b, p. 105)

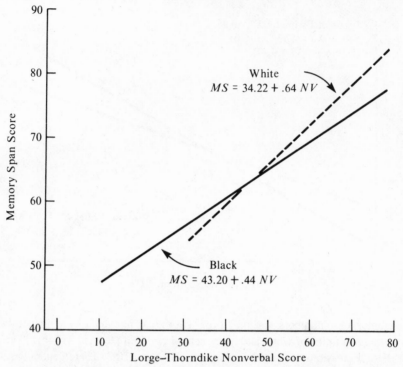

school grade means of whites and blacks differ by $.37\sigma$. Thus the largest average errors of prediction of black grades, using the white regression equation, are relatively large, so that it would be advisable to use separate regression equations for blacks and whites or to include the quantitized racial dichotomy and its interaction with test scores as a moderator variable in a multiple regression equation for predicting final school grade.

I venture the generalization that slope bias will be manifested in black–white regression comparisons whenever the criterion involves a much less *g*-loaded type of performance than the predictor test. In other words, highly *g*-loaded cognitive tests are very likely to show slope bias in black–white comparisons when the criterion performance to be predicted includes a large component of level I memory ability or is relatively lacking in level II abstract-conceptual ability. The best remedy for this condition is to include other less *g*-loaded but criterion-correlated variables in the prediction equation, along with race as a moderator variable, as explained in Chapter 9 (pp. 417–418).

We see this generalization demonstrated again in a sample of marine corps recruits undergoing training in Service Support Schools for several relatively low *g*-loaded jobs: food service, supply, and transport personnel (Farr et al., 1971, pp. 85–97). The training course lasted less than three weeks. There were ninety-nine whites and eighty-four blacks. The white–black mean difference on the predictor test (AFQT) was $.94\sigma$, which is significant beyond the .01 level. The white–black mean difference on the criterion measure (class standing) was only .35σ, which is quite nonsignificant ($t = 0.25$). The correlation between AFQT and class standing was .47 ($p < .01$) for whites and .05 (n.s.) for blacks (a significant difference in validities). The slopes of the white and black regression lines differ significantly ($p < .05$). It is instructive to compare the regression on another predictor test that is less conceptually complex than the AFQT, namely, the Fundamental Achievement Series (FAS), which is a test of elementary verbal and numerical skills. On this simpler test the white–black difference was only .72σ (as compared with .94σ on the AFQT). The correlations of FAS with class standing were .30 and .11 for whites and blacks, respectively; and, although the white–black slope differences were in the same direction as for the AFQT, they were of nonsignificant magnitude.

Another study (Farr et al., 1971, pp. 114–149) complements the previous study in its consistency with our level I–level II hypothesis. This study involves forty-six white and forty-eight black sophomore students at the University of Maryland who took part in an experiment specially designed to test an aspect of the level I–II hypothesis. The students undertook a five-hour unit of programmed instruction in elementary statistics. This subject matter is quite abstract and conceptual.

The criterion measure in this training unit was a thirty-item multiple-choice achievement test designed to measure applications of *concepts and principles* to *new* situations which were not included in the programmed instruction. This criterion test, therefore, is a highly *g*-loaded level II measure. Two main criterion measures were used: posttest scores and residual gain scores (i.e., the difference between *actual* posttest scores and the predicted posttest score as predicted from the pretest score on the thirty-item achievement test).

The predictor variables of particular interest were two level I tests—memory span for numbers and paired-associates learning (ten nonsense syllable/common noun pairs)— and a measure of level II or general intelligence (Wonderlic Personnel Test). The mean white minus black differences (in standard deviation units) and their two-tailed significance levels are

Level I tests	Memory for Numbers	$+0.37\sigma$,	$p > .05$
	Paired Associates	-0.39σ,	$p > .05$
Level II test	Wonderlic Personnel Test	$+1.70\sigma$,	$p < .001$

The mean white minus black differences (in σ units) and their significance levels on the criterion measures are

Pretest achievement scores	$+1.30\sigma$,	$p < .001$
Posttest achievement scores	$+1.27\sigma$,	$p < .001$
Residual gain	$+0.78\sigma$,	$p < .001$

The validity coefficients of the predictor tests are shown in Table 10.6.

None of the validity coefficients in Table 10.6 differs significantly between whites and blacks. Only the Wonderlic showed significant validities, except for predicting the blacks' residual gain score, which was nonsignificant ($p > .05$). As for the regressions, the two level I predictors (Memory for Numbers and Paired Associates) both showed significant ($p < .01$) intercept bias but no slope bias. On these tests the differences

Table 10.6.   Validity coefficients for whites and· blacks.

	Criterion Variable			
	Posttest Score		Residual Gain	
Predictor Score	White	Black	White	Black
Memory for Numbers	.12	.04	.18	−.01
Paired Associates	.05	−.01	−.05	−.09
Wonderlic Personnel Test	.43[a]	.48[a]	.41[a]	.20

[a] $p < .01$.

between the standard error of estimates for whites and blacks is nonsignificant or of borderline significance ($.05 < p < .10$). Marked white–black differences between intercepts but not slopes has been found in other studies involving the regression of level II measures on level I measures. For example, Figure 10.5 shows the regression of Lorge–Throndike Nonverbal Intelligence Test raw scores on Memory for Numbers scores in a large sample of black and white children in Grades 4 to 6. In summary, it appears that *when a level II test is used to predict level I performance, there is mainly slope bias* (Figure 10.4); and *when a level I test is used to predict level II performance, there is mainly intercept bias* (Figure 10.5). The Wonderlic Personnel Test, a level II predictor of the level II criterion, shows no significant white–black difference in slopes *or* intercepts. The standard error of estimate of the posttest scores, however, is slightly but significantly ($p < .05$) larger for whites, due to the greater variance and lesser validity of whites on this criterion measure.

What is the main practical consequence of the generalization noted, namely, that *g*-loaded or level II tests tend to show slope bias (with whites having the steeper slope) when predicting a performance criterion that is considerably less *g* loaded than the test? A good indication is to be found in a large-scale study of U.S. Navy trainees in Class A training schools for twenty-five various specialized jobs in the navy (Thomas, 1975). There was a total of 50,618 white and 2,239 black students. Final grades in the twenty-five training courses were predicted from a composite score consisting of the simple sum of two or three tests (including the General Classification Test in all but three courses) of the navy's Basic Test Battery consisting of the GCT and more highly specialized tests: Mechanical Knowledge and Comprehension, Shop Practices, Arithmetic Reasoning, and the Electronics Technician Selection Test (math, science, electricity, and radio knowledge). Adding one or two of the specialized tests to the GCT generally increases the predictive validity and reduces regression biases by increasing the similarity of ability factors common to both the predictor and criterion variables. Using these composite predictors, Thomas found one or another form of white–black regression bias in the prediction of final grades in thirteen out of the twenty-five courses. The equality of standard error of estimates, slopes, and intercepts were tested sequentially by the Gulliksen–Wilks chi squared test. There were nine courses for which the regressions showed a significant ($p < .05$) racial difference in standard error of estimates (blacks having larger standard errors of estimate in eight out of the nine courses); three courses with a significant difference in slopes (whites having a steeper slope in all courses); and one course with a significant difference in intercepts (whites higher). Because Thomas gives the minimum qualifying score on the predictor variable for assignment to each of the twenty-five navy class A schools, we can determine whether the selection bias in those cases showing significantly different regressions "favors" whites or blacks when the white regression equation is used. In every one of the thirteen courses with significantly unequal regressions, the bias "favors" the black selectees (i.e., the tests *over*predict) the blacks' final course grades. The reason is that the white and black regression line is above the black regression line; and in those cases where the regression lines are parallel, the white is above the black (i.e., intercept bias). In many cases, the amount of bias, though statistically significant with these large samples, is practically trivial. In every case, the bias is always in the direction of *over*predicting the average final grades of the black students who test above the minimum qualifying score.

AFQT and Job Knowledge versus Job Sample.   A study of the differential validity of the AFQT for predicting scores on an objective test of *job knowledge* as compared with scores on an objective measure of performance on a *job sample* (i.e., actually performing certain aspects of the job itself) showed that the AFQT *over*predicted blacks' job-knowledge scores more than their job-sample scores (Caylor, 1972). The four army job categories do not make very highly g-loaded demands: cook, mechanic, armor crewman, and supply specialist. Groups of whites and blacks in these jobs, matched on AFQT scores and number of months on the job, were compared on measures of job-knowledge and job-sample performance. The mean AFQT scores of these groups are quite low, falling into mental category IV. The average correlations between AFQT and job-knowledge scores were .47 for whites and .29 for blacks; correlations between AFQT and job-sample

Figure 10.5.   Regression of Lorge–Thorndike Nonverbal raw scores upon memory scores in white and black groups.   (From Jensen, 1974b, p. 106)

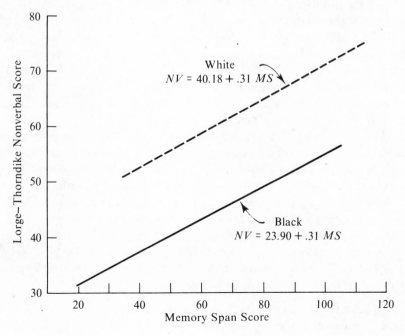

scores were .37 for whites and .20 for blacks. The AFQT is not an impressive predictor of job performance for either of these rather low-ability groups. But, again, we see that a predominantly g-loaded variable, the AFQT, shows appreciably lower correlations with much less g-loaded criterion variables for blacks than for whites. For both groups the AFQT predicts job *knowledge* better than it predicts job *performance*. Thus, it is apparent that verbal knowledge *about* a job and actually *doing* the job involve somewhat different ability factors. In the white and black groups matched on AFQT and months on job, the whites averaged a significantly ($p < .05$) .125σ higher than blacks on job-knowledge scores, but were only a nonsignificant .033σ higher on job-sample scores. Thus the AFQT appears slightly biased (overpredicting blacks' scores) on job knowlege but not on job performance.

   Officer Qualification Test. The OQT is used by the U.S. navy in the selection of applicants for attendance at the Officer Candidate School, from which graduation leads to a commission as ensign. The OQT is a heavily g-loaded test consisting of 115 multiple-choice items including verbal analogies, mechanical comprehension, and arithmetic reasoning, with a 90-minute time limit. Total scores are expressed in standardized form with a mean of 50 and a standard deviation of 10. The test has been accused of cultural bias, as a much larger proportion of white college graduates than of black college graduates exceed the OQT minimum qualifying score. Even for blacks and whites who pass the OQT and graduate from Officer Candidate School, there is a mean difference of about one standard deviation in OQT scores. The navy made a careful study of OQT with respect to possible bias in the prediction of the performance of blacks and whites in Officer Candidate School (Foley, 1971). The samples consisted of ninety-five blacks and ninety-five whites matched on OQT scores who had graduated from Officer Candidate School and an independent sample of 1,072 white graduates. The criterion was the OCS final grade, which is primarily a measure of academic achievement in OCS.

   It was found that the OQT validities differ significantly among the groups: blacks ($N = 95$), $r = .29$; matched whites ($N = 95$), $r = .48$; independent sample of whites ($N = 1,072$), $r = .38$. In the black and white samples perfectly matched on OQT scores, whites received significantly ($p < .005$) higher OCS final grades, on the average, than blacks, that is, the OQT *over*predicted black grades as compared with white grades. However, there was no significant difference in final grades between whites and blacks who were graduates from predominantly white colleges. Regression equations for predicting OCS final grades were computed for the total black sample ($N = 95$) and the independent (i.e., nonmatched) white sample ($N = 1,072$). The equations do not differ significantly ($F = 1.095$) in standard error of estimates or in slopes ($t < 1$), but do differ significantly in intercepts. Black final grades are significantly ($p < .05$) *over*predicted by the white regression equation, but only by a practically trivial amount (0.19σ)—just less than one-fifth of a standard deviation on the OCS final grade scale. (The overall white–black mean difference in OCS final grade was 0.72σ.) Thus, use of the white regression equation for all applicants can hardly be regarded as biased in any practical sense, and there is no evidence in this study that the minimum qualifying score of 55 on the OQT would exclude more blacks than whites who would succeed in OCS. However, the navy's report (Foley, 1971) of this study makes the following qualification:

   Since this study was based upon data for Negroes who had been accepted to and graduated from OSC, it was not possible to generalize the results reported herein to the larger group of Negro applicants to OSC who took the OQT but were not accepted. Whether the OQT is biased and serves to deny them the right to enter OCS, when in fact they are capable of performing successfully, cannot be answered with the data available.   (p. 14)

Airman Classification Battery.   The ACB is used for the assignment of enlisted personnel to various technical schools in the U.S. Air Force. Research has found that the validities are comparable for white and black males and women in the WAF (Gordon, 1953). There are negligible differences in the regressions of whites and blacks, and so the same minimum qualifying scores are applicable in the classification of white and black airmen. The male regression line, however, *under*predicts the performance of WAFs, who achieve higher school grades than male airmen having the same ACB aptitude index. This intercept bias in the case of WAFs warrants using a lower minimum qualifying score for female than for male enlisted personnel. In short, investigations revealed that the ACB was sex biased but not race biased.

Airman Qualifying Examination.   The AQE is a 200-item paper-and-pencil test given by Air Force Recruiting to all nonprior-service volunteers. The items involve arithmetic computation and reasoning, vocabulary, hidden figures, mechanical principles, shop practices, electrical and mechanical information, and the like. Four subtest composites are intended to measure general intelligence and aptitudes for administrative, mechanical, and electronics training. The largest study of white–black predictive bias using the AQE involved 18,103 "whites" (referred to as "non-Negroes" in the air force report) and 1,631 blacks (Guinn, Tupes, & Alley, 1970). In this study the predictor variables were composite aptitude indexes derived from a multiple regression equation including different combinations of AQE subtest scores. Different regression equations were developed to predict final grades in each of ten types of technical schools, for example, electrical repair, aircraft engine maintenance, aerospace control, air police, and electronics. No significant white–black slope bias was found for the regression equations of any of the ten school groups, but intercept bias was found in three of the ten schools. In these three schools, the blacks' final grades were significantly *over*predicted by average amounts varying from $.15\sigma$ to $.42\sigma$. When all students, regardless of race, were grouped into the two educational categories of high school graduates and nongraduates, the regression equations significantly *over*predicted the performance of the nongraduates in three schools by average amounts varying from $.21\sigma$ to $.57\sigma$. This study unfortunately did not test for racial differences in standard error of estimates, and the report does not provide the data needed to calculate these. (The report also includes detailed, but rather inconsistent, evidence on regional differences; in general, the common regression line tends slightly to overpredict final school grades for individuals from the North–Northwest area and underpredict for those from the Far West–Pacific Coast area.)

Bias in the Test Prediction of Civilian Job Performances

Single-group Validity and Differential Validity.   When the issue of test bias in personnel selection in civilian occupations first became a major concern, in the 1960s, the earliest researches focused on findings of single-group validity and differential validity as the primary indicators of bias. Single-group validity is demonstrated when one group shows a validity coefficient significantly larger than zero and the other group does not.

Differential validity is demonstrated when the two groups' validity coefficients differ significantly from one another. It must be emphasized that single-group validity and differential validity are independent; the latter cannot be inferred from the former, even when sample sizes are equal.

Boehm (1972) reviewed thirteen studies reporting single-group and differential validities in white–black comparisons.[5] The thirteen studies involved such occupations as medical technicians, telephone craftsmen, clerical workers, general maintenance, heavy vehicle operators, toll collectors, office personnel, machine shop trainees, administrative personnel, psychiatric aides, and welders. The studies employed a total of fifty-seven various predictor tests and thirty-eight criterion measures based mostly on supervisor's ratings of job performance or, less frequently, objective job knowledge and job sample tests. The average numbers of subjects per study were 135 whites and 101 blacks. The studies yielded altogether 160 white–black pairs of validity coefficients, which can be classified as follows:

	Number	Percent
Nonsignificant validity in both groups	100	62
Significant ($p < .05$) validity in both groups	27	17
Significant validity for whites only	20	13
Significant validity for blacks only	13	8
Significant differential validity	7	4

Single-group validity is a logically inappropriate indicator of test bias, as pointed out near the beginning of this chapter, so the only important finding in the preceding table, in terms of our inquiry, is differential validity, of which there were only 7 cases out of a possible 160, or 4 percent. But the number of differences significant at the .05 level expected by chance is 8. Thus these thirteen studies overall lend no support to the claim that tests are differentially valid for whites and blacks. It also appears that the findings of single-group and differential validity are closely linked to sample size. The more adequate the sample sizes in both groups, the less likely the appearance of single-group or differential validity. In none of the studies where N exceeded 100 in both white and black samples was there found any instance of either single-group or differential validity. Also, when the validity coefficients were determined for the combined white and black samples in each of the 120 instances where this information was given, in only 3 instances was the total group validity coefficient less than the validity for either racial group alone. In 117 (or 98 percent) of the cases, the combined-groups validity coefficient lies above or between those of the separate groups. This is statistically consistent with the hypothesis that the validities are the same in both populations, which, however, differ in central tendency on both the predictor and criterion variables.

An early study frequently cited as evidence of test bias is that of Kirkpatrick et al. (1968). On page 132, the authors give validity coefficients for whites ($N = 437$) and blacks ($N = 98$) on eight tests predicting two criterion measures (salary and performance ratings), that is, a total of sixteen validity coefficients. Not one pair shows significant ($p < .05$) differential validity. In fact, the average level of significance is $p = .65$, although there were eight instances of single-group validity. In seven out of the sixteen pairs of validity coefficients the black validity exceeds the white, which is very close to the chance value of eight if there were no difference between the population validities.

The evidence from the thirteen studies reviewed by Boehm (1972) leads one to hypothesize that with respect to white–black comparisons single-group validity is statistically artifactual and differential validity is a rare, or even nonexistent, phenomenon. Schmidt, Berner, and Hunter (1973) tested this hypothesis. They set up a "null model," hypothesizing that the test's validity coefficient is exactly the same for the white and black *populations* but would show single-group validity in various *sample* comparisons as a result of the absolute sample sizes of whites and blacks, the difference in sample sizes, and the overall average level of validity. Using this statistical model, which assumes no difference in the true population validity for blacks and whites, they then predicted the outcomes of nineteen studies of employment test validities in white and black samples, involving a total of eighty-six different predictors of seventy-four different criterion measures. (Twelve of the nineteen studies were the same as those included in Boehm's review of thirteen studies.[6]) There was a total of 410 white–black pairs of validity coefficients, which were classified as follows, with the percentages of the observed and the predicted outcomes in each category. The null model predicts the empirical outcomes very well indeed, as shown by the fact that the differences between the observed and predicted percentages do not even approach significance [$\chi^2 = 1.39$, n.s. ($p > .80$)].

	Observed	Predicted
Nonsignificant validities in both groups	59.5%	57.0%
Significant validities in both groups	12.9	15.5
Significant validity for whites only	18.3	18.4
Significant validity for blacks only	8.3	9.1

Schmidt, Berner, and Hunter also classified the validity coefficients into those based on subjective criteria (e.g., supervisor ratings) and those based on objective criteria (e.g., job-knowledge and work-sample tests), to see if their null model predicted the validity outcomes as well for both types of validity criteria. For both types, the frequencies of the observed and predicted outcomes do not differ significantly ($p > .20$ and $p > .50$ for subjective and objective criteria, respectively). The authors conclude:

> A conservative interpretation of these findings is that they cast serious doubt on the existence of single-group validity as a substantive phenomenon. The close fit of the null model likewise indicates that differential validity—which is much less frequently reported in the literature—is probably illusory in nature. (p. 8)

General Aptitude Test Battery. The GATB is a battery of twelve aptitude tests developed by the U.S. Employment Service for personnel selection in a wide variety of occupations. The battery measures nine aptitudes. Validation procedures have generally been exemplary. Occupational norms are established in terms of minimum qualifying scores for each of the significant aptitude measures that in combination predict job performance. For any particular occupation only those selector tests are used that, on cross-validation, significantly predict job performance in that occupation. The criterion measure is most often a supervisor's total ratings based on detailed rating scales consisting of thirty-five quite specific items relating to the employee's performance on the job.

All the validation studies presenting results separately for whites and blacks that were available from the U.S. Department of Labor at the time of writing are summarized in Table 10.7. The validity coefficients for white (W), black (B), and total groups are

Table 10.7. Predictive validity of U.S. Employment Service's General Aptitude Test Battery for whites (W) and blacks (B) in nine occupations. (From U.S. Employment Service Technical Reports, Manpower Administration, U.S. Department of Labor, Washington, D.C.)

Occupation Title	Selector Tests[1]	Sample Size		Validity Coefficient[2]			% Selected			% Failed Test and Passed Criterion			% Passed Test and Passed Criterion			U.S.E.S. Report No.
		W	B	W	B	Tot.	W	B	W − B	W	B	W − B	W	B	W − B	
Drafter	G-N-S-Q	221	40	.40	.32	.42	72	60	12	39	37	2	76	75	1	S-266 R'74
Electronics assembler	S-P-O-M	103	59	.39	.22	.32	73	49	24[a]	46	40	6	85	62	23[a]	S-310 R'74
Fork-lift truck operator	S-K	95	91	.28	.19	.28	84	52	32[a]	47	45	2	75	64	11	S-131 R'74
Key-punch operator	G-Q-M	205	120	.25	.23	.24	66	49	17[a]	48	47	1	71	68	3	S-180 R'74
Practical nurse	V-Q-K-M	119	73	.25	.29	.27	64	67	−3	51	42	9	75	71	4	S-270 R'75
Teacher aide (elem. sch.)	V-N-Q-K	161	91	.16	.32	.22	60	42	18[a]	55	40	15[b]	70	68	2	S-398 R'74
Bank teller	N-P-Q	168	78	.27	.20	.24	71	65	6	48	45	3	73	65	8	S-259 R-75
Hospital ward clerk	G-N-Q-K	99	81	.32	.28	.31	84	53	31[a]	44	45	−1	73	70	3	S-239 R'74
Production line welder	G-S-P-Q-K-F-M	59	57	.65	.54	.64	83	54	29[a]	30	35	−5	96	84	12[b]	S-447 R'69
Pooled samples		1,230	690	.30	.27	.29	71	51	20[a]	47	43	4	76	69	7[b]	

[1] G = general ability (g); V = verbal aptitude; N = numerical aptitude; S = spatial aptitude; P = form perception; Q = clerical perception, K = motor coordination; F = finger dexterity; M = manual dexterity.

[2] The validity coefficient is phi/phi max derived from a 2 × 2 contingency table: pass/fail on the test composite versus pass/fail on the criterion job performance rating.

[a] Difference significant at $p < .01$ (two-tailed test).

[b] Difference significant at $p < .05$ (two-tailed test).

502

based on phi/phi max (see Chapter 9, p. 431), which is directly comparable to the Pearson *r*, with a possible range from 0 to ±1.

The following points should be noted:

1. None of the white and black validity coefficients differs significantly for any occupation or for the pooled samples.

2. The minimum qualifying scores of the selector tests would result in the selection of a significantly higher percentage of white than of black applicants, the difference being 20 percent for the pooled samples. This differential selection simply reflects the mean white–black difference on the selector tests. Of course, for the purpose of the validation study, the job applicants were not selected or rejected on the basis of test scores.

3. "Failing" the test means earning less than the total minimum qualifying score on the selector tests. "Failing" the criterion means obtaining an overall rating of "marginal" or "unsatisfactory" performance on the job. Overall a slightly but nonsignificantly greater percentage of whites than of blacks who failed the test passed the criterion. (This difference was significant only for teacher aides.) Thus there is no evidence here that more blacks than whites who failed the tests would have succeeded on the criterion. In this sense the tests are unbiased.

4. Consistently more blacks than whites who passed the test failed on the criterion. This difference is significant for electronics assemblers and for welders in the pooled samples. This means that the test scores *over*predicted black performance, which again is the common finding of so many studies.

One of the studies (drafter) also involved "Spanish surname" (*N* = 30) and Oriental (*N* = 30) validation samples. The validity coefficients for these groups were .56 and .18, respectively. The other statistics are as follows:

Outcome	Spanish Surname	Orientals	White
% Selected	70	87	72
% Failed test and passed criterion	22	50	39
% Passed test and failed criterion	81	81	76

On each of the three outcomes, a chi squared test shows that the differences among the three ethnic groups are nonsignificant (.20 < *p* < .60). Thus there is no evidence here of test bias with respect to the selection of Spanish surname and Oriental groups when compared with nonminority whites. The statistical analysis is not very powerful, however, due to the rather small samples of the two minority groups, each with *N* = 30.

Regression Studies. Studies of the homogeneity of regressions are, of course, the most valuable method for assessing test bias. Fortunately, there are now numerous studies that use this method on employment selection tests comparing whites and blacks.

Ruch (1972) reanalyzed twenty such validity studies of paper-and-pencil tests in the literature that met the following criteria:[7]

1. Studies were conducted in a business or industrial (i.e., noneducational, nonmilitary) setting.

2. Separate statistics were available for blacks and whites.
3. Race was not confounded with some outside variable that would preclude meaningful interpretation.
4. Necessary data were reported to enable a test of homogeneity of regression between racial groups.

A variety of paper-and-pencil aptitude tests and a variety of job performance criteria were employed in these twenty studies, often several in one study. Thus there were altogether 618 white–black pairs of regressions to be statistically compared.

Ruch used the Gulliksen–Wilks (1950) method of testing the homogeneity of regressions between blacks and whites. This method sequentially tests for significant differences in standard error of estimates, slopes, and intercepts, in that order, and rejects the null hypothesis of homogeneity of regressions on the first parameter of the regression that shows a difference significant at the 5 percent level.

Of the 618 tests of significance between standard error of estimates, 72 (12 percent) were significant; of the remaining 546 tests for slopes, 64 (12 percent) were significant; and of the remaining 482 tests for intercepts, 87 (18 percent) were significant. There were altogether 395 (64 percent) pairs of regressions that showed no significant difference in standard errors, slopes, or intercepts. If there were really no significant differences between the populations, then, by chance, we should expect to find 530 (86 percent) that are nonsignificant at the 5 percent level, but only under the assumption that the 618 pairs of regressions are all derived from independent samples. Because many, however, were based on the same black and white samples, they are not statistically independent, and thus we cannot determine directly from these figures whether there are more significant differences than would be expected by chance. Ruch tried (incorrectly) to get around this problem by counting the number of significance tests in each study for each regression parameter that showed significance at $p < .05$ and determining whether that number was greater or less than would be expected by chance under the null hypothesis. Unfortunately, this does not solve the problem, because the significance tests within a given study do not involve independent samples, and the various predictor variables are highly intercorrelated as well as are the various criterion measures. So we really have no way to estimate how many significant differences would be due to chance if the null hypothesis is true. Statistical logic forces us to give up any hope of answering that question.

However, it is worth noting that in all twenty of these studies, not a single one shows biases for any given regression parameter that go in opposite directions for blacks and whites for different pairs of predictors and criteria. For example, if the regression lines for one pair of predictor criterion measures shows a significantly small slope for blacks, a significantly greater slope for blacks is never found for any other pair of predictor criterion measures used in that study. The same thing is true for standard error of estimates and for intercepts. This fact merely reflects the high degree of correlation that must exist among the predictor variables and among the criterion variables. Therefore, I believe that the best way to summarize all the results of these twenty independent regression studies is by the following procedure. In each study, for each regression parameter (i.e., standard error of estimate, slope, and intercept), there is one of three possible outcomes of the statistical test of the significance of the difference between blacks and whites: (1) nonsignificant ($p > .05$), (2) white significantly ($p < .05$) larger than black

(W > B), and (3) black significantly ($p < .05$) larger than white (B > W). Thus, for each study, we can determine which of these three possible outcomes occurs *at least once* for each parameter among all of the regressions computed between the various predictor and criterion variables used in the study. Notice that each study is counted *no less* and *no more* than *once* with respect to each one of the three regression parameters. The tabulations over all twenty studies are shown in Table 10.8. From this information we can ask, Do the biases that are significant tend consistently to favor whites and disfavor blacks over all twenty studies, or is the direction of these biases nonsignificantly different from random, favoring one group about as frequently as the other? If the direction of bias was merely random across all the studies, we should expect no significant differences between the frequencies of W > B and B > W shown in Table 10.8. A chi squared test (with 1 df) shows these differences to be nonsignificant (n.s.) for the standard error of estimate and the slope, but highly significant ($p < .01$) for the intercept. In other words, there is no evidence across studies of bias in standard error of estimates or slopes of which the effects on selection would consistently favor one group over the other. But there is a highly significant and consistent bias for intercepts, with the common finding of the white intercept being higher than the black. This means that, if the regression equation for whites is used to predict the criterion measure for blacks, it *over*predicts the blacks' average performance. Any selection procedure using the same regression equation for both whites and blacks, therefore, will be biased *against* white and *in favor* of blacks. That is the only statistically warranted overall conclusion regarding predictive test bias that can be drawn from the mass of regression data provided by the twenty independent studies included in Ruch's (1972) review. The remedy for intercept bias, of course, is a statistically simple one: include race (as a quantitized variable) among the predictors in the common regression equation.

   The ETS–U.S. Civil Service Commission Six-year Study.   This is the single most important investigation of test bias in the prediction of job performance to be found in the literature. It was a cooperative effort of the U.S. Civil Service Commission and the Educational Testing Service. It involved 1,400 government workers in three occupational categories (medical technicians, cartographic technicians, and inventory management specialists) for which quite thorough and objective assessments of job performance were possible and which employed sufficient numbers of minority workers to permit adequate statistical treatment of the data. The explicit major aim of the study, which extended over a six-year period, was, in the words of the project's director, Dr. Joel T. Campbell, ''to explore the real facts behind the oft-expressed belief that tests are biased against minority

Table 10.8.   Summary of statistical outcomes of tests of significance of the differences between whites and blacks in regression parameters in twenty independent studies.

Regression Parameter	Total	Nonsignificant	Significant ($p < .05$)		χ^2
			W > B	B > W	
Standard error of estimate	20	12	5	3	.50 n.s.
Slope	20	9	7	4	.82 n.s.
Intercept	20	8	11	1	8.33, $p < .01$

groups.'' In a technical critique of the study, Anastasi (1972, p. 79) commented, ''It is fortunate . . . that the general experimental design and the procedure for data gathering and analysis are such that they can be simply characterized as representing a high level of technical excellence. The study is in many ways a model for the validation of personnel selection tests.''

The basic design of the study can be described under five main headings: (1) job analysis, (2) test selection, (3) determination of the test's predictive validity for job performance by different ethnic groups, (4) comparison of different ethnic groups' regressions of job performance measures on test scores, and (5) analysis of bias in supervisors' ratings of job performance in terms of their regressions on objective measures of job knowledge and work samples.

First, a detailed job analysis was made of each occupation (medical technician, cartographic technician, and inventory management specialist). From this job analysis, the kinds of aptitudes deemed most important for each type of job were inferred. Tests designed to measure these aptitudes were selected from various available test batteries, mainly the kit of factored paper-and-pencil reference tests for measuring a variety of cognitive abilities derived by factor analysis of a multitude of highly diverse mental test items (French, Ekstrom, & Price, 1963). Thus each occupational group received a somewhat different combination of tests deemed the most relevant for the special aptitudes required by the particular occupation.

Three types of job performance criteria were used: (1) supervisor's rating scales, which were defined and anchored by behavioral descriptions of aspects of job performance, (2) work samples, and (3) job-knowledge tests. The job-knowledge tests sampled only knowledge that persons on the particular specialized job must have and that can be acquired on the job; they do not include cultural items that are irrelevant to performance of the job or to which minority employees are not exposed as much as the majority.

Care was taken to ensure adequate samples of majority and minority personnel employed in highly similar jobs under common supervision and who had followed similar career paths in attaining their current jobs. They had not been previously screened by employment tests, but there was naturally some degree of informal selection of these persons for a fair degree of suitability for their jobs, by self-selection for the job, interests, and education. All the jobs were at the skilled and technical level, and so the incumbents were far from being random samples of the three ethnic populations involved—blacks and whites in the study of medical technicians, and blacks, Mexican–Americans, and whites in the studies of cartographic technicians and inventory management specialists.

It is practically impossible to convey a full summary of the project's highly statistical 491-page final report (Campbell, Crooks, Mahoney, & Rock, 1973) or of the separate 152-page summary, conclusions, and discussions by outside experts (Crooks, 1972). So I shall simply quote verbatim each of the eleven main points chosen by Campbell, the project director, for the final summary of his conclusions (Campbell et al., 1973, pp. 423–425), accompanied by typical specific examples of the types of statistical analysis that substantiate these conclusions.

1. *''There is little in the data to support the hypotheses of differential validity for the wide variety of tests studied for the ethnic groups included in this study. Tests which were valid for one ethnic group were also valid for the other ethnic group(s). This held true where the tests were used to predict all three kinds of criterion measures.''*

Figure 10.6.   Validity coefficients of various tests for predicting job performance of white, black, and Mexican–American cartographic technicians. (From Campbell et al., 1973, p. 151)

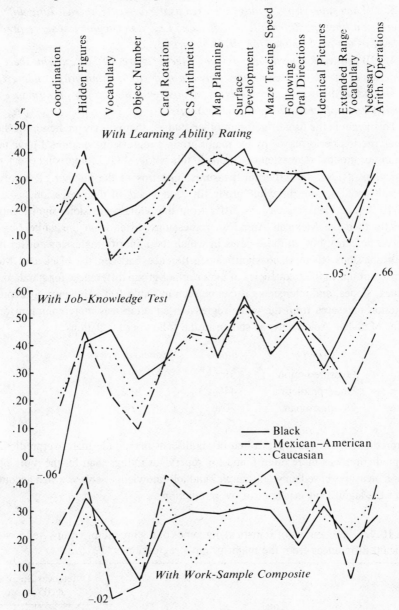

Figure 10.6 shows the correlation of the various aptitude tests with three different criterion measures for three ethnic groups. The same general similarity of validity coefficients across various tests for the different ethnic groups was also found for medical technicians and inventory management specialists.

2.   *"Tests valid against one kind of criterion were generally valid against other criteria also."*

This can be seen in Figure 10.6 in the similarity of validity profiles for the three different criteria: supervisor ratings of learning ability on the job, job-knowledge test, and work samples.

3. *"When supervisors' ratings are used as the criterion, there is little difference in the regression lines for different ethnic groups; i.e., a particular test score predicts the same level of job performance for all ethnic groups."*

4. *"When work samples or job knowledge tests are used as criteria, there usually are differences in the regression lines between majority and minority ethnic groups. In these instances, a given test score is associated with higher job performance for the Caucasian group than for the other two groups."*

This again is the usual finding in other studies, that is, *over*prediction of the minor group's criterion performance by the major group's regression equation. I have tabulated all the minor groups' regression equations in this whole study, comprising every possible combination of tests and criterion measures, in terms of the number of significant (*p* < .05) differences from the white group for each aspect of the regression, as shown in Table 10.9. The black regressions differ from the white regressions significantly more frequently than the Mexican–American regressions differ from the white (49 percent versus 33 percent); but, in those cases in which the minority regressions differ from the white regressions, there is no significant difference between the black and Mexican–American groups in the frequencies of major/minor group differences for standard error of estimates, slopes, and intercepts, as can be seen in Table 10.9. However, *over*prediction of criterion measures from the white regression equation was more common for blacks than for Mexican–Americans, as shown in the following tabulations:

Criterion	Black	Mexican–American
Overprediction	56%	22%
Underprediction	44%	70%
Nondiscrepant	0%	7%

Underprediction was much less often of significant magnitude than overprediction, and underprediction was more often found for supervisor ratings than for the more objective criterion measures based on work samples and job-knowledge scores, which accounted for most of the significant instances of overprediction.

Table 10.9.   Frequencies of statistical outcomes of testing minor groups' regressions for significant differences from the major group's regressions.

Minor Group	Total Regressions	Nonsignificant	Differences Significant at .05 Level		
			SE^1	Slope	Intercept
Blacks	118	60	25	5	28
Mexican–American	87	58	11	2	16
Total	205	118	36	7	44

[1]Standard error of estimate

Figure 10.7. Multiple *R* (predictive validity) weights derived from one racial group and than the black–white results shown in Figure 10.7.

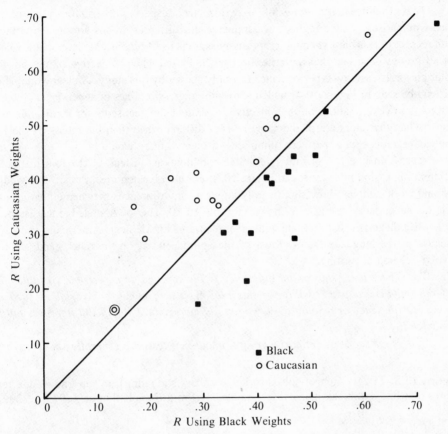

5. *"When test scores are combined by a multiple regression equation, there is no practical loss in predictability when the equation developed for one ethnic group is used for prediction of criterion scores for the other ethnic groups."*

In Figure 10.7 the multiple correlation validity coefficients (*R*) for each occupation and criterion are plotted so as to show the values of *R* for whites and blacks when the regression weights are based on the white and black samples. The distance between each point and the diagonal line represents the loss in the validity coefficient when regression weights from a different ethnic group are used. The corresponding results for Mexican-American/white comparisons are similar, but the data points are slightly more dispersed than the black–white results shown in Figure 10.7.

6. *"Supervisors' ratings were affected by interaction of ethnic group membership of the rater with the ethnic group membership of the ratee. Raters tended to give higher ratings to ratees of their own ethnic group. Ratings of Black job incumbents by Black supervisors had higher correlation with other measures than did ratings of Caucasian job incumbents by Black supervisors. In contrast, ratings of Caucasian job incumbents by Mexican-American supervisors had higher correlations with other measures than did* *their ratings of Mexican–Americans. Ratings by Caucasian raters of all three ethnic groups correlated about equally well with other measures.''*

These findings make *ratings* of job performance suspect as criteria for studies of test bias. Comparisons of the regression parameters for different groups are uninterpretable with respect to *test* bias when the criterion measure is itself biased, that is, not equivalent for all groups. The fact that the criterion itself is biased when subjective ratings are the criterion for assessing job performance is amply shown by this study. A clear example of this can be seen in Figure 10.8, which shows the regression lines of supervisors' subjective job-knowledge ratings on the objective job-knowledge test score for medical technicians, when the raters are of the same or of a different race than the ratees. If the job knowledge ratings were perfectly unbiased, of course, there would be only one and the same regression line for all four rater–ratee combinations instead of the four distinctly different regression lines we see in Figure 10.8. For all job categories, the job-knowledge test and work samples show significantly larger mean differences between ethnic groups than the supervisors' ratings, as shown in Table 10.10. The job-knowledge test is peculiarly difficult and most discrepant with other measures for Mexican–Americans, probably because of the language factor. Most of the aptitude tests, on the other hand, do not involve reading or writing.

7. *"There is no substantial difference in background or experience variables for different ethnic groups. Possibly for this reason, use of moderator variables such as length of experience or amount of education did not produce significant improvement in predictability.''*

8. *"Mean scores for minority groups on aptitude tests are generally about one-half*

Figure 10.8. Regression of job-knowledge supervisor ratings on job knowledge test scores of white and black medical technicians.   (From Campbell et al., 1973, p. 299)

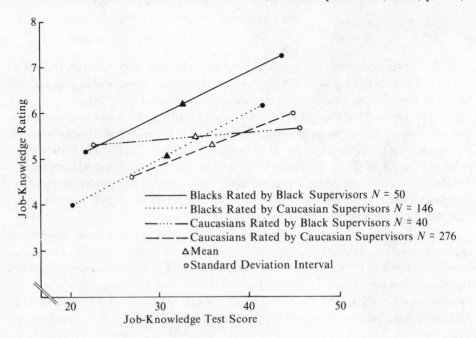

Table 10.10. Mean differences between whites (W) and blacks (B) or Mexican-Americans (M) expressed in standard deviation units.[1]

Occupation	Aptitude Tests		Overall Rating		Job-Knowledge Test		Work Sample		Sample Size		
	W-B	W-M	W-B	W-M	W-B	W-M	W-B	W-M	W	B	M
Medical technician	.55	NA	.10	NA	.44	NA	NA	NA	297	168	NA
Cartographic technician	.38	.51	.23	.06	.42	.87	.37	.39	240	101	101
Inventory management	.42	.27	.06	-.06	NA	NA	.56	-.02	194	112	72
Overall average[2]	.46	.40	.13	.01	.43	.87	.46	.21	731	381	173

NA–Not available.

[1] The mean raw score difference (white minus minority) divided by the average standard deviation of the two groups. The average standard deviation can be expressed as

$$[(N_A \sigma_A^2 + N_B \sigma_B^2)/(N_A + N_B)]^{1/2},$$ where N_A and N_B are the sample sizes of the two groups and σ_A and σ_B are the standard deviations.

[2] Weighted by N.

standard deviation below the mean scores for Caucasians. There are, however, a few instances where the mean for Mexican–Americans is above the mean for Caucasians."

The average differences in aptitude test scores, expressed in standard deviation units, are shown in the first two columns of Table 10.10.

9. *"Mean scores for minority groups on job knowledge tests and work samples are similarly about one-half standard deviation below the Caucasian mean score. There is one instance where the mean score for Mexican–Americans is above the mean score for Caucasians."*

The average white–minority differences on work samples are shown in Table 10.10. This is a point especially worth noting, because the popular belief has been that, even though some minority groups may score considerably below whites on aptitude tests, their actual job performance is on a par with whites. That is here shown to be untrue, insofar as the job-knowledge test and work-sample measures are indicative of job performance. These are at least the most objective indicators available. Job knowledge and work sample are more highly correlated with one another than either is correlated with supervisor ratings. The blacks are just as far below whites on the work-sample composite as on the aptitude tests composite. Thus the tests are a fair indicator of job performance for blacks and whites. The Mexican–Americans, however, are only about half as far below whites on the work sample as on the aptitude test.

10. *"In contrast to the differences on tests and work samples, the means of supervisors' ratings for minority groups are very close to those for Caucasians."*

This can be seen in Table 10.10 in the columns headed Overall Rating. Some part of the smaller group difference in ratings than in the more objective performance measures is probably due to the lower reliability of ratings. But reliability coefficients for these criterion measures are not provided in the report, and so we cannot test this hypothesis directly. However, we do have test reliabilities and the intercorrelations among various ratings from which one may infer their average reliability. The overall average reliability of the aptitude tests is about .82 and of the ratings about .75. The overall average differences for tests and ratings can be corrected for unreliability by dividing each one by the square root of its reliability. Obviously the slight differences in reliability cannot account for the much greater mean differences between the white and minority groups in aptitude scores than in supervisors' overall rating. Most likely the ratings are less valid and more biased indicators of job performance than are the job knowledge test and work samples. This supposition is strengthened by the finding of significant interactions between the race of the raters and race of ratees. (See point 6 earlier.)

11. *"Factor analyses of the test and criterion measures show very similar patterns for all groups."*

The factor analyses show that the factor structure of the aptitude tests is essentially the same for all three ethnic groups. These data are examined more closely in Chapter 11 (pp. 541–543) in connection with the analysis of test bias in terms of construct validity and factorial validity.

Why Is Black Performance Overpredicted by Tests?

The review of the evidence on predictive bias shows quite unequivocally that, when there is found to be significant bias in the prediction of blacks' criterion performance, the bias is most commonly *intercept bias, and virtually always the whites' intercept is higher than the blacks', thereby resulting in over*prediction of the blacks' criterion performance from the use of the whites' regression equation. The predictive bias, therefore, generally "favors" blacks when tests are used for selection without taking account of applicants' race.

We have also seen that such intercept bias and the consequent *over*prediction of blacks' criterion performance is much more common for the more complex, cognitively demanding criteria, such as academic performance, than for manual skills and the like. Even when scores on forward digit span (from the Wechsler Intelligence Scale for Children) are used to "predict" the cognitively more demanding backward digit span for blacks and whites, there is an intercept difference resulting in the overprediction of blacks' backward digit span from the white regression equation by an amount equal to half a standard deviation. Obviously there are factors involved in backward digit span on which blacks and whites differ that are not predicted by forward digit span (Jensen & Figueroa, 1975). (This is discussed further in Chapter 11, pp. 550–551.)

This common finding that mental tests *over*predict black performance comes as a surprise to many, since it has been the popular belief that blacks' mental test scores would *under*estimate their performance in college or in job training, job knowledge, or job performance. The fact that the opposite is much more often true thus seems puzzling.

No well-formulated psychological explanation of this phenomenon has been put forth, although there have been speculations in the literature invoking black–white differences in such factors as achievement motivation, interests, work and study habits, and personality traits involving persistence, emotional stability, and self-confidence—factors that are not measured by the more or less purely cognitive predictor tests but that enter into the criterion performance. Hypotheses of this type seem reasonable, but have not yet been empirically substantiated. They warrant more research. Such research, however, must take into account the statistical nature of the phenomenon of overprediction of black performance if it is to know precisely what it is that needs to be explained. It is surely nothing peculiar to the issue of black–white differences or test bias. For example, in predicting weight from height, women's weight is overpredicted by using the men's regression equation.

In general, overprediction of the minor group's performance from the major group's regression equation (or the common regression equation) is a consequence of a positive difference in intercepts, that is, the major group's regression line being above the minor group's. This positive difference in intercepts, or levels of the regression lines, of the two groups comes about when (1) the group mean difference on the criterion is greater than zero and in the same direction as the group mean difference on the predictor and also (2) the correlation (i.e., validity coefficient) between predictor and criterion multiplied by the group mean difference on the predictor in standard score units is *less* than the groups' mean difference on the criterion in standard score units. This can be seen more easily when it is expressed algebraically. Assuming that the regressions of the major and minor groups, *A* and *B,* do not differ in slopes b_{yx}, the difference in their intercepts in raw score form is

$$k_A - k_B = (\bar{Y}_A - \bar{Y}_B) - b_{yx} (\bar{X}_A - \bar{X}_B). \qquad \textbf{(10.1)}$$

Expressed in the form of standard scores (i.e., scores standardized in the combined groups), this becomes

$$k'_A - k'_B = (\bar{y}_A - \bar{y}_B - r_{xy}(\bar{x}_A - \bar{x}_B)). \tag{10.2}$$

Now it is clearly apparent that, if $\bar{y}_A - \bar{y}_B$ is greater than $r_{xy}(\bar{x}_A - \bar{x}_B)$, there will be a positive difference between the intercepts and, consequently, overprediction of the minor group from the major group's regression lines, amounting to $k_A - k_B$. Obviously if $\bar{y}_A - \bar{y}_B$ were as great as $\bar{x}_A - \bar{x}_B$, the correlation r_{xy} would need to be perfect for there to be no difference in intercepts. Thus in every case where the groups' difference on the criterion is as large or almost as large as on the predictor test, and the validity r_{xy} is not very high, there will be a positive difference in intercepts, hence overprediction. What it means, in so many words, is that the predictor variable does not account for enough of the variance in the criterion variable to account for the major–minor groups' mean difference on the criterion.

Now, because the criterion difference is a *given*, all our efforts to remedy the situation must focus on the second term of equation (10.2), namely, $r_{xy}(\bar{x}_A - \bar{x}_B)$. That is, we can alter or add elements to the predictor so as to increase r_{xy} (i.e., improve validity), and we can increase the mean difference $(\bar{x}_A - \bar{x}_B)$ on the predictor (i.e., make the test more discriminating). In other words, the more valid and the more discriminating we make the predictor test(s), the greater the reduction of the difference between intercepts. Thus, overprediction of the minor group's criterion performance can be seen to be a result of insufficient validity and discriminability of the predictor variable(s). What is needed to improve these properties is a problem for empirical research. It could involve adding other cognitive factors or personality factors, and the like, to the set of predictors—whatever will enhance r_{xy} and increase $\bar{x}_A - \bar{x}_B$. The easy way out, of course, is to add race as a quantitized variable, which will necessarily eliminate the intercept difference completely. But it will not give us any psychological insight as to the reason for the part of the criterion difference that is not predicted by the mental test variables. However, until we find out what the relevant psychological predictors are for which racial classification per se is merely a "stand-in" variable, we have no other choice, if we wish to improve predictive accuracy, but to include race (or other group membership) as a predictor variable along with the test scores or other predictive measures. On the other hand, if the overprediction of the minority group's criterion performance is not too extreme, it may seem reasonable to many to leave it uncorrected, thereby giving the benefit of the slight predictive bias to the presumably less advantaged group.

But, before resorting to these remedies, we should first establish that the difference in intercepts is not explainable by unreliability of measurement of the criterion and predictor variables. If the intercept difference is due mainly to unreliability, it can be easily overcome to a large extent by using "estimated true scores" on both the criterion and predictor. Whether or not this will reduce the intercept difference to nonsignificance can be determined by correcting the formula for the intercept difference for attenuation; thus,

$$\text{Corrected } (k'_A - k'_B) = \left(\frac{\bar{y}_A - \bar{y}_B}{\sqrt{r_{yy}}}\right) - \left(\frac{r_{xy}}{\sqrt{r_{xx}r_{yy}}}\right)\left(\frac{\bar{x}_A - \bar{x}_B}{\sqrt{r_{xx}}}\right) \tag{10.3}$$

If the resulting value differs significantly from zero, one or a combination of the above-suggested remedies is in order.

SUMMARY

Empirical studies of bias in tests' predictive validity for majority and minority groups (usually white and black) have been based mainly on (1) statistical comparison of the groups' validity coefficients and (2) comparison of the groups' regression equations (i.e., the regression of criterion measures on test scores) with respect to each of three parameters: intercepts, slopes, and standard error of estimates.

Numerous large-scale studies relevant to each of these statistical criteria of predictive bias are based on data from every major sphere in which standard tests are used for prediction and selection purposes: school and college, specialized training programs in the armed forces, and employment in a great variety of semiskilled and skilled occupations.

The total evidence on tests' predictive validity for whites and blacks in all these spheres reveals an overwhelming consistency of outcomes. In the first place, *differential* validity for the two racial groups is a virtually nonexistent phenomenon. The few instances of differential validity, against the total background of all studies failing to substantiate differential validity, can be explained in terms of sampling variation. The general finding is that tests' predictive validities are actually the same for blacks and whites, and probably for other native-born English-speaking groups as well, although the evidence on subpopulations other than whites and blacks is relatively scant.

The more rigorous criterion of bias is the equality of regression for the two groups. Here again the evidence is highly consistent. In the vast majority of studies, the regressions of criterion performance on test scores do not differ for blacks and whites. And, almost without exception, when the white and black regressions do differ significantly, the difference is in the *intercepts,* with the black intercept below the white. This *intercept bias* results in *over*prediction of the blacks' criterion performance when predictions for whites and blacks are based on the white or on the common regression line. In any selection procedure based on a common regression equation for all groups, such intercept bias *favors* selection of the group whose performance is *over*predicted. Thus, contrary to popular belief, the evidence shows that, when predictive test bias is found, it in fact most often *favors* blacks in any selection procedure that treats all test scores alike regardless of race. Thus tests, when used predictively in selection, are biased much more often in favor of blacks. Elimination or reduction of test bias in these cases would result in the selection of *fewer* black applicants, if the selection procedure were entirely color blind. Improvement of the reliability and validity of selection tests, and reduction of predictive bias, would not tend in the direction of equalizing the proportions of black and white selectees in any nonquota selection procedure based on test scores, but would have the opposite effect. A preponderance of evidence consistent with this conclusion is found for a variety of mental tests used in studies of predictive validity involving college grades, performance in armed forces training programs that have appreciable cognitive content, and objective measures of job knowledge and job performance in various skilled and semiskilled occupations.

It seems safe to conclude that most standard ability and aptitude tests in current use in education, in the armed forces, and in employment selection are not biased for blacks or whites with respect to criterion validity and that the little bias that has been found in some studies has been in a direction that actually favors the selection of blacks when the selection procedure is color blind.

NOTES

1. If test scores are X and criterion measures are Y, with means $\bar{X}$ and $\bar{Y}$ and standard deviations σ_X and σ_Y, and they are correlated r_{XY}, then the values of the parameters for the regression of Y on X are

$$\text{Slope:} \quad b_{YX} = r_{XY}\,(\sigma_Y/\sigma_X) \tag{10N.1}$$

$$\text{Intercept:} \quad k_Y = \bar{Y} - b_{YX}\bar{X} \tag{10N.2}$$

$$\text{Standard error of estimate:} \quad SE_{\hat{Y}} = \sigma_Y\,\sqrt{1 - r_{XY}^2} \tag{10N.3}$$

(To obtain the values of the parameters for the regression of X on Y, simply interchange X and Y in all the formulas.)

2. If A is the majority group and B is the minority, the regression equation for computing the predicted mean of group B on criterion measure Y is

$$\hat{\bar{Y}}_B = \bar{Y}_A - r_{X_A Y_A}\,(\sigma_{Y_A}/\sigma_{X_A})(\bar{X}_A - \bar{X}_B), \tag{10N.4}$$

where
$\hat{\bar{Y}}_B$ = predicted (i.e., estimated) mean of group B on criterion,
$\bar{Y}_A$ = obtained mean of group A on criterion,
$r_{X_A Y_A}$ = Pearson correlation between predictor (X) and criterion (Y) in group A,
σ_{Y_A} = standard deviation of criterion scores in group A,
σ_{X_A} = standard deviation of predictor scores in group A,
$\bar{X}_A$ = mean of predictor scores in group A, and
$\bar{X}_B$ = mean of predictor scores in group B.

3. Correction for attenuation of the regression equation (10N.4) is accomplished by dividing $r_{X_A Y_A}$ by r_{XX_A} (i.e., the reliability of text X in group A).

4. Further analysis and discussion of predictive bias in the tests used in the Coleman report, especially with respect to Mexican–Americans is found in Gordon (1975, pp. 98–102).

5. The studies included in Boehm's (1972) review are by Campbell, Pike, and Flaughter (1969); Grant and Bray (1970); Kirkpatrick et al. (1968); Lopez (1966); Mitchell, Albright, and McMurry (1968); Ruda and Albright (1968); Tenopyr (1967) Wollowick, Greenwood, and McNamara (1969); Wood (1969); U.S. Department of Labor (1969).

6. The additional studies used in the review by Schmidt, Berner, and Hunter (1973) that were not included in Boehm's (1972) review are by Campion and Freihoff (1970); Farr (1971); Farr et al. (1971); Gael and Grant (1972).

7. The twenty studies in Ruch's review are by Kirkpatrick et al. (1968); Farr et al. (1971); O'Leary et al. (1970); Tenopyr (1967); Campbell et al. (1969); Grant and Bray (1970); Gael and Grant (1972).

Chapter 11

Internal Criteria of Test Bias: Empirical Evidence

The preceding chapter reviewed empirical evidence on the degree to which tests behave similarly with respect to indices of *external* or predictive validity for different populations. The present chapter reviews evidence on the degree of similarity in various psychometric indices of *internal* characteristics of tests for different populations. These internal characteristics of psychometric tests have figured importantly in establishing the construct validity and factorial validity of tests, as well as in the process of test construction itself.

The essential rationale and methodology for using various internal psychometric features of tests for detecting test biases in different populations are explicated in Chapter 9. External and internal criteria of bias in combination can act as a series of sieves for the detection of bias in a given test when used in any two or more populations. The more such sieves through which a test is able to pass, the less credence we should have in an *a priori* hypothesis that the test is biased with respect to the populations in question. Note that the research question addressed by these methods concerns bias in some real test when used in two (or more) particular subpopulations. It is not a matter of trying to prove any *general* proposition concerning cultural bias in tests. Indeed, it may be granted as practically axiomatic that for any given test, two subpopulations can be found with respect to which the test can be shown to be biased; and that for any two subpopulations, some test can be found (or, if not, can be specially constructed) that can be shown to be biased. Merely to demonstrate empirically what can be granted as axiomatic adds little, if anything, to our knowledge of the degree of bias in an existing test for the populations on which it is being used.

It proved possible, for example, to construct two culturally biased tests of "general information," each comprised of twenty-five items specially written or selected for either rural or urban children and on which the direction of the average mean difference between rural and urban children is reversed on the two tests (Shimberg, 1929). The more urban-loaded test favored a large sample of urban children by 0.26σ over their rural counterparts, whereas the more rural-loaded test favored the rural children by 1.03σ over the urban. But the amount of groups (i.e., rural versus urban) $\times$ items interaction is sufficient on each of these two tests separately that they easily meet this internal criterion of bias. For example, one-fourth of the items on the rural-based test show disordinal interactions with groups. Thus it would be relatively easy to reverse the means of two groups simply by eliminating certain items. It has also been shown possible to devise a vocabulary test (the Black Intelligence Test of Cultural Homogeneity, or BITCH) based on black ghetto slang on which some samples of blacks score much higher than do most whites (Williams, 1972; see Chapter 14, pp. 679. Also the Draw-a-Horse test, after the fashion of Goodenough's Draw-a-Man test, with the scoring standardized on Pueblo Indian children, resulted in 11-year-old white boys' averaging 24 IQ points below Pueblo Indian children (DuBois, 1939; Norman, 1963). But what would be much more informative than these particular findings would be to determine if any of the present methods for detecting bias would reveal bias in these specially contrived tests. Finally, it should not go unnoticed that in every such example I have been able to find of a specially contrived test that shows a mean difference between two contrasting racial or ethnic groups that is in the opposite direction to the groups' mean difference on standard tests of intelligence, all the items of the contrived test involve exclusively either vocabulary knowledge sampled from an extremely limited or highly specialized lexicon (such as black ghetto slang), or sheer information items, or the drawing from memory of real objects that are especially familiar in a particular subculture. It has not yet been successfully demonstrated that specially contrived tests intended to equalize or reverse the particular ethnic group differences that are found on all standard tests of cognitive ability can be made up entirely of the kinds of items that best measure g, that is, items that involve some form of relation eduction, reasoning, or problem solving, and in which the items' contents (Spearman's *fundaments*) are highly familiar to all persons for whom the test is deemed appropriate, so that the items' contents per se are only a very minor source of variance in persons' test scores. When, in fact, tests are so designed to minimize variance due to content and maximize variance on relation eduction, reasoning, and problem solving, as in Raven's Progressive Matrices, Cattell's Culture Fair Tests of g, and the Leiter International Performance Scale, white–black mean differences are as large or larger than on the more common culturally and verbally loaded standard tests of cognitive ability.

Historical Precedents

It is interesting to note that, in the history of psychometrics, those who were first concerned about test bias focused on certain *internal* characteristics of tests as indicators of bias. The pioneers of mental testing, such as Binet, Stern, and Burt, in the early 1900s, were concerned with the causes of social-class differences in intelligence test performance and entertained the possibility that the tests themselves could be biased in certain ways that favored children of the upper classes and disfavored lower-class children. These and other early investigators looked at only one possible criterion of test bias, namely, the differential difficulty of various kinds of test items across social classes. In today's terminology, these investigators were searching essentially for group × item interactions, where the groups were different social classes. Their rationale was that, if each of the items comprising the test was assumed to measure one and the same trait, namely, general intelligence, and if some of the items were found to show consistently and markedly greater social-class differences in difficulty (as indexed by percentage passing the item) than the socially least discriminating items, this would mean that the most discriminating items were somehow peculiarly biased. Yet attempts to characterize these apparent item biases in terms of any categorical descriptive features of the multitude of diverse test items examined in this way led to remarkably little general consensus among investigators as to which types of items discriminated most or least between social classes. Herrick (in Eells et al., 1951, pp. 10–15) has summarized the nine earliest studies of this type, dating from 1911 to 1947. Each study lists the types of items that discriminate the least and the most between children of upper and lower social classes. But there is little agreement among results at this general level of item description. About the only types of items that are consistently never mentioned in the "most discriminating" category but are most frequently mentioned in the "least discriminating" category are items involving "rote memory" (with the exception of repetition of meaningful sentences) and items involving money. But it is most difficult to discern any clear consistency at the level of item description; it is too much like looking at a Rorschach inkblot. In reviewing this material, Herrick admits "some apparent inconsistency of findings," but goes on to give us his own conclusion, which I think can only be interpreted as his response to this "projective test" and should be viewed merely as a hypothesis rather than a conclusion:

> Nevertheless, it appears that these studies indicate that, in general, test items which are essentially linguistic or scholastic in nature show comparatively large differences in favor of children from high socioeconomic backgrounds, while test items which are primarily perceptual or "practical" in nature show either smaller differences or differences in favor of children from the lower socioeconomic backgrounds.   (p. 4)

There is little wonder as to the lack of consensus in these early studies. A major problem with these studies is that they did not recognize that item difficulties in terms of percentage passing the item cannot properly be compared across social classes at all levels of item difficulty. As pointed out in Chapter 9 (p. 439), percentage passing is not an interval scale. (The difference between 50 percent and 60 percent passing, for example, represents much less difference in item difficulty than the difference between 80 percent and 90 percent passing.) Percentage passing must be transformed to a normalized index of item difficulty (see p. 440) before meaningful social-class comparisons can be made throughout the full range of item difficulties. Also, social-class differences in item difficulty cannot be interpreted unless chronological age is taken into account, because the same test item may actually measure different mental factors or have significantly difference g loadings in different age groups. For example, the forward digit-span memory item correlates about .65 with Stanford–Binet IQ at 2 to 3 years of age, but only about .45 at age 10 (Terman & Merrill, 1960, Appendix B). Finally, it did not seem to occur to the early investigators that items' differential discriminability between social classes might be more closely related to certain latent characteristics of the items as revealed by factor analysis, such as the items' g loadings, than to those surface features of test items that can be discerned merely by inspection. For example, the seemingly rather similar Verbal Comprehension and Vocabulary subtests of the WISC are actually less alike in their g loadings than are Vocabulary and Block Designs. The surface features of test items are not dependable indicators of their factorial structure, and I suspect that this fact is in large part responsible for the failure of the early studies to reach any semblance of consensus concerning which features of test items discriminate the most and the least between social classes.

The Eells Study.   The first important advance in the analysis of social-class bias in tests, since the question was originally raised by Binet in 1911, was made by Kenneth Eells (1913–1973), in what is now generally regarded as a classic study in this field (Eells et al., 1951). (The "al." consist of members of Eells's dissertation committee and others in the University of Chicago's Department of Education who contributed brief introductory chapters to Eells's monograph.) Eells's famous monograph, entitled *Intelligence and Cultural Differences,* was based on his Ph.D. dissertation at the University of Chicago; it is one of the most massive and widely known doctoral studies in the history of psychology and education.

Eells's study was essentially an attempt to test the hypothesis that the main cause of the average IQ difference between children from upper- and lower-social-status backgrounds is to be found in the tests themselves, due to the predominantly upper-middle-class kinds of knowledge, vocabulary, and cognitive skills sampled by the test items, the contents of which presumably are much less frequently experienced by lower-status children. Eells clearly recognized other possible explanations for social-class differences in IQ, but he believed that the first one that should be investigated before the others were seriously entertained is the factor of cultural bias in the tests. He wrote:

> Do these differences prove that the children of high-status families inherit superior genetic constitutions, including superior mental equipment? Do they mean that the children of high-status families have lived in more stimulating environments so that their "mental alertness" has been developed more fully than that of children of low-status families? Or do they mean that the tests are heavily laden with materials with which high-status pupils have more opportunity for familiarity than do low-status pupils? In short—are the differences evidence of important differences in the pupils being measured, or are they evidence of important shortcomings in the measuring instruments?   (Eells et al., 1951, p. 162)

Eells examined this last question in terms of item analyses of the then most widely used standardized group IQ tests, comparing large samples of upper- and lower-status children on the item difficulties and the relative frequencies of errors among the multiple-choice distractors.

In 1946, Eells gave a battery of standard IQ tests to practically all the white pupils of ages 9, 10, 13, and 14, totaling nearly 5,000 children, in a midwestern industrial community of approximately 100,000 population. The test battery included such well-known tests as the Otis, Henmon–Nelson, Thurstone's Primary Mental Abilities, and the California Test of Mental Maturity. These tests altogether provided more than 650 items on which groups of upper and lower socioeconomic status (SES) could be compared. The index of SES was based on parental education and occupation, type of house, and residential area. On the basis of this index, the sample was divided into three SES levels, labeled high, middle, and low status. The low-status group was further divided into "ethnic" (at least one parent foreign born, except those from the British Isles, Canada, Germany, and Scandinavia) and "Old American" (both parents American born). Eells demonstrated correlations between IQ and his Index of Status Characteristics that are quite typical of those generally found in such studies, ranging from .20 to .43 for various tests and age levels, which amounts to some 8 to 23 IQ points difference between the high- and low-status groups.

The main analysis consisted of comparing the item difficulties of the more than 650 single test items across the high- and low-status groups and across the ethnic and Old American groups.

Eells's findings can be summarized in five main points.

1. *Status differences vary across test items.* The percentage passing each item was transformed to a normalized index of difficulty, thereby representing item difficulty on an interval scale, separately for each status group. All high–low status comparisons on items are based on the difference between the indexes of item difficulty of the high- and low-status groups (i.e., high minus low). These status differences in the index of difficulty for 658 items were found to be roughly normally distributed. It is difficult to say how widely the items vary in showing status differences, as we have no *a priori* expectation of the amount of variation against which we could compare the amount of variation actually found. (In this regard it would have been much more informative if Eells had matched high- and low-status pupils for total raw score on the tests and then looked at status differences on the individual items.) But the coefficient of variation (CV = 100σ/mean) of the distribution of status differences in the index of item difficulties is 70.5 for 9- and 10-year-olds and 41.9 for 13- and 14-year-olds. About half of the items for the younger group and 85 percent of the items for the older group showed status differences large enough to be significant at the 1 percent level. But more than a third of the items for the younger group and a tenth of the items for the older group show status differences too small to be significant at the 5 percent level. However, it should be noted that very few items showed *negative* status differences (i.e., more lower-status pupils got them correct); this occurred on only 5 percent of the items taken by the 9- and 10-year-olds and 0.6 percent of the items taken by the 13- and 14-year-olds. The fact of variation in status differences across items indicates very little by itself, without some external standard against which to compare it, and unfortunately Eells's study provides no such standard for comparison. A useful standard might be the distribution of index differences between two age groups, say, 9-year-olds and 10-year-olds, all of whom are of the same social status. (One could assure sameness of social background by using siblings reared together.)

2. *Ethnic differences do not vary across test items.* If *cultural* differences were to be found in this study, one might expect to find them most in the *ethnic* group as contrasted with the Old American group. Eells compared only the low-status ethnics with low-status Old Americans. (There were not enough high-status ethnics for statistical comparisons.) These groups differed only about 3 IQ points, on the average. Only 1.9 percent of the items showed index differences between these groups large enough to be significant at the 1 percent level, and more than 91.5 percent of the differences were too small to be significant at the 5 percent level. In short, the item analysis did not reveal any appreciable item index differences between two groups that, although presumably cultur- ally different, did not differ in overall IQ. (Eells tries to explain this finding by saying that his method of identifying ethnic pupils was not entirely satisfactory.) This finding raises the question of the range or variance of item index differences that would be found either for (1) two groups of Old Americans all of the same social status but differing as much in overall IQ as do the high- and low-status groups or (2) high- and low-status Old Ameri- cans of the same overall IQ. Although the mean status differences in item difficulty index between any two groups will of course be a direct function of their mean difference in IQ, the variance of the distribution of item index differences could well be more a function of a difference in overall ability than a difference in social status. These comparisons would have yielded a much more telling test of Eells's hypothesis that social-class differences in IQ are largely due to culturally biased test items than to any of the analyses that Eells provided. The failure to find greater than chance item differences between ethnics and Old Americans, groups that ostensibly differ in cultural background, is actually inconsistent with the culture-bias hypothesis. It is a point seldom mentioned in secondary accounts of Eells's work.

3. *Status differences are greater on the easier test items.* Status differences in the index of item difficulty are related to the difficulty level of the items. Contrary to Eells's expectation, the largest status differences were found on the easier items rather than on the more difficult ones, and this relationship was especially marked in the case of verbal items. This relationship held up throughout the full range of item difficulty, when the measure of item difficulty was based on either the high- or the low-status group. If item difficulty in general depends on relative unfamiliarity or strangeness of the vocabulary or information content of the item, one should expect that the more difficult items (i.e., items with the least familiar content) would show the largest status differences. But in fact just the opposite was found. Eells states:

> The hypothesis of cultural bias in the items . . . seems completely inadequate to explain the findings. The easier items may be presumed to be those which involve words and objects which are most likely to be familiar to all status groups, while the more difficult items are probably those which involve words and objects more likely to be familiar to high-status pupils alone. In terms of this hypothesis, therefore, one would expect results exactly the opposite of those found.   (p. 65)

4. *Status differences vary by type of test item.* When items were classified according to type of symbols used and type of question asked, the mean status differences were largest for verbal and smallest for picture, geometric design, and stylized drawing items. Also, the dispersion (i.e., standard deviation) of status differences was greater for verbal and pictorial items than for geometric designs, stylized drawings, number combinations, and letter combinations.

Eells explains the larger status differences shown by verbal items in terms of the academic or bookish vocabulary of many verbal items, which involve words, objects, or concepts with which high-status students have greater opportunity for becoming familiar. Eells notes, however, that there were many items that showed large status differences for which no particular explanation is apparent and through which runs no common feature, except that they were usually verbal. Because these were all group-administered tests, the verbal items necessarily depend on reading skill. Eells did not consider the question of how much the status differences on the verbal items could be attributed simply to the well-established social-status differences in reading skill, particularly reading comprehension, which itself is quite highly correlated with g.

Items showing the smallest status differences were nearly always nonverbal or involved simple everyday words not intended to test vocabulary. The one complete test showing the smallest status differences was the Spatial Visualization Ability Subtest of Thurstone's Primary Mental Abilities. (Later studies have also shown quite small SES differences on tests of spatial ability relative to IQ differences.) But the Spatial Ability test has the lowest g loading of any of the Primary Mental Abilities, which suggests the hypothesis that status differences are directly related to the item's g loading. It is a pity that Eells did not factor analyze the items (or scores based on subsets of highly similar items) and examine the relationship between items' factor loadings and status differences in item difficulty, but that would have been exceedingly costly in time and effort in the days before high-speed electronic computers.

Within either verbal or nonverbal classes of items no one type of item (e.g., analogies, opposites, classification, etc.) consistently showed larger or smaller status differences.

5. *Few differences arise in choice of error distractors.* The high- and low-status groups were also compared in the frequencies with which they made errors on the different multiple-choice distractors. Of the 315 multiple-choice items, 75 showed significantly different patterns of errors for the two groups. Eells could give a plausible explanation for a number of these error differences in terms of status differences in opportunity for familiarity with the content of the various error distractors. But most of the items did not readily yield to this kind of explanation. The errors of high-status children, more frequently than those of low-status children, consisted of choosing the one distractor that was most nearly correct or logically closest to the correct answer. Low-status children tended to spread their errors more evenly across the several distractors, as one would expect to find if they engaged in more random guessing. (There were no significant status differences in the proportions of all noncorrect responses that consisted of omissions.)

Choice of distractors has since been found to be related to mental age and chronological age in culturally homogeneous groups, in a way much like the status differences described by Eells. That is, when brighter or more mature children make errors on a multiple-choice test, they tend to make "better" or more sophisticated choices from among the several distractors. Moreover, as persons reach the more difficult items, they show a greater tendency to guess at the answers and the guesses become more random with the increasing difficulty of the items. Low-status pupils, for whom more items are in the high range of difficulty, thus have a greater opportunity to engage in "wild guessing."

Eells displays a small collection of items that show large status differences either in difficulty or in choice of distractors and for which an explanation in terms of greater familiarity with the item content in high-status homes seems very plausible. For example,

Pick out the ONE WORD that does not belong with the others:
    cello   harp   drum   violin   guitar
Sonata is a term used in
    drawing   drama   music   poetry   phonetics.

But one can find even more items with as large status differences as these for which there is no plausible explanation. Many of these items, however, require the pupil to perform some type of relation eduction, and such items are usually good measures of g. Thus it is ambiguous in Eells's results as to whether they reveal mainly status differences in familiarity with item content or differences in reading skill plus ability in relation eduction. Eells clearly perceived this uncertainty; he wrote, "The presence of such a large proportion of unexplained differences should lead to caution in accepting the idea that all status differences on test items can be readily accounted for in terms of the cultural bias of their content" (p. 357).

Despite this caution, Eells, following his mentor, the sociologist Allison Davis, of the University of Chicago, advocated the construction of culture fair tests based on the notion that the chief cause of social-class differences on existing tests was due to their culturally biased content. If the Davis–Eells theory is essentially correct, it should have an important practical consequence for test construction, namely, the possibility of making up intelligence tests that could eliminate, or even reverse, status differences and still preserve the essential psychometric properties of a good test, such as high reliability and compelling predictive, factorial, and construct validity. By means of item analysis, such as that used by Eells, one would eliminate all items showing significant status differences and, if necessary, make up new items to eliminate such differences. This idea was quite severely criticized on theoretical grounds shortly after publication of Eells's thesis (e.g., Lorge, 1966). But easily the most telling evidence against the Davis–Eells theory is the fact that no such test that eliminates SES differences has yet been devised, despite great efforts to do so by Davis and Eells themselves, and by others.

In 1951 Davis and Eells made up a test, the *Davis–Eells Games,* which they hoped would eliminate SES differences. The items, represented as games, consisted of cartoons of children doing ordinary things in familiar settings or settings more typical of a low-SES than of a middle-class environment. The test required no reading and had no time limit— features thought to favor low-SES relative to middle-SES children. Practical judgment and commonsense inferences are called for in solving most of the problems. One cartoon, for example, shows three panels, each depicting a boy trying to get over a high backyard fence. One boy is shown piling up boxes and rubbish cans in a most unstable fashion, one is futilely jumping, and one is stacking boxes in a stable fashion. The testee simply marks the picture that he or she thinks shows the best method for getting over the fence. Davis and Eells found that, to increase item difficulty with such familiar materials, to make them suitable for older or brighter children, they had to compose items calling for more and more complex inferences and judgments. As a result, the test involved the kind of relation eduction that characterizes *g,* and the test scores showed about the same SES differences as are found with conventional IQ tests (see Chapter 14, pp. 643–644). I suspect that it would be as difficult to make up a psychometrically defensible test of intelligence that eliminates SES differences as to make up an intelligence test that eliminates age differences. The *Davis–Eells Games* not only failed to achieve its main purpose, but it was deficient as well in various psychometric properties for an intelligence test, such as predictive validity for scholastic performance. Consequently, it was dropped from publication and is now merely a curio in the history of psychometrics.

The McGurk Study.   This, too, was a pioneer doctoral study, by psychologist Frank C. J. McGurk (1951). (McGurk has also written three articles—1953a, 1953b, 1967—on different aspects of this study.) McGurk's dissertation was concerned with testing the hypothesis that the poorer performance of blacks, as compared with that of whites, on most mental tests is the result of cultural bias in the tests. The questions posed by McGurk's study and the method for tackling them had been raised in somewhat less clear-cut form in several earlier studies, which inquired as to whether or not blacks performed relatively better on certain types of item content in mental tests than on some other types.

Bruce (1940), for example, had six psychologists classify the thirty-four subtests of the Kuhlman–Anderson intelligence scale into three categories of items: *information questions,* to which the answers depend on specific items of knowledge that the child must have already acquired before taking the test; *new situation questions,* which do not depend on any specific information but call on mental operations of a problem-solving nature during the examination; and *hybrid questions,* which combine features of the other two types of questions. Bruce found that the low mean IQ of blacks on the Kuhlman–Anderson test as a whole was not attributable to any particular type of items when so classified; blacks performed about the same on all types of items. Bean (1941, 1942) classified test items as verbal and nonverbal and concluded that the lower scores of southern blacks are not specifically a result of poorer vocabulary or poorer comprehension of verbal material per se. In fact, another study (Clarke, 1941) found that, when blacks and whites are *matched* both on chronological age and Stanford–Binet mental age, the blacks perform better than do the whites in the *verbal* items of the Stanford–Binet. In World War I, the U.S. Army used two mental tests for selection, the Alpha (a verbal test) and the Beta (a nonlanguage test). The mean white–black difference in σ units was greater on the combined scale (Alpha and Beta) than on Alpha alone (Alpers & Boring, 1944; Garrett, 1945, 1945b).

McGurk's (1951) doctoral study took a closer look at this type of question in terms of the rated "culture loading" of well-known standardized tests of intelligence, such as the Otis Test, Thorndike's CAVD, and the ACE test. A panel of 78 judges, including professors of psychology and sociology, educators, professional workers in counseling and guidance, and graduate students in these fields, were asked to classify each of 226 test items into one of three categories: I, least cultural; II, neutral; III, most cultural. Each rater was permitted to ascribe his own meaning to the word "cultural" in classifying the items. McGurk wanted to select the test items regarded as the most and the least "cultural" in terms of some implicit consensus as to the meaning of this term among psychologists, sociologists, and educators. Only those items were used on which at least 50 percent of the judges made the same classification or on which the frequency of classification showed significantly greater than chance agreement. The main part of the study then consisted of comparing blacks and whites on the 103 items claimed as the most cultural and the 81 items claimed as the least cultural according to the ratings described. The 184 items were administered to 90 high school seniors. From these data, items classed as "most cultural" were matched for difficulty (i.e., percentage passing) with items classed as "least cultural"; there were 37 pairs of items matched (± 2 percent) for difficulty.

These 37 pairs of matched items were then administered as a test to seniors in 14 high schools in Pennsylvania and New Jersey, totaling 2,630 whites and 233 blacks. Because there were so many more whites than blacks, it was possible for McGurk to obtain practically perfect matching of a white pupil with each of 213 black pupils. Each black pupil was paired with a white pupil in (1) the same curriculum, (2) the same school, and (3) enrollment in the same school district since first grade. The white–black pairs were also matched so that the white member of each pair was either equal to or lower than the black member on an eleven-item index of socioeconomic background (the Sims Scale). (Exact matching on the eleven items of the SES index was achieved, on the average, in 66 percent of the 213 matched black–white pairs.) The matched black and white groups averaged 18.2 and 18.1 years of age, respectively.

McGurk's findings can be summarized in five main points.

1. On the total test for the matched groups, the white–black mean difference, expressed in standard deviation units, is 0.50σ.

2. On the thirty-seven test items classified as "most cultural," the white–black mean difference is 0.30σ. On the thirty-seven test items classified as "least cultural," the white–black mean difference is 0.58σ. In other words, *the white–black difference on the "least cultural" items is almost twice as great as on the "most cultural" items.*

3. To determine if finding 2 was merely a result of differences in item difficulty between the most and least cultural items, McGurk obtained twenty-eight pairs of "most" and "least" cultural items matched (±5 percent) for difficulty (based on the percentage passing the items in the combined white–black samples). On these sets of most and least cultural items matched for difficulty, the white–black mean difference is 0.32σ on the "most cultural" items and 0.56σ on the "least cultural" items. In short, the results in finding 2 cannot be attributed to differences in item difficulty per se between the most and least cultural items. *Blacks perform relatively better on the items judged as the more culture loaded when item difficulty is held constant.* In 1951 this was considered a most surprising finding.

4. The item difficulties (percentage passing) separately for blacks and whites are correlated with each other .98 for the "most cultural" and .96 for the "least cultural" sets of difficulty-matched items. Thus there is a high degree of similarity in the items' relative difficulties for whites and blacks or, conversely, a practically negligible race $\times$ item interaction for both the most and the least culture-loaded items.

5. McGurk also wished to determine the way in which SES interacted with black–white differences on the sets of items judged as the most and the least cultural. The 25 percent of whites and blacks who ranked the highest and the 25 percent who ranked the lowest on the SES index were selected as the high-SES and low-SES groups for further analysis. There were fifty-three subjects of each race in each SES group. The results are summarized in Table 11.1 in terms of the mean difference expressed in standard deviation units.

The pattern of differences seen in Table 11.1 shows definite interactions among race, SES, and item type that are quite contrary to popular expectation. As one might expect, the most cultural items show a larger difference between high- and low-SES whites than the least cultural items. But just the opposite is true for blacks; the SES differences are greater for the *least* culture-loaded items. Also, the difference is considerably greater between whites and blacks matched for high SES than between whites and blacks matched for low SES, and this rather surprising result is even exaggerated on the most cultural items. This is quite inconsistent with the hypothesis that the white–black difference in test scores is due to the culture loading of the items, at least as the culture loading of test items is commonly judged.

One possible explanation for McGurk's seemingly paradoxical results is to be found in the fact that blacks perform better on tests involving rote learning and memory than on tests involving relation eduction or reasoning and problem solving, especially with content of an abstract nature. This is essentially the distinction between what I have labeled level I and level II abilities (Jensen, 1973c, 1974b).

In the most general terms, blacks perform relatively less well on test items that involve greater cognitive complexity. By cognitive complexity I mean the mental manipulation or transformation of the item input required to produce the correct output. Item complexity, in this sense, is quite distinct from item difficulty, which is defined as the percentage of subjects who can pass the item. It is hypothesized that the more culturally

Table 11.1.   Mean difference (in σ units) between high- and low-SES whites and blacks on the most and least cultural test items.   (From McGurk, 1951, Table 11, p. 30)

Groups[1]	Mean Difference in σ Units[2]	
	Most Cultural	Least Cultural
Low-SES White–Low-SES Black	0.14	0.50
High-SES White–High-SES Black	0.70	0.86
High-SES White–Low-SES White	1.14	0.85
High-SES Black–Low-SES Black	0.25	0.47
Overall: High–low SES	0.69	0.66
Overall: White–Black	0.32	0.69

[1]$N = 53$ in each subgroup.
[2]The mean difference in σ units is $(\overline{X}_A - \overline{X}_B)/\sqrt{\frac{1}{2}(\sigma_A^2 + \sigma_B^2)}$, where A and B are the two groups being compared. This formula applies only when groups A and B are of equal size.

loaded items at a given level of difficulty are not as cognitively complex as the less culturally loaded items at the same level of difficulty.

In general, the difficulty of the most culturally loaded items depends more on past learning and memory, whereas the difficulty of the least culturally loaded items depends more on the complexity of the reasoning needed to produce the correct answer. In other words, the most cultural items might be less *g* loaded than the least cultural items. For example, from McGurk's study there are two items of equal difficulty (28 percent passing) in the combined groups; the first item was placed by the judges in the "most cultural" category, the second in the "least cultural":

1. ABYSMAL   ::   (a) bottomless   (b) temporal   (c) incidental   (d) matchless
2. A hotel serves a mixture of three parts cream and two parts milk. How many pints of cream will it take to make 15 pints of this mixture?
   (a) 5   (b) 6   (c) $7\frac{1}{2}$ (d) 9   (e) 12

The mean white–black difference is 0.03σ on the first item and 0.38σ on the second. Many similar examples can be found in McGurk's (1951) report.

   Recent Studies of Verbal versus Nonverbal IQ Difference.   It has long been a common belief that blacks are more disfavored, relative to whites, by verbal tests than by nonverbal or performance tests. This is plausible in view of the seemingly greater scope for cultural factors to be involved in test items that depend on specific language usage, in contrast to nonverbal items.

   McGurk (1975) has reviewed virtually the entire published literature between 1951 and 1970 on the question of whether verbal or nonverbal intelligence tests show greater discrimination between the scores of blacks and whites. From 1,720 articles listed in *Psychological Abstracts* as dealing with "race" or "Negro," McGurk found 80 articles that contain objective test data comparing blacks and whites and 25 articles that compare blacks and whites on both verbal and nonverbal tests. McGurk determined the median overlap of the black and white distribution of scores on verbal and nonverbal tests. (Median overlap is the percentage of blacks whose test scores exceed the median of the whites' score distribution.) The average median overlap in all eighty studies is 15 percent (equivalent to an IQ difference of approximately 16 points). The verbal and performance subtests of the Wechsler show greater overlap for the verbal tests (see Table 11.2). The verbal and performance subtests of the Wechsler are well characterize by Sattler (1974):

> [T]he Verbal Scale is relatively highly structured, is dependent on the child's accumulated experience, and usually requires the child to respond automatically with what he already knows, whereas the Performance Scale is relatively less structured, is more dependent on the child's immediate problem solving ability, and requires the child to meet new situations and to apply past experience and previously acquired skills to a new set of demands.   (p. 206)

Contrary to popular expectation, as can be seen in Table 11.2, there is significantly greater black–white median overlap on the verbal than on the nonverbal tests.

McGurk did not consider the Stanford–Binet IQ test, probably because the verbal and nonverbal items are not scored separately as in the Wechsler tests. Kennedy, Van de Riet, and White (1963), however, did an item analysis of the 1960 revision of the Stanford–Binet given to 1,800 randomly sampled black children in five southeastern states. Examining the percentage of the sample passing each item, the authors concluded, "There does not seem to be any exceptionally high performance ability in contrast to low verbal ability for this sample, as suggested by authors" (p. 109). The largest and probably most representative white and black samples ever tested on the same verbal and nonverbal tests are those in the Coleman report (Coleman et al., 1966), which McGurk did not include in his review. The mean white–black difference (expressed in white σ units) on the tests of verbal ability given in grades 1, 3, 6, 9, and 12 is 1.02σ; on nonverbal ability the difference is 1.05σ. The difference of 0.03σ is trivial, for all practical purposes, but it fails to support the notion that blacks do worse on verbal than on nonverbal tests.

An especially valuable set of data for consideration of this question is found in a study by the U.S. Public Health Service (Roberts, 1971). As a part of the National Health Survey, a sample of 7,119 children was selected in such a way as to be representative of the roughly 24 million noninstitutionalized children 6 through 11 years of age in the United States. Approximately 1,000 children were examined in each age group. Approximately 14 percent of the sample were black. All children were given two subtests from the Wechsler Intelligence Scale for Children—Vocabulary and Block Design. This choice of

Table 11.2.   Average percentage of scores in black sample overlapping the white median score on various verbal and nonverbal IQ tests.   (From McGurk, 1975, p. 225)

Test	Number of Studies	Number of Subjects	Percentage Overlap		Significance Level of Difference
			Verbal	Nonverbal	
Wechsler Intelligence Scale for Children	10	1,692	18%	14%	.01
Wechsler Adult Intelligence Scale	5	506	19	16	.10
Wechsler–Bellevue Intelligence Scale	4	279	21	16	.20
Miscellaneous tests	6	1,202	19	14	.01
Total	25	3,679	19	15	.01

Figure 11.1. Average Vocabulary and Block Design raw scores on the Wechsler Intelligence Scale of white and black children by annual family income. The linear correlation between children's IQs and family income is .43 ± .027. (From Roberts, 1971)

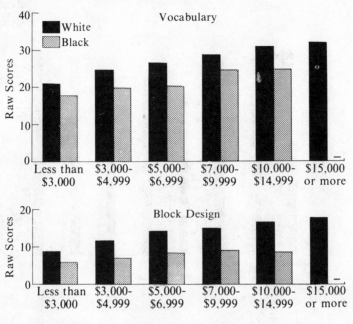

Annual Family Income

tests is ideal for two reasons: (1) The combined Vocabulary and Block Design tests correlate more highly (+.88) with the WISC Full Scale IQ than does any other combination of two subtests for both blacks and whites and (2) in a factor analysis done on the age 10 group, Vocabulary has the largest g loading (about .80) of any of the verbal subtests and Block Design has the largest g loading of any of the performance subtests. Vocabulary, however, is slightly more g loaded than is Block Design. The mean black–white difference, relative to the average standard deviation within groups, is approximately constant across all ages from 6 through 11 and appears at all economic and educational levels of the children's parents as shown in Figures 11.1 and 11.2.

The average white–black difference is 0.78σ on Vocabulary and 0.76σ on Block Design. The difference of 0.02σ is significant, but utterly trivial. It suggests that in large representative samples of American blacks there is probably little, if any, difference in level of performance on verbal and nonverbal tests, provided they have comparable g loadings. My perusal of all the available evidence leads me to the hypothesis that it is the item's g loading, rather than the verbal–nonverbal distinction per se, that is most closely related to the degree of white–black discrimination of the item. This observation was first made by Spearman (1927). In commenting on a study of 10 different mental tests administered to 120 black and 2,000 white American children of ages 10 to 14, Spearman noted that the blacks, on the average, showed poorer performance than whites on all ten tests, "but it was most marked in just those which are known to be most saturated with g" (p. 379). We shall examine this hypothesis more closely in the next section.

Figure 11.2. Average Vocabulary and Block Design raw scores on the Wechsler Intelligence Scale for white and black children in terms of education attained by parent (head of household). The linear correlation between children's IQs and the education of their parents is .48 ± .017. (From Roberts, 1971)

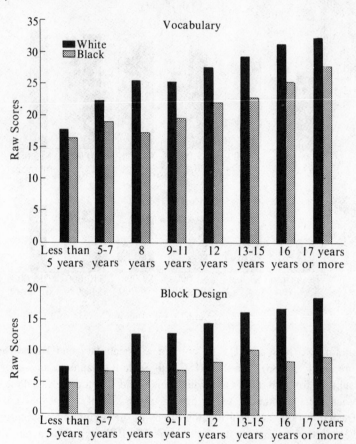

Years of Schooling Completed by Parent

Jensen (1974a) compared California elementary school whites ($N = 638$), blacks ($N = 381$), and Mexican–Americans ($N = 644$) on verbal and nonverbal tests that were perfectly matched on difficulty for white males ($N = 333$). The verbal test was the Peabody Picture Vocabulary (PPVT); the nonverbal test was Raven's Colored Progressive Matrices. These two tests seem ideal for examining our hypothesis. The PPVT consists of 150 plates each bearing four pictures; the examiner names one of the four pictures and asks the subject to point to the appropriate picture. The plates are presented in the order of the difficulty level of the stimulus words in terms of percentage passing in the normative sample. The level of item difficulty, and hence the rank order of the items' presentation, is quite closely related to the relative frequency of the occurrence of the stimulus words in the English language. Figure 11.3 shows the mean frequency of the PPVT stimulus words per million words, as tabulated in the Thorndike–Lorge (1944) general word count in American newspapers, magazines, and books. This indicates that the PPVT item difficulty is closely related to the rarity of the words in general usage in American English, and this is mainly what is meant by "culture loaded."

The contrasting test, in this respect, is the Raven Colored Progressive Matrices, which consists of thirty-six colored multiple-choice matrix items. This nonverbal test was specially designed to reduce item dependence on acquired knowledge and to keep cultural and scholastic content to a minimum while calling for reasoning ability. The difficulty level of the items is dependent on their degree of complexity, involving nonrepresentational figural material and the number of figural elements and abstract rules that must enter into the reasoning process required for correct solution. Examples of the PPVT and Progressive Matrices items are shown in Figure 11.4.

Because there are only 36 colored matrices items and 150 PPVT items, it was possible to obtain perfect matching of item difficulties on each of 35 pairs of matrices and PPVT items in the sample of white males, so that the means and standard deviations on these two subtests were identical in this sample.

We can then ask the crucial question: how large are the mean differences between these two contrasting tests, the PPVT and matrices, which were perfectly matched for difficulty on white males, when given to samples of blacks, Mexican–Americans, and white females of the same age?

It turns out that there is no significant mean difference between the matrices and PPVT scores *within* the groups of white females, black males, and black females. (In fact, white females show a larger difference than black males.) Both male and female

Figure 11.3. Mean Thorndike–Lorge word frequency of PPVT items (in forms A and B) as a function of item difficulty when items are ranked from 1 to 150 in *p* values (percentage passing) based on the normative sample.

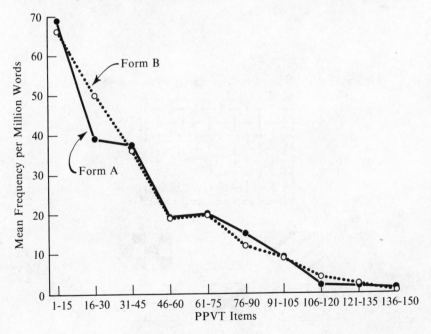

Figure 11.4A. Sample item of the Peabody Picture Vocabulary Test. The PPVT word for this item is "emerge."

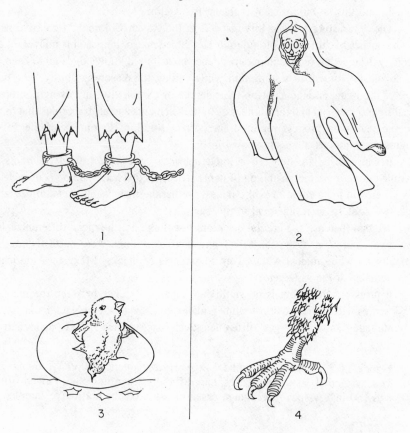

Figure 11.4B. Sample item of Raven's Progressive Matrices.

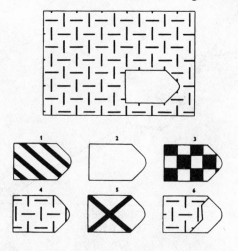

Mexican–American children, on the other hand, score significantly ($p < .01$) lower on the PPVT than on the matrices. Many of the Mexican–American children were from Spanish-speaking and bilingual homes, which may account for their obtaining significantly lower scores on the PPVT as compared with the matrices.

Thus, matrices and PPVT items intentionally matched on difficulty for white males are also thereby matched on difficulty for black males and females. The correlation between the p values (percentage passing) of the matched pairs of matrices and PPVT items is .94 for white females, .97 for black males, and .93 for black females. It appears from these findings that blacks perform no less well on a culturally loaded verbal test, the PPVT, than on a culture-reduced nonverbal test, the Colored Progressive Matrices, when these tests are perfectly equated in difficulty for whites.

All the findings reviewed here would seem to contradict the common belief that the majority of black children have a language different from standard American English, which supposedly handicaps them in taking IQ tests and in scholastic achievement. The fact that blacks perform at the same level on both verbal and nonverbal tests suggests that their overall lower test scores, relative to whites, is not attributable to a language deficit per se. By contrast, immigrant children, with little or no knowledge of English, score markedly higher on nonverbal than on standard verbal tests in English. Also, children who are born deaf and are therefore severely language deprived perform much less well on verbal than on nonverbal tests (Vernon, 1968). Moreover, a comprehensive review of the research pertaining to the "different language" hypothesis of the black IQ deficit found no evidence to support it. The authors concluded: "In general, no acceptable, replicated research has found that the dialect spoken by black children presents them with unique problems in comprehending standard English" (Hall & Turner, 1974, p. 79). These investigators argue that the explanation of the black IQ deficit must be sought elsewhere; they state that they "are convinced that more effort should be directed toward studying universals of cognitive development rather than toward relatively superficial performance differences such as spoken dialects" (p. 80).

Factor Analytic Evidence of Bias

A primary question in the investigation of bias is whether a given test (or battery of tests) really measures the *same* ability in both the major and minor groups.

Factor analysis obviously lends itself to the study of this question (see Chapter 9, pp. 446–450). If the pattern of correlations among all the units that make up the total score on a test differs significantly between the major and minor groups, the factorial structure of the scores, too, will differ, suggesting that the scores may have a different psychological meaning in the two groups. Factor analysis per se cannot tell us the cause of this difference; it merely shows that it exists. Whatever the cause, the fact of a significant group difference in factor structure or in factor loadings (even when the same factors emerge in both groups) is an indicator of bias according to our general definition of bias, namely, that the tests do not behave the same, psychometrically, in both groups.

I have collected all the recent data I can find in the literature that lends itself to a comparison of factors between two or more groups. I have included only those studies that involve standardized tests in current use and have large enough sample sizes for the statistical results to be worthwhile. In many cases, I have had to extract the factors from the authors' correlations myself, as the authors had not applied factor analysis or had used a type of analysis that was either inappropriate for our purpose or noncomparable with other studies.

In virtually all correlation matrices involving only ability tests, the general factor (or first principal component) accounts for the largest proportion of the total common factor variance and is also the largest source of variance in total scores on the test or battery as a whole. I have therefore focused my analyses on the first principal component, which, for the sake of brevity, I will henceforth refer to as the g factor. This should not be taken to imply that the g factor is identical from one set of data to another, although, in the abilities domain, there is generally a high degree of correlation between the g factors extracted from various batteries of tests. It should be kept in mind that g is sensitive to "psychometric sampling," that is, it varies, more or less, depending on the particular collection of variables that are included in the factor analysis.

Rotation of the factor axes to approximate simple structure, as by Kaiser's varimax, is most useful for identification of the group factors, that is, the common factor variance other than that accounted for by the g factor. Group factors are identified and described in terms of the characteristics of the few tests having the highest factor loadings on a given factor.

An important question is whether the same group factors emerge from the same set of variables when factor analyzed in samples from two or more different populations. At least with respect to white and black samples in the United States, in all the factor analyses of ability tests that I have found, the same clearly identifiable factors emerge in both racial groups.

I have used two simple methods for determining the similarity of a factor across the major and minor groups:

First, we do a chi squared test of the overall group difference in factor loadings on a given factor, as described in Chapter 9 (p. 449). This test is sensitive simultaneously to differences both in the *pattern* of factor loadings and in their *magnitudes*. If the value of χ^2 indicates a difference significant at the 5 percent level of confidence, we are justified in rejecting the null hypothesis, which states that the factor loadings do not differ between the major and minor groups. If we cannot reject the null hypothesis, no further analysis is called for. As in any statistical test, we cannot prove that any two things are the same; we can only state that they are or are not significantly different at some specified level of confidence, such as the conventional 5 percent level.

Second, if the χ^2 test reveals a significant difference, we then must look at the Pearson correlation between the two sets of factor loadings. The r is an index of the similarity in the *pattern* of factor loadings, regardless of the overall difference in their magnitudes. As we shall see, it is possible for the χ^2 test to be significant and yet for there to be a very high correlation between the factor loadings. A high r means, of course, that although the loadings may differ in overall magnitude between the groups, they maintain the same pattern in both groups. Conversely, the χ^2 may be nonsignificant and yet the r be low, indicating that the factor loadings overall are of similar magnitude but the pattern of loadings is quite different. This can easily occur on the g factor when *all* the variables entering into the factor analysis are quite highly g loaded, as is often the case, and especially when the samples of persons are small, which increases the sampling error of the factor loadings and plays havoc with the small relative differences among the loadings.

Finally, where the available data permit, I have examined Spearman's interesting hypothesis that the magnitudes of white–black mean differences on various mental tests are directly related to the tests' *g* loadings (Spearman, 1927, p. 379). This hypothesis is important to the study of test bias, because, if true, it means that the white–black difference in test scores is not mainly attributable to idiosyncratic cultural peculiarities in this or that test, but to a *general factor* that all the ability tests measure in common. A mean difference between populations that is related to one or more small group factors would seem to be explained more easily in terms of cultural differences than if the mean group difference is most closely related to a broad general factor common to a wide variety of tests. Unfortunately, none of the published data that I have been able to find lends itself ideally to testing the Spearman hypothesis, mainly because the reliability coefficient for each of the tests in the factor analysis either is not precisely known or is not given. (It is not sufficient merely to know the test's reliability in some other sample.) The reason that reliability coefficients are important for a rigorous test of the hypothesis, of course, is that both the tests' factor loadings and the mean white–black differences on the tests are attenuated by measurement error. Thus differences in the reliabilities of the various tests introduce some degree of spurious correlation between tests' factor loadings and the group mean differences (in σ units) on the tests. Without correction for attenuation of the loadings and mean differences, the results of my analyses of the data with respect to the Spearman hypothesis should be taken as only suggestive. But I doubt that the overall results would be seriously in error, as the reliabilities of most standard tests are more or less uniformly high and there is no reason to assume a systematic correlation between tests' reliabilities and their intrinsic *g* loadings (i.e., the *g* loading after correction for attenuation). Also, it should be obvious that the Spearman hypothesis cannot be appropriately tested on samples that were in any way specially selected with reference to any *g*-loaded characteristics.

Wechsler Intelligence Scale for Children.   A doctoral study by Nichols (1972) provides relevant data on seven subtests of the WISC, in addition to six other ability and achievement tests, given to large samples of white ($N = 1,940$) and black ($N = 1,460$) 7-year-olds in several large cities. The subjects were participants in a large-scale longitudinal study conducted by the National Institute of Neurological Disorders and Stroke of the U.S. National Institutes of Health. The subjects were enlisted in twelve public hospitals at the time of their mothers' pregnancy and are a fairly representative sample of the populations served by these large city hospitals, a population that Nichols describes as "skewed somewhat to the lower end" in social class.

Nichols notes (p. 83) that the intercorrelations among the thirteen tests are highly similar in the white and black samples, as indicated by a correlation of .954 between the two correlation matrices. Obviously the factor structure of these variables is bound to be highly similar for whites and blacks, and factor analysis bears this out. The *g* factor loadings extracted from these correlation matrices are shown in Table 11.3 along with the mean white–black difference expressed in σ units. The chi squared test of the overall significance of the white–black difference in *g* loadings of the thirteen tests yields a $\chi^2 = 1.31$, which is nonsignificant even with these very large samples. The correlation between the white and black *g* loadings is .98, which for $12 df$ (degrees of freedom) is significant beyond the .001 level of confidence.

Regarding the Spearman hypothesis referred to in the preceding section, the correla-

Table 11.3.   Mean difference (in σ units) between 7-year-old whites ($N = 1940$) and blacks ($N = 1460$), and tests' g loadings in each sample.   (Secondary analyses of data from Nichols, 1972, Tables 18, 19, 20)

Test	Mean W–B Difference[1]	Loading on g	
		White	Black
1. Bender–Gestalt	.69	.60	.61
2. WISC Information	.37	.67	.69
3. WISC Comprehension	.41	.47	.49
4. WISC Vocabulary	.85	.67	.71
5. WISC Digit Span	.45	.65	.63
6. WISC Picture Arrangement	.71	.64	.64
7. WISC Block Design	.66	.55	.58
8. WISC Coding	.17	.37	.31
9. I.T.P.A.[2]	.96	.75	.75
10. Draw-a-Man	.11	.49	.52
11. WRAT Spelling[3]	.73	.79	.78
12. WRAT Reading	.73	.78	.78
13. WRAT Arithmetic	.55	.79	.77
Percentage of total variance accounted for		41.6%	42.1%

[1]Mean white–black difference in σ units. The difference is

$$\sigma = \frac{(\overline{X}_W - \overline{X}_B)}{[(N_W \sigma_W^2 + N_B \sigma_B^2)/(N_W + N_B)]^{1/2}}$$

[2]Illinois Test of Psycholinguistic Abilities (Auditory–Vocal Association).
[3]Wide Range Achievement Tests.

tion between the mean white–black differences and the g loadings on the thirteen tests is .69 ($p < .01$) for whites and .71 ($p < .01$) for blacks. If we compare (1) the mean white–black difference (in σ units) on the six tests with the highest g loadings with (2) the mean white–black difference on the seven tests with the lowest g loadings, we have .70σ − .46σ = .24σ, which is a highly significant difference (noncorrelated $t = 6.92$, $df = 3398$, $p < .001$). Thus Spearman's hypothesis would seem to be borne out by these data. Certainly it is not contradicted. Yet there is a question, as the g loadings on some of these tests are not in marked agreement with their g loadings where they have been factor analyzed in other contexts. We are safest in concluding only that the white–black differences are quite highly correlated with the tests' g loadings in this particular battery, for both whites and blacks. Another way of describing these results is to say that those tests that best discriminate individual differences *among* whites are the same tests that best discriminate individual differences *among* blacks and are also the same tests that discriminate the most *between* whites and blacks.

The racial aspect of this finding, however, is ambiguous, being confounded with socioeconomic status. (This fact should not be interpreted to mean that SES is necessarily a cause of the observed mean white–black difference in test scores.) Nichols provides SES ratings and their correlations with each of the thirteen tests. The average correlation is only .25 for whites and .20 for blacks. But the more important points are that (1) SES correlates with the g factor .51 in the white sample and .42 in the black and (2) the correlations r_{xy} between $x = $ the correlation of SES with scores on a given test and $y = $

the mean white–black difference (in σ units) on the given test over the thirteen tests is .72 for whites and .79 for blacks. In other words, the tests' correlations with SES are related to he mean white–black test differences to a slightly greater degree than the tests' g loadings are related to the white–black difference. And within each racial group SES is more highly correlated with g than with any particular test. But this aside should not obscure the fact that there is nothing in this study that suggests that any of the thirteen tests in this battery is biased with respect to whites and blacks. The battery is factorially almost identical in the two races.

All twelve subtests of the WISC-R (i.e., the 1974 revision of the Wechsler Intelligence Scale for Children) were obtained on substantial random grade- and sex-matched samples of school children from four ethnic groups in Arizona: whites, $N = 252$; black, $N = 235$; Mexican–American, $N = 223$; and Native American Papago Indian, $N = 240$ (Reschly, 1978). When subjected to factor analysis (varimax rotation of the principal components), the usual verbal and performance factors emerged clearly in all four ethnic groups; a small third factor (memory) was evident in only the Anglo sample.

This is not unusual, because, in many factor analytic studies of the Wechsler tests, only the two rotated factors usually emerge (verbal and performance); the third factor (memory) is quite wavery from one sample to another. Reschly found that the two-factor solutions are "highly similar for the four ethnic groups." For example, the factor loadings on the verbal factor for the white group are correlated .95 with the loadings on the same factor in each of the ethnic groups, and the performance factor loadings for whites correlate .86 with those of blacks, .90 with Mexicans, and .78 with Indians. The χ^2 test shows no significant differences between the factor loadings of the whites and any of the ethnic minorities, for either the verbal or performance factors.

Because Reschly did not extract a g factor, I have done so from the original correlations sent to me by Reschly. The percentage of total variance accounted for by g in each group is white, 36.3 percent; black, 42.7 percent; Mexican, 35.8 percent; Indian, 35.2 percent. The three minority groups do not differ significantly from the white group on the g loadings ($\chi^2 < 1$ for every comparison). The six correlations of the g loadings among the four groups range from .81 to .93. The whites are correlated with the others: black, .87; Mexican, .90; Indian, .93. This study, then, much like the Nichols study, shows a very high degree of similarity of factor structures of the WISC-R for four quite distinct ethnic groups.

From longitudinal data on 11 WISC subtests given to 163 whites and 111 black children in Georgia in grades K, 1, 3, and 5, Miele (1979) extracted a g factor for each racial group at each grade level. The average percentage of variance accounted for by g is 35 percent for whites and 38 percent for blacks. At no grade level were the g factor loadings significantly different in blacks and whites (largest $\chi^2 = 2.42$, $p = .12$). Although we cannot reject the null hypothesis for these data, the white–black correlations between the factor loadings are very low and nonsignificant in grades K and 3 (.09 and .12, respectively), which appears to be due partly to the small variability among the various tests' g loadings at these grade levels. With such little variability, sampling fluctuations can easily obscure any intrinsic correlation. The correlations between the white and black g loadings in grades 1 and 5 are .67 and .77, respectively.

Correlations among eleven (out of the twelve) WISC subtests were obtained on random samples of white, black, and Mexican–American children of ages 7 and 10 years in the elementary schools of Riverside, California (Mercer & Smith, 1972). The sample sizes (N's) were as follows:

Group	Age 7	Age 10
White	100	90
Black	96	88
Mexican–American	64	48

I factor analyzed the correlation matrices. Verbal and performance factors clearly emerged from varimax rotation of the principal components in every ethnic group. The g factor (first principal component) was correlated across racial groups at each age level and the significance of the overall difference between the groups' g factor loadings was determined by a χ^2 test. The same was done for the rotated verbal and performance factors. The results are summarized in Table 11.4. It is a somewhat mixed picture. Sampling error is probably largely responsible; this study involves much smaller samples than any of the other factorial studies of the WISC. Of the eighteen group comparisons of factor loadings, six show significant differences, and three of these involve the loadings on the performance factor in grade 7, which differ significantly among all three ethnic groups. It appears that the loadings on the performance factor may be sensitive to age differences. While the 7-year-old black × Mexican correlation is $-.41$, at 10 years of age it jumps to .97; and the correlation between 7-year-old Mexicans and 10-year-old blacks is .50. These peculiarities are inexplicable from the available data. However, the g factor loadings, which are generally less subject to sampling error than are the rotated factors, are quite similar across groups. The percentages of the total variance accounted for by g in each group, shown as follows, do not differ significantly.

		Percentage of Total Variance	
	Group	Age 7	Age 10
	White	46.9%	46.1%
	Black	38.6	38.1
	Mexican–American	44.7	39.4

Fluid and Crystalized g.   Travis Osborne has provided data on twelve quite diverse tests given to white ($N = 608$) and black ($N = 246$) urban school children in Georgia. Eight of the tests are from the Educational Testing Service "Kit of Reference Tests for Cognitive Factors" (French et al., 1963). The tests fall into two categories similar to what Cattell (1971b) has characterized as "fluid" and "crystalized" intelligence, or g_f and g_c. The two categories of tests are as follows:

"Fluid"	*"Crystalized"*
Cube Comparisons	Calendar Test
Identical Pictures	Arithmetic
Formboard	Vocabulary (Wide Range)
Surface Development	Vocabulary (Heim)
Spatial	Spelling
Paper Folding	
Object Aperture	

Table 11.4.   Correlations between WISC subtest factor loadings in different ethnic groups and chi squared tests of the overall group difference in loadings.   (Based on my factor analyses of correlations given in Appendices I, II, and III in Mercer & Smith, 1972)

Groups Correlated	Age	*g*		Verbal		Performance	
		r	χ^2	*r*	χ^2	*r*	χ^2
White × Black	7	.13	2.87	.54	4.29[a]	.48	4.41[a]
	10	.36	4.58[a]	.59[a]	4.83[a]	.81[b]	2.03
White × Mexican	7	.56	2.00	.80[b]	2.76	.15	9.44[b]
	10	.64[a]	2.23	.85[b]	2.69	.82[b]	2.21
Black × Mexican	7	.53	1.82	.59[a]	3.78	−.41	13.39[b]
	10	.62[a]	2.83	.74[b]	3.59	.97[b]	0.58

[a] $p < .05$.   [b] $p < .01$.

The "fluid" tests are all nonverbal and nonscholastic and do not call on any specific knowledge acquired outside the testing situation.

I have factor analyzed this battery of twelve tests separately in the white and black samples. Chronological age (in months) was partialled out of all the intercorrelations. The rotated factors clearly divide up into g_f and g_c, which together account for 48.6 percent of the total variance in whites and 48.5 percent in blacks. The g_f accounts for 24.7 percent and 25.1 percent for whites and blacks, respectively; the corresponding figures for g_c are 23.9 percent and 23.4 percent. The loadings on g_f are correlated .81 ($p < .01$) between whites and blacks, and the loadings on g_c are correlated .93 ($p < .01$). Even with this high degree of similarity between the racial groups on g_f and g_c, the chi squared test shows the overall differences in factor loadings between the groups to be significantly different: for g_f, $\chi^2 = 7.76$, $p < .01$; and g_c, $\chi^2 = 4.36$, $p < .05$. But of course quite small differences in factor loadings can be statistically significant with such a large sample ($N = 854$).

The Spearman hypothesis was tested on these data for both g_f and g_c. The correlation between (1) the tests' loading on g_c and (2) the mean white–black difference on the tests is −.24 for the white g_c loadings and −.02 for the black; both r's are nonsignificant. The correlation between loadings on g_f and the mean white–black difference is +.56 ($p < .05$) for whites and +.42 ($p < .10$) for blacks. Thus, the mean white–black differences on the twelve tests are more highly related to the tests' loadings on g_f than on g_c. This finding contradicts the common notion that the white–black difference on tests largely involves differences in past learning as characterized by the "crystalized" component of variance in test scores. Instead, we find that the white–black differences on various tests are more closely related to the "fluid" component of test score variance.

Ability and Scholastic Achievement Tests.   I have factor analyzed a battery of 14 ability and scholastic achievement tests on a total of 607 white and 604 black pupils in grades 5–8 in a California school district. The tests were the Lorge–Thorndike Verbal IQ and Nonverbal IQ, Raven's Standard Progressive Matrices, the Figure Copying Test, three rote memory tests, and seven subtests of the Stanford Achievement Test, which measures achievement in the traditional school subjects. The *g* factor (first principal component) was extracted separately in each grade for each racial group. The correlation between the fourteen pairs of g loadings (corrected for attenuation) of whites and blacks in each grade from 5 through 8 are .70, .88, .64, and .87. Only in grade 5 is the overall difference between the white and black g loadings significant ($\chi^2 = 6.53$, $p < .02$). In grade 5 the g inexplicably accounts for more of the total variance in the white than in the black sample (45.3 percent versus 29.8 percent). The race difference in the percentage of variance accounted for by the g factor is negligible in grades 6 through 8, averaging 45.3 percent for whites and 44.4 percent for blacks. Overall, the picture is one of quite high similarity (i.e., average r of .79, $p < .01$) between g loadings of whites and blacks, with no significant differences in grades 6–8 (largest $\chi^2 = 1.66$, $p = .20$).

High School Seniors of Various Ethnicity.   Nearly 3,000 high school seniors desiring to enter an open-admission community college in New York City were given the College Entrance Examination Board Comparative Guidance and Placement Program battery, which consists of ten subtests designed to measure (1) vocabulary, (2) reading comprehension, (3) grammatical rules and usage, (4) quantitative reasoning, (5) following complex directions, (6) perceptual speed and accuracy, (7) inductive reasoning, (8) short-term memory, (9) spatial reasoning, and (10) information and concepts from broadly defined technical areas. All the tests were designed to "minimize the effects of formal classroom preparation and to emphasize material that should be familiar to all high school graduates" (Hennessy & Merrifield, 1976, p. 755).

Four ethnic groups are represented in this sample of high school seniors: 431 black, 163 Hispanic, 573 Jewish, and 1,818 Caucasian–gentile, representing a wide range of socioeconomic levels.

Because Hennessy and Merrifield were primarily concerned with ethnic differences in the structure of abilities, they partialed SES out of the correlations among all of the ability measures. The SES index was based on family income, the occupation of the main wage earner, and the educational level of both parents. (When SES was included in the factor analysis, it showed no loadings above .20 on any of the three ability factors that emerged. This small effect of SES, however, was statistically removed from the factor analyses discussed in the following paragraphs.)

For each group, three factors were extracted and subjected to oblique rotation to approximate simple structure. The factors were labeled Verbal, Reasoning, and Spatial-Technical Information. The first two factors are similar to Cattell's crystalized and fluid abilities. Two methods of assessing the similarity of factor structures across ethnic groups were used. The first consists of a least-squares prediction of the factor matrix of one group from that of another and then obtaining the mean squared deviations between the predicted and observed loadings of all three factors. The mean squared deviation score across all three factors in all four groups is not significantly different from zero, which indicates a very high degree of similarity of factor structures across the different ethnic groups. The second method of assessing similarity between groups is the intraclass correlation between pairs of groups' factor loadings on all three factors. The intraclass r, it should be noted, is simultaneously sensitive to differences in both the pattern and the overall absolute magnitude of the factor loadings, in contrast to the Pearson r, which indicates only the degree of pattern similarity. The intraclass correlations between the different ethnic groups, factor loadings on all three rotated factors and on the g factor loadings (provided in Hennessy, 1974, Tables 27–30), as well as the chi squared test of the significance of the overall group difference between g loadings are shown in Table 11.5. The percentage of the total variance accounted for by g is as follows: gentile, 74.3 percent; Jewish, 75.2 percent; black, 81.8 percent; and Hispanic, 78.4 percent. Hennessy and Merrifield conclude: "The overall conclusion from this study is that there are no meaningful differences in the factor structures for the four groups. . . . [W]hile there may be differences in the level of performance on the various tests between different ethnic groups, they seem to be measuring the same abilities across these groups" (p. 759).

The Spearman hypothesis that the white–black mean difference is directly related to the tests' g loadings can be tested on these data, using the SES-adjusted means (i.e., SES is statistically held constant for Caucasian-gentiles and blacks) provided by Hennessy (1974). I have correlated these mean white–black differences (in σ units) with the loadings on the g factor extracted from the pooled ethnic groups. (Given the high degree of similarity in the g loadings of the groups separately, as shown in Table 11.5, the pooled groups, with a total $N = 1973$, should yield highly stable g loadings.) This correlation is $+.74$ ($p < .01$). The mean white–black difference on the five tests with the highest g loadings is 0.77σ in contrast to 0.52σ for the difference on the five tests with the lowest g loadings—a difference of 0.25σ, which is significant beyond the .001 level, thus clearly bearing out Spearman's hypothesis. Hennessy computed factor scores (with SES statistically partialled out) for all subjects on the rotated factors. The three factors, labeled *Verbal* (likened to g_c), *Reasoning* (likened to g_f), and *Spatial–Technical Information* show mean white–black differences of 0.59σ, 0.92σ, and 0.33σ, respectively, a finding consistent with the greater white–black difference on g_f than on g_c for Georgia school children reported earlier in this chapter.

Factor Analysis of Tests in Adult Samples.   The *Six-Year Study* of test bias in the prediction of job performance, conducted by the Educational Testing Service (Campbell et al., 1973), provides the correlation matrices of aptitude test batteries given to samples of white, black, and Mexican–American adults employed as medical technicians (nine tests), cartographic technicians (thirteen tests), and inventory management specialists (twelve tests). The composition of the test batteries varied among the three occupational groups. Most of the tests were selected from the ETS *Kit of Reference Tests for Cognitive Factors*, in addition to four U.S. Civil Service Commission Tests and the Coordination Test of the Flanagan Industrial Test series. The following list of the various tests includes the initials of

Table 11.5. Intraclass correlation between different ethnic groups' factor loadings on rotated factors and on g factor and χ^2 test of group difference on g. (Data from Hennessy & Merrifield, 1976, Table 5; Hennessy, 1974, Tables 27–30)

Groups Correlated	Intraclass Correlation[1]		
	Rotated	g	χ^2
Caucasian–gentile × Black	.97	.91	5.06[a]
Caucasian–gentile × Hispanic	.95	.91	2.92
Caucasian–gentile × Jewish	.99	.98	2.31
Black × Hispanic	.95	.93	1.66
Black × Jewish	.97	.92	5.02[a]
Hispanic × Jewish	.99	.93	1.97

[1]All correlations are significant beyond the .001 level.   [a]$p < .05$.

the occupational groups to whom they were administered (M—medical technician, C—cartographic technician, I—inventory management specialist).

Vocabulary (M, C, I)	Subtraction and Multiplication (M, I)
Hidden Figures (M, C, I)	Necessary Arithmetic Operations
Pin-Dexterity (M)	(M, C, I)
Gestalt Completion (M)	Number Comparison (M, I)
Paper Folding (M)	Picture–Number Memory (M)
Object–Number (C, I)	Coordination (C)
U.S.C.S. Arithmetic (C)	Card Rotations (C)
Surface Development (C)	Map Planning (C)
Following Oral Directions (C, I)	Maze Tracing Speed (C)
Extended Range Vocabulary (C, IO)	Identical Pictures (C)
Nonsense Syllogisms (I)	Letter Sets (I)
Federal Service Entrance Exam (I)	Inference (I)

A g factor (first principal component) was extracted from the correlations among these tests in each ethnic group. The percentage of total variance accounted for by g was very similar across the three test batteries, averaging 41.3 percent for whites, 42.3 percent for blacks, and 40.5 percent for Mexican–Americans. The correlations between the various ethnic groups' g loadings and the chi squared test of the significance of the overall difference between the groups' g loadings are shown in Table 11.6. The overall average correlation between the ethnic groups' g loadings is .87, and only one out of the eight χ^2 tests of the difference in g loadings reaches the 5 percent level of significance. Thus, the general factor in these batteries of highly diverse tests is essentially the same factor in all three ethnic groups, and a properly weighted composite score from such a battery, therefore, can be considered a measure of the same general ability in all three groups.

Because all the individuals in these groups have been specially selected on variables relevant to successful performance in these occupations, their patterns of abilities are unlikely to be typical of the three ethnic populations, and so the data cannot be used meaningfully to test Spearman's hypothesis of the mean white–black differences being related to the tests' g loadings.

The 50-item *Wonderlic Personnel Test* was obtained on 204 white and 204 black young adult job applicants for entry level jobs in a company in New York City; no selection was made on age, education, or sex (Jensen, 1977a). The white and black means are close to the national norms on the WPT and differ by 0.89σ. The WPT is a test of general intelligence composed of items involving verbal, nonverbal, and logical reasoning and factual information. A principal components analysis was done separately on the matrix of forty-nine item intercorrelations in each random half of each racial group. (Item 50 was dropped, as there was no variance on this item in either racial group.) Thus the correlation between the groups' factor loadings could be determined both *within* and *between* the racial groups. The correlation within groups affords a baseline for assessing the correlation between groups. The correlation of the forty-nine g factor loadings across the random halves of the white sample is .69, and of the black sample it is .73. The correlation across whites and blacks (total samples) is .68 ($p < .01$). Thus the correlation of g loadings *between* races is about the same as *within* races.

A test was conducted of the hypothesis that the degree to which the items discrimi-nated between whites and blacks is correlated with the items' *g* loadings. For each group, the item *p* values were transformed to normalized *z* values, thereby ordering item diffi-culty on an interval scale. The difference between the white and black *z* scores is an index of the item's discrimination between the two groups. This item index of racial discrimina-tion is correlated with the items' *g* loadings .47 for whites and .62 for blacks, both correlations significant beyond the .01 level. These are quite high correlations when viewed against the correlation of the *z* scores between random halves of the same racial group, which is .49 for both whites and blacks. It is also noteworthy that five black and five white psychologists did no better than chance in distinguishing the eight most and the eight least racially discriminating items in the WPT simply by inspection.

In short, there is a substantial relationship between the size of the items' loadings on the general factor common to all items in the Wonderlic and the magnitude of the white–black difference on the items, and this is true whether the *g* factor is determined in the white or in the black samples. The items that best measure individual differences *within* each racial group are the same items, by and large, that discriminate the most *between* the racial groups.

White and black adults between 18 and 49 years of age were randomly selected in about equal numbers by race and sex from a probability sample of 1,027 households within the city of Detroit, sampled so as to yield a cross-section of each race group. Seven ability measures, administered to approximately half of each race sample by either a black or a white interviewer, were obtained on 179 whites and 186 blacks (Veroff, McClelland, & Marquis, 1971a). Complete intercorrelations among the ability measures for both racial

Table 11.6. Correlation between different ethnic groups' *g* loadings on battery of tests from ETS *Kit of Reference Tests for Cognitive Factors.* (Based on my factor analysis of correlation matrices given in Campbell et al., 1973, Appendix Tables III-A-III-D, pp. 467–473)

	Similarity of *g* Loadings	
Groups Correlated[1]	*r*	χ^2
Medical Technicians		
White (297) × Black (168)	.57	4.39[a]
Cartographic Technicians, Sample A		
White (51) × Black (38)	.82[b]	1.61
Cartographic Technicians, Sample B		
White (241) × Black (101)	.85[b]	1.54
White (241) × Mexican–American (99)	.92[b]	1.36
Black (101) × Mexican–American (99)	.79[b]	1.07
Inventory Management Specialists		
White (200) × Black (112)	.96[b]	0.84
White (200) × Mexican–American (72)	.89[b]	1.52
Black (112) × Mexican–American (72)	.92[b]	1.93

[1]Sample size in parentheses.   [a]$p < .05$.   [b]$p < .01$.

groups are presented for only six of the seven tests: Lorge–Thorndike Sentence Completion, Raven's Progressive Matrices, Ammons Quick Test, and the Digit Span, Coding (Digit Symbol), and Information subtests of the Wechsler Adult Intelligence Scale.

I factor analyzed these tests and compared the g loadings of whites and blacks. The percentage of total variance accounted for by g is 53.4 percent for whites and 49.8 percent for blacks, a nonsignificant difference. The correlation between the whites' and blacks' g loadings on the six tests is .82 ($p < .025$). The overall difference between white and black g loadings is nonsignificant ($\chi^2 = 1.37$).

We can check the Spearman hypotheses with the available information. Veroff et al. provide an analysis of variance on each test showing the F ratio for the race main effect; the rank order of these six F ratios is of course exactly the same as the rank order of the six tests' mean white–black differences expressed in σ units. So we may test the Spearman hypothesis by performing a rank order correlation ρ between the tests' g loadings and the F ratios indicating the magnitude of the mean white–black differences on the tests. The ρ is .66 for whites and .60 for blacks. Because with only 5 degrees of freedom ρ must be .83 or greater to be significant at the 5 percent level, in this case a statistically more powerful test of the Spearman hypothesis would be to compare the mean of the race effect F ratios for the three tests having the highest g loadings with the three tests having the lowest g loadings and perform a significance test on this difference. This is properly done by first transforming the F values to unit normal z values (see Paulson, 1942) and determining the significance of the difference between the average z's of the three highest and the three lowest g-loaded tests. This difference is highly significant ($p < .001$) for both blacks and whites, consistent with the Spearman hypothesis.

Socioeconomic Status.   Veroff et al. (1971) also classified the persons in their study into three SES categories, ignoring race: low, medium, and high SES, with N's of 79, 128, and 80, respectively. The g loadings of the six tests are rank correlated across SES groups as follows: low × medium, .89; low × high, .26; medium × high, .66. None of the SES groups differs significantly in g loadings (largest $\chi^2 = 3.52$, $.05 < p < .10$).

A total of 316 low-SES white, black, and Mexican–American children, averaging 5.3 years of age, from kindergartens serving very-low-income families in San Jose, California, were given a battery of 20 tests: Peabody Picture Vocabulary, Stanford–Binet, Wechsler Preschool and Primary Scale of Intelligence (Information, Vocabulary, Arithmetic, Similarities, Comprehension, Animal House, Picture Completion, Mazes, Geometric Designs, Block Design), Pictorial Test of Intelligence (Form Discrimination, Information–Comprehension, Similarities, Size and Numbers, Immediate Recall), and two subtests of the Illinois Test of Psycholinguistic Abilities. The authors (Southern & Plant, 1969) have provided the intercorrelations among all these tests for the total sample. The g factor accounts for 41.8 percent of the total variance. The highest g loading (.84) of any of the twenty tests is on the Stanford–Binet IQ, which should not be surprising, as it is the most heterogenous test of the whole lot. (A composite score based on all the WPPSI subtests would probably have at least as high a g loading as the Stanford–Binet.) The lowest g loading (.45) is on the memory subtest (Immediate Recall) of the Picture Test of Intelligence. Interestingly, it is the only test out of the twenty on which this low-SES group scored above the tests's standardization sample.

Although these data do not permit a comparison between the three ethnic groups, we can test the Spearman hypothesis by correlating the g loading of the twenty tests with the deviations (in σ units) of this "culturally disadvantaged" group's means from the published means of the standardization samples on the various tests. This correlation is .60 ($p < .01$). On the ten tests with the highest g loadings, the disadvantaged group averages .79σ below the norm, whereas, on the ten tests with the lowest g loadings, they average .37σ below the norm, a highly significant difference ($z = 7.41$, $p < .001$), consistent with Spearman's hypothesis.

Large samples of suburban ($N = 3,994$) and "inner-city" ($N = 1,501$) school children in Milwaukee took the Lorge–Thorndike Verbal and Nonverbal IQ scales and the Iowa Tests of Basic Skills, a scholastic achievement battery consisting of eleven subtests covering most of the traditional academic subject matter of the elementary school (Crano, 1974). The very same samples were tested in both grades 4 and 6, and the intercorrelations among all the tests, as well as the total IQ and composite achievement score, in both grade levels, totaling thirty variables in all, were used for the following analyses. The suburban children were mostly of middle and upper-middle SES and will henceforth be labeled Upper-SES. The inner-city children were in schools that qualified for aid under Title 1 of the Elementary and Secondary Education Act, intended to improve the education of the disadvantaged. This group is labeled Lower-SES. Although no information is given on the racial composition of these groups, the inner-city schools of Milwaukee are racially mixed, with a predominant percentage of blacks.

The general factor extracted from the intercorrelations among the thirty IQ and scholastic achievement variables accounts for 59.5 percent of the total variance in the Upper-SES and 51.4 percent in the Lower-SES group, a highly significant ($p < .001$) difference with these large samples. The tests with the largest g loadings in this battery, in both samples, are Composite Achievement and Verbal IQ. The correlation between the g loadings of the Upper- and Lower-SES groups is .83 ($p < .001$), indicating a high degree of similarity in the pattern of g loadings, although the overall difference between the g loadings of the Upper- and Lower-SES groups is highly significant ($\chi^2 = 28.8$, $p < .001$), since the Upper-SES sample has rather uniformly larger g loadings on nearly all the tests. A significant difference in the overall size of factor loadings, when the pattern of loadings is highly similar, suggests either (1) restriction of range in the Lower-SES sample, or (2) differential reliability in different ranges of the scale of scores on the various tests, or both.

This point is clearly illustrated in an important study by Humphreys and Taber (1973). From the massive data bank of Project TALENT, they selected for comparison four groups of ninth-grade boys, without regard to ethnic background, as follows:

		Socioeconomic Status	
		Lowest Quartile	*Highest Quartile*
IQ	*Highest Quartile*	Group *B* $N = 939$	Group *A* $N = 4,977$
	Lowest Quartile	Group *D* $N = 4,491$	Group *C* $N = 1,336$

A factor analysis was performed separately on each of the four samples on a battery of twenty-one diverse ability and scholastic achievement tests. In all groups, varimax rotation of the principal factors yielded six interpretable factors labeled Academic Achievement, Verbal Comprehension, Spatial Visualization, Clerical Speed, Rote Memorization, and Verbal Fluency. Concerning the rotated factors, Humphreys and Taber conclude:

> There were no important differences between either factors or factor loadings associated with differences in socioeconomic status. The same factors were also defined by groups high and low in intelligence, but there were fairly numerous large differences in sizes of loadings associated with the intelligence variable. When analyzed further most of these differences in loadings were explained by the characteristics of the scales of measurement. Some scales were too easy for the high intelligence groups and some too difficult for the low intelligence groups, thus producing differential reliability in different parts of the several scales. In a small number of variables, however, there is evidence for differences in factor loadings as a function of the intellectual level of the subjects that cannot be explained by the characteristics of the scales.   (1973, p. 114)

Table 11.7 shows the correlation between the various IQ × SES groups' factor loadings on the twenty-one tests for all six factors. Note that when IQ is constant and SES varies, the correlations are higher than when SES is constant and IQ varies. The average correlation over all factors for same IQ/different SES is .97, for same SES/different IQ is .84, and for different SES/different IQ is .85. This means that the *groups' differences in the tests' factor loadings are more related to the groups' differences in level of performance than to their differences in SES.* The fact that some of the tests fail to measure certain factors equally well at all levels of IQ is, of course, no less a psychometric defect than if they failed to do so across different levels of SES.

Similarity of Factor Structure between and within Families.   I have obtained data on seven tests administered to practically all the children aged 6–12 in 744 white and 414 black families in a California school district. The tests are Memory, Figure Copying, Pictorial Intelligence Test (Lorge–Thorndike Primary), Lorge–Thorndike Verbal IQ, and Nonverbal IQ, Vocabulary, and Reading Comprehension (Stanford Achievement Tests). One would prefer a larger and more diverse sample of psychometric variables for the comparison of factor structures across different groups, but these data were not collected originally with that purpose in mind. Yet the data will serve as an illustration of a method for testing an interesting hypothesis, namely, that the factorial structure of the tests is the same for children sharing the same family background as for children reared in different families. Any test score differences among children in the same family cannot be regarded as being due to differences in cultural background, whereas such differences between children from different families may or may not reflect cultural differences. Rejection of the hypothesis that test score differences between siblings reared together in the same family are factorially the same as differences between unrelated children reared in different families would, of course, favor the hypothesis that the tests are culture biased.

The differences *within* families can be factor analyzed by (1) obtaining for each test the difference between the age-standardized scores of every pair of siblings, (2) intercor-

Table 11.7. Correlations of factor loadings on twenty-one tests between groups as a function of IQ and SES. (Based on Humphreys & Taber, 1973, Table 1)

Groups Correlated	Rotated Factors[1]					
	AA	VC	SV	CS	RM	VF
A *B* Hi IQ/Hi SES × Hi IQ/Lo SES	.99	.98	.98	.98	.98	.95
C *D* Lo IQ/hi SES × Lo IQ/Lo SES	.99	.99	.98	.99	.35	.87
A *C* Hi IQ/Hi SES × Lo IQ/Hi SES	.57	.94	.93	.89	.28	.67
B *D* Hi IQ/Lo SES × Lo IQ/Lo SES	.58	.97	.97	.85	.86	.70
A *D* Hi IQ/Hi SES × Lo IQ/Lo SES	.61	.95	.96	.86	.85	.76
B *C* Hi IQ/Lo SES × Lo IQ/Hi SES	.54	.96	.95	.88	.39	.60

[1]AA = academic achievement; VC = verbal comprehension; SV = spatial visualization; CS = clerical speed; RM = rote memorization; VF = verbal fluency.
N.B.: Correlations greater than .423 are significant beyond the .05 level; correlations greater than .537 are signficant beyond the .01 level.

relating the sibling differences on the various tests, and (3) factor analyzing the correlation matrix. Such a *within*-family correlation matrix can contain no variance attributable to differences *between* families and, consequently, no variance due to socioeconomic or cultural factors. It can reflect only genetic variance and the microenvironmental variance among members of the same family. The differences *between* families can be factor analyzed by (1) obtaining for each test the mean of the age-standardized scores of all siblings in each family, then (2) intercorrelating the family means on the various tests, and (3) factor analyzing the correlation matrix.

The percentage of the total variance accounted for by the first principal component or *g* factor in each of the four matrices is

	White	*Black*
Between families	66.6%	61.0%
Within families	51.9	52.4

The between-families *g* accounts for a larger percentage of the total variance because the scores entering into the correlations are more reliable, being the *means* of two or more siblings on a given test. (The means of any two or more correlated measurements are always more reliable than the single measurements.) By the same token, the within-family correlations, based on the *differences* between siblings on a given test, are necessarily less reliable. (Differences between any two imperfectly reliable measurements are always less reliable than either of the single measurements.)

The pattern of *g* loadings on the seven tests is highly similar across the four groups, as shown by the cross-group correlations between the tests' *g* loadings:

		W b-f	W w-f	B b-f	B w-f
White between-families	*W b-f*	—	.95	.84	.97
White within-families	*W w-f*			.95	.94
Black between-families	*B b-f*				.88
Black within-families	*B w-f*				—

These correlations are statistically homogeneous; that is, they do not differ significantly from one another. Thus it appears that the *g* loadings of these seven tests show a very similar pattern regardless of whether they were extracted from the *within*-family correlations (which completely exclude cultural and socioeconomic effects in the factor analyzed variance) or from the *between*-families correlations, for either whites or blacks. The results are consistent with the hypothesis that the intelligence and achievement test score differences between children from different families, whether white or black, involve the same *g* factor as the test score differences between siblings reared together in the same family. This outcome would seem unlikely if the largest source of variance in these tests, reflected by their *g* loadings, were strongly influenced by whatever cultural differences that might exist between families and between whites and blacks.

We can also test the Spearman hypothesis on these data. Because the pattern of *g* loadings on the seven tests is so highly similar in both racial groups and for both the between- and within-family conditions, I have averaged the four sets of *g* loadings (via Fisher's *z* transformation) on each test and correlated these seven averages with the mean white–black differences (in σ units) on the seven tests. The correlation is $+.78$ ($p < .05$). Also, the mean white–black difference on the three most *g*-loaded tests is significantly ($p < .001$) greater than on the three least g-loaded tests, consistent with Spearman's hypothesis.

A Closer Look at the Spearman Hypothesis.   There is an obvious ambiguity in the interpretation of all the evidence presented relevant to Spearman's hypothesis, which states that the magnitude of the white–black difference on various tests is directly related to the tests' *g* loadings. The reason for the ambiguity is, of course, that a given test's *g* loading is not invariant when the test is factor analyzed among different collections of other tests. A test's *g* loading, in fact, can vary considerably depending on the composition of the battery of tests among which it is factor analyzed. The *g* factor itself is not invariant from one test battery to another, although the interbattery correlation on *g* is usually quite substantial when both batteries, even though they have no tests in common, consist of a dozen or more diverse tests of cognitive ability.

In suggesting this hypothesis, Spearman clearly had in mind not just the general factor in *any* collection of tests, but the *g* that he characterized specifically as the capacity for the "education of relations and correlates," that is, a capacity for abstract reasoning and problem solving involving the mental manipulation of words, symbols, and concepts. Only to the extent that the general factor extracted from a particular battery of tests can be assumed predominantly to represent Spearman's fundamental conception of *g* can it be claimed that the evidence presented heretofore substantiates Spearman's hypothesis regarding the nature of the white–black difference.

The alternative interpretation is that whites and blacks differ merely in overall level of performance on all test items (i.e., there is no race × items interaction), and those items (or subtests) that contribute the most to the true-score variance (by virtue of high reliability and optimal difficulty level) among individuals of either race thereby also show the largest mean differences between the races, and they are also the most heavily loaded on a general factor (i.e., the first principal component) that, by its mathematical nature, necessarily accounts for more of the variance than any other factor, regardless of the psychological nature of the first principal component extracted from the particular collection of tests. By this interpretation, the only condition needed to yield results at least superficially consistent with Spearman's hypothesis is that there be no appreciable race × items or race × tests interactions or, in other words, that the tests not be racially biased. A corollary of this alternative interpretation of the results we have examined is that the mean *difference between the races* has essentially the same factor composition as *individual differences within* each of the races.

These two interpretations are not at all incompatible. But the Spearman hypothesis in the strict sense intended by Spearman is not necessarily proved by the finding of a correlation between (1) various tests' *g* loadings with any particular battery and (2) the magnitude of the white–black mean differences on these tests. Probably the most compelling assemblage of evidence for the Spearman hypothesis, from the standpoint of factor analysis, is the massive data on the General Aptitude Test Battery of the U.S. Employment Service, which is discussed later (see Chapter 15, pp. 733–735).

To be able to decide in favor of the Spearman hypothesis in the strict sense requires some type of evidence that is independent of factor analysis and is based in part on a psychological judgment as to the extent to which any two (or more) tests differ along a dimension that we agree characterizes some essential feature of Spearman's psychological conception of *g*.

One such distinction that has held up in many studies is the contrast between tests of rote learning and short-term memory, on the one hand, and tests of reasoning and problem solving, on the other. The rote learning and short-term memory abilities are measured by tests such as digit memory span, serial and paired-associate learning, and immediate free recall of a set of familiar objects or common nouns. Reasoning, problem solving, and the use of concepts, which exemplify Spearman's definition of *g,* are measured by most tests of general intelligence and especially by verbal and figural analogies, number series, and progressive matrices. I have elsewhere (Jensen, 1968b) labeled these two classes of abilities level I and level II. Level I involves the registration and consolidation of stimulus inputs and the formation of simple associations. There is little transformation of the input and thus a high degree of correspondence between the form of the stimulus input and the form of the response output. Level II ability, on the other hand, involves self-initiated elaboration and transformation of the stimulus input before it eventuates in an overt response. The person must consciously manipulate the input to arrive at the correct output. Thus the crucial distinction between levels I and II involves a difference in the complexity of the transformations and mental manipulations required between the presentation of a given mental task to the person and his or her end response to it. Various cognitive tasks ranging along the level I–level II continuum would also correspond closely to their arrangement along the continuum of *g* loadings in the Spearman sense.

Numerous studies of the past decade have clearly demonstrated an interaction between race (white–black) and level I versus level II tests (Jensen, 1970b, 1970c, 1971a, 1973d, 1974b). Whites and blacks differ much less on the level I than on the level II abilities. Also, in factor analyses the level I tests have much smaller loadings on the g factor or first principal component than do the level II tests. These findings lend support to Spearman's hypothesis. A rather striking demonstration of this phenomenon consisted of comparing large groups of white and black children, 5 to 12 years of age, on forward and backward digit span (FDS and BDS). FDS and BDS are highly similar tasks, but BDS obviously requires more mental manipulation and transformation of the input. In FDS the examiner reads a series of digits at the rate of one digit per second, and the subject is required to repeat the string of digits in exactly the order in which they were presented. In BDS the subject is required to recall the digits in reverse order, which calls for mental transformation of the input order of the digits. Interestingly, it was found that BDS is significantly more highly correlated with the WISC-R Full Scale IQ than is FDS, in both the white and the black samples. (The Digit Span tests, of course, were not included in the WISC-R IQs.) This finding, along with the fact that the WISC-R Full Scale IQ is a good measure of Spearman's g, means that BDS is significantly more g loaded than is FDS. Also, the white–black mean difference (in σ units) was more than twice as great on BDS as on FDS. This marked interaction persists even when SES is controlled, as shown in Figure 11.5. The SES index is based on the occupation of the principal wage earner in the child's home as reported by the child's parent or guardian. Subsidiary studies indicated that these results could not be explained in terms of differences in task difficulty per se between FDS and BDS, race differences in test anxiety, or the race of the examiner (Jensen & Figueroa, 1975). Further evidence that the white–black difference is related more to task complexity (and hence Spearman's g) than to difficulty per se (as indexed by percentage passing) is shown in several studies of visual reaction time (RT), in which whites and blacks were found to differ much less on simple RT than on choice RT, with the white–black difference in mean RT increasing as a function of the number of response alternatives in the choice RT (see Chapter 14, pp. 704–706). The results are highly consistent with Spearman's hypothesis, if we interpret g as information processing capacity, in which individual differences can be revealed by varying the complexity of the stimuli that must be processed prior to the subject's final overt response.

The relevance of level I–level II abilities to the interaction of race with the *form* of the test items has been shown in two studies by Longstreth (1978). From the nature of the level I–level II distinction, Longstreth predicted that multiple-choice and essay types of tests should load higher than true–false tests on level II ability. This prediction is consistent with the interpretation of level II or g as information processing capacity. For example, the multiple-choice format, with its several available response alternatives, is informationally more loaded and complex, calling for more discriminative decisions, than the two-choice true–false format. Essay questions call for considerable internal processing, selection, reconstruction, mental manipulation, and transformation of information stored in memory, which are all level II functions.

Longstreth's prediction was borne out significantly and replicated in a second study in groups of white, black, Asian–American, and Mexican–American college students, who were given true–false, multiple-choice, and essay tests covering the content of a course in developmental psychology. In addition, the students were given a level I test (Forward Digit Span) and a level II test—the Cognitive Abilities Test (CAT), Nonverbal Battery (a successor to the Lorge–Thorndike Intelligence Test), which is highly loaded on Spearman's g). The multiple-choice and essay tests are correlated significantly higher

Figure 11.5. Scaled scores ($\overline{X} = 10$, $\sigma = 3$) of white and black children on WISC-R Forward and Backward Digit Span, as a function of SES (Lowest = 0). (From Jensen & Figueroa, 1975)

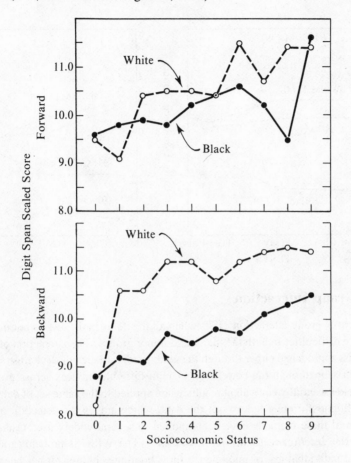

with each other than either one correlates with the true–false test, and the pattern of correlations indicates the multiple-choice and essay tests are more loaded on level II than on level I, whereas the true–false test comes close to level I.

If true–false items are less complex and therefore somewhat less *g* loaded than either multiple-choice or essay questions, we should expect an interaction between item types and race, if Spearman's hypothesis is valid, with a smaller white–black difference (expressed in σ units) on the true–false test than on the multiple-choice and essay tests. This is exactly what Longstreth found, as shown in the left panel of Figure 11.6. The right panel compares the four racial groups on the multiple-choice test alongside tests that are relatively pure level II and pure level I—the Cognitive Abilities Test and Forward Digit Span, respectively. These results are not only highly consistent with the Spearman hypothesis, but they also indicate an important point for the analysis of test items × group interactions in the study of test bias, namely, that some of the interaction may be due to the strictly formal characteristics of the test items, which should not be confused with *cultural* bias.

Figure 11.6.   Standard scores ($X = 0$, $\sigma = 1$) of white, black, Asian, and Mexican–American female university students on multiple-choice, essay, true–false, Cognitive Aptitude Test (CAT), and Forward Digit Span memory (FDS).   (From Longstreth, 1978.)

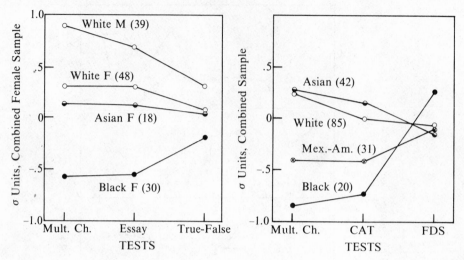

Item × Group Interaction

An item × group interaction exists when all the items in the test do not maintain the same relative difficulties in both the major and minor groups. The interaction of items and groups can be approached either through the analysis of variance of the items × groups × subjects matrix or through the correlation of item difficulty indices across groups. Both methods yield essentially equivalent results when applied to the same set of data. But each method highlights different features of the data, which aids in the detection of test bias. One or both of these methods have been applied to several widely used tests.

Wechsler Intelligence Scale for Children.   The WISC is probably the most frequently used individual test of intelligence for school-age children. It has been a popular target for accusations of culture bias, particularly with respect to black children, and therefore warrants thorough analysis.

The present analyses are based on longitudinal WISC data from white and black children in Georgia.[1] The subjects were selected from three Georgia counties representative of small rural, medium, and large industrial populations. The 163 white and 111 black

Table 11.8.   Mean white–black WISC difference in σ units ($\sigma = 15$) on WISC Georgia sample at four age levels.

Age	Verbal IQ	Performance IQ	Full Scale IQ
6	0.93	1.36	1.25
7	0.93	1.22	1.17
9	1.02	1.08	1.15
11	1.21	1.29	1.38
Mean	1.02	1.24	1.24

children were given the WISC at ages 6, 7, 9, and 11 years, at about the same time of each year. The whites averaged 1 month older than the blacks. There was some attrition of the sample over the 5 years, so that at age 11 there were only 128 whites and 97 blacks. The white and black IQs differ, on the average, slightly more than one standard deviation (σ = 15 IQ points), as shown in Table 11.8. The overall mean difference in Full Scale IQ is 18.6 points, which is quite typical of the average difference between whites and blacks in the southeastern United States (e.g., Kennedy, Van de Riet, & White, 1963).

Miele (1979) has analyzed these data with respect to test bias and summarizes the results as follows:

> The equivalence of the general factor in the two [racial] groups, the overwhelming correspondence in the rank order of item difficulty . . . the degree to which the race differences at any given grade level can be simulated by comparing the given group of White children with their performance in the previous grade or the given group of Black children with their performance in the subsequent grade force one to reject the hypothesis that the WISC is a culturally biased instrument for the groups examined.

Let us look at the evidence for the main points in Miele's summary.

1. *Rank Order of Item Difficulty.* All the items in nine of the WISC subtests were ranke for percentage passing, separately for boys and girls within each race, at each age level. (The Digit Span and Coding Tests were omitted, as they do not yield dichotomous item scores.) A total of 161 items were rank ordered within each race × sex group at each of four ages. The mean cross-racial rank order correlation for p values (within grades) is .96. For comparison, the rank correlation between the p values of boys and girls of the same race is .98 for whites and .97 for blacks.

I transformed all of the p values to delta (Δ) values, which is an interval scale index of item difficulty, and then obtained the cross-racial Pearson correlations between the Δ values at each age level. Also I determined the average white–black difference in item difficulty, expressed in white σ units. These results are shown in Table 11.9. Fewer items enter into these Δ correlations, since Δ values cannot be computed when p is 1 or 0 in either group. The correlations in Table 11.9 thus are based on only those items that have some variance *within* both racial groups. It can be seen that the cross-racial correlation of item difficulties is still quite high, averaging .94.

2. *Cultural Difference versus Mental Maturity Difference.* Miele obtained each item's correlation (Yule's Q) with (1) chronological age and (2) race. These correlations thus index the degree to which items (1) discriminate between the same children (of the

Table 11.9. Cross-racial Pearson correlation of WISC item delta values and the mean black–white difference in item difficulty expressed in normalized σ units.

Age	N Items	r	$(\overline{\text{W}}-\overline{\text{B}})/\sigma$
6	81	.93	.69
7	83	.94	.67
9	94	.94	.63
11	106	.96	.72
Mean	91	.94	.68

same race) at different ages and (2) the degree to which the items discriminate between whites and blacks of the same age. Miele found substantial correlations between these two indices, 1 and 2. That is, the items that discriminate most between whites and blacks at any given age are precisely those items that discriminate most between whites at a given age and the same whites at the next earlier age, or between blacks at a given age and the same blacks at the next higher age. Thus the observed white–black differences in item difficulty across the various WISC items can be *simulated* by comparing older and younger whites or younger and older blacks. (Note that the older and younger groups are the *same* children tested at different ages.) If the cross-racial variations in differences in item difficulties were due to *cultural* biases, it would seem a strange coincidence that they should be correlated with *age* differences *within* each racial group. Miele suggests that the more parsimonious interpretation of this finding, therefore, is that the pattern of white–black differences in item difficulty reflects differences in level of mental maturity (as measured by the WISC) rather than cultural differences per se. We will examine this hypothesis more closely in connection with item analysis of each of the subtests of the WISC.

Out of the 161 items of the WISC compared cross-racially at each of the four age levels, only 12 different items showed a reversal in difficulty, that is, blacks did better than whites on these 12 items. But in no case is the difference in percentage passing statistically significant. Most of these reversals occurred at one or the other extreme of the scale of difficulty, where the measure of item difficulty becomes more unreliable. This evidence is summarized in Table 11.10. It seems highly probable that, if we had very large racial samples, thereby minimizing sampling errors, there would be no item × race reversals whatever.

Let us look at the one item of the WISC that has been held up most often by critics of tests as an especially flagrant example of a culture-biased item for black children. It is the Comprehension subtest item no. 4: "What is the thing to do if a fellow (girl) much smaller than yourself starts to fight with you?" It has been argued that the majority of black children are typically taught to "fight back," and therefore the keyed correct response to this item runs counter to their cultural values. Yet, out of the 161 items of the WISC this is the forty-second *easiest* item for blacks (in all grades combined), but it is the forty-seventh easiest item for whites, which indicates that this item is relatively *easier* for blacks than for whites! As Miele (1979) notes, removing this item from the WISC would, in fact, penalize the black subjects. This nicely illustrates the fallibility of subjective analyses of bias by mere inspection of items. Only proper statistical item analysis methods can reliably establish bias.

Analysis of WISC Subtests.   At each age level a complete analysis of variance (ANOVA) was performed on the data matrix formed by the following variables: race × sex × items × subjects. All the subsequent analyses are based on these ANOVAs. As an example of what each ANOVA consists of, the ANOVA of the WISC Vocabulary subtest at age 6 is shown in Table 11.11. (It may be instructive for the reader to compare Table 11.11 with Table 9.4 and its accompanying text, which more fully explicates the interpretation of the ANOVA table.)

First, we notice that the item × race interaction is significant ($F = 33.62$, $p < .001$). In fact, *the item × race interaction is found to be significant beyond the .01 level for every subtest at every age.*

Table 11.10. WISC items showing disordinal interactions (i.e., black p > white p).

		Percentage Passing							
		Age 6		Age 7		Age 9		Age 11	
Item No.	Description	B	W	B	W	B	W	B	W
Info. 7	Pennies–Nickel			89.5%	82.0%				
Comp. 1	Cut finger					99.0%	98.5%		
Comp. 2	Lose ball (doll)					96.0	94.5		
Sim. 4	Knife–Glass	72.0%	68.0%						
Sim. 9	Paper–Coal					30.0	29.5	53.0%	44.0%
Sim. 10	Pound–Yard			4.0	0.0				
Voc. 3	Hat	100.0	99.5						
Pic. Comp. 11	Fish					51.0	50.0		
Pic. Comp. 13	Fly	2.0	1.0	5.0	2.5				
Pic. Comp. 15	Profile	1.0	0.5						
Pic. Comp. 18	Umbrella					1.0	0.0		
Pic. Arr.	Sleeper	1.0	0.5						

Table 11.11.   ANOVA of the WISC Vocabulary subtest at age 6.

Source of Variance	Sum of Squares	Degrees of Freedom	Mean Square	*F* Ratio	$\eta^2 \times 100$
Race	55.17	1	55.17	122.20[a]	0.84
Sex	0.89	1	0.89	1.98	0.01
Race × sex	0.78	1	0.78	1.73	0.01
Subjects (within groups)	121.89	270	0.45		1.85
Items	4,694.24	39	120.37	843.01[a]	71.30
Items × race	187.23	39	4.80	33.62[a]	2.84
Items × sex	13.42	39	0.34	2.41	0.20
Items × race × sex	6.96	39	0.18	1.25	0.11
Subjects × items (within groups)	1,503.47	10,530	0.14		22.84
Total	6,584.05	10,959			100.00

[a]$p < .001$.

Because the item × race interactions are significant, we must examine them further. (If they were nonsignificant, the analysis could stop right there.) How important are the interactions in relation to the observed racial differences in subtest means? We can evaluate the importance of the item × race interaction in terms of certain other indices derivable from the ANOVA.

As an example, we can look again at the results on the Vocabulary subtest. Only one of the forty items in the Vocabulary subtest shows a reversal of the rank order of item difficulties in the two racial groups. Most of the item × race interaction is due to unequal intervals between the various item difficulties in the two groups. The Spearman rank order correlation between the item p values of the whites and blacks is .97. The intraclass correlation r_i between the white and black values is .92; r_i reflects ordinal as well as disordinal interactions. The r_i is almost always equal to or lower than either the rank order correlation or the Pearson correlation for any given set of data. The reason that the intraclass correlation r_i is seldom higher than the rank order correlation ρ and never higher than the Pearson r is that (1) ρ reflects only differences in rank order, (2) r reflects discrepancies in rank order as well as inequality of the intervals between values that maintain the same rank order, and (3) the intraclass r_i is simultaneously sensitive not only to discrepancies in rank order and inequality of intervals, but also to differences in the means and variances of the two correlated variables. However, differences in means are not reflected in the r_i as computed from the ANOVA in the present example, as the overall mean race difference in item difficulty is removed in the race main effect of the ANOVA. The cross-racial intraclass r_i between item difficulties is obtained from the ANOVA as follows:

$$r_i = \frac{\text{Item MS} - \text{Item} \times \text{Race MS}}{\text{Item MS} + \text{Item} \times \text{Race MS}},$$

$$= \frac{120.37 - 4.80}{120.37 + 4.80} = .92.$$

A nonsignificant item $\times$ race interaction means that the r_i is not significantly less than 1. The r_i can be corrected for attenuation by dividing it by the reliability of the item difficulties, which is

$$r_{II} = \frac{\text{Item MS} - \text{Subjects} \times \text{Item MS}}{\text{Item MS} + \text{Subjects} \times \text{Item MS}},$$

$$= \frac{120.37 - 0.14}{120.37 + 0.14} = .998.$$

Obviously, with such high reliability of the item difficulties, correction for attenuation of the cross-racial r_i will have only a negligible effect. Because the item difficulty reliabilities are very high for most of the subtests, I have not corrected the cross-racial correlations for attenuation.

Another informative statistic that can be computed from the ANOVA is the point biserial correlation r_{pbi} of the test with race as a quantitized variable. The r_{pbi} is monotonically related to the difference (in σ units) between the means of the racial groups, with a mean difference of one standard deviation approximately equivalent to a r_{pbi} of .45. (See Chapter 9, p. 438, and Figure 4N.3.) The r_{pbi} is obtained as follows:

$$r_{pbi} = \sqrt{\frac{\text{Race SS}}{\text{Race SS} + \text{Subjects SS}}} \times \frac{2\sqrt{N_W N_B}}{(N_W + N_B)},$$

where N_W and N_B are the sample sizes of the white and black groups. For the Vocabulary subtest,

$$r_{pbi} = \sqrt{\frac{55.17}{55.17 + 121.89}} \times \frac{2\sqrt{163 \times 111}}{(163 + 111)} = .55.$$

The cross-racial correlations of item difficulties and the point biserial correlations of subtest with race, derived from ANOVA as in the Vocabulary subtest example, were obtained for each of the WISC subtests at each age level. The results are shown in Table 11.12. The overall average (grand mean) cross-racial correlation between item difficulties, when age is constant across racial groups, is .91. The r is clearly higher for some subtests (e.g., Information and Arithmetic) than for others (e.g., Block Design and Object Assembly). But the latter two subtests contain far fewer items than any of the others (Block Design, ten items; Object Assembly, four items), and, with as few as four items, the highest less-than-perfect rank order correlation possible is .80. Thus the cross-racial intraclass correlation between the item difficulties on the shorter tests will be more sensitive to any differences between the groups. In fact, at age 6, the cross-racial *rank order* correlations for Block Design and Object Assembly are .90 and 1.00, respectively, as compared with the intraclass correlations of .84 and .77. The Pearson r's are .94 and .99, respectively. Clearly, the intraclass r_i is the most comprehensive and sensitive index of cross-racial similarity in item difficulties. Despite this sensitivity to all features (except a difference in the overall mean) of the cross-racial discrepancies in item difficulties, most of the values of r_i are quite high, especially for the longer tests.

Table 11.12. Correlations between item difficulties in WISC subtests and subtest correlation (r_{pbi}) with race.

	Correlations between Item Difficulties														Subtest Correlation with Race			
	Correlated Race Groups[1]							Correlated Pseudorace Groups										
	Same Age				Age Lagged													
Subtest	W_6B_6	W_7B_7	W_9B_9	$W_{11}B_{11}$	W_6B_7	W_7B_9	W_9B_{11}	W_7W_6	W_9W_7	$W_{11}W_9$	B_7B_6	B_9B_7	$B_{11}B_9$	Age 6	Age 7	Age 9	Age 11
Information	.97	.99	.97	.94	.97	.97	.98	.96	.92	.95	.94	.95	.98	.38	.28	.41	.56
Comprehension	.94	.96	.97	.99	1.00	.98	.99	.96	.97	.98	.97	.98	.97	.40	.33	.33	.41
Similarities	.96	.91	.90	.87	.99	.95	.99	.89	.84	.87	.93	.98	.89	.29	.27	.44	.49
Arithmetic	.96	.99	.96	.94	.99	.96	.98	.96	.97	.91	.92	.92	.97	.22	.36	.47	.45
Vocabulary	.92	.92	.95	.94	.96	.97	.98	.98	.97	.94	.98	.96	.95	.55	.59	.56	.59
Picture Completion	.91	.98	.99	.97	.99	.97	.98	.99	.98	.97	.92	.97	.98	.52	.33	.37	.35
Picture Arrangement	.90	.55	.82	.95	.97	.99	.99	.49	.83	.96	.87	.53	.83	.41	.51	.46	.39
Block Design	.84	.89	.84	.66	.99	.99	.98	.87	.82	.77	.83	.88	.91	.41	.37	.37	.47
Object Assembly	.77	.75	.61	.79	.86	.79	.78	.87	.71	.47	.92	.80	.91	.48	.52	.39	.49
Mean	.91	.88	.93	.93	.98	.97	.98	.94	.92	.92	.93	.93	.95	.41	.40	.41	.47
Grand mean		.91				.98			.93			.94				.42	

[1]Capital letters designate racial groups, white (W) and black (B); subscripts designate age in years.

558

Age-lagged Cross-racial Correlations of Item Difficulties on WISC Subtests. Do the lower correlations, that is, those below, say, .95, reflect cultural differences between the two racial groups? Or are they merely a result of the group differences in mental age, as reflected by the mean race difference in Full Scale IQ? To find out, I have computed the r_i between whites and blacks of different age levels, comparing younger whites with older blacks. Whites at ages 6, 7, and 9 are compared with blacks at ages 7, 9, and 11. These age-lagged comparisons practically wipe out the mean racial difference in total scores on each of the subtests; that is, the age-lagged blacks have nearly the same mean score as whites of the next younger age.

Under this age-lagged condition, the cross-racial correlations between item difficulties are, in nearly all instances, appreciably higher than the same-age cross-racial correlations. The age-lagged cross-racial correlations, shown in Table 11.12, average .98, which is raised to .99 by correction for attenuation. The fact that the age-lagged cross-racial correlations are very high suggests that the somewhat lower correlations between the same age groups may be due to the white–black differences in mental age rather than to differential cultural biases in the various items.

The only test that still shows unimpressive age-lagged cross-racial correlations is the four-item Object Assembly test. Thus a closer look at the Object Assembly subtest data is called for. The percentage passing each item in each of the age-lagged groups is shown in Table 11.13. The correlations are generally substantial, but we cannot make much of their falling below unity, because with only four items even much lower cross-racial correlations in item difficulty would not be significantly different from unity. (With $N = 4$, the r would have to be below $+.22$ to be significantly different from .995 at the .05 level.) Also note that the cross-racial age groups W_9B_{11}, unlike the other age-lagged comparisons, are not closely matched for overall difficulty level on the Object Assembly items. Thus the question of bias in the Object Assembly subtest remains in doubt and will have to await cross-validation in other white and black samples, using the methods demonstrated here.

Simulated Cross-racial Correlations by Pseudorace Groups. The age-lagged cross-racial correlations are higher than the corresponding same-age cross-racial correlations, suggesting a mental maturity difference rather than a cultural difference between the same-age race groups. Therefore we should be able to simulate the same kind of mental maturity differences by comparing the very same children (of either race) at younger and older age levels. That is, we correlate the item difficulties of whites at age 6 with the item

Table 11.13. Percentage passing each item of the WISC Object Assembly as a function of race and age.

Item	W_6	B_7	W_7	B_9	W_9	B_{11}
1	67.0	64.0	85.0	82.5	91.5	100.0
2	20.5	11.0	34.0	34.0	58.5	93.0
3	11.5	8.0	24.5	14.5	37.5	93.0
4	9.0	6.0	27.5	9.0	44.0	95.0
Mean %	27	22	43	35	58	95
Rank order ρ		1.00		.80		.65
Pearson r		.99		.98		.87
Intraclass r_i		.86		.79		.78

difficulties of the same whites at age 7, and correlate age 7 with age 9, and age 9 with age 11. We do the same for blacks. When the ratio of the mental ages of the same-persons age-lagged group is approximately equal to the ratio of the mental ages of two same-age racial groups, we call the same-persons age-lagged groups "pseudorace" groups, as they mimic the actual mental-age difference between the actual racial groups when they are matched on chronological age. For example, using W and B to stand for white and black and subscripts to stand for age, the psuedorace comparisons W_7W_6 should simulate the true cross-racial comparison W_7B_7; and the pseudorace comparison B_7B_6 should simulate W_6B_6, and so forth.

The intraclass correlations between the item difficulties of these pseudorace groups are shown in Table 11.12. It can be seen that their overall average (.93 and .94) is closer to the actual same-age cross-racial correlation (.91) than to the age-lagged cross-racial correlation (.98).

As an index of the goodness of the pseudorace simulation of the cross-racial correlation on the various subtests, I have computed the Spearman rank order correlation between the nine true cross-racial correlations and their pseudorace simulated counterparts. These correlations are shown in Table 11.14. Also shown in Table 11.14 are the ratios of the mental ages for the actual race and the pseudorace comparisons, as explained in the table's footnote 1. It can be seen that there is a fair approximation of the black–white MA ratios by the pseudorace younger–older MA ratios.

The simulation of the item difficulty cross-racial correlation is quite good; four of the six rank order correlations are quite high and significant beyond the .01 level.

The fact that the cross-racial correlations can be improved by age lagging the racial groups, and that they can also be quite well simulated by creating pseudorace groups of the very same children at different ages within each racial group, is strongly consistent with the hypothesis that the imperfect cross-racial correlations between the item difficul-

Table 11.14. Rank order correlation between (A) the true cross-race correlations of item difficulties on nine WISC subtests and (B) the corresponding pseudorace correlations.

(A) Cross-Race Correlation	(B) Pseudorace Correlation	Correlation ρ between A and B	Ratio of Mental Ages[1]	
			(A) Black/White	(B) Younger/Older
W_6B_6	B_7B_6	.59	.81	.79
W_7B_7	W_7W_6	.78[a]	.84	.82
	B_9B_7	.50		.81
W_9B_9	W_9W_7	.89[a]	.84	.81
	$B_{11}B_9$	.95[a]		.82
$W_{11}B_{11}$	$W_{11}W_9$	.97[a]	.81	.79
Mean		.85[a]	.83	.81

[1]The MA of each age group is calculated as the WISC Full Scale (IQ/100) × the actual mean chronological age.
[a]$p < .01$.

ties are due to a racial difference in mental maturity at any given age rather than to differential effects of culture bias in various items within each of the WISC subtests.

The Group Difference / Interaction Ratio.   If the magnitude of the cross-group correlation between item difficulty indices is taken as an indicator of item biases when the correlation is significantly less than unity (or the group × item interaction is significant), we should also have an index showing the magnitude of the group mean difference on the test in relation to the magnitude of the group × items interaction. What we wish to determine is (*a*) how large is the group (e.g., race) difference relative to individual differences within groups, (*b*) how large is the group × item interaction relative to the individual × item interaction, and, most important, (*c*) how large is *a* relative to *b*? I once termed this final index the *a/b* ratio (Jensen, 1974a, p. 217); I now think it preferable to call it the group difference–interaction ratio (or GD/I ratio, for short). The less the item biases in a test, the larger should be the GD/I ratio. That is, large values of the GD/I ratio indicate that the group difference is large relative to the group × item interaction. Because test scores and item data are not an absolute scale, the mean group difference and group × item interaction must each be expressed in terms of the individual variation within groups.

Referring to the analysis of variance (see Table 11.11), the GD/I ratio for race may be expressed in three ways that are all exactly equivalent, in terms of the sum of squares (SS), the mean squares (MS), or the *F* ratios.

$$1. \ \ GD/I = \frac{\text{Race SS / Subjects SS}}{\text{Items} \times \text{Race SS / Subjects} \times \text{Items SS}} \ ,$$

$$2. \ \ GD/I = \frac{\text{Race MS / Items} \times \text{Race MS}}{\text{Subjects MS / Items} \times \text{Subjects MS}} \ ,$$

$$3. \ \ GD/I = \frac{\text{Race MS / Subjects MS}}{\text{Items} \times \text{Race MS / Subjects} \times \text{Items MS}} \ ,$$

$$4. \ \ GD/I = F_R/F_{I \times R} \ .$$

where F_R is the *F* ratio for the race main effect and $F_{I \times R}$ is the *F* ratio for the item × race interaction.

In the example of the ANOVA of the WISC Vocabulary subtest (Table 11.11), the GD/I ratio for race is 3.63.

The GD/I ratio need not be computed unless the item × group interaction is statistically significant. If it is not significant, there is no question of any bias according to this particular criterion. If the item × group interaction is significant, the GD/I ratio indicates how much larger the group main effect is than the group × item interaction. As GD/I approaches zero, the group mean difference becomes increasingly trivial and uninterpretable in terms of any unitary dimension measured by the test. That is, when GD/I is close to unity (or less than 1), we cannot discount the supposition that any significant difference between the groups is due to item biases. It is interesting that the only significant sex difference with a substantial GD/I ratio (4.91) in all these data is for Block Design at age 6. The overall average of GD/I for sex on every subtest at every age level (leaving out only Block Design at age 6) is 0.79, $\sigma = 0.79$. The mean sex differences are all very small and usually nonsignificant, and those that are significant are meaningless because of the low

GD/I ratio. That is, the item × sex interaction is so large relative to the sex main effect as to render the latter meaningless. It can be the result of item biases.

The GD/I ratios for race, by contrast, are quite large, averaging 5.47, as shown in Table 11.15. Values of GD/I greater than 2 clearly indicate that the mean difference between the groups cannot be attributed to an unfavorable balance of group × item biases and cannot be appreciably reduced by eliminating some items or adding new items selected at random from the same general population of items. When GD/I is close to 1, the possibility exists of reducing the group main effect to nonsignificance by eliminating or adding items of the same type, thereby balancing out the group × item biases and equalizing the group means. In fact, this is precisely what has been done in the construction of some tests in which a sex difference has been purposely eliminated by balancing item biases. This would not be possible if GD/I were not already close to unity and would be practically impossible if GD/I were originally greater than 2.

Notice in Table 11.15 that the age-lagged cross-race comparisons show very small values of GD/I, averaging 0.99. In other words, the black children's test results at a given age are very much like those of white children who are younger but have approximately the same mental age as the blacks.

Also, we can simulate the same-age cross-race GD/I ratios by means of the pseudorace groups, as shown in Table 11.15. The goodness of this age simulation of the race GD/I ratios for the various WISC subtests is indicated by the rank order correlation between the actual and the simulated ratios, as shown in Table 11.16. Again, it clearly appears that the test differences between whites and blacks of the same age closely resemble the same features as are found in comparing older and younger children of the same race. The race differences thus look more like differences in overall mental maturity rather than like cultural factors interacting with test items. If one were to claim culture bias from these data, one would also have to argue that the cultural biases closely simulate differences in mental maturity among white children or among black children. But this would seem to be a quite farfetched ad hoc hypothesis, especially in view of the great variety of items comprising the WISC.

Stanford–Binet Intelligence Scale. The Stanford–Binet has often been criticized for not having included any minority children in its original standardization in 1916 and again in 1937. The item selection procedures used in constructing the S–B have never included minority children of any kind, and it was not until publication of the 1972 revised IQ conversion tables, based on samples tested in 1971–1972, that the norms included some fairly representative proportion of blacks and Mexican–Americans. This 1972 updating of the S–B norms made no attempt (with but two minor exceptions) to change the S–B items, which came originally from the 1937 revision. (In the 1972 revision, at age II a female "doll card" was substituted for the male "doll card," and at age VII the word "charcoal" was permitted as a substitute for "coal" in the Similarities test.) In view of the fact that minorities were not considered in the item selection for the S–B, it should be especially interesting, therefore, to look for evidence of groups × items interaction or majority–minority correlations of S–B item difficulties.

There is a surprising dearth of such evidence on the S–B. I have found only two relevant studies. Paul Nichols (1972) provides an especially valuable set of data. His samples consist of 2,526 white and 2,514 black children in 12 cities, all tested on the S–B at 4 years of age. The mean S–B IQ difference of 15 points between these samples is close

Table 11.15. The group difference / interaction ratio for various contrasted groups on the WISC subtests.

Subtest	Contrasted Race Groups[1]							Contrasted Pseudorace Groups					
	Same-age Cross-race				Age-lagged Cross-race								
	W_6B_6	W_7B_7	W_9B_9	$W_{11}B_{11}$	W_6B_7	W_7B_9	W_9B_{11}	W_7W_6	W_9W_7	$W_{11}W_9$	B_7B_6	B_9B_7	$B_{11}B_9$
Information	3.82	4.94	5.59	6.99	0.19	3.61	0.63	6.39	6.12	6.49	5.64	4.74	4.19
Comprehension	5.59	3.41	5.01	15.38	2.16	0.11	0.36	2.16	3.31	17.93	5.12	5.49	5.29
Similarities	2.69	3.06	4.15	3.38	1.72	0.96	0.63	3.69	3.52	5.00	2.69	4.47	4.20
Arithmetic	2.22	4.75	3.45	4.07	3.93	2.62	0.01	4.50	7.40	3.26	3.17	3.82	3.36
Vocabulary	3.63	4.76	7.01	6.10	1.63	1.04	0.06	5.50	6.53	6.94	3.63	4.81	5.35
Picture Comp.	6.07	8.65	8.43	8.23	0.16	1.50	0.55	13.18	11.95	5.45	5.71	8.31	2.32
Picture Arr.	5.43	3.13	3.31	5.80	0.05	0.58	0.39	2.96	3.94	7.23	4.81	3.49	2.64
Block Design	3.44	3.77	3.10	3.44	0.02	0.04	1.75	3.05	2.74	3.50	3.68	3.37	2.56
Object Assembly	5.46	9.93	9.42	9.37	1.40	0.59	0.03	11.57	4.62	16.25	5.96	10.52	34.66
Mean	4.26	5.15	5.50	6.97	1.25	1.23	0.49	5.89	5.57	8.01	4.49	5.45	7.17
Grand mean		5.47				0.99			6.49			5.70	

[1]Capital letters designate racial groups, white (W) and black (B); subscripts designate age in years.

Table 11.16.   Rank order correlation between (A) the true cross-race group difference / interaction ratio on nine WISC subtests and (B) the corresponding pseudorace GD/I ratios.

(A) Cross-race GD/I Ratio	(B) Pseudorace GD/I Ratio	Correlation between A and B
W_6B_6	B_7B_6	.85[a]
W_7B_7	W_7W_6	.87[a]
	B_9B_7	.65[b]
W_9B_9	W_9W_7	.53
	$B_{11}B_9$	.48
$W_{11}B_{11}$	$W_{11}B_9$	.77[b]
Mean		.72[a]

[a] $p < .01$.   [b] $p < .05$.

to the difference typically found in most studies of American blacks (Jensen 1973b, pp. 62–66; Shuey, 1966). Because all the children were of preschool age, one should expect any cultural differences that might exist between the whites and blacks to be undiluted by the common environment provided by formal schooling. Another advantage in these data is that the S–B items for 4-year-olds (i.e., S–B items in the III- to V-year range) are an especially diverse collection of items; they are probably more heterogeneous in form and content than the items in any other age range of the S–B or than any set of the same number of consecutive items in any other standard test. Nichols (1972) presents the percentage of whites and blacks passing sixteen consecutive S–B items from age III-6 through V, shown in Table 11.17.

The rank order correlation between the white and black percentage passing (*p* values) is .99. When the *p* values are transformed to delta values, thereby representing item difficulties on an interval scale, the cross-racial correlation is .98. The scatter diagram of the delta values is shown in Figure 11.7. It can be seen that the regression is linear and that $.98^2$ or 96 percent of the variance in the black delta values can be predicted from the white delta values by the regression equation black $\Delta = 3.33 + 0.93$ white Δ. The overall mean black–white difference in item difficulty is 2.43Δ, or 0.61 σ units. The broken lines fall ± 1.96 standard errors of estimate (SE_E) from the regression line, which is the 95 percent confidence interval. An item falling outside that range may be considered biased; that is, its difficulty in the minor group cannot be predicted from the item's difficulty in the major group within the 95 percent confidence interval. By eliminating such items and replacing them with less biased items of comparable difficulty in either the major or minor group, the cross-group item difficulty correlation is increased and the 95 percent confidence interval becomes narrower. A more stringent criterion could be to use the 90 percent confidence interval (i.e., $\pm 1.64 SE_E$). The choice of confidence interval is a policy decision and will be governed by such factors as the resources available for improving the test.

The remarkable feature of the present S–B data is the high cross-racial correlation of the item difficulties. For comparison, we can split the white sample into two half-samples and obtain the item difficulty correlation *within* the white sample; and we do the same in the black sample. The respective rank order correlations in the white and black split-half samples (boosted by the Spearman–Brown formula for the correlation in the full-size sample) are both .99, which can be compared with the rank order correlation of .99 between whites and blacks. From this evidence it would be hard to argue that there are any appreciable black–white item biases in the S–B in the range of items appropriate for testing most 4-year-olds.

Nichols (1972, Table 16) also reports the point-biserial correlations between each of the sixteen S–B items and total IQ; the average r_{pbi} is .40 for whites and .42 for blacks. The Pearson correlation between the sixteen white and black r_{pbi}'s is .85, indicating a high degree of cross-racial similarity in the extent to which the items correlate with total IQ. Nichols also gives the point-biserial correlation of each of the sixteen items with an index of socioeconomic status; these average .13 for whites and .10 for blacks, and the cross-racial correlation between these sixteen pairs of correlations is .81, showing considerable white–black similarity in the extent to which the individual items correlate with SES within each racial group. I have computed the correlation (phi/phi max) of each test item (scored pass = 1, fail = 0) with race (quantitized as white = 1, black = 0). These correlations range from .20 to .60 with an average of .35, $\sigma = .12$, over the sixteen items.

Table 11.17. Stanford–Binet items and percentage passing by 2,526 white and 2,514 black 4-year-olds.   (Data from Nichols, 1972, Tables 13, 14, 15)

		% Passing	
Item	Description	White	Black
III-6, 1	Identify the larger of 2 balls.	89%	71%
III-6, 3	Match pictures of animals.	95	80
III-6, 4	Name common objects in pictures.	91	81
III-6, 6	Answer either "What do we do when we're thirsty?" or "Why do we have stoves?"	81	50
IV,1	Picture vocabulary: Name the objects on 14 of 18 cards.	47	23
IV, 2	Child is shown three objects (e.g., car, dog, shoe); one is hidden; child must then name the hidden object.	79	67
IV, 3	Opposite analogies: e.g., "Brother is a boy, sister is a _____." (Must answer 2 out of 5 correctly.)	59	35
IV, 4	Picture identification: e.g., "Which one do we cook on?"	69	41
IV-6, 2	Opposite analogies II. (Same as IV, but must answer 3 out of 5 correctly.)	34	12
IV-6, 3	Object similarities and differences: pick out object in picture that is different from others.	60	32
IV-6, 5	Follow instructions: e.g., "Put the pencil on the chair, go over and shut the door, and bring the box over here."	61	41
IV-6, 6	Answer either "What do we do with our eyes?" or "What do we do with our ears?"	49	31
V, 1	Must add at least 2 features to incomplete drawing of a man.	27	11
V, 3	Must know meaning of 2 of the following: *ball, hat, stove.*	57	32
V, 4	Copy a square. (Must have "square" corners.)	15	5
V, 6	Construct a rectangle from 2 triangular cards.	9	6

Figure 11.7. Regression of black item difficulties on white item difficulties of the 16 Stanford-Binet items described in Table 11.16. Item difficulties are expressed as delta (Δ) values, which is a normalized scale of the p values.

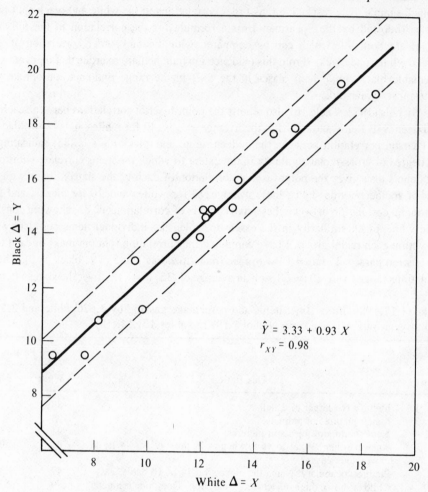

$$\hat{Y} = 3.33 + 0.93\ X$$
$$r_{XY} = 0.98$$

The items $\times$ race correlations are significantly correlated with the items $\times$ total IQ correlation (.74 for whites and .57 for blacks), indicating that the items that correlate the most with individual differences in total IQ *within* either race also correlate the most with the variable of race. The Pearson correlation between (1) item point-biserial correlations with race and (2) item point-biserial correlations with SES within each race is .69 for whites and .84 for blacks and indicates that race differences and SES differences (within races), whatever their causes, are hardly distinguishable among these sixteen S–B items.

Other evidence I have found as a basis for examining possible item biases in the S–B involves the Vocabulary test. The words in the S–B Vocabulary test are arranged in the order of their p values in the 1937 standardization based on an all-white sample. Kennedy, Van de Riet, and White (1963) obtained the S–B on 1,800 black school children in grades

1 through 6 in five southeastern states, with an overall average S–B IQ of 80.7, $\sigma = 12.4$. The sample was of predominantly low socioeconomic status. Kennedy et al. (p. 101) give the percentages of this large sample passing each of the first twenty-six words of the S–B Vocabulary test. The rank order correlation between the words' difficulty levels in the white standardization sample and in the black sample is .98, which is about as close agreement as one might expect to find even with a white sample tested more than twenty-five years after the standardization sample on which the order of difficulty of vocabulary words was determined. This high degree of cross-racial agreement seems quite remarkable, considering that one might reasonably expect Vocabulary to be perhaps the most prone to cultural bias.

Kennedy et al. (1963) also indicate the percentage of the black sample, separately for each of grades 1 through 6, passing each S–B item. Figure 11.8, which is based on these data, shows the average percentage passing the various S–B items as a function of the item's mental-age placement as determined in the 1937 standardization on a white population sample. It can be seen that at each grade level the percentage passing as a function of the item's mental-age placement in the original standardization sample is a

Figure 11.8. Mean percent of black children (sampled in five southeastern states) passing Stanford-Binet items as a function of the mental-age placement of the items in the white standardization sample.

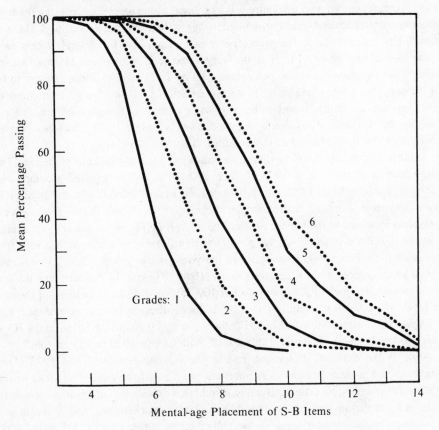

nearly perfect ogive of the normal curve. Thus the S–B item difficulties generally maintain the same relative positions in the *1963 black* sample as in the *1937 white* standardization sample.

Temporal Stability of Stanford–Binet Item Difficulty.   M. W. Smith (1974) proposed the hypothesis that, when the Stanford–Binet is administered to any population other than the original normative sample, the different population should score lower than the normative sample because of cultural biases, and this is true even for a group from the same general population as the original normative sample but tested at some later point in time. Smith argued that the lowering of test scores ''as time moves away from the moment when the test was standardized . . . may be due to changes in language and culture—an extreme example of this problem would be taking a test written in Middle English'' (p. 330).

Smith attempted to prove her hypothesis by comparing item difficulties (percentage passing) between the 1937 and 1960 norms for the Stanford–Binet. But this comparison is wholly fallacious and therefore can prove nothing. It cannot possibly show a *temporal* change in item difficulties between 1937 and 1960, since no new sample was tested in 1960. Apparently unknown to Smith, the 1960 normative group is *exactly the same* group of children as the 1937 standardization sample! The only essential difference between the 1937 and 1960 norms is that in the 1937 norms the IQ was calculated from MA/CA, whereas in 1960 the IQ is an age-standardized score with a mean of 100 and σ of 16. In the 1937 standardization, item difficulty was expressed as the percentage passing the item by children within each one-year *chronological-age* group; but in the 1960 S–B Manual, item difficulty is expressed as the percentage passing each item by children within each one-year *mental-age* group. But it is the very same total sample of children in each instance. Thus the decrease in the percentage passing from 1937 to 1960, pointed to by Smith in support of her hypothesis, is purely an artifact of the change in method of representing item difficulty, based on the very same normative sample each time. I have spelled out the reasons for this discrepancy elsewhere (Jensen, 1977c), as have Terman and Merrill in the 1960 Manual of the Stanford–Binet (pp. 28–31).

Smith's hypothesis is, if anything, contradicted by the available evidence. The restandardization of the S–B in 1972 (Terman & Merrill, 1973) involved a completely new sample, tested in 1971–1972, which included blacks and Spanish-surname children in proportion to their numbers in the sampled normative population drawn from several geographical locations in the United States. The interesting finding is that the percentage passing the S–B items in any given age group has significantly increased in the thirty-five years between 1937 and 1972, especially in the younger age groups (2 to 7 years), but also, to a lesser degree, in the older age groups (16 to 18 years). In standardizing the test anew, of course, the mean IQ is always set at 100, with a σ of 16, regardless of the raw score level of performance. But, if the 1972 standardization sample is assigned IQs according to the norms established in 1937, the mean and standard deviation of the IQ at various age levels are as shown in Table 11.18, with an overall mean IQ of 106.3.

What is the explanation for this rise in the IQ between 1937 and 1972? One possibility is that the standardization samples are not drawn from equivalent strata of the population in the same proportions. But how would that explain the differential amount of increase in IQ at various age levels? Possibly there are larger families, and consequently more children at the younger ages, in the higher-status families in 1972 than in 1937.

Table 11.18.   Means and standard deviations of IQs of the 1972 Stanford–Binet standardization sample when scored according to the 1937 norms.   (From Terman & Merrill, 1973, Table 11, p. 359)

Age	Mean	Standard Deviation
2–0	110.4	15.7
2–6	110.6	15.9
3–0	110.7	16.0
3–6	110.8	16.1
4–0	110.7	16.2
4–6	110.4	16.3
5–0	109.7	16.4
5–6	108.4	16.6
6–0	107.1	16.7
7–0	105.0	17.0
8–0	103.3	17.2
9–0	102.1	17.2
10–0	101.9	16.9
11–0	102.2	16.6
12–0	102.5	16.4
13–0	102.9	16.5
14–0	103.3	16.8
15–0	103.9	17.2
16–0	104.7	17.6
17–0	105.7	17.9
18–0	106.9	18.0

These kinds of fluctuations in sampling have not been fully examined or ruled out. The authors of the 1972 standardization, however, believe that these upward trends in S–B performance are "genuine, important and highly relevant shifts in performance characteristics of children in these age groupings" (Terman & Merrill, 1973, p. 359). The authors explain the upward shift in test performance in terms of the difference in cultural background between the 1930s and 1970s:

> This shows up most acutely in the case of preschool children, whose cultural environment has probably changed the most radically. In the 1930's, radio was new and relatively limited in its impact on small children, whereas in the 1970's television is omnipresent and viewed for hours each day by the typical preschooler. The impact of television and radio, the increases in literacy and education of parents, and the many other cultural changes of almost 40 years would appear to have had their most impressive impact on the preschool group. Furthermore, the tendency to persist in schools through the end of secondary education has continued to grow, and the numbers of 15-, 16- and 17-year-olds who are still in school in the 1970's is clearly higher than it was in the 1930's. This is perhaps the reason for an apparent modest rise in the curve at the upper ages.   (Terman & Merrill, 1973, p. 360)

Such cross-generation shifts in absolute level of item difficulties would seem almost inevitable for certain culturally loaded test items, but it would be surprising if there were not differential effects for various items, so that the cross-generation cultural changes would result in some alteration in the relative difficulties of items. If there were found to be no appreciable cross-generation change in items' relative difficulties, but a substantial change in overall difficulty level, one would be forced to hypothesize either (1) sampling bias in the cross-generation samples or (2) a change in some extraordinarily *general* environmental factor(s) that uniformly influences *all* kinds of test items. Perhaps nutritional differences between generations or changes in the rate of maturation, from whatever complex causes, might qualify as such general environmental factors. But it seems hardly likely that cultural factors per se would cause such a uniform shift in all item difficulties.

Smith's other claim is that any population group other than that on which the test was originally standardized must necessarily score lower than the standardization group. This hypothesis is clearly contradicted by numerous studies, the most recent evidence coming from the standardization of the Wechsler Intelligence Scale for Children (WISC) in Japan (Lynn, 1977). The Japanese translation of the verbal subtests of the WISC makes comparisons questionable, but five of the WISC performance subtests (all but Picture Completion) were used unaltered in their original form. Children at every age from 5 to 15 in the Japanese standardization sample, when scored on the U.S. norms, obtain higher average scores on the WISC Performance scale than did the U.S. normative samples in the corresponding age groups. The Performance IQ of the Japanese averages from 1 to 10.5 IQ points higher, with an overall mean of 3.1 points, than the U.S. norm in various age groups, being highest in the younger groups. The WISC, it should be recalled, was originally standardized on U.S. whites only, and it is this normative group with which the Japanese sample is compared. Similar results were found in the Japanese standardization of the Wechsler Adult Intelligence Scale (WAIS) and the Wechsler Preschool and Primary Intelligence Scale (WPPSI). Lynn summarizes: "In all, the Japanese standardizations yield 18 readings of Japanese mean IQs and all are higher [overall by 6.6 IQ points] than those of the American counterparts" (p. 70). Lynn concludes:

> [T]he Japanese results . . . clearly show that a population quite far removed from white middle class American can actually do better in these tests than the Americans themselves. The Japanese results suggest that tests like the performance scales of the Wechsler may be considerably more culture fair than many critics have been willing to allow. In any event, it seems hardly possible to advance test bias as an explanation for the high mean Japanese IQ.   (p. 71)

Contrasting Tests: Picture Vocabulary and Matrices.   One could hardly pick two more highly contrasting tests for the study of cultural bias than the Peabody Picture Vocabulary Test (PPVT) and Raven's Progressive Matrices. The PPVT and the Raven stand at diametrically opposite poles on the continuum of culture loadedness. The PPVT is perhaps the most obviously culture-loaded test among the more widely used measures of IQ. In contrast, the Raven is generally regarded as one of the most "culture-reduced" tests, being wholly nonverbal and expressly designed to reduce item dependence on acquired knowledge and cultural and scholastic content while getting at basic processes of intellectual ability.

Item difficulty in a culture-loaded test such as the PPVT is highly related to the rarity of the item, that is, the frequency or probability of encountering the informational content of the item in the so-called core culture in which the test was devised and standardized. Thus there is a close correspondence between the rank order of difficulty of the PPVT items and the rank order of the frequency of occurrence of the stimulus words (per million words) in American newspapers, magazines, and books (Jensen, 1974a, pp. 192–194) showing that PPVT item difficulty is closely related to the degree of rarity of the words in general usage in American English (see Figure 11.3). Rarity, more than complexity of mental processes, determines the difficulty of PPVT items. For example, there appears to be nothing conceptually more difficult about *culver* (the last and hardest item of the PPVT) than about *table* (the first and easiest item); these nouns differ vastly in rarity, however.

Item difficulty in a nonverbal culture-reduced test such as the Raven depends on the complexity of the items (abstract figural material) and the number of elements involved in the reasoning required for the correct solution.

It should be instructive, therefore, to compare the PPVT and the Raven with respect to the analysis of item × group interaction. I have done this with large representative samples of elementary school children from three ethnic groups (white, $N = 638$; black, $N = 381$; Mexican–American, $N = 644$) in a California school district. The study was replicated for the Raven in grades 3 to 8 in another California school district, with representative samples of 1,585 whites, 1,238 blacks, and 1,396 Mexican–Americans. Replication with the PPVT and Raven in still another California school district involved only whites ($N = 144$) and blacks ($N = 144$) in grades K, 1, and 3, randomly drawn from the two most contrasting neighborhood schools in the whole country with respect to socioeconomic status. The details of all these studies are presented elsewhere (Jensen, 1974a).

Item bias was examined both by means of cross-group correlation of item difficulties and by the item × group interaction in the analysis of variance.

The item difficulties (*p* values) of the PPVT and Raven were rank order correlated between ethnic groups, with the results in the various studies shown in Table 11.19. These correlations, which are not corrected for attenuation, are all very high. The average correlation between males and females *within* each of the ethnic groups is shown for comparison; the correlations indicate that there is no greater item × ethnic group interaction than item × sex (same ethnicity) interaction. The Raven has consistently higher correlations than the PPVT, as one might expect, but the difference is practically negligi-

Table 11.19. Cross-group rank order correlations of item difficulties on PPVT and Raven in three independent studies.

Groups Correlated[2]	Study A PPVT	Study A Raven	Study B Raven	Study C[1] PPVT[3]	Study C[1] Raven[4]
White × Black	.98	.98	.96	.86	.95
White × Mexican	.97	.99	.98		
Black × Mexican	.98	.99	.99		
Male × Female[5]	.98	.99	—[a]	—[a]	—[a]

[1]In study C, whites (all high SES) and blacks (all low SES) in grades K–3 selected at the extremes of socioeconomic status.
[2]Correlations obtained separately for each sex and then averaged.   [3]Based only on fifteen items (46–60).
[4]Based only on items 1–12.   [5]Average rank order correlation between the sexes *within* each ethnic group.
[a]Not obtained.

ble. The lowest correlations were obtained in the white and black groups selected at the extremes of socioeconomic status, but it should be noted that these correlations are based on smaller samples and on fewer items (because of the smaller range of p values larger than zero).

There are a number of indications that the "lowness" of these extremely high correlations is due mostly to the groups' overall differences in ability levels. When the Raven p values are determined within each school grade separately, it is seen from the white–black cross-racial × cross-grade correlations of the p values that whites resemble blacks who are two grades higher (i.e., about two years older) more than they resemble blacks of the same age or other whites who are two years older. In fact, grade 4 whites are more like grade 6 blacks ($r = .98$) than grade 4 whites are like grade 6 whites ($r = .81$). This result seems much less consistent with the hypothesis of a cultural difference than with the hypothesis of a difference in rates of intellectual development, unless we make the unlikely assumption that the test manifestations of cultural differences are indistinguishable from the test manifestations of general developmental difference within a culturally homogeneous group.

Another indication that the Raven item × group interaction is more a function of developmental lag than of cultural differences per se was obtained by factor analyzing the intercorrelations among all the Raven items and then getting the cross-racial × cross-grades correlations between the items' loadings on the first principal component. Blacks and whites in grade 4 correlate .52, but grade 4 whites and grade 5 blacks correlate .65, and grade 4 whites and grade 6 blacks correlate .85. The Mexicans do not fit this developmental lag hypothesis; they show their highest correlation for item factor loadings with whites of the same grade level: for example, grade 4 whites and grade 4 Mexicans correlate .75, whereas grade 4 whites and grade 6 Mexicans correlate $-.02$.

The group × item interaction in the analysis of variance gives essentially the same picture of these data. Also, it was possible to simulate quite closely the results of the white–black ANOVA for both PPVT and Raven by making up pseudorace groups composed entirely of younger (ages 6 to 9 years) and older (ages 8 to 11 years) whites. The simulation was not quite as good in the case of Mexicans. The values of eta squared × 100 (i.e., the percentage of the total variance accounted for) of the item × group interaction in the ANOVA of the PPVT and the Raven are as shown in Table 11.20. Note that by comparing younger white with older ethnic groups we can appreciably reduce the size of the item × group interaction as expressed by eta squared. An interaction quite comparable to that found in the white–black ANOVA is produced by doing an ANOVA on older and younger whites (i.e., the pseudorace comparison).

The interaction ratios, GD/I (see pp. 561–562), which indicate the magnitude of the group mean difference on the test as a whole relative to the item × group interaction, are as follows:

Groups in ANOVA	PPVT	Raven
White and black	7.10	17.32
White and Mexican	8.55	18.13
White (ages 6–9) and white (ages 8–11)	7.97	18.26

Note that the GD/I ratios for the Raven are more than double those for the PPVT. This is what we should expect in comparing the GD/I ratio of a culture-reduced test with that of a

Table 11.20. Item × groups interaction for various group comparisons in ANOVA.

Groups Compared in ANOVA	$\eta^2 \times 100$ for Items × Groups Interaction	
	PPVT	Raven
White and black (same age)	0.89[a]	0.87[a]
White and Mexican (same age)	1.50[a]	0.47[a]
White (ages 6–9) and black (ages 8–11)	0.12	0.22
White (ages 6–9) and Mexican (ages 8–11)	0.30	0.26
White (ages 6–9) and white (ages 8–11)	1.10[a]	0.94[a]

[a] *F* for the I × G interaction is significant beyond the .01 level.

culture-loaded test, if the mean group difference is real and not an artifact of test bias. Yet the ratios are very high for both the Raven and the PPVT and indicate that no amount of item elimination or sampling of other items from the same general population of such items would stand a chance of equalizing or reversing the white–black or white–Mexican mean difference on either test. These high GD/I ratios reflect the fact that the direction of the majority–minority difference is not reliably reversed on any item in either the PPVT or the Raven.

It should be interesting to see how much we can reduce the majority–minority difference on the PPVT by selecting from among the 150 PPVT items those that discriminate the majority–minority groups the least, as compared with those that discriminate the most. I made up separate subtests of the two types of items, then compared the majority–minority mean differences on the most and the least discriminating subscales. The PPVT subscale made up of the thirty-three items with the highest white–black discrimination showed a mean white–black difference of 1.28σ; the subscale composed of the thirty-one least discriminating items showed a mean white–black difference of 1.07σ. (The corresponding figures for the most and least discriminating subscales for the whites versus Mexican contrasts are 1.79σ and 1.45σ.) All these mean differences expressed in σ units are actually *larger* than the mean majority–minority differences on the full PPVT expressed in σ units, since the specially contrived subscales have considerably smaller within-group standard deviations. The most and least discriminating subscales correlate with each other .91 (for the black scales) and .88 (for the Mexican scales) in the combined ethnic groups. When Spearman–Brown corrected for length of the test, these correlations between subscales are as high as the split-half reliabilities of the whole PPVT, indicating that the two subscales still measure the same ability as the whole PPVT. Also, the most and least discriminating PPVT subscales show approximately the same correlations (averaging .63) with total scores on the Raven, which is further evidence that the most and least ethnically discriminating PPVT items are factorially equivalent.

Another investigation comparing the rank order of PPVT item difficulties in random samples of fourth- and fifth-grade white and black children enrolled in regular classes in the public schools in Middletown, Connecticut, found "no statistically significant difference in the correlation between item order and item difficulty for groups of different race or sex" (Berry, 1977, p. 40).

Thus we see that even the highly culture-loaded PPVT shows only slightly more item bias, as revealed by indices of items × ethnic groups interaction, than the culture-reduced Raven; and neither test shows any appreciable item bias for large samples of American-born black and Mexican–American children. The scant item × group interaction that exists is largely attributable to group differences in overall level of ability on the tests and can be simulated by comparing ethnically homogeneous groups of older and younger children. If culture bias is claimed to exist for these tests in these groups, it must also be argued that the bias involves *all* the items of the PPVT and the Raven about equally. This seems unlikely for a *cultural* effect in any meaningful sense of the term; the uniformity of the group differences across virtually all items of these tests seems more likely attributable to other factors—factors that could be reasonably hypothesized to have a much more general influence on overall rate of mental development.

Wonderlic Personnel Test.   The WPT is widely used for personnel selection and placement in business and industry. It is a group-administered paper-and-pencil test of general intelligence comprised of fifty highly diverse verbal, numerical, and spatial items. The distribution of total raw scores on the WPT is approximately normal in the adult population. The very large normative samples of white and black adults show an average raw score difference of 1σ. The obvious cultural–educational loading of the WPT items makes it suspect as possibly culture biased for the American black population.

To investigate this possibility, I have applied the prescribed correlation and ANOVA methods to the WPT items in two independent large samples of white and black applicants for the same jobs (Jensen, 1977a). (Sample 1, $N = 544$ whites and 544 blacks; sample 2, $N = 204$ whites and 204 blacks.) The mean white–black difference in total scores is 1.05σ in sample 1 and 0.87σ in sample 2.

The cross-racial correlation between item difficulties is .932 in sample 1 and .956 in sample 2. The same-race correlation between item difficulties in samples 1 and 2 is .98 for both whites and blacks; thus there is a slightly greater cross-race than within-race group × item interaction. But the difference is largely due to the overall group difference in ability level, as shown by the ANOVA performed on the larger sample (sample 1). The item × race interaction yields a small but statistically significant η^2 ($\times$ 100) of 1.04. But, if we perfectly match pairs of whites and blacks on total scores (there are 127 such perfectly matched pairs in sample 1) and do the ANOVA on the white and black groups matched on total score, the η^2 ($\times$ 100) for the items × race interaction drops to a nonsignificant 0.29. If the WPT items are culture biased for blacks, one should expect that whites and blacks with the same total score would obtain their scores in different ways, so that, even when the main effect of race is reduced to zero in the ANOVA, the item × race interaction would remain. This expectation is clearly not borne out.

On the other hand, we can simulate the item × race interaction by selecting a pseudorace group of all white subjects whose total score distribution closely approximates the total score distribution of blacks. The ANOVA of these pseudorace white groups, which differ in means by 1σ, yields a comparably significant items × pseudorace interaction, with the associated eta squared ($\times$ 100) = 0.94, which is only 0.10 less than the eta squared ($\times$ 100) for the actual white and black groups.

The interaction ratio, GD/I, for the WPT in sample 1 is 10.84, which is about intermediate between that of the PPVT and the Raven in the previous study and is so high as to indicate that no subscale of items selected from the WPT (or from a similar population of items) could possibly equalize or reverse the white and black means.

The WPT items were classified by item type into three categories to form three subscales: verbal (V), numerical (N), and logical reasoning (R). The V, N, and R scores were determined for every subject, and an ANOVA of the race × VNR scales was performed to determine if there is a significant race × scales interaction. The interaction is significant (the white–black difference is slightly less on the numerical than on the verbal and reasoning scales), but its eta squared is only one-twentieth as large as the eta squared for the race main effect. When the same ANOVA was done on whites and blacks matched on total score, the race × VNR scales interaction diminishes to nonsignificance. This finding contradicts the popular belief that, because verbal content presumably allows wider scope for cultural bias, blacks should perform relatively less well on verbal items than on other types of items.

Scholastic Achievement Tests.   The ANOVA item × group interaction or the cross-group correlation of item difficulties have seldom been applied to standardized tests of scholastic achievement. I have found only one such study, which fortunately is a very good one, by Arneklev (1975). The scholastic measures are five subtests of the Comprehensive Tests of Basic Skills (Form Q, Level 3), published by the California Test Bureau (1968); it is one of the most widely used batteries for measuring achievement and skills in the basic school subjects: Reading Vocabulary, Reading Comprehension, Arithmetic Computation, Arithmetic Concepts, and Arithmetic Applications. These five subtests were given to white, black, and Asian pupils in the eighth grade in schools of Tacoma, Washington. The Asian sample, however, is much too small (twenty-five males, thirty females) to allow reliable item p values, which should never be based on a sample of less than one hundred. So I shall confine description to only the data on whites and blacks.

The mean white–black difference in item difficulties (percentage passing) on all five achievement subtests is 18.4 percent, or a difference of 1.15σ, which is close to the white–black difference generally found on intelligence tests.

Arneklev obtained the cross-racial correlations and cross-sex correlations between item difficulties on each subtest. He used three different indices of item difficulty; p values, logits of the p values, that is, $\log (1 - p)/p$, which transforms the p values to an interval scale, and a scale of item difficulty derived from the Rasch model. Because the cross-race and cross-sex correlations are very similar regardless of the method used for scaling item difficulty, I shall report only the results based on the familiar item p values.

Arneklev also determined the standard error of estimate, SE_E, of the white sample's estimated or predicted p values, as predicted from the actual regression of the white p values on black p values. An item was identified as significantly biased when its actual p value differed from the predicted p values (i.e., the regression line) by $\pm 2SE_E$ or more, which means the item's actual p value differs from its predicted p value by an amount that is significant beyond the .05 level of confidence. It can therefore be regarded as a "significantly biased" item. Of course, 5 percent of the items must necessarily meet this criterion, and so the items designated as significantly biased are simply the *most* biased 5 percent of all the items in the test. Bias, after all, is a continuum, and any given criterion for defining bias in terms of the SE_E deviation from the regression line is quite arbitrary;

the .05 level is merely conventional. If we wanted to be even more stringent (against the test), we could adopt the .10 level or even the .20 level.

An item whose p value falls $2SE_E$ or more *above* the regression line (i.e., the regression of white p values on black p values) is biased in "*favor*" of whites; that is, it is a relatively *easier* item, in comparison with all other items, for whites than for blacks. An item whose p value falls $2SE_E$ or more *below* the regression line is biased "*against*" whites; that is, it is a relatively more difficult item, in comparison with all other items, for whites than for blacks. An item that significantly "favors" or "disfavors" whites will almost always have the opposite effect for blacks, but not necessarily; that can only be precisely determined by considering the other regression line, that is, the regression of the blacks' item p values on the whites' p values. This is illustrated in Figure 11.9. (Arneklev's study does not provide these regressions, but they can easily be derived from the other statistics given in his report.)

The results of Arneklev's analyses are shown in Table 11.21. We see that the cross-racial correlations of item p values in the various subtests are all quite high and scarcely differ from the same-race cross-sex correlations (last two columns), the overall averages of the cross-race and cross-sex correlations being .94 and .937, respectively. The last row of Table 11.21 shows the total number of significantly biased items (i.e., those with p values $\pm 2SE_E$ or more from the regression line) in all five subtests. There are 183 items in all, and so the number of items designated as biased at the .05 level of significance that should be expected is 5 percent of 183, which is 9.15. (*Note:* This is not the number that should be expected "by chance," i.e., sampling error, but the number that necessarily falls beyond the 95 percent confidence limits in the distribution of the deviations of obtained values from predicted values.) The actual numbers of biased items found in the cross-racial comparisons is nine for males and nine for females.

But we should beware of the common false inference that, when item biases are revealed by correlation of p values or items × groups interaction in the ANOVA, the biases necessarily "favor" the group with the higher overall mean or "disfavor" the group with the lower mean on the test as a whole. The item biases can work in *either*

Table 11.21.   Cross-race and cross-sex (same-race) correlations between item p values of the Comprehensive Tests of Basic Skills.   (From Arneklev, 1977)

Subtest[2]	Groups Correlated[1]			
	Wm × Bm	Wf × Bf	Wm × Wf	Bm × Bf
Vocabulary (40)	.92	.95	.96	.91
Reading Comprehension (45)	.92	.92	.95	.89
Arithmetic Computation (48)	.96	.96	.97	.97
Arithmetic Concepts (30)	.95	.95	.88	.91
Arithmetic Applications (20)	.90	.92	.95	.89
Mean	.94	.94	.95	.92
Number of Biased Items	9	9	8	6

[1]W = white, B = black, m = male, f = female. *N*'s are Wm = 1,027, Wf = 931, Bm = 128, and Bf = 150.
[2]Number of items in each subtest in parentheses.

Figure 11.9.   Hypothetical graph showing the two regression lines (the thin solid lines) for the correlation between the item difficulties (*p* values) of a test in groups A and B. The 95% confidence interval (i.e., $\pm 2SE_{Est.}$) around each regression line is indicated by the heavy solid lines for the regression of A on B, and by the broken lines for the regression of B on A. Items that fall within the unshaded area bounded by the confidence intervals are regarded as unbiased for both groups A and B. Items that fall within the upper left unshaded area are regarded as biased items favoring group A and disfavoring group B. Biased items falling in the lower right unshaded area favor group B and disfavor group A. The four shaded areas indicate item biases that either favor or disfavor one group but not both: (1) disfavors B, (2) disfavors A, (3) favors A, (4) favors B.

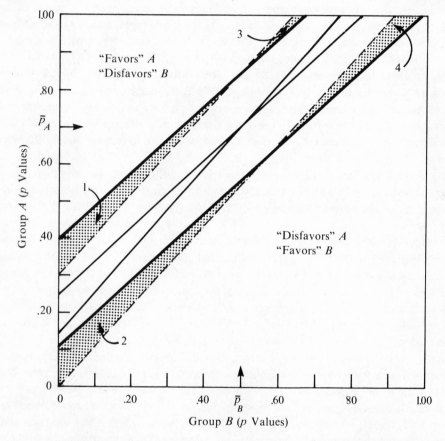

Group *B* (*p* Values)

direction. For example, in the Arneklev study, out of the total of fifteen different items designated as significantly biased in the cross-racial analyses, twelve are biased in the direction that "disfavors" whites and only three are biased in the direction that "favors" whites. In this case, elimination of the fifteen biased items from the test would have the net effect of slightly *increasing* the mean white–black difference in total scores.

   Figure 11.9 illustrates in general terms this type of item regression analysis, showing the various regions into which the item *p* values may fall and be classified as either "unbiased" or "significantly biased" at the .05 level, with respect to one or both groups. The two regression lines are drawn so as to represent a cross groups' correlation of .90

between the item p values, with $2SE_E = 14$ around each regression line. (The SE_E is based on a p values' standard deviation of 16 in each group, which is close to the standard deviation of p values found in Arneklev's study.)

College Aptitude Tests.   Although the cross-group correlation of item p values and item × group interaction had their first application in the detection of bias in college aptitude tests, these methods have not been widely used in college aptitude testing since the first studies that introduced the methods.

Cardall and Coffman (1964) were the first to look for item biases in the widely used Scholastic Aptitude Test (SAT) by means of analysis of variance and by correlating item difficulties, separately for the Verbal and Math subtests, across groups from three areas: (1) the rural Midwest, (2) New York City, and (3) the Southeast, which was an all-black sample. The difficulties of the SAT Verbal and Math items show significantly lower correlations between the white and black groups (1 × 3 and 2 × 3) than within each of the three groups. The cross-racial correlation of item difficulties is slightly higher for Math items ($r = .89$) than for Verbal items ($r = .84$). The average correlation *within* groups is .98. Because the white and black groups differ in overall score, however, it is uncertain how much of the lower correlation between the item difficulties of whites and blacks is attributable to differences in level of ability and how much to racial–cultural differences per se.

Angoff and Ford (1973) controlled for level of ability, using the same item correlation method on the Preliminary Scholastic Aptitude Test (PSAT). They correlated item difficulties across white and black groups that were matched for ability and also across randomly selected groups of whites and blacks. All groups were from a large urban area in the Southwest. The Verbal PSAT item difficulties were correlated across black and white groups matched on the Math PSAT; and the Math PSAT item difficulties were correlated across black and white groups matched on the Verbal PSAT. The correlations of item difficulties between the randomly selected white and black groups range from .859 to .948; the correlations for the matched white and black groups are slightly higher—.923 to .959—indicating that some of the racial difference in the relative difficulties of items in the randomly selected groups of whites and blacks is due to their differences in level of ability. Finally, these correlations between the racial groups matched on ability should be compared with the *within*-race correlations of item difficulties: .978 between two black samples and .987 between two white samples. The implication of these results is that differences in ability level account for some, but not all, of the race × item interaction in the PSAT Verbal and Math tests. One wonders how much race × item interaction would remain (i.e., how far below 1 the cross-racial correlation of item difficulties would be) if black and white groups were matched for scores on the *same* test (Verbal or Math) on which the item difficulties were correlated across the racial groups. Because the correlation between Verbal and Math scores is generally in the range of .60 to .70, white and black groups that are selected so as to be matched on Verbal scores will not, because of regression effects, be matched on Math scores, on the average; and white and black groups that are selected so as to be matched on Math scores will not be matched on Verbal scores.

The use of analysis of variance, with the item × group interaction as a method for detecting bias, was used by Cleary and Hilton (1968) in separate analyses of variance of the Verbal and Math subtests of the PSAT, comparing large white and black samples from integrated schools in metropolitan areas. They found statistically significant but practially negligible item × race interactions, accounting for 0.9–1.8 percent of the total variance. The authors concluded that, "given the stated definition of bias, the PSAT for practical purposes is not biased for the groups studied" (p. 74). Stanley (1969) later showed that what little item × race interaction existed in these data was due to just a few items that were too difficult for both racial groups, resulting in a high guessing rate and hence little reliable discrimination between the groups. On most of the items of the PSAT, blacks scored rather uniformly lower than whites.

Tests of Highly Specific Occupational Knowledge.   The U.S. Navy has applied the method of cross-race correlation of item difficulties to a large number of tests based on content that is highly specific to navy occupational skills, for example, aviation machinist's mate, boatswain's mate, boiler technician, commissaryman, hospital corpsman, and machinist's mate. The tests are so specialized that the results of these studies do not warrant detailed description here.

One study (Robertson & Montague, 1976) obtained cross-racial correlations of item difficulties on twenty-four navy tests for typical white and black samples of Navy personnel and for white and black groups matched on total scores, and found that "total test score appears to account largely, but not completely, for racial differences in relative item difficulty" (p. 18). Another navy study (Robertson & Royle, 1975) found significant race × item interactions on various occupational exams, with whites and blacks showing greater similarity of item *p* values on *"applied"* than on *"theoretical"* types of item content. A study by Robertson, Royle, and Morena (1977), involving comparisons of white and black navy personnel on various specialized tests of technical knowledge, tried to make up tests that would minimize white–black differences by using only those items from the total item pool that were most similar in difficulty for blacks and whites. They found that

> selecting items that were similar in difficulty for both blacks and whites . . . did reduce mean score differences between blacks and whites but it also reduced item differentiation [i.e., difference in item *p* values between high and low scores *within* each racial group] and test reliability. . . . Developing tests by using items similar in difficulty for blacks and whites is not feasible since it reduces test quality. However, developing tests by eliminating excessively difficult items would improve test quality and benefit blacks.   (p. viii)

Most of the items of similar difficulty for whites and blacks were concentrated in the most difficult range of item difficulty where guessing is most prevalent and item reliability and discrimination are poor.

Item Characteristic Curves and the SAT.   The item characteristic curve (ICC) is undoubtedly the most sensitive, detailed, and powerful method for examining item bias. (See Chapter 9, p. 442, for a theoretical description of the ICC.) Unfortunately, the ICC has been used scarcely at all so far in the study of test bias. The most likely reason is that the ICC, to be applied properly, requires very large samples over a fairly wide range of ability to obtain reliable estimates of the ICC for every item in a test. The sample sizes needed for the ICC are generally beyond the resources of most individual researchers. But they are within the capacity of, say, the armed forces or test publishers who have access to the item data from large representative samples of the populations for whom the test is intended. Consequently it is not surprising that the two studies of item bias using the ICC method that I have seen reference to in the literature were done by the California Test Bureau with respect to the California Achievement Tests (Green & Draper, 1972) and by the Educational Testing Service with respect to the Verbal SAT (Lord, 1976). In each report, examples of rather marked group differences in the ICCs for specific items are shown for illustrative purposes, but little specific information is provided concerning the proportion of all items in these tests that show significantly different ICCs for majority and minority groups. The impression one is left with is that markedly different ICCs for the major and minor groups are the rare exceptions rather than the general finding for the items in these tests. In comparing several quite discrepant ICC curves for the Verbal SAT items in black and white samples, Lord (1976, p. 29) states, "It would seem desirable to exclude such items from our tests as far as possible. Let me emphasize that the [ICC] curves shown here were picked simply because they did show a definite difference between black groups and white groups. Most of the items in the Verbal SAT do not show large biases of this kind." In the near future we hope to see detailed reports of such studies of bias in various standard tests based on comparison of the ICCs in major and minor groups.

Item Selection Method

This method begins with a large pool of items devised to measure the ability, knowledge, or skills that we wish our finished test to measure. Standard criteria for item selection are then applied in a tryout of all the items in the pool, separately in representative samples of the major and minor populations in which we intend to use the test. Those items that are selected for both the major and minor groups by this procedure are defined as unbiased items, and items that are selected for one group but not for the other are defined as biased. The method can be applied to an existing standardized test by using all the items in a test as the pool from which item selection is made, using the same selection criteria separately in the major and minor groups, and determining what proportion of the items in, say, the best half (or any other fraction of the item pool) of all of the items for each group are common to both groups. By "best" items is simply meant the items most qualified, according to the item selection criteria, to be selected from the total pool of items in making up a test of any given length comprised of fewer items than the number in the pool. An item pool that is unbiased with respect to the major and minor groups should yield up very much the same set of items when these items are selected by the same criteria *within* each group. To the extent that this does not occur, the item pool may be regarded as biased for the groups in question. In other words, we are asking to what extent the item selection procedure, applied to a given item pool separately for the major and minor groups, results in different tests for the major and minor groups.

Certain controls may be needed in this method to make it a valid criterion of bias, such as using subgroups of the major and minor populations matched on overall ability, and using pseudogroups made up of subsamples of the same population (major or minor) but differing in means and standard deviations to the same degree as the true major and minor groups. These are necessary precautions because, even within a culturally homogeneous population, the "best" items measuring an ability in one range of the total ability continuum may not be the "best" items for measuring the ability in a different range.

The item selection method, but without the suggested controls, was applied by Green (1972) to item data of the California Achievement Tests (1970 edition), a comprehensive battery of general scholastic achievement tests involving vocabulary, reading comprehension, grammar, and mathematics (computation, concepts, and word problems). The subjects were more than 200,000 pupils in grades 1, 2, 5, 8, and 10 from about 400 schools in 10 states. Seven groups were used in the item selection procedure:

1. Northern, suburban, high-SES white
2. Southern, suburban, high-SES white
3. Southwestern, city and suburban, high-SES white
4. Southern, rural, low-SES white
5. Northern, central city, low-SES black
6. Southern, rural, low-SES black
7. Southwestern, city, low-SES Mexican–American

For each group, the item selection routine was applied to each subtest of the CAT at each grade to select the "best" half of the items for a given group. The "best" items were defined as those with the highest item × test correlations. The index of bias with respect to any given pair of groups is the proportion of the total number of items selected in each group that are classed as biased, that is, the items that were not selected as the "best" half of the items for *both* groups of the given pair. This can be understood more easily in terms of the following classes of items resulting from the item selection procedure:

A. Items selected in *both* groups, that is, the "best" half of the items that are common to both groups
B. Items selected in one group but not in the other group, i.e., "biased" items
C. Items not selected in either group, i.e., the "worst" half of the items that are common to both groups

The index of bias is $B/(A + B)$, which can vary from 0 to 1. The total number of items in the pool from which the "best" half of the items are selected for each group is $T = A + B + C$. The total number of items selected in each group (i.e., $A + B$) may vary from $T/2$ to T.

The detailed results of this analysis reported by Green (1972, pp. 7–10) can be most easily summarized in terms of averages over subtests and grades. If we compare the three high-SES white groups with the two low-SES black groups, the average index of bias is .37, that is, 37 percent of the selected items are classed as biased. But there is a good deal of sampling error in the item selection procedure, so this figure of .37 must be compared with the average index of bias resulting from the contrasts among the three high-SES white groups, which is .26. The average index based on the contrasts between the two low-SES black groups is also .26. The high-SES white × low-SES Mexican–American contrast yields the highest average bias index, .38, which is close to the white–black index of .37. In other words, the average index of bias for any of the cross-ethnic group comparisons is .11 or .12 higher than the average index *within* ethnic groups. The average index for low-SES whites versus high-SES whites is .31; for blacks versus Mexican–Americans, .28; and for low-SES whites versus Mexican–Americans, .24. Thus the index of bias for the contrasting ethnic and social-class groups seem quite low when compared with the index *within* racially and socioeconomically homogeneous groups, which can be viewed as the size of the index due to sampling error. However, as Green

(1972, p. 13) points out, because the item pool (which was all the items in the full CAT) consisted of already highly selected items (based on majority samples), there was probably less room for the creation of biased item sets constituting a larger proportion of the total item pool, when items were selected as "best" for different ethnic groups, than would have been the case if the item pool has been more heterogeneous in those item characteristics that originally determined their selection for the full CAT. But, if this is true, it only means, of course, that the item selection method that selected the "best" CAT items for the majority thereby at the same time also selected, for the most part, the "best" items for the minority groups. This is probably true in general.

Subtests can be made up of the items classed as "biased" by the procedure just described; there are two such biased subtests for each pair of contrasted groups, that is, subtest *A* composed of the items selected as "best" for group *A* (but not "best" for group *B*), and subtest *B* composed of the items selected as "best" for group *B* (but not "best" for group *A*). How alike are the subtests *A* and *B* in the abilities they measure? This was determined by correlating the two biased subtests in each group. The correlations range from $-.17$ to $+.82$ with a median of about .50. This is a quite low correlation, considering that the KR-20 reliability (i.e., self-correlation) of the total test (i.e., the total item pool in this case) is close to .90 for every group. But another point must also be taken into consideration here. Because many of the biased subtests were comprised of relatively few items with restricted variances and low item–test correlations and consequently low reliabilities, it is necessary that the correlations between the biased subtests be corrected for attenuation. After correction for attenuation, the correlations between the biased subtests range from $-.30$ to $+1.00$, with a median r near .80 (.84 for high-SES whites and .77 for low-SES blacks). (This analysis is reported by Green and Draper, 1972.) Thus it appears that the biased subtests measure largely, but not entirely, the same thing.

How much is the mean majority–minority difference affected by the direction of the bias in these tests? Recall that one of the biased subtests is comprised of the "best" items for the majority (but not for the minority) group and that the other subtest is comprised of the "best" items for the minority (but not for the majority). Data provided by Green and Draper (1972, Table 8) permit comparison of the mean percentage of high-SES whites and low-SES blacks passing the items of the two biased subtests derived from the full Reading Comprehension test of the CAT:

		Test Derived on			
		Whites	*Blacks*	% Diff.	σ Diff.
Test Taken by	*Whites*	67.7%	81.9%	14.2	.45σ
	Blacks	37.6%	52.5%	14.9	.38σ
	% Diff.	30.1%	29.4%		
	σ Diff.	.78σ	.85σ		

The sigma difference is probably the more valid comparison, since it expresses the group difference on an interval scale, which the percentages do not.

The smallest white–black difference (67.7 percent $-$ 52.2 percent, or $.40\sigma$) is found when each group takes the test that was derived as "best" for each group. But it should be noted that these "best" tests for each group are not composed of the same items or of items of the same level of difficulty; the black-derived test is clearly an easier test for both groups.

Blacks do 14.9 percent (or $.38\sigma$) better on the black-derived test than on the white-derived test, but whites also do 14.2 percent (or $.45\sigma$) better on the black-derived tests. Thus when both groups are given the same test, the mean white–black difference in item difficulty is only slightly affected by whether the subtest was derived on the white or on the black group. The mean white–black difference on the full test, as compared with the white–black difference on the "unbiased" subtests comprised of items selected as "best" in both groups, is probably about the same size as the differences shown in the table, although unfortunately Green presents no data on this point. He does, however, present evidence that the minority groups, significantly more often than the majority groups, showed some gain in score on the "best" half-test over the full test, but a cross-validation of this analysis showed that the minority gain held up in only two of the six CAT subtests (Green & Draper, 1972, p. 13–14). From these results the authors concluded that biased "best"-item tests as here defined do not necessarily yield relatively higher or lower scores for black or white groups than do other item sets from the same item pool.

Green (1972, p. 13) concludes:

> The amount of relative improvement in score that a minority group could expect to gain by using tests built with tryout groups like itself does not appear to be very large. This relative improvement is most unlikely to overcome any large discrepancy between typical scores in that group and those in more favored groups.

Reliability as a Criterion of Bias

A test may be regarded as biased if the scores are substantially less reliable for one group than for another.

In the study by Green (1972) of the California Achievement Test, described in the preceding section, the average (over all CAT subtests and grades) internal consistency reliabilities (KR-20) are .92 for whites, .91 for blacks, and .90 for Mexican–Americans—a nonsignificant difference.

The KR-20 reliabilities of the Peabody Picture Vocabulary Test (PPVT) and Raven's Colored Progressive Matrices were determined by Jensen (1974a) in large samples of white, black, and Mexican–American school children, with the following results:

		PPVT	*Raven*
White	Male	.96	.90
	Female	.96	.91
Black	Male	.97	.86
	Female	.95	.86
Mexican–American	Male	.96	.90
	Female	.95	.87

The ethnic group and sex differences in reliabilities are obviously negligible. The Raven has lower reliability only because it contains fewer items than the PPVT. When corrected for length of test, the Raven actually has higher KR 20 reliability than the PPVT. This is perhaps best expressed in terms of the average item intercorrelation, which, averaged over all groups, is .165 for the PPVT and .180 for the Raven.

The Wonderlic Personnel Test in large samples of white and black adults has reliabilities of .88 for whites and .86 for blacks—a negligible difference (Jensen, 1977a).

Error Distractor Analysis

As explained in Chapter 9 (p. 452), test bias may be indicated when the major and minor groups differ significantly in the relative frequencies with which their incorrect responses to any given test items are distributed across the several multiple-choice distractors.

As far as I can determine, this method of detecting bias has been applied in only one study involving the PPVT and the Raven Standard Progressive Matrices (Jensen, 1974a). Each PPVT item has one possible correct response and three distractors. A chi squared test of white-black differences in the relative frequencies of choosing one of the three distractors reveals significant differences on 26 percent of the PPVT items, and they are the same items in both random halves of the total samples. But oddly enough, the mean white-black difference in percentage passing the items on which the groups show significantly different choices of error distractors is not appreciably different from the racial difference in percentage passing on the items that do not show a racial difference in choice of distractors. The same thing was found to be true for the Raven, with 12 percent of the items showing significant differences in relative frequency of distractor choice. Apparently whatever biases determine the choice of distractor do not necessarily affect the difficulty of the item.

The choice of distractors on the Raven is related to age. Some errors can be regarded as more "sophisticated" than others, and older children tend to make the more "sophisticated" errors. When white children in grades 3 and 4 are compared with black children in grades 5 and 6, the white-black difference in choice of distractors largely disappears. The distractors most commonly chosen by blacks of a given age are the same distractors that are more frequently chosen by whites who average about two years younger. Thus the tendency to be "taken in" by a particular distractor appears to be more a function of mental age than of racial-cultural background. The Mexican-Americans differ less from whites than do blacks in choice of Raven distractors, probably because, in this sample, Mexican-Americans score intermediately between whites and blacks on the Raven.

Correlation between Raw Scores and Age

The rationale and limitations of this criterion of bias are given in Chapter 9 (pp. 424–426). It has seldom been used. Jensen (1974a) gives the following correlations (Pearson r) of PPVT and Raven Colored Progressive Matrices raw scores with age (in months) in large ethnic samples of children ranging from 6 to 12 years of age:

	PPVT	*Raven*
White	.787	.722
Black	.728	.660
Mexican–American	.671	.702

Both minority group r's differ significantly ($p < .05$) from the white on the PPVT, but none of the differences is significant on the Raven. In all groups the raw scores on both the PPVT and Raven increase linearly with age between 6 and 12 years.

SUMMARY

Criteria of culture bias in tests based on the statistical detection of group differences in a variety of internal psychometric features of tests and their factor structure and construct validity, as described in general terms in Chapter 9, are here applied to data on a variety of current standard tests of ability and achievement. Detailed examination of this massive collection of evidence, most of it relating to culture bias in test score differences between whites and blacks, quite unequivocally supports the following general conclusions.

White, black, and Mexican-American samples all show generally the same internal consistency reliability and the same correlation of raw test scores with chronological age.

Neither social-class nor racial (i.e., white–black) differences in item difficulty are consistently related to the judged degree of culture loading of the test items. In fact, white–black differences are larger on the least culture-loaded items than on the most culture loaded, in the generally accepted sense of this term. It is argued that the explanation of this surprising finding lies in the fact that the more culture-loaded items are generally less highly loaded on the g factor (i.e., mainly reasoning ability) than the less culture-loaded items, and the white–black difference is mainly a difference in g rather than in group factors that are specific to certain types of items.

White–black differences are generally slightly larger on nonverbal than on verbal tests. This race $\times$ verbal–nonverbal interaction fails to appear, however, when verbal and nonverbal items are perfectly matched for difficulty in the white group. Verbal and nonverbal items that are matched for difficulty in the white group show no significant difference in difficulty in the black group. In those cases where blacks show significant verbal–nonverbal differences, compared with whites, the effect is consistent with the interpretation that the verbal and nonverbal items differ in their loadings on g, which is the main source of racial variance.

Factor analyses of test batteries in white and black samples show the same factorial structure in both racial groups. Loadings of the various tests on the first principal component or general factor rarely differ significantly across black and white samples, which is strong evidence that the tests measure the same general factor of ability in both racial groups.

One of the most important findings of cross-racial factor analytic studies of a variety of cognitive tests is their complete consistency with the hypothesis, originally advanced by Spearman, that the magnitudes of the white–black differences (expressed in standard deviation units) on various tests is directly related to the tests' g loadings. We have found no exception to this generalization in any of the large-scale factor analyses of test batteries in white and black samples. This finding is also supported by evidence that is independent of factor analysis, such as the finding that white–black differences are greater on tests and test items that depend more on reasoning, transformation, or mental manipulation of the item's elements than on sheer memory or recall of acquired information. The evidence clearly substantiates the generalization that the mean white–black difference in scores on various tests is mainly a difference in g, the factor common to a great variety of cognitive tests, rather than a difference due to the culture-specific content of tests. In factor analytic studies that have employed tests that permit a factorial distinction between fluid and crystalized general intelligence (g_f and g_c), the mean white–black differences are greater on the more g_f-loaded tests than on the g_c-loaded tests.

The hypothesis attributing white–black differences to culture bias should lead one to expect a sizable race × items interaction in tests with highly varied item content that show mean white–black differences. That is, the order of item difficulties should be expected to differ between racial groups. However, it is found that even on tests with such heterogeneous item types as the Stanford–Binet and Wechsler scales, the rank order of item difficulties is highly similar (as indicated by cross-racial correlations over .95) in white and black samples. Analysis of variance reveals that the variance due to race × items interaction is very small (and often nonsignificant) as compared with the overall mean difference between the races. Moreover, where significant race × item interactions are found, it is shown that they can be simulated by the interaction between items and age differences *within* each racial group. That is, the items that discriminate most between whites and blacks are the same items that discriminate most between older and younger children *within* each racial group. Thus it appears that the small race × item interaction, when found, can be more parsimoniously interpreted as due to differences in mental maturity than to differences in cultural experience. This finding is consistent with a general cognitive "developmental lag" hypothesis of the white–black difference in test performance. The purely ad hoc counterhypothesis, namely, that cultural differences perfectly simulate age differences in item difficulties for a great diversity of test items observed *within* each racial group, seems too farfetched to command serious consideration. Two sociologists, Gordon and Rudert (1979), have cogently summarized this point as follows:

> The absence of race-by-item interaction in all of these studies places severe constraints on models of the test score difference between races that rely on differential access to information. In order to account for the mean difference, such models must posit that information of a given difficulty among whites diffuses across the racial boundary to blacks in a solid front at all times and places, with no items leading or lagging behind the rest. Surely, this requirement ought to strike members of a discipline that entertains hypotheses of idiosyncratic culture lag and complex models of cultural diffusion (e.g., "two-step flow of communication") as unlikely. But this is not the only constraint. Items of information must also pass over the racial boundary at all times and places in order of their level of difficulty among whites, which means that they must diffuse across race in exactly the same order in which they diffuse across age boundaries, from older to younger, among both whites and blacks. These requirements imply that diffusion across race also mimics exactly the diffusion of information from brighter to slower youngsters of the same age within each group. Even if one postulates a vague but broad kind of "experience" that behaves in exactly this manner, it should be evident that it would represent but a thinly disguised tautology for the mental functions that IQ tests are designed to measure. (pp. 179–180)

In general, for children and adults alike, it is found that those test items that best discriminate individual differences in general mental ability among whites are the same items that best discriminate differences in general ability among blacks, and they are also the same items that discriminate the most *between* whites and blacks.

All the main findings of this examination of internal and construct validity criteria of culture bias either fail to support, or else diametrically contradict, the expectations that follow from the hypothesis that most current standard tests of mental ability are culturally biased for American-born blacks. However, the available evidence is inadequate to permit strong conclusions regarding the results of applying these internal and construct validity criteria of culture bias to other minority groups, particularly Hispanic, American Indians, and Asians. Where the same analyses have been applied to Mexican-American samples, the results are much the same as for blacks, especially on nonverbal tests (on which Mexican-Americans generally score higher than blacks), whereas some verbal tests show possible bias for Mexican-Americans that is not demonstrable in the black samples. Test bias has not been studied in Asian-Americans, probably because overall they have shown little consistent or appreciable differences from majority whites in scores on most standardized tests. This of course does not necessarily mean that tests are unbiased for Asian-Americans, but only that tests have not been an important concern to this minority group.

NOTE

1. I am grateful to R. T. Osborne, director of the Testing and Evaluation Center of the University of Georgia, for obtaining and providing these data.

Chapter 12

External Sources of Bias

External sources of bias are those that do not involve the test per se but result from factors in the external testing situation that interact with individual or group differences to produce a systematic bias in the test scores of individuals or groups. Some of the external factors on which research has been focused are (1) "test sophistication," that is, the effects of prior practice or coaching on similar tests; (2) interpersonal effects involving the attitude, expectancy, and dialect of the examiner and the manner of giving test instructions, motivating and rewarding behavior on the part of the examiner; (3) individual versus group administration and the effects of general classroom morale and discipline on test performance; (4) timed versus untimed tests; (5) the race and sex of the examiner, which may interact with the race and sex of the subjects; and (6) biased scoring of test performance due to halo effects.

We shall not be concerned here with sources of variance in test scores that are more remote from the test situation itself, such as hereditary factors, health history, nutrition, general cultural environment, and educational background. It is assumed that unbiased scores on most tests reflect some differentially weighted amalgam of all these factors.

Test Sophistication, Effects of Practice and Coaching

Test sophistication (also called "test-wiseness") is a possible source of bias in test scores when the persons taking a test have had different amounts of practice or coaching on similar tests.

Because tests differ widely, it is hardly possible to give a simple or general description of what constitutes test sophistication, although its effect on test scores can be definitely determined by a proper experimental design. In paper-and-pencil objective tests, for example, test sophistication would include such things as familiarity with the use of separate answer sheets, carefully reading the instructions before beginning the test, considering *all* the alternatives in a multiple-choice item and not just picking the first one that looks right, not spending too much time on doubtful or puzzling items, checking over completed items when time permits, concentrating full attention on one item at a time rather than wasting time by scanning ahead or looking around to see how far other examinees have gotten in the test booklet, and so on. Test sophistication probably also involves increased self-confidence and lessened anxiety or bewilderment in the test situation.

Practice Effects.   Test sophistication has been studied as a dependent variable in experiments on the effects of practice and coaching on the scores of particular tests, comparing treatment and control groups. Practice involves taking the same or similar tests two or more times at various intervals, without any implication of special instructions or specific coaching in test taking. There is a fairly extensive research literature on this topic, which has been quite thoroughly reviewed by the British psychologist Philip E. Vernon (1938, 1954a, 1954b, 1960, Ch. 8) and others (James, 1953; Wiseman & Wrigley, 1953; Yates, 1953). The evidence that emerges rather consistently from these studies can be summarized succinctly in twelve points.

1. Practice effects are naturally greatest for naïve subjects, that is, those who have not been tested before.
2. Retesting of naïve subjects on the *identical* test, after a short interval, shows gains of about 2 to 8 IQ points for various tests, averaging about 5 IQ points. (Regardless of the tests used in the various studies reviewed here, gains are converted to a scale with $\sigma = 15$, which is the usual σ for IQ.)
3. There is considerable variability in practice effects among individuals. Bright subjects tend to gain more from practice than dull subjects.
4. The curve of practice gains is very negatively accelerated with repeated practice; that is, there are rapidly diminishing returns of repeated practice on the same or similar tests, yet slight gains have been shown on up to five repetitions, beyond which there is no further improvement. Practice gain between the first and second test experience is usually as great or greater than the total of all further gains from subsequent practice trials.
5. For naïve subjects, age makes little difference in the amount of practice effect. There are more examples of large practice effects in young children, however, simply because fewer of them than of older children or adults have had prior experience with tests.
6. Practice effects differ, on the average, for various types of tests, showing the smallest gains for information, vocabulary, and verbal tests generally and the largest gains for nonverbal and performance tests, probably because the materials of the latter tests are less familiar to most subjects than are verbal and informational questions.
7. Practice effects are greater for tests comprised of heterogeneous types of items than for homogeneous tests.
8. Practice effects are about 10 to 25 percent less for untimed tests than for speeded tests.
9. For naïve subjects, practice gains are greater on group-administered paper-and-pencil tests than on individually administered tests.
10. Practice effects show surprisingly little "transfer of training," with the gradient of practice gains falling off steeply from identical tests to parallel forms, to similar tests, to different types of tests. The average practice gain from Form M to Form L of the Stanford–Binet, for example, is only 2 or 3 points. Parallel forms of group tests show average practice gains of 3 to 4 points after one practice session and 5 to 6 points after several practice sessions. One large-

scale study showed a total gain of 6 IQ points over the course of eight parallel forms given to London school children (Watts, Pidgeon, & Yates, 1952).

11. Practice effects are not appreciably diminished by improving the usual test instructions or by giving a short practice test on easy items prior to the actual test. There seems to be no substitute for taking an actual test under normal test conditions for a practice effect to be manifested.

12. The practice effect is quite lasting; about three quarters of the gain found after one week is maintained up to six months, and half remains after one year.

Since the 1950s, virtually all children in the public schools have been increasingly exposed to standardized scholastic aptitude and achievement tests, from the primary grades through high school and college, so that exceedingly few pupils by age 10 or so could be regarded as naïve in respect to tests. Because of the concern of teachers and parents, the least able pupils or those with special learning problems are apt to be tested the most, especially on individual tests given by a school psychologist. Therefore, it seems most likely that in the present day very little of the variance in standardized aptitude or achievement test scores can be attributed to individual or group differences in test sophistication, with the exception of recent immigrants and persons who have had little or no formal schooling or who have gone to quite atypical schools.

Even by the third grade in a typical American school, practice gains across four group-administered IQ tests are quite small, probably because of prior exposure to similar tests. A study of third-graders showed a mean gain from the first to the second testing session of 2.7 IQ points and from the second to the third session, 1.0 IQ point. These small practice gains in IQ, as measured against a control group that received only the one pretest, diminished to nonsignificance after five months (Kreit, 1968).

Coaching Effects. Coaching consists of someone instructing the testee in the "tricks of the trade" in test taking, including how to analyze test questions and problems, instructions and demonstrations in working through typical test problems, distributing one's time most efficiently, and doing many typical practice problems with a tutor or manual providing immediate informative feedback. Self-coaching is possible with the aid of commercially published booklets of practice tests of various types.

The most remarkable fact about the effects of direct coaching on test-taking techniques is how little effect it actually has, over and above the practice effects already described. Coaching on a specific test, consisting of teaching the person the answers to items, can of course produce any desired amount of gain for almost any normal person, given enough coaching time. But that is the trivial case. What are the effects of coaching on parallel forms, or similar tests, or on test-taking techniques in general? The most consistent findings from numerous studies can be summarized as follows:

1. Coaching is quite ineffective unless accompanied by practice at taking complete tests under regular test conditions. According to Vernon, the leading expert on the topic, "coaching without practice is singularly ineffective, regardless of how protracted it is" (1960, p. 131).

2. The typical gain from several hours of coaching plus practice gain on a similar test is about 9 IQ points, or a coaching gain of 4 or 5 points over and above the

gain due solely to the practice effect of taking a similar test once or twice previously.

3. The coaching effect is greatest for naïve subjects and diminishes with prior test-taking experience. Even with equal prior testing experience, there are substantial individual differences in gains from coaching; the moderately bright tend to gain most.

4. Coaching gains are greater on nonverbal and performance-type items than on verbal and information items. Also, numerical reasoning and arithmetic problems are more susceptible to coaching gains than are items based on verbal knowledge and reasoning.

5. Age and sex show no consistent interaction with coaching effects.

6. The effects of coaching are highly specific, with little transfer to other types of tests, and at times there is even *negative* transfer to dissimilar tests.

7. The maximum effects of coaching are achieved quickly; further gain does not result from coaching prolonged beyond the first few hours. One study found three hours to be optimal.

8. A study of educationally disadvantaged children in Israel found that coaching on a nonverbal intelligence test substantially improved the test's validity, that is, correlation with teachers' marks and with the Verbal IQ of the WISC (Ortar, 1960).

9. The effects of coaching seem to fade considerably faster than the effects of practice per se. A study by Greene (1928) shows the decline over time in the gains on Stanford–Binet IQ from coaching children on the very same test items or on similar items; the control children were tested at the same times as the experimental groups, but they were never coached, and so their gains represent only practice effect.

	Mean IQ Gain When Retested after			
Condition	*3 Weeks*	*3 Months*	*1 Year*	*3 Years*
Coached on test itself	29.1	17.5	12.6	4.3
Coached on similar test	7.9	7.6	5.6	1.5
Control, not coached	5.0	2.6	3.3	0.6

For pupils with normal school experience from first grade to high school, direct coaching by teachers or private tutors and individual practice at home have a negligible effect on aptitude tests such as those typically required for college admission. The College Entrance Examination Board has studied this matter extensively, as the parents of many college applicants have been willing to pay high fees to have their children coached by "experts" in hopes of raising their Scholastic Aptitude Test (SAT) score and improving their chances of getting into college. The best evidence indicates that these coaching efforts are a waste of time and money as far as SAT performance is concerned (see Karmel & Karmel, 1978, pp. 151–153). The one possible exception is in the case of persons taking the SAT who have been out of school for some time; not coaching on the test per se, but a "brush up" on high school mathematics, particularly algebra, may significantly boost the SAT–Math score. The commercially published practice booklets for the SAT, available in most college bookstores, may be useful in providing many pages of math problems typical of those in the SAT for practice in brushing up on basic mathematical operations. Aside from that, the magnitudes of gains from coaching or home drill on practice test booklets are small at best and seem to be unrelated to the particular method or amount of coaching or to the student's level of ability. Favorable testimonials on the effects of coaching have capitalized on the rather wide range of change scores, from one form of the test to another and from one time to another, resulting from uncontrolled errors of measurement, when a large number of persons are tested. The average *systematic* gain resulting from coaching and drill actually amounts to less than one-tenth of a standard deviation. Whatever intellectual abilities and academic skills are measured by the SAT apparently are acquired slowly throughout the individual's whole development from early childhood to maturity, and a person's overall level of intellectual functioning cannot, at that time, be markedly enhanced by a crash course of intensive coaching and drill in the mechanics of test taking.

Practice and Coaching Effects, Interaction with Race and Social Class.   There is a remarkable paucity of evidence on this subject, but the few studies that exist are quite solid and generally negative.

Baughman and Dahlstrom (1968, pp. 165–169) found a practice gain of 2 IQ points on retesting white children of kindergarten age on the same form of the Stanford–Binet; black children showed no gain at all on the retest. Neither group attended kindergarten. Groups of white and black children attending kindergarten and tested on the Stanford–Binet in the fall and spring showed gains of 7.3 and 1.1 IQ points, respectively; this general result was replicated in three samples. The Primary Mental Abilities Tests, on the other hand, showed a slightly greater (1.7) retest gain for black than for white kindergarten children. The authors attribute this differential gain to the fact that the PMA tasks appear to resemble more closely the learning activities of the kindergarten than do the Stanford–Binet items. White children who did not attend kindergarten showed a larger average PMA retest gain (from fall to spring) than black children who did not attend kindergarten.

Costello (1970) gave a randomly selected group of black preschool children the Peabody Picture Vocabulary Test and the Stanford–Binet and retested them on the same tests a few months later. Their retest scores were compared with those of a comparable randomly selected group of black children who had received no pretest. There were no significant practice effects on either the PPVT or Stanford–Binet, whether in total score or on the ceiling item (i.e., the hardest item scored as correct).

White lower-class and white middle-class elementary school children were the subjects in an experiment to test the prediction that lower-class subjects would show larger gains than middle-class subjects on Raven's Colored Progressive Matrices as a result of prior familiarization and coaching with feedback on a set of Raven-like items specially designed to illustrate the essential features of matrix problems and distractors (Turner, Hall & Grimmett, 1973). Half of each social-class group was given the familiarization training and half served as controls. The result: Familiarization and feedback training significantly ($p < .05$) improved the performance of lower- and middle-class children about equally; the predicted interaction of SES and prior training did not materialize. In addition to scoring the number of correct responses to the Raven, item latencies (i.e., solution time) were obtained on every item. Mean item latency showed a significant social-class main effect (middle SES *slower* than low SES) but nonsignificant effects of prior familiarization and its interaction with SES.

The correlation between average item latency and total score on the Raven is about +.60 for both SES groups (control condition). The positive correlation suggests that the low-SES subjects (who have lower total scores and shorter item latencies) are more impulsive than the middle-SES subjects. Another study, using adult subjects, found a nonsignificant correlation ($r = -0.06$) between item latencies and total Raven score (White, 1973). It is evident from White's report that the correlation between item latency and total score is complexly determined.

The hypothesis that extra practice and extra testing time would improve the mental ability test scores of blacks more than of whites was examined by Dubin, Osburn, and Winick (1969). Black ($N = 235$) and white ($N = 232$) high school students were given parallel forms of the Employee Aptitude Survey under timed and untimed conditions. (this test involves numerical ability, spatial visualization, and verbal reasoning.) Whites outperformed blacks on each form of the test under timed and untimed conditions. The practice effect (measured by the difference between the first and second parallel forms) enhanced the scores of whites and blacks about equally. The untimed test condition also raised white and black scores about equally. The same thing was found for both practice and timing effects when the racial groups were divided into high- and low-SES groups; that is, low- and high-SES groups of both races gained equally from the practice and from the more lenient timing. The authors concluded that "the testing procedure itself does not discriminate between racial groups nor between culturally advantaged and disadvantaged subjects" (p. 19).

A well-designed study by Dyer (1970) examined the effects of practice and coaching on the mental test performance of white ($N = 174$) and black ($N = 152$) students attending predominantly white or predominantly black colleges in the South. "The schools selected included neither the best white schools nor the worst black schools and drew students from roughly the same geographical areas" (p. 124). (Dyer also varied race of the examiner, but that aspect of her study is described later in this chapter.)

Dyer hypothesized that some of the differences in test scores between white and black students can be attributed to differences in test sophistication. Whites and blacks can be viewed as situated on different parts of a "test learning" curve, with the relatively test-sophisticated whites situated in the high and negatively accelerated part of the curve and the relatively test-unsophisticated blacks near the bottom of the curve. Thus one should predict that practice and coaching in test taking would raise the scores of blacks more than of whites. To test this prediction, Dyer used three equivalent forms (equated for difficulty) of a standardized test of reasoning ability consisting of letter series, number series, figure analogies, figure series, and arithmetic problem solving—all multiple-choice tests using separate answer sheets in the fashion of most standardized high school and college aptitude tests. A random half of each racial group was given the three equivalent forms of the test on three occasions (at two week intervals) with *standard instructions*. The other half of each racial group was also tested on three occasions but were given *special instructions* immediately preceding each test. The special instructions were designed to teach the students all the "tricks of the trade" in test taking, with emphasis on the particular types of items used in the standard test. The coaching materials

Figure 12.1. Three-way interaction of race, type of instructions, and practice. (From Dyer, 1970, p. 100)

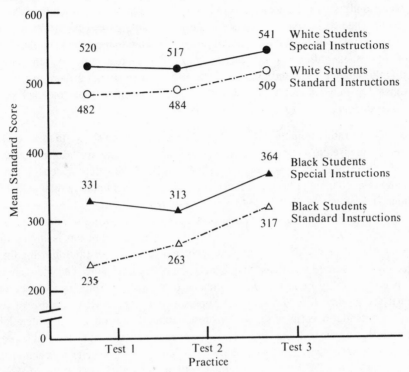

included over seventy practice items, with immediate feedback on the correct answers, accompanied by explanations of the correct answers. The oral instructions were accompanied with illustrations on the blackboard and on specially prepared graphic materials displaying the various types of items in the test.

The results are shown in Figure 12.1. Analysis of variance reveals statistically significant effects of practice (i.e., the overall difference between tests 1, 2, and 3) and of special instructions. Also the hypothesis of a practice × race interaction is borne out significantly ($p < .01$), but the instruction × race interaction is nonsignificant. In brief, blacks showed a significantly greater gain from practice, but not from coaching, than did whites. The practice × race interaction, however, is quite small as compared with the race main effect (i.e., the overall race difference). (In the ANOVA the mean square for the race main effect is 381 times as large as the mean square for the practice × race interaction; 49.6 percent of the total variance in the whole experiment is attributable to the race main effect. The point-biserial correlation of race with total test scores in Dyer's sample is 0.74.) Dyer's conclusions:

Some minimal support for the basic hypothesis was found. The special instructions and practice did make a greater difference for black students than for white, but the differential gains were small and not useful in a practical sense in view of the very large differences found between the black and white students. Differences attributed to race amounted to two standard deviations. Differential scores attributed to the special conditions amounted to only about $\frac{1}{4}$ SD. Both black and white students tested by black administrators obtained slightly higher scores than those tested by white administrators, thus no part of the difference in black and white scores could be attributed to the race of the examiner. No sizable part of the difference in test scores could be attributed to verbal or reading problems since scores on the only part of the test including verbal material, an arithmetic reasoning section, showed a slightly smaller difference in scores than the other parts. Furthermore, the tests showed a higher correlation with reported grade point average for black than for white students.   (1970, p. 125)

Despite the rather minimal effects of practice and coaching shown in these studies, it would seem unwise to recommend that practice and coaching on tests be ignored or disdained. There is no evidence of deleterious effects of practice or coaching on test scores, and brief coaching plus a full-length practice test given under regular examination conditions (i.e., not announced as a practice test) helps to equalize test sophistication among persons with differing amounts of past experience in taking standardized tests or who differ in the recency of taking tests. When the supply of applicants is ample, little is to be gained from the use of coaching and practice tests by the institution using the tests for selection, but some individuals may benefit from this procedure, and there are indications that the validity of test scores is enhanced by thus minimizing variance due to individual (or group) differences in test sophistication. Where the purpose of testing emphasizes potential benefits to the persons tested more than economic considerations by the institution using the test scores for selection or other decisions of considerable personal consequence to the testees, a standardized procedure of brief special instruction in test taking plus a ''for real'' practice session on a full-length parallel form of the final test can be recommended. This would seem especially appropriate when there is evidence that applicants have had diverse educational backgrounds or different amounts of prior experience with tests of the type in question.

Race of Examiner

It is often claimed that the race of the examiner (i.e., tester) is an important source of bias in the testing of minority groups. The popular belief is that persons perform better on mental tests when the examiner is of the same race as the subject than when the examiner and the subject are of different races. How well do these propositions stand up in light of all the investigations intended to test their validity?

A thorough search of the literature has turned up a total of thirty studies, published between 1936 and 1977, addressed to this question. The studies can be classified into three main categories in terms of the experimental design involved: (1) *inadequate designs,* (2) *adequate but incomplete designs,* and (3) *adequate and complete designs.*

To be an *adequate* design, an experiment on the effect of the race of examiner (E) on test scores should meet the following two minimum requirements: (1) at least two (or more) Es of each race and (2) random assignment of subjects (Ss) to Es. These requirements seem obvious. If there is only one E of each race, the variable of race is wholly confounded with the other personal attributes of each E. Randomization is needed to rule out the possibility of any selection bias that might result in a spurious (i.e., noncausal) correlation between Es and the trait being measured. Any study that does not meet these minimal requirements of experimental design is classified as *inadequate*. When it is not clear whether the study meets these requirements, I have given it the benefit of the doubt and classified it as adequate.

An adequate design is termed *incomplete* if the Ss are sampled from only one racial population. A *complete* design involves Ss sampled from two (or more) racial groups. In the terminology of analysis of variance, this is a nested factorial design, with individual Es "nested" within race of E. In the ideal experiment, the same Ss need not be (and preferably should not be) tested on the same test by more than one E; in other words, it is a $2 \times 2 \times 2$ factorial design without repeated measurements. The proper design can be represented as follows:

Race of Examiners

		Majority		Minority	
		E_1	E_2	E_3	E_4
Race of Subjects	Majority				
	Minority				

Only two examiners of each race are shown here, which is the minimum for an adequate design, although, of course, any larger number of Es is possible and desirable. (The number of Es of each race need not be the same, but it makes the analysis simpler if they are.) The analysis of variance summary table for the above design (with N Ss in each of the eight cells) is as follows:

	Source of Variance	df
Main Effects		
A	Between races of Ss	1
B	Between races of Es	1
C	Between Es (within race of Es)	2
Interactions		
$A \times B$		1
$A \times C$		2
Error		
Within cell		$2 \times 2 \times 2 \times (N - 1)$

For this design, the one and only correct error term for testing the significance of each of the main effects and each of the interactions is the *within-cell MS* (mean square).

It is, of course, the $A \times B$ interaction (i.e., S's race $\times$ E's race) that is of crucial interest, for if the interaction is significant it means that the size of the mean difference between the majority and minority groups is determined to some extent by the race of the examiner(s). The popular hypothesis states that (1) the mean racial difference in test scores will be largest when each racial group is tested by an examiner of a different race from that of the groups and (2) the racial difference in scores will be smallest when each racial group is tested by an E of its own race.

If this hypothesis is true, the race of S's $\times$ race of E's interaction should be significant in the analysis of variance. If the interaction is significant, then one must inquire further as to its direction and magnitude, which are more important in terms of its practical consequences than is statistical significance per se. Significance merely informs us that there is a real effect that warrants further examination.

A relevant but hardly definitive study by Shuey (1966) is not classifiable in terms of the criteria just cited, because it is a survey of existing studies rather than a true experiment. It does not involve random assignment of Ss to Es and therefore could have some unknown bias. Shuey compared all the reported studies up to 1965 (nineteen studies in all) of the IQ of southern black children in elementary schools where the testing was done by a black tester, with the IQ reported in all studies of black school children in the South, where the vast majority were tested by white examiners. Shuey concluded:

> The 2,360 elementary school children tested by Negroes earned a mean IQ of 80.9 as compared with a combined mean of 80.6 earned by more than 30,000 Southern Negro school children, an undetermined but probably a large number of whom were tested by white investigators. The present writer also calculated the combined mean IQ achieved by 1,796 Southern colored high school pupils who were tested by Negro adults. This was 82.9 as compared with a mean of 82.1 secured by nearly 9,000 Southern colored high school students, many of whom were examined by white researchers. From these comparisons it would seem that the intelligence score of a Negro school child or high school pupil has not been adversely affected by the presence of a white tester.   (1966, p. 507)

Inadequate Designs

Canady (1936): On the first administration of the 1916 Stanford–Binet, black and white Ss obtained significantly higher IQs when tested by Es (one black and twenty whites) of their own race, whereas on retest Ss obtained significantly higher IQs when tested by Es of the other race. Sattler (1966) has presented a detailed reanalysis and critique of Canady's study and points out the inconclusiveness of the results because of methodological deficiencies.

Passamanick and Knoblock (1955): A white E tested forty 2-year-old black Ss on the Gesell Developmental Examination and is claimed to have obtained lower "verbal responsiveness" scores than presumably would have been obtained by a black E. But no Ss were tested by a black E for comparison.

Forrester and Klaus (1964): Twenty-four black kindergartners obtained nonsignificantly higher Stanford–Binet IQs when tested by a female black E than when tested by a female white E.

La Crosse (1964): A white E obtained significantly lower Stanford–Binet retest scores when testing black Ss who had been previously tested by two black Es. The same white E obtained significantly higher retest scores with white Ss previously tested by three white Es.

Pettigrew (1964): White Es (number not reported) are said to have obtained fewer correct responses than black Es (number not reported) from northern black Ss given two tests (identifying six famous men and giving synonyms). No statistical tests of significance are reported.

Lipsitz (1969): Lorge–Thorndike group-administered test–retest by one black E and one white E showed no significant race of E or interaction effects in eastern black and white fourth-, fifth-, and sixth-graders in private schools (unrepresentative samples).

Caldwell and Knight (1970): Stanford–Binet test–retest on forms L and M, with one black female E and one male E, produced no significant effect of E on the IQs of sixth-grade southern black children (all boys).

Scott, Hartson, and Cunningham (1976): One black E and five white Es gave the Iowa Test of Preschool Development to twenty-eight black and thirty-seven white children of ages 2 years and 7 months to 2 years and 9 months. Race of E × race of S interactions were generally nonsignificant, but on measures of large motor skills and expressive language blacks scored higher with white Es than with the black E. The authors concluded that same-race Es do not improve Ss' test performance.

Summary of Inadequate Designs. All the studies noted here, being wholly inadequate experiments, really cannot prove anything. But we may obtain a "box score" for the eight studies based on their authors' conclusions with respect to the hypothesis that black Ss perform better when tested by a black E than when tested by a white E. Three of the studies (Passamanick & Knoblock; La Crosse; Pettigrew) seem to favor the hypothesis; four seem to disconfirm the hypothesis (Forrester & Klaus; Lipsitz; Caldwell & Knight; Scott et al., and one seems to confirm the hypothesis on original testing and disconfirm it on retesting (Canady). Thus the "box score" with respect to the hypothesis in these eight inadequate studies is $3\frac{1}{2}$ "pro" to $4\frac{1}{2}$ "con."

Adequate but Incomplete Designs

Smith and May (1967): Four white Es and two black Es gave the Illinois Test of Psycholinguistic Abilities to 171 black children averaging 6 years of age. Race of E had no consistent effect on scores.

Pelosi (1968): Six black Es and six white Es tested young adult black males enrolled in a Neighborhood Youth Corps on the Wechsler Adult Intelligence Scale, the Purdue Pegboard, and the IPAT Culture Fair Test; there were no significant effects of race of E.

Costello (1970): Two white Es and two black Es giving the Peabody Picture Vocabulary Test to black preschoolers resulted in no significant race of E effect.

Dill (1972): Three black Es and three white Es gave the Torrance Tests of Creative Thinking to 120 black second-graders. Race of E showed no significant effects.

Moore and Retish (1974): Three white Es and three black Es (all women) tested forty-two black preschoolers (about 5 years of age) on the Wechsler Preschool and Primary Scale of Intelligence in a test–retest design, counterbalancing race of E. The race of E effect is significant ($p < .05$), with Ss obtaining a higher (by about $5\frac{1}{2}$ IQ points) mean IQ when tested by black Es.

Summary of Adequate but Incomplete Designs. These designs using Es of two races and Ss of one race can test the hypothesis of a main effect of the race of E on Ss' test scores but, of course, cannot test the hypothesis that the mean test score *difference* between Ss of different races is influenced by the race of E, a hypothesis that can be tested only by a design that includes the interaction of race of E × race of S.

Of the five studies in the adequate–incomplete category, four show no significant effect of race of E on Ss' test performance (Pelosi; Costello; Dill; Smith & May), and one shows a significant effect of race of E (Moore & Retish).

Adequate and Complete Designs

Miller and Phillips (1966): Three black Es and three white Es (all women) tested black and white preschool children in a Head Start program in the South on the Stanford–Binet and the Peabody Picture Vocabulary Test. Neither the main effect of race of E nor the interaction of race of E × race of S is significant.

Abramson (1969): In this well-designed but incorrectly analyzed study, two white Es and two black Es tested white and black kindergarten and first-grade children in an integrated urban school on the Peabody Picture Vocabulary Test. Abramson indeed reported a significant ($F = 40.69$, $df = 1, 2$, $p < .05$) interaction of E's race × S's race for the first-graders but not for the kindergartners. However, Abramson used the wrong error term in the analysis of variance for testing both the main effects and their interaction, which in fact are all nonsignificant. Because the full ANOVA is presented by Abramson, we can calculate the proper significance tests, in which case the interaction of E's race × S's race is quite nonsignificant (for first-graders, $F = 0.42$, $df = 1, 72$; for kindergartners, $F = 0.85$, $df = 1, 80$).

Crown (1970): Two white Es and two black Es tested twenty-eight black and twenty-eight white kindergartners in public schools in Florida on the Wechsler Preschool and Primary Scale of Intelligence. Black Es produced significantly higher scores for *both* white and black Ss, but the race of E × race of S interaction is nonsignificant.

Dyer (1970): Three white Es and three black Es (all men) administered tests of reasoning ability to white and black students in southern colleges. Race of E shows a significant ($p < .05$) effect, with black Es producing slightly higher scores for Ss of both races. (I say "slightly" because the mean square for the main effect of race of S is more than eighty times greater than the main effect of race of E.) The interaction of race of E × race of S is nonsignificant ($F < 1$).

Gould and Klein (1971): Two white Es and two black Es tested thirty-eight white Ss and forty-six black Ss (high school students) on the Verbal Reasoning and Abstract Reasoning subtests of the Differential Aptitude Tests under timed and untimed conditions. Hence the experimental design is a 2 (race of E) × 2 (race of S) × 2 (timed versus untimed) factorial. Both on the Verbal Reasoning and the Abstract Reasoning tests, the main effect of S's race is significant ($p < .01$). But the main effect of race of E and the race of E × race of S interaction are nonsignificant for both tests. Timed versus untimed conditions produced no significant interactions involving race of E or race of S.

Veroff, McClelland, and Marquis (1971a, 1971b): Eight white Es and six black Es tested large samples of white ($N = 179$) and black ($N = 186$) adults on seven different tests (Wechsler Digit Span, Lorge–Thorndike Sentence Completion, Raven Matrices, Ammons Quick Test, Wechsler Information, Wechsler Digit Symbol, Picture Order). Analysis of covariance was used to control for S's amount of formal education (1971b, Appendix 4, p. 26). Black Es generally elicited higher test scores for Ss of both races; this main effect of race of E is significant ($p < .05$) for Sentence Completion, Raven, and Information. The race of E × race of S interaction is nonsignificant for every one of the seven tests.

Yando, Zigler, and Gates (1971): Six white *E*s and six black *E*s gave the Peabody Picture Vocabulary Test (PPVT) to seventy-two white and seventy-two black second-graders. Race of *E* was not significant.

Solkoff (1972): Four white *E*s and four black *E*s (all women) administered the Wechsler Intelligence Scale for Children to 112 black children (equal *N*s of boys and girls within each racial group) 8 to 11 years of age from low-SES areas of the city (presumably Buffalo, New York). There are significant ($p < .05$) race of *E* main effects (white $E <$ black *E*) for the Comprehension and Picture Completion subtests and for the Verbal IQ, Performance IQ, and Full Scale IQ. The interaction of race of $E \times$ race of *S*s is significant ($p < .05$) only for the Information subtest. The WISC Verbal IQ, Performance IQ, and Full Scale IQ all show a nonsignificant race of $E \times$ race of *S* interaction.

Savage and Bowers (1972): Ten white *E*s and ten black *E*s gave the WISC Block Design and Digit Span subtests to 120 white and 120 black children in grades 1, 3, and 5. Scores on Block Design were significantly higher with same-race *E*s, but the race of *E* showed no significant effects on Digit Span.

France (1973): Tape recordings of four white *E*s and four black *E*s administering the PPVT were used to test 128 white and 124 black children ages 6 to 12 years. Race of *E* (i.e., *E*'s recorded voice) had no effect on the performance of black *S*s, but white *S*s performed better with white *E*s' recorded voices than with black *E*s' recorded voices.

Wellborn, Reid, and Reichard (1973): Three white *E*s and three black *E*s gave the Wechsler Intelligence Scale for Children (WISC) to twenty-four white and twenty-four black second- and third-graders. Race of *E* showed no significant effects.

Jensen (1974c): Twelve white *E*s and eight black *E*s administered four group tests to all the white and black children (about 5,400 whites and 3,600 blacks) from kindergarten through sixth grade in the public schools of Berkeley, California. The tests are the Lorge–Thorndike (Verbal and Nonverbal) Intelligence Test, Figure Copying, Memory for Numbers (digit span), Listening–Attention Test, and Speed and Persistence Test (Making Xs). Analysis of variance was performed on each test at each grade level and also averaged over all grades. Because the sample sizes are very large, even quite small effects are significant. The Lorge–Thorndike Nonverbal IQ shows no overall race of $E \times$ race of *S* interaction, but the interaction is significant for Verbal IQ, although the net effect of the interaction amounts to only 3.2 percent (or less than 1 IQ point) of the mean white-black difference in Verbal IQ. The Figure Copying Test (a measure of *g*) shows a significant interaction amounting to 11.4 percent of the mean white–black difference. The Speed and Persistence Test, a measure of motivation or effort in the testing situation, showed a significant interaction amounting to more than the mean white–black difference, which does not differ significantly from zero on this test. White *E*s elicited significantly better performance from white *S*s than from black *S*s. The Listening–Attention Test and Memory for Numbers Test both show a nonsignificant main effect for race of *E* and for the interaction of race of $E \times$ race of *S*. Conclusions were as follows:

> The present results on group-administered tests . . . show unsystematic and, for all practical purposes, probably negligible effects of race of *E* on the mental test scores of the white and black school children. Moreover, the direction of the relatively slight race of *E* effects does not consistently favor *S*s of either race. The magnitudes of race of *E* effects are in all cases very small relative to the mean difference

between the racial groups, except for the one noncognitive test, Making Xs, which is a measure of motivation or speed and persistence under the conditions of group testing. On this test, both white and black S in all grades performed significantly and substantially (about 0.4 to 0.8σ) better with white Es than with black Es. This shows that some types of performance are capable of systematically reflecting race of E effects and it tends to highlight the relative lack of such effects on the cognitive ability tests.   (Jensen, 1974c, p. 12)

As a part of the same study (but not reported in Jensen, 1974c), one subject was selected at random from each classroom in the Berkeley schools to be tested individually on the Lorge–Thorndike IQ Test by either one of the white Es or one of the black Es. Analysis of variance showed a nonsignificant main effect of race of E for both nonverbal and verbal IQ and a nonsignificant race of E × race of S interaction for nonverbal IQ, but a significant ($p < .01$) interaction for verbal IQ. The interaction, however, works just the opposite of the popular expectation: the mean white–black difference in verbal IQ is *greater* (by 3.2 IQ points) when the Ss are tested by Es of their own race than when tested by Es of a different race.

Marwit and Neumann (1974): Two white Es and two black Es gave the Reading Comprehension subtest of the California Reading Test to fifty-three white and sixty black second-graders. The only significant effect of race of E was that black Ss performed better with white Es than with black Es.

Solkoff (1974): Two white Es and two black Es gave the WISC to fifty-four white and fifty-four black children averaging 10 years of age. The main effect of race of E was nonsignificant, whereas, on the subscales showing a significant race of E × race of S interaction, Ss performed *better* with Es of a *different* race.

Ratusnik and Koenigsknecht (1977): Three white Es and three black Es gave the Draw-a-Man test to seventy-two white and seventy-two black children averaging $4\frac{1}{2}$ years of age. There was a significant race of E × race of S interaction. Black Ss averaged 6 IQ points higher with black Es than with white Es; whites averaged 3 IQ points higher with white Es than with black Es.

Samuel (1977): Four white Es and four black Es (two of each sex) tested 208 white and 208 black junior and senior high school students (all girls) on the Wechsler Intelligence Scale for Children. The ANOVA shows nonsignificant effects for the race of E and for the interaction of race of E × race of S. In fact, the mean square for the main effect of race of S is 150 times greater than the mean square for the race of E × race of S interaction. Samuel also found that S's SES does not interact significantly with race of E, nor is the triple interaction of S's SES × race of E × race of S significant.

Summary of Adequate and Complete Designs.   With respect to the interaction of race of E × race of S for tests of cognitive ability, ten out of sixteen of the studies show nonsignificant effects. The remaining six studies show significant but practically negligible or inconsistent effects of race of E on different tests, or the race of E by race of S interaction has the effect of *reducing* the overall mean difference between racial groups (three studies).

Viewing the results of all these studies together, it seems safe to conclude that the evidence lends no support to the popular notion that the race of the examiner is an important source of variance between whites and blacks on tests of mental ability. (Comprehensive reviews of studies of racial experimenter effects on a variety of other psychological variables besides standard tests of mental ability are presented by Sattler, 1970, 1973.)

Sex of Examiner

The literature on the effects of the sex of the examiner on intelligence test performance has been well reviewed by Sattler (1974, p. 63) and, more recently, by Rumenik, Capasso, and Hendrick (1977). The evidence regarding the effects of examiner's sex on test scores is generally nondescript, showing no large or directionally consistent effects, although main effects and interactions are occasionally significant for particular subtests or part scores (e.g., verbal or performance), but not for overall IQ. Although no systematic trend emerges from the rather inadequate studies of this topic, the evidence suggests that female Es tend to elicit slightly better performance than male Es both from male and female Ss.

The rather informal nature of some of these studies leads one to suspect that the statistically significant findings, which are often contradictory and make no sense theoretically, may be Type I errors* resulting from the fact that, when significant E effects are occasionally found in any available data, they are more likely to be reported in the literature than when no significant effects are found. However, a recent study (Samuel, 1977), which seems much less likely to have this disadvantage, but is not included in the reviews by Sattler (1974) and Rumenik et al. (1977), involves only female Ss (black and white) tested on the WISC by male and female (black and white) Es in a proper factorial design. The main effect of sex of E is significant ($p < .001$): Ss obtained higher IQs when tested by a female E. Also the race of E × sex of S interaction is significant ($p < .05$): black female testers elicit slightly higher IQs than white female testers. The second-order interaction (sex of E × race of E × race of S) is nonsignificant. Altogether, the main effect of sex of E and all its interactions with race of E and race of S account for only 3.9 percent of the total variance in WISC Full Scale IQs in this experiment, as compared with individual differences (within groups), which account for 68.8 percent of the total variance, and the main effect of race of S, which accounts for 12.5 percent of the total variance.

Thus the evidence, unimpressive as it is, does not indicate that the sex of E is a potent factor, at least in IQ testing.

Language and Dialect of Examiner

Black Dialect. Many blacks, particularly those from poor socioeconomic backgrounds, speak a nonstandard dialect distinctly different from standard English. Therefore it seems plausible that some part of the average difference between blacks and whites on mental tests might be attributable to the discrepancy between the dialect to which black Ss are accustomed and the standard English spoken by the examiner. (E), whether the E is black or white. Deficient performance on a test could result from the S's failure fully to understand either the E's oral directions or the verbal test items themselves when presented in standard English.

The consensus of a number of studies, however, indicates that, although black children produce somewhat different speech, they comprehend standard English at least as well as they comprehend their own nonstandard dialect and that they develop facility in understanding the standard language at an early age (Eisenberg, Berlin, Dill, & Sheldon, 1968; Hall & Turner, 1971, 1974; Harms, 1961; Krauss & Rotter, 1968; Peisach, 1965; Weener, 1969).

The effect of black dialect as compared with standard English on the IQs of black lower-class children was investigated in three studies by Quay (1971, 1972, 1974), who had the Stanford–Binet translated into black ghetto dialect by a linguistics specialist in black dialect. No significant difference (the difference actually amounts to less than 1 IQ point) was found between the nonstandard dialect and standard English forms of the Stanford–Binet when administered by two black Es to one hundred black children in a Head Start program in Philadelphia (Quay, 1971). The same results were found in a second study in which black 4-year-olds were obtained from "an extremely deprived, physically and socially isolated community" (Quay, 1972). Moreover, in this study the item difficulties (i.e., percentage passing each item) of the individual Stanford–Binet items were compared for the two versions of the test, the dialect version and the standard version. The two versions showed no significant differences in item difficulties. In Quay's third study, essentially the same procedure was repeated, but this time 104 Philadelphia black children at two age levels (grades 3 and 6) were tested to ascertain whether the language condition (dialect versus standard English) might show an interaction with Ss' age. Ss' sex was also taken into account in the 2 (language) $\times$ 2 (age level of S) $\times$ 2 (sex of S) design. The only significant effect in the ANOVA is Ss' age, with the younger Ss having higher IQs. Not E's language (black dialect versus standard English), or S's sex or the interaction of S's language $\times$ S's sex is significant. The black dialect and the standard English forms of the Stanford–Binet yielded mean IQs of 84.58 ($\sigma = 10.47$) and 84.52 ($\sigma = 11.08$), respectively. Item difficulties (proportion passing) were compared across the language conditions; six out of seventy-two comparisons showed significant ($p < .05$) differences, but about four significant differences would be expected by chance. On three of these significant differences black dialect was easier, and on the other three standard English was easier. Quay interpreted all these differences as due to chance, as they are inconsistent in direction and occur haphazardly on the nonverbal as well as on the verbal items. Quay concluded that black children are not penalized by the use of standard English in test administration.

In a factorial design, Crown (1970) varied not only the language of test administration (black dialect versus standard English), but also the race of E (two black Es and two white Es) and the race of S (twenty-eight black and twenty-eight white kindergartners in Florida) on the Wechsler Preschool and Primary Scale of Intelligence. ANOVA reveals no significant difference overall between the black dialect and standard English conditions, and there are no significant interactions of language with race of E or race of S.

Testing Bilingual Subjects.   The testing of bilingual persons in the United States today concerns mainly the Spanish-speaking, principally Mexican–Americans, who number more than six million, concentrated largely in Arizona, California, Colorado, New Mexico, and Texas. According to the U.S. Commission on Civil Rights, about 50 percent of Mexican–Americans entering first grade speak only Spanish (*Education Yearbook*. 1973–1974, p. 415). Obviously, verbal tests given in English to such children can only yield meaningless or at best highly questionable scores if interpreted as measures of general cognitive ability rather than as merely a short-term predictor of scholastic performance where English is the medium of instruction. The same thing can be said, of course, in the case of other non-English-speaking or bilingual groups, such as the Puerto Ricans, American Indians, and Orientals. Standard tests, when used with these groups, are found to have as high predictive validity as for the exclusively English-speaking population only when the criterion being predicted is scholastic achievement in typical American schools, measured close in time to the predictor test. (The relevant evidence is discussed in Chapter 10.) The question to be considered here, however, is a rather different one: What effect does the language of the examiner or of the test itself have on the performance of children from a non-English-speaking or bilingual background?

Most studies addressed to this question involve Spanish-speaking Mexican–Americans and Puerto Ricans. Reviews and bibliographies are provided by Darcy (1963), Sattler (1974, Ch. 14), and Zirkel (1973). Most of the findings based on the Spanish-speaking groups regarding the effects of language on mental test scores can probably be safely generalized to other non-English-speaking groups in the United States, such as Orientals and American Indians, and to the Asian immigrants in Britain. Where this is known not to be the case, I shall so indicate. Ignoring all the sheer surmise that abounds in this literature, the actual empirical evidence can be summarized in seven points.

1. The language of the test and of the examiner *does* make a difference, as indicated by the fact that all non-English-speaking or bilingual groups—groups as racially and culturally diverse as Mexican–American, Puerto Rican, American Indian, Chinese, and Japanese—obtain higher scores on every kind of nonverbal and performance test than on any kind of verbal test presented in English, oral or written. It seems most unlikely that the general finding in such diverse groups would be entirely the result of an inherent deficiency in these groups' verbal ability relative to their nonverbal ability. Moreover, other evidence (given in the following paragraphs) suggests that the discrepancy between verbal and nonverbal scores *within* groups is mainly a language effect rather than a difference in abilities per se. This generalization, of course, does not necessarily apply to the nature of the mean difference *between* groups, on either verbal or nonverbal tests.

2. On standard (English language) tests of scholastic achievement, pupils from foreign language backgrounds perform relatively better on arithmetic items than on language items.

3. Mexican–Americans generally score higher on the Wechsler and the Stanford–Binet IQ tests when these are given in Spanish than when given in English. The results are not consistent in all studies, but seem to depend partly on the particular form of the Spanish translation and the form of Spanish spoken by *E,* since there are quite important variations between the Spanish of Spain, of Mexico, and of Puerto Rico, especially among the low-SES segments of these populations. Translation of a verbal test is generally a tricky and risky affair, because some English words have no exact counterpart in Spanish and because Spanish counterparts may have quite different levels of difficulty (i.e., a common word in the one language may be an unusual word in the other language). Verbal tests in a foreign language should be composed by native speakers and should be subjected to the same item analysis and standardization procedures for the target population as are applied when verbal tests in English are constructed for English-speaking populations. For reasons that can only be speculative at present, American verbal tests translated into

Japanese, with but few modifications aside from mere translation, yield scores in Japanese populations that equal or exceed the American norms, whereas the same tests when translated into Spanish yield lower scores for Puerto Ricans (for whom the translation was specifically intended) and Mexican–Americans (for whom the translation may not be entirely suitable). It is puzzling why the Wechsler tests should translate more comparably into Japanese than into Spanish, if indeed that is the explanation. But it should be noted that the Japanese also score higher than Puerto Ricans and Mexican–Americans (and even white English-speaking Americans) on nonverbal and performance tests (Lynn, 1977). This phenomenon might even reflect an actual average superiority of the Japanese in g.

4. The language spoken by E makes less difference on performance tests and nonlanguage tests in general than on verbal tests, oral or written. In nonlanguage tests, apparently, the oral directions per se given by E are so simple, relative to the test's overall level of item difficulty, that Ss' comprehension of the directions for taking the test contributes almost nothing to the variance in test scores, whether the directions are spoken in English or in Spanish. Most Ss can easily infer what is required of nonverbal test items through pantomime demonstration by E or by inspection of sample items or the easiest beginning items of the test itself.

5. On nonverbal tests with directions given in Spanish, Mexican–Americans score lower than "Anglo" whites and Orientals, but the discrepancy is markedly reduced when the groups are roughly equated for socioeconomic status. In many studies, the language factor is confounded with SES. But, even when SES is equated in Mexican–American and "Anglo" groups, the mean difference in scores is still considerably greater on verbal than on nonverbal tests. Figure 12.2 shows statistically independent (i.e., orthogonal) factor score means on (1) verbal IQ and scholastic achievement, (2) nonverbal IQ, (3) rote memory (in English), and (4) a composite index of SES, for large samples of white "Anglo," Mexican–American, and black children in grades 4 to 6 in a California school district (Kern County). The mean differences on each factor score represent differences between the ethnic groups that have been statistically equated on all three of the other factor scores.

6. Mexican–American children from bilingual homes (i.e., Spanish and English spoken by the parents) generally perform better on standard tests than do children from homes in which Spanish is spoken exclusively.

7. The language of the test (or of the E) makes less difference the longer Ss have attended English language schools, and the disparity between verbal and nonverbal test scores diminishes with increasing number of years in school. In many cases, after several years of schooling, English far overtakes Spanish as the most proficient language for Mexican–American pupils, especially when it comes to taking tests that involve scholastic knowledge and skills.

Recommendations for the Testing of Bilingual Persons. Verbal IQ tests given in English afford about as good validity for the short-range prediction of scholastic achievement in the case of bilingual children as for other children from exclusively English-speaking homes. The verbal test scores of bilingual children, however, should not be interpreted beyond their function as merely a short-term predictive index of the pupil's probable achievement in a typical school setting where English is the medium of instruction. For bilingual children, never should long-term (i.e., more than a year) educational predictions or placement in special classes, particularly classes for the educably mentally

Figure 12.2.   Mean factor scores (mean $= 50$, $\sigma = 10$ within each grade level) for four variables, comparing white, black, and Mexican–American samples in grades 4, 5, and 6. The factor scores are orthogonal; that is, the scores on any one factor reveal differences between subjects who are statistically equated on the three other factors.   (From Jensen, 1971a, Table 6)

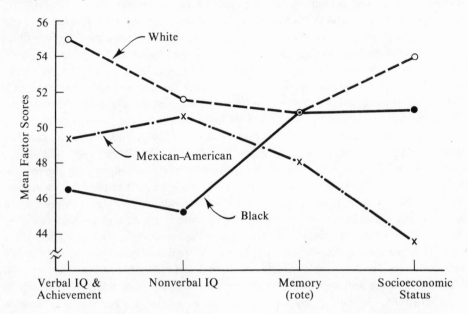

retarded or the educationally subnormal, be based on standard verbal tests administered in English. Nonverbal and performance tests (in addition to social adjustment criteria) are essential and should be given primary consideration in making placement recommendations or diagnoses of educational problems. If the results of testing are of importance to the individual, the bilingual child should be tested in *both* languages by an *E* who is fluent in the *S*'s primary language and its particular localisms, and the test should be scored in terms of the total number of correct responses in *either* language, with proper corrections for guessing, if the answers are multiple choice. School psychologists who have made this a general practice in testing bilingual children report that the maximum score attained in both languages is usually not more than 5 to 10 points higher than in either language alone, but occasionally the difference is considerably greater, thus making this precaution worthwhile if any important decision concerning the individual child is to be based on the test results.

Examiner Expectancy or Self-fulfilling Prophecy Effect.   It was once a popular claim that a child's performance on an IQ test is influenced by the teacher's or examiner's prior expectation concerning the child's ability level. The prior expectation, it was believed, would somehow be communicated to the child or would shape his cognitive development or test performance, thereby acting as a self-fulfilling prophecy—a favorable expectation leading to better IQ test performance and a poor expectation leading to poor performance. If teachers hold lower expectations for most minority pupils than for most majority pupils, it was believed, this might explain, at least in part, the commonly observed lower mean IQ of some minority groups.

This belief was given wide currency in the past decade by the publication of *Pygmalion in the Classroom* (1968) by Robert Rosenthal and Lenore Jacobson. In this study, elementary school teachers were given, at the beginning of the school term, the names of several children in each class who, according to a special pretest, were predicted to show a marked spurt in cognitive development during the coming school year. Actually these experimental group children had been selected from the class purely at random, and so any significant gain in IQ at the end of the school year, as compared with the nonexpectancy or control children in the class, would be attributed to the effect of the teacher's expectations for the specially selected children. And that is what the study purported to show: the pupils for whom the teachers were given positive expectancies apparently obtained significantly greater gains on an IQ test throughout the school term than did the control children for whom the teachers were given no prior expectation of a cognitive spurt. The study, however, was remarkably weak methodologically, and it has failed to stand up under critical scrutiny (e.g., Elashoff & Snow, 1971; Snow, 1969; Thorndike; 1968). This study, it is now generally recognized, provides no support for the teacher expectancy or self-fulfilling prophecy effect on IQ. But it has at least provided an apt and enduring label for the hypothesized outcome—the *Pygmalion effect.* Just as Ovid's myth of Pygmalion's creation of the beautiful Galatea endures because of its wish-fulfilling appeal to human emotions, so too does the myth of the expectancy effect on IQ persist for much the same reason, despite a dozen attempts to replicate the expectancy effect, all without success. In the attempts experimentally to detect effects of teacher expectancy on children's IQs, the null hypothesis has remained consistently unyielding (Anderson & Rosenthal, 1968; Clairborn, 1969; Conn, Edwards, Rosenthal, & Crowne, 1968; Deitz & Purkey, 1969; Dusek & O'Connell, 1973; Evans & Rosenthal, 1969; Fielder, Cohen, & Finney, 1971; Fleming & Anttonen, 1971; Flowers, 1968; Ginsburg, 1970; Gozali & Meyen, 1970; José & Cody, 1971; Pitt, 1956). The study by Deitz and Purkey (1969) is especially interesting from our standpoint, as it revealed no expectancy effect based on pupil's race.

In brief, I have not found in the literature a single bona fide study showing an expectancy effect for IQ. There are three studies of which the outcomes can be interpreted as consistent with the expectancy hypothesis, but these studies do not involve IQ or aptitude test scores, and they are all based on rather small and atypical samples or on atypical teacher–pupil interactions: Meichenbaum, Bowers, and Ross (1969) on delinquent girls; Beez (1973) on Head Start pupils in a 10-minute instructional interaction with experimenters; and Seaver (1973), which is the most interesting study of the lot. Based on naturally induced teacher expectancies (teacher's prior experience with the pupil's older sibling), Seaver's study shows significant expectancy effects on four out of six subscales of the Stanford Achievement Test (but, strangely, not on pupils' grades) in a privileged suburban school population. An IQ test was included in this study, but, oddly, the IQ was not tested for the teacher expectancy effect.

It should not seem surprising that the teacher expectancy effect has failed to materialize with respect to IQ. After all, even much more direct instruction on the test, tutoring, and compensatory education programs have failed to yield appreciable gains in IQ. Why should as subtle a condition as the teacher's expectation about the child's intelligence have a greater effect? Teacher expectations may in fact be quite realistic. From observing their pupils for a few months in class, most teachers can make fairly accurate judgments of the pupils' IQs. For example, I asked teachers in eight elementary school classes (grades 4, 5, 6) at the end of the school year to rate each pupil's intelligence on a five-point scale. None of the pupils had been given any standardized tests prior to the teachers' assessments. The teacher ratings showed the following correlations with various tests: Lorge–Thorndike Verbal IQ, 0.66; Lorge–Thorndike Nonverbal IQ, 0.58; Raven's Standard Progressive Matrices, 0.49; Rote Memory Test, 0.44. The teachers' ratings had a factor loading of 0.79 on the general factor (first principal component) extracted from the intercorrelations among the tests (Jensen, 1973b, pp. 263–264).

I have found seven studies that have looked at the expectancy effect exerted by examiners in the test situation itself. Five of the studies show no significant effects of E's prior expectation on the subjects' test scores (Dangel, 1970; Ekren, 1962; Gillingham, 1970; Samuel, 1977; Saunders & Vitro, 1971). Two studies show significant expectancy effects (Hersh, 1971; Schroeder & Kleinsasser, 1972). These two positive studies differ from the others in that the sample sizes are much smaller and that each E tested only two Ss, one of whom was always designated as a low-expectancy S. In no study where Es tested more than two Ss were there found any significant effects of examiner expectation.

The study by Samuel (1977) is the most powerful and most informative, as it employs 8 Es and 416 Ss in a completely balanced factorial design involving six factors: (1) *examiner expectation* (in which the E even tells the S that he or she is expected to score below average or above average on the basis of previous tests and school grades), (2) *atmosphere* (formal, evaluative versus relaxed, game-like), (3) *socioeconomic status of S, race of S* (white–black), (5) *race of E* (white–black), and (6) *sex of E*. The Ss were junior high and high school pupils under 16 years of age. The IQ test consisted of four performance subscales of the WISC: Picture Completion, Picture Arrangement, Block Design, and Coding. There were no significant effects of examiner expectation on the IQs, and this factor showed no significant first- or second-order interactions with any of the other factors in the design. The total amount of variance attributable to expectancy and all of its interactions with the other factors (altogether thirty interaction terms) is 6.4 percent, as compared with 12.5 percent for just the main effect of race of S and 68.5 percent for individual differences (within cells). Atmosphere (evaluative versus game-like) also showed no significant main effect or first- or second-order interactions, and the main effect of atmosphere plus all thirty interactions accounts for only 6.8 percent of the total IQ variance. It seems safe to conclude that the atmosphere and examiner expectancy effects are negligible on the WISC Performance IQ.

Bias in the Scoring of Tests

In the scoring of test responses, one must distinguish between nonsystematic, or random, errors and systematic errors. Only systematic errors in scoring constitute scoring bias, in contrast to random errors of measurement. The distinction is an important one, as the usual methods for determining a test's reliability will certainly detect random errors of measurement but may not detect *systematic* errors in scoring, that is, scoring bias. The problem of scoring bias is virtually nonexistent with respect to objectively scored tests, such as most machine- or stencil-scored group-administered paper-and-pencil tests. But scoring bias can enter into individually administered tests, particularly verbal tests, in which the S's response to each item must be subjectively judged in terms of the general scoring criteria, with the aid of a few typical examples of passing and failing responses provided in the test manual.

The fact of the high internal consistency reliability and high test–retest reliability of most standard individual tests (see Chapter 7), which are at least as high as for objectively scored tests, surely indicates that there is relatively little nonsystematic scoring error in individual, subjectively scored tests when scored by well-trained examiners. But what about scoring *bias,* that is, the scorer's tendency, when in doubt, consistently to overrate (or underrate) a given S's responses?

The research addressed to this question leaves little doubt that halo effects do occur in the scoring of subjects' responses on individual tests such as the Stanford–Binet and the Wechsler, at least under the rather contrived and artificial conditions of the experiments that characterize most of these investigations. The most common paradigm is for the investigator to make up, say, a fictitious Wechsler test protocol, showing the fictitious S's complete verbal responses to every item, including a number of intentionally ambiguous responses, that is, responses that cannot easily be judged by any of the formal scoring criteria and on which a panel of well-trained judges actually show considerable disagreement in scoring. Es (usually students in a college course on mental testing) are then given the protocol to score, along with some type of "background" information on the S who supposedly took the test. This information is varied as the experimental treatment: Es are led to believe, from other information, that the S is either "bright" or "dull" or that the ambiguous responses are included either in a test protocol with many obviously correct responses (making for an overall IQ of about 130) or in a protocol with many erroneous responses (making for an overall IQ of about 90). Under these conditions of high or low expectancy, Es tend significantly to overrate the ambiguous responses for the high-expectancy Ss and to underrate them for the low-expectancy Ss (Egeland, 1969; Sattler & Winget, 1970; Sattler, Hillix, & Neher, 1970; Simon, 1969). The halo effects, though statistically significant, are generally surprisingly small. The scoring of ambiguous responses is much more subject to a halo effect from the quality of the S's ability level, as indicated by the quality of the S's nonambiguous responses to all of the other items in the test, than by any extraneous information, such as IQs from previous testings, provided about the S. Also, there is some evidence that Es who rate Ss as likeable and "warm" in a 10-minute interview situation prior to scoring the S's (artificial) WAIS protocol, containing ambiguous verbal responses tended significantly to overrate the S's responses, as compared with E's rating of responses given by Ss whom E regards as less liked and less warm (Donahue & Sattler, 1971).

These studies unfortunately do not answer the question of the magnitude of halo effects in scoring actual noncontrived test protocols, in which there may be considerably fewer ambiguous responses and less room for scoring bias. In any case, the studies fail to consider the more crucial question of whether the halo effect on the scoring of ambiguous responses increases or decreases the validity of the resulting total test scores. The most telling experimental paradigm, which has never been applied, would be to substitute a small number of ambiguous responses made in authentic test protocols ranging widely in total score and note the degree of discrepancy between the ratings given to the substituted ambiguous responses and the ratings given to the S's actual responses on those items. Just on probabalistic grounds, it is likely that the halo effect, on the average, *enhances* the scoring validity of highly ambiguous responses.

Ethnic Group and SES Bias in Scoring.   I have found only one study on scoring bias as a function of race (Jacobs & DeGraaf, 1972). It is a well-designed, completely counterbalanced factorial study involving race of S (white–black), race of E, and expectancy (high versus low ability). Sixteen Es of each race viewed a videotape of the WISC being administered to a white and black child, both 10 years of age and both of similar IQ (about 90). (A better design would have included at least two children of each race.) Es were provided with fictitious referral material on each child; half the referral materials, relevant to Ss and distributed to Es in a perfectly counterbalanced fashion, were intended to induce low expectation (previous test results reported with IQs of about 70 and scholastic problems) or high expectation (previous IQs about 113 and excellent student). From observing the videotape and reading the referral materials, the psychologists were asked to score the S's WISC protocols. The resulting IQs were subjected to an analysis of variance. Taking $p < .05$ as the level of significance, the only significant effect on Full Scale IQ was for expectancy, with the high expectancy averaging an IQ of 89.6 and the low expectancy an IQ of 87.9—a difference of 1.7 IQ points. There were no significant effects for race of S (88.6 versus 88.6) or race of E (88.8 versus 88.6) and no significant interactions among any of the factors. The expectancy effect was more marked on the Verbal than on the Performance subscales. Thus there is no significant race of E × race of S scoring bias, and in fact, there was a tendency (though nonsignificant) for the expectancy effect to be greater when E and S were of the same race; the expectancy effect was practically nil when E and S were of different races. Certainly nothing in this study suggests there is any scoring bias associated with either the S's race or the E's race or their interaction.

When it comes to interpreting the subjects' IQs, studies indicate that psychologists give higher estimates (by about 3 to 5 IQ points) of "true" or "effective" intelligence for black and Mexican–Americans Ss than for white Ss with the same measured IQ (Nalven, Hofmann, & Bierbryer, 1969; Sattler & Kuncik, 1976). (Effects are small and inconsistent with respect to the S's SES.) This may mean either that many clinical and school psychologists accept the popular belief that IQ tests underestimate the "effective intelligence" of minority Ss or that the psychologists' estimates of "effective intelligence" give more weight to ability factors, such as memory, which contribute very little to the variance in actual IQ scores. The latter explanation seems unlikely, however, in view of the finding that clinicians who are asked to estimate "effective intelligence" from various patterns of WISC subtest scores actually give more weight to those WISC subtests that are in fact most g loaded (Sattler & Kuncik, 1976).

Bias Due to Situational and Procedural Conditions

Timed Tests.   Spearman (1927) differentiated experimentally between two types of speed factors that enter into performance on timed tests (or enter into the total amount of time needed to complete an untimed test). This distinction was corroborated in later studies (Line & Kaplan, 1932).

One speed factor is intrinsic to g and is inseparable from g; it involves the speed of mental operations, or "speed of cognition," as Spearman referred to it. It is reflected in the speed with which a person recalls relevant information for answering a question or for solving a problem and the speed of mentally manipulating the elements of the problem in working toward its solution. Persons who score high on *g*-loaded tests, even when they are untimed, evince faster mental operations in this respect—call it cognitive speed or *g*-intrinsic speed.

The other form of speed was likened by Spearman to a general attitude or preference for speed in performing any task. It might be called *personal tempo* to distinguish it from *cognitive speed*. Personal tempo can be experimentally distinguished from cognitive speed by means of test items that are within everyone's capability of performing correctly and in which the only source of individual differences is the time required. A slower personal tempo results in fewer such easy items being completed in a given amount of time. If all persons were given enough time on a test composed entirely of such easy items, there would be no variance in total scores. Moreover, a pure measure of speed differences, in the absence of any cognitive difficulty posed by the items, has virtually no *g* loading. This personal tempo factor, however, may enter into the variance on timed tests, as slower persons will spend more time getting through the easier items that nearly everyone can do and have less time left for working on the harder items. A timed test, therefore, can penalize persons with a slower personal tempo. It has been claimed that this is a factor in the lower scores of blacks, in particular, and of persons of low SES, in general (e.g., Klineberg, 1928).

No evidence has been adduced, however, that shows that the personal tempo factor, as contrasted to cognitive speed, contributes appreciably to the average difference in test performance between various racial and socioeconomic groups.

In the first place, we find no consistent variation in the size of the white–black difference in terms of timed versus untimed tests, as one should expect to find if the personal tempo factor per se contributed substantially to the white–black difference in cognitive ability tests.

In the second place, tests of personal tempo do not show a significant white–black difference. The Making X's Test is a measure of speed that has virtually no *g* loading in children beyond age 7, excluding the severely mentally retarded. This test is described in Chapter 5 (p. 136). Briefly, the person is asked to make as many X's in rows of "boxes" (totaling 150) as he can in 90 seconds, first under neutral, nonmotivating instructions and then under motivating instructions that emphasize speed. The subject's scores are the numbers of X's made within 90 seconds under each condition. Nearly all subjects make X's faster under the speed instructions than under the neutral instructions, and there are highly reliable individual differences in personal tempo as measured by this test.

When the Making X's Test was given to all of the white ($N = 3,770$) and black ($N = 2,643$) children in grades 1 to 6 in a California school district, the mean white–black difference, in standard deviation units, was $+.03\sigma$ with neutral instructions and $-.02\sigma$ with speed instructions (Jensen, 1974c). Neither difference is significant. In the same groups, however, the mean white–black difference on the Lorge–Thorndike Nonverbal IQ is $+1.47\sigma$. Obviously the personal tempo factor measured by the Making X's Test contributes virtually nothing to the white–black IQ difference.

A direct examination of the effect of time limits on the testing of whites and blacks, and of low- and high-SES groups within each race, was made by Dubin, Osburn, and Winick (1969). They hypothesized that (1) extra practice on an equivalent form of the test would be more advantageous to blacks than to whites, (2) extended testing time would favor blacks more than whites, and (3) blacks would benefit even more from the combination of extra practice and extended testing time. The same hypotheses were applied also to low- and high-SES groups within each race. The hypotheses were tested on samples of white ($N = 232$) and black ($N = 235$) high school pupils, who were given practice tests and final tests of verbal, numerical, and spatial reasoning under short and long time limits. None of the preceding hypotheses was borne out significantly. Both whites and blacks obtained higher scores to about the same degree as a result of the practice and the extended time limit. The authors concluded:

> The results failed to support the hypotheses that Negroes would be favored by extra practice and/or extra testing time. Apparently, the administration of highly speeded tests given without extra practice did not handicap the average Negro S nor Ss in lower socioeconomic classes. In a more general sense the results imply that the testing procedure itself was not a major factor in discriminating between Negro and white Ss or between culturally advantaged and culturally disadvantaged Ss. (p. 22)

A study of one hundred white–Anglo and one hundred Mexican–American adult male job applicants taking the Cattell Culture Free Intelligence Test under speeded and untimed conditions showed a statistically significant, but practically negligible, effect of the speeded versus untimed conditions (Knapp, 1960). Both groups obtained higher mean scores under the untimed than under the speed condition, with Mexican–Americans showing a slight advantage. The percentage of variance accounted for by the group difference (Anglo versus Mexican–American) is 28 percent; test condition (speeded versus untimed), 7 percent; interaction of groups $\times$ conditions, 0.4 percent.

In summary, the evidence indicates that the condition of timed versus untimed tests (also referred to as speeded versus power tests) of mental ability is a negligible factor in the observed mean differences in test scores between majority and minority groups.

Examiner's Instructions and Attitude. The literature on mental testing includes many studies that show rather small, but often statistically significant, effects of a variety of testing conditions stemming from the examiner's manner of administering the test and E's general rapport with the subject. These conditions, which have been experimentally manipulated in numerous studies, involve the use of incentives and rewards, both material and verbal: motivation-inducing instructions; the emotional tone of the testing situation— friendly, warm, casual versus formal, cool, aloof; dispensing of praise and encouragement; interspersing very easy items with more difficult items to reduce the subject's feeling of failure, and control of any factors in the test situation that might affect the degree of effort and concentration applied by the subject. Good introductions to the relevant literature are provided by Anastasi (1976, Ch. 2), Sattler (1974, Ch. 6), and Sattler and Theye (1967).

Of more central relevance to the question of cultural bias in testing is the degree to which any of the preceding conditions may interact with different cultural groups to produce differences in their performance on mental tests. This has been researched only with respect to groups characterized as ''culturally disadvantaged'' or low SES and with respect to comparisons of blacks and whites. This literature generally lends no support to the notion that the conditions of testing contribute significantly to the social-class and racial differences observed on most tests.

The effects of *incentives* are consistently negative, with the exception of one study.

Klugman (1974) found that a money incentive, as compared with verbal praise, for correct answers on the Stanford–Binet by white and black children, ages 7 to 14, raised the blacks' mean IQ by a significant 4 points, but produced a nonsignificant effect on the IQs of whites. But Tiber and Kennedy (1964) found no significant white–black or SES differences in Stanford–Binet IQ among 7–9-year-olds as a function of four different incentive conditions: praise, reproof, candy reward, and no incentive. Sweet (1969) found no differential effects of money rewards for correct answers or verbal feedback as to the correctness of answers on the WISC verbal subscale scores of white and black children 6 to 13 years of age. And Cohen (1970) found no interaction of verbal praise and candy rewards with race (white versus black) on the WISC Block Design performance of second- and fifth-graders. Also, Quay (1971) found no differential effects of praise versus candy on the Stanford–Binet IQs of one hundred 4-year-old black children in Project Head Start. Quay found less than 1 IQ point difference from the effects of a money incentive on Binet IQs of ninety-two low-SES black children about 9 years of age. The experimental groups were given 5 cents for each Binet item passed. The control children were tested in the usual manner specified in the test manual.

In a study of four of the nonverbal performance tests of the General Aptitude Test Battery given to white ($N = 121$) and black ($N = 99$) delinquent male youths, there were no significant interactions of race with three different incentive conditions: material reward ("ducats" redeemable for canteen goods), verbal praise and encouragement, and no incentive (i.e., merely bare instructions for taking the test) (Wenk, Rozynko, Sarbin, & Robison, 1971).

Other *modifications of testing procedures* have shown negative or inconclusive effects with respect to interactions with race. Samuel (1977) varied the testing atmosphere (relaxed, game-like versus formal, evaluative) in administering the WISC to 208 white and 208 black junior and senior high school pupils under 16 years of age. There was no significant main effect of the testing conditions and no significant interactions with race of Ss, race of Es, sex of Es, or E's expectation of S's IQ level. Zigler and Butterfield (1968) administered the Stanford–Binet to low-SES white and black preschoolers in a manner intended to optimize performance without actually giving the subjects test-relevant information. For example, the easiest items were presented first to maximize initial successes, and, whenever a child failed two items in succession, much easier items from earlier age levels were then given to assure a feeling of success, and encouragement was given generously. This score-optimizing testing procedure yielded IQs about 6 points higher than the IQs obtained from a control group under the standard administration procedure. However, the results were not analyzed separately by race, and also we have no way of knowing, from this study, whether the same amount of IQ gain would occur in more advantaged groups when tested under the same optimizing conditions. The same question remains unanswered by a study of a modified procedure for the administration of the Peabody Picture Vocabulary Test, which resulted in raising the scores, as compared with the standard administration procedure, in a group of black preschoolers (Ali & Costello, 1971). About all that such single-group studies demonstrate is the fact that marked departures from the standard administration procedures can have some effect on the average level of obtained scores. The modified method of administration, however, may not interact with any socially defined groups. Also, its effect on the test's practical validity remains unknown.

Bias Arising from Motivational, Attitudinal, and Personality Factors

Test Anxiety. There is a considerable literature on the role of anxiety in test performance. The key references to this literature are provided in reviews by Anastasi (1976, pp. 37–38), Matarazzo (1972, pp. 439–449), I. G. Sarason (1978), S. B. Sarason et al. (1960), and Sattler (1974, p. 324). In brief, many studies have reported generally low but significant *negative* correlations between various measures of the subject's anxiety level, such as the Taylor Manifest Anxiety Scale and the Sarason Test Anxiety Scale, and performance on various mental ability tests. Many nonsignificant correlations are also reported, although they are in the minority, and are usually rationalized by the investigators in various ways, such as atypical samples, restriction of range on one or both variables, and the like (e.g., Spielberger, 1958). I suspect that this literature contains a considerably larger proportion of "findings" that are actually just Type I errors (i.e., rejection of the null hypothesis when it is in fact true) than of Type II errors (i.e., failure to reject the null hypothesis when it is in fact false). Statistically significant correlations are more often regarded as a "finding" than are nonsignificant results, and Type I errors are therefore more apt to be submitted for publication. Aside from that, sheer correlations are necessarily ambiguous with respect to the direction of causality. Persons who, because of low ability, have had the unpleasant experience of performing poorly on tests in the past may for that reason find future test situations anxiety provoking—hence a negative correlation between measures of test anxiety and ability test scores.

Test anxiety has not figured prominently among the variables hypothesized to account for cultural or racial group differences in test scores. The lack of published studies on this point, in fact, further strengthens the suspicion that null results are seldom reported when found. Yet the few null results that are published are quite clear-cut.

For example, one of the most sensitive indicators of anxiety level is pulse rate, and we note that the Sarason Test Anxiety Scale contains the item "I sometimes feel my heart beating very fast during important tests." Noble (1969) measured the pulse rates of groups of white and black elementary school children immediately before and after being individually tested and found no race difference in pre- or posttest pulse rate.

The Sarason Test Anxiety Scale given to black and white children between the ages of 8 and 11 showed no significant race difference, no significant interactions with S's race $\times$ E's race, and no significant correlations with WISC Full Scale IQ (Solkoff, 1972).

A questionnaire measure of manifest anxiety, the N (neuroticism) scale of the Junior Eysenck Personality Inventory, administered to large samples of white, black, and Mexican–American children in grades 4 to 8 in a California school district, showed significant but very small (less than 1 point) group differences, with whites having *higher* anxiety scores. In all groups the N scale showed nonsignificant and negligible correlations with verbal and nonverbal IQ and tests of scholastic achievement (Jensen, 1973e).

Among the various subtests of the Stanford–Binet and the Wechsler IQ tests, digit span is generally claimed to be the most sensitive to the adverse effects of anxiety, which interferes with the subject's concentration and short-term retention. An enforced 10-second delay in recall depresses digit-span retention, due to the interference of extraneous thoughts, which are presumably increased by test anxiety. (For example, the Test Anxiety Scale contains items expressing this form of distractability while taking a test.) Therefore it was predicted that, if whites and blacks differ in test anxiety, there should be an interaction between race and immediate versus delayed recall of aural digit series. No significant interaction was found in the digit-span performance of white ($N = 4,467$) and black ($N = 3,610$) California school children in grades 2 to 8 (Jensen & Figueroa, 1975).

In summary, there appears to be no consistent or appreciable differential effect of anxiety on the test performance of whites and blacks.

Achievement Motivation.   Achievement motivation (now conventionally abbreviated n-Ach, standing for "need for achievement") is a general striving to perform one's best in any activity in which a standard of excellence applies or in which one judges the quality of one's own performance in terms of success or failure. It has been hypothesized that cultural groups differ in their level of achievement motivation, which could be one cause of the observed differences in test performance and scholastic achievement (Chapman & Hill, 1971, pp. 91–103). Achievement motivation is hypothesized to influence test performance in two main ways: first, by determining the level of interest, striving, and effort that persons invest in the development of their intellectual skills throughout all their experience prior to being confronted with a mental test and, second, by determining the level of attention, concentration, effort, and persistence applied in the test situation itself. The most highly developed theoretical formulations of the relationship of n-Ach to intellectual performance and scholastic achievement are attributable to the work of John W. Atkinson and his associates (Atkinson, 1974; Atkinson, Lens, & O'Malley, 1976).

The research literature on this topic is voluminous, but remarkably unenlightening. The reader may gain some impression of the lack of consensus among researchers and among empirical finding in this field by perusal of the quite comprehensive compendium of research findings and conclusions relating to every aspect of n-Ach compiled by Chapman and Hill (1971). For almost every empirical finding or author's conclusion there is a counterfinding or counterconclusion by another researcher. It seems apparent that n-Ach either is not a very robust psychological construct, in the sense, say, that g is, or the theoretical construct of n-Ach is exceedingly complex and individual differences in n-Ach are so complexly determined and seemingly interact so strongly with so many contextual variables as to allow ad hoc explanations or rationalizations of virtually any given empirical finding. Moreover, the objective measurement of n-Ach, usually by means of projective techniques and questionnaires, has not yet been fully standardized in the research literature, and often it is not clear that different investigators are measuring one and the same construct.

Conclusions, therefore, regarding the role of achievement motivation as a factor in systematic group biases in testing are virtually impossible in terms of the empirical evidence. Of course there is plenty of armchair theorizing, but the most sweeping generalizations seem to be the least empirically substantiated. Overall, I find little in the research literature that leads one to believe that n-Ach is a potent source of individual or group differences in most cognitive tests, particularly intelligence tests. In reviewing the relevant literature, Heckhausen (1967) concluded that most studies do not show statistically significant correlations between measures of achievement motivation and intelligence test scores. Later studies specially directed at this question also failed to find any significant relationship of n-Ach to intelligence test scores (Mingione, 1968) or to school grades and standardized achievement test scores (de Charmes & Carpenter, 1968) among culturally disadvantaged school children. However, there is some evidence of significant correlations between achievement motivation and academic grades at the high school and college level (Atkinson, Lens, & O'Malley, 1976) and low but significant correlations (.12 to .37) with a cognitive ability measure (Sentence Completion Test) in white and black adults (Veroff, McClelland, & Marquis, 1971a). In the study by Veroff et al., the measure of achievement motivation was a significant independent predictor (along with age, intelligence, and SES background) of the amount of formal education attained by adulthood for black males and white females but not for black females or white males. From the data provided by Veroff et al., I have estimated that the correlation of .16 between race and achievement motivation drops to .04 when "intelligence" (Sentence Completion Test) is partialed out, and the correlation of .45 between race and "intelligence" drops to .42 when achievement motivation is partialled out, which suggests that about 7 percent of the mean white–black difference on the Sentence Completion Test is associated with the achievement motivation measure. Of course, no causal connection can be inferred from this correlation analysis; but I suspect that a higher achievement orientation is more a product of high ability than the reverse.

Self-esteem. If individual or group differences in feelings of self-esteem or self-confidence have a greater effect on test scores than on the external criteria that the test is intended to predict or the construct that the test is supposed to measure, the variable of self-esteem would be a source of bias in mental testing. So far, in the literature, no empirical case has been made for self-esteem as a source of test bias, although it has been hypothesized to be among the factors contributing to the lower scores of blacks on cognitive tests (e.g., Roen, 1960).

A recent comprehensive review of studies of white–black differences in measures of own-race preference and self-esteem concluded that blacks evince significantly lower self-esteem, as measured by a variety of questionnaires, than do whites (Shuey, 1978). But IQ is not considered in any of these studies, except one (Posner, 1969). Posner found that both white and black children with very low IQs (50–75) show lower self-esteem than children of average or superior IQ, but there was no significant white–black difference in self-esteem in these samples.

Thus self-esteem as a source of test bias remains in the limbo of untested hypotheses. The first question to be answered in testing the hypothesis is whether self-esteem acts as a suppressor variable differentially in terms of race (or other group membership) in the predictive validity of mental tests and whether including an index of self-esteem in a multiple regression equation, along with the variables of mental test score and group membership, significantly increases predictive power (as indicated by R^2). If self-esteem acts as a suppressor variable in the multiple regression equation (along with ability and group membership), it should carry a negative weight. In other words, the correlation between the ability test scores and the criterion should be improved by partialing out self-esteem, if self-esteem is, in fact, a source of test bias. I have not found in the literature any data relevant to self-esteem that lend themselves to this type of analysis.

Reflection–Impulsivity. This is another trait that may contribute to test bias but has been inadequately studied in this context. Persons have been found to differ in a variety of measures of reflection-impulsivity. Reflective persons tend to delay responses in answering test items involving an initial uncertainty, and as a result their performance gains in accuracy. The payoff of a reflective attitude is greatest in tasks that call for careful analysis of possible response alternatives, as is characteristic, for example, of multiple-choice nonverbal tests such as the Raven Matrices. Impulsive persons, on the other hand, typically respond quickly, with little reflection or analysis, at the expense of a higher rate of erroneous responses. Reflection–impulsivity, as a trait, is usually measured by means of Kagan's Matching Familiar Figures Test (MFFT). In this test, the subject is asked to mark the one figure, out of a set of several highly similar distractors, that perfectly matches a "target" figure.

The literature on reflection–impulsivity is comprehensively reviewed by Messer (1976). Impulsivity as measured by the MFFT shows a median correlation of about $-.30$ with various IQ test scores, and the correlation would be substantially higher when corrected for attenuation, as the MFFT scores have only moderate test–retest stability. I suspect, however, that much of this correlation may be due to an intrinsic relationship between g and reflectivity, that is, one of the manifestations of g ability is reflectiveness. More complex cognitive machinery is set into motion by a complex or ambiguous stimulus in a high-g person than in a low-g person. Experimental manipulations of reflection–impulsivity have shown rather weak and inconsistent results. The correlation between social class and impulsivity disappears when IQ is controlled. As far as I can determine from the literature, nothing really is known about racial differences in reflection–impulsivity.

SUMMARY

A number of situational variables external to the tests themselves that have been hypothesized to influence test performance were examined as possible sources of bias in the testing of different racial and social-class groups. The evidence is wholly negative for every such variable on which empirical studies are reported in the literature. That is, no variables in the test situation, but extraneous to the tests, have been identified that contribute significantly to the observed average test score differences between social classes and racial groups.

Practice effects in general are small, amounting to a gain of about 5 IQ points between the first and second test and becoming much less thereafter. Special coaching on test-taking skills may add another 4 to 5 IQ points (over the practice effect) on subsequent tests if these are highly similar to the test on which subjects were coached. However, neither practice effects nor coaching interacts significantly with race or social class. These findings suggest that experience with standard tests is approximately equal across different racial and social-class groups. None of the observed racial or social-class differences in test scores is attributable to differences in amount of experience with tests per se.

A review of thirty studies addressed to the effect of the race of the tester on test scores reveals preponderantly nonsignificant and negligible effects of the examiner's race on the test performance of white and black children. The evidence conclusively contradicts the hypothesis that subjects (of either race) perform better when tested by a person of the same race than when tested by a person of a different race. In brief, the race of examiner × race of subject interaction is not substantiated.

Also, the sex of the examiner is not a potent factor in IQ testing.

The language style or dialect of the examiner has no effect on the IQ performance of black children or adults, who do not score higher on verbal tests translated and administered in black ghetto dialect than in standard English. On the other hand, all major bilingual populations in the United States score slightly but significantly lower on verbal tests (in standard English) than on nonverbal tests, suggesting that a specific language factor is involved in their lower scores on verbal tests. This depression of verbal scores in bilingual groups does not impair the tests' short-range predictive validity for scholastic performance when English is the medium of instruction. But the construct validity of verbal tests should be regarded as suspect for bilingual persons. Properly translated tests (which involve psychometric equating of item difficulties in addition to mere translation) may often get around this problem, but are not guaranteed to do so. Test users should especially note statistically significant discrepancies between verbal and nonverbal scores in bilingual subjects, for whom failure to use nonverbal tests is clearly a form of psychometric malpractice.

The teacher's or tester's expectation concerning the child's level of ability has no demonstrable effect on the child's performance on IQ tests. I have found no bona fide study in the literature that shows a significant expectancy effect (or ''Pygmalion effect'') for IQ.

Significant but small halo effects on the *scoring* of subjectively scored tests (e.g., some of the verbal scales of the Wechsler) have been found in some studies, but these halo effects have not been found to interact with either the race of the scorer or the race of the subject.

Speeded versus unspeeded tests do not interact with race or social class, and the evidence contradicts the notion that speed or time pressure in the test situation contributes anything to the average test score differences between racial groups or social classes. The same conclusion is supported by evidence concerning the effects of varying the conditions of testing with respect to instructions, examiner attitudes, incentives, and rewards.

Test anxiety has not been found to have differential effects on the test performances of blacks and whites. Studies of the effects of achievement motivation and self-esteem on test performance also show largely negative results in this respect.

In summary, as yet no factors in the testing procedure itself have been identified as sources of bias in the test performances of different racial groups and social classes.

Chapter 13

Sex Bias

Sex differences in selection rates are often seen in selection situations in which mental tests, usually along with other information, are used for making selection decisions—in special school programs for the retarded and the gifted, in college admissions, and in personnel selection. We should like to know to what extent the tests themselves contribute to the observed sex differences in selection rates.

Just as in the case of racial and social-class differences, the question has two main aspects: true differences in ability *versus* artifactual differences due to bias in the tests—in this case, *sex bias*. The null hypothesis of "no difference" is not assumed *a priori* to be either true or false. No line of scientific evidence or reasoning based thereon would warrant any such *a priori* assumption. It is the task of psychometrics and differential psychology to distinguish between true differences in abilities and artifactual differences resulting from bias in the measuring instruments.

The question of sex bias in mental tests arises from consideration of the fact that boys and girls, from an early age, are socialized in traditional masculine and feminine roles, involving differences in types of toys, games, experiences, learning opportunities, and developed skills. Varieties of test items are certainly not all independent of these experiential sex differences, and any given test could consist of a biased sample of the total possible pool of masculine- and feminine-slanted items. If, as is usually the case, tests are made up by men, do they include more masculine than feminine types of items?

In terms of the predictive validity of tests, we are not concerned with the *origins* of sex differences in abilities. Our concern is only to establish that the observed sex difference (or the *absence* of a sex difference) in ability test scores is not merely a result of test bias. Test bias can, of course, obscure a true difference as well as produce an artifactual difference where no true difference exists. If women are not so good as men in mathematics only because women have not taken so much math in high school or college, it is still a real difference with practical implications in certain situations, and any good test of mathematics achievement should reflect such a difference. From the standpoint of validity, it does not matter that the difference is acquired rather than innate. If test bias can be ruled out as the cause of sex differences in certain abilities, the further problem of explaining those sex differences lies outside the scope of this book. For comprehensive reviews of the state of the art on that topic, the reader is referred elsewhere (Maccoby, 1966; Maccoby & Jacklin, 1974). However, I shall briefly summarize the conclusions that

I think we may justifiably draw from the total mass of empirical evidence relating to sex differences in tested abilities.

Sex Differences in Tested Abilities

Table 13.1 summarizes the outcomes of all studies of sex differences in various abilities that have appeared in the literature since 1966. The essential details of each study are provided by Maccoby and Jacklin (1974). The overall picture that emerges is essentially the same as was found in an earlier review of studies published before 1966 (Maccoby, 1966).

The most striking feature of Table 13.1 is that, with the exception of tests of quantitative ability and of nonverbal tests of divergent thinking (of which there are fewer studies than for any other type of test), a *majority* of the studies find no sex differences large enough to be significant beyond the .05 level. Yet the sample sizes are generally adequate for even quite small differences, equivalent to a tenth of a standard deviation or less, to show up as statistically significant. The other striking feature of Table 13.1 is that, when significant sex differences *are* found, they never consistently favor males or females for any given type of ability, although for several abilities (indicated by a superscript *a*) there is a significant difference in the frequencies of study outcomes that significantly favors one or the other sex. The most extreme example of this is in tests of analytic visual–spatial ability, on which males tend to perform better than females.

All this immediately suggests that sex differences in the ability realm are a relatively small-magnitude phenomenon as compared with racial and social-class differences. The inconsistencies among studies also suggest that sex differences on mental tests are complexly determined and are conditional on a number of other factors, such as age of the subjects, educational level, regional differences, and secular trends. When such factors are uncontrolled across studies with respect to a small-magnitude phenomenon, there may be highly significant differences *within* any particular study but little consistent direction of the differences from one study to another.

Table 13.1.   Numbers of studies of sex differences and their outcomes on various types of tests published since 1966.

Type of Test	Significant[1] Difference in Favor of		
	Neither	Male	Female
General Intelligence	40	3	15[a]
Verbal Ability	81	13	37[a]
Quantitative Ability	15	16	4[a]
Visual–Spatial (nonanalytic)	24	9	2[a]
Visual–Spatial (analytic)	35	25	3[a]
Reasoning (nonverbal, nonspatial)	26	7	5
Piagetian Tests of Conceptual Level	41	6	4
Divergent Thinking[2] (verbal)	16	5	11
Divergent Thinking[2] (nonverbal)	7	8	8

[1]Significant beyond the .05 level.   [2]Popularly, but mistakenly, called "creativity."
[a]Sex difference frequencies significantly different beyond the .05 level by chi squared test with $1\,df$.

There is also the problem in this research of obtaining equally random or representative samples of males and females. The only difficulty in sampling school populations is that the extreme lower tail of the ability distribution is excluded from regular schools. At the high school level there is the risk of differential ability-related dropout rates for the sexes. Beyond high school age, large and equally representative samples of males and females are virtually impossible to obtain. Sex differences in the social and economic pressures for college attendance, as well as differences in the types of colleges that attract men or women students, make it impossible to generalize the results of studies of sex differences in college students to the general population. There has never existed any institutionalized system allowing for the large-scale mental measurement of the general adult female population such as existed in the military draft, which made it possible to test the entire noninstitutionalized male population of the United States between the ages of 18 and 26.

Let us now take a closer look at each of the several categories of tests listed in Table 13.1.

General Intelligence. The most widely used standardized tests of general intelligence have explicitly tried to minimize sex differences in total score by discarding those items that show the largest sex differences in the normative sample and by counterbalancing the number of remaining items that favor either sex. This is true, for example, of the Stanford–Binet and the Wechsler scales of intelligence. Such tests, therefore, obviously cannot be used to answer the question of whether there is in fact a true difference between males and females in general intelligence. The particular mix of various items in any omnibus type of test could make the sex difference go in either direction. The fact that the differences actually found in most studies hover close to zero only indicates that the test constructors have been reasonably successful in their attempts to balance out any overall sex difference by careful item selection. The practice of eliminating and counterbalancing items to minimize sex differences is based on the assumption that the sexes do not really differ in general intelligence.

McNemar (1942, Ch. 5) justifies this procedure, in the case of the Stanford–Binet, with the argument that test batteries of extensive scope and varied content, unselected with respect to sex, generally show very small and inconsistent sex differences in total scores from one sample to another. Also, the particular items that show large sex differences in percentage passing can usually be accounted for in terms of experiences or training that are typically associated more with one sex than with the other. McNemar makes another important observation regarding the extremely varied pool of Binet test items: no one *type* of item consistently favors either sex. The sex differences in item difficulty are apparently more a function of specific item *content* than of the types of basic abilities called for by the item. Yet with the very large standardization samples, even quite small sex differences in percentage passing an item show up as highly significant statistically. The 190-item Stanford–Binet test contains 12 items on which girls significantly (*p* < .01) surpass boys and 16 items on which boys significantly surpass girls. These items are sufficiently well balanced that the total IQ difference between the sexes in any large sample is practically negligible. The same is true of the Wechsler tests.

The fact that many more studies in Table 13.1 show tests of general intelligence favoring females is probably attributable to the general finding that females slightly outperform males on verbal items and in reading skills in the elementary school grades and that many general intelligence tests, particularly group tests, are heavily weighted on a verbal ability factor (in addition to g) and require reading.

Tests of general intelligence that were constructed entirely without reference to sex differences show hardly any larger or more consistent sex difference in total scores than tests constructed to minimize the difference. Raven's Progressive Matrices and Thurstone's Primary Mental Abilities are good examples of this.

The Raven Colored Progressive Matrices is a nonverbal test of reasoning ability heavily loaded on g and not much loaded on any other factors. The Peabody Picture Vocabulary Test (PPVT), in contrast, has its variance divided about equally between the g and V (verbal ability) factors. I perfectly matched each of 35 items of the Raven with each of 35 PPVT items on difficulty (percentage passing) on 333 white elementary school boys. The average item p value (percentage passing) for both the Raven and the PPVT in this sample is 66.7 percent. The same sets of 35 Raven and 35 PPVT items were administered to 305 girls in the same classes as the boys. The girls' average item p values are 64.8 percent and 61.6 percent for the Raven and PPVT, respectively, a nonsignificant difference (Jensen, 1974a). Interestingly, the girls differ less from boys on the nonverbal Raven than on the verbal PPVT. The p values of the Raven and PPVT items, of course, are correlated 1.00 for the boys, as the items were purposely matched on p values. The p values of the same Raven and PPVT items, however, are correlated .94 for the girls. Thus even on two such markedly different tests, the sex difference is quite small.

In the Wechsler Adult Intelligence Scale no explicit attempt was made to eliminate sex differences in the separate subtests, but the sex differences on the eleven subtests are sufficiently counterbalanced to make for practically negligible sex differences in Full Scale IQ (see Matarazzo, 1972, pp. 352–358). The men in the standardization groups significantly surpass women on Information, Comprehension, Arithmetic, Picture Completion, and Block Design; women significantly surpass men on Similarities, Vocabulary, and Digit Symbol. There are no sex differences on Digit Span, Picture Arrangement, and Object Assembly.

I have factor analyzed the WAIS standardization data to see how the sexes might differ in factor scores. Only three nontrivial principal components can be extracted from the intercorrelations among the eleven WAIS subtests: a large g factor accounting for over 50 percent of the total variance and two smaller group factors best labeled *Verbal* and *Performance*. The average g loading of the tests on which women surpass men is .73 and on which men surpass women is .70—a nonsignificant difference. Also, there is a nonsignificant correlation between the g loadings of the subtests and the magnitudes or directions of the sex difference in mean subtest scores. Thus it is quite apparent that the sexes do not differ at all in the g factor of the WAIS. This is true also when the g factor loadings are averaged on only the verbal subtests or on only the performance subtests. On the Verbal factor (which is completely uncorrelated with g), however, women significantly surpass men. The average of the V factor loadings on the tests on which women excell is .48 as compared with .38 on the tests on which men excell. The Performance factor shows just the opposite. The average P factor loading on the tests on which men excell is .26 as compared to .16 for the tests on which women excell—a significant difference. I suspect that these results represent true sex differences rather than sex bias artifacts. The absence of a sex difference on g, when V and P factors are removed, is entirely in line with the lack of any consistent sex difference on nonverbal–nonspatial tests of reasoning ability (see Table 13.1).

It is noteworthy that Spearman (1927, pp. 388–390) believed that there is no sex difference in *g*, but only in what he termed "special abilities" (now called group factors or primaries). "Special abilities" are what is left over (besides error variance) after *g* is removed. Spearman (1927, p. 229) observed, perhaps before anyone else, that the special ability factor most related to sex is the spatial–visualization factor. He noted that tests of spatial visualization have their total variance more evenly divided between *g* and the spatial factor in men than in women, for whom variance on spatial tests is more nearly all *g* variance, suggesting that fewer women than men call on any special ability in addition to *g* for solving spatial problems.

Verbal Ability. As indicated in Table 13.1, the evidence is mixed regarding sex differences in verbal ability. It becomes more clear as soon as we take age into account. Girls begin to talk a bit earlier than boys, but from then up until about age 10 or 11 years there is no clear superiority of either sex in verbal ability. From that age on up to maturity, however, girls begin, on the average, to surpass boys rather consistently on a wide variety of verbal tests that were not specially devised with reference to sex differences. In adolescence, girls average close to a quarter of a standard deviation higher than boys on verbal tasks (Maccoby & Jacklin, 1973, p. 39). This is equivalent to a point-biserial correlation of about 0.12 between sex and verbal ability. Boys begin to catch up slightly in later adolescence, but girls still remain ahead into maturity. The sex difference in verbal ability after puberty appears to be a genuine phenomenon and not just a measurement artifact.

Quantitative Ability. Developmentally, the trend of sex differences in quantitative or mathematical ability is just the opposite of verbal ability, but more exaggerated. Before puberty there is no sex difference. After puberty boys begin to forge ahead of girls, and the average difference by the end of high school varies from one-fifth to two-thirds of a standard deviation in various studies. The greater interstudy variability of the sex difference in mathematical ability than in verbal ability suggests either greater factorial heterogeneity in the tests of quantitative ability or a greater role of school-related factors contributing to the difference, or both. But the difference remains, whatever the cause. It is a real difference in the sense of not being an artifact of test bias. Reversing the "gender" of the quantitative test items' contents does not wipe out the male's superiority. On the average, men perform better than women even on quantitative test items couched in terms of traditionally feminine activities such as reducing a cooking recipe by some fraction, or figuring out the yardage needed for a certain dress pattern, or estimating the price per ounce of two unequal-sized jars of facial cream.

A modest difference in groups means, of course, results in large differences in the proportions of each group that fall above a high selection cutoff. Thus we find conspicuous disparity in the proportions of males and females with exceptional mathematical talent. For example, in 1972 a mathematical talent search was conducted in all the seventh, eighth, and ninth grades of the schools in the greater Baltimore area (Fox, 1976). Nationally standardized college-level tests of mathematical aptitude and achievement were given to all pupils who scored at or above the 95th percentile on grade-level tests of math ability. Of this highly select group 44 percent were girls, but 19 percent of the boys scored higher than the *highest*-scoring girl, and the highest-scoring girl and highest-scoring boy differ almost 2 standard deviations (190 points on the SAT-M, a college-level test of math aptitude). In another large survey of all junior high school pupils in the greater Baltimore area and suburbs of Washington, D.C., who scored above the 98th percentile on standardized grade-level achievement tests, the highest SAT-M score of any girl was 650, whereas 7 percent of the boys scored above 660 (Fox, 1976). The high-scoring girls in this mathematical talent search, it should be noted, had taken as much mathematics in school as the boys, and with apparently as much interest and motivation. The mathematical superiority of males may be mainly a result of the even more clear-cut sex difference in spatial–visualization ability, which is probably a potent mediator of mathematical aptitude.

Spatial Ability.   The largest and most consistently found sex difference is spatial visualization ability, especially on spatial tests that require analysis, that is, mentally breaking up a gestalt into smaller units in ways that facilitate spatial problem solving (e.g., the Block Designs test) or visually disembedding certain target figures from a larger, more complex figural pattern (e.g., the Embedded Figures Test), or mentally rotating, or turning over, or mirror imaging a complex geometric figure to determine if it matches a given target figure presented in a different orientation.

As in the case of verbal and quantitative abilities, the sex difference in spatial ability is not established consistently until about puberty, and it persists thereafter. Generally, in studies of adolescents or adults, only about one-fourth of the females exceed the male median on various tests of spatial visualization.

The cause of the verbal versus spatial–quantitative sex difference is still an open question scientifically. The amount of recent research on this topic involving noncultural, physiological, and genetic factors in the spatial–verbal differences between the sexes suggests that most students of the problem now give little importance to the once popular but patently superficial explanations in terms of differences in cultural sex-role socialization. All the attempts that I have seen to explain the observed sex differences in certain abilities along these lines, especially differences in spatial ability, appear fatuous when critically examined in light of the relevant evidence. The currently most authoritative students of this whole literature, in reviewing the evidence on the verbal–spatial sex difference, state: "We have not been able to locate any solid research which relates any sort of social pressure or parental socialization practices in adoelscence to specific patterns of abilities" (Maccoby & Jacklin, 1973, p. 48).

The most plausible noncultural type of evidence to date involves differential rates of maturation and hormonal factors that may affect different brain functions, rather than any factors that would suggest basic differences in the structure or "wiring" of male and female brains. For example, Waber (1976) found that early maturing adolescents, regardless of sex, perform better on verbal than on spatial tests, and the late maturing show just the opposite pattern. The generally earlier sexual maturation of girls might, therefore, explain the postpuberty sex difference in verbal–spatial abilities. Maturation rate is also related to greater lateralization (left cerebral hemisphere dominance) for speech, with late maturers showing the greater lateralization, making for less interference between left-hemisphere (verbal) and right-hemisphere (spatial) functions.

Sex linkage (more exactly, X-linkage) of spatial ability has been a highly plausible theory (Bock & Kolakowski, 1973), but the main line of empirical evidence for it (namely the distinctive pattern of same-sex versus different-sex parent–child and sibling correlations for X-linked traits) is presently not as consistent or compelling as it once seemed. The X-linkage theory still remains rather speculative, and only more and better evidence will resolve the issue. Lehrke (1978) invokes X-linkage to explain the greater variability of males in a host of traits, including general intelligence (see the discussion following). X-linkage has also been invoked in theoretical attempts to explain observed race × sex interactions with spatial and other abilities (Jensen, 1971b, 1975b, 1979; Stevens & Hyde, 1978.)

Although highly plausible and entirely sound in terms of genetic theory, these efforts remain only a speculative source of testable hypotheses, still lacking the many items of evidence needed for any theory to be regarded as substantiated. Probably the most widely extrapolated and controversial, but impressively argued, biologically based theory of sex differences in socially important behaviors has been expounded by Goldberg in a fascinating book, *The Inevitability of Patriarchy* (1973).

Psychomotor Abilities.   Noble (1978, pp. 351–362) has recently reviewed much of this evidence and reports some clearly real, but often small, sex differences in various perceptual–motor skills, such as color perception, aiming, dotting, finger dexterity, inverted alphabet printing, card sorting, rotary pursuit, and discrimination reaction time. But, as Noble states, "There is no consistent ascendancy of either sex over the other on all psychomotor tasks. . . . The causes of the differences are not really understood, but socialized sex-role explanations would seem the least plausible and the most ad hoc in many cases, e.g., in learning rotary pursuit skill, in which the sex difference *increases* with practice" (p. 353).

Sex Differences in Variability.   For abilities that show a real difference between the means of the distributions of ability in males and females, the often markedly unequal proportions of the two sexes falling above (or below) some high (or low) selection cutoff on the ability scale are to be expected as a consequence of the properties of the normal curve, which approximately fits the population distribution of most abilities. But highly significant sex differences at the extremes have been found on abilities that show no appreciable mean differences between the sexes, most importantly general intelligence. In his search for intellectually gifted children, Terman (1925), for example, found more boys than girls (in the ratio of 1.4 to 1) with Stanford–Binet IQs of 140 and above, despite the fact that in the initial screening, based on teachers' nominations prior to testing, teachers had overestimated the IQs proportionally more often for girls than for boys, so that when the IQs were actually tested, almost twice as many girls as boys failed to qualify for inclusion in Terman's gifted group. The evidence is more compelling for a comparable sex difference in the "mentally retarded" range of ability, that is, IQs below 70. This evidence has been well summarized by Lehrke (1978). Males in general show more innate or constitutional defects of almost every kind, physical and behavioral, as well as greater vulnerability to infectious diseases.

These large sex differences at the extremes of the IQ distribution can be comprehended by postulating a greater variability in males than in females. It would not take as much as 1 IQ point difference between the male and female standard deviations (i.e., about 13 percent greater IQ variance for males) to account for the large male–female sex ratios found at the gifted and retarded extremes of the IQ distribution. Because the sex difference in standard deviations is very small (about 1 IQ point), it flip-flops in either direction from one study to another when samples are too small for statistical significance or are subject to selection biases. It requires a sample size of at least 985 of each sex to detect a 1 IQ point difference in standard deviations as statistically significant at the 5 percent level of confidence. Thus a mere tally of the statistical significance of the outcomes of numerous studies on this point is useless if the samples are too small to reject the null hypothesis even if, in fact, it is false. I therefore put most stock in the largest, most representative sample ever tested in a single study on a group IQ test. The sample consisted of *all* children (excluding only the deaf and blind) in the age range $10\frac{1}{2}$ to $11\frac{1}{2}$ living in Scotland in 1932—a total N of 87,000 (Scottish Council for Research in Education, 1933). The sex difference in mean IQs was not statistically significant, even with this enormous N, but the sex difference in standard deviations (about 1 IQ point difference) was highly significant, being about 12 times larger than its standard error. Random samples of 500 children of each sex were drawn from this total age group of Scottish children, to be individually tested on the Stanford–Binet. Again, there was no sex difference in mean IQ, but there was a larger (about 1 IQ point) standard deviation for boys.

The sex difference in variability of general intelligence is most likely a real phenomenon, although the evidence apparently still leaves room for somewhat differing interpretations (e.g., Kuznets & McNemar, 1940; Maccoby & Jacklin, 1974, pp. 114–120; Lehrke, 1978).

Sex Bias in Predictive Validity

Differential Validity. Probably because the sex differences in tests of general ability and scholastic aptitude are so unimpressive, there is a dearth of studies of the differential predictive validity of various tests by sex or of the inequality of regressions of criterion measures on test scores. The few published studies virtually all involve test validity for predicting grades in college. I have come across no predictive validity studies involving sex differences at the grade school level, although there are such data in existence, much of it already computerized, on which such studies could easily be done.

I have found no studies that report *lower* validity coefficients for women than for men in predicting college grades. If anything, the difference is in the opposite direction. Both Seashore (1962) and Stanley (1967) came to this conclusion on the basis of very large surveys, reporting an average difference of about 0.10 in the validity coefficients obtained in male and female college samples. Stanley characterizes the usual explanation for the apparently greater predictability of female's academic performance as follows:

> Girls are reputed to be more conscientious students than boys, working more nearly in accordance with their basic abilities and skills. They are thought to be more attentive, meticulous, and compliant students than are boys, and hence less likely to underachieve academically. These differential characteristics, if really present, should cause girls' Scholastic Aptitude Test (SAT) scores to correlate higher with their grades in school than do boys' scores with their grades.   (1967, p. 49)

And this is exactly what Stanley found for freshman grades over a six-year period in thirteen predominantly white coeducational colleges in the South. The generalization did not hold up in three predominantly black colleges, in which SAT validities were about the same for men and women.

Though there can be no doubt of the statistical significance of these findings, considerable doubt as to their generality is raised in a study by Hewitt and Goldman (1975) involving large representative samples of men and women students in four highly selective liberal arts colleges of the University of California. Hewitt and Goldman found no consistent or significant sex difference in the predictive validites of the SAT. The validity coefficients are also about 0.10 *lower* than those found by Stanley, probably because of the greater restriction of range of SAT scores in the more selective college samples. The high selectivity of the colleges in their study may contain the clue to the difference between Hewitt and Goldman's findings and those of Seashore and Stanley, which were based on academically less selective colleges including a number of two-year junior colleges.

What Seashore and Stanley did not take into account in their analyses is the sex difference in the types of courses taken by men and women. If men and women are enrolled in different proportions in different curricula having different academic standards for assigning grades, the predictive validities of the SAT for men and women could be quite different. For the sex comparison of validities to be more than trivial, one must demonstrate either equal enrollments of men and women across all courses *or* equal bivariate frequency distributions of SAT scores and grades in every course. Other studies show that neither of these conditions prevails in most large coeducational colleges. My hunch is that the bivariate distributions of SAT and grades are much less uniform through-out the various courses in the colleges surveyed by Stanley than in those examined by Hewitt and Goldman, and thus the Stanley finding is essentially a within-college sampling artifact. The range of SAT scores is probably considerably smaller in the math and science courses more frequently taken by men than in the humanities and arts courses, with their higher proportion of women, and this particular difference in range is probably greater in the less selective colleges. It is the degree of restriction of range on the SAT in the courses in which students actually earn their grades that is the determiner of sex differences in SAT validity coefficients, so that mere demonstration of equality of variances on the SAT for *all* men and women students enrolled in the college is not a crucial item of information. Until the predictive validity of the SAT is determined separately for men and women *within* the same courses (and corrected for differences in range *within* courses), the notion that the sexes differ in academic predictability must be regarded as merely an untested hypothesis. In terms of differential test validity by sex, the null hypothesis has really not been challenged.

Inequality of Regressions. The regressions of overall college grade-point average (GPA) on SAT scores have been compared for men and women in ten coeducational colleges (Linn, 1973). In all ten colleges the regression equation for males (and con-sequently also the common regression line for males and females combined) *under*esti-mates the GPA of female students. This is all *intercept bias;* the slopes of the males' and females' regression lines do not differ significantly. That is, for any given score on the SAT, female college students, on the average, earn a higher GPA than is earned by male students. The amount of *under*prediction of female GPA as measured in standard devia-tion (σ) units is considerable, ranging from 0.24σ to 0.98σ in the ten colleges, with a mean of 0.55σ. Men and women students show considerably greater differences in GPA than in SAT scores. Thus it appears that the SAT is a seriously biased predictor, *under*-estimating women's academic potential and *over*estimating men's, when the common regression equation is used for predicting college grades. This finding has often been "explained" in terms of females' being academic "overachievers" compared with men with the same academic aptitude.

The fact is, however, that this apparent sex bias of the SAT is most probably entirely illusory, a mere artifact of the failure to control for differences in the difficulty levels and grading standards of the many college courses that enroll markedly disproportionate numbers of men and women. Hewitt and Goldman (1975) used the SAT to predict GPAs of more than 13,000 students in four major universities. The usual intercept bias clearly appeared when the regressions were compared for men and women. But, when sex differences in choice of major field were statistically controlled, the sex difference in regression intercepts was eliminated or drastically reduced. When major field is taken into account, the male–female intercept difference accounts for only 0.1 percent to 0.5 percent of the total variance in GPA in the four colleges, with an average of 0.37 percent that, although statistically significant, is a practically trivial amount of variance. Thus much if not most of the apparent "overachievement" of college women is accounted for by sex differences in major field choice.

Sex Bias in Selection.   Even when test bias itself is completely ruled out, there may still appear to be a sex bias in selection. No general statement is justified concerning these cases, as the determining circumstances differ in every institution. Therefore each case must be investigated in its own right. The greatest risk is that investigators often may be too unsophisticated in complex data analysis to avoid easy deception by the surface-level appearance of the data, which can be riddled with subtle artifacts.

A beautiful case study of such deceptive first appearances is presented by Bickel, Hammel, and O'Connell (1975) in the case of apparent sex bias in graduate admissions at the University of California in Berkeley. These authors show that out of 4,321 female and 8,442 male applicants for graduate study at Berkeley in fall 1973, about 44 percent of the males and 35 percent of the females were actually admitted—a *prima facie* case of discrimination against women, assuming that men and women applicants have equal Graduate Record Examination scores and undergraduate GPAs, which are the main criteria for selection. But then Bickel et al. methodically proceed, through a series of proper analyses, to demonstrate that, in fact, there is evidence of a small but statistically significant selection bias in *favor* of women! They point out that the chances of getting into a graduate program are strongly associated with the tendency of men and women to apply for admission to different departments in different proportions. A higher proportion of women than of men apply to departments that are hard to get into (for either men *or* women), and a lower proportion of women than of men apply to departments that are easy to get into, and this phenomenon is more pronounced in departments with the largest numbers of applicants. These tend to be the departments in which students take longer to complete their graduate work, thereby leaving fewer openings in any given year for new students, and hence a smaller proportion of each year's applicants can be admitted than in less "crowded" departments. *Within* departments, selection bias actually tends slightly to favor women (possibly because of the affirmative action policy adopted by the university), whereas the overall *campuswide* selection ratios for men and women misleadingly give the appearance of sex bias favoring men. Would-be investigators of sex bias in institutional settings will surely profit from thorough study of the exemplary didactic article by Bickel et al. (1975).

Sex × Item Interaction

When a test is made up intentionally to minimize the overall sex difference in total score by counterbalancing item difficulties that favor either sex, we should naturally expect to find a significant sex × item interaction, as explained in Chapters 9 (pp. 432–436) and 11 (pp. 553–558). Also, if the counterbalancing of items is successful, we should expect the variance contributed by the overall mean sex difference to be very small relative to the sex × item interaction variance.

Sex × Item Interaction in WISC. This is precisely what was found for the Wechsler Intelligence Scale for Children. These data are described in Chapter 11 (pp. 553–556). Although the sex × item interaction is statistically significant, it is minute relative to the individual differences variance. The correlation between the item p values (percentage passing) for same-age boys and girls on 161 items of the WISC (omitting the Digit Span and Coding subtests, because they do not lend themselves to determination of p values) is .98 for whites and .97 for blacks. What this means is that the differences between male and female item p values are quite small, so that counterbalancing items results in no large differences in the rank order of the items' p values for boys and girls. Also, the GD/I ratio (i.e., the F for sex divided by the F for the sex × item interaction; see Chapter 11, p. 561) is less than 1 for every subtest at every age level (except Block Design at age 6). This means that whatever little sex difference there is on any subtest, or on Full Scale IQ, could be due to the imperfect counterbalancing of the items rather than represent any real sex difference. When the GD/I ratio is less than 1, the elimination of just a few items from the whole test could completely eliminate or reverse the sex difference in the overall mean test score.

Contrast between Sex and Race Item Interaction. The question may be raised as to why it should not be possible to eliminate the white–black racial differences on our standard IQ tests in the same way that sex differences are eliminated or minimized. The answer is twofold.

1. The race × item interaction is scarcely greater than the sex × item interaction *within* each racial group, but the average racial difference in item p values is very much greater than the average sex difference in p values. That is, the overall mean sex difference is very small relative to the sex × item interaction, whereas the overall mean race difference is very large relative to the race × item interaction, and this merely reflects the fact that the *direction* of the racial groups' difference is consistently the same on every item in the whole test. (The few exceptions always involve items with extremely high or extremely low p values; these item discriminations at the two extremes of difficulty are usually statistically unreliable and, in any case, contribute the least to the total variance in test scores.) This is true not only for the finally selected items in the test (in which the rather small sex differences in item p values have been counterbalanced) but also for the entire pool of trial test items from which the final selections are made or for tests in which item selection did not take sex or race into account.

2. So far, no one has been able to identify or make up a large and diverse pool of test items that measure g (i.e., relation eduction) but do not show significant racial differences or show racial differences going in both directions so as to permit racial counterbalancing in the item selections for the final test. All attempts to do this have proved unsuccessful. At most, the usual race difference is only slightly reduced, rather than eliminated or reversed, by such attempts, and always at a great loss in reliability and predictive validity.

Sex × Item Interactions in the SAT.   Strassberg, Rosenberg, and Donlon (1975) examined the SAT-V and SAT-M for items that showed significant sex differences in difficulty. Out of the ninety items of the SAT-V, twelve items showed a significant sex difference (nine in favor of males, three in favor of females); and out of the sixty items of the SAT–M, seven items showed a significant sex difference (five in favor of males, two in favor of females). Inspection of these items revealed no obvious explanation for the sex differences. The Educational Testing Service, the publisher of the Scholastic Aptitude Test, has undertaken a comparison of the SAT item characteristic curves (ICC) for men and women, but the results are not yet available (Wild & Dwyer, 1978, p. 17). The ICC analysis should reveal the full extent of sex bias at the item level.

Peabody Picture Vocabulary Test.   The sex × item interaction in the PPVT is minimal, as indicated by the rank order correlation between the item p values of boys and girls over the 150 items of the PPVT. These correlations (corrected for attenuation) are .988, .992, and .983 in large samples of white, Mexican–American, and black school children, respectively (Jensen, 1974a).

Raven Matrices.   The same analyses (as for the PPVT) were performed on Raven's Colored Progressive Matrices, which gave correlations (corrected for attenuation) between the item p values of boys and girls of .996, .998, and 1.00 for whites, Mexican–Americans, and blacks, respectively (Jensen, 1974a). It should be noted that neither sex nor race were considered in the construction or standardization of the Raven matrices. Yet it shows less sex bias than any other standardized test in terms of sex × item interaction. (The same thing may be said for race bias in the Raven.) This is probably because the Raven is such a relatively nonscholastic- and noncultural-content-loaded test; it measures virtually nothing other than relation eduction, the purest form of Spearman's g.

Broader Aspects of Sex Bias

Males and females undoubtedly differ in more ways, physically and psychologically, than have yet been substantiated by research. The only personality difference between the sexes that is now virtually beyond scientific dispute is the male's greater aggressiveness, in all its forms (Maccoby & Jacklin, 1974, Ch. 7). This difference and probably other as yet less well-established basic personality differences, in addition to certain unquestioned physical differences (particularly in sheer muscular strength), surely must interact with "ideal" sex ratio, in terms of the average sex differences and the amount of overlap in the various traits most relevant to successful performance in the particular occupation.

With few exceptions, we have no idea what this sex ratio should be for most occupations or careers. What can be said with considerable assurance from the research on sex differences in abilities is that, as far as *abilities* are concerned, the "ideal" sex ratio for the vast majority of occupations in modern industrial societies is much closer to 1 than the actual sex ratios observed in various occupations today, making allowance for the different overall employment rates of males and females. The causes of the great disparities in sex ratios we see in most occupations and educational curricula are much more a result of traditional sociocultural sex-role modeling and typecasting of males and females for different vocational aspirations than a result of basic differences in cognitive abilities. Strongly ingrained attitudes and self-acceptance of different sex roles in the world of work are now far more important factors in maintaining the status quo of educational and occupational sex ratios than overt, externally imposed sex discrimination per se.

The use of psychological tests in educational and occupational selection and vocational counseling should, if anything, help to overcome the traditional but artificial inequality of sexes in various job opportunities and in gaining the specific training needed for them. The great variation in sex ratios for many occupations in different countries shows how circumstantially artificial these sex ratios are. For example, in the United States only about 9 percent of physicians and dentists are women, whereas in the Soviet Union the figure is close to 50 percent.

Vocational Interest Inventories. The one type of psychological "test" that may well be the most sex biased is vocational interest inventories, when these have been standardized on the *past or present* distribution of males and females in various occupations. These vocational interest inventories are based on the empirically demonstrated fact that, given adequate ability and training, a person whose pattern of interests matches the pattern of persons who are successful in a particular occupation is more likely to succeed in that occupation and to be happy in it than is a person with a markedly different pattern of interests. Often the interests questioned seem vocationally neutral, with no obvious relationship to the occupation for which they are keyed. But expression of the interest in fact discriminates reliably between "successful" and "unsuccessful" persons in the particular occupation. There may be such interest questions as "Would you prefer to (a) play golf (b) play tennis, (c) go hiking, (d) go swimming?" or "Would you prefer going to (a) a symphony concert, (b) a good movie, (c) a baseball game, (d) a dinner party?"

There is nothing wrong with this type of questionnaire, in principle. The only trouble is that the older interest inventories on the market were devised using criterion groups comprised mostly or entirely of men in certain occupations. It seems most unlikely that the interest patterns of successful men and successful women in a given occupation will not differ. Therefore, the use of current standard occupational interest inventories in vocational counseling for females might very well steer many females away from pursuing careers in which they could be successful. The vocational interest inventories need to be reworked, taking proper account of sex. Recommendations along these lines are provided in a set of *Guidelines for Assessing Sex Bias and Sex Fairness in Career Interest Inventories* issued by the Career Education Program of the National Institute of Education in Washington, D.C.

SUMMARY

Sex difference in measured mental abilities is a small-magnitude phenomenon. Sex differences in test scores are apparently complexly determined, which makes for a great amount of sampling variation and inconsistency of results among studies that are not based on especially large and representative samples. However, the total evidence permits several generalizations that can be made with considerable confidence.

Some intelligence tests have been deliberately constructed to minimize or eliminate a sex difference in IQ by eliminating or balancing items that significantly favor either sex. Such tests, of course, cannot answer the question of sex differences in ability. However, examination of tests that were not constructed with reference to sex, along with factor analyses of test batteries that permit the comparison of males and females on factor scores, indicate that the sexes do not differ in *g,* the general intelligence factor. Sex differences on single items or on homogenous subtests are differences in item-specific characteristics or in group factors uncorrelated with *g.* But there is no evidence of a mean sex difference in *g.* However, there appears to be a true difference (of about 1 IQ point) in the standard deviation of IQ, with males showing the greater variability. This fact accounts for the generally observed greater frequencies of males in the extreme upper and lower ranges of the IQ distribution.

The two types of ability (independent of *g*) that consistently show a significant sex difference (in favor of males) that cannot be attributed to test bias are analytic spatial–visualization ability and mathematical or quantitative reasoning ability. These two abilities seem to be closely linked, and the observed sex difference may be due to some single factor common to both spatial and quantitative abilities. Various hypotheses of these differences have been propounded, but none has gained unequivocal empirical support or general acceptance by students of sex differences. In recent years, hypotheses involving biological factors associated with sex differences have shown ascendance over explanations invoking purely cultural and psychological factors in sex-role socialization.

As for sex bias in mental tests, it seems to be a rare, even nonexistent, phenomenon in properly controlled studies. Studies of sex bias are largely concentrated on the predictive validity of college aptitude tests. Validity coefficients, that is, the correlations of aptitude test scores with college grade-point averages (GPA), are most often slightly higher (by about 0.10) for women than for men, but this difference is most probably an artifact of differences in the types of courses taken by men and women. Studies that control for major field find negligible male–female differences in tests' predictive validity.

When the regressions of GPA on test scores are compared for men and women, there is frequently found to be *intercept* bias; that is, the common regression line *under*estimates the GPA of females and *over*estimates the GPA of males. This gives the appearance of test bias against females. Again, however, this bias is an artifact of the different courses enrolled in by men and women. The intercept bias is diminished to negligible magnitude when regressions are compared for men and women in the same majors. A given test score does not predict the same GPA in different fields of study, and, where various fields enroll men and women in different proportions, systematic biases are introduced into the regressions of GPA on test scores. A larger proportion of women tend to enroll in those courses with somewhat "easier" grading standards, which causes their GPAs to be *under*predicted when the prediction is based on either the male or the common regression equation. It is recommended that separate regression equations be used for men and women or that major field be taken into consideration, in college selection.

Because sex differences in mental abilities are exceedingly small compared with the relatively great differences in the representation of males and females in various types of educational programs and occupations, it is suggested that the use of tests in selection should promote greater equality of the sexes for educational and occupational opportunities.

Chapter 14

Culture-reduced Tests and Techniques

One could conceivably construct a test of general mental ability that would have a high degree of validity for all the siblings in one family but that would yield random scores close to the chance guessing level for all other persons attempting the test. The content of the test items could be drawn exclusively from the particular family's private experiences, their private stories, jokes, anecdotes, and family secrets, their uncomplimentary nicknames for relatives and neighbors never uttered outside the immediate family, their idiosyncratic "bathroom words," and the like. Scores on such a test might well reflect differences in mental "brightness" among all the children within the particular family; but they would tell us next to nothing about the brightness of the children in any other family, except perhaps the children of the next-door neighbors, who might have picked up a bit of the item content through their close association and thereby score a little better than chance.

At the other extreme, one might imagine a test that could validly rank order some important aspects of mental ability of all primates, both between and within species and subspecies, including *Homo sapiens*. Graded variations of discrimination learning-set tasks and of detour and oddity problems might well serve this purpose.

Thus we have drawn the two theoretical extremes of a continuum extending from the most to the least "culturally specific" tests. Presumably our existing standard mental tests can be ordered along this hypothetical continuum, of course with none of them anywhere near approaching either extreme. There is no definite point on the continuum that divides "culture-loaded" from "culture-free" tests. As we move in one direction along the continuum, tests become more "culture specific," and, as we move in the opposite direction, they become more "culture reduced." So-called cross-cultural tests are not an isolated category of tests; they are merely tests that lie further in the "culture-reduced" direction than some other tests. A simple way to tell whether a given test item lies further along the continuum in the culture-reduced than in the culture-specific direction is to ask "Would Archimedes (287–212 B.C.) and Plato (427–347 B.C.) be likely to pass this item, even if suitably translated?" I imagine they would have little trouble with Raven's matrices or the WAIS Block Designs, but I figure they could not possibly get more than four out of the twenty-nine WAIS Information items right. They could no doubt answer "Who wrote the *Iliad?*" (with a p value of 21 percent in the American standardization group) but not "What are the colors of the American flag?" (p value of 100 percent)!

Operationally, we can think of the degree of "culture reducedness" of a test in terms of the "cultural distance" over which a test maintains substantially the same psychometric properties of reliability, validity, item–total score correlation, and rank order of item difficulties. Some tests maintain their essential psychometric properties over a much wider cultural distance than others, and to the extent that they do so they are referred to as "culture reduced." Certain culture-reduced tests, such as Raven's Progressive Matrices and Cattell's Culture Fair Test of *g,* have at least shown *equal* average scores for groups of people of remotely different cultures and unequal scores of people of the same culture and high loadings on a "fluid" *g* factor *within* two or more different cultures. Such tests apparently span greater cultural distances than do tests that involve language and specific informational content and scholastic skills.

In reality the picture is still more complicated than I have depicted in terms of a single linear continuum going from least to most culture reduced. "Cultural distance" is multidimensional, and so *all* the properties of a particular test may not span any given cultural distance. A verbal test, for example, may be accurately translated into the language of a different culture and therefore it would span the cultural distance in terms of language, but the translated words may have quite different connotations in a different cultural context that might affect item difficulties and item validities, and therefore the test would fail to span the cultural distance at the conceptual level. Or, if speed of response affects the scores, and speed of work is part of the cultural tradition in one population but not in another, the test may fail to span the cultural distance for that reason, even though it may be a nonlanguage test or a language test with perfect translation at both the denotative and connotative levels.

Obviously, the wider the multidimensional cultural distance, the more complex and intractible is the problem of cross-cultural testing. Constructing a single test that maintains all its essential psychometric properties when administered to Arctic Eskimos and Kalahari Bushmen may or may not be possible, but a detailed consideration of the many problems introduced by such a possibility is far beyond the scope of this book. Readers interested in the variety of theoretical approaches and empirical studies in such cross-cultural testing will find an excellent introduction in several other books (Biesheuvel, 1969; Brislin, Lonner, & Thorndike, 1974; Cole, Gay, Glick, & Sharpe, 1971; Cronbach & Drenth, 1972; Schwartz & Krug, 1972).

Cross-cultural Predictive versus Construct Validity

An important distinction that conceptually divides the problem of cross-cultural testing to make it somewhat more tractable is to be clear about whether one's purpose in testing involves *predictive* validity or *construct* validity. If the problems of predictive validity increase arithmetically as a function of cultural distance, the problems of construct validity increase geometrically. Many arguments would be spared if this distinction were brought forth more clearly. A quite highly culture-specific test may derive much of its validity for predicting a particular criterion from its cultural specificity per se. A culture-specific test involving knowledge of English grammar, spelling, punctuation, and musical terminology may well be a good predictor of success as a copy editor of an English-language music magazine, regardless of the cultural and language backgrounds of the persons taking the test. Many existing tests will have adequate cross-cultural validity for many purposes in this predictive sense. For some other educational or occupational criteria, tests may have to be revamped, or entirely new tests constructed, to achieve adequate cross-cultural predictive validity. In any case, demonstrating useful cross-cultural validity for a particular educational or occupational criterion is invariably much easier than establishing a test's construct validity across remote cultures. Establishing the cross-cultural validity of a psychological construct, such as *g,* involves much more than simply revamping an existing test. It calls for a whole program of research.

We may gain some insight into the factors that determine the cultural distance that a test can span by looking at some of the ways that have been proposed for constructing culture-reduced tests.

Ways of Reducing the Culture Loading of Tests

Tests that are generally regarded as more or less culture loaded usually differ in some of the following ways:

Culture Loaded	*Culture Reduced*
Paper-and-pencil tests	Performance tests
Printed instructions	Oral instructions
Oral instructions	Pantomime instructions
No preliminary practice	Preliminary practice items
Reading required	Purely pictorial
Pictorial (objects)	Abstract figural
Written response	Oral response
Separate answer sheet	Answers written on test itself
Language	Nonlanguage
Speed tests	Power tests
Verbal content	Nonverbal content
Specific factual knowledge	Abstract reasoning
Scholastic skills	Nonscholastic skills
Recall of past-learned information	Solving novel problems
Content graded from familiar to rare	All item content highly familiar
Difficulty based on rarity of content	Difficulty based on *complexity* of relation eduction

These "dimensions" on which tests differ all seem quite obvious, but it cannot be taken for granted that changing a test on any one or a combination of these dimensions will necessarily make the test less culturally biased for any particular cultural group or for predicting any particular criterion. These questions must be answered empirically for each case. In general, however, the culture-reduced test features indicated here tend to widen the cultural distance over which a test will maintain its psychometric properties and practical usefulness.

Universality of Fundaments. Spearman's principle of "the indifference of the indicator" originally emphasized the importance of constructing test items out of *fundaments* that are equally familiar to all persons on whom the test is to be used. The fundaments constitute the elemental content of the test items, and it should be possible to demonstrate empirically that no significant part of the variance in test scores is attributable to individual differences in ability to recognize or distinguish the fundaments per se. The verbal analogy item

> *Cat* is to *kitten* as *dog* is to   *bark   big   chase   fight   puppy   run.*

assumes that all these words (i.e., the fundaments) are familiar to all persons taking the test and that the only source of true-score variance arises from individual differences in ability for relation eduction. The indicated method for achieving a more culture-reduced test, according to Spearman, therefore, is to keep the fundaments as universally familiar as possible while preserving the essential element of relation eduction or analogical reasoning. Cultures may also differ in their emphasis on analogical reasoning, in which case a test based on this form of item is problematic in construct bias, even when all the fundaments entering into the analogies or other relations are universally familiar.

Cattell (1940) has suggested a list of highly, but not absolutely, universal fundaments that would span nearly all cultures and provide a common basis on which operations of reasoning could be performed:

Common Objects	*Common Processes*
The human body and its parts	Breathing, choking, coughing, sneezing
Footprints, etc.	Eating, drinking, defecating, urinating
Trees (except for Eskimos)	Sleeping
Four-legged animals	Birth and death
Earth and sky	Running, walking, climbing, jumping
Clouds, sun, moon, stars, lightning	Striking, stroking
Fire and smoke	Sensing: seeing, hearing, smelling,
Water and its transformations	tasting, touching
Parents and children (growth)	Emotional experiences: anger, fear, grief,
	etc.

Cattell later abandoned this approach in favor of using abstract figural material as a basis for relation eduction—figures made up of universally recognized elements such as dots, lines, curves, circles, squares, triangles, shaded versus unshaded areas, and so on. Cattell (1971a, p. 23) believes that it is desirable that the fundaments should not only be nonverbal and nonpictorial, but that they should not even possess names. This principle has been applied to a large extent in the construction of Cattell's own Culture Fair Test of *g*, which is reviewed later in this chapter. The same principle applies to Raven's Progressive Matrices. The figural elements in the Cattell and Raven tests have been analyzed from the standpoint of the purely topological concepts employed in these tests. They all can be found in the designs on pottery, baskets, carvings, face paintings, body paintings, blankets, and clothing of a majority of primitive cultures (Kidd & Rivoire, 1965).

The elimination of verbal items usually lowers a test's predictive validity when the criterion involves verbal ability, such as scholastic performance. In such cases, cross-cultural tests are more effective if they include verbal items that are appropriately translated and standardized within the particular culture. Translation of a test from one language to another is risky and should always be done in connection with proper psychometric equating methods. Words and concepts do not all lend themselves to equivalent meanings, familiarity, connotation, or difficulty level when translated into the language of another culture. Even some of the items of the Peabody Picture Vocabulary Test, standardized in Tennessee, are grossly inappropriate when used in London, England. We have found some PPVT items that differ more than fifty places in the rank order of item difficulties from London to California school children of the same age and general ability. Words like *bronco, thermos,* and *caboose,* for example, are extremely more "difficult" in the English population than in the United States.

The cross-cultural equating of vocabulary and other verbal items when translated is accomplished by retaining only those items (or substituting new items) that maintain the same absolute difficulty level (*p* values) in both cultures, or the same rank order of difficulty, and have the same item × total score correlations in both cultures. In other words, the translated items may be regarded as equivalent forms. When this procedure has been applied to translated tests, it has been found that the tests retain virtually the same psychometric properties of reliability and predictive validity in their respective language groups. A good example of the application of such procedures is found in the development of a Spanish version of the Scholastic Aptitude Test (SAT) (Angoff & Modu, 1973). Although such psychometric equating of translated and adapted tests across different language groups results in psychometrically equivalent forms of the test *within* each language, one should not be under the illusion that such psychometrically equated tests also permit meaningful comparisons of the average ability level *across* groups. This becomes possible, however, if both tests include a number of "anchor" items that independent evidence leads one to believe are equally fair and appropriate measures of the whole test's first principal component in both language groups. But that is a tall order and is seldom striven for in producing psychometrically equated tests. Their purpose usually is merely to provide comparable predictive validity within each language group rather than to make absolute comparisons of the groups in the construct measured by the tests.

These cautions about translated tests should not be misconstrued to imply that simple translation of test items has drastic effects on item biases as reflected in the groups × items interaction. Thorndike (1973-1974) reports a study involving the simple translation of a thirty-item reading comprehension test from English into seven other languages. The test was given in the national language to age-matched school children in eleven different countries. The single-item difficulties of the thirty items were intercorrelated among the eleven countries. The fifty-five resulting correlation coefficients ranged from 0.80 (France × Germany) to 0.98 (England × Scotland), with a mean of 0.88. The average correlation, excluding pairs of countries in which the same language is spoken, was 0.86. It can be seen that even the subtleties of a reading comprehension test survive translation quite well and that the items maintain highly similar relative difficulties across different language and national groups. Thorndike notes that the difficulty of a reading comprehension test item lies "not in the verbiage or syntax of a specific language, but in the structure of ideas with which the item deals. At age 13, when these youngsters were tested, reading is no longer—to any substantial degree—a decoding problem, these results would seem to say. It is a thinking problem" (p. 145).

Rarity versus Complexity. The two main dimensions along which test items vary in difficulty are *rarity* and *complexity*. Rarity refers to the general frequency of occurrence or exposure of the item's fundaments. (For example, the words *pigeon* and *culver* in a vocabulary test differ in difficulty, that is, percentage passing, solely because of the difference in the frequency of their usage in our language.) Complexity refers to the amount of mental manipulation of the fundaments required to produce the correct response. Most tests of vocabulary and general information are good examples of increasing item difficulty along the rarity dimension. Tests involving figure analogies, matrices, block designs, arithmetic operations, and the like are examples of increasing item difficulty along the complexity dimension. Performances on both types of tests are highly correlated within a culturally homogeneous population. But the rarity dimension is an exceedingly poor option for item selection in the development of cross-cultural tests. Where cultural differences are even suspected among the groups to be tested, tests based on the rarity principle should be assiduously eschewed. I find a good many of the items in some of our most widely used and up-to-date standardized tests highly offensive from this standpoint. One need not look far to find such examples. The Peabody Picture Vocabulary Test is based entirely on the rarity principle, as are the Information and Vocabulary subtests of the Wechsler scales. I find it impossible to justify their continued use even within a culturally homogeneous population. The presence of sheer rarity items in present-day intelligence tests seems as anachronistic as isinglass windows in a modern automobile. Also, the poor ''face validity'' of items based on the rarity principle makes the tests that include such items easy targets for public ridicule. Such items are quite unnecessary for the measurement of g, if that is one's aim. However, this does not imply that specialized tests of information and vocabulary may not have very high predictive validity for certain criteria. Vocabulary is perhaps the single best measure of V, the verbal ability factor, after g is partialled out; and V is an important source of variance in scholastic performance and in some occupations.

Instructions and Procedures.   The first essential of culture fair testing is to ensure that all persons fully understand the requirements of each type of task involved in the test. This cannot be emphasized strongly enough, especially for group-administered tests. It is too often assumed that what were putatively clear and simple instructions for the standardization group will be clear and simple for some other group. When it comes to test instructions, nothing should be taken for granted. I have been surprised more often than not by the apparent difficulty that some subjects have in understanding what they are supposed to do in the face of certain classes of test items, even after being given seemingly clear and simple instructions. Moreover, the subject's eager assent when asked if he or she fully understands the instructions is a poor indicator of his or her actual understanding. It is a defective testing procedure indeed that imposes greater cognitive demands on understanding the instructions than on working the test items themselves.

The best way to ensure understanding of the task demands is to use a series of practice items that begin with the easiest possible exemplars of the type of item in the test proper. The practice items and their correct answers can be explained verbally or by pantomine, accompanied by enlarged visual displays of the practice items. The first half-dozen or so items in the test can incorporate all the essential task requirements of later items but can be made so simple that failures on the first few items may be viewed as an indicator of failure to understand the task requirements. Separate scores based on just these easiest items at the beginning of the test (or each section of new item types) should be recorded for all subjects as a means of spotting the low scorers on the whole test who might not have understood the instructions.

If equivalent forms of the test are available, it is desirable to use one form strictly for practice and instruction.

Separate answer sheets, which facilitate machine scoring, can be a serious impediment for persons who are not accustomed to using them. Their extra demands for comprehension, attention, and clerical accuracy can add an extraneous source of individual differences that the test per se is not intended to measure. Separate answer sheets should not be used with persons who have not had preliminary practice with them.

The importance of a speed factor in testing has been greatly exaggerated as a source of cultural differences. However, unless a speed factor is considered an integral aspect of the test's construct validity or predictive validity, there is no good reason for not trying to minimize it in testing culturally heterogeneous groups. Most culture-reduced tests are either untimed or have liberal time limits. A notable exception is the Cattell Culture Fair Test. My own experience with this test leads me to believe its relatively few items of each type and its short time limits (about three minutes) for each section of the test constitute its main weakness, especially when it is used with so-called culturally disadvantaged children. However, it can be given without time limit and the test manual provides norms for unspeeded administration, but these seem rather dubious in terms of the size and representativeness of the samples.

Some low-scoring subjects finish a test before many of the high-scoring subjects. This has led some commentators to suggest that the subjects are rushing through the test, marking their answer sheets haphazardly, to escape as quickly as possible from a discomforting situation. In most cases, however, this superficial explanation is belied by the fact that the low-scoring fast-finishers show as high internal consistency reliability and retest reliability as anyone else. Moreover, they make the very same errors on retest, which indicates that their answers are not really haphazard. It appears that they are able to answer more quickly (though often erroneously) because their information processing is superficial. A correct response to some of the Raven matrices items, for example, requires the simultaneous mental manipulation of three or four different fundaments, which takes some time. The easier and much less time-consuming manipulation of only one or two of these fundaments will dependably lead to selection of one of the error distractors, and that is what we generally see in the cognitively less able subjects. The erroneous answers on the Raven are every bit as explainable in terms of the cognitive processing that led to them as are the correct answers. We find that encouraging subjects to take more time than they normally need to finish the test at their own pace, however, results in no appreciable gain in total score. Superficial but erroneous solutions are usually not recognized as such by the subject himself.

Initial Selection and Editing of Items.   To hear some test critics, one would think that there is a conspiracy among test constructors and publishers to produce tests that are as biased as possible against certain minority groups. Nothing could be further from the truth. No professional psychometrician has ever tried to make a biased test, and in recent years, especially, the major test publishers have taken considerable pains to ensure selection of culturally fair items in constructing ability and achievement tests. It is now routine practice for test publishers to hire item writers from various minority groups to produce test items that, in their judgment, will be fair and appropriate in terms of the cultural background of the particular minority group with which they have personal familiarity.

All test items in the major tests published today, for example, by the Educational Testing Service, the Psychological Corporation, the Iowa Testing Program, the American College Testing Program, and others, are submitted to panels of minority psychologists, sociologists, anthropologists, and educators for critical scrutiny. Items that may seem in any way culturally biased with respect to any ethnic minority, or that may be perceived as offensive by any segment of the population, are eliminated even before the tryouts of the items to determine their statistical and psychometric suitability in representative samples of the population for which the test is intended.

   Ethnic and Socioeconomic Cultural Factors Generally Overrated.   It was noted in Chapters 10 and 11 that, when tests that differ quite widely along the culture-reduced continuum are taken by various native-born ethnic minorities and different socioeconomic groups, there is remarkably little variation in any group's mean score, in relation to majority norms, across the more and less culture-reduced tests. Even tests constructed with little or no consideration for culture reduction show highly comparable reliability and validity for minority and majority groups alike. These facts are often interpreted to mean that even the most culture-reduced tests we possess are still, in some mysterious way, as culture biased for certain minorities as any of our much less culture-reduced tests. The counterinterpretation, which is much more parsimoniously in accord with the total body of evidence on this topic, is that practically all our present standardized tests, culture reduced or not, span as wide or wider a range of cultural distance as is found among any native-born, English-speaking racial and socioeconomic groups within the United States today. The differences between the ordinary culture-loaded tests and the more culture-reduced tests, therefore, show up markedly only in foreign language groups and across quite remote cultures. One simple example: recent immigrant Chinese children from Hong Kong, tested after about six months of school attendance in California, score markedly lower than native-born Oriental children on the usual IQ and achievement tests, but on the Lorge–Thorndike Nonverbal IQ, Raven's matrices, and Figure Copying Tests they score on a par with American-born Orientals and slightly above native-born whites in the same city. In this case the culture-reduced tests make a big difference. Within two to three years of school attendance the immigrant children perform on a par with their native-born peers on the verbal culture-loaded tests as well. Eskimos inhabiting the icy wastes above the Artic circle score at or above white Scottish and white Canadian norms on Raven's matrices, Piagetian tests, and the Embedded Figures Test (Berry, 1966; MacArthur, 1968, 1969). These Eskimos, of course, would be at almost a total loss on our usual culture-loaded tests. This shows that some of our culture-reduced tests were capable of spanning quite remote cultural distances. The fact that ordinary tests and culture-reduced tests make no difference when applied to various segments of the U.S. population, provided that they are English-speaking native-born, can mean only that these groups do not differ culturally in ways that interact with mental tests of varying degrees of culture reducedness.

   To the extent that tests are culture loaded and depend on specific items of acquired information, they seem to contaminate to some degree the most *g*-loaded, relation-eduction aspect of the test score variance. Groups that differ primarily on this factor show a slightly greater mean difference in scores when performance is made *less* dependent on the specific knowledge involved in each test item. Gentile (1968) gave a verbal analogies test to high-, middle-, and low-SES groups of junior high school students under two conditions: (1) with definitions (both oral and printed) given for each of the specific words used in each verbal analogy item and (2) with no definition given. One of the ten analogy items was

> *Fire* is to *ashes* as   (a) *tree* is to *leaves*.
>   (b) *winter* is to *ice*.
>   (c) *Christmas* is to *holly*.
>   (d) *event* is to *memories*.

Providing definitions made the test significantly easier for all three SES groups, but it also *increased* the differences between the groups slightly but nonsignificantly. The higher on the SES scale students were, the more that providing definitions helped to improve their performance. Gentile concluded that definition deficiencies in analogy tests cannot be considered primarily responsible for the poor performance of students of lower socioeconomic standing.

Arvey and Mussio (reported in Arvey, 1972) gave a verbal analogy test to 266 female clerical Civil Service employees divided into "high" and "low" socioeconomic groups on the basis of father's education and a questionnaire concerning cultural experiences. The words used in the analogies were common, familiar, and simple, such as

> *Cat* is to *dog* as *kitten* is to   *tiger   puppy   wolf   rat   animals*.

Each verbal analogy in the test had a parallel *pictorial* analogy, for example, pictures of a cat, a dog, a kitten, and so on. The high- and low-SES groups differed significantly on both tests, but slightly *more* on the *pictorial* than on the verbal form of the test. Arvey (1972, p. 442) concluded that the use of a pictorial analogy test does not decrease the differences between the culturally disadvantaged and a more advantaged group.

Group-administered Culture-reduced Tests

Davis–Eells Games

Although now defunct, this test is a classic example of a careful attempt to construct a culture- or status-fair test of general reasoning ability based on the premise that the relatively poor performance of low-SES groups on conventional IQ tests is largely due to their highly verbal, abstract, or schoolish content. The authors' aim, therefore, was to eliminate these properties as much as possible and substitute instead cartoon pictures of persons engaged in familiar, easily recognizable situations. The examiner asks plainly worded questions about each cartoon, and the answer depends on some reasoning concerning a valid interpretation of the pictured situation. One of the items of the Games is shown in Figure 14.1.

The Games proved to be remarkably unsuccessful in achieving its authors' main aim. A majority of studies found that the Games IQ discriminated between social-class groups in the same direction and to about the same degree as conventional tests (e.g., Angelino & Shedd, 1955; Coleman & Ward, 1955; Fowler, 1957; Noll, 1958; Geist, 1954). The same is true also for ethnic group differences (Ludlow, 1956), rural versus urban (Tate & Voss, 1956), and poor readers (Justman & Aronov, 1955). The Games gives an appreciable advantage, however, to bilingual (mostly Spanish-speaking) children (Altus, 1956). As for white–black differences, Ludlow (1956) found that blacks obtained slightly *lower* IQs on the Games than on the California Test of Mental Maturity, the

Figure 14.1.   An item of the Davis–Eells Games. The examiner reads aloud the following: ''This picture shows a woman; it shows a man with a bump on his head; and it shows a broken window. A boy is outside the window. Look at the picture and find out the thing that is true. (1) The man fell down and hit his head. (2) The ball came through the window and hit the man's head. (3) The picture does not show how the man got the bump on his head. Nobody can tell because the picture doesn't show how the man got the bump.'' The subject checks one of the numbers beside the cartoon; 2 is keyed as the best answer.

Hennon–Nelson, and the Cattell Culture Fair Test, Form A. To find out if the Games reveals more ability in low-SES children who score low on conventional IQ tests, Rosenblum, Keller, and Papania (1955) gave the Games to thirty very-low-SES white and black boys with very low Stanford–Binet, WISC, and California Mental Maturity IQs (55 to 75). The group's mean IQs on the various tests were Games, 64.7; Binet, 65.9; WISC, 66.5; CMM, 66.5. The authors concluded ''for this population the Davis–Eells Games do not tend to reveal a 'hidden intellectual potential'—by virtue of their elimination of culturally unfair items—not tapped by other intelligence tests presumed to be culturally biased'' (p. 54).

Thus the Games is much the same as other IQ tests with respect to revealing differences between various ethnic and social-class groups in our population. But the Games was soon abandoned largely because it is much more cumbersome to administer in the classroom than conventional tests and, more important, because it proved to be relatively deficient in reliability and in predictive validity for scholastic performance. The Games possessed virtually no utility, although it played a uniquely instructive role in the history of psychometrics, for which Allison Davis and Kenneth Eells will be long remembered.

Raven's Progressive Matrices

Students working in Spearman's laboratory in the Psychology Department of the University of London, around 1930, discovered that certain nonverbal and nonpictorial perceptual analogy items, based on simple geometric forms, showed substantial loadings on *g* when factor analyzed along with other more conventional tests of reasoning ability (Fortes, 1930; Line, 1931). This apparently was the origin of culture-reduced tests based on perceptual analogic and inductive reasoning. The first ones to cast this principle into the form of a matrix in which the perceptual analogies were two-dimensional—simultaneously involving both horizontal and vertical transformations— were an eminent British geneticist, Lionel Penrose, and a British psychologist and student of Spearman, J. C. Raven (Penrose & Raven, 1936). Most of the credit for this ingenious invention probably belongs to Penrose, but Raven (1938) is fully re-sponsible for publishing the first Progressive Matrices Test and its subsequent improve-ments and extensions (Raven, 1947, 1960). Raven's Progressive Matrices (RPM) has become undoubtedly the best-known, most extensively researched, and most widely used of all culture-reduced tests. It has probably been used in more extreme cross-cultural studies than any other test and has penetrated every part of the globe, in developed and undeveloped nations, with the possible exceptions of the Soviet Union and mainland China. A remarkably thorough annotated bibliography (with periodic supplements) on the RPM has been compiled by J. H. Court of the Flinders University of South Australia (1972, 1974, 1976). At last count, the bibliography on the RPM contained nearly nine hundred items.

Raven describes the Progressive Matrices as "a test of a person's present capacity to form comparisons, reason by analogy, and develop a logical method of thinking regard-less of previously acquired information" (Raven, 1938, p. 12). Typical matrices are shown on pages 157 and 532. The variety of forms, relationships, and transformations is practically unlimited. Figures may increase or decrease in size, elements may be added or subtracted, shaded or unshaded, rotated, flipped, mirror imaged, or show many other progressive changes in pattern. In every case, one "cell" of the total matrix (always in the lower right corner) is missing, and the subject must select the best one of the six multiple-choice alternatives to fill the empty cell.

The RPM can be individually administered or group administered, using reusable test booklets and separate answer sheets. The RPM is generally given as a power test, with a liberal time limit or no time limit at all. Most persons are able to finish the form of the RPM appropriate for their age or ability level within an hour, and only negligible gains result by allowing more time. Most subjects who have sufficient time to attempt every item arrive at "solutions" that are not based on sheer guessing (even when wrong), and subjects subjectively feel that they have solved all the problems. Beyond that, additional time is of little use.

Three forms of the RPM are now in use. *Standard Progressive Matrices* (SPM) is the most widely used, as it covers the widest range of ability, being suitable for ages 6 years to adult, although the *Colored Progressive Matrices* is preferable for most children under about 10 years of age, and the *Advanced Progressive Matrices* is required for superior adults.

Standard Progressive Matrices consists of sixty matrix items grouped into five sets of twelve items each. Each set involves different principles of varying the matrix patterns, and within each set the items become progressively more difficult. Thus after every twelfth item, the subject is always confronted by a quite simple item. This staves off discouragement and keeps subjects interested.

The test instructions are so simple and the task requirements so obvious to most subjects beyond five or six years of age that they can even be given by pantomine. It is therefore useful with foreign language groups and the deaf, who perform up to the norms on the RPM, in contrast to their generally poor performance on verbal IQ tests (Vernon, 1968). With even minimal instructions, it is rare to find a subject (above the severely retarded range) who is in doubt as to what to do with the first couple of items. A form-board version of the test, with removable multiple-choice "blocks" that can be actually inserted in the blank space, can be used with young children and the mentally retarded, who may find it difficult to "catch on" with the booklet form of the test. I have found the form-board version a good instructional practice test for getting "disadvantaged" preschoolers of ages 4 and 5 into the booklet form of the Colored Matrices.

Colored Progressive Matrices (CPM) is most useful for children from about 4 to 10 years of age, except gifted children, who, beyond 6 or 7 years of age should be given the SPM. The CPM, as its name implies, consists of colored matrices. They are easier, on the whole, than the SPM, and are less steeply graded in difficulty. The CPM consists of three sets of twelve items each, with items increasing very gradually in difficulty within each set. Elementary school children usually finish the whole test in 30 to 40 minutes. Unless one is merely screening for mental retardation, children who score above 30 on the CPM should be given the SPM, as some scores above 30 are underestimates of the child's ability, due to the ceiling effect. Because of the large proportion of bright children in upper- and middle-SES schools, we have found the CPM unsuitable beyond the third grade (about age 8). In schools in "disadvantaged" neighborhoods, on the other hand, the CPM shows little if any ceiling effect even up to the eighth grade (age 12 or 13), although many gifted youngsters risk being overlooked if the SPM is not also given to those who score above 30 on the CPM.

The CPM has also been found useful with mentally retarded older children and adults and with older persons who have undergone some mental decline.

Advanced Progressive Matrices (APM) consists of thirty-six matrix items of considerably greater difficulty than those of the SPM. In fact, the difficulty level of the APM is such as to make it unsuitable for persons scoring below about 50 on the SPM. For the general adult population the APM has much too small a range of scores to be useful. The APM is intended for intellectually superior youths and adults, university students, and the like, for whom the SPM is too easy. Berkeley undergraduates, for example, on the SPM are all bunched in the narrow range of scores from 50 to 60, with a mean of 55 and a standard deviation of less than 3, whereas on the APM they are spread over nearly the full possible range, with very few attaining the maximum possible score.

All three forms of the RPM are published in the United States by the Psychological Corporation in New York, with sales carefully restricted to qualified psychologists.

Factorially the Progressive Matrices apparently measures g and little else (Burke, 1958). The loadings that are occasionally found on other "perceptual" and "performance"-type factors, independently of g, are usually so trivial and inconsistent from one analysis to another as to suggest that the RPM does not reliably measure anything but g in the general population. The internal consistency reliability of the RPM is close to .90 in most studies. Many other tests also measure *g* to a high degree, but few, if any, have so little loading as the Raven on any of the main group factors—Verbal, Numerical, Spatial, and Memory. It is a common misconception that the RPM is a measure of "perceptual ability" or "spatial–visualization" ability. In fact, the Raven has very meager loadings on these factors, when *g* is excluded. Another misconception is that the RPM, when factor analyzed at the item level, involves more than a single factor. This erroneous impression has come about through improper orthogonal rotations of the principal components—a method that can artificially create the appearance of several factors even in correlation matrices that are artificially constructed so as to contain only one factor plus random "error." Some of the small spurious factors that emerge from factor analysis of the inter-item correlations are not really ability factors at all but are "difficulty" factors, due to varying degrees of restriction of variance on items of widely differing difficulty levels and to nonlinear regressions of item difficulties on age and ability (McDonald, 1965). When proper account is taken of these psychometric artifacts, the RPM seems to measure only a single factor of mental ability, which is best called *g*. The raw inter-item correlation matrix on large unselected samples closely approximates the appearance of a "simplex," which means that all the intercorrelations can be "explained" most parsimoniously in terms of a single factor plus random errors of measurement.

Although consideration of sex differences did not enter into the construction of the RPM, it turns out that it does not significantly favor either sex. The sex differences occasionally reported are attributable to sampling errors, and no true sex differences have been reliably demonstrated (Court & Kennedy, 1976).

Although the RPM has been popular in psychometric, cognitive, and cross-cultural research, it has not gained general favor in applied settings. There are two main reasons for this. First, the test is too "pure," factorially, to be as good a predictor of most practical criteria, such as scholastic and vocational performance, as are factorially more complex tests, especially those that include a large verbal component. The RPM's correlations with conventional IQ tests are mostly in the range from .50 to .75. It seems to correlate least with the highly verbal and culture-loaded Peabody Picture Vocabulary Test. In a California school population including about equal numbers of white, black, and Mexican–American pupils, the correlation (with age in months partialed out) between RPM and PPVT is 0.53 (Jensen, 1974a). Predictive validities of the RPM generally run about .10 to .20 lower than for conventional tests of scholastic aptitude and vocational aptitudes. For this reason Raven has recommended using, in addition to the RPM, the Mill Hill Vocabulary Scale (with the SPM) or the Crichton Vocabulary Scale (with the CPM). As a highly suitable verbal companion to the APM, I suggest Terman's *Concept Mastery Test*. The second drawback to the Raven tests is their lack of adequate standardization norms in the United States. In clinical practice and in educational and vocational counseling, the psychologist requires adequate normative data for the useful interpretation of an individual's score. The British norms provided in the Raven manuals are crude and inadequate for this purpose. The best one can do at present is to look up the statistics on appropriate reference groups used in various studies reported in the literature, but this is hardly satisfactory.

Actually, the RPM, for all its ingenuity and virtues, could stand considerable psychometric improvement, in addition to a proper standardization. There are some peculiar gaps in the total sequence of item difficulties; item p values should be more smoothly graded between the easiest and hardest items. There are far too few items in each form of the test, and, for homogeneous age groups, the items are too widely spaced in difficulty to yield smooth raw score distributions or percentile scores without marked gaps. Too few of the items are actually discriminative within any 12-month age group, so that only a very few items can make the difference between a wide range of percentiles or IQs. This psychometric deficiency could be remedied by the creation of many more items finely graded in difficulty. Two or more equivalent forms at each level would also be a boon for practical uses where retesting after special instruction and practice would have diagnostic or predictive value. In selecting African tribesmen for training to work with industrial machinery, for example, the CPM was found to have better predictive validity (0.51) after subjects had taken two similar practice tests (Ombredane, Robaye, & Plumail, 1956).

Because the RPM is an excellent culture-reduced measure of fluid g, one of its chief values is for screening illiterate, semiliterate, bilingual, and otherwise educationally disadvantaged or socially depressed populations for potential academic talent that might easily remain undetected by parents and teachers or by the more conventional culture-loaded tests of scholastic aptitude. It is probably the surest instrument we now possess for discovering intellectually gifted children from disadvantaged backgrounds, so that they can be given the special attention needed for the full realization of their ability in school and in the world of work.

Cattell Culture Fair Intelligence Tests

The CFI series is both a forerunner and outgrowth of Raymond B. Cattell's theory of fluid and crystalized intelligence, or g_f and g_c. The CFI was designed to come as close as possible to measuring g_f, that aspect of mental performance that depends minimally on past learned knowledge and skills (see Chapter 6, pp. 234–236). The theoretical rationale for this nonverbal, nonpictorial test, first spelled out by Cattell in 1940, has been refined and elaborated in light of Cattell's subsequent research on g_f and g_c (Cattell, 1940; 1963; 1971a; 1971b, Ch. 5). The CFI has a more explicitly developed theoretical rationale underlying it than perhaps any other test of intelligence, and for the interested reader there is really no adequate substitute for Cattell's own writings, particularly the references cited here, in addition to the test manuals (published by the Institute for Personality and Ability Testing, or IPAT, in Champaign, Illinois).

The CFI tests are paper-and-pencil group-administered speeded tests with strict time limits for each subtest. There are three main scales, which together span a mental-age range from 2 years to "superior adult."

Scale 1, intended for children of ages 4 to 8 and mentally defective adults, is comprised of eight subtests, each with short time limits varying from 2 to 4 minutes. Scale 1 takes altogether some 40 to 60 minutes to administer, but subjects spend only 22 minutes of the total time in actually doing the test. Thus a relatively small behavior sample is obtained for the total amount of time it takes to give the test. The manual recommends that for younger children the test be given in two sittings to avoid fatigue. Listening to the lengthy instructions for each subtest, however, may be more fatiguing than actually doing the tests. It certainly puts a high premium on a test-taking factor that might be termed "listening attention," and probably the test inadvertently involves more sheer verbal comprehension than even the Stanford–Binet. This is anomalous for a purportedly "culture fair'' test. Some of the subtests must be administered individually. This scale is the only one of the three that includes some subtests that involve culture-loaded pictorial and verbal material, although the items were selected so as to be highly familiar, at least in Western industrialized societies. However, Archimedes and Plato would almost surely fail at least several of these pictorial items, which seems undesirable in a test labeled ''culture fair.''

Scale 2 (for ages 8 to 13 and average unselected adults) and *Scale 3* (for high school, college, and superior adults) consist entirely of ''content-free'' abstract figural materials forming sets of problems in series progression, classification, matrices, and discovering common topological properties. There are two equivalent forms (A and B) of scales 2 and 3, and, for persons who are unsophisticated in test taking, Cattell recommends using one form as a preliminary practice test. In my own experience, this is absolutely essential for using scales 2 and 3 with any culturally or educationally disadvantaged groups.

The four subtests of scales 2 and 3 are each highly speeded, with time limits varying from $2\frac{1}{2}$ to 4 minutes. The subject's total working time is only $12\frac{1}{2}$ minutes, but the test takes about a half an hour to give. Again, there is little actual subject performance time in relation to total administering time.

A few years ago, in trying to decide on whether to use the Raven Progressive Matrices or the CFI in conducting a large-scale testing program in schools enrolling a large proportion of ''culturally disadvantaged'' black and Mexican–American pupils, we tried out both tests (as well as the Lorge–Thorndike Intelligence Test) in several elementary school classrooms, using Scale 2 of the CFI. As it turned out, there were great difficulties with the CFI that were not at all in evidence with the Raven or the Lorge–Thorndike (Verbal and Nonverbal). With the CFI, about one-half to two-thirds of the total administration time was spent on verbal instructions for taking the test. On every subtest, reading the instructions, and often having to repeat them because of the puzzled looks on many children's faces, took much longer than the brief time allowed for the subjects to actually *do* the test. The lengthy instructions so bored many of the children that they ''turned off,'' and, when they were told to ''begin,'' they had no idea what to do. Apparently they could not infer the task requirements from the easiest items. White middle-class subjects had much less trouble in this respect, which led us to believe that the CFI may be the last test we would want to select for the ''disadvantaged.'' The lack of attention to the detailed instructions, and the evident frustration of having ''Pencils down!'' called after only $2\frac{1}{2}$ to 4 minutes of working on a subtest, resulted in unusual pile-ups of chance-level scores for many children. The same groups performed fairly well on the Raven, with minimal pantomine and verbal instructions taking altogether about 1 minute, and there were virtually no suspiciously low or chance-level scores. The children became quickly engrossed in the Raven and worked on it raptly, usually attempting all the items within a 50-minute time limit. The whole procedure of the CFI, in contrast, is much more ''test-like,'' with its tedious, long-winded oral explanations and repeated commands of ''Do not turn the page until told to do so,'' ''Stop!,'' ''Pencils down!,'' ''Ready? Go!,'' etc. For too many scholastically alienated pupils, an officious procedure only leads to bewilderment and confusion, and perhaps even noncooperation. So we abandoned the CFI for our testing program and retained the Raven and Lorge–Thorndike, which both worked quite well in this population. *Individual* administration of the CFI to low-SES, bilingual Mexican–American children, however, has apparently worked quite well (Kidd, 1962). If the CFI is to be used as a group test with disadvantaged children, they should probably be tested in smaller groups (say, ten or twelve) than the average classroom, to maintain better attention, with Form A used in an informal instructional atmosphere on the first day and Form B given on the second day with greatly abbreviated instructions. The time limits should probably be increased for certain groups, but then the published norms would not be applicable.

The deficiency of the CFI described here is probably partly responsible for the rather low equivalent forms reliability. Forms A and B of Scale 2 are correlated between .58 and .72 in various age groups, which is rather low by ordinary standards (Krug, 1967). The equivalent forms' reliabilities are slightly lower (.50 to .70) for Scale 3.

The standardization samples and procedures are not very fully described in the IPAT manuals, and they leave some doubts. One would like to see a complete raw score frequency distribution based on a large representative sample of some clearly specified population. The Nonverbal part of the Lorge–Thorndike IQ test (recently renamed the Cognitive Abilities Test) is quite similar to Cattell's CFI and could serve the same purpose if one needs a nonverbal, highly g-loaded test with superb standardization.

Krug (1967) has summarized much of the data on the psychometric properties of the CFI. It shows moderate correlations (.20–.50) with scholastic achievements—higher r's with arithmetic, lower with language, and the predictive validities are fairly impressive for certain groups and criteria. Correlations with other intelligence tests are mostly in the .50 to .70 range. Most emphasis, however, is rightly put on the CFI's factorial validity. In various factor analytic studies the CFI has g loadings of around .80, similar to Raven's matrices. Cattell has argued, however, that the CFI's g is more pure than the Raven's g, as the latter is based on only one type of test item and therefore contains a matrices-specific factor. The CFI total score, on the other hand, is based on four different types of culture-reduced items, so that the specific factors are averaged out, making the total score both a broader and purer measure of fluid g (see Cattell, 1971b, p. 82, note 3).

The CFI has been tried on many culturally different groups outside the United States, with quite comparable scores even across some linguistically and culturally quite dissimilar groups, for example, children in America, England, France, Hong Kong, and Taiwan. Lynn (1978) has reviewed many of the far-flung international comparisons made with the CFI and other culture-reduced tests.

The CFI generally shows slightly lower correlations with socioeconomic status than culture-loaded or verbal tests, and some bilingual immigrant groups score higher on the CFI than on conventional IQ tests. But the CFI does not necessarily reduce the magnitude of the racial differences found with other tests or yield higher scores, on the average, in native-born culturally disadvantaged groups, particularly blacks.

The fact that the CFI does not wipe out racial and social-class differences has been improperly used as a criticism of the test—as if the *sine qua non* for a culture-reduced test be that it eliminate all group differences! This common misconception has been repeated again and again in textbook discussions of the CFI (and other culture-reduced tests) and even in some supposedly technical reviews in Buros's *Mental Measurements Yearbook*.

Two studies, in particular, lend some insight into how the CFI compares with the more conventional tests when used with the two largest ethnic minorities in the United States—blacks and Mexican–Americans.

Kidd (1962) individually administered the CFI (Scale 2) and the Stanford–Binet (Form L) to one hundred upper- and lower-SES "Anglo" and Mexican–American school children, ages 10-0 to 11-0 years, in Arizona. Some of Kidd's statistical analyses are faulty and can be ignored for our purposes, but the basic data appear sound and are worth reporting. Overall mean IQs were 93.88, $\sigma = 19.85$, on the CFI and 104.57, $\sigma = 18.43$, on the Stanford–Binet. This discrepancy of over 10 IQ points is probably due to differences in the standardization reference groups for the CFI and Stanford–Binet. Such a large discrepancy raises further doubts about the standardization of the CFI, or the Stanford–Binet, or both. Kidd peculiarly fails to present means or standard deviations for the separate SES and ethnic groups, but it is possible to infer the mean differences (in standard deviation or σ units) between the groups from her analysis of variance tables.[1]

Groups	Stanford–Binet	Cattell CFI
Upper SES − Lower SES	$.88\sigma$	$.40\sigma$
"Anglo" − Mexican	$.73\sigma$	$.69\sigma$

It can be seen that the CFI considerably reduces the difference on the SES variable but not on the ethnic variable. Neither the CFI nor the Stanford–Binet IQ shows a significant ethnic × SES interaction, and neither test shows a significant sex difference.

The correlations between the CFI and Stanford–Binet IQs are reported to range from .636 to .745 in each of the four SES × ethnic groups with a *mean r* of .683. (This was misleadingly labeled as "Total Group." The analysis of variance in Kidd's Table 3, which I have not made use of, is incorrect, using the wrong error term in computing all the F ratios. Besides that, Kidd's whole ANOVA design of Table 3 is very wrong and her use of normalized T scores I find completely baffling. And t tests are improperly used for post hoc comparisons. The journal referees must have been on holiday.)

"Disadvantaged" or "culturally deprived" black sixth-graders ($N = 89$) in New Haven, Connecticut schools were given Cattell's CFI (Set 2) along with a conventional test of scholastic aptitude (Academic Promise Test) (Willard, 1968). The Academic Promise Test (APT) raw scores are normed to an IQ scale corresponding to WISC IQs, with mean = 100, $\sigma = 16$. In the disadvantaged black group the CFI gave a mean IQ of 94.4, σ of 16.0; the APT gave a mean IQ of 90.8, σ of 12.2. The correlation between CFI and APT IQs in this group is .55. The correlations of CFI and APT IQs with a test of reading achievement are .57 and .75, respectively, with arithmetic achievement of .50 and .73, respectively. This difference in correlations should not be surprising, as the APT has verbal and numerical subtests that are quite similar to scholastic achievement tests of reading and arithmetic.

Also tested by Willard (1968) were eighty-three "disadvantaged" black children in special classes, with a mean Stanford–Binet IQ of 68.1, $\sigma = 6.4$ (misprinted in Willard's Table IV as 63.1). The CFI (Set 2) in this group has a mean of 70.0, σ of 10.2. This is a small mean difference (1.9 IQ points), which led Willard (p. 35) to the incredible conclusion that "nonverbal intelligence seems to be of no major advantage in the school situation" and led one reviewer to conclude that "black children of low socioeconomic level . . . did no better on this test [i.e., CFI] than on the Stanford–Binet" (Anastasi, 1976, p. 291). These conclusions, however, misleadingly overlooked a most salient feature of Willard's data in the complete frequency distributions of both CFI and

Stanford–Binet IQs: No child in the special classes had a Stanford–Binet IQ above 81, whereas 17 percent of these children have CFI IQs *above* 81, and the distribution of CFI IQs ranges continuously without a single gap all the way up to IQ 98! The frequency distribution of IQs for the CFI reveals another notable feature, similar to what I myself had found when I tried to use the CFI with "culturally deprived" children in this age group: a piling up of subjects at the lowest possible IQ on the CFI at this age—17 percent of the group all piled up at precisely IQ 57! Obviously these children really cannot be said to have taken the test. They probably "turned off" during the lengthy verbal instructions. What IQs would these children have obtained had they actually taken culture-reduced tests? At the very least, eleven out of these fourteen children with lowest possible CFI IQs of 57 had Stanford–Binet IQs of 60 or above. Not to have noticed this gross anomaly in the distribution of CFI IQs was an egregious oversight by the school psychologist who obtained these results. Willard does not report the correlation between CFI and Stanford–Binets in this group, but we can estimate the intraclass correlation roughly from the frequency distribution of CFI–SB IQ differences (Willard's Table V);[1] the estimated intraclass correlation is +.22, which is so low as to indicate that the Stanford–Binet and CFI rank order these children quite differently. I would regard the results of both tests in such circumstances as suspect, but more especially the CFI scores, because of the marked pile-up at the lowest possible score. This anomaly in the CFI distribution reinforces my suspicion that the CFI is probably unsuitable for low-IQ culturally disadvantaged children of elementary school age. Its use is much too risky in the hands of school psychologists who cannot "read" their data.

Rulon's Semantic Test of Intelligence

Rulon's STI is an ingenious culture-reduced test that, as far as I can determine, has never been published commercially. Therefore, it has been seldom used, and the research literature on the test, outside one article by Rulon and Schweiker (1953), is nil. The STI was developed for testing illiterates in the U.S. Army. Rulon aimed to devise a completely nonverbal test, not even requiring any verbal instructions, that would nevertheless measure presumably the basic elements of *verbal* ability, that is, the cognitive processes involved in learning almost any natural language. Rulon was dissatisfied with the abstract nonverbal tests generally used for testing illiterates; he believed that they did not get at the same kinds of intellectual ability that is involved in *verbal* intelligence tests (Rulon, 1966). The STI is his proposed remedy for this lack. It attempts to measure verbal ability by means of a purely nonlanguage test. Rulon (1966, p. 475) notes: "The appearance of validity of the material is not merely superficial, since the operations required of the examinee are the simpler linguistic or semantic operations, not just operations thought up for the purpose of constructing a test. These operations are undoubtedly related to the operations of reading any language." The test is undoubtedly highly *g* loaded, but it would be most interesting to determine how loaded it is on a purely *verbal* factor (independent of *g*) when factor analyzed among a battery of the usual verbal and nonverbal tests. If it measures only *g,* it only duplicates what many other nonlanguage tests can do and, therefore, is not of great interest in its own right. If it substantially measures a *verbal* factor as well, however, it would be of great scientific interest and practical value. It would mean we could measure *g* + *V* (the main factorial composition of most ordinary intelligence and scholastic aptitude tests) with one and the same test across different language and cultural groups. The possibility merits further research with the STI.

Figure 14.2. Items of Rulon's Semantic Test of Intelligence.

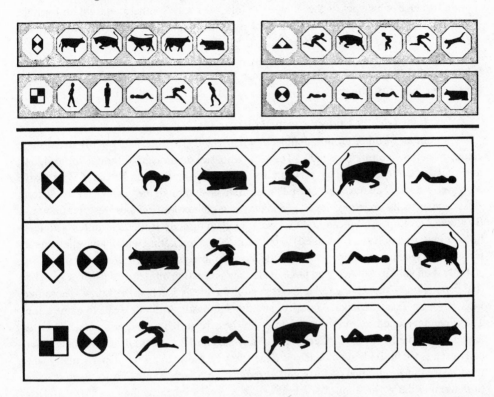

Figure 14.2 shows how the STI works. The meanings of each of the abstract symbols on the far left in the shaded rectangles above must be induced from the set of five pictures to the right of it. It is a matter of finding the common element in all five of the pictures. The meanings of the four symbols are *cow, man, jumping, lying down*. Given this information in the shaded rectangles, the subject must then decode the combinations of two symbols in each of the three items (rows) below, and circle the correct picture, for example, *cow jumping, cow lying down,* and *man lying down*. Items are made more difficult by adding more symbols, up to four-symbol "sentences," for example, *woman kicks dog lying down*. The same symbols are repeated over and over in various combinations throughout the test, so that the subject gradually becomes more and more "literate" in this new set of symbols.

Rulon took pains to depict only objects and concepts that are universally familiar in all Western cultures, even the most primitive. In addition to pictures of men, women, children, and common domesticated animals, there are simple objects like bowls, stools, and trees. Depicted actions are standing, walking, running, jumping, sitting, pushing, dragging, lifting, beating, chasing, and the like. The brief instructions are given by pantomime, with the examiner pointing to the pictures and doing some very easy example items to give subjects the idea. No words in any language are spoken in the administration of the STI. Rulon claimed considerable potential for the STI:

> It has been found possible to construct a test of substantial difficulty which does not seem to offer any reward for visual acuity or pure visual perception. Also it seems

possible now to produce such a test using such materials so as not to give any advantage whatever to the Northern child over the Southern, the white over the colored, or the time-server in school over the bright youngster with less schooling.   (Rulon, 1966, p. 476)

It is a pity that in the twenty-seven years since Rulon invented the STI its putative virtues have never been investigated.

Psychometrically Underdeveloped Group Tests

A number of other group-administered paper-and-pencil tests explicitly make some claims to being "culture reduced." They are all based on nonverbal, nonpictorial figural materials, often quite similar to Cattell's Culture Fair Test or Raven's Progressive Matrices. And they all have one other characteristic in common: they are what I would term "psychometrically underdeveloped," and the research literature on these tests is almost nil. By "underdeveloped" I mean that they have jumped directly from their author's conception (or imitation of Raven or Cattell) to publication and marketing without the elaborate intervening stages of psychometric refinement—item analyses, factor analyses, reliability, stability, and validity studies, and large-scale standardization on clearly defined representative populations—that characterize the best published tests, such as the Lorge–Thorndike, the California Test of Mental Maturity, and the Scholastic Aptitude Test, to name a few. The underdeveloped culture-reduced tests are best regarded as experimental. Their inadequate standardization, or often a lack of any standardization at all, makes them practically useless for individual guidance. But they may be useful in research, particularly when used in combination, such as for solidly establishing a large fluid g factor against which to determine the g_f loading of some new test or measurement technique. All these tests appear to be quite highly g_f loaded. However, those who are looking for a highly g_f-loaded group test that also has well-developed psychometric properties and adequate standardization are advised to avoid these experimental tests and consider using instead the nonverbal parts of the Lorge–Thorndike Intelligence Test or the California Test of Mental Maturity.

Another problematic feature shared by all these tests is that, although the *materials* are nonverbal, the oral or written instructions for taking the tests are verbal and at times rather *complexly* verbal. None of the tests gets along with such minimal verbal instructions as are required for the Raven.

What follow are brief comments on the best-known underdeveloped culture-reduced tests. The numbers in parentheses after each test refer to the volume and review numbers in Buros's *Mental Measurements Yearbook* in which interested readers will find technical information about each of these tests, their cost, publisher, intended age groups, and so on, along with detailed critical reviews by test experts. References to studies of black Americans on some of these tests can be found in Shuey's (1966) comprehensive review.

D-48 or *Domino Test* (6:454) is probably the least imitative of the lot. All the test "items" consist of pictured arrangements of from four to fourteen dominoes in a progressive series; the last domino in the series is left blank, and the subject has to fill in the correct number of dots on the domino to continue the series according to the same rule governing the preceding sequence of dominoes. Interestingly, the name of the psychologist involved in the test's development is George Domino. One may wonder how cross-cultural the game of dominoes is. The test is factorially very homogeneous, with a *g* loading purportedly close to .90, which is about the same as its split-half reliability. One might suspect a numerical ability factor as well.

The D-48 has been used in Belgium, France, Italy, and the United States, with highly similar means for all national groups matched on age and educational level. Thus language differences seem to make little, if any, difference in scores. The D-48 has quite good predictive validity for school grades. The standardization is inadequate as a basis for assigning IQs or percentile equivalents in any American (or perhaps *any*) population.

The *Figure Reasoning Test* (6:457) is almost like an equivalent form of Raven's Progressive Matrices and, indeed, is reported to correlate .93 with the Raven, while its split-half reliability is .96. It also correlates quite highly with conventional IQ tests. Thus it appears to be a good nonverbal measure of *g*. The test does not seem to have enough "top" (i.e., very difficult items) to spread out the brightest subjects or enough easy items for discriminating among the retarded. This attractive matrices test of forty-five items, which takes only 30 minutes, is a useful *g* measure in studies or selection situations in which raw scores rather than excellently derived normative scores are all that are needed.

The *Lowry–Lucier Reasoning Test Combination* (6:468) uses serial relationships among days of the week and classical matchstick problems, suitable for ages 5 to 16. The scores are claimed to be less correlated with SES than are scores on conventional tests. It has correlations with other tests and school grades in the same range as found for most culture-reduced tests, which is to say slightly lower than most good conventional tests. The standardization is inadequate, and the test itself needs further psychometric study and development.

The *Purdue Non-Language Test* (6:491) is based on the oddity problem; one geometric figure out of every set of five figures (forty-eight sets in all) has to be picked out as the "odd" one because of some uniquely distinguishing figural characteristic. Oddity-type problems, in general, are known to be quite *g* loaded, so the idea of a whole oddity test is a good one, although any *particular* test based on oddity must of course be evaluated psychometrically on its own. The existing information on the PNT is very inadequate for such evaluation and at this stage the test is best regarded as "experimental," as it is characterized in the test manual. Recommended only for further research.

The *Safran Culture Reduced Intelligence Test* (7:384) is a nonverbal inductive reasoning test based on figure series, in which the subject must select from multiple-choice alternatives the one figure that continues the series according to the induced rule. The rather complex verbal directions for the test could be a problem in disadvantaged or bilingual groups, like the administration difficulties described for such groups in connection with Cattell's Culture Fair Intelligence Test, and it has inadequate norms. Reported correlations with other tests and criteria are much like those for the Raven, the Cattell, and the Lorge–Thorndike Nonverbal IQ.

The *WLW Culture Fair Inventory* (7:399) is an untimed thirty-item reasoning test based on figural materials in oddity problems, series completion, matrices, paper form board, and block counting. It is a very poorly made test; the "art work" and printing are bad. Some of the intricate items seem to depend as much on sheer visual acuity as on reasoning ability. There is no standardization, psychometric information, or research on this test worth mentioning. In view of the availability of a number of similar yet far superior tests, the WLW–CFI is best forgotten altogether.

Individually Administered Culture-reduced Tests

Leiter International Performance Scale

This extremely ingenious and elaborate test, which originated in 1929 as Russell Leiter's master's thesis, is remarkably underdeveloped psychometrically, considering its seemingly great promise and the fact that it has been around since 1929. A sample "item" is shown on page 164. Items involve matching a great variety of forms, colors, and pictures, and are suitable for ages 2 to 12 years. The pictorial material can hardly be called "culture reduced" and some of it is now quite dated. I think these relatively few obviously culture-loaded items could be omitted to advantage. The resulting raw scores then could not be converted to MAs or IQs, but the test's poor norms (based on 289 middle-class white children) are now almost worthless anyway.

The Leiter's greatest virtue perhaps is that it is truly a nonlanguage test. Not a word need be uttered by either the examiner or the subject. The large kit of test materials is extensive, which makes the test probably the most expensive of all psychological tests. Because the scores are correlated about .80 with the WISC Performance IQ in a middle-class population, there would be no benefit gained from using the test with most normal middle-class children. The Leiter, however, lends itself well to testing foreign language, bilingual , deaf, and otherwise language-handicapped children and children with whom it is difficult to establish rapport in individual tests requiring considerable examiner–subject interaction. Aside from the fact that the Leiter is clearly highly *g* loaded, little is known about its factor structure. Item analysis information is lacking, but I suspect item difficulties are not graded smoothly enough and there are too few items of a given type within a one-year mental-age range. Thus too few of the items will be reliably discriminating within any culturally homogeneous group of age-matched subjects. The norms are so inadequate as to make it inadvisable to use the test for determining a subject's IQ or percentile rank. So it is hard to see how the Leiter can be a clinically useful instrument. The subject's raw score and observed performance can only provide a basis for subjective evaluation by the clinician. It would take a great investment of time, money, and psychometric research expertise to develop the Leiter into an objective, clinically useful, language-free, culture-reduced test.

Although it is labeled "international," surprisingly little cross-national or cross-cultural research has been done with the Leiter in the more than forty years since it was first published. (For bibliography and reviews, see Buros, *4*:349; *5*:406; *6*:526.)

Kohs Block Designs

Devised in 1923 by S. C. Kohs, a shortened version of this test has become the familiar Block Designs subtest of the Wechsler scales. The subject copies various designs of graded difficulty (i.e., complexity) using colored blocks. The test ostensibly requires analytic and synthetic reasoning and is the most heavily *g* loaded of all the performance tests in the Wechsler scales—about .70 after correction for attenuation. The Block Design test is also loaded moderately on a spatial–visualization factor and probably for this reason shows a larger sex difference (favoring men) than most other subtests.

The Block Design and Vocabulary scales combined correlate more highly with total Wechsler IQ than any of the other fifty-five possible combinations of two subscales. There are too few items in the Kohs Block Design Test to yield the psychometric properties that would justify its use as an intelligence test by itself, and its *g* is contaminated by a spatial factor and, if given under speeded conditions, by sheer manual dexterity. It has proved a valuable part of performance test batteries, however, and shows lower correlations with the amount of the subjects' formal education than most other tests, even though it is more *g* loaded than many tests that are more highly correlated with amount of schooling. The test can be given without the use of language.

Porteus Maze Test

Invented in 1914, this is one of the oldest mental tests still in use. Its extensive use in many cross-cultural studies is rivaled only by Raven's Progressive Matrices. Probably no other test has been given to more remotely different cultural groups all around the world. Extensive bibliographies and critical accounts of the Porteus Maze Test (PMT) can be found in Buros (6:532; 7:419) and in Porteus's fascinating auto-biographical and heavily anecdotal book (1965) on his fifty years' work with the maze test. This book also reviews many of the cross-cultural studies with the PMT, as does Lynn (1978, pp. 263–266).

The PMT consists altogether of twenty-eight mazes graded in difficulty from extremely easy (for age 3) to quite complicated (adult level). One of the mazes is shown on page 163. Mental-age and IQ conversion tables are given in Porteus (1965), but little confidence can be placed in these, as the test is very inadequately standardized. Porteus and others have been exceedingly casual about the psychometric aspects of the PMT. Despite the extensive literature on the PMT, there is really not much psychometric information of the kind needed by test users.

The PMT requires no language by either the examiner or the subject, and one of its best features is that it quickly engages subjects' interest and effort. This has been found in a number of primitive cultures, including the Aborigines of Central Australia. The PMT score also reflects effects of psychosurgery (lobotomy and leucotomy), which suggests that it measures some function of the frontal lobes of the brain, the so-called organs of foresight. Conventional IQ tests are generally not as sensitive to the psychological effects of psychosurgery.

Porteus himself was so much the clinician and psychological anthropologist and so little the psychometrician and systematic researcher that we have comparatively little "hard knowledge" about the PMT. We can glean something psychometrically about maze performance in general from the fact that the Wechsler Intelligence Scale for Children (WISC) and the Wechsler Preschool and Primary Scale of Intelligence (WPPSI) both include a maze subtest. Because the WISC and WPPSI Full Scale IQs are good *g* measures in the normative samples, it is instructive to look at the correlations of the Mazes subscale with the FS IQ. The average *r* over different age groups for the WISC is +.48 and for the WPPSI, +.54. These *r*'s may be compared with the average *r* between each of the ten or eleven other subscales and FS IQ: for the WISC, +.57, and for the WPPSI, +.63. Thus it can be seen that the maze test is not quite as good a measure of *g* as are the other subtests, on the average. This is true even after correction for attenuation. The PMT correlates about +.60 with Stanford–Binet IQ.

In addition to measuring *g*, the PMT has been found to measure a spatial-visualization factor, which probably accounts for Porteus's repeated finding that men average slightly higher scores than women.

More important, however, Porteus believes that the PMT measures a kind of social or practical competence and adaptive capacity that is not measured by conventional IQ tests. This competence factor becomes especially important in the assessment of the mentally retarded, some of whom score markedly higher in the PMT than on the Stanford–Binet or Wechsler tests. There is evidence that the PMT discriminates reliably between ''mentally retarded'' persons who become more or less self-sufficient in the community and those in constant need of care and supervision, even when both these groups have about the same Binet IQs. In one study of black adolescents who scored in the retarded IQ range on conventional tests, higher PMT scores distinguish those who were described as being socially alert and socially effective and having a high general activity level, higher vocational ability, sports ability, good physical appearance, and accurate social judgment (Cooper, York, Daston, & Adams, 1967). This type of finding, along with the fact that the PMT has been found to correlate $+.75$ with the Knox Cube Test, which is a measure of immediate visual and auditory memory with very little g component, leads me to believe the PMT is more a measure of what I have termed level I ability than of level II, or g. For this reason it is a valuable adjunct to the usual IQ test for predicting the social and practical adaptiveness of persons who are borderline (or below) on the more highly g-loaded tests. If only there were more trustworthy norms for the PMT and more validity information for typical groups for whom the PMT might be most useful!

Rational Learning Test

This simple, long-forgotten test devised by Peterson (1928) is worth mentioning because of its quite different approach to culture-reduced testing. The test would have been more accurately named the Rote Learning Test. It measures simple associational learning in the test situation itself. The fundaments of the test consist of no more than a simple knowledge of counting (1, 2, 3, etc.) and of the order of letters in the alphabet, although numbers beyond 5 and letters beyond E are not called for. (However, more numbers and letters could be used to make the test more difficult.) From a prearranged ''code,'' such as $A = 4$, $B = 1$, $C = 5$, $D = 2$, $E = 3$, the examiner says each letter in succession and the subject has to guess which number goes with it; the examiner reinforces a correct guess by saying ''Right,'' and then says the next letter in the series, which is repeated in the same way until the subject is able to give all the correct numbers in succession twice through. The whole procedure is subject paced. A record is made of the subject's entire performance, so that a learning curve (errors per repetition) can be plotted; and total time to mastery is also recorded. A simple foretest, using only $A = 1$, $B = 3$, $C = 2$, is given to ensure that the subject understands the task requirements.

Peterson believed the RLT is much more culture reduced than most tests, because ''it keeps well within the range of the experience of all subjects, however meager this experience may have been, so far as its demands on knowledge and skills are concerned'' (Peterson, 1928, p. 334). This seems a bit overstated; as a foretest the subject should be asked to count from 1 to 20 and to say the alphabet. For any subjects who could not do these things easily, I would regard the test as suspect.

Peterson collected considerable data on this test, including adult norms, on whites and blacks. The test shows systematic age differences and has some predictive validity for scholastic performance, although less than ordinary IQ tests. It correlates .30 to .50 with various IQ tests. It also correlated quite well (.63) with a teacher's estimates of the intelligence of thirty-three sixth-grade pupils. Although there are consistent white–black mean differences on the RLT, they are somewhat smaller than on conventional IQ tests. All these findings are quite typical of what I have found in my own research on level I abilities, that is, simple rote learning and memory. It seems safe to say that Peterson's RLT is a level I test. Such tests have only modest g loadings, but that very fact may be their chief virtue. Used in conjunction with a highly g-loaded test, they stand the chance of revealing an ability that is different from g but possibly of practical importance, especially in the assessment of persons who are below average on highly g-loaded tests (see Jensen, 1973a, pp. 204–293; 1973c, pp. 51–85). However, this is a promise that has not yet really been fulfilled in fact and may finally prove to be a false hope. Only further research will tell.

Rote learning tests such as the RLT unfortunately have at least two easily recognized psychometric disadvantages. (1) Because pure guessing is involved in the early trials, this adds a large chance element to the scores; this of course is error variance, which militates against achieving high reliability. The RLT, for example, has test–retest reliabilities in the .55 to .75 range, which is very low compared with conventional IQ tests. (2) Any particular learning task involves considerable task-specific variance, due to the interaction of numerous procedural variables in addition to the specific content of what is to be learned, so that even a quite time-consuming learning task behaves, in an item analysis and factor analytic sense, much like a *single item* in a test such as the Stanford–Binet. No clear factorial structure (other than the ubiquitous g) has ever emerged from factor analyzing batteries of diverse learning tasks. A composite score based on a large variety of such learning tests may well measure no other factor but g, plus a large "error" component made up of task specificity and true random error (due to the necessity of guessing on early trials in selective learning tasks). If this is true, as I am slowly and reluctantly coming to believe it most probably is, it could mean that level I tests, as I have labeled them, will have very little general validity or practical predictive utility outside whatever little g they may reflect, which can be measured much more efficiently by other tests.

Queensland Test

The QT was developed for selecting persons who are likely "to be able to learn rapidly the complex skills of Western urbanized cultures, from among groups who had had little contact with that culture" (McElwain & Kearney, 1970, p. 1). The QT has been used most extensively in studies of the indigenes of Papua–New Guinea and the Australian Aborigines, and comparative data have been obtained on Australians of European descent. The research and development that went into the QT are easily the most impressive of any culture-reduced test that I know of, and the psychometric information provided in the test manual (McElwain & Kearney, 1970) is an example of what one would like to see for other culture-reduced tests (but which usually is woefully deficient). In developing the QT, a great many types of performance test items were tried out, and only those that maintained good psychometric qualities across the most diverse cultural groups were retained. As a result of the cross-cultural anthropological and psychometric sophistication that were lavished on the QT's development, it is very likely the best culture-reduced individually administered test available today.

It is a pity that this excellent test is so little known in the United States. If suitable American norms were obtained, the QT would be a most valuable adjunct in the individual assessment of foreign-language-speaking, culturally disadvantaged, and other minority children who have scholastic problems. It is less culture loaded than the Performance Scales of the Wechsler tests, and it has been shown to maintain its essential psychometric properties across groups from even the most extremely diverse cultures, such as the

Aborigines of the Australian Outback, whose experiential background is probably more remote from that of modern American and European city dwellers than that of any other peoples on earth.

The QT consists of five essentially untimed performance subtests: Knox cube imitation, copying bead patterns, pass-along test, form-board assembly, and pattern matching (like Kohs's block design but using flat colored tiles instead of blocks). Administering the tests requires no langauge on the part of the examiner or the subject; subtests are preceded by demonstrations and practice items. The test is most suitable for ages 8 to adult. There is an almost perfectly linear regression of QT raw scores on chronological age between ages 8 to 14 in a great variety of populations.

Factor analyses of the QT indicate that it measures mostly *g*. Other standard non-verbal tests of intelligence show correlations with the QT of between 0.70 and 0.80 in various samples. The QT correlates 0.69 to 0.76 with Raven's matrices. Verbal IQ tests show lower correlations (0.49 to 0.62) with the QT. The Pattern Matching subtest is the most highly *g* loaded. The Knox cube imitation subtest, a measure of short-term memory, has the lowest *g* loading and appears to be mainly a measure of level I ability. Its inclusion somewhat dilutes the *g* saturation of the QT total score. Interestingly, the Knox cubes score shows the smallest mean difference of any of the subtests between Aborigines and Europeans. The QT correlates with school marks to about the same degree as Raven's matrices, but not as highly as conventional verbal scholastic aptitude tests.

Drawing Tests

Draw-a-Man Test

The task of drawing a man was first included as part of a children's intelligence test by Sir Cyril Burt (1921). He had noticed that children's drawings steadily improved with age in detail and complexity and that retarded children of a given age produced cruder drawings characteristic of much younger children. Because certain features of children's drawings, quite independently of their artistic merits, show marked and consistent developmental trends, these features can be quantified along a mental-age scale.

Florence Goodenough (1926), following Burt, developed the first standard administration and scoring procedure and extensive norms for children's drawings of a man. Points are assigned to the child's drawing for various features that had been found empirically to discriminate reliably between successive age groups and also between groups of children (of the same age) who were accelerated and children who were held back a grade or more in school. The total point score can be converted to mental age and IQ.

Goodenough's Draw-a-Man became a popular test with clinicians. It is easy to administer, it serves as a good "ice breaker" for beginning a testing session, children readily take to it, and an expert can score the child's product in a few minutes. Dale Harris (1963) provides a thorough review of the research on this test. Extensive bibliographies and critical reviews of the Goodenough Draw-a-Man and the Harris revision of it are to be found in Buros (*4*:292; *5*:335; *6*:460; *7*:352). Harris has also revised the procedures and extended the norms. There are now large-scale normative data—some of the best ever obtained for any psychological test—extending over the age range from 3 to 1*7* (Harris, 1963; Harris & Pinder, 1974).

The test works best, however, below about age 12 or 13. Above that age it becomes increasingly less discriminating among age groups, because of the marked negative acceleration of the "growth" curves of raw scores as a function of age. Between about 6 and 12 years of age, the raw scores increase as an almost perfectly linear function of age.

In the Harris revision, called the Goodenough–Harris Drawing Test (GHDT), the child is asked to draw a picture of a man, of a woman, and of himself. (See page 166.) Scoring reliabilities are generally above .90. Retest reliabilities are around .70.

The correlations of the GHDT with other standard IQ tests, such as the Stanford–Binet and Wechsler, show about the same range and central tendency as the correlations of the separate Wechsler *subscales* with Full Scale IQ. In other words, the GHDT is psychometrically very much like a homogeneous *subtest* of one of the better standard test batteries. By itself it is not a particularly good measure of *g*, especially beyond age 12, yet it is as *g* loaded as any single Wechsler subscale and more *g* loaded than some, for example, Digit Span and Coding. The factor structure of the GHDT is substantially the same for blacks, whites, and Mexican–Americans in the southwestern United States (Merz, 1970).

It is important to note that ratings of the *artistic* quality of the drawings show almost no correlation with the mental age or IQ scores derived from the drawings. The scored features do not involve artistic ability per se, but reflect developmental differences in drawing body proportions, attachment of limbs and head, and only certain details of facial features, hands, and clothing. A Rembrandt could not score much higher on the Draw-a-Man Test than the average 16-year-old.

Like many other developmental tasks, all drawing tests without exception show negative acceleration of scores (and usually decreasing variance) with increasing age of the subjects. Walking ability, for example, shows this; nearly all the individual differences variance in walking ability is found between 10 and 20 months of age. On the Draw-a-Man Test, the mean raw score difference between ages 6 and 11 is about 13 points, as compared with about 4 points difference between ages 12 and 17.

Drawing the human figure clearly reveals developmental aspects of mental ability. But how culture loaded is this performance? It is commonly believed that human figure drawing is more culture fair than many other tests, because all persons, from an early age, see the human figure frequently. I would agree that, *within* a particular culture, nearly all children have a high degree of exposure to adults (clothed in one way or another). But there is probably not equal exposure to *pictorial* representations of the human figure. To the extent that aspects of clothing enter into the scoring (as in fact they do), the scores would be cross-culturally suspect, at least outside Western societies.

Various items of evidence lead me to believe that human figure drawing is no more culture fair, and probably even less so, in the true cross-cultural sense, than many other nonverbal tests. A series of studies by Wayne Dennis (1957, 1958) of children in the Middle East suggests how sensitive the Draw-a-Man Test is to cultural differences. (For a review, see McWhinnie, 1971.) If human drawing tests are to be used cross-culturally, it is clear that aspects of clothing should not be confounded with other developmental characteristics of the drawings. It is this aspect, more than anything else, that makes the Draw-a-Man (or Woman) a quite highly culture-loaded test. Dennis (1968) also found systematic changes over a ten-year period in the drawings of black children in the United States. In 1957, black children almost invariably drew a *white* man when asked to "draw a man"; but in 1968, some 20 percent of black children drew a *black* man—a clear indication of cultural change. Another indication of the test's "cultural" sensitivity is the fact that teen-age boys and girls show virtually no difference in drawing a man but show a marked difference (in favor of girls) of about half a standard deviation in drawing a woman (Harris & Pinder, 1974).

Most of the American white–black comparisons on the Draw-a-Man Test have been reviewed by Shuey (1966). In most of the studies the black mean IQ is between 80 and 90, averaging about one standard deviation below the white mean, as is found on most other standard IQ tests. However, in one of the largest studies, blacks averaged about 10 IQ points lower than the white norms on the Draw-a-Man Test but about 20 points lower on the Stanford–Binet (Shuey, 1966, p. 83).

The white–black differences in Draw-a-Man scores found in school-age children in the same communities sharing the same styles of male attire would seem difficult to explain in terms of cultural differences. These, and similar findings with other developmental scales and other quite different kinds of drawing and copying tests, suggest the hypothesis that there is a genuine developmental lag in black children in the mental functions reflected by these drawing tests. The high degree of consistency of the average white–black difference over such a variety of developmental tasks (excluding purely sensory–motor devlopment), throughout the age range from childhood to maturity, would seem to strain any purely cultural explanation.

Figure Copying Tests

Copying geometric figures was included in Binet's first intelligence test published in 1905—copying a square (placed at age 5) and a diamond (at age 6). Figure copying proved a highly valid type of item and was retained throughout all subsequent revisions of the Binet and the Stanford–Binet scales. An advantage of copying a geometric figure over drawing a person is that geometric copying allows much less scope for idiosyncratic performance. The task requirements are completely unambiguous (i.e., "try to copy this figure to look as much like the model as possible"). The figures to be copied are simple geometric forms that have been frequently perceived by all persons living in a "carpentered world" involving straight lines, circles, triangles, squares, and so on. In terms of their *content*, geometric figure copying tests are surely among the most culture fair tests. This is even more true for children of school age, who have experience with paper and pencil.

Examples of such tests are the Figure Copying Test developed at Yale University's Gesell Institute of Child Study (Ilg & Ames, 1964, pp. 63–129) and the Bender Gestalt Test, which is well known to clinicians for its sensitivity to brain damage and other abnormal conditions (Koppitz, 1964; Pascal & Suttell, 1951). The figures used in these tests are shown on page 165.

Essential requirements in administering such tests are that there be no time limit, so that the subject can attempt every figure, and that the subject be provided with a pencil *and eraser,* so as to be able to make changes or improvements in his or her attempts to copy the model exactly. There should be as few as possible external distractions or impediments to achieving a perfect performance.

The most interesting thing about the Gesell Figure Copying Test (FCT) is that the ten figures (each presented on a separate page of the test booklet) are rank ordered in difficulty along an age scale that extends over a mental-age range from about 3 to 12 years, more or less, depending on the particular population sampled. Figure copying tests are not highly related to intelligence outside this age range. The total variance shrinks with increasing age, as more and more children can satisfactorily copy all the figures. Between kindergarten and fourth grade, however, figure copying scores correlate highly with other IQ measures. Our factor analyses of the FCT scores, along with a variety of other cognitive tests, show it to be as highly g loaded as its reliability and variance permit, and it is not appreciably loaded on any other factor. It clusters closely with Raven's matrices and the Lorge–Thorndike Nonverbal IQ. When factor analyzed along with thirty-nine other highly diverse mental tests given to sixty mentally retarded young adults (mean Stanford–Binet IQ of 39), the FCT has a loading of $+0.75$ on the g factor (first principal component) and has no significant loading on any of the other eight components (with eigenvalues greater than 1). Stanford–Binet IQ has a g loading of .73 in this same analysis. In the range of mental ages appropriate for the difficulty levels of these figural items, the FCT is a nearly pure measure of g.

Each figure of the FCT, as we have used this test, is rated on a three-point scale in terms of its resemblance to essential features of the model, so that the total range of scores goes only from 0 to 20, which is a psychometric limitation. But we have found that a much more refined scoring system does not result in higher g loadings or in correlations with scholastic achievement, even when the scoring reliability of the crude and refined scoring systems are the same (above .90). Even a two-point scale for each figure would not be appreciably less informative than the three-point scale. The essential aspect of scoring is: Is the drawing accurate in all essential features? It does not have to be especially neat or draftsman-like. By this simple criterion, virtually 100 percent of university students obtain "perfect" scores on the FCT. Interestingly, a child's performance is practically indistinguishable from a college student's on *some* of the items, whereas on the remainder the child's failures are conspicuous. Typically, a child will do the first few items (the number depending on his mental age) up to an adult standard and will completely fail the next item and all subsequent items in the series.

We have given the FCT to over 10,000 children, 5 to 12 years of age, of different ethnic groups attending the same integrated elementary schools in California. We find pronounced group differences at every age, with Orientals (Chinese and Japanese) scoring highest, followed closely by whites, then Mexican–Americans, and, last, blacks. The range of the group means is almost two standard deviations between Orientals and blacks, as can be seen in Figure 14.3. Black children in the fourth grade (ages 9–10) perform on a par with Oriental children in the first grade and slightly below white children in the second grade. The Mexican–American group, although lowest in socioeconomic status, is intermediate between Orientals and blacks and nearly on a par with whites. Considering that performance on the FCT is most highly related to learning "readiness" for the typical scholastic tasks of the primary grades (Ilg & Ames, 1964), these results are not irrelevant to the commonly observed ethnic difference in early school learning of the "three R's." The relatively high performance of the Mexican group on the FCT, compared with their relatively poor early scholastic performance, suggests that a language factor may be depressing the highly verbal scholastic skills. A considerable proportion of the Mexican–American pupils come from non-English-speaking homes.

The developmental difficulties in copying the figures are of a conceptual nature and have virtually nothing to do with perceptual acuity or manual dexterity. The child who draws a perfect square and triangle shows that he can draw straight lines and accurate angles. Why, then, with any amount of time and effort, can he not draw a diamond or a cube? Obviously, the child has to be able to formulate, in some abstract, analytic sense,

Figure 14.3. Figure Copying Test scores of Oriental (O), white (W), Mexican-American (M), and black (B) groups from socioeconomically urban, largely middle- to upper-middle-class (U) communities and rural, largely lower- to middle-class (L) communities. The six groups are ranked from highest (SES 1) to lowest (SES 6) on a composite index of socioeconomic status.

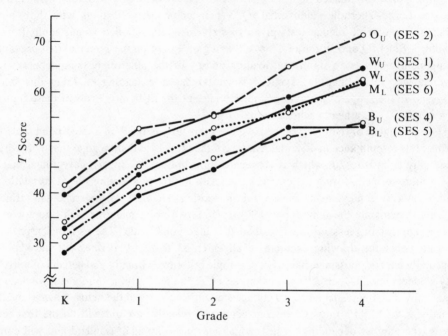

the *concept* of the figure he is trying to copy. It is the child's analytic concept of the figure that governs the performance. The analytic concept for each figure shows a fairly regular developmental progression from earlier to later ages. Two of my research assistants sorted hundreds of drawings of different age groups in terms of the types of difficulties or distortions evinced by the drawings. They found that certain modal types of difficulty appear at different ages. Some examples of the age sequences of modal difficulties are shown in Figure 14.4.

The interesting thing is that all the different ethnic and social-class groups show the same types of difficulties in exactly the same sequence but that they simply reach the same modal difficulties at *different ages*, as if their analytic–conceptual development is merely progressing at different rates. The drawings of black children at ages 6 to 7 are indistinguishable from the drawings of white and Oriental children of ages 5 to 6. This would seem a highly improbable finding if figure copying skill is largely determined by cultural influences. It is hard to imagine what form such influences would take, as we have found that direct instruction on the figure copying test has almost no effect on a child's score. It is surprisingly difficult to train a child to copy any figure that he or she cannot accurately copy spontaneously. I have succeeded in teaching some children to copy the next figure in the scale *following* the first figure that the child could not copy correctly. Say that the child gets figures 1 to 4 all right and fails on figure 5; we then train the child to draw figure 6. This training does not subsequently improve the child's success with figure 5. Yet over 90 percent of the children who can correctly draw figure 6 without special instruction have no trouble with figure 5. Apparently one can, with difficulty, train the specifics of copying a particular figure but not the underlying dimension of analytic conceptual ability on which figure copying ability depends, and which is reflected in the Guttman-like scale of difficulty of these Gesell figures. I therefore regard the FCT as one of the most culture-reduced tests of intellectual development for children below about 10 or 12 years of age (depending on social and ethnic groups) who are attending school and have had some little experience with paper and pencil.

There are no large-scale published norms on the FCT, although the test is clinically useful in the assessment of school readiness when used in the manner described by Ilg and Ames (1964). The FCT should never be used alone, because when scored on a twenty-point scale it is psychometrically crude, and, at any given age, a difference of two or three points can make for a considerable difference in percentile scores.

A ten-item figure copying test is one of the subscales of the Wechsler Preschool and Primary Scale of Intelligence (WPPSI). Its correlation with the Full Scale IQ is +0.58. (The average correlation of each of the other WPPSI subtests with Full Scale IQ is +0.61.) The highest correlations of figure copying scores with FS IQ (+0.64) are at ages 5 and 6.

Some figure copying tests require the subject to inspect the model for, say, 10 seconds, and then draw it from memory (e.g., the Graham and Kendall Memory-for-Designs Test). We have tried this procedure with the FCT and find that it makes the test more difficult but that it does not alter its essential psychometric characteristics. It still measures conceptual–analytic ability much more than memory, and, in fact, drawing from memory seems to accentuate the test's g loading.

Figure 14.4. Developmental changes in children's figure copying, going from lesser to greater maturity. The models are on the extreme left.

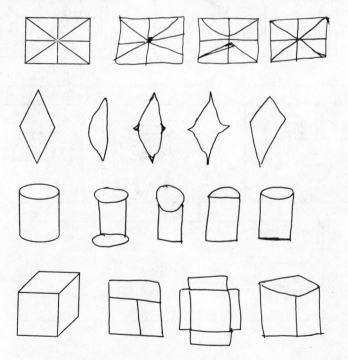

Figure 14.5.   Examples of thirteen developmentally ordered categories of basic features of children's drawings.   (From Eisner, 1967)

1. No horizon line present. Morphemes "floating," not standing on the edge of the paper.
2. Morphemes standing on the bottom edge of the paper. No horizon line drawn.
3. Some morphemes standing on the bottom edge of the paper, others floating in space.
4. Morphemes standing on bottom edge of paper and horizon line drawn.
5. Partial horizon line drawn.
6. Two or more horizon lines drawn.

7. Horizon line drawn. Morphemes floating above horizon line.
8. Horizon line drawn. Morphemes standing on horizon line.
9. Horizon line drawn. Some morphemes standing on horizon line, others floating above.
10. Morphemes overlap ground but do not overlap horizon line.
11. Morphemes standing on bottom edge of paper and overlapping horizon line.
12. Morphemes clearly overlapping horizon line.
13. Horizon line drawn. Morphemes overlapping each other.
14. Unclassifiable with respect to above categories.

Free Drawing

Children's intellectual maturity is also reflected in their "free drawings," that is, drawings that allow great latitude as to content, style, and so on. Certain elemental features of such drawings show definite developmental trends. Elliot W. Eisner (1967), a professor of art education at Stanford, in thoroughly reviewing the research literature on differences in children's free drawings as a function of age, formulated the sequence of the few basic features of children's free drawings that showed the clearest developmental trend. On the basis of these features (and their combinations, which are also developmentally sequenced), he made up thirteen ordered categories into which children's drawings could be developmentally classified. The "score" on a given picture, therefore, is simply the number of the category (ordered 1 to 13, plus an "unclassifiable" category). These developmentally ordered categories involve the horizon line and the placement of other figures with respect to it and with respect to each other. Examples and generic definitions of the categories are shown in Figure 14.5. Eisener's scaling of these categories is actually quite crude; a more sophisticated method of optimally age scaling the categories would surely result in greater developmental discriminability and greater differentiation of SES groups than does Eisner's overly simple ordinal scale. It is fundamentally a statistical problem in discriminant analysis. One advantage of Eisner's *a priori* scale, of course, is that it was made up completely independently of the data to which it was applied, and therefore it does not "capitalize on chance" or thereby make it absolutely essential to cross-validate the scale.

To elicit drawings that might display these features, Eisner asked subjects simply to "Make a crayon drawing of you and your friends playing in the school yard." Each child was given a new box of crayons and a 12″ × 18″ sheet of paper, and was allowed 20 minutes to complete the drawing. Eisner secured drawings under these conditions from approximately 1,600 school children in grades 1, 3, 5, and 7. Half of the children were from low-SES (79 percent black) and half from high-SES (74 percent white) homes in slum and suburban communities, respectively. Eisner had hypothesized that

> the qualities available to individuals living in a slum area were more diverse and imposing than the qualities permeating the environment of the upper-middle-class suburban child . . . the perceptual abilities of children living in slums might be more highly developed . . . than those of their middle-class contemporaries, and since perceptual ability is related to drawing ability, in the area of drawing, children from the slums might not be as disadvantaged as they are in the discursive academic areas. (1967, p. 77)

Figure 14.6.   Mean drawing scores of upper- and lower-SES groups as a function of school grade level.   (From Eisner, 1967, p. 126)

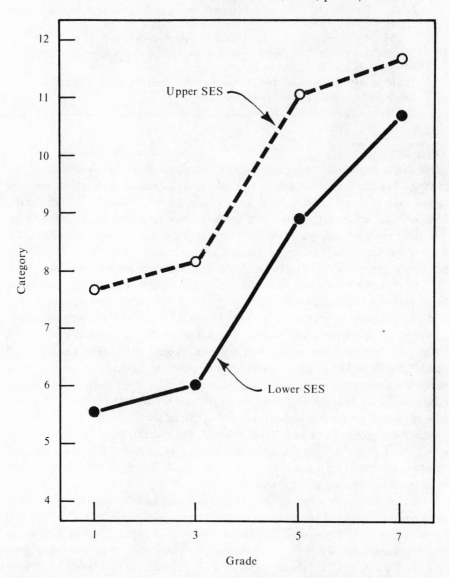

The maturity (i.e., the mean category number) of drawing scores for the low- and high-SES groups differ overall by 0.67σ in favor of the high-SES group. The scores increase monotonically with age in both SES groups, as shown in Figure 14.6. It can be seen that the average low-SES seventh-grader performs approximately on a par with the high-SES fifth-grader; and the low-SES fifth-grader's performance is on a par with the high-SES third-grader. This is about the same amount of grade lag as is found between such SES groups in most tests of scholastic aptitude and achievement. There is some evidence of a ceiling effect in the high-SES group at grade 7, and so the SES groups tend to converge in this older age range. The correlation between the drawing scores and reading scores of fifth- and seventh-graders is 0.44. The correlation between drawing scores and IQ is 0.34.

If these drawing scores were very sensitive to environmental influences, one should expect to find an appreciable sex difference, because, as Eisner notes, girls have more interest in art and more favorable attitudes and more information about it than boys. Yet the drawing scores of boys and girls do not differ significantly.

The fact of a large and highly significant SES difference in maturity of drawings, along with the fact of a parallel increase in scores of both the low- and high-SES groups, as a function of age, is again consistent with the hypothesis of a relative lag in the low-SES children's rate of mental development.

Piagetian Tests

A type of "test" item that seems to be very culture reduced has originated in the ingenious researches on children's cognitive development by the famous Swiss psychologist Jean Piaget (born 1896). Piaget's theories and experiments on the nature of mental development represent a life's work and are far too extensive for even brief review in the present context. For an introduction to the complex and fascinating world of Piaget, the reader is referred to Flavell's (1963) excellent textbook. The adaptation of psychometric methodology to Piagetian theory is introduced in a symposium (in which Piaget himself was a participant) edited by Green, Ford, and Flamer (1971).

Piaget's research mainly concerns careful description of the psychological characteristics of the rather distinctive stages of cognitive development through which all normal human beings pass from birth to maturity. Piaget distinguishes four main stages or developmental landmarks in the course of intellectual growth, which are *invariant* in sequence for all humans. There are individual and group differences in the ages at which these cognitive developmental landmarks are reached, but their *order* is invariant. If the theory is correct, therefore, it should be possible to devise *ordinal scales* of cognitive development that are broadly cross-cultural. Piaget views the fundamental aspects of development represented in his four stages as the result of interactions between innate, biological, maturational programs in the nervous system and highly universal experiential factors available to virtually all normally reared children. However, each stage of cognitive development is a structured whole; mental development fundamentally does not consist of a mere accretion of specific bits of knowledge and skills. Piaget's four main stages are

1. The *sensory–motor* stage, from birth to the onset of language (i.e., age 1 to 2 years), a period of perceptual learning, conditioning, development of sensory–motor coordination and object permanence, and completely stimulus-bound "cognition."
2. The *preoperational* stage, from about age 2 to 6 or 7 years, a period of symbolic play and cognitive egocentrisim; that is, the child views everything only in terms of his own relationship to it.
3. The stage of *concrete operations,* from 7 or 8 to 11 or 12, which, in Piaget's view, is the first manifestation of true intelligence, that is, the capacity to perform mental operations related to concrete objects, such as *numeration* (e.g., a number of eggs can be matched with a number of egg cups), *seriation* (e.g., a

number of cubes of different sizes can be arranged in order from smallest to largest), *classification* (e.g., a pile of large, medium, and small blocks colored red, yellow, and blue can be sorted into three groups in terms of color *or* size or into six groups in terms of color *and* size), and *conservation*, or the ability to conceive the invariant structure of classes, relations, and numbers (e.g., a given quantity of liquid is conceived of as remaining the same *amount* of liquid whether it is poured into a broad, shallow bowl or into a tall, thin flask).

4. The stage of *formal operations* (onset between 11 and 13 years of age) is the final level of operational thinking, involving logical reasoning, which is not dependent on the mental manipulation of concrete objects, and propositional, conditional, combinational, and inferential thinking. The level of formal operations includes the capacity for thinking in terms of hypothetical possibilities, abstractions, and imaginary conditions, as well as the capacity for mental manipulation of nonpictorial symbols for things and for abstract relationships. Some adults never attain the stage of formal operations, but it is not known precisely the percentage of any particular population that fails to reach this final level of cognitive development.

Piaget's quite inadvertent contribution to psychometrics stems from his invention of numerous ingeniously simple "tasks" with which children can be confronted under rather informal clinical interview conditions and that reveal the particular stage of the child's cognitive development. A given child can be clearly in one of the four stages or in a transitional stage, in which he or she performs some, but not all, of the types of tasks that characterize a given stage. The sequence of characteristic tasks *within* a stage, however, is an ordinal scale *between* stages; that is, a child who performs any task at one stage can perform *most* of the tasks of an earlier stage. There is really no chance of having "missed out" on learning something at an earlier stage, because what is actually assessed at any stage is not items of acquired *knowledge* in the ordinary sense, but unconscious cognitive structures or schemas that develop through the child's interaction with those most common aspects of the environment that are universally available to virtually *all* biologically normal children.

Because the stage of concrete operations is characterized by the first levels of mental operations that we think of as true intelligence, the tasks that mark this stage have received the most attention and elaboration by Piagetian psychologists. There are now a great many Piagetian tasks that can be used to determine whether a child has developed *concrete* operations or is still preoperational; these tasks are, of course, most discriminative between the ages of about 5 or 6 to 8 or 9 years, the period when most children make the transition from preoperational to concrete operations.

The best known of these concrete operations tasks are those involving the *conservation of quantity*—volume and number. The child fills two identical beakers to exactly the same level and satisfies himself that they contain equal amounts of liquid. The examiner then pours one beaker into a broad, shallow bowl and the other into a tall, thin cylinder. The preoperational child is then convinced that the amounts of liquid have become unequal. He claims that the tall cylinder now contains more than the shallow bowl. No amount of verbal instruction and demonstration will really convince him otherwise. Suppose that an examiner shows a preoperational child a *half*-full glass of Coke and a full glass of the same and asks him which one he would prefer. The child says, "The full one." Why? "It has more Coke in it, of course." Then the examiner, in full view of the child, pours the *full* glass into the broad, shallow bowl and pours the *half*-full glass into the tall, thin cylinder. "Now take your choice," he says. "You may drink it this time." The preoperational child unhesitatingly picks the tall cylinder, even though he has clearly seen the examiner pour the *half*-full glass of Coke into it. "Why did you pick that one?" the examiner asks. "It's got more Coke," the child replies, as if the answer is perfectly obvious. A child who has already attained the stage of concrete operations, however, would not be "taken in" by this. He would immediately and intuitively "know" that pouring a liquid into a different-shaped jar does not change the *quantity* of liquid. He is able to conserve quantity.

The same kind of thing is done with two rows of pennies (or gumdrops or any other small, uniform, desirable objects). One row contains six pennies, and the other row contains eight. When they are all placed with the pennies touching each other and with one row above the other, the child readily agrees there are more pennies in the eight-pennies row than in the six-pennies row. He is told he can take either row to keep for himself. He naturally expresses his preference for the row of eight pennies. But, before the examiner lets the child take the pennies, he spreads out the row containing only six pennies, so it is now about twice as long as the row of eight pennies, and says, "Now take your choice." The child now takes the long six-penny row! It looks like "more" to him. The same thing occurs with a round ball of clay, which, when flattened out like a pancake, is interpreted by the preoperational child as consisting of *more* clay than the small round ball of clay. Virtually no children under the age of 5 show the concept of conservation (Hood, 1962).

Another favorite Piagetian indicator of the concrete operations stage is the "horizontality of liquid" task, illustrated in Figure 14.7. A child is shown a bottle of red liquid (A). An opaque card is then placed in front of the bottle, and the bottle is tilted (B). Then the child is given a full-scale outline drawing of the bottle and is asked to draw the level of the red liquid as it will appear when the card is removed (C). Most children under 8 or 9 years

Figure 14.7. Piaget's tilted water bottle test for assessing child's concept of the horizontality of water level.

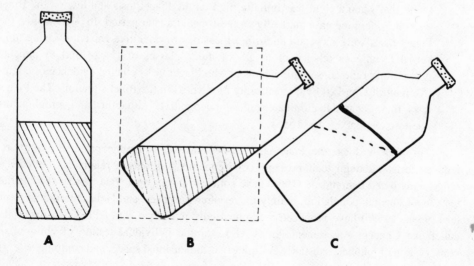

A   B   C

of age draw a line more or less parallel to the bottom of the bottle, as shown in C, whereas older children more often correctly draw a horizontal line. Many children under 8 years do not markedly improve their drawing even after they have been shown the liquid in the tilted bottle.

Because the experiential elements involved in these Piagetian tasks are so universally available to observation by virtually all children and get at the most fundamental kinds of mental operations that are sequentially ordered in the mental development of all children, Piagetian psychologists believe these tasks are much less culture loaded than most of the items in conventional IQ tests. It would indeed be difficult to argue with this position. The Piagetian tasks are also apparently much less susceptible to influence by specific instruction than ordinary IQ tests (Kohlberg, 1968, pp. 1029–1044; Sigel & Olmsted, 1970). Kohlberg (1968) made these observations:

> An integrated Montessori program for Headstart children aged 3 and 4 led to a mean 14-point increase in Stanford–Binet IQ in the first 6 months. No significant further increase in IQ was found during the remaining $1\frac{1}{2}$ years in which the children were in the program. The initial IQ increases could not be considered actual increases in general cognitive–structural development, since they were not paralleled by any significant increases in performance upon Piaget cognitive–structural tasks. The primary cause of the IQ increase was an improvement in attention and rapport with adults. Increases in rated attention in the classroom (as well as in the test situation) were marked during the first 6 months, and individual improvement in rated attention correlated .63 with improvement in Stanford–Binet IQs during this period. In addition to attention, verbalization showed a sharp initial spurt indicating that the IQ changes were more a result of changes in cognitive motivation than a change in cognitive capacity. These changes in turn had a ceiling rather than moving continuously upward, and the motivational changes themselves did not lead to a later increase in cognitive capacity because of increased general learning.   (p. 1051)

> It was found that Piaget tests were more stable than Binet tests, i.e., they yielded test–retest reliabilities between a 2-to-4 month period in the 0.90's. It was also found that when a child was initially high on the Piaget tests and low on the Binet tests, he would increase markedly on the Binet at a later period. In other words, the Piaget tasks were more situation-free measures of cognitive capacity. Using non-verbal techniques (choice of length of gum, glasses of Coca-Cola) to indicate possession of the conservation concept, the Piaget tasks elicited evidence of cognitive maturity masked by distractibility or shyness in the Binet situation. The Piaget tests, then, seemed to eliminate some ''noncognitive'' situational and verbal factors due to experience.   (p. 1055)

For such reasons, the Piagetian ''tests'' have considerable promise as culture-reduced tests, although their present scope encompasses only a relatively limited age range. Pinard and Laurendeau (1964) have collected norms on a wide variety of Piagetian tests in a Canadian population, mainly for research purposes; and Goldschmidt and Bentler (1968a, 1968b) have produced a commercially published set of Piagetian materials, called the Concept Assessment Kit (CAK), for the individual testing of children on conservation of number, substance, weight, two-dimensional space, and continuous (e.g., liquid) and discontinuous (e.g., kernals of corn) quantities. In the CAK the various Piagetian tasks are "psychometrized" in the fashion of the Stanford–Binet or WISC, with two parallel forms, and zero, one, or two points are assigned to the subject's performance on each of the six tasks, with a total score range (on each parallel form) of zero to twelve points. This, of course, does not permit a very spread-out distribution of scores in the age range for which the test is recommended, namely, ages 4 to 7 years. (Some Piagetian experts believe that the test works best in the age range from about 5 to 8.) The norms provided with the CAK are based on 560 children in the Los Angeles area and appear to slightly overrepresent the lower middle class. One would like to see a more widely representative standardization. The test as a whole has exceptionally high (about 0.95) parallel-form and retest reliabilities when these are determined in a three-year age range. (Detailed reviews of the CAK are to be found in Buros 7:437 and the *Journal of Educational Measurement*, 1969, *6*, 263–269.)

Two questions are of particular interest from the standpoint of psychometrics: (1) Do Piaget's tests measure a different mental ability than the *g* measured by conventional IQ tests? and (2) Do minority children and "culturally disadvantaged" children perform better on the Piagetian tests, relative to majority children, than on conventional IQ tests?

Piaget (1947, p. 154) believes that his tests measure the same mental ability as is measured by psychometric instruments such as the Stanford–Binet; his criticism of the conventional tests is not that they fail to measure an individual's level of intelligence, but that they do so in a less revealing way, giving only a measure of total "yield" without revealing the cognitive structures and schema that constitute the stages of mental development, as are revealed by the Piagetian tasks. The fact that Piaget was correct in this matter is shown by the fact that the correlations between summed scores on the Piaget tests and Binet scores are in the .70's for children of a given age (Kohlberg, 1968, p. 1052). Table 14.1 shows the correlations between various standard intelligence and achievement tests and various Piagetian batteries consisting of from five to ten Piagetian tests all assessing concrete operations. The correlations range from .18 to .84, with a mean of about .50. The correlations are highly variable for several reasons: (1) they are based on composite scores from different numbers (from 5 to 10) of Piagetian items, (2) different age ranges are involved in the various studies, and the Piagetian tests correlate higher with IQ in the transitional age ranges with respect to the stages of mental development, (3) age is controlled in some studies and not in others, and (4) there is considerable statistical sampling error when sample sizes are not exceptionally large, as is often the case in Piagetian studies. (With a sample size of one hundred, two-thirds of the correlations will fall between +.42 and +.57 purely due to sampling error, when the true correlation in the population is +.50.)

These important points must be taken into account in interpreting the correlations of Piagetian tests with other measures.

First, each Piagetian task is psychometrically equivalent to a *single* item in an ordinary test, and the variance on single items contains so much error and specificity that single items of a test cannot correlate very highly with any other measure. The inter-correlations of single Piagetian items are, in fact, remarkably high compared with inter-correlations among single items in psychometric tests. A study by Tuddenham (1970, Table 3.2, p. 67) shows inter-item correlations ranging from +0.15 to +0.65, with a median of +0.40, for six Piagetian tasks. The average inter-item correlation on Raven's

Table 14.1. Correlation (r) between Piagetian tests and various measurements of intelligence and scholastic achievement.

Variable	r	Study
Intelligence Tests		
Stanford–Binet MA	.38	Beard, 1960
WISC MA	.69	Kuhn, 1976
WISC Full Scale IQ	.43	Elkind, 1961
WISC Verbal IQ	.47	Eklind, 1961
WISC	.69–.84	Hathaway, 1972
Raven's Matrices	.60	Tuddenham, 1970
Peabody Picture Vocabulary Test	.21	Tuddenham, 1970
Peabody Picture Vocabulary Test	.47	Gaudia, 1972
Peabody Picture Vocabulary Test	.28	De Avila & Havassy, 1974
Peabody Picture Vocabulary Test	.31	Klippel, 1975
Lorge-Thorndike MA	.62	Kaufman, 1970, 1971
Lorge-Thorndike IQ	.55	Kaufman, 1970, 1971
Gesell School Readiness Test	.64	Kaufmann, 1970, 1971
IQ–Unspecified Test	.24–.34	Dodwell, 1962
Mean r	*.49*	
Scholastic Achievement		
Reading (SAT)	.58	Kaufmann & Kaufmann, 1972
Reading (SAT)	.42	Garfinkle, 1975
Arithmetic (SAT)	.50	Garfinkle, 1975
Arithmetic (SAT)	.60	Kaufman & Kaufman, 1972
Mathematics (MAT)	.18–.41	De Vries, 1974
Arithmetic Grades	.52	Goldschmidt, 1967
Composite Achievement (SAT)	.64	Kaufman & Kaufman, 1972
Composite Achievement (California Achievement Test)	.63	Dudek et al., 1969
Mean r	*.55*	

Colored Progressive Matrices is only $+0.20$. The average item intercorrelation on the Stanford–Binet is $+0.43$, which is not significantly different than for the Piagetian items. This is remarkable, considering that Piagetian tests were not selected with reference to any psychometric criteria whatsoever, whereas one of the criteria for item selection in the Stanford–Binet is a high item by total score correlation (which is related to the average inter-item correlation as follows: $\bar{r}_{ij} = \bar{r}_{it}^2$).

Second, the Piagetian scores are usually based on very few items (five to ten or so), so that the score is almost certain to contain more specific and error variance than tests consisting of a great many items. All the reliable common factor variance in any multi-item test is comprised of twice the sum of the item covariances; the error and specific variance consists of the sum of the item variances. Consequently, tests with few items, such as the Piaget tests, are at a disadvantage psychometrically. Despite this fact, the Piagetian tests correlate very substantially with other tests of intelligence and achievement.

Third, it is instructive to look at a principal components analysis of Piagetian items. A study by Garfinkle (1975, Table 28, p. 88) provides intercorrelations among fourteen Piagetian tasks administered to ninety-six kindergarten and first-grade children. The mean inter-item correlation is $+0.34$. I have done a principal components analysis of the intercorrelations among the fourteen Piagetian tasks. The first principal component (i.e., the *g* factor of this Piagetian battery) accounts for 40 percent of the total variance in these fourteen items. (The eigenvalue of the first principal component of these fourteen *items* is almost exactly the same as the eigenvalue of the first principal component of the eleven WISC *subscales*.) The communalities (which are close to the squared multiple correlation of each item with every other item) of the fourteen Piagetian *items* range from .41 to .80, with a mean of .61, which is comparable to what we find for Wechsler *subtests* (each comprised of at least several items). These findings for *single items* are absolutely re-markable from a psychometric standpoint—a fact scarcely recognized by most Piagetian psychologists.

But what makes this evidence even more striking testimony to Piaget's genius in devising test items that get at the most fundamental aspects of intellectual development is the fact that the general factor of the Piagetian battery is almost pure *g* in the Spearman sense. Vernon (1965) factor analyzed a large number of Piagetian tests along with many standard IQ tests and found a large general factor—unquestionably Spearman's *g*—common to both types of tests. The non-*g* variance in the separate Piagetian tests seems to be largely task specific, having little in common with other Piagetian tasks or with conventional psychometric measures. But this should not be surprising, as there is considerable item-specific variance (in addition to true measurement error) in practically all single test items of whatever type.

I should point out that a number of factor analytic studies of Piagetian tests along with other measures commit an egregious psychological error by orthogonally rotating the factors (or principal components) by some method such as varimax, which prohibits the emergence of the large general factor in all such tests. About the only wholly correct factor analysis of Piagetian tests I have found in the literature is the one by Philip Vernon (1965), a well-known expert in factor analysis and psychometrics. Many developmental psychologists, with no special training in factor analysis or psychometrics, simply select the most popular computer program, Kaiser's varimax, for doing their factor analyses. As applied to factor extraction in the abilities domain, this is flatly *wrong*, not mathemati-cally, but psychologically and scientifically. In the abilities domain, either oblique rota-tion should be done to permit the hierarchical extraction of *g*, or the *g* factor should be extracted (as the first principal factor) prior to rotation of the remaining factors. (In the latter procedure, one additional factor should be extracted prior to rotation.) It will be a great day for psychology when we no longer have to read studies in which the author automatically applies the varimax computer program (which is expressly intended to "rotate away" a general factor) and then points out that "factor analysis" fails to reveal a general factor in his test data!

Do Piagetian tests show social-class and ethnic group differences within the United States? Yes. Children from low-SES backgrounds are about as far behind on Piagetian tests as on conventional IQ tests (Almy, 1970; Almy, Chittenden, & Miller, 1966; Fig-urelli & Keller, 1972; Tuddenham, 1970; Wasik & Wasik, 1971).

Some five hundred blacks, whites, and Orientals (Chinese and Japanese) in grades 1 to 3 (ages 6 to 8) in three California communities were tested by Tuddenham (1970) with a battery of ten Piagetian tests. Black children performed less well than whites on every item, whereas Orientals outperformed whites on seven of the ten items and did not differ appreciably on the remaining three. The white–black differences, reported by Tuddenham in terms of percentage passing each item, can be converted to normalized sigma (σ) differences. The average white–black σ difference for the ten items is 0.74σ, which can be compared with the average white–black σ difference of 0.61σ for single Stanford–Binet items in large samples of 4-year-olds (see Chapter 11, p. 564). A quite typical example is the horizontality-of-water-level test (see Figure 14.7), which was "passed" by 43 percent of Orientals, 35 percent of whites, and 13 percent of blacks.

In short, the Piagetian items are somewhat *more* racially discriminating than the Stanford–Binet items as concerns white–black comparisons. On the other hand, Orientals generally score about the same as whites on conventional IQ tests, but they score *higher* than whites on the Piagetian tests. (We found that the same thing was true for the Gesell Figure Copying Test.) Also, there is some evidence, though not so conclusive, that Mexican–American children differ much less, if at all, from majority children on Piagetian tests (De Avila & Havassy, 1974; Eimers, 1971), which is also consistent with our findings on the Figure Copying Test. Gaudia (1972) compared 126 very-low-SES white, black, and American Indian children in grades 1 to 3 on a battery of Piagetian conservation tests. The whites and Indians did not differ significantly, although both groups scored about a year below the age norms for these tests; the blacks lagged significantly ($p < .001$) behind the whites and Indians in the acquisition of conservation, with the lag greatest in the older age groups. Expressed as a percentage of the highest possible conservation score, the means of the three age-matched ethnic groups are white = 51, American Indian = 51, black = 30.

In all such comparisons of group means, one must take into account the small number of items of the Piagetian tests, which tends greatly to attenuate mean differences expressed in σ units or standard score units. When this is properly taken into account, in terms of *item* discriminabilities and inter-item correlations, it turns out that the Piagetian tests show *larger* white–black differences than the Stanford–Binet or other conventional IQ tests. I figure the white–black mean difference in σ units would be about 20 percent larger than the Stanford–Binet IQ difference on Piagetian tests of comparable length to the Stanford–Binet. But, while Piagetian tests tend to magnify the white–black difference, they tend to diminish the differences between whites and Mexicans and Indians, and Orientals tend to surpass whites in Piagetian performance. Interestingly, Arctic Eskimos surpass white urban Canadian children on Piagetian tests, and Canadian Indians do almost as well as Eskimos (Vernon, 1965; MacArthur, 1968, p. 48). Obviously it is not necessary to have lived in a Western or middle-class urban culture to perform up to Western middle-class levels on Piagetian tests.

Developmental Preference Test

This developmental test is especially interesting because it has no "right" or "wrong" answers, but only preferences that are known to change systematically with age. As children mature mentally, they show changing preferences for color, form, number, and size, in that sequence, in attending to the attributes of objects. The order of preference for children of kindergarten age (5 or 6 years) is (1) form, (2) color, (3) number, and (4) size.

Groups of white and black kindergarten children were each shown twelve different stimulus displays of the type shown in Figure 14.8. The figures on the four cards differ simultaneously in color (green, red, blue, yellow), shape, size, and number. The examiner gives the small card at the top to the child and asks the child to put it down on any one

Figure 14.8. An item of the color–form–number–size test. The letters (which do not appear on the actual test) indicate the colors of the figures.

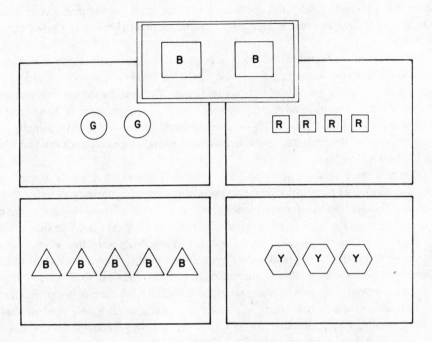

of the four cards with which he or she thinks it goes best. It is made clear that there is no "right" answer. Thus, the child can match the target card on the basis of color, form, number, or size. White and black children of the same age differ in the relative frequencies of their preferences, in accord with the developmental prediction; that is, the black children show a significantly higher percentage of the less mature preferences (Toki, 1971):

	Color	Form	Number	Size
White	10.2%	73.5%	14.9%	1.5%
Black	28.9	56.5	12.5	2.1

In view of the consistent racial differences in these highly diverse developmental tasks, I venture the hypothesis that typical black and white children will show consistent differences in growth rates and in orderly sequential development on all age-related tasks involving abstraction, judgment, mental manipulation—in short, the essence of g or level II ability.

Tests Constructed Specifically for Blacks

Because all existing tests of intelligence and scholastic aptitude have shown mean differences of about one standard deviation between representative samples of American whites and blacks beyond 4 years of age, attempts have been made to construct aptitude tests specifically for the black population in the hope that such specially devised tests would yield a more valid index of blacks' mental ability. A corollary expectation is that such tests would show little or no difference in average scores between blacks and whites.

Listening Comprehension Test

The psychometrically most impressive attempt in this vein was made by the American Institutes for Research, under the sponsorship of the College Entrance Examination Board. The study was reported in stages by Orr and Graham (1968) and Carver (1968–1969, 1969).

The investigators hypothesized that a large part of the low performance of blacks on conventional scholastic aptitude tests is the result of blacks' *reading deficiency* and blacks' disinterest in the content of the standard tests. The aim, then, was to construct a wholly aural test that requires no reading and calls for the comprehension of content that is of great interest to black children. To focus the interest aspect of the test optimally, the target population of the projected test was narrowed to eighth-grade disadvantaged black males in Washington, D.C.

The first stage of developing the test consisted of having a young black male interview a number of boys from the target population regarding their chief interests and their most frequent topics of conversation outside of school. (Interviewees were not approached through the schools.) Interviews with twenty boys revealed that they all had television sets at home and great interest in programs involving adventure stories, spies, cowboys, soldiers, detectives, and sports events (particularly football and basketball). Certain comic books were another common interest. When the boys were asked "If you could make up your own movie, what would it be about?" the topics most frequently mentioned were soldier, great Negro, comedy, detective, secret agent, football, baseball. The Listening Comprehension Test (LCT), therefore, was made up of content about sports, adventure, war, cowboys, detectives, and so on. The whole test was tape recorded in the style of a radio program; there would be a short episode about one of the topics and then the "announcer" would ask several comprehension questions about the contents of the episode. The "announcer" was a native of the target population area, so his voice and accent might lead to sympathetic identification by the testees.

The test items went through tryouts and all the standard psychometric procedures of test development. Only items with p values (i.e., percentage passing) between 10 percent and 90 percent were retained, except for a few very easy items at the beginning of the test. The Kuder–Richardson internal consistency reliability was .89. The LCT also correlated in the range of .64 to .78 with various standard aptitude tests (Carver, 1969, Table 2). The test was also tried on white low- and middle-income eighth-grade boys and showed comparable correlations with standard aptitude tests (SCAT and STEP). Blacks expressed a definite preference for the LCT over the standard tests; whites showed more mixed preferences. Carver (1968–1969, p. 12) concluded that the method of test development and the correlations of the test with other validated measures "supported the conclusion that the new test was reliable and valid as a listening comprehension test for eighth-grade boys, black and white, of all socioeconomic levels. It also appears to be an adequate indicator of verbal aptitude among these boys."

The final test was given to large samples of eighth-grade black and white boys, who were classed as low income if their family's annual income (in 1968) was judged to be less than $5,000; all others were classed as middle income. Table 14.2 compares the race and income groups on the new Listening Comprehension Test and a conventional aptitude test, the School and College Ability Test (SCAT-II), in sigma units (i.e., σ = the average standard deviation within the four race–income groups). It can be seen that the LCT shows somewhat smaller differences between SES levels (within races) and between whites and

Table 14.2. Mean differences (in σ units[1]) between race and income groups on the Listening Comprehension Test (LCT) and the School and College Ability Test (SCAT–II). (From Carver, 1969, Table 2)

Contrasted Groups	LCT	SCAT–II
Middle-income whites − Middle-income blacks	+0.83	+1.01
Middle-income whites − Low-income blacks	+1.32	+1.81
Low-income whites − Middle-income blacks	+0.17	−0.07
Low-income whites − Low-income blacks	+0.66	+0.72
Middle-income whites − Low-income whites	+0.66	+1.08
Middle-income blacks − Low-income blacks	+0.50	+0.80

[1]A σ unit is the average (i.e., root mean square) within-group (race–income level) standard deviation.

blacks than the more conventional paper-and-pencil test, the SCAT-II. The overall race difference is 0.63σ on the LCT and 0.75σ on the SCAT. The overall difference between income levels is 0.58σ on the LCT and 0.94σ on the SCAT. The difference of 0.12σ between the LCT and the SCAT with respect to the race difference seemed too small for the American Institutes of Research to consider the LCT a success (see Carver, 1968–1969), and so further work on the LCT was abandoned. Because the item types and content of the SCAT are considerably more diverse than on the LCT, I would hypothesize that the SCAT total score is more highly *g* loaded than the LCT score, and therefore the slightly smaller racial difference on the LCT could be explained in terms of Spearman's hypothesis that the magnitude of the white–black difference is directly related to the test's *g* loading. In any case, it is evident that a large-scale attempt, using sound psychometric methods, to develop a test specially for blacks resulted in a test on which blacks score much lower than whites even when the groups are roughly matched on SES.

Black Intelligence Test of Cultural Homogeneity

The BITCH-100, as it is better known, is a highly culture-specific test devised and published by Robert L. Williams (1972a, 1972b), especially for testing the intelligence of black Americans. The BITCH appears to be an offshoot of an earlier (unpublished) black intelligence test known as the Dove Counterbalance Intelligence Test. The "Dove" items tested one's knowledge of black ghetto slang, a typical item being:

If a judge finds you *holding wood* (in California), what's the most he can give you?
  (a) indeterminant (life)   (d) a year in the county
  (b) a nickle   (e) $100
  (c) a dime   [Answer c is keyed as correct.]

The BITCH is similarly composed entirely of words, terms, and expressions peculiar to the black culture. Williams is quoted (Matarazzo & Wiens, 1977, p. 58) as claiming that the BITCH test samples "the various idioms, patois, argots, idialects [*sic*], and social dialects of black people." The actual items of a published test, of course, cannot be quoted, but some sample items from the S.O.B. Test ("son of the original BITCH Test") have been printed in *Psychology Today* (May 1974, p. 101) and are highly typical of the content of the BITCH, in which all the items are presented in a multiple-choice vocabulary format. In the following samples an asterisk indicates the keyed answer:

1. *The Bump*
   - (a) A result of a forceful blow
   - (b) A suit
   - (c) A car
   - *(d) A dance

2. *Running a game*
   - (a) Writing a bad check
   - (b) Looking at something
   - (c) Directing a contest
   - *(d) Getting what one wants

3. *To get down*
   - (a) To dominate
   - (b) To travel
   - (c) To lower a position
   - *(d) To have sexual intercourse

4. *Cop an attitude*
   - (a) Leave
   - *(b) Become angry
   - (c) Sit down
   - (d) Protect a neighborhood

In case anyone might wonder if the BITCH Test was intended as a spoof, it should be noted that the National Institute of Mental Health awarded its author $153,000 to develop it (*Science Digest,* August 1975, p. 8).

The standardization of the one hundred-item BITCH Test was based on one hundred white and one hundred black high school students ages 16 to 18 in St. Louis, Missouri. The mean scores of the whites and blacks in the standardization samples are fifty-one and eighty-seven items answered correctly out of one hundred, respectively. The retest reliabilities were .84 for whites and .88 for blacks.

The only published research I have found on the BITCH is a study by Matarazzo and Wiens (1977), who gave the BITCH, along with the Wechsler Adult Intelligence Scale (WAIS), to black ($N = 17$) and white ($N = 116$) young adult applicants for the police force in Portland, Oregon. The mean white–black difference (in σ units based on these samples) on the WAIS Full Scale IQ is $+1.62\sigma$ (white mean IQ = 116.7, black mean IQ = 104.6). On the BITCH Test, the black mean of 84.9 exceeds the white mean of 63.7 by 2.83σ. In fact, the white and black distributions of BITCH scores show almost no overlap at all: the *lowest* BITCH score obtained by any black is 79 and the highest BITCH score obtained by any white is 80. With so little overlap, the point-biserial correlation between the racial dichotomy and BITCH scores turns out to be 0.97!

The correlations between the BITCH and the WAIS can be summarized as follows:

	Whites (N = 116)	Blacks (N = 17)
WAIS Verbal IQ	+.16	−.04
WAIS Performance IQ	+.09	+.13
WAIS Full Scale IQ	+.16	+.04
Years of education	+.02	−.33

Correlation of BITCH with

None of the correlations differs significantly from zero, and none of the eleven WAIS subscales shows a significant correlation with the BITCH in either the white or black samples. The black sample had an average of more than $2\frac{1}{2}$ years of college education, so that group can hardly be called educationally disadvantaged. Nor are they disadvantaged on the WAIS with an overall mean IQ about twenty points higher than blacks in general. Yet their BITCH scores fall below the average of the black standardization samples of 16-

to 18-year-old high school pupils. This, added to the fact that in the police applicant group the BITCH correlates essentially zero with the WAIS Full Scale IQ as well as with every one of the WAIS subtests, suggests the reasonable conclusion that the BITCH is an exceedingly poor test of general intelligence, if indeed it measures any *g* at all, in either the black or white populations. If the BITCH has validity for any purpose, it remains to be discovered. At present the most that can be said for it is that it is *prima facie* a test of a person's knowledge of black ghetto slang and of what Matarazzo and Wiens refer to as "street wiseness." Whether it is even a psychometrically good test of black slang and "street wiseness" is not known.

Black Intelligence Test
Like the BITCH, the BIT was designed specifically to measure information, vocabulary, and phraseology more or less peculiar to the black culture (Boone & Adesso, 1974). (In a personal communication, Boone states that the name of the BIT has now been changed to BEAT—for Black Environmental Adjustment Test—"to reflect the environmental bias of the test.") The BIT has four types of items: historical information about blacks (ten items), comprehension of nonstandard English (ten items) similarities (ten items), and vocabulary (twenty items). That the test is not very homogeneous can be seen from the extraordinarily low KR-20 reliabilities of 0.51 and 0.42 in black and white samples of one hundred persons each (personal communication from Boone, Feb. 1977). (The KR-20 reliability of most standard tests is over 0.90.) A KR-20 of 0.51 for a fifty-item test means that the average item intercorrelation is only 0.02. (The average item intercorrelation in the Stanford–Binet is about 0.40.)

In a study by Boone and Adesso (1974) of the BIT (or BEAT) obtained on one hundred white and one hundred black students in the University of Wisconsin, Milwaukee, the BIT correlated near zero (0.009) with the Vocabulary subtest of a standard intelligence test, so in this respect, too, the BIT is very much like the BITCH.

Whites score considerably lower than blacks on the BIT, but any other statistical conclusions from the Boone and Adesso (1974) article would seem risky to expound on, as I find altogether thirteen numerical errors in their two ANOVA tables, in which the *F* ratios are off by as much as factors of 10 and 100.

The *p* values (percentage passing) for blacks and whites of each of the fifty BIT items were provided by Boone so that I could determine the cross-racial correlation of item *p* values as an index of item $\times$ group interaction (see Chapter 9, pp. 432–439). The correlation is +0.52, which indicates a large amount of race $\times$ item interaction. This method, therefore, clearly detects the marked cultural bias that was built into this test. The correlation of +0.52 may be compared with the white–black correlation of item *p* values for the Stanford–Binet ($r = +0.98$), WISC ($r = +0.96$), Raven's matrices ($r = +0.98$, PPVT ($r = +0.98$), and the Wonderlic Personnel Test ($r = +0.94$).

Like the BITCH, the BIT (or BEAT) as yet has no demonstrated construct validity or predictive validity for any criterion of ability in the black culture.

Adaptive Behavior Inventories

Adaptive behavior inventories (ABIs) are intended to assess an individual's effectiveness in coping with the natural and social demands of his or her environment. These inventories are not tests in the usual sense, but are standardized interviews with the subject's parent or someone who has a close day-to-day acquaintance with the subject and can answer questions about the subject's typical behavior in a variety of specific areas.

ABIs are most often used in the assessment of the mentally retarded and were originally designed expressly for that purpose. I include a brief discussion of ABIs in this chapter not because they are in any way culture-reduced tests, but because there have been so many misconceptions recently surrounding these inventories—misconceptions that have confused the ABIs with the controversy over ethnic biases in mental tests. The chief misconception is that measures of adaptive behavior are in opposition to, or alternatives to, IQ tests, as if to imply that the ABI does a better job of assessing an individual's intelligence than an IQ test, especially if the individual belongs to a disadvantaged minority. The fact is that ABIs are intended to assess something quite distinct from IQ. This makes the ABI a valuable *supplement* to other kinds of tests, including the IQ, when used in the clinical assessment of children and adults suspected of mental subnormality.

The lower a person's IQ, the greater the probability of a diagnosis of "mental retardation." But the diagnosis of retardation depends on consideration of factors other than just the IQ. For this reason, we find a rather widely overlapping *range* of IQs, rather than a single clear-cut point, which separates the "retarded" from the "normal." Elsewhere (Jensen, 1970c, 1971c) I have distinguished between the main categories of mental retardation, and I believe that many misconceptions about IQ in relation to retardation would be cleared up by clearly recognizing these distinctions.

The first major distinction is between *organic* and *familial* retardation (Zigler, 1967). *Organic* includes all types of retardation with a known physical cause: brain damage, single-gene defects, and chromosomal abnormalities. *Familial* retardation is a part of normal biological variation—the lower tail of the normal distribution of *g* in the population; it is mental retardation in physically normal persons, just as shortness of stature is found in physically normal persons (as contrasted to the glandular and other physical abnormalities of midgets and dwarfs). Only about one-fourth of all retarded persons are of the organic type.

The other major distinction, which is less clear-cut and is really a continuum rather than a dichotomy, is between *primary* and *secondary* familial retardation. It so happens that some familial retardates are retarded in *g* or the level II ability largely measured by IQ tests, but are *not* below the average range in rote learning and memory abilities (i.e., level I abilities); and some familial retardates are as far below the average in level I as in level II ability. I refer to the combination of low level I and low level II abilities as *primary* familial retardation, and to the combination of average (or above) level I and low level II as *secondary* retardation. Primary and secondary retardates, even with the same low IQs, can be quite different socially. Having average (or above) level I abilities is a considerable asset in getting along in the world despite a low IQ, and so secondary retardates are much less likely to be found in institutions for the retarded. Low-IQ persons with good level I abilities can often become dependable, employable, self-supporting citizens. They are capable of many useful jobs with minimal educational requirements and little demand for *g*. Persons who are deficient in level I as well as level II are much more seriously handicapped, socially and in the world of work. They are more often perceived by others as retarded, and they usually remain dependent on their parents or social agencies.

IQ tests do not distinguish these main categories of intellectual retardation, as they measure essentially only one dimension of mental ability, namely, *g* or level II ability. Tests of short-term memory and rote learning ability are needed to supplement the clinical assessment of retardation, along with measures of the person's attained level of socially adaptive behavior or competence in the ordinary tasks of getting along in the world. These factors, even more than IQ, determine the extent to which the person needs special help or supervision in managing his or her life. Adaptive behavior assessments may also indicate certain deficiencies that may be remedied through proper training to a degree that they no longer constitute a severe social handicap.

IQ tests have come under severe attack because of their role in the "labeling" of some school children as "retarded" and the fact that the label is attached to disproportionate numbers of black and Mexican–American children (Mercer, 1972, 1973). (A thorough critical review of Mercer's writings on this topic is provided by Gordon, 1975.) Actually, the tests themselves are not to blame, but the label of "retarded" may well be unfortunate. Such a diagnosis, when properly made in the school setting, indeed corresponds to a marked handicap in scholastic performance. Children so diagnosed by a competent clinician simply do not keep up with the general run of children in the regular classroom, but fall further and further behind in scholastic attainments. There is no question that they are educationally retarded or, to use the British term, "educationally subnormal." Other terminology might be preferable to "retarded," however, as the term "retardation" has both pathological and social connotations that extend far beyond the area of scholastic performance. In this Mercer is correct in noting that many children, especially minority children, who are labeled as "retarded" in school (and in fact *are* retarded in terms of IQ and in the more *g*-loaded scholastic subjects) are not perceived by their family, friends, neighbors, and co-workers as retarded once they get out of the academic setting. On leaving school many of them assume normal roles in the community. The reason, of course, is that the *g* measured by IQ tests is the chief ability involved in scholastic performance, particularly in the more academic subjects, whereas outside of school there are many socially respectable roles and gainful jobs that require only a modest level of *g*-type abilities. If the person is otherwise physically normal and is socially well adjusted, he or she can get along quite well in many minimally *g*-loaded settings, despite a very real and markedly handicapping disability in the ordinary school environment. It should also be realized that behavior that is perceived as "retarded" in one social context may appear quite normal in another. Whether we like it or not, the school setting, by its nature, constantly exposes *g*-type ability, and schooling unfortunately becomes a succession of failures and punishing experiences for many of those who, for whatever reasons, are genuinely and perennially low in *g*. A child with an IQ below 80 is under a severe handicap in school. Even outside of school, his or her intellectual behavior would be a source of anguish in a family or social group where the average IQ is say, 115 or 120. But within a social group where the average IQ is 80 or 85, a person with an IQ of 70 or 75 scarcely stands out as intellectually deviant. It is this *relativism* of the *social interpretation* of a low IQ that has led to so much misunderstanding. The actual level of *intellectual* capability associated with a given IQ differs little, if at all, from one social group to another, but the *perception* of a given level of intellectual capability and its *social meaning* may vary greatly for different groups in the population.

The ***Vineland Social Maturity Scale*** (VSMS), devised by Doll (1953, 1965), was the first major adaptive behavior inventory and has been a model for subsequent inventories. It is an interview questionnaire of 117 items, grouped by one-year age levels, like the Stanford–Binet, and yielding a "social age" and a "social quotient," which is social age divided by chronological age, with a standardization mean of 100 and standard deviation of 10. The examiner asks the subject's parent (or guardian) questions regarding the subject's actual behavior in common specific situations involving general self-help, eating and dressing, self-direction, assumption of various responsibilities, communication, independence in getting around, socialization, and work.

The subject's social maturity age (SA) or social quotient (SQ) is usually compared with his MA or IQ on tests such as the Stanford–Binet or Wechsler. The difference between SQ and IQ has important diagnostic and prognostic implications. A person with nearly average SQ would not be regarded as mentally retarded despite a quite low IQ. But this should not be misconstrued to mean that the person will function as well as the average person in situations that call for the kind of ability measured by the IQ. Mercer and others unfortunately have promulgated the false notion that, because some persons obtain higher SQs than IQs, the IQ must be in error, and their usual interpretation is that the IQ is more culturally biased than the SQ or other adaptive behavior measure. Actually, adaptive behavior scales are probably more culturally loaded than IQ tests. Inventory items concerning the child's crossing city streets alone, shopping alone, going about town alone, going into public restrooms alone, staying out at night without parental supervision, and the like reflect as much or more about parental attitudes and restrictions as about the child's degree of social maturity. Many adaptive behavior inventory items are not about what the child *can* or *cannot* do, but about what his or her parents *permit* or *prohibit*. There are marked social-class and ethnic cultural differences in many of these activities. A group × items interaction analysis of any of the current adaptive behavior inventories would most likely reveal a greater amount of such interaction variance among various SES and ethnic groups than do most IQ tests.

The interpretation of the IQ–SQ absolute difference must take into consideration the *size* of the difference *d*, as relatively small differences can be due to chance. It is a well-known principle in psychometrics that the *difference* between two scores is less reliable than either score alone, and the difference therefore always has a larger standard error than either of the separate scores. The reliability of a difference score *d* between variables X and Y is

$$r_d = \frac{r_{xx} + r_{yy} - 2r_{xy}}{2 - 2r_{xy}},$$

where r_{xx} and r_{yy} are the reliabilities of X and Y and where r_{xy} is the correlation between X and Y. Hurst (1962) provides tables showing the size of d = IQ–SQ (for Stanford–Binet IQ and Vineland SQ) needed for a given level of statistical confidence over a likely range of reliabilities and intercorrelations of these two measures. To conclude, at the 10 percent level of confidence, that a *true* difference exists between IQ and SQ, the observed differences must range from seven to twenty-two points (with a mean of 10.5), depending on the reliabilities of the two tests, within a realistic range of reliabilities.

The correlation between SQ and IQ is substantial. In five quite diverse samples reported by Hurst (1962), the correlations between Stanford–Binet IQ and Vineland SQ range between +0.41 and +0.82, and the correlations between MA and SA, with CA partialed out, range from +0.56 to +1.00. KaDell (1960) factor analyzed the Vineland and Stanford–Binet items together in a group of one hundred 11- and 12-year-old institutionalized retarded children, excluding those with physical or emotional disabilities and those with IQs below 20. The correlation between SQ and IQ in this group is +0.62. The general factor of the Vineland and Stanford–Binet items intercorrelation matrix accounts for 60 percent of the total variance of both tests. The average g loadings of the Vineland and Stanford–Binet items are +0.62 and +0.89, respectively. Clearly, SQ and IQ have considerable factorial variance in common, which is mostly g. I suspect, however, that the g component of SQ is probably somewhat *less* in noninstitutionalized populations in which considerably more of the item variance would be attributable to differences in parental attitudes, demands, and restrictiveness or permissiveness. The factorial variance that is *unique* to the Vineland Social Maturity Scale involves motor skills, self-help, and cooperative behavior. Thus "social maturity," as measured by the Vineland (and probably most other adaptive behavior scales), is far from being independent of g, although of course it includes other factors besides g.

The Vineland Scale has been superseded to a large extent by the well-constructed **Adaptive Behavior Scale** (ABS) developed by the American Association on Mental Deficiency (1974). The ABS is more specifically adapted to assessment of the retarded and includes more items tapping abnormal behaviors than the Vineland. However, assessment of normal socialization, self-sufficiency, and many aspects of competency are very broadly covered by the ABS. (For detailed reviews of the ABS, see Buros 7:37.)

The **Fairview Self-Help Scale** (Ross, 1970) is a downward extension of the adaptive behavior inventory to accommodate the lower levels of mental deficiency. It is useful in assessing the ward behavior and the supervisional needs of severely retarded institutionalized persons. It assesses capabilities in the areas of ambulation, speech, dressing, grooming, eating skills, toilet training, socialization, and understanding. Among normal children from 1 to 120 months of age, scores on the Fairview are correlated (eta) 0.95 with age in months. (Scores are negatively accelerated and asymptotic at 120 months.) Even at this very simple behavioral level the Fairview total scores are correlated between 0.77 and 0.87 with IQ in various groups.

The **Adaptive Behavior Inventory for Children** (ABIC) is designed for use in the school setting, especially with the culturally disadvantaged, as part of Mercer's System of Multicultural Pluralistic Assessment (SOMPA). Recently published by the Psychological Corporation, it is still too new to have been subjected to independent critical evaluation.

Scales for measuring social maturity (Edgerton, Ullman, & Sylvester, 1971) and functional competence (Northcutt et al., 1975) in important areas of modern living have been developed for use with normal and "marginal" adults, but too little information is as yet available for evaluation of their psychometric properties. In a national survey based on a theoretically well-developed "functional competence" scale of the minimal knowledge and skills in several areas regarded as essential for economic independence above the poverty level in adult life, Northcutt et al. (1975) find that approximately one-fifth of U.S. adults are functioning with difficulty. Functioning "with difficulty" at this level of competency is associated with inadequate income of poverty level or less, inadequate education of eight years of school or less, and unemployment or occupations of low job status.

Laboratory Techniques

Two laboratory techniques—choice reaction time and evoked electrical potentials of the brain—have been found to be correlated with conventional tests of intelligence. To the extent that these techniques in fact are capable of measuring *g*, they would seem to stand as far toward the culture-reduced extreme of the continuum of culture loading as any psychological measurements we yet know of. Both reaction time and evoked potentials are totally free of any cultural or intellectual content. This fact would make even very modest correlations with IQ of great interest for the potential future development of these techniques. I doubt that they have any practical utility at the present time because of certain rather severe psychometric deficiencies in their present state of development. I regard them as embryo techniques for further experimental and psychometric research and development and as tools to be used in research aimed at achieving a more complete theoretical understanding of the essential nature of intelligence.

Reaction Time

The study of reaction time (RT) has a long and checkered history. It was introduced to psychology more than a century ago by F. C. Donders, and the experimental study of RT became so prominent in the last quarter of the nineteenth century that E. G. Boring, in his *History of Experimental Psychology* (1950, p. 145), characterized it as the period of "mental chronometry." Galton was the first to suggest that RT might reflect general mental ability, and he invented his own device for measuring RT and included it in his battery of anthropometric measurements that were administered to thousands of Londoners at Galton's laboratory in the South Kensington Museum of Natural Science (Galton, 1908, p. 248). But Galton measured only *simple* RT to an auditory stimulus, and it seemd not to be significantly correlated with any important characteristics in normal adults. (In *simple* RT the subject makes a single reaction to a single stimulus, as contrasted to *choice* RT in which the subject must make differential responses depending on which one, or a combination, of two or more stimuli is presented.)

Shortly before the turn of the century, James McKeen Cattell, the first American to earn a Ph.D. in psychology (from Wundt's laboratory in Leipzig), returned to the United States, after a two-year postdoctoral stint under Galton, to introduce to American psychology the first battery of "mental tests"—so christened by Cattell—along the lines of Galtonian "brass instrument" psychology (Cattell, 1890). (James McKeen Cattell was no relation to Raymond B. Cattell. However, J. McK. Cattell's daughter, Psyche Cattell, became a psychologist; she is perhaps best known as the author of the Catell Infant Intelligence Scale.) Cattell's battery of "mental tests" included a specially constructed chronometer for measuring a person's RT to sound.

Working under Cattell's direction in the Psychological Laboratory of Columbia University, at the turn of the century, Wissler (1901) became the first psychologist actually to compute a Pearsonian coefficient of correlation between RT and "intelligence." What he found was a disappointment: a correlation of only -0.02, based on 227 male students in Columbia College. The meager result of an apparently carefully executed study, which was conducted in the country's then most prestigious psychological laboratory, was so singularly unimpressive and became so widely cited as to throw a pall over the investigation of RT as a potential means for measuring intelligence. This failure of RT as a measure of intelligence, followed so soon by the conspicuous practical appeal of Binet's new scale of intelligence, published just four years after Wissler's RT study, completely turned the direction of psychometrics away from the seemingly unpromising path indicated by Galton and James McKeen Cattell.

Historic hindsight, of course, reveals the extreme psychometric naïveté of the Cattell and Wissler study of RT and intelligence. They had used only *simple* RT to sound, with each subject's RT score based on an average of only three to five trials. The subjects were Ivy League students highly selected for general mental ability. The measure of intelligence was course grades. No attention was paid to attenuation of the correlation due to unreliability of the measurements or to restriction of the range of talent. (We have determined that the average of three trials of simple RT has a test–retest reliability of only 0.35 for Berkeley students.)

A quarter of a century later, Peak and Boring (1926) revived RT and made sure this time to obtain sufficiently reliable measures of *simple* RT by obtaining one hundred trials on each subject. Also, by that time, some standardized intelligence tests had been developed, and for the first time in history the correlation between actual intelligence test scores and RT could be computed. However, the fact that Peak and Boring reported the phenomenal correlations of $-.90$ and -1.00, respectively, did nothing to revive psychologists' interest in RT as a potential measure of intelligence. These correlations are based on a total N of 5! Even Peak and Boring themselves were apparently not enthusiastic enough about their finding to follow it up in studies using more impressive sample sizes, although they noted the potential significance of such work, saying:

> It is needless to point out that, if the relation of intelligence (as the tests have tested it) to reaction time of any sort can finally be established, great consequences, both practical and scientific, would follow. Practically we should have a precise and economical way of testing a fundamental and socially important individual difference. (1926, p. 93)

Just a year later there was published what, by modern standards, is perhaps the first technically respectable study of RT and intelligence, by Vernon Lemmon, working in Cattell's lab at Columbia under the direction of Henry Garrett. Using simple and choice RT and a variety of mental tests given to some one hundred Columbia College students, Lemmon (1927–1928) found some significant and orderly, though modest, relationships. As far as I can determine, he was the first to discover the higher correlation of intelligence (Thorndike Intelligence Test) with *choice* RT than with *simple* RT: -0.25 ($p < .01$) versus -0.08 (n.s.), although the difference is barely significant (one-tailed $p < .10$). Lemmon's general conclusions, which he wrote, it should be recalled, in the heyday of J. McK. Cattell and E. L. Thorndike, seem so relevant to our present problem that they are worth quoting at length:

> It is possible that the *quality* of intelligence may depend upon the number of connections, but also upon the *speed* with which these connections are formed. Nerve centers (e.g., association centers) cannot remain excited indefinitely at maximum intensity; consequently in the case of a person who forms connections slowly it is possible that the excitation of the first association centers to be affected will have diminished and disappeared before the later centers come into play. Thus

only a limited number of centers are cooperating at any one time. The person who forms connections quickly, however, is apt to have more association centers interacting at once, since the later centers are aroused before the earlier ones had a chance to lose their effectiveness. But the most intelligent response is, in general, the one in the determination of which the greatest number of factors have been taken into consideration. In neural terms this may well mean the response in the determination of which the greatest number of association centers have cooperated, and the number of simultaneously active centers may in turn depend to some extent upon the speed with which nervous impulses are conducted from center to center and through synapses within the centers. Conduction speed may play a similar role in learning of the higher types.

The fact that intelligence and learning correlate less well with the simple than with the discriminative reactions is consistent with the hypothesis just presented, for the discriminative reactions probably involve more nerve centers of the association type than does the simple reaction. In the case of memory, however, the correlation with simple reaction is greater than with the discriminative reactions. This may imply that the centers involved in memory are different from those which are most important in intelligent responses and in learning of the higher types, and more like those involved in the simple reaction. (1927–1928, p. 35)

Apparently after 1926 the psychometric Zeitgeist was so completely dominated by the atheoretical testing movement that sprang from the success of the Binet tests that psychology completely abandoned RT and all other Galtonian ''brass instrument'' laboratory techniques as means of investigating the nature of intelligence. This sad fate of RT in the development of psychometrics may well be viewed by future historians of science as a case *par excellence* of throwing out the baby with the bath water. But psychometricians, then as now, were more interested in finding large correlations and making practical predictions with their IQ tests than in advancing our scientific understanding of intelligence itself.

RT continued to be used in studies of the mentally retarded, the brain damaged, and of various pathological conditions and the effects of drugs. But, because of the almost exclusive concentration of RT research in these areas, it became commonly believed that RT is correlated with intelligence only when abnormalities are present that lower IQ as well as slow RT—a not very exciting finding from the standpoint of understanding normal variation in intelligence.

It was not until the 1960s that RT again came into its own in general experimental psychology, along with recent developments of information processing theory and experimental cognitive psychology. In these areas we have seen a rebirth of what Boring termed ''mental chronometry.'' RT has been resurrected as the chief instrumentality for the measurement and analysis of cognitive processes, as can be seen in the recent researches of Hunt (1976), Posner (1969), Robert Sternberg (1977), and Saul Sternberg (1966, 1975). However, RT still has had almost no impact in the fields of psychometrics and individual differences.

Nevertheless, it is now clearly established that RT, particularly *choice* RT, has some significant relationship to psychometric *g*. I can best illustrate this in terms of an experimental arrangement, originally suggested by Roth (1964; cited by Eysenck, 1967), with which I have been working. I have modified Roth's procedure so as to measure RT and MT (movement time) independently, as Roth's procedure confounds the two and thereby reduces the precision of measurement of RT.

The apparatus for measuring the subject's RT and MT is shown in Figure 14.9. It consists of a panel, $13'' \times 17''$, painted flat black and tilted at a 30° angle. At the lower center of the panel is a red push button, $\frac{1}{2}$ inch in diameter, called the "home" button. Arranged in a semicircle above the home button are eight red push buttons, all equidistant (six inches) from the home button. Half an inch above each button (except the home button) is a $\frac{1}{2}$ inch faceted green light. Different flat black panels can be fastened over the whole array so as to expose arrays having either one, two, four, six, or eight light–button combinations (or any other number of light–button combinations involving from one to eight response alternatives).

The subject is instructed to place the index finger of the preferred hand on the home button; then an auditory warning signal is sounded (a high-pitched tone of 1 second duration), followed (after a continuous random interval of from 1 to 4 seconds) by one of the green lights going on, which the subject must turn off as quickly as possible by touching the microswitch button directly below it. The particular light that goes on in each trial is random and hence unpredictable by the subject. RT is the time the subject takes to remove his or her finger from the home button after a green light goes on. MT is the interval between removing the finger from the home button and touching the button that turns off the green light. RT and MT are thus experimentally independent. On each trial RT and MT are registered in milliseconds by two electronic timers.

Figure 14.9. Subject's console of the Reaction Time–Movement Time apparatus. Red push buttons are indicated by circles, faceted green lights by crossed circles.

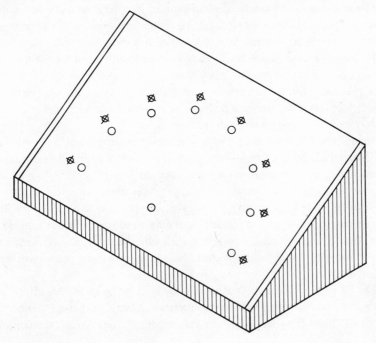

In our experiments subjects are given either fifteen or thirty trials on each light–button combination; we find that fifteen trials give quite satisfactory split-half reliabilities, generally over .90, for RT and MT or other parameters derived from these. We use the subject's *median* RT or MT over trials; we find the median has higher reliability than the mean, and the subject's median has the added advantage of being less correlated with the subject's standard deviation over trials. Also, because the frequency distributions of individual's RTs and MTs are skewed (positively), the median is the better measure of central tendency.

Before showing some typical results, let me list some advantages of this setup.

1. RT and MT are measurements on an *absolute* scale, as is the slope of the median RT as a function of task complexity (i.e., the number of light–button combinations), and also intraindividual variability as measured by the standard deviation about the subject's own mean. An absolute scale of measurement is especially important in developmental studies, as well as for rigorous theory construction and the comparison of experimental parameters across various studies.

2. The demands of the task are extremely simple throughout the total range of difficulty (one to eight light–buttons). Virtually all subjects beyond 3 years of age have no trouble understanding the task requirements with minimal verbal instructions and demonstration by the experimenter. We have tested subjects ranging in Stanford–Binet IQ from about 15 to 150, or above. For persons below 15 or 20 we find there are problems, especially at the levels of difficulty beyond simple RT (i.e., one light–button). Thus, unlike nearly all other ability tests, which must be varied in content or complexity to accommodate different ages and ability levels, this task remains the same over an extremely wide range of age and ability. This is a great advantage for developmental and gerontological studies.

3. The task makes absolutely no short-term or long-term memory demands, and it presupposes no specific knowledge or cognitive content above the level of complying with the instructions, which present no difficulty to the average 3-year-old.

4. No learning seems to be involved in performance, except for the most retarded subjects, with IQs below about 40. They show some improvement over the first few minutes of practice. Normal subjects do not show any systematic change in level of performance throughout the whole test. Even when tested every other day for a month, subjects show no systematic changes in performances.

5. The RT and MT internal consistency reliabilities are quite high (>.90) even with as few as fifteen trials per each light–button condition, and the reliability can be made as high as one wishes by simply averaging a greater number of trials. We have obtained reliabilities up to .99 in fairly homogeneous college samples.

6. A relatively few "cognitive" processes would seem to be involved in performance. Association, learning, and memory scanning would seem to be excluded. To the extent that the RT measurements correlate with other tests involving these cognitive processes, it suggests that the correlation is based on some even more basic processes common to both tests.

7. The RT measurements do not seem to be affected by conscious effort, provided that the subject merely complies with the instructions. At any given time, subjects seem to try their "best." Instructing the subject to "try harder," "beat your last attempt," or to "relax and not try as hard" has no effect on the subject's RT. When subjects are instructed to attempt voluntarily to fake less than their "best" RT performance, they are remarkably unsuccessful. The subject's least conscious intention to respond less quickly than his or her "best" RT puts the RT into an entirely different distribution with a median about eight standard deviations removed from the median of the distribution of the subject's normal, unfaked RT. Faked RTs do not even fall within the normal distribution of individual differences in RT.

Performing normally, subjects have no subjective awareness of the "goodness" of their performance on any single trial. We have asked subjects repeatedly to guess whether their RT was faster or slower than their RT on the immediately preceding trial, which came just a few seconds earlier. Invariably their guesses are no better than chance. Subjects also evince disbelief when shown that their RT is much slower for the eight-button task than for the one-button task. Paradoxically, most subjects imagine their RT is much faster than their MT, when in fact MT is generally almost twice as fast as RT.

I believe that the reason for this inability subjectively to estimate one's RT on a given trial or voluntarily to fake one's RT is found in the research of Libet and his co-workers (1965, 1971), who have demonstrated by means of studies involving direct stimulation of the cerebral cortex that the latency of conscious awareness of stimulation to peripheral sense organs is about 500 milliseconds, which is longer than the longest RTs normally made by subjects doing the eight-button task on our apparatus. Only the severely mentally retarded have longer RTs. This means that normal subjects' reactions occur well before the subject becomes consciously aware of the stimulus that initiates his response. RT is therefore not under voluntary control, and it is therefore also unaffected by conscious effort or "motivation" in the usual sense of that term. This is not to say, however, that RT may not be affected by some form of "arousal" at the neurophysiological level.

There may be a number of disadvantages in this setup that we have not yet perceived. But there is one disadvantage that we are already aware of and have explicitly investigated. For some time I had wondered about the reason for the apparent ceiling to the correlations we get between the RT parameters and scores on various standardized *g*-loaded tests. Neither I nor anyone else, to my knowledge, has been able to get correlations larger than about -0.40 to -0.50 between choice RT and IQ, with typical correlations in the -0.30 to -0.40 range, using reasonable-sized samples. Correction for attenuation, using internal consistency or split-half reliabilities, raises these correlations only to about -0.35 to -0.45. So we did a study to look at test–retest reliability, testing ten college students every other day for a month. It turns out that an individual's median RT is highly unstable from day to day and, therefore, that subjects within a fairly homogeneous sample show considerable shifts in rank order of RT "ability" from one day to the next. Interestingly, simple RT has the highest day-to-day stability, almost as high as the split-half reliability on any single day. But, sadly, the parameters of the RT performance that correlate the highest with IQ scores also show the lowest day-to-day reliability, such that the highest correlations we can theoretically expect between our RT parameters obtained in a single testing session and any external criterion measures should be about .55 to .60 at most. Interestingly, MT has much greater temporal stability than RT; the day-to-day intercorrelations for MT are as high as the split-half reliability on any one day. The reasons for this temporal instability of RT, especially choice RT, are not known. But my wife and I, in testing each other on RT every day for two weeks, found considerable fluctuations in our RTs at different times of the day, tending to slow down from morning until late afternoon. For one thing, there is evidence that body temperature influences RT, and a person's temperature varies throughout the day and night (Kamiya, 1961). To the degree that choice RT reflects what Raymond B. Cattell terms "fluid *g*" we should expect a person's fluid *g* to fluctuate considerably from one time to another (Cattell, 1971b, Ch. 5).

The temporal instability of RT measurements might militate against the practical usefulness of RT as a test of *g* (or whatever it measures), but this finding is really not discouraging from a theoretical standpoint, and it may even afford one more facet of po'ential theoretic importance.

Parameters of the RT –MT Test. I can best describe the main parameters of the RT and MT measurements that we are looking at in relationship to psychometric *g* in terms of data on fifty university undergraduates (twenty-five males and twenty-five females) who were given fifteen trials on each of the one-, two-, four-, and eight-light–button tasks in a single testing session. Figure 14.10 shows the mean of the median RTs and MTs in milliseconds, plotted as a function of the number of "bits" of information conveyed by the stimulus display. Because we found no significant sex differences in the RT parameters, the RT data for males and females were combined. A bit—from *b(inary) (dig)it*—is the logarithm to the base 2 of the number of choice alternatives. One bit of information reduces the total amount of uncertainty of choice by one-half; thus, if there is no choice (i.e., no uncertainty as to which light bulb will go on, as in the one-light–button task), there is no information or 0 bit conveyed by the stimulus. A display of two light bulbs has 1 degree of uncertainty as to which one will go on, thus conveying 1 bit of information; four lights convey 2 bits, and eight lights 3 bits of information.

Note in Figure 14.10 that RT or decision time increases as a linear function of the number of bits. This fact was originally discovered by Hick (1952) and replicated by Hyman (1953) and has become known as Hick's law. We have never found a significant departure from Hick's law in any group we have tested, with the exception of the severely retarded. Hick's law is not just the result of taking a group average. It holds for every individual, with rare exceptions. *Within* individuals in this particular sample, the average linear correlation between median RT and bits is .93, which is as high a correlation as the reliability of the RT measures will permit. Hick's law is a most robust and striking psychological phenomenon, which, I believe, may be of key importance in discovering the nature of *g*, conceived of as the capacity for information processing. Also it is important to note that MT does not follow Hick's law. MT, which is much faster than RT, does not differ systematically as a function of bits.

It is generally found that the standard deviation of RT over trials increases as a function of bits. Figure 14.10 also shows the mean ± 1 standard deviation of fifteen RT trials at each level of task complexity. As we shall see, it is a theoretically important point that *within* individuals the standard deviation of RT increases monotonically as a function of bits.

Thus the most important parameters of the performance of each subject are the *intercept* and *slope* of the regression of median RT on bits, the *mean of the standard deviations* of RT at the four levels of task complexity, and the *slope* of the regression of the standard deviations of RT on bits; also the *mean median* MT and the standard deviation of MT. These parameters, it should be noted, are all experimentally or athematically *independent* of one another. (Which is not to imply that they are uncorrelated.)

We have found, in general, that the RT but not the MT parameters are significantly correlated with scores on standard intelligence tests in adults and that *both* the RT and MT parameters are correlated with intelligence in children and retarded adults.

The six RT and MT parameters listed above, along with tests of verbal serial rote learning, digit-span memory, the Raven Advanced Progressive Matrices, the Terman Concept Mastery Test (a high-level test of verbal ability), and the Extraversion, Neuroticism, and Lie scales of the Eysenck Personality Inventory were subjected to a principal components analysis. The loadings of the variables on the first principal component,

Figure 14.10. Mean median RT and MT, and the mean standard deviation of RT, as a function of task complexity scaled in bits, based on a sample ($N = 50$) of university undergraduates. Note the linear regression of RT on bits.

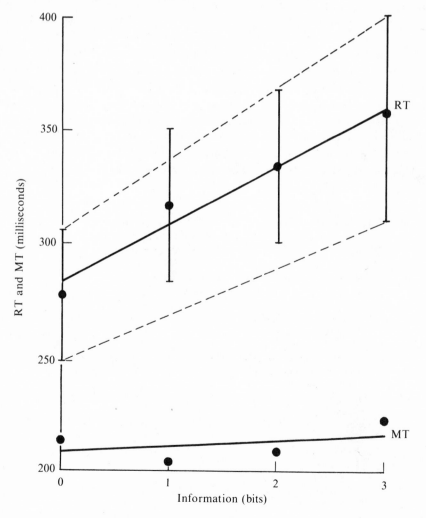

which represents the general factor (not necessarily Spearman's *g*) of this battery, are shown in Table 14.3.

The slope, standard deviation, and slope of standard deviation of RT show the highest loadings, along with the intelligence tests, especially the Raven, which is generally acknowledged as the best measure of Spearman's *g* among all of these variables. The loadings on these measures are all significant beyond the .001 level. The fact that the Raven has a loading above .70 on this factor, despite the restricted range of mental ability of university students, strongly suggests that this factor may be interpreted as Cattell's fluid *g*. The zero-order correlations of RT *intercept* and *slope* with Raven matrices scores are +.15 (n.s.) and −.41 ($p < .01$), respectively. So RT slope and the slope of the RT standard deviation seem to be more involved with fluid *g* than any of the other experimental variables. Lesser slope of RT as a function of bits goes with higher ability on *g*-loaded tests. Also the standard deviation of RT (i.e., trial-to-trial intra-individual variability) is *negatively* correlated with *g*.

In a sample of thirty-nine ninth-grade girls, however, the Raven Standard Progressive Matrices scores are correlated about −.40 ($p < .01$) with both the intercept and slope of RT and also with median MT. Figure 14.11 shows the median RT and MT for these data, plotted separately for the low, middle, and high thirds of the group in Raven scores. We do not yet know why our university students show no correlation of MT with *g*, whereas children, as well as adults of lower intelligence, do show a correlation between MT and IQ. It seems puzzling that there should be any correlation between intelligence test scores and MT, when MT is unrelated to amount of information. This is just one of the many questions we still have to investigate further. My first hunch is that below a certain mental age, two decision processes, rather than one, are involved in the RT–MT performance. RT is a more pure measure of decision time for all subjects, whereas MT may reflect some amount of decision time, as well as sheer movement time, in persons of lower

Table 14.3. Loadings on the first principal component of a number of RT, MT, and psychometric variables.

Variable	Loading[1]
RT intercept	+.42
RT slope	−.65
RT mean standard deviation	−.50
RT slope of standard deviation	−.73
MT mean median	−.18
MT mean standard deviation	−.08
Serial rote learning (errors)	−.07
Digit-span memory	+.41
Raven matrices	+.73
Concept Mastery Test	+.57
Eysenck Personality Inventory	
Extraversion	−.32
Neuroticism	+.09
Lie Scale	−.19

[1]For loadings greater than .36, $p < .01$; for loadings greater than .46, $p < .001$.

The group differences in intercepts and slopes of the regressions of R
Figure 14.13 are, of course, confounded with the group differences in age
level. But we can safely make one generalization from our data: the interce
and intraindividual variability of RT decrease with age from childhood to
groups of similar IQ level. This has also been found by other investigators
different methods for measuring RT (Connolly, 1970; Surwillo, 1971). When
are corrected for attenuation, the consistently strongest (negative) correlation
RT parameters with *g* is the mean standard deviation of RT, which is a
trial-to-trial intraindividual variability in RT. This measure is also positivel
with RT intercept and slope. I think it has the most important implications for
a theory that will explain the correlations of all these RT parameters with *g*.

Figure 14.13. RT as function of bits, illustrating Hick's law, in diverse gro
in age and intelligence: (A) university students (*N* = 155); (B) ninth-grade girl
(C) sixth-graders in a high-SES–high-IQ school (*N* = 50); (D) and (E) white
and black (*N* = 99), respectively, male vocational college freshmen with ap
equal scholastic aptitude test scores; (F) severely mentally retarded young adul
mean IQ 39); and (G) mildly retarded and borderline young adults (*N* = 46)

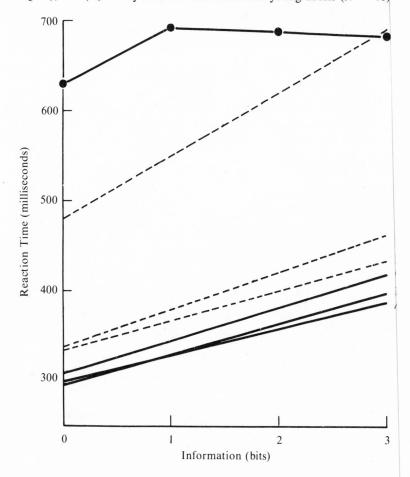

Figure 14.11.   Mean RT and MT as a function of bits for the high (H), middle (M), and low (L) thirds of a sample (*N* = 39) of ninth-grade girls on the
Raven Standard Progressive Matrices scores.   (From Jensen & Munro, 1979)

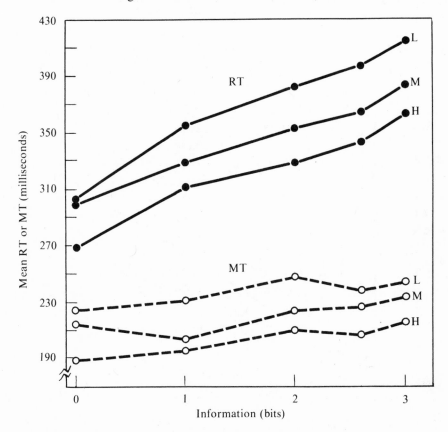

mental age. In a group of retarded young adults, we found that MT is often as slow or even
slower than RT. We never find this in normal adults or even in children of average IQ.

Figure 14.12 illustrates, once again, one of the most important generalizations about
g, namely, that a task correlates more highly with *g* as the task's complexity is increased.
The correlation between Raven matrices scores and RT are here plotted as a function of
task complexity scaled in bits, for university students and ninth-graders.

Figure 14.13 shows RT as a function of bits in samples from seven quite different
populations with regard to age, general intelligence level, and background. Note that all
the groups except the severely mentally retarded (with a mean Stanford–Binet IQ of 39)
illustrate Hick's law. In no other groups have we found a significant departure from linear
regression of RT on bits, and so, for the sake of graphical clarity, I have plotted only the
regression lines without the data points. The departure from linearity in the retarded
sample is due mostly to the severely retarded, with IQs below 25. As I mentioned earlier,
these subjects also showed something we have never found in any normal group—slower
MT than RT. In the severely retarded group (*N* = 60), a simple sum of the RT and MT
parameters is correlated − .54 (*p* < .001) with *g* factor scores based on a factor analysis of
fifteen various psychometric tests that are appropriate for the severely retarded. More than

Figure 14.12. The correlation of Raven matrices scores with
stimulus complexity scale in bits for (A) female ninth-graders ($N =$
students ($N = 50$), who, probably because they are more highly sel
more restricted in variability on *g*, show the smaller correlations.

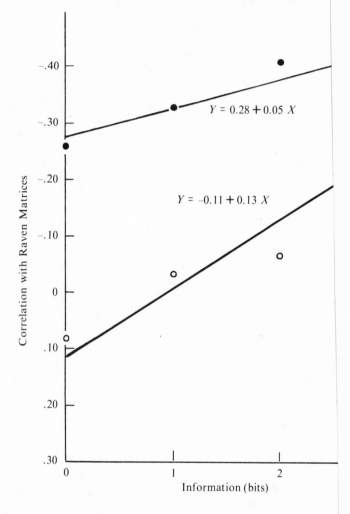

a month after the RT testing of the retarded sample, Edward Sch
measures of average evoked potential (AEP) on these subjects. (See th
potential following.) AEP correlates .33 with the simple sum of the I
ters (after they are each converted to *z* scores), and AEP correlates .3
g factor scores (both $p < .05$). The fact that the RT and AEP measure:
with each other insofar as they both correlate with *g* is shown by the f:
correlation RT and AEP together predict *g* factor scores not signific:
RT alone.

In brief, significant correlations between measurements from ou
and scores on psychometric tests of mental ability are found at all
selected university students to institutionalized retardates.

considerable interest that intraindividual variability of EEG evoked potentials, like intraindividual variability of RT, decreases with age up to maturity and is negatively
correlated (about $-.50$) with IQ in adults (Callaway, 1975, pp. 72–74).

Related RT Phenomena. Hick's law has a counterpart in the time required for
scanning short-term memory, which I shall label the "Sternberg effect," after Saul
Sternberg (1966, 1976), who discovered the phenomenon shown in Figure 14.14. It has
been replicated many times under various conditions. The subject is presented with a
series of digits or letters containing from one to seven items; this is immediately followed
by presentation of a single probe item, and the subject's RT (decision time) as to whether
the probe item was present or absent in the list increases linearly as a function of the
number of *items* in the list. (This is also true for lists of eight to twenty items, although the
intercept of RT is much higher than for lists of one to seven items; Burrows & Okada,
1975). It is especially noteworthy that RT increases *linearly* with the number of items in
the set in the case of short-term memory scanning, (i.e., the Sternberg effect), whereas

Figure 14.14. RT for scanning a letter series in short-term memory for the presence or
absence of a single probe letter as a function of list length and RT to name the next item
that follows the probe letter in the list. Note that RT is a linear function of the *number of
items* in the list rather than of $\log_2$ of the number of alternatives (i.e., bits) as in Figures
14.10, 14.12, and 14.13.   (From Sternberg, 1966)

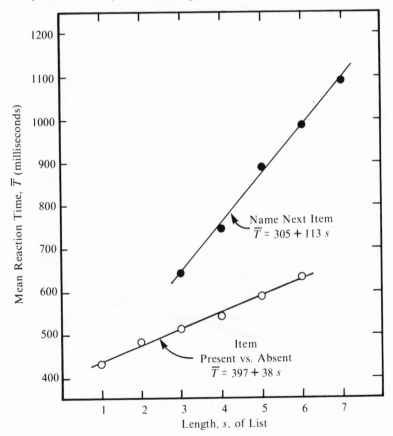

RT increases *logarithmically* with the number of stimulus alternatives in a simultaneous visual display (i.e., Hick's law). An essential difference between the Hick and the Sternberg phenomena is that the former involves mental processing speed for stimuli presented from *outside* the sensorium whereas the latter involves speed of retrieval from short-term memory. (RT for long-term memory search also seems to be linearly related to set size; Sternberg, 1975, pp. 23–25.) On the other hand, RT for *naming* pictures of familiar objects (e.g., book, chair, typewriter), which involves both processing of external stimuli and long-term memory scan, decreases logarithmically as a function of the Thorndike–Lorge word frequency of the object names (Oldfield & Wingfield, 1965). This would seem an important lead to investigating the relationship of RT to vocabulary, which is one of the most g-loaded measures of verbal ability.

Hunt (1976) has found a relationship between speed of retrieving highly overlearned codes (letters of the alphabet) and scores on the verbal part of the Scholastic Aptitude Test (SAT-V) among university students. The subject is presented letters that are either physically the same (e.g., *AA*) or physically different (e.g., *AB*), or physically different but have the same name (e.g., *Aa*). When a pair of letters is presented, the subject responds as quickly as possible by pressing one of two push buttons labeled ''same'' or ''different''—''same'' meaning the pair of letters have the same name. University students take about 75 milliseconds longer to react to *Aa* than to *AA*. The average length of the processing time needed for stimulus decoding is negatively correlated with SAT-V scores, as shown in Figure 14.15.

When the slope of the RT measures (over items or bits) corresponding to the Hick, Sternberg, and Hunt paradigms are combined in a multiple regression equation to predict Raven matrices scores in three groups of school children, ages 9, 13, and 17, they yield multiple R's of .59, .57, and .60, respectively (Keating & Bobbitt, 1978). Spiegel and Bryant (1978) have found with ninety-four sixth-graders that the mean RT and the slope of RT (in simple tasks of varying complexity) are correlated with both verbal and nonverbal Lorge–Thorndike IQs (r's ranging from $-.43$ to $-.62$) and with reading and math scholastic achievement test scores (r's of $-.30$ to $-.53$).

Blind-Alley Hypotheses. Many hypotheses may be suggested to explain the observed relationships between RT parameters and psychometric g, but several of these hypotheses, I believe, are hopeless blind alleys, which are listed as follows:

1. *Visual Scanning.* Speed of *visual* or ocular scanning of the lights on the display panel of the RT apparatus has been most definitely ruled out as a cause of the linear increase in RT as a function of number of bits. The slope of the linear regression of RT on bits measures some *central* processing time; it is clearly not a peripheral sensory–motor phenomenon. When visual scanning is completely eliminated by having the subject focus his or her vision on a single white spot against a black background onto which is projected a single stimulus (e.g., a colored spot or simple geometric form) that the subject must identify by naming or by pushing a button as quickly as possible, the subject's RT increases linearly with the number of bits in the total set of stimuli from which the single stimulus was sampled. It takes longer to identify a *red* spot, for example, when the other possible alternatives are yellow, blue, and green than when the other possible alternative is only *one* of these colors. (See Bosco, 1970, and my comments, p. 706.)

Figure 14.15. Time required to recognize name or physical identity of letter pairs by university students who score in the upper (high) or lower (low) quartile on the SAT–Verbal.   (After Hunt, 1976, Table 1, p. 244)

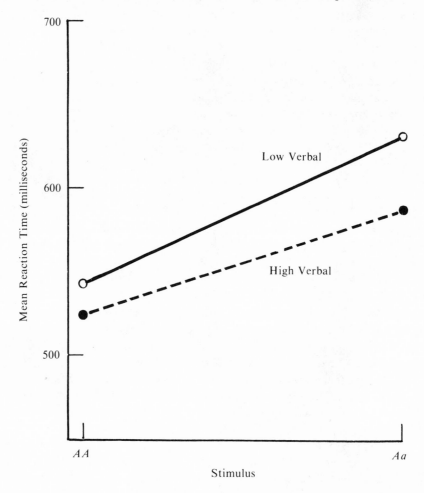

2. *Cognitive Strategy Differences*. The RT experiment completely refutes the notion that individual differences in *g* are largely the result of individual differences in learned strategies, in any acceptable sense of that term. RTs for processing up to 3 bits of information are much too short to allow a strategy explanation of the individual differences in RT. Access to even the simplest overlearned codes, such as the time needed to discriminate between *AA* and *Aa* in Hunt's (1976) experiment, takes more than twice the amount of time that is needed to process one bit of information in the light–button RT paradigm. Individual differences in cognitive strategies may account for some of the variance on some tests, most likely certain types of scholastic achievement tests, particularly tests involving mathematical skills, but differences in acquired strategies can hardly account for the *g*-loaded individual differences in RT in the studies I have reviewed. In general, the explanation of *g* in terms of common strategies is strongly contradicted by the ubiquity of *g* in extremely diverse tasks, provided only that they involve some degree of complexity in cognitive processing.

3. *Speed of Test Performance.* The correlation between RT and intelligence test scores is not a result of a test-taking speed factor that is presumably common to both tasks. In our own studies, tests have never been given under speeded conditions, and, in some of the tests, such as figure copying, retarded persons take no more time than normal persons; they simply do not perform as well on the more complex figures. In no test that we have correlated with RT does the speed of response enter into the subject's test score. We have found that measures of sheer speed of working in a test situation, such as the Making X's Test in which the subject makes X's in three hundred "boxes" under neutral or speed instructions, show negligible correlations with intelligence test scores even on timed tests. Apparently only some fraction of the total amount of time a subject spends in taking a standard test is spent in the kind of mental processing that is measured in our RT tasks.

The determinants of overall speed in test taking are complex and are less correlated with total test score (or with *g*) than is RT measured independently in a much less complex task situation. In a sample of fifty university students, in fact, we found a correlation of 0.00 between total time spent to complete the Raven matrices test and total score on the test. Even when the subject's solution time is precisely measured separately for each item of the matrices, the average solution time over all items is nonsignificantly correlated (-0.06) with Raven IQ in a group of ninety-three adult males (White, 1973). I predict, however, that, if one averages the solution times of test items over subjects, the noncognitive time components of performance will average out, leaving a nearly perfect correlation between the average cognitive processing time for each item and the item difficulties as measured by the percentage (*p*) of subjects (or a normalized transformation of *p*) giving the correct answer. I also venture to hypothesize that the types of test items for which the values are the most highly predictable from a knowledge of the average response latencies to the separate items (when gotten correct) will be the most highly *g* loaded. An item's *g* loading as well as its average cognitive processing time would be a function of the number or the importance of the neural processes that are involved in the item's solution. Individual differences in the common processes involved in different items make for inter-item correlations and correlations among whole tests, and hence they are the basis of *g*. Thus even wholly noncognitive and purely neurophysiological variables, such as the amplitude and latency of average evoked cortical potentials, show individual differences that are correlated with psychometric *g* (Schafer & Marcus, 1973; Shucard & Horn, 1972).

4. *Motivational Differences.* Any close observer of many normal children, college students, and retarded adults while they are taking the RT–MT test would hardly be inclined to attribute the large differences in RT and MT among them to differences in motivation, effort, incentive, or interest in the task. If anything, children and retardates appear somewhat more motivated than normal adults. Also, it seems most likely that motivation, if it has any influence at all, would affect RT about equally across different levels of stimulus complexity (i.e., the intercept of RT), which would not explain the correlation between the *slope* of RT and *g*. Because motivation is not substantially correlated with IQ and is hardly involved in cortical evoked potentials, it is most unlikely that it is the common factor among these measures and the correlated RT parameters.

Promising Clues to a Theory of the Correlation between RT and g. The main clues to developing a theory of these phenomena, I conjecture, are to be found in the relationships among *intercept, slope,* and *intraindividual variability* (or standard deviation) of the RT measurements as a function of the amount of information processed. These variables are all correlated with one another, and they are also correlated with age and with individual differences in highly g-loaded tests. A theoretical model must comprehend all these facts, as well as account for the difference between Hick's law and the Sternberg effect.

Consider the binary tree, which might be thought of as one element in a neural network, shown in Figure 14.16. The fundamental units of the nervous system, the nerve cells, are essentially binary conductors; that is, they either discharge or they do not. The all-or-none law is basic in neurophysiology. After discharge, nerve cells are momentarily refractory to further excitation. Conduction across synapses, of course, depends on the simultaneous cooperation of many nerve cells.

When there are eight sets of neural elements on "ready" for a choice decision, the path of stimulation to any one of the elements must pass through $\log_2 8 = 3$ levels of the binary tree to reach the final "exit" to response. If only four choices were available, then only four elements would be on "ready" and stimulation would enter at the four-element level of the binary tree and have to pass through only $\log_2 4 = 2$ levels to "exit." Then, if the speed of conduction through the levels of the pathway at any one time is constant for an individual, the RT should be an increasing linear function of $\log_2 N =$ bits of information, where N is the number of choices or number of excitatory elements on "ready." The fact that the time for retrieval from memory stores increases as a *linear* function of the number of choices (i.e., size of memory set), rather than as a function of bits, suggests that there are perhaps different "wiring" systems involved in the Sternberg and the Hick phenomena: In terms of Figure 14.16, it is as if in memory scanning the pathway of excitation moves horizontally across a single level of the binary tree prior to exit. This would result in a linear relationship between set size and RT. Incidentally, the *slopes* of

Figure 14.16. Hierarchical binary tree illustrating relationship of the number of choice elements to bits.

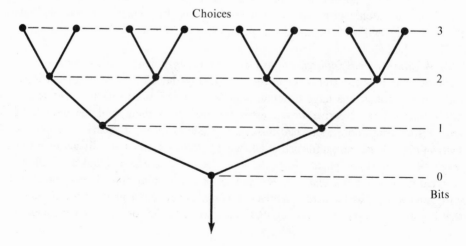

Figure 14.17. Oscillation or waves of excitatory potential above and below threshold (horizontal lines) for excitation, showing faster and slower waves and stimuli (S_1, S_2, S_3) entering at different points in time.

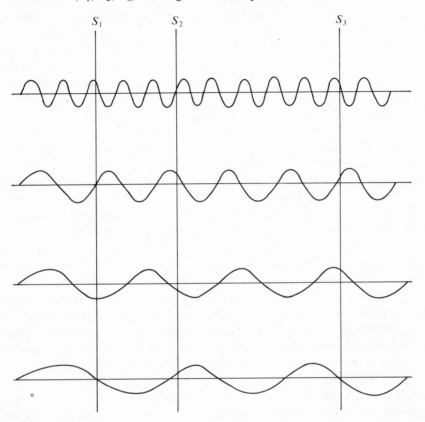

RT in the Hick and Sternberg effects are quite similar, at least in the range of one to eight elements.

But why should the standard deviation of the individual's RT over trials be correlated with the individual's mean RT? And why should the standard deviation of RT increase with the number of bits of information transmitted? Assume that nearly all the delay in the speed of conduction occurs at the nodes (possibly synapses) connecting the elements of the binary tree shown in Figure 14.17. And assume that the refractoriness of these nodes to excitation has a regular periodic oscillation above and below a threshold for excitation, as depicted in Figure 14.17. Also assume that there are individual differences (as well as day-to-day fluctuations for a given individual) in the frequency of oscillation, as depicted by the fast and slow waves in Figure 14.17. Notice that when a stimulus (S_1) begins when the excitatory wave is above threshold, both fast and slow waves will respond equally fast. But, if the stimulus (S_2) begins in a trough of the wave, the faster wave will have the shorter latency of response. By this reason alone, higher frequency of oscillation should produce a shorter mean RT and a smaller standard deviation of RT over trials. If we think of such a wave as operating at each node of the binary tree, with the probability .50 that the stimulation will enter at the excitatory phase of each node, the mean and standard deviation of RT will both increase as a function of the number of nodes in the path through which the stimulation is conducted. Slower waves should produce a correspondingly higher mean and standard deviation of RT.

If we have learned nothing else of fundamental importance from these reaction time studies as yet, they have surely proved beyond reasonable doubt that the *g* of standard psychometric tests of mental ability reflects individual differences in cognitive processes that are far more general and far more profound than anything suggested by the popular notion of IQ tests as reflecting only differences in cognitive contents and skills that persons have chanced to learn in school or acquire in a cultured home.

SES and Race Differences in RT Parameters.   As yet there is too little systematic evidence to afford any definitive generalizations about the relative magnitudes of racial and social-class differences on the various parameters of RT. All that can be said with assurance at present is that, when RT measures have been obtained on different SES groups and on whites and blacks, statistically significant differences have been found in the theoretically expected direction.

For example, in terms of the RT–MT apparatus already described, white and black groups of 18- to 19-year-old male vocational students (groups D and E, respectively, in Figure 14.13) who had very nearly the same distributions of scores on a scholastic aptitude test showed no significant mean difference (3 milliseconds) in RT intercepts, but a significant ($p < .01$) difference in the slopes of the regression of RT on bits. That is to say, the two groups did not differ appreciably on the one-light–button task (simple RT with 0 bit of information), but differed very significantly (31 milliseconds, significant at $p < .001$) on the eight-light-button task (choice RT with 3 bits of information). The white–black difference increases approximately 10 milliseconds per bit. The groups also differ significantly in intraindividual variability (i.e., the mean of every subject's trial-to-trial standard deviation about his own mean RT), and blacks show a greater rate of increase in intraindividual variability as a function of bits. Although no theoretical prediction could have been made concerning the magnitudes of these differences, the *directions* of the differences are predictable from the theoretical position described in the preceding section, making the reasonable assumption that the black and white samples are from populations that differ on *g*-loaded tests. These particular samples are not representative of the white and black populations; both groups had rather restricted range, with no very low IQs (i.e., none below about 80) and few very high IQs (above 115), but the white group was at about the population average for whites whereas the black group was nearly a standard deviation above the mean of the general population of blacks. Under these conditions the black sample's RT means should be expected to regress further away from the white group's RT means as task complexity (i.e., number of bits of information) increases, and that is just what was found. More representative samples of whites and blacks would be theoretically expected to show considerably larger differences than those found in the present study, but this prediction remains to be tested with this same RT method.

A different apparatus measuring four-choice (i.e., 2 bits) RT was used for testing quite representative samples of white and black children ($N = 106$ in each group) in rural Georgia, matched for age and sex (Noble, 1969). Each child was given 160 trials. The results, plotted as mean response speed (the reciprocal of RT), are shown in Figure 14.18. The overall white–black difference is significant ($p < .01$). It can be seen that there is a slight practice effect; the groups hardly differ on the early trials, but with practice the

Figure 14.18. Mean response speed in successive twenty-trial blocks on a four-choice reaction time test. Each curve is based on 106 children. (From Noble, 1969)

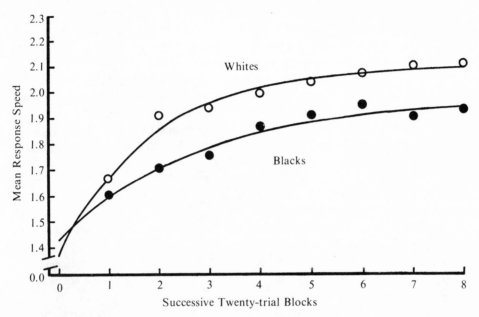

group difference is increased and soon becomes stabilized. If motivational or attitudinal factors were acting to depress the RT of the black children, it would be hard to explain why the groups should differ so little in the early trials.

The only other RT studies I have found involving whites and blacks were performed in Africa. Poortinga (1971) tested black and white (forty of each) undergraduate university students between 18 and 24 years of age; anyone who had failed more than one year in their school career prior to university was excluded. The black sample was considered to be representative of all black African university students in South Africa. Visual and auditory four-choice and eight-choice RT tasks were used. Subjects were given one hundred trials on each task. The blacks averaged significantly slower RTs than whites, with the mean difference (in standard deviation units) ranging from 1.2σ to 1.5σ. There were significant practice effects (over five two-trial blocks) for both groups, but no significant interaction between race and practice effect. It seems especially interesting, theoretically, that Poortinga found no significant difference between the racial groups on *simple* RT, both visual and auditory, on which the black–white mean RT differences are only 0.02σ and 0.20σ, respectively. A problematic aspect of Poortinga's results, however, would seem to be that the choice auditory RT correlates significantly ($r = -0.45$, $p < .01$) with Raven's matrices in the white but not in the black African group ($r = -0.07$, n.s.). But then it should be noted, too, that the r of -0.45 does not differ very significantly ($z = 1.76$, two-tailed $p = .08$,) from the r of -0.07, and both white and black groups show a nonsignificant correlation of Raven matrices with visual choice RT. So this apparent anomaly can hardly have much theoretical significance unless it is replicated in experiments on other samples.

As for social-class differences in information processing speed, the only study that I have found is by Bosco (1970), using a purely visual form of reaction time known as *metacontrast* or *masking*. When a visual stimulus is presented for a standard duration, followed by a "blank" interval, and then by a second stimulus (greater in retinal area than the first stimulus) of standard duration, the observer either will or will not be able to name the first stimulus (e.g., a letter of the alphabet), depending on the duration of the "blank" interval between the first and second stimuli (called the "test signal" and the "masking" stimulus, respectively). If the blank interval is too short, the test signal is "wiped out" and the observer's guess as to what it was is no better than chance. There are reliable individual differences in the shortness of the blank interstimulus interval that observers can tolerate without "losing" the test signal. The duration of the shortest interval for which the observer can still identify the test signal is called the "information processing rate."

Using this technique, Bosco (1970) found significant ($p < .01$) differences in information processing rate between urban low- and middle-SES children in grades 1, 3, and 6. Race and SES are confounded (low SES = 28 white, 62 black; middle SES = 88 white, 2 black). The test signals were four simple figures: *circle, square, triangle,* and a five-pointed *star*. According to Bosco, "None of the children . . . had difficulty identifying the four stimuli during the preliminary part of the testing. Even the disadvantaged first graders responded correctly and promptly" (p. 61). With four stimuli each having equal probability of occurrence, there are only 2 bits of information transmitted. The mean difference between the low- and middle-SES groups in information processing rate was much greater than the mean differences between grades. Middle-SES children in the *first* grade had a slightly *faster* information processing rate than low-SES children in the *sixth* grade. At first grade, low-SES children needed more than twice as much visual processing time as was needed by middle-SES children. By sixth grade, low-SES children needed only about 30 percent more time. With only 2 bits of information, the task becomes almost too simple for sixth-graders, as there is considerable restriction of the range of scores with increasing age for such a simple task. Even so, the rate of information processing in sixth-graders showed correlations (around 0.20) with various scholastic achievement measures. If the task employed more *bits* of information (e.g., by using the sixteen most easily discriminable letters of alphabet = 4 bits) one should expect a slower information processing rate and higher correlations between rates and scholastic achievement or *g*-loaded tests. The stimuli used in this metacontrast method can be so extremely culture reduced that the method warrants much further research and development. I suspect that it taps the same basic source of individual differences variance as other RT tests, namely, the person's speed of information processing. Over a very few trials, the absolute differences in information processing rate (or increments in RT as a function of bits) may seem quite small, although statistically significant. But the operation of such small differences in all of the person's encounters with the environment multiplied over *years* can make for noticeable large cumulative differences in the total amount of information acquired and the complexity of cognitive problems that can be dealt with successfully.

Critical Flicker Frequency

This phenomenon theoretically would seem to be related to RT and especially to metacontrast, and therefore might be of value for the measurement and study of intelligence. A stroboscopic light flashes on and off at a rate such as to produce a distinct flicker to the observer. The rate is then gradually increased up to a point at which the observer reports that the flicker *fuses* and appears as a steady light. Readings are also taken from the opposite direction, going from a steady light to the observer's report of the point at which the perception of flicker first appears. Averaged over a number of trials, to ensure reliability, this threshold between the perception of flicker and the perception of a steady light is termed the *critical flicker frequency,* or CFF. (It is also known as the *flicker fusion threshold.*)

There are highly reliable individual differences in CFF. Are they related to intelligence? The evidence is inconsistent. One would hardly expect large correlations, as the cognitive complexity and information conveyed by the stimulus is practically zero. But the same basic hypothesized neural oscillation mechanism underlying RT could well be reflected in CFF.

The first principal component of a battery of thirteen diverse tests including CFF given to fifty normal adults by Halstead (1947, p. 40), in his study of "biological intelligence," shows a loading of +0.47 ($p < .01$) for CFF; Henmon–Nelson IQ is loaded +0.69 on the same component. (It is interesting that the maximal frequency of brain waves that can be experimentally induced in monkeys and normal humans by means of intermittent photic stimulation is directly related to the CFF; Halstead, 1947, p. 70.)

From a sample of ninety-eight fifth-grade children who had been given the Cattell Culture Fair Intelligence Test, three groups of fourteen children each were selected so as to represent low, middle, and high scores on the Cattell test. CFF was measured on the forty-two children so selected. The correlation between CFF and the Cattell Culture Fair Test turned out to be +0.43, $p < .01$; the WISC on these children, however, did not correlate significantly with CFF (Barratt, Clark, & Lipton, 1962). These investigators also found a correlation of +0.24, $p < .05$, between CFF and the Cattell test in seventy college sophomores, but in the same group the Otis Quick Scoring Mental Ability Test correlated *negatively* ($r = -0.33$, $p < .01$) with CFF. This contradictory result seems wholly inexplicable, since I doubt that any components measured by the Cattell and Otis tests (which measure mainly fluid and crystalized g, respectively) would be negatively correlated with one another. Such contradictory results cry out for replication and further experimental analysis.

An earlier review (Landis & Hamwi, 1956) of studies of the correlation between CFF and IQ reports a number of significant but also of nonsignificant correlations. The results overall look unimpressive, but, then, so do the studies on which they are based. In all cases, the finding of a CFF × IQ correlation is quite incidental to the main purpose of the study. The samples are small and usually consist of psychiatric patients and persons who have undergone psychosurgery. (CFF was in vogue in neurologic and psychiatric research some twenty years ago.) Under such conditions, despite the authors' conclusion that the observed correlations between CFF and IQ could be interpreted as "examples of random fluctuation," I would not be so quick to shut the door on the potential value of CFF in research on the nature of intelligence. I expect that CFF, in conjunction with RT and metacontrast, will prove to have important theoretic connections with g.

Average Evoked Potentials

If reaction time measurements are far toward the extreme of culture reducedness, then it would seem that measurements of the brain's electrical potentials recorded from electrodes attached to the person's scalp should be even more extremely culture reduced. Indeed brain electrical potentials are not *cognitive* processes at all. Moreover, a person has no awareness or voluntary control of his brain's electrical activity. If some reliable and stable measure of the brain's "neural efficiency" could be derived from recordings of the brain's electrical potentials and was found to be nontrivially correlated with IQ, it would be of potentially great scientific importance. As Enoch Callaway has half-facetiously remarked, "Such a true measure of neural efficiency would be the finding of the Holy Grail for those who have sought the ephemeral physiological basis for Spearman's g and Cattell's g_f" (1975, p. 61). Indeed an excellent example of the theoretical elaboration of this exciting possibility has been provided by Cattell himself (1971b, pp. 190–197), and one can scarcely find a better brief introduction to this subject than in those few pages by Cattell. More detailed technical aspects of measuring the brain's electrical activity under various conditions and a fine-grained (though at times confusing) review of much of the empirical evidence can be found in the book by Callaway (1975), which, in any case, is a "must" for all serious students of this topic.

The average evoked potential, or AEP as it is most commonly referred to in the literature, is the cumulation or summation of a large number of single electrical discharges of the cerebral cortex, recorded at about fifty millionths of a volt by electrodes attached to the scalp in response to very brief intermittent visual or auditory stimuli. Methods differ widely, but, typically, the subject, with two or more small electrodes gummed to his scalp, usually at the vertex (as well as to an ear lobe in some procedures), is seated in a relaxed position in a small, quiet room free of all distraction, while either a visual or auditory stimulus of very short duration (e.g., a flash of light or a "click" or "beep") is presented at random intervals every few seconds. The subject generally does nothing but sit and wait for these intermittent stimuli, usually in a single session lasting anywhere from 5 to 15 minutes or so. Throughout all this, the experimenter can view the subject's "brain waves" on an oscilloscope. However, there is so much "noise" in the electrical waves of the idling brain that its minute electrical reactions to the intermittent stimuli can hardly be seen, if at all, against the great amount of background "noise," which appears as merely a jumble of rapid waves. But each of the brain's reactions (so-called evoked potentials) to the stimuli, from the instant of occurrence of each stimulus and for a few seconds thereafter, are cumulatively recorded by a computer; that is, they are summated with each previous evoked potential (EP). This has the effect of "averaging out" the random "noise" of the idling brain, and with each successive "trial" it gradually increases the signal–noise ratio up to the point that the brain's characteristic EP response can be clearly discerned in the average evoked potential (AEP), which is then printed out graphically by the computer. The complex technology behind all this is completely understood only by specialists in electrophysiology, electronics, and computer hardware. For our purposes, it suffices to note that there are quite distinctive individual differences in certain features of the AEP. The most commonly used parameters in statistical analyses are (1) the AEP *latency* (analogous to reaction time), that is, the time (in milliseconds) elapsing between the onset of the stimulus and the brain's EP (measured to the peaks of the first, second, etc. "waves" following the stimulus); (2) the AEP *amplitude,* that is, the height (in microvolts) of the graphically recorded waves; (3) the EP *variability,* that is, the standard deviations of the latency and amplitude of EP measures about the subject's AEP (i.e., AEP is the *mean* of the EP measures); and (4) the difference in AEP latencies and amplitudes obtained under *automatic* presentation of stimuli (as described earlier) and under *self-stimulation,* in which the subject directly controls the presentation of the stimuli by pressing a telegraph key or pulling the trigger of a toy pistol that is electrically connected to the stimulus-producing mechanism. The subject's sequence of self-stimulations can be recorded and played back to him or her on another occasion under the automatic presentation condition to ensure the identical interstimulus intervals under both conditions.

Chalke and Ertl (1965) were the first to discover correlations between AEP measures and IQ test scores. Callaway tersely summarizes this breakthrough and its aftermath:

> Short visual AEP latencies were found associated with high IQ, and a simple straightforward hypothesis was advanced: Fast minds should have higher IQs—fast brains should produce short-latency AEPs, and fast minds should be the companions of fast brains. The subsequent history of latency/IQ correlations is anything but simple. There have been replications and failures to replicate. There have been correlations of the opposite sort observed for auditory AEPs, with long latencies appearing to be associated with high IQ. There have been a variety of technical modifications and innovations.   (1975, pp. 42–43)

The AEP and IQ research picture soon becomes a thicket of seemingly inconsistent and confusing findings, confounded variables, methodological differences, statistically questionable conclusions, unbridled theoretical speculation, and, not surprisingly, considerable controversy, which, at times, unfortunately has been rather more acrimonious than most scientific debates. As we well know, the topic of IQ frequently sparks the emotions. But the intrinsic aspects of the controversy actually concerned technical problems with the research. John Ertl, the field's chief innovator, received the brunt of the most highly publicized criticisms. Some of his public claims were probably extravagant or misleading in terms of the ambiguities in the evidence. But it is interesting that, a full decade after Ertl's pioneer researches in this field, Callaway, a leading expert in the field and no mean critic himself, writes the following: "Taking everything into consideration, there are a lot of problems; yet Ertl's data remain quite impressive" (1975, p. 45).

Ertl and Schafer (1969) reported correlations between AEP latencies and IQs (WISC, Peabody, and Otis) ranging from -0.10 to -0.35, with a mean r of -0.28 ($p < .001$), in a random sample of some 570 children from grades 3 to 8 in 39 Ottawa schools. Similar correlations have been reported in a number of studies by other investigators, most notably the well-designed study by Shucard and Horn (1972), which showed significant correlations in the range from -0.15 to -0.32 between visual AEP latencies and measures of fluid g and crystalized g. But there have also been a number of failures that seem hard to explain (see Callaway, 1975, pp. 45–48). Visual and auditory AEPs seem to yield quite different, even contrary, results, *visual* latencies usually being *negatively* correlated with IQ and *auditory* latencies being *positively* correlated. The directions of correlations also seem to flip-flop according to whether the IQs of the sample involved in the study are distributed mostly in the below-average range or mostly in the above-average range of IQs. AEPs are affected by more variables than meet the eye, and it appears that measurements of this complex phenomenon have not yet been brought completely under experimental control. There is a notable lack of standardization of techniques and procedures, but I view this as inevitable and probably desirable in the initial exploratory phase of a new science. Surely the state of the art can hardly be regarded at present as more than exploratory and experimental. So far, the consistently highest correlations of AEP with IQ are found with scores derived from the difference in amplitudes of auditory AEPs produced by self-stimulation and automatic stimulation, a technique developed by Schafer and Marcus (1973). Brighter subjects show a greater reduction of AEP amplitude under the self-stimulation condition relative to the automatic stimulation condition.

Two studies reported in the literature that involve racial comparisons on the AEP seem so shaky, even in the opinion of their authors, that I am loath to put any emphasis on the results (Engel & Henderson, 1973; Callaway, 1975—see esp. "Racial factors" in the index). The reports of these results do not include sufficient information for independent critical assessment (e.g., Callaway does not give significance tests or the standard deviations that would be needed to calculate these). However, what these two studies do seem to suggest, if their results are not due to sampling errors or other artifacts (which Callaway suggests may well be the case), is that the variance component of conventional psychometric tests that is correlated with the AEP may not discriminate appreciably between blacks and whites or may even discriminate in an *opposite* direction to the total score on the conventional IQ tests. Unfortunately, these findings are so questionable, in terms of sampling and other rather atypical features of the data *within* the racial groups, that they have stirred little interest. If the results could be replicated in large representative samples, they would be of considerable scientific interest and would undoubtedly occasion much puzzlement, more debate, and, we should hope, still further investigations into the enigmatic AEP.

On the other hand, Ertl (1978) obtained EEG records on large samples of white (N = 2,805) and black (N = 2,955) children of ages $5\frac{1}{2}$ to $7\frac{1}{2}$ years and found significant age differences in EEG characteristics, which he interpreted as maturational changes, within each racial group. Moreover, these age-dependent EEG indices (frequency, hemispheric synchronization, alpha percentage, and their interrelationships) revealed statistically significant differences between white and black children, showing a "maturational lag for the black children and a slight developmental acceleration for females as compared with males." However, Ertl claims that the maturational lag of black children in the EEG parameters has no implications for IQ differences, because in another study these particular EEG measures did not correlate significantly with IQ. Thus more questions are raised than are answered by the existing research on racial differences in the electrical activity of the brain. About all that we can conclude at present is that significant differences have been found, but their meaning and implications for cognitive development are not at all understood.

Overall, there can now be no doubt that the relationship of AEP to IQ is an authentic phenomenon, albeit quite puzzling, in terms of the total current research evidence for it. We have to learn much more about it before we can develop an adequate theory of the phenomenon or can integrate it fruitfully with psychometric research on individual and group differences. It seems premature to speculate on its practical use in clinical and educational diagnosis and prediction. The AEP surely suggests all these possibilities, which however await further research and development. Such investigation warrants high priority in psychometrics and differential psychology.

Computerized Testing

Computerized testing (CT) consists of a two-way interchange between the person being tested and the computer. In principle, CT is no more nor less culture reduced than any other form of testing. It all depends on the test items that are programmed into the computer. Although there is a rapidly growing literature on CT, to which interested readers can be introduced by pursuing the references provided by Anastasi (1976, pp. 302–305), I mention the topic here briefly only because of claims for its usefulness in overcoming bias in the testing of minorities. Before getting to that, however, a few words are in order about the general advantages and disadvantages of CT.

The main disadvantage is that CT requires elaborate and costly equipment that, for many mass-testing purposes, may not seem warranted. For a given test program, the number of subjects who can be tested per hour is a function of the available number of computer display response consoles through which the subject "interacts" with the computer. This is expensive hardware and has all the usual disadvantages of any complex equipment.

The advantages of CT are great from a purely psychometric standpoint. The main advantage is that CT is *adaptive* to the ability level of the person being tested. Right on the spot, CT in effect tailors the test to fit the person in such a way as quickly to maximize the desired psychometric parameters. Testing time *per subject,* therefore, can be drastically shortened while yielding as much (or more) psychometric information as the ordinary group test. The reason, of course, is that, in CT, subjects need to spend only a minimal amount of time on test items that lie outside the optimally discriminating range of item difficulties for the particular subject's level of ability. In an ordinary test, many of the abler subjects have to "wade through" a large number of items that are too easy for them and therefore yield no discriminations among the abler subjects. Similarly, the less able subjects soon run out of the easy items that are appropriate for their ability level and are faced with too many overly difficult items; this often results in a lot of guessing at the answers, which adulterates total scores and damages reliability. By contrast, in CT the subject is quickly routed to items of the most suitable difficulty level for the reliable, fine-grained discrimination of individual differences. The subject's own performance on each item determines which item the computer will present next. Many more items can be programmed into the computer than could be included in a paper-and-pencil test, but only a small fraction of the item pool is given to any one subject, who need not waste any time on items that are too easy or too difficult. By reference to the *item characteristic curves* (ICC; see Chapter 9, pp. 442–444) of each item in the normative population, it is possible precisely to place the performance level of any given computer-tested individual on the full scale of the population distribution for the ability in question.

CT also has the advantage of being able to record the subject's response latency to each item, which can be an additional source of reliable discrimination that contributes to the tests' validity. Also, all the data from the subject's performance goes directly into the computer for whatever statistical processing may be desired.

In addition to all the foregoing advantages, it has been alleged that CT has the virtue of reducing test bias by eliminating biasing interaction effects between examiner and subjects, or experimenter bias in general. (In Chapter 13 such supposed biasing effects

Figure 14.19.   Mean subtest performance for each administration procedure for blacks and whites. (A perfect score on these subtests is 50.)   (From Johnson & Mihal, 1973)

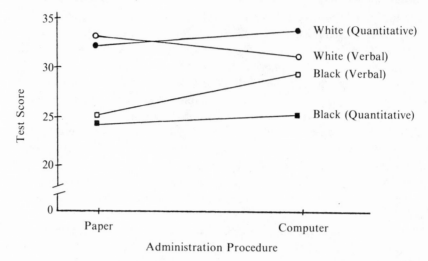

were seen to be trivial or nonexistent in mental testing.) One study of the computerized testing of whites and blacks has been performed to test this hypothesis (Johnson & Mihal, 1973). Two parallel forms of the School and College Ability Test (SCAT) were used— one for the computerized administration, the other for the normal procedure of administering a paper-and-pencil test. Subjects were tested under both procedures in a counterbalanced order. The subjects were ten black and ten white boys in the seventh and eighth grades of an inner-city high school in Rochester, New York. The results are rather difficult to interpret, as they show a significant race × procedure interaction for the Verbal but not for the Quantitative SCAT score. From the ANOVAs and the one graph presented by Johnson and Mihal (1973), shown in Figure 14.19, one can estimate[2] the white–black differences in σ units (σ based on subjects within groups). The white–black σ differences are as follows:

	Administration Procedure	
SCAT Score	*Normal*	*Computerized*
Verbal	$+0.97\sigma$	$+0.23\sigma$
Quantitative	$+1.13\sigma$	$+1.51\sigma$

All the white–black differences are typical and highly significant except for the Verbal score under computerized administration. Although the observed interaction is statistically significant, three elements lead me to suspect that it is a chance result: (1) the effect of computerized administration is seen only for blacks and then on only the verbal part of the test, (2) the sample of blacks is very small ($N = 10$), and (3) in the more than five years since the publication of the study, the results have not been replicated. Until someone takes such a tentative finding seriously enough to do the kind of research needed to establish it as an authentic phenomenon, it must be consigned to the limbo of doubtful findings.

SUMMARY

Various mental tests may be ordered on a continuum going from highly *culture loaded,* at the one extreme, to highly *culture reduced,* at the other extreme. This continuum reflects the "cultural distance" over which a test maintains essentially the same psychometric properties. Tests can be made less culture bound by various means, such as by using only fundaments that are as universally familiar as possible and by eliminating the use of language, scholastic and cultural content, and specialized skills. Culture-reduced tests emphasize variation in cognitive *complexity* of the problems, rather than rarity of the contents of test items, as a means of varying item difficulty.

A number of purportedly culture-reduced tests of the past and present are critically evaluated. None of these attempts to create highly culture-reduced tests, when psychometrically sound, has succeeded in eliminating, or even appreciably reducing, the mean differences between certain subpopulations (races and social classes) in the United States that have been noted to differ markedly on the more conventional culture-loaded tests. On the other hand, some culture-reduced tests show negligible differences between certain widely diverse linguistic, national, and cultural groups, which suggests that these tests are indeed capable of measuring general ability across quite wide cultural distances. The fact that such culture-reduced tests do not show smaller mean differences between blacks and whites (in the United States) than do conventional culture-loaded IQ tests suggests that the racial difference in test scores is not due to cultural factors per se.

Most of the currently published culture-reduced tests can be characterized as "psychometrically underdeveloped." Without exception, they have been less adequately standardized on large, representative samples of any population than are the currently most popular standardized tests of the conventional type.

Drawing and figure copying tests show social-class and racial differences of comparable magnitude to conventional IQ tests, but they highlight a psychologically important finding, namely, the differences in performance between blacks and whites on these tests are qualitatively indistinguishable from the types of developmental differences observed between younger and older children all of the same race and socioeconomic background. Thus the race differences observed in drawing and copying tests are more parsimoniously interpreted as differences in rate of mental maturation than as cultural differences.

Consistent with this mental maturation hypothesis are the findings of racial differences on Piagetian tests, which were specially designed to reveal certain developmental landmarks in the course of mental growth. The Piagetian tests based on the concept of conservation of substance, number, volume, and so on, are generally viewed as more culture reduced than conventional tests. The contents of these tests (e.g., balls of clay, jars of liquid, etc.) are universally familiar. Yet the white–black differences on Piaget's tests are of about the same magnitude as on such conventional standardized IQ tests as the Stanford–Binet and Wechsler. Factor analyses show that Piagetian tests are highly *g* loaded.

Adaptive behavior inventories are not less culture loaded than conventional IQ tests. Although correlated with IQ to a considerable extent, adaptive behavior inventories are best regarded as a complement to, rather than as a substitute for, IQ tests in the clinical diagnosis of mental retardation.

Laboratory methods of mental measurement, such as complex reaction time, flicker fusion threshold, and electroencephalographic recordings of the average latency and amplitude of brain potentials show small but reliable correlations with conventional IQ scores, which indicates that conventional IQ tests indeed measure something more profound than the popular notion of IQ as reflecting merely knowledge or skills acquired in school or in a cultured home. Such laboratory tests, of course, stand at the extreme of culture reducedness. However, these laboratory techniques are as yet virtually useless for any practical purposes in their current experimental stage of development. Their promise seems to be more as tools for gaining a clearer scientific understanding of the nature of mental ability than as alternatives to conventional psychometric tests.

Computerized testing has advantages over conventional tests in the precision and efficiency of measurement, although the hardware requirements may make it an unfeasible substitute for ordinary paper-and-pencil tests in large-scale group testing. Computerized testing per se is not any more culture reduced than are conventional tests.

NOTES

1. From the frequency distribution of the differences between two sets of scores having similar means and standard deviations, such as IQs from different tests, one can roughly estimate the intraclass correlation r_i between the two sets of scores, X and Y, as follows: Obtain the average *absolute* difference $\bar{d}$ (i.e., treat all differences as *positive*) and use the following formula:

$$r_i \approx 1 - \left(\frac{|\bar{d}|\sqrt{\pi}}{2\bar{\sigma}}\right)^2 \quad \text{or} \quad 1 - \left(\frac{|\bar{d}|}{1.13\bar{\sigma}}\right)^2,$$

where σ is the average standard deviation of the two distributions, X and Y:

$$\bar{\sigma} = \sqrt{(\sigma_X^2 + \sigma_Y^2)/2}.$$

2. The sum of squares for a group difference main effect (where there is only one degree of freedom) divided by the total sum of squares gives the squared point-biserial correlation between the dichotomized group variable (e.g., ethnicity) and the dependent variable (e.g., test scores). From this squared point-biserial correlation, we can estimate the mean difference $\bar{d}$ between the groups in σ units from the following formula:

$$\bar{d} = \frac{4}{\sqrt{\dfrac{1}{r_{pps}^2} - 1}}.$$

highly with achievement tests or that scholastic achievement cannot be quite accurately predicted by the IQ. But, because the achievement itself is the school's main concern, I see no need to measure anything other than the achievement itself—with two exceptions, to which I will come shortly.

The economics of routine IQ testing of all children in school makes little sense. The value of the information gained from mass IQ testing cannot justify the sheer monetary cost, even ignoring for the moment the possible abuses of this practice. The pupils' IQs are entered into their school records and, for the most part, are never looked at again. Often they are recorded by the pupils' teachers, who as often as not misunderstand the psychometric nature or meaning of the IQ. A teacher needs to know whether a pupil has or has not learned what was taught. A teacher does not need to know a child's IQ.

Teacher Abuses of Tests.   It would be unreasonable to expect school teachers to be experts in psychometrics, test construction, and the psychological interpretation of test results. That is not their job. However, they should be trained to administer group-standardized tests and to appreciate the importance of doing it properly. This means following the directions precisely—to ensure that the scores are obtained under the same conditions of administration that pertained in the standardization of the test. In some schools, unfortunately, teachers' attitudes toward standardized tests are so negative that test administration can be entrusted to them only with considerable risk, even after they have received proper instruction in test administration.

The commonest teacher abuse of standardized tests is failure to give adequate or standard instructions and to follow carefully the prescribed time limits. In my experience in school testing I have come across teachers who have allowed pupils a full week to do a test with a prescribed 30-minute time limit, or who have started the test too late in the school period and have had to cut short the time limit by nearly one-half. Others have given out some of the answers, or have altered the questions to make them easier, or have read aloud the reading comprehension test items to give a better chance to pupils who could not read. And so on. I have found all the abuses that one could well imagine and some that one would not imagine, such as the instance of one teacher's filling in the correct answers to all the items that were left unanswered on the test papers by the pupils in her class. Fortunately, such abuses are the exception rather than the rule, but they occur often enough to render test scores from teacher-administered group-standardized tests highly suspect. It is a shame if such scores are ever recorded anywhere, yet they surely are, in many cases.

How much error variance in standardized test scores is typically attributable to poor test administration by teachers? No one knows exactly, but the quite high grade-to-grade correlations of IQ and achievement suggest that the errors could not be very great. Yet it is doubtful that teacher-administered tests are as reliable as they could be. In a large school system, to my personal knowledge, a battery of group-administered achievement tests was given by the classroom teachers one year and the same achievement tests were given the following year by a staff of carefully trained and closely supervised psychometrists, who made every effort to administer the tests under highly uniform conditions, timed with stopwatches. The school population and curriculum had not changed from the one year to the next. The overall mean achievement scores for the school district did not differ appreciably in going from the teacher-administered to the psychometrist-administered tests, but the teacher-administered tests showed about 25 percent *greater variance* in scores than the test results obtained by psychometrists. Most of this 25 percent increase in variance is therefore variance attributable mainly to differences among teachers in the ways that they administered the tests. Specific investigation of some of the most deviant class means on the achievement tests revealed some of the teacher abuses of test administration procedures that I have just described.

No remedy is needed for this condition if no real use is made of the test scores. But, then, why give tests at all? However, if the results of standardized group testing are to be used in ways that are beneficial to pupils and teachers, either one of two precautions should be considered by school authorities. Either the classroom teachers periodically should be given special in-service instruction in group test administration and their test administration procedures should be periodically monitored in the classroom by a testing supervisor as a continuation of the teacher's instruction in testing; or a staff of specially trained testers should be employed by the school system to administer all standardized tests.

Scoring Tests.   Most standardized tests today use special answer sheets that can be machine scored. These machine-scored answer sheets afford much less chance for error than teacher-scored tests, especially if the raw score (number correct) has to be converted to some form of standard score or grade equivalent by means of a conversion table or formula. At a summer workshop on group testing for teachers, I once assigned the mere scoring and conversion of raw scores (by formula) of a standard IQ test to the fifty or so students in the workshop. Despite prior instruction, several of the students turned in grossly misscored tests; conversion errors were larger and more common than were errors in tallying raw scores. I am wary of teacher-scored tests and would not enter them in any school records without checking them. Of course, the practice, which one still sees occasionally, of having pupils score their own or each other's tests is absolutely egregious if any use at all of the scores is intended.

IQs and School Grades.   There is a substantial correlation between IQ and course grades assigned by teachers, even when there has been no chance of "contamination" of grades by the teacher's knowledge of pupils' IQs. However, I have come across instances of direct contamination, where the teacher has done such a poor job of evaluating pupils' actual achievement in the subject matter of the course and the teacher had so little confidence in his or her own estimate of pupils' performances that the teacher used the pupils' IQs, as recorded in the school records, as the basis for assigning course grades. It is hard to know to what extent a teacher's knowledge of pupils' IQs affects the grading of pupils' achievements. IQ contamination of school grades should be assiduously avoided. The easiest method of avoidance is to not use IQ tests at all for the general run of pupils in school and to not give teachers access to the IQs of the few pupils who have been individually tested by the school psychologist for special diagnostic purposes (which I include under legitimate uses of IQ tests).

Standardized achievement tests, provided that they adequately sample the curriculum that was actually taught, provide a sound basis for pupil evaluation and grading. Teachers should be aware that standardized achievement tests (and test items) are generally much better for a broad assessment of achievement than tests that teachers make up themselves. Test construction, involving item writing, tryout, psychometric analysis of items, and standardization on representative groups, is a highly technical specialty far beyond the training and resources of most teachers and most school systems. Frequent use of informal teacher-made tests should be an essential part of the instructional process. But these should be supplemented periodically for broader evaluations of pupils' achievement of instructional objectives by professionally designed norm-referenced and criterion-referenced standardized tests.

A possibly valuable innovation for achievement testing would be for test publishers to provide packs of well-designed individual achievement test items that could be used by teachers (or schools) to make up achievement tests that specifically sample the teacher's instructional objectives and the subject matter that has actually been taught. For the teacher's information, each item would be accompanied by item statistics information, such as the percentage of pupils passing the item at any given grade level in the standardization sample and the item correlation with total score on the whole achievement battery, the total matrix of item intercorrelations, interval scaling of item difficulties, and the like. Such tailor-made achievement test modules could well be used in pretest–posttest fashion for measuring pupil progress in each main instructional unit throughout the school year. The aim of such testing is not to assign pupils a numerical score per se, but to determine, for the teacher's and pupil's information, which elements of the intended curriculum have been mastered and which elements still require gains in the pupil's proficiency. Obtaining pure test scores per se, that is, test scores divorced from specific instructional objectives without information as to the specific scholastic attainments or the lack thereof that went into the pupil's achievement test score, seems to me to be a waste of school resources.

Ability Grouping.   Also referred to as tracking, streaming, homogeneous grouping, or achievement grouping, this practice was more common in the past than in recent years. Its advantages were largely administrative; many teachers felt that it was easier to teach homogeneous ability groups, especially when class sizes were large. Recent reviews of research on the effects of ability grouping come to largely negative or at best ambiguous and noncommittal conclusions. The most thorough and well-considered review that I have found in the literature, for example, concludes:

> Briefly, we find that ability grouping . . . shows no consistent positive value for helping students generally, or particular groups of students, to learn better. Taking all students into account, the balance of findings is chiefly of no strong effect either favorable or unfavorable. Among the studies showing significant effects the slight preponderance of evidence showing the practice favorable for the learning of high ability students is more than offset by evidence of unfavorable effects on the learning of average and low ability groups, particularly the latter. Finally, these instances of special benefit under ability grouping have generally involved substantial modification of materials and methods, which may well be the influential factors wholly apart from grouping.   (Findley & Bryan, 1971, p. 54)

There is no compelling evidence that would justify ability grouping in the elementary grades. I believe that schools should aim to keep pupils of as wide a range of abilities as is feasible in regular classes. This practice has become known as "mainstreaming." Grouping into separate classes on the basis of either IQ or achievement test scores not only stigmatizes the pupils in some classes as slow learners, but limits the educational aspirations and opportunities of those children placed in the slow groups, making it still more difficult to catch up or keep up with their age-mates if they are capable of doing so.

Grouping is usually based on a pupil's weakness in some scholastic area and tends to overlook the pupil's particular strengths, which can be cultivated as a source of self-esteem in a regular classroom, despite the pupil's difficulties with certain aspects of the curriculum.

Individual differences in mental ability and achievement become much greater and more visible, in an absolute sense, at the high school level. But this wide range of differences can be accommodated by offering highly differentiated curricula in the high school, without stigmatizing effects. Expert guidance, of course, is called for in pupils' choice of courses, based on up-to-date assessments of prior achievement in the specific prerequisite knowledge and skills for certain courses. This is not the same as tracking, but is educational guidance in terms of the pupil's developed capabilities for a particular course. It makes little sense to assign a pupil who has not mastered the rudiments of arithmetic to a high school course in algebra. But, where there is any doubt about the pupil's prerequisite ability and the probability of his or her success in an elected course, I believe the best "test" is the student's performance in the course itself. The margin of error based on predictions of future performance from test scores of any kind are large enough that, when at all feasible, I would let the motivated student try, even if he then fails, rather than tell him that he should not try because of his low score on a test. Remedial courses (not necessarily labeled as such) can be provided for students who are deficient in prerequisites, and demonstrating a prescribed level of competency on the prerequisite knowledge or skills can be a legitimate criterion for admission to more advanced courses. With such arrangements, the issue of tracking is irrelevant at the high school level. And it seems unnecessary and undesirable at the elementary school level.

Special education should not be confused with tracking or homogeneous grouping. It is another matter altogether. A small percentage of the school population have physical, mental, or emotional handicaps of such severity that they can hardly benefit at all from the instruction they would receive in regular classes, and they would more likely suffer psychological harm from frustration and social exclusion by their abler classmates. Unfortunately, many young children can be surprisingly cruel to age-mates who are markedly deviant. Such conspiciously deviant children require special educational attention beyond the resources of the regular classroom. The recommendation for such special services should be based on a thorough examination and diagnosis by medical and psychological experts, making use of all the relevant techniques of psychological examination, which includes an individual IQ test.

Teacher Referral and IQ Testing.   One of the legitimate uses of IQ testing is in the diagnosis of a pupil's educational problems when a teacher refers the pupil to the school psychologist. Such referral is made when the pupil shows persistent deviant behavior in class, or consistently fails to achieve, or makes abnormally slow progress in scholastic subjects. Because there can be various causes, some remediable, for these conditions, a thorough physical and psychological diagnosis of the problem is called for. This should not be the teacher's responsibility. It is the teacher's duty simply to provide the proper school authority (usually the school psychologist) with a clear, objective behavioral description of the pupil's particular problems. Stigmatizing labels should be avoided by all school personnel. There is no technical need for general labels; they are usually misleading and harmful.

Once the presence of possible sensory–motor defects or other physical abnormalities have been evaluated by a medical examination, individual psychological testing by a qualified psychologist is an essential part of the diagnostic work-up. This includes an individual IQ test, such as the WISC, and often other more specialized cognitive ability tests as well. The value of the information provided by such instruments in the diagnosis and possible remediation of education problems is highly dependent on the training, experience, and intelligence of the psychologist using them. The same thing can be said of the medical diagnostician who measures a patient's temperature, pulse rate, and blood pressure. It goes without saying that the various measurements must be obtained as accurately as possible, but equally important is the diagnostic and prescriptive evaluation based on the measurements. Evaluation of the evidence is a complex matter of professional expertise, the explication of which falls largely outside the scope of this book, except insofar as it involves the consideration of the psychometrics of test bias. But this is only a narrow aspect of educational and psychological evaluation, for which minimal qualification depends on at least three years of appropriate graduate training at the doctoral level.

Use of IQ Tests in Educational Research.   Group and individual IQ tests (or scholastic aptitude tests) undoubtedly measure an important psychological variable of great relevance to children's scholastic performance. They can therefore be valuable in quantitative or statistical research studies of various school populations, experimental instructional programs, and the evaluation of schools. Because IQ is the single best indicator of the scholastic learning abilities of pupils, it can be informative, in the kinds of research just mentioned, to examine pupils' scholastic achievement following a course of instruction designed to impart such achievement in relation to the pupils' IQs by means of regression analysis. This seems to me the best way to compare the achievement results of different instructional methods, of different teachers, or of classrooms or schools. Pupil achievements on specifically taught scholastic material is measured against the much broader base of pupil abilities and cumulative achievements measured by IQ tests. When different classes or different schools with the same distributions of IQs show appreciably different distributions of achievement scores, further investigation is called for to determine why the classes (or schools) differ in educational output (i.e., pupils' achievement) despite equal inputs of aptitude (i.e., pupils' ability level).

Group IQ tests (or their equivalent) serve a necessary and legitimate function in such investigations. But such investigations can be carried out most efficiently without resorting to routine teacher-administered IQ testing of all children in the entire school system. A well-designed study can obtain much better test data at much less cost in time and money by appropriate sampling procedures that select only a relatively small percentage of the total school population for testing. With small samples from each grade in school, the group tests can be administered under optimal conditions by trained psychometrists, so that one can have confidence in the results. Test scores so obtained would not be entered into the pupils' school records or used for any individual decisions. Test protocols would be immediately coded in a way to eliminate pupil identity, and only the coded data or the derived group statistics relevant to the research questions the study was designed to answer would be made available to anyone concerned.

Identifying Academic Talent.   The most compelling argument for not doing away with IQ testing completely is that IQ tests, particularly those of the nonverbal, culture-reduced type, may be better able to identify academic talent at the early stage of schooling in certain segments of the school population than typical scholastic achievement tests. Academic talent not yet realized in formal achievements can go unrecognized most easily in children from an educationally and culturally disadvantaged home background. Parents may not always recognize high intellectual ability in their own children, and often the teacher's perceptions of certain pupils' intellectual abilities are obscured by the veneer of social class or a culturally impoverished background. Suitable tests can "read through" the veneer of environmental advantages or disadvantages better than any other means we yet know of and can reveal academic potential where it might otherwise go undetected and therefore remain undeveloped. School grades and teachers' estimates of ability reflect social and cultural factors in pupils' homes more than IQ test scores do. There is considerably less risk of unrecognized ability in middle-class majority children than in children from poor homes and from minority and immigrant groups, for whom academic potential, when it is found, requires more fostering and encouragement by the school for its full development than in the case of middle-class white children, whose parents are usually keen to promote whatever talents their children may have. If scholastic ability of a level required for higher education is valued by a minority group, such ability should be identified as early in a child's school career as possible, to ensure its fostering and further development. A larger percentage of minority youths, with sufficiently developed academic skills for successful college attendance than we see today, may become available in the future through the identification and development of academically talented minority children early in their school careers. Years of educational neglect or disinterest cannot suddenly be overcome, at age 18 or so, when youths seek admission to college.

So I think that group IQ tests may prove more valuable to the educational welfare of disadvantaged minorities than to the white middle class. IQ tests could be used with the disadvantaged in a positive way only, to identify the potential academic achievers (say, IQs over 100) among them. Group-administered tests could be machine scored or scored by a clerical staff not connected with the school, and only the high-potential pupils would be identified for the school's use. The rest of the data could be disregarded. High-potential pupils who are markedly underachieving scholastically should warrant special attention.

Teachers could also be taught more about recognizing potential high achievers from their classroom achievements as well as from their extracurricular activities and social skills, and these indications could be further substantiated by referral for appropriate testing of such pupils.

Identification of high academic potential should not imply any lack of the school's concern with the less academically gifted, though unfortunately there is that risk. Without caution, the technology of psychological and educational measurement may run ahead of our wisdom in applying it.

Communicating Test Results.   For most teachers, parents, and pupils, the results of an achievement test, when closely geared to the material that has been taught, are more constructively informative and much less apt to be misunderstood than an IQ or an aptitude test score. This is especially true if the achievement test results can be described in criterion-referenced terms, that is, in terms of precisely what kinds of knowledge and skills the pupil has or has not attained after a period of systematic instruction. Such criterion-referenced description may also be accompanied by normative information that places the pupil's performance in terms of its average grade equivalent or in terms of its percentile rank among the pupil's age peers who have received approximately the same instruction. This information is easily communicated and easily understood by almost everyone. Although IQs are highly correlated with achievement measures, and usually have more general and more long-range predictive validity and are less influenced by a number of other factors that determine scholastic achievement in any given grade, the IQ is further removed from the specific scholastic performances that are the teacher's chief concern. Therefore, the IQ is not so directly helpful as is information about the pupil's actual achievement in what he or she has presumably been taught. Teachers, parents, and pupils have only the vaguest notions of the meaning of the IQ, and they often have erroneous conceptions. Brief explanations are of little use. Essentially the same information that the IQ conveys to the psychologist can be conveyed to teachers, pupils, and parents in terms of the pupil's percentile rank in scholastic achievement measures cumulated over a period of time. The pupil's performance on the achievement tests can be directly examined and reasonably understood by the layman. If a teacher, pupil, or parent wishes to know the reason for special concern about any particular pupil, he can be shown not only the pupil's overall percentile rank among age peers, but even the percentage of the pupil's age group who pass each item on the achievement test. Such direct inspection of a pupil's test papers, accompanied by normative data, is much more understandable and meaningful information to the layman than an IQ score could possibly be without a full course of instruction on the nature and measurement of general intelligence. Therefore, I see no value in the general use of IQ tests for all pupils. In the special instances where pupils with learning problems are referred to the school psychologist for examination including an IQ test, I would say the same thing. The IQ will be useful to the psychologist, but cannot be usefully communicated, as such, to the teacher, pupil, or parent. Description of the pupil's educational problem should be given in terms of scholastic performance per se, and its trend over the pupil's years in school. It is part of the school psychologist's job to try and find, through examination, any factors in the school or home situations that might feasibly be altered to the benefit of the pupil's scholastic progress, personal development, and self-esteem. Beyond that, the school psychologist, in his official role, should not be called on to *explain* to anyone the basic causes of any given pupil's level of performance. The reality of individual differences simply must be recognized, and their complex causes can be described in general terms. But there is little value in these generalities in dealing with any given individual. In most cases we cannot determine the causes of deviation anyway; we can only measure or describe the end products of the whole complex chain of causes. Among these, of course, are genetic factors. But, where it comes to anything really important in life, most persons resist the idea of sheer luck as a determining factor. Yet we know that our own genetic make-up and that of our children, for better or worse, is largely a matter of luck. Insofar as our genes are concerned, we are all products of a random lottery. Such is the way of nature. No one is to be praised for one's good luck in this lottery, or blamed for one's bad luck. Human worth, dignity, and self-esteem come from one's trying to make the best of it—for oneself, for one's children, and for others.

Abuses by the Media in Reporting Test Results. It is a quite common occurrence for the media periodically to report the results of testing in the various school districts throughout the state. Average percentile ranks on various scholastic achievement tests are given for each school district, often accompanied by remonstrations in newspaper editorials about the marked differences in achievement levels between school districts. The differences between schools in average test scores are the occasion for praise and blame of schools and educators, as if they were solely responsible for the variation among schools' average levels of achievement. The public is badly informed by such misguided praise and blame. We have known for years that much of the variation in level of scholastic achievement among schools is predictable from a number of demographic characteristics of the populations that they serve. But the schools themselves can have no control over such community characteristics as socioeconomic level, racial composition, average educational and occupational level of the adult population, and the like. This fact is seldom mentioned, much less emphasized, as it should be, by the media. Schools' average IQ and scholastic achievement scores can be predicted for a wide range of communities, with a multiple correlation of about 0.60, from census variables such as the educational level of the adult population, percentage of home ownership, quality of housing, proportion of native-born whites, rate of female employment, and proportion of professional workers (Thorndike, 1951). To ignore such findings while reporting differences between the average achievement levels of schools is a disservice to the schools and to the public.

Minimum Competency Testing for School Graduation. MCT is currently a topic of great discussion and debate by educators, lawmakers, and the general public. The basic idea of MCT is that a high school student, on graduation, should not be given a diploma but only a certificate of attendance, if he or she has failed to pass a test demonstrating "minimal competency" in basic academic skills and their practical application to typical "real-life" demands. Basic skills mean reading and arithmetic and such practical demands as figuring out a map, writing a check, calculating the cost of groceries, and filling out a job application. The drive for MCT stems from the alarming numbers of high school graduates who today are judged deficient in these basic skills generally deemed essential for economic self-sufficiency in any modern industrial society. To discriminate the "competent" from the "incompetent" in terms of educational attainments, and to make the high school diploma signify more than merely a certificate of attendance, an increasing number of school systems and states throughout the United States have been officially adopting the requirement of MCT for all graduating high school seniors. The states of Arizona and Oregon already have such a provision, and it is about to become law in New York and Florida.

The first trial of MCT, in Florida in 1978, raised a public furor. It was reported that some 77 percent of blacks, 39 percent of Hispanics, and 24 percent of whites "failed" the arithmetic test; and 26 percent of blacks, 7 percent of Hispanics, and 3 percent of whites "failed" in "communications" (reading and writing). MCT only confirmed what was already known or should have been known.

Although the results of MCT undoubtedly highlight a serious educational problem, I cannot see MCT as in any way contributing to the solution of the problem. It appears to me to be an unnecessary stigmatizing practice, with absolutely no redeeming benefits to individual pupils or to society. I say this not because I do not believe that individual differences in scholastic attainments cannot be reliably measured, but because I see no utility whatsoever in drawing an arbitrary, imaginary line between "minimal competence" and "incompetence." "Competence" is an entirely relative concept. What is competence for one purpose may be incompetence for another. There can be no single all-purpose demarcation between "competence" and "incompetence." The notion is psychometrically nonsensical.

Each school or college admitting high school graduates should determine its own standards of academic competence for admission, based on whatever criteria best serve its purpose. The same thing applies to employers who wish to hire high school graduates. They are free to use whatever tests or other selection criteria yield the kinds of employees they desire, consistent with fair selection and fair employment policies. Every college and every job requires different minimal competencies, which are best determined by each particular college or employer. So who would possibly benefit from the extremely costly and occupationally and socially stigmatizing minimal competency testing of all graduating high school pupils? MCT is surely one of the most futile proposals to come along in public education in many a decade.

This is not to say that teachers, pupils, and parents should not have explicit objective evidence of the pupil's attainments in basic scholastic skills and other skills most generally required for assuming adult responsibilities. But this information on every pupil should be provided at least every year, beginning with the first grade. When attainment after a unit of study is below par, the pupils who lag in any area should be so informed and helped Repetition of the particular units should be routinely required for failing students for them to attain the levels of knowledge and skill that are actually prerequisite for more advanced units of study in the same area, even if, for some pupils, it means repeating a whole grade. In high school, course offerings should be sufficiently diverse that students over a wide range of academic abilities will find courses of study and training (not necessarily *academic* courses) that will be of tangible benefit to them when they leave school. The role of standardized tests in this process is to monitor pupil achievement periodically so as to assure its fullest development, to whatever level that might be for a given individual. It is an abuse of tests to use them to assign general labels of "competent" or "incompetent."

Confidentiality of Test Results.   It should be explicitly understood that standard tests of scholastic aptitudes and achievements are an integral part of the school's instructional program and may be used by the school as deemed appropriate without the permission of parents. However, the results of such tests should be treated as personal and confidential information available only to the pupil, teacher, and parents. Test results should leave the school files for statistical treatment or other research purposes only in a coded format, with personal identities removed. Test results of identified pupils should not be transmitted to other agencies outside the local school system without written permission of the pupil's parent or legal guardian. An excellent set of detailed recommendations regarding the management of pupils' tests and records is the *Guideline for the Collection, Maintenance, and Dissemination of Pupil Records* (1970), published by the Russell Sage Foundation.

Individual psychological evaluation should be undertaken only with parental consent, and the results should be treated in accord with the principles of confidentiality spelled out in the American Psychological Association's *Ethical Standards for Psychologists* (1972) and *Standards for Educational and Psychological Tests* (1974). The same confidentiality applies to the results of a psychological examination, including test results, as applies generally to personal information in medical records or a lawyer's records of a client's legal consultation. The right of pupils and their parents to know everything placed in their cumulative records in school underlines the importance of maintaining records with scrupulous accuracy and an objectivity that eschews generalized labels and far-reaching inferences.

College Selection

The use of tests for prediction and selection becomes crucial once students have completed the amount of schooling required by law or are beyond school age. The need for prediction and selection for college admissions is obvious. Colleges vary widely in their purposes and in their academic demands and standards. Because all applicants cannot be admitted to any one type of college, selective admissions are a necessity. The aim of selection is to match a student's goals and aptitudes to the type of college in which the student would be most likely to benefit. College entrance examinations, such as the nationally used Scholastic Aptitude Test, now serve the purpose of college admissions officers remarkably well for the statistical prediction of a student's probable success in any given college. Fortunately, students who do not meet the entrance requirements of their first-choice college have many other options, and the student's demonstrated ability in the first year or two of a college with less stringent admission standards may gain the student's admission to an academically more demanding college. No injustice is done by the use of standardized academic aptitude tests for college admission. In fact, quite the contrary, because nationally standardized tests yield valid predictive information that is much less determined by local school standards than course grades, rank in graduating class, or teacher recommendations. Many would-be academic failures in college are steered away from colleges that are unsuitable for their level of aptitude and preparation and find admission to more appropriate colleges. On the other hand, because of the Scholastic Aptitude Test, some students (and their parents) discover, for the first time, that the student's academic promise actually exceeds their expectations and aspirations. I suspect that this surprise occurs more often to students whose parents have had little formal education. It seems safe to say that the use of aptitude tests in college selection has had more beneficial effects for individuals and for society in general, and has been subject to fewer abuses, than any other use of tests.

Tests in Vocational Guidance

Test results used in vocational counseling and guidance should be presented to the client in terms of where his or her scores fall in relation to the median, range, and form of the frequency distributions on particular aptitudes of persons who are successfully engaged in various occupations. There is enough inexactness in such probabilistic prediction, however, that test results should not be used by counselors to actively discourage persons whose vocational aim seems too high in terms of probabilistic prediction from their aptitude scores. When ambition is high, I think it is better, when at all feasible, to let the person's performance on the criterion itself be the test of capability. Most persons come to realize their own strengths and deficiencies through perception of their success or failure in achieving a standard of performance or in meeting the competition, and the individual's own perception is more valid than a test's prediction or an outsider's impression, because the individual knows the degree of his or her own efforts. An important aspect of attaining maturity consists in getting to know one's own capabilities in relation to the effort that one is willing to make, and this must come from actually making the effort to achieve one's goals. The statistical predictive power of standardized tests should not be used to limit one's own discovery of one's abilities, by putting them to the actual test of attempting the performances that seem worthy of one's best effort. No one with an ambition should let a test score substitute for this kind of direct self-knowledge. Failing after an honest effort is not fun, but it has always seemed far preferable to me than forever wondering if one might have succeeded in realizing an ambition if one had made a real effort. But that is only an opinion with which others may well disagree.

Personnel Selection

Mandatory universal education is largely responsible for making the traditional high school diploma a mere certificate of attendance without any discriminating significance in the world of work. Employers who are concerned with the qualifications of job applicants, therefore, have turned increasingly to the use of tests of one kind or another, in addition to certain other types of information, for the selection and advancement of employees. This trend will continue. Tests have clearly proven themselves as an effective and efficient selection device, with generally greater validity than school records, recommendations, and interviews, especially in the case of applicants without previous relevant work experience. Today the use of selection tests is routine at the hiring-in level for most jobs in government, the military, business, and industry.

Uses or abuses of testing in personnel selection that contradict the principles set forth in Title VII of the Civil Rights Act of 1964, which made it unlawful to discriminate on the basis of race, color, religion, sex, or national origin, have been fully recognized in the *Guidelines on Employee Selection Procedures* issued by the Equal Employment Opportunity Commission (EEOC) in 1966 (*Federal Register,* 1970, *35* (1949), 12333–12336). The main point made by the EEOC *Guidelines* is that the use of any test that adversely affects the hiring or promotion of the classes protected by Title VII of the Civil Rights Act must be justified by objective empirical evidence of the test's content validity, predictive validity, or criterion validity for the particular groups in question and that suitable alternative selection procedures are unavailable. Obviously, a test is used *unfairly* if it discriminates between certain groups but is not related to the actual job performance of those groups.

The EEOC *Guidelines* and the OFCC *Guidelines for Reporting Criterion-Related and Content Validity,* issued by the Office of Federal Contract Compliance (*Federal Register,* 1974, *39* (12), 2094–2096), spell out in detail the minimal standards for test validation. The essence of these *Guidelines* is that the test should show statistically significant and practically substantial correlation with "important elements of work behavior which comprise or are relevant to the job or jobs for which candidates are being evaluated." In other words, a test that statistically discriminates between majority and minority groups in a direction unfavorable to the *minority* group (many would prefer it said *any* group) must not be used for selection or promotion of employees unless the test scores can be shown to be significantly correlated with *specific criterion measures* of satisfactory performance of the *particular job* in question for *both* minority and majority employees. Moreover, the correlation between test scores and criterion performance must be of sufficient magnitude to have "practical significance." "Practical significance" is a complex judgment based on the size of the validity coefficient, the selection ratio, and the amount of economic and human risk involved in hiring an unqualified applicant (a "false positive"). (The interrelationship among these factors in determining the efficacy of a selection procedure is discussed in Chapter 8, pp. 306–310.) Hiring an unqualified airline *pilot,* for example, constitutes greater economic and human risk than hiring an unqualified airline *steward.*

The EEOC and OFCC *Guidelines* are quite comprehensive and appear thoroughly reasonable and sound, ethically and psychometrically, as far as they go; but they fail to emphasize a most important distinction revealed by research on the predictive validity of tests in personnel selection. This is the distinction between the prediction of performance *during job training* and performance *after the completion of training.* Because often the training phase of the newly hired on a job is not formally demarcated, we should extend this distinction to the *initial* phase of job performance and *later* job performance. This distinction, I think, is especially important for minority hiring. Its importance arises from the finding that, for many jobs that typically do not involve traditional academic knowledge and skills, tests generally have considerably higher validity coefficients for predicting performance *during* job training than for predicting actual job performance *after training.* The reason, briefly, is that the validity of most selection tests is mainly related to the tests' *g* loadings, and the training phase on most jobs is more *g* loaded than job performance after training. After training, certain aptitudes other than *g* become more important, although some of these non-*g* aptitudes are so highly job specific that they are not measured to an important degree by any available standardized tests. However, certain differential aptitude tests, such as those in the General Aptitude Test Battery devised by the U.S. Employment Service, are better predictors of posttraining job performance than are more highly *g*-loaded tests. Facility in learning from verbal instructions, from passive observation of demonstrations, and from rather abstract diagrams and training manuals is more highly predictable from predominantly *g*-loaded tests (which means most vocational aptitude tests) than is the actual job performance that is being trained. Therefore, tests that are validated on the performance of employees during the training phase immediately following hiring will show higher validity and result in greater discrimination, to the disadvantage of certain minorities, than could be justified by the test's validity coefficients obtained after the completion of training.

The whole issue, of course, hinges on the duration and cost of the training required for a particular job, as well as on the ultimate success–failure ratio of trainees as a function of their test scores. When training is costly and prolonged for even the best trainees, the use of selection tests to predict success in training seems quite justified. Such extensive and costly training is not required for many jobs, however, and most employees will be able to complete the necessary training satisfactorily, although there will be considerable individual differences in the facility and speed of getting through the training, and these individual differences can be predicted by tests. Research has shown that training procedures can be modified in ways that make success less dependent on *g.* Because the relevance of *g* success in many jobs involves mainly the job-training phase and not the quality of job performance after the successful completion of training, greater efforts are called for to seek job-training methods that minimize the correlation between ability successfully to complete training and scores on aptitude tests. This, of course, is a wholly unrealistic expectation for those "high-level" jobs in which not only the training for the job but the performance of the job itself constantly makes demands of a highly *g*-loaded nature.

Aptitude Patterns or Profiles

When scores on a variety of separate tests are obtained on individuals or on certain subgroups of the population (e.g., race, sex), different patterns or profiles of scores are often observed. Reliably distinctive patterns of test scores can be found for individuals and for the mean scores of population groups.

Individual profiles of standard scores on the eleven Wechsler subscales are well known to clinicians. A most common abuse of Wechsler profiles is the overinterpretation of individual differences in profiles. Pattern or profile interpretation is generally unwarranted because (1) only very large pattern deviations are reliable, and (2) even when these occur their psychological meaning is unclear and at best should be only the occasion for questioning the results and for further inquiry. Profile deviations are suspect since, although there are eleven subtests in the Wechsler scale, only two or at most three factors besides *g* are measured by the whole battery, and each subtest has more *g* variance than variance on any other factor. The Wechsler factors other than *g* are Verbal, Performance, and (only in some samples) short-term memory; these factors combined account for less of the total variance than does the *g* factor. In fact, even the diagnostic meaning of a significant difference between the Verbal and Performance IQs is not clear, except in the cases of persons with specific language handicaps, unfamiliarity with English, or little schooling. In general, the Wechsler tests yield but *one* excellent and meaningful index—a highly *g*-loaded measure of general intelligence in the Full Scale IQ; but little else can be validly derived from the Wechsler subscale scores, contrary to much of the clinical folklore that has accumulated around this test. In general practice, the Wechsler tests, like the Stanford–Binet, should be used only to measure an individual's IQ, and no other pretensions should be made.

Subpopulation Profile Differences. A celebrated study by Lesser, Fifer, and Clark (1965), partially replicated by Stodolsky and Lesser (1967), provides an example of apparent ability profile differences among racial–cultural groups. Four different aptitude tests (the Hunter College Aptitude Scales) measuring Verbal, Reasoning, Number, and Spatial Visualization abilities were obtained on first-grade pupils from four ethnic groups (Chinese, Jewish, black, and Puerto Rican), with each group divided into lower- and middle-socioeconomic status. The raw scores on each test were converted to normalized standardized scores within the combined samples. The means of the standardized scores of the four ethnic groups on each of the aptitude tests are shown in Figure 15.1. The distinctive *patterns* for each group, interestingly, remain almost identical for the middle- and lower-SES halves of each ethnic group; only the overall *level* of the profile, not its distinctive pattern, changes as a function of SES.

But are the distinctive patterns of the different ethnic groups really a "fact of nature"? Do they represent anything of fundamental significance about the "*pattern* of ability" in any one ethnic group? *No, they do not.* There are four main reasons why not.

First, the distinctive *shape* of any one group's profile is wholly a function of the particular groups that happen to be included with it when the raw test scores are trans-

Figure 15.1.   Patterns of normalized aptitude scores for each ethnic group. (From Lesser, Fifer, & Clark, 1965, p. 64)

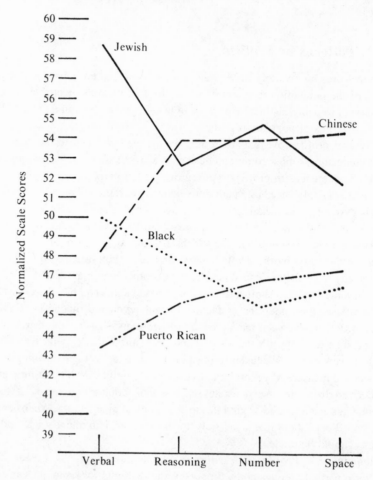

formed to standardized scores (and, in this case, also normalized scores) within the combined groups. Leave out any one of the groups and all the remaining groups' profiles will change. Add another ethnic group and all the other groups' profiles will change. Use only two groups (*any* two groups) and their standard score profiles will necessarily be perfect mirror images of one another, like mountains reflected in a lake.

Second, if the raw scores are transformed to comparable scales by some other method than normalized–standardized scores, such as by expressing each score as a percentage of the total number of test items answered correctly, the groups' distinctive profiles are altered to some other shapes. In other words, the distinctive shapes of the group profiles are not only a function of the particular groups involved, but of the particular method of score transformation. Constructing profiles from the raw scores on such tests would, of course, be even more meaningless, because the different tests have different numbers of items and also probably different average difficulty levels. Points 1 and 2 were first noted by Feldman (1973; see also reply by Lesser, 1973).

Third, the various tests are all intercorrelated (average $r = 0.43$), and they have different g loadings. (Although one should not take a factor analysis based on as few as four variables very seriously, the g loadings extracted from the intercorrelations among the four measures for the combined groups in the Lesser, Fifer, and Clark study, for what little they are worth, are Verbal, .55; Reasoning, .86; Number, .69; Space, .54.) Because the several groups also differ in g, and because different published tests of verbal, reasoning, number, and spatial aptitudes have different g loadings, there is little reason to expect that they should all show the same or even similar patterns for the several ethnic groups. This problem is compounded if the intercorrelations among the tests differ significantly between groups, as may well be the case if there are real differences in the groups' variance due to ceiling or floor effects on tests that may not accommodate the full range of talent in every group.

Fourth, different reliabilities of the tests or different reliabilities in different groups can alter the profiles, as the magnitudes of mean differences in standard scores between groups are affected by test reliability.

Because of these limitations, differential "patterns of ability" are more arbitrary artifacts of the particular groups, tests, and methods used than they are "facts of nature." The interpretations of such ethnic group profiles in the forms in which they are presented in all the published studies that I have seen on this topic are virtually meaningless. Certainly they can tell us nothing about any given group's "pattern of abilities" in any absolute sense.

Another point that needs to be made about such group profiles, aside from their artifactual nature, is that the profile for any given group usually comes nowhere near representing the profiles of the majority of the members of the given group. For example, fewer than one-fourth of the individuals in the four ethnic samples of the Lesser, Fifer, and Clark study can be correctly sorted into their respective ethnic groups on the basis of the resemblance of their individual profiles to the groups' profiles (Feldman, 1973). Thus a particular groups' profile, even if it were psychologically meaningful, would be an exceedingly poor indicator of the pattern of abilities of any individual member of the group. If one takes the overall *level* of group profiles into account, of course, the percentages of individuals who can be correctly sorted into their ethnic groups is considerably higher.

The question of group differences in patterns of ability (also referred to as group $\times$ ability interaction) is indeed an interesting and important one, but to the best of my knowledge it has not yet been properly researched on any comprehensive scale. The minimum methodological requirements for such research are the following.

1. A number of highly homogeneous differential aptitude tests should have each aptitude represented by at least three tests that have (a) the same item homogeneity (i.e., average inter-item correlation) and internal consistency reliability in each of the tests and in each of the groups being compared; (b) essentially the same factorial composition and the same relative magnitudes of factor loadings in each of the groups (i.e., the matrix of test intercorrelations should not differ significantly between groups); and (c) the same distributions of item difficulties for one particular *reference* group (e.g., white Anglo middle-class males), so that all the tests will have approximately the same mean and standard deviation in the reference group.

2. The various aptitude tests, which will inevitably be intercorrelated, should be factor analyzed in the reference group to yield orthogonal (i.e., uncorrelated) factors; the *general factor* should be extracted first, with the remaining (significant) factors (in addition to the next largest factor) orthogonally rotated to approximate simple structure. (The rotation is useful for factor interpretation.) The factor structure should be the same in the comparison groups as in the reference group.

3. All persons in all groups are given *uncorrelated factor scores* on g and on the aptitude factors that emerge from the factor analysis of the original test scores *in the reference group* (not in the combined groups). The several factor scores will of necessity all have the same mean and standard deviation in the reference group, and so the factor score abilities "profile" of the reference group will always be a straight line.

4. The group profiles of mean factor scores are interpreted as deviations from the reference group. This is necessitated by the fact that there can be no such thing as an ability profile in any absolute sense; any ability profile is merely the result of group comparisons. So that the combined various comparison groups do not determine the pattern of any one group, we must compare each group with one arbitrarily selected reference group. Profiles of different groups can then be meaningfully compared.

To my knowledge no study of ethnic group ability profiles has yet been made that observes these methodological desiderata.

White–Black Profile Differences.   Sufficient data are now available, however, to make two important empirical generalizations about ethnic group profiles with considerable confidence.

The first generalization is that the average aptitude profiles of blacks as compared with whites do not resemble the profiles of middle-SES groups as compared with low-SES groups within either racial group. Therefore, whatever factors cause the *pattern* of aptitude differences between blacks and whites are not the same as the factors involved in the *pattern* of differences between social-class groups. This conclusion, of course, does not rule out the possibility that the same factors may be responsible for the overall *level* of the aptitude profiles according to race and social class. But the *pattern* of black–white differences cannot be explained in terms of SES variables. (The most impressive study of this point is by Humphreys, Fleishman, and Lin, 1977.)

The second generalization is that the mean white–black difference that is observed on a great variety of tests is primarily a difference in g rather than a difference in test-specific elements or in so-called group factors. This was originally hypothesized by Spearman (1927, pp. 379–380), and it is highly consistent with the results of each of six independent factor analytic studies, which are described in Chapter 11. This impressively consistent finding underlines the importance of using uncorrelated factor scores instead of various aptitude test scores for the study of differential patterns of ability. Because few major aptitude tests are more highly loaded on the specific aptitude (or group factor) that they are intended to measure than they are loaded on g, and because white–black differences on tests are proportional to their g loadings, the profile of aptitudes for blacks will be a completely confounded amalgam of g and specific aptitudes. With our present evidence and the lack of any proper profile studies, as described here, it would be difficult to make a compelling argument that blacks and whites differ on any abilities *other* than g in both its fluid and crystalized aspects.

The General Aptitude Test Battery (GATB) of the U.S. Employment Service (U.S. Department of Labor, 1970) is a source of evidence relevant to this point. The nine aptitudes measured by GATB are general intelligence (G), verbal aptitude (V), numerical aptitude (N), spatial aptitude (S), form perception (P), clerical aptitude (Q), motor coordination (K), finger dexterity (F), and manual dexterity (M). I have estimated the g loadings on each of these nine aptitudes in two different ways. First, from the intercorrelations among the aptitudes in each of five large samples (total $N = 27,365$) given in the GATB *Manual,* I have extracted g (i.e., the first principal factor). The correlations of the nine g factor loadings across the five samples are so high as to justify averaging them over the five samples. (The profile of these averaged g factor loadings on the nine aptitudes has a profile reliability of 0.97.) Second, the GATB *Manual* gives the correlations in large samples between each of the nine aptitude scores and total IQ (or some equivalent score) on each of twelve well-known standard tests of IQ or general intelligence, which are presumably highly g loaded (ACE Psychological Examination, California Test of Mental Maturity, Cattell Culture Fair Test of g, Raven Colored Progressive Matrices, DAT-Reasoning, Henmon–Nelson, Lorge–Thorndike, Otis, Beta, School and College Aptitude Test, Wechsler Adult Intelligence Scale, Wonderlic Personnel Test). I averaged the twelve correlations between each of the nine GATB aptitudes and the twelve IQ tests. (The profile reliability of this nine-point profile of averaged correlations is 0.97.) Because the g loadings of the aptitudes as well as their correlations with the IQ tests are affected to some degree by the differing reliabilities (ranging from 0.67 to 0.87) of the nine aptitude variables, we must subject the g loadings and correlations to correction for attenuation, using the reliabilities of the aptitude tests provided in the GATB *Manual* (p. 255). It so happens that the least g-loaded tests also have the lowest reliabilities, and so correction for attenuation is essential to rule out the possibility that the differences between the aptitudes' g loadings or their correlations with the IQ tests are not merely the result of their differing reliabilities. So from here on I shall be dealing only with g loadings and correlations that have been corrected for attenuation.

Now, if the g of the nine aptitudes extracted by factor analysis is essentially the same g as is measured by a variety of standard tests of IQ or general intelligence, we should expect a considerable degree of resemblance between the profile of g loadings on each of the nine aptitudes and the profile of average correlations with IQ for each of the nine aptitudes. In fact, there is considerable resemblance between these two profiles, the correlation between them being 0.95. These profiles are shown in Figure 15.2.

Finally, from the GATB data provided by the U.S. Employment Service, it was possible to determine the average white–black difference on each of the nine GATB aptitudes. Twenty-four various occupational groups were tested, including 2,631 whites and 1,521 blacks. In each occupational group the white–black mean difference was divided by the average within-groups standard deviation, so that each white–black (W–B) difference is expressed in σ units. These differences, then, were averaged over the twenty-four occupational groups for each of the nine aptitudes. Because σ differences are also attenuated by test reliability, just as are g loadings and correlations, the W–B σ differences were corrected for attenuation by dividing each σ difference by the square root of the particular aptitude test's reliability. The nine-point profile of these average white–black σ differences (averaged over the twenty-four occupations) has a profile reliability of 0.99. The profile of white–black differences (in σ units corrected for attenuation) on the

Figure 15.2. Profiles of (1) the correlations of each of the nine GATB aptitudes with IQ, (2) the g factor loadings of each aptitude, and (3) the mean white–black difference (in σ units) on each of the aptitudes.

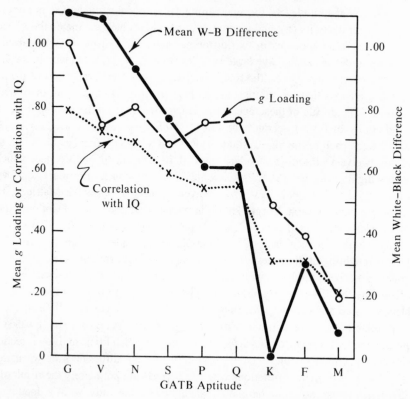

nine aptitudes is shown in Figure 15.2. Notice its marked similarity to the profiles of g loadings and IQ correlations. An index of the degree of similarity among the three profiles is the correlation (Pearson r) between pairs of profiles:

$$g \text{ loading} \times \text{correlation with IQ:} \quad r = 0.95 \ (0.98)$$
$$g \text{ loading} \times \text{white–black difference:} \quad r = 0.88 \ (0.90)$$
$$\text{Correlation with IQ} \times \text{white–black difference:} \quad r = 0.98 \ (1.00)$$

These profile intercorrelations are almost as high as the reliabilities of each of the profiles would permit. The profile intercorrelations after correction for attenuation are shown in parentheses. The results strongly bear out Spearman's hypothesis that the magnitude of white–black differences on various ability tests is proportional to the test's g loading. The one aptitude that shows the largest discrepancy between the otherwise highly similar profile of g loadings and mean white–black differences, as shown in Figure 15.2, is aptitude K: Motor Coordination. Although its g loading in this battery is almost $+0.50$, there is zero difference between the white and black means. This would happen only if blacks, on average, were superior to whites on the non-g factor(s) measured by the coordination test.

Does this finding have any implications for personnel selection in different occupations? Certainly not for any individual. But there are statistical implications for populations when aptitude batteries such as the GATB are used in selecting employees in various occupations. The GATB *Manual* presents the validity coefficients of each of the nine aptitudes for samples in 446 occupational categories. The validity coefficients are the correlations between aptitude scores and some criterion of job performance, which in most cases is supervisors' ratings. It is apparent that, as we should expect, the various aptitudes have different degrees of relevance or validity for various occupations. For some occupations the validities of the aptitudes closely parallel the aptitude tests' *g* loadings, whereas for some other occupations the reverse is true. For many occupations there is practically no relationship at all between the most relevant aptitudes for the occupation and the aptitude tests' *g* loadings. This finding implies that blacks, on the whole, would be at a relatively smaller disadvantage in selection in a variety of occupations if selection were based on differential aptitude tests weighted in accord with their validities for the particular jobs for which applicants are being selected. Any single omnibus type of test will inevitably be much more highly *g* loaded, to the relative disadvantage of black applicants, than would a properly weighted (e.g., by a multiple regression equation) battery of differential aptitude tests for each occupation. In selection for many occupations for which the validities are almost negligible on the more *g*-loaded aptitudes, blacks, as a group, should be at hardly any disadvantage relative to whites. The low validity of many of the special aptitude tests for certain jobs also suggests that other selection criteria should be sought that are more valid than the aptitude test scores, and not too much weight should be given to the present test scores.

To get some idea of how valid the GATB aptitudes are for occupations in general, I have obtained the means and standard deviations of the nine aptitude validity coefficients for the first 300 occupations listed (in alphabetical order) in the GATB *Manual*'s tabulation of aptitude validity coefficients for 466 occupations. To get some idea of the reliability of the profile of these average validities, I obtained the means and standard deviations of the validity coefficients separately for the first 150 occupations and for the second 150 occupations listed, and the grand mean of all 300, as shown in Table 15.1. The correlation

Table 15.1. Means and standard deviations of the validity coefficients of GATB aptitudes for three hundred occupations.

Aptitude	First 150		Second 150		Combined Mean
	Mean	SD	Mean	SD	
G	.28	.16	.27	.17	.272
V	.21	.16	.19	.17	.200
N	.26	.15	.25	.16	.251
S	.20	.16	.19	.16	.198
P	.22	.15	.22	.17	.219
Q	.22	.15	.21	.15	.216
K	.20	.15	.20	.16	.201
F	.19	.16	.21	.17	.200
M	.21	.16	.21	.19	.209
Average	.22	.16	.22	.17	.218

between the mean validity coefficients of the first and second 150 occupations is 0.96, indicating a very high reliability (0.98) of the profile for the combined occupations. The correlation of the combined profile of validities with the aptitudes' g loadings is 0.65; with the aptitudes' average correlations with IQ tests, 0.61; and with the mean white-black differences on the aptitudes, 0.60. However, in absolute values, the average validities differ but little across the various aptitudes, and they are all about equally variable, as indicated by the quite uniform standard deviations. The various aptitudes, however, are very differentially valid for various occupations, a fact that is hidden by the "flatness" of the *average* validity profile for occupations in general. What the "flatness" of the average profile means is that no *particular* aptitude is outstandingly more important than any others for all occupations in general, although aptitude G (general intelligence) has a slight edge over the others. An inevitable statistical consequence of the "fair" or "color-blind" use of an unbiased differential aptitude battery in employment selection will be unequal selection rates of blacks in various occupations, with relatively fewer blacks selected into those occupations with relevant aptitude validities that most closely parallel the g loadings of the aptitude tests. Various occupations differ in their g loadings as do various tests. But the color-blind use of weighted differential aptitudes in employment selection should result, overall, in selection decisions that are relatively more advantageous for blacks than any other color-blind or nonquota selection procedure we know of, with the possible exception of a random lottery.

Misguided Expectations

Psychological tests are not simply to be regarded as good *in principle*. They are good only to the extent that they can serve useful and beneficial purposes and can do so more objectively, reliably, and efficiently than other available means. Good psychological decisions, educational decisions, and personnel selection decisions require sound evidence, and some of the most useful and reliable evidence can be gotten from well-designed and properly interpreted standardized tests.

Some people criticize tests, particularly IQ tests, because they do not measure a number of valued human characteristics—characteristics that the tests were never intended to measure: honesty, compassion, commitment to democratic values, cooperativeness, ambition, soul, creativeness, a well-integrated personality—to mention but a few of the human virtues that IQ tests have been criticized for not taking into account. But such criticisms seem altogether too simple-minded to deserve further comment.

Some persons, too, are rankled by their noticing the obvious fact, which we should all take for granted, that IQ tests do not always rank persons in the order of their unique values to one personally, or in terms of one's love, affection, or esteem for the particular persons. These complex personal sentiments obviously have little dependence on any single trait as measured by a unidimensional test; such sentiments are often not even highly correlated among themselves. We all can think of persons we may greatly respect or admire for an outstanding talent or achievement, but for whom we have little or no liking, personally; and everyone knows persons who have no recognizably superior traits or accomplishments, but who are infinitely precious to one personally. It is wholly unreasonable to expect that the psychological test scores of those whom we know personally should parallel our idiosyncratic sentiments toward them.

People also fail too often to distinguish clearly between tests per se and the *uses* of tests. Too often, legitimate criticisms in the one aspect get confused with the other, and neither aspect is thereby improved. Psychological tests, as with any other useful instruments, *can* of course be misused. However, I believe that the evidence will bear out the conclusion that tests have been well used far more often than they have been misused, although this book has not tried to press that particular argument. It has primarily examined the possible sources of bias in the strictly psychometric aspects of tests.

The overall results of this examination should be most reassuring to all native-born English-speaking minority persons. The overwhelming *negative* evidence with respect to claims of psychometric bias in today's most widely used standardized tests implies, for one thing, that the individual can realize that, insofar as a standard test is a reliable and valid indicator of present ability for other individuals in general, it is equally so for that individual, regardless of his or her racial origin. In short, the tests themselves appear to be color blind. The same thing can be said regarding the individual's sex. Generally speaking, for most tests, the score obtained by a given individual is that individual's *own* score; it does not include, at the psychometric level, any "component" identifiable with the individual's race or sex that could be added to or subtracted from the individual's score to make it a more valid or trustworthy score for any of the legitimate uses of test scores.

Whatever the causes of the statistical differences between the test scores of various racial groups within the United States, the preponderance of evidence leads to the conclusion that the tests themselves do not contribute to the differences. The observed racial group differences are *real* in the sense that they are not merely an artifact of the measuring instruments. Once that point has been determined for any standard test, through empirical investigations such as those reviewed in this book, and the proper uses and limitations of the test are duly noted, the psychometricians and the test publishers should be under no obligation to *explain* the causes of the statistical differences between groups. The problem of explaining the causes of group differences, aside from possible psychometric artifacts, is not the primary or sole responsibility of the constructors, publishers, or users of tests. The search for causes is an awesomely complex task calling for the collaborative endeavor of at least several specialized fields of science in addition to psychometrics. The state of our scientific knowledge on these matters at present only justifies an agnostic stance on the part of psychometricians, publishers, and users of tests, whatever else their personal sentiments may dictate. It is most unbecoming to persons in these fields defensively to belittle tests and the benefits of testing to society, merely because the causes of certain group differences in mental ability have not yet been established by a scientific consensus or because of the far-reaching social consequences of such differences. Tests only *reveal* differences; they neither create them nor explain their causes. Scientific uncertainty concerning the causes of group differences in no way mitigates their important educational, economic, and social consequences. Nor would any of these consequences be lessened in the least by abolishing psychological tests.

For many years now it has been practically axiomatic among people in the testing field that the fact of statistical differences between racial populations should not be permitted to influence the treatment accorded to *individuals* of any race—in education, employment, legal justice, and political and civil rights. The well-established finding of a wide range of individual differences in IQ and other abilities within all major racial populations, and the great amount of overlap of their frequency distributions, absolutely contradicts the racist philosophy that persons of different races should be treated differently, one and all, only by reason of their racial origins. Those who would accord any treatment to *individuals* solely by virtue of their race will find no rational support in any of the scientific findings from psychological testing or present-day theories of differential psychology. That much seems certain. Righting the past wrongs of racial discrimination cannot be furthered by blaming the mental tests (which we admittedly should continue to improve and to use more wisely), but by prohibiting racial discrimination in any form, by legal sanctions when necessary, and by seeking equal educational opportunities for members of those minority groups that have been denied them in the past, so they can compete fairly, as individuals, in selection for employment, technical training, or higher education, without condescending dispensations.

SUMMARY

Group-administered tests of IQ or scholastic aptitude are probably overused in schools, especially at the elementary school level. There is no routine purpose served by group IQ tests that cannot be better served by standardized achievement tests that are closely matched to the instructional program. Teachers need to know how well their pupils have learned what they have been taught in school; they do not need to know their pupils' IQs. Criterion-referenced tests are of more direct benefit to teachers and pupils than are norm-referenced tests.

The main faults with mental testing generally involve abuses and inadequacies in the *use* of tests rather than bias or other psychometric deficiencies in the tests themselves. Teacher-administered standardized tests are worse than useless if they are not given scrupulously under the prescribed conditions with regard to instructions and time limits. Because there is no assurance of this, school authorities should not base important decisions regarding individual pupils on teacher-administered tests.

A legitimate use of IQ tests is in the individual testing, by qualified psychologists, of pupils who are referred for educational diagnosis by the teacher when the pupil is experiencing unusual problems in scholastic performance. An expertly administered, scored, and interpreted individual IQ test, along with other relevant information on the pupil's background and scholastic performance, can aid the school psychologist, working with the pupil's teacher, toward improving the pupil's benefits from attending school.

Probably the most compelling argument for using group IQ tests, particularly of the culture-reduced type, for routine testing of all pupils at the elementary level is in screening the school population to discover academic talent in children from disadvantaged backgrounds. Academic talent in such children is more apt to go unnoticed by parents and teachers and needs early fostering to develop to its fullest realization in the more advanced levels of scholastic achievement that are prerequisite for a college education.

Ability grouping at the elementary school level is more a convenience for teachers than a benefit to pupils. With the exception of the severely handicapped who could not benefit from attendance in a regular classroom, it seems best to accommodate all children in regular unstreamed classes, despite the fact that the range of scholastic aptitude will be great within each class. The drawbacks of tracking, streaming, or ability grouping at the elementary level outweigh the advantages. At the high school level, differences in academic aptitude become more highly manifest. But ability grouping should not be an issue in high schools with sufficiently diverse curricula to accommodate different levels and types of abilities, to which entrance is based on pupils' demonstrated achievements in prerequisite knowledge and skills rather than on IQ or scholastic aptitude scores.

Group IQ tests can serve a legitimate function as a control variable in research on scholastic achievement in different schools, instructional programs, and the like.

Test results in vocational guidance should be interpreted to the client in probabilistic terms. Test scores never compel. They only indicate *probabilities* of success under specified conditions. When at all feasible, the predictive use of tests should not deprive individuals of gaining direct self-knowledge of their own capabilities through making their best efforts to achieve in the criterion performance itself. We all like to think that we can do a better job, when we really try our best, than our test scores predict. Ideally, all persons should have the opportunity to learn their own limitations and strengths through the reality of their actual performance. But in some highly skilled occupations and the courses of training required for them, this is neither feasible nor desirable, and the best predictors, usually in the form of objective measurements of achievements in prerequisite knowledge and skills, must be relied upon for the selection of the aspirants who are statistically the most likely to succeed.

The use of tests in personnel selection can be justified only if there is a correlation between test scores and quality of performance on the job or in succeeding in a job-training program. Aptitude tests generally correlate more highly with training criteria, such as course grades and learning rate, than with job performance after training is successfully completed. The validities of aptitude tests should be determined separately for training or early job performance criteria and for later job performance criteria. Economic considerations involving the duration and costliness of the job-training phase will determine the relative weights of the two types of validity in the selection process.

Patterns or profiles of differential aptitudes, both for individuals and for group means, are generally overinterpreted. Critical examination reveals that there is actually less information, psychometrically, in differential abilities profiles than meets the eye. The distinctive patterns of aptitudes found for various racial or cultural groups are largely an artifact of the factorial compositions of the particular aptitude tests and of the particular combination of groups being compared. Better methods are suggested for studying individual and group differences in various aptitudes. Analysis of the nine aptitude scores of the General Aptitude Test Battery (GATB) of the U.S. Employment Service shows most clearly that the pattern of white–black differences across the nine aptitudes is mostly a function of the g loadings of the aptitude measures. The magnitudes of the white–black differences on the various aptitudes closely parallel the aptitudes' g loadings and the aptitudes' correlations with standard IQ tests. This finding, in conjunction with the finding that different aptitudes often have quite different predictive validities for different jobs, suggests that employment selection for any given job that is based on an index of the best weighted composite of differential aptitude scores not only increases the validity of the selection procedures for all applicants, but also favors the selection of minority applicants more than would the use of any single omnibus test that emphasizes the g factor. Although g has a higher overall predictive validity than any other *single* aptitude, its validity for any *particular* job is not so high as a best-weighted composite of a number of different aptitude measurements.

Tests are often criticized because of misguided expectations concerning what they are intended to measure. Good tests of abilities do not measure human worth in any absolute sense, but they do provide indices that are correlated with certain types of performance generally deemed important for achieving responsible and productive roles in our present-day society.

Most current standardized tests of mental ability yield unbiased measures for all native-born English-speaking segments of American society today, regardless of their sex or their racial and social-class background. The observed mean differences in test scores between various groups are generally not an artifact of the tests themselves, but are attributable to factors that are causally independent of the tests. The constructors, publishers, and users of tests need to be concerned only about the psychometric soundness of these instruments and must apply appropriate objective methods for detecting any possible biases in test scores for the groups in which they are used. Beyond that, the constructors, publishers, and users of tests are under no obligation to explain the *causes* of the statistical differences in test scores between various subpopulations. They can remain agnostic on that issue. Discovery of the causes of the observed racial and social-class differences in abilities is a complex task calling for the collaboration of several specialized fields in the biological and behavioral sciences, in addition to psychometrics.

Whatever may be the causes of group differences that remain after test bias is eliminated, the practical applications of sound psychometrics can help to reinforce the democratic ideal of treating every person according to the person's *individual* characteristics, rather than according to his or her sex, race, social class, religion, or national origin.

Glossary

Absolute value: The positive value of a real number regardless of its sign (i.e., whether positive or negative).

Analysis of variance (often abbreviated ANOVA):   A statistical method, developed by Sir Ronald A. Fisher (1890–1962) for analyzing the total variance (see **Variance**) of a set of measurements into a number of additive components of variance.

Attenuation: The weakening or lowering of accuracy of any descriptive statistic by errors of measurement. It is usually applied to correlation coefficients, which are moved to some extent toward zero by errors of measurement in one or both of the correlated variables. A correlation coefficient is *corrected for attenuation* by dividing it by the geometric mean of the reliabilities of the two correlated variables, that is, $\sqrt{r_{xx}r_{yy}}$. A correlation that has been corrected for attenuation indicates the degree of correlation that would theoretically obtain between the two variables if each could be measured without error.

Ceiling effect: When a test is too easy for some individuals in the group taking the test, there is a pile-up of scores at the top of the possible range of scores. This is the *ceiling effect*. These top-scoring persons would be spread out over a wider range of scores if the test contained more "top," that is, more difficult items. By preventing the ablest individuals from scoring even higher if only there were more difficult items, the ceiling effect restricts the total variance in test scores and attenuates the test's possible correlation with other variables.

Content validity: With reference to tests of scholastic achievement or specific occupational skills, a rating or assessment of the accuracy and adequacy with which the test as a whole samples the domain of knowledge or skill in question, as judged by a consensus of experts in that particular field.

Correlation: An index of the degree of relationship between two variables, expressed as a *coefficient of correlation,* which is a dimensionless number ranging from 0 to ± 1. There are several types of correlation coefficients that are appropriate under various conditions:

> **Interclass correlation** (Pearson r) is appropriate when the two correlated variables, X and Y, are continuous variables and there is no reason to assume that X and Y have the same mean or the same standard deviation in the population.

> **Intraclass r** is called for when X and Y are assumed to have the same mean and standard deviation in the population. It can also be applied to three or more variables,

indicating the overall correlation among all the variables. It is most often used for indexing the reliability of tests and the degree of resemblance between relatives (e.g., twins, siblings, etc.) on a given trait.

Rank order correlation (rho or ρ) is appropriate when X and Y are not scalar measurements or scores but merely ranks, that is, 1, 2, 3, . . ., N, on a given trait or dimension. (Also referred to as the *Spearman correlation*.)

Point-biserial correlation is called for when one variable is truly dichotomous (e.g., male–female) and the other is continuous (e.g., height).

Biserial correlation is called for when one variable is expressed as a dichotomy (e.g., pass–fail) but may reasonably be assumed to be continuously distributed and the other variable is continuous.

Phi coefficient is used when both X and Y are dichotomous variables.

Criterion contamination: A source of error in estimates of a test's predictive validity, resulting, for example, from some knowledge of a person's test score entering into the rating of his performance on the criterion (e.g., a supervisor's rating of job performance being favorably or unfavorably influenced by the supervisor's knowledge of the person's score on the selection test).

Criterion-referenced test: A test designed to describe a person's "score" or level of performance specifically in terms of the kinds of knowledge, skills, or tasks that he or she can accomplish (e.g., he can perform arithmetic problems involving addition, subtraction, multiplication, and short division, but fails on long division and fractions) rather than in terms of the person's relative standing among his or her age peers, as in the case of a norm-referenced or standardized test (see **Standardized test**).

Cutoff score: The test score above which or below which applicants are accepted or rejected in a selection procedure.

Face validity: The appearance that a test (or test item) measures the trait or ability that it is intended to measure, as judged by inspection of the test (or item).

Factor analysis: A class of various mathematical techniques for transforming a matrix of intercorrelations (or covariances) among a number of different variables (measurements, tests, etc.) to a *factor matrix,* which expresses the correlation (then called a *factor loading* or *saturation*) of each test with each of a number of hypothetical factors. Thus the intercorrelations among a large number of tests may all be "explained" (i.e., accounted for within the limits of sampling error) by a relatively small number of factors or principal components (axes). Individuals can be given scores on each factor, called *factor scores*. Factors (or their axes) may be *orthogonal* (i.e., uncorrelated) or *oblique* (i.e., correlated), depending on the method of extracting and rotating factors.

Floor effect (sometimes called *basement effect*):   The opposite of the *ceiling effect*, that is, when a test does not have items easy enough to discriminate among the least able members of the group being tested and there is consequently a pile-up of scores at the low end of the scale.

Frequency distribution: The actual number of observations (i.e., measurements, scores, etc.) occurring within each uniform interval on some scale of measurement. In the *relative frequency distribution* the frequency within each interval is expressed as a proportion (or percentage) of the total number of observations.

Guttman scale (named after the American–Israeli psychometrician Louis Guttman, born 1916): Any homogeneous or unidimensional scale based on a number of test items in which the pattern of right and wrong item responses of any given individual is completely reproducible simply from a knowledge of the individual's scale score on the whole test. In other words, in an ideal Guttman scale, the items can be ordered such that persons who answer a given question correctly all have higher ranks on the scale than persons who answer the same question incorrectly. (See Guttman, 1950.)

Halo effect: The tendency, in rating a person on a certain trait, to be influenced by some other trait or general impression of the person. This tendency is a common source of error in ratings.

Homoscedasticity: Equality of the standard deviations in all the rows (and columns) of a correlation scatter diagram, making for a linearly symmetrical bivariate frequency distribution.

Index of forecasting efficiency: The percentage reduction in errors of prediction of variable y from variable x. It is equal to $100 \, (1 - \sqrt{1 - r_{xy}^2})$.

Item analysis: A number of statistical or quantitative procedures used in psychometrics or test construction for determining the suitability of any specific test item for inclusion in a particular test. It consists of such procedures as determining the item's difficulty level (percentage passing) in a specified population sample, the item's correlation with total score on the whole test, the item's correlation with the criterion, and estimating the parameters of the item characteristic curve (i.e., the function relating the probability of a correct response to an item with a hypothetical latent trait scale, such as intelligence).

Measurement error: The deviation of an obtained measure from the true value, where the hypothetical true value is assumed to be the mean of an infinite number of measurements of the same thing.

Moderator variable: If the size of the correlation r_{xy} between variables x and y is a function of a third variable z, then z is said to be a moderator variable. The variable z may be group membership (e.g., male–female), a status variable (e.g., socioeconomic status), or scores on some other test.

Monotonic: A characteristic of the function relating a dependent variable y to an independent variable x, in which the values of y continuously increase (or decrease) with increases (or decreases) in the values of x.

Null hypothesis: The hypothesis that two (or more) populations do not differ on a given parameter (e.g., mean, standard deviation, correlation, etc.).

Ogive: The cumulative frequency distribution (of a unimodal distribution), plotted with the measurement scale or scores on the abscissa and the number (or percentage) of observations falling below a given score on the ordinate.

Power test: An untimed test, or one in which the time limit is lenient and is a negligible source of variance in test scores, and in which the items are steeply graded in difficulty, so that very few persons can get all the items right, given any amount of time.

Predictive validity: The degree of accuracy with which a test score (or combination of test scores) can estimate a person's performance on some criterion (e.g., scholastic achievement, grade-point average, rated job performance, etc.). The *validity coefficient* is the correlation (Pearson *r*) between the predictor variable (e.g., test scores) and the criterion measurements.

Quantitize (also *quantize*):   To quantify, or to express a qualitative, nonmetrical, or discrete variable (e.g., sex or ethnic group) quantitatively by assigning numerical values (e.g., 0 and 1) to each of the qualitative categories.

Raw score: The actual number of items scored as "correct" (or in the keyed direction) on a test. This number may be "corrected" for guessing in the case of true–false and multiple-choice items.

Reliability: The consistency of a measurement; the proportion of true variance (as contrasted to variance due to measurement error) in a set of measurements or scores.

Sampling error: The deviation from the population value of some descriptive statistic (e.g., mean, median, standard deviation, *r,* etc.) computed on a random sample from the population. The magnitude of this error is generally inversely proportional to $\sqrt{N-1}$, where *N* is the number of observations in the sample.

Selection ratio: $A/(A + R)$, where *A* is the number of applicants accepted and *R* is the number of applicants rejected in a selection procedure.

Simplex: A correlation matrix in which the variables can be ordered such that the correlations are largest near the main diagonal and consistently decrease the farther away they are from the main diagonal. Such a matrix of intercorrelations can usually be accounted for in terms of single factor plus random error.

Standard deviation: A measure of dispersion of a frequency distribution. Symbolized by σ, it is equal to the positive square root of the variance (see **Variance**).

Standard error of measurement: A measure of the range on the scale of measurement within which the hypothetical true score for any given obtained score falls with a probability of .6826, on the assumption that errors of measurement are normally distributed. The standard error of measurement is the standard deviation of the errors of measurement and is estimated (from large samples) by the following formula:

$$SE_{\text{meas}} = s\sqrt{1 - r_{xx}},$$

where *s* is the sample standard deviation of variable *x* and r_{xx} is the reliability coefficient.

Standard score (also *standardized score*):   A score that expresses the person's relative standing with respect to some normative population. The simplest standard score is the *z* score, the distribution of which has a mean of 0 and a standard deviation of 1. It is $z = (X - \overline{X})/\sigma$, where *X* is the person's raw score, $\overline{X}$ is the mean of all scores in the reference group, and σ is the standard deviation of the raw scores in the reference group. A number of other standard scores, such as the *T* score and the IQ, are linear transformations of the *z* score as defined above: $T = 10z + 50$ and $IQ = 15z + 100$.

Standardized test (also called *norm-referenced* test):   A test for which items were selected by the usual methods of item analysis (see **Item analysis**) with reference to a particular population sample or normative group (e.g., age group or grade level) and for which the *raw scores* can be converted to *standard scores* that express the person's relative standing in the normative group. (See **Raw score** and **Standard score**.)

Suppressor variable: If the correlation r_{xy} between variables x and y is increased by partialing out variable z (i.e., $r_{xy \cdot z} > r_{xy}$), then variable z is termed a suppressor variable. Suppressor variables are sometimes used to improve the predictive validity of test scores. Suppressor variables have negative weights in a multiple regression equation.

Type I error: In statistical inference, rejecting the null hypothesis when in fact it is true. *Type II error* is accepting the null hypothesis when in fact it is false.

Validity: The degree of accuracy with which a test measures what it is intended to measure. (See **Predictive validity** and **Validity coefficient**.)

Validity coefficient: The coefficient of correlation between scores on a given test and some external criterion, for example, school grades, ratings of job performance, etc.

Variance: An index of dispersion or variation in a set of measurements. Symbolized as V or s^2 or σ^2, it is the arithmetic average of the squared deviations of all the individual scores from the overall mean, that is, $\sigma^2 = \Sigma(X - \bar{X})^2/N$. It is, of course, the square of the standard deviation, σ. The sample estimate s^2 of the population variance σ^2 is obtained by $s^2 = \Sigma(X - \bar{X})^2/(N - 1)$.

References

Abramson, T. The influence of examiner race on first-grade and kindergarten subjects' Peabody Picture Vocabulary Test scores. *Journal of Educational Measurement,* 1969, *6,* 241–246.

Ali, F., & Costello, J. Modification of the Peabody Picture Vocabulary Test. *Developmental Psychology,* 1971, *5,* 86–91.

Almy, M., & Associates. *Logical Thinking in Second Grade.* New York: Teachers College Press, 1970.

Almy, M.; Chittenden, E.; & Miller, P. *Young Children's Thinking.* New York: Teachers College Press, 1966.

Alpers, T. G., & Boring, E. G. Intelligence test scores of northern and southern white and Negro recruits in 1918. *Journal of Abnormal and Social Psychology,* 1944, *39,* 471–474.

Altus, G. T. Some correlates on the Davis-Eells tests. *Journal of Consulting Psychology,* 1956, *20,* 227–232.

American Association on Mental Deficiency. *Adaptive Behavior Scale: Manual.* Washington, D.C.: The Association, 1974.

Anastasi, A. Sources of bias in the prediction of job performance: Technical critiques. In L. A. Crooks (Ed.), *An Investigation of Sources of Bias in the Prediction of Job Performance—A Six-year Study.* Proceedings of an invitational conference. Princeton, N.J.: Educational Testing Service, 1972.

Anastasi, A. *Psychological Testing* (4th ed.). New York: Macmillan, 1976.

Anderson, D. F., & Rosenthal, R. Some effects of interpersonal expectancy and social interaction on institutionalized retarded children. *Proceedings of the 76th Annual Convention of the American Psychological Association,* 1968, *3,* 479–480. (Summary)

Anderson, J. The prediction of adjustment over time. In I. Iscoe & H. Stevenson (Eds.), *Personality Development in Children.* Austin: University of Texas Press, 1960.

Angelino, H., & Shedd, C. L. An initial report of a validation study on the Davis-Eells tests of general intelligence or problem-solving ability. *Journal of Psychology,* 1955, *40,* 35–38.

Angoff, W. H. Group membership as a predictor variable: A comment on McNemar. *American Psychologist,* 1976, *31,* 612.

Angoff, W. H., & Ford, F. F. Item–race interaction on a test of scholastic aptitude. *Journal of Educational Measurement,* 1973, *10,* 95–106.

Angoff, W. H., & Modu, C. C. Equating the scales of the Prueba de Aptitude Académica and the Scholastic Aptitude Test. Research Report 3. New York: College Entrance Examination Board, 1973.

Arneklev, B. L. *Data Related to the Question of Bias in Standardized Testing.* Tacoma, Wash.: Office of Evaluation, Tacoma Public Schools, 1975.

Arvey, R. D. Some comments on culture fair tests. *Personnel Psychology,* 1972, *25,* 433–448.

Ash, P., & Kroeker, L. P. Personnel selection, classification, and placement. *Annual Review of Psychology* 1975, *26,* 481–507.

Atkinson, J. W. Motivational determinants of intellective performance and cumulative achievement. In J. W. Atkinson, J. O. Raynor, et al., *Motivation and Achievement,* Ch. 20. Washington, D.C.: Winston (distr. by Halsted Press), 1974.

Atkinson, J. W.; Lens, W.; & O'Malley, P. M. Motivation and ability: Interactive psychological determinants of intellective performance, educational achievement, and each other. In W. H. Sewell, R. M. Hauser, & D. L. Featherman (Eds.), *Schooling and Achievement in American Society,* pp. 29–60. New York: Academic Press, 1976.

Bajema, C. J. A note on the interrelations among intellectual ability, educational attainment, and occupational achievement: A follow-up study of a male Kalamazoo public school population. *Sociology of Education*, 1968, *41*, 317-319.

Baker, F. B. Advances in item analysis. *Review of Educational Research*, 1977, *47*, 151-178.

Baker, J. R. *Race.* New York: Oxford University Press, 1974.

Baldwin, W. K. The social position of the educable mentally retarded child in the regular grades in the public schools. *Exceptional Child*, 1958, *25*, 106-108.

Ball, R. S. The predictability of occupational level from intelligence. *Journal of Consulting Psychology*, 1938, *2*, 184-186.

Barbe, W. B. Peer relationships of children of different intelligence levels. *School and Society*, 1954, *80*, 60-62.

Barratt, E. S.; Clark, M.; & Lipton, J. Critical flicker frequency in relation to a culture fair measure of intelligence. *American Journal of Psychology*, 1962, *75*, 324-325.

Bartlett, C. J., & O'Leary, B. S. A differential prediction model to moderate the effects of heterogeneous groups in personnel selection and classification. *Personnel Psychology*, 1969, *22*, 1-17.

Bass, A. R. The "equal-risk" model: A comment on McNemar. *American Psychologist*, 1976, *31*, 611-612.

Baughman, E. E., & Dahlstrom, W. G. *Negro and White Children: A Psychological Study in the Rural South*. New York: Academic Press, 1968.

Bayley, N. On the growth of intelligence. *American Psychologist*, 1955, *10*, 805-818.

Bean, K. L. Negro responses to certain intelligence test items. *Journal of Psychology*, 1941, *12*, 191-198.

Bean, K. L. Negro responses to verbal and nonverbal test material. *Journal of Psychology*, 1942, *13*, 343-353.

Beard, R. M. The nature and development of concepts. *Education Review*, 1960, *13*, 12-26.

Beez, W. V. Influences of biased psychological reports on teacher behavior and pupil performance. *Proceedings of the 76th Annual Convention of the American Psychological Association*, 1968, *3*, 605-606. (Summary)

Bell, E. F. Do bar examinations serve a useful purpose? *American Bar Association Journal*, December 1971, *57*, 1215-1218.

Bennett, G. K.; Seashore, H. G.; & Wesman, A. G. *Manual for the Differential Aptitude Test* (4th ed.). New York: Psychological Corporation, 1966.

Bereiter, C. Individualization and inequality (Review of A. R. Jensen, *Educational Differences*, 1974). *Contemporary Psychology*, 1975, *20*, 455-456.

Bereiter, C. IQ differences and social policy. In N. F. Ashline, T. R. Pezullo, & C. I. Norris (Eds.), *Education, Inequality, and National Policy*, pp. 137-155. Lexington, Mass.: Lexington Books, 1976.

Berman, A. Delinquency as a learning disability. *Science News*, 1978, *114*, 180-181.

Bernal, E. M., Jr. A response to "Educational Uses of Tests with Disadvantaged Subjects." *American Psychologist*, 1975, *30*, 93-95.

Berry, G., Jr. An investigation of the item ordering of the Peabody Picture Vocabulary Test by sex and race. Doctoral dissertation, University of Connecticut, 1977.

Berry, J. W. Temne and Eskimo perceptual skills. *International Journal of Psychology*, 1966, *1*, 207-222.

Bickel, P. J.; Hammel, E. A.; & O'Connell, J. W. Sex bias in graduate admissions: Data from Berkeley. *Science*, 1975, *187*, 398-404.

Biesheuvel, S. (Ed.). *Methods for the Measurement of Psychological Performance*. International Biological Program (IBP) Handbook No. 10. Oxford, England: Blackwell, 1966.

Binet, A. *Les Idées modernes sur les enfants*. Paris: E. Flammarion, 1910.

Binet, A., & Simon, T. Méthodes nouvelles pour le diagnostic du niveau intellectuel des anormaux. *L'Année Psychologique*, 1905, *11*, 191-244.

Binet, A., & Simon, T. *The Development of Intelligence in Children*. Trans. by Elizabeth S. Kite. Baltimore: Williams & Wilkins, 1916.

Bischof, L. J. *Intelligence: Statistical Concepts of Its Nature*. New York: Doubleday, 1954.

Bitterman, M. E. The evolution of intelligence. *Scientific American*, 1965, *212*, 92-100.

Bitterman, M. E. The comparative analysis of learning. *Science*, 1975, *188*, 699-709.

Block, N. J., & Dworkin, G. IQ: Heritability and inequality. Part I. *Philosophy and Public Affairs*, 1974, *3*, 331–409.

Blommers, P., & Lindquist, E. F. *Elementary Statistical Methods in Psychology and Education*. Boston: Houghton Mifflin, 1960.

Bloom, B. S. *Stability and Change in Human Characteristics*. New York: Wiley, 1964.

Bock, R. D., & Kolakowski, D. Further evidence of sex-linked major-gene influences on human spatial visualizing ability. *American Journal of Human Genetics*, 1973, *25*, 1–14.

Boehm, V. R. Negro–white differences in validity of employment and training selection procedures: Summary of research evidence. *Journal of Applied Psychology*, 1972, *56*, 33–39.

Boney, J. D. Predicting the academic achievement of secondary school Negro students. *Personnel and Guidance Journal*, 1966, *44*, 700–703.

Boone, J. A., & Adesso, V. J. Racial differences on a Black Intelligence Test. *Journal of Negro Education*, 1974, *43*, 429–436.

Boring, E. G. Intelligence as the tests test it. *New Republic*, 1923, *35*, 35–37.

Boring, E. G. *A History of Experimental Psychology* (2nd ed.). New York: Appleton-Century-Crofts, 1950.

Bosco, J. J. *Social Class and the Processing of Visual Information*. Final Report, Project No. 9-E-041. Washington, D.C.: U.S. Office of Education, May 1970.

Bowers, J. The comparison of GPA regression equations for regularly admitted and disadvantaged freshmen at the University of Illinois. *Journal of Educational Measurement*, 1970, *7*, 219–225.

Bowles, S., & Gintis, H. I.Q. in the U.S. class structure. *Social Policy*, Nov.–Dec. 1972, Jan.–Feb. 1973.

Bray, D. W., & Moses, J. L. Personnel selection. *Annual Review of Psychology*, 1972, *23*, 545–576.

Brim, O. G., Jr. American attitudes towards intelligence tests. *American Psychologist*, 1965, *20*, 125–130.

Brislin, R. W.; Lonner, W. J.; & Thorndike, R. M. *Cross-cultural Research methods*. New York: Wiley, 1974.

Brogden, H. E. On the interpretation of the correlation coefficient as a measure of predictive efficiency. *Journal of Educational Psychology*, 1946, *37*, 65–76.

Brown, C. W., & Ghiselli, E. E. Per cent increase in proficiency resulting from use of selective devices. *Journal of Applied Psychology*, 1953, *37*, 341–345.

Brown, W. W., & Reynolds, M. O. A model of IQ, occupation, and earnings. *American Economic Review*, 1975, *65*, 1002–1007.

Bruce, M. Factors affecting intelligence test performance of whites and Negroes in the rural South. *Archives of Psychology, New York*, 1940, no. 252.

Burke, H. R. Raven's Progressive Matrices: A review and critical evaluation. *Journal of Genetic Psychology*, 1958, *93*, 199–228.

Buros, O. K. (Ed.). *Mental Measurements Yearbook* (7 vols.). Highland Park, N.J.: Gryphon Press, 1938–1972.

Burrows, D., & Okada, R. Memory retrieval from long and short lists. *Science*, 1975, *188*, 1031–1033.

Burt, C. *Mental and Scholastic Tests* (3rd ed.). London: P. S. King, 1921.

Burt, C. *The Young Delinquent*. New York: Appleton, 1925.

Burt, C. *The Factors of the Mind*. London: University of London Press, 1940.

Burt, C. *The Factors of the Mind: An Introduction to Factor Analysis in Psychology*. New York: Macmillan, 1941.

Burt, C. The distribution of intelligence. *British Journal of Psychology*, 1957, *48*, 161–175.

Burt, C. Factor analysis and its neurological basis. *British Journal of Mathematical and Statistical Psychology*, 1961, *14*, 53–71.

Burt, C. Is intelligence distributed normally? *British Journal of Mathematical and Statistical Psychology*, 1963, *16*, 175–190.

Burt, C. Quantitative genetics in psychology. *British Journal of Mathematical and Statistical Psychology*, 1971, *24*, 1–21.

Burt, C. The inheritance of general intelligence. *American Psychologist*, 1972, *27*, 175–190.

Caldwell, M. B., & Knight, D. The effect of Negro and white examiners on Negro intelligence test performance. *Journal of Negro Education*, 1970, *39*, 177–179.

Callaway, E. *Brain Electrical Potentials and Individual Psychological Differences*. New York: Grune & Stratton, 1975.

Campbell, J. T.; Crooks, L. A.; Mahoney, M. H.; & Rock, D. A. *An Investigation of Sources of Bias in the Prediction of Job Performance—A Six-year Study*. ETS Report PR-73-37. Princeton, N.J.: Educational Testing Service, 1973.

Campbell, J. T.; Pike, L. W.; & Flaugher, R. L. *Prediction of Job Performance for Negro and White Medical Technicians: A Regression Analysis of Potential Test Bias: Predicting Job Knowledge Scores from an Aptitude Battery*. ETS Report PR-69-6. Princeton, N.J.: Educational Testing Service, 1969.

Campion, J. E., & Freihoff, E. C. *Unintentional Bias When Using Racially Mixed Employee Samples for Test Validation*. Experimental Publication System, Ms. No. 285-2. Washington, D.C.: American Psychological Association, 1970.

Canady, H. G. The effect of "rapport" on the IQ: A new approach to the problem of racial psychology. *Journal of Negro Education*, 1936, *5*, 209–219.

Caplan, N. S. Intellectual functioning. In H. C. Quay (Ed.), *Juvenile Delinquency: Research and Theory*, pp. 100–138. Princeton, N.J.: Van Nostrand, 1965.

Cardall, C., & Coffman, W. E. *A Method for Comparing the Performance of Different Groups on the Items in a Test*. Research Bulletin 64-61. Princeton, N.J.: Educational Testing Service, 1964.

Carver, R. P. Designing an aural aptitude test for Negroes: An experiment that failed. *College Board Review*, Winter 1968–1969, *70*, 10–14.

Carver, R. P. Use of a recently developed listening comprehension test to investigate the effect of disadvantagement upon verbal proficiency. *American Educational Research Journal*, 1969, *6*, 263–270.

Cattell, J. McK. Mental tests and measurements. *Mind*, 1890, *15*, 373–380.

Cattell, R. B. A culture-free intelligence test, Part I. *Journal of Educational Psychology*, 1940, *31*, 161–179.

Cattell, R. B. *Personality*. New York: McGraw-Hill, 1950.

Cattell, R. B. *Factor Analysis: An Introduction and Manual for the Psychologist and Social Scientist*. New York: Harper, 1952.

Cattell, R. B. Theory of fluid and crystalized intelligence: A critical experiment. *Journal of Educational Psychology*, 1963, *54*, 1–22.

Cattell, R. B. The structure of intelligence in relation to the nature–nurture controversy. In R. Cancro (Ed.), *Intelligence: Genetic and Environmental Influences*, pp. 3–30. New York: Grune & Stratton, 1971. (a)

Cattell, R. B. *Abilities: Their Structure, Growth, and Action*. Boston: Houghton Mifflin, 1971. (b)

Cattell, R. B. *The Scientific Use of Factor Analysis in Behavioral and Life Sciences*. New York: Plenum, 1978.

Cattell, R. B., & Butcher, H. J. *The Prediction of Achievement and Creativity*. New York: Bobbs-Merrill, 1968.

Caylor, J. S. Selection testing for job proficiency: Some illustrated empirical problems in assessing fairness. Paper presented at the annual convention of the American Psychological Association, September, 1972. (Human Resources Research Organization, Presidio of Monterey, Calif.)

Centra, J. A.; Linn, R. L.; & Parry, M. E. Academic growth in predominantly Negro and predominantly white colleges. *American Educational Research Journal*, 1970, *1*, 83–98.

Chalke, F. C. R., & Ertl, J. Evoked potentials and intelligence. *Life Sciences*, 1965, *4*, 1319–1322.

Chapman, M., & Hill, R. A. (Eds.). *Achievement Motivation: An Analysis of the Literature*. Philadelphia: Research for Better Schools, Inc., 1971.

Clairborn, W. L. Expectancy effects in the classroom: A failure to replicate. *Journal of Educational Psychology*, 1969, 60, 377–383.

Clark, K. B., & Plotkin, L. *The Negro Student at Integrated Colleges*. National Scholarship Service and Fund for Negro Students, 1963.

Clark, K.. & Plotkin, L. Aptitude test bias. (Letters) *Science*, 1971, *174*, 1278–1279.

Clarke, D. P. Stanford–Binet Scale L response patterns in matched racial groups. *Journal of Negro Education*, 1941, *10*, 230–238.

Cleary, T. A. Test bias: Prediction of grades of Negro and white students in integrated colleges. *Journal of Educational Measurement*, 1968, *5*, 115–124.

Cleary, T. A., & Hilton, T. L. An investigation of item bias. *Educational and Psychological Measurement*, 1968, *28*, 61–75.

Cleary, T. A.; Humphreys, L. G.; Kendrick, S. A.; & Wesman, A. Educational uses of tests with disadvantaged students. *American Psychologist*, 1975, *30*, 15–41.

Cleary, T. A., & Stanley, J. C. Test bias. (Letters) *Science*, 1972, *176*, 113–114.

Cohen, D. K. Does IQ matter? *Commentary*, April 1972.

Cohen, L. The effects of material and non-material reinforcement upon performance of the WISC Block Design subtest by children of different social classes: A follow-up study. *Psychology*, 1970, *7*, 41–47.

Cole, M.; Gay, J.; Glick, J. A.; & Sharpe, D. W. *The Cultural Context of Learning and Thinking*. New York: Basic Books, 1971.

Cole, N. S. Bias in selection. *Journal of Educational Measurement*, 1973, *10*, 237–255.

Coleman, J. S. et al. *Equality of Educational Opportunity*. Washington, D.C.: U.S. Office of Education, 1966. (a)

Coleman, J. S. et al. *Equality of Educational Opportunity, Supplemental Appendix 9.10*. Washington, D.C.: U.S. Office of Education, 1966. (b)

Coleman, W., & Ward, A. W. A comparison of Davis–Eells and Kuhlman–Finch scores of children from high- and low-socioeconomic status. *Journal of Educational Psychology*, 1955, *46*, 463–469.

Conn, L. K.; Edwards, C. N.; Rosenthal, R.; & Crowne, D. Perception of emotion and response to teachers' expectancy by elementary school children. *Psychological Reports*, 1968, *22*, 27–34.

Connolly, K. Response speed, temporal sequencing, and information processing in children. In K. Connolly (Ed.), *Mechanisms of Motor Skill Development*. New York: Academic Press, 1970.

Cooper, C. D.; York, M. W.; Daston, P. G.; & Adams, H. B. The Porteus Test and various measures of intelligence with southern Negro adolescents. *American Journal of Mental Deficiency*, 1967, *71*, 787–792.

Costello, J. Effects of pretesting and examiner characteristics on test performance of young disadvantaged children. *Proceedings of the 78th Annual Convention of the American Psychological Association*, 1970, *5*, 309–310.

Court, J. H. *Researchers' Bibliography for Raven's Progressive Matrices and Mill Hill Vocabulary Scales* (3 eds. and supplements). Adelaide, South Australia: Flinders University, 1972, 1974, 1976.

Court, J. H., & Kennedy, R. J. Sex as a variable in Raven's Standard Progressive Matrices. *Proceedings of the 21st International Congress of Psychology*, Paris, 1976.

Cox, C. M. *Genetic Studies of Genius*, Vol. 2., *The Early Mental Traits of Three Hundred Geniuses*. Stanford, Calif.: Stanford University Press, 1926.

Crano, W. D. Causal analyses of the effects of socioeconomic status and initial intellectual endowment on patterns of cognitive development and academic achievement. In D. R. Green (Ed.), *The Aptitude–Achievement Distinction*, pp. 223–253. Monterey, Calif.: California Test Bureau (distr. by McGraw-Hill), 1974.

Crano, W. D.; Kenny, D. A.; & Campbell, D. T. Does intelligence cause achievement? A cross-lagged panel analysis. *Journal of Educational Psychology*, 1972, *63*, 258–275.

Cronbach, L. J. *Essentials of Psychological Testing* (2nd ed.). New York: Harper, 1960.

Cronbach, L. J. Intelligence? Creativity? A parsimonious reinterpretation of the Wallach–Kogan data. *American Educational Research Journal*, 1968, *5*, 491–511.

Cronbach, L. J. *Essentials of Psychological Testing* (3rd ed.). New York: Harper & Row, 1970.

Cronbach, L. J. Can mental tests contribute to social justice? Paper presented at a symposium on psychological tests, Sociedad Mexicana de Psicología, June 29–30, 1973.

Cronbach, L. J. Five decades of public controversy over mental testing. *American Psychologist*, 1975, *30*, 1–14.

Cronbach, L. J. Appendix I: Measuring mental ability: Lingering questions and loose ends. In B. D. Davis & P. Flaherty (Eds.), *Human Diversity: Its Causes and Social Significance*. Cambridge, Mass.: Ballinger, 1976.

Cronbach, L. J., & Drenth, P. J. D. (Eds.). *Mental Tests and Cultural Adaptation*. The Hague Mouton, 1972.

Crooks, L. A. (Ed.). *An Investigation of Sources of Bias in the Prediction of Job Performance—A Six-year Study*. Proceedings of an invitational conference. Princeton, N.J.: Educational Testing Service, 1972.

Crow, J. F. Review of *Educability and Group Differences* by A. R. Jensen. *American Journal of Human Genetics*, 1975, *27*, 130–133.

Crown, P. J. The effects of race of examiner and standard vs. dialect administration of the Wechsler Preschool and Primary Scale of Intelligence on the performance of Negro and white children. Doctoral dissertation, Florida State University, 1970.

Dangel, H. L. The biasing effect of pretest information on the WISC scores of mentally retarded children. Doctoral dissertation, Pennsylvania State University, 1970. (University Microfilms, no. 71-16, 588)

Darcy, N. T. Bilingualism and measurement of intelligence: Review of a decade of research. *Journal of Genetic Psychology*, 1963, *103*, 259–282.

Darlington, R. B. Another look at "culture fairness." *Journal of Educational Measurement*, 1971, *8*, 71–82.

Davis, J. A., & Kerner-Hoeg, S. *Validity of Preadmissions Indices for Blacks and Whites in Six Traditionally White Public Universities in North Carolina*. ETS Report PR-71-15. Princeton, N.J.: Educational Testing Service, 1971.

Davis, J. A., & Temp, G. Is the SAT biased against black students? *College Board Review*, Fall 1971, pp. 4–9.

Dawes, R. M. Graduate admission variables and future success. *Science*, 1975, *187*, 721–723.

DeAvila, E. A., & Havassy, B. *Intelligence of Mexican American Children: A Field Study Comparing NeoPiagetian and Traditional Capacity and Achievement Measures*. Austin, Texas: Dissemination Center for Bilingual Bicultural Education, 1974.

DeCharms, R., & Carpenter, V. Measuring motivation in culturally disadvantaged school children. *Journal of Experimental Education*, 1968, *37*, 31–41.

Deitz, S. M., & Purkey, W. W. Teacher expectation of performance based on race of student. *Psychological Reports*, 1969, *24*, 694.

Dennis, W. Performance of Near Eastern children on the Draw-a-Man Test. *Child Development*, 1957, *28*, 427–430.

Dennis, W. Handwriting conventions as determinants of human figure drawing. *Journal of Consulting Psychology*, 1958, *22*, 293–295.

Dennis, W. Racial change in Negro drawings. *Journal of Psychology*, 1968, *69*, 129–130.

Denniston, C. Accounting for differences in mean IQ. *Science*, 1975, *187*, 161–162.

DeVries, R. Relationships among Piagetian achievement and intelligence assessments. *Child Development*, 1974, *45*, 746–756.

Dill, J. R. A study of the influence of race of the experimenter and verbal reinforcement on creativity test performance of lower-socioeconomic-status black children. Doctoral dissertation, New York University, 1971. (*Dissertation Abstracts International*, 1972, *32*, 6071B; University Microfilms, no. 72-11, 449)

Dillon, H. J. *Early School Leavers: A Major Educational Problem*. New York: National Child Labor Committee, 1949.

Dixon, W. J. & Massey, F. J., Jr. *Introduction to Statistical Analysis*. New York: McGraw-Hill, 1951.

Dodwell, P. C. Relations between the understanding of the logic of classes and of cardinal number in children. *Canadian Journal of Psychology*, 1962, *16*, 152–160.

Doll, E. A. *The Measurement of Social Competence*. Minneapolis: Educational Test Bureau, 1953.

Doll, E. A. *Vineland Social Maturity Scale: Manual of Directions* (rev. ed.). Minneapolis: Educational Test Bureau, 1965.

Donahue, D., & Sattler, J. M. Personality variables affecting WAIS scores. *Journal of Consulting and Clinical Psychology*, 1971, *36*, 441.

Dreger, R. M., & Miller, K. S. Comparative psychological studies of Negroes and whites in the United States. *Psychological Bulletin*, 1960, *57*, 361-402.

Dreger, R. M., & Miller, K. S. Comparative psychological studies of Negroes and whites in the United States: 1959-1965. *Psychological Bulletin Monograph Supplement*, 1968, *70* (3, pt. 2).

Dubin, J. A.; Osburn, H.; & Winick, D. M. Speed and practice: Effects on Negro and white test performances. *Journal of Applied Psychology*, 1969, *53*, 19-23.

DuBois, P. H. A test standardized on Pueblo Indian children. *Psychological Bulletin*, 1939, *36*, 523. (Abstract)

Dudek, S. F.; Lester, E. P.; Goldberg, J. S., & Dyer, G. B. Relationship of Piaget measures to standard intelligence and motor scales. *Perceptual and Motor Skills*, 1969, *28*, 351-362.

Duncan, O. D. Ability and achievement. *Eugenics Quarterly*, 1968, *15*, 1-11.

Dunnette, M. D. Critics of psychological tests: Basic assumptions: How good? *Psychology in the Schools*, 1963, *1*, 63-69.

Durning, K. P. Preliminary assessment of the Navy Memory for Numbers Test. Master's thesis, San Diego State College, 1968.

Dusek, J. B., & O'Connell, E. J. Teacher expectancy effects on the achievement test performance of elementary school children. *Journal of Educational Psychology*, 1973, *65*, 371-377.

Dyer, P. J. Effects of test conditions on Negro-white differences in test scores. Doctoral dissertation, Columbia University, 1970.

Ebbinghaus, H. Über eine neue Methode zur Prüfung geistiger Fähigkeiten und ihre Anwendung bei Schulkindern. *Zeitschrift für Psychologische und Physiologische Sinnesorgane*, 1897, *13*, 401-459.

Ebel, R. L. What do educational tests test? *Educational Psychologist*, 1973, *10*, 76-79.

Eckland, B. K. Academic ability, higher education, and occupational mobility. *American Sociological Review*, 1965, *30*, 735-746.

Edgerton, H. A.; Ullmann, C. A.; & Sylvester, R. W. The Performance Index: A measure of maturity of young adult males. *Measurement and Evaluation in Guidance*, Winter 1971, *3*, 213-219.

Education Yearbook. New York: Macmillan, 1973-1974.

Eells, K. et al. *Intelligence and Cultural Differences*. Chicago: University of Chicago Press, 1951.

Egeland, B. Examiner expectancy: Effects on the scoring of the WISC. *Psychology in the Schools*, 1969, *6*, 313-315.

Eimers, S. V. Assessment of the concept of conservation among Mexican–American and Caucasian first- and second-grade children. Master's thesis, California State college, Long Beach, 1971.

Einhorn, H. J., & Bass, A. R. Methodological considerations relevant to discrimination in employment testing. *Psychological Bulletin*, 1971, *75*, 261-269.

Eisenberg, L.; Berlin, C.; Dill, A.; & Sheldon, F. Class and race effects on the intelligibility of monosyllables. *Child Development*, 1968, *39*, 1077-1089.

Eisner, E. W. *A Comparison of the Developmental Drawing Characteristics of Culturally Advantaged and Culturally Disadvantaged Children*. Final Report, Project No. 3086. Washington, D.C.: U.S. Office of Education, September 1967.

Ekren, U. W. The effect of experimenter knowledge of a subject's scholastic standing on the performance of a reasoning task. Master's thesis, Marquette University, 1962.

Elashoff, J. D., & Snow, R. E. *"Pygmalion" Reconsidered*. Worthington, Ohio: Charles A. Jones Publishing Co., 1971.

Elkind, D. The development of quantitative thinking. *Journal of Genetic Psychology*, 1961, *98*, 36-46.

Elster, R. S., & Dunnette, M. D. The robustness of Tilton's measure of overlap. *Educational and Psychological Measurement*, 1971, *31*, 685-697.

Engel, R., & Henderson, N. B. Visual evoked responses and IQ scores at school age. *Developmental and Medical Child Neurology*, 1973, *15*, 136-145.

Epperson, D. C. Some interpersonal and performance correlates of classroom alienation. *School Review*, 1963, *71*, 360-375.

Ertl, J. P. EEG, race, sex, and maturation. *Creative Science and Technology*, 1978, *2*. 25-27.

Ertl, J., & Schafer, E. W. P. Brain response correlates of psychometric intelligence. *Nature*, 1969, *223*, 421–422.

Estes, W. K. *Learning Theory and Mental Development*. New York: Academic Press, 1970.

Evans, J. T., & Rosenthal, R. Interpersonal self-fulfilling prophecies: Further extrapolations from the laboratory to the classroom. *Proceedings of the 77th Annual Convention of the American Psychological Association*, 1969, *4*, 371–372. (Summary)

Eysenck, H. J. Primary mental abilities. *British Journal of Educational Psychology*, 1939, *9*, 270–265.

Eysenck, H. J. Intelligence assessment: A theoretical and experimental approach. *British Journal of Educational Psychology*, 1967, *37*, 81–98.

Eysenck, H. J. *The I.Q. Argument*. Freeport, N.Y.: Library Press, 1971.

Falconer, D. S. *An Introduction to Quantitative Genetics*. New York: Ronald Press, 1960.

Farr, J. L. The use of work sample and culture-fair tests in the prediction of job success with racially mixed groups. Paper presented at the meeting of the American Psychological Association, Washington, D.C., September 1971.

Farr, J. L.; O'Leary, B. S.; Pfeiffer, C. M.; Goldstein, I. L.; & Bartlett, C. J. *Ethnic Group Membership as a Moderator in the Prediction of Job Performance: An Examination of Some Less Traditional Predictors*. AIR Technical Report No. 2. Washington, D.C.: American Institutes for Research, September 1971.

Feldman, D. Problems in the analysis of patterns of abilities. *Child Development*, 1973, *44*, 12–18.

Fiedler, W. R.; Cohen, R. D.; & Finney, S. An attempt to replicate the teacher expectancy effect. *Psychological Reports*, 1971, *29*, 1223–1228.

Figurelli, J. K., & Keller, H. R. The effects of training and socioeconomic class upon the acquisition of conservation concepts. *Child Development*, 1972, *43*, 293–298.

Findley, W. G. (Ed.). *The Impact and Improvement of School Testing Programs*. 62nd Yearbook of the National Society for the Study of Education, Part II. Chicago: University of Chicago Press, 1963.

Findley, W. G., & Bryan, M. M. *Ability Grouping: 1970*. Athens: Center for Educational Improvement, College of Education, University of Georgia, 1971.

Fisher, J. The twisted pear and the prediction of behavior. *Journal of Consulting Psychology*, 1959, *23*, 400–405.

Fisher, R. A. *Statistical Methods for Research Workers* (14th ed.). New York: Hafner Press, 1970.

Fishman, J. A.; Deutsch, M.; Kogan, L.; North, R.; & Whiteman, M. Guidelines for testing minority group children. *Journal of Social Issues*, 1964, *20*, 127–145. (Supplement to the April issue, no. 2)

Flavell, J. *The Developmental Psychology of Jean Piaget*. New York: Van Nostrand, 1963.

Fleming, E. S., & Anttonen, R. G. Teacher expectancy as related to the academic and personal growth of primary-age children. *Monographs of the Society for Research in Child Development*, 1971, *36* (5, serial no. 145).

Flowers, C. E. Effects of an arbitrary accelerated group placement on the tested academic achievement of educationally disadvantaged students. Doctoral dissertation, Teachers College, Columbia University, 1966. (Cited in Rosenthal & Jackson, 1968.)

Foley, P. P. *Validity of the Officer Qualification Test for Minority Group Applicants to Officer Candidate School*. Washington, D.C.: Naval Personnel Research and Development Laboratory, January 1971.

Ford, J. D., Jr., & Meyer, J. K. *Training in Computer Flow Charting Using Programmed Instruction: Eliminating the Effects of Mathematics Aptitude upon Achievement*. Technical Bulletin STB 67-10. San Diego, Calif.: U.S. Naval Personnel Research Activity, November 1966.

Forrester, B. J., & Klaus, R. A. The effect of race of the examiner on intelligence test scores of Negro kindergarten children. *Peabody Papers in Human Development*, 1964, *2*, 1–7.

Fortes, M. A new application of the theory of noegenesis to the problems of mental testing. Doctoral dissertation, University of London, 1930.

Fowler, W. L. A comparative analysis of pupil performance on conventional and culture-controlled mental tests. *Yearbook of the National Council on Measurements Used in Education*, 1957, *14*, 8–19.

Fox, D. G. An investigation of the biographical correlates of race. Master's thesis, University of Utah, 1972.

Fox, L. H. Sex differences in mathematical precocity: Bridging the gap. In D. P. Keating (Ed.), *Intellectual Talent: Research and Development,* pp. 183–214. Baltimore: Johns Hopkins Press, 1976.

Fox, W. L., & Taylor, J. E. Adaptation of training to individual differences. Paper presented at the North Atlantic Treaty Organization Conference on "Manpower Research in the Defense Context," August 14–18, 1967, London, England. (Human Resources Research Organization, Division No. 3, Presidio of Monterey, Calif.)

Fox, W.; Taylor, J.; & Caylor, J. Aptitude level and the acquisition of skills and knowledge in a variety of military training tasks. Human Resources Research Organization Technical Report 69-6. Washington, D.C.: Chief of Research and Development, Department of the Army, May 1969.

France, K. Effects of "white" and of "black" examiner voices on IQ scores of children. *Developmental Psychology,* 1973, *8,* 144.

French, J. W.; Ekstrom, R. B.; & Price, L. A. *Kit of Reference Tests for Cognitive Factors.* Princeton, N.J.: Educational Testing Service, 1963.

Fricke, B. G. *Report to the Faculty: Grading, Testing, Standards, and All That.* Ann Arbor: Evaluation and Examinations Office, University of Michigan, 1975.

Fryer, W. B. Employment discrimination: Statistics and preferences under Title VII. *Virginia Law Review,* 1973, *59,* 463–491.

Funches, D. L. Correlation between secondary school transcript averages of freshmen at Jackson State College. *College and University,* 1967, *43,* 52–54.

Gael, S., & Grant, D. L. Employment test validation for minority and nonminority telephone company service representatives. *Journal of Applied Psychology,* 1972, *56,* 135–139.

Gallagher, J. J. Social status of children related to intelligence propinquity and social perception. *Elementary School Journal,* 1958, *58,* 225–231.

Galton, F. *Hereditary Genius: An Inquiry into Its Laws and Consequences.* London: Macmillan, 1869.

Galton, F. *Memories of My Life.* London: Methuen, 1908.

Gardner, J. W. *Excellence.* New York: Harper, 1961.

Garfinkle, A. S. Development of a Battery of Piagetian Logico-Mathematical Concepts. Master's thesis, University of Colorado, 1975.

Garrett, H. E. A note on the intelligence scores of Negroes and whites in 1918. *Journal of Abnormal and Social Psychology,* 1945, *40,* 344–346. (a)

Garrett, H. E. Comparison of Negro and white recruits on the army tests given in 1917–1918. *American Journal of Psychology,* 1945, *58,* 480–495. (b)

Garrett, H. E. *Great Experiments in Psychology* (3rd ed.). New York: Appleton-Century-Crofts, 1951.

Garrett, H. E.; Bryan, A. I.; & Perl, R. E. The age factor in mental organization. *Archives of Psychology,* 1935, no. 176.

Gaudia, G. Race, social class, and age of achievement of conservation on Piaget's tasks. *Developmental Psychology,* 1972, *6,* 158–165.

Gavurin, E. I. The relationship of mental ability to anagram solving. *Journal of Psychology,* 1967, *66,* 227–230.

Geist, H. Evaluation of culture-free intelligence. *California Journal of Educational Research,* November 1954, *5,* 209–214.

Gentile, J. R. Sociocultural level and knowledge of definitions in the solution of analogy items. *American Educational Research Journal,* 1968, *5,* 626–638.

Getzels, J. W., & Jackson, P. W. *Creativity and Intelligence.* New York: Wiley, 1962.

Ghiselli, E. E. The measurement of occupational aptitude. *University of California Publications in Psychology,* 1955, *8* (2), 101–216.

Ghiselli, E. E. *The Validity of Occupational Aptitude Tests.* New York: Wiley, 1966.

Gillingham, W. H. *An investigation of examiner influence on Wechsler Intelligence Scale for Children scores.* Doctoral dissertation, Michigan State University, 1970. (University Microfilms, no. 70-20, 458)

Ginsburg, R. E. *An Examination of the Relationship between Teacher Expectancies and Students' Performance on a Test of Intellectual Functioning.* Doctoral dissertation, University of Utah, 1970. (University Microfilms, no. 71-922)

Glueck, S., & Glueck, E. *Unraveling Juvenile Delinquency*. Cambridge, Mass.: Harvard University Press, 1950.

Goldberg, S. *The Inevitability of Patriarchy*. New York: Morrow, 1973.

Goldman, R. D., & Hewitt, B. N. An investigation of test bias for Mexican–American college students. *Journal of Educational Measurement*, 1975, *12*, 187–196.

Goldman, R. D., & Hewitt, B. N. The Scholastic Aptitude Test "explains" why college men major in science more often than college women. *Journal of Counseling Psychology*, 1976, *23*, 50–54.

Goldman, R. D., & Richards, R. The SAT prediction of grades for Mexican–American versus Anglo-American students of the University of California, Riverside. *Journal of Educational Measurement*, 1974, *11*, 129–135.

Goldman, R. D.; Schmidt, D. E.; Hewitt, B. N.; & Fisher, R. Grading practices in different major fields. *American Educational Research Journal*, 1974, *11*, 343–357.

Goldman, R. D., & Slaughter, R. E. Why college grade-point average is difficult to predict. *Journal of Educational Psychology*, 1976, *68*, 9–14.

Goldschmid, M. L. Different types of conservation and non-conservation and their relation to age, sex, IQ, MA, and vocabulary. *Child Development*, 1967, *38*, 1229–1246.

Goldschmid, M. L., & Bentler, P. M. The dimensions and measurement of conservation. *Child Development*, 1968, *39*, 787–802. (a)

Goldschmid, M. L., & Bentler, P. M. *Concept Assessment Kit: Conservation, Manual, and Keys*. San Diego, Calif.: Educational and Industrial Testing Service, 1968. (b)

Goodenough, F. L. *Measurement of Intelligence by Drawings*. New York: Harcourt, Brace & World, 1926.

Goodman, F. I. De facto school segregation: A constitutional and empirical analysis. *California Law Review*, 1972, *60*, 275–437.

Gordon, M. A. *A Study in the Applicability of the Same Minimum Qualifying Scores for Technical Schools to White Males, WAF, and Negro Males*. Technical Report 53-34. Lackland AFB, Texas: Personnel Research Laboratory, November 1953.

Gordon, R. A. Examining labeling theory: The case of mental retardation. Paper presented at the Third Vanderbilt University Sociology Conference, Nashville, Tennessee, October 28–29, 1974.

Gordon, R. A. Examining labeling theory: The case of mental retardation. In W. R. Grove (Ed.), *The Labeling of Deviance: Evaluating a Perspective*, pp. 83–146. New York: Halsted Press, 1975. (a)

Gordon, R. A. Crime and cognition: An evolutionary perspective. Paper presented at the Second International Symposium on Criminology at the International Center of Biological and Medico-Forensic Criminology, São Paulo, Brazil, August 7, 1975. (b)

Gordon, R. A. Prevalence: The rare datum in delinquency measurement and its implications for the theory of delinquency. In M. W. Klein (Ed.), *The Juvenile Justice System*, pp. 201–284. Beverly Hills, Calif.: Sage Publications, 1976.

Gordon, R. A., & Rudert, E. E. Bad news concerning IQ tests. *Sociology of Education*, 1979, *52*, 174–190.

Goslin, D. A. *The Search for Ability: Standardized Testing in Social Perspective*. New York: Science Editions (Wiley), 1966.

Goslin, D. A. Standardized ability tests and testing. *Science*, 1968, *159*, 851–855.

Gould, L., & Klein, E. Performance of black and white adolescents on intellectual and attitudinal measures as a function of race of tester. *Journal of Consulting and Clinical Psychology*, 1971, *37*, 195–200.

Gozali, J., & Meyen, E. L. The influence of the teacher expectancy phenomenon on the academic performances of educable mentally retarded pupils in special classes. *Journal of Special Education*, 1970, *4*, 417–424.

Grant, D. L., & Bray, D. W. Validation of employment tests for telephone company installation and repair occupations. *Journal of Applied Psychology*, 1970, *54*, 7–14.

Green, D. R. *Racial and Ethnic Bias in Test Construction*. Monterey, Calif.: California Test Bureau (distr. by McGraw-Hill), 1972.

Green, D. R. (Ed.). *The Aptitude–Achievement Distinction*. Monterey, Calif.: California Test Bureau (distr. by McGraw-Hill), 1974.

Green, D. R., & Draper, J. F. Exploratory studies of bias in achievement tests. Paper presented at annual meeting of American Psychological Association, Honolulu, Hawaii, September 1972.

Green, D. R.; Ford, M. P.; & Flamer, G. B. (Eds.). *Measurement and Piaget*. New York: McGraw-Hill, 1971.

Green, R. L., & Farquhar, W. W. Negro academic motivation and scholastic achievement. *Journal of Educational Psychology*, 1965, *56*, 241–243.

Greene, K. B. The influence of specialized training on tests of general intelligence. In *Twenty-seventh Yearbook of the National Society for the Study of Education*, pp. 421–428. Bloomington, Indiana: Public School Publishing Co., 1928.

Gross, A. L., & Su, W. Defining a "fair" or "unbiased" selection model: A question of utilities. *Journal of Applied Psychology*, 1975, *60*, 345–351.

Grunzke, N.; Guinn, N.; & Stauffer, G. *Comparative Performance of Low-Ability Airmen*. Technical Report 70-4. Lackland AFB, Texas: Air Force Human Resources Laboratory, 1970.

Guilford, J. P. The difficulty of a test and its factor composition. *Psychometrika*, 1941, *6*, 67–77.

Guilford, J. P. *Psychometric Methods*. New York: McGraw-Hill, 1954.

Guilford, J. P. *Fundamental Statistics in Psychology and Education* (3rd ed.). New York: McGraw-Hill, 1956.

Guilford, J. P. Three faces of intellect. *American Psychologist*, 1959, *14*, 469–479.

Guilford, J. P. Zero correlations among tests of intellectual abilities. *Psychological Bulletin*, 1964, *61*, 401–404.

Guilford, J. P. *The Nature of Human Intelligence*. New York: McGraw-Hill, 1967.

Guinn, N.; Tupes, E. C.; & Alley, W. E. *Cultural Subgroup Differences in the Relationships between Air Force Aptitude Composites and Training Criteria*. Technical Report 70-35. Brooks Air Force Base, Texas: Air Force Human Resources laboratory, September 1970.

Gulliksen, H. *Theory of Mental Tests*. New York: Wiley, 1950.

Gulliksen, H., & Wilks, S. S. Regression tests for several samples. *Psychometrika*, 1950, *15*, 91–114.

Guttman, L. The basis for scalogram analysis. In S. A. Stouffer, L. Guttman, E. A. Suchman, P. F. Lazarsfeld, S. A. Star, & J. A. Clausen, *Studies in Social Psychology in World War II*, Vol. 4, *Measurement and Prediction*, pp. 60–90. New York: Science Editions (Wiley), 1950.

Hakstian, A. R., & Cattell, R. B. The checking of primary ability structures of a broader basis of performances. *British Journal of Educational Psychology*, 1974, *44*, 140–154.

Hall, V. C., & Turner, R. R. Comparison of imitation and comprehension scores between two lower-class groups and the effects of two warm-up conditions on imitation of the same groups. *Child Development*, 1971, *42*, 1735–1750.

Hall, V. C., & Turner, R. R. The validity of the "different language explanation" for poor scholastic performance by black students. *Review of Educational Research*, 1974, *44*, 69–81.

Halstead, W. C. *Brain and Intelligence*. Chicago: University of Chicago Press, 1947.

Halverson, C. F., Jr., & Waldrop, M. F. Relations between preschool activity and aspects of intellectual and social behavior at age $7\frac{1}{2}$. *Developmental Psychology*, 1976, *12*, 107–112.

Harlow, H. F. Learning set and error factor theory. In S. Koch (Ed.), *Psychology: A Study of a Science*, Vol. 2, pp. 492–537. New York: McGraw-Hill, 1959.

Harlow, H. F., & Harlow, M. K. The mind of man. In *Yearbook of Science and Technology*. New York: McGraw-Hill, 1962.

Harman, H. H. *Modern Factor Analysis* (2nd ed.). Chicago: University of Chicago Press, 1967.

Harms, L. S. Listener comprehension of speakers of three status groups. *Language and Speech*, 1961, *4*, 109–112.

Harrell, T. W., & Harrell, M. S. Army General Classification Test scores for civilian occupations. *Educational and Psychological Measurement*, 1945, *5*, 229–239.

Harris, D. B. *Children's Drawings as Measures of Intellectual Maturity: A Revision and Extension of the Goodenough Draw-a-Man Test*. New York: Harcourt, Brace, & World, 1963.

Harris, D. B., & Pinder, G. D. *The Goodenough–Harris Drawing Test as a Measure of Intellectual Maturity of Youths*. Vital and Health Statistics, Series 2, no. 138. Washington, D.C.: Government Printing Office, 1974.

Harrison, G. A.; Weiner, J. S.; Tanner, J. M.; & Barnicot, N. A. *Human Biology: An Introduction to Human Evolution, Variation, and Growth*. London: Oxford University Press, 1964.

Hathaway, W. E. The degree, nature and temporal stability of the relations between traditional psychometric and Piagetian developmental measures of mental development. Doctoral dissertation, University of Pennsylvania, 1972.

Healy, W., & Bronner, A. F. *New Light on Delinquency and Its Treatment*. New Haven, Conn.: Yale University Press, 1936.

Hebb, D. O. *The Organization of Behavior: A Neuropsychological Theory*. New York: Wiley, 1949.

Heckhaussen, H. *The Anatomy of Achievement Motivation*. New York: Academic Press, 1967.

Hennessy, J. J. Structure and patterns of mental abilities in several ethnic groups. Doctoral dissertation, New York University, 1974. (University Microfilms, no. 74-24, 997.)

Hennessy, J. J., & Merrifield, P. R. A comparison of the factor structures of mental abilities in four ethnic groups. *Journal of Educational Psychology*, 1976, *68*, 754-759.

Hersh, J. B. Effects of referral information on testers. *Journal of Consulting and Clinical Psychology*, 1971, *37*, 116-122.

Hewer, V. H. Are tests fair to college students from homes with low socioeconomic status? *Personnel and Guidance Journal*, 1965, *43*, 764-769.

Hewitt, B. N., & Golman, R. D. Occam's razor slices through the myth that college women overachieve. *Journal of Educational Psychology*, 1975, *67*, 323-330.

Hick, W. On the rate of gain of information. *Quarterly Journal of Experimental Psychology*, 1952, *4*, 11-26.

Hills, J. R. Prediction of college grades for all public colleges of a state. *Journal of Educational Measurement*, 1964, *1*, 155-159.

Hills, J. R., & Stanley, J. C. Easier test improves prediction of black students' college grades. *Journal of Negro Education*, 1970, *39*, 320-324.

Hirsch, N. D. M. An experimental study upon three hundred school children over a six-year period. *Genetic Psychology Monographs*, 1930, *7*, no. 6.

Hirschi, T., & Hindelang, M. J. Intelligence and delinquency: A revisionist review. *American Sociological Review*, 1977, *42*, 571-587.

Hoffman, B. *The Tyranny of Testing*. New York: Crowell-Collier, 1962.

Hollingworth, L. S. *Children above 180 IQ*. New York: Harcourt, Brace, & World, 1942.

Hollingworth, L. S., & Cobb, M. V. Children clustering at 165 I.Q. and children clustering at 146 I.Q. compared for three years of achievement. In *Nature and Nurture*, Part II, pp. 3-33. 27th Yearbook of the National Society for the Study of Education, 1928.

Holtzman, W. H. The changing world of mental measurement and its social significance. *American Psychologist*, 1971, *26*, 546-553.

Holzinger, K. *Preliminary Report on Spearman-Holzinger Unitary Trait Study*, Nos. 1-8. Chicago: University of Chicago Press, 1935.

Honigfeld, G. "Neurological efficiency," perception, and personality. *Perceptual and Motor Skills*, 1962, *15*, 531-553.

Honzik, M. P. Consistency and change in intellectual functioning and personality characteristics during the life span. *Proceedings of the 20th International Congress of Psychology, pp. 224-225*. Tokyo, 1972.

Hood, B. H. An experimental study of Piaget's theory of the development of number in children. *British Journal of Psychology*, 1962, *53*, 273-286.

Hooton, E. A. *The American Criminal*. Vol. 1. Cambridge, Mass.: Harvard University Press, 1939.

Horn, J. L. Intelligence: Why it grows, why it declines. *Trans-Action*, 1967, 523-531.

Horn, J. L. Psychometric studies of aging and intelligence. In S. Gershon & A. Raskin (Eds.). *Genesis and Treatment of Psychologic Disorders in the Elderly, pp. 19-45*. New York: Raven, 1975.

Horn, J. L., & Cattell, R. B. Age differences in fluid and crystalized intelligence. *Acta Psychologica*, 1967, *26*, 107-129.

Hotelling, H. Analysis of a complex of statistical variables into principal components. *Journal of Educational Psychology*, 1933, 24, 417-441, 498-520.

Hull, C. L. *Aptitude Testing*. New York: World Book Co., 1928.

Humphreys, L. G. Factor analysis: Psychological applications. In D. L. Sills (Ed.), *International*

Encyclopedia of the Social Sciences, Vol. 5, pp. 281–287. New York: Macmillan & Free Press, 1968.

Humphreys, L. G. Theory of intelligence. In R. Cancro (Ed.), *Intelligence: Genetic and Environmental Influences,* pp. 31–55. New York: Grune & Stratton, 1971.

Humphreys, L. G. Statistical definitions of test validity for minority groups. *Journal of Applied Psychology,* 1973, *58* (1), 1–4.

Humphreys, L. G. Addendum. *American Psychologist,* 1975, *30,* 95–96.

Humphreys, L. G. Relevance of genotype and its environmental counterpart to the theory, interpretation, and nomenclature of ability measures. *Intelligence,* 1978, *2,* 181–193.

Humphreys, L. G.; Fleishman, A. I.; & Lin, P-C. Causes of racial and socioeconomic differences in cognitive tests. *Journal of Research in Personality,* 1977, *11,* 191–208.

Humphreys, L. G.; Levy, J.; & Taber, T. Predictability of academic grades for students of high and low academic promise. *Educational and Psychological Measurement,* 1973, *33,* 385–392.

Humphreys, L. G., & Taber, T. Ability factors as a function of advantaged and disadvantaged groups. *Journal of Educational Measurement,* Summer 1973, *10,* 107–115.

Hunt, E. Varieties of cognitive power. In L. B. Resnick (Ed.). *The Nature of Intelligence,* pp. 237–259. Hillsdale, N.J.: Erlbaum, 1976.

Hunt, J. McV. *Intelligence and Experience.* New York: Ronald Press, 1961.

Hunter, J. E., & Schmidt, F. L. A critical analysis of the statistical and ethical implications of various definitions of "test bias." *Psychological Bulletin,* 1976, *83,* 1053–1071.

Hurley, J. R. Parental acceptance-rejection and children's intelligence. *Merrill–Palmer Quarterly of Behavior and Development,* 1965, *11,* 19–31.

Hurst, J. G. The meaning and use of difference scores obtained between the performance on the Stanford–Binet Intelligence Scale and the Vineland Social Maturity Scale. *Journal of Clinical Psychology,* 1962, *18,* 153–160.

Hyman, R. Stimulus information as a determinant of reaction time. *Journal of Experimental Psychology,* 1953, *45,* 188–196.

Ilg, F. L., & Ames, L. B. *School Readiness.* New York: Harper & Row, 1964.

Izard, C. E. Personality correlates of sociometric status. *Journal of Applied Psychology,* 1959, *43,* 89–93.

Jackson, C. D. On the report of the Ad Hoc Committee on Educational Uses of Tests with Disadvantaged Students: Another psychological view from the Association of Black Psychologists. *American Psychologist,* 1975, *30,* 86–90.

Jacobs, J. F., & DeGraaf, C. A. *Expectancy and Race: Their Influences upon the Scoring of Individual Intelligence Tests.* Final Report, Project No. 1-E-096. Washington, D.C.: U.S. Department of Health, Education, and Welfare, March 14, 1972.

James, W. S. Symposium on the effects of coaching and practice in intelligence tests: II. Coaching for all recommended. *British Journal of Educational Psychology,* 1953, *23,* 155–162.

Jencks, C. *Inequality: A Reassessment of the Effect of Family and Schooling in America.* New York: Basic Books, 1972.

Jensen, A. R. Social class, race, and genetics: Implications for education. *American Educational Research Journal,* 1968, *5,* 1–42. (a)

Jensen, A. R. Patterns of mental ability and socioeconomic status. *Proceedings of the National Academy of Sciences,* 1968, *60,* 1330–1337. (b)

Jensen, A. R. IQ's of identical twins reared apart. *Behavior Genetics,* 1970, *1,* 133–148. (a)

Jensen, A. R. Hierarchical theories of mental ability. In B. Dockrell (Ed.), *On Intelligence,* pp. 119–190. Toronto: Ontario Institute for Studies in Education, 1970. (b)

Jensen, A. R. A theory of primary and secondary familial mental retardation. In N. R. Ellis (Ed.), *International Review of Research in Mental Retardation,* Vol. 4, pp. 33–105. New York: Academic Press, 1970. (c)

Jensen, A. R. Do schools cheat minority children? *Educational Research,* 1971, *14,* 3–28. (a)

Jensen, A. R. The race × sex × ability interaction. In R. Cancro (Ed.), *Contributions to Intelligence,* pp. 107–161. New York: Grune & Stratton, 1971. (b)

Jensen, A. R. A two-factor theory of familial mental retardation. Proceedings of the Fourth International Congress of Human Genetics, *Excerpta Medica.* Amsterdam, 1971. (c)

Jensen, A. R. *Genetics and Education.* London: Methuen (New York: Harper & Row), 1973. (a)

Jensen, A. R. *Educability and Group Differences*. London: Methuen (New York: Harper & Row), 1973. (b)

Jensen, A. R. *Educational Differences*. London: Methuen, 1973. (c)

Jensen, A. R. Level I and Level II abilities in three ethnic groups. *American Educational Research Journal*, 1973, *4*, 263-276. (d)

Jensen, A. R. Personality and scholastic achievement in three ethnic groups. *British Journal of Educational Psychology*, 1973, *43*, 115-125. (e)

Jensen, A. R. How biased are culture-loaded tests? *Genetic Psychology Monographs*, 1974, *90*, 185-244. (a)

Jensen, A. R. Interaction of Level I and Level II abilities with race and socioeconomic status. *Journal of Educational Psychology*, 1974, *66*, 99-111. (b)

Jensen, A. R. The effect of race of examiner on the mental test scores of white and black pupils. *Journal of Educational Measurement*, 1974, *11*, 1-14. (c)

Jensen, A. R. Ethnicity and scholastic achievement. *Psychological Reports*, 1974, *34*, 659-668. (d)

Jensen, A. R. The meaning of heritability in the behavioral sciences. *Educational Psychologist*, 1975, *11*, 171-183. (a)

Jensen, A. R. A theoretical note on sex linkage and race differences in spatial ability. *Behavior Genetics*, 1975, *5*, 151-164. (b)

Jensen, A. R. The problem of genotype–environment correlation in the estimation of heritability from monozygotic and dizygotic twins. *Acta Geneticae Medicae et Gemellologiae*, 1976, *25*, 86-99.

Jensen, A. R. An examination of culture bias in the Wonderlic Personnel Test. *Intelligence*, 1977, *1*, 51-64. (a)

Jensen, A. R. Cumulative deficit in IQ of blacks in the rural South. *Developmental Psychology*, 1977, *13*, 184-191. (b)

Jensen, A. R. An unfounded conclusion in M. W. Smith's analysis of culture bias in the Stanford–Binet intelligence scale. *Genetic Psychology Monographs*, 1977, *130*, 113-115. (c)

Jensen, A. R. Sex linkage and race differences in spatial ability: A reply. *Behavior Genetics*, 1978, *8*, 213-217.

Jensen, A. R. *g:* Outmoded theory or unconquered frontier? *Creative Science and Technology*, 1979, *2*, 16-29.

Jensen, A. R., & Figueroa, R. A. Forward and backward digit-span interaction with race and IQ: Predictions from Jensen's theory. *Journal of Educational Psychology*, 1975, *67*, 882-893.

Jensen, A. R., & Munro, E. Reaction time, movement time, and intelligence. *Intelligence*, 1979, *3*, 121-126.

Jerison, H. J. *Evolution of the Brain and Intelligence*. New York: Academic Press, 1973.

Jinks, J. L., & Fulker, D. W. Comparison of the biometrical genetical, MAVA, and classical approaches to the analysis of human behavior. *Psychological Bulletin*, 1970, *73*, 311-349.

Johnson, D. F., & Mihal, W. L. Performance of blacks and whites in computerized vs. manual testing environments. *American Psychologist*, 1973, *28*, 694-699.

José, J., & Cody, J. J. Teacher–pupil interaction as it relates to attempted changes in teacher expectancy of academic ability and achievement. *American Educational Research Journal*, 1971, *8*, 39-49.

Justman, J., & Aronov, M. The Davis–Eells Games as a measure of the intelligence of poor readers. *Journal of Educational Psychology*, 1955, *46*, 418-422.

KaDell, M. B. A factor analysis of the Vineland Social Maturity Scale and the Stanford–Binet Intelligence Scale. Master's thesis, University of Minnesota, 1960.

Kagan, J. Controversies in intelligence: The meaning of intelligence. In D. W. Allen & E. Seifman (Eds.), *The Teacher's Handbook*, pp. 655-662. Glenview, Ill.: Scott, Foresman, 1971.

Kagan, J; Moss, H. A.; & Sigel, I. Psychological significance of styles of conceptualization. In J. C. Wright & J. Kagan (Eds.), Basic cognitive processes in children. *Monographs of the Society for Research in Child Development*, 1963, *28* (2, serial no. 86).

Kaiser, H. F. The varimax criterion for analytic rotation in factor analysis. *Psychometrika*, 1958, *23*, 187-200.

Kaiser, H. F.; Hunka, S., & Bianchini, J. C. Relating factors between studies based upon different individuals. *Multivariate Behavioral Research*, 1971, *6*, 409-422.

Kallingal, A. The prediction of grades for black and white students of Michigan State University. *Journal of Educational Measurement,* 1971, *8,* 263-265.

Kamiya, J. Behavioral, subjective, and psychological aspects of drowsiness and sleep. In D. W. Fiske & S. R. Maddi (Eds.), *Functions of Varied Experience,* pp. 145-174. Homewood, Ill.: Dorsey, 1961.

Karlsson, J. L. *Inheritance of Creative Intelligence.* Chicago: Nelson-Hall, 1978.

Karmel, L. J., & Karmel, M. O. *Measurement and Evaluation in the Schools* (2nd ed.). New York: Macmillan, 1978.

Karn, M. N., & Penrose, L. S. Birth weight and gestation time in relation to maternal age, parity, and infant survival. *Annals of Eugenics,* 1952, *16,* 147-164.

Kaufman, A. S. Comparisons of tests built from Piaget's and Gesell's tasks: An analysis of their psychometric properties and psychological meaning. Doctoral dissertation, Teachers College, Columbia University, 1970.

Kaufman, A. S. Piaget and Gesell: A psychometric analysis of tests built from their tasks. *Child Development,* 1971, *42,* 1341-1360.

Kaufman, A. S. Factor analysis of the WISC-R at eleven age levels between 6½ and 16½ years. *Journal of Clinical and Consulting Psychology,* 1975, *43,* 135-147.

Kaufman, A. S., & Kaufman, N. L. Tests built from Piaget's and Gesell's tasks as predictors of first-grade achievement. *Child Development,* 1972, *43,* 521-535.

Keating, D. P., & Bobbitt, B. Individual and developmental differences in cognitive processing components of mental ability. *Child Development,* 1978, *49,* 155-169.

Kemp, L. C. D. Environmental and other characteristics determining attainments in primary schools. *British Journal of Educational Psychology,* 1955, *25,* 66-77.

Kendall, M. G. *The Advanced Theory of Statistics,* Vol. 1 (3rd ed.). New York: Hafner, 1960.

Kennedy, W. A.; Van de Riet, V.; & White, J. C., Jr. A normative sample of intelligence and achievement of Negro elementary school children in the southeastern United States. *Monographs of the Society for Research on Child Development,* 1963, *28,* no. 6.

Keys, N. *The Improvement of Measurement through Cumulative Testing.* New York: Teachers College, Columbia University, 1928.

Kidd, A. The culture fair aspects of Cattell's test of *g*: Culture-free. *Journal of Genetic Psychology,* 1962, *101,* 343-362.

Kidd, A. H., & Rivoire, J. L. The culture fair aspects of the development of spatial perception. *Journal of Genetic Psychology,* 1965, *106,* 101-111.

Kirkpatrick, J. J.; Ewen, R. B.; Barrett, R. S.; & Katzel, R. A. *Testing and Fair Employment.* New York: New York University Press, 1968.

Klineberg, O. An experimental study of speed and other factors in "racial" differences. *Archives of Psychology,* 1928, no. 93.

Klippel, M. D. Measurement of intelligence among three New Zealand ethnic groups. *Journal of Cross-Cultural Psychology,* 1975, *6,* 365-376.

Klugman, S. F. The effects of money incentive versus praise upon the reliability and obtained scores of the Revised Stanford-Binet Test. *Journal of Genetic Psychology,* 1944, *30,* 255-269.

Knapp, R. R. The effects of time limits on the intelligence test performance of Mexican and American subjects. *Journal of Educational Psychology,* 1960, *51,* 14-20.

Knox, H. A. A scale based on the work at Ellis Island for estimating mental defect. *Journal of the American Medical Association,* 1914, *62,* 741-747.

Kogan, N., & Pankove, E. Long-term predictive validity of divergent-thinking tests: Some negative evidence. *Journal of Educational Psychology,* 1974, *66,* 802-810.

Kolhberg, L. Early education: A cognitive-developmental view. *Child Development,* 1968, *39,* 1013-1062.

Kohlberg, L. *Stages in the Development of Moral Thought and Action.* New York: Holt, Rinehart, & Winston, 1969.

Kohnberg, L.; LaCrosse, J.; & Ricks, D. The predictability of adult mental health from childhood behavior. In B. Wolman (Ed.), *Handbook of Child Psychopathology.* New York: McGraw-Hill, 1970.

Koppitz, E. M. *The Bender-Gestalt Test for Young Children.* New York: Grune & Stratton, 1964.

Krauss, R. M., & Rotter, G. S. Communication abilities of children as a function of status and age. *Merrill-Palmer Quarterly,* 1968, *14,* 161-173.

Krebs, E. G. The Wechsler Preschool and Primary Scale of Intelligence and prediction of reading achievement in first grade. Doctoral dissertation, Rutgers State University, 1969.

Kreit, L. H. The effects of test-taking practice on pupil test performance. *American Educational Research Journal*, 1968, *5*, 616–625.

Kreze, A.; Zelina, M.; Juhás, J.; & Garbara, M. Relationship between intelligence and relative prevalence of obesity. *Human Biology*, 1974, *46*, 109–113.

Krug, S. E. Psychometric properties of the culture-fair scales: Reliability and validity. *IPAT Information Bulletin*, 1967, no. 14.

Kuder, G. F., & Richardson, M. W. The theory of the estimation of test reliability. *Psychometrika*, 1937, *2*, 135–138.

Kuhn, D. Relation of two Piagetian stage transitions to IQ. *Journal of Developmental Psychology*, 1976, *12*, 157–161.

Kuznets, G. M., & McNemar, O. Sex differences in intelligence-test scores. In G. M. Whipple (Ed.), *39th Yearbook of the National Society for the Study of Education*, Part I, pp. 211–220. Bloomington, Ill.: Public School Publishing Co., 1940.

LaCrosse, J. E. Examiner reliability on the Stanford–Binet Intelligence Scale (Form L–M) in a design employing white and Negro examiners and subjects. Master's thesis, University of North Carolina, 1964.

Landis, C., & Hamwi, V. Critical flicker frequency, age, and intelligence. *American Journal of Psychology*, 1956, *69*, 459–461.

Lavin, D. E. *The Prediction of Academic Performance*. New York: Science Editions (Wiley), 1965.

Lawler, J. M. *IQ, Heritability, and Racism*. New York: International Publishers, 1978.

Lawley, D. N., & Maxwell, A. E. *Factor Analysis as a Statistical Method*. London: Butterworth, 1963.

Laycock, F., & Caylor, J. S. Physiques of gifted children and their less gifted siblings. *Child Development*, 1964, *35*, 63–74.

Learned, W. S., & Wood, B. D. *The Student and His Knowledge*. New York: Carnegie Foundation for the Advancement of Teaching, 1938.

Lehrke, R. G. Sex linkage: A biological basis for greater male variability. In R. T. Osborne, C. E. Noble, & N. Weyl (Eds.), *Human Variation: The Biopsychology of Age, Race, and Sex*, pp. 171–198. New York: Academic Press, 1978.

Leland, H.; Shellhaas, M.; Nihira, K.; & Foster, R. Adaptive behavior: A new dimension in the classification of the mentally retarded. *Mental Retardation Abstracts*, 1967, *4*, 359–387.

Lemmon, V. W. The relation of reaction time to measures of intelligence, memory, and learning. *Archives of Psychology*, 1927–1928, *15*, 5–38.

Lesser, G. S. Problems in the analysis of patterns of abilities: A reply. *Child Development*, 1973, *44*, 19–20.

Lesser, G. S.; Fifer, F.; & Clark, H. Mental abilities of children from different social-class and cultural groups. *Monographs of the Society for Research in Child Development*, 1965, *30* (whole no. 4).

Lewis, D. *Quantitative Methods in Psychology*. New York: McGraw-Hill, 1960.

Li, C. C. *Path Analysis: A Primer*. Pacific Grove, Calif.: Boxwood Press, 1975.

Libet, B. Cortical activation in conscious and unconscious experience. *Perspectives in Biology and Medicine*, 1965, *9*, 77–86.

Libet, B.; Alberts, W. W.; Wright, E. W., Jr.; & Feinstein, B. Cortical and thalamic activation in conscious sensory experience. In *Neurophysiology Studied in Man*, pp. 157–168. Proceedings of a symposium held in Paris at the Faculté des Sciences, July 20–22, 1971, Amsterdam: Excerpta Medica, 1971.

Lindvall, C. M. *Measuring Pupil Achievement and Aptitude*. New York: Harcourt, Brace, & World, 1967.

Line, W. The growth of visual perception in children. *British Journal of Psychology Monograph Supplement*, 1931, no. 15.

Line, W., & Kaplan, E. The existence, measurement, and significance of a speed factor in the abilities of public school children. *Journal of Experimental Education*, 1932, *1*, 1–8.

Linn, R. L. Fair test use in selection. *Review of Educational Research*, 1973, *43*, 139–161.

Lipsitz, S. Effect of the race of the examiner on results of intelligence test performance of Negro and white children. Master's thesis, Long Island University, 1969.

Little, V. L., & Baily, K. G. Potential intelligence or intelligence test potential? A question of empirical validity. *Journal of Consulting and Clinical Psychology,* 1972, *39,* 168.

Loehlin, J. C.; Lindzey, G.; & Spuhler, J. N. *Race Differences in Intelligence.* San Francisco: W. H. Freeman, 1975.

Lohnes, P. R. Evaluating the schooling of intelligence. *Educational Researcher,* 1973, *2,* 6–11.

Lohnes, P. R., & Gray, M. M. Intelligence and the cooperative reading studies. *Reading Research Quarterly,* 1972, *8,* 52–61.

Longstreth, L. E. Level I–Level II abilities as they affect performance of three races in the college classroom. *Journal of Educational Psychology,* 1978, *70,* 289–297.

Lopez, F. M., Jr. Current problems in test performance of job applicants. *Personnel Psychology,* 1966, *19,* 10–18.

Lord, F. M. Test theory and the public interest. In *Testing and the Public Interest,* pp. 17–30. Proceedings of the 1976 Invitational Conference on Testing Problems. Princeton, N.J.: Educational Testing Service, 1976.

Lorge, I. Difference or bias in tests of intelligence. In A. Anastasi (Ed.), *Testing Problems in Perspective.* Washington, D.C.: American Council on Education, 1966.

Ludlow, H. G. Some recent research on the Davis–Eells Game. *School and Society,* 1956, *84,* 146–148.

Lynn, R. The intelligence of the Japanese. *Bulletin of the British Psychological Society,* 1977, *30,* 69–72.

Lynn, R. Ethnic and racial differences in intelligence: International comparisons. In R. T. Osborne, C. E. Noble, & N. Weyl (Eds.), *Human Variation: The Biopsychology of Age, Race, and Sex,* pp. 261–286. New York: Academic Press, 1978.

MacArthur, R. Some differential abilities of northern Canadian native youth. *International Journal of Psychology,* 1968, *3,* 43–51.

MacArthur, R. S. Some cognitive abilities of Eskimo, white, and Indian–Métis pupils aged 9 to 12 years. *Canadian Journal of Behavioral Science,* 1969, *1,* 50–59.

Maccoby, E. E. (Ed.). *The Development of Sex Differences.* Stanford, Calif.: Stanford University Press, 1966.

Maccoby, E. E., & Jacklin, C. N. Sex differences in intellectual functioning. In *Assessment in a Pluralistic Society,* pp. 37–55. Proceedings of the 1972 Invitational Conference on Testing Problems. Princeton, N.J.: Educational Testing Service, 1973.

Maccoby, E. E., & Jacklin, C. N. *The Psychology of Sex Differences.* Stanford, Calif.: Stanford, University Press, 1974.

MacKinnon, D. W., & Hall, W. B. Intelligence and creativity. In H. W. Peter (Chm.) Colloquium 17: The measurement of creativity. *Proceedings, XVIIth International Congress of Applied Psychology,* Liege, Belgium, 25–30 July, 1971, Vol. 2, pp. 1883–1888. Brussels: Editest, 1972.

Manpower Administration, U.S. Department of Labor, *Manual for the USES General Aptitude Test Battery,* Section III: Development. Washington, D.C.: U.S. Employment Service, 1970.

Marascuilo, L. *Statistical Methods for Behavioral Science Research.* New York: McGraw-Hill, 1971.

Marwit, S. J., & Neumann, G. Black and white children's comprehension of standard and nonstandard English passages. *Journal of Educational Psychology,* 1974, *66,* 329–332.

Matarazzo, J. D. *Wechsler's Measurement and Appraisal of Adult Intelligence* (5th ed.). Baltimore: Williams & Wilkins, 1972.

Matarazzo, J. D., & Wiens, A. N. Black Intelligence Test of Cultural Homogeneity and Wechsler Adult Intelligence Scale scores of black and white police applicants. *Journal of Applied Psychology,* 1977, *62,* 57–63.

Maxwell, A. E. Factor analysis: Statistical aspects. In D. L. Sills (Ed.), *International Encyclopedia of the Social Sciences,* Vol. 5, pp. 275–281. New York: Macmillan & Free Press, 1968.

Maxwell, A. E. Factor analysis: Thomson's sampling theory recalled. *British Journal of Mathematical and Statistical Psychology,* 1972, *25,* 1–21.

Mayeske, G. W. *On the Explanation of Racial–Ethnic Group Differences in Achievement Test Scores*. Washington, D.C.: U.S. Office of Education.

McCall, R. B. Intelligence quotient pattern over age: Comparisons among siblings and parent–child pairs. *Science,* 1970, *170,* 644–648.

McCall, R. B. Childhood IQ's as predictors of adult educational and occupational status. *Science,* 1977, *197,* 482–483.

McCarthy, D. *Manual for the McCarthy Scales of Children's Abilities*. New York: Psychological Corporation, 1970.

McClearn, G. E., & DeFries, J. C. *Introduction to Behavioral Genetics*. San Franciso: W. H. Freeman, 1973.

McClelland, D. C. *Talent and Society*. New York: Van Nostrand, 1958.

McDonald, R. P. Difficulty factors and nonlinear factor analysis. *British Journal of Mathematical and Statistical Psychology,* 1965, *18,* 11–23.

McElwain, D. W., & Kearney, G. E. *Queensland Test Handbook*. Hawthorn, Victoria: Australian Council for Educational Research, 1970.

McGaw, B., & Jöreskog, K. G. Factorial invariance of ability measures in groups differing in intelligence and socioeconomic status. *British Journal of Mathematical and Statistical Psychology,* 1971, *24,* 154–168.

McGurk, F. C. J. *Comparison of the Performance of Negro and White High School Seniors on Cultural and Noncultural Psychological Test Questions*. Washington, D.C.: Catholic University Press, 1951. (Microcard)

McGurk, F. C. J. On white and Negro test performance and socio-economic factors. *Journal of Abnormal and Social Psychology,* 1953, *48,* 448–450. (a)

McGurk, F. C. J. Socioeconomic status and culturally-weighted test scores of Negro subjects. *Journal of Applied Psychology,* 1953, *37,* 276–277. (b)

McGurk, F. C. J. The culture hypothesis and psychological tests. In R. E. Kuttner (Ed.), *Race and Modern Science,* pp. 367–381. New York: Social Science Press, 1967.

McGurk, F. C. J. Race differences—twenty years later. *Homo,* 1975, *26,* 219–239.

McKelpin, J. P. Some implications of the intellectual characteristics of freshmen entering a liberal arts college. *Journal of Educational Measurement,* 1965, *2,* 161–166.

McNemar, Q. *The Revision of the Stanford–Binet Scale*. Boston: Houghton Mifflin, 1942.

McNemar, Q. *Psychological Statistics*. New York: Wiley, 1949.

McNemar, Q. Lost: Our intelligence? Why? *American Psychologist,* 1964, *19,* 871–882.

McNemar, Q. On so-called test bias. *American Psychologist,* 1975, *30,* 848–851.

McNemar, Q. Reply to Bass and Angoff. *American Psychologist,* 1976, *31,* 612–613.

McWhinnie, H. J. Review of recent literature on figure drawing tests as related to research problems in art education. *Review of Educational Research,* 1971, *41,* 131–142.

Meehl, P. E. *Clinical vs. Statistical Prediction*. Minneapolis: University of Minnesota Press, 1954.

Meichenbaum, D. H.; Bowers, K. S.; & Ross, R. R. A behavioral analysis of teacher expectancy effect. *Journal of Personality and Social Psychology,* 1969, *13,* 306–316.

Mercer, J. R. IQ: The lethal label. *Psychology Today,* 1972, *6,* 44–47, 95–97.

Mercer, J. R. *Labeling the Retarded*. Berkeley, Calif.: University of California Press, 1973.

Mercer, J. R., & Smith, J. M. *Subtest Estimates of the WISC Full Scale IQ's for Children*. Vital and Health Statistics, Series 2, no. 47. Washington, D.C.: Government Printing Office, March 1972.

Merrill, M. A. *Problems of Child Delinquency*. Boston: Houghton Mifflin, 1947.

Merz, W. R. A factor analysis of the Goodenough–Harris Drawing Test across four ethnic groups. *Dissertation Abstracts International,* 1970, *31,* 1627A.

Messé, L. A.; Crano, W. D.; Messé, S. R.; & Rice, W. Evaluation of the predictive validity of tests of mental ability for classroom performance in elementary grades. *Journal of Educational Psychology,* 1979, *71,* 233–241.

Messer, S. B. Reflection-impulsivity: A review. *Psychological Bulletin,* 1976, *83,* 1026–1052.

Miele, F. Cultural Bias in the WISC. *Intelligence,* 1979, *3,* 149–164.

Miles, T. R. Contributions to intelligence testing and the theory of intelligence: I. On defining intelligence. *British Journal of Educational Psychology,* 1957, *27,* 153–165.

Miller, J. O., & Phillips, J. A preliminary evaluation of the Head Start and other metropolitan

Nashville kindergartens. Unpublished manuscript, Demonstration and Research Center for Early Education, George Peabody College for Teachers, Nashville, Tenn., 1966.

Mingione, A. Need for achievement in Negro, white, and Puerto Rican children. *Journal of Consulting and Clinical Psychology,* 1968, *32,* 94–95.

Mitchell, M. D.; Albright, L. E.; & McMurry, F. D. Biracial validation of selection procedures in a large southern plant. *Proceedings of the 76th Annual Convention of the American Psychological Association,* 1968, *3,* 575–576. (Summary)

Moore, C. L., & Retish, P. M. Effect of the examiner's race on black children's Wechsler Preschool and Primary Scale of Intelligence IQ. *Developmental Psychology,* 1974, *10,* 672–676.

Mueller, C. G. Numerical transformations in the analysis of experimental data. *Psychological Bulletin,* 1949, *46,* 198–223.

Munday, L. Predicting college grades in predominantly Negro colleges. *Journal of Educational Measurement,* 1965, *2,* 157–160.

Munsinger, H. The adopted child's IQ: A critical review. *Psychological Bulletin,* 1975, *82,* 623–659.

Mussen, P.; Harris, S.; Rutherford, E.; & Keasey, C. B. Honesty and altruism among preadolescents. *Developmental Psychology,* 1970, *3,* 169–194.

Nalven, F. B.; Hoffman, L. J.; & Bierbryer, B. The effects of subjects' age, sex, race, and socioeconomic status on psychologists' estimates of "true IQ" from WISC scores. *Journal of Clinical Psychology,* 1969, *25,* 271–274.

Nelson, B. Education power: Talent search helps poor realize their potential. *Science,* 1969, *163,* 53–56.

Nias, A. H. W., & Kay, H. Immediate memory of a broadcast feature program. *British Journal of Educational Psychology,* 1954, *24,* 154–160.

Nichols, P. L. The effects of heredity and environment on intelligence test performance in 4- and 7-year-old white and Negro sibling pairs. Doctoral dissertation, University of Minnesota, 1972.

Nihira, K.; Foster, R.; Shellhaas, M.; & Leland, H. *Adaptive Behavior Scales, Manual.* Washington, D.C.: American Association of Mental Deficiency, 1969.

Nissen, H. W. Phylogenetic comparison. In S. S. Stevens (Ed.), *Handbook of Experimental Psychology,* pp. 347–386. New York: Wiley, 1951.

Noble, C. E. Race, reality, and experimental psychology. *Perspectives in Biology and Medicine,* 1969, *13,* 10–30.

Noble, C. E. Learning, psychomotor. In *Encyclopaedia Britannica* (15th ed., 1974), pp. 748–754.

Noble, C. E. Age, race, and sex in the learning and performance of psychomotor skills. In R. T. Osborne, C. E. Noble, & N. Weyl (Eds.), *Human Variation: The Biopsychology of Age, Race, and Sex,* pp. 287–378. New York: Academic Press, 1978.

Noll, V. H. Relation of scores on Davis–Eells Test of General Intelligence to social status, school achievement, and other intelligence test results. *American Psychologist,* 1958, *13,* 394.

Norman, R. D. Intelligence tests and the personal world. *New Mexico Quarterly,* 1963, *33,* 153–184.

Northcutt, N. et al. *Adult Functional Competency: A Summary.* Austin: Industrial and Business Training Bureau, Adult Performance Level Project, University of Texas, March 1975.

Office of the Surgeon General. *Supplement to Health of the Army: Results of the Examination of Youths for Military Service, 1968.* Washington, D.C.: Medical Statistics Agency, Department of the Army, June 1969.

Oldfield, R. C., & Wingfield, A. Response latencies in naming objects. *Quarterly Journal of Experimental Psychology,* 1965, *17,* 273–281.

O'Leary, B. S.; Farr, J. L.; & Bartlett, C. J. *Ethnic Group Membership as a Moderator of Job Performance.* Washington, D.C.: American Institutes for Research, 1970.

Ombredane, A.; Robaye, F.; & Plumail, H. Résultats d'une application répetée du matrix-couleur à une population de Novis Conglais. *Bulletin du Centre d'Etudes et Recherches Psychotechnique,* 1956, *6,* 129–147.

Ornstein, A. C. Are quotas here to stay? *National Review,* 1974, 480–482.

Orr, D. B., & Graham, W. R. Development of a listening comprehension test to identify educational potential among disadvantaged junior high school students. *American Educational Research Journal,* 1968, *5,* 167–180.

Ortar, G. R. Improving test validity by coaching. *Educational Research,* 1960, *2,* 137–142.

Osborne, R. T., & Suddick, D. E. Blood type gene frequency and mental ability. *Psychological Reports,* 1971, *29,* 1243–1249.

Osler, S. F., & Trautman, G. E. Concept attainment: II. Effect of stimulus complexity upon concept attainment at two levels of intelligence. *Journal of Experimental Psychology,* 1961, *6,* 9–13.

Pasamanick, B., & Knobloch, H. Early language behavior in Negro children and the testing of intelligence. *Journal of Abnormal and Social Psychology,* 1955, *50,* 401–402.

Pascal, G. R., & Suttell, B. J. *The Bender–Gestalt Test: Quantification and Validity for Adults.* New York: Grune & Stratton, 1951.

Paterson, D. G. *Physique and Intellect.* New York: Century, 1930.

Paulson, E. An approximate normalization of the analysis of variance distribution. *Annals of Mathematical Statistics,* 1942, *13,* 233–235.

Peak, H., & Boring, E. G. The factor of speed in intelligence. *Journal of Experimental Psychology,* 1926, *9,* 71–94.

Peisach, E. C. Children's comprehension of teacher and peer speech. *Child Development,* 1965, *36,* 467–480.

Pelosi, J. W. A study of the effects of examiner race, sex, and style on test responses of Negro examinees. Doctoral dissertation, Syracuse University, 1968.

Penrose, L. S., & Raven, J. C. A new series of perceptual tests: Preliminary communication. *British Journal of Medical Psychology,* 1936, *16,* 97–104.

Perlberg, A. Predicting academic achievement of engineering and science college students. *Journal of Educational Measurement,* 1967, *4,* 241–246.

Petersen, N. S. *An Expected Utility Model for "Optimal" Selection.* Iowa Testing Programs Occasional Paper No. 10, 1975.

Petersen, N. S., & Novick, M. R. An evaluation of some models for culture-fair selection. *Journal of Educational Measurement,* 1976, *13,* 3–29.

Peterson, J. Comparisons of white and Negro children in the rational learning test. *27th Yearbook of the NSSE,* Part I, 1928, pp. 333–341.

Peterson, R. E. Predictive validity of a brief test of academic aptitude. *Educational and Psychological Measurement,* 1968, *28,* 441–444.

Pettigrew, T. F. *A Profile of the Negro American.* Princeton, N.J.: Van Nostrand, 1964.

Pfeifer, C. M., Jr., & Sedlacek, W. E. The validity of academic predictors for black and white students at a predominantly white university. *Journal of Educational Measurement,* 1971, *8,* 253–261.

Piaget, J. *The Psychology of Intelligence.* London: Routledge & Kegan Paul, 1947.

Pinard, A., & Laurendeau, M. A scale of mental development based on the theory of Piaget. *Journal of Research Science in Teaching,* 1964, *2,* 253–260.

Pinneau, S. R. *Changes in Intelligence Quotient: Infancy to Maturity.* Boston: Houghton Mifflin, 1961.

Pitcher, B., & Schrader, W. B. Summary of results from 1968–1969 LSAT Validity Study Service. LSAT Council, June 1969. (Mimeo)

Pitt, C. C. V. An experimental study of the effects of teacher's knowledge or incorrect knowledge of pupil IQ's on teachers' attitudes and practices and pupils' attitudes and achievement. *Dissertation Abstracts,* 1956, *16,* 2387–2388.

Poland, H. V. The relationship between self-concept and supervisory and peer ratings of success in nurses' training. *Dissertation Abstracts,* 1961, *22* (4), 1260.

Poortinga, Y. H. *Cross-cultural Comparison of Maximum Performance Tests: Some Methodological Aspects and Some Experiments with Simple Auditory and Visual Stimuli.* Johannesburg: National Institute for Personnel Research, 1971.

Poortinga, Y. H. Cross-cultural comparison of maximum performance tests: Some methodological aspects and some experiments with simple auditory and visual stimuli. *Psychologia Africana,* Monograph Supplement No. 6, 1971.

Porteus, S. D. *Porteus Maze Test: Fifty Years' Application.* Palo Alto, Calif.: Pacific Books, 1965.

Posner, C. A. Some effects of genetic and cultural variables on self-evaluations of children. Doctoral dissertation, Illinois Institute of Technology, 1969. (Cited by Shuey, 1978.)

Posner, M. I. Abstraction and the process of recognition. In G. H. Bower & J. T. Spence (Eds.), *The Psychology of Learning and Motivation,* Vol. 3, pp. 43–100. New York: Academic Press, 1969.

Quay, L. C. Language, dialect, reinforcement, and the intelligence test performance of Negro Children. *Child Development,* 1971, *42,* 5–15.

Quay, L. C. Negro dialect and Binet performance in severely disadvantaged black four-year-olds. *Child Development,* 1972, *43,* 245–250.

Quay, L. C. Language dialect, age, and intelligence-test performance in disadvantaged black children. *Child Development,* 1974, *45,* 463–468.

Ratusnik, D. L., & Koenigsknecht, R. A. Biracial testing: The question of clinicians' influence on children's test performance. *Language, Speech, and Hearing Services in Schools,* 1977, *8,* 5–14.

Raven, J. C. *Progressive Matrices: A Perceptual Test of Intelligence,* 1938, Individual Form. London: H. K. Lewis, 1938.

Raven, J. C. *Coloured Progressive Matrices.* London: H. K. Lewis, 1947.

Raven, J. C. *Guide to the Standard Progressive Matrices.* London: H. K. Lewis, 1960.

Reschly, D. WISC-R factor structures among Anglos, blacks, Chicanos, and Native American Papagos. *Journal of Consulting and Clinical Psychology,* 1978, *46,* 417–422.

Reschly, D. J., & Sabers, D. L. An examination of bias in predicting MAT scores from WISC-R scores for four ethnic–racial groups. *Journal of Educational Measurement,* 1979, *16,* 1–9.

Reuning, H. Psychological studies of Kalahari Bushmen. In L. J. Cronbach & P. J. D. Drenth (Eds.), *Mental Tests and Cultural Adaptation,* pp. 171–181. The Hague: Mouton, 1972.

Roberts, J. *Intellectual Development of Children by Demographic and Socioeconomic Factors.* DHEW Publication No. 72-1012. Washington, D.C.: Government Printing Office, 1971.

Roberts, J., & Baird, J. T., Jr. *Behavior Patterns in Children in School.* DHEW Publication No. 72-1042. Washington, D.C.: Government Printing Office, 1972.

Robertson, D. W., & Montague, W. E. *Comparative Racial Analysis of Enlisted Advancement Exams: Relative Item–Difficulty between Performance-Matched Groups.* Technical Report 76-34. San Diego, Calif.: Navy Personnel Research and Development Center, April 1976.

Robertson, D. W., & Royle, M. H. *Comparative Racial Analysis of Enlisted Advancement Exams: Item–Difficulty.* Technical Report 76-6. San Diego, Calif.: Navy Personnel Research and Development Center, July 1975.

Robertson, D. W.; Royle, M. H.; & Morena, D. J. *Comparative Racial Analysis of Enlisted Advancement Exams: Item Differentiation.* Technical Report 77-16. San Diego, Calif.: Navy Personnel Research and Development Center, February 1977.

Roen, S. R. Personality and Negro–white intelligence. *Journal of Abnormal and Social Psychology,* 1960, *61,* 148–150.

Rosenblum, S.; Keller, J. E.; & Papania, N. Davis–Eells ("culture-fair") test performance of lower-class retarded children. *Journal of Consulting Psychology,* 1955, *19,* 51–54.

Rosenthal, R., & Jacobson, L. *Pygmalion in the Classroom.* New York: Holt, Rinehart, & Winston, 1968.

Ross, R. T. *Fairview Self-help Scale: Manual.* Fairview, Calif.: Fairview State Hospital, 1970.

Roth, E. Die Geschwindigkeit der Verarbeitung von Information und ihr Zusammenhang mit Intelligence. *Zeitschrift für Experimentelle und Angewandte Psychologie,* 1964, *11,* 616, 622.

Ruch, W. W. A reanalysis of published differential validity studies. Paper presented at meeting of American Psychological Association, Honolulu, Hawaii, September 1972.

Ruda, E., & Albright, L. E. Racial differences on selection instruments related to subsequent job performance. *Personnel Psychology,* 1968, *21,* 31–41.

Rulon, P. J. A semantic test of intelligence. In A. Anastasi (Ed.), *Testing Problems in Perspective,* pp. 472–480. Washington, D.C.: American Council on Education, 1966.

Rulon, P. J., & Schweiker, R. F. *Validation of a Nonverbal Test of Military Trainability.* Cambridge, Mass.: Graduate School of Education, Harvard University, 1953.

Rumenik, D. K.; Capasso, D. R.; & Hendrick, C. Experimenter sex effects in behavioral research. *Psychological Bulletin,* 1977, *84,* 852–877.

Russell Sage Foundation. *Guidelines for the Collection, Maintenance, and Dissemination of Pupil Records.* New York: The Foundation, 1970.

Samuda, R. J. *Racial Discrimination through Mental Testing: A Social Critic's Point of View.* ERIC document no. 42. New York: Teachers College, Columbia University, May 1973.

Samuel, W. Observed IQ as a function of test atmosphere, tester expectation, and race of tester: A replication for female subjects. *Journal of Educational Psychology,* 1977, *69,* 593–604.

Samuels, S. J., & Dahl, R. D. Relationships among IQ, learning ability, and reading achievement. In J. L. Johns (Ed.) *Literacy for Diverse Learners,* pp. 31–38. Newark, Del.: International Reading Association, 1973.

Sarason, I. G. The Test Anxiety Scale: Concepts and research. In C. D. Spielberger and I. G. Sarason (Eds.), *Stress and Anxiety,* Vol. 5. Washington, D.C.: Hemisphere, 1978.

Sarason, S. B.; Davison, K. S.; Lighthall, F. F.; Waite, R. R.; & Ruebush, B. K. *Anxiety in Elementary School Children.* New York: Wiley, 1960.

Sattler, J. M. Racial "experimenter effects" in experimentation, testing, interviewing, and psychotherapy. *Psychological Bulletin,* 1970, *73,* 137–160.

Sattler, J. M. Racial experimenter effects. In K. S. Miller & R. M. Dreger (Eds.), *Comparative Physiological, Psychological, and Sociological Studies of Negroes and Whites in the United States.* New York: Seminar Press, 1973.

Sattler, J. M. *Assessment of Children's Intelligence.* Philadelphia: Saunders, 1974.

Sattler, J. M. Intelligence testing of ethnic minority group and culturally disadvantaged children. In L. Mann & D. Sabatino (Eds.), *The First Review of Special Education,* vol. 2, pp. 161–201. Philadelphia: The JSE Press, 1973.

Sattler, J. M.; Hillix, W. A.; & Neher, L. A. Halo effect in examiner scoring of intelligence test responses. *Journal of Consulting and Clinical Psychology,* 1970, *34,* 172–176.

Sattler, J. M., & Kuncik, T. M. Ethnicity, socioeconomic status, and pattern of WISC scores as variables that effect psychologists' estimates of "effective intelligence." *Journal of Clinical Psychology,* 1976, *32,* 362–366.

Sattler, J. M., & Theye, F. Procedural, situational, and interpersonal variables in individual intelligence testing. *Psychological Bulletin,* 1967, *68,* 347–360.

Sattler, J. M., & Winget, B. M. Intelligence testing procedures as affected by expectancy and IQ. *Journal of Clinical Psychology,* 1970, *26,* 446–448.

Saunders, B. T., & Vitro, F. T. Examiner expectancy and bias as a function of the referral process in cognitive assessment. *Psychology in the Schools,* 1971, *8,* 168–171.

Savage, J. E., Jr., & Bowers, N. D. *Testers' Influence on Children's Intellectual Performance.* Washington, D.C.: U.S. Office of Education, 1972. (ERIC microfiche no. 064 329)

Schafer, E. W. P., & Marcus, M. M. Self-stimulation alters human sensory brain responses. *Science,* 1973, *181,* 175–177.

Schmidt, F. L. Racial differences in some cognitive and motivational correlates of peer evaluations. Unpublished manuscript, 1972.

Schmidt, F. L.; Berner, J. G.; & Hunter, J. E. Racial differences in validity of employment tests: Reality or illusion? *Journal of Applied Psychology,* 1973, *58,* 5–9.

Schmidt, F. L., & Hunter, J. E. Development of a general solution to the problem of validity generalization. *Journal of Applied Psychology,* 1977, *62,* 529–540.

Schroeder, H. E., & Kleinsasser, L. D. Examiner bias: A determinant of children's verbal behavior on the WISC. *Journal of Consulting and Clinical Psychology,* 1972, *39,* 451–454.

Schwartz, P. A., & Krug, R. E. *Ability Testing in Developing Countries: A Handbook of Principles and Techniques.* New York: Praeger, 1972.

Scott, R.; Hartson, J.; & Cunningham, M. Race of examiner as a variable in test attainments of preschool children. *Perceptual and Motor Skills,* 1976, *42,* 1167–1173.

Scottish Council for Research in Education. *The Intelligence of Scottish Children: A National Survey of an Age-Group.* London: University of London Press, 1933.

Seashore, H. G. Women are more predictable than men. *Journal of Counseling Psychology,* 1962, *9,* 261–270.

Seaver, W. B. Effects of naturally induced teacher expectancies. *Journal of Personality and Social Psychology,* 1973, *28,* 333–342.

Seligman, D. How "equal opportunity" turned to employment quotas. *Fortune,* 1973, *87* (3), 160–168.

Shimberg, M. E. An investigation into the validity of norms with special reference to urban and rural groups. *Archives of Psychology,* 1929, no. 104.

Shucard, D. W., & Horn, J. L. Evoked cortical potentials and measurement of human abilities. *Journal of Comparative and Physiological Psychology*, 1972, *78* (1), 59–68.

Shucard, D. W.; Horn, J. L.; & Metcalf, D. An objective procedure for the hand scoring of scalp average evoked potentials. *Behavioral Research Methodology and Instruction*, 1971, *3* (1), 5–7.

Shuey, A. M. *The Testing of Negro Intelligence* (2nd ed.). New York: Social Science Press, 1966.

Shuey, A. M. Own-race preference and self-esteem in young Negroid and Caucasoid children. In R. T. Osborne, C. E. Noble, & N. Weyl (Eds.), *Human Variation: The Biopsychology of Age, Race, and Sex*, pp. 199–260. New York: Academic Press, 1978.

Shulman, H. M. *A Study of Problem Boys and Their Brothers*. Albany: New York State Crime Commission, 1929.

Shulman, H. M. Intelligence and delinquency. *Journal of Criminal Law and Criminology*, 1951, *41*, 763–781.

Siebert, L. A. Otis IQ scores of delinquents. *Journal of Clinical Psychology*, 1962, *18*, 517.

Sigel, I. W., & Olmsted, P. Modification of cognitive skills among lower-class black children. In J. Hellmuth (Ed.), *Disadvantaged Child*, Vol. 3, pp. 300–338. New York: Brunner-Mazel, 1970.

Simon, B. *Intelligence, Psychology, and Education: A Marxist Critique*. London: Lawrence & Wishart, 1971.

Simon, W. E. Expectancy effects in the scoring of vocabulary items: A study of scorer bias. *Journal of Educational Measurement*, 1969, *6*, 159–164.

Smith, H. W., & May, T. Influence of the examiner on the ITPA scores of Negro children. *Psychological Reports*, 1967, *20*, 499–502.

Smith, M. W. Alfred Binet's remarkable questions: A cross-national and cross-temporal analysis of the cultural biases built into the Stanford–Binet Intelligence Scale and other Binet tests. *Genetic Psychology Monographs*, 1974, *89*, 307–334.

Snow, R. Unfinished Pygmalion. *Contemporary Psychology*, 1969, *14*, 197–199.

Solkoff, N. Race of experimenter as a variable in research with children. *Developmental Psychology*, 1972, *7*, 70–75.

Solkoff, N. Race of examiner and performance on the Wechsler Intelligence Scale for Children: A replication. *Perceptual and Motor Skills*, 1974, *39*, 1063–1066.

Southern, M. L., & Plant, W. T. A factor analysis of scholastic aptitudes of culturally disadvantaged kindergarteners. Paper presented at the meeting of the Western Psychological Association, Vancouver, British Columbia, June 1969.

Sowell, T. Are quotas good for blacks? *Commentary*, 1978, *65*, 39–43.

Spearman, C. "General intelligence": Objectively determined and measured. *American Journal of Psychology*, 1904, *15*, 201–292.

Spearman, C. *The Nature of "Intelligence" and the Principles of Cognition*. London: Macmillan, 1923.

Spearman, C. *The Abilities of Man*. New York: Macmillan, 1927.

Spearman, C. *Creative Mind*. New York: Cambridge, 1930.

Spearman, C., & Jones, L. L. W. *Human Ability*. London: Macmillan, 1950.

Spiegel, M. R., & Bryant, N. D. Is speed of processing information related to intelligence and achievement? *Journal of Educational Psychology*, 1978, *70*, 904–910.

Spielberger, C. D. On the relationship between manifest anxiety and intelligence. *Journal of Consulting Psychology*, 1958, *22*, 220–224.

Standards for Educational and Psychological Tests. Washington, D.C.: American Psychological Association, 1974.

Stanley, J. C. Further evidence via the analysis of variance that women are more predictable academically than men. *Ontario Journal of Educational Research*, 1967, *10*, 49–56.

Stanley, J. C. Plotting ANOVA interactions for ease of visual interpretation. *Educational and Psychological Measurement*, 1969, *29*, 793–797.

Stanley, J. C. Predicting college success of the educationally disadvantaged. *Science*, 1971, *171*, 640–647. (a)

Stanley, J. C. Predicting college success of educationally disadvantaged students. In S. J. Wright (Ed.), *Barriers to Higher Education*. New York: College Entrance Examination Board, 1971. (b)

Stanley, J. C. Reliability. In R. L. Thorndike (Ed.), *Educational Measurement* (2nd ed.), pp. 356-442. Washington, D.C.: American Council on Education, 1971.

Stanley, J. C.; Keating, D. P.; & Fox, L. H. (Eds.). *Mathematical Talent: Discovery, Description, and Development.* Baltimore: Johns Hopkins University Press, 1974.

Stanley, J. C., & Porter, A. C. Correlation of Scholastic Aptitude Test scores with college grades for Negroes versus whites. *Journal of Educational Measurement,* 1967, *4,* 199-218.

Stenhouse, D. *The Evolution of Intelligence.* London: Allen & Unwin, 1973.

Sternberg, R. J. *Intelligence, Information Processing, and Analogical Reasoning: The Componential Analysis of Human Abilities.* Hillsdale, N.J.: Erlbaum, 1977.

Sternberg, S. High-speed scanning in human memory. *Science,* 1966, *153,* 652-654.

Sternberg, S. Memory scanning: New findings and current controversies. *Quarterly Journal of Experimental Psychology,* 1975, *27,* 1-32.

Stevens, M. E., & Hyde, J. S. A comment on Jensen's note on sex linkage and race differences in spatial ability. *Behavior Genetics,* 1978, *8,* 207-211.

Stoddard, G. D. *The Meaning of Intelligence.* New York: Macmillan, 1943.

Stodolsky, S. S., & Lesser, G. Learning patterns in the disadvantaged. *Harvard Educational Review,* 1967, *37,* 546-593.

Storms, L. H. Rationales for the "twisted pear." *Journal of Consulting Psychology,* 1960, *24,* 552-553.

Strassberg-Rosenberg, B., & Donlon, T. F. Content influences on sex differences in performance on aptitude tests. *National Council on Measurement in Education,* 1975.

Surwillo, W. W. Human reaction time and period of the EEG in relation to development. *Psychophysiology,* 1971, *8,* 468-482.

Sweet, R. C. Variations in the intelligence test performance of lower-class children as a function of feedback or monetary reinforcement. Doctoral dissertation, University of Wisconsin, 1969. (University Microfilms, no. 70-3721.)

Symonds, P. M. Factors influencing test reliability. *Journal of Educational Psychology,* 1928, *19,* 73-87.

Tate, M. W. Individual differences in speed of response in mental test materials of varying degrees of difficulty. *Educational and Psychological Measurement,* 1948, *8,* 353-374.

Tate, M. W., & Voss, C. E. A study of the Davis-Eells test of intelligence. *Harvard Educational Review,* 1956, *26,* 374-387.

Taylor, H. C., & Russell, J. T. The relationship of validity coefficients to the practical effectiveness of tests in selection: Discussion and tables. *Journal of Applied Psychology,* 1939, *23,* 565-578.

Temp, G. Test bias: Validity of the SAT for blacks and whites in thirteen integrated institutions. *Journal of Educational Measurement,* 1971, *8,* 245-251.

Tenopyr, M. L. Race and socioeconomic status as moderators in predicting machine-shop training success. Paper presented in symposium, American Psychological Association, Washington, D.C., 1967.

Terman, L. M. *The Measurement of Intelligence.* Boston: Houghton Mifflin, 1916.

Terman, L. M. Intelligence and its measurement, Part II. *Journal of Educational Psychology,* 1921, *12,* 127-133.

Terman, L. M. *Genetic Studies of Genius,* Vol. 1, *Mental and Physical Traits of a Thousand Gifted Children.* Stanford, Calif.: Stanford University Press, 1925.

Terman, L. M., & Merrill, M. A. *Measuring Intelligence.* Boston: Houghton Mifflin, 1937.

Terman, L. M., & Merrill, M. A. *Stanford-Binet Intelligence Scale: Manual for the Third Revision, Form L-M.* Boston: Houghton Mifflin, 1960.

Terman, L. M., & Merrill, M. A. *Stanford-Binet Intelligence Scale: 1972 Norms Edition.* Boston: Houghton Mifflin, 1973.

Terman, L. M., & Oden, M. *The Gifted Group at Mid-life.* Stanford, Calif.: Stanford University Press, 1959.

Thomas, C. L., & Stanley, J. C. *The Effectiveness of High School Grades for Predicting College Grades of Negro Students: An Exploratory Study.* New York: Teachers College, Columbia University, 1969. (Mimeo)

Thomas, P. J. *An Investigation of Possible Test Bias in the Navy Basic Test Battery.* Technical Bulletin STB 73-1. San Diego, Calif.: Naval Personnel and Training Research Laboratory, August 1972.

Thomas, P. J. *Racial Differences in the Prediction of Class "A" School Grades*. Technical Bulletin NPRDC-TR-75-39. San Diego, Calif.: Navy Personnel Research and Development Center, June 1975.

Thomson, G. H. *The Factorial Analysis of Human Ability* (5th ed.). Boston: Houghton Mifflin, 1951.

Thorndike, E. L. Reading as reasoning: A study of mistakes in paragraph reading. *Journal of Educational Psychology,* 1917, *8,* 323–332.

Thorndike, E. L. Intelligence and its measurement, Part I. *Journal of Educational Psychology,* 1921, *12,* 124–127.

Thorndike, E. L. *The Measurement of Intelligence*. New York: Teachers College, Columbia University, 1927.

Thorndike, E. L.; Lay, W., & Dean, P. R. The relation of accuracy in sensory discrimination to general intelligence. *American Journal of Psychology,* 1909, *20,* 364–369.

Thorndike, E. L., & Lorge, I. *The Teacher's Word Book of 30,000 Words*. New York: Teachers College, Columbia University, 1944.

Thorndike, R. L. The effect of the interval between test and retest on the constancy of the IQ. *Journal of Educational Psychology,* 1933, *24,* 543–549.

Thorndike, R. L. Community variables as predictors of intelligence and academic achievement. *Journal of Educational Psychology,* 1951, *42,* 321–338.

Thorndike, R. L. *The Concepts of Over- and Underachievement*. New York: Teachers College Press, 1963. (a)

Thorndike, R. L. Some methodological issues in the study of creativity. In *Proceedings of the 1962 Invitational Conference on Testing Problems,* pp. 40–54. Princeton, N.J.: Educational Testing Service, 1963. (b)

Thorndike, R. L. Reivew of *Pygmalion in the Classroom,* by R. Rosenthal and L. Jacobson. *American Educational Research Journal,* 1968, *5,* 708–711.

Thorndike, R. L. Concepts of culture-fairness. *Journal of Educational Measurement,* 1971, *8,* 63–70. (a)

Thorndike, R. L. Memorandum on the use of the Lorge–Thorndike Tests in California. February 26, 1971. (Mimeo) (b)

Thorndike, R. L. Reading as reasoning. *Reading Research Quarterly,* 1973–1974, *9* (2), 135–147.

Thorndike, R. L.; Fleming, C. W.; Hildreth, G., & Stanger, M. Retest changes in the I.Q. in certain superior schools. In National Society for the Study of Education, *39th Yearbook,* 1940, pp. 351–361.

Thorndike, R. L., & Hagen, E. *Ten Thousand Careers*. New York: Wiley, 1959.

Thurstone, L. L. Intelligence and its measurement. *Journal of Educational Psychology*, 1921, *12,* 201–207.

Thurstone, L. L. A method of scaling psychological and educational tests. *Journal of Educational Psychology,* 1925, *16,* 433–451.

Thurstone, L. L. The mental-age concept. *Psychological Review,* 1926, *33,* 268–278.

Thurstone, L. L. The absolute zero in intelligence measurement. *Psychological Review,* 1928, *35,* 175–197.

Thurstone, L. L. *Primary Mental Abilities*. Psychometric Monographs, No. 1. Chicago: University of Chicago Press, 1938.

Thurstone, L. L. *Multiple Factor Analysis*. Chicago: University of Chicago Press, 1947.

Tiber, N., & Kennedy, W. A. The effects of incentives on the intelligence test performance of different social groups. *Journal of Consulting Psychology,* 1964, *28,* 187–189.

Tilton, J. W. Measurement of overlapping. *Journal of Educational Psychology,* 1937, *28,* 656–662.

Timm, N. H. *Multivariate Analysis with Applications in Education and Psychology*. Monterey, Calif.: Brooks/Cole, 1975.

Toki, E. Kindergarten children's preferences for color, form, size, and number stimuli. Master's thesis, University of California, Berkeley, 1971.

Tuddenham, R. D. The nature and measurement of intelligence. In L. Postman (Ed.), *Psychology in the Making: Histories of Selected Research Problems,* pp. 469–525. New York: Knopf, 1962.

Tuddenham, R. D. A "Piagetian" test of cognitive development. In W. B. Dockrell (Ed.), *On Intelligence,* pp. 49–70. London: Methuen, 1970.

Tuddenham, R. D., & Snyder, M. M. Physical growth of California boys and girls from birth to eighteen years. *University of California Publications in Child Development,* 1954, *1,* 183–364.

Turner, R., Hall, V., & Grimmett, S. Effects of familiarization feedback on the performance of lower-class and middle-class kindergarteners on the Raven Colored Progressive Matrices. *Journal of Educational Psychology,* 1973, *65,* 356–363.

Tyler, L. E. *The Psychology of Human Differences* (3rd ed.). New York: Appleton-Century-Crofts, 1965.

Tyler, L. E. *Individual Differences: Abilities and Motivational Directions.* Englewood Cliffs, N.J.: Prentice-Hall, 1974.

U.S. Department of Labor, Manpower Administration. *Development of USES Aptitude Test Battery for Welder, Production Line (welding) 810.884.* U.S. Training and Employment Service Technical Report S-447. Washington, D.C.: The Department, 1969.

U.S. Department of Labor, Manpower Administration. *Manual for the USES General Aptitude Test Battery.* Washington, D.C.: U.S. Employment Service, 1970.

Van Valen, L. Brain size and intelligence in man. *American Journal of Physical Anthropology,* 1974, *40,* 417–423.

Vane, J. R. Relation of early school achievement to high school achievement when race, intelligence, and socioeconomic factors are equated. *Psychology in the Schools,* 1966, *3,* 124–129.

Vernon, M. Fifty years of research on the intelligence of deaf and hard-of-hearing children: A review of literature and discussion of implications. *Journal of Rehabilitation of the Deaf,* 1968, *1,* 1–12.

Vernon, P. E. Intelligence test sophistication. *British Journal of Educational Psychology,* 1938, *8,* 237–244.

Vernon, P. E. Research on personnel selection in the Royal Navy and the British Army. *American Psychologist,* 1947, *2,* 35–51.

Vernon, P. E. *The Structure of Human Abilities.* New York: Wiley, 1950.

Vernon, P. E. Practice and coaching effects in intelligence tests. *Educational Forum,* March 1954, pp. 269–280. (a)

Vernon, P. E. Symposium on the effects of coaching and practice in intelligence tests: V. Conclusions. *British Journal of Educational Psychology,* 1954, *24,* 57–63. (b)

Vernon, P. E. *Intelligence and Attainment Tests.* London: University of London Press, 1960.

Vernon, P. E. Creativity and intelligence. *Educational Research,* 1964, *6,* 163–169.

Vernon, P. E. Environmental handicaps and intellectual development, Part II and Part III. *British Journal of Educational Psychology,* 1965, *35,* 1–22.

Vernon, P. E. *Intelligence and Cultural Environment.* London: Methuen, 1969.

Veroff, J.; McClelland, L.; & Marquis, K. *Measuring Intelligence and Achievement Motivations in Surveys.* Ann Arbor: Survey Research Center, Institute for Social Research, University of Michigan, October 1971. (a)

Veroff, J.; McClelland, L.; & Marquis, K. *Measuring Intelligence and Achievement Motivation in Surveys.* Appendices 3–6. Ann Arbor: Survey Research Center, Institute for Social Research, University of Michigan, October 1971. (b)

Viaud, G. *Intelligence: Its Evolution and Forms.* London: Hutchinson, 1960.

Vineburg, R., & Taylor, E. N. *Performance in Four Army Jobs by Men at Different Aptitude (AFQT) Levels: 3. The Relationship of AFQT and Job Experience to Job Performance.* Human Resources Research Organization Technical Report 72-22. Washington, D.C.: Chief of Research and Development, Department of the Army, August 1972.

von Neumann, J., & Morgenstern, O. *Theory of Games and Economic Behavior* (3rd ed.). Princeton, N.J.: Princeton University Press, 1953.

Wald, A. *Statistical Decision Functions.* New York: Wiley, 1950.

Wallach, M., & Kogan, N. *Modes of Thinking in Young Children.* New York: Holt, Rinehart, & Winston, 1965.

Waller, J. H. Achievement and social mobility: Relationships among IQ score, education, and occupation in two generations. *Social Biology,* 1971, *18,* 252–259.

Warden, C. J. Animal intelligence. *Scientific American,* June 1951, pp. 3–6.

Warden, C. J.; Jenkins, T. N.; & Warner, L. H. *Introduction to Comparative Psychology.* New York: Ronald, 1934.

Warren, H. C. *Dictionary of Psychology*. Boston: Houghton Mifflin, 1934.

Wasik, B. H., & Wasik, J. L. Performance of culturally deprived children on the *Concept Assesssment Kit—Conservation. Child Development*, 1971, *42*, 1586-1950.

Watts, A. F.; Pidgeon, D. A., & Yates, A. *Secondary School Entrance Examinations*. London: Newnes, 1952.

Wechsler, D. *Measurement of Adult Intelligence* (3rd ed.). Baltimore: Williams & Wilkins, 1944.

Wechsler, D. *The Measurement and Appraisal of Adult Intelligence* (4th ed.). Baltimore: Williams & Wilkins, 1958.

Wechsler, D. *Manual for the Wechsler Intelligence Scale for Children—Revised*. New York: Psychological Corporation, 1974.

Wechsler, D. Intelligence defined and undefined: A relativistic appraisal. *American Psychologist*, 1975, *30*, 135-139.

Weener, P. D. Social dialect differences and the recall of verbal messages. *Journal of Educational Psychology*, 1969, *60*, 194-199.

Wellborn, E. S.; Reid, W. R.; & Reichard, G. L. Effect of examiner race on test scores of black and white children. *Education and Training of the Mentally Retarded*, 1973, *8*, 194-196.

Wenk, E. A.; Rozynko, V. V.; Sarbin, T. R.; & Robison, J. O. The effect of incentives upon aptitude scores of white and Negro inmates. *Journal of Research in Crime and Delinquency*, 1971, *8*, 53-64.

Wesman, A. G. *Better Than Chance*. Test Service Bulletin No. 45. New York: Psychological Corporation, 1953.

White, P. O. Individual differences in speed, accuracy, and persistence: A mathematical model for problem solving. In H. J. Eysenck (Ed.), *The Measurement of Intelligence*, pp. 246-260. Baltimore: Williams & Wilkins, 1973.

White, S. H. et al. *Federal Programs for Young Children: Review and Recommendations*, Vol. 1, *Goals and Standards of Public Programs for Children*. Washington, D.C.: Department of Health, Education, and Welfare, 1973.

Wild, C. L., & Dwyer, C. A. *Sex Bias in Selection*. Research Memorandum. Princeton, N.J.: Educational Testing Service, February 1978.

Willard, L. A comparison of culture fair test scores with group and individual intelligence test scores of disadvantaged Negro children. *Journal of Learning Disabilities*, 1968, *1*, 584-589.

Williams, R. L. Abuses and misuses in testing black children. *Counseling Psychologist*, 1971, *2*, 62-77.

Williams, R. L. *The BITCH Test (Black Intelligence Test of Cultural Homogeneity)*. St. Louis, Mo.: Black Studies Program, Washington University, 1972. (a)

Williams, R. L. The BITCH-100: A culture-specific test. Paper presented at the annual convention of the American Psychological Association, Honolulu, Hawaii, September 1972. (b)

Williams, R. L. Scientific racism and IQ: The silent mugging of the black community. *Psychology Today*, May 1974, pp. 32-41.

Wilson, K. M. *Contributions of SAT's to Prediction of Freshman Grades: CRC–Member Colleges (Women Only)*. Poughkeepsie, N.Y.: College Research Center, 1970.

Wilson, R. S. Twins: Early mental development. *Science*, 1972, *175*, 914-917.

Wing, C. W., Jr., & Ktsanes, V. *The Effect of Certain Cultural Background Factors on the Prediction of Student Grades in College*. New York: College Entrance Examination Board, August 1960.

Wing, H. D. A factorial study of musical tests. *British Journal of Psychology*, 1941, *31*, 341-355.

Wiseman, S. *Education and Environment*. Manchester, England: Manchester University Press, 1964.

Wiseman, S. (Ed.) *Intelligence and Ability*. Baltimore: Penguin, 1967.

Wiseman, S., & Wrigley, J. The comparative effects of coaching and practice on the results of verbal intelligence tests. *British Journal of Psychology*, 1953, *44*, 83-94.

Wissler, C. The correlation of mental and physical tests. *Psychological Review Monograph Supplement 3*, no. 6, 1901, (whole no. 16).

Wober, D. P. Sex differences in cognition: A function of maturational rate? *Science*, 1976, *192*, 572-574.

Wollowick, H. B.; Greenwood, J. M.; & McNamara, W. J. Psychological testing with a minority group population. *Proceedings of the 77th Annual Convention of the American Psychological Association*, 1969, *4*, 609-610. (Summary)

Womer, F. B. National assessment says. *Measurement in Education,* 1970, *2,* 1–8.

Wonderlic, E. F., & Wonderlic, C. F. *Wonderlic Personnel Test: Negro Norms.* Northfield, Ill.: E. F. Wonderlic & Associates, 1972.

Wood, M. T. Validation of a selection test against a turnover criterion for racial and sex subgroups of employees. Paper presented at the meeting of the Midwestern Psychological Association, Chicago, May 1969.

Woodrow, H. The effect of practice on groups of different initial ability. *Journal of Educational Psychology,* 1938, *29,* 268–278. (a)

Woodrow, H. The effect of practice on test intercorrelations. *Journal of Educational Psychology,* 1938, *29,* 561–572. (b)

Woodrow, H. The relation between abilities and improvement with practice. *Journal of Educational Psychology,* 1938, *29,* 215–230. (c)

Woodrow, H. Factors in improvement with practice. *Journal of Psychology,* 1939, *7,* 55–70. (a)

Woodrow, H. The application of factor analysis to problems of practice. *Journal of General Psychology,* 1939, *21,* 457–460. (b)

Woodrow, H. The relation of verbal ability to improvement with practice in verbal tests. *Journal of Educational Psychology,* 1939, *30,* 179–186. (c)

Woodrow, H. Interrelations of measures of learning. *Journal of Psychology,* 1940, *10,* 49–73.

Woodrow, H. The ability to learn. *Psychological Review,* 1946, *53,* 147–158.

Yamamoto, K. Role of creative thinking and intelligence in high school achievement. *Psychological Record,* 1964, *14,* 783–789.

Yando, R.; Zigler, E.; & Gates, M. The influence of Negro and white teachers rated as effective or noneffective on the performance of Negro and white lower-class children. *Developmental Psychology,* 1971, *5,* 290–299.

Yates, A. Symposium on the effects of coaching and practice in intelligence tests: An analysis of some recent investigations. *British Journal of Educational Psychology,* 1953, *23,* 147–154.

Zeaman, D., & House, B. J. The relation of IQ and learning. In R. M. Gagné (Ed.), *Learning and Individual Differences,* pp. 192–217. Columbus, Ohio: Merrill, 1967.

Zigler, E. Familial mental retardation: A continuing dilemma. *Science,* 1967, *155,* 292–298.

Zigler, E., & Butterfield, E. C. Motivational aspects of changes in IQ test performance of culturally deprived nursery school children. *Child Development,* 1968, *39,* 1–14.

Zigler, E.; Levine, J.; & Gould, L. Cognitive processes in the development of children's appreciation of humor. *Child Development,* 1966, *37,* 507–518.

Zirkel, P. A. Spanish-speaking students and standardized tests. In *Education Yearbook 1973–1974,* pp. 299–307. New York: Macmillan, 1973.

Indexes

NAME INDEX

SUBJECT INDEX